RHYTHM & BLUES

TOP R&B
ALBUMS

Billboard.   **1965-1998**

Chart Data Compiled From *Billboard's* R&B Albums Charts, 1965-1998.

ISBN 0-89820-134-9

Record Research Inc.
P.O. Box 200
Menomonee Falls, Wisconsin 53052-0200   U.S.A.

Phone: 414-251-5408
Fax: 414-251-9452
E-Mail: record@execpc.com
Web Site: http://www.recordresearch.com

CONTENTS

Most Charted Albums   Most Weeks At The #1 Position
Most Top 40 Albums   Most Gold & Platinum Albums
Most Top 10 Albums   Most Consecutive #1 Albums
Most #1 Albums   Longest Album Chart Careers

AUTHOR'S NOTE

I have long looked forward to publishing this first-ever compilation of research of *Billboard's* R&B albums chart. Finally, here in **Top R&B Albums** is the complete history, back to 1965, of R&B's best-selling albums from soul to funk to disco to rap. What fun it was to peruse the hits and misses of Stax soul, urban contemporary, New Jack Swing and cool jazz, and to note the following characteristics of *Billboard's* R&B albums chart.

* Artists never wearing out their welcome on the chart are The Isley Brothers, Aretha Franklin and The Temptations. Regular charters on smaller labels included Clarence Carter, Johnnie Taylor, and Little Milton.

* Jazz maintained a regular presence through the years thanks to Billy Cobham, Hugh Masekela, The Rippingtons, Freddie Hubbard, Miles Davis, George Howard, Gerald Albright, Najee, and Jimmy Smith.

* Another constant has been the long-play contributions of vocal groups such as the Chi-Lites, TLC, The Dramatics, The Supremes, The Dells, Xscape, The Stylistics, Boyz II Men, SWV, and All-4-One.

* Bass groups in the early '90s who tested the limits of subwoofers were Bass Boy, Bass Outlaws, Bass Patrol, DJ Magic Mike, and Techmaster P.E.B.

* With the exponential growth of rap in the '90s came the proliferation of labels founded by newer artists. Albums from the stable of Master P's No Limit label and Puff Daddy's Bad Boy label frequented the Top 10 of the chart.

* The R&B Albums chart witnessed the mainstream revival of gospel music with the popularity of Kirk Franklin, the Winans family, William Becton, Commissioned, and Take 6.

* Making rather curious appearances on the chart in the late '60s and early '70s were Led Zeppelin, The Osmonds, Vanilla Fudge, and MC5.

* Zapp, Ohio Players, Bar-Kays, Dazz Band, Mtume, and the Parliament/Funkadelic aggregation fueled the fire of funk.

* Suppliers of smooth grooves included Luther Vandross, Peabo Bryson, Roberta Flack, Sade, Freddie Jackson, Randy Crawford, R. Kelly, Anita Baker, and Barry White.

* Infusing humor on to the chart were comedians Bill Cosby, Skillet & Leroy, Richard Pryor, Moms Mabley, Eddie Murphy, Blowfly, and Redd Foxx.

* Representers of reggae included Third World, Buju Banton, Shabba Ranks, Bob Marley, and Mega Banton.

* And, only here will you find chart listings for author Alex Haley, actor Philip Michael Thomas, and NBA veteran Wayman Tisdale.

These are only a handful of thousands of findings. I invite you to pore over this ripe, new research and launch your own new discoveries. And so with great pleasure, I present to you the premiere edition of **Top R&B Albums**.

JOEL WHITBURN

1965-1998
SYNOPSIS OF THE *BILLBOARD* R&B ALBUMS CHART

Date	Positions	Chart Title
1/30/65 (chart debut)	10	HOT R&B LP's
6/5/65	10	TOP SELLING R&B LP's
3/12/66	20	TOP SELLING R&B LP's
8/6/66	25	TOP SELLING R&B LP's
4/15/67	30	TOP SELLING R&B LP's
1/13/68	30	BEST SELLING R&B LP's
4/6/68	50	BEST SELLING RHYTHM & BLUES LP's
8/23/69	50	BEST SELLING SOUL LP's
8/26/72 to 10/7/72		No *Soul LPs* Charts Published
10/14/72	50	BEST SELLING SOUL LP's
7/7/73	60	BEST SELLING SOUL LP's
7/14/73	60	SOUL LP's
11/25/78	75	SOUL LPs
6/26/82	75	BLACK LPs
10/20/84	75	TOP BLACK ALBUMS
9/3/88	100	TOP BLACK ALBUMS
10/27/90	100	TOP R&B ALBUMS
12/5/92*	100	TOP R&B ALBUMS

The research of this book begins on January 30, 1965, with *Billboard* magazine's first R&B Albums chart. Every album that hit the R&B Albums chart from 1965 through 1998 appears in this book.

From 1976 through 1991, *Billboard* did not publish an issue on the final week of the year. The last published chart of the year was considered "frozen" and all chart positions of that final issue remained the same for the unpublished week. This frozen chart data is included in our tabulations. Since 1992, *Billboard* has compiled an R&B Albums chart for the last week of the year, even though an issue is not published. This chart is available through *Billboard's* computerized information network or by mail. Our tabulations include this unpublished chart data.

Billboard's compilation of the R&B Albums chart has always been based on album sales. For over 30 years, *Billboard* tallied the R&B Albums chart from rankings of best-selling albums as reported by a representative sampling of stores nationwide.

*On December 5, 1992, *Billboard* ushered in a new era in the compilation of its sales-based R&B Albums chart. *Billboard* now compiles the R&B Albums chart based on actual units sold data as collected by point-of-sale scanning machines which read the album's UPC bar code. The music research firm SoundScan, Inc. provides *Billboard* with the actual sales of all albums from a continually revised representative sampling of stores.

All dates within *Top R&B Albums* refer to the issue dates of *Billboard* magazine. Keep in mind that the R&B Albums chart reports on albums sales from the seven-day period ending approximately 13 days prior. For example, *Billboard* compiled its *Top R&B Albums* chart dated November 28, 1998 (Saturday) from sales reports covering a seven-day period ending November 15, 1998 (Sunday).

The Artist Section lists by artist name, alphabetically, every album that charted on *Billboard* magazine's R&B Albums chart from January 30, 1965 through December 26, 1998. (See page vi for a chart synopsis.) Each artist's charted hits are listed in chronological order and are sequentially numbered. Listed below each Top 10 album are its tracks in order of their appearance on the album. (See page ix for further explanation.)

EXPLANATION OF COLUMNAR HEADINGS

DEBUT: Date album first charted

PEAK: Highest charted position (highlighted in bold type)

WKS: Total weeks charted

Gold: RIAA-certified gold or platinum album

Pop #: Peak position attained on *Billboard's* Pop Albums charts

$: Current value of near-mint commercial copy

LABEL & NUMBER: Original label and number of album when charted

EXPLANATION OF SYMBOLS

★59★   Number next to an artist name denotes an artist's ranking among the Top 200 R&B Album Artists of All Time

[1]   Superior number to the right of the #1 or #2 peak position is the total weeks the album held that position

+   Plus symbol after the debut date indicates that album peaked in the year after it first charted

↑   Arrow symbol after the weeks charted total indicates that the album was still on the chart as of the July 31, 1999 research cut-off date

●   RIAA-certified gold album (500,000 units sold)

▲   RIAA-certified platinum album (1,000,000 units sold)

       The Recording Industry Association of America (RIAA) began certifying gold albums in 1958, platinum albums in 1976 and multi-platinum albums in 1984. Some record labels have never requested RIAA certification for albums which would have qualified for these awards.

       A superscript number to the right of the platinum triangle indicates album was awarded multi-platinum status (ex.: ▲³ indicates an album was certified triple platinum and sold three million units).

LETTER(S) IN BRACKETS AFTER TITLES

C - Comedy

E - Earlier Recordings/Releases

G - Greatest Hits

I - Instrumental Recording

K - Compilation

L - Live Recording

M - Mini Album (12" EP or lower-priced CD)

N - Novelty

OC - Original Cast

R - Reissue or re-release **with a new label number** of a previously charted album or Christmas re-release of album with or without the same label number

S - Movie Soundtrack

T - Talk/Spoken Word Recording

TV - Television Program Soundtrack

X - Christmas

TOP ALBUMS AT A GLANCE

All Top 10 albums are shaded with a gray background.

❶ marks all #1 albums.

For an artist that charted five or more albums, their highest-charting album is underlined. Ties are broken based on peak position, weeks at peak position and total weeks charted.

Listed under the biographies of prolific artists are their Top 3 or Top 5 albums:

Top 3 albums are listed if the artist charted at least 10 albums
Top 5 albums are listed if the artist charted at least 20 albums

ARTIST & TITLE NOTES

Below every artist name are notes about the artist. To conserve space in some artist biographies, the abbreviation "b:" for "born on" or "born in" and the abbreviation "d:" for "died on" are used. Directly under some album titles are notes indicating guest artists, the location of live recordings, the names of famous producers, etc. Duets and other important name variations are shown in bold capital letters. All movie, TV and album titles, and other major works, appear in italics.

Highlighted in bold type are the names of artists mentioned in the biographies and title notes (but not in Top 10 albums tracks listings) of other R&B Albums artists, if those mentioned artists had their own album listing elsewhere in this book. For example, **Janet Jackson**'s name is shown in bold type in Paula Abdul's biography. A name appears in bold only the first time it is referenced in an artist's biography.

As always, we gladly welcome any corrections/updates to our artist biographies or title notes (please include solid verification).

ARTIST'S TOP YEAR

The year of an artist's peak popularity (based primarily on yearly chart performance) appears to the right of the artist's name. Again, the top year is a reflection of chart performance and may not always include an artist's highest peaking chart hit or their hit with the most weeks charted.

ARTIST'S CONSECUTIVE TOP 10 ALBUMS

The peak positions of an artist's string of <u>five or more consecutive Top 10 albums</u> are shaded in a box, so you can quickly spot their hot streaks. A string is not broken by special releases, such as Christmas, Greatest Hits, Compilation, Live, Duet, and Soundtrack albums.

ARTIST PHOTOS / THE TOP 200 ARTISTS

A picture of each of the Top 50 artists appears next to their listing in the artist section with their overall ranking to the right of their name. The overall ranking of the Top 51–200 artists appear to the left of their names. The artist ranking system is explained on page 312.

LISTING OF TRACKS

Below each Top 10 album is a listing of its tracks in order of their appearance on the album.

All tracks that charted on *Billboard's* R&B Singles chart are highlighted in bold type with their peak position listed to the right in bold, italicized type. Only the version that charted appears in bold with its peak position; other versions of a chart hit do not.

If a song hit the charts as a B-side and never achieved its own highest position, then "flip" is listed to the right in bold, italicized type.

If the spelling on an R&B Singles-chart hit differs from the spelling listed on the album, we show the title's spelling as it appears on the single (and thus, as it appears in our *Top R&B Singles* book).

Tracks were taken from the vinyl releases of albums that charted prior to 1990.

For albums that charted from 1990 through 1998, the listed tracks refer to the album's release on compact disc.

If a track's spelling on the album label and album jacket conflict, the spelling from the label is usually shown unless the label spelling is proven incorrect.

ALBUM PRICING

The dollar amounts listed in the price column are estimates of the dealer-asking prices for *near-mint* commercial copies. Our prices are based on averages from sources around the country and the album's chart action. Albums that charted very low on the chart are generally worth more than a million-selling hit album. Chances are few were pressed; and, with the passage of time, these low-charting albums become quite scarce.

The prices shown apply only to near-mint vinyl albums or compact discs. A near-mint album is almost perfect. It is of extremely high grade and contains only a few tiny blemishes. Only careful scrutiny will reveal the minimal flaws of a near-mint album.

For albums that charted from 1965 through 1989, the album pricing corresponds to the *vinyl album* configuration. From 1990 on, the pricing refers to the *compact disc* configuration.

Prior to 1969, most albums were issued concurrently in both mono and stereo. When format is not specified by the manufacturer's prefix and/or number, the price reflects a low average of mono and stereo copies. In most cases, there is little or no difference between the two. Keep in mind that for some '60s albums, the stereo pressing is considerably rarer and thus more valuable than the mono. Conversely, several late '60s albums can be much more valuable in mono than in stereo.

Early limited pressings or variations from the original commercial release, such as promotional copies, mistakes or differentiations on the label, colored vinyl, etc. can vastly increase or, in <u>very</u> rare cases, decrease the price of the record. The price listed is for pressings of the album during its chart run. These prices do not apply to promotional copies that can be priced anywhere from slightly to significantly higher than the commercial releases.

Record prices vary from dealer to dealer. It is not unusual for prices of the same record of identical grade to fluctuate widely. Always remember that an album's true value is dependent on the demand for it and its availability.

ALBUMS BY ARTIST

Lists, alphabetically by artist name, every album that charted on *Billboard's* R&B Albums chart from January 30, 1965 through December 26, 1998.

DEBUT	PEAK	WKS	Gold	Album Title	Pop #	$	Label & Number

A

A+   '96
Born Andre Levins in 1983 in Hempstead, New York. Male rapper.

| 9/14/96 | 36 | 8 | | The Latch-Key Child .... | | $8 | Kedar/Universal 53005 |

AALIYAH   '97
Pronounced: ah-lee-yah. Born Aaliyah Haughton on 1/16/79 in Brooklyn, New York; raised in Detroit. Female singer/rapper.

| 6/11/94 | 3 | 41 | ▲ 1 | Age Ain't Nothing But A Number | 18 | $8 | Blackground 41533 |

produced by R. Kelly

Throw Your Hands Up • **Back & Forth** *[1]* • Age Ain't Nothing But A Number *[35]* • Down With The Clique • **At Your Best (You Are Love)** *[2]* • No One Knows How To Love Me Quite Like You Do • I'm So Into You • Street Thing • Young Nation • Old School • I'm Down

| 9/14/96+ | 2¹ | 71 | ▲² 2 | One In A Million | 18 | $8 | Blackground 92715 |

Beats 4 Da Streets • Hot Like Fire • One In A Million • A Girl Like You • **If Your Girl Only Knew** *[1]* • Choosey Lover • Got To Give It Up • 4 Page Letter • Everything's Gonna Be Alright • Giving You More • I Gotcha' Back • Never Givin' Up • Heartbroken • Never Comin' Back • Ladies In Da House • **The One I Gave My Heart To** *[8]* • Came To Give Love

AALON   '77
Born Aalon Butler. Male singer/songwriter/guitarist.

| 10/8/77 | 45 | 7 | | Cream City .... | | $10 | Arista 4127 |

ABBOTT, Gregory   '86
Born on 4/2/54 in New York City. Singer/songwriter.

| 10/4/86 | 5 | 38 | ● 1 | Shake You Down | 22 | $8 | Columbia 40437 |

I Got The Feelin' (It's Over) *[5]* • Say You Will • **Shake You Down** *[1]* • You're My Angel • Magic • Wait Until Tomorrow • Rhyme And Reason • I'll Find A Way

| 6/11/88 | 17 | 16 | 2 | I'll Prove It To You .... | 132 | $8 | Columbia 44087 |

ABDUL, Paula   '89
Born on 6/19/62 in Los Angeles. Singer/choreographer. Former cheerleader for the NBA's Los Angeles Lakers. Choreographed **Janet Jackson**'s *Control* videos and TV's *The Tracey Ullman Show*. Married to actor Emilio Estevez from 1992-94.

| 8/6/88+ | 10 | 97 | ▲⁷ 1 | Forever Your Girl | 1¹⁰ | $8 | Virgin 90943 |

(It's Just) The Way That You Love Me *[10]* • Knocked Out *[8]* • **Opposites Attract** *[3]* • State Of Attraction • I Need You • Forever Your Girl *[54]* • **Straight Up** *[2]* • Next To You • Cold Hearted • One Or The Other

| 6/9/90 | 65 | 14 | ▲ 2 | Shut Up And Dance (The Dance Mixes) .... [K] | 7 | $8 | Virgin 91362 |

remixes of her hits

| 6/1/91 | 31 | 27 | ▲³ 3 | Spellbound .... | 1² | $8 | Captive/Virgin 91611 |

ABOVE THE LAW   '93
Rap trio from Pamona, California: Don Hutchinson, Kevin Gulley and Anthony Stewart. Hutchinson is the nephew of **Willie Hutch**.

4/21/90	14	26	1	Livin' Like Hustlers	75	$8	Ruthless 46041
8/10/91	37	13	2	Vocally Pimpin' .... [M]	120	$6	Ruthless 47934
2/20/93	6	25	3	Black Mafia Life	37	$8	Ruthless 24477

Black Triangle • Never Missin' A Beat • Why Must I Feel Like Dat • Commin' Up • Pimpology 101 • Call It What U Want • Harda U R Tha Doppa U Faal • Game Wreck-Oniz-Iz Game • Pimp Clinic • **V.S.O.P.** *[97]* • Process Of Elimination (Untouchakickamurdaqtion) • G's & Macaronies • G-Rupies Best Friend • Mee Vs. My Ego

7/30/94	15	27	4	Uncle Sam's Curse	113	$8	Ruthless 5524
11/2/96	16	6	5	Time Will Reveal	80	$8	Tommy Boy 1154
3/14/98	27	8	6	Legends	142	$8	Tommy Boy 1233

ABRAMS, Colonel   '86
Born Colonel Abrams in Detroit; raised in New York City. Singer/songwriter.

| 1/25/86 | 13 | 34 | 1 | Colonel Abrams .... | 75 | $8 | MCA 5682 |
| 9/5/87 | 25 | 16 | 2 | You And Me Equals Us .... | | $8 | MCA 42029 |

ACE JUICE   '90
Male rap duo from Oakland: Ace Roberson and Juice Sneed.

| 1/6/90 | 43 | 12 | | Ace Juice .... | | $8 | Capitol 90925 |

ACE SPECTRUM   '74
Vocal group from New York City: Ed Zant, Aubrey Johnson, Elliot Isaac and Rudy Gay.

| 6/15/74 | 28 | 15 | 1 | Inner Spectrum .... | 209 | $12 | Atlantic 7299 |
| 8/16/75 | 35 | 8 | 2 | Low Rent Rendezvous .... | 138 | $12 | Atlantic 18143 |

ACKLIN, Barbara   '68
Born on 2/28/43 in Chicago. Died of pneumonia on 11/27/98 (age 55). Singer/songwriter. Formerly married to Eugene Record of **The Chi-Lites**.

| 10/5/68 | 48 | 4 | | Love Makes A Woman .... | 146 | $25 | Brunswick 754137 |

ADAMS, Gayle   '82
Born in Washington, DC. Female singer/songwriter.

| 3/20/82 | 55 | 5 | | Love Fever .... | | $8 | Prelude 14104 |

ADAMS, Oleta   '91
Born on 5/4/62 in Seattle. Female singer/pianist.

8/25/90+	11	53	● 1	Circle Of One	20	$8	Fontana 846346
8/21/93	20	26	2	Evolution	67	$8	Fontana 514965
11/25/95	49	4	3	Moving On	194	$8	Fontana 528684

3

ADC BAND   '79

Disco group: Audrey Matthews (vocals), Michael Judkins (vocals, keyboards), Pervis Johnson (guitar), Kublah Khan (congas), Mark Patterson (bass) and Artwell Matthews (drums).

12/9/78+	16	13		1 Long Stroke	139	$10	Cotillion 5210
9/1/79	62	8		2 Talk That Stuff		$10	Cotillion 5216
6/14/80	69	7		3 Renaissance		$10	Cotillion 5221

★195★   **ADDERLEY, Cannonball**   '67

Born Julian Adderley on 9/15/28 in Tampa, Florida. Died of a stroke on 8/8/75 (age 46). Alto saxophonist. His quintet consisted of brother Nat Adderley (cornet), Joe Zawinul (keyboards), Walter Booker (bass) and Roy McCurdy (drums). Zawinul later formed **Weather Report**.

THE CANNONBALL ADDERLEY QUINTET:

2/25/67	❶[1]	20		1 Mercy, Mercy, Mercy! [I-L]	13	$15	Capitol 2663

recorded at the Club De Lisa in Chicago
Fun • Games • **Mercy, Mercy, Mercy** [2] • Sticks • Hippodelphia • Sack O'Woe

6/10/67	18	7		2 Why Am I Treated So Bad! [I-L]	148	$15	Capitol 2617
2/3/68	26	2		3 74 Miles Away - Walk Tall [I-L]	186	$15	Capitol 2822

above 2 recorded in Hollywood

3/21/70	7	23		4 Country Preacher [I-L]	136	$15	Capitol 404

recorded in Chicago; introduction by Rev. Jesse Jackson
Walk Tall • **Country Preacher** [29] • Hummin' • Oh Babe • Afro-Spanish Omelet • The Scene

CANNONBALL ADDERLEY:

7/22/72	11	5		5 Soul Zodiac	74	$15	Capitol 11025 [2]

featuring the Nat Adderley Sextet; narration by Rick Holmes

5/18/74	48	4		6 Love, Sex And The Zodiac [I]		$12	Fantasy 9445
12/7/74+	45	8		7 Pyramid [I]		$12	Fantasy 9455
8/16/75	24	12		8 Phenix [I]	121	$15	Fantasy 79004 [2]
11/8/75	59	2		9 Big Man		$15	Fantasy 79006 [2]

concept album based on the life of John Henry

AFRIQUE   '73

Instrumental session group featuring **David T. Walker** (guitar) and Chuck Rainey (bass).

6/23/73	33	9		Soul Makossa [I]	152	$12	Mainstream 394

AFRO-BLUES QUINTET PLUS ONE, The   '66

Instrumental group: Jack Fulks (saxophone), Joe De Aguero (vibes), Bill Henderson (piano), Moses Obligacion (congas), Norm Johnson (bass) and Michael Davis (drums).

8/6/66	23	3		Introducing The Afro-Blues Quintet Plus One [I]		$20	Mirwood 3002

AFRO-RICAN   '90

Rap trio from Miami: Derrick Rahming, Juan Arroyo and Mark Rice.

12/2/89+	79	10		Against All Odds		$8	Luke Skyywalker 109

AFROS, The   '90

Rap trio from New York City: Hurricane, Kool Tee and DJ Kippy-O.

9/15/90	57	22		Kickin' Afrolistics		$8	Columbia 46802

AFTER 7   '90

Vocal trio from Indianapolis: Keith Mitchell with brothers Kevon and Melvin Edmonds. Keith is the cousin of producer L.A. Reid. Kevon and Melvin are the brothers of **Babyface**.

9/16/89+	3	78	▲	1 After 7	35	$8	Virgin 91061

Don't Cha' Think [25] • Heat Of The Moment [5] • Can't Stop [1] • My Only Woman [36] • Love's Been So Nice • One Night • Ready Or Not [1] • Sayonara

9/12/92	8	50	●	2 Takin' My Time	76	$8	Virgin 86349

All About Love • Kickin' It [6] • Can He Love U Like This [22] • Truly Something Special [49] • Baby I'm For Real [5] • No Better Love • Takin' My Time • G.S.T. • Love By Day, Love By Night • He Said, She Said

8/5/95	7	31	●	3 Reflections	40	$8	Virgin 40547

produced by **Babyface** and **Jon B.**
'Til You Do Me Right [5] • Cryin For It • Save It Up • **Damn Thing Called Love** [33] • How Did He Love You • What U R 2 Me • **How Do You Tell The One** [60] • Sprung On It • How Could You Leave • Givin Up This Good Thing • I Like It Like That • Honey (Oh How I Need You)

3/29/97	24	15		4 The Very Best Of After 7 [G]	97	$8	Virgin 42756

A-G-2-A-KE   '98

Rap trio from Milwaukee: 88 Keyz, G-Mone and Mac Fee.

9/12/98	37	5		Mil-Ticket		$8	Rap-A-Lot 46144

AHMAD   '94

Born Ahmad Ali Lewis in 1975 in Los Angeles. Male rapper.

6/11/94	48	15		Ahmad		$8	Giant 24548

AKINYELE   '96

Pronounced: Ah-kin-el-e. Born Akinyele Adams in New York City. Male rapper.

9/4/93	83	1		1 Vagina Diner		$8	Interscope 92236
8/31/96	18	47		2 Put It In Your Mouth (a.k.a. fella) [M]	127	$6	Stress 11142

ALBRIGHT, Gerald   '88

Born in 1957 in Los Angeles. Saxophonist.

12/12/87+	21	25		1 Just Between Us [I]	181	$8	Atlantic 81813
11/26/88+	53	22		2 Bermuda Nights [I]		$8	Atlantic 81919
12/15/90+	50	23		3 Dream Come True [I]		$8	Atlantic 82087
3/12/94	25	29		4 Smooth [I]	151	$8	Atlantic 82552
11/15/97	59	3		5 Live To Love [I]		$8	Atlantic 83050
10/17/98	36	27		6 Pleasures Of The Night	169	$8	Verve Forecast 557613

WILL DOWNING & GERALD ALBRIGHT

AL B. SURE! '88

Born Al Brown in 1969 in Boston; raised in Mt. Vernon, New York. Singer/songwriter.

DEBUT	PEAK	WKS	Gold	Album Title	Pop #	$	Label & Number
5/21/88	❶[7]	57	▲	1 **In Effect Mode**	20	$8	Warner 25662

Nite And Day [1] • Oooh This Love Is So • **Killing Me Softly** [14] • Naturally Mine • **Rescue Me** [3] • Off On Your Own (Girl) [1] • If I'm Not Your Lover [2] • Just A Taste Of Lovin'

| 11/10/90 | 4 | 37 | ● | 2 **Private Times...And The Whole 9!** | 20 | $8 | Warner 26005 |

Hotel California • Touch You • So Special • I Want To Know • No Matter What You Do • Shades Of Grey • Private Times • **Missunderstanding** [1] • Channel J • Had Enuf? [28] • Just For The Moment • Sure! Thang • You Excite Me • Ooh This Jazz Is So

| 10/10/92 | 2[1] | 26 | | 3 **Sexy Versus** | 41 | $8 | Warner 26973 |

Right Now [1] • U & I • Playing Games • **Natalie** [56] • Ooh 4 You Girl • Kick In The Head • Turn You Out • See The Lady • Thanks 4 A Great Time Last Nite • **I Don't Wanna Cry** [83] • Die For You • I'll Never Hurt You Again • Papes In The End

ALEEM '86

Trio from New York City: twin brothers Taharqa (guitar) and Tunde-Ra (keyboards) Aleem with Leroy Burgess (vocals).

| 4/26/86 | 45 | 8 | | Casually Formal .... | | $8 | Atlantic 81622 |

ALEEM FEATURING LEROY BURGESS

ALFONZO '83

Born Alfonzo Jones in Los Angeles.

| 2/19/83 | 50 | 8 | | Alfonzo .... | | $10 | Larc 8101 |

ALI, Tatyana '98

Born on 1/24/79 in Long Island, New York. Singer/actress. Played "Ashley" on TV's *The Fresh Prince Of Bel-Air*.

| 9/12/98 | 47 | 14 | | Kiss The Sky .... | 106 | $8 | MJJ Music 68656 |

ALKAHOLIKS, Tha '95

Rap trio from Los Angeles: James Robinson, Rico Smith and Eric Brooks.

9/11/93	23	18		1 21 & Over	124	$8	Loud/RCA 66280
3/18/95	12	12		2 Coast II Coast	50	$8	Loud/RCA 66446
9/13/97	15	8		3 Likwidation	57	$8	Loud/RCA 67435

ALL CITY '98

Rap duo from New York City: J. Mega and Greg Valentine.

| 11/21/98 | 42 | 3 | | Metropolis Gold .... | | $8 | MCA 11829 |

ALLEN, Donna '89

Born in Key West, Florida; raised in Tampa. Former cheerleader for the NFL's Tampa Bay Buccaneers.

| 2/14/87 | 33 | 25 | | 1 Perfect Timing .... | 133 | $8 | 21 Records 90548 |
| 12/10/88+ | 28 | 25 | | 2 Heaven On Earth .... | | $8 | Oceana 91028 |

ALLEN, Rance '91

Born in 1949 in Detroit. Singer/guitarist/keyboardist. His group included his brothers Steven (bass) and Tom (drums) Allen.

8/2/75	35	5		1 A Soulful Experience		$12	Truth 4207
6/9/79	74	2		2 Straight From The Heart		$10	Stax 4109
10/20/79	69	2		3 Smile		$10	Stax 4127
8/10/91	33	16		4 Phenomenon		$8	Bellmark 71806

THE RANCE ALLEN GROUP (above 2)

ALL-4-ONE '94

Male vocal group from Los Angeles: Jamie Jones, Delious Kennedy, Alfred Nevarez and Tony Borowiak.

4/30/94	12	45	▲[2]	1 All-4-One	7	$8	Blitzz/Atlantic 82588
6/24/95	31	24	▲	2 And The Music Speaks	27	$8	Blitzz/Atlantic 82746
12/23/95+	87	3		3 An All-4-One Christmas .... [X]	91	$8	Blitzz/Atlantic 82846

ALLFRUMTHA I '98

Male rap duo from Inglewood, California: Binky and Squeak.

| 5/23/98 | 32 | 5 | | AllFrumTha I .... | 168 | $8 | Priority 50588 |

ALLURE '97

Female vocal group from New York City: Alia Davis, Akissa Mendez, Lalisha McLean and Linnie Belcher.

| 5/24/97 | 23 | 38 | ● | Allure .... | 108 | $8 | Crave 67848 |

ALMIGHTY RSO, The '96

Rap group from Dorchester, Massachusetts: Anthony Johnson, Marco Ennis, Raymond Scott and DJ Deff Jeff. RSO: Real Solid Organization.

| 10/15/94 | 97 | 1 | | 1 Revenge Uv Da Badd Boyz .... | | $8 | RCA 66444 |
| 12/7/96 | 52 | 2 | | 2 Doomsday: Forever RSO .... | | $8 | Rap-A-Lot 42270 |

ALPERT, Herb '87

Born on 3/31/35 in Los Angeles. Trumpeter/songwriter/producer. Formed A&M record label in 1962 and Almo Sounds label in 1994. Charted 27 pop albums from 1962-87.

| 10/13/79 | 6 | 31 | ▲ | 1 Rise .... [I] | 6 | $10 | A&M 4790 |

1980 • **Rise** [4] • Behind The Rain • **Rotation** [20] • Street Life [65] • Love Is • Angelina • Aranjuez (Mon Amour)

7/26/80	26	11		2 Beyond .... [I]	28	$8	A&M 3717
8/22/81	39	10		3 Magic Man .... [I]	61	$8	A&M 3728
8/21/82	52	6		4 Fandango .... [I]	100	$8	A&M 3731
9/24/83	49	9		5 Blow Your Own Horn .... [I]	120	$8	A&M 4949
4/4/87	5	30	●	6 Keep Your Eye On Me .... [I]	18	$8	A&M 5125

Keep Your Eye On Me [3] • Hot Shot • **Diamonds** [1] • Traffic Jam • Cat Man Do • Pillow • Our Song • **Making Love In The Rain** [7] • Rocket To The Moon • Stranger On The Shore

| 4/6/91 | 51 | 15 | | 7 North On South St. .... [I] | | $8 | A&M 5345 |

ALSTON, Gerald '90
Born on 11/8/42 in North Carolina. Lead singer of **The Manhattans** from 1971-88.

12/10/88+	18	33		1 Gerald Alston		$8	Motown 6265
10/20/90	14	33		2 Open Invitation		$8	Motown 6298
11/21/92	62	2		3 Always In The Mood		$8	Motown 6353
10/15/94	93	1		4 First Class Only		$8	Street Life 75441

AMERICA'S MOST WANTED '91
Rap trio from Los Angeles: Tyrell Brewer, Charles Mack and Chris Wilson.

3/16/91	66	14		Criminals		$8	Triad 2222

AMG '92
Born Jason Lewis in New York City. Male rapper.

12/14/91+	20	35	●	1 Bitch Betta Have My Money	63	$8	Select 21642
6/24/95	22	7		2 Ballin' Outta Control	100	$8	Select 21654

AMMONS, Gene '71
Born Eugene Ammons on 4/14/25 in Chicago. Died of cancer on 8/6/74 (age 49). Tenor saxophonist. Nicknamed "Jug." Son of boogie-woogie pianist Albert Ammons.

5/8/71	33	6		1 The Black Cat!	[I]	$15	Prestige 10006
1/29/72	35	7		2 My Way	[I]	$15	Prestige 10022

ANDERSON, Carl '86
Born on 2/27/45 in Lynchburg, Virginia. Singer/actor. Played "Judas" in the original Broadway cast and movie version of *Jesus Christ Superstar*.

9/13/86	49	8		1 Carl Anderson	87	$8	Epic 40410
7/14/90	50	9		2 Pieces Of A Heart		$8	GRP 9612

ANGELOU, Maya — see ASHFORD & SIMPSON

ANGIE & DEBBIE '93
Duo of sisters Angie and Debbie Winans. Part of the gospel family group **The Winans**.

9/11/93	73	7		Angie & Debbie		$8	Capitol 95582

ANNE G. '89
Born in Tennessee. Singer/keyboardist.

5/20/89	67	8		On A Mission		$8	Atlantic 81946

ANOTHA LEVEL '94
Rap group from Los Angeles: Ced Twice, Stenge, Bambino, Stix and Stones.

5/14/94	60	9		On Anotha Level		$8	Priority 53867

ANOTHER BAD CREATION '91
Male vocal group from Atlanta: Chris Sellers, Dave Shelton, Romell Chapman, with brothers Marliss and Demetrius Pugh. Group appeared in the movie *The Meteor Man*.

3/9/91	2⁴	35	▲	**coolin' at the PLAYGROUND ya' know!**	7	$8	Motown 6318

Parents • Playground [4] • Mental (So Pay Attention) • Little Soldiers • My World [77] • Iesha [6] • Spydermann • That's My Girl • Jealous Girl [25] • ABC

ANQUETTE '89
Born Anquette Allen in Miami. Female rapper.

12/3/88+	41	27		Respect		$8	Luke Skyywalker 103

ANTOINETTE '89
Born Antoinette Patterson. Female rapper.

6/24/89	47	18		1 Who's The Boss?		$8	Next Plateau 1015
7/7/90	66	10		2 Burnin' At 20 Below		$8	Next Plateau 1021

APACHE '93
Born Anthony Teaks in Jersey City, New Jersey. Male rapper.

2/27/93	15	12		Apache Ain't Shit	69	$8	Tommy Boy 1068

APOLLONIA 6 '84
Female R&B trio formed by **Prince**. Led by Patty "Apollonia" Kotero (co-star of movie *Purple Rain* and cast member of TV's *Falcon Crest*, 1985-86). With former **Vanity 6** members Brenda Bennett and Susan Moonsie.

10/27/84	24	21		Apollonia 6	62	$8	Warner 25108

ARABIAN PRINCE '90
Born Michael Lezan in Compton, California. Former member of **Bobby Jimmy & The Critters**.

12/2/89+	55	16		Brother Arab	193	$8	Orpheus 75614

ARMATRADING, Joan '80
Born on 12/9/50 in St. Kitts, West Indies; raised in Birmingham, England. Singer/songwriter/guitarist.

6/14/80	52	12		Me Myself I	28	$10	A&M 4809

ARMSTRONG, Vanessa Bell '93
Born on 10/2/53 in Detroit. Gospel singer.

3/13/93	75	5		1 Something On The Inside		$8	Jive 41468
9/2/95	77	1		2 The Secret Is Out		$8	Verity 43011

ARPEGGIO '79
One-woman, three-man disco studio group.

3/17/79	43	9		Let The Music Play	75	$10	Polydor 6180

DEBUT	PEAK	WKS	Gold	Album Title	Pop #	$	Label & Number

ARRESTED DEVELOPMENT   '92

Hip-hop group from Atlanta: Todd "Speech" Thomas, Dionne Farris, Aerle Taree, Tim Barnwell, Montsho Eshe, Donald Jones and Baba Oje. Won the 1992 Best New Artist Grammy Award.

DEBUT	PEAK	WKS	Gold	Album Title	Pop #	$	Label & Number
4/18/92	3	73	▲⁴	1 3 Years, 5 Months & 2 Days In The Life Of ...	7	$8	Chrysalis 21929

title refers to the length of time between group's formation and the signing of its recording contract
Man's Final Frontier • Mama's Always On Stage • People Everyday [2] • Blues Happy • Mr. Wendal [6] • Children Play With Earth • Raining Revolution • Fishin' 4 Religion • Give A Man A Fish • U • Eve Of Reality • Natural [90] • Dawn Of The Dreads • Tennessee [1] • Washed Away

| 4/10/93 | 38 | 9 | ● | 2 Unplugged .... [L] | 60 | $8 | Chrysalis 21994 |

recorded on January 6, 1993

| 7/2/94 | 20 | 10 | | 3 Zingalamaduni | 55 | $8 | Chrysalis 29274 |

title is Swahili for "Beehive of Culture"

ARRINGTON, Steve   '83

Born in Dayton, Ohio. Singer/drummer. Former member of Slave.

| 3/5/83 | 12 | 31 | | 1 Steve Arrington's Hall Of Fame: I | 101 | $8 | Atlantic 80049 |
| 2/18/84 | 36 | 11 | | 2 Positive Power | 141 | $8 | Atlantic 80127 |

STEVE ARRINGTON'S HALL OF FAME (above 2)

| 4/27/85 | 32 | 31 | | 3 Dancin' In The Key Of Life | 185 | $8 | Atlantic 81245 |
| 10/10/87 | 50 | 7 | | 4 Jam Packed | | $8 | Manhattan 46903 |

ARTIFACTS   '94

Rap duo from Newark, New Jersey: El The Sensai and Tame One.

| 11/12/94 | 17 | 5 | | 1 Between A Rock And A Hard Place | 137 | $8 | Big Beat 92397 |
| 5/3/97 | 25 | 6 | | 2 That's Them | 134 | $8 | Big Beat 92753 |

ARTISTS UNITED AGAINST APARTHEID   '85

Benefit group of 49 superstar artists formed to protest the South African apartheid government; proceeds went to political prisoners in South Africa. Organized by Steve Van Zant and Arthur Baker.

| 11/30/85 | 28 | 19 | | Sun City | 31 | $8 | Manhattan 53019 |

ART N' SOUL   '96

Trio from Oakland: Tracy (vocals, bass), Lattrel (keyboards) and Dion (drums).

| 4/13/96 | 36 | 10 | | Touch Of Soul | | $8 | Big Beat 92655 |

ART OF NOISE, The   '84

British techno-pop trio: Anne Dudley (keyboards), J.J. Jeczalik (keyboards, programmer) and Gary Langan (engineer).

3/31/84	21	22		1 Into Battle With The Art Of Noise		$8	Island 96974
6/30/84	22	14		2 (Who's Afraid Of?) The Art Of Noise!	85	$8	Island 90179
5/31/86	49	11		3 In Visible Silence	53	$8	Chrysalis 41528

ASHFORD & SIMPSON   ★55★   '85

Husband-and-wife vocal/songwriting duo: Nickolas Ashford (b: 5/4/43 in Fairfield, South Carolina) and Valerie Simpson (b: 8/26/48 in New York City). Joined staff at Motown and wrote and produced for many of the label's top stars. They married in 1974. Valerie's brother, Ray Simpson, was the lead singer of the Village People.

1) Solid 2)Is It Still Good To Ya 3)Stay Free

10/20/73+	18	17		1 Gimme Something Real	156	$10	Warner 2739
7/27/74	21	12		2 I Wanna Be Selfish	195	$10	Warner 2789
4/10/76	35	14		3 Come As You Are	189	$10	Warner 2858
1/29/77	30	17		4 So So Satisfied	180	$10	Warner 2992
10/15/77	10	39	●	5 Send It	52	$10	Warner 3088

By Way Of Love's Express [35] • Let Love Use Me • Don't Cost You Nothing [10] • Send It [15] • Top Of The Stairs • Too Bad • Bourgie Bourgie • I Waited Too Long

| 9/9/78 | ❶¹ | 33 | ● | 6 Is It Still Good To Ya | 20 | $10 | Warner 3219 |

It Seems To Hang On [2] • Is It Still Good To Ya [12] • The Debt Is Settled • Ain't It A Shame • Get Up And Do Something • You Always Could • Flashback [70] • As Long As It Holds You

| 9/1/79 | 3 | 27 | ● | 7 Stay Free | 23 | $10 | Warner 3357 |

Found A Cure [2] • Stay Free • Dance Forever • Nobody Knows [19] • Crazy • Finally Got To Me • Follow Your Heart

| 8/23/80 | 8 | 23 | | 8 A Musical Affair | 38 | $10 | Warner 3458 |

Love Don't Make It Right [6] • Rushing To • I Ain't Asking For Your Love • Make It To The Sky • We'll Meet Again • You Never Left Me Alone • Get Out Your Handkerchief [65] • Happy Endings [35]

| 10/24/81 | 45 | 8 | | 9 Performance .... [L] | 125 | $12 | Warner 3524 [2] |

3 of 4 sides recorded live

| 6/5/82 | 5 | 26 | | 10 Street Opera | 45 | $8 | Capitol 12207 |

Love It Away [20] • Make It Work Again • Mighty Mighty Love • I'll Take The Whole World On • Working Man • Who Will They Look To • Street Corner [9] • Times Will Be Good Again

| 9/17/83 | 14 | 28 | | 11 High-Rise | 84 | $8 | Capitol 12282 |
| 11/17/84+ | ❶⁴ | 43 | | 12 Solid | 29 | $8 | Capitol 12366 |

Solid [1] • Outta The World [4] • The Jungle • Honey I Love You • Babies [29] • Closest To Love • Cherish Forever More • Tonight We Escape (We Make Love)

9/27/86	12	21		13 Real Love	74	$8	Capitol 12469
3/18/89	28	20		14 Love Or Physical	135	$8	Capitol 46946
11/2/96	49	12		15 Been Found		$8	Hopsack & Silk 4512

ASHFORD & SIMPSON WITH MAYA ANGELOU
Angelou is a famed female poet/novelist

ASSAULT & BATTERY   '92

| 2/15/92 | 63 | 12 | | Assault & Battery | | $8 | Attitude 14001 |

ASWAD   '88

British reggae trio: Brinsley Forde (vocals), Courtney Hemmings (keyboards) and Tony Gad (drums). Aswad is Arabic for "black."

| 9/3/88 | 41 | 13 | | Distant Thunder | 173 | $8 | Mango 9810 |

DEBUT	PEAK	WKS	Gold	Album Title		Pop #	$	Label & Number
				ATLANTA DISCO BAND, The '76				
				Disco studio group from Atlanta assembled by producer Dave Crawford. Includes members of **MFSB**.				
1/31/76	46	6		Bad Luck		172	$10	Ariola America 50004
	★95★			**ATLANTIC STARR** '82				
				Group from White Plains, New York: brothers Wayne (vocals, keyboards), Jonathan (trumpet) and David (vocals, guitar) Lewis, with **Sharon Bryant** (vocals), Clifford Archer (bass) and Porter Carroll (drums). **Barbara Weathers** replaced Bryant in 1984. Porscha Martin replaced Weathers in 1989. Rachel Oliver replaced Martin in 1991. Aisha Tanner replaced Oliver in 1993.				
				1)*Brilliance* 2)*As The Band Turns* 3)*All In The Name Of Love*				
8/19/78	21	21		1 Atlantic Starr		67	$10	A&M 4711
6/2/79	65	3		2 Straight To The Point		142	$10	A&M 4764
3/14/81	5	38		3 Radiant		47	$8	A&M 4833
				When Love Calls *[5]* • Does It Matter • Think About That • **Send For Me** *[16]* • Mystery Girl • Am I Dreaming • Under Pressure • My Turn Now				
3/27/82	❶³	38		4 Brilliance		18	$8	A&M 4883
				Love Me Down *[14]* • Sexy Dancer • Love Moves • Your Love Finally Ran Out • Circles *[2]* • Let's Get Closer • **Perfect Love** *[32]* • You're The One				
11/12/83	10	36		5 Yours Forever		91	$8	A&M 4948
				Yours Forever • **Touch A Four Leaf Clover** *[4]* • More, More, More *[11]* • I Want Your Love • **Second To None** *[50]* • Island Dream • Who Could Love You Better? • More Time For Me • Tryin'				
5/18/85+	3	74	●	6 As The Band Turns		17	$8	A&M 5019
				Freak-A-Ristic *[6]* • Cool, Calm, Collected *[33]* • One Love • In The Heat Of Passion • If Your Heart Isn't In It *[4]* • Silver Shadow *[13]* • Let's Start It Over • **Secret Lovers** *[4]* • Thank You				
5/2/87	4	32	●	7 All In The Name Of Love		18	$8	Warner 25560
				One Lover At A Time *[10]* • You Belong With Me • Females • Don't Take Me For Granted • **Always** *[1]* • Let The Sun In • Thankful *[65]* • All In The Name Of Love *[51]* • My Mistake				
5/20/89	26	22		8 We're Movin' Up		125	$8	Warner 25849
11/23/91+	25	30		9 Love Crazy		134	$8	Reprise 26545
6/11/94	80	2		10 Time			$8	Arista 18723
				AUDIO TWO '88				
				Rap duo from New York City: brothers Kirk and Gene Robinson.				
5/28/88	45	13		1 What More Can I Say?		185	$8	First Priority 90907
6/16/90	74	6		2 I Don't Care-The Album			$8	First Priority 91358
				AUGER, Brian '70				
				Born on 7/18/39 in Bihar, India; raised in London. Jazz-rock keyboardist.				
9/26/70	46	2		1 Befour		184	$12	RCA Victor 4372
				BRIAN AUGER & THE TRINITY				
10/13/73	59	2		2 Closer To It!		64	$10	RCA Victor 0140
11/8/75	51	3		3 Reinforcements		115	$10	RCA Victor 1210
				BRIAN AUGER'S OBLIVION EXPRESS (above 2)				
				AURRA '82				
				Male-female vocal duo from Dayton, Ohio: Curt Jones and Starleana Young. Young was a member of **Slave**. Duo later changed name to Déjà. Mysti Day replaced Young in 1988.				
5/30/81	22	21		1 Send Your Love		103	$10	Salsoul 8538
2/20/82	12	18		2 A Little Love		38	$10	Salsoul 8551
2/26/83	36	10		3 Live And Let Live		208	$10	Salsoul 8559
10/31/87	27	24		4 Serious		186	$8	Virgin 90601
6/3/89	96	2		5 Made To Be Together			$8	Virgin 91060
				DÉJÀ (above 2)				
				AUSTIN, Patti '83				
				Born on 8/10/48 in New York City. R&B-jazz singer/actress. Former session and commercial jingle singer.				
7/26/80	62	4		1 Body Language		208	$10	CTI 36503
10/10/81+	16	55		2 Every Home Should Have One		36	$8	Qwest 3591
7/9/83	65	3		3 In My Life			$10	CTI 9009
3/31/84	25	17		4 Patti Austin		87	$8	Qwest 23974
11/23/85+	25	36		5 Gettin' Away With Murder		182	$8	Qwest 25276
9/3/88	56	14		6 The Real Me			$8	Qwest 25696
4/28/90	45	15		7 Love Is Gonna Getcha		93	$8	GRP 9603
12/7/91+	75	11		8 Carry On			$8	GRP 9660
	★109★			**AVERAGE WHITE BAND** '75				
				Vocal/instrumental group from Scotland: Alan Gorrie (vocals, bass), Onnie McIntyre (guitar, vocals), Hamish Stuart (guitar, vocals), Malcolm Duncan (saxophone), Roger Ball (saxophone, keyboards) and Robbie McIntosh (drums). McIntosh died of a drug overdose on 9/23/74 (age 24), replaced by Steve Ferrone. Disbanded in 1983. Group re-formed in 1988 with Gorrie, McIntyre, Ball and Alex Ligertwood (former lead singer with Santana).				
				1)*AWB* 2)*Cut The Cake* 3)*Soul Searching*				
12/28/74+	❶³	24	●	1 AWB		1¹	$10	Atlantic 7308
				You Got It • Got The Love • **Pick Up The Pieces** *[5]* • Person To Person • Work To Do • Nothing You Can Do • Just Wanna Love You Tonight • Keepin' It To Myself • I Just Can't Give You Up • There's Always Someone Waiting				
4/12/75	39	5		2 Put It Where You Want It ....[E]		39	$10	MCA 475
				first released in 1973 as *Show Your Hand* on MCA 345 ($20)				
6/21/75	❶¹	16	●	3 Cut The Cake		4	$10	Atlantic 18140
				Cut The Cake *[7]* • School Boy Crush *[22]* • It's A Mystery • Groovin' The Night Away • If I Ever Lose This Heaven *[25]* • Why • High Flyin' Woman • Cloudy • How Sweet How Can It Get • When They Bring Down The Curtain				
7/17/76	2²	26	▲	4 Soul Searching		9	$10	Atlantic 18179
				Love Your Life • I'm The One • **A Love Of Your Own** *[35]* • **Queen Of My Soul** *[21]* • Soul Searching • Goin' Home • Everybody's Darling • Would You Stay • Sunny Days (Make Me Think Of You) • Digging Deeper				

DEBUT	PEAK	WKS	Gold	Album Title	Pop #	$	Label & Number
				AVERAGE WHITE BAND — Cont'd			
1/22/77	9	16	●	5 Person To Person .... [L]	28	$12	Atlantic 1002 [2]
				recorded in Philadelphia, Pittsburgh and Cleveland			
				Person To Person • Cut The Cake • If I Ever Lose This Heaven • **Cloudy** [55] • T.L.C. • I'm The One • Pick Up The Pieces • Love Your Life • School Boy Crush • I Heard It Through The Grapevine			
7/30/77	14	19		6 Benny And Us	33	$10	Atlantic 19105
				AVERAGE WHITE BAND & BEN E. KING			
4/1/78	12	15	●	7 Warmer Communications	28	$10	Atlantic 19162
4/7/79	30	12		8 Feel No Fret	32	$10	Atlantic 19207
5/31/80	38	16		9 Shine	116	$10	Arista 9523
8/14/82	49	5		10 Cupid's In Fashion	202	$10	Arista 9594
2/4/89	69	6		11 Aftershock		$10	Track 58830
				AWESOME DRÉ **'89**			
				Born Andre Acker in Los Angeles. Male rapper.			
7/8/89	52	15		You Can't Hold Me Back		$8	Bentley 12001
				AWESOME DRÉ & THE HARDCORE COMMITTEE			
	★75★			**AYERS, Roy** **'77**			
				Born on 9/10/40 in Los Angeles. Singer/vibraphone player/keyboardist. With **Herbie Mann** from 1966-70.			
				1)Lifeline 2)Everybody Loves The Sunshine 3)Vibrations			
1/31/76	13	22		1 Mystic Voyage	90	$10	Polydor 6057
8/14/76	10	19		2 Everybody Loves The Sunshine	51	$10	Polydor 6070
				Hey Uh-What You Say Come On • **The Golden Rod** [70] • Keep On Walking • You And Me My Love • The Third Eye • It Ain't Your Sign It's Your Mind • People And The World • Everybody Loves The Sunshine • Tongue Power • Lonesome Cowboy			
1/15/77	11	14		3 Vibrations	74	$10	Polydor 6091
6/25/77	9	27		4 Lifeline	72	$10	Polydor 6108
				ROY AYERS UBIQUITY (all of above)			
				This Side Of Sunshine • **Running Away** [19] • Gotta Find A Lover • I Still Love You • Lifeline • Cincinnati Growl • Fruit • Sanctified Feeling • Stranded In The Jungle • Together			
3/18/78	15	14		5 Let's Do It	33	$10	Polydor 6126
8/19/78	16	29		6 You Send Me	48	$10	Polydor 6159
1/6/79	45	6		7 Step In To Our Life		$10	Polydor 6179
				ROY AYERS/WAYNE HENDERSON			
5/26/79	25	20		8 Fever	67	$10	Polydor 6204
12/22/79+	22	21		9 No Stranger To Love	82	$10	Polydor 6246
6/28/80	62	5		10 Prime Time	205	$10	Polydor 6276
				ROY AYERS/WAYNE HENDERSON			
11/15/80	47	6		11 Love Fantasy	157	$10	Polydor 6301
8/15/81	43	10		12 Africa, Center Of The World	197	$10	Polydor 6327
3/20/82	45	6		13 Feeling Good	160	$10	Polydor 6348
1/5/85	50	13		14 In The Dark .... [I]	201	$8	Columbia 39422
11/23/85+	31	32		15 You Might Be Surprised		$8	Columbia 40022
9/10/88	60	9		16 Drive		$8	Ichiban 1028
6/3/89	60	11		17 Wake Up		$8	Ichiban 1040
7/1/95	71	3		18 Naste		$8	RCA 66613
				AZ **'95**			
				Born Anthony Cruz in Brooklyn, New York. Male rapper. Member of **The Firm**.			
10/28/95	❶¹	29		1 Doe Or Die	15	$8	EMI 32631
				Uncut Raw • **Gimme Yours** [51] • Ho Happy Jackie • Rather Unique • I Feel For You • **Sugar Hill** [12] • Mo Money, Mo Murder (Homicide) • **Do Or Die** [69] • We Can't Win • Your World Don't Stop			
4/18/98	5	16		2 Pieces Of A Man	22	$8	Noo Trybe 56715
				New Life • I'm Known • How Ya Livin' • Trading Places • What's The Deal • Love Is Love • The Pay Back • Just Because • Sosa • It's A Boy Thing • Pieces Of A (Black) Man • Last Dayz • Whatever Happened (The Birth) • Trial Of The Century • Betcha Don't Know			
				AZTECA **'73**			
				Latin jazz-rock ensemble led by brothers Pete (vocals) and Thomas "Coke" (timbales) Escovedo. Pete is the father of **Sheila E.**; Coke died on 7/13/86 (age 45).			
1/27/73	38	4		Azteca	151	$12	Columbia 31776
				AZ YET **'96**			
				Vocal group from Philadelphia: Dion Allen, Darryl Anthony, Marc Nelson, Shawn Rivera and Kenny Terry.			
11/16/96	18	41	●	Az Yet	60	$8	LaFace 26034

B

DEBUT	PEAK	WKS	Gold	Album Title	Pop #	$	Label & Number
	★148★			**BABYFACE** **'89**			
				Born Kenneth Edmonds on 4/10/59 in Indianapolis. Singer/songwriter/producer/multi-instrumentalist. Former member of **Manchild** and **The Deele**. Brother of Kevon and Melvin Edmonds of **After 7**. Co-founded the LaFace record label with songwriter/producer L.A. Reid.			
5/23/87	28	30		1 Lovers By Babyface		$8	Solar 72552
8/5/89	❶¹¹	66	▲²	2 Tender Lover	14	$8	Solar 45288
				It's No Crime [1] • Tender Lover [1] • Let's Be Romantic • Can't Stop My Heart • My Kinda Girl [3] • Whip Appeal [2] • Soon As I Get Home • Given A Chance • Sunshine • Where Will You Go			

BABYFACE — Cont'd

DEBUT	PEAK	WKS	Gold	Album Title	Pop #	$	Label & Number
9/4/93	2²	87	▲³	3 For The Cool In You	16	$8	Epic 53558

For The Cool In You [10] • Lady, Lady • **Never Keeping Secrets [3]** • Rock Bottom • **And Our Feelings [8]** • Saturday • When Can I See You [6] • Illusions • A Bit Old-Fashioned • You Are So Beautiful • I'll Always Love You • Well Alright

DEBUT	PEAK	WKS	Gold	Album Title	Pop #	$	Label & Number
11/16/96	4	47	▲²	4 The Day	6	$8	Epic 67293

Every Time I Close My Eyes [5] • Talk To Me • I Said I Love You • When Your Body Gets Weak • Simple Days • All Day Thinkin' • Seven Seas • The Day (That You Gave Me A Son) • How Come, How Long • **This Is For The Lover In You [2]**

DEBUT	PEAK	WKS	Gold	Album Title	Pop #	$	Label & Number
12/13/97	33	11	●	5 MTV Unplugged NYC 1997	[L] 106	$8	Epic 68779
12/12/98+	34	5		6 Christmas With Babyface	[X] 101	$8	Epic 69617

BABY HUEY '71

Born James Ramey in 1954 in Richamond, Indiana. Died of natural causes on 10/28/70 (age 26).

| 4/10/71 | 38 | 6 | | The Baby Huey Story/The Living Legend | 214 | $30 | Curtom 8007 |

BACK YARD '97

Rap group: Gingus, Carlos, Wincie, Bruce, Mike, Bubba, Leroy, Keith, Paul and Eric.

| 11/22/97 | 69 | 1 | | Hood Related | | $12 | Future 1025 [2] |

BADAROU, Wally '86

Born in Paris of West African parentage. Producer/multi-instrumentalist.

| 4/5/86 | 61 | 7 | | Echoes | [I] | $8 | Island 90495 |

BAD AZZ '98

Born in 1975 in Los Angeles. Male rapper.

| 10/17/98 | 32 | 7 | | Word On Tha Streets | 182 | $8 | Priority 50741 |

BADU, Erykah '97

Born Erica Wright on 2/26/71 in Dallas. Female singer.

| 3/1/97 | ❶⁴ | 64 | ▲² | 1 Baduizm | 2¹ | $8 | Kedar/Universal 53027 |

Rimshot • **On&On [1]** • Apple Tree • Otherside Of The Game • Sometimes • Next Lifetime • Afro • Certainly • 4 Leaf Clover • No Love • Drama

| 11/29/97 | ❶³ | 43 | ▲ | 2 Live | [L] 4 | $8 | Kedar/Universal 53109 |

recorded on October 1, 1997 at Sony Studios in New York City
Rimshot • Otherside Of The Game • On&On • Apple Tree • Ye Yo • Searching • Medley: Boogie Nights/All Night • Certainly • Stay • Tyrone • Next Lifetime

BAHAMADIA '96

Born Antonia Reed in Philadelphia. Female rapper.

| 4/20/96 | 13 | 19 | | Kollage | 126 | $8 | Chrysalis 35484 |

BAILEY, Philip '85

Born on 5/8/51 in Denver. Co-lead singer for **Earth, Wind & Fire**.

| 9/10/83 | 19 | 30 | | 1 Continuation | 71 | $8 | Columbia 38725 |
| 11/24/84+ | 10 | 35 | | 2 Chinese Wall | 22 | $8 | Columbia 39542 |

Photogenic Memory [61] • I Go Crazy • **Walking On The Chinese Wall [56]** • For Every Heart That's Been Broken • Go • **Easy Lover [3]** • Show You The Way To Love • Time Is A Woman • Woman • Children Of The Ghetto

| 5/31/86 | 30 | 15 | | 3 Inside Out | 84 | $8 | Columbia 40209 |
| 4/16/94 | 100 | 1 | | 4 Philip Bailey | | $8 | Zoo 11051 |

| ★91★ | | | | **BAKER, Anita** '88 | | | |

Born on 12/20/57 in Toledo, Ohio; raised in Detroit. Lead female vocalist of **Chapter 8** from 1976-83.

| 7/9/83 | 12 | 50 | | 1 The Songstress | 139 | $10 | Beverly Glen 10002 |

also see #5 below

| 4/12/86 | ❶³ | 108 | ▲⁵ | 2 Rapture | 11 | $8 | Elektra 60444 |

Sweet Love [2] • You Bring Me Joy • **Caught Up In The Rapture [6]** • Been So Long • Mystery • **No One In The World [5]** • Same Ole Love (365 Days A Year) [8] • Watch Your Step [23]

| 11/5/88 | ❶⁸ | 46 | ▲³ | 3 Giving You The Best That I Got | 1⁴ | $8 | Elektra 60827 |

Priceless • **Lead Me Into Love [4]** • Giving You The Best That I Got [1] • Good Love • Rules • Good Enough • **Just Because [1]** • You Belong To Me

| 7/28/90 | 3 | 46 | ▲ | 4 Compositions | 5 | $8 | Elektra 60922 |

Talk To Me [3] • Perfect Love Affair • Whatever It Takes • **Soul Inspiration [16]** • Lonely • No One To Blame • More Than You Know • Love You To The Letter • Fairy Tales [8]

| 12/21/91+ | 90 | 6 | | 5 The Songstress | [R] | $8 | Elektra 61116 |

reissue of #1 above

| 10/1/94 | ❶⁴ | 53 | ▲² | 6 Rhythm Of Love | 3 | $8 | Elektra 61555 |

Rhythm Of Love • The Look Of Love • **Body & Soul [4]** • Baby • I Apologize [8] • Plenty Of Room • **It's Been You [32]** • You Belong To Me • Wrong Man • Only For A While • Sometimes I Wonder Why • My Funny Valentine

B ANGIE B '91

Born Angela Boyd in Norton, Mississippi. Dance singer.

| 5/4/91 | 12 | 43 | | B Angie B | 133 | $8 | Bust It/Capitol 95236 |

BANKS, Ant '97

Born Anthony Banks in Oakland. Male rapper/producer.

| 4/17/93 | 22 | 15 | | 1 Sittin' On Somethin' Phat | 123 | $8 | Jive 41496 |
| 7/2/94 | 10 | 12 | | 2 The Big Badass | 80 | $8 | Jive 41534 |

The Big Badass • 2 Kill A G • Streets Of Oakland • The Drunken Fool • Parlayin' • Clownin' Wit Da Crew • Fuckin' Wit Banks • Straight Hustlin' • Pimp Style Gangstas • The Loot • Packin' A Gat • Hard As Hell

| 11/11/95 | 36 | 4 | | 3 Do Or Die | | $8 | Jive 41575 |
| 7/26/97 | 4 | 13 | | 4 Big Thangs | 20 | $8 | Priority 50698 |

Big Thangs • Coolin In The Luff • Can't Stop • West Riden' • Hard Knox • Gamblin' Wit Ice T • 4 Tha Hustlas • Time Is Tickin' • Cutaluff • Hoo-Ride Ant Banks • Make Money • Playa Paraphernalia • Fien • You Want Me Back

BANKS, Ron '84

Born on 5/10/51 in Detroit. Former lead singer of **The Dramatics**.

| 1/28/84 | 62 | 8 | | Truly Bad | | $8 | CBS Associated 39148 |

DEBUT	PEAK	WKS	Gold	Album Title	Pop #	$	Label & Number

BANTON, Buju '95
Born Mark Myrie in Jamaica. The name Buju Banton is taken from the Jamaican word for breadfruit.

| 8/21/93 | 29 | 30 | | 1 **Voice Of Jamaica** | 159 | $8 | Mercury 518013 |
| 8/5/95 | 27 | 38 | | 2 **'Til Shiloh** | 148 | $8 | Loose Cannon 524119 |

BANTON, Mega '94
Male dancehall/reggae singer from Jamaica.

| 4/23/94 | 100 | 1 | | **First Position** | | $8 | VP 1343 |

BARBIERI, Gato '77
Born Leandro Barbieri on 11/28/34 in Rosario, Argentina. Jazz tenor saxophonist.

| 3/12/77 | 49 | 3 | | **Caliente!** [I] | 75 | $8 | A&M 4597 |
| | | | | title is Spanish for hot | | | |

| | ★61★ | | | **BAR-KAYS** '79 | | | |

Funk group from Memphis: Larry Dodson (vocals), Barry Wilkins (guitar), Ronnie Caldwell (organ), Phalon Jones (saxophone), James Alexander (bass) and Carl Cunningham (drums). Four of group's earlier members died in plane crash that also killed **Otis Redding** on 12/10/67 in Madison, Wisconsin.

  1)Injoy 2)Nightcruising 3)As One

7/26/69	40	4		1 **Gotta Groove**		$30	Volt 6004
2/13/71	12	23		2 **Black Rock**	90	$25	Volt 6011
6/2/73	45	3		3 **Do You See What I See?**	212	$25	Volt 8001
11/20/76+	8	24		4 **Too Hot To Stop**	69	$10	Mercury 1099

Too Hot To Stop *[8]* • Cozy • Bang, Bang (Stick 'Em Up) • **Spellbound** *[29]* • **Shake Your Rump To The Funk** *[5]* • You're So Sexy • Summer Of Our Love • Whitehouseorgy

| 11/19/77+ | 7 | 30 | ● | 5 **Flying High On Your Love** | 47 | $10 | Mercury 1181 |

Shut The Funk Up • Standing On The Outside • Woman Of The Night • Whatever It Is • Can't Keep My Hands Off You • **Let's Have Some Fun** *[11]* • **Attitudes** *[22]* • You Can't Run Away • Flying High On Your Love

11/18/78	21	20		6 **Money Talks**	72	$10	Stax 4106
12/23/78+	15	24		7 **Light Of Life**	86	$10	Mercury 3732
11/10/79	2³	27	●	8 **Injoy**	35	$10	Mercury 3781

More And More • **Move Your Boogie Body** *[3]* • Running In And Out Of My Life • Girl I'm On Your Side • Loving You Is My Occupation • **Today Is The Day** *[25]* • You've Been • Up In Here

| 12/20/80+ | 6 | 22 | | 9 **As One** | 57 | $10 | Mercury 3844 |

Boogie Body Land *[7]* • Say It Through Love • Work It Out • **Body Fever** *[42]* • As One • Take The Time To Love Somebody • Open Your Heart • Deliver Us

| 11/21/81+ | 6 | 35 | ● | 10 **Nightcruising** | 55 | $10 | Mercury 4028 |

Nightcruising • **Hit And Run** *[5]* • Feels Like I'm Falling In Love • **Freaky Behavior** *[27]* • Touch Tone • Unforgettable Dream • Traffic Jammer • Backseat Driver

| 11/20/82 | 9 | 36 | | 11 **Propositions** | 51 | $10 | Mercury 4065 |

Propositions • Tripping Out • Anticipation • Busted • **Do It (Let Me See You Shake)** *[9]* • **She Talks To Me With Her Body** *[13]* • I Can't Believe You're Leaving Me • You Made A Change In My Life

| 4/21/84 | 7 | 44 | | 12 **Dangerous** | 52 | $8 | Mercury 818478 |

Dangerous • **Dirty Dancer** *[17]* • Make Believe Lover • Dance, Party, Etc. • **Freakshow On The Dance Floor** *[2]* • Lovers Should Never Fall In Love • Loose Talk • **Sexomatic** *[12]*

9/21/85	11	19		13 **Banging The Wall**	115	$8	Mercury 824727
10/24/87	25	21		14 **Contagious**	110	$8	Mercury 830305
2/18/89	36	16		15 **Animal**		$8	Mercury 836774
6/5/93	80	4		16 **The Best Of Bar-Kays** [G]		$8	Mercury 514823

BARRABAS '75
Disco group: Jo Tejada (vocals), Ricky Morales (guitar), Juan Vidal (keyboards), Ernesto Duarte (percussion), Miguel Morales (bass) and Daniel Louis (drums).

| 8/23/75 | 51 | 4 | | **Heart Of The City** | 149 | $10 | Atco 118 |

BARRY, Claudja '79
Born in Jamaica; raised in Toronto. Disco singer/actress. Acted in the musicals *Hair* and *Catch My Soul*.

| 6/23/79 | 73 | 5 | | **Boogie Woogie Dancin' Shoes** | 101 | $10 | Chrysalis 1232 |

BARTZ, Gary '80
Born in Baltimore. Session saxophonist.

| 5/24/80 | 71 | 2 | | **Bartz** | | $10 | Arista 4263 |

BASIC BLACK '90
Group from Los Angles: Darryl Adams (vocals), Walter Scott and Lloyd Turner (keyboards) and Kelvin Bradshaw (drums).

| 9/1/90 | 24 | 35 | | **Basic Black** | 178 | $8 | Motown 6307 |

BASIE, Count '68
Born William Basie on 8/21/04 in Red Bank, New Jersey. Died of cancer on 4/26/84 (age 79). Legendary big-band leader/pianist/organist. Won the Grammy's Trustees Award in 1981.

3/26/66	20	1		1 **Arthur Prysock/Count Basie**	107	$20	Verve 8646
5/18/68	18	5		2 **Manufacturers of Soul**	195	$20	Brunswick 754134
				JACKIE WILSON/COUNT BASIE			

BASS, Fontella '66
Born on 7/3/40 in St. Louis. Singer/pianist. Married to trumpet player Lester Bowie. Aunt of **David Peaston**.

| 3/12/66 | 6 | 8 | | **The 'New' Look** | 93 | $80 | Checker 2997 |

Our Day Will Come • How Glad I Am • Oh No, Not My Baby • **Rescue Me** *[1]* • Gee Whiz • I'm A Woman • Since I Fell For You • Impossible • You've Lost That Lovin' Feelin' • Soul Of The Man • Come And Get These Memories • I Know

BASS BOY '92
Born in Sarasota, Florida. Mixer/scratcher of bass-heavy samples.

| 5/30/92 | 82 | 12 | | **I Got The Bass** | 160 | $8 | Newtown 2209 |

11

BASSEY, Shirley '73
Born on 1/8/37 in Cardiff, Wales.

DEBUT	PEAK	WKS	Gold	Album Title	Pop #	$	Label & Number
12/5/70	29	6		1 Shirley Bassey Is Really "Something"	105	$15	United Artists 6765
6/30/73	34	7		2 Never, Never, Never	60	$10	United Artists 055
10/13/73	20	13		3 Live At Carnegie Hall ....[L]	136	$15	United Artists 111 [2]
				featuring Woody Herman's band; recorded May 11-12, 1973			
11/8/75	54	6		4 Good, Bad But Beautiful	186	$10	United Artists 542

BASS OUTLAWS '93
Hardcore bass group from Sarasota, Florida.

DEBUT	PEAK	WKS	Gold	Album Title	Pop #	$	Label & Number
12/5/92+	48	24		Illegal Bass ....[I]	165	$8	Newtown 2210

BASS PATROL '92
Rap duo from Sanford, Florida: Brian "DJ Fury" Graham and Robert "RX Lord" Lewis.

DEBUT	PEAK	WKS	Gold	Album Title	Pop #	$	Label & Number
5/2/92	63	23		1 The Kings Of Bass		$8	Joey Boy 3004
7/24/93	72	6		2 Nothin But Bass		$8	Joey Boy 3009

BASS 305 '93

DEBUT	PEAK	WKS	Gold	Album Title	Pop #	$	Label & Number
1/16/93	92	2		Digital Bass		$8	DMR 41260

BEASLEY, Walter '93
Born in Los Angeles. Jazz saxophonist/singer/songwriter.

DEBUT	PEAK	WKS	Gold	Album Title	Pop #	$	Label & Number
2/27/88	72	3		1 Walter Beasley ....[I]		$8	Polydor 833866
2/20/93	56	11		2 Intimacy ....[I]		$8	Mercury 512592

BEASTIE BOYS '87
White rap-punk trio from Brooklyn, New York: Adam Horovitz, Adam Yauch and Michael Diamond.

DEBUT	PEAK	WKS	Gold	Album Title	Pop #	$	Label & Number
11/29/86+	2[4]	40	▲[8]	1 Licensed To Ill	1[7]	$8	Def Jam 40238
				Rhymin & Stealin • It's The New Style [22] • She's Crafty • Posse In Effect • Slow Ride • Girls • Fight For Your Right • No Sleep Till Brooklyn • Paul Revere [34] • Hold It, Now Hit It [55] • Brass Monkey [83] • Slow And Low • Time To Get Ill			
8/19/89	24	13	▲[2]	2 Paul's Boutique	14	$8	Capitol 91743
				album named after a store in Brooklyn			
5/16/92	37	29	▲[2]	3 Check Your Head	10	$8	Capitol 98938
6/18/94	2[1]	33	▲[3]	4 Ill Communication	1[1]	$8	Grand Royal 28599
				Sure Shot • Tough Guy • B-Boys Makin' With The Freak Freak • Bobo On The Corner • Root Down • Sabotage • Get It Together • Sabrosa • The Update • Futterman's Rule • Alright Hear This • Eugene's Lament • Flute Loop • Do It • Ricky's Theme • Heart Attack Man • The Scoop • Shambala • Bodhisattva Vow • Transitions			

BEATLES, The '70
Rock group from Liverpool, England: John Lennon and George Harrison (guitars), Paul McCartney (bass) and Ringo Starr (drums). All shared vocals with Lennon and McCartney the main singers/songwriters. Widely considered the most popular and influential rock group of all-time. Won the 1964 Best New Artist Grammy Award. Lennon was shot to death on 12/8/80 (age 40). Group inducted into the Rock and Roll Hall of Fame in 1988. Charted 41 pop albums from 1964-96.

DEBUT	PEAK	WKS	Gold	Album Title	Pop #	$	Label & Number
1/24/70	38	7	▲[9]	Abbey Road	1[11]	$25	Apple 383
				named after the London recording studio where the album was recorded			

BEATNUTS, The '94
Rap trio from New York City: Les Fernandez, Jerry Tineo and Bert Smalls.

DEBUT	PEAK	WKS	Gold	Album Title	Pop #	$	Label & Number
5/8/93	50	9		1 Intoxicated Demons		$8	Violator 1114
7/9/94	28	9		2 The Beatnuts	182	$8	Relativity 1179
7/12/97	38	13		3 Stone Crazy	154	$8	Relativity 1508
2/28/98	52	3		4 The Beatnuts Remix EP: The Spot ....[M]		$6	Relativity 1621

BECK FAMILY, The '79
Family vocal group from Philadelphia: Joanna Beck, with brothers Tony, Tyrone and Menelick Beck, with cousins Nick Mundy and Donald Wilson.

DEBUT	PEAK	WKS	Gold	Album Title	Pop #	$	Label & Number
5/12/79	72	2		Dancin' On The Ceiling		$8	LeJoint 17001

BECTON, William '95
Born in Washington, DC. Gospel singer/arranger/producer.

DEBUT	PEAK	WKS	Gold	Album Title	Pop #	$	Label & Number
7/1/95	25	44		1 Broken		$8	WEB 9145
11/1/97	90	4		2 Heart Of A Love Song		$8	CGI 161318
				WILLIAM BECTON & FRIENDS (above 2)			

BEE GEES '78
Trio of brothers from Manchester, England: Barry and twins Robin and Maurice Gibb. Inducted into the Rock and Roll Hall of Fame in 1997. Charted 27 pop albums from 1967-97.

DEBUT	PEAK	WKS	Gold	Album Title	Pop #	$	Label & Number
10/2/76	23	29	▲	1 Children Of The World	8	$10	RSO 3003
6/11/77	25	17	▲	2 Here At Last...Bee Gees...Live ....[L]	8	$12	RSO 3901 [2]
				recorded on their 1976 tour			
1/7/78	❶[6]	38	▲[15]	3 Saturday Night Fever ....[S]	1[24]	$12	RSO 4001 [2]
				Stayin' Alive [Bee Gees] [4] • How Deep Is Your Love [Bee Gees] • Night Fever [Bee Gees] [8] • More Than A Woman [Bee Gees] • If I Can't Have You [Yvonne Elliman] [60] • A Fifth Of Beethoven [Walter Murphy] [10] • More Than A Woman [Tavares] [36] • Manhattan Skyline [David Shire] • Calypso Breakdown [Ralph McDonald] • Night On Disco Mountain [David Shire] • Open Sesame [Kool & The Gang] • Jive Talkin' [Bee Gees] [4] • You Should Be Dancing [Bee Gees] [4] • Boogie Shoes [K.C. & The Sunshine Band] [29] • Salsation [David Shire] • K-Jee [MFSB] • Disco Inferno [Trammps] [9]			
2/24/79	9	22	▲	4 Spirits Having Flown	1[6]	$10	RSO 3041
				Tragedy [44] • Too Much Heaven [10] • Love You Inside Out [57] • Reaching Out • Spirits (Having Flown) • Search, Find • Stop (Think Again) • Living Together • I'm Satisfied • Until			

BEENIE MAN '98
Born in 1973 in Jamaica. Reggae singer/rapper. Beenie is Jamaican slang for little.

DEBUT	PEAK	WKS	Gold	Album Title	Pop #	$	Label & Number
3/14/98	35	23		Many Moods Of Moses	151	$8	VP 1513

DEBUT	PEAK	WKS	Gold	Album Title	Pop #	$	Label & Number

BELL, Archie, & The Drells   '76
Born on 9/1/44 in Henderson, Texas. The Drells consisted of James Wise, Lee Bell and Willie Parnell.

DEBUT	PEAK	WKS		Album Title	Pop #	$	Label & Number
5/25/68	15	22		1 Tighten Up	142	$30	Atlantic 8181
2/8/69	28	4		2 I Can't Stop Dancing		$30	Atlantic 8204
12/27/75+	11	20		3 Dance Your Troubles Away	95	$12	TSOP 33844
1/22/77	47	3		4 Where Will You Go When The Party's Over		$10	Philadelphia I. 34323
10/6/79	37	9		5 Strategy		$10	Philadelphia I. 36096

BELL, Madeline   '68
Born in England. Singer/actress. Former lead singer of group Blue Mink.

5/11/68	46	2		I'm Gonna Make You Love Me		$20	Philips 271

BELL, William   '77
Born William Yarborough on 7/16/39 in Memphis.

6/21/69	49	4		1 Bound To Happen		$30	Stax 2014
4/2/77	15	13		2 Coming Back For More	63	$10	Mercury 1146
5/17/86	39	27		3 Passion		$8	Wilbe 3001
8/15/92	96	3		4 Bedtime Stories		$8	Wilbe 4128

BELL & JAMES   '79
Duo of Leroy Bell and Casey James. Began as songwriting team for Bell's uncle, producer Thom Bell.

1/6/79	17	23		1 Bell & James	31	$10	A&M 4728
11/3/79	36	6		2 Only Make Believe	125	$10	A&M 4784

BELL BIV DeVOE   '90
Trio of **New Edition** members: Ricky Bell, Michael Bivins and Ronnie DeVoe.

4/7/90	❶[1]	70	▲[4]	1 Poison	5	$8	MCA 6387

She's Dope! [9] • B.B.D. (I Thought It Was Me)? [1] • Let Me Know Something?! • Do Me! [4] • Word To Tha Mutha! • Poison [1] • Ain't Nut'in' Changed! • When Will I See You Smile Again? [3] • I Do Need You

9/21/91	18	25	●	2 WBBD - Bootcity! The Remix Album	[K]	18	$8	MCA 10345
7/10/93	6	23	●	3 Hootie Mack		19	$8	MCA 10682

Nickel • Above The Rim [81] • Lovely • Ghetto Booty • Hootie Mack • From The Back • Show Me The Way • The Situation • Something In Your Eyes [6] • Please Come Back • Lost In The Moment

BELLE, Regina   '89
Born on 7/15/63 in Englewood, New Jersey.

6/20/87	14	38		1 All By Myself	85	$8	Columbia 40537
9/16/89	❶[1]	55	●	2 Stay With Me	63	$8	Columbia 44367

Baby Come To Me [1] • When Will You Be Mine • Dream Lover • What Goes Around [3] • Make It Like It Was [1] • Good Lovin' • It Doesn't Hurt Anymore • This Is Love [7] • (It's Gonna Take) All Our Love • Medley: Someday We'll All Be Free/Save The Children

3/6/93	13	37	●	3 Passion	63	$8	Columbia 48826
9/23/95	18	16		4 Reachin' Back	115	$8	Columbia 66813
10/10/98	42	6		5 Believe In Me		$8	MCA 11777

BENDER, Chris   '92
Born on 8/2/72 in Boston. Shot to death on 11/3/91 (age 19). Male singer.

7/18/92	92	4		Draped		$8	EastWest 91708

BENÉT, Eric   '97
Born on 10/5/69 in Milwaukee. Singer/songwriter.

10/12/96+	38	45		True To Myself	174	$8	Warner 46270

BENOIT, David   '94
Born in Hermosa Beach, California. Jazz keyboardist.

4/23/94	73	5		The Benoit/Freeman Project	[I]	118	$8	GRP 9739

BENSON, George ★28★   '76
Born on 3/22/43 in Pittsburgh. Singer/songwriter/guitarist. Session player for **Brother Jack McDuff** and **Jimmy Smith**. Member of **Fuse One**.

1)Breezin' 2)Give Me The Night 3)Weekend In L.A.

4/26/69	38	2		1 Shape Of Things To Come	[I]		$20	A&M 3014
8/23/69	43	3		2 Tell It Like It Is	[I]	145	$20	A&M 3020
4/17/76	❶[6]	46	▲[3]	3 Breezin'		1[2]	$10	Warner 2919

Breezin' [55] • This Masquerade [3] • Six To Four • Affirmation • So This Is Love? • Lady

6/26/76	18	18		4 Good King Bad	[I]	51	$12	CTI 6062
11/6/76	27	8		5 Benson & Farrell	[I]	100	$12	CTI 6069

GEORGE BENSON & JOE FARRELL

2/12/77	2[3]	28	▲	6 In Flight	9	$10	Warner 2983

Nature Boy • The Wind And I • The World Is A Ghetto • Gonna Love You More [41] • Valdez In The Country • Everything Must Change [34]

2/12/77	43	4		7 George Benson In Concert-Carnegie Hall	[I-L]	122	$12	CTI 6072

recorded on January 11, 1975

13

DEBUT	PEAK	WKS	Gold	Album Title	Pop #	$	Label & Number

BENSON, George — Cont'd

| 2/11/78 | ❶² | 30 | ▲ 8 | Weekend In L.A. [L] | 5 | $12 | Warner 3139 [2] |

recorded September 30-October 2, 1977 at the Roxy in Hollywood

Weekend In L.A. • **On Broadway** *[2]* • Down Here On The Ground • California P.M. • **The Greatest Love Of All** *[2]* • It's All In The Game • Windsong • Ode To A Kudu • **Lady Blue** *[39]* • We All Remember Wes • We As Love

| 3/24/79 | 4 | 26 | ● 9 | Livin' Inside Your Love | 7 | $12 | Warner 3277 [2] |

Livin' Inside Your Love • Hey Girl • Nassau Day • Soulful Strut • Prelude To Fall • A Change Is Gonna Come • **Love Ballad** *[3]* • You're Never Too Far From Me • Love Is A Hurtin' Thing • Welcome Into My World • Before You Go • **Unchained Melody** *[55]*

| 8/9/80 | ❶⁴ | 37 | ▲ 10 | Give Me The Night | 3 | $8 | Warner 3453 |

Love X Love *[9]* • Off Broadway • Moody's Mood • **Give Me The Night** *[1]* • What's On Your Mind • Dinorah, Dinorah • Love Dance • Star Of A Story • Midnight Love Affair • **Turn Out The Lamplight** *[33]*

| 11/28/81+ | 5 | 32 | ● 11 | The George Benson Collection [G] | 14 | $10 | Warner 3577 [2] |

Turn Your Love Around *[1]* • **Love All The Hurt Away** *[6]* • **Give Me The Night** *[1]* • Cast Your Fate To The Wind • **Never Give Up On A Good Thing** *[16]* • **On Broadway** *[2]* • White Rabbit • **This Masquerade** *[3]* • **Love Ballad** *[3]* • Nature Boy • Last Train To Clarksville • Livin' Inside Your Love • Here Comes The Sun • **Breezin'** *[55]* • Moody's Mood • We Got The Love • **The Greatest Love Of All** *[2]*

| 6/25/83 | 6 | 33 | ● 12 | In Your Eyes | 27 | $8 | Warner 23744 |

Feel Like Making Love • **Inside Love (So Personal)** *[3]* • **Lady Love Me (One More Time)** *[21]* • Love Will Come Again • In Your Eyes • Never Too Far To Fall • Being With You • Use Me • Late At Night • In Search Of A Dream

2/9/85	20	34	● 13	20/20	45	$8	Warner 25178
9/20/86	21	27	● 14	While The City Sleeps...	77	$8	Warner 25475
7/11/87	28	22	● 15	Collaboration [I]	59	$8	Warner 25580

GEORGE BENSON/EARL KLUGH

10/1/88	17	26	16	Twice The Love	76	$8	Warner 25705
7/10/93	50	23	17	Love Remembers		$8	Warner 26685
8/17/96	33	20	18	That's Right [I]	150	$8	GRP 9823
6/27/98	47	17	19	Standing Together		$8	GRP 9906

BENTON, Brook '70

Born Benjamin Franklin Peay on 9/19/31 in Camden, South Carolina. Died of spinal meningitis on 4/9/88 (age 56). Singer/songwriter.

| 2/21/70 | 4 | 21 | | Brook Benton Today | 27 | $15 | Cotillion 9018 |

Rainy Night In Georgia *[1]* • **My Way** *[25]* • Life Has Its Little Ups And Downs • Can't Take My Eyes Off You • We're Gonna Make It • A Little Bit Of Soap • Baby • Where Do I Go From Here? • Desertion • I've Gotta Be Me

BERRY, Chuck '72

Born Charles Edward Anderson Berry on 10/18/26 in St. Louis. Singer/songwriter/guitarist. Acclaimed as one of rock and roll's most influential artists. Won Grammy's Lifetime Achievement Award in 1984. Inducted into the Rock and Roll Hall of Fame in 1986.

| 7/1/72 | 8 | 33 | ● 1 | The London Chuck Berry Sessions [L] | 8 | $20 | Chess 60020 |

side 1: studio; side 2: recorded at the Lanchester Arts Festival in Coventry, England (with **Average White Band** backing)

Let's Boogie • Mean Old World • I Will Not Let You Go • London Berry Blues • I Love You • Reelin' & Rockin' • **My Ding-A-Ling** *[42]* • Johnny B. Goode

| 9/22/73 | 58 | 2 | 2 | Chuck Berry/Bio | 175 | $20 | Chess 50043 |

B.G., The '97

Born in New Orleans. Male rapper. B.G.: Baby Gangsta. Member of **Hot Boy$**.

| 7/19/97 | 40 | 7 | 1 | It's All On U | | $8 | Cash Money 9613 |
| 11/15/97 | 20 | 5 | 2 | It's All On U Vol. 2 | 184 | $8 | Cash Money 9616 |

B.G. KNOCC OUT & DRESTA '95

Male rap duo from New York City.

| 9/2/95 | 15 | 11 | | Real Brothas | 128 | $8 | OutBurst 527899 |

BIG BROTHER & THE HOLDING COMPANY '68

Rock group from San Francisco: **Janis Joplin** (vocals), James Gurley and Sam Andrew (guitars), Peter Albin (bass) and David Getz (drums). Joplin died of a drug overdose on 10/4/70 (age 27).

| 10/14/67 | 28 | 2 | 1 | Big Brother & The Holding Company | 60 | $30 | Mainstream 6099 |
| 10/12/68 | 7 | 23 | ● 2 | Cheap Thrills | 1⁸ | $20 | Columbia 9700 |

Combination Of The Two • I Need A Man To Love • Summertime • Piece Of My Heart • Turtle Blues • Oh, Sweet Mary • Ball And Chain

BIG BUB '97

Born Frederick Lee Drakeford in Englewood, New Jersey. Male singer/rapper. Former member of **Today**.

| 10/31/92 | 30 | 37 | 1 | Comin' At Cha | | $8 | EastWest 92180 |
| 11/8/97 | 15 | 22 | 2 | Timeless | 104 | $8 | Kedar/Universal 53074 |

BIG ED '98

Born in Richmond, California. Male rapper.

| 9/19/98 | 3 | 11 | | The Assassin | 16 | $8 | No Limit 50729 |

My Entourage • I'm Yo Soldier • Rodeo • Make Some Room • We Some • Go 2 War • Life • Uh Oh • I Miss 'Em • Buck 'Em • Just Me & U • We Represent • The Assassin • Shake'm Up • Come Home With Me • Come Get Me • Scriptures

BIG L '95

Born Larry Coleman in Harlem, New York. Male rapper.

| 4/15/95 | 22 | 10 | | Lifestylez Ov Da Poor & Dangerous | 149 | $8 | Columbia 53795 |

BIG MELLO — see BONE HARD PRODUCTIONS

BIG MIKE '97

Born Michael Barnett on 9/27/71 in New Orleans. Member of **Convicts** and **The Geto Boys**.

| 7/16/94 | 4 | 42 | ● 1 | Somethin' Serious | 40 | $8 | Rap-A-Lot 53907 |

Comin From The Swamp • World Of Mind • Ghetto Love • Creepin - Rollin • Smoke Em & Choke Em • Havin Thangs • On Da Real • Playa Playa • Southern Thang • Somethin' Serious • Get Over That • Fire • Daddy's Gone (With Mr. Scarface) • On Da 1

| 4/26/97 | 3 | 19 | | Still Serious | 16 | $8 | Rap-A-Lot 44099 |

Playas To Governors • Seal It With A Kiss • Southern Dialect • Candy's 4 Babies • 'Burban & Impalas • All A Dream • It's Alright • Grey Skies • Everybody Wants A Name • Southern Comfort (On & On) • Still Serious • Black Lacquer

DEBUT	PEAK	WKS	Gold	Album Title	Pop #	$	Label & Number

BIG NOYD   '97
Born Terrance Perry in New York City. Male rapper.

12/28/96+	59	12		Episodes Of A Hustla		$8	Tommy Boy 1156

BIG PUNISHER   '98
Male rapper from New York City.

5/9/98	❶²	33	▲	Capital Punishment	5	$8	Loud/RCA 67512

Beware • Super Lyrical • **Still Not A Player** *[6]* • The Dream Shatterer • **Punish Me** *[87]* • You Ain't A Killer • Caribbean Connection • Glamour Life • Capital Punishment • Uncensored • **I'm Not A Player** *[19]* • Twinz (Deep Cover 98) • Boomerang • **You Came Up** *[49]* • Tres Leches (Triboro Trilogy) • Fast Money • Parental Discretion

BIG TYMERS   '98
Rap duo: Mannie Fresh and Brian "Baby" Williams.

3/7/98	25	12		1 How You Luv That?	168	$8	Cash Money 9617
10/10/98	17	34↑		2 How You Luv That? Vol. 2	105	$8	Cash Money 53170

BIONIC BOOGIE   '78
Disco studio group assembled by producer Gregg Diamond.

4/22/78	59	2		Bionic Boogie	88	$8	Polydor 6123

BIZ MARKIE   '89
Born Marcel Hall on 4/8/64 in New York City. Male rapper.

3/26/88	19	39		1 Goin' Off	90	$8	Cold Chillin' 25675
11/4/89	9	26	●	2 The Biz Never Sleeps	66	$8	Cold Chillin' 26003

THE DIABOLICAL BIZ MARKIE
Dedication • Check It Out • The Dragon • Spring Again • **Just A Friend** *[37]* • She's Not Just Another Woman (Monique) • Mudd Foot • A Thing Named Kim • Me Versus Me • My Man Rich • I Hear Music • Biz In Harmony • Things Get A Little Easier

9/21/91	44	10		3 I Need A Haircut	113	$8	Cold Chillin' 26648
7/10/93	43	6		4 All Samples Cleared		$8	Cold Chillin' 45261

BIZZY BONE   '98
Born Charles Scruggs in Cleveland. Member of **Bone Thugs-N-Harmony**.

10/24/98	2¹	22	●	Heaven'z Movie	3	$8	Mo Thugs 1670

Roll Call • Thugz Cry • Marchin' On Washington • Yes Yes Y'All • Menensky Mobbin' • Waitin' For Warfare • Mr. Majesty II • Brain On Drugs • On The Freeway • Demons Surround Me • (The Roof Is) On Fire • Nobody Can Stop Me • Social Studies

BLACK, David   '92
Born in San Francisco. Singer/songwriter.

8/8/92	41	17		Loving Ain't Easy		$8	Bust It/Capitol 98015

BLACK BOX   '90
Male Italian dance trio of producer Daniele Davoli and musicians Mirko Limoni and Valerio Semplici. Videos feature French model Katrin Quinol as lead singer; however, **Martha Wash** is the uncredited lead vocalist on the album below.

8/18/90	16	51	●	Dreamland	56	$8	RCA 2221

BLACKBYRDS, The   '76
★162★
Group from Washington, DC. Core members: **Donald Byrd** (trumpet), Joe Hall (vocals, bass), Kevin Toney (vocals, keyboards) and Keith Killgo (vocals, drums).

6/22/74	14	26		1 The Blackbyrds	96	$15	Fantasy 9444
12/7/74+	5	36		2 Flying Start	30	$15	Fantasy 9472

I Need You • The Baby • Love Is Love • Blackbyrds' Theme • **Walking In Rhythm** *[4]* • Future Children, Future Hopes • April Showers • Spaced Out

7/5/75	19	10		3 Cornbread, Earl and Me .... [S]	150	$15	Fantasy 9483
11/29/75+	3	31	●	4 City Life	16	$15	Fantasy 9490

Rock Creek Park *[37]* • Thankful 'Bout Yourself • City Life • All I Ask • **Happy Music** *[3]* • Love So Fine • **Flyin' High** *[22]* • Hash And Eggs

12/4/76+	6	29	●	5 Unfinished Business	34	$15	Fantasy 9518

Time Is Movin' *[15]* • In Life • Enter In • You've Got That Something • **Party Land** *[30]* • Lady • Unfinished Business

10/15/77	8	28	●	6 Action	43	$12	Fantasy 9535

Supernatural Feeling *[19]* • Lookin' Ahead • Mysterious Vibes • Something Special • Street Games • **Soft And Easy** *[20]* • Dreaming About You

12/23/78+	43	9		7 Night Grooves .... [G]	159	$12	Fantasy 9570
1/10/81	40	16		8 Better Days	133	$12	Fantasy 9602

BLACK EYED PEAS   '98
Rap trio from Los Angeles: William, Apldeap and Taboo.

7/18/98	37	14		Behind The Front	129	$8	Interscope 90152

BLACK FLAMES, The   '90
Vocal trio from Newark, New Jersey: John Sykes, Nate Burgess and Donald Richardson.

7/21/90	70	15		The Black Flames		$8	Columbia 44030

BLACKFOOT, J.   '84
Born John Colbert on 11/20/46 in Greenville, Mississippi; raised in Memphis. Former member of **The Soul Children**.

1/21/84	16	20		1 City Slicker		$10	Sound Town 8002
8/15/87	67	3		2 U-Turn		$10	Edge 001

BLACKGIRL   '94
Female vocal trio from Atlanta: Nycolia Turman, Pamela Copeland and Rochelle Stuart.

5/28/94	46	14		Treat U Right		$8	Kaper/RCA 66359

BLACK HEAT   '75
Dance group: Brad Owens (vocals, guitar), John Gray (keyboards), Ray Green (percussion), Ray Thompson (sax), Rodney Edwards (trumpet), Namon Jones (bass) and Esco Cromer (drums).

5/18/74	58	2		1 No Time To Burn	201	$12	Atlantic 7294
4/12/75	51	4		2 Keep On Burnin'		$12	Atlantic 18128

DEBUT	PEAK	WKS	Gold	Album Title	Pop #	$	Label & Number
				BLACK IVORY '72			
				Vocal trio from New York City: Leroy Burgess, Stuart Bascombe and Russell Patterson. Burgess later joined **Aleem**.			
3/11/72	13	19		1 Don't Turn Around	158	$12	Today 1005
12/30/72+	26	13		2 Baby, Won't You Change Your Mind	188	$12	Today 1008
				BLACK MENACE '95			
8/19/95	48	9		Drama Time		$8	Big Boy 0017
				BLACK MOON '94			
				Rap trio from Brooklyn, New York: Kenyatta Blake, 5 Ft. Excellerator and Edward Pewgarde.			
10/30/93+	33	44		1 Enta Da Stage		$8	Wreck 02002
11/2/96	33	7		2 Diggin' In Dah Vaults [K]		$8	Wreck/Nervous 20232
				BLACK SHEEP '92			
				Rap duo from the Bronx, New York: Andre Titus and William McLean.			
11/16/91+	15	41	●	1 A Wolf In Sheep's Clothing	30	$8	Mercury 848368
12/24/94	24	8		2 Non-Fiction	107	$8	Mercury 522685
				BLACK STAR '98			
				Rap duo from New York City: Mos Def and Talib Kweli.			
10/17/98	13	10		Black Star	53	$8	Rawkus 1158
				MOS DEF & TALIB KWELI ARE BLACK STAR			
				BLACKstreet '96			
				Hip-hop group: Teddy Riley, Chauncey Hannibal, Levi Little and David Hollister. Riley, a prolific producer and originator of the "new jack swing" sound, was a member of Kids At Work and **Guy**. Hollister is the cousin of **K-Ci & JoJo**. Hollister and Little left in late 1995, replaced by Eric Williams and Mark Middleton.			
7/9/94	7	64	▲	1 BLACKstreet	51	$8	Interscope 92351
				Baby Be Mine [17] • U Blow My Mind • I Like The Way You Work • Good Life • Physical Thing • Make U Wet • **Booti Call** [14] • Love's In Need • Joy [12] • Before I Let You Go [2] • Falling In Love Again • **Tonight's The Night** [27] • Happy Home • Wanna Make Love • Givin' You All My Lovin'			
9/21/96	❶⁵	68	▲⁴	2 Another Level	3	$8	Interscope 90071
				This Is How We Roll • No Diggity [1] • Fix [17] • Good Lovin' • Let's Stay In Love • Don't Leave Me • Never Gonna Let You Go • I Wanna Be Your Man • (Money Can't) Buy Me Love • I Can't Get You (Out Of My Mind) • I'll Give It To You • Happy Song (Tonite) • The Lord Is Real (Time Will Reveal)			
				BLAC MONKS '94			
				Rap group from Houston.			
5/14/94	65	13		1 Secrets Of The Hidden Temple		$8	Rap-A-Lot 53898
6/6/98	74	1		2 No Mercy		$8	Rap-A-Lot 45787
				BLAHZAY BLAHZAY '96			
				Rap duo from Brooklyn, New York: Out Loud and P.F. Cuttin'.			
8/31/96	34	6		Blah, Blah, Blah		$8	Fader/Mercury 124093
				BLANCHARD, Terence '90			
				Born on 3/13/62 in New Orleans. Jazz trumpeter.			
9/1/90	21	18		1 Mo' Better Blues [S]	63	$8	Columbia 46792
				THE BRANFORD MARSALIS QUARTET FEATURING TERENCE BLANCHARD			
12/5/92	92	1		2 Malcolm X The Original Motion Picture Score [I-S]		$8	Columbia 53190
				BLAND, Bobby ★41★ '75			
				Born on 1/27/30 in Rosemark, Tennessee. Blues singer. Nicknamed "Blue." Member of legendary blues band the Beale Streeters in 1949. Inducted into the Rock and Roll Hall of Fame in 1992.			
				1)Together For The First Time...Live 2)His California Album 3)Dreamer 4)Together Again...Live 5)Get On Down With Bobby Bland			
10/15/66	17	7		1 The Soul Of The Man		$100	Duke 79
7/8/67	29	3		2 The Best Of Bobby Bland [G]		$25	Duke 84
4/6/68	38	4		3 A Touch Of The Blues		$25	Duke 88
9/13/69	24	14		4 Spotlighting The Man		$25	Duke 89
12/8/73+	3	22		5 His California Album	136	$15	Dunhill/ABC 50163
				BOBBY BLUE BLAND			
				This Time I'm Gone For Good [5] • Up And Down World • It's Not The Spotlight • (If Loving You Is Wrong) I Don't Want To Be Right • Goin' Down Slow [17] • The Right Place At The Right Time • Help Me Through The Day • Where Baby Went • Friday The 13th Child • I've Got To Use My Imagination			
7/27/74	5	31		6 Dreamer	172	$15	Dunhill/ABC 50169
				Ain't No Love In The Heart Of The City [9] • I Wouldn't Treat A Dog (The Way You Treated Me) [3] • Lovin' On Borrowed Time • The End Of The Road • I Ain't Gonna Be The First To Cry • Dreamer • Yolanda [21] • Twenty-Four Hour Blues • Cold Day In Hell • Who's Foolin' Who			
10/26/74+	2¹	16	●	7 Together For The First Time...Live [L]	43	$20	Dunhill/ABC 50190 [2]
				B.B. KING & BOBBY BLAND			
				3 O'Clock Blues • It's My Own Fault • Driftin' Blues • That's The Way Love Is • I'm Sorry • I'll Take Care Of You • Don't Cry No More • Don't Answer The Door • Medley: Good To Be Back Home/Driving Wheel/Rock Me Baby/Black Night/Cherry Red/It's My Own Fault/3 O'Clock Blues/Worried Life Blues/Chains Of Love/Gonna Get Me An Old Woman • Why I Sing The Blues • Goin' Down Slow • I Like To Live The Love			
9/6/75	14	12		8 Get On Down With Bobby Bland	154	$12	ABC 895
7/17/76	9	15		9 Together Again...Live [L]	73	$12	ABC/Impulse 9317
				BOBBY BLAND & B.B. KING			
				Let The Good Times Roll [20] • Medley: Stormy Monday Blues/Strange Things Happen • Feel So Bad • Medley: Mother-In-Law Blues/Mean Old World • Everyday (I Have The Blues) • Medley: The Thrill Is Gone/I Ain't Gonna Be The First To Cry			

DEBUT	PEAK	WKS	Gold	Album Title	Pop #	$	Label & Number

BLAND, Bobby — Cont'd

DEBUT	PEAK	WKS	Gold	Album Title	Pop #	$	Label & Number
5/21/77	47	10		10 Reflections In Blue	185	$12	ABC 1018
6/17/78	31	16		11 Come Fly With Me	185	$12	ABC 1075
9/22/79	34	21		12 I Feel Good, I Feel Fine	187	$10	MCA 3157
12/6/80+	29	24		13 Sweet Vibrations		$10	MCA 5145

BOBBY "BLUE" BLAND

9/12/81	52	11		14 Try Me, I'm Real	207	$10	MCA 5233
7/10/82	22	36		15 Here We Go Again	201	$10	MCA 5297
7/23/83	50	16		16 Tell Mr. Bland		$10	MCA 5425
8/25/84	35	20		17 You've Got Me Loving You		$10	MCA 5503
12/14/85+	45	24		18 Members Only		$8	Malaco 7429
12/20/86+	65	9		19 After All		$8	Malaco 7439
3/5/88	71	2		20 Blues You Can Use		$8	Malaco 7444
8/12/89	26	70		21 Midnight Run		$8	Malaco 7450
1/4/92	50	32		22 Portrait Of The Blues		$8	Malaco 7458

BOBBY "BLUE" BLAND (above 2)

| 9/25/93 | 80 | 5 | | 23 Years Of Tears | | $8 | Malaco 7469 |

B-LEGIT THE SAVAGE   '96

Born Brandt Jones in San Francisco. Male rapper. Member of **The Click**. Cousin of **E-40**.

| 3/6/93 | 41 | 19 | | 1 Tryin' To Get A Buck | | $8 | Sick Wid' It 712 |
| 12/14/96 | 15 | 20 | | 2 The Hemp Museum | 55 | $8 | Sick Wid' It 41593 |

BLEU, Mikki   '92

Born in Houston. Male singer.

| 5/16/92 | 98 | 2 | | Gimme The Keys | | $8 | Ultrax 030293 |

★107★   **BLIGE, Mary J.**   '94

Born Mary Jane Blige on 1/11/71 in New York City.

| 8/15/92 | ❶⁷ | 64 | ▲² | 1 What's The 411? | 6 | $8 | Uptown/MCA 10681 |

Leave A Message • **Reminisce** [6] • **Real Love** [1] • **You Remind Me** [1] • **Sweet Thing** [11] • **Love No Limit** [5] • **I Don't Want To Do Anything** [86] • Slow Down • **My Love** [23] • Changes I've Been Going Through • What's The 411?

| 12/25/93+ | 22 | 25 | | 2 What's The 411? Remix   [K] | 118 | $8 | Uptown/MCA 10942 |

remixes of all but 2 songs from #1 above

| 12/17/94 | ❶⁸ | 85 | ▲³ | 3 My Life | 7 | $8 | Uptown/MCA 11156 |

Mary Jane (All Night Long) • **You Bring Me Joy** [29] • I'm The Only Woman • My Life • You Gotta Believe • I Never Wanna Live Without You • **I'm Goin' Down** [13] • Be With You • Mary's Joint • Don't Go • **I Love You** [flip] • No One Else • **Be Happy** [6]

| 5/3/97 | ❶⁴ | 75 | ▲³ | 4 Share My World | 1¹ | $8 | MCA 11606 |

I Can Love You [2] • **Love Is All We Need** [flip] • Round And Round • Share My World • Seven Days • It's On • Missing You • **Everything** [5] • Keep Your Head • Can't Get You Off My Mind • Get To Know You Better • Searching • Our Love • **Not Gon' Cry** [1]

| 8/15/98 | 7 | 19 | ● | 5 The Tour   [L] | 21 | $8 | MCA 11848 |

Real Love • You Remind Me • Reminisce • Sweet Thing • Mary Jane (All Night Long) • Love No Limit • Summer Madness • My Life • You Gotta Believe • Slow Down • Mary's Joint • I'm The Only Woman • Share My World • I'm Goin' Down • Thank You Lord • I Can Love You • Keep Your Head • Everything • Seven Days • Not Gon' Cry • Missing You • Day Dreaming • Misty Blue

BLIND FAITH   '69

British rock supergroup: Eric Clapton (vocals, guitar), **Steve Winwood** (vocals, keyboards), Rick Grech (bass) and Ginger Baker (drums). Grech died on 3/17/90 (age 43).

| 9/20/69 | 40 | 3 | ▲ | Blind Faith | 1² | $20 | Atco 304 |

original album cover depicted a prepubescent nude girl ($30); quickly withdrawn and replaced by a photo of the band

BLONDIE   '81

Techno-pop group from New York City: Debbie Harry (vocals), Chris Stein and Frank Infante (guitars), Jimmy Destri (keyboards), Nigel Harrison (bass) and Clem Burke (drums).

| 3/21/81 | 25 | 7 | ▲ | Autoamerican | 7 | $10 | Chrysalis 1290 |

BLOODS & CRIPS   '93

Rap group from Los Angeles made up of members of two rival street gangs. Features a revolving lineup of rappers.

3/27/93	18	56		1 Bangin' On Wax	86	$8	Dangerous 19138
10/1/94	20	9		2 Bangin' On Wax 2...the saga continues	139	$8	Dangerous 6715
10/21/95	40	6		3 Damu Ridas		$8	Dangerous 6738

BLOODS

| 10/21/95 | 44 | 10 | | 4 Nationwide Rip Ridaz | | $8 | Dangerous 6739 |

CRIPS

BLOODSTONE   '73

Group from Kansas City, Missouri: Charles Love (vocals, guitar), Willis Draffen (guitar), Harry Williams and Roger Durham (percussion), Charles McCormick (bass) and Melvin Webb (drums). Durham died after falling off a horse in 1973. Webb died of diabetes in 1973; replaced by Eddie Summers. Group acted in the 1975 movie *Train Ride To Hollywood*.

| 5/5/73 | 2¹ | 36 | | 1 Natural High | 30 | $12 | London 620 |

You Know We've Learned • Who Has The Last Laugh Now • Peter's Jones • That's The Way We Make Our Music • Damn That Rock 'N' Roll Medley: Bo Diddley/Diddley Daddy • **Natural High** [4] • I Need Your Love • Tell It To My Face • Ran It In The Ground • **Never Let You Go** [7]

| 12/29/73+ | 6 | 21 | | 2 Unreal | 110 | $12 | London 634 |

Outside Woman [2] • What Did You Do To Me? • Unreal • Everybody Needs Love • Something • Keep Our Own Thing Together • Let Me Ride • The Traffic Cop (Dance) • Moulded Oldies Medley: Hound Dog/Searchin'/So Fine

8/3/74	13	21		3 I Need Time	141	$12	London 647
3/1/75	22	9		4 Riddle Of The Sphinx	147	$12	London 645
7/24/76	51	3		5 Do You Wanna Do A Thing?		$12	London 671
7/10/82	11	25		6 We Go A Long Way Back	95	$10	T-Neck 38115

17

BLOOD, SWEAT & TEARS '69
Rock-jazz fusion group from New York City. Numerous personnel changes. David Clayton-Thomas was lead singer from 1969-71.

DEBUT	PEAK	WKS	Gold	Album Title	Pop #	$	Label & Number
4/26/69	15	38	▲³	1 Blood, Sweat & Tears	1⁷	$15	Columbia 9720
8/22/70	35	6	●	2 Blood, Sweat & Tears 3	1²	$15	Columbia 30090

BLOUNT, Tanya '94
Born in Washington, DC. Female singer.

9/3/94	58	12		Natural Thing		$8	Polydor 521514

BLOW, Kurtis '80
Born Kurtis Walker on 8/9/59 in New York City. Influential rapper.

10/18/80	10	11		1 Kurtis Blow	71	$8	Mercury 3854

Rappin' Blow • The Breaks [58] • Way Out West • Throughout Your Years [31] • Hard Times [75] • All I Want In This World (Is To Find That Girl) • Takin' Care Of Business

7/18/81	35	10		2 Deuce	137	$8	Mercury 4020
10/9/82	38	8		3 Tough ....[M]	167	$6	Mercury 505
8/20/83	36	9		4 Party Time?	203	$8	Mercury 812757
9/22/84	18	42		5 Ego Trip	83	$8	Mercury 822420
10/19/85+	18	28		6 America	153	$8	Mercury 826141
10/25/86	16	20		7 Kingdom Blow	196	$8	Mercury 830215
9/3/88	84	4		8 Back By Popular Demand		$8	Mercury 834692

BLOWFLY '80
Born Clarence Reid on 2/14/45 in Cochran, Georgia. X-rated singer/songwriter/producer.

7/26/80	26	15		1 Blowfly's Party [X-Rated] ....[N]	82	$10	Weird World 2034
6/29/91	76	7		2 The Twisted World Of Blowfly ....[N]		$8	Oops! 3007

BLU, Peggi '87
Born in Lumberton, North Carolina.

8/15/87	71	2		Blu Blowin'		$8	Capitol 12550

BLUE MAGIC '74
Vocal group from Philadelphia: brothers Vernon and Wendell Sawyer, with Theodore Mills, Keith Beaton and Richard Pratt (left in 1981).

2/9/74	4	43		1 Blue Magic	45	$12	Atco 7038

Sideshow [1] • Look Me Up [36] • What's Come Over Me [11] • Just Don't Want To Be Lonely • Stop To Start [14] • Welcome To The Club • Spell [30] • Answer To My Prayer • Tear It Down

1/11/75	14	14		2 The Magic Of The Blue	71	$12	Atco 103
10/4/75	9	11		3 Thirteen Blue Magic Lane	50	$12	Atco 120

The Loneliest House On The Block • Chasing Rainbows [17] • Born On Halloween • Haunted (By Your Love) • I Like You • Magic Of The Blue • We're On The Right Track • Stop And Get A Hold Of Yourself • What's Come Over Me [11]

9/25/76	44	4		4 Mystic Dragons	170	$12	Atco 140
4/23/83	52	7		5 Magic #		$10	Mirage 90074
4/15/89	48	22		6 From Out Of The Blue		$8	Columbia 45092

BLUES BOY WILLIE '91
Born William McFalls in 1946 in Memphis, Texas. Blues singer/harmonica player.

1/26/91	57	21		1 Be-Who?		$8	Ichiban 1064
9/28/91	86	9		2 Be Who 2		$8	Ichiban 1119

BOBBY JIMMY & THE CRITTERS '86
Comedic rap group from Los Angeles: Russ Parr ("Bobby Jimmy"), Michael Lezan ("Arabian Prince"), Buckwheat and Bo.

10/18/86	30	15		1 Roaches: The Beginning ....[N]	200	$8	Macola 0933
9/12/87	49	6		2 Back And Proud ....[N]		$8	Macola 0989
3/24/90	67	5		3 Hip Hop Prankster ....[N]		$8	Priority 57117

BOBBY M '83
Born Bobby Militello in Detroit. Saxophonist.

1/22/83	53	9		Blow		$10	Gordy 6023

BOBCAT '89
Born Robert Ervin in Los Angeles. Male rapper.

7/29/89	72	8		Cat Got Ya Tongue		$8	Arista 8596

BOBO, Willie '66
Born William Correa on 2/28/34 in New York City. Died on 9/15/83 (age 49). Latin-jazz percussionist.

4/9/66	16	4		Spanish Grease ....[I]	137	$20	Verve 8631

BOFILL, Angela ★166★ '83
Born in 1954 in New York City. Singer/songwriter.

2/17/79	20	27		1 Angie	47	$10	GRP 5000
11/10/79+	10	33		2 Angel of the Night	34	$10	GRP 5501

I Try • People Make The World Go 'Round • Angel Of The Night [67] • Rainbow Child (Little Pas) • What I Wouldn't Do (For The Love Of You) [18] • The Feelin's Love • Love To Last • The Voyage

11/21/81+	13	28		3 Something About You	61	$8	Arista 9576
2/5/83	6	44		4 Too Tough	40	$8	Arista 9616

Too Tough [5] • Ain't Nothing Like The Real Thing • Tonight I Give In [12] • You Could Come Take Me Home • Love You Too Much • Is This A Dream • Song For A Rainy Day • I Can See It In Your Eyes • Accept Me (I'm Not A Girl Anymore) • Rainbow Inside My Heart

12/3/83+	20	25		5 Teaser	81	$8	Arista 8198
11/24/84	39	15		6 Let Me Be The One		$8	Arista 8258
11/2/85	53	11		7 Tell Me Tomorrow		$8	Arista 8396
11/26/88+	38	20		8 Intuition		$8	Capitol 48335
2/27/93	51	7		9 I Wanna Love Somebody		$8	Jive 41510

BOHANNON, Hamilton '78
Born on 3/7/42 in Newnan, Georgia. Drummer for **Stevie Wonder** from 1965-67.

9/28/74	49	7		1 Keep On Dancin'			$15	Dakar 76910
5/17/75	28	18		2 Insides Out			$15	Dakar 76916
1/17/76	21	12		3 Bohannon			$15	Dakar 76917
6/19/76	47	3		4 Dance Your Ass Off			$15	Dakar 76919
6/11/77	46	8		5 Phase II		203	$12	Mercury 1159
6/24/78	14	33		6 Summertime Groove		58	$12	Mercury 3728
2/24/79	34	8		7 Cut Loose			$12	Mercury 3762
3/22/80	72	2		8 Music In The Air			$12	Mercury 3813

BOLIVAR, John '88
Born in Atlanta. Jazz flutist/saxophonist.

12/3/88	97	2		Bolivar ....[I]			$8	Optimism 3204

BOND, Angelo '75
Born in Detroit. Male singer/songwriter.

9/13/75	60	1		Bondage		179	$10	ABC 889

BONDS, Gary (U.S.) '81
Born Gary Anderson on 6/6/39 in Jacksonville, Florida. Singer/songwriter.

5/16/81	34	14		Dedication		27	$10	EMI America 17051

BONE HARD PRODUCTIONS '94
Rap group from Houston: Curtis "Big Mello" Davis, Sleepy, Crazy C and Harvey Love.

9/19/92	96	2		1 Bone Hard Zaggin			$8	Rap-A-Lot 57175
				BONE HARD PRODUCTIONS Starring BIG MELLO				
7/9/94	44	4		2 Wegonefunkwichamind			$8	Rap-A-Lot 53897
				BONE HARD PRODUCTIONS Featuring BIG MELLO				

★137★ BONE THUGS-N-HARMONY '95
Male rap group from Cleveland: brothers Steven ("Layzie Bone") and Stanley ("Flesh-N-Bone") Howse, with Anthony Henderson ("Krayzie Bone"), Byron McCane ("Wish Bone") and Charles Scruggs ("Bizzy Bone"). Previously known as **Bone Enterprise**.

7/9/94	2²	119	▲²	1 Creepin On Ah Come Up ....[M]		12	$10	Ruthless 5526
				Mr. Ouija • **thuggish-ruggish-Bone** [17] • No Surrender • Down Foe My Thang • Creepin On Ah Come Up • **Foe Tha Love Of $** [33] • Moe Cheese				
7/15/95	29	17		2 Faces Of Death ....[E]		188	$8	Stoney Burke 70020
				BONE ENTERPRISE recordings from 1993				
8/5/95	❶³	105	▲⁴	3 E. 1999 Eternal		1²	$8	Ruthless 5539
				East 1999 [39] • Eternal • Crept And We Came • Down '71 (The Getaway) • Mr. Bill Collector • Budsmokers Only • **Tha Crossroads** [1] • Me Killa • Land Of The Heartless • No Shorts, No Losses • **1st Of Tha Month** [12] • Buddah Lovaz • Die Die Die • Mr. Ouija 2 • Mo' Murda • Shotz To Tha Double Glock				
8/16/97	❶¹	34	▲⁴	4 The Art Of War		1¹	$12	Ruthless 6340 [2]
				Handle The Vibe • **Look Into My Eyes** [4] • Body Rott • It's All Mo' Thug • Ready 4 War • Ain't Nothin Changed • Clog Up Yo Mind • It's All Real • Mind Of A Souljah • If I Could Teach The World [20] • Family Tree • Thug Luv • Hatin Nation • 7 Sign • Wasteland Warriors • U Ain't Bone • Gett Cha Thug On • All Original • Let The Law End • Whom Die They Lie • Friends (How Many Of Us Are Them) • Evil Paradise				
12/12/98	12	26	●	5 The Collection Volume One ....[G]		32	$8	Ruthless 69715

BONEY JAMES '97
Born James Oppenheim in Massachusetts; raised in New York and Los Angeles. Male saxophonist.

8/9/97	49	40	●	Sweet Thing ....[I]		112	$8	Warner 46548

BOOGIE BOYS, The '85
Rap trio from New York City: William Stroman, Joe Malloy and Rudy Sheriff.

8/31/85	10	29		1 City Life		53	$8	Capitol 12409
				Runnin' From Your Love • Do Or Die • Break Dancer • **A Fly Girl** [6] • City Life • Party Asteroid • **You Ain't Fresh** [60] • Shake And Break				
8/2/86	25	21		2 Survival Of The Freshest		124	$8	Capitol 12488
3/26/88	46	8		3 Romeo Knight		117	$8	Capitol 46917

BOOGIE DOWN PRODUCTIONS '89
Rap group from Bronx, New York. Founded by Lawrence Parker ("KRS-One") and Scott Sterling (shot to death on 8/25/87, age 24). Group includes a revolving lineup of rappers.

10/31/87	73	5		1 Criminal Minded			$10	B Boy 4787
5/7/88	18	27	●	2 By All Means Necessary		75	$8	Jive 1097
7/29/89	7	23	●	3 Ghetto Music: The Blueprint Of Hip Hop		36	$8	Jive 1187
				The Style You Haven't Done Yet • **Why Is That?** [48] • The Blueprint • Jack Of Spades • Jah Rulez • Breath Control • Who Protects Us From You? • You Must Learn • Hip Hop Rules • Bo! Bo! Bo! • Gimme Dat (Woy) • Ghetto Music • World Peace				
9/1/90	9	25	●	4 Edutainment		32	$8	Jive 1358
				Blackman In Effect • Ya Know The Rules • Beef • House Nigga's • **Love's Gonna Get'cha** [46] • 100 Guns • Ya Strugglin' • Breath Control II • Edutainment • The Homeless • The Kenny Parker Show • Original Lyrics • The Racist • 7 Dee Jays • 30 Cops Or More				
4/6/91	25	14		5 Live Hardcore Worldwide ....[L]		115	$8	Jive 1425
				recorded in New York, Paris and London				
3/14/92	20	17		6 Sex And Violence		42	$8	Jive 41470

BOOGIEMONSTERS '94
Male rap group from Virginia: Vex, Mondo, Myntric and Yodared. The latter two left in 1996.

8/27/94	42	10		1 Riders Of The Storm: The Underwater Album			$8	Pendulum 29607
7/5/97	47	3		2 God Sound			$8	EMI 56045

BOOKER, Chuckii   '92
Born in Los Angeles. Singer/songwriter/multi-instrumentalist.

| 6/10/89 | 18 | 28 | | 1 CHUCKii | | 116 | $8 | Atlantic 81947 |
| 10/10/92 | 13 | 31 | | 2 Niice N' Wiild | | | $8 | Atlantic 82410 |

★97★   **BOOKER T. & THE MG'S**   '71
Interracial instrumental group formed by sessionmen from Stax Records in Memphis: Booker T. Jones (keyboards; b: 11/12/44 in Memphis), Steve Cropper (guitar), Donald "Duck" Dunn (bass) and Al Jackson (drums). Jackson was murdered on 10/1/75 (age 39); replaced by Willie Hall. Cropper and Dunn had been in the **Mar-Keys**. MG stands for Memphis Group. Group inducted into the Rock and Roll Hall of Fame in 1992. Jones also recorded duets with his wife, Priscilla Coolidge (sister of Rita).
   1)Melting Pot 2)Hip Hug-Her 3)Uptight

| 12/3/66+ | 18 | 6 | | 1 And Now...Booker T. & The MG's | [I] | | $60 | Stax 711 |
| 6/24/67 | 4 | 18 | | 2 Hip Hug-Her | [I] | 35 | $50 | Stax 717 |

Hip Hug-Her *[6]* • Soul Sanction • Get Ready • More • Double Or Nothing • Carnaby St. • Slim Jenkins' Joint • Pigmy • Groovin' *[10]* • Booker's Notion • Sunny

4/6/68	17	26		3 Doin' Our Thing	[I]	176	$50	Stax 724
10/5/68	14	12		4 Soul Limbo	[I]	127	$25	Stax 2001
2/8/69	7	31		5 Uptight	[I-S]	98	$25	Stax 2006

Johnny, I Love You • Cleveland Now • Children, Don't Get Weary • Tank's Lament • Blues In The Gutter • We've Got Johnny Wells • Down At Ralph's Joint • Deadwood Dick • Run Tank Run • **Time Is Tight** *[7]*

| 6/14/69 | 10 | 19 | | 6 The Booker T. Set | [I] | 53 | $25 | Stax 2009 |

The Horse • Love Child • Sing A Simple Song • Lady Madonna • **Mrs. Robinson** *[35]* • This Guy's In Love With You • Light My Fire • Michelle • You're All I Need To Get By • I've Never Found A Girl • It's Your Thing

| 5/2/70 | 19 | 18 | | 7 McLemore Avenue | [I] | 107 | $25 | Stax 2027 |

version of **The Beatles'** *Abbey Road* album; McLemore is the street outside the Stax studios

| 11/21/70+ | 18 | 13 | | 8 Booker T. & The MG's Greatest Hits | [G-I] | 132 | $15 | Stax 2033 |
| 1/16/71 | 2² | 38 | | 9 Melting Pot | [I] | 43 | $15 | Stax 2035 |

Melting Pot *[21]* • Back Home • Chicken Pox • Fuquawi • Kinda Easy Like • Hi Ride • L.A. Jazz Song • Sunny Monday

| 11/24/73 | 49 | 5 | | 10 Chronicles | | | $12 | A&M 4413 |

BOOKER T. & PRISCILLA

3/9/74	56	4		11 The MG's			$15	Stax 3024
7/16/77	59	2		12 Universal Language	[I]	209	$12	Asylum 1093
11/28/81	49	7		13 I Want You			$10	A&M 4874

BOOKER T.

BOOM, Taka   '79
Born Yvonne Stevens in 1954 in Chicago. Former member of **The Undisputed Truth**. Sister of **Chaka Khan** and Mark Stevens of **The Jamaica Boys**.

| 6/9/79 | 48 | 6 | | Taka Boom | | 171 | $10 | Ariola 50041 |

BOOT CAMP CLIK   '97
Collective of rap acts: BDI, **Cocoa Brovaz**, **Heltah Skeltah**, O.G.C., The Reps, B.T.J's, Swan & Boogie Brown, F.L.O.W. and Illa Noyz.

| 5/31/97 | 4 | 16 | | For The People | | 15 | $8 | Priority 50646 |

1-900 Get Da Boot • Down By Law • Night Riders • Headz Are Reddee • Watch Your Step • Illa Noyz • Rag Time • Blackout • Ohkeedoke • Rugged Terrain • The Dugout • Go For Yours • Likkle Youth Man Dem • Last Time

BOOTSY'S RUBBER BAND — see COLLINS, William "Bootsy"

BOO-YAA T.R.I.B.E.   '90
Rap group from Los Angeles: Samoan brothers Ted, Donald, David, Danny, Paul and Roscoe Devoux.

| 4/21/90 | 33 | 24 | | New Funky Nation | | 117 | $8 | 4th & B'way 444017 |

BORN JAMERICANS   '94
Dancehall reggae duo: Horace Payne and Norman Howell.

| 6/25/94 | 36 | 19 | | 1 Kids From Foreign | | 188 | $8 | Delicious Vinyl 92349 |
| 6/14/97 | 65 | 4 | | 2 Yardcore | | | $8 | Delicious Vinyl 5018 |

B.O.S.E.   '90
B.O.S.E.: Bass Overdrive System Experts.

| 2/3/90 | 78 | 6 | | Spread The Word | [I] | | $8 | Rockwell 3316 |

BOSS   '93
Born Lichelle Laws in 1973 in Southfield, Michigan. Female rapper.

| 6/12/93 | 3 | 27 | | Born Gangstaz | | 22 | $8 | DJ West/Chaos 52903 |

Deeper *[28]* • Comin' To Getcha • Mai Sista Izza Bitch • Thelma & Louise • Drive By • Progress Of Elimination • Livin' Loc'd • Recipe Of A Hoe *[73]* • Catch A Bad One • Born Gangsta • 1-800-Body-Bags • Diary Of A Mad Bitch • 2 To Da Head • I Don't Give A Fuck

BOUNTY KILLER   '96
Born Rodney Pryce in Jamaica. Dancehall reggae singer.

| 10/5/96 | 27 | 26 | | 1 My Xperience | | 145 | $8 | TVT/VP 1461 |
| 11/21/98 | 39 | 3 | | 2 Next Millennium | | | $8 | Blunt 6370 |

BOWIE, David   '83
Born David Jones on 1/8/47 in London. Pop-rock singer/actor. Charted 33 pop albums from 1972-97. Inducted into the Rock and Roll Hall of Fame in 1996.

| 6/18/83 | 21 | 22 | ▲ | Let's Dance | | 4 | $10 | EMI America 17093 |

BOY GEORGE   '89
Born George O'Dowd on 6/14/61 in Bexleyheath, England. Lead singer of **Culture Club**.

| 4/8/89 | 34 | 20 | | High Hat | | 126 | $8 | Virgin 91022 |

BOYS, The   '89
Vocal group from Northridge, California: brothers Khiry, Hakeem, Tajh and Bilal Abdul-Samad.

DEBUT	PEAK	WKS	Gold	Album Title	Pop #	$	Label & Number
10/29/88+	3	54	▲	1 **Messages From The Boys**	33	$8	Motown 6260

Dial My Heart [1] • Lucky Charm [1] • A Little Romance [29] • Sunshine • Love Gram • Just For The Fun Of It • Personality • Be My Girl • Happy [57] • Let's Dance

DEBUT	PEAK	WKS	Gold	Album Title	Pop #	$	Label & Number
10/27/90	24	36	●	2 The Boys	108	$8	Motown 6302
5/30/92	45	12		3 The Saga Continues...	191	$8	Motown 6336

★132★ BOYZ II MEN   '91
Vocal group from Philadelphia: Wanya Morris, Michael McCary, Shawn Stockman and Nathan Morris.

DEBUT	PEAK	WKS	Gold	Album Title	Pop #	$	Label & Number
6/8/91	❶²	122	▲⁹	1 **Cooleyhighharmony**	3	$8	Motown 6320

Please Don't Go [8] • Lonely Heart • This Is My Heart • Uhh Ahh [1] • It's So Hard To Say Goodbye To Yesterday [1] • Motownphilly [4] • Under Pressure • Sympin [72] • Little Things • Your Love

DEBUT	PEAK	WKS	Gold	Album Title	Pop #	$	Label & Number
10/23/93	6	16	▲²	2 **Christmas Interpretations** [X]	19	$8	Motown 6365

Let It Snow [17] • Share Love • You're Not Alone • A Joyous Song • Why Christmas • Cold December Nights • Do They Know • Who Would Have Thought • Silent Night

DEBUT	PEAK	WKS	Gold	Album Title	Pop #	$	Label & Number
9/17/94	❶²	89	▲¹²	3 **II**	1⁵	$8	Motown 0323

Thank You [17] • All Around The World • U Know • Vibin' [27] • I Sit Away • Jezzebel • Khalil • Trying Times • I'll Make Love To You [1] • On Bended Knee [2] • 50 Candles • Water Runs Dry [4] • Yesterday

DEBUT	PEAK	WKS	Gold	Album Title	Pop #	$	Label & Number
11/25/95+	15	18	▲	4 The Remix Collection [K]	17	$8	Motown 0584
10/11/97	❶¹	54	▲²	5 **Evolution**	1¹	$8	Motown 0819

Doin' Just Fine • Never • 4 Seasons Of Loneliness [2] • Girl In The Life Magazine • A Song For Mama [1] • Can You Stand The Rain • Can't Let Her Go • Baby C'mon • Come On • All Night Long • Human II (Don't Turn Your Back On Me) • To The Limit • Dear God

BRAINSTORM   '77
Disco group from Detroit: Belita Woods, Charles Overton, Jeryl Bright, Larry Sims, Gerald Kent, Trenita Womack, Lamont Johnson, Willie Wooten and Renell Gonsalves.

DEBUT	PEAK	WKS	Gold	Album Title	Pop #	$	Label & Number
3/12/77	31	24		1 Stormin'	145	$8	Tabu 2048
4/8/78	53	5		2 Journey To The Light		$8	Tabu 35327

BRAND NEW HEAVIES, The   '91
Funk group from London: N'Dea Davenport (vocals), Simon Bartholomew (guitar), Andrew Levy (bass) and Jan Kincaid (drums). Davenport left in 1996; replaced by Siedah Garrett.

DEBUT	PEAK	WKS	Gold	Album Title	Pop #	$	Label & Number
4/27/91	17	49		1 **The Brand New Heavies**		$8	Delicious Vinyl 846874
8/29/92	49	10		2 Heavy Rhyme Experience: Vol. 1	139	$8	Delicious Vinyl 92178
4/9/94	26	21		3 Brother Sister	95	$8	Delicious Vinyl 92319
3/9/96	70	3		4 Excursions: Remixes & Rare Grooves [K]		$8	Delicious Vinyl 35535
5/31/97	29	12		5 Shelter	118	$8	Delicious Vinyl 5019

BRAND NUBIAN   '93
Rap trio from New Rochelle, New York: Maxwell Dixon ("Grand Puba"), Derek Murphy ("Sadat X") and Lorenzo DeChalus ("Lord Jamar"). Dixon left in 1992, replaced by Terence Perry ("Sincere Allah").

DEBUT	PEAK	WKS	Gold	Album Title	Pop #	$	Label & Number
1/12/91	34	40		1 **One For All**	130	$8	Elektra 60946
2/20/93	4	16		2 **In God We Trust**	12	$8	Elektra 61381

Allah U Akbar • Ain't No Mystery • Meaning Of The 5% • Pass The Gat • Black Star Line • Allah And Justice • The Godz... • The Travel Jam • Brand Nubian Rock The Set • Love Me Or Leave Me Alone [68] • Steal Ya 'Ho • Steady Bootleggin' • Black And Blue • Punks Jump Up To Get Beat Down [42]

DEBUT	PEAK	WKS	Gold	Album Title	Pop #	$	Label & Number
11/19/94	13	18		3 Everything Is Everything	54	$8	Elektra 61682
10/17/98	12	19		4 Foundation	59	$8	Arista 19024

BRANDY   '98
Born Brandy Norwood on 2/11/79 in McComb, Mississippi; raised in California. Singer/actress. Regular on TV's *Thea* in 1993 and star of TV's *Moesha* since 1996. Sister of **Ray J**.

DEBUT	PEAK	WKS	Gold	Album Title	Pop #	$	Label & Number
10/15/94+	6	87	▲⁴	1 **Brandy**	20	$8	Atlantic 82610

Movin' On • Baby [1] • Best Friend [7] • I Wanna Be Down [1] • Brokenhearted [2] • I'm Yours • Sunny Day • As Long As You're Here • Always On My Mind • Love Is On My Side • Give Me You

DEBUT	PEAK	WKS	Gold	Album Title	Pop #	$	Label & Number
6/27/98	2²	58↑	▲⁴	2 **Never S-a-y Never**	2¹	$8	Atlantic 83039

Angel In Disguise [17] • The Boy Is Mine [1] • Learn The Hard Way • Almost Doesn't Count [16] • Top Of The World • U Don't Know Me (Like U Used To) • Never Say Never • Truthfully • Have You Ever? [2] • Put That On Everything • Happy • One Voice • Tomorrow • (Everything I Do) I Do It For You

★144★ BRASS CONSTRUCTION   '76
Multi-ethnic disco group from New York City: Randy Muller (vocals, keyboards), Joe Wong (guitar), Wayne Parris, Morris Price, Jesse Ward and Mickey Grudge (horn section), Sandy Billups (congas), Wade Williamston (bass) and Larry Payton (drums). Muller later formed **Skyy**.

DEBUT	PEAK	WKS	Gold	Album Title	Pop #	$	Label & Number
2/14/76	❶³	31	▲	1 **Brass Construction**	10	$10	United Artists 545

Movin' [1] • Peekin' • Changin' [24] • Love • Talkin' • Dance

DEBUT	PEAK	WKS	Gold	Album Title	Pop #	$	Label & Number
11/20/76+	3	24	●	2 **Brass Construction II**	26	$10	United Artists 677

Ha Cha Cha (Funktion) [8] • Get To The Point (Summation) • Sambo (Progression) • Screwed (Conditions) • The Message (Inspiration) [42] • Now Is Tomorrow (Anticipation) • Blame It On (Introspection) • What's On Your Mind (Expression) [69]

DEBUT	PEAK	WKS	Gold	Album Title	Pop #	$	Label & Number
11/19/77	16	28	●	3 Brass Construction III	66	$10	United Artists 775
11/25/78	24	10		4 Brass Construction IV	174	$10	United Artists 916
12/8/79+	18	27		5 Brass Construction 5	89	$10	United Artists 977
9/20/80	32	10		6 Brass Construction 6	121	$10	United Artists 1060
5/1/82	21	20		7 Attitudes	114	$8	Liberty 51121
5/28/83	29	13		8 Conversations	176	$8	Capitol 12268
7/28/84	31	20		9 Renegades		$8	Capitol 12327

BRAXTON, Toni   '93
Born on 10/7/68 in Severn, Maryland. Female singer. Recorded in 1990 with her younger sisters as **The Braxtons**. Won the 1993 Best New Artist Grammy Award.

| 7/31/93 | **❶**³ | 105 | ▲⁸ | 1 Toni Braxton | 1² | $8 | LaFace 26007 |

Another Sad Love Song [2] • **Breathe Again** [4] • Seven Whole Days • Love Affair • Candlelight • Spending My Time With You • **Love Shoulda Brought You Home** [2] • **I Belong To You** [6] • How Many Ways [11] • **You Mean The World To Me** [3] • Best Friend

| 7/6/96 | **❶**¹ | 92 | ▲⁷ | 2 Secrets | 2¹ | $8 | LaFace 26020 |

Come On Over Here • **You're Makin' Me High** [1] • There's No Me Without You • **Un-Break My Heart** [2] • Talking In His Sleep • How Could An Angel Break My Heart • Find Me A Man • **Let It Flow** [flip] • Why Should I Care • **I Don't Want To** [flip] • I Love Me Some Him [9] • In The Late Of Night

BRAXTONS, The   '96
Vocal trio of sisters from Severn, Maryland: Tamar, Trina and Towanda Braxton. Began as a quintet, with Traci and **Toni Braxton**. Toni went solo in 1992; Traci went solo in 1995.

| 8/31/96 | 26 | 8 | | So Many Ways | 113 | $8 | Atlantic 82875 |

BREAKWATER   '80
Disco group from Philadelphia: Gene Robinson (vocals), Lincoln Gilmore (guitar), Kae Williams (keyboards), John Braddock (percussion), Vince Garnell and Greg Scott (horns), Steve Green (bass) and James Jones (drums).

| 3/3/79 | 36 | 15 | | 1 Breakwater | 173 | $10 | Arista 4208 |
| 5/17/80 | 33 | 18 | | 2 Splashdown | 141 | $10 | Arista 4264 |

BRECKER BROTHERS, The   '75
Duo of Philadelphia-born brothers Randy (b: 11/27/45; trumpet) and Michael (b: 3/29/49; reeds) Brecker. Former members of **Spyro Gyra**. Michael was also with **Members Only**.

| 5/17/75 | 25 | 12 | | 1 The Brecker Brothers | [I] | 102 | $10 | Arista 4037 |
| 3/6/76 | 32 | 11 | | 2 Back To Back | 82 | $10 | Arista 4061 |

BREEZE   '89
Born Morgan Rodriguez in New York City. Male rapper.

| 8/19/89 | 60 | 11 | | The Young Son Of No One | | $8 | Atlantic 81995 |

BRENDA & THE TABULATIONS   '67
Vocal group from Philadelphia: Brenda Payton (d: 6/14/92), Jerry Jones, Eddie Jackson and Maurice Coates.

| 6/24/67 | 19 | 6 | | Dry Your Eyes | 191 | $40 | Dionn 2000 |

BRICK   '77
Disco-jazz group from Atlanta: Jimmy Brown (sax), Reggie Hargis (guitar), Don Nevins (keyboards), Ray Ransom (bass) and Eddie Irons (drums). All share vocals.

| 11/6/76+ | **❶**¹ | 24 | | 1 Good High | 19 | $10 | Bang 408 |

Here We Come • **Music Matic** [82] • **Dazz** [1] • Can't Wait • Southern Sunset • Good High • Brick City • Sister Twister • **That's What It's All About** [48]

| 9/10/77 | **❶**² | 33 | | 2 Brick | 15 | $10 | Bang 409 |

Ain't Gonna' Hurt Nobody [7] • Living From The Mind • Happy • We Don't Wanna' Sit Down (We Wanna' Git Down) • Dusic [2] • Hello • Honey Chile • Fun • Good Morning Sunshine

5/19/79	25	12		3 Stoneheart	100	$10	Bang 35969
7/19/80	31	27		4 Waiting On You	179	$10	Bang 36262
9/5/81	13	15		5 Summer Heat	89	$10	Bang 37471

BRIDES OF FUNKENSTEIN, The   '78
Female singers from **George Clinton**'s corporation. Duo in 1978 of Dawn Silva and Lynn Mabry. Trio in 1980 of Silva, Sheila Horn and Jeanette McGruder.

| 10/28/78 | 17 | 16 | | 1 Funk Or Walk | 70 | $15 | Atlantic 19201 |
| 3/1/80 | 49 | 6 | | 2 Never Buy Texas From A Cowboy | 93 | $10 | Atlantic 19261 |

BRIDGES, Alicia   '78
Born on 7/15/53 in Lawndale, North Carolina. Disco singer/songwriter.

| 10/14/78 | 30 | 20 | | Alicia Bridges | 33 | $10 | Polydor 6158 |

BRIDGEWATER, Dee Dee   '79
Born on 5/27/50 in Memphis; raised in Flint, Michigan. Jazz singer/actress. Appeared on Broadway in The Wiz.

| 6/9/79 | 57 | 3 | | Bad For Me | 182 | $10 | Elektra 188 |

BRIGHTER SIDE OF DARKNESS   '73
Vocal group from Chicago: Darryl Lamont, Ralph Eskridge, Randolph Murphy and Larry Washington.

| 4/14/73 | 35 | 5 | | Love Jones | 202 | $12 | 20th Century 405 |

BRISTOL, Johnny   '74
Born on 2/3/39 in Morganton, North Carolina. Singer/songwriter/producer.

| 9/7/74 | 7 | 19 | | 1 Hang On In There Baby | 82 | $12 | MGM 4959 |

Woman, Woman • **Hang On In There Baby** [2] • Reachin' Out For Your Love • **You And I** [20] • Take Care Of You For Me • I Got Cha Number • It Don't Hurt No More • Memories Don't Leave Like People Do • Love Me For A Reason

| 4/19/75 | 29 | 6 | | 2 Feeling The Magic | | $12 | MGM 4983 |
| 2/5/77 | 43 | 6 | | 3 Bristol's Creme | 154 | $10 | Atlantic 18197 |

BROOKINS, Robert   '89
Singer/songwriter/producer.

| 1/14/89 | 37 | 18 | | Let It Be Me | | $8 | MCA 42250 |

BROOKLYN, BRONX & QUEENS BAND, The   '81
Group from New York City: Lucious Floyd (vocals), Abdul Walli Mohammed (guitar), Kevin Nance (keyboards), PeeWee Ford (bass) and Dwayne Perdue (drums). New lineup in 1982 included Nance and Perdue with Kevin Robinson (vocals), Cheili Minucci (guitar) and Tony Bridges (bass).

| 8/22/81 | 19 | 18 | | 1 The Brooklyn, Bronx & Queens Band | 109 | $8 | Capitol 12155 |
| 8/28/82 | 32 | 12 | | 2 All Night Long | | $8 | Capitol 12212 |

THE B.B. & Q. BAND

BROOM, Bobby '81
Born in New York City. Jazz guitarist.

DEBUT	PEAK	WKS	Gold	Album Title	Pop #	$	Label & Number
8/29/81	50	9		Clean Sweep	[I] 203	$10	Arista/GRP 5504

BROTHA LYNCH HUNG '97
Born in Los Angeles. Male rapper.

8/7/93	91	5		1 24 Deep		$8	Black Market 24
3/18/95	26	33		2 Season Of Da Siccness - The Resurrection	162	$8	Black Market 53967
10/18/97	9	10		3 Loaded	28	$8	Black Market 50648

Sicc Made House • My Soul To Keep • Die 1 By 1 • One A Da Las Sicc Niggaz • Situation • Heataz • Did It And Did It • Went Way • Thatz What I Said • Feel My Nature Rize • One Mo Pound • On My Brief Case • Secondz A Way

BROTHERHOOD CREED '92
Rap duo from Los Angeles: Tyrone Ward and Sean McDuffie.

5/16/92	29	27		Brotherhood Creed		$8	Gasoline Alley 10574

★111★ BROTHERS JOHNSON, The '78
Duo of brothers from Los Angeles: George (guitar; b: 5/17/53) and Louis (bass; b: 4/13/55) Johnson. With **Billy Preston**'s band from 1973-75.

3/13/76	❶[4]	38	▲	1 Look Out For #1	9	$10	A&M 4567

I'll Be Good To You [1] • Thunder Thumbs And Lightnin' Licks • Get The Funk Out Ma Face [4] • Tomorrow • Free And Single [26] • Come Together • Land Of Ladies • Dancin' And Prancin' • The Devil

5/21/77	2[3]	32	▲	2 Right On Time	13	$10	A&M 4644

Runnin' For Your Lovin' [20] • Free Yourself, Be Yourself • "Q" • Right On Time • Strawberry Letter 23 [1] • Brother Man • Never Leave You Lonely • Love Is [50]

8/12/78	❶[7]	26	▲	3 Blam!!	7	$10	A&M 4714

Ain't We Funkin' Now [45] • So Won't You Stay • Blam!! • Blast Off • Ride-O-Rocket [45] • Mista' Cool • It's You Girl • Streetwave

3/8/80	❶[2]	32	▲	4 Light Up The Night	5	$10	A&M 3716

Stomp! [1] • Light Up The Night [16] • You Make Me Wanna Wiggle • Treasure [36] • This Had To Be • All About The Heaven • Smilin' On Ya • Closer To The One That You Love • Celebrations

7/25/81	10	16		5 Winners	48	$10	A&M 3724

The Real Thing [11] • Dancin' Free [51] • Sunlight • Teaser • Caught Up • In The Way • I Want You • Do It For Love • Hot Mama • Daydreamer Dream

1/8/83	23	14		6 Blast! (The Latest And The Greatest)	[G] 138	$10	A&M 4927

side 1: new songs; side 2: greatest hits

8/4/84	20	15		7 Out Of Control	91	$10	A&M 4965

BROTHER TO BROTHER '76
Group from St. Louis: Michael Burton (vocals), Billy Jones, Frankie Prescott and Yogi Horton.

12/14/74	45	4		1 In The Bottle		$15	Turbo 7013
5/22/76	33	12		2 Let Your Mind Be Free		$15	Turbo 7015

★142★ BROWN, Bobby '88
Born on 2/5/69 in Roxbury, Massachusetts. Singer/songwriter/producer. Former member of **New Edition**. Appeared in the movies *Ghostbusters II*, *Panther* and *A Thin Line Between Love & Hate*. Married **Whitney Houston** on 7/18/92. The B. Brown Posse consisted of Brown with rappers Stylz, Coop B, Harold Travis, Smoothe Sylk and Dede O'Neal.

11/29/86+	12	28	▲	1 King Of Stage	88	$8	MCA 5827
7/16/88	❶[11]	80	▲[7]	2 Don't Be Cruel	1[6]	$8	MCA 42185

Don't Be Cruel [1] • My Prerogative [1] • Roni [2] • Rock Wit'cha [3] • Every Little Step [1] • I'll Be Good To You • Take It Slow • All Day All Night • I Really Love You Girl

12/9/89+	7	23	▲	3 Dance!...Ya Know It!	[K] 9	$8	MCA 6342

contains remixes of his hits

Roni • Rock Wit'cha • Girl Next Door • Don't Be Cruel • Every Little Step • On Our Own • Baby, I Wanna Tell You Something • My Prerogative • Seventeen

9/12/92	❶[2]	45	▲[2]	4 Bobby	2[1]	$8	MCA 10417

Humpin' Around [1] • Two Can Play That Game • Get Away [3] • Til The Ehnd Of Time • Good Enough [5] • Pretty Little Girl • Lovin' You Down • One More Night • Something In Common • That's The Way Love Is [9] • College Girl • Storm Away • I'm Your Friend

5/15/93	96	2		5 B. Brown Posse		$8	MCA 10785
12/11/93	72	8		6 Remixes N The Key Of B	[K]	$8	MCA 10974

contains remixes of his hits

11/22/97	15	7		7 Forever	61	$8	MCA 11691

BROWN, Chuck, & The Soul Searchers '79
Funk group from Washington, DC: Chuck Brown (vocals, guitar), John Buchanan (synthesizer), Don Tillery (trumpet), Leroy Fleming (sax), Gregory Gerran (congas), Curtis Johnson (organ), Jerry Wilder (bass) and Ricky Wellman (drums).

2/10/79	5	17	●	Bustin' Loose	31	$10	Source 3076

Bustin' Loose [1] • Never Gonna Give You Up • If It Ain't Funky • I Gotcha Now • Could It Be Love • Game Seven [81] • Berro Sombaro

BROWN, Dennis '82
Born on 2/1/57 in Kingston, Jamaica. Died of a collapsed lung on 7/1/99 (age 42). Reggae singer/songwriter.

5/15/82	36	10		Love Has Found Its Way		$8	A&M 4886

BROWN, Foxy '96
Born Inga Marchand on 9/6/79 in New York City. Female rapper. Took her name from the action movie character played by actress Pam Grier. Member of **The Firm**.

12/7/96	2[4]	46	▲	Ill Na Na	7	$8	Violator 533684

Chicken Coop • Letter To The Firm • Foxy's Bells • Get Me Home • The Promise • The Set Up • If I... • The Chase • Ill Na Na • No One's • Fox Boogie • I'll Be [5]

BROWN, Horace '96
Born in Charlotte, North Carolina.

7/6/96	18	19		Horace Brown	145	$8	Motown 0625

BROWN, James ★3★ '74

Born on 5/3/33 in Barnwell, South Carolina; raised in Augusta, Georgia. Acclaimed as one of the most influential "soul" artists of all-time. Various nicknames include "The Godfather of Soul" and "The Hardest Working Man in Show Business." Inducted into the Rock and Roll Hall of Fame in 1986. On 12/15/88, received a six-year prison sentence after leading police on an interstate car chase; released from prison on 2/27/91. Won Grammy's Lifetime Achievement Award in 1992.

1)The Payback 2)It's A Mother 3)Hell 4)Live At The Apollo, Volume II 5)Papa's Got A Brand New Bag

4/17/65	9	3		**1 Grits & Soul** [I]	124	$40	Smash 67057

Grits • Tempted • There • After You're Through • Devil's Hideaway • Who's Afraid Of Virginia Woolf? • Infatuation • Wee Wee • Mister Hip • Headache

9/11/65	2³	20		**2 Papa's Got A Brand New Bag**	26	$40	King 938

Papa's Got A Brand New Bag *[1]* • **Mashed Potatoes U.S.A.** *[21]* • Cross Firing • Love Don't Love Nobody • I Stay In The Chapel Every Night (Just Won't Do Right) • And I Do Just What I Want • This Old Heart • **Baby, You're Right** *[2]* • **Have Mercy Baby** *[92]* • You Don't Have To Go • Doin' The Limbo

11/27/65	3	11		**3 James Brown Plays James Brown - Today & Yesterday** [I]	42	$40	Smash 67072

Papa's Got A Brand New Bag • Oh Baby Don't You Weep • **Try Me** *[34]* • Sidewinder • **Out Of Sight** *[24]* • Maybe The Last Time • Every Beat Of My Heart • Hold It • A Song For My Father

1/29/66	2¹	15		**4 I Got You (I Feel Good)**	36	$50	King 946

I Got You (I Feel Good) *[1]* • **Lost Someone** *[2]* • **Night Train** *[5]* • You've Got The Power • Love Don't Love Nobody • Think • Good, Good Loving • I Can't Help It (I Just Do-Do-Do) • I've Got Money • **Three Hearts In A Tangle** *[18]* • Suds • Dancin' Little Thing

5/21/66	11	6		**5 James Brown Plays New Breed** .... [I]	101	$40	Smash 67080
9/10/66	11	15		**6 It's A Man's Man's Man's World**	90	$50	King 985
11/26/66	24	3		**7 Handful Of Soul** .... [I]	135	$40	Smash 67084
4/29/67	7	9		**8 Raw Soul**	88	$50	King 1016

Bring It Up *[7]* • **Don't Be A Drop-Out** *[4]* • Till Then • Tell Me That You Love Me • Yours And Mine • **Money Won't Change You** *[11]* • Only You • **Let Yourself Go** *[5]* • The Nearness Of You • Nobody Knows • Stone Fox

6/17/67	5	15		**9 Live At The Garden** [L]	41	$80	King 1018

Out Of Sight • Bring It Up • Try Me • Let Yourself Go • Hip Bag '67 • Prisoner Of Love • It May Be The Last Time • I Got You (I Feel Good) • Ain't That A Groove • Please, Please, Please • Bring It Up

7/8/67	27	3		**10 James Brown Plays The Real Thing** .... [I]	164	$40	Smash 67093
9/16/67	5	14		**11 Cold Sweat**	35	$50	King 1020

Cold Sweat *[1]* • Fever • **Kansas City** *[21]* • Stagger Lee • Good Rockin' Tonight • Mona Lisa • I Want To Be Around • Nature Boy • Come Rain Or Come Shine • I Loves You Porgy • Back Stabbin'

3/9/68	13	10		**12 James Brown Presents His Show Of Tomorrow**		$50	King 1024
3/23/68	4	15		**13 I Can't Stand Myself (When You Touch Me)**	17	$50	King 1030

I Can't Stand Myself (When You Touch Me) *[4]* • **There Was A Time** *[3]* • **Get It Together** *[11]* • Baby, Baby, Baby, Baby • Time After Time • The Soul Of J.B. • Why Did You Take Your Love Away From Me • Need Your Love So Bad • You've Got To Change Your Mind • Funky Soul #1

5/18/68	8	15		**14 I Got The Feelin'**	135	$50	King 1031

I Got The Feelin' *[1]* • Maybe I'll Understand • You've Got The Power • Maybe Good-Maybe Bad • Shhhhhhh (For A Little While) • Just Plain Funk • If I Ruled The World • Stone Fox • It Won't Be Me • Here I Go

8/17/68	20	6		**15 James Brown Plays Nothing But Soul** .... [I]	150	$50	King 1034
9/7/68	2³	44		**16 Live At The Apollo, Volume II** [L]	32	$70	King 1022 [2]

recorded at the Apollo Theater in New York City

I'll Go Crazy • Try Me • Think • I Don't Mind • Lost Someone • Please, Please, Please • You've Got The Power • I Found Someone • Why Do You Me • I Want You So Bad • I Love You, Yes I Do • Why Does Everything Happen To Me • Bewildered • Please Don't Go • Night Train • Out Of Sight • Try Me • Bring It Up • Let Yourself Go • There Was A Time • Little Groove Maker Me • Cold Sweat

4/12/69	6	19		**17 Say It Loud-I'm Black And I'm Proud**	53	$50	King 1047

Say It Loud - I'm Black And I'm Proud *[1]* • **I Guess I'll Have To Cry, Cry, Cry** *[15]* • **Goodbye My Love** *[9]* • Shades Of Brown • **Licking Stick - Licking Stick** *[2]* • I Love You • Then You Can Tell Me Goodbye • Let Them Talk • Maybe I'll Understand • I'll Lose My Mind

5/24/69	14	16		**18 Gettin' Down To It**	99	$50	King 1051
8/23/69	4	27		**19 James Brown plays & directs The Popcorn** [I]	40	$40	King 1055

The Popcorn *[11]* • Why Am I Treated So Bad • In The Middle • **Soul Pride** *[33]* • A New Shift • Suds • The Chicken • The Chase

8/30/69	2⁵	28		**20 It's A Mother**	26	$40	King 1063

Mother Popcorn *[1]* • Mashed Potato Popcorn • I'm Shook • Popcorn With A Feeling • The Little Groove Maker Me • Any Day Now • If I Ruled The World • You're Still Out Of Sight • Top Of The Stack

2/14/70	5	19		**21 Ain't It Funky** [I]	43	$40	King 1092

Ain't It Funky Now *[3]* • Fat Wood • Cold Sweat • **Give It Up Or Turnit A Loose** *[1]* • Nose Job • Use Your Mother • After You Done It

4/18/70	12	14		**22 Soul On Top**	125	$40	King 1100

with the Louie Bellson Orchestra

6/13/70	11	17		**23 It's A New Day So Let A Man Come In**	121	$40	King 1095
10/3/70	4	31		**24 Sex Machine**	29	$50	King 1115 [2]

not a live album; audience effects are dubbed in

Get Up (I Feel Like Being Like A) Sex Machine *[2]* • **Brother Rapp** *[2]* • Bewildered • I Got The Feelin' • Give It Up Or Turnit A Loose • I Don't Want Nobody To Give Me Nothing • Licking Stick - Licking Stick • Low Down Popcorn • Spinning Wheel • If I Ruled The World • There Was A Time • It's A Man's Man's World • Please, Please, Please • I Can't Stand Myself (When You Touch Me) • Mother Popcorn

1/30/71	4	20		**25 Super Bad**	61	$40	King 1127

not a live album; audience effects are dubbed in

Super Bad *[1]* • Let It Be Me • Sometime • A Man Has To Go Back To The Crossroads • Giving Out Of Juice • By The Time I Get To Phoenix

DEBUT	PEAK	WKS	Gold	Album Title	Pop #	$	Label & Number
				BROWN, James — Cont'd			
5/1/71	26	4		26 Sho Is Funky Down Here..[I]	137	$40	King 1110
9/11/71	4	21		27 **Hot Pants**	22	$40	Polydor 4054
				Blues & Pants • Can't Stand It • **Escape-ism** *[6]* • Hot Pants (She Got To Use What She Got To Get What She Wants) *[1]*			
12/25/71+	7	27		28 **Revolution Of The Mind - Live At The Apollo, Volume III** [L]	39	$60	Polydor 3003 [2]
				recorded at the Apollo Theater in New York City			
				It's A New Day So Let A Man Come In And Do The Popcorn • Bewildered • Sex Machine • Escape-ism • Make It Funky • Try Me • Medley: I Can't Stand It/Mother Popcorn/I Got The Feelin' • Give It Up Or Turnit A Loose • Super Bad • Get Up, Get Into It, Get Involved • Soul Power • Hot Pants (She Got To Use What She Got To Get What She Wants)			
6/24/72	13	12		29 **James Brown Soul Classics**..............................[G]	83	$25	Polydor 5401
7/22/72	10	18		30 **There It Is**	60	$40	Polydor 5028
				There It Is *[4]* • King Heroin *[6]* • I'm A Greedy Man *[7]* • Who Am I • **Talking Loud And Saying Nothing** *[1]* • Public Enemy #1 • I Need Help (I Can't Do It Alone) • Never Can Say Goodbye			
12/2/72+	8	19		31 **Get On The Good Foot**	68	$60	Polydor 3004 [2]
				Get On The Good Foot *[1]* • The Whole World Needs Liberation • Your Love Was Good For Me • Cold Sweat • Recitation By Hank Ballard • I Got A Bag Of My Own *[3]* • Nothing Beats A Try But A Fail • **Lost Someone** *[2]* • Funky Side Of Town • Please, Please • Ain't It A Groove • My Part/Make It Funky • Dirty Harri			
3/3/73	2²	23		32 **Black Caesar** [S]	31	$50	Polydor 6014
				Down And Out In New York City *[13]* • Blind Man Can See It • Sportin' Life • Dirty Harri • The Boss • Make It Good To Yourself • Mama Feelgood • Mama's Dead • White Lightning (I Mean Moonshine) • Chase • Like It Is, Like It Was			
7/21/73	15	15		33 **Slaughter's Big Rip-Off**...........................[S]	92	$50	Polydor 6015
10/13/73	30	15		34 **Soul Classics Vol. II**.............................[G]	202	$25	Polydor 5402
12/22/73+	❶²	37	●	35 <u>The Payback</u>	34	$50	Polydor 3007 [2]
				The Payback *[1]* • Doing The Best I Can • Take Some-Leave Some • Shoot Your Shot • Forever Suffering • Time Is Running Out Fast • **Stoned To The Bone** *[4]* • Mind Power			
8/31/74	2⁴	22		36 **Hell**	35	$80	Polydor 9001 [2]
				Coldblooded • Hell • **My Thang** *[1]* • Sayin' It And Doin' It • Please, Please, Please • When The Saints Go Marching In • These Foolish Things • Stormy Monday • A Man Has To Go Back To The Cross Road Before He Finds Himself • Sometime • I Can't Stand It '76" • Lost Someone • Don't Tell A Lie About Me And I Won't Tell The Truth On You • **Papa Don't Take No Mess** *[1]*			
2/1/75	5	11		37 **Reality**	56	$40	Polydor 6039
				Reality *[19]* • Funky President (People It's Bad) *[4]* • Further On Up The Road • Check Your Body • Don't Fence Me In • All For One • I'm Broken Hearted • The Twist • Who Can I Turn To			
6/7/75	10	9		38 **Sex Machine Today**	103	$40	Polydor 6042
				Sex Machine *[16]* • I Feel Good • Problems • Dead On It • Get Up Off Of Me • Deep In It			
10/11/75	22	7		39 **Everybody's Doin' The Hustle & Dead On The Double Bump**...............	193	$40	Polydor 6054
1/17/76	25	8		40 **Hot**..		$40	Polydor 6059
8/14/76	14	10		41 **Get Up Offa That Thing**.....................................	147	$40	Polydor 6071
1/15/77	20	13		42 **Bodyheat**...	126	$40	Polydor 6093
8/27/77	31	7		43 **Mutha's Nature**...		$40	Polydor 6111
4/15/78	30	22		44 **Jam/1980's**..	121	$40	Polydor 6140
2/3/79	58	3		45 **Take A Look At Those Cakes**..............................		$30	Polydor 6181
7/21/79	37	9		46 **The Original Disco Man**..................................	152	$30	Polydor 6212
3/29/80	68	3		47 **People**...		$30	Polydor 6258
10/25/86+	39	23		48 **Gravity**..	156	$12	Scotti Brothers 40380
6/25/88	15	21		49 **I'm Real**...	96	$12	Scotti Brothers 44241
7/13/91	89	7		50 **Star Time**..[K]		$30	Polydor 331 [4]
8/17/91	51	10		51 **Love Over-Due**...		$8	Scotti Brothers 75225
4/3/93	99	1	▲	52 **20 All-Time Greatest Hits**............................[G]		$8	Polydor 511326
				BROWN, Jocelyn　　　　　'87			
				Born in North Carolina. Singer with the disco groups **Inner Life** and **Salsoul Orchestra**.			
5/23/87	65	4		**One From The Heart**..		$8	Warner 25445
				BROWN, Mel　　　　　'71			
				Born on 10/7/39 in Jackson, Mississippi. Jazz guitarist.			
5/29/71	39	2		**I'd Rather Suck My Thumb**.................................		$15	Impulse 9186
				BROWN, Nappy　　　　　'89			
				Born Napoleon Brown Culp on 10/12/29 in Charlotte, North Carolina. Male singer. Had the #2 hit "Don't Be Angry" in 1955.			
5/6/89	80	9		**Deep Sea Diver**..		$8	Meltone 1502
				BROWN, Norman　　　　　'94			
				Born in Los Angeles. Jazz guitarist.			
10/24/92	51	12		1 **Just Between Us**..[I]		$8	MoJazz 7000
6/4/94	21	39		2 **After The Storm**...[I]	140	$8	MoJazz 0301
7/6/96	31	15		3 **Better Days Ahead**......................................[I]	162	$8	MoJazz 0545
				BROWN, Odell, & The Organ-Izers　　　　　'67			
				Jazz group from Nashville.			
8/5/67	13	10		1 **Mellow Yellow**...[I]	173	$20	Cadet 788
6/21/69	32	3		2 **Odele Brown Plays Otis Redding**.....................[I]		$20	Cadet 823
				BROWN, Peter　　　　　'78			
				Born on 7/11/53 in Blue Island, Illinois. Disco singer/keyboardist/producer.			
1/28/78	9	38		1 **A Fantasy Love Affair**	11	$10	Drive 104
				Fantasy Love Affair • Do Ya Wanna Get Funky With Me *[3]* • You Should Do It *[25]* • The Singer's Become A Dancer • For Your Love • **Dance With Me** *[5]* • It's True What They Say About Love • Without Love			
1/19/80	71	2		2 **Stargazer**..	206	$10	Drive 108

BROWN, Randy   '79
Singer/songwriter from Memphis.

DEBUT	PEAK	WKS	Gold	Album Title	Pop #	$	Label & Number
9/30/78+	46	9		1 Welcome To My Room		$10	Parachute 9005
3/31/79	48	7		2 Intimately		$10	Parachute 9012
3/29/80	50	13		3 Midnight Desire		$10	Chocolate City 2010

BROWN, Shirley   '75
Born on 1/6/47 in West Memphis, Arkansas; raised in East St. Louis.

2/1/75	11	18		1 Woman To Woman	98	$12	Truth 4206
11/11/89	66	19		2 Fire & Ice		$8	Malaco 7451
6/15/91	63	23		3 Timeless		$8	Malaco 7459
4/29/95	67	9		4 Diva Of Soul		$8	Malaco 7476

BROWNE, Tom   '80
Born in 1959 in New York City. Jazz-funk trumpeter. Member of **Fuse One**.

9/8/79	50	12		1 Browne Sugar [I]	147	$10	GRP 5003
8/2/80	**❶**[1]	32	●	2 Love Approach [I]	18	$10	GRP 5008

Funkin' For Jamaica (N.Y.) [1] • Her Silent Smile • Forever More • Dreams Of Lovin' You • Nocturne • Martha • Moon Rise • Weak In The Knees

2/21/81	5	23		3 Magic	37	$10	GRP 5503

Let's Dance [59] • Magic • I Know • Midnight Interlude • God Bless The Child • Night Wind • Thigh's High (Grip Your Hips And Move) • Making Plans

12/26/81+	20	17		4 Yours Truly	97	$10	GRP 5507
11/19/83	24	23		5 Rockin' Radio [I]	147	$8	Arista 8107
12/1/84	49	14		6 Tommy Gun [I]		$8	Arista 8249

BROWNSTONE   '95
Female vocal trio from Los Angeles: Monica Doby, Nichole Gilbert and Charmayne Maxwell. Doby left group for health reasons in June 1995; replaced by Kina Cosper.

1/28/95	4	44	▲	1 From The Bottom Up	29	$8	MJJ Music 57827

Party Wit Me • Grapevyne [6] • If You Love Me [2] • Sometimes Dancin' • I Can't Tell You Why [22] • Don't Cry For Me • **Pass The Lovin'** [58] • Fruit Of Life • True To Me • Wipe It Up • Deeper Feelings (Ooh La La) • Half Of You

7/12/97	16	18		2 Still Climbing	51	$8	MJJ Music 67524

BRUNSON, Tyrone   '83
Born in Washington, DC. Singer/bassist. Nicknamed "Tystick."

3/26/83	25	18		1 Sticky Situation		$8	Believe In A D. 38140

TYRONE (TYSTICK) BRUNSON

4/21/84	63	4		2 Fresh		$8	Believe In A D. 39197

BRYANT, Ray   '66
Born Raphael Bryant on 12/24/31 in Philadelphia. Jazz pianist.

6/18/66	5	19		1 Gotta Travel On [I]	111	$20	Cadet 767

Gotta Travel On • Erewhon • Smack Dab In The Middle • Monkey Business • All Things Are Possible • It Was A Very Good Year • Bag's Groove • Midnight Stalkin' • Little Soul Sister

4/15/67	18	7		2 Slow Freight [I]	193	$20	Cadet 781

BRYANT, Rusty   '71
Jazz tenor saxophonist. Died on 3/25/91 (age 61). Father of **Stevie Woods**.

2/27/71	35	7		Soul Liberation		$15	Prestige 7798

BRYANT, Sharon   '89
Born on 8/14/56 in Westchester County, New York. Lead singer of **Atlantic Starr** from 1976-84.

8/5/89	27	38		Here I Am	139	$8	Wing 837313

BRYSON, Peabo   ★51★   '91
Born Robert Peabo Bryson on 4/13/51 in Greenville, South Carolina. Male singer.
1)Can You Stop The Rain 2)Crosswinds 3)I Am Love

10/2/76	48	8		1 Peabo		$15	Bullet 7000
2/11/78	11	37	●	2 Reaching For The Sky	49	$10	Capitol 11729
12/23/78+	3	35	●	3 Crosswinds	35	$10	Capitol 11875

Crosswinds [28] • I'm So Into You [2] • Smile • She's A Woman [44] • Point Of View • Spread Your Wings • Don't Touch Me • Love Is Watching You

12/15/79+	7	20		4 We're The Best Of Friends	44	$10	Capitol 12019

NATALIE COLE/PEABO BRYSON
Gimme Some Time [8] • This Love Affair • I Want To Be Where You Are • Your Lonely Heart • What You Won't Do For Love [16] • We're The Best Of Friends • Medley: Let's Fall In Love/You Send Me • Love Will Find You

5/3/80	13	25		5 Paradise	79	$10	Capitol 12063
12/27/80+	10	19		6 Live & More [L]	52	$12	Atlantic 7004 [2]

ROBERTA FLACK & PEABO BRYSON
recorded at the Holiday Star Theater in Merrillville, Indiana
Medley: Only Heaven Can Wait (For Love)/You Are My Heaven • **Make The World Stand Still** [13] • Feel The Fire • God Don't Like Ugly • If Only For One Night • **Love Is A Waiting Game** [46] • Reaching For The Sky • Killing Me Softly With His Song • More Than Everything • Feel Like Makin' Love • When Will I Learn • Don't Make Me Wait Too Long • Back Together Again • Medley: Love In Every Season/I Believe In You

12/5/81+	6	31		7 I Am Love	40	$8	Capitol 12179

I Am Love • Move Your Body • Split Decision • Impossible • There's No Guarantee [36] • Love Is On The Rise • **Let The Feeling Flow** [6] • Get Ready To Cry • You

12/11/82+	8	28		8 Don't Play With Fire	55	$8	Capitol 12241

Go For It • Give Me Your Love [22] • Don't Play With Fire • **We Don't Have To Talk (About Love)** [16] • Remember When (So Much In Love) [54] • Turn It On • Words • Let Me Be The One You Need

| --- | --- | --- | --- | --- | --- | --- | --- |
				BRYSON, Peabo — Cont'd			
8/20/83	8	44	●	9 Born To Love	25	$8	Capitol 12284
				PEABO BRYSON/ROBERTA FLACK			
				Tonight, I Celebrate My Love [5] • Blame It On Me • Heaven Above Me • Born To Love • **Maybe** [68] • I Just Came Here To Dance • Comin' Alive • You're Looking Like Love To Me [41] • Can We Find Love Again			
6/23/84	12	26		10 Straight From The Heart	44	$8	Elektra 60362
8/4/84	55	11		11 The Peabo Bryson Collection [G]	168	$8	Capitol 12348
7/6/85	40	15		12 Take No Prisoners	102	$8	Elektra 60427
11/1/86	45	10		13 Quiet Storm		$8	Elektra 60484
3/5/88	42	11		14 Positive	157	$8	Elektra 60753
6/17/89	27	29		15 All My Love		$8	Capitol 90641
6/29/91	❶²	47	●	16 Can You Stop The Rain	88	$8	Columbia 46823
				Lost In The Night [43] • Can You Stop The Rain [1] • Closer Than Close [10] • Shower You With Love [47] • I Can't Imagine • I Wish You Love • You Don't Have To Beg • I Wanna Be With You • I Just Had To Fall • Soul Provider • If It's Really Love			
7/2/94	54	5		17 Through The Fire		$8	Columbia 52911
	★197★			**B.T. EXPRESS** '75			
				Disco group from Brooklyn, New York. Core members: Barbara Joyce (female vocals; left by 1977), brothers Louis (vocals, bass) and Bill (sax) Risbrook, Richard Thompson (guitar), Carlos Ward (flute) and Dennis Rowe (congas). Keyboardist Michael Jones, who was in the group from 1976-79, later recorded solo as **Kashif**.			
11/30/74+	❶¹	26	●	1 Do It ('Til You're Satisfied)	5	$12	Roadshow 5117
				Express [1] • If It Don't Turn You On (You Oughta' Leave It Alone) • Once You Get It • Everything Good To You (Ain't Always Good For You) • Mental Telepathy • Do It ('Til You're Satisfied) [1] • Do You Like It • That's What I Want For You Baby • This House Is Smokin'			
8/9/75	❶²	17		2 Non-Stop	19	$12	Roadshow 41001
				Peace Pipe [flip] • Give It What You Got [5] • Discotizer • Still Good-Still Like It • Close To You [31] • You Got It-I Want It • Devil's Workshop • Happiness • Whatcha Think About That?			
6/5/76	11	18		3 Energy To Burn	43	$10	Columbia 34178
5/28/77	39	3		4 Function at the Junction	111	$10	Columbia 34702
2/25/78	16	14		5 Shout!	67	$10	Columbia 35078
5/10/80	29	16		6 B.T. Express 1980	164	$10	Columbia 36333
6/5/82	49	6		7 Keep It Up		$10	Coast To Coast 38001
				BUCKSHOT LeFONQUE '95			
				Instrumental group: **Branford Marsalis** (saxophone), Carl Burnett (guitar), Frank McComb (keyboards), Russell Gunn (trumpet), Reginald Veal (bass) and Rocky Bryant (drums).			
4/1/95	94	2		Buckshot LeFonque [I]		$8	Columbia 57323
				BUGNON, Alex '90			
				Born in Montreux, Switzerland. Keyboardist. Nephew of **Donald Byrd**.			
3/18/89	34	31		1 Love Season	127	$8	Orpheus 75602
6/2/90	32	20		2 Head Over Heels [I]	131	$8	Orpheus 75615
10/19/91	74	23		3 107 Degrees In The Shade [I]		$8	Orpheus 47979
6/19/93	39	13		4 This Time Around [I]		$8	Orpheus 52995
10/14/95	51	5		5 Tales From The Bright Side [I]		$8	RCA 66665
				BURCH, Vernon '75			
				Born in Washington, DC. Singer/songwriter/guitarist. Appeared as **Marvin Gaye** in the 1980 movie *Hollywood Nights*.			
3/8/75	46	4		1 I'll Be Your Sunshine		$12	United Artists 342
5/1/82	50	7		2 Playing Hard To Get		$10	Spector 70005
				BURDON, Eric — see WAR			
				BURKE, Solomon '65			
				Born in 1936 in Philadelphia. Former gospel singer. Preached and broadcast from own church in Philadelphia from 1945-55 as the "Wonder Boy Preacher." Church was founded for him by his grandmother.			
7/10/65	6	5		1 The Best Of Solomon Burke [G]	141	$30	Atlantic 8109
				Got To Get You Off My Mind [1] • The Price [57] • Down In The Valley [20] • I'm Hanging Up My Heart For You [15] • If You Need Me [2] • Just Out Of Reach (Of My Two Open Arms) [7] • Cry To Me [5] • Everybody Needs Somebody To Love [58] • Home In Your Heart • **Tonight's The Night** [2] • I Really Don't Want To Know • Words			
6/7/75	54	6		2 Music To Make Love By		$15	Chess 60042
				BURRELL, Kenny '66			
				Born on 7/31/31 in Detroit. Jazz guitarist.			
12/10/66	21	3		The Tender Gender [I]	146	$20	Cadet 772
				BURTON, Jenny '85			
				Born on 11/18/57 in New York City.			
3/3/84	50	7		1 In Black And White	181	$8	Atlantic 80122
3/16/85	45	14		2 Jenny Burton		$8	Atlantic 81238
				BUSHWICK BILL '95			
				Born Richard Shaw on 12/8/66 in Kingston, Jamaica. Member of **The Geto Boys**. Lost his right eye in a shooting on 5/10/91.			
10/17/92	15	24		1 Little Big Man	32	$8	Rap-A-Lot 57189
7/29/95	3	17		2 Phantom Of The Rapra	43	$8	Rap-A-Lot 40512
				Phantom's Theme • Wha Cha Gonna Do? • Times Is Hard • Who's The Biggest [88] • Ex-Girlfriend • Only God Knows • Already Dead • The Bushwicken • Subliminal Criminal • Inhale Exhale • Mr. President			
12/5/98	84	1		3 No Surrender...No Retreat		$8	Ichiban 8174

BUSTA RHYMES '97

Born Trevor Smith in 1972 in New York City. Male rapper. Member of **Leaders Of The New School** and Flipmode Squad.

4/13/96	❶[1]	25	▲	1 **The Coming**	6	$8	Elektra 61742

The Coming • Do My Thing • **Everything Remains Raw** *[flip]* • Abandon Ship • **WOO-HAH!! Got You All In Check** *[6]* • **It's a Party** *[27]* • Hot Fudge • I'll Vibe • Flipmode Squad Meets Def Squad • Still Shining • Keep It Movin' • The Finish Line • The End Of The World

9/27/97	❶[1]	46	▲	2 **When Disaster Strikes...**	3	$8	Elektra 62064

The Whole World Lookin' At Me • Survival Hungry • When Disaster Strikes • So Hardcore • Get High Tonight • **Turn It Up** *[7]* • Put Your Hands Where My Eyes Could See • There's Not A Problem My Squad Can't Fix • We Could Take It Outside • Rhymes Galore • Things We Be Doin' For Money • One • **Dangerous** *[4]* • The Body Rock • Get Off My Block

BUST DOWN '92

Born in New Orleans. Male rapper.

1/11/92	56	25		Nasty Bitch (Chapter 1)		$8	Effect 3005

BUSY BEE '88

Born in New York City. Male rapper.

9/10/88	48	9		Running Thangs		$8	Uni 2

★65★ BUTLER, Jerry '69

Born on 12/8/39 in Sunflower, Mississippi. Member of **The Impressions** from 1957-58. Nicknamed "The Ice Man." Worked as the Cook County Commissioner in Illinois.
1)The Ice Man Cometh 2)Ice On Ice 3)You & Me 4)The Spice Of Life 5)Thelma & Jerry

2/11/67	23	2		1 The Soul Artistry Of Jerry Butler		$20	Mercury 21105
4/6/68	40	6		2 Jerry Butler's Golden Hits Live ... *[L]*	178	$15	Mercury 61151

recorded in September 1967 at Morgan State College in Baltimore

8/24/68	25	9		3 The Soul Goes On	195	$15	Mercury 61171
1/4/69	2[1]	50		4 **The Ice Man Cometh**	29	$15	Mercury 61198

Hey, Western Union Man *[1]* • Can't Forget About You, Baby • Only The Strong Survive *[1]* • How Can I Get In Touch With You • Just Because I Really Love You • **Lost** *[15]* • **Never Give You Up** *[4]* • **Are You Happy** *[9]* • (Strange) I Still Love You • Go Away-Find Yourself • I Stop By Heaven

9/27/69	4	30		5 **Ice On Ice**	41	$15	Mercury 61234

Moody Woman *[3]* • A Brand New Me • Been A Long Time • Close To You Love • Since I Lost You Lady • **What's The Use Of Breaking Up** *[4]* • When You're Alone • I Forgot To Remember • **Got To See If I Can't Get Mommy (To Come Back Home)** *[21]* • Don't Let Love Hang You Up *[12]* • Walking Around In Teardrops

5/16/70	10	17		6 **You & Me**	172	$15	Mercury 61269

I Could Write A Book *[15]* • A One Woman Man • Tammy Jones • Real Good Man • Something • Ordinary Joe • Life's Unfortunate Sons • No Money Down • Winter Of A Loving Heart • You And Me

6/27/70	31	12		7 The Best Of Jerry Butler ... *[G]*	167	$15	Mercury 61281
2/6/71	25	10		8 Jerry Butler Sings Assorted Sounds	186	$15	Mercury 61320
9/18/71	25	25		9 The Sagittarius Movement	123	$15	Mercury 61347
6/24/72	17	19		10 The Spice Of Life	92	$20	Mercury 7502 [2]
7/7/73	43	14		11 The Love We Have, The Love We Had	201	$15	Mercury 660

JERRY BUTLER & BRENDA LEE EAGER

12/22/73+	22	14		12 Power Of Love		$15	Mercury 689
10/19/74	55	3		13 Sweet Sixteen		$15	Mercury 1006
8/14/76	49	6		14 Love's On The Menu		$12	Motown 850
3/5/77	22	15		15 Suite For The Single Girl	146	$12	Motown 878
6/18/77	20	11		16 Thelma & Jerry	53	$12	Motown 887

THELMA HOUSTON & JERRY BUTLER

11/25/78	42	12		17 Nothing Says I Love You Like I Love You	160	$10	Philadelphia I. 35510
8/2/80	71	3		18 The Best Love		$10	Philadelphia I. 36413
12/4/82	60	3		19 Ice 'N Hot		$10	Fountain 821
11/28/92	92	1		20 Time & Faith		$8	Ichiban 1151

BUTLER, Jonathan '87

Born in Capetown, South Africa. Singer/songwriter/guitarist.

5/17/86	46	19		1 Introducing Jonathan Butler	101	$8	Jive 8408
6/13/87	13	50	●	2 Jonathan Butler	50	$10	Jive 1032 [2]
10/29/88+	17	52		3 More Than Friends	113	$8	Jive 1136
9/15/90	58	16		4 Heal Our Land		$8	Jive 1361
10/1/94	32	13		5 Head To Head		$8	Mercury 522682
9/27/97	57	16		6 Do You Love Me?		$8	N2K Encoded 10005

BWP '91

Female rap duo from New York City: Lyndah and Tanisia Michelle. BWP: Bytches With Problems.

3/9/91	34	20		The Bytches		$8	No Face 47068

BY ALL MEANS '90

Trio from Los Angeles: Lynn Roderick (female vocals), James Varner (male vocals, piano) and Billy Sheppard (guitar).

8/6/88	40	24		1 By All Means		$8	Island 90898
12/2/89+	36	29		2 Beyond A Dream	160	$8	Island 91319
5/23/92	55	13		3 It's Real		$8	Motown 6344

★158★ BYRD, Donald '73

Born on 12/9/32 in Detroit. Trumpeter/flugelhorn player. Founded **The Blackbyrds** in 1973. Uncle of **Alex Bugnon**.
1)Black Byrd 2)Street Lady 3)Places And Spaces

3/22/69	29	6		1 Slow Drag		$20	Blue Note 84292
2/14/70	50	2		2 Fancy Free		$20	Blue Note 84319
5/5/73	2[1]	32		3 **Black Byrd**	36	$15	Blue Note 047

Flight Time • **Black Byrd** *[19]* • Love's So Far Away • Mr. Thomas • Sky High • Slop Jar Blues • Where Are We Going?

BYRD, Donald — Cont'd

4/6/74	6	36		4 Street Lady [I]	33	$15	Blue Note 140

Lansana's Priestess • Miss Kane • Sister Love • Street Lady • Witch Hunt • Woman Of The World

3/29/75	7	18		5 Stepping Into Tomorrow [I]	42	$15	Blue Note 368

Stepping Into Tomorrow • Design A Nation • We're Together • Think Twice • Makin' It • Rock And Roll Again • You Are The World • I Love The Girl

11/22/75+	6	26		6 Places And Spaces	49	$15	Blue Note 549

Change (Makes You Want To Hustle) • Wind Parade • Dominoes • Places And Spaces • You And Music • Night Whistler • Just My Imagination

1/15/77	46	2		7 Donald Byrd's Best [G]	167	$15	Blue Note 700
2/12/77	12	12		8 Caricatures	60	$15	Blue Note 633
12/1/79	71	3		9 Donald Byrd And 125th Street, N.Y.C.	204	$10	Elektra 247
9/19/81	15	21		10 Love Byrd	93	$10	Elektra 531

DONALD BYRD AND 125th STREET, N.Y.C. (above 2)

C

CAESAR, Shirley   '77

Born on 10/13/38 in Durham, North Carolina. Billed as the "First Lady Of Gospel Music."

7/23/77	36	16		1 First Lady		$10	Roadshow 744
2/20/93	95	1		2 He's Working It Out For You		$8	Word 80738

CALDWELL, Bobby   '79

Born on 8/15/51 in New York City; raised in Miami. Singer/songwriter/multi-instrumentalist.

11/25/78+	7	28		1 Bobby Caldwell	21	$10	Clouds 8804

Special To Me • My Flame [40] • Love Won't Wait • Can't Say Goodbye [36] • Come To Me • What You Won't Do For Love [6] • Kalimba Song • Take Me Back To Then • Down For The Third Time

4/12/80	46	15		2 Cat In The Hat	113	$10	Clouds 8810
4/24/82	41	12		3 Carry On	133	$8	Polydor 6347
10/3/92	65	9		4 Stuck On You		$8	Sin-Drome 8893
6/8/96	23	15		5 Soul Survivor		$8	Sin-Drome 8910

CALIFORNIA RAISINS, The   '88

Studio group assembled by producer Ross Vanelli (brother of **Gino Vanelli**). Based on the claymation characters of a California Raisin Growers TV commerical. Features lead singer **Buddy Miles**.

12/3/88	82	6		Sweet, Delicious, & Marvelous	140	$8	Priority 9755

CALLOWAY   '90

Duo of brothers Reginald and Vincent Calloway from Cincinnati. Both were members of **Midnight Star**.

1/6/90	42	36		1 All The Way	80	$8	Solar 75310
4/18/92	89	4		2 Let's Get Smooth		$8	Solar 75326

CAMEO ★35★   '86

Soul-funk aggregation founded in 1974 by Larry Blackmon (producer, vocals, drums) as The New York City Players. Varying members included Gregory Johnson, Tomi Jenkins, brothers Nathan and Arnett Leftenant, Wayne Cooper, Gary Dow, Eric Durham, Anthony Lockett, **Charlie Singleton**, Jeryl Bright, Thomas Campbell, Stephen Moore, Aaron Mills and Kevin Kendricks. Blackmon, Johnson, Dow, Durham, Lockett and the Leftenants also recorded as East Coast. In mid-'80s, Blackmon relocated group to Atlanta and formed own label, Atlanta Artists. By 1986, group pared to trio of Blackmon, Jenkins and Nathan Leftenant (left by 1992 and Singleton returned).

1)Word Up! 2) She's Strange 3)Cameosis

7/2/77	16	25		1 Cardiac Arrest	116	$12	Chocolate City 2003
2/11/78	15	25		2 We All Know Who We Are	58	$12	Chocolate City 2004
10/21/78	16	17		3 Ugly Ego	83	$12	Chocolate City 2006
7/21/79	4	34	●	4 Secret Omen	46	$12	Chocolate City 2008

Energy • I Just Want To Be [3] • Find My Way • Macho • The Rock • Sparkle [10] • New York

5/17/80	❶²	29	●	5 Cameosis	25	$12	Chocolate City 2011

Cameosis • Shake Your Pants [8] • Please You • We're Goin' Out Tonight [11] • I Care For You • On The One • Why Have I Lost You

11/15/80	6	37	●	6 Feel Me	44	$12	Chocolate City 2016

Throw It Down • Your Love Takes Me Out • Keep It Hot [4] • Feel Me [27] • Is This The Way • Roller Skates • Better Days

6/20/81	2³	24	●	7 Knights Of The Sound Table	44	$12	Chocolate City 2019

Knights By Nights • Freaky Dancin' [3] • I Never Knew • Use It Or Lose It • The Sound Table • Don't Be So Cool • I'll Always Stay • I Like It [25]

4/24/82	6	32	●	8 Alligator Woman	23	$12	Chocolate City 2021

Just Be Yourself [12] • Soul Army • Flirt [10] • Enjoy Your Life • Alligator Woman [54] • Secrets Of Time • I Owe It All To You • For You

5/7/83	14	22		9 Style	53	$10	Atlanta Artists 811072
3/17/84	❶²	32	●	10 She's Strange	27	$10	Atlanta Artists 814984

She's Strange [1] • Love You Anyway • Talkin' Out The Side Of Your Neck [21] • Tribute To Bob Marley • Groove With You • Hangin' Downtown [45] • Leve Toi!

CAMEO — Cont'd

| 7/20/85 | 2³ | 33 | ● | 11 Single Life | 58 | $10 | Atlanta Artists 824546 |

Attack Me With Your Love [3] • Single Life [2] • I've Got Your Image • A Good-Bye [76] • I'll Never Look For Love • Urban Warrior • Little Boys - Dangerous Toys

| 9/27/86 | ❶⁵ | 52 | ▲ | 12 Word Up! | 8 | $10 | Atlanta Artists 830265 |

Word Up [1] • Candy [1] • Back And Forth [3] • Don't Be Lonely • She's Mine • Fast, Fierce & Funny • You Can Have The World

| 11/5/88 | 10 | 35 | | 13 Machismo | 56 | $10 | Atlanta Artists 836002 |

You Make Me Work [4] • I Like The World • Promiscuous • In The Night • Skin I'm In [5] • Pretty Girls [52] • Honey • Soul Tightened • DKWIG

7/21/90	18	18		14 Real Men...Wear Black	84	$8	Atlanta Artists 846297
6/5/93	44	19		15 The Best Of Cameo	[G]	$8	Mercury 514824
12/24/94+	83	4		16 In The Face Of Funk		$8	Way 2 Funky 3003

CAMERON, Rafael   '80

Born in 1951 in Georgetown, Guyana. Disco singer.

7/19/80	18	33		1 Cameron	67	$10	Salsoul 8535
7/11/81	29	18		2 Cameron's In Love	101	$10	Salsoul 8542
8/21/82	43	9		3 Cameron All The Way		$10	Salsoul 8553

CAMPBELL, Tevin   '93

Born on 11/12/78 in Waxahachie, Texas. Male singer.

| 12/7/91+ | 5 | 70 | ▲ | 1 T.E.V.I.N. | 38 | $8 | Qwest 26291 |

Round And Round [3] • Over The Rainbow And On To The Sun • Tell Me What You Want Me To Do [1] • Lil' Brother • Alone With You [1] • Strawberry Letter 23 [40] • One Song • Just Ask Me To [9] • Goodbye [2] • Perfect World • Confused [33] • Look What We'd Have (If You Were Mine) • She's All That

| 11/13/93 | 3 | 58 | ▲² | 2 I'm Ready | 18 | $8 | Qwest 45388 |

Can We Talk [1] • Don't Say Goodbye Girl [28] • The Halls Of Desire • I'm Ready [2] • What Do I Say • Uncle Sam • Paris • Always In My Heart [6] • Shhh • Brown Eyed Girl • Infant Child

| 7/13/96 | 11 | 17 | | 3 Back To The World | 46 | $8 | Qwest 46003 |

CAMP LO   '97

Hip-hop duo from the Bronx, New York: Salahadeen Wallace and Saladine Wilds.

| 2/22/97 | 5 | 25 | | Uptown Saturday Night | 27 | $8 | Profile 1470 |

Krystal Karrington • Luchini aka (This Is It) [21] • Park Joint • B-Side To Hollywood • Killin' Em Softly • Sparkle • Black Connection • Swing • Rockin' It • Say Word • Negro League • Nicky Barnes • Black Nostaljack • Coolie High [62]

CAM'RON   '98

Born Cameron Giles in 1978 in New York City. Male rapper.

| 8/1/98 | 2¹ | 14 | ● | Confessions Of Fire | 6 | $8 | Untertainment 68976 |

Glory • 357 [88] • Rockin' And Rollin' • Wrong Ones • Death • Horse & Carriage [9] • Me, My Moms & Jimmy • Prophecy • We Got It • D Rugs • Feels Good [54] • A Pimp's A Pimp • Confessions • Fuck You • Me & My Boo • Shanghai • Who's Nice

C & C MUSIC FACTORY   '91

Dance group led by producers/songwriters Robert Clivilles (percussion) and David Cole (keyboards). Featured vocalists include Freedom Williams, Deborah Cooper (of Fatback, Change) and Martha Wash. Cole died of spinal meningitis on 1/24/95 (age 32).

| 1/12/91 | 11 | 49 | ▲⁵ | 1 Gonna Make You Sweat | 2⁷ | $8 | Columbia 47093 |
| 3/14/92 | 85 | 7 | | 2 Greatest Remixes Vol. I | [K] 87 | $8 | Columbia 48840 |

CLIVILLES + COLE

| 8/27/94 | 39 | 12 | | 3 Anything Goes! | 106 | $8 | Columbia 66160 |

CANDYMAN   '90

Born on 6/25/68 in Los Angeles. Male rapper.

| 11/3/90 | 18 | 27 | ● | Ain't No Shame In My Game | 40 | $8 | Epic 46947 |

CANIBUS   '98

Born Germaine Williams in New Jersey. Male rapper.

| 9/19/98 | 2¹ | 10 | ● | Can-I-Bus | 2¹ | $8 | Universal 53136 |

Patriots • Get Retarded • Niggonometry • Second Round K.O. [13] • What's Going On • I Honor U • Hype-nitis • How We Roll • Channel Zero • Let's Ride • Buckingham Palace • Rip Rock

CANNED HEAT   '69

Blues-rock group from Los Angeles. Bob "The Bear" Hite (vocals, harmonica), Alan "Blind Owl" Wilson and Henry Vestine (guitars), Larry Taylor (bass) and Frank Cook (drums). Wilson died of a drug overdose on 9/3/70 (age 27). Hite died of a drug-related heart attack on 4/6/81 (age 36). Vestine died of heart failure on 10/20/97 (age 52).

| 2/8/69 | 45 | 2 | | Living The Blues | [L] 18 | $25 | Liberty 27200 [2] |

the second album was recorded live at the Kaleidoscope in Hollywood

CAPITOLS, The   '66

Vocal trio from Detroit: Sam George, Donald Norman and Richard Mitchell. George was murdered on 3/17/82 (age 39).

| 7/30/66 | 10 | 7 | | Dance The Cool Jerk | 95 | $40 | Atco 190 |

Cool Jerk [2] • My Girl • I Got My Mojo Working • Please Please Please • In The Midnight Hour • Good Lovin' • Love Makes The World Go Round • Zig Zaggin' • Dog & Cat • Hello Stranger • Tired Running From You • The Kick

CAPLETON   '95

Born Clifton Bailey on 4/13/67 in Islington, St. Mary, Jamaica. Male reggae singer.

| 11/25/95 | 65 | 10 | | Prophecy | | $8 | African Star 529264 |

CAPONE-N-NOREAGA '97
Rap duo from Queens, New York: Kiam "Capone" Holley and Victor "Noreaga" Santiago.

6/28/97	4	32		1 The War Report	21	$8	Penalty 3041

Bloody Money • Driver's Seat • **Stick You** *[84]* • Parole Violators • Iraq (See The World) • Live On Live Long • Neva Die Alone • T.O.N.Y. (Top Of New York) *[56]* • Channel 10 • Capone Bone • Halfway Thugs • L.A., L.A. • **Illegal Life** *[84]* • Black Gangstas • Closer *[63]*

7/18/98	❶¹	33	●	2 N.O.R.E.	3	$8	Penalty 3077

NOREAGA
The Jump Off • Banned From TV • I Love My Life • **N.O.R.E.** *[59]* • Hed • It's Not A Game • Fiesta • 40 Island • The Way We Live • The Change • **SuperThug** *[15]* • Da Story • Mathematics (Esta Loca) • The Assignment • Body In The Trunk • One Love

CAPPADONNA '98
Born Darryl Hill in New York City. Male rapper.

4/4/98	❶¹	15	●	The Pillage	3	$8	Razor Sharp 67947

Slang Editorial • Pillage • Run • Blood On Blood War • Supa Ninjaz • MCF • Splish Splash • Oh-Donna • Milk The Cow • South Of The Border • Check For A Nigga • Dart Throwing • Young Hearts • Everything Is Everything • Pump Your Fist • Black Boy

CAPTAIN SKY '79
Born Daryl Cameron on 7/10/57 in Chicago. Singer/songwriter/producer.

1/13/79	30	32		1 The Adventures Of Captain Sky	157	$10	AVI 6042
12/1/79	49	4		2 Pop Goes The Captain		$10	AVI 6077
8/2/80	69	4		3 Concerned Party #1	210	$10	TEC 1202

CARA, Irene '82
Born on 3/18/59 in Bronx, New York. Singer/actress/dancer/pianist. Acted in such movies as *Fame*, *D.C. Cab* and *The Cotton Club*.

2/6/82	39	12		1 Anyone Can See	76	$10	Network 60003
12/17/83+	45	30		2 What A Feelin'	77	$8	Geffen 4021

CAREY, Mariah '93
★74★
Born on 3/27/70 of in Long Island, New York. Singer/songwriter/producer. Daughter of former opera singer Patricia Carey. Won the 1990 Best New Artist Grammy Award. Married to Tommy Mottola, president of Sony Music Entertainment, from 1993-98.
1)Music Box 2)Daydream 3)Mariah Carey

7/7/90	3	68	▲⁸	1 Mariah Carey	1¹¹	$8	Columbia 45202

Vision Of Love *[1]* • There's Got To Be A Way • **I Don't Wanna Cry** *[2]* • Someday *[3]* • Vanishing • All In Your Mind • Alone In Love • You Need Me • Sent From Up Above • Prisoner • **Love Takes Time** *[1]*

10/12/91	6	44	▲⁴	2 Emotions	4	$8	Columbia 47980

Emotions *[1]* • And You Don't Remember • **Can't Let Go** *[2]* • **Make It Happen** *[7]* • If It's Over • You're So Cold • So Blessed • To Be Around You • Till The End Of Time • The Wind

6/20/92	16	44	▲³	3 MTV Unplugged EP	[L-M]	3	$6	Columbia 52758

recorded on March 16, 1992

9/18/93	❶²	86	▲¹⁰	4 Music Box	1⁸	$8	Columbia 53205

Dreamlover *[2]* • Hero *[5]* • **Anytime You Need A Friend** *[22]* • Music Box • Now That I Know • **Never Forget You** *[7]* • Without You *[flip]* • Just To Hold You Once Again • I've Been Thinking About You • All I've Ever Wanted

12/3/94	4	7	▲⁴	5 Merry Christmas	[X]	3	$8	Columbia 64222

Silent Night • All I Want For Christmas Is You • O Holy Night • Christmas (Baby Please Come Home) • Miss You Most (At Christmas Time) • Joy To The World • Jesus Born On This Day • Santa Claus Is Comin' To Town • Medley: Hark! The Herald Angels Sing/Gloria (In Excelsis Deo) • Jesus Oh What A Wonderful Child

10/21/95	❶¹	74	▲⁹	6 Daydream	1⁶	$8	Columbia 66700

Fantasy *[1]* • Underneath The Stars • **One Sweet Day** *[2]* • Open Arms • **Always Be My Baby** *[1]* • I Am Free • When I Saw You • Long Ago • Melt Away • Forever • Looking In

10/4/97	3	54	▲⁴	7 Butterfly	1¹	$8	Columbia 67835

Honey *[2]* • Butterfly • **My All** *[4]* • The Roof • Fourth Of July • **Breakdown** *[4]* • Babydoll • Close My Eyes • Whenever You Call • Fly Away • The Beautiful Ones • Outside

12/5/98	6	34	▲³	8 #1's	[G]	4	$8	Columbia 69670

Sweetheart • **When You Believe** *[33]* • Whenever You Call • My All *[4]* • Honey *[2]* • **Always Be My Baby** *[1]* • One Sweet Day *[2]* • Fantasy *[1]* • Hero *[5]* • Dreamlover *[2]* • I'll Be There *[11]* • Emotions *[1]* • I Don't Wanna Cry *[2]* • Someday *[3]* • Love Takes Time *[1]* • Vision Of Love *[1]* • I Still Believe *[3]*

CARLTON, Carl '81
Born in 1952 in Detroit. Singer/songwriter.

1/18/75	22	11		1 Everlasting Love	132	$12	ABC 857
1/31/76	49	4		2 I Wanna Be With You		$12	ABC 910
7/25/81	3	27		3 Carl Carlton	34	$10	20th Century 628

Sexy Lady • Let Me Love You 'Til The Morning Comes • Don't You Wanna Make Love • **This Feeling's Rated X-Tra** *[57]* • **She's A Bad Mama Jama (She's Built, She's Stacked)** *[2]* • I've Got That Boogie Fever • **I Think It's Gonna Be Alright** *[65]* • Fighting In The Name Of Love

10/23/82	21	9		4 The Bad C.C.	133	$10	RCA Victor 4425
10/19/85	36	6		5 Private Property		$8	Casablanca 822705

CARMAN, Pauli '86
Male singer. Former member of **Champaign**.

8/9/86	66	3		Dial My Number		$8	Columbia 40336

CARN, Jean '86
Born Sarah Jean Perkins in Columbus, Georgia.

2/12/77	46	12		1 Jean Carn	122	$12	Philadelphia I. 39394
7/8/78	55	2		2 Happy To Be With You		$12	Philadelphia I. 34986
12/1/79+	42	19		3 When I Find You Love		$12	Philadelphia I. 36196
8/15/81	38	17		4 Sweet And Wonderful	176	$10	TSOP 36775
6/19/82	37	12		5 Trust Me	210	$10	Motown 6010
8/2/86	9	20		6 Closer Than Close	162	$8	Omni 90492

Closer Than Close *[1]* • Flame Of Love *[21]* • Break Up To Make Up • Lucky Charm • **Everything Must Change** *[79]* • Anything For Money • Candy Love • It Must Be Love • Sexy Eyes

DEBUT	PEAK	WKS	Gold	Album Title	Pop #	$	Label & Number
				CARN, Jean — Cont'd			
4/16/88	40	13		7 You're A Part Of Me		$8	Atlantic 81811
				JEAN CARNE (above 2)			
				CARR, James **'67**			
				Born on 6/13/42 in Memphis.			
3/25/67	25	2		You Got My Mind Messed Up		$150	Goldway 3001
	★119★			**CARTER, Clarence** **'71**			
				Born on 1/14/36 in Montgomery, Alabama. Singer/songwriter/guitarist. Blind since age one. Formerly married to **Candi Staton**.			
				1)The Best Of Clarence Carter 2)Patches 3)Dr. C.C.			
10/19/68	49	2		1 This Is Clarence Carter	200	$30	Atlantic 8192
2/22/69	22	15		2 The Dynamic Clarence Carter	169	$30	Atlantic 8199
8/9/69	35	4		3 Testifyin'	138	$30	Atlantic 8238
10/3/70	18	11		4 Patches	44	$30	Atlantic 8267
5/29/71	11	13		5 The Best Of Clarence Carter [G]	103	$20	Atlantic 8282
1/5/74	41	9		6 Sixty Minutes With Clarence Carter		$15	Fame 186
9/13/75	58	2		7 Loneliness & Temptation		$15	ABC 896
12/27/80+	28	26		8 Let's Burn	189	$10	Venture 1005
7/12/86+	20	49		9 Dr. C.C.		$10	Ichiban 1003
11/21/87	34	33		10 Hooked On Love		$10	Ichiban 1016
1/7/89	52	20		11 Touch Of Blues		$10	Ichiban 1032
11/3/90	48	23		12 Between A Rock And A Hard Place		$8	Ichiban 1068
7/20/91	74	14		13 The Best Of Clarence Carter - The Dr's Greatest Prescriptions .... [G]		$8	Ichiban 1116
9/12/92	73	12		14 Have You Met Clarence Carter...Yet?		$8	Ichiban 1141
				CARTER, Ron **'75**			
				Born on 5/4/37 in Ferndale, Michigan. Jazz bassist. Member of **Miles Davis**'s band from 1963-68.			
4/12/75	37	7		1 Spanish Blue ....[I]		$12	CTI 6051
12/20/75	52	3		2 Anything Goes ....[I]		$12	Kudu 25
				CASE **'96**			
				Born in New York City. Male singer/songwriter.			
8/31/96	7	11		**Case**	42	$8	Def Jam 533134
				More To Love [36] • Don't Be Afraid • I Gotcha • Crazy • What's Wrong? • Rain • Touch Me Tease Me [4] • The Day That I Die • Fallin' • Cryin' Over Time			
				CA$HFLOW **'86**			
				Funk-rap group from Atlanta: Kary Hubbert (vocals), James Duffie and Regis Ferguson (keyboards), and Gaylord Parsons (drums). Ferguson left in 1987, replaced by Simeo Overall.			
4/26/86	15	27		1 Ca$hflow	144	$8	Atlanta Artists 826028
9/3/88	84	4		2 Big Money		$8	Atlanta Artists 832187
				CASHMERE **'85**			
				Trio from Chicago: Dwight Dukes (vocals, guitar), McKinley Horton (keyboards) and Daryl Burgee (drums). Dukes was formerly in **Heaven & Earth**.			
3/2/85	52	13		Cashmere		$8	Philly World 90243
				CASH MONEY & MARVELOUS **'89**			
				Duo of DJ Jerome "Cash Money" Hewlett and rapper Marvin "Marvelous" Berryman.			
1/21/89	20	20		Where's The Party At?		$10	Sleeping Bag 42016
				CASTOR, Jimmy **'72**			
				Born on 6/22/43 in New York City. Singer/songwriter/saxophonist/arranger. Castor replaced Frankie Lymon in The Teenagers, in 1957. Formed The Jimmy Castor Bunch in 1972, with Harry Jensen (guitar), Gerry Thomas (keyboards, trumpet), Doug Gibson (bass), Lenny Fridie (congas) and Bobby Manigault (drums).			
				THE JIMMY CASTOR BUNCH:			
4/29/72	11	17		1 It's Just Begun	27	$15	RCA Victor 4640
6/9/73	49	2		2 Dimension III		$15	RCA Victor 0103
3/1/75	34	13		3 Butt Of Course	74	$10	Atlantic 18124
11/22/75	30	8		4 Supersound		$10	Atlantic 18150
9/18/76	29	6		5 E-Man Groovin'	132	$10	Atlantic 18186
				CASUAL **'94**			
				Born Jonathan Owens. Male rapper.			
2/19/94	22	8		Fear Itself	108	$8	Jive 41520
				C-BO **'95**			
				Born Shawn Thomas in Oakland. Male rapper.			
7/17/93	53	22		1 Gas Chamber		$8	AWOL 719
8/27/94	22	11		2 The Autopsy		$8	AWOL 7196
6/24/95	4	23		3 Tales From The Crypt	99	$8	AWOL 7197
				Jackin' And Assassin' • Murder That He Ritt • Free Style • Hard Core • Want To Be A "G" • Stompin' In My Steel Toes • Birds In The Kitchen • 187 Dance • Groovin' On A Sunday • Who Ride • Take It How You Want Too • Ain't No Sunshine			
11/25/95	35	21		4 The Best Of C-BO ....[G]		$8	AWOL 7199
2/22/97	12	13		5 One Life 2 Live	65	$8	AWOL 7201
3/14/98	4	12		6 Til My Casket Drops	41	$8	AWOL 45496
				Ride Til' We Die • Deadly Game • Major Pain & Mr. Bossalini • Money By The Ton • 40 & C-BO • Hard Labor • Raised In Hell • Can We All Ball • Desparado Outlaws • Real Niggas • Professional Ballers • Big Gangsta • All I Ever Wanted • Boo You! • No Pain No Gain • Till My Casket Drops • 357			
				CELI BEE & THE BUZZY BUNCH **'77**			
				Puerto Rican disco band led by female vocalist Celinas Soto.			
5/14/77	39	4		Celi Bee & The Buzzy Bunch	169	$8	APA 77001

CELLA DWELLAS '96
Rap duo from Brooklyn, New York: Ug and Phantasm.

| 4/13/96 | 21 | 9 | | Realms 'N Reality | 160 | $8 | Loud/RCA 66521 |

CELLY CELL '96
Born Michael McCarver in Vallejo, California. Male rapper.

| 4/9/94 | 34 | 18 | | 1 Heat 4 Yo Azz | | $8 | Sick Wid' It 1724 |
| 5/18/96 | 4 | 24 | | 2 Killa Kali | 26 | $8 | Sick Wid' It 41577 |

Round 2 • What U Niggaz Thought • 4 Tha Scrilla • It's Goin' Down • Can't Tell Me Shit • Tha Bullet • Red Rum • Skanlezz Call • Skanlezz Azz Butchez • Remember Where You Came From • Killa Kali • Playerizm • Funk Season

| 8/15/98 | 17 | 9 | | 3 The G Filez | 53 | $8 | Sick Wid' It 41622 |

CENTRAL LINE '82
Group from London: Linton Beckles (vocals, drums), Henry Defoe (guitar), Lipson Francis (keyboards) and Camelle Hinds (bass).

| 1/9/82 | 23 | 16 | | Central Line | 145 | $10 | Mercury 4033 |

CENTURY 22 '86
Trio from Los Angeles: George Shaw (vocals, keyboards), Frank Potenza (guitar) and Stan Smith (drums).

| 12/28/85+ | 54 | 9 | | Flight 2201 | | $10 | TBA 209 |

CENTURY 22 featuring GEORGE SHAW

CERRONE '78
Born Jean-Marc Cerrone in 1952 in St. Michel, France. Composer/producer/drummer.

3/12/77	55	6		1 Love In C Minor	153	$10	Cotillion 9913
8/6/77	52	3		2 Cerrone's Paradise	162	$10	Cotillion 9917
2/4/78	56	3		3 Cerrone 3 - Supernature	129	$10	Cotillion 5202
11/11/78	49	9		4 Cerrone IV - The Golden Touch	118	$10	Cotillion 5208

CHAD '87
Born in New York City. Singer/songwriter/producer.

| 11/21/87 | 64 | 4 | | Fast Music, Love & Promises | | $8 | RCA Victor 6610 |

CHAIRMEN OF THE BOARD '70
Vocal group from Detroit: General Johnson, Danny Woods, Harrison Kennedy and Eddie Curtis.

5/2/70	27	10		1 Give Me Just A Little More Time	133	$40	Invictus 7300
11/21/70	16	21		2 In Session	117	$40	Invictus 7304
11/2/74	52	4		3 Skin I'm In		$40	Invictus 32526

CHAMBERS BROTHERS, The '68
Group from Mississippi: brothers George (bass), Willie (guitar), Lester (harmonica) and Joe (guitar) Chambers, with Brian Keenan (drums).

| 2/3/68 | 6 | 37 | ● | 1 The Time Has Come | 4 | $20 | Columbia 9522 |

All Strung Out Over You • People Get Ready • I Can't Stand It • Romeo And Juliet • In The Midnight Hour • So Tired • Uptown • Please Don't Leave Me • What The World Needs Now Is Love • Time Has Come Today

| 11/2/68 | 24 | 9 | | 2 A New Time-A New Day | 16 | $20 | Columbia 9671 |
| 1/17/70 | 17 | 20 | | 3 Love, Peace And Happiness [L] | 58 | $25 | Columbia 20 [2] |

record 2: live at Bill Graham's Fillmore East

| 3/27/71 | 36 | 4 | | 4 New Generation | 145 | $15 | Columbia 30032 |
| 2/9/74 | 44 | 10 | | 5 Unbonded | | $12 | Avco 11013 |

CHAMPAIGN '83
Interracial group from Champaign, Illinois: Pauli Carman and Rena Jones (lead vocals), Leon Reeder (guitar), Michael Day and Dana Walden (keyboards), and Rocky Maffit (drums).

| 3/21/81 | 14 | 22 | | 1 How 'Bout Us | 53 | $8 | Columbia 37008 |
| 4/2/83 | 9 | 29 | | 2 Modern Heart | 64 | $8 | Columbia 38284 |

Let Your Body Rock [62] • Try Again [2] • Party Line • Cool Running • Walkin' • Keep It Up • Love Games • Get It Again • International Feel

| 11/3/84 | 45 | 19 | | 3 Woman In Flames | 184 | $8 | Columbia 39365 |
| 4/13/91 | 72 | 8 | | 4 Champaign IV | | $8 | Malaco 7461 |

CHANDLER, Gene '66
Born Eugene Dixon on 7/6/37 in Chicago. Singer/songwriter/producer.

| 12/25/65+ | 5 | 19 | | 1 Gene Chandler - Live On Stage In '65 [L] | 124 | $50 | Constellation 1425 |

recorded at the Regal Theater in Chicago
Rainbow '65 [2] • If You Can't Be True • Soul Hootenanny • Monkey Time • What Now • Just Be True • Ain't No Use • Bless Our Love • A Song Called Soul

10/17/70	35	8		2 The Gene Chandler Situation	178	$15	Mercury 61304
11/25/78+	12	20		3 Get Down	47	$10	Chi-Sound 578
8/25/79	50	8		4 When You're #1	153	$10	20th Century 598
6/7/80	11	23		5 Gene Chandler '80	87	$10	20th Century 605

CHANGE '81
European-American studio group formed in Italy by producers Jacques Fred Petrus and Mauro Malavasi. Led by Paolo Gianolio (guitar) and David Romani (bass). Luther Vandross sang lead on several songs for group's first charted album. Later group, based in New York, included lead vocals by James Robinson and Deborah Cooper (later with C & C Music Factory).

| 4/26/80 | 10 | 35 | ● | 1 The Glow Of Love | 29 | $10 | RFC 3438 |

A Lover's Holiday [5] • It's A Girl's Affair • Angel In My Pocket • The Glow Of Love [49] • Searching [23] • End, The

| 4/18/81 | 9 | 27 | | 2 Miracles | 46 | $10 | Atlantic 19301 |

Paradise [7] • Hold Tight [40] • Your Move • Stop For Love • On Top • Heaven Of My Life • Miracles

5/8/82	14	17		3 Sharing Your Love	66	$10	Atlantic 19342
4/2/83	34	10		4 This Is Your Time	161	$10	Atlantic 80053
4/21/84	15	19		5 Change of Heart	102	$10	Atlantic 80151
5/11/85	64	3		6 Turn On Your Radio	208	$10	Atlantic 81243

CHANGING FACES '94
Female vocal duo from New York City: Charisse Rose and Cassandra Lucas.

| 9/10/94 | ❶¹ | 34 | ● 1 | **Changing Faces** | 25 | $8 | Big Beat 92369 |

Stroke You Up *[2]* • Foolin' Around *[9]* • Lovin' Ya Boy • One Of Those Things • **Keep It Right There** *[49]* • Am I Wasting My Time • Feeling All This Love • Thoughts Of You • Come Closer • Baby Your Love • Movin' On • Good Thing • All Is Not Gone

| 6/28/97 | 6 | 21 | ● 2 | **All Day, All Night** | 21 | $8 | Big Beat 92720 |

G.H.E.T.T.O.U.T. *[1]* • My Lovely • Thinkin' About You • I Apologize • Time After Time • All Of My Own • All Day, All Night • My Heart Can't Take Much More • **I Got Somebody Else** *[49]* • Goin' Nowhere • No Stoppin' This Groove • All That • Baby Tonight

CHANNEL LIVE '95
Rap duo from New Jersey: Tuffy and Hakeem.

| 4/8/95 | 9 | 11 | | **Station Identification** | 58 | $8 | Capitol 28968 |

Station Identification • Lock It Up • What! (Cause And Effect) • **Mad Izm** *[27]* • Reprogram • Sex For The Sport • Down Goes The Devil • Build & Destroy • Alpha & Omega • Homicide Ride • Who U Represent

CHANSON '78
Disco studio group. Lead vocals by James Jamerson, Jr. and David Williams. Jamerson's father was a prominent Motown bassist. Group name is French for song.

| 11/11/78 | 23 | 20 | | **Chanson** | 41 | $10 | Ariola 50039 |

CHAPMAN, Tracy '88
Born on 3/20/64 in Cleveland. Singer/songwriter/guitarist. Won the 1988 Best New Artist Grammy Award.

| 6/25/88 | 29 | 40 | ▲⁴ 1 | **Tracy Chapman** | 1¹ | $8 | Elektra 60774 |
| 11/4/89 | 72 | 6 | ▲ 2 | **Crossroads** | 9 | $8 | Elektra 60888 |

CHAPTER 8 '88
Group from Detroit: **Anita Baker** and Gerald Lyles (vocals), Michael Powell (guitar), Courtlen Hale (sax), Vernon Fails (keyboards), David Washington (bass) and Derek Dickerson (drums). Baker left in 1983, replaced by Valerie Pinkston.

| 10/20/79 | 70 | 4 | 1 | **Chapter 8** | | $10 | Ariola America 50056 |
| 9/17/88 | 54 | 13 | 2 | **Forever** | | $8 | Capitol 46947 |

CHARLENE '82
Born Charlene D'Angelo on 6/1/50 in Hollywood.

| 11/27/82 | 48 | 7 | | **Used To Be** | 162 | $8 | Motown 6027 |

CHARLES, Ray ★48★ '66
Born Ray Charles Robinson on 9/23/30 in Albany, Georgia. To Greenville, Florida, while still an infant. Partially blind at age five, completely blind at seven (glaucoma). Studied classical piano and clarinet at State School for Deaf and Blind Children, St. Augustine, Florida, 1937-45. With local Florida bands; moved to Seattle in 1948. Formed own band in 1954. Inducted into the Rock and Roll Hall of Fame in 1986. Won Grammy's Lifetime Achievement Award in 1987.

1)Crying Time 2)A Portrait Of Ray 3)Ray's Moods 4)Ray Charles Invites You To Listen 5)Ray Charles Live In Concert

| 4/3/65 | 9 | 4 | 1 | **Ray Charles Live In Concert** [L] | 80 | $20 | ABC-Paramount 500 |

recorded at the Shrine Auditorium in Los Angeles
Swing A Little Taste • I Gotta Woman • Margie • You Don't Know Me • Hide Nor Hair • Baby, Don't You Cry • Makin' Whoopee • Hallelujah I Love Her So • Don't Set Me Free • What'd I Say

| 3/5/66 | ❶¹ | 29 | 2 | **Crying Time** | 15 | $20 | ABC-Paramount 544 |

Crying Time *[5]* • No Use Crying • **Let's Go Get Stoned** *[1]* • Going Down Slow • Peace Of Mind • Tears • Drifting Blues • We Don't See Eye To Eye • You're In For A Big Surprise • You're Just About To Lose Your Clown • Don't You Think I Ought To Know • You've Got A Problem

| 10/1/66 | 7 | 20 | 3 | **Ray's Moods** | 52 | $15 | ABC 550 |

What-Cha Doing In There (I Wanna Know) • Please Say You're Fooling • By The Light Of The Silvery Moon • You Don't Understand • Maybe It's Because Of Love • Chitlins With Candied Yams • Granny Wasn't Grinning That Day • She's Lonesome Again • Sentimental Journey • A Born Loser • It's A Man's World • A Girl I Used To Know

| 3/25/67 | 14 | 11 | ● 4 | **A Man And His Soul** [G] | 77 | $20 | ABC 590 [2] |
| 7/15/67 | 9 | 14 | 5 | **Ray Charles invites you to Listen** | 76 | $15 | ABC/TRC 595 |

She's Funny That Way (I Got A Woman Crazy For Me) • How Deep Is The Ocean (How High Is The Sky) • You Made Me Love You (I Didn't Want To Do It) • **Yesterday** *[9]* • I'll Be Seeing You • **Here We Go Again** *[5]* • All For You • Love Walked In • Gee, Baby Ain't I Good To You • People

| 4/20/68 | 5 | 28 | 6 | **A Portrait Of Ray** | 51 | $12 | ABC/TRC 625 |

Never Say Naw • The Sun Died • Am I Blue • Yesterdays • When I Stop Dreamin' • I Won't Leave • Sweet Young Thing Like You • The Bright Lights & You Girl • **Understanding** *[13]* • Eleanor Rigby *[30]*

5/10/69	25	11	7	**I'm All Yours-Baby!**	167	$12	ABC/TRC 675
7/12/69	34	14	8	**Doing His Thing**	172	$12	ABC/TRC 695
6/13/70	37	7	9	**My Kind Of Jazz** [I]	155	$12	Tangerine 1512
10/10/70	34	10	10	**Love Country Style**	192	$12	ABC/TRC 707
6/5/71	16	19	11	**Volcanic Action Of My Soul**	52	$12	ABC/TRC 726
12/11/71	32	6	12	**A 25th Anniversary in Show Business Salute to Ray Charles** [G]	152	$15	ABC 731 [2]

record 1: Atlantic hits; record 2: ABC hits

5/20/72	22	13	13	**A Message From The People**	52	$12	ABC/TRC 755
1/27/73	43	5	14	**Through The Eyes Of Love**	186	$12	ABC/TRC 765
5/12/73	42	5	15	**Ray Charles Live** [L-R]	182	$15	Atlantic 503 [2]

record 1: recorded on July 5, 1958 at the Newport Jazz Festival; record 2: reissue of his 1960 album *Ray Charles In Person*

5/11/74	34	6	16	**Come Live With Me**	206	$12	Crossover 9000
6/28/75	34	15	17	**Renaissance**	175	$12	Crossover 9005
1/31/76	55	4	18	**My Kind Of Jazz Part 3**		$12	Crossover 9007
12/11/76	43	5	19	**Porgy & Bess**	138	$15	RCA Victor 1831 [2]

RAY CHARLES/CLEO LAINE

DEBUT	PEAK	WKS	Gold	Album Title	Pop #	$	Label & Number
				CHARLES, Ray — Cont'd			
10/29/77	23	21		20 True To Life	78	$12	Atlantic 19142
10/14/78	35	3		21 Love & Peace		$12	Atlantic 19199
11/10/79	59	4		22 Ain't It So	204	$12	Atlantic 19251
4/17/93	53	13		23 My World	145	$8	Warner 26735
				CHARLES, Sonny '83			
				Born in Fort Wayne, Indiana. Leader of **The Checkmates, Ltd.**			
12/4/82+	14	16		The Sun Still Shines	136	$10	Highrise 102
				CHARLES & EDDIE '92			
				Vocal duo of Charles Pettigrew (from Philadelphia) and Eddie Chacon (from Oakland, California).			
12/5/92	81	4		Duophonic	153	$8	Capitol 97150
				CHEATHAM, Oliver '83			
				Born in Detroit.			
7/9/83	52	7		Saturday Night		$8	MCA 5410
				CHECKMATES, LTD., The '68			
				Interracial group from Fort Wayne, Indiana: **Sonny Charles** (vocals), Bobby Stevens, Harvey Trees, Bill Van Buskirk and Marvin Smith.			
4/6/68	36	3		Checkmates Ltd. Live At Caesar's Palace [L]		$30	Capitol 2840
				CHER '79			
				Born Cherilyn Sarkisian on 5/20/46 in El Centro, California. From 1963 until their divorce in 1974, in successful recording duo with husband, Sonny Bono, as Sonny & Cher. Own TV series with Bono from 1971-77.			
3/3/79	32	16	●	Take Me Home	25	$10	Casablanca 7133
				CHERRELLE '86			
				Born Cheryl Norton in 1958 in Los Angeles. Cousin of **Pebbles**.			
6/16/84	27	27		1 Fragile	144	$8	Tabu 39144
11/23/85+	9	44		2 High Priority	36	$8	Tabu 40094
				You Look Good To Me [26] • **Artificial Heart** [18] • New Love • Oh No It's U Again • **Saturday Love** [2] • Will You Satisfy? • Where Do I Run To • High Priority			
11/26/88+	15	29		3 Affair	106	$8	Tabu 44148
3/21/92	43	16		4 The Woman I Am		$8	Tabu 4005
				CHERRY, Ava '80			
				Born in Chicago. Female singer.			
2/23/80	66	6		Ripe!!!	206	$10	RSO 3072
				CHERRY, Neneh '89			
				Born Neneh Karlsson on 8/10/64 in Stockholm, Sweden; raised in New York City. Stepdaughter of jazz trumpeter Don Cherry.			
6/24/89	62	11		Raw Like Sushi	40	$8	Virgin 91252
	★139★			**CHIC** '78			
				Pronounced: sheek. Disco group formed in New York City by prolific producers Bernard Edwards (bass) and Nile Rodgers (guitar). Featured drummer Tony Thompson and vocalists Luci Martin and Norma Jean Wright. Wright began solo career in 1978 as **Norma Jean**; replaced by Alfa Anderson. Rodgers joined **The Honeydrippers** in 1984. Thompson joined the Power Station in 1985 and Edwards became their producer. Wright along with supporting Chic member Raymond Jones formed **State Of Art** in 1991. Rodgers and Edwards regrouped as Chic in 1992 with female lead vocalists/South Carolina natives Sylvester Logan Sharp and Jenn Thomas. Edwards died of pneumonia on 4/18/96 (age 43).			
12/24/77+	12	31	●	1 Chic	27	$8	Atlantic 19153
12/2/78	❶[11]	38	▲	2 C'est Chic	4	$8	Atlantic 19209
				Chic Cheer • Le Freak [1] • Savoir Faire • Happy Man • **I Want Your Love** [5] • At Last I Am Free • Sometimes You Win • (Funny) Bone			
8/25/79	2[2]	17	▲	3 Risque	5	$8	Atlantic 16003
				Good Times [1] • A Warm Summer Night • **My Feet Keep Dancing** [42] • **My Forbidden Lover** [33] • Can't Stand To Love You • Will You Cry (When You Hear This Song) • What About Me			
12/22/79+	44	9		4 Les Plus Grands Succes De Chic - Chic's Greatest Hits [G]	88	$8	Atlantic 16011
8/2/80	8	19		5 Real People	30	$8	Atlantic 16016
				Open Up • **Real People** [51] • I Loved You More • I Got Protection • **Rebels Are We** [8] • Chip Off The Old Block • 26 • You Can't Do It Alone			
12/19/81+	36	14		6 Take It Off	124	$8	Atlantic 19323
12/4/82	47	9		7 Tongue In Chic	173	$8	Atlantic 80031
4/4/92	39	17		8 Chic-Ism		$8	Warner 26394
				CHICAGO '71			
				Jazz-oriented rock group from Chicago: Peter Cetra (vocals, bass), Terry Kath (guitar), Robert Lamm (keyboards), James Pankow (trombone), Lee Loughnane (trumpet), Walt Parazaider (reeds) and Danny Seraphine (drums). Kath died of a self-inflicted gunshot on 1/23/78 (age 31).			
2/13/71	22	14	▲	1 Chicago III	2[2]	$25	Columbia 30110 [2]
8/5/72	33	11	▲[2]	2 Chicago V	1[9]	$20	Columbia 31102
				CHILD, Jane '90			
				Born in Toronto, Canada. Singer/songwriter/pianist.			
5/26/90	40	11		Jane Child	49	$8	Warner 25858

DEBUT	PEAK	WKS	Gold	Album Title	Pop #	$	Label & Number
	★82★			**CHI-LITES, The** '72			

Vocal group from Chicago: Eugene Record, Robert Lester, Marshall Thompson and Creadel Jones. Jones left in 1973, first replaced by Stanley Anderson, then Willie Kensey. Doc Roberson replaced Kensey in 1975. Record (husband of **Barbara Acklin**) went solo in 1976, and David Scott and Danny Johnson were added. Vandy Hampton replaced Johnson in 1977. Re-formed in 1980 with all four original members. Jones retired in 1983, group continued as a trio. By 1990, Anthony Watson replaced Record.
1)A Lonely Man 2)Give More Power To The People 3)Chi-Lites

DEBUT	PEAK	WKS	Gold	Album Title	Pop #	$	Label & Number
9/13/69	16	7		1 Give It Away	180	$25	Brunswick 754152
8/7/71	3	34		2 (For God's Sake) Give More Power To The People	12	$25	Brunswick 754170

Yes I'm Ready (If I Don't Get To Go) • We Are Neighbors [17] • I Want To Pay You Back (For Loving Me) [35] • Have You Seen Her [1] • (For God's Sake) Give More Power To The People [4] • Love Uprising • Troubles A'Comin' • You Got Me Walkin' • What Do I Wish For

DEBUT	PEAK	WKS	Gold	Album Title	Pop #	$	Label & Number
4/29/72	❶5	32		3 A Lonely Man	5	$25	Brunswick 754179

Oh Girl [1] • Living In The Footsteps Of Another Man • Love Is • Being In Love • A Lonely Man [25] • The Man & The Woman (The Boy & The Girl) • Ain't Too Much Of Nothin' • Inner City Blues (Make Me Wanna Holler) • The Coldest Days Of My Life [8]

DEBUT	PEAK	WKS	Gold	Album Title	Pop #	$	Label & Number
10/21/72	4	17		4 The Chi-Lites Greatest Hits [G]	55	$25	Brunswick 754184

Oh Girl [1] • I Wanna Pay You Back • I Like Your Lovin' (Do You Like Mine) • Give It Away [10] • Let Me Be The Man My Daddy Was [15] • Love Uprising • The Coldest Days Of My Life [8] • Have You Seen Her [1] • (For God's Sake) Give More Power To The People [4] • Are You My Woman? (Tell Me So) [8] • We Are Neighbors [17] • Living In The Footsteps Of Another Man • I'm Ready If I Don't Get To Go • 24 Hours Of Sadness [30] • A Lonely Man [25]

DEBUT	PEAK	WKS	Gold	Album Title	Pop #	$	Label & Number
3/31/73	4	15		5 A Letter To Myself	50	$25	Brunswick 754188

A Letter To Myself [3] • Too Late To Turn Back Now • Just Two Teenage Kids (Still In Love) • Sally • Someone Else's Arms • We Need Order [13] • Love Comes In All Sizes • My Heart Just Keeps On Breakin' [46] • You Smiled The Same Old Way

DEBUT	PEAK	WKS	Gold	Album Title	Pop #	$	Label & Number
9/8/73	3	23		6 Chi-Lites	89	$25	Brunswick 754197

Homely Girl [3] • Go Away Dream • Too Good To Be Forgotten • I Found Sunshine [17] • I Never Had It So Good (And Felt So Bad) • Marriage License • I Forgot To Say I Love You Till I'm Gone • One Man Band • Bet You'll Never Be Sorry • Stoned Out Of My Mind [2]

DEBUT	PEAK	WKS	Gold	Album Title	Pop #	$	Label & Number
7/13/74	12	13		7 Toby	181	$25	Brunswick 754200
7/19/75	41	12		8 Half A Love		$25	Brunswick 754204
11/29/80+	42	19		9 Heavenly Body	179	$15	Chi-Sound 619
2/27/82	31	16		10 Me And You	162	$15	Chi-Sound 635
5/14/83	15	18		11 Bottom's Up	98	$12	Larc 8103
7/21/90	77	7		12 Just Say You Love Me		$8	Ichiban 1057
				CHILL DEAL BOYZ, The '92			
3/14/92	70	7		Hip Hop Ain't Nothin' But A Party .... [M]		$6	Pump 15187
				CHILL ROB G '90			
				Born Robert Frazier in Jersey City, New Jersey. Male rapper.			
1/20/90	60	29		Ride The Rhythm		$8	Wild Pitch 2002
				CHIMES, The '90			
				Trio from Scotland: Pauline Henry (vocals), Mike Peden (bass) and James Locke (drums).			
6/9/90	71	13		The Chimes	162	$8	Columbia 46008
				CHINO XL '96			
				Born Derrick Barbosa in East Orange, New Jersey. Male rapper.			
4/27/96	56	6		Here To Save You All		$8	American 43038
				CHOCOLATE MILK '76			
				Group from New Orleans: Frank Richard (vocals), Mario Tio (guitar), Amadee Castanell (saxophone), Joe Foxx (trumpet), Robert Dabon (keyboards) and Dwight Richards (drums).			
10/11/75	34	7		1 Action Speaks Louder Than Words	191	$10	RCA Victor 1188
3/20/76	18	9		2 Chocolate Milk		$10	RCA Victor 1399
6/10/78	34	8		3 We're All In This Together	171	$10	RCA Victor 2331
3/31/79	52	15		4 Milky Way	161	$10	RCA Victor 3081
9/6/80	69	2		5 Hipnotism		$10	RCA Victor 3569
12/5/81+	22	18		6 Blue Jeans	162	$10	RCA Victor 3896
12/11/82	50	16		7 Friction		$10	RCA Victor 4412
				CHOICE '90			
				Born Kim Davis in Houston. Female rapper.			
9/15/90	46	33		1 The Big Payback		$8	Rap-A-Lot 105
4/18/92	83	14		2 Stick-N-Moove		$8	Rap-A-Lot 57172
				CHOICE FOUR, The '76			
				Vocal group from Washington, DC: Bobby Hamilton, Ted Maduro, Pete Marshall and Charles Blagmore.			
4/17/76	43	3		On Top Of Clear		$10	RCA Victor 1400
				CHRISTIÓN '97			
				Vocal duo from Oakland: Kenny Ski and Allen Anthony.			
11/22/97	23	18		Ghetto Cyrano	146	$8	Roc-A-Fella 536281
				CHRISTOPHER, Gavin '86			
				Born in Chicago. Male singer/songwriter/producer.			
7/5/86	36	14		1 One Step Closer	74	$8	Manhattan 53024
3/19/88	48	10		2 Gavin		$8	EMI-Manhattan 46998
				CHUBB ROCK '91			
				Born Richard Simpson on 5/28/68 in Jamaica; raised in Brooklyn, New York. Male rapper. Acted in the movie *Private Times*.			
5/14/88	54	12		1 Chubb Rock Featuring Hitman Howie Tee		$8	Select 21614
7/29/89	28	21		2 And The Winner Is...		$8	Select 21631
				CHUBB ROCK With Howie Tee			
11/24/90+	22	29		3 Treat 'Em Right	73	$8	Select 9063
6/8/91	13	49		4 The One	71	$8	Select 21640

CHUBB ROCK — Cont'd

DEBUT	PEAK	WKS	Gold	Album Title	Pop #	$	Label & Number
9/26/92	24	13		5 I Gotta Get Mine Yo! - Book Of Rhymes	127	$8	Select 61299
6/14/97	45	4		6 The Mind		$8	Select 21659

CHUCK D '96
Born Carlton Ridenhour on 8/1/60 in New York City. Leader of **Public Enemy**.

11/9/96	47	2		Autobiography Of Mistachuck	190	$8	Mercury 532944

CHUNK '93

11/6/93	90	1		Break 'Em Off A Chunk		$8	Murder One 1874

CHUNKY A '90
Chunkston Arthur Hall is actually actor/comedian Arsenio Hall. Born on 2/12/57 in Cleveland. Hosted own late night talk show (1989-1994) and starred in own sitcom (1997). Acted in the movies *Coming To America* and *Harlem Nights*.

12/16/89+	41	15		Large And In Charge [N]	71	$8	MCA 6354

CISSEL, Chuck '80
Born in Tulsa, Oklahoma. Singer/actor. Made numerous commercials and appeared in many Broadway shows.

2/16/80	39	9		Just For You	204	$10	Arista 4257

C.J. & CO. '77
Disco group from Detroit: Cornelius Brown, Curtis Durden, Joni Tolbert, Connie Durden and Charles Clark.

7/2/77	12	19		Devil's Gun	60	$10	Westbound 6100

CLARK, Rhonda '89
Born in St. Louis; raised in Flint, Michigan. Female singer.

10/21/89	69	6		Between Friends		$8	Tabu 40882

CLARKE, Stanley ★182★ '81
Born on 6/30/51 in Philadelphia. Jazz bassist. Member of **Return To Forever** and **Fuse One**.
1)The Clarke/Duke Project 2)Journey To Love 3)Modern Man

11/8/75	8	14		1 Journey To Love [I]	34	$10	Nemperor 433

Silly Putty *[94]* • Journey To Love • Hello Jeff • Song To John • Medley: Concerto For Jazz/Rock Orchestra

5/6/78	25	9		2 Modern Man [I]	57	$10	Nemperor 35303
7/21/79	36	20		3 I Wanna Play For You [I-L]	62	$12	Nemperor 35680 [2]

half is studio and half is live

6/21/80	40	15		4 Rocks, Pebbles And Sand	95	$8	Epic 36506
5/2/81	7	27		5 The Clarke/Duke Project	33	$8	Epic 36918

STANLEY CLARKE/GEORGE DUKE
Wild Dog • Louie Louie • **Sweet Baby** *[6]* • I Just Want To Love You *[49]* • Never Judge A Cover By It's Book • Let's Get Started • Winners • Touch And Go • Finding My Way • Atlanta

8/28/82	25	9		6 Let Me Know You	114	$8	Epic 38086
11/26/83	44	11		7 The Clarke/Duke Project II	146	$8	Epic 38934

STANLEY CLARKE/GEORGE DUKE

4/28/84	52	25		8 Time Exposure	149	$8	Epic 38688
8/25/90	52	14		9 3		$8	Epic 46012

STANLEY CLARKE/GEORGE DUKE

9/11/93	54	27		10 East River Drive [I]		$8	Epic 47489

CLARK-SHEARD, Karen '97
Born in Detroit. Gospel singer. Daughter of Dr. Mattie Moss Clark. Member of the Clark Sisters gospel group.

11/22/97	28	46		Finally Karen		$8	Island 524397

CLAY D. AND THE NEW GET FUNKY CREW '92
Born Clayton Dixon in Miami. Prolific rap producer. The New Get Funky Crew includes Mikeal Jones, Ernest Ruffin and John Rose.

5/2/92	66	12		We're Goin' Off		$8	Pandisc 8815

CLAY, Otis '92
Born on 2/11/42 in Waxhaw, Mississippi.

7/25/92	75	9		I'll Treat You Right		$8	Bullseye Blues 9520

CLAYTON, Merry '71
Born Mary Clayton in Los Angeles. Session singer. Acted in the 1987 movie *Maid To Order*.

11/20/71	36	9		1 Merry Clayton	180	$12	Ode 77012
9/6/75	50	5		2 Keep Your Eye On The Sparrow	146	$12	Ode 77030

CLICK, The '95
All-star rap group: E-40, B-Legit The Savage, Suga T and D-Shot.

4/24/93	87	11		1 Down & Dirty		$8	Sick Wid' It 707
11/25/95	3	29	●	2 Game Related	21	$8	Sick Wid' It 41562

Wolf Tickets • **Hurricane** *[31]* • Out My Body • World Went Crazy • Actin' Bad • Get Chopped • We Don't Fuck Wit' Dat • Be About Yo' Paper • Boss Baller • **Scandalous** *[49]* • Learn About It • If I Took Your Boyfriend • Rock Up My Birdie • Hot Ones • Echo Thru The Ghetto

CLIFF, Jimmy '92
Born James Chambers on 4/1/48 in St. James, Jamaica. Reggae singer/composer. Starred in the movies *The Harder They Come* and *Club Paradise*.

10/10/92	60	6		Breakout		$8	JRS 35808

CLIFFORD, Linda '78
Born in Brooklyn, New York. Disco singer.

5/6/78	9	24		1 If My Friends Could See Me Now	22	$15	Curtom 5021

If My Friends Could See Me Now *[68]* • You Are, You Are • **Runaway Love** *[3]* • Broadway Gypsy Lady • I Feel Like Falling In Love Again • Please Darling, Don't Say Goodbye • Gypsy Lady

4/7/79	19	15		2 Let Me Be Your Woman	26	$12	RSO 3902 [2]
12/1/79	47	8		3 Here's My Love	117	$10	RSO 3067

DEBUT	PEAK	WKS	Gold	Album Title	Pop #	$	Label & Number
				CLIFFORD, Linda — Cont'd			
7/5/80	53	4		4 The Right Combination	180	$10	RSO 3084
				LINDA CLIFFORD/CURTIS MAYFIELD			
10/11/80	47	9		5 I'm Yours	160	$10	RSO 3087
12/15/84+	49	11		6 Sneakin' Out		$8	Red Label 10000
				CLINTON, George **'83**			
				Born on 7/22/40 in Kannapolis, North Carolina. Highly prolific and influential funk music singer/songwriter/producer. Formed the seminal groups **Parliament** and **Funkadelic**. Those groups featured several influential musicians and spawned several offshoot groups including **Bootsy's Rubber Band**, **The Brides Of Funkenstein** and the **P-Funk All Stars**.			
12/18/82+	3	41		1 Computer Games	40	$8	Capitol 12246
				Get Dressed [73] • Medley: Man's Best Friend/Loopzilla • Pot Sharing Tots • Computer Games • **Atomic Dog** [1] • Free Alterations • One Fun At A Time			
1/14/84	18	29		2 You Shouldn't-Nuf Bit Fish	102	$8	Capitol 12308
7/20/85	17	17		3 Some Of My Best Jokes Are Friends	163	$8	Capitol 12417
5/24/86	17	18		4 R&B Skeletons In The Closet	81	$8	Capitol 12481
9/2/89	75	7		5 The Cinderella Theory	192	$8	Paisley Park 25994
10/30/93	31	11		6 Hey Man...Smell My Finger	145	$8	Paisley Park 25518
6/29/96	27	9		7 T.A.P.O.A.F.O.M. - The Awesome Power Of A Fully-Operational Mothership	121	$8	550 Music/Epic 67144
				GEORGE CLINTON & THE P-FUNK ALLSTARS			
11/16/96	46	8		8 Greatest Funkin' Hits .... [K]	138	$8	Capitol 33911
				contains remixes of his greatest hits			
				CLIVILLÉS & COLE — see C & C Music Factory			
				C-LOC **'98**			
				Male rapper from New Orleans. Member of **Concentration Camp II**.			
10/10/98	52	2		Ya Heard Me		$8	No Limit 50732
				CLUB NOUVEAU **'87**			
				Dance group from Sacramento, California. Formed and fronted by Jay King (producer/owner of King Jay Records; produced the **Timex Social Club**; early lineup: vocalists Valerie Watson and **Samuelle** Prater with Denzil Foster and Thomas McElroy. Prater, Foster and McElroy left in 1988, replaced by David Agent and Kevin Irving. Agent left in 1989. Foster and McElroy formed a prolific production duo and also recorded as FMob.			
12/20/86+	2⁴	44	▲	1 Life, Love & Pain	6	$8	Warner 25531
				Jealousy [8] • Why You Treat Me So Bad [2] • Lean On Me [2] • Promises Promises • Situation #9 [4] • Heavy On My Mind [42] • Let Me Go • Pump It Up			
6/18/88	44	8		2 Listen To The Message	98	$8	Warner 25687
12/2/89+	39	19		3 Under A Nouveau Groove		$8	Warner 25991
6/20/92	80	10		4 A New Beginning		$8	JVK 19101
				C-MURDER **'98**			
				Born Corey Miller in New Orleans. Male rapper. Brother of **Master P** and **Silkk The Shocker**.			
3/28/98	❶¹	31	●	Life Or Death	3	$8	No Limit 50723
				Second Chance • Akickdoe! • Constantly In Danger • Don't Play No Games • Show Me Luv • Picture Me • On The Run • Gettin' Paid • Only The Strong Survive • The Truest Shit • Makin Moves • Soldiers • Cluckers • Life Or Death • Where I'm From • G's & Macks • Riders • Watch Yo Enemies • Duck & Run • Ghetto Ties • Survival Of The Fittest • Dreams			
				COBHAM, Billy **'75**			
				Born on 5/16/44 in Panama; raised in New York City. Jazz-rock drummer. Formerly with **Miles Davis**.			
5/11/74	19	8		1 Crosswinds .... [I]	23	$12	Atlantic 7300
1/11/75	12	10		2 Total Eclipse .... [I]	36	$12	Atlantic 18121
11/22/75	32	5		3 A Funky Thide Of Sings .... [I]	79	$10	Atlantic 18149
				COCKER, Joe **'70**			
				Born John Robert Cocker on 5/20/44 in Sheffield, England. Blues-rock singer.			
9/19/70	23	11	●	Mad Dogs & Englishmen .... [L-S]	2¹	$20	A&M 6002 [2]
				recorded March 27-28, 1970 at the Fillmore East in New York City			
				COCOA BROVAZ **'98**			
				Rap duo from New York City: Tek and Steele. Formerly known as Smif-N-Wessun. Members of **Boot Camp Clik**.			
1/28/95	5	21		1 Dah Shinin'	59	$8	Wreck 2005
				SMIF-N-WESSUN			
				Timz N Hood Chek • Wrektime • Wontime • **Wrekonize** [95] • Sound Bwoy Bureill • K.I.M. • **Bucktown** [61] • Stand Strong • Shinin...Next Shit • Cession At Da Doghillee • Hellucination • Home Sweet Home • Wipe Ya Mouf • Let's Git It On • P.N.C.			
4/11/98	3	16		2 The Rude Awakening	21	$8	Duck Down 50699
				Off The Wall • Still Standin Strong • **Won On Won** [94] • Blown Away • Money Talks • The Cash • Black Trump • Dry Snitch • Game Of Life • Back 2 Life • Bucktown USA • Hold It Down • Spanish Harlem • Myah Angelow • Memorial			
				COFFEY, Dennis, And The Detroit Guitar Band **'72**			
				Born in Detroit. Session guitarist for Motown.			
11/6/71+	13	22		1 Evolution .... [I]	36	$12	Sussex 7004
4/15/72	37	12		2 Goin' For Myself .... [I]	90	$12	Sussex 7010
1/17/76	31	8		3 Finger Lickin Good .... [I]	147	$10	Westbound 212

COLE, Natalie ★38★   '77
Born on 2/6/50 in Los Angeles. Daughter of **Nat "King"** Cole. Married for a time to her record producer, Marvin Yancey. Later married Andre Fischer, former drummer of **Rufus**. Won the 1975 Best New Artist Grammy Award. Hosted own syndicated variety TV show *Big Break* in 1990.

1)Unpredictable 2)Inseparable 3)Natalie

| 8/9/75 | ❶¹ | 50 | ● | 1 **Inseparable** | 18 | $10 | Capitol 11429 |

Needing You • Joey • **Inseparable** [1] • I Can't Say No • **This Will Be** • Something For Nothing • I Love Him So Much • How Come You Won't Stay Here • Your Face Stays In My Mind • You

| 5/22/76 | 3 | 32 | ● | 2 **Natalie** | 13 | $10 | Capitol 11517 |

Mr. Melody [10] • Heaven Is With You • **Sophisticated Lady (She's A Different Lady)** [1] • No Plans For The Future • Can We Get Together Again • Keep Smiling • Good Morning Heartache • Not Like Mine • Touch Me • Hard To Get Along

| 2/26/77 | ❶³ | 29 | ▲ | 3 **Unpredictable** | 8 | $10 | Capitol 11600 |

This Heart • Still In Love • **Party Lights** [9] • **I've Got Love On My Mind** [1] • Unpredictable You • Peaceful Living • Be Mine Tonight • I Can't Breakaway • Your Eyes • I'm Catching Hell

| 12/17/77+ | 5 | 37 | ▲ | 4 **Thankful** | 16 | $10 | Capitol 11708 |

Lovers • **Our Love** [1] • La Costa • Nothing Stronger Than Love • Be Thankful • I Can't Stay Away • **Annie Mae** [6] • Keeping A Light

| 7/22/78 | 9 | 15 | ● | 5 **Natalie...Live!** | [L] | 31 | $12 | Capitol 11709 [2] |

recorded August 1977 at the Universal Amphitheatre in Los Angeles and March 1978 at the Latin Casino in Cherry Hill, New Jersey
Sophisticated Lady (She's A Different Lady) • Que Sera, Sera • Lovers • I'm Catching Hell (Living Here Alone) • Mr. Melody • This Will Be • Party Lights • I've Got Love On My Mind • **Lucy In The Sky With Diamonds** [53] • Inseparable • Cry Baby • Can We Get Together Again • I Can't Say No • Something's Got A Hold On Me • Be Thankful • Our Love

| 4/7/79 | 11 | 18 | ● | 6 I Love You So | 52 | $10 | Capitol 11928 |
| 12/15/79+ | 7 | 20 | | 7 **We're The Best Of Friends** | 44 | $10 | Capitol 12019 |

NATALIE COLE/PEABO BRYSON
Gimme Some Time [8] • This Love Affair • I Want To Be Where You Are • Your Lonely Heart • What You Won't Do For Love [16] • We're The Best Of Friends • Medley: Let's Fall In Love/You Send Me • Love Will Find You

6/21/80	17	22		8 Don't Look Back	77	$10	Capitol 12079
9/19/81	37	10		9 Happy Love	132	$10	Capitol 12165
9/17/83	54	7		10 I'm Ready	182	$8	Epic 38280
6/22/85	48	16		11 Dangerous	140	$8	Modern 90270
7/18/87+	8	65		12 Everlasting	42	$8	Manhattan 53051

Everlasting • **Jump Start** [2] • The Urge To Merge • Split Decision • When I Fall In Love [31] • Pink Cadillac [9] • I Live For Your Love [4] • In My Reality • I'm The One • More Than The Stars

| 5/27/89 | 21 | 28 | | 13 Good To Be Back | 59 | $8 | EMI 48902 |
| 7/6/91 | 5 | 79 | ▲⁷ | 14 **Unforgettable With Love** | 1⁵ | $8 | Elektra 61049 |

The Very Thought Of You • Paper Moon • Route 66 • Mona Lisa • L-O-V-E • This Can't Be Love • Smile • Lush Life • That Sunday That Summer • Orange Colored Sky • Medley: For Sentimental Reasons/Tenderly/Autumn Leaves • Straighten Up And Fly Right • Avalon • Don't Get Around Much Anymore • Too Young • Nature Boy • Darling, Je Vous Aime Beaucoup • Almost Like Being In Love • Thou Swell • Non Dimenticar • Our Love Is Here To Stay • **Unforgettable** [10]

7/3/93	14	23	●	15 Take A Look	26	$8	Elektra 61496
12/3/94	20	7	●	16 Holly & Ivy	[X]	36	$8	Elektra 61704
10/12/96	11	18	●	17 Stardust	20	$8	Elektra 61946

COLE, Nat "King"   '65
Born Nathaniel Adams Coles on 3/17/17 in Montgomery, Alabama; raised in Chicago. Died of lung cancer on 2/15/65 (age 47). Legendary singer/pianist. Father of **Natalie** Cole. Acted in several movies. Hosted own TV variety series (1956-57). Won Grammy's Lifetime Achievement Award in 1990.

| 3/20/65 | 8 | 4 | | 1 L-O-V-E | 4 | $20 | Capitol 2195 |

L-O-V-E • The Girl From Ipanema • Three Little Words • There's Love • My Kind Of Girl • Thanks To You • Your Love • More • Coquette • How I'd Love To Love You • Swiss Retreat

| 8/23/69 | 46 | 3 | | 2 Close-Up | 197 | $15 | Capitol 252 [2] |

reissue of albums *Ballads Of The Day* (Capitol 680) and *Nat King Cole's Top Pops* (Capitol 1891)

COLEMAN, Durell   '85
Born in Roanoke, Virginia. Male singer.

| 9/28/85 | 33 | 26 | | Durell Coleman | 155 | $8 | Island 90293 |

COLEMAN, Gary B.B.   '87
Born in 1947 in Paris, Texas. Blues guitarist.

| 4/11/87 | 74 | 2 | | Nothin' But The Blues | | $10 | Ichiban 1005 |

COLLEGE BOYZ, The   '92
Male rap group from Los Angeles: Rom, Squeak, The Q and DJ B-Selector.

| 4/25/92 | 25 | 31 | | 1 Radio Fusion Radio | 118 | $8 | Virgin 91658 |
| 10/22/94 | 80 | 2 | | 2 Nuttin' Less, Nuttin' Mo' | | $8 | Virgin 39839 |

COLLINS, "Bootsy" — see COLLINS, William "Bootsy"

COLLINS, Lyn   '72
Born on 6/12/48 in Lexington, Texas. Former member of the **James Brown** Revue. Nicknamed "The Female Preacher."

| 10/14/72 | 34 | 6 | | Think (About It) | | $25 | People 5602 |

COLLINS, Phil   '85
Born on 1/30/51 in London. Pop singer/songwriter/drummer. Lead singer of rock group Genesis from 1975-96.

| 5/25/85 | 27 | 29 | ▲¹⁰ | No Jacket Required | 1⁷ | $8 | Atlantic 81240 |

39

DEBUT	PEAK	WKS	Gold	Album Title	Pop #	$	Label & Number

COLLINS, Tyler   '90
Born in Harlem, New York; raised in Detroit. Female singer.

| 1/6/90 | 22 | 41 | | Girls Nite Out | 85 | $8 | RCA 9642 |

★161★   **COLLINS, William "Bootsy"**   '78
Born on 10/26/51 in Cincinnati. Singer/bass player. Member of **James Brown**'s group from 1969-71. Joined Funkadelic/Parliament aggregation in 1972. Later led **Bootsy's Rubber Band** including brother Phelps Collins, Frank Waddy, Joel "Razor Sharp" Johnson, Gary "Mudbone" Cooper and Robert "P-Nut" Johnson. Collins featured his alter-egos "Bootzilla" and "Casper" in stage shows.

| 4/10/76 | 10 | 31 | | 1 **Stretchin' Out In Bootsy's Rubber Band** | 59 | $15 | Warner 2920 |

Stretchin' Out (In A Rubber Band) [18] • Psychoticbumpschool [69] • Another Point Of View • I'd Rather Be With You [25] • Love Vibes • Physical Love • Vanish In Our Sleep

| 2/5/77 | ❶¹ | 26 | ● | 2 **Ahh...The Name Is Bootsy, Baby!** | 16 | $15 | Warner 2972 |

Ahh...The Name Is Bootsy, Baby! [18] • **The Pinocchio Theory [6]** • Rubber Duckie • Preview Side Too • What's A Telephone Bill? • Munchies For Your Love • **Can't Stay Away [19]** • We Want Bootsy

| 3/4/78 | ❶³ | 25 | ● | 3 **Bootsy? Player Of The Year** | 16 | $15 | Warner 3093 |

Bootsy? (What's The Name Of This Town) • May The Force Be With You • Very Yes • **Bootzilla [1]** • Hollywood Squares [17] • Roto-Rooter • As In (I Love You)

| 7/14/79 | 9 | 15 | | 4 **This Boot Is Made For Fonk-n** | 52 | $15 | Warner 3295 |

BOOTSY'S RUBBER BAND (all of above)
Under The Influence Of A Groove • **Bootsy Get Live [38]** • Oh Boy Gorl • **Jam Fan (Hot) [13]** • Chug-A-Lug (The Bunn Patrol) • Shejam (Almost Bootsy Show)

| 12/6/80+ | 30 | 14 | | 5 **Ultra Wave** | 70 | $15 | Warner 3433 |

BOOTSY

| 5/22/82 | 18 | 16 | | 6 **The One Giveth, The Count Taketh Away** | 120 | $15 | Warner 3667 |

WILLIAM "BOOTSY" COLLINS

| 10/15/88 | 58 | 8 | | 7 **What's Bootsy Doin'?** | | $10 | Columbia 44107 |
| 8/27/94 | 59 | 6 | | 8 **Back In The Day: The Best Of Bootsy** [G] | | $8 | Warner Archives 26581 |

BOOTSY COLLINS (above 2)

COLLINS, Willie   '86
Born in North Carolina.

| 6/28/86 | 59 | 9 | | **Where You Gonna Be Tonight?** | | $8 | Capitol 12442 |

COLOR ME BADD   '91
Vocal group from Oklahoma City: Bryan Abrams, Sam Watters, Mark Calderon and Kevin Thornton.

| 8/17/91 | 10 | 47 | ▲³ | 1 **C.M.B.** | 3 | $8 | Giant 24429 |

I Wanna Sex You Up [1] • All 4 Love • Heartbreaker • **I Adore Mi Amor [1]** • Groove My Mind • Roll The Dice • Slow Motion • **Thinkin' Back [31]** • Color Me Badd [56] • Your Da One I Onena Love

| 12/4/93 | 20 | 18 | ● | 2 **Time And Chance** | 56 | $8 | Giant 24524 |
| 6/1/96 | 39 | 4 | | 3 **Now & Forever** | 113 | $8 | Giant 24622 |

COLOUR CLUB   '96
Vocal trio: Lisa Taylor, Les Pierce and Bernard Wise.

| 8/10/96 | 42 | 3 | | **In The Flow** | | $8 | Vertex/JVC 3004 |

COLTRANE, Alice   '74
Born Alice McLeod on 8/27/37 in Detroit. Jazz keyboardist. Married to John Coltrane until his death on 7/17/67.

| 11/9/74 | 33 | 7 | | **Illuminations** [I] | 79 | $12 | Columbia 32900 |

TURIYA ALICE COLTRANE/DEVADIP CARLOS SANTANA

COMING OF AGE   '93
Male vocal group from Los Angeles: Terrance Quaites, Israel Spencer, Ivan Shaw, Tee Kese and Marthony Tabb. Quaites recorded as **TQ**.

| 10/16/93 | 43 | 11 | | **Coming Of Age** | | $8 | Zoo 11064 |

COMMISSIONED   '94
Contemporary Christian vocal group: Fred Hammond, Marvin Sapp, Karl Reid, Mitchell Jones and Maxx Frank.

| 4/9/94 | 65 | 10 | | **Matters Of The Heart** | | $8 | Benson 1078 |

COMMODORES ★23★   '77
Group from Tuskegee, Alabama: Lionel Richie (vocals, saxophone), William King (trumpet), Thomas McClary (guitar), Milan Williams (keyboards), Ronald LaPread (bass) and Walter "Clyde" Orange (drums). Richie left in 1982.

1)Commodores 2)Natural High 3)Hot On The Tracks

| 8/31/74 | 22 | 6 | | 1 **Machine Gun** | 138 | $15 | Motown 798 |
| 3/22/75 | 7 | 25 | | 2 **Caught In The Act** | 26 | $10 | Motown 820 |

Wide Open • **Slippery When Wet [1]** • The Bump • I'm Ready • **This Is Your Life [13]** • Let's Do It Right • Better Never Than Forever • Look What You've Done To Me • You Don't Know That I Know

| 11/15/75 | 7 | 30 | | 3 **Movin' On** | 29 | $10 | Motown 848 |

Hold On • Free • Mary, Mary • **Sweet Love [2]** • (Can I) Get A Witness • Gimme My Mule • Time • Cebu

| 7/10/76 | ❶⁶ | 31 | | 4 **Hot On The Tracks** | 12 | $10 | Motown 867 |

Let's Get Started • Girl, I Think The World About You • High On Sunshine • **Just To Be Close To You [1]** • **Fancy Dancer [9]** • Come Inside • Thumpin' Music • Quick Draw • Can't Let You Tease Me

| 4/9/77 | ❶⁸ | 44 | | 5 **Commodores** | 3 | $10 | Motown 884 |

Squeeze The Fruit • Funny Feelings • Heaven Knows • Zoom • Won't You Come Dance With Me • **Brick House [4]** • Funky Situation • Patch It Up • **Easy [1]**

DEBUT	PEAK	WKS	Gold	Album Title	Pop #	$	Label & Number

COMMODORES — Cont'd

DEBUT	PEAK	WKS		Album Title	Pop #	$	Label & Number
11/19/77	2[7]	26	6	Commodores Live!	[L] 3	$12	Motown 894 [2]

recorded during their 1977 American tour • Won't You Come Dance With Me • Slippery When Wet • Come Inside • Just To Be Close To You • Funny Feelings • Fancy Dancer • Sweet Love • Zoom • Easy • I Feel Sanctified • Brick House • Too Hot Ta Trot

| 6/3/78 | ❶[8] | 32 | ▲ 7 | Natural High | 3 | $10 | Motown 902 |

Fire Girl • X-Rated Movie • **Flying High [21]** • **Three Times A Lady [1]** • Such A Woman • Say Yeah • I Like What You Do • Visions

| 11/18/78 | 24 | 17 | 8 | Commodores' Greatest Hits | [G] 23 | $10 | Motown 912 |
| 8/18/79 | ❶[3] | 38 | 9 | Midnight Magic | 3 | $10 | Motown 926 |

Gettin' It • Midnight Magic • You're Special • **Still [1]** • **Wonderland [21]** • Sexy Lady • Lovin' You • **Sail On [8]** • 12:01 A.M.

| 6/28/80 | 3 | 39 | ▲ 10 | Heroes | 7 | $10 | Motown 939 |

Got To Be Together • Celebrate • **Old-Fashion Love [8]** • **Heroes [27]** • All The Way Down • Sorry To Say • Wake Up Children • Mighty Spirit • **Jesus Is Love [34]**

| 7/18/81 | 4 | 40 | ▲ 11 | In The Pocket | 13 | $10 | Motown 955 |

Lady (You Bring Me Up) [5] • Saturday Night • Keep On Taking Me Higher • **Oh No [5]** • **Why You Wanna Try Me [42]** • This Love • Been Loving You • Lucy

12/4/82+	12	30	12	All The Great Hits	[G] 37	$10	Motown 6028
6/11/83	50	7	13	Commodores Anthology	[G] 141	$12	Motown 6044 [2]
10/1/83	26	17	14	Commodores 13	103	$8	Motown 6054
2/23/85	❶[3]	36	● 15	Nightshift	12	$8	Motown 6124

Animal Instinct [22] • **Nightshift [1]** • I Keep Running • Lay Back • Slip Of The Tongue • Play This Record Twice • **Janet [65]** • The Woman In My Life • Lightin' Up The Night

| 11/15/86+ | 17 | 21 | 16 | United | 101 | $8 | Polydor 831194 |

COMMON SENSE '97
Born Rasheed Lynn in Chicago. Male rapper.

3/6/93	70	6	1	Can I Borrow A Dollar		$8	Relativity 1084
10/22/94	27	16	2	Resurrection	179	$8	Relativity 1208
10/18/97	12	20	3	One Day It'll All Make Sense	62	$8	Relativity 1535

COMMON

COMPTON'S MOST WANTED '94
Rap group from Los Angeles fronted by MC Eiht.

7/14/90	32	22	1	It's A Compton Thang	133	$8	Orpheus 75627
8/10/91	23	17	2	Straight Checkn 'Em	92	$8	Orpheus 47926
10/17/92	20	38	3	Music To Driveby	66	$8	Orpheus 52984
8/6/94	❶[5]	25	● 4	We Come Strapped	5	$8	Epic Street 57696

Niggaz That Kill • Def Wish III • Take 2 With Me • All For The Money • Compton Cyco • Niggaz Make The Hood Go Round • Nuthin' But High • We Come Strapped • Can I Still Kill It • Goin' Out Like Geez • Nuthin' But The Gangsta • Hard Times • Compton Bomb • 2 Tha Westside

| 4/27/96 | 3 | 19 | 5 | Death Threatz | 16 | $8 | Epic Street 67139 |

MC EIHT FEATURING CMW (above 2)
Def Wish IV (Tap That Azz) • Ain't Nuthin 2 It • Killin Nigguz • Run 4 Your Life • Endoness • Thuggin It Up • Love 4 Tha Hood • Fuck Em All • Late Nite Hype Part 2 • Set Trippin • Collect My Stripez • Fuck Your Hood • You Can't See Me • Drugs & Killin • Killin Season

| 11/2/96 | 88 | 2 | 6 | Killafornia Organization | | $8 | Killa Cali/Thug 3003 |

KILLAFORNIA ORGANIZATION FEATURING COMPTONS MOST WANTED

COMRADS, The '97
Rap duo from Los Angeles: K-Mac and Gangsta.

| 7/26/97 | 33 | 4 | | The Comrads | 113 | $8 | Street Life 75507 |

CONCENTRATION CAMP II '98
Gathering of solo rappers: C-Loc, Young Bleed, Lay Lo, Lucky Knuckles and Boo The Boss Playa.

| 5/30/98 | 24 | 9 | | Da Holocaust | 84 | $8 | Priority 53536 |

★87★ CON FUNK SHUN '78
Funk group from Vallejo, California: Michael Cooper (vocals, guitar), Danny Thomas (keyborads), Karl Fuller, Paul Harrell and Felton Pilate (horns), Cedric Martin (bass), and Louis McCall (drums).
1)Secrets 2)Touch 3)Candy

| 10/1/77+ | 6 | 30 | ● 1 | Secrets | 51 | $8 | Mercury 1180 |

DooWhaChaWannaDoo • Who Has The Time • Tears In My Eyes • **Ffun [1]** • Secrets • **Confunkshunizeya [31]** • I'll Set You Out O.K. • Indian Summer Love

| 6/17/78 | 10 | 25 | ● 2 | Loveshine | 32 | $8 | Mercury 3725 |

So Easy [28] • Magic Woman • **Shake And Dance With Me [5]** • Make It Last • Loveshine • When The Feeling's Right • I Think I Found The Answer • Wanna Be There • Can't Go Away

| 5/26/79 | 7 | 25 | ● 3 | Candy | 46 | $8 | Mercury 3754 |

Fire When Ready • **Chase Me [4]** • Not Ready • **Da Lady [60]** • Candy • **(Let Me Put) Love On Your Mind [24]** • Main Slice • Images

| 4/19/80 | 7 | 21 | ● 4 | Spirit Of Love | 30 | $8 | Mercury 3806 |

Got To Be Enough [8] • **By Your Side [27]** • Curtain Call • Early Morning Sunshine • Spirit Of Love • **Happy Face [87]** • All Up To You • Juicy • Honey Wild • Lovestruck 1980

| 12/20/80+ | 7 | 26 | 5 | Touch | 51 | $8 | Mercury 4002 |

Too Tight [8] • **Lady's Wild [42]** • Give Your Love To Me • Pride And Glory • Kidnapped! • Welcome Back To Love • Touch • Can't Say Goodbye • Play Widit

| 12/26/81+ | 17 | 26 | 6 | Con Funk Shun 7 | 82 | $8 | Mercury 4030 |
| 11/20/82+ | 9 | 48 | 7 | To The Max | 115 | $8 | Mercury 4067 |

Ms. Got-The-Body [15] • Let's Ride And Slide • Everlove • Hide And Freak • **You Are The One [47]** • Take It To The Max • Love's Train • **Ain't Nobody, Baby [31]** • T.H.E. Freak

| 11/26/83+ | 12 | 28 | 8 | Fever | 105 | $8 | Mercury 814447 |

CON FUNK SHUN — Cont'd

DEBUT	PEAK	WKS		Album Title	Pop #	$	Label & Number
5/18/85	9	36	9	Electric Lady	62	$8	Mercury 824345

Turn The Music Up • Rock It All Night • **I'm Leaving Baby** [12] • **Tell Me What (I'm Gonna Do)** [47] • **Electric Lady** [4] • Don't Go (I Want You Back) • Circle Of Love • Pretty Lady

7/26/86	25	16	10	Burnin' Love	121	$8	Mercury 826963
6/5/93	43	12	11	The Best Of Con Funk Shun .... [G]		$8	Mercury 510275
11/16/96	74	2	12	Live For Ya A** .... [L]		$8	Intersound 9220

recorded at the Concourse Exhibition Center in San Francisco

CONLEY, Arthur   '67
Born on 4/1/46 in Atlanta.

5/13/67	10	7		Sweet Soul Music	93	$30	Atco 215

Sweet Soul Music [2] • Take Me (Just As I Am) • Who's Foolin' Who • There's A Place For Us • I Can't Stop (No, No, No) • Wholesale Love • I'm A Lonely Stranger • I'm Gonna Forget About You • Let Nothing Separate Us • Where You Lead Me

★170★   CONNORS, Norman   '76
Born on 3/1/48 in Philadelphia. Jazz drummer. Featured vocalists are **Michael Henderson**, **Jean Carn** and **Phyllis Hyman**.

1)You Are My Starship 2)This Is Your Life 3)Romantic Journey

11/9/74	51	6	1	Slewfoot		$12	Buddah 5611
8/16/75	35	19	2	Saturday Night Special	150	$10	Buddah 5643
5/15/76	5	33	● 3	You Are My Starship	39	$10	Buddah 5655

We Both Need Each Other [23] • Betcha By Golly Wow [29] • Bubbles • **You Are My Starship** [4] • Just Imagine • So Much Love • The Creator Has A Master Plan

4/9/77	24	17	4	Romantic Journey	94	$10	Buddah 5682
5/20/78	20	24	5	This Is Your Life	68	$10	Arista 4177
12/9/78+	44	9	6	The Best Of Norman Connors & Friends .... [G]	175	$10	Buddah 5716
7/7/79	34	12	7	Invitation	137	$10	Arista 4216
10/25/80	30	23	8	Take It To The Limit	145	$10	Arista 9534
12/5/81	51	6	9	Mr. C	197	$10	Arista 9575
4/16/88	39	13	10	Passion		$8	Capitol 48515
4/10/93	70	8	11	Remember Who You Are		$8	MoJazz 7003

CONSCIOUS DAUGHTERS, The   '94
Female rap duo from Oakland: Carla Green and Karryl Smith.

1/22/94	25	25	1	Ear To The Street	126	$8	Scarface 53877
3/23/96	29	7	2	Gamers		$8	Priority 53994

CONTROLLERS, The   '86
Vocal group from Fairfield, Alabama: brothers Reginald and Larry McArthur, with Lenard Brown and Ricky Lewis.

3/15/80	47	3	1	Next In Line		$10	Juana 200,005
10/20/84	47	8	2	The Controllers		$8	MCA 5514
6/14/86	25	18	3	Stay		$8	MCA 5681
11/7/87	72	1	4	For The Love Of My Woman		$8	MCA 42043

CONVICTS   '91
Rap duo from New Orleans: Mike Barnett ("Big Mike") and Chris Barriere. Big Mike later joined the **Geto Boys**.

8/17/91	52	17		Convicts		$8	Rap-A-Lot 57152

COOKE, Sam   '65
Born on 1/22/31 in Clarksdale, Mississippi; raised in Chicago. Died from a gunshot wound on 12/11/64 (age 33); shot by a female motel manager under mysterious circumstances. Son of a Baptist minister. Father of Linda Womack (of **Womack & Womack**). Uncle of **R.B. Greaves**. Inducted into the Rock and Roll Hall of Fame in 1986.

1/30/65	❶³	27	1	Sam Cooke At The Copa [L]	29	$35	RCA Victor 2970

The Best Things In Life Are Free • Bill Bailey • Nobody Knows You When You're Down And Out • Frankie And Johnny • Medley: Try A Little Tenderness/(I Love You) For Sentimental Reasons/You Send Me • If I Had A Hammer • When I Fall In Love • Twistin' The Night Away • This Little Light Of Mine • Blowin' In The Wind • Tennessee Waltz

1/30/65	5	5	2	The Best Of Sam Cooke [G]	22	$35	RCA Victor 2625

You Send Me [1] • Only Sixteen [13] • Everybody Likes To Cha Cha Cha [2] • (I Love You) For Sentimental Reasons [15] • Wonderful World [2] • Summertime • Chain Gang [2] • Cupid [20] • Twistin' The Night Away [1] • Sad Mood [23] • Having A Party [4] • Bring It On Home To Me [2]

2/13/65	❶⁴	15	3	Shake	44	$30	RCA Victor 3367

Shake [2] • Yeah Man • Win Your Love For Me • Love You Most Of All • Meet Me At Mary's Place • It's Got The Whole World Shakin' [15] • A Change Is Gonna Come [9] • I'm In The Mood For Love • You're Nobody 'Til Somebody Loves You • Comes Love • I'm Just A Country Boy • (Somebody) Ease My Troublin' Mind

8/7/65	7	2	4	The Best Of Sam Cooke, Volume 2 [G]	128	$30	RCA Victor 3373

Frankie And Johnny [4] • That's Where It's At [93] • Another Saturday Night [1] • Little Red Rooster [7] • Shake [2] • Baby, Baby, Baby • Good News [11] • Cousin Of Mine [40] • A Change Is Gonna Come [9] • Tennessee Waltz [35] • Basin Street Blues • Love Will Find A Way

COOKIE CREW, The   '89
Rap trio based in London: DJ Biznezz with Debbie Pryce (born in Barbados) and Susan Banfield (born in Jamaica). Banfield is the sister of John Banfield of **The Pasadenas**.

5/20/89	93	5		Born This Way		$8	FFRR 828134

COOL C   '89
Born Christopher Roney in Philadelphia. Male rapper.

9/23/89	51	13	1	I Gotta Habit		$8	Atlantic 82020
10/20/90	72	6	2	Life In The Ghetto		$8	Atlantic 82149

COOLIO '94
Born Artis Ivey in 1963 in Los Angeles. Male rapper. Former member of **WC And The MAAD Circle**.

8/6/94	5	22	▲ 1	It Takes A Thief	8	$8	Tommy Boy 1083

Fantastic Voyage [12] • County Line [97] • Mama, I'm In Love Wit A Gangsta • Hand On My Nutsac • Ghetto Cartoon • Smokin' Stix • Can-O-Corn • U Know Hoo! • It Takes A Thief • Bring Back Somethin Fo Da Hood • N Da Closet • On My Way To Harlem • Sticky Fingers • Thought You Knew • Ugly Bitches • I Remember [83]

11/25/95+	14	44	▲² 2	Gangsta's Paradise	9	$8	Tommy Boy 1141
9/13/97	49	8	● 3	My Soul	39	$8	Tommy Boy 1180

COOPER, Michael '88
Born on 11/15/52 in Vallejo, California. Singer/songwriter/guitarist/producer. Leader of **Con Funk Shun**.

1/16/88	21	28	1	Love Is Such A Funny Game	98	$8	Warner 25653
9/16/89+	27	28	2	Just What I Like		$8	Reprise 25923
2/20/93	56	12	3	Get Closer		$8	Reprise 26686

COOP M.C. '95

3/25/95	62	2		Home Of The Killas		$8	On The Rise 2

COREA, Chick '76
Born Anthony Armando Corea on 6/11/42 in Chelsea, Massachusetts. Jazz-rock pianist. Member of **Return To Forever**.

3/20/76	32	7		The Leprechaun	[I] 42	$10	Polydor 6062

CORNELIUS BROTHERS & SISTER ROSE '72
Family group from Dania, Florida. Consisted of Edward, Carter and Rose Cornelius. Billie Jo was added in 1973. Carter died on 11/7/91 (age 43).

8/5/72	12	16	1	Cornelius Brothers & Sister Rose	29	$15	United Artists 5568
1/5/74	32	10	2	Big Time Lover		$15	United Artists 121
4/3/76	60	2	3	Greatest Hits	[G]	$12	United Artists 593

★94★ **COSBY, Bill** '67
Born on 7/12/38 in Philadelphia. Comedian/actor. Starred on TV's *I Spy* and *The Cosby Show*. Acted in several other TV shows and movies.
1)Revenge 2)To Russell, My Brother, Whom I Slept With 3)Bill Cosby Sings/Silver Throat

6/10/67	❶²	23	● 1	Revenge	[C] 2¹	$15	Warner 1691

Revenge • Two Daughters • Two Brothers • The Tank • Smoking • Wives • Cool Covers • Old Weird Harold • Fat Albert • Planes

7/29/67	18	20	▲ 2	Bill Cosby Is A Very Funny Fellow, Right!	[C] 21	$15	Warner 1518
8/19/67	21	6	▲ 3	Wonderfulness	[C] 7	$15	Warner 1634
9/9/67	15	12	4	Bill Cosby Sings/Silver Throat	[C] 18	$12	Warner 1709
2/24/68	22	5	5	Bill Cosby Sings/Hooray For The Salvation Army Band!	[C] 74	$12	Warner 1728
4/13/68	6	29	● 6	To Russell, My Brother, Whom I Slept With	[C] 7	$12	Warner 1734

Baseball • Conflict • The Losers • The Apple • To Russell, My Brother, Whom I Slept With

11/2/68	18	16	● 7	200 M.P.H.	[C] 16	$12	Warner 1757
2/15/69	21	17	8	It's True! It's True!	[C] 37	$12	Warner 1770
7/19/69	40	4	9	8:15 12:15	[C] 62	$15	Tetragrammaton 5100 [2]

title: times of shows at Harrah's Lake Tahoe

9/6/69	34	19	▲ 10	The Best Of Bill Cosby	[C-K] 51	$12	Warner 1798
10/25/69	50	4	11	Bill Cosby	[C] 70	$10	Uni 73066
6/5/76	23	12	12	Bill Cosby Is Not Himself These Days (Rat Own, Rat Own, Rat Own)	[N] 100	$8	Capitol 11530
12/18/82+	33	16	13	Bill Cosby "Himself"	[C-S] 64	$8	Motown 6026

excerpts of his filmed one-man show in Ontario, Canada

7/5/86	45	8	● 14	Those Of You With Or Without Children, You'll Understand	[C] 26	$8	Geffen 24104

COUNTS, The '72
Funk group from Detroit: Mose Davis (vocals), Demetrus Cates, Raoul Keith Mangrum, Andrew Gibson and Leroy Emmanuel.

5/27/72	35	8	1	What's Up Front That-Counts	193	$30	Westbound 2011
11/10/73	45	8	2	Love Signs		$25	Aware 2002
4/19/75	58	3	3	Funk Pump		$20	Aware 2006

COUP, The '94
Rap trio from Oakland: Boots, E Roc and DJ Pam The Funkstress.

5/22/93	83	7	1	Kill My Landlord		$8	Wild Pitch 89047
11/5/94	62	2	2	Genocide & Juice		$8	Wild Pitch 29273

COVAY, Don '73
Born on 3/24/38 in Orangeburg, South Carolina. Singer/songwriter.

8/18/73	45	5		Super Dude I	204	$12	Mercury 653

COVER GIRLS, The '88
Female dance trio from New York City: Louise Sabater, Caroline Jackson and Sunshine Wright.

2/27/88	74	2		Show Me	64	$8	Fever 4

COX, Deborah '98
Born on 7/13/74 in Toronto, Canada.

10/28/95	25	36	● 1	Deborah Cox	102	$8	Arista 18781
10/17/98	14	42↑	● 2	One Wish	72	$8	Arista 19022

CPO '90
Rap duo from Compton, California: Lil' Nation and DJ Train. CPO: Capital Punishment Organization.

9/15/90	33	17		To Hell And Black		$8	Capitol 94522

CRAIG G '91
Born Craig Curry in 1972 in New York City. Male rapper.

5/25/91	97	2		Now, That's More Like It		$8	Atlantic 82196

CRAWFORD, Hank '76
Born on 12/21/34 in Memphis. Jazz alto saxophonist. Member of the **Ray Charles** band from 1958-63.

DEBUT	PEAK	WKS		Album Title	Pop #	$	Label & Number
5/6/72	42	7		1 Help Me Make It Through The Night .... [I]		$12	Kudu 06
2/24/73	49	2		2 We Got A Good Thing Going .... [I]		$12	Kudu 08
2/28/76	17	13		3 I Hear A Symphony .... [I]	159	$12	Kudu 26
1/29/77	42	4		4 Hank Crawford's Back .... [I]	167	$12	Kudu 33

★186★ CRAWFORD, Randy '81
Born Veronica Crawford on 2/18/52 in Macon, Georgia; raised in Cincinnati. Female singer.
1)Secret Combination 2)Rich And Poor 3)Windsong

DEBUT	PEAK	WKS		Album Title	Pop #	$	Label & Number
7/7/79	63	6		1 Raw Silk		$10	Warner 3283
5/24/80	30	17		2 Now We May Begin	180	$10	Warner 3421
5/30/81	12	22		3 Secret Combination	71	$10	Warner 3541
6/26/82	24	23		4 Windsong	148	$10	Warner 23687
11/5/83	41	11		5 Nightline	164	$10	Warner 23976
7/26/86	53	9		6 Abstract Emotions	178	$8	Warner 25423
11/18/89+	19	41		7 Rich And Poor	159	$8	Warner 26002
5/9/92	49	12		8 Through The Eyes Of Love		$8	Warner 26736
5/4/96	40	21		9 Naked And True		$8	Bluemoon 92662
2/28/98	70	14		10 Every Kind Of Mood - Randy, Randi, Randee		$8	Bluemoon 92785

CRAY, Robert, Band '87
Born on 8/1/53 in Columbus, Georgia. Blues singer/guitarist.

DEBUT	PEAK	WKS		Album Title	Pop #	$	Label & Number
1/24/87	21	35	▲²	1 Strong Persuader	13	$8	Mercury 830568
9/10/88	80	11	●	2 Don't Be Afraid Of The Dark	32	$8	Mercury 834923
10/27/90	89	5	●	3 Midnight Stroll	51	$8	Mercury 846652
				THE ROBERT CRAY BAND FEATURING THE MEMPHIS HORNS			
				The Memphis Horns: Wayne Jackson (trumpet) and Andrew Love (sax)			
12/5/92	80	5		4 I Was Warned	103	$8	Mercury 512721
				ROBERT CRAY			

CREAM '68
British rock supergroup: Eric Clapton (vocals, guitar), Jack Bruce (vocals, bass) and Ginger Baker (drums). Inducted into the Rock and Roll Hall of Fame in 1993.

DEBUT	PEAK	WKS		Album Title	Pop #	$	Label & Number
8/17/68	11	26	●	Wheels Of Fire .... [L]	1⁴	$40	Atco 700 [2]
				record 1: studio; record 2: Live At The Fillmore			

CREATIVE SOURCE '74
Vocal group from Los Angeles: Don Wyatt, Celeste Rhodes, Steve Flanagan, Barbara Berryman and Barbara Lewis.

DEBUT	PEAK	WKS		Album Title	Pop #	$	Label & Number
11/10/73+	21	16		1 Creative Source	152	$15	Sussex 8027
10/5/74	28	9		2 Migration		$15	Sussex 8035
12/13/75	49	3		3 Pass The Feelin' On		$12	Polydor 6052

CREEDENCE CLEARWATER REVIVAL '70
Rock group from El Cerrito, California: brothers John (vocals, guitar) and Tom (guitar) Fogerty, with Stu Cook (keyboards, bass) and Doug Clifford (drums). Tom Fogerty died on 9/6/90 (age 48). Group inducted into the Rock and Roll Hall of Fame in 1993.

DEBUT	PEAK	WKS		Album Title	Pop #	$	Label & Number
4/5/69	41	10	▲²	1 Bayou Country	7	$15	Fantasy 8387
9/27/69	26	20	▲³	2 Green River	1⁴	$15	Fantasy 8393
1/17/70	28	11	▲²	3 Willy and the Poorboys	3	$15	Fantasy 8397
8/22/70	11	22	▲⁴	4 Cosmo's Factory	1⁹	$15	Fantasy 8402
1/23/71	28	9	▲	5 Pendulum	5	$15	Fantasy 8410

CRIME BOSS '97
Born Thurston Slaughter in Houston. Male rapper.

DEBUT	PEAK	WKS		Album Title	Pop #	$	Label & Number
3/11/95	11	29		1 All In The Game	113	$8	Suave House 0003
4/26/97	6	9		2 Conflicts & Confusion	25	$8	Suave House 1566
				CRIME BOSS Featuring The Fedz			
				Conflicts & Confusion • No Friends • Chemical Imbalance • Warning • Back To The Streets • Life Is Crying • What Does It Mean (To Be A Real Crime Boss) • Close Range • Please Stop • Get Up In Your Ass • Death Notes • Get Mine			
9/5/98	81	2		3 Still At Large		$8	Crime Lab 8409

CRIMINAL NATION '90
Interracial rap group from Seattle: Mark Womack, Eugene DeHostos, Clifton Jones, Darren Robinson and Cleetus Brooks.

DEBUT	PEAK	WKS		Album Title	Pop #	$	Label & Number
12/1/90	73	13		1 Release The Pressure		$8	Nastymix 70240
9/5/92	75	9		2 Trouble In The Hood		$8	Nastymix 7107

CRIPS — see BLOODS & CRIPS

CRISS, Sonny '76
Born William Criss on 10/23/27 in Memphis. Committed suicide on 11/19/77 (age 50). Alto saxophonist.

DEBUT	PEAK	WKS		Album Title	Pop #	$	Label & Number
4/3/76	51	5		Warm & Sonny		$12	ABC/Impulse 9312

CROPPER, Steve — see KING, Albert

CROSBY, STILLS & NASH '69
Folk-rock trio formed in Los Angeles: David Crosby (guitar), Stephen Stills (guitar, keyboards, bass) and Graham Nash (guitar). Crosby had been in The Byrds, Stills had been in Buffalo Springfield, and Nash was with The Hollies. Won the 1969 Best New Artist Grammy Award. Trio inducted into the Rock and Roll Hall of Fame in 1997.

DEBUT	PEAK	WKS		Album Title	Pop #	$	Label & Number
9/6/69	35	4	▲³	Crosby, Stills & Nash	6	$20	Atlantic 8229

CROSS, Christopher '83
Born Christopher Geppert on 5/3/51 in San Antonio, Texas. Singer/songwriter. Won the 1980 Best New Artist Grammy Award.

DEBUT	PEAK	WKS		Album Title	Pop #	$	Label & Number
2/26/83	52	7	●	Another Page	11	$8	Warner 23757

DEBUT	PEAK	WKS	Gold	Album Title	Pop #	$	Label & Number

CROUCH, Andraé '77
Born on 7/1/42 in Los Angeles. Top gospel choir leader.

3/5/77	41	9		1 This Is Another Day		$12	Light 5683
12/15/79+	46	22		2 I'll Be Thinking Of You		$12	Light 5763
11/7/81	51	5		3 Don't Give Up	208	$10	Warner 3513

CROWN HEIGHTS AFFAIR '75
Disco group from New York City: Phil Thomas (vocals), William Anderson (guitar), Bert Reid, James Baynard and Raymond Reid (horn section), Howard Young (keyboards), Muki Wilson (bass) and Raymond Rock (drums).

10/25/75	28	7		1 Dreaming A Dream	121	$10	De-Lite 2017
7/31/76	59	2		2 Foxy Lady		$10	De-Lite 2021
12/4/76+	41	20		3 Do It Your Way	207	$10	De-Lite 2022
8/5/78	56	3		4 Dream World	205	$10	De-Lite 9506
3/31/79	40	6		5 Dance Lady Dance	207	$10	De-Lite 9512
3/22/80	50	10		6 Sure Shot	148	$10	De-Lite 9517

CRU '97
Rap trio from New York City: Chadio, Yogi and Mighty Ha.

| 9/13/97 | 26 | 6 | | Da Dirty 30 | 102 | $8 | Violator 537607 |

CRUCIAL CONFLICT '96
Hip-hop group from Chicago: Wildstyle, Kilo, Cold Hard and Never.

| 7/20/96 | 5 | 33 | ● | 1 The Final Tic | 12 | $8 | Pallas 53006 |

Don't Let It • Final Tic • Showdown • Desperado • Life Ain't The Same • Hay [10] • Trigger Happy • 1-900-Off-Your Square • Lil Advice • Tell It To The Judge • Ride The Rodeo • To The Left • Just Getting My Money • Get Up

| 11/21/98 | 10 | 17 | | 2 Good Side Bad Side | 38 | $8 | Pallas 53163 |

The Bidness • Scummy • Roll Somethin • To Bogish • Let It Go • Like This • Young Guns • Universal Love • Faceless Ones • Swing It Over Here • Airplane • Pump It Up • Back Against The Wall • Come On • I'm Bout To Explode • Ghetto Queen • Raw Dope Anthem

CRUSADERS, The ★40★ '79
Instrumental jazz-oriented group from Houston: **Joe Sample** (keyboards), **Wilton Felder** (reeds), Nesbert **Stix Hooper** (drums) and **Wayne Henderson** (trombone). First known as **The Jazz Crusaders**. Henderson left in 1975; Hooper left in 1983.

1)Street Life 2)Southern Comfort 3)The 2nd Crusade 4)Free As The Wind 5)Those Southern Knights

| 8/3/68 | 30 | 9 | | 1 Lighthouse '68 | [I-L] | | $20 | Pacific Jazz 20131 |

recorded at The Lighthouse in Hermosa Beach, California

| 2/22/69 | 38 | 6 | | 2 Powerhouse | | 184 | $20 | Pacific Jazz 20136 |
| 8/29/70+ | 12 | 31 | | 3 Old Socks, New Shoes...New Socks, Old Shoes | | 90 | $15 | Chisa 804 |

THE JAZZ CRUSADERS (above 3)

3/18/72	29	21		4 Crusaders 1	[I]	96	$20	Blue Thumb 6601 [2]
10/14/72	45	4		5 Hollywood			$15	MoWest 1181
3/24/73	4	26		6 The 2nd Crusade	[I]	45	$20	Blue Thumb 7000 [2]

Don't Let It Get You Down [31] • Take It Or Leave It • Gotta Get It On • Where There's A Will There's A Way • Look Beyond The Hill • Journey From Within • Ain't Gon' Change A Thang • A Message From The Inner City • A Search For Soul • No Place To Hide • Tomorrow Where Are You? • Tough Talk • Do You Remember When?

10/27/73	19	13		7 At Their Best	[I-K]	203	$15	Motown 796
11/17/73	33	9		8 Unsung Heroes	[I]	173	$12	Blue Thumb 6007
4/20/74	16	24		9 Scratch	[I-L]	73	$10	Blue Thumb 6010
11/16/74	3	24	●	10 Southern Comfort	[I]	31	$12	Blue Thumb 9002 [2]

Stomp And Buck Dance [41] • Greasy Spoon • Get On The Soul Ship (It's Sailing) • Super-Stuff • Double Bubble • The Well's Gone Dry • Southern Comfort • Time Bomb • When There's Love Around • Lilies Of The Nile • Whispering Pines • A Ballad For Joe (Louis)

| 8/30/75 | 9 | 13 | | 11 Chain Reaction | [I] | 26 | $10 | Blue Thumb 6022 |

Creole [84] • Chain Reaction • I Felt The Love • Mellow Out • Rainbow Visions • Hallucinate • Give It Up • Hot's It • Sugar Cane • Soul Caravan

| 5/29/76 | 9 | 18 | | 12 Those Southern Knights | [I] | 38 | $10 | Blue Thumb 6024 |

Spiral • Keep That Same Old Feeling [21] • My Mama Told Me So • 'Til The Sun Shines • And Then There Was The Blues [92] • Serenity • Feeling Funky

| 12/18/76 | 41 | 4 | | 13 The Best Of The Crusaders | [G-I] | 122 | $12 | Blue Thumb 6027 [2] |
| 6/18/77 | 8 | 22 | | 14 Free As The Wind | [I] | 41 | $10 | Blue Thumb 6029 |

Free As The Wind [84] • I Felt The Love • The Way We Was • Nite Crawler • Feel It [63] • Sweet 'N' Sour • River Rat • It Happens Everyday

| 7/29/78 | 18 | 18 | ● | 15 Images | [I] | 34 | $10 | Blue Thumb 6030 |
| 6/9/79 | 3 | 36 | ● | 16 Street Life | [I] | 18 | $8 | MCA 3094 |

Street Life [17] • My Lady • Rodeo Drive (High Steppin') • Carnival Of The Night • The Hustler • Night Faces

7/12/80	14	19		17 Rhapsody And Blues	[I]	29	$8	MCA 5124
10/10/81	29	11		18 Standing Tall	[I]	59	$8	MCA 5254
7/10/82	30	17		19 Royal Jam	[L]	144	$10	MCA 8017 [2]

recorded September 1981 at the Royal Festival Hall in London; with B.B. King and The Royal Philharmonic Orchestra

| 4/28/84 | 20 | 26 | | 20 Ghetto Blaster | | 79 | $8 | MCA 5429 |
| 12/13/86+ | 49 | 14 | | 21 The Good And Bad Times | [I] | | $8 | MCA 5781 |

CULTURE CLUB   '84

Pop group from London: George "Boy George" O'Dowd (vocals), Roy Hay (guitar, keyboards), Michael Craig (bass) and Jon Moss (drums). Won the 1983 Best New Artist Grammy Award.

3/12/83	24	37	▲ 1	Kissing To Be Clever	14	$8	Epic 38398
2/11/84	7	29	▲⁴ 2	Colour By Numbers	2⁶	$8	Epic 39107

Karma Chameleon [67] • It's A Miracle [75] • Black Money • Changing Every Day • That's The Way (I'm Only Trying To Help You) • Church Of The Poison Mind • **Miss Me Blind** [8] • Mister Man • Stormkeeper • Victims

12/15/84	55	12	▲ 3	Waking Up With The House On Fire	26	$8	Virgin 39881

CUTLASS, Frankie   '97

Born Francis Parker in Puerto Rico. Hip-hop producer.

3/1/97	32	14		Politics & Bullsh*t	129	$8	Relativity 1548

CYMANDE   '73

Afro-rock band from the West Indies: Ray King (vocals), Peter Serreo (sax), Mike Rose (flute), Pablo Gonsales (congas), Joe Dee (percussion), Derek Gibbs (sax), Pat Patterson (guitar) and Sam Kelly (drums).

1/6/73	24	14	1	Cymande	85	$12	Janus 3044
7/7/73	41	4	2	Second Time Round	180	$12	Janus 3054

CYMONE, Andre   '85

Born Andre Simon Anderson in Minneapolis. Former bass player of **Prince**'s band, The Revolution.

12/4/82+	49	18	1	Livin' In The New Wave		$8	Columbia 38123
10/15/83	31	7	2	Survivin' In The 80's	185	$8	Columbia 38902
9/21/85	28	13	3	A.C.	121	$8	Columbia 40037

★176★   **CYPRESS HILL**   '93

Rap trio from Los Angeles: Senen Reyes (older brother of **Mellow Man Ace**), Louis Freese and Lawrence Muggerud (former member of The 7A3). Band named for Cypress Street in the Southgate section of Los Angeles. Appeared in the movie *The Meteor Man*. Freese was also a member of **The Psycho Realm**.

10/12/91+	4	102	▲ 1	Cypress Hill	31	$8	Ruffhouse 47889

Pigs • How I Could Just Kill A Man • Hand On The Pump • Hole In The Head • Ultraviolet Dreams • Light Another • The Phuncky Feel One • Break It Up • Real Estate • Stoned Is The Way Of The Walk • Psycobetabuckdown • Something For The Blunted • Latin Lingo • The Funky Cypress Hill Shit • Tres Equis • Born To Get Busy

8/7/93	❶⁴	43	▲² 2	Black Sunday	1²	$8	Ruffhouse 53931

I Wanna Get High • **We Ain't Goin' Out Like That** [86] • **Insane In The Brain** [27] • When The Ship Goes Down • Lick A Shot • Cock The Hammer • Lil' Putos • Legalize It • Hits From The Bong • What Go Around Come Around, Kid • A To The K • Hand On The Glock • Break 'Em Off Some

11/18/95	3	34	▲ 3	Cypress Hill III (Temples Of Boom)	3	$8	Ruffhouse 66991

Spark Another Owl • **Throw Your Set In The Air** [60] • Stoned Raiders • **Illusions** [87] • Killa Hill Niggas • **Boom Biddy Bye Bye** [73] • No Rest For The Wicked • Make A Move • Killafornia • Funk Freakers • Locotes • Red Light Visions • Strictly Hip Hop • Let It Rain • Everybody Must Get Stoned

8/31/96	15	11	4	Unreleased & Revamped (EP) [E-M]	21	$6	Ruffhouse 67780

contains remixes and previously unreleased songs

10/24/98	11	17	● 5	IV	11	$8	Ruffhouse 69037

D

DA BRAT   '94

Born Shawntae Harris in Chicago. Female rapper.

7/16/94	❶¹	56	▲ 1	Funkdafied	11	$8	So So Def 66164

Da Shit Ya Can't Fuck Wit • **Fa All Y'all** [18] • Fire It Up • **Funkdafied** [2] • May Da Funk Be Wit 'Cha • Ain't No Thang • Come And Get Some • Mind Blowin' • **Give It 2 You** [11]

11/16/96	5	26	● 2	Anuthatantrum	20	$8	So So Def 67813

Anuthatantrum • My Beliefs • **Sittin' On Top Of The World** [18] • Let's All Get High • West Side • Just A Little Bit More • Keepin' It Live • **Ghetto Love** [11] • Lyrical Molestation • Live It Up • Make It Happen

DA BUSH BABEES   '96

Rap trio from Brooklyn, New York: Mr. Man, Lee Major and Light.

12/24/94	83	4	1	Ambushed		$8	Reprise 45449
11/2/96	75	2	2	Gravity		$8	Warner 46229

        BUSH BABEES

DADDY FREDDY   '91

Born in Kingston, Jamaica. Male rapper.

7/13/91	74	10		Stress		$8	Chrysalis 21844

DADDY-O   '93

Born Glenn Bolton in Brooklyn, New York. Male rapper. Former member of **Stetsasonic**.

11/20/93	86	1		You Can Be A Daddy, But Never Daddy-O		$8	Island 518203

DAEMYON, Jerald   '96

Born in Detroit. Classically trained violinist.

1/13/96	35	24		Thinking About You [I]	195	$8	GRP 9829

DA KAPERZ   '98

11/7/98	68	7		Da Kaperz		$8	Fully Loaded 8010

da'KRASH   '88

Funk group from St. Louis: Robert Jordan (vocals), Brian Tate, Edgar Hinton, Dee Dee James and Gabriel Acevedo.

3/19/88	29	10		da'KRASH	184	$8	Capitol 48355

DA LENCH MOB '92
Rap trio from Los Angeles: Terry Gray, DeSean Cooper and Shorty. Cooper left in 1993, replaced by Maulkie.

10/10/92	4	26	● 1	**Guerillas In Tha Mist**	24	$8	Street Know. 92206

Capital Punishment In America • Buck Tha Devil • Lost In Tha System • You & Your Heroes • All On My Nut Sac • Guerillas In Tha Mist • Lenchmob Also In Tha Group • Ain't Got No Class • Freedom Got An A.K. • Ankle Blues • Who Ya Gonna Shoot Wit That • Lord Have Mercy • Inside Tha Head Of A Black Man

11/19/94	14	5	2	Planet Of Da Apes	81	$8	Street Know. 53939

DALIA '97

1/25/97	89	1		Dalia		$8	Mercury 642330

DAMIAN DAME '91
Male/female duo: Damian from Battle Creek, Michigan, with Houston-born Debra "Deah Dame" Hurd (d: 7/4/94 in a car crash, age 36).

6/8/91	21	44		Damian Dame		$8	LaFace 26000

DANA DANE '87
Born in New York City. Male rapper.

8/29/87	2²	33	● 1	**Dana Dane With Fame**	46	$8	Profile 1233

Dedication • **Cinderfella Dana Dane** [11] • **This Be The Def Beat** [30] • Dana Dane With Fame • **Delancey Street** [44] • We Wanna Party • **Nightmares** [21] • Keep The Groove • Love At First Sight

11/3/90	23	24	2	Dana Dane 4-Ever	150	$8	Profile 1298
4/15/95	42	4	3	Rollin' Wit Dana Dane		$8	Maverick 45770

D&D PROJECT, The '95
Rap producers Douglas Gramma and David Lotwin.

6/10/95	39	10		The D&D Project		$8	Arista 18780

D'ANGELO '96
Born Michael D'Angelo Archer on 2/11/74 in Richmond, Virginia. Singer/songwriter.

7/22/95+	4	80	▲	**Brown Sugar**	22	$8	EMI 32629

Brown Sugar [5] • Alright • Jonz In My Bonz • **Me And Those Dreamin' Eyes Of Mine** [25] • Shit, Damn, Motherfucker • Smooth • **Cruisin'** [10] • When We Get By • **Lady** [2] • Higher

D'ARBY, Terence Trent '88
Born on 3/15/62 in New York City. Singer/songwriter/producer.

11/7/87+	❶³	59	▲² 1	**Introducing The Hardline According To Terence Trent D'Arby**	4	$8	Columbia 40964

If You All Get To Heaven • **If You Let Me Stay** [19] • **Wishing Well** [1] • I'll Never Turn My Back On You (Father's Words) • **Dance Little Sister** [9] • Seven More Days • Let's Go Forward • Rain • **Sign Your Name** [2] • As Yet Untitled • Who's Lovin' You

12/2/89	75	10	2	Terence Trent D'Arby's Neither Fish Nor Flesh	61	$8	Columbia 45351

DARK SUN RIDERS '96
Rap group: Jason "Brother J" Hunter (of **X-Clan**), Ultraman, Master China, D.J. Mate and The Rhythm Antenna.

3/16/96	85	1		Seeds Of Evolution		$8	Island 524159

DARK SUN RIDERS Featuring Brother J

DAS EFX '92
Rap duo from Brooklyn, New York: Andre "Dray" Weston and Willie "Skoob" Hines. DAS is an acronym for Dray And Skoob (which is "books" spelled backward).

4/25/92	❶⁵	46	▲ 1	**Dead Serious**	16	$8	EastWest 91827

Mic Checka [22] • Jussummen • They Want EFX [5] • Looseys • Dum Dums • East Coast • If Only • Brooklyn To T-Neck • Klap Ya Handz • Straight Out The Sewer [66]

12/4/93	6	26	2	**Straight Up Sewaside**	20	$8	EastWest 92265

Undaground Rappa • Gimme Dat Micraphone • Check It Out • **Freakit** [24] • Rappaz • **Baknaffek** [98] • Kaught In Da Ak • Wontu • Krazy Wit Da Books • It'z Lik Dat • Host Wit Da Most

10/7/95	4	17	3	**Hold It Down**	22	$8	EastWest 61829

No Diggedy • Knockin' Niggaz Off • Here We Go • **Real Hip-Hop** [48] • Here It Is • **Microphone Master** [39] • 40 & A Blunt • Buck-Buck • Can't Have Nuttin' • Alright • Hold It Down • Dedicated • Ready To Rock Rough Rhymes • Represent The Real • Comin' Thru • Hardcore Rap Act • Bad News

4/11/98	10	7	4	**Generation EFX**	48	$8	EastWest 62063

Raw Breed • Shine • Somebody Told Me • Set It Off • No Doubt • Rap Scholar • Generation EFX • Rite Now • Whut Goes Around • Make Noize • New Stuff • Take It Back • Change

DAVENPORT, N'dea '98
Born in Atlanta. Former lead singer of **The Brand New Heavies**.

7/18/98	56	5		N'dea Davenport		$8	Delicious Vinyl 27021

DAVINA '98
Born in Detroit. Female singer.

4/25/98	34	12		Best Of Both Worlds	180	$8	Loud/RCA 67536

DAVIS, Betty '74
Female singer. Formerly married to **Miles Davis**.

9/15/73	54	5	1	Betty Davis	202	$15	Just Sunshine 5
4/20/74	46	6	2	They Say I'm Different		$15	Just Sunshine 3500
12/27/75+	54	3	3	Nasty Girl	202	$12	Island 9329

DAVIS, Mary '90
Born in Savannah, Georgia. Lead singer with **The S.O.S. Band** from 1980-86.

3/31/90	82	4		Separate Ways		$8	Tabu 40978

DAVIS, Miles '70
Born on 5/26/26 in Alton, Illinois. Died of a stroke on 9/28/91 (age 65). Innovative jazz trumpeter who influenced the jazz fusion movement. Formerly married to **Betty Davis** and actress Cicely Tyson. Won Grammy's Lifetime Achievement Award in 1990.

DEBUT	PEAK	WKS	Gold	Album Title	Pop #	$	Label & Number
11/8/69	40	5		1 In A Silent Way ....[I]	134	$20	Columbia 9875
5/16/70	4	27	●	2 Bitches Brew ....[I]	35	$15	Columbia 26 [2]
				Pharaoh's Dance • Bitches Brew • Spanish Key • John McLaughlin • Miles Runs The Voodoo Down • Sanctuary			
6/12/71	47	1		3 A Tribute To Jack Johnson ....[I-S]	159	$12	Columbia 30455
				movie is a biography of the world heavyweight boxing champ (1908-1915)			
1/4/75	33	6		4 Get Up With It ....[I]	141	$15	Columbia 33236 [2]
				a Duke Ellington tribute album			
8/8/81	13	18		5 The Man With The Horn ....[I]	53	$10	Columbia 36790
7/6/85	63	5		6 You're Under Arrest ....[I]	111	$10	Columbia 40023
11/22/86	61	11		7 Tutu ....[I]	141	$8	Warner 25490
8/1/92	28	22		8 Doo-Bop ....[I]	190	$8	Warner 26938
8/28/93	86	3		9 Live At Montreux ....[I-L]		$8	Warner 45221
				MILES DAVIS & QUINCY JONES			
				recorded on July 8, 1991 at the Montreux Jazz Festival in Switzerland			

DAVIS, Rainy '87
Born Denise Lorraine Davis in Brooklyn, New York. Singer/songwriter.

DEBUT	PEAK	WKS	Gold	Album Title	Pop #	$	Label & Number
3/28/87	61	8		Sweetheart		$8	Columbia 40635

DAVIS, Tyrone ★56★ '79
Born on 5/4/38 in Greenville, Mississippi; raised in Saginaw, Michigan. Worked as valet/chauffeur for **Freddie King** until 1962. His younger sister, Jean Davis, was a member of the group **Facts Of Life**.
1)In The Mood With Tyrone Davis 2)Turn Back The Hands Of Time 3)Tyrone Davis 4)Turning Point 5)Love And Touch

DEBUT	PEAK	WKS	Gold	Album Title	Pop #	$	Label & Number
3/15/69	12	18		1 Can I Change My Mind	146	$40	Dakar 9005
7/11/70	9	14		2 Turn Back The Hands Of Time	90	$40	Dakar 9027
				Turn Back The Hands Of Time [1] • The Waiting Was Not In Vain • **Let Me Back In** [12] • Love Bones • **I'll Be Right Here** [8] • Something You Got • Undying Love • Just Because Of You • If It's Love That You're After • I Keep Coming Back			
7/29/72	42	2		3 I Had It All The Time	182	$40	Dakar 76901
12/30/72+	42	4		4 Greatest Hits ....[G]		$40	Dakar 76902
6/2/73	24	20		5 Without You In My Life	174	$40	Dakar 76904
1/26/74	28	11		6 It's All In The Game		$40	Dakar 76909
4/26/75	55	2		7 Home Wrecker		$40	Dakar 76915
2/14/76	10	13		8 Turning Point		$40	Dakar 76918
				So Good (To Be Home With You) [9] • Turning Point [1] • Forever • I Can't Bump (instrumental) • Saving My Love For You • Ever Lovin' Girl • Don't Let It Be Too Late • I Can't Bump (vocal) • Turn Back The Hands Of Time			
10/2/76	12	18		9 Love And Touch	89	$12	Columbia 34268
6/25/77	17	8		10 Let's Be Closer Together		$12	Columbia 34654
4/8/78	18	11		11 I Can't Go On This Way		$12	Columbia 35304
3/31/79	9	26		12 In The Mood With Tyrone Davis	115	$12	Columbia 35723
				In The Mood [6] • You Know What To Do • I Can't Wait • Keep On Dancin' • I Don't Think You Heard Me • **Ain't Nothing I Can Do** [72] • All The Love I Need • We Were In Love Then			
12/15/79+	40	12		13 Can't You Tell It's Me		$12	Columbia 36230
10/4/80	39	8		14 I Just Can't Keep On Going		$12	Columbia 36598
12/25/82+	10	27		15 Tyrone Davis	137	$10	Highrise 103
				Are You Serious [3] • I'm So Excited • Overdue • **A Little Bit Of Loving (Goes A Long Way)** [49] • Let Me Be The One • You've Got To (Save Me) • Where Did We Lose • The Fool In Me			
11/12/83	46	25		16 Something Good		$10	Ocean-Front 101
5/28/88	37	36		17 Flashin' Back		$10	Future 1003
3/30/91	39	53		18 I'll Always Love You		$8	Ichiban 1103
5/30/92	53	27		19 Something's Mighty Wrong		$8	Ichiban 1135
10/22/94	88	1		20 For The Good Times		$8	Life 78002
12/7/96+	85	8		21 Simply Tyrone Davis		$8	Malaco 7483

DAVY D '87
Born David Reeves in Queens, New York. Male rapper.

DEBUT	PEAK	WKS	Gold	Album Title	Pop #	$	Label & Number
8/8/87	34	15		Davy's Ride		$8	Def Jam 40657

DAY, Morris '85
Born in Springfield, Illinois; raised in Minneapolis. Lead singer of **The Time**. Acted in the movies *Purple Rain*, *The Adventures Of Ford Fairlane* and *Graffiti Bridge*.

DEBUT	PEAK	WKS	Gold	Album Title	Pop #	$	Label & Number
10/26/85	7	37		1 Color Of Success	37	$8	Warner 25320
				Color Of Success [15] • The Character [34] • The Oak Tree [3] • Love Sign • Don't Wait For Me • Medley: Love/Addiction			
3/19/88	7	17		2 Daydreaming	41	$8	Warner 25651
				Daydreaming [26] • Yo' Luv • Fishnet [1] • A Man's Pride • Are You Ready • **Love Is A Game** [71] • Moonlite (Passionlite) • Sally			

DAYNE, Taylor '88
Born Leslie Wundermann on 3/7/63 in Long Island, New York. Female singer.

DEBUT	PEAK	WKS	Gold	Album Title	Pop #	$	Label & Number
2/6/88	27	45	▲²	Tell It To My Heart	21	$8	Arista 8529

DA YOUNGSTA'S '93
Rap trio from Philadelphia: brothers Taji and Qu'ran Goodman, with Tarik Dawson.

DEBUT	PEAK	WKS	Gold	Album Title	Pop #	$	Label & Number
5/8/93	25	11		1 The Aftermath	126	$8	EastWest 92245
10/8/94	45	4		2 No Mercy		$8	EastWest 92370

DAYTON '82
Funk group from Dayton, Ohio: Chris Jones (male vocals), Jennifer Matthews (female vocals), Shawn Sandridge (guitar), Craig Robinson (bass) and Kevin Hurt (drums).

DEBUT	PEAK	WKS	Gold	Album Title	Pop #	$	Label & Number
8/14/82	36	8		Hot Fun		$10	Liberty 51126

DEBUT	PEAK	WKS	Gold	Album Title	Pop #	$	Label & Number

DAYTON FAMILY, The   **'96**
Rap group from Flint, Michigan: brothers Eric and Ira Dorsey, with Matt Hinkle and Raheen Peterson.

| 10/29/94+ | 38 | 46 | | 1 What's On My Mind?.. | | $8 | Po Broke 5433 |
| 10/12/96 | 7 | 27 | | 2 F.B.I. | 45 | $8 | Relativity 1544 |

F.B.I.: Fuck Being Indicted
79th & Halstead • Hand That Rocks The Cradle • F.B.I. • Real With This • Player Haters • Eyes Closed • What's On My Mind •
Killer G's • Posse Is Dayton Ave. • Blood Bath • Newspaper • Stick & Move • Ghetto

★145★   **DAZZ BAND**   **'82**
Funk group from Cleveland. Formerly known as **Kinsman Dazz**. Core members: Skip Martin (vocals), Eric Fearman (guitar), Bobby Harris
(sax), Pierre DeMudd (trumpet), Kevin Frederick (keyboards), and brothers Michael (bass) and Isaac (drums) Wiley. Martin left in 1988 to
join **Kool & The Gang**, replaced by Terry Stanton.
1)Keep It Live 2)Joystick 3)On The One

| 11/25/78 | 52 | 6 | | 1 Kinsman Dazz.. | 203 | $12 | 20th Century 574 |
| 9/22/79 | 62 | 6 | | 2 Dazz.. | | $12 | 20th Century 594 |

KINSMAN DAZZ (above 2)

| 6/27/81 | 36 | 20 | | 3 Let The Music Play.................................... | 154 | $10 | Motown 957 |
| 3/27/82 | ❶¹ | 37 | ● | 4 Keep It Live | 14 | $10 | Motown 6004 |

Let It Whip [1] • Gamble With My Love • I'll Keep On Lovin' You • Just Can't Wait 'Till The Night • Shake What You Got • **Keep It
Live (On The K.I.L.L.) [20]** • Just Believe In Love • Can We Dance • Let Me Love You Until

2/12/83	12	24		5 On The One..	59	$10	Motown 6031
12/17/83+	12	36		6 Joystick..	73	$10	Motown 6084
11/3/84	18	30		7 Jukebox..	83	$10	Motown 6117
8/31/85	24	12		8 Hot Spot...	98	$10	Motown 6149
8/30/86	37	12		9 Wild And Free..	100	$8	Geffen 24110
10/15/88	91	3		10 Rock The Room.......................................		$8	RCA Victor 6928
8/10/96	42	15		11 Under The Streetlights..............................		$8	Lucky 010
8/8/98	99	1		12 Here We Go Again....................................		$8	Platinum 9338

D.E.A.   **'98**

| 10/31/98 | 96 | 1 | | Screwed 4 Life.. | | $8 | Dead End 0001 |

DeBARGE   **'82**
Family group from Grand Rapids, Michigan: El DeBarge (male vocals, keyboards), **Bunny DeBarge** (female vocals), Mark (trumpet), James
(keyboards) and Randy (bass) DeBarge. Brothers Bobby and Tommy were in **Switch**. James was briefly married to **Janet Jackson** in 1984.

| 10/16/82+ | 3 | 73 | ● | 1 All This Love | 24 | $8 | Gordy 6012 |

I'll Never Fall In Love Again • **Stop! Don't Tease Me [46]** • I Like It [2] • Can't Stop • All This Love [5] • It's Getting Stronger •
Life Begins With You • I'm In Love With You

| 10/29/83+ | 4 | 48 | ● | 2 In A Special Way | 36 | $8 | Gordy 6061 |

Be My Lady • Stay With Me • **Time Will Reveal [1]** • Need Somebody • **Love Me In A Special Way [11]** • Queen Of My Heart •
Baby, Won't Cha Come Quick • I Give Up On You • A Dream

| 3/30/85 | 3 | 49 | ● | 3 Rhythm Of The Night | 19 | $8 | Gordy 6123 |

Prime Time • **The Heart Is Not So Smart [29]** • Who's Holding Donna Now [2] • Give It Up • Single Heart • You Wear It
Well [7] • The Walls (Came Tumbling Down) • Share My World • **Rhythm Of The Night [1]**

DeBARGE, Bunny   **'87**
Born on 3/15/55 in Grand Rapids, Michigan. Member of **DeBarge**.

| 3/7/87 | 50 | 11 | | In Love.. | 172 | $8 | Motown 6217 |

DeBARGE, Chico   **'97**
Born Jonathan DeBarge in 1966 in Grand Rapids, Michigan. DeBarge sibling, but not a member of the group **DeBarge**.

11/1/86	25	32		1 Chico DeBarge......................................	90	$8	Motown 6214
10/31/87	63	15		2 Kiss Serious..		$8	Motown 6249
12/6/97	14	64	●	3 Long Time No See....................................	86	$8	Kedar/Universal 53088

DeBARGE, El   **'86**
Born Eldra DeBarge on 6/4/61 in Grand Rapids, Michigan. Member of **DeBarge**.

| 6/14/86 | 8 | 37 | ● | 1 El DeBarge | 24 | $8 | Gordy 6181 |

Who's Johnny [1] • Secrets Of The Night • I Wanna Hear It From My Heart • **Someone [32]** • When Love Has Gone Away •
Private Line • Love Always [7] • Lost Without Her Love • Thrill Of The Chase • Don't Say It's Over

| 3/18/89 | 35 | 28 | | 2 Gemini.. | | $8 | Motown 6264 |
| 6/18/94 | 24 | 21 | | 3 Heart, Mind & Soul.................................. | 137 | $8 | Reprise 45375 |

DEEE-LITE   **'90**
Dance trio based in New York City: Super DJ Dmitry Brill (from Kiev, Soviet Union), Jungle DJ Towa "Towa" Tei (from Tokyo, Japan) and
vocalist Lady Miss Kier (Kier Kirby from Youngstown, Ohio). Group's name inspired by the tune "It's De-lovely" from the 1936 Cole Porter
musical *Red, Hot & Blue*. Brill and Kier are married.

| 10/13/90 | 34 | 28 | ● | World Clique... | 20 | $8 | Elektra 60957 |

DEELE, The   **'88**
Group from Cincinnati: Darnell "Dee" Bristol and Carlos "Satin" Greene (lead vocals), Stanley Burke, Kenny "**Babyface**" Edmonds (former
member of **Manchild**), Kevin Roberson and Mark "L.A. Reid" Rooney.

| 12/17/83+ | 9 | 37 | | 1 Street Beat | 78 | $8 | Solar 60285 |

Body Talk [3] • Surrender [66] • **Just My Luck [25]** • Sexy Love • Street Beat • Video Villain • Crazy 'Bout 'Cha • Working (9 To
5)

| 6/22/85 | 29 | 14 | | 2 Material Thangz..................................... | 155 | $8 | Solar 60410 |
| 9/5/87+ | 5 | 40 | ● | 3 Eyes Of A Stranger | 54 | $8 | Solar 72555 |

Two Occasions [4] • **Shoot 'em Up Movies [10]** • Let No One Separate Us • Eyes Of A Stranger • **Can-U-Dance [48]** • She
Wanted • Hip Chic • So Many Thangz

DEF DAMES   **'90**
Female rap duo from Bakersfield, California: Marilyn Smith and Yolanda Sugart.

| 3/10/90 | 76 | 28 | | 2 - 4 - The Bass...................................... | | $8 | Sedona 7521 |

DEF JEF '90
Born Jeffrey Fortson in Harlem, New York. Male rapper.

| 1/6/90 | 59 | 11 | | Just A Poet With Soul .... | | | $8 | Delicious Vinyl 3001 |

DEF SQUAD '98
All-star rap trio: **Keith Murray**, **Redman** and **Erick Sermon**.

| 7/18/98 | ❶¹ | 12 | | El Niño | | 2¹ | $8 | Def Jam 558343 |

Check N' Me Out • Countdown • **Full Cooperation** [51] • Ride Wit' Us • Rhymin' Wit' Biz • The Game (Freestyle) • Can U Dig It? • You Do, I Do • Ya'll Niggas Ain't Ready • Say Word! • No Guest List • Def Squad Delite

DÉJA — see AURRA

DE LA SOUL '89
Psychedelic-rap trio from Long Island, New York: Kelvin Mercer, David Jolicoeur and Vincent Mason.

| 3/11/89 | ❶⁵ | 36 | ● | 1 **3 Feet High And Rising** .... | | 24 | $8 | Tommy Boy 1019 |

The Magic Number • Change In Speak • Cool Breeze On The Rocks • Can U Keep A Secret? • Jenifa Taught Me (Derwin's Revenge) • Ghetto Thang • Transmitting Live From Mars • Eye Know • Take It Off • A Little Bit Of Soap • Tread Water • Potholes In My Lawn • **Say No Go** [32] • Do As De La Does • Plug Tunin' (Last Chance To Comprehend) • De La Orgee • **Buddy** [18] • Description • **Me Myself And I** [1] • This Is A Recording 4 Living In A Full Time Era (L.I.F.E.) • I Can Do Anything (Delacratic) • D.A.I.S.Y. Age

| 6/8/91 | 24 | 19 | ● | 2 **De La Soul Is Dead** .... | | 26 | $8 | Tommy Boy 1029 |
| 10/9/93 | 9 | 24 | | 3 **Buhloone Mindstate** | | 40 | $8 | Tommy Boy 1063 |

Eye Patch • En Focus • Patti Dooke • I Be Blowin' • Long Island Wildin' • **Ego Trippin'** [74] • Paul's Revenge • 3 Days Later • Area • I Am I Be • In The Woods • **Breakadawn** [30] • Dave Has A Problem...Seriously • Stone Age

| 7/13/96 | 4 | 18 | | 4 **Stakes Is High** | | 13 | $8 | Tommy Boy 1149 |

Supa Emcees • **The Bizness** [53] • Wonce Again Long Island • Dinninit • Brakes • Dog Eat Dog • Baby Baby Baby Baby Ooh Baby • Long Island Degrees • Betta Listen • **Itzsoweezee (Hot)** [60] • 4 More • Big Brother Beat • Down Syndrome • Pony Ride • **Stakes Is High** [70] • Sunshine

DELEGATION '79
Soul-disco trio based in England: Jamaicans Ricky Bailey and Ray Patterson, with Texan, Bruce Dunbar.

| 2/17/79 | 8 | 17 | | 1 **The Promise Of Love** | | 84 | $12 | Shadybrook 010 |

The Promise Of Love • You've Been Doing Me Wrong • Mr. Heartbreak • Let Me Take You To The Sun • Back Door Love • Where Is The Love • Soul Trippin' • **Oh Honey** [6] • Someone Oughta Write A Song (About You Baby) [45] • Love Is Like A Fire

| 5/24/80 | 69 | 8 | | 2 **Delegation** .... | | | $10 | Mercury 3821 |

DELFONICS, The '70
Vocal trio from Philadelphia: brothers William and Wilbert Hart, with Randy Cain. Cain left in 1971, replaced by **Major Harris**.

| 6/1/68 | 15 | 14 | | 1 **La La Means I Love You** .... | | 100 | $80 | Philly Groove 1150 |
| 2/22/69 | 8 | 19 | | 2 **Sound Of Sexy Soul** | | 155 | $80 | Philly Groove 1151 |

Ready Or Not Here I Come (Can't Hide From Love) [14] • Let It Be Me • Hot Dog Baby • Loving Him • Ain't That Peculiar • With These Hands • Face It Girl, It's Over • Going Out Of My Head • My New Love • **Somebody Loves You** [41] • Scarborough Fair • Everytime I See My Baby

| 11/22/69+ | 7 | 35 | | 3 **The Delfonics Super Hits** | [G] | 111 | $40 | Philly Groove 1152 |

La - La - Means I Love You [2] • I'm Sorry [15] • With These Hands • You're Gone • Somebody Loves You [41] • **You Got Yours And I'll Get Mine** [6] • Ready Or Not Here I Come (Can't Hide From Love) [14] • Let It Be Me • Loving Him • My New Love • Break Your Promise [12]

| 8/8/70 | 4 | 22 | | 4 **The Delfonics** | | 61 | $40 | Philly Groove 1153 |

Didn't I (Blow Your Mind This Time) [3] • Funny Feeling [48] • **When You Get Right Down To It** [12] • Baby I Love You • How Could You • Trying To Make A Fool Of Me [8] • Down Is Up, Up Is Down • Over And Over [9] • Think About Me • I Gave To You

| 6/24/72 | 15 | 9 | | 5 **Tell Me This Is A Dream** .... | | 123 | $40 | Philly Groove 1154 |
| 5/4/74 | 34 | 7 | | 6 **Alive & Kicking** | | 205 | $40 | Philly Groove 1501 |

DELINQUENT HABITS '96
Rap trio from Los Angeles: Kemo, Ives and O.G. Style.

| 6/22/96 | 31 | 10 | | **Delinquent Habits** .... | | 74 | $8 | Loud/RCA 66929 |

DELINQUENTS, The '97
Rap duo from Oakland: Vidal Provost and Glen Jones.

| 6/7/97 | 84 | 2 | | **Big Moves** .... | | | $8 | Priority 50680 |

DELLS, The ★43★ '69
Vocal group formed at Thornton Township High School in Harvey, Illinois: Johnny Carter (lead), Marvin Junior (baritone lead), Verne Allison (tenor), Mickey McGill (baritone) and Chuck Barksdale (bass). First recorded as the El-Rays for Checker in 1953. Original lead, Johnny Funches, left in 1960.

1)Love Is Blue 2)There Is 3)Freedom Means 4)Like It Is, Like It Was 5)The Dells Greatest Hits

| 5/18/68 | 4 | 39 | | 1 **There Is** | | 29 | $40 | Cadet 804 |

There Is [11] • Stay In My Corner [1] • Wear It On Our Face [27] • Please Don't Change Me Now • Show Me • The Change We Go Thru (For Love) • Higher And Higher • Close Your Eyes • Run For Cover • Love Is So Simple • When I'm In Your Arms • **O-O, I Love You** [22]

| 3/1/69 | 9 | 20 | | 2 **The Dells Musical Menu/Always Together** | | 146 | $40 | Cadet 822 |

Always Together [3] • Hallways Of My Mind [44] • Believe Me • I Want My Momma • Agatha Van Thurgood • Hallelujah Baby • Good-Bye Mary Ann • **Does Anybody Know I'm Here** [15] • Make Sure (You Have Someone Who Loves You) • I Can't Do Enough [20]

| 6/14/69 | 9 | 29 | | 3 **The Dells Greatest Hits** | [G] | 102 | $40 | Cadet 824 |

Stay In My Corner [1] • Always Together [3] • There Is [11] • Love Is So Simple • Please Don't Change Me Now • Wear It On Our Face [27] • Make Sure (You Have Someone Who Loves You) • O-O, I Love You [22] • Does Anybody Know I'm Here [15] • Hallways Of My Mind [44] • The Change We Go Thru (For Love) • I Can't Do Enough [20]

DEBUT	PEAK	WKS	Gold	Album Title	Pop #	$	Label & Number

DELLS, The — Cont'd

DEBUT	PEAK	WKS			Pop #	$	Label & Number
8/23/69	**3**	34	4	Love Is Blue	54	$40	Cadet 829

Medley: I Can Sing A Rainbow/Love Is Blue • Oh, What A Night [1] • On The Dock Of The Bay [13] • A Little Understanding • One Mint Julep • A Whiter Shade Of Pale • Summer Place • **The Glory Of Love** [30] • Honey • Medley: Wichita Lineman/By The Time I Get To Phoenix

2/28/70	**7**	18	5	Like It Is, Like It Was	126	$40	Cadet 837

I'm Not Afraid Of Tomorrow • Oh What A Day [10] • Come Out, Come Out • **Open Up My Heart** [5] • Darling Dear • Since I Fell For You • Nadine [flip] • **Long Lonely Nights** [27] • Off Shore

8/14/71	**4**	20	6	Freedom Means	81	$25	Cadet 50004

Freedom Means • Rather Be With You • **The Love We Had (Stays On My Mind)** [8] • One Less Bell To Answer • It's All Up To You [23] • Medley: If You Go Away/Love Story • Make It With You • Free And Easy • Melody Man • Freedom Theme

7/29/72	32	4	7	The Dells Sing Dionne Warwicke's Greatest Hits	162	$25	Cadet 50017
11/18/72	33	12	8	Sweet As Funk Can Be		$25	Cadet 50021
6/30/73	10	13	9	Give Your Baby A Standing Ovation	99	$25	Cadet 50037

Give Your Baby A Standing Ovation [3] • Ain't No Sunshine • You Don't Care • Share • Love Can Make It Easier • **The Glory Of Love** [30] • Stand Up And Show The World • Soul Strollin' • Closer

11/3/73+	15	28	10	The Dells	202	$25	Cadet 50046
3/23/74	15	25	11	The Dells vs. The Dramatics	156	$25	Cadet 60027
9/28/74	13	13	12	The Mighty Mighty Dells	114	$25	Cadet 60030
3/1/75	47	7	13	The Dells Greatest Hits Volume 2 ....[G]	210	$20	Cadet 60036
11/29/75+	31	8	14	We Got To Get Our Thing Together	207	$20	Cadet 60044
6/12/76	47	5	15	No Way Back		$15	Mercury 1084
5/7/77	40	6	16	They Said It Couldn't Be Done, But We Did It	208	$15	Mercury 1145
1/21/78	45	6	17	Love Connection	204	$15	Mercury 3711
9/2/78	55	3	18	New Beginnings	169	$12	ABC 1100
2/17/79	71	6	19	Face To Face	203	$12	ABC 1113
8/9/80	23	25	20	I Touched A Dream	137	$12	20th Century 618
4/14/84	49	8	21	One Step Closer		$10	Private I 39309
3/11/89	92	2	22	The Second Time		$10	Veteran 1988

DEL THE FUNKYHOMOSAPIEN   '93
Born Teren Jones in Oakland. Male rapper. Cousin of Ice Cube.

2/1/92	48	13	1	I Wish My Brother George Was Here		$8	Elektra 61133
12/11/93	27	10	2	No Need For Alarm	125	$8	Elektra 61529

DEMUS, Chaka, & Pliers   '93
Jamaican male dancehall reggae duo of DJ Chaka Demus and vocalist Everton "Pliers" Banner.

6/26/93	70	11		All She Wrote		$8	Mango 9930

DEODATO   '75
Born Eumir De Almeida Deodato on 6/21/42 in Rio de Janeiro, Brazil. Keyboardist/producer.

9/15/73	16	16	1	Deodato 2 ....[I]	19	$12	CTI 6029
5/18/74	28	6	2	Whirlwinds ....[I]	63	$10	MCA 410
9/20/75	15	9	3	First Cuckoo ....[I]	110	$10	MCA 491
9/13/80	53	8	4	Night Cruiser ....[I]	186	$10	Warner 3467

DEREK B   '88
Born Derek Boland in London. Male rapper.

8/6/88	56	13		Bullet From A Gun		$8	Profile 1266

DeSARIO, Teri   '80
Born in Miami. Singer/songwriter.

2/16/80	57	8		Moonlight Madness	80	$10	Casablanca 7178

DES'REE   '98
Born Des'ree Weeks in London to West Indian parents. Female singer.

9/5/98	72	4		Supernatural	185	$8	550 Music/Epic 69508

DESTINY'S CHILD   '98
Female R&B vocal group from Houston: Beyonce, Kelly, LaTavia and LeToya.

3/7/98	14	27	●	Destiny's Child	67	$8	Columbia 67728

DETROIT EMERALDS   '71
Vocal trio from Little Rock, Arkansas: brothers Abrim and Ivory Tilmon, with James Mitchell. Abrim Tilmon died of a heart attack in 1982.

5/8/71	23	14	1	Do Me Right	151	$40	Westbound 2006
3/25/72	37	7	2	You Want It, You Got It	78	$40	Westbound 2013
4/14/73	27	7	3	I'm In Love With You	181	$40	Westbound 2018

DETROIT'S MOST WANTED   '92

4/13/91	83	6	1	Tricks Of The Trades		$8	Bryant 30010
4/4/92	58	18	2	Tricks Of The Trades Vol. II		$8	Bryant 4126

DeVAUGHN, William   '74
Born in 1948 in Washington DC. Singer/songwriter/guitarist.

8/3/74	10	19	1	Be Thankful For What You Got	165	$12	Roxbury 100

Give The Little Man A Great Big Hand [51] • We Are His Children • Blood Is Thicker Than Water [10] • Kiss And Make Up • **Be Thankful For What You Got** [1] • Sing A Love Song • You Can Do It • Something's Being Done

8/2/80	74	3	2	Figures Can't Calculate		$10	TEC 1200

DEVIN   '98
Born Devin Copeland in Houston. Male rapper.

7/4/98	27	16		The Dude	177	$8	Rap-A-Lot 45938

DEBUT	PEAK	WKS	Gold	Album Title	Pop #	$	Label & Number

DFC   '94
Rap duo from Flint, Michigan: Alpha Breed and T Double E. DFC: Da Funk Clan.

| 4/9/94 | 7 | 19 | | 1 Things In Tha Hood | 71 | $8 | Assault 92320 |

Piece Of Mind • Put Your Locs On • **Caps Get Peeled** [78] • Mo' Love • **Things In Tha Hood** [98] • Pass The Hooter • 2-2 The Chest • Death B-4 Dishonesty • Hand's On My Nine • Roll With The Clan • Digga Bigga Ditch • You Can Get The Dick • Da Bomb

| 1/3/98 | 92 | 1 | | 2 Whole World's Rotten | | $8 | Penalty 3047 |

DIAMOND   '97
Born Joseph Kirkland in the Bronx, New York. Male rapper.

| 10/24/92 | 47 | 22 | | 1 Stunts, Blunts And Hip Hop | | $8 | Chemistry 513934 |

DIAMOND AND THE PSYCHOTIC NEUROTICS

| 11/29/97 | 40 | 4 | | 2 Hatred, Passions And Infidelity | | $8 | Mercury 534900 |

DIBANGO, Manu   '73
Born on 2/10/34 in Cameroon, Africa. Saxophonist/pianist.

| 6/30/73 | 11 | 12 | | 1 Soul Makossa [I] | 79 | $12 | Atlantic 7267 |
| 2/23/74 | 27 | 12 | | 2 Makossa Man [I] | | $12 | Atlantic 7276 |

DIEGO, Don   '92
Born Donald Bables in Plano, Texas. Saxophonist.

| 2/15/92 | 70 | 24 | | Razz [I] | | $8 | Ultrax 050293 |

DIGABLE PLANETS   '93
Rap trio from Washington DC: Ishmael Butler, Mary Ann Vierra and Craig Irving.

| 2/27/93 | 5 | 32 | ● | 1 Reachin' (A New Refutation Of Time And Space) | 15 | $8 | Pendulum 61414 |

It's Good To Be Here • Pacifics • **Where I'm From** [60] • What Cool Breezes Do • Time & Space (A New Refutation Of) • **Rebirth Of Slick (Cool Like Dat)** [6] • Last Of The Spiddyocks • Jimmi Diggin Cats • La Femme Fetal • Escapism (Gettin' Free) • Appointment At The Fat Clinic • **Nickel Bags (Of Funk)** [93] • Swoon Units • Examination Of What

| 11/5/94 | 13 | 17 | | 2 Blowout Comb | 32 | $8 | Pendulum 30654 |

DIGITAL UNDERGROUND   '91
Hip-hop group from Oakland: Eddie Humphrey and Ron Brooks (vocals), Gregory Jacobs (keyboards) and Chopmaster J (samples, percussion). Varying members include Tupac **"2Pac"** Shakur, Earl Cook, Clee Askew, Saafir The Saucee Nomad and Michael Boston. Group appeared in the movie *Nothing But Trouble*. Brooks later formed **Raw Fusion**.

| 4/14/90 | 8 | 30 | ▲ | 1 Sex Packets | 24 | $8 | Tommy Boy 1026 |

The Humpty Dance [7] • The Way We Swing • Rhymin' On The Funk • The New Jazz • Underwater Rimes • Gutfest '89 • The Danger Zone • Freaks Of Industry • **Doowutchyalike** [29] • Sex Packets • Street Scene • Packet Man

| 2/9/91 | 7 | 22 | ● | 2 This Is An E.P. Release [M] | 29 | $6 | Tommy Boy 964 |

Same Song • Tie The Knot • The Way We Swing • Nuttin' Nis Funky • Packet Man • Arguin' On The Funk

11/9/91	23	28	●	3 Sons Of The P	44	$8	Tommy Boy 1045
10/23/93	16	7		4 The Body-Hat Syndrome	79	$8	Tommy Boy 1080
6/22/96	26	9		5 Future Rhythm	113	$8	Critique 15452
9/26/98	91	1		6 Who Got The Gravy?		$8	Interscope 92061

DILLINGER, Daz   '98
Born Delmar Arnaud in Los Angeles. Male rapper. Member of **Tha Dogg Pound**. Cousin of **Snoop Doggy Dogg**.

| 4/11/98 | 2[1] | 17 | | Retaliation, Revenge And Get Back | 8 | $8 | Death Row 53524 |

Gang Bangin Ass Criminal • Its Going Down • Playa Partners • It Might Sound Crazy • Our Daily Bread • In California • Initiated • Oh No • Retaliation, Revenge And Get Back • O.G. • Baby Mama Drama • Only For U • Ridin High • The Ultimate Come Up • Thank God For My Life

DINO   '89
Born Dino Esposito on 7/20/63 in Encino, California; raised in Hawaii and Connecticut.

| 4/1/89 | 47 | 31 | ● | 24/7 | 34 | $8 | 4th & B'way 444011 |

DISCO RICK — see DOGS

DISCO TEX & HIS SEX-O-LETTES   '75
Disco studio group assembled by producer Bob Crewe. Featuring lead singer Joseph "Sir Monti Rock III" Montanez.

| 5/17/75 | 20 | 8 | | Disco Tex & His Sex-O-Lettes | 36 | $12 | Chelsea 505 |

DIS 'N' DAT   '94
Rap duo of sisters Tishea "Dis" and Tenesia "Dat" Bennett.

| 10/29/94 | 53 | 18 | | Bumpin' | | $8 | Epic Street 57625 |

DIVINE   '98
Female vocal trio from New Jersey: Nikki Bratcher, Kia Thornton and Tonia Tash.

| 11/14/98 | 40 | 23 | | Fairy Tales | 126 | $8 | Pendulum 12325 |

DIVINE STYLER   '90
Born in 1971 in Brooklyn, New York. Male rapper.

| 2/10/90 | 62 | 11 | | Word Power | | $8 | Epic 45299 |

DIVINE STYLER Featuring The Scheme Team

DJ DMD   '98
Born Dorie Dorsey in Port Arthur, Texas. Male DJ.

| 4/26/97 | 80 | 6 | | 1 Eleven | | $8 | Inner Soul 4518 |
| 11/21/98 | 28 | 20↑ | | 2 Twenty-Two: P.A. World Wide | | $8 | Inner Soul 62428 |

DJ DMD and The Inner Soul Clique

DJ FURY   '92
Born Brian Graham in Sanford, Florida. One-half of the **Bass Patrol**.

| 7/25/92 | 71 | 16 | | 1 Furious Bass | | $8 | On Top 9011 |
| 1/16/93 | 83 | 6 | | 2 Bass Man | | $8 | Joey Boy 3006 |

				DJ HONDA '98			
				Born in Hokkaido, Japan. Hip-hop DJ.			
8/3/96	90	1		1 DJ Honda		$8	Relativity 1549
4/11/98	57	5		2 H II		$8	Relativity 1613
				D.J. JAZZY JEFF & THE FRESH PRINCE '88			
				Rap duo from Philadelphia: D.J. Jeff Townes and rapper **Will Smith**. Smith starred in the hit TV sitcom *The Fresh Prince of Bel Air* and acted in several movies.			
3/7/87	24	33		1 Rock The House	83	$8	Jive 1026
5/7/88	5	47	▲³	2 He's The D.J., I'm The Rapper	4	$10	Jive 1091 [2]
				A Nightmare On My Street [9] • Here We Go Again • **Brand New Funk [76]** • Time To Chill • Charlie Mack-The First Out The Limo • As We Go • **Parents Just Don't Understand [10]** • Pump Up The Bass • Let's Get Busy Baby • Another Special Announcement • Live At Union Square, November 1986 • D.J. On The Wheels • My Buddy • Rhythm Trax-House Party Style • He's The D.J., I'm The Rapper • Hip Hop Dancer's Theme • Jazzy's In The House • Human Video Game			
11/25/89	19	20	●	3 And In This Corner................................	39	$8	Jive 1188
8/3/91	5	31	▲	4 Homebase	12	$8	Jive 1392
				I'm All That • **Summertime [1]** • **The Things That U Do [43]** • This Boy Is Smooth • **Ring My Bell [22]** • A Dog Is A Dog • Caught In The Middle (Love & Life) • Trapped On The Dance Floor • Who Stole The D.J. • You Saw My Blinker • Dumb Dancin'			
10/30/93	39	12	●	5 Code Red...	64	$8	Jive 41489
6/13/98	93	1		6 Greatest Hits.....................................[G]	144	$8	Jive 41640
				JAZZY JEFF & FRESH PRINCE (above 2)			
				D.J. JIMI '93			
				Born Jimi Payton in New York City. Male DJ.			
12/5/92+	57	16		It's Jimi		$8	Avenue 9105
				DJ JUBILEE '98			
5/9/98	61	3		Take It To The St. Thomas		$8	Take Fo' 206
				DJ KOOL '96			
				Born John Bowman in Washington DC. Male rapper.			
10/20/90	60	20		1 The Music Ain't Loud Enuff		$8	Creative Funk 7000
7/23/94+	84	5		2 20 Minute Work Out		$8	CLR 7201
4/6/96	21	42		3 Let Me Clear My Throat	161	$8	CLR 7209
				D.J. LAZ '92			
				Born Lazaro Mendez on 12/2/68 in Miami. Male rapper.			
3/7/92	86	5		D.J. Laz		$8	Pandisc 8817
				D.J. MAGIC MIKE '93			
				Born Michael Hampton in Orlando, Florida. Rap producer.			
12/23/89+	60	26	▲	1 D.J. Magic Mike And The Royal Posse		$8	Cheetah 9401
7/14/90	42	59		2 Bass Is The Name Of The Game	157	$8	Cheetah 9403
1/5/91	51	27	●	3 Back To Haunt You!	153	$8	Cheetah 9404
				VICIOUS BASE Featuring D.J. MAGIC MIKE!			
11/30/91+	31	25	●	4 Ain't No Doubt About It	72	$8	Cheetah 9405
7/25/92	64	10		5 Twenty Degrees Below Zero	149	$8	Cheetah 9412
				D.J. MAGIC MIKE & M.C. MADNESS (above 2)			
3/27/93	26	16	●	6 Bass: The Final Frontier	67	$8	Magic 9413
3/27/93	40	10		7 This Is How It Should Be Done	107	$8	Magic 9411
6/4/94	83	3		8 Represent		$8	Crap 9423
				DJ POOH '97			
				Born Mark Jordan in Los Angeles. Rap producer.			
8/2/97	34	8		Bad Newz Travels Fast	116	$8	Big Beat 92752
				DJ QUIK '95			
				Born David Blake in Compton, California. Male rapper.			
2/23/91	9	45	▲	1 Quik Is The Name	29	$8	Profile 1402
				Sweet Black Pussy • **Tonite [13]** • **Born And Raised In Compton [16]** • Deep • Tha Bombudd • Dedication • Quik Is The Name • Loked Out Hood • 8 Ball • Quik's Groove • Tear It Off • I Got That Feelin' • Skanless			
8/8/92	13	30	●	2 Way 2 Fonky	10	$8	Profile 1430
3/11/95	❶²	27	●	3 Safe + Sound	14	$8	Profile 1462
				Street Level Entrance • Get At Me • Diggin' U Out • **Safe + Sound [56]** • Somethin' 4 Tha Mood • Don't You Eat It! • Can I Eat It? • Itz Your Fantasy • Ho In Yo • Dollaz + Sense • Let You Havit • Summer Breeze • Quik's Groove III • Sucka Free • Keep Tha "P" In It • Hoorah 4 Tha Funk			
12/12/98	13	34↑		4 Rhythm-al-ism	63	$8	Profile 19034
				DJ SCREW '96			
4/6/96	52	10		3 N The Mornin'		$8	Big Tyme 1130
				DJ SMURF AND P.M.H.I. '95			
				Born in Atlanta. Male rapper.			
7/8/95	98	1		Versastyles		$8	Wrap 8145
				DJ SQUEEKY PRESENTS: TOM SKEEMASK '98			
				Duo from Memphis. Tom Skeemask is the rapper. DJ Squeeky is the producer.			
4/4/98	75	2		2 Wild For The World		$8	Relativity 1649
				DJ TAZ '97			
				Born Tino Santron McInytosh in Atlanta. Male DJ/rapper.			
8/30/97	93	1		...Worldwide		$8	EMI 57878
				DMG '93			
				Born in Houston. Male rapper. DMG: Detri-Mental-Gangsta.			
8/28/93	40	20		Rigormortiz		$8	Rap-A-Lot 53862

D-MOB   '90
British dance group headed by producer Danny D. Lead singer Cathy Dennis went solo in late 1990.

| 2/10/90 | 60 | 10 | | A Little Bit Of This, A Little Bit Of That | 82 | $8 | FFRR 828159 |

DMX   '98
Born Earl Simmons in Yonkers, New York. Male rapper. DMX is short for Dark Man X.

| 6/6/98 | ❶² | 61↑ | ▲³ | It's Dark And Hell Is Hot | 1¹ | $8 | Def Jam 558227 |

Ruff Ryders' Anthem [33] • Fuckin' Wit' D • Look Thru My Eyes • Get At Me Dog [19] • Let Me Fly • X-Is Coming • Damien •
How's It Goin' Down? [19] • Crime Story • Stop Being Greedy [45] • ATF • For My Dogs • I Can Feel It • The Convo • Niggaz
Done Started Something

D-NICE   '90
Born Derrick Jones in 1970 in New York City.

| 8/11/90 | 12 | 29 | | 1 Call Me D-Nice | 75 | $8 | Jive 1202 |
| 12/14/91+ | 27 | 18 | | 2 To Tha Rescue | 137 | $8 | Jive 41466 |

D.O.C., The   '89
Born Tray Curry in Dallas. Male rapper.

| 8/19/89 | ❶² | 36 | ▲ | 1 No One Can Do It Better | 20 | $8 | Ruthless 91275 |

It's Funky Enough [12] • Mind Blowin' • Lend Me An Ear • Comm. Blues • Let The Bass Go • Beautiful But Deadly • The D.O.C.
& The Doctor • No One Can Do It Better • Whirlwind Pyramid • Comm. 2 • The Formula [76] • Portrait Of A Master Piece • The
Grand Finale

| 2/10/96 | 5 | 12 | | 2 Helter Skelter | 30 | $8 | Giant 24627 |

Return Of Da Livin' Dead [67] • From Ruthless 2 Death Row (Do We Part) • Secret Plan • Komurshell (Mo' Hair) • 4 My
Doggz • .45 Automatic • Sonz O' Light • Bitchez • Da Hereafter • Erotix Shit • Welcome To The New World • Killa Instinc • Brand
New Formula • Crazy Bitchez

DR. BUZZARD'S ORIGINAL SAVANNAH BAND   '78
Big-band swing/disco band formed in New York City by brothers Stony Browder (guitar) and Thomas "August Darnell" Browder (bass).
Featuring Cory Daye (vocals), Andy Hernandez (vibraphone) and Mickey Sevilla (drums). Darnell and Hernandez left in 1980 to form Kid
Creole & The Coconuts.

| 9/18/76+ | 31 | 27 | ● | 1 Dr. Buzzard's Original Savannah Band | 22 | $12 | RCA Victor 1504 |
| 3/4/78 | 23 | 7 | | 2 Dr. Buzzard's Original Savannah Band Meets King Penett | 36 | $12 | RCA Victor 2402 |

DR. DRE   '93
Born Andre Young on 2/18/65 in Compton, California. Rapper/prolific producer. Co-founder of N.W.A. and World Class Wreckin' Cru.
Founded Death Row Records in 1992. Half-brother of Warren G.

| 1/2/93 | ❶⁸ | 105 | ▲³ | 1 The Chronic | 3 | $8 | Death Row 57128 |

The Chronic • Dre Day [6] • Let Me Ride [34] • The Day The Niggaz Took Over • Nuthin' But A "G" Thang [1] • Deeez
Nuuuts • Bitches Ain't Shit • Lil' Ghetto Boy • A Nigga Witta Gun • Rat-Tat-Tat-Tat • The $20 Sack Pyramid • Lyrical Gangbang •
High Powered • The Doctor's Office • Stranded On Death Row • The Roach

| 10/8/94 | 14 | 11 | | 2 Concrete Roots - Anthology | [K] | 43 | $8 | Hitman 51170 |
| 6/8/96 | 18 | 8 | | 3 First Round Knock Out | [K] | 52 | $8 | Triple X 51226 |

DOCTOR DRE & ED LOVER   '94
Rap duo from New York City: Andre "Doctor Dre" Brown and James "Ed Lover" Roberts. Hosted own show on MTV. Starred in the movie
Who's The Man? Doctor Dre not to be confused with prolific artist/producer Andre "Dr. Dre" Young.

| 11/26/94 | 91 | 1 | | Back Up Off Me! | | $8 | Relativity 1230 |

DOCTOR ICE   '89
Born Fred Reeves in 1966 in New York City. Male rapper. Former member of UTFO.

| 10/28/89 | 81 | 6 | | The Mic Stalker | | $8 | Jive 1249 |

DR. JOHN   '73
Born Malcolm Rebennack on 11/20/42 in New Orleans. Singer/pianist.

| 8/25/73 | 28 | 5 | | In The Right Place | 24 | $12 | Atco 7018 |

DOCTOR J.R. KOOL   '85

| 8/3/85 | 23 | 12 | | The Complete Story of Roxanne...The Album | 113 | $10 | Compleat 1014 |

DOCTOR J.R. KOOL & The Other Roxannes

DOG, Tim   '92
Born Timothy Blair in the Bronx, New York. Male rapper.

| 11/30/91+ | 34 | 22 | | 1 Penicillin On Wax | 155 | $8 | Ruffhouse 48707 |
| 5/1/93 | 53 | 4 | | 2 Do Or Die | | $8 | Ruffhouse 53237 |

DOGG POUND, Tha   '95
Rap duo from Los Angeles: Delmar "Daz Dillinger" Arnaud and Ricardo "Kurupt" Brown. Arnaud is a cousin of Snoop Doggy Dogg.

| 11/11/95 | ❶² | 43 | ▲² | Dogg Food | 1¹ | $8 | Death Row 50546 |

Dogg Pound Gangstaz • Respect • New York, New York • Smooth • Cyco-Lic-No (Bitch Azz Niggaz) • Ridin', Slipin' And Slidin' •
Big Pimpin 2 • Let's Play House [21] • I Don't Like To Dream About Gettin Paid • Do What I Feel • If We All Fuck • Some Bomb
Azz Pussy • A Doggy Day Afternoon • Reality • One By One • Sooo Much Style

DOGS, The   '90
Rap group from Miami: "Disco Rick" Taylor, Tony T., Ant and Peanut. Taylor was a member of Gucci Crew II. By 1992, reduced to a duo of
Ant and Peanut.

| 5/5/90 | 37 | 25 | | 1 The Dogs | | $8 | Joey Boy 2003 |
| 1/26/91 | 73 | 8 | | 2 The Negro's Back | | $8 | Joey Boy 2004 |

DISCO RICK FEATURING THE DOGS

| 6/15/91 | 55 | 16 | | 3 Beware Of The Dogs | | $8 | Joey Boy 2006 |

THE DOGS Featuring Disco Rick

| 11/28/92 | 95 | 2 | | 4 K-9 Bass | | $8 | Joey Boy 2007 |

DOLBY, Thomas   '83
Born on 10/14/58 in Cairo, Egypt, of British parentage. Pop synthesizer player.

| 7/9/83 | 45 | 5 | | The Golden Age Of Wireless | 13 | $10 | Capitol 12271 |

DEBUT	PEAK	WKS	Gold	Album Title	Pop #	$	Label & Number

DOMINO '94
Born Shawn Ivy in St. Louis; raised in Long Beach, California. Male rapper.

12/25/93+	10	32	●	1 Domino	39	$8	OutBurst 57701

Diggady Domino • **Getto Jam** *[4]* • A.F.D. • Do You Qualify • Jam • Money Is Everything • **Sweet Potatoe Pie** *[13]* • Raincoat • Long Beach Thang • That's Real

| 6/29/96 | 34 | 6 | | 2 Physical Funk | 152 | $8 | OutBurst 531033 |

DONALD-D '90
Born in the Bronx, New York; raised in Los Angeles. Male rapper.

| 11/11/89+ | 78 | 19 | | Notorious | | $8 | Rhyme Syndicate 45298 |

DONALDSON, Lou '67
Born on 11/1/26 in Badin, North Carolina. Jazz alto saxophonist.

11/4/67	15	10		1 Alligator Bogaloo	[I]	141	$20	Blue Note 84263
4/6/68	44	4		2 Mr. Shing-A-Ling	[I]		$20	Blue Note 84271
10/26/68	45	3		3 Midnight Creeper	[I]	182	$20	Blue Note 84280
3/29/69	27	11		4 Say It Loud!	[I]	153	$20	Blue Note 84299
9/27/69	35	12		5 Hot Dog	[I]	158	$20	Blue Note 84318
7/25/70	39	5		6 Everything I Play Is Funky	[I]	190	$15	Blue Note 84337
9/22/73	49	4		7 Sassy Soul Strut	[I]	176	$15	Blue Note 109
9/21/74	44	8		8 Sweet Lou	[I]	185	$15	Blue Note 259

DON-e '92
Born Donald McLean in London. Multi-instrumentalist of West Indian heritage.

| 9/26/92 | 69 | 7 | | Unbreakable | | $8 | Gee Street 512725 |

DOOBIE BROTHERS, The '80
Rock group from San Jose, California: **Michael McDonald** (vocals, keyboards), Patrick Simmons (vocals, guitar), John McFee (guitar), Cornelius Bumpus (sax), Tiran Porter (bass) and Chet McCracken (drums).

| 10/18/80 | 31 | 18 | ▲ | One Step Closer | 3 | $10 | Warner 3452 |

DO OR DIE '96
Male rap trio: AK 47, N.A.R.D. and Belo Zero.

| 9/21/96 | 3 | 36 | ● | 1 Picture This | 27 | $8 | Neighborhood W. 42058 |

Alpha And Omega • Shut 'Em Down • **Po Pimp** *[15]* • Kill Or Be Killed • Paperchase • Playa Like Me And You • Promise • 6 Million • Search Warrant • Anotha One Dead And Gone • Money Flow

| 4/25/98 | 3 | 19 | ● | 2 Headz Or Tailz | 13 | $8 | Rap-A-Lot 45612 |

Headz • Just Ballin • Pimpology • Lil Sum Sum • Nobody's Home • Still Po Pimpin' • All In The Club • Can I • Choppin Up That Paper • Gangsta Shit • Bustin Back • Ultimate Shutdown • Who Am I • Caine House • Under Surveillance • Dead Or Alive • Tailz

DORSEY, Lee '66
Born Irving Lee Dorsey on 12/24/24 in New Orleans. Died of emphysema on 12/1/86 (age 61). Male singer.

| 10/29/66 | 13 | 8 | | The New Lee Dorsey | 129 | $30 | Amy 8011 |

DOUBLE EXPOSURE '76
Vocal group from Philadelphia: James Williams, Leonard Davis, Charles Whittington and Joseph Harris.

| 8/28/76 | 40 | 8 | | Ten Percent | 129 | $12 | Salsoul 5503 |

DOUG E. FRESH & THE GET FRESH CREW '88
Rap trio formed in 1985 by Doug E. Fresh (b: Douglas Davis on 9/17/66 in New York City) with Barry Bee and Chill Will. Early records featured **Slick Rick** as M.C. Ricky D.

| 12/27/86+ | 21 | 34 | | 1 Oh, My God! | | $8 | Reality 9649 |
| 6/4/88 | 7 | 54 | | 2 The World's Greatest Entertainer | 88 | $8 | Reality 9658 |

Guess? Who? • Ev'rybody Got 2 Get Some • D.E.F. = Doug E. Fresh • On The Strength • **Keep Risin' To The Top** *[4]* • Greatest Entertainer • I'm Gettin' Ready • **Cut That Zero** *[66]* • The Plane (So High) • Ev'rybody Loves A Star • Crazy 'Bout Cars • Africa (Goin' Back Home)

5/30/92	47	16		3 Doin' What I Gotta Do		$8	Bust It/Capitol 98358
				DOUG E. FRESH & THE NEW GET FRESH CREW			
10/14/95	81	2		4 Play		$8	Gee Street 444069
				DOUG E. FRESH			

DOUGLAS, Carl '75
Born in 1942 in Jamaica; raised in California. Singer/songwriter.

| 12/28/74+ | ❶[1] | 12 | | Kung Fu Fighting And Other Great Love Songs | 37 | $12 | 20th Century 464 |

Kung Fu Fighting *[1]* • Witchfinder General • When You Got Love • Changing Times • I Want To Give You My Everything • Dance The Kung Fu *[8]* • Never Had This Dream Before • I Don't Care What People Say • Blue Eyed Soul

DOUGLAS, Carol '75
Born Carol Strickland on 4/7/48 in Brooklyn, New York. Female singer.

| 3/22/75 | 37 | 5 | | The Carol Douglas Album | 177 | $12 | Midland Int'l. 0931 |

DOVE SHACK '95
Rap trio from Long Beach, California: Bo-Rock, C-Knights and 2 Scoop.

| 9/9/95 | 13 | 11 | | This Is The Shack | 68 | $8 | G Funk/RAL 527933 |

DOWNING, Will '91
Born in Brooklyn, New York. Singer/songwriter/producer.

12/9/89+	62	18		1 Come Together As One		$8	Island 91286
4/13/91	22	36		2 A Dream Fulfilled		$8	Island 848278
8/21/93	24	58		3 Love's The Place To Be	166	$8	Mercury 518086
11/25/95	23	30		4 Moods	139	$8	Mercury 528755
11/15/97	30	21		5 Invitation Only	127	$8	Mercury 536350
10/17/98	36	27		6 Pleasures Of The Night	169	$8	Verve Forecast 557613
				WILL DOWNING & GERALD ALBRIGHT			

DEBUT	PEAK	WKS	Gold	Album Title	Pop #	$	Label & Number

DOZIER, Lamont '74
Born on 6/16/41 in Detroit. Singer/songwriter/producer. With brothers Brian and Eddie Holland in highly successful songwriting/production team for Motown. Trio left Motown in 1968 and formed own Invictus/Hot Wax label. Holland-Dozier-Holland were inducted into the Rock and Roll Hall of Fame in 1990.

12/22/73+	11	21		1 Out Here On My Own	136	$12	ABC 804
12/28/74+	27	10		2 Black Bach	186	$12	ABC 839
7/17/76	59	1		3 Right There		$10	Warner 2929
8/6/77	59	3		4 Peddlin' The Music		$10	Warner 3039
7/20/91	28	19		5 Inside Seduction		$8	Atlantic 82228

DRAMATICS, The ★76★ '72
Vocal group from Detroit: **Ron Banks**, William Howard, Larry Demps, Willie Ford and Elbert Wilkins. Howard and Wilkins left in 1973, replaced by L.J. Reynolds and Lenny Mayes. Reynolds left in late 1979, replaced by Craig Jones until 1986 when Jones left and Reynolds returned.
1)Whatcha See Is Whatcha Get 2)Do What You Wanna Do 3)The Dramatic Jackpot

| 1/15/72 | 5 | 28 | | 1 Whatcha See Is Whatcha Get | 20 | $25 | Volt 6018 |

Get Up And Get Down *[16]* • Thank You For Your Love • Hot Pants In The Summertime • **Whatcha See Is Whatcha Get** *[3]* • In The Rain *[1]* • Gimme Some (Good Soul Music) • Fall In Love, Lady Love • Mary Don't Cha Wanna

10/27/73	11	18		2 A Dramatic Experience	86	$25	Volt 6019
3/23/74	15	25		3 The Dells vs. The Dramatics	156	$25	Cadet 60027
5/11/74	36	13		4 Dramatically Yours		$25	Volt 9501
3/29/75	9	21		5 The Dramatic Jackpot	31	$15	ABC 867

(I'm Going By) The Stars In Your Eyes *[22]* • Good Things Don't Come Easy • Trying To Get Over Losing You • I Cried All The Way Home • Never Let You Go • A Thousand Shades Of Blue • Me Myself And I • I Dig Your Music • **Me And Mrs. Jones** *[4]* • How Do You Feel

| 11/15/75 | 10 | 15 | | 6 Drama V | 93 | $15 | ABC 916 |

You're Fooling You *[10]* • She's A Rainmaker • I Was The Life Of The Party • Things Are Changing • I'm Gonna Love You To The Max • **Treat Me Like A Man** *[49]* • Just Shopping (Not Buying Anything) • Come Out Of Your Thing • I'll Make It So Good

| 10/23/76+ | 11 | 30 | | 7 Joy Ride | 103 | $15 | ABC 955 |
| 8/13/77 | 10 | 25 | | 8 Shake It Well | 60 | $15 | ABC 1010 |

Shake It Well *[4]* • You Make The Music (I Just Dance Along) • My Ship Won't Sail Without You • Come Inside • Spaced Out Over You • That Heaven Kind Of Feeling • (I Like) Makin' You So Happy • **Ocean Of Thoughts And Dreams** *[17]* • Music Is Forever

| 5/13/78 | 6 | 24 | ● | 9 Do What You Wanna Do | 44 | $15 | ABC 1072 |

Why Do You Want To Do Me Wrong • **Do What You Want To Do** *[56]* • Disco Dance Contest • California Sunshine • Jane • Stop Your Weeping *[22]* • I Want You • Yo' Love (Can Only Bring Me Happiness)

5/12/79	15	24		10 Anytime, Anyplace		$15	ABC 1125
3/8/80	14	16		11 10 1/2	61	$10	MCA 3196
12/6/80	38	24		12 The Dramatic Way		$10	MCA 5146
6/12/82	40	13		13 New Dimension		$10	Capitol 12205
6/3/89	80	9		14 Positive State Of Mind		$10	Volt 3402

DREAMBOY '84
Group from Oak Park, Michigan: Jeff Stanton (vocals), Jeff Bass (guitar), Jimi Hunt (keyboards), Paul Stewart (bass) and George Twymon (drums).

| 12/17/83+ | 32 | 25 | | 1 Dreamboy | [M] 168 | $8 | Qwest 23988 |
| 11/24/84 | 45 | 16 | | 2 Contact | | $10 | Qwest 25163 |

DRE DOG '95
Born in San Francisco. Male rapper.

| 4/29/95 | 79 | 3 | | I Hate You With A Passion | | $8 | In-A-Minute 8800 |

DRENNON, Eddie, & B.B.S. Unlimited '76
Disco group from New York City.

| 3/13/76 | 53 | 3 | | Collage | [I] | $12 | Friends & Co. 108 |

DREW, Patti '70
Born on 12/29/44 in Charleston, South Carolina. Former lead singer of The Drew-Vels.

| 3/28/70 | 49 | 3 | | Wild Is Love | | $20 | Capitol 408 |

DRIFTERS, The '68
Vocal group from New York City. The group's lead singers included Clyde McPhatter, **Ben E. King**, Rudy Lewis and Johnny Moore. Lewis died on 5/20/64 (age 27). McPhatter died on 6/13/72 (age 39). Moore died on 12/30/98 (age 64). Many personnel changes throughout career and several groups have used the name in later years. Inducted into the Rock and Roll Hall of Fame in 1988.

| 4/20/68 | 33 | 4 | | The Drifters' Golden Hits | [G] 122 | $30 | Atlantic 8153 |

D.R.S. '93
Male vocal group from Sacramento, California: Endo, Pic, Jail Bait, Deuce Deuce and Blunt. D.R.S.: Dirty Rotten Scoundrels.

| 11/20/93 | 6 | 17 | ● | Gangsta Lean | 34 | $8 | Capitol 81445 |

Mama Didn't Raise No Punk • Strip • **Skoundrels Get Lonely** *[87]* • Gangsta Lean *[1]* • 44 Ways • Nigga Wit A Badge • Sickness • Bonnie & Clyde • Do Me, Baby • Trust Me • Make It Rough

DRU DOWN '96
Born in Oakland. Male rapper.

| 9/24/94 | 46 | 22 | | 1 Explicit Games | | $8 | C-Note 1222 |
| 9/21/96 | 14 | 11 | | 2 Can You Feel Me | 54 | $8 | Relativity 1531 |

| --- | --- | --- | --- | --- | --- | --- | --- |

DRU HILL '98
Male vocal group from Baltimore: Mark Andrews, James Green, Tamir Ruffin and Larry Anthony. Green left in March 1999. Group named after Druid Hill Park in Baltimore.

DEBUT	PEAK	WKS	Gold	Album Title	Pop #	$	Label & Number
12/7/96+	5	82	▲	1 Dru Hill	23	$8	Island 524306

Anthem • Nothing To Prove • **Tell Me** [5] • Do U Believe? • Whatever U Want • Satisfied • April Showers • All Alone • **Never Make A Promise** [1] • So Special • **In My Bed** [1] • Love's Train • Share My World • 5 Steps

| 11/14/98 | 2¹ | 38↑ | ▲² | 2 Enter The Dru | 2¹ | $8 | Island 524542 |

Real Freak • **How Deep Is Your Love** [1] • This Is What We Do • Holding You • I'm Wondering • You Are Everything • I'll Be The One • One Good Reason • Angel • What Do I Do With The Love • **Beauty** [53] • **These Are The Times** [5] • **The Love We Had (Stays On My Mind)** [48] • What Are We Gonna Do

D-SHOT '97
Born Donald Stevens in San Francisco. Male rapper. Member of **The Click**. Brother of **E-40**.

DEBUT	PEAK	WKS	Gold	Album Title	Pop #	$	Label & Number
7/17/93	52	15		1 Shot Calla		$8	Sick Wid' It 715
8/16/97	21	8		2 Six Figures	81	$8	Shot/Jive 41602

DUBB, J. '95

| 10/14/95 | 42 | 6 | | Game Related | | $8 | Relentless 530 |

DUICE '93
Male rap duo: Los Angeles-born LA Sno and Barbados-born Creo-D.

| 1/30/93 | 26 | 33 | ● | Dazzey Duks | 84 | $8 | TMR/Bellmark 71000 |

DUKE, Doris '70
Born Doris Curry in Sandersville, Georgia. Gospel singer.

| 3/28/70 | 39 | 9 | | I'm A Loser | | $15 | Canyon 7704 |

DUKE, George ★81★ '77
Born on 1/12/46 in San Rafael, California. Singer/songwriter/keyboardist/percussionist.
1)Reach For It 2)Don't Let Go 3)The Clarke/Duke Project

DEBUT	PEAK	WKS	Gold	Album Title	Pop #	$	Label & Number
1/3/76	36	12		1 I Love The Blues, She Heard My Cry	169	$12	MPS/BASF 25671
10/29/77	4	21	●	2 Reach For It	25	$10	Epic 34883

The Beginning • Lemme At It • Hot Fire • **Reach For It** [2] • Just For You • Omi (Fresh Water) • Searchin' My Mind • Watch Out Baby! • Diamonds • The End

| 6/3/78 | 5 | 18 | | 3 Don't Let Go | 39 | $10 | Epic 35366 |

We Give Our Love • Morning Sun • **Dukey Stick** [4] • Starting Again • Yeah, We Going • The Way I Feel • **Movin' On** [68] • Don't Let Go • The Future

3/17/79	17	11		4 Follow The Rainbow	56	$10	Epic 35701
11/17/79	18	19		5 Master Of The Game	125	$10	Epic 36263
6/21/80	40	13		6 A Brazilian Love Affair	119	$10	Epic 36483
5/2/81	7	27		7 The Clarke/Duke Project	33	$8	Epic 36918

STANLEY CLARKE/GEORGE DUKE
Wild Dog • Louie Louie • **Sweet Baby** [6] • I Just Want To Love You [49] • Never Judge A Cover By It's Book • Let's Get Started • Winners • Touch And Go • Finding My Way • Atlanta

3/6/82	17	17		8 Dream On	48	$8	Epic 37532
5/7/83	46	7		9 Guardian Of The Light	147	$8	Epic 38513
11/26/83	44	11		10 The Clarke/Duke Project II	146	$8	Epic 38934

STANLEY CLARKE/GEORGE DUKE

5/4/85	52	6		11 Thief In The Night	183	$8	Elektra 60398
9/27/86	56	10		12 George Duke		$8	Elektra 60480
5/20/89	87	7		13 Night After Night		$8	Elektra 60778
8/25/90	52	14		14 3		$8	Epic 46012

STANLEY CLARKE/GEORGE DUKE

10/24/92+	36	37		15 Snapshot		$8	Warner 45026
2/11/95	33	22		16 Illusions		$8	Warner 45755
4/12/97	65	7		17 Is Love Enough?		$8	Warner 46494

DUKE BOOTEE '84
Born Edward Fletcher in Elizabeth, New Jersey. Male rapper.

| 6/9/84 | 57 | 6 | | Bust Me Out | | $10 | Mercury 818667 |

DUNLAP, Gene '81
Born in Detroit. Drummer/guitarist/keyboardist. Member of **Earl Klugh**'s group. The Ridgeways vocal group consisted of sisters Gloria, Esther and Gracie with brother Tommy Ridgeway.

| 3/21/81 | 39 | 12 | | 1 It's Just The Way I Feel | 202 | $10 | Capitol 12130 |

GENE DUNLAP Featuring The Ridgeways

| 2/6/82 | 68 | 2 | | 2 Party In Me | | $10 | Capitol 12190 |

DUPRI, Jermaine '98
Born in 1972 in Atlanta. Rapper/producer.

| 8/1/98 | ❶² | 38 | ▲ | Jermaine Dupri Presents Life In 1472 - The Original Soundtrack | 3 | $8 | So So Def 69087 |

Turn It Out • **Money Ain't A Thang** [10] • Get Your Shit Right • Fresh • Sweetheart • Jazzy Hoes • Don't Hate On Me • **Going Home With Me** [57] • You Get Dealt Wit • **The Party Continues** [14] • All That's Got To Go • Protector's Of 1472 • Lay You Down • Three The Hard Way

DYNAMICS, The '73
Vocal group from Detroit: Samuel Stevenson, Isaac Harris, George White and Fred Baker.

| 12/8/73 | 52 | 3 | | What A Shame | | $12 | Black Gold 5001 |

DYNAMIC SUPERIORS, The '75
Vocal group from Washington DC: Tony Washington, George Spann, George Peterbark, Michael McCalphin and Maurice Washington.

| 2/22/75 | 36 | 12 | | 1 The Dynamic Superiors | 201 | $12 | Motown 822 |
| 8/23/75 | 36 | 6 | | 2 Pure Pleasure | 130 | $12 | Motown 841 |

DYNASTY '80

Vocal trio from Los Angeles: Kevin Spencer, Linda Carriere and Nidra Beard. Carriere left in 1987, replaced by William Shelby.

DEBUT	PEAK	WKS		Album Title	Pop #	$	Label & Number
10/6/79	72	2	1	Your Piece Of The Rock		$10	Solar 3398
7/26/80	11	36	2	Adventures In The Land Of Music	43	$10	Solar 3576
9/26/81	42	7	3	The Second Adventure	119	$10	Solar 20
12/25/82+	54	5	4	Right Back At Cha!		$10	Solar 60176
8/6/88	68	5	5	Out Of Control		$8	Solar 72559

DYSON, Ronnie '70

Born on 6/5/50 in Washington DC; raised in Brooklyn, New York. Died of heart failure on 11/10/90 (age 40). Acted in the Broadway musical *Hair* and the movie *Putney Swope*.

DEBUT	PEAK	WKS		Album Title	Pop #	$	Label & Number
9/12/70	12	21	1	(If You Let Me Make Love To You Then) Why Can't I Touch You?	55	$12	Columbia 30223
4/14/73	34	8	2	One Man Band	142	$12	Columbia 32211
10/16/76	30	5	3	The More You Do It		$12	Columbia 34350
11/5/77	45	6	4	Love In All Flavors		$12	Columbia 34866
10/22/83	53	4	5	Brand New Day		$10	Cotillion 90119

E

EARLAND, Charles '70

Born on 5/24/41 in Philadelphia. Keyboardist/saxophonist.

DEBUT	PEAK	WKS		Album Title	Pop #	$	Label & Number
6/6/70	7	43	1	Black Talk! [I]	108	$15	Prestige 7758

Black Talk • The Mighty Burner • Here Comes Charlie • Aquarius • More Today Than Yesterday

12/19/70+	12	17	2	Black Drops [I]	131	$15	Prestige 7815
5/1/71	22	9	3	Living Black! [I-L]	176	$15	Prestige 10009

recorded at the Key Club in Newark, New Jersey

3/20/76	20	14	4	Odyssey	155	$12	Mercury 1049
6/25/77	56	3	5	Revelation		$12	Mercury 1149
3/27/82	48	12	6	Earland's Jam [I]	208	$10	Columbia 37573

EARTH, WIND & FIRE ★12★ '81

Los Angeles-based group formed by Chicago-bred producer/songwriter/vocalist/percussionist/kalimba player **Maurice White**. In 1969, White, former session drummer for Chess Records and member of **The Ramsey Lewis Trio**, formed the Salty Peppers; recorded for Capitol. Maurice's brother Verdine White was the group's bassist. Eighteen months later, the brothers hired a new band and recorded as Earth, Wind & Fire (named for the three elements of Maurice's astrological sign). Co-lead singer **Philip Bailey** joined in 1971. Group generally contained eight to 10 members, with frequent personnel shuffling. Appeared in the movies *That's the Way of the World* (1975) and *Sgt. Pepper's Lonely Hearts Club Band* (1978). Elaborate stage shows featured an array of magic acts and pyrotechnics.

1)Raise! 2)All 'N All 3)Gratitude 4)That's The Way Of The World 5)I Am

DEBUT	PEAK	WKS		Album Title	Pop #	$	Label & Number
5/8/71	24	17	1	Earth, Wind & Fire	172	$20	Warner 1905

also see #6 below

2/5/72	35	9	2	The Need Of Love	89	$20	Warner 1958

also see #6 below

1/6/73	15	31	3	Last Days And Time	87	$15	Columbia 31702
6/9/73	2³	49	● 4	Head To The Sky	27	$12	Columbia 32194

Evil [25] • Keep Your Head To The Sky [23] • Build Your Nest • The World's A Masquerade • Clover • Zanzibar

4/13/74	●¹	36	▲ 5	Open Our Eyes	15	$12	Columbia 32712

Mighty Mighty [4] • Devotion [23] • Fair But So Uncool • Feelin' Blue • **Kalimba Story [6]** • Drum Song • Tee Nine Chee Bit • Spasmodic Movements • Caribou • Open Our Eyes

9/14/74	29	10	6	Another Time	97	$20	Warner 2798 [2]

reissue of #1 and #2 above

3/22/75	●⁵	33	▲² 7	That's The Way Of The World [S]	1³	$12	Columbia 33280

Shining Star [1] • That's The Way Of The World [5] • Happy Feelin' • All About Love • Yearnin', Learnin' • Reasons • Africano • See The Light

12/6/75+	●⁶	29	▲² 8	Gratitude [L]	1³	$15	Columbia 33694 [2]

contains some studio cuts
Medley: Africano/Power • Yearnin' Learnin' • Devotion • Sun Goddess • Reasons • Sing A Message To You • Shining Star • New World Symphony • Sunshine • **Sing A Song [1]** • Gratitude • Celebrate • **Can't Hide Love [11]**

10/16/76	2⁸	28	▲² 9	Spirit	2²	$12	Columbia 34241

Getaway [1] • On Your Face [26] • Imagination • Spirit • **Saturday Nite [4]** • Earth, Wind & Fire • Departure • Biyo • Burnin' Bush

12/10/77	●⁹	36	▲³ 10	All 'N All	3	$12	Columbia 34905

Serpentine Fire [1] • Fantasy [12] • Jupiter • Love's Holiday • I'll Write A Song For You • Magic Mind • Runnin' • Be Ever Wonderful

12/9/78+	3	21	▲⁴ 11	The Best Of Earth, Wind & Fire, Vol. I [G]	6	$10	ARC 35647

Got To Get You Into My Life [1] • Fantasy [12] • Can't Hide Love [11] • Love Music • Getaway [1] • That's The Way Of The World [5] • September [1] • Shining Star [1] • Reasons • Sing A Song [1]

6/23/79	●¹	37	▲² 12	I Am	3	$10	ARC 35730

In The Stone [23] • Can't Let Go • After The Love Has Gone [2] • Let Your Feelings Show • Boogie Wonderland [2] • Star [47] • Wait • Rock That! • You And I [29]

EARTH, WIND & FIRE — Cont'd

DEBUT	PEAK	WKS		Album Title	Pop #	$	Label & Number
11/29/80	2⁵	22	● 13	**Faces**	10	$12	ARC 36795 [2]

Let Me Talk [8] • Turn It Into Something Good • Pride • **You** [10] • Sparkle • Back On The Road • Song In My Heart • You Went Away • And Love Goes On [15] • Sailaway • Take It To The Sky • Win Or Lose • Share Your Love • In Time • Faces

| 11/14/81 | ❶¹¹ | 29 | ▲ 14 | **Raise!** | 5 | $10 | ARC 37548 |

Let's Groove [1] • Lady Sun • My Love • Evolution Orange • Medley: Kalimba Tree/You Are A Winner • I've Had Enough • **Wanna Be With You** [15] • The Changing Times

| 3/12/83 | 4 | 25 | ● 15 | **Powerlight** | 12 | $8 | Columbia 38367 |

Fall In Love With Me [4] • Spread Your Love [57] • **Side By Side** [15] • Straight From The Heart • The Speed Of Love • Freedom Of Choice • Something Special • Hearts To Heart • Miracles

| 12/3/83 | 8 | 21 | 16 | **Electric Universe** | 40 | $8 | Columbia 38980 |

Magnetic [10] • Touch [23] • Moonwalk [67] • Could It Be Right • Spirit Of A New World • Sweet Sassy Lady • We're Living In Our Own Time • Electric Nation

| 11/28/87 | 3 | 31 | ● 17 | **Touch The World** | 33 | $8 | Columbia 40596 |

System Of Survival [1] • Evil Roy [22] • **Thinking Of You** [3] • You And I [29] • New Horizons • Money Tight • Every Now And Then • Touch The World • Here Today And Gone Tomorrow • Victim Of The Modern Heart

12/17/88	74	5	● 18	**The Best Of Earth, Wind & Fire, Vol. II** ...... [G]	190	$8	Columbia 45013
2/24/90	19	20	19	**Heritage**	70	$8	Columbia 45268
10/2/93	8	24	20	**Millennium**	39	$8	Reprise 45274

Even If You Wonder • **Sunday Morning** [20] • Blood Brothers • Kalimba • **Spend The Night** [42] • Divine • **Two Hearts** [88] • Honor The Magic • Love Is The Greatest Story • The "L" Word • Just Another Lonely Night • Super Hero • Wouldn't Change A Thing About You • Love Across The Wire • Chicago (Chi-Town) Blues • Kalimba Blues

| 11/16/96 | 75 | 3 | 21 | **Greatest Hits Live** ...... [G-L] | | $8 | Pyramid 72621 |

recorded on April 20, 1995 in Japan

| 8/16/97 | 50 | 11 | 22 | **In The Name Of Love** .... | | $8 | Pyramid 72864 |

EAST COAST FAMILY   '92

Grouping of artists assembled by Michael Bivins (**New Edition**, **Bell Biv DeVoe**). Features Bivins, **Another Bad Creation**, **Boyz II Men**, **M.C. Brains**, and **Yo-Yo**.

| 8/22/92 | 12 | 27 | ● | **East Coast Family Volume One** .... | 54 | $8 | Biv 10 6352 |

EASTON, Sheena   '85

Born on 4/27/59 in Glasgow, Scotland. Singer/actress.

| 2/16/85 | 26 | 13 | ▲ 1 | **A Private Heaven** .... | 15 | $8 | EMI America 17132 |
| 12/3/88+ | 29 | 25 | ● 2 | **The Lover In Me** .... | 44 | $8 | MCA 42249 |

EAZY-E   '93

Born Eric Wright on 9/7/63 in Compton, California. Died of AIDS on 3/26/95 (age 31). Rapper/producer. Formerly with **N.W.A.** Founded the Ruthless record label.

11/26/88+	12	53	▲² 1	**Eazy-Duz-It**	41	$8	Ruthless 57100
12/26/92+	15	23	● 2	**5150 Home 4 Tha Sick** ...... [M]	70	$6	Ruthless 53815
10/30/93	❶¹	40	▲ 3	**It's On (Dr. Dre) 187um Killa** ...... [M]	5	$6	Ruthless 5503

187 is slang for murder
Exxtra Special Thankz • **Real Muthaphuckkin G's** [31] • Any Last Werdz • Still A Nigga • Gimmie That Nutt • It's On • Boyz N Tha Hood • Down 2 Tha Last Roach

| 12/16/95 | 19 | 15 | 4 | **Eternal E** ...... [K] | 84 | $8 | Ruthless 50544 |
| 2/17/96 | ❶¹ | 19 | ● 5 | **Str8 Off Tha Streetz Of Muthaphukkin Compton** | 3 | $8 | Ruthless 5504 |

First Power • Ole School Shit • Sorry Louie • **Just Tah Let U Know** [30] • Sippin On A 40 • Nutz On Ya Chin • Muthaphuckkin Real • Lickin, Suckin, Phukkin • Hit The Hooker • My Baby'z Mama • Creep N Crawl • Wut Would You Do • Gangsta Beat 4 Tha Street • Eternal E

EBONEE WEBB   '81

Funk group from Memphis: Michael Winston (vocals), Thomas Brown (guitar), Gregg Davis and Leon Thomas (keyboards), Ronald Coleman (trumpet), Charles Liggins (percussion), Ken Coleman (bass) and Roy Munn (drums).

| 9/5/81 | 21 | 20 | 1 | **Ebonee Webb** | 157 | $10 | Capitol 12148 |
| 3/19/83 | 45 | 9 | 2 | **Too Hot** .... | | $10 | Capitol 12250 |

EBONYS, The   '74

Vocal group from Camden, New Jersey: Jenny Holmes, David Beasley, James Tuten and Clarence Vaughan.

| 2/16/74 | 33 | 11 | | **The Ebonys** | | $12 | Philadelphia I. 32419 |

ECKSTINE, Billy   '66

Born on 7/8/14 in Pittsburgh. Died of heart failure on 3/8/93 (age 78). Highly influential balladeer. Nicknamed "Mr. B."

| 1/15/66 | 8 | 13 | | **The Prime Of My Life** | | $25 | Motown 632 |

The Prime Of My Life • Maybe Today • Who Can I Turn To • Down To Earth • Feeling Good • Had You Been Around • Loe Is Gone • Just Loving You • Climb Ev'ry Mountain • Fantasy • This Is All I Ask

ECSTASY, PASSION & PAIN   '74

Dance group from New York City: Barbara Roy (vocals, guitar), Billy Gardner (keyboards), Alan Tizer (percussion), Joe Williams (bass) and Althea "Cookie" Smith (drums).

| 9/21/74 | 38 | 6 | | **Ecstasy, Passion, And Pain** .... | | $12 | Roulette 3013 |

EDDIE F. AND THE UNTOUCHABLES   '94

Rap producer Eddie Ferrell. The Untouchables consist of rap producers **Puff Daddy**, **Pete Rock**, Dave Hall, Nevelle Hodge, Kenny Smoove and Kenny Greene.

| 11/5/94 | 70 | 5 | | **Let's Get It On** .... | | $8 | Motown 0313 |

ED O. G & DA BULLDOGS   '91

Rap group from Boston: Edward Anderson, T-Nyne, Gee Man and DJ Cruz. ED O. G: Every Day, Other Girls. BULLDOGS: Black United Leaders Living Directly On Groovin' Sounds.

| 3/30/91 | 21 | 32 | 1 | **Life Of A Kid In The Ghetto** ...... | 166 | $8 | PWL America 848326 |
| 2/5/94 | 36 | 7 | 2 | **Roxbury 02119** .... | | $8 | Chemistry 518161 |

DEBUT	PEAK	WKS	Gold	Album Title	Pop #	$	Label & Number

EDWARDS, Dennis '84
Born on 2/3/43 in Birmingham, Alabama. Lead singer of The Contours until 1968. Lead singer of **The Temptations** from 1968-77, 1980-84 and 1987-present.

2/25/84	2²	35		1 **Don't Look Any Further**	48	$10	Gordy 6057

I'm Up For You • **Don't Look Any Further** *[2]* • **(You're My) Aphrodisiac** *[15]* • Can't Fight It • Another Place In Time • Shake Hands (Come Out Dancin') • I Thought I Could Handle It • Just Like You • Let's Go Up

7/27/85	36	20		2 Coolin' Out	205	$10	Gordy 6148

E-40 '95
Born Earl Stevens in Vallejo, California. Male rapper. Member of **The Click** with sister **Suga T**, brother **D-Shot** and cousin **B-Legit The Savage**.

1/23/93	80	12		1 Federal		$8	Sick Wid' It 711
10/16/93	13	50		2 The Mail Man	131	$8	Sick Wid' It 7340
4/1/95	2¹	34	●	3 **In A Major Way**	13	$8	Sick Wid' It 41558

Chip In Da Phone • Da Bumble • Sideways • Spittin' • **Sprinkle Me** *[24]* • Outta Bounds • Dusted 'n' Disgusted • **1-Luv** *[51]* • Smoke 'n' Drank • Dey Ain't No • Fed • H.I. Double L. • Bootsee • It's All Bad

11/16/96	2¹	24	●	4 **Tha Hall Of Game**	4	$8	Jive 41591

Record Haters • **Rappers' Ball** *[flip]* • Growing Up • Million Dollar Spot • Mack Minister • I Wanna Thank U • The Story • My Drinking Club • Ring It • Pimp Talk • Keep Pimpin' • I Like What You Do To Me • **Things'll Never Change** *[19]* • Circumstances • It Is What It Is • Smebbin'

8/29/98	4	14	●	5 **The Element Of Surprise**	13	$12	Sick Wid' It 41645 [2]

The Element Of Surprise • Trump Change • All Tha Time • Dump, Bust, Blast • Hope I Don't Go Back • $999,999 + $1 = A Mealticket • Money Scheme • Zoom • Mayhem • Personal • My Hoodlums & My Thugs • Do It To Me • Lieutenant Roast A Botch • It's On, On Sight • From The Ground Up • Flashin' • Doin' Dirt Bad • Broccoli • Jump My Bone • Back Against The Wall • To Da Beat • Dirty Deeds • Ballin' Outta Control • One More Gen

EGYPTIAN LOVER, The '87
Born Greg Broussard in Los Angeles. Techno-funk singer.

1/26/85	44	9		1 On The Nile	146	$8	Egyptian Empire 00663
2/14/87	37	20		2 One Track Mind		$8	Egyptian Empire 00773
9/17/88	99	2		3 Filthy		$8	NuBeat 9723
2/17/90	72	13		4 Get Into It		$8	Egyptian Empire 00993

EIGHTBALL & MJG '95
Rap duo from Houston: Rodney Ellis ("**Eightball**") and Marlon Jamal Goodwin ("**MJG**").

9/4/93+	40	59		1 Comin' Out Hard		$8	Suave 0001
6/18/94	11	43		2 On The Outside Looking In	106	$8	Suave 0002
11/18/95	2¹	51	●	3 On Top Of The World	8	$8	Suave House 1521

Pimp In My Own Rhyme • What Can I Do • For Real • Funk Mission • Kick That Shit • Friend Or Foe • Hand Of The Devil • Top Of The World • What Do You See • In The Line Of Duty • All In My Mind • Comin' Up • **Space Age** *[58]* • Break'em Off

12/6/97	4	18	●	4 No More Glory	20	$8	Suave House 53105

MJG

Keep Your Mind • Hip Hop Voodoo • Good Damm Man • Shine And Recline • That Girl • Slippin' • Take No Shit • Pimpin Ain't Easy • Black Mac Is Back • No More Glory • What Is This • Don't Hold Back • Reflections • Hard But Fair • Middle Of The Night

6/6/98	3	19	▲²	5 Lost	5	$15	Suave 53127 [3]

EIGHTBALL

Put Tha House On It • All 4 Nuthin' • Bounce Wit Me • Drama In My Life • My Homeboy's Girlfriend • Stompin' And Pimpin' • Backyard Mississippi • If I Die • The Artist Pays The Price • Get Money • Ghetto Luv • All On Me • Lost • 360 Degrees • Let's Ride • Time • Coffee Shoppe • Pure Uncut • Down And Out • Put Your Hands Up • Ball And Bun • I Don't Wanna Die • My First Love • Gett Bucked • This Is Dedicated • Ill Hill Niggas • Been Done Some Shit • How We Roll • Scummie • What You Weigh Me • Many Know • Incarcerated Minds • Class In Session • Baby Baby • The Moocher • All The Way • Can't Stop

8TH DAY, The '71
Group from Detroit: Melvin Davis (male vocals, drums), Lynn Harter (female vocals), Michael Anthony and Bruce Nazarian (guitars), Jerry Paul (percussion), Carole Stallings (electric violin), Anita Sherman (vibes) and Tony Newton (bass).

8/28/71	42	6		The 8th Day	131	$15	Invictus 7306

ELBERT, Donnie '72
Born on 5/25/36 in New Orleans; raised in Buffalo, New York. Died on 1/26/89 (age 52). Singer/multi-instrumentalist.

12/18/71+	45	8		Where Did Our Love Go	153	$25	All Platinum 3007

EL CHICANO '70
Latin group from Los Angeles: Jerry Salas (vocals), Mickey Lespron (guitar), Andre Baeza (congas) and Bobby Espinosa (organ). Salas and Baeza later formed **Tierra**.

6/20/70	17	15		Viva Tirado	[I] 51	$15	Kapp 3632

EL COCO '77
Disco group from Los Angeles led by producers Laurin Rinder and Michael Lewis.

12/25/76	52	2		1 Let's Get It Together		$10	AVI 6006
11/5/77	35	20		2 Cocomotion	82	$10	AVI 6012
11/25/78	73	2		3 Dancing In Paradise	208	$10	AVI 6044

ELECTRIC INDIAN, The '69
Instrumental group assembled from top Philadelphia studio musicians. Some members later joined **MFSB**.

11/22/69	46	5		Keem-O-Sabe	[I] 104	$15	United Artists 6728

11/5 '96
Rap trio from San Francisco: Taydatay, Hennessy and Maine-O. Group name is slang for heroin.

2/4/95	76	3		1 Fiendin 4 Tha Funk		$8	Dogday 3000
8/3/96	33	7		2 A-1 Yola		$8	Dogday 3200

ELEVENTH HOUR, The '76
Disco group featuring lead singers Michael Gray and Kenneth Kerr.

4/24/76	32	5		Hollywood Hot		$12	20th Century 511

ELLIOTT, Missy "Misdemeanor"   **'97**
Born in Portsmouth, Virginia. Female rapper/songwriter.

| 7/26/97 | **❶**[1] | 41 | ▲ | **Supa Dupa Fly** | | 3 | $8 | EastWest 62062 |

Hit 'Em Wit Da Hee • **Sock It 2 Me** [4] • **The Rain (Supa Dupa Fly)** [flip] • Beep Me 911 • They Don't Wanna Fuck Wit Me • Pass Da Blunt • Friendly Skies • Best Friends • Don't Be Commin' (In My Face) • Izzy Izzy Ahh • Why You Hurt Me • I'm Talkin' • Gettaway

ELLIS, Terry   **'95**
Born on 9/5/66 in Houston. Female singer. Member of **En Vogue**.

| 12/2/95 | 27 | 21 | | Southern Gal | | 116 | $8 | EastWest 61857 |

★155★   **EMOTIONS, The**   **'77**
Female vocal trio from Chicago: sisters Wanda, Sheila and Jeanette Hutchinson. Jeanette replaced by cousin Theresa Davis in 1970, and later by sister Pamela Hutchinson. Jeanette returned to the group in 1978.
1)Rejoice 2)Flowers 3)Sunbeam

| 7/12/69 | 43 | 4 | | 1 So I Can Love You | | | $25 | Volt 6008 |
| 8/14/76 | 5 | 31 | ● | 2 Flowers | | 45 | $10 | Columbia 34163 |

I Don't Wanna Lose Your Love [13] • Me For You • You've Got The Right To Know • We Go Through Changes • Special Part • No Plans For Tomorrow • How Can You Stop Loving Someone • **Flowers** [16] • God Will Take Care Of You

| 7/2/77 | **❶**[7] | 32 | ▲ | 3 Rejoice | | 7 | $10 | Columbia 34762 |

Best Of My Love [1] • A Feeling Is • A Long Way To Go • Key To My Heart • Love's What's Happenin' • How'd I Know That Love Would Slip Away • **Don't Ask My Neighbors** [7] • Blessed • Rejoice

12/3/77+	39	18		4 Sunshine [E]		88	$10	Stax 4100
8/19/78	12	21	●	5 Sunbeam		40	$10	Columbia 35385
12/15/79	35	13		6 Come Into Our World		96	$10	ARC 36149
9/26/81	46	8		7 New Affair		168	$10	ARC 37456
4/28/84	33	18		8 Sincerely		206	$10	Red Label 001
5/4/85	54	10		9 If I Only Knew		203	$10	Motown 6136
3/30/96	77	1		10 Best Of My Love: The Best Of The Emotions [G]			$8	Legacy 64832

ENCHANTMENT   **'78**
Vocal group from Detroit: Ed Clanton, Bobby Green, Davis Banks, Emanuel Johnson and Joe Thomas.

| 2/5/77 | 11 | 39 | | 1 Enchantment | | 104 | $10 | United Artists 682 |
| 1/28/78 | 8 | 20 | | 2 Once Upon A Dream | | 46 | $10 | Roadshow 811 |

Sunny Shine Feeling • If You're Ready (Here It Comes) [14] • It's You That I Need [1] • You're The One • You Must Be An Angel • Up Higher • Silly Love Song • Angel In My Life • Trying To Get Over (With You)

| 3/17/79 | 25 | 18 | | 3 Journey To The Land Of...Enchantment | | 145 | $10 | Roadshow 3269 |
| 12/6/80 | 65 | 6 | | 4 Soft Lights, Sweet Music | | 202 | $10 | RCA Victor 3824 |

ENTOUCH   **'89**
Male duo of Eric McCain (from Mt. Vernon, New York) and Free (from the Bronx, New York).

| 7/29/89 | 32 | 38 | | All Nite | | 177 | $8 | Vintertainment 60858 |

EN VOGUE   **'92**
Female vocal group from Oakland: Dawn Robinson, **Terry Ellis**, Cindy Herron and Maxine Jones. Herron married pro baseball player Glenn Braggs in 1993. Robinson left in early 1997.

| 4/28/90 | 3 | 74 | ▲ | 1 Born To Sing | | 21 | $8 | Atlantic 82084 |

Party • Strange • **Lies** [1] • Hip Hop Bugle Boy • **Hold On** [1] • Part Of Me • **You Don't Have To Worry** [1] • Time Goes On • Just Can't Stay Away • **Don't Go** [3] • Luv Lines • Waitin' On You

| 4/11/92 | **❶**[2] | 84 | ▲[3] | 2 Funky Divas | | 8 | $8 | EastWest 92121 |

This Is Your Life • **My Lovin' (You're Never Gonna Get It)** [1] • Hip Hop Lover • **Free Your Mind** [23] • Desire • **Giving Him Something He Can Feel** [1] • It Ain't Over Till The Fat Lady Sings • **Give It Up, Turn It Loose** [16] • Yesterday • Hooked On Your Love • **Love Don't Love You** [31] • What Is Love

| 10/9/93 | 16 | 21 | | 3 Runaway Love [M] | | 49 | $6 | EastWest 92296 |
| 7/5/97 | 8 | 21 | ▲ | 4 EV3 | | 8 | $8 | EastWest 62057 |

Whatever [8] • **Don't Let Go (Love)** [1] • Right Direction • Damn I Wanna Be Your Lover • **Too Gone, Too Long** [25] • You're All I Need • Let It Flow • Sitting By Heaven's Door • Love Makes You Do Thangs • What A Difference A Day Makes • Eyes Of A Child • Does Anybody Hear Me

★167★   **EPMD**   **'88**
Rap duo from Long Island, New York: **Erick Sermon** and Parrish ("PMD") Smith. EPMD: Erick and Parrish Makin' Dollars.

| 6/18/88 | **❶**[3] | 39 | ● | 1 Strictly Business | | 80 | $8 | Fresh 82006 |

Strictly Business [25] • I'm Housin' • Let The Funk Flow • **You Gots To Chill** [22] • It's My Thing • You're A Customer • The Steve Martin • Get Off The Bandwagon • D.J. K La Boss • Jane

| 8/19/89 | **❶**[2] | 30 | ● | 2 Unfinished Business | | 53 | $8 | Fresh 82012 |

So Wat Cha Sayin' [23] • Total Kaos • Get The Bozack • Jane II • Please Listen To My Demo • It's Time To Party • Who's Booty • The Big Payback • Strictly Snappin' Necks • Knick Knack Patty Wack • You Had Too Much To Drink • It Wasn't Me, It Was The Fame

| 2/2/91 | **❶**[2] | 27 | ● | 3 Business As Usual | | 36 | $8 | Def Jam/RAL 47067 |

I'm Mad • Hardcore • **Rampage** [30] • Manslaughter • Jane 3 • For My People • Mr. Bozack • **Gold Digger** [14] • Give The People • Rap Is Outta Control • Brothers On My Jock • Underground • Hit Squad Heist • Funky Piano

| 8/15/92 | 5 | 30 | ● | 4 Business Never Personal | | 14 | $8 | RAL 52848 |

Boon Dox • Nobody's Safe Chump • Can't Hear Nothing But The Music • Chill • **Head Banger** [75] • Scratch Bring It Back • **Crossover** [14] • Cummin' At Cha • Play The Next Man • It's Going Down • Who Killed Jane

| 10/4/97 | 4 | 19 | ● | 5 Back In Business | | 16 | $8 | Def Jam 536389 |

Richter Scale [62] • The Joint [42] • Never Seen Before • Intrigued • Last Man Standing • Get Wit This • Do It Again • You Gots To Chill '97 • Put On • K.I.M. • Dungeon Master • Jane 5

DEBUT	PEAK	WKS	Gold	Album Title	Pop #	$	Label & Number

ERIC B. & RAKIM   '88
Rap duo: DJ Eric Barrier (from Elmhurst, New York) and rapper William "Rakim" Griffin (from Long Island, New York).

| 8/15/87 | 8 | 43 | ▲ | 1 Paid In Full | 58 | $8 | 4th & B'way 444005 |

I Ain't No Joke *[38]* • Eric B. Is On The Cut • My Melody • **I Know You Got Soul** *[64]* • Move The Crowd • **Paid In Full** *[65]* • As The Rhyme Goes On • Chinese Arithmetic • **Eric B. Is President** *[48]* • Extended Beat

| 8/20/88 | 7 | 26 | ● | 2 Follow The Leader | 22 | $8 | Uni 3 |

Follow The Leader *[16]* • Microphone Fiend • Lyrics Of Fury • Eric B. Never Scared • Just A Beat • Put Your Hands Together • To The Listeners • No Competition • R, The *[79]* • Musical Massacre • Beats For The Listeners

| 7/7/90 | 10 | 20 | ● | 3 Let The Rhythm Hit 'Em | 32 | $8 | MCA 6416 |

Let The Rhythm Hit 'Em *[23]* • No Omega • In The Ghetto *[82]* • Step Back • Eric B. Made My Day • Run For Cover • Untouchables • Mahogany • Keep 'Em Eager To Listen • Set 'Em Straight

| 7/11/92 | 9 | 21 | | 4 Don't Sweat The Technique | 22 | $8 | MCA 10594 |

What's On Your Mind (House Party II Rap Theme) *[34]* • Teach The Children • Pass The Hand Grenade • Casualties Of War • Rest Assured • Punisher, The • Relax With Pep • Keep The Beat • What's Going On • **Juice (know the ledge)** *[38]* • Don't Sweat The Technique *[14]* • Kick Along

| 4/8/95 | 96 | 1 | | 5 Eric B. .... | | $8 | Nine 70001 |
| 11/15/97 | ❶[1] | 23 | ● | 6 The 18th Letter | 4 | $8 | Universal 53113 |

RAKIM
The 18th Letter (Always And Forever) • It's Been A Long Time • Remember That • The Saga Begins • Guess Who's Back • Stay A While • New York (Ya Out There) • Show Me Love • The Mystery (Who Is God?) • When I'm Flowin

ERUPTION   '78
Techno-funk group of Jamaican natives based in London: Precious Wilson and Lintel (vocals), brothers Gregory and Morgan Petrineau (guitars), Horatio McKay (keyboards) and Eric Kingsley (drums).

| 4/8/78 | 44 | 7 | | Eruption .... | 133 | $12 | Ariola 50033 |

ESCORTS, The   '73
Vocal group formed and recorded at Rahway State Prison in New Jersey: Reginald Haynes, Laurence Franklin, Robert Arrington, William Dugger, Stephen Carter, Frank Heard and Marion Murphy.

| 6/30/73 | 41 | 10 | | 1 All We Need Is One More Chance .... | | $15 | Alithia 9104 |
| 5/25/74 | 57 | 3 | | 2 Three Down And Four To Go .... | | $15 | Alithia 9106 |

ESCOVEDO, Coke   '76
Born Thomas Escovedo on 4/30/41 in Los Angeles. Died on 7/13/86 (age 45). Latin singer/percussionist. Member of **Azteca**. Uncle of **Sheila E.**

| 11/29/75 | 44 | 5 | | 1 Coke .... | 195 | $12 | Mercury 1041 |
| 6/5/76 | 37 | 6 | | 2 Comin' At Ya! .... | 190 | $12 | Mercury 1085 |

E.S.G.   '95
Born Cedric Hill in Houston. Male rapper. E.S.G.: Everday Street Gangsta.

| 9/30/95 | 29 | 8 | | 1 Sailin' Da South .... | | $8 | Perrion 53973 |

E.S.G. Featuring Screwed Mix

| 4/18/98 | 67 | 2 | | 2 Return Of The Living Dead .... | | $8 | Blackhearted 1001 |

ESHAM   '96
Born Esham Smith in Detroit. Male rapper.

| 5/25/96 | 38 | 6 | | 1 Dead Flowerz .... | | $8 | Reel Life 1040 |
| 3/22/97 | 57 | 3 | | 2 Bruce Wayne Gothom City 1987 .... | | $8 | Gothom 850 |

ESTEFAN, Gloria   '88
Born Gloria Fajardo on 12/1/57 in Havana, Cuba; raised in Miami. Formed Miami Sound Machine with her husband, percussionist Emilio Estefan.

| 6/18/88 | 55 | 14 | ▲[3] | 1 Let It Loose | 6 | $8 | Epic 40769 |

GLORIA ESTEFAN & MIAMI SOUND MACHINE

| 8/19/89 | 80 | 8 | ▲[3] | 2 Cuts Both Ways | 8 | $8 | Epic 45217 |
| 2/23/91 | 64 | 10 | ▲[2] | 3 Into The Light .... | 5 | $8 | Epic 46988 |

ESTUS, Deon   '89
Born in Detroit. Singer/bassist.

| 4/15/89 | 44 | 15 | | Spell .... | 89 | $8 | Mika 835713 |

ETERNAL   '94
Female vocal group from London: sisters Esther and Vernette Bennett, with Louise Nurding and Kelle Bryan.

| 3/26/94 | 59 | 8 | | Always & Forever .... | 152 | $8 | EMI 28212 |

E.U.   '89
Funk group from Washington DC. Led by singer/bassist Gregory Elliot. E.U.: Experience Unlimited.

| 4/8/89 | 22 | 34 | | 1 Livin' Large .... | 158 | $8 | Virgin 91021 |
| 1/5/91 | 92 | 4 | | 2 Cold Kickin' It .... | | $8 | Virgin 91379 |

EURYTHMICS   '84
Synth/pop duo: Annie Lennox (from Aberdeen, Scotland) and David Stewart (from England).

| 9/3/83 | 36 | 10 | ● | 1 Sweet Dreams (Are Made Of This) .... | 15 | $8 | RCA Victor 4681 |
| 3/3/84 | 36 | 20 | ▲ | 2 Touch .... | 7 | $8 | RCA Victor 4917 |

EVANS, Adriana   '97
Born in San Francisco. Female singer.

| 5/17/97 | 33 | 14 | | Adriana Evans .... | | $8 | RCA 67509 |

EVANS, Faith   '95
Born on 6/10/73 in New York City. Married to **The Notorious B.I.G.** until his death on 3/9/97.

| 9/16/95 | 2[1] | 53 | ▲ | 1 Faith | 22 | $8 | Bad Boy 73003 |

No Other Love • Fallin' In Love • **Ain't Nobody** *[14]* • Love Don't Live Here Anymore • **Come Over** *[56]* • **Soon As I Get Home** *[3]* • All This Love • **You Used To Love Me** *[4]* • Give It To Me • You Don't Understand • Don't Be Afraid • Reasons

| 11/14/98 | 3 | 38↑ | ● | 2 Keep The Faith | 6 | $8 | Bad Boy 73016 |

Love Like This *[2]* • **All Night Long** *[3]* • Sunny Days • My First Love • Anything You Need • No Way • Life Will Pass You By • Keep The Faith • Never Gonna Let You Go • Caramel Kisses • Lately I

| --- | --- | --- | --- | --- | --- | --- | --- |

EVERETT, Betty   '69
Born on 11/23/39 in Greenwood, Mississippi. Singer/pianist.

| 5/31/69 | 44 | 3 | | There'll Come A Time | | $25 | Uni 73048 |

EX-GIRLFRIEND   '91
Female vocal group from New York City: Julia Roberson, Monica Boyd, Tisha Hunter and Stacy Francis.

| 8/17/91 | 37 | 26 | | X Marks The Spot | | $8 | Reprise 26547 |

EXPOSÉ   '87
Female vocal trio from Miami: Ann Curless, Gioia Bruno and Jeanette Jurado. Bruno left in 1992, replaced by Kelly Moneymaker.

3/7/87	20	61	▲²	1 Exposure	16	$8	Arista 8441
7/15/89	94	5	●	2 What You Don't Know	33	$8	Arista 8532
12/5/92	93	1	●	3 Exposé	135	$8	Arista 18577

EXTRA PROLIFIC   '94
Hip-hop duo from San Francisco: Mike G. and Duane Lee.

| 11/12/94 | 46 | 1 | | Like It Should Be | | $8 | Jive 41532 |

F

FACEMOB   '96
Rap group from Houston: Devin, DMG, Sha-Riza, Smit-D and 350.

| 8/24/96 | 6 | 14 | | The Other Side Of The Law | 51 | $8 | Rap-A-Lot 41336 |

In The Flesh • Bank Robbery • Da Coldest • Millions • Tales From The Hood • Respect Rude • Stay True • The Other Side • Black Woman • Rivals

FACTS OF LIFE   '77
Vocal trio: Jean Davis (younger sister of **Tyrone Davis**), Keith William and Chuck Carter.

| 4/23/77 | 33 | 5 | | 1 Sometimes | 146 | $12 | Kayvette 802 |
| 6/10/78 | 54 | 6 | | 2 A Matter Of Fact | | $12 | Kayvette 803 |

FAGEN, Donald   '82
Born on 1/10/48 in Passaic, New Jersey. Founding memeber of **Steely Dan**.

| 11/13/82 | 24 | 17 | ● | The Nightfly | 11 | $10 | Warner 23696 |

FAIR, Yvonne   '75
Born in Virginia. Died on 3/6/94 (age 51). Toured with **James Brown** Revue. Appeared in the movie *Lady Sings The Blues*.

| 9/13/75 | 57 | 1 | | The Bitch Is Black | | $12 | Motown 832 |

FAITH, HOPE & CHARITY   '75
Vocal trio from Tampa, Florida: Brenda Hilliard, Albert Bailey and Diane Destry. **Zulema** was an early member (left in 1971).

| 8/23/75 | 24 | 11 | | Faith, Hope & Charity | 100 | $12 | RCA Victor 1100 |

FALCO   '86
Born Johann Holzel on 2/19/57 in Vienna, Austria. Died in a car crash on 2/6/98 (age 40). Male singer/songwriter.

| 3/22/86 | 18 | 16 | ● | Falco 3 | 3 | $8 | A&M 5105 |

FAMILY, The   '85
Group from Minneapolis: Susannah Melvoin, with former **Time** members Paul "St. Paul" Peterson, Jerome Benton and Jellybean Johnson. Melvoin is the sister of Wendy Melvoin (of **Wendy and Lisa**).

| 9/7/85 | 17 | 30 | | The Family | 62 | $8 | Paisley Park 25322 |

FAMILY STAND, The   '90
Trio from New York City: Sandra St. Victor (vocals), Peter Lord (keyboards) and V. Jeffrey Smith (guitar, bass, drums).

| 6/16/90 | 56 | 17 | | Chain | | $8 | Atlantic 82036 |

FANTASTIC FOUR   '75
Vocal group from Detroit: brothers Robert and Joseph Pruitt, with James Epps and Toby Childs.

| 6/7/75 | 33 | 13 | | Alvin Stone (The Birth And Death Of A Gangster) | 99 | $15 | Westbound 201 |

FATAL   '98
Born in New York City. Male rapper.

| 4/18/98 | 10 | 11 | | In The Line Of Fire | 50 | $8 | Relativity 1622 |

M.O.B. • **Everyday** *[79]* • Friday • I Know The Rules • Outlaws • Time's Wastin' • What's Your Life Worth? • Getto Star • Take Your Time • The World Is Changing

FATBACK   ★129★   '80
Funk group: Bill Curtis (vocals, drums), Johnny King (guitar), Saunders McCrae (keyboards), Earl Shelton, George Williams, George Adam, and Richard Cromwell (horns), and Johnny Flippin (bass).
1)Hot Box 2)Fatback XII 3)14 Karat

| 1/24/76 | 37 | 15 | | 1 Raising Hell | 158 | $15 | Event 6905 |
| 8/21/76 | 31 | 8 | | 2 Night Fever | 182 | $12 | Spring 6711 |

THE FATBACK BAND (above 2)

4/23/77	54	2		3 NYCNYUSA (Nik-Ne-Yoo-Sa)		$12	Spring 6714
7/1/78	17	20		4 Fired Up 'N' Kickin'	73	$10	Spring 6718
3/17/79	57	5		5 Brite Lites/Big City		$10	Spring 6721
9/29/79	16	21		6 Fatback XII	89	$10	Spring 6723
4/5/80	7	31	●	7 Hot Box	44	$10	Spring 6726

Hot Box • Come And Get The Love • Love Spell • **Gotta Get My Hands On Some (Money)** *[6]* • **Backstrokin'** *[3]* • Street Band

| 11/8/80 | 16 | 15 | | 8 14 Karat | 91 | $10 | Spring 6729 |
| 6/20/81 | 17 | 12 | | 9 Tasty Jam | 102 | $10 | Spring 6731 |

FATBACK — Cont'd

DEBUT	PEAK	WKS	Gold	Album Title	Pop #	$	Label & Number
1/23/82	68	2		10 Gigolo	148	$10	Spring 6734
7/10/82	28	13		11 On The Floor	204	$10	Spring 6736
4/16/83	27	21		12 Is This The Future?		$10	Spring 6738
2/4/84	64	4		13 With Love		$10	Spring 6741
7/21/84	67	3		14 Phoenix		$8	Cotillion 90168

FAT BOYS   '87

Rap trio from Brooklyn, New York: Mark "Prince Markie Dee" Morales, Darren "Human Beat Box" Robinson and Damon "Kool Rock" Wimbley. First known as Disco 3. Starred in the 1987 movie *Disorderlies*. Robinson died of heart failure on 12/10/95 (age 28).

DEBUT	PEAK	WKS	Gold	Album Title	Pop #	$	Label & Number
12/1/84+	6	42	●	1 Fat Boys	48	$8	Sutra 1015

Jail House Rap [17] • Stick 'Em • Can You Feel It [38] • Fat Boys [65] • The Place To Be • Human Beat Box [flip] • Don't Dog Me

DEBUT	PEAK	WKS	Gold	Album Title	Pop #	$	Label & Number
8/17/85	11	36	●	2 The Fat Boys Are Back!	63	$8	Sutra 1016
5/24/86	10	22		3 Big & Beautiful	62	$8	Sutra 1017

Sex Machine [23] • Go For It • Breakdown • Double-O Fat Boys • Big And Beautiful • Rap Symphony (In C-Minor) • Human Beat Box, Part 3 • In The House [51] • Beat Box Is Rockin'

DEBUT	PEAK	WKS	Gold	Album Title	Pop #	$	Label & Number
6/13/87	4	35	▲	4 Crushin'	8	$8	Tin Pan Apple 831948

Crushin' • Medley: Protect Yourself/My Nuts • Rock Ruling • Making Noise • Boys Will Be Boys • Falling In Love [16] • Fat Boys Dance • Wipeout [10] • Between The Sheets • Hell, No!

DEBUT	PEAK	WKS	Gold	Album Title	Pop #	$	Label & Number
7/16/88	30	21	●	5 Coming Back Hard Again	33	$8	Tin Pan Apple 835809
10/21/89	52	8		6 On And On	175	$8	Tin Pan Apple 838867
12/21/91+	89	5		7 Mack Daddy		$8	Emperor 4118

FATHER DOM   '92

Born in 1973 in Oakland, California. Male rapper.

DEBUT	PEAK	WKS	Gold	Album Title	Pop #	$	Label & Number
4/11/92	80	8		Father Dom		$8	Wrap 8105

FATHER MC   '91

Born Timothy Brown in New York City. Dancehall reggae singer. Dropped the MC from his name in mid-1993.

DEBUT	PEAK	WKS	Gold	Album Title	Pop #	$	Label & Number
11/24/90+	23	30		1 Father's Day	62	$8	Uptown/MCA 10061
9/12/92	34	30		2 Close To You	185	$8	Uptown/MCA 10542
1/8/94	55	9		3 Sex Is Law		$8	Uptown/MCA 10937

FATHER

FAT JOE   '98

Born Joseph Cartagena in the Bronx, New York. Male rapper.

DEBUT	PEAK	WKS	Gold	Album Title	Pop #	$	Label & Number
8/28/93	46	11		1 Represent		$8	Relativity 1175

FAT JOE DA GANGSTA

DEBUT	PEAK	WKS	Gold	Album Title	Pop #	$	Label & Number
11/11/95	7	27		2 Jealous One's Envy	71	$8	Relativity 1239

Bronx Tale • Success • Envy [44] • Fat Joe's In Town • Part Deux • King NY • The Shit Is Real • Fat Joe's Way • Respect Mine • Watch Out • Say Word • Dedication • Bronx Keeps Creating It

DEBUT	PEAK	WKS	Gold	Album Title	Pop #	$	Label & Number
9/12/98	2¹	20	●	3 Don Cartagena	7	$8	Mystic 92805

The Crack Attack • Triplets • Find Out • Don Cartagena [40] • My World • John Blaze • Walk On By • Dat Gangsta Shit • Bet Ya Man Can't (Triz) [54] • Misery Needs Company • The Hidden Hand • My Prerogative • Good Times • Terror Squadians

FAT LARRY'S BAND   '80

Funk group from Philadelphia led by "Fat Larry" James (died on 12/5/87, age 38).

DEBUT	PEAK	WKS	Gold	Album Title	Pop #	$	Label & Number
9/27/80	72	3		Stand Up		$10	Fantasy 9599

FAT PAT   '98

Born Patrick Hawkins in Houston. Shot to death on 2/3/98 (age 27). Male rapper.

DEBUT	PEAK	WKS	Gold	Album Title	Pop #	$	Label & Number
3/21/98	39	5		1 Ghetto Dreams		$8	Wreckshop 1111
10/24/98	40	3		2 Throwed In Da Game		$8	Wreckshop 1112

FAT PAT & THE WRECKSHOP FAMILY

FATTBURGER   '86

Jazz group from San Diego: Carl Evans, Mark Hunter, Kevin Koch, Steve Laury, Hollis Gentry and Tom Aros.

DEBUT	PEAK	WKS	Gold	Album Title	Pop #	$	Label & Number
10/11/86	39	11		One Of A Kind	[I]	$8	Golden Boy 2001

FAZE   '91

Vocal group from Miami: Dave Johnson, Edward Faison, Robert Wright, Fernandez Cherry and Wayne Morrison.

DEBUT	PEAK	WKS	Gold	Album Title	Pop #	$	Label & Number
11/16/91	93	5		Love Games		$8	Bahia 3078

FAZE-O   '78

Funk group from Chicago: Robert Neal (vocals), Ralph Aikens (guitar), Keith Harrison (keyboards), Frederick Crum (bass) and Roger Parker (drums).

DEBUT	PEAK	WKS	Gold	Album Title	Pop #	$	Label & Number
2/18/78	19	20		1 Riding High	98	$10	She 740
11/4/78	40	7		2 Good Thang	145	$10	She 741
9/29/79	48	8		3 Breakin' The Funk		$10	She 742

FELDER, Wilton   '85

Born on 8/31/40 in Houston. Reed player. Co-founder of The Crusaders.

DEBUT	PEAK	WKS	Gold	Album Title	Pop #	$	Label & Number
12/23/78+	33	16		1 We All Have A Star	173	$10	ABC 1109
11/1/80	14	31		2 Inherit The Wind	142	$8	MCA 5144
5/14/83	55	6		3 Gentle Fire	[I]	$8	MCA 5406
3/9/85	10	20		4 Secrets	[I] 81	$8	MCA 5510

Secrets • (No Matter How High I Get) I'll Still Be Lookin' Up To You [2] • La Luz • The Truth Song • I Found You • Mr. Scoots

FELICIANO, Jose   '68
Born on 9/8/45 in Puerto Rico; raised in New York City. Blind since birth. Virtuoso acoustic guitarist. Composed score for TV's *Chico & The Man*. Won the 1968 Best New Artist Grammy Award.

7/20/68	3	35	●	1 **Feliciano!**	2³	$15	RCA Victor 3957

California Dreamin' • **Light My Fire** *[29]* • Don't Let The Sun Catch You Crying • In My Life • And I Love Her • Nena Na Na • (There's) Always Something There To Remind Me • Just A Little Bit Of Rain • Sunny • Here, There And Everywhere • The Last Thing On My Mind

12/7/68+	4	15		2 **Souled**	24	$15	RCA Victor 4045

Younger Generation • I'll Be Your Baby Tonight • Sleep Late, My Lady Friend • And The Sun Will Shine • She's Too Good To Me • Hey! Baby • Hitchcock Railway • My World Is Empty Without You • You've Got A Lot Of Style • The Sad Gypsy • **Hi-Heel Sneakers** *[44]*

7/19/69	15	12	●	3 **Feliciano/10 To 23**	16	$15	RCA Victor 4185
1/30/82	61	4		4 **Jose Feliciano**		$10	Motown 953

FELONY, Jayo   '98
Born James Savage in New York City. Male rapper.

10/7/95	65	6		1 **Take A Ride**		$8	JMJ/RAL 124038
9/12/98	8	10		2 **Whatcha Gonna Do**	46	$8	Def Jam 558792

Nobody On Dry Land • How Angry • Whatcha Gonna Do • Easy To Get In • Nitty Gritty • I'm Deadly • Lovely • Bumpin' Bullet Loco • Love Don't Love • Finna Shit On 'Em • Hustle In My Genes • End Of The World • Justice Against Y'all Oppressors

FERRELL, Rachelle   '93
Born in Philadelphia. Female singer/keyboardist.

10/31/92+	25	124	●	**Rachelle Ferrell**	161	$8	Manhattan 93769

FEVER   '79
Disco group from Ohio: Clydene Jackson (vocals), Dale Reed (saxophone), Joe Bomback (keyboards) and Dennis Waddington (bass).

12/8/79	67	2		**Fever**	205	$10	Fantasy 9580

FEW GOOD MEN, A   '95
Vocal group from Atlanta: Aaron Hilliard, David Morris, Tony Amey and Demail Burks.

10/14/95	53	4		**Take A Dip**		$8	LaFace 26021

FIELDS, Richard "Dimples"   '82
Born in San Francisco. Male singer/songwriter/producer.

7/18/81	5	20		1 **Dimples**	33	$10	Boardwalk 33232

I Like Your Lovin • Let Me Take You In My Arms Tonight • Let The Lady Dance • Lovely Lady • In The Still Of The Night (I'll Remember) • She's Got Papers On Me • **I've Got To Learn To Say No!** *[42]* • **Earth Angel** *[81]* • Don't Ever Take Your Love

2/27/82	3	26		2 **Mr. Look So Good!**	63	$10	Boardwalk 33249

If It Ain't One Thing...It's Another *[1]* • After I Put My Lovin' On You • Baby Work Out • Mr. Look So Good • **Taking Applications** *[35]* • (Woman At Home And) A Freak On The Side • Sincerely • The Lady Is Bad

12/4/82+	40	17		3 **Give Everybody Some!**		$10	Boardwalk 33258
8/4/84	51	8		4 **Mmm...**		$8	RCA Victor 5169
8/22/87	58	7		5 **Tellin' It Like It Is**		$8	Columbia 40859

FIEND   '98
Born Rickey Jones in New Orleans. Male rapper.

5/16/98	❶¹	25	●	**There's One In Every Family**	8	$8	No Limit 50715

Take My Pain • Going Out With A Blast • Do You Know? • Big Timer • Who Got The Fire • All I Know • I Swore • Only A Few • The Baddest • The Streets Ain't Safe • All In A Week • I.C.U. • On A Mission • Slangin' • At All Times • Walk Like A "G" • We Survivors • What Cha Mean • Do You Wanna Be A Rider • For The N.O. • Live Me Long

5TH DIMENSION, The   '69
★90★

Vocal group from Los Angeles: Marilyn McCoo, Billy Davis, Jr., Florence LaRue, Lamont McLemore and Ron Townson. McCoo and Davis were married in 1969 and recorded as a duo since 1976.

1)The Age Of Aquarius 2)Portrait 3)Greatest Hits

7/29/67	10	16	●	1 **Up, Up And Away**	8	$15	Soul City 92000

Up-Up And Away • Another Day, Another Heartache • Which Way To Nowhere • California My Way • Misty Roses • Go Where You Wanna Go • Never Gonna Be The Same • Pattern People • Rosecrans Blvd. • Learn How To Fly • Poor Side Of Town

6/22/68	43	4		2 **The Magic Garden**	105	$15	Soul City 92001
8/24/68	10	18		3 **Stoned Soul Picnic**	21	$15	Soul City 92002

Sweet Blindness *[45]* • It'll Never Be The Same Again • The Sailboat Song • It's A Great Life • **Stoned Soul Picnic** *[2]* • California Soul *[49]* • Lovin' Stew • Broken Wing Bird • Good News • Bobbie's Blues (Who Do You Think Of?) • The Eleventh Song (What A Groovy Day!)

6/7/69	2²	20	●	4 **The Age Of Aquarius**	2²	$15	Soul City 92005

Aquarius/Let The Sunshine In (The Flesh Failures) *[6]* • Blowing Away • Skinny Man • **Wedding Bell Blues** *[23]* • Don'tcha Hear Me Callin' To Ya • The Hideaway • **Workin' On A Groovy Thing** *[15]* • Let It Be Me • Sunshine Of Your Love • The Winds Of Heaven • Those Were The Days

5/16/70+	6	32	●	5 **Portrait**	20	$12	Bell 6045

Puppet Man • One Less Bell To Answer *[4]* • Feelin' Alright? • This Is Your Life • A Love Like Ours • Save The Country *[41]* • Medley: The Declaration/A Change Is Gonna Come/People Gotta Be Free • Dimension 5ive

5/30/70	8	21	●	6 **The 5th Dimension/Greatest Hits**	[G]	5	$12	Soul City 33900

Aquarius/Let The Sunshine In (The Flesh Failures) *[6]* • The Girls' Song • Stoned Soul Picnic *[2]* • The Worst That Could Happen • Wedding Bell Blues *[23]* • California Soul *[49]* • Up-Up And Away • Blowin' Away • Carpet Man • Workin' On A Groovy Thing *[15]* • Paper Cup • Sweet Blindness *[45]*

3/27/71	10	17	●	7 **Love's Lines, Angles And Rhymes**	17	$12	Bell 6060

Time And Love • Love's Lines, Angles And Rhymes *[28]* • What Does It Take (To Win Your Love)? • Guess Who • Viva Tirado • Light Sings • The Rainmaker • He's A Runner • The Singer • Every Night

11/6/71	13	24	●	8 **The 5th Dimension/Live!!**	[L]	32	$15	Bell 9000 [2]
4/15/72	21	16		9 **Individually & Collectively**	58	$12	Bell 6073
10/14/72	10	17	●	10 **Greatest Hits On Earth**	[G]	14	$12	Bell 1106

(Last Night) I Didn't Get To Sleep At All *[28]* • Stoned Soul Picnic *[2]* • One Less Bell To Answer *[4]* • Aquarius/Let The Sunshine In (The Flesh Failures) *[6]* • Wedding Bell Blues *[23]* • Save The Country *[41]* • Love's Lines, Angles And Rhymes *[28]* • Puppet Man • Up, Up And Away • Never My Love *[45]* • Together Let's Find Love *[22]*

DEBUT	PEAK	WKS	Gold	Album Title	Pop #	$	Label & Number
				5TH DIMENSION, The — Cont'd			
4/7/73	25	6		11 Living Together, Growing Together	108	$12	Bell 1116
1/25/75	55	2		12 Soul & Inspiration	202	$12	Bell 1315
9/13/75	30	7		13 Earthbound	136	$10	ABC 897
				5TH WARD BOYZ '94			
				Rap trio from Houston: Andre Barnes, Eric Taylor and Lo Life.			
5/22/93	19	24		1 Ghetto Dope	176	$8	Rap-A-Lot 53859
3/12/94	13	15		2 Gangsta Funk	105	$8	Rap-A-Lot 53844
12/2/95	35	21		3 Rated G	189	$8	Rap-A-Lot 40758
12/6/97	26	22		4 Usual Suspects	180	$8	Rap-A-Lot 45117
				5TH WARD JUVENILEZ '95			
				Rap trio from Houston.			
7/8/95	28	7		Deadly Groundz	200	$8	Underground 40531
				52ND STREET '86			
				British group.			
6/21/86	23	18		Children Of The Night		$8	MCA 5738
				FINESSE & SYNQUIS '88			
				Female rap duo from Queens, New York.			
9/10/88	61	11		Soul Sisters		$8	Uptown/MCA 42177
				FINEST HOUR '89			
				Vocal group from Boston: Joe Burks, Troy Sanders, Jamal Seymour and Carlos Munoz.			
9/23/89	79	7		Make That Move		$8	Polydor 839517
				FIRM, The '97			
				All-star rap group: **Nas**, Foxy Brown, AZ and Nature.			
11/1/97	❶¹	29		The Firm - The Album	1¹	$8	Aftermath 90136
				Firm Fiasco • Phone Tap • Executive Decision • Firm Family • Firm All Stars • Fuck Somebody Else • Hardcore • Untouchable • Five Minutes To Flush • Desparados • Firm Biz • I'm Leaving • Throw Your Guns			
				FIRST CHOICE '74			
				Female vocal trio from Philadelphia: Joyce Jones, Rochelle Fleming and Annette Guest. Jones left in 1977, replaced by Debbie Martin.			
9/29/73	55	3		1 Armed And Extremely Dangerous	184	$15	Philly Groove 1400
11/9/74	36	8		2 The Player	143	$15	Philly Groove 1502
4/17/76	53	5		3 So Let Us Entertain You	204	$15	Warner 2934
4/28/79	58	3		4 Hold Your Horses	135	$12	Gold Mind 9502
				FIRST CIRCLE '87			
				Group from New York City: Albert Lee (vocals), Larry Marsden (guitar), Richard Sinclair (percussion), Anthony McEwan (bass) and Glenn Everette (drums).			
5/23/87	73	2		Boys' Night Out		$8	EMI America 17268
				FISCHER, Lisa '91			
				Born in Brooklyn, New York. Former session singer.			
5/25/91	5	30		So Intense	100	$8	Elektra 60889
				Save Me [7] • Get Back To Love • How Can I Ease The Pain [1] • So Intense [15] • Wildflower • Some Girls • So Tender • Send The Message Of Love • Chain Of Broken Hearts • Last Goodbye			
				FIT, The '88			
				Duo of producer/multi-instrumentalist Chuck Gentry and singer Vince Ebo.			
4/16/88	68	4		Just Havin' Fun		$8	A&M 5183
				FIVE XI '93			
				Vocal duo: Rod Marcel (from Miami) and Lawrence Tolbert (from Gary, Indiana). Five XI: Five Eleven.			
7/31/93	84	1		Five XI		$8	RCA 66144
				FIVE SPECIAL '79			
				Vocal group from Detroit: Bryan Banks, Greg Finley, Steve Harris, Steve Boyd and Mike Petillo. Banks is the brother of **Ron Banks**.			
8/4/79	20	16		1 Five Special	118	$10	Elektra 206
6/7/80	46	10		2 Special Edition		$10	Elektra 270
				FIVE STAIRSTEPS, The '67			
				Group from Chicago: brothers Clarence, James, Dennis and Keni Burke, with their sister Aloha. Later joined by their five-year-old brother Cubie. Clarence, James, Dennis and Keni later became **The Invisible Man's Band**.			
3/4/67	8	13		1 The Five Stairsteps	139	$25	Windy C 6000
				Danger! She's A Stranger [16] • The Girl I Love • Come Back [15] • The Touch Of You • You Waited Too Long [16] • Playgirl's Love • World Of Fantasy [12] • Oooh, Baby Baby [34] • Don't Waste Your Time • You Don't Love Me • Behind Curtains			
1/20/68	20	8		2 Our Family Portrait	195	$20	Buddah 5008
5/3/69	22	10		3 Love's Happening	198	$20	Curtom 8002
				5 STAIRSTEPS & CUBIE (above 2)			
5/30/70	12	20		4 Stairsteps	83	$15	Buddah 5061
12/12/70+	47	4		5 Step by Step by Step	199 [K]	$15	Buddah 5068
3/13/76	37	8		6 2nd Ressurection	203	$12	Dark Horse 22004
				STAIRSTEPS (above 3)			
				FIVE STAR '86			
				Family vocal group from England: Deniece, Doris, Lorraine, Stedman and Delroy Pearson.			
8/31/85+	14	55		1 Luxury Of Life	57	$8	RCA Victor 8052
9/20/86	22	27		2 Silk & Steel	80	$8	RCA Victor 5901
11/19/88	91	5		3 Rock The World		$8	RCA 8531

FLACK, Roberta ★44★ '71
Born on 2/10/39 in Asheville, North Carolina; raised in Arlington, Virginia. Played piano from an early age. Music scholarship to Howard University at age 15; classmate of **Donny Hathaway**. Worked as a high school music teacher in North Carolina. Discovered by jazz musician **Les McCann**. Signed to Atlantic in 1969.

1)First Take 2)Roberta Flack & Donny Hathaway 3)Killing Me Softly

DEBUT	PEAK	WKS	Gold	Album Title	Pop #	$	Label & Number
1/31/70+	**❶**²	44	●	**1 First Take**	1⁵	$10	Atlantic 8230
				Angelitos Negros • Our Ages Or Our Hearts • I Told Jesus • Hey, That's No Way To Say Goodbye • **The First Time Ever I Saw Your Face** *[4]* • Tryin' Times • Ballad Of The Sad Young Men			
9/5/70+	**4**	73	●	**2 Chapter Two**	33	$10	Atlantic 1569
				Reverend Lee • Do What You Gotta Do • Just Like A Woman • Let It Be Me • Gone Away • Until It's Time For You To Go • The Impossible Dream • Business Goes On As Usual			
12/11/71+	**4**	34	●	**3 Quiet Fire**	18	$10	Atlantic 1594
				Go Up Moses • Bridge Over Troubled Water • Sunday And Sister Jones • See You Then • **Will You Still Love Me Tomorrow** *[38]* • To Love Somebody • Let Them Talk • Sweet Bitter Love			
5/13/72	**2**⁵	26	●	**4 Roberta Flack & Donny Hathaway**	3	$10	Atlantic 7216
				I (Who Have Nothing) • **You've Got A Friend** *[8]* • Baby I Love You • Be Real Black For Me • **You've Lost That Lovin' Feelin'** *[30]* • For All We Know • **Where Is The Love** *[1]* • When Love Has Grown • Come Ye Disconsolate • Mood			
9/1/73	**2**¹	17	●	**5 Killing Me Softly**	3	$10	Atlantic 7271
				Killing Me Softly With His Song *[2]* • **Jesse** *[19]* • No Tears (In The End) • I'm The Girl • River • Conversation Love • When You Smile • Suzanne			
4/5/75	**5**	18		**6 Feel Like Makin' Love**	24	$10	Atlantic 18131
				Feelin' That Glow *[25]* • I Wanted It Too • I Can See The Sun In Late December • Some Gospel According To Matthew • **Feel Like Makin' Love** *[1]* • Mr. Magic • Early Ev'ry Midnite • Old Heartbreak Top Ten • She's Not Blind			
1/7/78	**5**	29	●	**7 Blue Lights In The Basement**	8	$10	Atlantic 19149
				Why Don't You Move In With Me • **The Closer I Get To You** *[1]* • Fine, Fine Day • This Time I'll Be Sweeter • **25th Of Last December** *[52]* • After You • I'd Like To Be Baby To You • Soul Deep • Love Is The Healing • Where I'll Find You			
9/30/78	37	9		**8 Roberta Flack**	74	$10	Atlantic 19186
3/29/80	**4**	26	●	**9 Roberta Flack Featuring Donny Hathaway**	25	$10	Atlantic 16013
				Only Heaven Can Wait (For Love) • God Don't Like Ugly • **You Are My Heaven** *[8]* • Disguises • **Don't Make Me Wait Too Long** *[67]* • **Back Together Again** *[18]* • Stay With Me			
12/27/80+	10	24		**10 Live & More**	[L]	52	$12	Atlantic 7004 [2]
				ROBERTA FLACK & PEABO BRYSON			
				recorded at the Holiday Star Theater in Merrillville, Indiana			
				Medley: Only Heaven Can Wait (For Love)/You Are My Heaven • **Make The World Stand Still** *[13]* • Feel The Fire • God Don't Like Ugly • If Only For One Night • **Love Is A Waiting Game** *[46]* • Reachin' For The Sky • Killing Me Softly With His Song • More Than Everything • Feel Like Makin' Love • When Will I Learn • Don't Make Me Wait Too Long • Back Together Again • Medley: Love In Every Season/I Believe In You			
7/11/81	48	10		**11 Bustin' Loose**	[S]	161	$8	MCA 5141
6/19/82	16	32		**12 I'm The One**	59	$8	Atlantic 19354
8/20/83	8	44	●	**13 Born To Love**	25	$8	Capitol 12284
				PEABO BRYSON/ROBERTA FLACK			
				Tonight, I Celebrate My Love *[5]* • Blame It On Me • Heaven Above Me • Born To Love • **Maybe** *[68]* • I Just Came Here To Dance • Comin' Alive • **You're Looking Like Love To Me** *[41]* • Can We Find Love Again			
11/26/88+	24	27		**14 Oasis**	159	$8	Atlantic 81916

FLATLINERZ '94
Rap trio from New York City: Redrum, Tempest and Gravedigger.

11/26/94	65	1		**U.S.A.**		$8	Def Jam 523601

FLESH-N-BONE '96
Born Stanley Howse in Cleveland. Male rapper. Member of **Bone Thugs-N-Harmony**.

12/7/96	8	16	●	**T.H.U.G.S. - Trues Humbly United Gatherin' Souls**	23	$8	Mo Thugs 533938
				T.H.U.G.S. • Reverend Run Sermon • World So Cruel • Northcoast • Nothin But Da Bone In Me • The Silence Isn't Over • Crazy By The Flesh • Mystic Spirits • Coming 2 Serve You • Live Soil • Sticks And Stones • Empty The Clip • No Mercy • Playa Hater			

FLIPMODE SQUAD '98
Rap collective from New York City: **Busta Rhymes**, **Rampage**, Rah-Digga, Serious and Spliff Star.

10/3/98	3	18	●	**The Imperial**	15	$8	Elektra 62238
				To My People • Settin' It Off • Run For Cover • I Got Your Back • This Is What Happens • Everybody On The Line Outside • Last Night • Where You Think You Goin' • We Got U Opin • Straight Spittin • Money Talks • **Cha Cha Cha** *[61]* • Hit Em Wit Da Heat • Do For Self • Everything			

FLOATERS, The '77
Vocal group from Detroit: brothers Paul and Ralph Mitchell, Charles Clark, Larry Cunningham and Jonathan Murray.

6/25/77	**❶**³	25	▲	**1 The Floaters**	10	$10	ABC 1030
				Float On *[1]* • **You Don't Have To Say You Love Me** *[28]* • Got To Find A Way • I Bet You Get The One You Love • Everything Happens For A Reason • Take One Step At A Time • No Stronger Love • I Am So Glad I Took My Time			
4/22/78	27	9		**2 Magic**	131	$10	ABC 1047

FLOYD, Eddie '70
Born on 6/25/35 in Montgomery, Alabama; raised in Detroit.

8/16/69	49	3		**1 Rare Stamps**		$25	Stax 2011
7/18/70	41	5		**2 California Girl**		$25	Stax 2029

DEBUT	PEAK	WKS	Gold	Album Title	Pop #	$	Label & Number

FLOYD, King '71
Born on 2/13/45 in New Orleans. Singer/songwriter.

| 6/5/71 | **19** | 10 | | King Floyd .... | 130 | $15 | Chimneyville 9047 |

FORCE M.D.'S '87
Vocal group from Staten Island, New York: brothers Steve and Antoine Lundy, Jesse Lee Daniels, Trisco Pearson and Charles Richard "Mercury" Nelson. Daniels left in 1987. Nelson died of a heart attack on 3/10/95 (age 30). M.D.: Musical Diversity.

11/17/84	**28**	23		1 Love Letters	185	$8	Tommy Boy 1003
2/1/86	**14**	39		2 Chillin'..	69	$8	Tommy Boy 1010
8/15/87	**12**	38		3 Touch And Go....................................	67	$8	Tommy Boy 25631
9/29/90	**74**	16		4 Step To Me		$8	Tommy Boy 25893

FORD, Pennye '85
Born on 6/11/64 in Cincinnati. Member of The S.O.S. Band (1987-89) and Snap!.

| 2/2/85 | **39** | 8 | | Pennye... | | $8 | Total Exp. 5704 |

FOREIGNER '85
British-American rock group: Lou Gramm (vocals), Mick Jones (guitar), Rick Wills (bass) and Dennis Elliott (drums).

| 3/2/85 | **49** | 11 | ▲² | Agent Provocateur .... | 4 | $8 | Atlantic 81999 |

FOR LOVERS ONLY '94
Male vocal trio: Terry Weeks (from Florida), DeFrantz Forrest (from Southbend, Indiana) and Michael Dickerson (from Arkansas).

| 5/28/94 | **78** | 1 | | For Lovers Only .... | | $8 | Motown 6371 |

FOR REAL '94
Female vocal group from Los Angeles: Josina Elder, Wendi Williams, LaTanyia Baldwin and Necia Bray.

| 4/30/94 | **80** | 4 | | 1 It's A Natural Thang | | $8 | A&M 0156 |
| 11/2/96 | **100** | 1 | | 2 Free | | $8 | Rowdy 37013 |

FORTÉ, John '98
Born in Brooklyn, New York. Male rapper.

| 8/1/98 | **28** | 6 | | Poly Sci .... | 84 | $8 | Ruffhouse 68639 |

4 BY FOUR '87
Vocal group from Queens, New York: brothers Damen and Lance Heyward, with Steve Gray and Jeraude Jackson.

| 6/27/87 | **28** | 29 | | 4 By Four .... | 141 | $8 | Capitol 12560 |

415 '91
Rap trio from Oakland: Richie Rich, D-Loc and D.J. Daryl. 415 is their area code.

| 11/30/91 | **90** | 3 | | Nu Niggaz On Tha Blokkk................... | | $8 | Priority 57163 |

FOURPLAY '93
All-star group: Lee Ritenour (guitar), Bob James (keyboards), Nathan East (bass) and Harvey Mason (drums).

10/26/91+	**16**	28	●	1 Fourplay .... [I]	97	$8	Warner 26656
9/4/93	**15**	41	●	2 Between The Sheets............................ [I]	70	$8	Warner 45340
12/2/95	**79**	6	●	3 Elixir .... [I]	90	$8	Warner 45922
6/27/98	**44**	11		4 .... [I]	146	$8	Warner 46921

4 P.M. (FOR POSITIVE MUSIC) '95
Male vocal group from Baltimore: brothers Rene and Roberto Pena, with Larry McFarland and Marty Ware.

| 3/4/95 | **96** | 1 | | Now's The Time .... | 126 | $8 | Next Plateau 828579 |

4.0 '97
Pronounced: Four Point Oh. Vocal group from Atlanta: Tony Hightower, Sammy Crumbley, Jason Sylvain and Ron Jackson.

| 10/11/97 | **100** | 1 | | 4.0... | | $8 | Savvy 9034 |

FOUR TOPS ★13★ '65
Legendary vocal group from Detroit: Levi Stubbs (lead singer), Renaldo Benson, Lawrence Payton and Abdul Fakir. Group has had no personnel changes since its formation. Stubbs is the brother of Joe Stubbs (of 100 Proof Aged In Soul). Stubbs was the voice of the killer plant in the 1986 movie *Little Shop of Horrors*. Payton died on 6/20/97 (age 59). Group inducted into the Rock and Roll Hall of Fame in 1990.

1)Four Tops 2)Four Tops Live! 3)The Four Tops Greatest Hits 4)Four Tops Reach Out 5)Still Waters Run Deep

| 2/27/65 | **❶³** | 18 | | 1 Four Tops | 63 | $30 | Motown 622 |

Baby I Need Your Loving [11] • Without The One You Love (Life's Not Worth While) [43] • Where Did You Go • Ask The Lonely [9] • Your Love Is Amazing • Sad Souvenirs • Don't Turn Away • Tea House In China Town • Left With A Broken Heart • Love Has Gone • Call On Me

| 12/4/65 | **3** | 20 | | 2 Four Tops Second Album | 20 | $25 | Motown 634 |

I Can't Help Myself [1] • Love Feels Like Fire • Is There Anything That I Can Do • Something About You [9] • It's The Same Old Song [2] • Helpless • Just As Long As You Need Me • Darling, I Hum Our Song • I Like Everything About You • Since You've Been Gone • Stay In My Lonely Arms • I'm Grateful

| 8/27/66 | **3** | 18 | | 3 4 Tops On Top | 32 | $25 | Motown 647 |

I Got A Feeling • Brenda • Loving You Is Sweeter Than Ever [12] • Shake Me, Wake Me (When It's Over) [5] • Until You Love Someone • There's No Love Left • Matchmaker • Michelle • In The Still Of The Night • Bluesette • Quiet Nights Of Quiet Stars • Then

| 12/17/66+ | **❶¹** | 33 | | 4 Four Tops Live! | [L] | 17 | $25 | Motown 654 |

recorded at the Roostertail Club in Detroit
It's The Same Old Song • It's Not Unusual • Baby I Need Your Loving • Reach Out I'll Be There • I'll Turn To Stone • I Left My Heart In San Francisco • You Can't Hurry Love • Ask The Lonely • Climb Ev'ry Mountain • The Girl From Ipanema • If I Had A Hammer • I Can't Help Myself • I Like Everything About You

| 4/8/67 | **15** | 10 | | 5 4 Tops On Broadway......................... | 79 | $25 | Motown 657 |

DEBUT	PEAK	WKS	Gold	Album Title	Pop #	$	Label & Number
				FOUR TOPS — Cont'd			
8/12/67	3	52		6 Four Tops Reach Out	11	$25	Motown 660

Reach Out I'll Be There [1] • Walk Away Renee [15] • 7 Rooms Of Gloom [10] • If I Were A Carpenter [17] • Last Train To Clarksville • I'll Turn To Stone [50] • I'm A Believer • Standing In The Shadows Of Love [2] • Bernadette [3] • Cherish • Wonderful Baby • What Else Is There To Do (But Think About You)

DEBUT	PEAK	WKS	Gold	Album Title	Pop #	$	Label & Number
9/30/67	2⁵	46		7 The Four Tops Greatest Hits [G]	4	$20	Motown 662

Baby I Need Your Loving [11] • It's The Same Old Song [2] • Reach Out I'll Be There [1] • Ask The Lonely [9] • Standing In The Shadows Of Love [2] • Loving You Is Sweeter Than Ever [12] • I Can't Help Myself [1] • Without The One You Love (Life's Not Worth While) [43] • 7 Rooms Of Gloom [10] • Something About You [9] • Bernadette [3] • Shake Me, Wake Me (When It's Over) [5]

DEBUT	PEAK	WKS	Gold	Album Title	Pop #	$	Label & Number
10/5/68	7	19		8 Yesterday's Dreams	91	$20	Motown 669

Yesterday's Dreams [31] • Can't Seem To Get You Out Of My Mind • I'm In A Different World [23] • We've Got A Strong Love (On Our Side) • By The Time I Get To Phoenix • Remember When • Sunny • Never My Love • Daydream Believer • Once Upon A Time • The Sweetheart Tree • A Place In The Sun

DEBUT	PEAK	WKS	Gold	Album Title	Pop #	$	Label & Number
7/19/69	18	31		9 Four Tops Now!	74	$20	Motown 675
12/13/69+	30	11		10 Soul Spin	163	$20	Motown 695
4/4/70	3	48		11 Still Waters Run Deep	21	$20	Motown 704

Still Water (Love) [4] • Reflections • It's All In The Game [6] • Everybody's Talking • Love Is The Answer • I Wish I Were Your Mirror • Elusive Butterfly • Bring Me Together • L.A. (My Town) • Still Water (Peace)

DEBUT	PEAK	WKS	Gold	Album Title	Pop #	$	Label & Number
10/24/70	20	8		12 Changing Times	109	$20	Motown 721
10/31/70	18	19		13 The Magnificent 7	113	$20	Motown 717
				SUPREMES & FOUR TOPS			
6/26/71	18	6		14 The Return Of The Magnificent Seven	154	$20	Motown 736
				SUPREMES & FOUR TOPS			
10/9/71	22	9		15 Four Tops Greatest Hits, Vol. 2 [G]	106	$20	Motown 740
2/5/72	21	4		16 Dynamite	160	$20	Motown 745
				SUPREMES & FOUR TOPS			
10/14/72	4	15		17 Nature Planned It	50	$20	Motown 748

I Am Your Man • (It's The Way) Nature Planned It [8] • I'll Never Change • She's An Understanding Woman • I Can't Quit Your Love • Walk With Me, Talk With Me, Darling • Medley: Hey Man/We Got To Get You A Woman • You Gotta Forget Him Darling • If You Let Me • Happy (Is A Bumpy Road) • How Will I Forget You

DEBUT	PEAK	WKS	Gold	Album Title	Pop #	$	Label & Number
11/18/72+	6	29		18 Keeper Of The Castle	33	$12	Dunhill/ABC 50129

Keeper Of The Castle [7] • Ain't No Woman (Like The One I've Got) [2] • Put A Little Love Away • Turn On The Light Of Your Love • When Tonight Meets Tomorrow • Love Music • Remember What I Told You To Forget • (I Think I Must Be) Dreaming • The Good Lord Knows • Jubilee With Soul • Love Makes You Human

DEBUT	PEAK	WKS	Gold	Album Title	Pop #	$	Label & Number
5/19/73	35	6		19 The Best Of The 4 Tops [G]	103	$15	Motown 764 [2]
9/22/73	8	31		20 Main Street People	66	$12	Dunhill/ABC 50144

I Just Can't Get You Out Of My Mind [18] • It Won't Be The First Time • Sweet Understanding Love [10] • Am I My Brothers Keeper • Are You Man Enough [2] • Whenever There's Blue • Too Little Too Late • Peace Of Mind • One Woman Man • Main Street People

DEBUT	PEAK	WKS	Gold	Album Title	Pop #	$	Label & Number
4/27/74	22	21		21 Meeting Of The Minds	118	$12	Dunhill/ABC 50166
8/24/74	42	9		22 Anthology [K]	203	$25	Motown 809 [3]
11/9/74	29	8		23 Live & In Concert [L]	92	$12	Dunhill/ABC 50188
6/14/75	24	6		24 Night Lights Harmony	148	$12	ABC 862
10/23/76	26	16		25 Catfish	124	$12	ABC 968
11/5/77	54	5		26 The Show Must Go On		$12	ABC 1014
12/16/78	73	2		27 At The Top	208	$12	ABC 1092
9/12/81	5	23		28 Tonight!	37	$10	Casablanca 7258

When She Was My Girl [1] • Don't Walk Away • Tonight I'm Gonna Love You All Over [32] • Who's Right, Who's Wrong • Let Me Set You Free [71] • From A Distance • Something To Remember • All I Do • I'll Never Ever Leave Again

DEBUT	PEAK	WKS	Gold	Album Title	Pop #	$	Label & Number
9/18/82	45	7		29 One More Mountain		$10	Casablanca 7266
11/12/83	47	11		30 Back Where I Belong	202	$10	Motown 6066
6/29/85	33	18		31 Magic	140	$8	Motown 6130
9/24/88	66	25		32 Indestructible	149	$8	Arista 8492
				IV XAMPLE '95			

R&B group from Los Angeles: Lucious, Bobby C, Andre Allen and Runni Rae.

DEBUT	PEAK	WKS	Gold	Album Title	Pop #	$	Label & Number
5/13/95	69	8		For Example		$8	MCA 11220
				FOX, Samantha '89			

Born on 4/15/66 in England. Dance singer. Former topless model.

DEBUT	PEAK	WKS	Gold	Album Title	Pop #	$	Label & Number
12/17/88+	41	16	●	I Wanna Have Some Fun	37	$8	Jive 1150
				FOXX, Inez & Charlie '68			

Brother-sister vocal duo from Greensboro, North Carolina. Charlie died of leukemia on 9/18/98 (age 58).

DEBUT	PEAK	WKS	Gold	Album Title	Pop #	$	Label & Number
3/16/68	29	2		Inez & Charlie Foxx's Greatest Hits, Past & Present		$40	Dynamo 8002
				FOXX, Jamie '94			

Actor/comedian/singer. Cast member of TV's In Living Color. Acted in several movies.

DEBUT	PEAK	WKS	Gold	Album Title	Pop #	$	Label & Number
8/6/94	12	16		Peep This	78	$8	Fox 66436
				FOXX, Redd '76			

Born John Elroy Sanford on 12/9/22 in St. Louis. Died of a heart attack on 10/11/91 (age 68). Comedian/actor. Star of TV's Sanford & Son.

DEBUT	PEAK	WKS	Gold	Album Title	Pop #	$	Label & Number
1/3/76	14	14		You Gotta Wash Your Ass [C]	87	$10	Atlantic 18157
				FOXY '78			

Latino dance group from Miami: Ish Ledesma (vocals, guitar), Richie Puente (percussion), Charlie Murciano (keyboards), Arnold Pasiero (bass) and Joe Galdo (drums). Puente is son of famous bandleader Tito Puente.

DEBUT	PEAK	WKS	Gold	Album Title	Pop #	$	Label & Number
7/22/78	3	29		1 Get Off	12	$12	Dash 30005

Tena's Song • Ready For Love • Madamoiselle • You • Get Off [1] • Lucky Me • Goin' Back To You • It's Happening

DEBUT	PEAK	WKS	Gold	Album Title	Pop #	$	Label & Number
4/21/79	10	16		2 Hot Numbers	29	$12	Dash 30010

Head Hunter • Devil Boogie • Give Me A Break • Nobody Will Ever Take Me Away From You • Chicapbon-Chicapbon • Hot Number [4] • Lady • Give Me That Groove • Lady Of The Streets

DEBUT	PEAK	WKS	Gold	Album Title	Pop #	$	Label & Number

FRANKIE   **'97**
Born George Franklin Jackson in Washington DC.

9/27/97   93   1   **My Heart Belongs To You** .... $8   Chucklife/Epic 67634

FRANKLIN, Aretha ★2★   **'68**
Born on 3/25/42 in Memphis; raised in Buffalo and Detroit. Revered as the all-time Queen of Soul Music. Daughter of famous gospel preacher Rev. Cecil L. Franklin, pastor of Detroit's New Bethel Baptist Church. Signed to Columbia Records in 1960 by legendary talent scout John Hammond. Dramatic turn in style and success after signing with Atlantic in 1966 and working with producer Jerry Wexler. Her sisters Carolyn and Erma also recorded. Married to her manager/cowriter Ted White, 1961-69, and actor Glynn Turman, 1978-84. Won Grammy's Living Legends Award (1990) and Lifetime Achievement Award (1994). Inducted into the Rock and Roll Hall of Fame in 1987.

1)Aretha Now 2)Aretha: Lady Soul 3)I Never Loved A Man The Way I Love You 4)Jump To It 5)Aretha Live At Fillmore West

1/30/65	9	1		1 **Runnin' Out Of Fools**	84	$30	Columbia 9081

Mockingbird • How Glad I Am • Walk On By • Every Little Bit Hurts • The Shoop Shoop Song (It's In His Kiss) • You'll Lose A Good Thing • I Can't Wait Until I See My Baby's Face • It's Just A Matter Of Time • **Runnin' Out Of Fools** *[57]* • My Guy • Two Sides Of Love • One Room Paradise

8/7/65	8	3		2 **Yeah!!!**	[L] 101	$25	Columbia 9151

This Could Be The Start Of Something • Once In A Lifetime • Misty • More • There Is No Greater Love • Muddy Water • If I Had A Hammer • Impossible • Today I Love Ev'rybody • Without The One You Love • Trouble In Mind • Love For Sale

7/30/66	8	8		3 **Soul Sister**	132	$25	Columbia 9321

Until You Were Gone • You Made Me Love You (I Didn't Want To Do It) • Follow Your Heart • Ol' Man River • Sweet Bitter Love • A Mother's Love • Swanee • (No, No) I'm Losing You • **Take A Look** *[28]* • **Can't Just See Me** *[96]* • Cry Like A Baby *[27]*

4/8/67	❶[14]	66	●	4 **I Never Loved A Man The Way I Love You**	2[3]	$15	Atlantic 8139

Respect *[1]* • Drown In My Own Tears • I Never Loved A Man (The Way I Love You) *[1]* • Soul Serenade • Don't Let Me Lose This Dream • Baby, Baby, Baby • Dr. Feelgood • Good Times • **Do Right Woman-Do Right Man** *[37]* • Save Me • A Change Is Gonna Come

6/17/67	10	11		5 **Aretha Franklin's Greatest Hits**	[G] 94	$20	Columbia 9473

Rock-A-Bye Your Baby With A Dixie Melody • **Today I Sing The Blues** *[10]* • **Cry Like A Baby** *[27]* • Without The One You Love • **One Step Ahead** *[18]* • Evil Gal Blues • **Runnin' Out Of Fools** *[57]* • Try A Little Tenderness • Sweet Bitter Love • God Bless The Child • If Ever I Would Leave You • Elusive Butterfly

8/26/67	❶[5]	28		6 **Aretha Arrives**	5	$15	Atlantic 8150

(I Can't Get No) Satisfaction • You Are My Sunshine • Never Let Me Go • 96 Tears • Prove It • Night Life • That's Life • I Wonder • Ain't Nobody (Gonna Turn Me Around) • Going Down Slow • **Baby I Love You** *[1]*

11/11/67	22	4		7 **Take A Look**	[E] 173	$20	Columbia 9554
2/24/68	❶[16]	53	●	8 **Aretha: Lady Soul**	2[2]	$15	Atlantic 8176

Chain Of Fools *[1]* • Money Won't Change You • People Get Ready • Niki Hoeky • **A Natural Woman (You Make Me Feel Like)** *[2]* • **(Sweet Sweet Baby) Since You've Been Gone** *[1]* • Good To Me As I Am To You • Come Back Baby • Groovin' • Ain't No Way *[9]*

7/13/68	❶[17]	35	●	9 **Aretha Now**	3	$15	Atlantic 8186

Think *[1]* • **I Say A Little Prayer** *[3]* • **See Saw** *[9]* • Night Time Is The Right Time • **You Send Me** *[28]* • You're A Sweet Sweet Man • I Take What I Want • Hello Sunshine • A Change • I Can't See Myself Leaving You *[3]*

11/30/68	2[3]	21		10 **Aretha In Paris**	[L] 13	$15	Atlantic 8207

recorded on May 7, 1968 at the Olympia Theatre in Paris
(I Can't Get No) Satisfaction • Don't Let Me Lose This Dream • Soul Serenade • Night Life • Baby, I Love You • Groovin' • A Natural Woman (You Make Me Feel Like) • Come Back Baby • Dr. Feelgood • (Sweet Sweet Baby) Since You've Been Gone • I Never Loved A Man (The Way I Love You) • Chain Of Fools • Respect

2/15/69	❶[4]	32		11 **Aretha Franklin: Soul '69**	15	$15	Atlantic 8212

Rock-A-Bye Your Baby With A Dixie Melody • Today I Sing The Blues • Cry Like A Baby • Without The One You Love • One Step Ahead • Evil Gal Blues • Runnin' Out Of Fools • Try A Little Tenderness • Sweet Bitter Love • God Bless The Child • If Ever I Would Leave You • Elusive Butterfly

4/26/69	29	9		12 **Soft And Beautiful**	[E]	$15	Columbia 9776
7/19/69	❶[4]	36		13 **Aretha's Gold**	[G] 18	$15	Atlantic 8227

I Never Loved A Man (The Way I Love You) *[1]* • Do Right Woman-Do Right Man *[37]* • **Respect** *[1]* • Dr. Feelgood • Baby I Love You *[1]* • A Natural Woman (You Make Me Feel Like) *[2]* • Chain Of Fools *[1]* • **(Sweet Sweet Baby) Since You've Been Gone** *[1]* • Ain't No Way *[9]* • Think *[1]* • You Send Me *[28]* • The House That Jack Built *[2]* • I Say A Little Prayer *[3]* • See Saw *[9]*

2/14/70	2[3]	31		14 **This Girl's In Love With You**	17	$15	Atlantic 8248

Son Of A Preacher Man • Share Your Love With Me *[1]* • Dark End Of The Street • Let It Be • **Eleanor Rigby** *[5]* • This Girl's In Love With You • It Ain't Fair • **The Weight** *[3]* • **Call Me** *[1]* • Sit Down And Cry

9/19/70	2[1]	26		15 **Spirit In The Dark**	25	$15	Atlantic 8265

Don't Play That Song *[1]* • **The Thrill Is Gone** *[flip]* • Pullin' • You And Me *[flip]* • **Spirit In The Dark** *[3]* • When The Battle Is Over • One Way Ticket • Try Matty's • That's All I Want From You • Oh No Not My Baby • Why I Sing The Blues

6/5/71	❶[5]	37	●	16 **Aretha Live At Fillmore West**	[L] 7	$15	Atlantic 7205

Respect • Love The One You're With • Bridge Over Troubled Water • Eleanor Rigby • Make It With You • Don't Play That Song • Dr. Feelgood • Spirit In The Dark • Reach Out And Touch (Somebody's Hand)

10/2/71	3	25		17 **Aretha's Greatest Hits**	[G] 19	$15	Atlantic 8295

Spanish Harlem *[1]* • Chain Of Fools *[1]* • Don't Play That Song *[1]* • I Say A Little Prayer *[3]* • Dr. Feelgood • Let It Be • Do Right Woman-Do Right Man *[37]* • Bridge Over Troubled Water *[1]* • Respect *[1]* • Baby I Love You *[1]* • A Natural Woman (You Make Me Feel Like) *[2]* • I Never Loved A Man (The Way I Love You) *[1]* • You're All I Need To Get By *[3]* • Call Me *[1]*

2/19/72	2[6]	27	●	18 **Young, Gifted & Black**	11	$15	Atlantic 7213

Oh Me Oh My (I'm A Fool For You Baby) *[9]* • Day Dreaming *[1]* • Rock Steady *[2]* • Young, Gifted And Black • All The King's Horses *[7]* • A Brand New Me • **April Fools** *[flip]* • I've Been Loving You Too Long • First Snow In Kokomo • The Long And Winding Road • Didn't I (Blow Your Mind This Time) • Border Song (Holy Moses) *[5]*

6/24/72	2[1]	19	▲2	19 **Amazing Grace**	[L] 7	$15	Atlantic 906 [2]

recorded at the New Temple Missionary Baptist Church in Los Angeles
Mary, Don't You Weep • Medley: Precious Lord, Take My Hand/You've Got A Friend • Old Landmark • Give Yourself To Jesus • How I Got Over • What A Friend We Have In Jesus • Amazing Grace • Precious Memories • Climbing Higher Mountains • God Will Take Care Of You • **Wholy Holy** *[49]* • You'll Never Walk Alone • Never Grow Old

DEBUT	PEAK	WKS	Gold	Album Title	Pop #	$	Label & Number
				FRANKLIN, Aretha — Cont'd			
7/14/73	2³	21		20 **Hey Now Hey (The Other Side Of The Sky)**	30	$12	Atlantic 7265
				Hey Now Hey (The Other Side Of The Sky) • Somewhere • So Swell When You're Well • **Angel** [1] • Sister From Texas • Mister Spain • That's The Way I Feel About Cha • Moody's Mood • Just Right Tonight			
3/16/74	❶¹	38		21 **Let Me In Your Life**	14	$12	Atlantic 7292
				Let Me In Your Life • Every Natural Thing • Ain't Nothing Like The Real Thing [6] • I'm In Love [1] • Until You Come Back To Me (That's What I'm Gonna Do) [1] • The Masquerade Is Over • With Pen In Hand • Oh Baby • Eight Days On The Road • If You Don't Think • A Song For You			
12/28/74+	6	12		22 **With Everything I Feel In Me**	57	$12	Atlantic 18116
				Without Love [6] • Don't Go Breaking My Heart • When You Get Right Down To It • You'll Never Get To Heaven • **With Everything I Feel In Me** [20] • I Love Every Little Thing About You • Sing It Again - Say It Again • All Of These Things • You Move Me			
11/22/75	9	14		23 **You**	83	$12	Atlantic 18151
				Mr. D.J. (5 For The D.J.) [13] • It Only Happens (When I Look At You) • I'm Not Strong Enough To Love You Again • Walk Softly • You Make My Life • Without You • The Sha-La Bandit • **You** [15] • You Got All The Aces • As Long As You Are There			
6/19/76	❶¹	28	●	24 **Sparkle**	[S] 18	$12	Atlantic 18176
				Sparkle • **Something He Can Feel** [1] • Hooked On Your Love [flip] • Look Into Your Heart [10] • I Get High • Jump [17] • Loving You Baby • Rock With Me			
12/25/76+	29	8		25 **Ten Years Of Gold**	[G] 135	$12	Atlantic 18204
6/18/77	6	23		26 **Sweet Passion**	49	$12	Atlantic 19102
				Break It To Me Gently [1] • When I Think About You [16] • What I Did For Love • No One Could Ever Love You More • A Tender Touch • Touch Me Up • Sunshine Will Never Be The Same • Meadows Of Springtime • I've Got The Music In Me • Sweet Passion			
5/13/78	12	13		27 **Almighty Fire**	63	$12	Atlantic 19161
10/6/79	25	10		28 **La Diva**	146	$12	Atlantic 19248
10/25/80+	6	37		29 **Aretha**	47	$10	Arista 9538
				Come To Me [39] • Can't Turn You Loose • United Together [3] • Take Me With You • Whatever It Is • What A Fool Believes [17] • Together Again • Love Me Forever • School Days • Look To The Rainbow			
9/5/81	4	23		30 **Love All The Hurt Away**	36	$10	Arista 9552
				Love All The Hurt Away [6] • Hold On I'm Comin' • Living In The Streets • There's A Star For Everyone • You Can't Always Get What You Want • It's My Turn [29] • Truth And Honesty • Search On • Whole Lot Of Me • Kind Of Man			
8/14/82	❶⁷	38	●	31 **Jump To It**	23	$10	Arista 9602
				Jump To It [1] • Love Me Right [22] • If She Don't Want Your Lovin' • This Is For Real [63] • (It's Just) Your Love • I Wanna Make It Up To You • It's Your Thing • Just My Daydream			
8/6/83	4	26		32 **Get It Right**	36	$10	Arista 8019
				Get It Right [1] • Pretender • Every Girl (Wants My Guy) [7] • When You Love Me Like That • I Wish It Would Rain • Better Friends Than Lovers • I Got Your Love • Giving In			
7/27/85	3	51	▲	33 **Who's Zoomin' Who?**	13	$8	Arista 8286
				Freeway Of Love [1] • Another Night [9] • Sweet Bitter Love • Who's Zoomin' Who [2] • Sisters Are Doin' It For Themselves [66] • Until You Say You Love Me • Ain't Nobody Ever Loved You [30] • Push • Integrity			
11/15/86+	7	39	●	34 **Aretha**	32	$8	Arista 8442
				Jimmy Lee [2] • I Knew You Were Waiting (For Me) [5] • Do You Still Remember • Jumpin' Jack Flash [20] • Rock-A-Lott [25] • An Angel Cries • He'll Come Along • If You Need My Love Tonight [88] • Look To The Rainbow			
12/26/87+	25	22		35 **One Lord, One Faith, One Baptism**	[L] 106	$10	Arista 8497 [2]
				recorded at the New Bethel Baptist Church in Detroit			
5/27/89	21	26		36 **Through The Storm**	55	$8	Arista 8572
7/27/91	28	20		37 **What You See Is What You Sweat**	153	$8	Arista 8628
1/2/93	99	1		38 **Queen of Soul: The Atlantic Recordings**	[K]	$30	Rhino 71063 [4]
				includes a 79 page booklet			
3/12/94	23	42	▲	39 **Greatest Hits (1980-1994)**	[G] 85	$8	Arista 18722
4/11/98	7	22	●	40 **A Rose Is Still A Rose**	30	$8	Arista 18987
				A Rose Is Still A Rose [5] • Never Leave You Again • In Case You Forgot • **Here We Go Again** [24] • Every Lil' Bit Hurts • In The Morning • I'll Dip • How Many Times • Watch My Back • Love Pang • The Woman			
				FRANKLIN, Kirk **'96**			
				Born in 1970 in Dallas. Gospel singer/choir leader.			
12/24/94+	6	108	▲	1 **Kirk Franklin and the family**	[L] 58	$8	GospoCentric 2119
				recorded on July 25, 1992 at Grace Temple Church in Fort Worth, Texas			
				Why We Sing • He's Able • Silver & Gold • Call On The Lord • Real Love • He Can Handle It • A Letter From My Friend • The Family Worship Medley • Speak To Me • Till We Meet Again			
5/11/96	3	73	▲	2 **Whatcha Lookin' 4**	[L] 23	$8	GospoCentric 72127
				KIRK FRANKLIN and The Family (above 2)			
				Savior More Than Life • Whatcha Lookin' 4 • Melodies From Heaven • Conquerors • Don't Take Your Joy Away • When I Think About Jesus • Mama's Song • Jesus Paid It All • I Love You Jesus • Washed Away • Where The Spirit Is • Let Me Touch You • Anything 4 U			
10/10/98	4	43↑	▲	3 **The Nu Nation Project**		$8	GospoCentric 90178
				Revolution [59] • Lean On Me [26] • Something About The Name Jesus • Riverside • He Loves Me • Gonna Be A Lovely Day • Praise Joint • Hold Me Now • You Are • If You've Been Delivered • Smile Again • Love • My Desire • Blessing In The Storm • I Can			
				FRANKLIN, Rodney **'80**			
				Born on 9/16/58 in Berkeley, California. Jazz pianist.			
4/5/80	25	18		1 **You'll Never Know**	[I] 104	$10	Columbia 36122
11/29/80	62	3		2 **Rodney Franklin**	[I] 207	$10	Columbia 36747
12/5/81	47	8		3 **Endless Flight**	204	$10	Columbia 37154
12/11/82+	45	22		4 **Learning To Love**	190	$10	Columbia 38198
3/3/84	54	9		5 **Marathon**	187	$10	Columbia 38953
				FRANKS, Michael **'82**			
				Born on 9/18/44 in La Jolla, California. Singer/songwriter.			
2/6/82	30	16		**Objects Of Desire**	45	$10	Warner 3648

FRAZE '97
Born in Miami. Male rapper.

4/26/97	82	4	Ruff Ride - The Album..	$8	Before Dawn 2011

FREAK NASTY '97
Born Carlito Timmons in Puerto Rico; raised in New Orleans. Male rapper.

7/15/95	92	1	1 Freak Nasty		$8	Hotlanta 4195
2/1/97	68	22	2 Controversee...That's Life...And That's The Way It Is..............	132	$8	Power 2111

FREEMAN, Russ, & The Rippingtons '94
Born on 2/11/60 in Nashville. Guitarist/songwriter/producer. Leader of jazz-pop group, The Rippingtons.

4/23/94	73	5	1 The Benoit/Freeman Project..	[I]	118	$8	GRP 9739
9/17/94	62	1	2 Sahara	[I]	192	$8	GRP 9781
3/16/96	77	3	3 Brave New World	[I]		$8	GRP 9835

FREE MOVEMENT, The '72
Vocal group from Los Angeles: brothers Adrian and Claude Jefferson, Godoy Colbert, Cheryl Conley, Jennifer Gates and Josephine Brown.

2/12/72	26	7	I've Found Someone Of My Own	167	$15	Columbia 31136

FREESTYLE '90
Techno group from Miami: Garfield Baker, Byron Smith, Harris Vereen and Darryl Hawkins.

7/21/90	62	10	Freestyle		$8	Pandisc 8810

FRESH KID ICE '92
Born Christopher Wong Won in Trinidad, West Indies. Male rapper. Member of 2 Live Crew.

9/26/92	56	10	The Chinaman		$8	Effect 3007

FRIENDS OF DISTINCTION, The '70
Vocal group from Los Angeles: Floyd Butler, Harry Elston, Jessica Cleaves and Barbara Jean Love.

5/10/69	10	43	1 Grazin'	35	$15	RCA Victor 4149

Grazing In The Grass [5] • I've Never Found A Girl (To Love Me Like You Do) • I Really Hope You Do • Sweet Young Thing Like You • Going In Circles [3] • Eli's Comin' • Help Yourself (To All Of My Lovin') • Baby I Could Be So Good At Loving You • And I Love Him • Peaceful • Lonesome Mood

10/25/69	14	15	2 Highly Distinct	173	$15	RCA Victor 4212
4/4/70	9	15	3 Real Friends	68	$15	RCA Victor 4313

Love Or Let Me Be Lonely [13] • Lady Mae • It Don't Matter To Me • My Mind Is A Camera • Out In The Country • Any Way You Want Me • Crazy Mary • Just A Little Lovin' • Long Time Comin' My Way • On & On

11/28/70	42	5	4 Whatever	179	$15	RCA Victor 4408

FROST — see KID FROST

FUGEES '96
Hip-hop trio from East Orange, New Jersey: Lauryn Hill, Wyclef Jean and Pras Michel. Fugees is short for refugees.

7/2/94	62	14	1 Blunted On Reality		$8	Ruffhouse 57462

FUGEES (TRANZLATOR CREW)

3/2/96	❶[8]	63	▲[6]	2 The Score	1[4]	$8	Ruffhouse 67147

How Many Mics • Ready Or Not • Zealots • The Beast • Fu-Gee-La [13] • Family Business • Killing Me Softly • The Score • The Mask • Cowboys • No Woman, No Cry • Manifest • Mista Mista

12/14/96	50	11	3 Bootleg Versions	[K]	127	$8	Ruffhouse 67904

FULL BLOODED '98
Male rapper from New Orleans.

12/19/98	20	4	Memorial Day	112	$8	No Limit 50027

FULL FORCE '86
Rap group from Brooklyn, New York: brothers Brian, Paul Anthony and Lou George, with their cousins Gerry Charles, Junior Clark and Curt Bedeau. Assembled and produced Lisa Lisa & Cult Jam. Production work for numerous others.

11/9/85+	29	41	1 Full Force	160	$8	Columbia 40117
8/16/86	19	28	2 Full Force get busy 1 time!	141	$8	Columbia 40395
11/28/87+	28	27	3 Guess Who's Comin' To The Crib?	126	$8	Columbia 40894
9/16/89	61	21	4 Smoove...		$8	Columbia 45216

FULSON, Lowell '76
Born on 3/31/21 in Tulsa, Oklahoma. Died on 3/7/99 (age 77). Blues singer/guitarist.

2/21/76	56	3	The Ol' Blues Singer		$15	Granite 1006

FUNKADELIC '78
★69★

Ensemble of nearly 40 musicians assembled by George Clinton that also recorded as Parliament. Members included brothers Phelps and William "Bootsy" Collins, Eddie Hazel, Bernie Worrell and Frank Waddy. Singers Clarence "Fuzzy" Haskins, Calvin Simon and Grady Thomas split from Clinton and recorded the 1981 album Connections & Disconnections (see #15 below). Parliament/Funkadelic inducted into the Rock and Roll Hall of Fame in 1997.

1)One Nation Under A Groove 2)Uncle Jam Wants You 3)Funkadelic

3/28/70	8	30	1 Funkadelic	126	$50	Westbound 2000

also see #10 below
Mommy, What's A Funkadelic? • I'll Bet You [22] • Music For My Mother [50] • I Got A Thing, You Got A Thing, Everybody's Got A Thing [30] • Good Old Music • Qualify & Satisfy • What Is Soul

11/7/70	11	10	2 Free Your Mind...And Your Ass Will Follow	92	$50	Westbound 2001
8/7/71	14	24	3 Maggot Brain	108	$50	Westbound 2007
6/24/72	22	9	4 America Eats Its Young	123	$60	Westbound 2020 [2]
7/21/73	21	20	5 Cosmic Slop	112	$50	Westbound 2022
8/10/74	13	12	6 Standing On The Verge Of Getting It On	163	$50	Westbound 1001

also see #8 below

3/8/75	50	5	7 Funkadelic's Greatest Hits	[G]		$50	Westbound 1004
4/19/75	43	4	8 Standing On The Verge Of Getting It On	[R]		$25	Westbound 208

reissue of #6 above

7/5/75	14	13	9 Let's Take It To The Stage	102	$50	Westbound 215

DEBUT	PEAK	WKS	Gold	Album Title	Pop #	$	Label & Number
				FUNKADELIC — Cont'd			
1/3/76	58	2		10 Funkadelic .... [R]		$30	Westbound 216
				reissue of #1 above			
10/2/76	14	15		11 Tales Of Kidd Funkadelic	103	$50	Westbound 227
11/27/76	12	14		12 Hardcore Jollies	96	$25	Warner 2973
10/7/78	❶[4]	25	▲	13 One Nation Under A Groove	16	$25	Warner 3209
				One Nation Under A Groove [1] • Groovallegiance • Who Says A Funk Band Can't Play Rock?! • Promentalshitbackwashpsychosis Enema Squad (The Doo Doo Chasers) • Into You • Cholly (Funk Getting Ready To Roll!) [43] • Maggot Brain • Lunchmeataphobia (Think! It Ain't Illegal Yet!) • P.E. Squad (Doo Doo Chasers)			
10/20/79	2[3]	19	●	14 Uncle Jam Wants You	18	$25	Warner 3371
				Freak Of The Week • (not just) Knee Deep [1] • Uncle Jam [53] • Field Maneuvers • Holly Wants To Go To California • Foot Soldiers (Star-Spangled Funky)			
3/28/81	45	8		15 Connections & Disconnections	151	$10	LAX 37087
8/29/81	41	5		16 The Electric Spanking Of War Babies	105	$25	Warner 3482
				FUNKDOOBIEST　　　　　　　　　　'93			
				Rap trio from Los Angeles: Ralph Medrano, Jason Vasquez and Tyrone Pachenco.			
5/22/93	19	11		1 Which Doobie U B?	56	$8	Epic 53212
7/22/95	35	4		2 Brothas Doobie	115	$8	Immortal 64195
2/28/98	90	2		3 Troubleshooters		$8	Buzz Tone 67550
				FUNK INC.　　　　　　　　　　'75			
				Instrumental group from Indianapolis: Steve Weakley (guitar), Bobby Watley (organ), Eugene Barr (sax), Cecil Hunt (congas) and Jimmy Munford (drums).			
2/26/72	45	4		1 Funk Inc. .... [I]	211	$12	Prestige 10031
12/22/73+	31	13		2 Superfunk .... [I]		$12	Prestige 10071
1/11/75	30	7		3 Priced To Sell .... [I]		$12	Prestige 10087
				FUNK MOBB　　　　　　　　　　'96			
				Rap trio: Mac Shawn, K-One and G-Note.			
8/3/96	46	4		It Ain't 4 Play		$8	Sick Wid' It 45006
				FU-SCHNICKENS　　　　　　　　　　'92			
				Rap trio from Brooklyn, New York: Poc Fu, Chip Fu and Moc Fu.			
3/21/92	13	36	●	1 F.U. "Don't Take It Personal"	64	$8	Jive 41472
11/12/94	19	11		2 Nervous Breakdown	81	$8	Jive 41519
				FUSE ONE　　　　　　　　　　'82			
				All-star group: George Benson, Tom Browne, Stanley Clarke, Ronnie Foster, Eric Gale, Wynton Marsalis, Ndugu, Stanley Turrentine and Dave Valentin.			
2/13/82	44	10		Silk .... [I]	139	$10	CTI 9006
				FUZZ, The　　　　　　　　　　'71			
				Female vocal trio from Washington DC: Sheila Young, Barbara Gilliam and Val Williams.			
9/18/71	43	6		The Fuzz	196	$15	Calla 2001

G

DEBUT	PEAK	WKS	Gold	Album Title	Pop #	$	Label & Number
				GABLE, Eric　　　　　　　　　　'89			
				Singer from New Orleans.			
8/12/89	25	38		1 Caught In The Act		$8	Orpheus 75603
11/9/91	44	24		2 Can't Wait To Get You Home		$8	Orpheus 47927
1/29/94	55	10		3 Process Of Elimination		$8	Orpheus 52996
				GAINES, Rosie　　　　　　　　　　'95			
				Born in Pittsburg, California. Singer/songwriter/keyboardist.			
7/1/95	99	1		Closer Than Close		$8	Motown 0462
				GALE, Eric　　　　　　　　　　'77			
				Session guitarist. Member of Fuse One and Stuff. Died of cancer on 5/25/94 (age 55).			
5/28/77	56	2		Ginseng Woman	148	$10	Columbia 34421
				GAMBINO FAMILY　　　　　　　　　　'98			
				Male rap duo from New Orleans: Gotti and Feno.			
11/7/98	3	7		Ghetto Organized	17	$8	No Limit 50718
				I'm A Baller • Childhood Years • Make'm Bleed • Desperado • Drama In My City • Trapped In A Storm • Only G's Ride • Clean Sweep • Ghetto Wayz • So Much Drama • Studio B • Young Gunz • Losing My Faith • Memories • 2 All My Thug Niggaz • Don't Cry • Mafiosos • U Neva Know			
				GAME RELATED　　　　　　　　　　'96			
2/3/96	62	2		Soak Game		$8	Big K 1234
				GANGSTA BASS ALLIANCE　　　　　　　　　　'90			
				Rap duo from Miami: James Bevelle and Rodney Robinson			
7/28/90	82	7		Work Me Down (To Da' Draws)		$8	Boomtown 3320
				GANGSTA BOO　　　　　　　　　　'98			
				Female rapper. Former member of Prophet Posse and Three 6 Mafia.			
10/17/98	15	31		Enquiring Minds	46	$8	Relativity 1685

DEBUT	PEAK	WKS	Gold	Album Title	Pop #	$	Label & Number

GANGSTA PAT   '97

1/19/91	87	5	1 #1 Suspect	$8	On Top 9005
8/12/95	98	1	2 Deadly Verses	$8	Triad 2102
2/15/97	68	2	3 Homicidal Lifestyle	$8	Triad 2114

GANG STARR   '98

Rap duo from Brooklyn, New York: Christopher "DJ Premier" Martin and Keith "Guru" Elam.

2/24/90	83	5	1 No More Mr. Nice Guy		$8	Wild Pitch 2001
2/9/91	19	28	2 Step In The Arena	121	$8	Chrysalis 21798
5/23/92	14	28	3 Daily Operation	65	$8	Chrysalis 21910
3/26/94	2[1]	22	4 Hard To Earn	25	$8	Chrysalis 28435

A Long Way To Go • **Code Of The Streets** [83] • Brainstorm • Tonz 'O' Gunz • The Planet • Aiiight Chill... • Speak Ya Clout • Dwyck • Words From The Nutcracker • **Mass Appeal** [42] • Blowin' Up The Spot • Suckas Need Bodyguards • Now You're Mine • Mostly Tha Voice • F.A.L.A. • Comin' For Datazz

4/11/98	❶[1]	22	●	5 Moment Of Truth	6	$8	Noo Trybe 45585

You Know My Steez [32] • Robbin Hood Theory • Work • Royalty • Above The Clouds • JFK 2 LAX • Itz A Set Up • Moment Of Truth • B.I. Vs. Friendship • **The Militia** [68] • The Rep Grows Bigga • What I'm Here 4 • She Knowz What She Wantz • New York Strait Talk • My Advice 2 You • Make 'Em Pay • The Mall • Betrayal • Next Time • In Memory Of...

GANKSTA NIP   '93

Born Rowdy Lewayne on 8/28/69 in Houston. Male rapper.

4/11/92	63	15	1 The South Park Psycho		$8	Rap-A-Lot 57160
7/17/93	30	12	2 Psychic Thoughts (Are What I Conceive?)	151	$8	Rap-A-Lot 53860
3/9/96	32	5	3 Psychotic Genius		$8	Rap-A-Lot 41335
7/18/98	57	3	4 Interview With A Killa		$8	Rap-A-Lot 45967

GAP BAND, The ★49★   '82

Funk trio of brothers from Tulsa, Oklahoma: Ronnie (vocals, horns, keyboards), Robert (vocals, bass) and **Charlie Wilson** (vocals, drums). Named for three streets in Tulsa: Greenwood, Archer and Pine.

1)Gap Band IV 2)The Gap Band III 3)Gap Band VI

4/28/79	10	26		1 The Gap Band	77	$10	Mercury 3758

Shake [4] • You Can Count On Me • **Open Up Your Mind (Wide)** [13] • Messin' With My Mind • Baby Baba Boogie • I'm In Love • Got To Get Away • I Can Sing

12/22/79+	3	31	●	2 The Gap Band II	42	$10	Mercury 3804

Steppin' (Out) [10] • No Hiding Place • **I Don't Believe You Want To Get Up And Dance (Oops, Up Side Your Head)** [4] • Nothin' Comes To Sleepers • Who Do You Call • You Are My High • **Party Lights** [36] • The Boys Are Back In Town • Gash Gash Gash

1/10/81	❶[6]	37	▲	3 The Gap Band III	16	$10	Mercury 4003

When I Look In Your Eyes • **Yearning For Your Love** [5] • Burn Rubber (Why You Wanna Hurt Me) [1] • Nothin' Comes To Sleepers • Are You Living • Sweet Caroline • **Humpin'** [60] • The Way • Gash Gash Gash

6/19/82	❶[9]	55	▲	4 Gap Band IV	14	$8	Total Exp. 3001

Early In The Morning [1] • Season's No Reason To Change • Lonely Like Me • **Outstanding** [1] • Stay With Me • **You Dropped A Bomb On Me** [2] • I Can't Get Over You • Talkin' Back

9/17/83	2[4]	39	●	5 Gap Band V - Jammin'	28	$8	Total Exp. 3004

Where Are We Going? • Shake A Leg • **I'm Ready (If You're Ready)** [74] • You're My Everything • Jammin' In America • Smile • Party Train [3] • **Jam The Motha** [16] • I Expect More • You're Something Special • Someday

1/12/85	❶[2]	40		6 Gap Band VI	58	$8	Total Exp. 5705

Video Junkie • Weak Spot • I Believe • **I Found My Baby** [8] • Beep A Freak [2] • Don't You Leave Me • **Disrespect** [18] • The Sun Don't Shine Everyday

3/23/85	46	10	▲	7 Gap Gold/Best of the Gap Band [G]	103	$8	Total Exp. 824343
1/18/86	6	32		8 Gap Band VII	159	$8	Total Exp. 5714

Desire [46] • Going In Circles [2] • **Automatic Brain** [78] • L'il Red Funkin' Hood • Ooh, What A Feeling • I Want A Real Love • Bumpin' Gum People • I Know We'll Make It • I Need Your Love

5/31/86	61	8	9 The 12" Collection [K]		$8	Mercury 826808
1/10/87	29	23	10 Gap Band 8		$8	Total Exp. 2700
9/3/88	74	6	11 Straight From The Heart		$8	Total Exp. 2710
12/2/89+	20	37	12 Round Trip	189	$8	Capitol 90799
7/13/96	54	8	13 Live & Well [L]		$8	Intersound 9183

recorded on February 29, 1996 at the Fox Theater in Atlanta

GARRETT, Siedah   '88

Born in Hollywood, California. Female singer/songwriter. Joined **The Brand New Heavies** in 1996.

8/6/88	41	12	Kiss Of Life	$8	Qwest 25689

GARY'S GANG   '79

Disco group from Queens, New York: Gary Turnier (drums) and Eric Matthew (vocals, guitar), Al Lauricella and Rino Minetti (keyboards), Bill Catalano (percussion), Bob Forman (sax) and Jay Leon (trombone).

3/24/79	27	9	Keep On Dancin'	42	$10	Columbia 35793

GAYE, Marvin ★6★   '73

Born Marvin Pentz Gay, Jr. on 4/2/39 in Washington DC. Fatally shot by his father after a quarrel on 4/1/84 (age 44) in Los Angeles. Sang in his father's Apostolic church. In vocal groups the Rainbows, the Marquees and the Moonglows. Session work as a drummer at Motown; married to Berry Gordy's sister Anna, 1961-75. First recorded under own name for Tamla in 1961. In seclusion for several months following the death of **Tammi Terrell** in 1970. Problems with drugs and the IRS led to his moving to Europe for three years. Father of **Nona Gaye**. Inducted into the Rock and Roll Hall of Fame in 1987. Won Grammy's Lifetime Achievement Award in 1996.

1)Let's Get It On 2)What's Going On 3)Midnight Love 4)Marvin Gaye Live At The London Palladium 5)Marvin Gaye Live!

DEBUT	PEAK	WKS		Album Title	Pop #	$	Label & Number
2/13/65	4	7		**1 How Sweet It Is To Be Loved By You**	128	$40	Tamla 258

You're A Wonderful One [15] • How Sweet It Is To Be Loved By You [4] • Try It Baby [15] • Baby Don't You Do It [27] • Need Your Lovin' (Want You Back) • One Of These Days • No Good Without You • Stepping Closer To Your Heart • Need Somebody • Me And My Lonely Room • Now That You've Won Me • Forever

6/25/66	8	17		**2 Moods Of Marvin Gaye**	118	$40	Tamla 266

I'll Be Doggone [1] • Little Darling, I Need You • **Take This Heart Of Mine [16]** • Hey Diddle Diddle • One More Heartache [4] • **Ain't That Peculiar [1]** • Night Life • You've Been A Long Time Coming • Your Unchanging Love [7] • You're The One For Me • I Worry 'Bout You • One For My Baby (And One For The Road)

4/22/67	24	2		**3 Take Two**		$40	Tamla 270
				MARVIN GAYE & KIM WESTON			
9/30/67	19	3		**4 Marvin Gaye/Greatest Hits, Vol.2** ....[G]	178	$30	Tamla 278
10/7/67	7	22		**5 United**	69	$30	Tamla 277
				MARVIN GAYE & TAMMI TERRELL			

Ain't No Mountain High Enough [3] • You Got What It Takes • If I Could Build My Whole World Around You [2] • Somethin' Stupid • **Your Precious Love [2]** • Hold Me Oh My Darling • Two Can Have A Party • Little Ole Boy, Little Ole Girl • If This World Were Mine [27] • Sad Wedding • Give A Little Love • Oh How I'd Miss You

9/21/68	4	19		**6 You're All I Need**	60	$30	Tamla 284
				MARVIN GAYE & TAMMI TERRELL			

Ain't Nothing Like The Real Thing [1] • Keep On Lovin' Me Honey [11] • You're All I Need To Get By [1] • Baby Don'tcha Worry • You Ain't Livin' Till You're Lovin' • Give In, You Just Can't Win • When Love Comes Knocking At My Heart • Come On And See Me • I Can't Help But Love You • That's How It Is (Since You've Been Gone) • I'll Never Stop Loving You Baby • Memory Chest

10/12/68	2²	30		**7 In The Groove**	63	$20	Tamla 285

You [7] • Tear It On Down • **Chained [8]** • I Heard It Through The Grapevine [1] • At Last (I Found A Love) • Some Kind Of Wonderful • Loving You Is Sweeter Than Ever • Change What You Can • It's Love I Need • Every Now And Then • You're What's Happening (In The World Today) • There Goes My Baby

6/7/69	❶²	32		**8 M.P.G.**	33	$20	Tamla 292

Too Busy Thinking About My Baby [1] • This Magic Moment • **That's The Way Love Is [2]** • The End Of Our Road [7] • Seek And You Shall Find • Memories • Only A Lonely Man Would Know • It's A Bitter Pill To Swallow • More Than A Heart Can Stand • Try My True Love • I Got To Get To California • It Don't Take Much To Keep Me

6/14/69	16	10		**9 Marvin Gaye And His Girls** ....[K]	183	$20	Tamla 293
				with **Tammi Terrell**, Mary Wells and Kim Weston			
2/7/70	17	16		**10 That's The Way Love Is**	189	$20	Tamla 299
6/13/70	17	8		**11 Marvin Gaye & Tammi Terrell Greatest Hits** ....[G]	171	$20	Tamla 302
10/31/70	19	12		**12 Marvin Gaye Super Hits** ....[G]	117	$20	Tamla 300
6/19/71	❶⁹	53	●	**13 What's Going On**	6	$15	Tamla 310

also see #26 below

What's Going On [1] • What's Happening Brother • Flyin' High (In The Friendly Sky) • Save The Children • God Is Love • **Mercy Mercy Me (The Ecology) [1]** • Right On • Wholy Holy • **Inner City Blues (Make Me Wanna Holler) [1]**

12/23/72+	3	21		**14 Trouble Man**	[I-S]	14	$15	Tamla 322

Main Theme From Trouble Man • "T" Plays It Cool • Poor Abbey Walsh • The Break In (Police Shoot Big) • Cleo's Apartment • **Trouble Man [4]** • Theme From Trouble Man • "T" Stands For Trouble • Main Theme From Trouble Man • Life Is A Gamble • Deep In It • Don't Mess With Mister "T" • There Goes Mister "T"

9/15/73	❶¹¹	46		**15 Let's Get It On**	2¹	$15	Tamla 329

also see #27 below

Let's Get It On [1] • Please Don't Stay (Once You Go Away) • If I Should Die Tonight • Keep Gettin' It On • Come Get To This [3] • Distant Lover • You Sure Love To Ball [13] • Just To Keep You Satisfied

11/17/73+	7	27		**16 Diana & Marvin**	26	$15	Motown 803

You Are Everything • Love Twins • **Don't Knock My Love [25]** • You're A Special Part Of Me [4] • Pledging My Love • Just Say, Just Say • Stop, Look, Listen (To Your Heart) • I'm Falling In Love With You • **My Mistake (Was To Love You) [15]** • Include Me In Your Life

4/27/74	10	27		**17 Marvin Gaye Anthology**	[K]	61	$30	Motown 791 [3]

Stubborn Kind Of Fellow [8] • Hitch Hike [12] • Pride And Joy [2] • Once Upon A Time [19] • Can I Get A Witness [15] • What's The Matter With You Baby [17] • You're A Wonderful One [15] • Try It Baby [15] • Baby Don't You Do It [27] • What Good Am I Without You [61] • Forever • How Sweet It Is To Be Loved By You [4] • It Takes Two [4] • I'll Be Doggone [1] • Pretty Little Baby [16] • Ain't That Peculiar [1] • Ain't No Mountain High Enough [3] • One More Heartache [4] • Take This Heart Of Mine [16] • Your Precious Love [2] • Little Darling, I Need You [10] • Your Unchanging Love [7] • If This World Were Mine [27] • You [7] • If I Could Build My Whole World Around You [2] • Chained [8] • Ain't Nothing Like The Real Thing [1] • How Can I Forget [18] • I Heard It Through The Grapevine [1] • Good Lovin' Ain't Easy To Come By [11] • Too Busy Thinking About My Baby [1] • That's The Way Love Is [2] • You're All I Need To Get By [1] • The End Of Our Road [7] • What's Going On [1] • Mercy Mercy Me (The Ecology) [1] • Inner City Blues (Make Me Wanna Holler) [1] • Save The Children • You're The Man [7] • Trouble Man [4]

7/27/74	❶²	34		**18 Marvin Gaye Live!**	[L]	8	$15	Tamla 333

recorded at the Alameda County Coliseum in Oakland

Trouble Man • Inner City Blues (Make Me Wanna Holler) • **Distant Lover [12]** • Jan • Medley: I'll Be Doggone/Try It Baby/Can I Get A Witness/You're A Wonderful One/Stubborn Kind Of Fellow/How Sweet It Is To Be Loved By You • Let's Get It On • What's Going On

4/10/76	❶¹	26		**19 I Want You**	4	$15	Tamla 342

I Want You [1] • Come Live With Me Angel • **After The Dance [14]** • Feel All My Love Inside • I Wanna Be Where You Are • All The Way Around • Since I Had You • Soon I'll Be Loving You Again

10/9/76	17	6		**20 Marvin Gaye's Greatest Hits** ....[G]	44	$15	Tamla 348

DEBUT	PEAK	WKS	Gold	Album Title	Pop #	$	Label & Number

GAYE, Marvin — Cont'd

| 4/9/77 | ❶² | 30 | | 21 **Marvin Gaye Live At The London Palladium** [L] | 3 | $15 | Tamla 352 [2] |

Trouble Man • Inner City Blues (Make Me Wanna Holler) • Distant Lover • Jan • Medley: I'll Be Doggone/Try It Baby/Can I Get A Witness/You're A Wonderful One/Stubborn Kind Of Fellow/How Sweet It Is (To Be Loved By You) • Let's Get It On • What's Going On • Medley: You're All I Need To Get By/Ain't Nothing Like The Real Thing/Your Precious Love/It Takes Two/Ain't No Mountain High Enough • Distant Lover • **Got To Give It Up** [1]

| 1/13/79 | 4 | 26 | | 22 **Here, My Dear** | 26 | $15 | Tamla 364 [2] |

Here, My Dear • I Met A Little Girl • When Did You Stop Loving Me, When Did I Stop Loving You • Anger • Is That Enough • Everybody Needs Love • Time To Get It Together • Sparrow • Anna's Song • **A Funky Space Reincarnation** [23] • You Can Leave, But It's Going To Cost You • Falling In Love Again

| 2/7/81 | 6 | 22 | | 23 **In Our Lifetime** | 32 | $10 | Tamla 374 |

Praise [18] • Life Is For Learning • Love Party • Funk Me • Far Cry • Love Me Now Or Love Me Later • **Heavy Love Affair** [61] • In Our Lifetime

| 11/20/82 | ❶⁸ | 43 | ▲² | 24 **Midnight Love** | 7 | $10 | Columbia 38197 |

Midnight Lady • **Sexual Healing** [1] • Rockin' After Midnight • **'Til Tomorrow** [31] • Turn On Some Music • Third World Girl • Joy [78] • My Love Is Waiting

4/28/84	26	11	▲	25 **Every Great Motown Hit Of Marvin Gaye** [G]	80	$10	Motown 6058
5/5/84	62	3		26 **Motown Superstar Series Volume 15** [K]	208	$10	Motown 115
5/26/84	49	5		27 **What's Going On** [R]		$10	Motown 5339
				reissue of #13 above			
5/26/84	62	2		28 **Let's Get It On** [R]		$10	Motown 5192
				reissue of #15 above			
6/15/85	8	8		29 **Dream Of A Lifetime**	41	$10	Columbia 39916

Sanctified Lady [2] • Savage In The Sack • Masochistic Beauty • **It's Madness** [55] • Ain't It Funny (How Things Turn Around) • Symphony • Life's Opera • Dream Of A Lifetime

4/26/86	48	9		30 **Motown Remembers Marvin Gaye**	193	$10	Tamla 6172
6/11/88	69	5		31 **A Musical Testament 1964-1984** [K]		$12	Motown 6255 [2]
1/26/91	67	11		32 **The Marvin Gaye Collection** [K]		$30	Motown 6311 [4]

GAYE, Nona   **'92**
Born in Washington DC. Daughter of **Marvin Gaye**.

| 11/14/92 | 84 | 3 | | **Love For The Future** | | $8 | Third Stone 92181 |

GAYNOR, Gloria   **'79**
Born on 9/7/49 in Newark, New Jersey. Disco singer.

3/15/75	21	7		1 **Never Can Say Goodbye**	25	$10	MGM 4982
10/11/75	32	7		2 **Experience Gloria Gaynor**	64	$10	MGM 4997
8/28/76	40	5		3 **I've Got You**	107	$10	Polydor 6063
2/3/79	4	28	▲	4 **Love Tracks**	4	$10	Polydor 6184

Stoplight • Anybody Wanna Party? [16] • Please, Be There • Goin' Out Of My Head • **I Will Survive** [4] • You Can Exit • I Said Yes • Substitute [78]

| 10/27/79 | 56 | 5 | | 5 **I Have A Right** | 58 | $10 | Polydor 6231 |

GENERAL GRANT — see GRANT, General

GENIUS/GZA   **'95**
GZA pronounced: Jiz-ah. Born Gary Grice on 8/22/66 in Brooklyn, New York. Male rapper. Member of **Wu-Tang Clan**.

| 11/18/95 | 2¹ | 38 | ● | **Liquid Swords** | 9 | $8 | Geffen 24813 |

Liquid Swords [33] • Duel Of The Iron Mic • Living In The World Today • Gold • **Cold World** [57] • Labels • 4th Chamber • **Shadowboxin'** [41] • Killah Hills 10304 • Investigative Reports • Hell's Wind Staff • I Gotcha Back • Basic Instructions Before Leaving Earth

GENTRY, Bobbie   **'67**
Born Roberta Streeter on 7/27/44 in Chickasaw County, Mississippi; raised in Greenwood, Mississippi. Singer/songwriter. Won the 1967 Best New Artist Grammy Award.

| 10/14/67 | 5 | 12 | ● | **Ode To Billie Joe** | 1² | $15 | Capitol 2830 |

Mississippi Delta • I Saw An Angel Die • Chickasaw County Child • Sunday Best • Niki Hoeky • Papa, Won't You Let Me Go To Town With You • Bugs • Hurry, Tuesday Child • Lazy Willie • **Ode To Billie Joe** [8]

GEORGIO   **'87**
Born Georgio Allentini in Los Angeles; raised in San Francisco. Singer/songwriter/keyboardist/guitarist.

| 4/25/87 | 27 | 54 | | 1 **Sexappeal** | 117 | $8 | Motown 6229 |
| 12/24/88+ | 55 | 22 | | 2 **Georgio** | | $8 | Motown 6263 |

GERARDO   **'91**
Born Gerardo Mejia III on 4/16/65 in Guayaquil, Ecuador; raised in Glendale, California. Rapper/actor. Acted in the movies *Can't Buy Me Love* and *Colors*.

| 3/2/91 | 64 | 19 | ● | **Mo' Ritmo** | 36 | $8 | Interscope 91619 |

GERONIMO, Mic   **'97**
Born in Queens, New York. Male rapper.

| 12/2/95 | 48 | 9 | | 1 **The Natural** | | $8 | Blunt/TVT 4910 |
| 11/22/97 | 20 | 14 | | 2 **Vendetta** | 112 | $8 | Blunt/TVT 4930 |

GET FRESH GIRLS, The   **'91**
Rap duo from Miami: Katrina Bryant and Regina Bailey.

| 8/24/91 | 77 | 9 | | **Trickin' (I Seen Your Boyfriend)** | | $8 | Breakaway 1001 |

GETO BOYS, The   **'93**

| | ★159★ | | | | | | |

Rap group from Houston: Richard "Bushwick Bill" Shaw, William "Willie D" Dennis, Brad "Scarface" Jordan, and Collins "DJ Ready Red" Lyaseth (left group in early 1991; replaced by "Big Mike" Barnett).

12/23/89+	19	37		1 **Grip It! On That Other Level**	166	$8	Rap-A-Lot 103
				THE GHETTO BOYS			
11/3/90	67	10		2 **The Geto Boys**	171	$8	Rap-A-Lot 24306

DEBUT	PEAK	WKS	Gold	Album Title	Pop #	$	Label & Number
				GETO BOYS, The — Cont'd			
7/20/91	5	41	▲	3 **We Can't Be Stopped**	24	$8	Rap-A-Lot 57161

Rebel Rap Family • We Can't Be Stopped • Homie Don't Play That • Another Nigger In The Morgue • Chuckie • **Mind Playing Tricks On Me** *[10]* • I'm Not A Gentleman • Gotta Let Your Nuts Hang • Fuck A War • Ain't With Being Broke • Quickie • Punk-Bitch Game • The Other Level • Trophy

DEBUT	PEAK	WKS	Gold	Album Title	Pop #	$	Label & Number
12/5/92	31	23		4 Best Uncut Dope	[K] 147	$8	Rap-A-Lot 57183
3/27/93	❶²	42	●	5 **Till Death Do Us Part**	11	$8	Rap-A-Lot 57191

Geto • It Ain't • **Crooked Officer** *[70]* • No Nuts No Glory • **Six Feet Deep** *[37]* • Murder Avenue • Raise Up • Murder After Midnight • Straight Gangstaism • Cereal Killer • This Is For You • Street Life • Bring It On

DEBUT	PEAK	WKS	Gold	Album Title	Pop #	$	Label & Number
4/13/96	❶¹	30	●	6 **The Resurrection**	6	$8	Rap-A-Lot 41555

Ghetto Prisoner • Still • **The World Is A Ghetto** *[37]* • Open Minded • Killer For Scratch • Hold It Down • Blind Leading The Blind • First Light Of The Day • Time Taker • Geto Boys and Girls • Geto Fantasy • I Just Wanna Die • Niggas And Flies • A Visit With Larry Hoover • Point Of No Return

DEBUT	PEAK	WKS	Gold	Album Title	Pop #	$	Label & Number
12/5/98	5	22		7 **Da Good Da Bad & Da Ugly**	26	$8	Rap-A-Lot 46780

Dawn 2 Dusk • Livin' 4 The Moment • Niggas Ain't Doin' Shit • Eye 4 An Eye • Bitches & Ho's • Why U Playin' • Like Some Ho's • I Don't Fuck With You • Do Yo Time • Free • Thugg Niggaz • They Bitches • Big Faces • Gangsta (Put Me Down) • Street Game • Retaliation • Gun In My Mouth

DEBUT	PEAK	WKS	Gold	Album Title	Pop #	$	Label & Number
				GHETTO COMMISSION **'98**			
				Rap group from New Orleans.			
11/28/98	12	6		Wise Guys	59	$8	No Limit 50011
				GHETTO MAFIA **'98**			
				Male rap duo from Decatur, Georgia: Wicked and Nino.			
5/21/94	79	6		1 Draw The Line		$8	Funk Town 4184
11/11/95	65	2		2 Full Blooded Niggaz		$8	Triad 2105
2/15/97	49	22		3 Straight From The Dec		$8	Down South 0514
11/7/98	34	33		4 On Da Grind	169	$8	Rap Artist 2061
				GHETTO TWIINZ **'98**			
				Rap duo of twin sisters Tonya and Tremethia Jupiter from New Orleans.			
1/20/96	37	14		1 Surrounded By Criminals		$8	Big Boy 0020
				GHETTO TWINZ			
7/19/97	36	17		2 In That Water		$8	Rap-A-Lot 44438
10/10/98	35	6		3 No Pain/No Gain	191	$8	Rap-A-Lot 46259
				GHOSTFACE KILLAH **'96**			
				Born Dennis Coles in Brooklyn, New York. Member of **Wu-Tang Clan**.			
11/16/96	❶¹	33	●	**Ironman**	2¹	$8	Razor Sharp 67729

Iron Maiden • Wildflower • The Faster Blade • 260 • Assassination Day • Poisonous Darts • Winter Warz • Box In Hand • Fish • Camay • Daytona 500 • Motherless Child • Black Jesus • After The Smoke Is Clear • All That I Got Is You • The Soul Controller • Marvel

DEBUT	PEAK	WKS	Gold	Album Title	Pop #	$	Label & Number
				GHO$TT **'98**			
12/5/98	46	1		Gho$tt		$8	Thump Street 9976
				GIBB, Andy **'78**			
				Born Andrew Roy Gibb on 3/5/58 in Manchester, England. Died of an inflammatory heart virus on 3/10/88 (age 30). Moved to Australia when six months old, then back to England at age nine. Youngest brother of **The Bee Gees**. Hosted TV's *Solid Gold* from 1981-82.			
7/8/78	18	12	▲	1 Shadow Dancing	7	$10	RSO 3034
3/8/80	67	4	●	2 After Dark	21	$10	RSO 3069
	★196★			**GILL, Johnny** **'90**			
				Born on 5/22/66 in Washington, D.C. Joined **New Edition** in 1988. His brother Randy and cousin Jermaine Mickey are members of **II D Extreme**.			
7/30/83	64	3		1 Johnny Gill		$10	Cotillion 90103
3/17/84	27	25		2 Perfect Combination	139	$10	Cotillion 90136
				STACY LATTISAW & JOHNNY GILL			
3/23/85	51	9		3 Chemistry		$10	Cotillion 90250
5/5/90	❶³	67	▲²	4 Johnny Gill	8	$8	Motown 6283

Rub You The Right Way *[1]* • Fairweather Friend *[2]* • Wrap My Body Tight *[1]* • Feels So Much Better • Never Know Love • My, My, My *[1]* • Lady Dujour • Just Another Lonely Night • Giving My All To You • Let's Spend The Night

DEBUT	PEAK	WKS	Gold	Album Title	Pop #	$	Label & Number
6/26/93	4	46	●	5 Provocative	14	$8	Motown 6355

Provocative • **The Floor** *[11]* • Where No Man Has Gone Before • **I Got You** *[35]* • A Cute, Sweet, Love Addiction • **Long Way From Home** *[42]* • Tell Me How U Want It • Mastersuite • **Quiet Time To Play** *[25]* • I Know Where I Stand

DEBUT	PEAK	WKS	Gold	Album Title	Pop #	$	Label & Number
10/26/96	7	38	●	6 Let's Get The Mood Right	32	$8	Motown 0646

Let's Get The Mood Right *[17]* • Touch • Maybe • Having Illusions • Bring It On • Take Me (I'm Yours) • **Love In An Elevator** *[59]* • **It's Your Body** *[19]* • Someone To Love • 4 U Alone • Love U Right • Simply Say I Love U • I Know You Want Me • So Gentle

DEBUT	PEAK	WKS	Gold	Album Title	Pop #	$	Label & Number
				GILMORE, Joey **'89**			
				Born on 6/4/44 in Ocala, Florida. Blues singer.			
11/11/89	80	12		So Good To Be Bad		$8	Pandisc 8807
				GILSTRAP, Jim **'76**			
				Born in Texas. Former session singer.			
6/19/76	36	12		Love Talk		$12	Roxbury 105
				GINUWINE **'97**			
				Born Elgin Lumpkin in Washington DC. Male singer/dancer.			
10/26/96+	14	75	▲²	Ginuwine...The Bachelor	26	$8	550 Music/Epic 67685

GIOVANNI, Nikki '71
Born on 6/7/43 in Knoxville, Tennessee. Female poet.

| 8/21/71 | 15 | 18 | | 1 Truth Is On Its Way ....[T] | 165 | $15 | Right-On 5001 |

NIKKI GIOVANNI & The New York Community Choir

| 8/18/73 | 51 | 4 | | 2 Like A Ripple On A Pond ....[T] | | $15 | Niktom 4200 |

GLENN, Garry '87
Born in Detroit. Singer/songwriter/producer/keyboardist.

| 10/17/87 | 70 | 2 | | Feels Good To Feel Good .... | | $8 | Motown 6234 |

GLP '94

| 6/4/94 | 90 | 2 | | Straight Out The Labb.. | | $8 | Getlow 002 |

GOD'S PROPERTY '97
Funk-rap-gospel collective of 50 young singers (ages 16-26) founded in Dallas by Linda Searight.

| 6/7/97 | ❶⁵ | 77 | ▲² | God's Property .... | 3 | $8 | B-Rite 90093 |

Stomp • My Life Is In Your Hands • It's Rainin' • More Than I Can Bear • Up Above My Head • Love • Sweet Spirit • Faith • You Are The Only One • So Good • The Storm Is Over Now • He Will Take The Pain Away

GOLDY '94
Born Mhisani Miller. Male rapper.

| 11/26/94 | 28 | 12 | | In The Land Of Funk... | | $8 | Jive 41554 |

GONZALEZ '79
British disco group featuring vocals by Linda Taylor and Alan Marshall.

| 2/10/79 | 52 | 10 | | Shipwrecked .... | 67 | $10 | Capitol 11855 |

GOODFELLAZ '97
Vocal trio from New York City: Angel Vasquez, DeLouie Avant and Ray Vencier.

| 5/10/97 | 70 | 3 | | Goodfellaz .... | | $8 | Avatar/Polydor 533396 |

GOOD GIRLS, The '90
Female vocal trio from Westchester, California: Joyce Tolbert, DeMonica Santiago and Shireen Crutchfield.

| 12/9/89+ | 32 | 30 | | All For Your Love .... | | $8 | Motown 6278 |

GOODIE MOB '98
Male rap group from Atlanta: Cee-Lo, Khujo, T-Mo and Big Gipp.

| 11/25/95+ | 8 | 47 | ● | 1 Soul Food .... | 45 | $8 | LaFace 26018 |

Free • Thought Process • Red Dog • **Dirty South** *[53]* • **Cell Therapy** *[17]* • Sesame Street • Guess Who • Serenity Prayer • Fighting • Blood • Live At The O.M.N.I. • Goodie Bag • **Soul Food** *[31]* • Funeral • I Didn't Ask To Come • Rico • The Coming • Cee-Lo • The Day After

| 4/25/98 | 2¹ | 27 | ● | 2 Still Standing .... | 6 | $8 | LaFace 26047 |

The Experience • **Black Ice (Sky High)** *[48]* • Fly Away • The Damm • They Don't Dance No Mo' • Beautiful Skin • Gutta Butta • Ghetto-ology • Distant Wilderness • Greeny Green • I Refuse Limitation • See You When I See You • Inshallah • Just About Over • Still Standing

GOODY GOODY '78
Disco studio group from Philadelphia with lead vocals by Denise Montana.

| 10/7/78 | 50 | 2 | | Goody Goody .... | 210 | $10 | Atlantic 19197 |

GP WU '98
Rap group from New York City: Pop The Brown Hornet, Down Low Recka, June Luva and Rubberbands.

| 2/14/98 | 44 | 7 | | Don't Go Against The Grain .... | | $8 | MCA 11587 |

GQ '79
Vocal group from the Bronx, New York: Emmanuel Rahiem LeBlanc (lead singer), Keith Crier, Herb Lane and Paul Service (left in 1980).

| 3/31/79 | 2⁵ | 38 | ▲ | 1 Disco Nights .... | 13 | $10 | Arista 4225 |

Disco Nights (Rock-Freak) *[1]* • Make My Dreams A Reality *[8]* • It's Your Love • Spirit • This Happy Feeling • Wonderful • Boogie Oogie Oogie • I Do Love You *[5]*

| 4/12/80 | 9 | 22 | | 2 Two .... | 46 | $10 | Arista 9511 |

Standing Ovation *[12]* • Is It Cool • Someday (In Your Life) • Lies • GQ Down • Don't Stop This Feeling • Reason For The Season • Sitting In The Park *[9]* • It's Like That

| 11/21/81 | 18 | 17 | | 3 Face To Face .... | 140 | $10 | Arista 9547 |

★117★ GRAHAM, Larry '80
Born on 8/14/46 in Beaumont, Texas; raised in Oakland, California. Bass player with **Sly & The Family Stone** from 1966-72. In 1973, formed Hot Chocolate (not to be confused with the English group of the same name); band later renamed **Graham Central Station**. Consisted of Graham (vocals, bass), Hershall Kennedy and Robert Sam (keyboards), Willie Sparks and Patrice Banks (percussion), and David Vega (guitar). Graham went solo in 1980.

1)One In A Million You 2)Ain't No 'Bout-A-Doubt It 3)Mirror

GRAHAM CENTRAL STATION:

2/16/74	20	20		1 Graham Central Station	48	$10	Warner 2763
10/19/74	22	9		2 Release Yourself	51	$10	Warner 2814
8/9/75	4	21	●	3 Ain't No 'Bout-A-Doubt It	22	$10	Warner 2876

The Jam *[15]* • Your Love *[1]* • It's Alright *[19]* • I Can't Stand The Rain • It Ain't Nothing But A Warner Brothers Party • Ole Smokey • Easy Rider • Water • Luckiest People

| 6/26/76 | 7 | 17 | | 4 Mirror .... | 46 | $10 | Warner 2937 |

Entrow *[21]* • Love *[14]* • Mirror • Do Yah • Save Me • I Got A Reason • Priscilla • Forever

| 4/30/77 | 12 | 16 | | 5 Now Do U Wanta Dance .... | 67 | $10 | Warner 3041 |

LARRY GRAHAM & GRAHAM CENTRAL STATION:

| 6/10/78 | 18 | 18 | | 6 My Radio Sure Sounds Good To Me .... | 105 | $10 | Warner 3175 |
| 6/30/79 | 44 | 9 | | 7 Star Walk .... | 136 | $10 | Warner 3322 |

DEBUT	PEAK	WKS	Gold	Album Title	Pop #	$	Label & Number

LARRY GRAHAM:

DEBUT	PEAK	WKS	Gold	Album Title	Pop #	$	Label & Number
6/21/80	2²	36	●	8 One In A Million You	26	$8	Warner 3447

One In A Million You [1] • Stand Up And Shout About Love • Sweetheart • There's Something About You • Forever Yours • I'm So Glad It's Summer Again • **When We Get Married** [9] • Time For You And Me • I Just Can't Stop Dancing • Sunshine, Love And Music

DEBUT	PEAK	WKS	Gold	Album Title	Pop #	$	Label & Number
8/8/81	8	17		9 Just Be My Lady	46	$8	Warner 3554

Just Be My Lady [4] • Loving You Is Beautiful • **Guess Who** [69] • Our Love Keeps Growing Strong • Can't Nobody Take Your Place • No Place Like Home • Baby, You Are My Sunshine • I Just Love You • Feels Like Love • Remember When

DEBUT	PEAK	WKS	Gold	Album Title	Pop #	$	Label & Number
6/26/82	15	20		10 Sooner Or Later	142	$8	Warner 3668
8/6/83	52	13		11 Victory	173	$8	Warner 23878

GRAND DADDY I.U. '94
Born in Long Island, New York. Male rapper.

DEBUT	PEAK	WKS	Gold	Album Title	Pop #	$	Label & Number
3/16/91	91	6		1 Smooth Assassin		$8	Cold Chillin' 26341
7/9/94	88	1		2 Lead Pipe		$8	Cold Chillin' 57866

GRAND FUNK RAILROAD '71
Hard-rock trio from Flint, Michigan: Mark Farner (vocals, guitar), Mel Schacher (bass) and Don Brewer (drums).

DEBUT	PEAK	WKS	Gold	Album Title	Pop #	$	Label & Number
12/12/70+	17	13	▲²	Live Album [L]	5	$15	Capitol 633 [2]

GRANDMASTER FLASH '82
Born Joseph Saddler in Barbados; raised in the Bronx, New York. Pioneer rap DJ/producer. The Furious Five consisted of Melvin "Grandmaster Melle Mel" Glover, Nathaniel "Kidd Creole" Glover (not the August Darnell character), Guy "Rahiem" Williams, Keith "Cowboy" Wiggins and Scorpio. Wiggins died on 9/8/89.

DEBUT	PEAK	WKS	Gold	Album Title	Pop #	$	Label & Number
10/23/82	8	29		1 The Message	53	$12	Sugar Hill 268

GRANDMASTER FLASH & THE FURIOUS FIVE
She's Fresh • It's Nasty (Genius Of Love) [22] • Scorpio [30] • It's A Shame (Mt. Airy Groove) • Dreamin • You Are • The Message [4]

DEBUT	PEAK	WKS	Gold	Album Title	Pop #	$	Label & Number
3/9/85	35	26		2 They Said It Couldn't Be Done	201	$10	Elektra 60389
4/26/86	27	13		3 The Source	145	$10	Elektra 60476
4/18/87	43	12		4 Ba-Dop-Boom-Bang	197	$10	Elektra 60723

GRANDMASTER MELLE MEL '84
Born Melvin Glover in New York City. Under Glover's direction, the Furious Five included Keith "Cowboy" Wiggins, King Lou, Scorpio, Grandmaster E-Z Mike and Dynamite.

DEBUT	PEAK	WKS	Gold	Album Title	Pop #	$	Label & Number
10/13/84	43	9		Grandmaster Melle Mel And The Furious Five		$12	Sugar Hill 9205

GRANDMASTER SLICE & IZZY CHILL '90
Interracial rap duo.

DEBUT	PEAK	WKS	Gold	Album Title	Pop #	$	Label & Number
12/16/89+	60	24		Shall We Dance		$8	Creative Funk 7001

GRAND PUBA '95
Born Maxwell Dixon on 3/4/66 in the Bronx; raised in New Rochelle, New York. Former member of **Brand Nubian** and **Masters Of Ceremony**.

DEBUT	PEAK	WKS	Gold	Album Title	Pop #	$	Label & Number
11/7/92	14	23		1 Reel To Reel	28	$8	Elektra 61314
7/8/95	5	16		2 2000	48	$8	Elektra 61619

Very Special • I Like It (I Wanna Be Where You Are) [68] • A Little Of This [90] • Keep On • Back Stabbers • 2000 • Amazing • Don't Waste My Time • Play It Cool • Playin The Game • Change Gonna Come

GRANT, Angel '98
Born in New York City. Female singer.

DEBUT	PEAK	WKS	Gold	Album Title	Pop #	$	Label & Number
6/20/98	89	1		Album		$8	Flyte Tyme 53130

GRANT, Eddy '83
Born Edmond Montague Grant on 3/5/48 in Plaisance, Guyana. Moved to London in 1960. Singer/songwriter/guitarist.

DEBUT	PEAK	WKS	Gold	Album Title	Pop #	$	Label & Number
4/16/83	13	29	●	1 Killer On The Rampage	10	$8	Portrait 38554
7/21/84	53	9		2 Going For Broke	64	$8	Portrait 39261

GRANT, General '98
Born in Trinidad. Male rapper.

DEBUT	PEAK	WKS	Gold	Album Title	Pop #	$	Label & Number
10/3/98	37	9		Mr. Energizer		$8	PolyBeat 46055

GRAVEDIGGAZ '94
Male rap group: Robert "RZA" Diggs (of **Wu-Tang Clan**), Poetic, Paul Huston (of **Stetsasonic**) and Arnold Hamilton.

DEBUT	PEAK	WKS	Gold	Album Title	Pop #	$	Label & Number
8/27/94	6	15		1 6 Feet Deep	36	$8	Gee Street 524016

Just When You Thought It Was Over • Constant Elevation • Nowhere To Run, Nowhere To Hide • Defective Trip (Trippin') • 2 Cups Of Blood • Blood Brothers • 360 Questions • 1-800 Suicide • Diary Of A Madman [57] • Mommy, What's A Gravedigga? • Bang Your Head • Here Comes The Gravediggaz • Graveyard Chamber • Deathtrap • 6 Feet Deep • Rest In Peace

DEBUT	PEAK	WKS	Gold	Album Title	Pop #	$	Label & Number
11/1/97	7	16		2 The Pick, The Sickle And The Shovel	20	$8	Gee Street 32501

Dangerous Mindz • Da Bomb • Unexplained • Twelve Jewelz • Fairytalez • Never Gonna Come Back • Pit Of Snakes • The Night The Earth Cried • Elimination Process • Repentance Day • Hidden Emotions • What's Goin' On • Deadliest Biz

GRAY, Dobie '79
Born Lawrence Darrow Brown on 7/26/40 in Brookshire, Texas. Male singer.

DEBUT	PEAK	WKS	Gold	Album Title	Pop #	$	Label & Number
2/3/79	72	3		Midnight Diamond	174	$10	Infinity 9001

GREAR, James, & Co. '98
Gospel singer from Minneapolis.

DEBUT	PEAK	WKS	Gold	Album Title	Pop #	$	Label & Number
4/18/98	34	20		Don't Give Up		$8	Born Again 1018

GREAVES, R.B. '70
Born Ronald Bertram Greaves on 11/28/44 in Georgetown, British Guyana; raised in California. Nephew of **Sam Cooke**.

DEBUT	PEAK	WKS	Gold	Album Title	Pop #	$	Label & Number
1/10/70	24	13		R.B. Greaves	85	$20	Atco 311

GREEN, Al ★20★   '72
Born on 4/13/46 in Forrest City, Arkansas. Singer/songwriter. With gospel group the Greene Brothers. To Grand Rapids, Michigan, in 1959. First recorded for Fargo in 1960. In group The Creations from 1964-67. Sang with his brother Robert Green and Lee Virgins in the group Soul Mates from 1967-68. Went solo in 1969. Returned to gospel music in 1980. Inducted into the Rock and Roll Hall of Fame in 1995.

1)Let's Stay Together 2)I'm Still In Love With You 3)Call Me 4)Al Green Is Love 5)Livin' For You

4/3/71+	15	32		1 Al Green Gets Next To You	58	$20	Hi 32062
2/19/72	❶10	38	●	2 Let's Stay Together	8	$15	Hi 32070

Let's Stay Together [1] • La-La For You • So You're Leaving • What Is This Feeling (Who Loves Me Like You Do) • How Can You Mend A Broken Heart • Judy • It Ain't No Fun To Me • Old Time Lovin • I've Never Found A Girl

10/14/72	37	6		3 Al Green [E]	162	$15	Bell 6076

first released in 1967 as *Back Up Train* on Hot Line 1500 ($50)

10/28/72	❶5	53	▲	4 I'm Still In Love With You	4	$15	Hi 32074

I'm Still In Love With You [1] • I'm Glad You're Mine • **Love And Happiness [92]** • What A Wonderful Thing Love Is • Simply Beautiful • Oh, Pretty Woman • For The Good Times • **Look What You Done For Me [2]** • One Of These Good Old Days

1/13/73	3	27		5 Green Is Blues [E]	19	$15	Hi 32055

recorded and first released in 1969
One Woman • Talk To Me • My Girl • The Letter • I Stand Accused • Gotta Find A New World • What Am I Gonna Do With Myself • Tomorrow's Dream • Get Back Baby • Get Back • Summertime

5/19/73	❶2	32	●	6 Call Me	10	$15	Hi 32077

Call Me (Come Back Home) [2] • Have You Been Making Out O.K. • Stand Up • I'm So Lonesome I Could Cry • Your Love Is Like The Morning Sun • **Here I Am (Come And Take Me) [2]** • Funny How Time Slips Away • **You Ought To Be With Me [1]** • Jesus Is Waiting

12/29/73+	❶1	37	●	7 Livin' For You	24	$15	Hi 32082

Livin' For You [1] • Home Again • Free At Last • **Let's Get Married [3]** • So Good To Be Here • My Sweet Sixteen • Unchained Melody • My God Is Real • Beware

12/7/74+	❶1	31	●	8 Al Green Explores Your Mind	15	$15	Hi 32087

Sha-La-La **(Make Me Happy) [2]** • Take Me To The River • God Blessed Our Love • The City • One Nite Stand • I'm Hooked On You • Stay With Me Forever • Hangin' On • School Days

3/29/75	3	14		9 Al Green/Greatest Hits [G]	17	$15	Hi 32089

also see #19 below
Tired Of Being Alone [7] • Call Me (Come Back Home) [2] • I'm Still In Love With You [1] • Here I Am (Come And Take Me) [2] • How Can You Mend A Broken Heart • Let's Stay Together [1] • I Can't Get Next To You [11] • You Ought To Be With Me [1] • Look What You Done For Me [2] • Let's Get Married [3]

9/27/75	❶2	13		10 Al Green Is Love	28	$15	Hi 32092

L-O-V-E (Love) [1] • Rhymes • The Love Sermon • There Is Love • Could I Be The One • Love Ritual • I Didn't Know • Oh Me, Oh My **(Dreams In My Arms) [7]** • I Gotta Be More (Take Me Higher) • I Wish You Were Here

3/20/76	12	13		11 Full Of Fire	59	$15	Hi 32097
11/27/76+	12	13		12 Have A Good Time	93	$15	Hi 32103
7/9/77	33	5		13 Al Green's Greatest Hits, Volume II [G]	134	$15	Hi 32105
12/24/77+	29	20		14 The Belle Album	103	$15	Hi 6004
1/6/79	44	14		15 Truth N' Time		$15	Hi 6009
3/20/82	62	9		16 Higher Plane		$12	Myrrh 6674
4/11/87	25	25		17 Soul Survivor	131	$10	A&M 5150
6/17/89	60	13		18 I Get Joy		$10	A&M 5228
8/19/95	34	97	▲	19 Al Green/Greatest Hits [G-R]	127	$8	Right Stuff 30800

reissue of #9 above

11/25/95+	57	15		20 Your Heart's In Good Hands		$8	MCA 11350
2/28/98	78	4		21 More Greatest Hits [G]		$8	Right Stuff 57074

GREEN, Grant   '70
Born on 6/6/31 in St. Louis. Jazz guitarist.

6/6/70	49	1		1 Carryin' On [I]		$25	Blue Note 84327
9/5/70	24	14		2 Green Is Beautiful [I]		$25	Blue Note 84340
10/16/71	31	13		3 Visions [I]	151	$15	Blue Note 84373

GREGORY, Dick   '70
Born on 10/12/32 in St. Louis. Comedian/civil rights activist.

1/17/70	41	7		1 The Light Side: The Dark Side [C]	23	$20	Poppy 60001 [2]
12/15/73+	48	7		2 Caught In The Act [C]		$20	Poppy 176 [2]

GREY & HANKS   '79
Vocal duo from Chicago: Zane Grey and Len Ron Hanks.

2/10/79	20	12		1 You Fooled Me	97	$10	RCA Victor 3069
2/9/80	60	7		2 Prime Time	195	$10	RCA Victor 3477

GRIFFIN, Billy   '84
Born on 8/15/50 in Baltimore. Replaced **Smokey Robinson** in **The Miracles** in 1972. Went solo in 1982.

4/14/84	63	3		Respect		$10	Columbia 38924

GROOVE THEORY   '95
Male-female duo: Bryce Wilson (keyboards) and Amel Larrieux (vocals). Wilson was a member of **Mantronix**.

11/11/95	14	47	●	Groove Theory	69	$8	Epic 57421

GROUND ZERO   '91
Rap duo from San Francisco: Michael Thomas and Erik Hicks.

11/16/91	81	3		Future Of The Funk E.P. [M]		$6	Lethal Beat 112

DEBUT	PEAK	WKS	Gold	Album Title		Pop #	$	Label & Number

GROUP HOME　　　　　　'95
Rap duo from New York City: Melachi The Nutcracker and Lil' Dap.

| 12/9/95 | 34 | 17 | | Livin' Proof .... | | | $8 | Payday 124079 |

GRUSIN, Dave　　　　　　'83
Born on 6/26/34 in Littleton, Colorado. Jazz pianist. Composed several movie soundtracks and TV themes.

| 4/9/83 | 54 | 6 | | Dave Grusin and the NY/LA Dream Band .... [I-L] | 181 | $10 | GRP 1001 |
| | | | | with Steve Gadd, Eric Gale and Lee Ritenour | | | |

GUCCI CREW II　　　　　　'89
Rap trio from Miami: "Disco Rick" Taylor, Cleveland Bell and Victor May. Taylor later formed The Dogs.

9/3/88	95	1		1 So Def, So Fresh, So Stupid		$8	Gucci 3303
1/7/89	35	29		2 What Time Is It? It's Gucci Time		$8	Gucci 3309
9/23/89	42	20		3 Everybody Wants Some	173	$8	Gucci 3314
9/8/90	58	12		4 G4		$8	Gucci 3327

GUCE　　　　　　'95

| 9/23/95 | 94 | 2 | | Pure Pressure .... | | $8 | Riot 4222 |

GUESSS　　　　　　'94
Male vocal duo from St. Louis: Darryl Gerdine and Ronnie Irons.

| 3/5/94 | 63 | 11 | | Guesss .... | | $8 | Warner 45481 |

GURU　　　　　　'93
Born Keith Elam on 7/18/66 in Boston. Rapper from the duo Gang Starr. Guru stands for Gifted Unlimited Rhymes Universal.

| 6/5/93 | 15 | 26 | | 1 Jazzmatazz Volume 1 .... | 94 | $8 | Chrysalis 21998 |
| 8/5/95 | 16 | 14 | | 2 Jazzmatazz Volume II The New Reality .... | 71 | $8 | Chrysalis 34290 |

GUTHRIE, Gwen　　　　　　'86
Born on 7/9/50 in Newark, New Jersey. Died of cancer on 2/4/99 (age 48). Singer/songwriter.

9/18/82	28	15		1 Gwen Guthrie	208	$10	Island 90004
4/6/85	55	6		2 Just For You		$10	Island 90252
8/10/85	47	8		3 Padlock .... [M]		$6	Garage Island 2001
9/13/86	20	14		4 Good To Go Lover	89	$8	Polydor 829532

GUY　　　　　　'89
Vocal trio from New York City: brothers Aaron Hall and Damion "Crazy Legs" Hall, with Teddy Riley. Riley was a member of Kids At Work. Disbanded in 1991. Riley formed BLACKstreet in 1993.

7/16/88+	❶⁵	73	▲²	1 Guy	27	$8	Uptown/MCA 42176
				Groove Me [4] • Teddy's Jam [5] • Don't Clap...Just Dance • You Can Call Me Crazy • Piece Of My Love • I Like [2] • 'Round And 'Round (Merry Go 'Round Of Love) [24] • Spend The Night [15] • Goodbye Love • My Business			
12/1/90+	❶³	51	▲	2 The Future	16	$8	MCA 10115
				Her • I Wanna Get With U [4] • Do Me Right [2] • Teddy's Jam 2 • Let's Chill [3] • Tease Me Tonite • D-O-G Me Out [8] • Total Control • Gotta Be A Leader • The Future • Let's Stay Together [16] • Where Did The Love Go • Yearning For Your Love • Smile • Long Gone			

GUY, Jasmine　　　　　　'90
Born on 3/10/64 in Boston; raised in Atlanta. Actress/singer. Played "Whitley Gilbert" on TV's A Different World.

| 11/10/90 | 38 | 25 | | Jasmine Guy .... | 143 | $8 | Warner 26021 |

H

HALEY, Alex　　　　　　'77
Born on 8/11/21 in Ithaca, New York. Died of a heart attack on 2/10/92 (age 70). Author of Roots.

| 4/23/77 | 46 | 2 | | Alex Haley Tells The Story Of His Search For Roots .... [T] | | $12 | Warner 3036 |

HALF PINT　　　　　　'93
Born Dion Hamilton in Miami.

| 5/29/93 | 65 | 9 | | Watch Me Grow .... | | $8 | On Top 9013 |

HALL, Aaron　　　　　　'93
Born on 8/10/64 in Brooklyn, New York. Member of Guy which included his younger brother Damion "Crazy Legs" Hall.

10/16/93	7	77	▲	1 The Truth	47	$8	Silas/MCA 10810
				Do Anything • Open Up • Get A Little Freaky With Me [48] • Pick Up The Phone • Don't Be Afraid [1] • Until I Found You • You Keep Me Crying • Let's Make Love [36] • When You Need Me [30] • I Miss You [2] • Until The End Of Time			
11/7/98	11	18		2 Inside Of You	55	$8	MCA 11778

HALL, Damion "Crazy Legs"　　　　　　'94
Born Albert Damion Hall on 6/6/68 in Brooklyn, New York. Member of Guy which included his older brother Aaron Hall.

| 5/14/94 | 22 | 9 | | Straight To The Point .... | 147 | $8 | Silas/MCA 10996 |

HALL, Daryl, & John Oates　　　　　　'83
Pop duo formed at Temple University in Philadelphia. Daryl Hall was born on 10/11/48 in Philadelphia. John Oates was born on 4/7/49 in New York City.

10/18/75	50	5	●	1 Daryl Hall & John Oates	17	$10	RCA Victor 1144
12/4/76+	33	11	●	2 Bigger Than Both Of Us	13	$10	RCA Victor 1467
1/9/82	11	18	▲	3 Private Eyes	5	$8	RCA Victor 4028
2/26/83	8	29	▲²	4 H2O	3	$8	RCA Victor 4383
				Maneater [78] • Crime Pays • Art Of Heartbreak • One On One [8] • Open All Night • Family Man [81] • Italian Girls • Guessing Games • Delayed Reaction • At Tension • Go Solo			
12/3/83+	26	32	▲²	5 Rock 'N Soul, Part 1 .... [G]	7	$8	RCA Victor 4858

81

DEBUT	PEAK	WKS	Gold	Album Title	Pop #	$	Label & Number
				HALL, Daryl, & John Oates — Cont'd			
11/17/84+	25	37	▲²	6 Big Bam Boom...	5	$8	RCA Victor 5309
10/5/85	41	12	●	7 Live At The Apollo with David Ruffin & Eddie Kendrick ....[L]	21	$8	RCA Victor 7035
				recorded at the re-opening of New York's Apollo Theater; side 1 features guest vocalists Ruffin and Kendrick			
5/28/88	30	18	▲	8 ooh yeah!...	24	$8	Arista 8539
				HALL, Randy　　　　　　　　**'84**			
				Singer/songwriter/guitarist.			
9/8/84	30	17		I Belong To You...		$8	MCA 5504
				HAMILTON, Chico　　　　　　　　**'66**			
				Born Foreststorn Hamilton on 9/21/21 in Los Angeles. Jazz drummer.			
4/9/66	14	7		1 El Chico...[I]		$20	Impulse 9102
4/20/74	51	3		2 The Master...[I]		$12	Stax 7501
				HAMILTON, JOE FRANK & REYNOLDS　　　　**'76**			
				Pop vocal trio of Dan Hamilton, Joe Frank Carollo and Tommy Reynolds. Hamilton died on 12/23/94 (age 48).			
12/6/75+	46	12		Fallin' In Love...	82	$10	Playboy 407
				HAMMOND, Johnny　　　　　　　　**'71**			
				Born John Robert Smith on 12/16/33 in Louisville, Kentucky. Jazz organist.			
7/31/71	15	24		1 Breakout...[I]	125	$15	Kudu 01
1/8/72	34	4		2 What's Going On...[I]		$15	Prestige 10015
4/22/72	43	9		3 Wild Horses/Rock Steady...[I]	174	$15	Kudu 04
★68★				**HANCOCK, Herbie**　　　　　　　　**'74**			
				Born on 4/12/40 in Chicago. Jazz electronic keyboardist. Pianist with the **Miles Davis** band, 1963-68. Won an Oscar in 1987 for his *Round Midnight* movie score. Also scored the 1988 movie *Colors*. Hancock's vocals are synthesized through the use of a Vocoder machine. Backed by the **Headhunters**.			
				1)*Head Hunters* 2)*Thrust* 3)*Man-Child*			
2/2/74	2²	46	▲	1 Head Hunters　　　　　　　　　　[I]	13	$12	Columbia 32731
				Chameleon *[18]* • Watermelon Man • Sly • Vein Melter			
9/14/74	31	13		2 Treasure Chest...[E-I]	158	$15	Warner 2807 [2]
				contains recordings from 1969-70			
10/5/74	2²	26		3 Thrust　　　　　　　　　　[I]	13	$12	Columbia 32965
				Palm Grease *[45]* • Actual Proof • Butterfly • Spank-A-Lee			
12/7/74+	38	9		4 Death Wish...[I-S]		$12	Columbia 33199
10/25/75	6	9		5 Man-Child...[I]	21	$12	Columbia 33812
				Hang Up Your Hang Ups • Sun Touch • The Traitor • Bubbles • Steppin' In It • Heartbeat			
9/11/76	8	9		6 Secrets...[I]	49	$12	Columbia 34280
				Doin' It *[83]* • People Music • Cantelope Island • Spider • Gentle Thoughts • Swamp Rat • Sansho Shima			
5/7/77	24	5		7 V.S.O.P..[I-L]	79	$12	Columbia 34688 [2]
				V.S.O.P.: Very Special Onetime Performance; recorded on June 29, 1976 at the Newport Jazz Festival			
7/29/78	31	9		8 Sunlight...	58	$12	Columbia 34907
3/17/79	16	26		9 Feets Don't Fail Me Now..	38	$12	Columbia 35764
4/19/80	19	24		10 Monster...	94	$10	Columbia 36415
11/22/80	46	11		11 Mr. Hands...[I]	117	$10	Columbia 36578
10/10/81	40	10		12 Magic Windows...	140	$10	Columbia 37387
5/29/82	31	18		13 Lite Me Up...	151	$10	Columbia 37928
9/10/83	10	60	▲	14 Future Shock...[I]	43	$10	Columbia 38814
				Rockit *[6]* • Future Shock • TFS • Earth Beat • Autodrive *[26]* • Rough			
9/1/84	34	13		15 Sound-System...[I]	71	$10	Columbia 39478
6/11/88	65	5		16 Perfect Machine...[I]		$10	Columbia 40025
				HANDY, John　　　　　　　　**'76**			
				Born on 2/3/33 in Dallas. Jazz saxophonist.			
5/22/76	10	19		1 Hard Work　　　　　　　　　　[I]	43	$12	ABC/Impulse 9314
				Hard Work *[13]* • Blues For Louis Jordan • Young Enough To Dream • Love For Brother Jack • Didn't I Tell You • Afro Wiggle • You Don't Know			
4/8/78	28	4		2 Where Go The Boats...[I]		$10	Warner 3170
				HARD BOYS, The　　　　　　　　**'92**			
				Male rap trio from Atlanta: Kerry Taylor, Charles Hood and Darrell Gilbert.			
3/28/92	42	29		1 A-Town Hard Heads...		$8	A.E.I. 4120
7/13/96	67	2		2 Trapped In The Game...		$8	Power 92674
				HARDCASTLE, Paul　　　　　　　　**'85**			
				Born on 12/10/57 in London. Keyboardist/producer. Member of **The Jazzmasters**.			
3/30/85	30	24		1 Rain Forest...[I]	63	$8	Profile 1206
4/16/94	35	13		2 Hardcastle...	182	$8	JVC 2033
				HAREWOOD, Dorian　　　　　　　　**'88**			
				Born on 8/6/51 in Dayton, Ohio. Actor/singer. Appeared in several TV shows and movies.			
11/12/88	72	10		Love Will Stop Calling...		$8	Emeric 1001
				HARLEY, Rufus　　　　　　　　**'68**			
				Born on 5/20/36 in Raleigh, North Carolina. Jazz multi-instrumentalist.			
9/14/68	32	4		A Tribute To Courage...		$15	Atlantic 1504
				HARMONY　　　　　　　　**'90**			
				Born Pamela Scott in Brooklyn, New York. Female rapper.			
11/17/90	77	10		Let There Be Harmony...		$8	Virgin 91394

DEBUT	PEAK	WKS	Gold	Album Title	Pop #	$	Label & Number

HARP, Everette   **'94**
Born in Houston. Male saxophonist.

| 10/10/92 | 54 | 15 | | 1 Everette Harp ....[I] | | $8 | Manhattan 96242 |
| 7/30/94 | 44 | 11 | | 2 Common Ground ....[I] | | $8 | Blue Note 89297 |

HARRELL, Grady   **'89**
Born in Los Angeles. Male singer.

| 5/6/89 | 34 | 14 | | Come Play With Me .... | | $8 | RCA 8341 |

★108★   **HARRIS, Eddie**   **'68**
Born on 10/20/36 in Chicago. Died of cancer on 11/5/96 (age 60). Jazz tenor saxophonist.
1)Swiss Movement 2)The Electrifying Eddie Harris 3)Plug Me In

11/5/66	23	2		1 Mean Greens ....[I]		$15	Atlantic 1453
3/16/68	2[1]	45		2 **The Electrifying Eddie Harris** ....[I]	36	$15	Atlantic 1495
				Theme In Search Of A Movie • Listen Here [11] • Judie's Theme • Sham Time • Spanish Bull • I Don't Want No One But You			
8/3/68	10	21		3 **Plug Me In** ....[I]	120	$15	Atlantic 1506
				Live Right Now • It's Crazy • Ballad (For My Love) • Lovely Today • Theme In Search Of A T.V. Commercial • Winter Meeting			
2/22/69	29	15		4 Silver Cycles ....[I]	199	$15	Atlantic 1517
8/16/69	11	17		5 High Voltage ....[I-L]	122	$15	Atlantic 1529
				recorded at the Village Gate in New York City and at Shelly's Manne-Hole in Hollywood			
12/13/69+	2[3]	33		6 **Swiss Movement** [I-L]	29	$15	Atlantic 1537
				LES McCANN & EDDIE HARRIS			
				recorded June 1969 at the Montreaux Jazz Festival in Switzerland			
				Compared To What [35] • Cold Duck [44] • Kathleen's Theme • You Got It In Your Soulness • The Generation Gap			
6/6/70	40	5		7 Come On Down! ....[I]		$15	Atlantic 1554
6/12/71	14	18		8 Second Movement ....[I]	41	$15	Atlantic 1583
				EDDIE HARRIS & LES McCANN			
1/1/72	33	4		9 Eddie Harris Live At Newport ....[I-L]	164	$12	Atlantic 1595
4/5/75	36	9		10 I Need Some Money ....[I]	125	$12	Atlantic 1669
10/11/75	26	7		11 Bad Luck Is All I Have ....[I]	133	$12	Atlantic 1675
3/27/76	44	5		12 That Is Why You're Overweight ....[I]		$12	Atlantic 1683

HARRIS, Gene   **'76**
Born in Benton Harbor, Michigan. Jazz pianist.

7/26/69	36	5		1 Elegant Soul ....[I]		$15	Blue Note 84301
				GENE HARRIS & The Three Sounds			
1/3/76	56	2		2 Nexus ....[I]		$12	Blue Note 519

HARRIS, Major   **'75**
Born on 2/9/47 in Richmond, Virginia. Member of **The Delfonics** from 1971-74.

| 3/8/75 | 12 | 20 | | 1 My Way .... | 28 | $15 | Atlantic 18119 |
| 2/14/76 | 33 | 10 | | 2 Jealously .... | 153 | $15 | Atlantic 18160 |

HARRIS, Robin   **'90**
Born on 8/30/53 in Los Angeles. Died on 3/18/90 (age 36). Male movie actor/comedian. Acted in the movie *House Party*.

| 10/13/90 | 28 | 28 | | Bé-Bé's Kids ....[C] | | $8 | Wing 841960 |

HARRIS, Sam   **'84**
Born in Oklahoma. Singer/actor.

| 10/6/84 | 29 | 18 | ● | Sam Harris .... | 35 | $8 | Motown 6103 |

HARRISON, George   **'71**
Born on 2/24/43 in Liverpool, England. Lead guitarist of **The Beatles**.

| 1/23/71 | 27 | 7 | ▲[2] | All Things Must Pass .... | 1[7] | $40 | Apple 639 [3] |

HARTMAN, Dan   **'80**
Born on 12/8/50 in Harrisburg, Pennsylvania. Died of a brain tumor on 3/22/94 (age 43). Multi-instrumentalist/songwriter/producer. Member of the Edgar Winter Group from 1972-76.

| 1/5/80 | 67 | 2 | | Relight My Fire .... | 189 | $10 | Blue Sky 36302 |

HARVEY, Dee   **'92**
Born in Memphis. Male singer.

| 2/22/92 | 80 | 7 | | Just As I Am .... | | $8 | Motown 6330 |

HARVEY, Steve   **'97**
| 10/11/97 | 67 | 6 | | Live...Down South Somewhere ....[C] | | $8 | Island 524415 |

HATHAWAY, Donny   **'72**
Born on 10/1/45 in Chicago; raised in St. Louis. Committed suicide by jumping from the 15th floor of New York City's Essex House hotel on 1/13/79 (age 33). Singer/songwriter/keyboardist/producer/arranger. His wife Eulalah was a classical singer. Their daughter **Lalah Hathaway** began recording career in 1990.

10/10/70+	33	10		1 Everything Is Everything	73	$12	Atco 332
5/15/71	6	25		2 Donny Hathaway	89	$12	Atco 360
				Giving Up [21] • A Song For You • Little Girl • He Ain't Heavy, He's My Brother • Magnificent Sanctuary Band • She Is My Lady • I Believe In Music • Take A Love Song • Put Your Hand In The Hand			
3/11/72	4	34	●	3 **Donny Hathaway Live** [L]	18	$12	Atco 386
				recorded at the Bitter End in New York City			
				What's Going On • The Ghetto • Hey Girl • You've Got A Friend • Little Ghetto Boy [25] • We're Still Friends • Jealous Guy • Voices Inside (Everything Is Everything)			
5/13/72	2[5]	26	●	4 **Roberta Flack & Donny Hathaway**	3	$12	Atlantic 7216
				I (Who Have Nothing) • You've Got A Friend [8] • Baby I Love You • Be Real Black For Me • You've Lost That Lovin' Feelin' [30] • For All We Know • Where Is The Love [1] • When Love Has Grown • Come Ye Disconsolate • Mood			
7/21/73	18	15		5 Extension Of A Man	69	$12	Atco 7029
9/23/78	51	4		6 The Best Of Donny Hathaway ....[G]		$12	Atco 107

HATHAWAY, Donny — Cont'd

| 9/20/80 | 68 | 5 | | 7 In Performance .... [L] | 201 | $10 | Atlantic 19278 |

recorded at the Bitter End and Carnegie Hall in New York City and at the Troubador in Los Angeles

HATHAWAY, Lalah　　　　　　　　　**'90**

Born in 1969 in Chicago. Daughter of the late **Donny Hathaway**. Her mother is classical singer Eulalah Hathaway.

| 9/1/90 | 18 | 44 | | 1 Lalah Hathaway .... | 191 | $8 | Virgin 91382 |
| 6/18/94 | 40 | 11 | | 2 A Moment .... | | $8 | Virgin 39542 |

HAVENS, Richie　　　　　　　　　**'71**

Born on 1/21/41 in Brooklyn, New York. Folk singer/guitarist.

| 5/29/71 | 35 | 6 | | Alarm Clock... | 29 | $12 | Stormy Forest 6005 |

HAVOC & PRODEJE　　　　　　　　　**'95**

Rap duo from Los Angeles: Havoc Da Mouthpiece and Prodeje. Both were members of **South Central Cartel**.

| 1/14/95 | 59 | 12 | | Kickin' Game .... | | $8 | GWK 6718 |

HAWKINS, Edwin, Singers　　　　　　　　　**'69**

Hawkins (b: August 1943) formed gospel group with Betty Watson in Oakland in 1967 as the Northern California State Youth Choir. Member Dorothy Morrison went on to a solo career.

| 5/17/69 | 5 | 19 | | 1 Let Us Go Into The House Of The Lord | 15 | $20 | Pavilion 10001 |

Let Us Go Into The House Of The Lord • Jesus, Lover Of My Soul • To My Father's House • I'm Going Through • **Oh Happy Day** [2] • I Hear The Voice Of Jesus • Early In The Morning • Joy, Joy

7/7/73	57	2		2 New World		$15	Buddah 5131
9/21/74	57	4		3 Live .... [L]		$15	Buddah 5606
1/15/77	40	11		4 Wonderful		$12	Birthright 4005

HAYES, Isaac ★10★　　　　　　　　　**'71**

Born on 8/20/42 in Covington, Tennessee. Singer/songwriter/keyboardist/producer/actor. Session musician for **Otis Redding** and other artists on the Stax label. Teamed with songwriter **David Porter** to compose many classic songs. Voice of "Chef" on TV's *South Park*.

1)Shaft 2)To Be Continued 3)Hot Buttered Soul 4)The Isaac Hayes Movement 5)Black Moses

| 7/12/69 | ❶10 | 68 | ● | 1 Hot Buttered Soul | 8 | $20 | Enterprise 1001 |

Walk On By [13] • Hyperbolicsyllabicsequedalymistic • One Woman • **By The Time I Get To Phoenix** [37]

| 4/18/70 | ❶7 | 53 | | 2 The Isaac Hayes Movement | 8 | $20 | Enterprise 1010 |

I Stand Accused [23] • One Big Unhappy Family • I Just Don't Know What To Do With Myself • Something

| 12/12/70 | ❶11 | 46 | | 3 To Be Continued | 11 | $20 | Enterprise 1014 |

Ike's Rap • Our Day Will Come • The Look Of Love • Ike's Mood • You've Lost That Lovin' Feelin' • Runnin' Out Of Fools

| 8/14/71 | ❶14 | 68 | ● | 4 Shaft | [I-S] | 1¹ | $20 | Enterprise 5002 [2] |

Theme From Shaft [2] • Bumpy's Lament • Walk From Regio's • Ellie's Love Theme • Shaft's Cab Ride • **Do Your Thing** [3] • The End Theme • Cafe Regio's • Early Sunday Morning • Be Yourself • A Friend's Place • Soulsville • No Name Bar • Bumpy's Blues • Shaft Strikes Again

| 12/18/71+ | ❶7 | 40 | | 5 Black Moses | 10 | $20 | Enterprise 5003 [2] |

Never Can Say Goodbye [5] • (They Long To Be) Close To You • Nothing Takes The Place Of You • Man's Temptation • Never Gonna Give You Up • Help Me Love • Need To Belong To Someone • Good Love 6-9969 • Your Love Is So Doggone Good • For The Good Times • I'll Never Fall In Love Again • Part-Time Love • A Brand New Me • Going In Circles

| 3/25/72 | 25 | 13 | | 6 In The Beginning .... [E] | 102 | $15 | Atlantic 1599 |

first released in 1968 as *Presenting Isaac Hayes* on Enterprise 100 ($30)

| 5/26/73 | ❶2 | 23 | ● | 7 Live At The Sahara Tahoe .... [L] | 14 | $15 | Enterprise 5005 [2] |

Theme From Shaft • Medley: The Come On/Light My Fire • Medley: Ike's Rap V/Never Can Say Goodbye • Windows Of The World • The Look Of Love • Ellie's Love Theme • Use Me • Do Your Thing • Theme From The Men • It's Too Late • Rock Me Baby • Stormy Monday Blues • Type Thang • The First Time Ever I Saw Your Face • Medley: Ike's Rap VI/Ain't No Sunshine • Feelin' Alright

| 11/3/73 | 2³ | 21 | ● | 8 Joy | 16 | $12 | Enterprise 5007 |

Joy [7] • I Love You That's All • A Man Will Be A Man • The Feeling Keeps On Coming • I'm Gonna Make It (Without You)

| 7/27/74 | 17 | 10 | | 9 Truck Turner .... [I-S] | 156 | $15 | Enterprise 7507 [2] |
| 6/28/75 | ❶2 | 19 | ● | 10 Chocolate Chip | 18 | $15 | HBS 874 |

That Loving Feeling • Body Language • **Chocolate Chip** [13] • I Want To Make Love To You So Bad • **Come Live With Me** [20] • I Can't Turn Around

8/30/75	57	2		11 The Best Of Isaac Hayes .... [G]	165	$12	Enterprise 7510
1/24/76	19	11		12 Disco Connection	85	$12	HBS 923
2/28/76	11	13		13 Groove-A-Thon	45	$12	HBS 925
7/31/76	18	7		14 Juicy Fruit (Disco Freak)	124	$12	HBS 953
2/26/77	20	11		15 A Man And A Woman .... [L]	49	$12	HBS 996 [2]

ISAAC HAYES & DIONNE WARWICK

12/10/77	26	14		16 New Horizon	78	$10	Polydor 6120
11/11/78+	15	20		17 For The Sake Of Love	75	$10	Polydor 6164
9/29/79	9	29	●	18 Don't Let Go	39	$10	Polydor 6224

Don't Let Go [11] • What Does It Take • **A Few More Kisses To Go** [89] • Fever • Someone Who Will Take The Place Of You

| 10/27/79 | 17 | 24 | | 19 Royal Rappin's .... | 80 | $10 | Polydor 6229 |

MILLIE JACKSON & ISAAC HAYES

5/17/80	26	17		20 And Once Again	59	$10	Polydor 6269
11/29/86+	32	21		21 U-Turn		$8	Columbia 40316
10/15/88	70	6		22 Love Attack		$8	Columbia 40941
6/10/95	75	3		23 Branded		$8	Pointblank 40335

DEBUT	PEAK	WKS	Gold	Album Title		Pop #	$	Label & Number

HAYWOOD, Leon   '66
Born on 2/11/42 in Houston. Singer/keyboardist.

7/2/66	**19**	2		1 Soul Cargo			$50	Fat Fish 2525
6/29/74	**35**	11		2 Keep It In The Family			$12	20th Century 440
8/23/75	**21**	11		3 Come And Get Yourself Some		140	$10	20th Century 476
5/17/80	**22**	12		4 Naturally		92	$10	20th Century 613
7/2/83	**48**	5		5 It's Me Again			$10	Casablanca 810304

HEADHUNTERS   '75
Herbie Hancock's backing group: Blackbird McKnight (guitar), Bennie Maupin (sax), **Bill Summers** (percussion), Paul Jackson (bass) and Mike Clark (drums).

| 4/19/75 | **34** | 6 | | Survival Of The Fittest .... [I] | | 126 | $10 | Arista 4038 |

HEATH BROTHERS, The   '81
Jazz duo: brothers Jimmy (reeds) and Percy (bass) Heath.

| 6/20/81 | **54** | 4 | | Expressions Of Life .... [I] | | 202 | $10 | Columbia 37126 |

HEATHER B.   '96
Born Heather Gardener on 11/13/70 in Jersey City, New Jersey. Female rapper. One of the first-season cast members of MTV's *The Real World* in 1992.

| 6/29/96 | **36** | 5 | | Takin Mine .... | | | $8 | EMI 38383 |

HEATWAVE   '78
Multi-national, interracial group formed in Germany. Core members: Johnnie and Keith Wilder (vocals), Eric Johns and William Jones (guitars), Rod Temperton and Calvin Duke (keyboards), Derek Bramblz (bass) and Ernest Berger (drums). Johnnie Wilder became a paraplegic due to a car accident in 1979, but continued singing with the group. Temperton left in late 1978 and became a prolific songwriter.

| 7/23/77 | **5** | 42 | ▲ | 1 Too Hot To Handle | | 11 | $12 | Epic 34761 |

Too Hot To Handle • **Boogie Nights [5]** • Ain't No Half Steppin' • **Always And Forever [2]** • Super Soul Sister • All You Do Is Dial • Lay It On Me • Sho'nuff Must Be Luv • Beat Your Booty

| 4/29/78 | **2**[4] | 28 | ▲ | 2 Central Heating | | 10 | $12 | Epic 35260 |

Put The Word Out • Send Out For Sunshine • Central Heating • Happiness Togetherness • **The Groove Line [3]** • **Mind Blowing Decisions [49]** • The Star Of A Story • Party Poops • Leavin' For A Dream

5/19/79	**16**	16	●	3 Hot Property		38	$10	Epic 35970
12/20/80+	**24**	14		4 Candles		71	$10	Epic 36873
7/3/82	**21**	14		5 Current		156	$10	Epic 38065

HEAVEN & EARTH   '79
Vocal group from Chicago: brothers Dwight and James Dukes, with Keith Steward and Dean Williams. Steward joined **Cashmere** in 1982.

| 9/22/79 | **45** | 10 | | Fantasy .... | | | $10 | Mercury 3763 |

HEAVY D & THE BOYZ   '89

★136★

Born Dwight Meyers on 5/24/67 in Jamaica; raised in Mt. Vernon, New York. Male rapper. Former president of Uptown Records. The Boyz consisted of Glen Parrish, Troy Dixon and Eddie Ferrell. Dixon died on 7/15/90 (age 22) from an accidental fall in Indianapolis.

| 10/31/87+ | **10** | 36 | | 1 Living Large... | | 92 | $8 | MCA 5986 |

The Overweight Lovers In The House • Nike • Chunky But Funky • Dedicated • Here We Go • On The Dance Floor • Moneyearnin' Mount Vernon • I'm Gonna Make You Love Me • Overweighter • I'm Getting Paid • Rock The Bass • **Mr. Big Stuff [60]** • Don't You Know [12]

| 7/8/89 | **❶**[2] | 51 | ▲ | 2 Big Tyme | | 19 | $8 | Uptown/MCA 42302 |

We Got Our Own Thang [10] • You Ain't Heard Nuttin Yet • **Somebody For Me [8]** • Mood For Love • Ez Duz It, Do It Ez • A Better Land • **Gyrlz, They Love Me [12]** • More Bounce • Big Tyme • Flexin' • Here We Go Again, Y'all • Let It Flow

| 7/27/91 | **5** | 55 | ▲ | 3 Peaceful Journey | | 21 | $8 | Uptown/MCA 10289 |

Now That We Found Love [5] • Let It Rain • I Can Make You Go Oooh • Sister Sister • Don't Curse • Peaceful Journey [54] • The Lover's Got What U Need • Cuz He'z Alwayz Around • **Is It Good To You [13]** • Letter To The Future • Swinging With Da Hevster • Body And Mind • Do Me, Do Me • **Somebody For Me [8]**

| 1/30/93 | **7** | 27 | ● | 4 Blue Funk | | 40 | $8 | Uptown/MCA 10734 |

Truthful [57] • **Who's The Man? [52]** • Talk Is Cheap • Girl • It's A New Day • Who's In The House • Love Sexy • Slow Down • Silky • Here Comes The Heavster • Blue Funk • Yes Y'All • A Buncha Niggas

| 6/11/94 | **❶**[1] | 43 | ▲ | 5 Nuttin' But Love | | 11 | $8 | Uptown/MCA 10998 |

Friends & Respect • Sex Wit You • **Got Me Waiting [3]** • **Nuttin' But Love [18]** • Something Goin' On • This Is Your Night • Take Your Time • Spend A Little Time On Top • Keep It Goin' • **Black Coffee [15]** • Move On • Lord's Prayer

| 5/10/97 | **3** | 29 | ● | 6 Waterbed Hev | | 9 | $8 | Uptown 53033 |

HEAVY D
Big Daddy [5] • Keep It Comin • You Can Get It • Waterbed Hev • Shake It • I'll Do Anything • Don't Be Afraid • Can You Handle It • Wanna Be A Player • Get Fresh Hev

HEBB, Bobby   '66
Born on 7/26/41 in Nashville. Singer/songwriter/multi-instrumentalist.

| 9/10/66 | **21** | 4 | | Sunny .... | | 103 | $25 | Philips 212 |

HELTAH SKELTAH   '96
Male rap duo from Brooklyn, New York: Rock and Ruck. Members of **Boot Camp Clik**.

| 6/29/96 | **5** | 22 | | 1 Nocturnal | | 35 | $8 | Duck Down 50532 |

Letha Brainz Blo • Undastand • Who Dat? • Sean Price • Clan's, Posse's, Crew's & Clik's • **Therapy [77]** • Place To Be • Soldiers Gone Psyco • The Square (Triple R) • **Da Wiggy [flip]** • Gettin Ass Gettin Ass • **LaFlaur LeFlah Eshkoshka [51]** • Prowl • Grate Unknown • **Operation Lock Down [64]**

| 10/31/98 | **8** | 7 | | 2 Magnum Force | | 34 | $8 | Duck Down 53543 |

Worldwide (Rock The World) • Call Of The Wild • Gunz 'N Onez (Iz U Wit Me) • Perfect Jab • Chicka Woo • **I Ain't Havin' That [58]** • Brownsville II Long Beach • Magnum Force • Sean Wigginz • Forget Me Nots • Black Fonzirelliz • Do The Knowledge • MFC Lawz • Hold Your Head Up • Gang's All Here

HENDERSON, Finis   '83
Pronounced: FINE-us. Male singer from Chicago.

| 7/9/83 | **42** | 14 | | Finis .... | | 208 | $10 | Motown 6036 |

★183★ HENDERSON, Michael '78

Born in 1951 in Yazoo City, Mississippi. Singer/bass player. Featured vocalist for **Norman Connors**.

11/6/76+	10	26		1 **Solid**	173	$10	Buddah 5662

Make Me Feel Better • Time • Let Love Enter • Treat Me Like A Man • Solid • **Be My Girl** *[23]* • **You Haven't Made It To The Top** *[80]* • Valentine Love • Stay With Me This Summer

8/13/77	18	17		2 **Goin' Places**	49	$10	Buddah 5693
7/15/78	5	32	●	3 **In The Night-Time**	38	$10	Buddah 5712

Take Me I'm Yours *[3]* • We Can Go On • Happy • **In The Night-Time** *[15]* • Whisper In My Ear • Am I Special • Yours Truly, Indiscreetly • One To One

7/28/79	17	17		4 **Do It All**	64	$10	Buddah 5719
8/23/80	6	27		5 **Wide Receiver**	35	$10	Buddah 6001

You're My Choice • Make Me Feel Like • **Reach Out For Me** *[78]* • **Wide Receiver** *[4]* • I Don't Need Nobody Else • What I'm Feeling (For You) • Ask The Lonely • There's No One Like You • **Prove It** *[27]*

9/19/81	14	17		6 **Slingshot**	86	$10	Buddah 6002
6/11/83	41	8		7 **Fickle**	169	$10	Buddah 6004
4/19/86	30	14		8 **Bedtime Stories**		$8	EMI America 17181

HENDERSON, Wayne '79

Born on 9/24/39 in Houston. Trombone player. Original member of **The Crusaders**.

6/17/78	56	2		1 **Living On A Dream**		$10	Polydor 6145
1/6/79	45	6		2 **Step In To Our Life**		$10	Polydor 6179
6/28/80	62	5		3 **Prime Time**	205	$10	Polydor 6276

ROY AYERS/WAYNE HENDERSON (above 2)

★89★ HENDRIX, Jimi '68

Born on 11/27/42 in Seattle. Died of a drug overdose in London on 9/18/70 (age 27). Legendary psychedelic-blues guitarist. Began career as a studio guitarist. Created The Jimi Hendrix Experience with Noel Redding (bass) and Mitch Mitchell (drums). Formed new group in 1969, Band of Gypsys, with **Buddy Miles** (drums) and Billy Cox (bass). The Jimi Hendrix Experience was inducted into the Rock and Roll Hall of Fame in 1992. Won Grammy's Lifetime Achievement Award in 1992.

1)Electric Ladyland 2)Axis: Bold As Love 3)The Cry Of Love

10/14/67+	10	69	▲4	1 **Are You Experienced?**	5	$50	Reprise 6261

Purple Haze • Manic Depression • Hey Joe • Love Or Confusion • May This Be Love • I Don't Live Today • The Wind Cries Mary • Fire • Third Stone From The Sun • Foxey Lady • Are You Experienced?

2/17/68	6	16	▲	2 **Axis: Bold As Love**	3	$25	Reprise 6281

EXP • Up From The Skies • Spanish Castle Magic • Wait Until Tomorrow • Ain't No Telling • Little Wing • If 6 Was 9 • You Got Me Floatin' • Castles Made Of Sand • She's So Fine • One Rainy Wish • Little Miss Lover • Bold As Love

11/2/68	5	19	▲2	3 **Electric Ladyland**	1 2	$30	Reprise 6307 [2]

...And The Gods Made Love • Have You Ever Been (To Electric Ladyland) • Crosstown Traffic • Voodoo Chile • Little Miss Strange • Long Hot Summer Night • Come On • Gypsy Eyes • Burning Of The Midnight Lamp • Rainy Day, Dream Away • 1983...(A Merman I Should Turn To Be) • Moon, Turn The Tides...Gently Gently Away • Still Raining, Still Dreaming • House Burning Down • All Along The Watchtower • Voodoo Chile (Slight Return)

8/23/69	22	17	▲2	4 **Smash Hits** [G]	6	$25	Reprise 2025 [2]

THE JIMI HENDRIX EXPERIENCE (all of above)

5/23/70	14	49	▲2	5 **Band Of Gypsys** [L]	5	$20	Capitol 472

recorded on December 31, 1969 at the Fillmore East in New York City

10/3/70	15	9	●	6 **Monterey International Pop Festival** [L-S]	16	$20	Reprise 2029

THE JIMI HENDRIX EXPERIENCE/OTIS REDDING
recorded June 1967 and featured in the movie *Monterey Pop*; side 1: Hendrix; side 2: Redding

3/13/71	6	15	▲	7 **The Cry Of Love**	3	$20	Reprise 2034

Freedom • Drifting • Ezy Ryder • Night Bird Flying • My Friend • Straight Ahead • Astro Man • Angel • In From The Storm • Belly Button Window

10/16/71	9	18	●	8 **Rainbow Bridge**	15	$20	Reprise 2040

Dolly Dagger • Earth Blues • Pali Gap • Room Full Of Mirrors • Star Spangled Banner • Look Over Yonder • Hear My Train A Comin' • Hey Baby (New Rising Sun)

3/18/72	12	19	●	9 **Hendrix In The West** [L]	12	$20	Reprise 2049
10/14/72	49	2		10 **Rare Hendrix** [E]	82	$15	Trip 9500

recorded on June 10, 1966

7/28/73	46	4		11 **sound track recordings from the film Jimi Hendrix** [L-S]	89	$25	Reprise 6481 [2]
5/14/94	38	9	●	12 **Blues** [E]	45	$8	MCA 11060

recorded from 1966-70

9/3/94	45	3		13 **Jimi Hendrix: Woodstock** [L]	37	$8	MCA 11063

recorded in 1969

HENDRYX, Nona '83

Born on 8/18/45 in Trenton, New Jersey. Member of **Patti LaBelle & The Blue-Belles** from 1961-77.

4/9/83	25	31		1 **Nona**	83	$10	RCA Victor 4565
4/28/84	40	13		2 **The Art of Defense**	167	$10	RCA Victor 4999
5/23/87	30	14		3 **Female Trouble**	96	$8	EMI America 17248

HERNANDEZ, Patrick '79

Born on 4/6/49 in Paris of a Spanish father and Austrian/Italian mother. Rock-disco singer.

8/11/79	53	10		**Born To Be Alive**	61	$10	Columbia 36100

HERSCHELWOOD HARDHEADZ '98

Rap group from Houston: Lil Keke, Duke, Knocky and Archie.

9/19/98	54	3		**A Million Dollars Later**		$8	Jam Down 481003

HESITATIONS, The '68

Vocal group from Cleveland. Leader George "King" Scott was accidentally killed by a bullet from a gun owned by group member Fred Deal in February 1968.

2/24/68	30	2		**The new Born Free**	193	$25	Kapp 3548

DEBUT	PEAK	WKS	Gold	Album Title	Pop #	$	Label & Number

HEWETT, Howard   '90
Born on 10/1/57 in Akron, Ohio. Lead singer of **Shalamar** from 1979-85.

9/20/86	14	48		1 I Commit To Love	159	$8	Elektra 60487
4/30/88	30	34		2 Forever and Ever	110	$8	Elektra 60779
4/14/90	8	34		3 Howard Hewett	54	$8	Elektra 60904

When Will It Be • **Show Me** *[2]* • If I Could Only Have That Day Back *[14]* • **Let Me Show You How To Fall In Love** *[67]* • I Do • The More I Get (The More I Want) • Let's Get Deeper • Shadow • I Know You'll Be Comin' Back • Don't Give In • Jesus

12/5/92	73	3		4 Allegiance		$8	Elektra 61393
12/3/94+	29	36		5 It's Time	181	$8	Caliber 1008

HI-C   '92
Born in Louisiana; raised in California. Male rapper.

3/7/92	53	15		1 Skanless	152	$8	Skanless 61235
10/16/93	63	5		2 Swing'n		$8	Skanless 3011

HICKS, D'atra   '89
Born in Harlem, New York. Female singer/actress.

9/9/89	63	10		D'atra Hicks		$8	Capitol 46990

HICKS, Marva   '91
Born in Petersburg, Virginia. Female singer/actress.

3/30/91	46	24		Marva Hicks		$8	Polydor 847209

HIDDEN STRENGTH   '76
Jazz-funk group: Roy Herring (vocals), Grover Underwood and Ken Sullivan (keyboards), Ray Anderson (trombone), Robert Leach (sax), Alvin Brown (bass) and Al Thomas (drums).

5/29/76	58	2		Hidden Strength	208	$12	United Artists 555

HIEROGLYPHICS   '98
Rap group from Oakland: A Plus, Tajai, Del, Pep Love, Jay Biz, Opio, Phesto, Casual, Domino and Toure.

4/11/98	88	1		3rd Eye Vision		$8	Hiero Imperium 8473

HI-FIVE   '91
Male vocal group from Waco, Texas: **Tony Thompson**, Roderick Clark, Russell Neal, Marcus Sanders and Toriano Easley (left group after release of first album, replaced by Treston Irby).

11/24/90+	❶¹	56	●	1 Hi-Five	38	$8	Jive 1328

I Just Can't Handle It *[10]* • Just Another Girlfriend *[41]* • **I Like The Way (The Kissing Game)** *[1]* • Rag Doll • I Can't Wait Another Minute *[1]* • Too Young • Merry-Go-Round • The Way You Said Goodbye • Sweetheart • Know Love

8/29/92	9	33	●	2 Keep It Goin' On	82	$8	Jive 41474

She's Playing Hard To Get *[2]* • Quality Time *[3]* • She Said • Fly Away • A Little Bit Older Now • **Mary, Mary** *[50]* • Let's Get It Started (Keep It Goin' On) • Video Girl • Whenever You Say

11/13/93	23	17		3 Faithful	105	$8	Jive 41528

HIGH FASHION   '82
Vocal trio from New York City: **Meli'sa Morgan**, **Alyson Williams** and Erick McClinton.

7/24/82	51	5		Feelin' Lucky		$10	Capitol 12214

HIGH INERGY   '77
Female vocal group from Pasadena, California: sisters Barbara and Vernessa Mitchell, with Linda Howard and Michelle Rumph. Vernessa left in 1978; group continued as a trio.

10/22/77	6	21		1 Turnin' On	28	$10	Gordy 978

Love Is All You Need *[20]* • **You Can't Turn Me Off (In The Middle Of Turning Me On)** *[2]* • Some Kinda Magic • Searchin' (I've Got To Find My Love) • Ain't No Love Left (In My Heart For You) • Let Me Get Close To You • Save It For A Rainy Day • Could This Be Love • High School

7/22/78	46	6		2 Steppin' Out	42	$10	Gordy 982
5/26/79	72	2		3 Shoulda Gone Dancin'	147	$10	Gordy 987
9/20/80	70	3		4 Hold On	208	$10	Gordy 996
6/18/83	62	3		5 Groove Patrol	206	$10	Motown 6041

HIGHLAND PLACE MOBSTERS   '92
Rap group led by Dallas Austin (producer of **Boyz II Men**, **Another Bad Creation** and **TLC**). With singers Theophilus Glass and Derrick Culbreath, and rapper Melvin Davis.

9/5/92	72	8		1746DCGA30035		$8	LaFace 26004

title is code for the address of the house that band shared: 1746 Highland Place, Decatur, Georgia 30035

HILL, Lauryn   '98
Born in 1975 in South Orange, New Jersey. Singer/actress. Member of **The Fugees**. Acted on TV's *As The World Turns* and in the movie *Sister Act 2*.

9/12/98	❶⁶	47↑	▲⁵	The Miseducation Of Lauryn Hill	1⁴	$8	Ruffhouse 69035

Lost Ones • Ex-Factor *[7]* • To Zion *[77]* • Doo Wop (That Thing) *[2]* • Superstar • Final Hour • When It Hurts So Bad • I Used To Love Him • Forgive Them Father • Every Ghetto, Every City • **Nothing Even Matters** *[25]* • Everything Is Everything • The Miseducation Of Lauryn Hill • **Can't Take My Eyes Off Of You** *[45]* • Tell Him

HILL, Z.Z.   '84
Born Arzel Hill on 9/30/35 in Naples, Texas. Died of a heart attack on 4/27/84 (age 48). Blues singer.

2/13/82	17	93		1 Down Home	209	$10	Malaco 7406
12/18/82+	16	51		2 The Rhythm & The Blues	165	$10	Malaco 7411
12/10/83+	15	51		3 I'm A Blues Man	170	$10	Malaco 7415
11/10/84	35	21		4 Bluesmaster		$10	Malaco 7420
7/13/85	61	5		5 In Memorium 1935-1984	[K]	$10	Malaco 7426

HINDSIGHT   '88
Male duo from London: Camelle Hinds and Henri Defoe.

4/23/88	75	1		Days Like This		$8	Virgin 90633

DEBUT	PEAK	WKS	Gold	Album Title	Pop #	$	Label & Number

HINES, Gregory   **'88**
Born on 2/14/46 in New York City. Dancer/actor/singer. Acted in several movies and Broadway musicals.

| 8/6/88 | 53 | 11 | | Gregory Hines .... | | $8 | Epic 40671 |

HIROSHIMA   **'80**
Jazz-pop group from Los Angeles. Founded by Dan Kuramoto. Most members are of Japanese ancestry.

1/26/80	20	22		1 Hiroshima	51	$10	Arista 4252
11/22/80	31	17		2 Odori	72	$10	Arista 9541
9/10/83	50	9		3 Third Generation .... [I]	142	$8	Epic 38708
9/5/87	54	11	●	4 Go	75	$8	Epic 40679

HITMAN HOWIE TEE — see CHUBB ROCK

HODGES, JAMES AND SMITH   **'74**
Female vocal trio from Detroit: Patricia Hodges, Denita James and Jessica Smith.

| 2/2/74 | 51 | 6 | | 1 Incredible .... | | $12 | 20th Century 425 |
| 7/5/75 | 58 | 2 | | 2 Power In Your Love .... | | $12 | 20th Century 475 |

HO FRAT HO!   **'92**
Male rap group from San Francisco: King Ho, Heavy Ho, Lo Ho, X-Ho and Mighty Ho.

| 8/8/92 | 63 | 12 | | Ho Frat Ho! .... | | $8 | Bust It/Capitol 95384 |

HOLIDAY, Billie   **'73**
Born Eleanor Gough on 4/7/15 in Philadelphia. Died on 7/17/59 (age 44). Legendary jazz singer. Nicknamed: "Lady Day." Subject of the 1972 movie *Lady Sings The Blues* starring Diana Ross. Won Grammy's Lifetime Achievement Award in 1987.

2/10/73	28	13		1 The Billie Holiday Story .... [K]	85	$20	Decca 161 [2]
				recordings from 1944-50			
2/24/73	28	9		2 Strange Fruit .... [K]	108	$15	Atlantic 1614
				recordings from 1939 and 1944			

HOLIDAY, Jimmy   **'66**
Born on 7/24/34 in Durant, Mississippi; raised in Waterloo, Iowa. Died of heart failure on 2/15/87 (age 52). Singer/songwriter.

| 12/31/66 | 25 | 2 | | Turning Point .... | | $30 | Minit 40005 |

HOLIDAY, Tasha   **'97**
Born in Atlantic City, New Jersey. Female singer. Descendant of **Billie Holiday**.

| 4/12/97 | 91 | 3 | | Just The Way You Like It .... | | $8 | MCA 11460 |

HOLLIDAY, Jennifer   **'83**
Born on 10/19/60 in Riverside, Texas. Singer/actress. Appeared in several Broadway musicals.

10/22/83	6	26		1 Feel My Soul	31	$8	Geffen 4014
				Just Let Me Wait *[24]* • I Am Ready Now • This Game Of Love (I'm Never Coming Down) • I Am Love *[2]* • Shine A Light • Just For A While • My Sweet Delight • Change Is Gonna Come • This Day			
9/14/85	34	31		2 Say You Love Me	110	$8	Geffen 24073
8/17/91	29	35		3 I'm On Your Side	184	$8	Arista 18578
9/28/96	50	5		4 The Best Of Jennifer Holliday .... [G]		$8	Geffen 25004

HOLLOWAY, Loleatta   **'75**
Born in Chicago. Female disco singer.

| 6/7/75 | 47 | 4 | | 1 Cry To Me .... | | $20 | Aware 2008 |
| 11/4/78 | 47 | 2 | | 2 Queen Of The Night .... | 187 | $20 | Gold Mind 9501 |

HOLMAN, Eddie   **'70**
Born on 6/3/46 in Norfolk, Virginia. Singer/songwriter.

| 1/31/70 | 10 | 16 | | I Love You .... | 75 | $30 | ABC 701 |
| | | | | I Love You *[30]* • It's All In The Game • Since My Love Has Gone • I Cried • I'll Be Forever Loving You • Since I Don't Have You • Hey There Lonely Girl *[4]* • Let Me Into Your Life • Four Walls • Don't Stop Now *[24]* • Am I A Loser | | | |

HOLMES, Cecil, Soulful Sounds   **'73**
Born in New York City. Songwriter/producer. Former executive with Buddah record label.

| 4/28/73 | 42 | 3 | | 1 The Black Motion Picture Experience .... [I] | 141 | $12 | Buddah 5129 |
| 10/27/73 | 47 | 3 | | 2 Soulful Sounds .... [I] | | $12 | Buddah 5139 |

HOLMES, Richard "Groove"   **'66**
Born on 5/2/31 in Camden, New Jersey. Died of cancer on 6/29/91 (age 60). Jazz organist.

5/7/66	3	27		1 Soul Message .... [I]	89	$15	Prestige 7435
				Groove's Groove • Dahoud • Misty *[12]* • Song For My Father • The Things We Did Last Summer • Soul Message			
8/6/66	17	5		2 Tell It Like It Is .... [I]		$15	Pacific Jazz 10105
10/8/66	3	15		3 Living Soul .... [I-L]	143	$15	Prestige 7468
				Living Soul • Blues For Yna Yna • The Girl From Ipanema • Gemini • Over The Rainbow			

HOME TEAM   **'92**
Rap duo from Brooklyn, New York: brothers Debonaire and Drugzie. Debonaire was a member of **Poison Clan**.

| 11/7/92 | 50 | 5 | | Via Satellite From Saturn .... | | $8 | Luke 120 |

HONEY CONE, The   **'71**
Female vocal trio from Los Angeles: Carolyn Willis, Edna Wright and Shellie Clark.

6/26/71	14	11		1 Sweet Replies	137	$15	Hot Wax 706
12/4/71+	15	21		2 Soulful Tapestry	72	$15	Hot Wax 707
10/14/72	41	5		3 Love, Peace & Soul	189	$15	Hot Wax 713

HONEYDRIPPERS, The   **'85**
All-star rock group: singer Robert Plant, with guitarists Jimmy Page, Jeff Beck and Nile Rodgers. Plant and Page were members of **Led Zeppelin**. Rodgers was a member of **Chic**.

| 1/5/85 | 67 | 7 | ▲ | Volume One .... [M] | 4 | $6 | Es Paranza 90220 |

DEBUT	PEAK	WKS	Gold	Album Title	Pop #	$	Label & Number

HOODRATZ   **'93**
Rap duo from Queens, New York: Mark Eason and Lamont Lake.

| 9/11/93 | 79 | 3 | | Sneeke Muthafukaz.. | | $8 | Epic 53227 |

HOOKER, John Lee   **'71**
Born on 8/22/17 in Clarksdale, Mississippi. Legendary blues singer/guitarist. Inducted into the Rock and Roll Hall of Fame in 1991.

| 5/29/71 | 38 | 2 | | Endless Boogie.. | 126 | $20 | ABC 720 [2] |

HOOPER, Stix   **'79**
Born Nesbert Hooper on 8/15/38 in Houston. Drummer for **The Crusaders.**

| 10/20/79 | 49 | 17 | | The World Within ....[I] | 166 | $10 | MCA 3180 |

HORNE, Jimmy "Bo"   **'78**
Born on 9/28/49 in West Palm Beach, Florida. Singer/dancer.

| 6/3/78 | 23 | 16 | | 1 Dance Across The Floor.. | 122 | $10 | Sunshine Sound 7801 |
| 9/29/79 | 42 | 9 | | 2 Goin' Home For Love.. | | $10 | Sunshine Sound 7805 |

HORNE, Lena   **'82**
Born on 6/30/17 in Brooklyn, New York. Singer/actress. Won Grammy's Lifetime Achievement Award in 1989.

| 1/23/82 | 64 | 3 | | Lena Horne: The Lady And Her Music............................[OC] | 112 | $12 | Qwest 3597 [2] |

HOT   **'77**
Female vocal trio from Los Angeles: Gwen Owens, Cathy Carson and Juanita Curiel.

| 6/4/77 | 28 | 17 | | Hot .... | 125 | $10 | Big Tree 89522 |

HOT BOY$ **'97**
Rap group from New Orleans: **The B.G., Juvenile, Lil' Wayne** and **Young Turk.**

| 10/11/97 | 37 | 38 | | Get It How U Live!!.. | | $8 | Cash Money 9614 |

HOT CHOCOLATE   **'79**
Interracial group formed in London: Errol Brown (vocals), Harvey Hinsley (guitar), Larry Ferguson (keyboards), Patrick Olive (bass) and Tony Connor (drums).

| 11/29/75+ | 34 | 15 | | 1 Hot Chocolate.. | 41 | $12 | Big Tree 89512 |
| 1/20/79 | 18 | 11 | | 2 Every 1's A Winner .... | 31 | $10 | Infinity 9002 |

HOUSE OF PAIN   **'94**
White rap group from Los Angeles: Erik Schrody, Danny O'Connor and Leor DiMant.

8/15/92	16	46	▲	1 House Of Pain..	14	$8	Tommy Boy 1056
7/16/94	12	13	●	2 Same As It Ever Was	12	$8	Tommy Boy 1089
11/9/96	31	5		3 Truth Crushed To Earth Shall Rise Again	47	$8	Tommy Boy 1161

HOUSTON, Thelma   **'77**
Born on 5/7/46 in Leland, Mississippi. Disco singer/actress.

| 10/4/69 | 50 | 2 | | 1 Sunshower.. | | $25 | Dunhill/ABC 50054 |
| 1/8/77 | 5 | 24 | | 2 Any Way You Like It .... | 11 | $12 | Tamla 345 |

Any Way You Like It • **Don't Leave Me This Way** [1] • Don't Know Why I Love You • Come To Me • Don't Make Me Pay (For Another Girl's Mistake) • Sharing Something Perfect Between Ourselves • **If It's The Last Thing I Do** [12] • Differently

| 6/18/77 | 20 | 11 | | 3 Thelma & Jerry .... | 53 | $10 | Motown 887 |

        THELMA HOUSTON & JERRY BUTLER

11/26/77	29	8		4 The Devil In Me	64	$10	Tamla 358
11/25/78	74	2		5 Ready To Roll		$10	Tamla 361
6/6/81	51	6		6 Never Gonna Be Another One	144	$8	RCA Victor 3842
1/12/85	30	17		7 Qualifying Heat		$8	MCA 5527

| | ★57★ | | | **HOUSTON, Whitney**   **'92** | | | |

Born on 8/9/63 in Newark, New Jersey. Daughter of Cissy Houston and cousin of **Dionne Warwick**. Began singing career at age 11 with the gospel group New Hope Baptist Junior Choir. As a teen, worked as a backing vocalist for **Chaka Khan** and **Lou Rawls**. Pursued modeling career in 1981, appearing in *Glamour* magazine and on the cover of *Seventeen*. Married **Bobby Brown** on 7/18/92. Starred in the movies *The Bodyguard, Waiting To Exhale* and *The Preacher's Wife*.

| 4/6/85 | ❶[6] | 116 | ▲[12] | 1 Whitney Houston | 1[14] | $8 | Arista 8212 |

You Give Good Love [1] • Thinking About You [10] • Someone For Me • **Saving All My Love For You** [1] • Nobody Loves Me Like You Do • **How Will I Know** [1] • All At Once • Take Good Care Of My Heart • **Greatest Love Of All** [3] • Hold Me [5]

| 6/27/87 | 2[7] | 75 | ▲[9] | 2 Whitney | 1[11] | $8 | Arista 8405 |

I Wanna Dance With Somebody (Who Loves Me) [2] • Just The Lonely Talking Again • **Love Will Save The Day** [5] • Didn't We Almost Have It All [2] • Where You Are • Love Is A Contact Sport • You're Still My Man • For The Love Of You • Where Do Broken Hearts Go [2] • I Know Him So Well

| 12/1/90 | ❶[8] | 53 | ▲[4] | 3 I'm Your Baby Tonight | 3 | $8 | Arista 8616 |

I'm Your Baby Tonight [1] • My Name Is Not Susan [8] • All The Man That I Need [1] • Lover For Life • Anymore • Miracle [2] • I Belong To You [10] • Who Do You Love • We Didn't Know [20] • After We Make Love • I'm Knockin'

| 12/5/92 | ❶[8] | 122 | ▲[16] | 4 The Bodyguard | [S] | 1[20] | $8 | Arista 18699 |

I Will Always Love You [1] • I Have Nothing [4] • I'm Every Woman [5] • Run To You [31] • Queen Of The Night • Jesus Loves Me • Even If My Heart Would Break [Kenny G & Aaron Neville] • Someday (I'm Coming Back) [Lisa Stansfield] • It's Gonna Be A Lovely Day [S.O.U.L. S.Y.S.T.E.M.] [44] • (What's So Funny 'Bout) Peace, Love And Understanding [Curtis Stigers] • Theme From The Bodyguard [Alan Silvestri] • Trust In Me [Joe Cocker & Sass Jordan]

| 12/14/96+ | ❶[2] | 49 | ▲[3] | 5 The Preacher's Wife | [S] | 3 | $8 | Arista 18951 |

I Believe In You And Me [4] • Step By Step [29] • Joy • Hold On, Help Is On The Way • I Go To The Rock • I Love The Lord • Somebody Bigger Than You And I [flip] • You Were Loved • **My Heart Is Calling** [35] • Who Would Imagine A King • He's All Over Me • The Lord Is My Shepherd • Joy To The World

| 12/5/98 | 7 | 35↑ | ▲[2] | 6 My Love Is Your Love | 13 | $8 | Arista 19037 |

It's Not Right But It's Okay • Heartbreak Hotel [1] • My Love Is Your Love • **When You Believe** [33] • If I Told You That • In My Business • I Learned From The Best • Oh Yes • Get It Back • Until You Come Back • I Bow Out • You'll Never Stand Alone

HOWARD, Adina '95
Born on 11/14/74 in Grand Rapids, Michigan. Female singer.

3/18/95	7	33	●	**Do You Wanna Ride?**	39	$8	Mecca Don 61757

You Got Me Humpin' • **Freak Like Me** [2] • If We Make Love Tonight • I Wants Ta Eat • You Can Be My Nigga • **It's All About You** [58] • Let's Go To Da Sugar Shack • Do You Wanna Ride? • You Don't Have To Cry • **My Up And Down** [32] • Horny For Your Love • Coolin' In The Studio • Baby Come Over

★140★ HOWARD, George '87
Born on 9/15/56 in Philadelphia. Died of cancer on 3/22/98 (age 41). Jazz saxophonist.
1)A Nice Place To Be 2)Love Will Follow 3)A Home Far Away

4/16/83	58	12		1 Asphalt Gardens [I]		$10	Palo Alto 8035
6/2/84	39	22		2 Steppin' Out [I]	178	$8	TBA 201
5/18/85	47	25		3 Dancing in the Sun [I]	169	$8	TBA 205
3/29/86	22	26		4 Love Will Follow [I]	142	$8	TBA 210
12/20/86+	22	29		5 A Nice Place To Be [I]	109	$8	MCA 5855
6/4/88	33	12		6 Reflections [I]	109	$8	MCA 42145
3/24/90	39	14		7 Personal [I]	128	$8	MCA 6335
3/23/91	32	17		8 Love And Understanding [I]	131	$8	GRP 9629
5/23/92	33	19		9 Do I Ever Cross Your Mind [I]	137	$8	GRP 9669
8/7/93	32	16		10 When Summer Comes [I]		$8	GRP 9724
8/20/94	28	13		11 A Home Far Away [I]	180	$8	GRP 9780
3/16/96	38	16		12 Attitude Adjustment [I]		$8	GRP 9839
2/14/98	96	2		13 Midnight Mood [I]		$8	GRP 9902

HOWARD, Miki '90
Born in Chicago. Female singer/songwriter. Former lead singer of **Side Effect**. Portrayed **Billie Holiday** in the movie *Malcolm X*.

12/20/86+	19	35		1 Come Share My Love	171	$8	Atlantic 81688
11/28/87+	13	34		2 Love Confessions	145	$8	Atlantic 81810
11/18/89+	4	43		3 Miki Howard	112	$8	Atlantic 82024

If You Still Love Her • Come Home To Me [53] • Until You Come Back To Me (That's What I'm Gonna Do) [3] • Ain't Nuthin' In The World [1] • Love Under New Management [2] • I'll Be Your Shoulder • Love Me All Over • Mister • Just The Way You Want Me To • Who Ever Said It Was Love

10/3/92	7	29		4 Femme Fatale	110	$8	Giant 24452

Good Morning Heartache • This Bitter Earth • Hope That We Can Be Together Soon • Shining Through • But I Love You • **Ain't Nobody Like You** [1] • I've Been Through It • **Release Me** [43] • Thank You For Talkin' To Me Africa • Cigarette Ashes On The Floor • New Fire From An Old Flame

1/29/94	72	3		5 Miki Sings Billie - A Tribute To Billie Holiday		$8	Giant 24521

HOWLIN' WOLF '71
Born Chester Arthur Burnett on 6/10/10 in West Point, Mississippi. Died on 1/10/76 (age 65). Legendary blues singer/guitarist.

4/12/69	49	4		1 This Is Howlin' Wolf's New Album		$25	Cadet Concept 319
9/11/71	28	10		2 The London Howlin' Wolf Sessions	79	$20	Chess 60008
3/23/74	49	5		3 Back Door Wolf		$20	Chess 50045

H-TOWN '93
Vocal trio from Houston: brothers Shazam and John Conner with Darryl Jackson.

4/24/93	❶¹	37	▲	1 Fever For Da Flavor	16	$8	Luke 126

Can't Fade Da H • Treat U Right • Fever For Da Flavor • Sex Me • H-Town Bounce • **Keepin' My Composure** [46] • Lick U Up [21] • **Knockin' Da Boots** [1] • Won't U Come Back • **Baby I Wanna** [87]

11/26/94	21	42	●	2 Beggin' After Dark	98	$8	Luke 212
11/15/97	12	33		3 Ladies Edition	53	$8	Relativity 1596

★177★ HUBBARD, Freddie '75
Born on 4/7/38 in Indianapolis. Jazz trumpeter.
1)The Baddest Hubbard 2)Windjammer 3)Liquid Love

7/8/67	21	7		1 Backlash [I]		$20	Atlantic 1477
7/4/70	40	7		2 Red Clay [I]		$15	CTI 6001
3/20/71	34	14		3 Straight Life [I]		$15	CTI 6007
1/8/72	25	7		4 First Light [I]		$15	CTI 6013
3/31/73	21	9		5 Sky Dive [I]	165	$12	CTI 6018
1/26/74	36	10		6 Keep Your Soul Together [I]	186	$12	CTI 6036
11/2/74+	23	17		7 High Energy [I]	153	$10	Columbia 33048
12/14/74+	16	12		8 The Baddest Hubbard [I-K]	127	$12	CTI 6047
4/26/75	32	9		9 Polar AC [I]	167	$12	CTI 6056
8/2/75	21	9		10 Liquid Love [I]	149	$10	Columbia 33556
9/4/76	17	10		11 Windjammer [I]	85	$10	Columbia 34166

HUES CORPORATION, The '75
Vocal trio from Los Angeles: H. Ann Kelley, Bernard Henderson and Fleming Williams. Tom Brown replaced Williams in late 1974. Karl Russell replaced Brown in early 1975.

11/3/73	59	2		1 Freedom For The Stallion	20	$10	RCA Victor 0323
12/7/74+	20	10		2 Rockin' Soul		$10	RCA Victor 0775
7/12/75	40	6		3 Love Corporation	147	$10	RCA Victor 0938

HUFF, Leon '80
Born on 4/8/42 in Camden, New Jersey. Keyboardist/producer. Formed Philadelphia International record label with partner Kenny Gamble.

11/8/80	63	6		Here To Create Music [I]	204	$10	Philadelphia I. 36758

HUGHES, Rhetta '69
Singer/actress. Starred in Broadway's *Dreamgirls*.

3/29/69	47	3		Relight My Fire		$15	Tetragrammaton 111

DEBUT	PEAK	WKS	Gold	Album Title	Pop #	$	Label & Number

HUMAN LEAGUE, The   '86
Electro-pop trio from Sheffield, England: Philip Oakey, Joanne Catherall and Susanne Sulley.

| 10/18/86 | 28 | 19 | | Crash | 24 | $8 | A&M 5129 |

HUMPHREY, Bobbi   '75
Born Barbara Ann Humphrey on 4/25/50 in Dallas. Jazz flutist.

| 4/6/74 | 18 | 25 | | 1 Blacks and Blues ....[I] | 84 | $10 | Blue Note 142 |
| 12/14/74+ | 5 | 16 | | 2 Satin Doll | 30 | $10 | Blue Note 344 |

New York Times • Satin Doll • San Francisco Lights • Ladies Day • Fun House [82] • My Little Girl • Rain Again • You Are The Sunshine Of My Life

11/22/75+	24	11		3 Fancy Dancer ....[I]	133	$10	Blue Note 550
11/6/76	43	5		4 Bobbi Humphrey's Best ....[G-I]	208	$10	Blue Note 699
7/9/77	44	3		5 Tailor Made		$10	Epic 34704
6/17/78	34	11		6 Freestyle	89	$10	Epic 35338
8/25/79	64	6		7 The Good Life		$10	Epic 35607
6/10/89	67	9		8 City Beat		$8	Malaco 1502

HUMPHREY, Paul   '71
Born on 10/12/35 in Detroit. Session drummer. The Cool Aid Chemists: Clarence MacDonald, David T. Walker and Bill Upchurch.

| 5/29/71 | 31 | 13 | | Paul Humphrey & The Cool Aid Chemists | 170 | $15 | Lizard 20106 |

HUNTER, Alfonzo   '97
Born in Chicago. Singer/saxophonist.

| 11/16/96+ | 44 | 25 | | Blacka Da Berry | | $8 | Def Squad/EMI 52827 |

HUNTSBERRY, Howard   '88
Born in Pacoima, California. Former lead singer of Klique. Portrayed Jackie Wilson in the 1987 movie La Bamba.

| 10/1/88 | 47 | 10 | | With Love | | $8 | MCA 42217 |

HURBY'S MACHINE   '88
Rap producer Hurby "Luv Bug" Azor.

| 2/20/88 | 28 | 15 | | The House That Rap Built | | $10 | Sound Check 1009 |

HUTCH, Willie   '73
Born Willie Hutchinson in 1946 in Los Angeles; raised in Dallas. Producer/songwriter. Uncle of Don Hutchinson of Above The Law.

5/5/73	17	23		1 The Mack ....[S]	114	$12	Motown 766
10/6/73	15	19		2 Fully Exposed	183	$12	Motown 784
5/4/74	36	10		3 Foxy Brown ....[S]	179	$12	Motown 811
12/21/74+	41	17		4 The Mark Of The Beast		$12	Motown 815
7/19/75	24	20		5 Ode To My Lady	150	$12	Motown 838
3/13/76	22	9		6 Concert In Blues	163	$12	Motown 854
11/20/76	54	4		7 Color Her Sunshine		$12	Motown 871
6/18/77	26	22		8 Havin' A House Party		$12	Motown 874
11/25/78	63	3		9 In Tune		$10	Whitfield 3226

HUTCHERSON, Bobby   '71
Born in 1941 in Los Angeles. Jazz vibraphonist.

| 7/17/71 | 42 | 9 | | San Francisco ....[I] | | $15 | Blue Note 84362 |

HUTSON, Leroy   '76
Born on 6/4/45 in Newark, New Jersey. Member of The Impressions from 1971-73.

3/9/74	36	7		1 The Man!		$12	Curtom 8020
5/17/75	46	5		2 Hutson		$12	Curtom 5002
3/13/76	21	7		3 Feel The Spirit	170	$12	Curtom 5010
12/4/76+	26	13		4 Hutson II		$12	Curtom 5011
10/27/79	69	7		5 Unforgettable		$10	RSO 3062

H.W.A.   '91
Female rap trio: sisters Kim and Tanya Kenner, with Dion Devoux. H.W.A.: Hoes Wit Attitude.

| 11/17/90+ | 38 | 18 | | 1 Livin' In A Hoe House | | $8 | Drive-By 15131 |
| 3/12/94 | 71 | 6 | | 2 Az Much Ass Azz U Want | | $8 | Ruthless 5506 |

HYMAN, Dick   '69
Born on 3/8/27 in New York City. Composer/conductor/pianist/arranger.

| 4/27/68 | 49 | 2 | | 1 Mirrors - Reflections Of Today ....[I] | 179 | $15 | Command 924 |

DICK HYMAN AND "THE GROUP"

| 7/26/69 | 35 | 17 | | 2 Moog - The Electric Eclectics of Dick Hyman ....[I] | 30 | $15 | Command 938 |

HYMAN, Phyllis   ★127★   '91
Born on 7/6/50 in Philadelphia; raised in Pittsburgh. Committed suicide on 6/30/95 (age 44). Singer/actress/model.
1)Prime Of My Life 2)You Know How To Love Me 3)Living All Alone

5/7/77	49	7		1 Phyllis Hyman	107	$12	Buddah 5681
2/10/79	15	19		2 Somewhere In My Lifetime	70	$10	Arista 4202
11/24/79+	10	26		3 You Know How To Love Me	50	$10	Arista 9509

You Know How To Love Me [12] • Some Way • Under Your Spell [37] • This Feeling Must Be Love • But I Love You • Heavenly • Hold On • Give A Little More • Complete Me

8/1/81	11	24		4 Can't We Fall In Love Again	57	$10	Arista 9544
6/25/83	20	16		5 Goddess Of Love	112	$10	Arista 8021
9/13/86+	11	63		6 Living All Alone	78	$8	Philadelphia I. 53029
7/20/91	10	49		7 Prime Of My Life	117	$8	Philadelphia I. 11006

When You Get Right Down To It [10] • I Found Love [70] • Don't Wanna Change The World [1] • Prime Of My Life • When I Give My Love (This Time) • I Can't Take It Anymore • Walk Away • Living In Confusion [9] • Meet Me On The Moon • What Ever Happened To Our Love

DEBUT	PEAK	WKS	Gold	Album Title	Pop #	$	Label & Number
				HYMAN, Phyllis — Cont'd			
11/25/95	12	24		8 I Refuse To Be Lonely	67	$8	Philadelphia I. 11040
4/13/96	47	5		9 Loving You, Losing You		$8	RCA 66838
11/16/96	78	1		10 The Legacy Of Phyllis Hyman		$8	Arista 18938
8/15/98	66	7		11 Forever With You		$8	Philadelphia I. 30902

■

★83★				**ICE CUBE** '91			

Born O'Shea Jackson on 6/15/69 in Los Angeles. Male rapper/actor. Former member of **N.W.A**. Acted in the movies *Boyz N The Hood*, *Trespass*, *Higher Learning* and *Friday*. Cousin of **Del Tha Funkee Homosapien**.

DEBUT	PEAK	WKS	Gold	Album Title	Pop #	$	Label & Number
6/9/90	6	32	▲	1 AmeriKKKa's Most Wanted	19	$8	Priority 57120

Better Off Dead • The Nigga Ya Love To Hate • Amerikkka's Most Wanted • What They Hittin' Foe? • You Can't Fade Me • Once Upon A Time In The Projects • Turn Off The Radio • Endangered Species (Tales From The Darkside) • A Gangsta's Fairytale • I'm Only Out For One Thang • Get Off My Dick And Tell Yo Bitch To Come Here • The Drive-By • Rollin' Wit The Lench Mob • Who's The Mack? • It's A Man's World • The Bomb

1/5/91	5	32	▲	2 Kill At Will [M]	34	$6	Priority 7230

Endangered Species (Tales From The Darkside) • Jackin' For Beats • Get Off My Dick And Tell Yo Bitch To Come Here • The Product • Dead Homiez • JD's Gaffilin' • I Gotta Say What Up!!!

11/23/91	❶³	44	▲	3 Death Certificate	2¹	$8	Priority 57155

The Funeral • The Wrong Nigga To Fuck Wit • My Summer Vacation • **Steady Mobbin'** *[30]* • Robin Lench • Givin' Up The Nappy Dug Out • Look Who's Burnin' • A Bird In The Hand • Man's Best Friend • Alive On Arrival • Death • The Birth • I Wanna Kill Sam • Horny Lil' Devil • Black Korea • True To The Game • Color Blind • Doing Dumb Shit • Us • No Vaseline

12/5/92	❶¹	56	▲	4 The Predator	1¹	$8	Priority 57185

The First Day Of School • When Will They Shoot? • I'm Scared • **Wicked** *[47]* • Now I Gotta Wet 'Cha • The Predator • **It Was A Good Day** *[7]* • We Had To Tear This Mothafucka Up • Fuck 'Em • Dirty Mack • Don't Trust 'Em • Gangsta's Fairytale 2 • **Check Yo Self** *[1]* • Who Got The Camera? • Integration • Say Hi To The Bad Guy

12/18/93	❶¹	51	▲	5 Lethal Injection	5	$8	Priority 53876

The Shot • **Really Doe** *[30]* • Ghetto Bird • **You Know How We Do It** *[21]* • Cave Bitch • **Bop Gun (One Nation)** *[37]* • What Can I Do? • Lil Ass Gee • Make It Ruff, Make It Smooth • Down For Whatever • Enemy • When I Get To Heaven

12/10/94	3	35	●	6 Bootlegs & B-Sides [K]	19	$8	Priority 53921

Robbin' Hood (Cause It Ain't All Good) • What Can I Do? • 24 Wit An L • You Know How We Do It • 2 N The Morning • Check Yo Self • You Don't Wanna Fuck Wit These • Lil Ass Gee • My Skin Is My Sin • It Was A Good Day • U Ain't Gonna Take My Life • When I Get To Heaven • D'Voidofpopniggafiedmegamix

1/3/98	32	13		7 Featuring...Ice Cube [K]	116	$8	Priority 51037

contains Ice Cube's guest raps on hits by other artists

12/5/98	2¹	31	▲	8 War & Peace Vol. I (The War Disc)	7	$8	Priority 50700

Ask About Me • **Pushin' Weight** *[12]* • Dr. Frankenstein • Fuck Dying • War & Peace • Ghetto Vet • Greed • MP • Cash Over Ass • The Curse Of Money • The Peckin' Order • Limos, Demos & Bimbos • Once Upon A Time In The Projects 2 • If I Was Fuckin' You • X-Bitches • Extradition • 3 Strikes You In • Penitentiary

				ICE-T '88			

Born Tracy Morrow on 2/16/58 in Newark, New Jersey. Male rapper/actor. In the movies *New Jack City*, *Who's The Man?*, *Trespass* and *Tank Girl*. Formed own Rhyme Syndicate record label.

8/8/87	26	31	●	1 Rhyme Pays	93	$8	Sire 25602
10/8/88	6	32	●	2 Power	35	$8	Sire 25765

Power • Drama • Heartbeat • The Syndicate • Radio Suckers • **I'm Your Pusher** *[13]* • Personal • Girls L.G.B.N.A.F. • **High Rollers** *[76]* • Grand Larceny • Soul On Ice

11/4/89	11	27	●	3 Freedom Of Speech...Just Watch What You Say	37	$8	Sire 26028

ICE-T The Iceberg

6/8/91	9	22	●	4 O.G. Original Gangster	15	$8	Sire 26492

Home Of The Bodybag • First Impression • Ziplock • Mic Contract • Mind Over Matter • **New Jack Hustler (Nino's Theme)** *[49]* • Ed • Bitches 2 • Straight Up Nigga • O.G. Original Gangster • The House • Evil E-What About Sex? • Fly By • Midnight • Fried Chicken • M.V.P.s • Lifestyles Of The Rich And Infamous • Body Count • Prepared To Die • Escape From The Killing Fields • Street Killer • Pulse Of The Rhyme • The Tower • Ya Shoulda Killed Me Last Year

4/10/93	9	13	●	5 Home Invasion	14	$8	Rhyme Syndicate 53858

Warning • It's On • Ice M.F. T • Home Invasion • G Style • Addicted To Danger • Question And Answer • Watch The Ice Break • Race War • That's How I'm Livin' • I Ain't New Ta This • Pimp Behind The Wheels • Gotta Lotta Love • Shit Hit The Fan • Depths Of Hell • 99 Problems • Funky Gripsta • Message To The Soldier • Ain't A Damn Thing Changed

6/22/96	19	8		6 VI: Return Of The Real	89	$8	Rhyme Syndicate 53933
				ILL AL SKRATCH '94			

Male rap duo from New York City: ILL (I Lyrical Lord) and Al Skratch.

8/20/94	22	16		1 Creep Wit' Me	137	$8	Mercury 522661
5/10/97	55	4		2 Keep It Movin'		$8	Mercury 532945
				ILLEGAL '93			

Male rap duo from Atlanta: Malik Edwards and Jamal Phillips.

9/11/93	19	13		The Untold Truth	119	$8	Rowdy 37002
				IMAGINATION '84			

Dance trio from London: Leee John (vocals), Ashley Ingram (keyboards, bass) and Errol Kennedy (drums).

3/6/82	46	14		1 Body Talk		$10	MCA 5271
11/13/82	45	11		2 In The Heat Of The Night		$10	MCA 5373
3/3/84	44	8		3 New Dimension	205	$10	Elektra 60316

DEBUT	PEAK	WKS	Gold	Album Title	Pop #	$	Label & Number

IMMATURE   '96
Vocal trio from Los Angeles: Marques Houston, Jerome Jones and Kelton Kessee.

8/20/94	26	45	●	1 Playtyme Is Over	88	$8	MCA 11068
12/23/95+	14	36	●	2 We Got It	76	$8	MCA 11385
10/11/97	20	31		3 The Journey	92	$8	MCA 11668

I.M.P.   '93
Rap group from San Francisco: cousins Rob V and Cougnut, with Stingy, C-Fresh and Lou-E-Lou.

| 5/29/93 | 100 | 1 | | Back In The Days | | $8 | In-A-Minute 8200 |

IMPRESSIONS, The   ★50★   '65
Vocal group from Chicago: **Jerry Butler**, **Curtis Mayfield**, Sam Gooden and brothers Arthur and Richard Brooks. Butler left in 1958, replaced by Fred Cash. The Brooks brothers left in 1962, leaving Mayfield as the trio's leader. Mayfield left in 1970 for a solo career, replaced by **Leroy Hutson**. In 1973, Hutson was replaced by Reggie Torian and Ralph Johnso. Group inducted into the Rock and Roll Hall of Fame in 1991.

1)People Get Ready 2)The Impressions Greatest Hits 3)We're A Winner

| 1/30/65 | 4 | 2 | | 1 **Keep On Pushing** | 8 | $30 | ABC-Paramount 493 |

Keep On Pushing [10] • I've Been Trying [35] • I Ain't Supposed To • Dedicate My Song To You • Long Long Winter • Somebody Help Me • **Amen** [17] • I Thank Heaven • **Talking About My Baby** [12] • Don't Let It Hide • I Love You (Yeah) • I Made A Mistake

| 3/6/65 | ❶² | 13 | | 2 **People Get Ready** | 23 | $30 | ABC-Paramount 505 |

Woman's Got Soul [9] • Emotions • Sometimes I Wonder • We're In Love • Just Another Dance • Can't Work No Longer • **People Get Ready** [3] • I've Found That I've Lost • Hard To Believe • See The Real Me • Get Up And Move • **You Must Believe Me** [15]

| 3/13/65 | 2² | 12 | | 3 **The Impressions Greatest Hits** [G] | 83 | $30 | ABC-Paramount 515 |

It's All Right [1] • Gypsy Woman [2] • Grow Closer Together • Little Young Lover • You've Come Home • Never Let Me Go • Minstrel And Queen • I Need Your Love • I'm The One Who Loves You • Sad, Sad Girl And Boy • As Long As You Love Me • Twist And Limbo

| 9/11/65 | 4 | 11 | | 4 **One By One** | 104 | $25 | ABC-Paramount 523 |

Twilight Time • I Wanna Be Around • Nature Boy • Just One Kiss From You • I Want To Be With You • Answer Me, My Love • It's Not Unusual • Without A Song • Falling In Love With You • My Prayer • Mona Lisa • Lonely Man

| 3/12/66 | 4 | 15 | | 5 **Ridin' High** | 79 | $25 | ABC-Paramount 545 |

Ridin' High • No One Else • Gotta Get Away • I Need To Belong To Someone • Right On Time • I Need A Love • Too Slow • Man's Temptation • That's What Mama Say • Let It Be Me • I'm A Tellin' You

| 7/15/67 | 16 | 13 | | 6 The Fabulous Impressions | 184 | $20 | ABC 606 |
| 3/2/68 | 4 | 20 | | 7 **We're A Winner** | 35 | $20 | ABC 635 |

We're A Winner [1] • Moonlight Shadows • Let Me Tell The World • I'm Gettin' Ready • Nothing Can Stop Me • No One To Love • Little Brown Boy • **I Loved And I Lost** [9] • Romancing To The Folk Song • Up Up And Away

| 9/14/68 | 23 | 15 | | 8 The Best Of The Impressions [G] | 172 | $20 | ABC 654 |
| 11/16/68+ | 5 | 26 | | 9 **This Is My Country** | 107 | $15 | Curtom 8001 |

They Don't Know • Stay Close To Me • I'm Loving Nothing • Loves Happening • Gone Away • You Want Somebody Else • So Unusual • My Woman's Love • **Fool For You** [3] • **This Is My Country** [8]

5/10/69	21	25		10 The Young Mods' Forgotten Story	104	$15	Curtom 8003
2/21/70	23	11		11 Best Of The Impressions [G]		$15	Curtom 8004
10/10/70	22	4		12 Check Out Your Mind		$15	Curtom 8006
3/20/71	23	6		13 16 Greatest Hits [G]	180	$15	ABC 727
3/24/73	31	9		14 Preacher Man	204	$12	Curtom 8016
5/18/74	16	28		15 Finally Got Myself Together	176	$12	Curtom 8019
7/20/74	26	15		16 Three The Hard Way [S]	202	$12	Curtom 8602
7/12/75	13	16		17 First Impressions	115	$12	Curtom 5003
3/13/76	24	6		18 Loving Power	195	$12	Curtom 5009

IMPROMP2   '95
Jazz/rap duo of Johnny Britt and Sean E. Mac.

| 6/24/95 | 52 | 17 | | 1 You're Gonna Love It | | $8 | MoJazz 0541 |
| 4/12/97 | 72 | 5 | | 2 Can't Get Enough | | $8 | MoJazz 0748 |

INCOGNITO   '95
British trio: **Maysa** Leak (female vocals), Jean Paul Maunick (guitar) and Patrick Clahar (sax).

3/6/93	74	12		1 Tribes, Vibes & Scribes		$8	Talkin Loud 514198
4/9/94	54	47		2 Positivity		$8	Talkin Loud 522036
6/24/95	29	20		3 100 Degrees And Rising	149	$8	Talkin Loud 528000

INCREDIBLE BONGO BAND, The   '73
Studio band assembled in Canada by producer Michael Viner.

| 8/25/73 | 58 | 3 | | Bongo Rock | 197 | $12 | Pride 0028 |

INDEEP   '83
Dance group led by writer/producer Michael Cleveland with female singers Reggie Megliore and Rose Marie Ramsey.

| 7/2/83 | 43 | 10 | | Last Night A D.J. Saved My Life! | | $10 | Sound Of N.Y. 1201 |

INDEPENDENTS, The   '73
Vocal group from Chicago: Chuck Jackson, Maurice Jackson, Helen Curry and Eric Thomas.

| 1/20/73 | 18 | 28 | | 1 The First Time We Met | 127 | $25 | Wand 694 |
| 12/14/74 | 42 | 4 | | 2 Discs Of Gold [G] | 209 | $25 | Wand 699 |

DEBUT	PEAK	WKS	Gold	Album Title	Pop #	$	Label & Number

INDO G   '98
Born in Memphis. Male rapper. Member of **Prophet Posse**.

| 9/12/98 | 32 | 5 | | Angel Dust | 105 | $8 | Relativity 1683 |

INFORMATION SOCIETY   '88
Techno-dance group from Minneapolis: Kurt Valaquen (vocals), Paul Robb (songwriter), Amanda Kramer (keyboards) and James Cassidy (bass).

| 9/17/88 | 78 | 9 | ● | Information Society | 25 | $8 | Tommy Boy 25691 |

INGRAM, James   '84
Born on 2/16/56 in Akron, Ohio. Singer/songwriter/multi-instrumentalist. Former member of the group Revelation Funk.

| 11/19/83+ | 10 | 41 | ● | 1 It's Your Night | 46 | $8 | Qwest 23970 |

Party Animal [21] • Yah Mo B There [5] • She Loves Me (The Best That I Can Be) [59] • Try Your Love Again • Whatever We Imagine • One More Rhythm • There's No Easy Way [14] • It's Your Night • How Do You Keep The Music Playing

9/20/86	37	13		2 Never Felt So Good	123	$8	Qwest 25424
6/17/89	44	24		3 It's Real	117	$8	Warner 25924
6/12/93	74	3		4 Always You		$8	Warner 45275

INGRAM, Luther   '72
Born on 11/30/44 in Jackson, Tennessee. Singer/songwriter.

| 1/8/72 | 21 | 15 | | 1 I've Been Here All The Time | 175 | $15 | Koko 2201 |
| 10/14/72 | 5 | 23 | | 2 If Loving You Is Wrong I Don't Want To Be Right | 39 | $15 | Koko 2202 |

(If Loving You Is Wrong) I Don't Want To Be Right [1] • I'll Be Your Shelter (In Time Of Storm) [9] • Always [11] • Dying & Crying • Help Me Love • I'm Trying To Sing A Message To You • I Remember • I'll Love You Until The End [39] • Love Ain't Gonna Run Me Away [23] • I Can't Stop

| 3/21/87 | 61 | 3 | | 3 Luther Ingram | | $10 | Profile 1226 |

INNER CIRCLE   '93
Reggae group from Kingston, Jamaica: Calton Coffie (vocals), Touter Harvey, Lancelot Hall, brothers Ian and Roger Lewis, and Lester Adderly.

| 5/22/93 | 41 | 47 | ▲ | Bad Boys | 64 | $8 | Big Beat 92261 |

INNER CITY   '90
Techno-funk group led by producer/songwriter/mixer Kevin Saunderson (from Detroit) and female singer Paris Grey (from Glencove, Illinois).

| 2/17/90 | 58 | 6 | | Big Fun | 162 | $8 | Virgin 91242 |

INNER LIFE   '80
Vocal group: **Jocelyn Brown**, Krystal Davis, Janet Wright and Dennis Collins.

| 1/12/80 | 47 | 11 | | I'm Caught Up | | $10 | Prelude 12175 |

INNOCENCE   '91
British dance group: singer Gee Morris with producers Anna Jolley, Mark Jolley and Brian Harris.

| 5/25/91 | 54 | 15 | | Belief | | $8 | Chrysalis 21797 |

INSANE POETRY   '92
Rap trio from Los Angeles: Psycho, DJ Streek and Em'Dee.

| 11/7/92 | 98 | 4 | | Grim Reality | | $8 | Nastymix 7108 |

INSTANT FUNK   '79
Funk group from Philadelphia. Core members: James Carmichael (vocals), Kim Miller (guitar), Dennis Richardson (keyboards), Raymond Earl (bass) and Scotty Miller (drums).

| 2/10/79 | ❶[1] | 22 | ● | 1 Instant Funk | 12 | $10 | Salsoul 8513 |

I Got My Mind Made Up (You Can Get It Girl) [1] • Crying [41] • Never Let It Go Away • Don't You Wanna Party • Wide World Of Sports • Dark Vader • You Say You Want Me To Stay • I'll Be Doggone

12/1/79	23	14		2 Witch Doctor	129	$10	Salsoul 8529
10/11/80	62	10		3 The Funk Is On	130	$10	Salsoul 8536
4/10/82	43	8		4 Looks So Fine	147	$10	Salsoul 8545
2/19/83	38	20		5 Instant Funk V		$10	Salsoul 8558

INTELLIGENT HOODLUM   '90
Born Percy Chapman in Long Island, New York. Male rapper.

| 8/25/90 | 52 | 26 | | 1 Intelligent Hoodlum | | $8 | A&M 5311 |
| 7/10/93 | 57 | 3 | | 2 Tragedy - Saga Of A Hoodlum | | $8 | A&M 5389 |

INTRO   '93
Vocal trio from New York City: Kenny Greene, Clinton Wike and Jeff Sanders.

| 4/24/93 | 11 | 59 | ● | 1 Intro | 65 | $8 | Atlantic 82463 |
| 11/18/95 | 16 | 21 | | 2 New Life | 86 | $8 | Atlantic 82662 |

INTRUDERS, The   '68
Vocal group from Philadelphia: Sam Brown, Eugene Daughtry, Phil Terry and Robert Edwards. Daughtry died on 12/25/94 (age 55).

1/13/68	23	3		1 The Intruders Are Together		$40	Gamble 5001
7/13/68	11	17		2 Cowboys To Girls	112	$40	Gamble 5004
2/1/69	19	14		3 The Intruders Greatest Hits ......[G]	144	$40	Gamble 5005
12/19/70	48	2		4 When We Get Married		$40	Gamble 5008
5/19/73	12	15		5 Save The Children	133	$20	Gamble 31991
7/28/73	51	4		6 Super Hits ......[G]	205	$20	Gamble 32131
5/31/75	41	4		7 Energy Of Love		$15	TSOP 33149

INVISIBLE MAN'S BAND, The   '80
Vocal group evolved from **The Five Stairsteps**. Consisted of brothers Clarence, Kenneth, Dennis and James Burke.

| 6/7/80 | 19 | 17 | | The Invisible Man's Band | 90 | $10 | Mango 9537 |

IRBY, Joyce "Fenderella"   '89
Born in Florida. Former member of **Klymaxx**.

| 5/13/89 | 19 | 24 | | Maximum Thrust | | $8 | Motown 6267 |

ISIS   '91
Born Lin Que Ayoung in Queens, New York. Female rapper.

12/1/90+   **52**   22   Rebel Soul .... $8   4th & B'way 444030

ISLEY BROTHERS, The ★7★   '80
Trio of brothers from Cincinnati: O'Kelly, Rudolph and Ronald Isley. Moved to New York in 1957 and first recorded for Teenage Records. Trio added their younger brothers Ernie (guitar, drums) and Marvin (bass, percussion) Isley and brother-in-law Chris Jasper (keyboards) in September 1969. Formed own T-Neck label the same year. Ernie, Marvin and Chris began recording as the trio **Isley Jasper Isley** in 1984. O'Kelly died of a heart attack on 3/31/86 (age 48); Ronald and Rudolph continued on as The Isley Brothers through 1990. Ernie, Marvin and Ronald reunited as The Isley Brothers in 1991. Ronald married **Angela Winbush** on 6/26/93. Group inducted into the Rock and Roll Hall of Fame in 1992.

1)Go All The Way 2)The Heat Is On 3)Showdown 4)Go For Your Guns 5)Between The Sheets

DEBUT	PEAK	WKS		Album Title	Pop #	$	Label & Number
7/16/66	**15**	6		1 This Old Heart Of Mine	140	$30	Tamla 269
4/26/69	**2**[2]	24		2 It's Our Thing	22	$20	T-Neck 3001

I Know Who You Been Socking It To • Somebody Been Messin' • Save Me • I Must Be Losing My Touch • Feel Like The World • **It's Your Thing [1]** • Give The Women What They Want • Love Is What You Make It • Don't Give It Away • He's Got Your Love

11/22/69	**20**	7		3 The Brothers: Isley	180	$20	T-Neck 3002
9/25/71	**13**	24		4 Givin' It Back	71	$15	T-Neck 3008
7/1/72	**5**	26		5 Brother, Brother, Brother	29	$15	T-Neck 3009

Brother, Brother • Put A Little Love In Your Heart • Sweet Seasons • Keep On Walkin' • **Work To Do [11]** • **Pop That Thang [3]** • Lay-Away [6] • It's Too Late [39] • Love Put Me On The Corner

3/24/73	**14**	14		6 The Isleys Live [L]	139	$20	T-Neck 3010 [2]
9/8/73	**2**[1]	38	▲	7 3 + 3	8	$12	T-Neck 32453

That Lady [2] • Don't Let Me Be Lonely Tonight • If You Were There • You Walk Your Way • Listen To The Music • **What It Comes Down To [5]** • Sunshine (Go Away Today) • **Summer Breeze [10]** • The Highways Of My Life

12/8/73+	**24**	8		8 Isleys' Greatest Hits [G]	195	$12	T-Neck 3011
9/28/74	**❶**[1]	29	●	9 Live It Up	14	$12	T-Neck 33070

Live It Up [4] • Brown Eyed Girl • Need A Little Taste Of Love • Lover's Eve • **Midnight Sky [8]** • Hello It's Me • Ain't I Been Good To You

6/28/75	**❶**[4]	25	▲	10 The Heat Is On	1[1]	$12	T-Neck 33536

Fight The Power [1] • The Heat Is On • Hope You Feel Better Love • **For The Love Of You [10]** • Sensuality • Make Me Say It Again Girl

3/20/76	**49**	4		11 The Best...Isley Brothers [G]		$15	Buddah 5652 [2]
5/29/76	**❶**[1]	27	●	12 Harvest For The World	9	$12	T-Neck 33809

Harvest For The World [9] • People Of Today • **Who Loves You Better [3]** • (At Your Best) You Are Love • Let Me Down Easy • So You Wanna Stay Down • You Still Feel The Need

4/16/77	**❶**[2]	33	▲	13 Go For Your Guns	6	$12	T-Neck 34432

The Pride [1] • Footsteps In The Dark • Tell Me When You Need It Again • Climbin' Up The Ladder • **Voyage To Atlantis [50]** • Livin' In The Life [4] • Go For Your Guns

10/22/77	**40**	8		14 Forever Gold [G]	58	$12	T-Neck 34452
4/29/78	**❶**[3]	24	▲	15 Showdown	4	$12	T-Neck 34930

Showdown • **Groove With You [16]** • Ain't Givin' Up No Love • Rockin' With Fire • **Take Me To The Next Phase [1]** • Coolin' Me Out • Fun And Games • Love Fever

11/25/78	**70**	3		16 Timeless [G]	204	$12	T-Neck 35650 [2]
6/16/79	**3**	30		17 Winner Takes All	14	$12	T-Neck 36077 [2]

I Wanna Be With You [1] • Liquid Love • **Winner Takes All [38]** • Let's Fall In Love • How Lucky I Am • You're The Key To My Heart • You're Beside Me • Let Me In Your Life • Love Comes And Goes • Go For What You Know • Mind Over Matter • Life In The City • **It's A Disco Night (Rock Don't Stop) [27]** • (Can't You See) What You Do To Me?

4/19/80	**❶**[5]	27	▲	<u>18 Go All The Way</u>	8	$10	T-Neck 36305

Go All The Way • Say You Will • Pass It On • **Here We Go Again [11]** • Don't Say Goodnight (It's Time For Love) [1] • The Belly Dancer

3/21/81	**3**	24	●	19 Grand Slam	28	$10	T-Neck 37080

Tonight Is The Night (If I Had You) • **I Once Had Your Love (And I Can't Let Go) [57]** • Hurry Up And Wait [17] • Young Girls • Party Night • Don't Let Up • Who Said? [20]

10/31/81	**8**	23		20 Inside You	45	$10	T-Neck 37533

Inside You [10] • Baby Hold On • Don't Hold Back Your Love • First Love • Love Merry-Go-Round • **Welcome Into My Heart [45]** • Love Zone

8/21/82	**9**	18		21 The Real Deal	87	$10	T-Neck 38047

The Real Deal [14] • Are You With Me? • Stone Cold Lover • **It's Alright With Me [59]** • All In My Lover's Eyes [67] • I'll Do It All For You • Under The Influence

6/4/83	**❶**[1]	31	▲	22 Between The Sheets	19	$10	T-Neck 38674

Choosey Lover [6] • Touch Me • I Need Your Body • **Between The Sheets [3]** • Let's Make Love Tonight • Ballad For The Fallen Soldier • Slow Down Children • Way Out Love • Gettin' Over • Rock You Good

12/7/85	**19**	27		23 Masterpiece	140	$10	Warner 25347
6/20/87	**5**	24		24 Smooth Sailin'	64	$10	Warner 25586

Everything Is Alright • Dish It Out • It Takes A Good Woman • Send A Message • **Smooth Sailin' Tonight [3]** • Somebody I Used To Know • Come My Way [71] • I Wish [74]

THE ISLEY BROTHERS Featuring Ronald Isley:

9/2/89	**4**	37		25 Spend The Night	89	$10	Warner 25940

Spend The Night (Ce Soir) [3] • You'll Never Walk Alone [25] • One Of A Kind [38] • Real Woman • Come Together • If You Ever Need Somebody • Baby Come Back Home

6/20/92	**19**	18		26 Tracks Of Life	140	$8	Warner 26620
10/2/93	**34**	33		27 Live! [L]		$8	Elektra 61538
8/27/94	**67**	9		28 Beautiful Ballads [K]		$8	Legacy 57860

DEBUT	PEAK	WKS	Gold	Album Title	Pop #	$	Label & Number

ISLEY BROTHERS Featuring Ronald Isley — Cont'd

DEBUT	PEAK	WKS		Album Title	Pop #	$	Label & Number
6/1/96	2¹	71	▲ 29	Mission To Please	31	$8	Island 524214

Floatin' On Your Love [14] • Whenever You're Ready • **Let's Lay Together** [24] • **Tears** [12] • Can I Have A Kiss (For Old Times' Sake)? • Mission To Please You • Holding Back The Years • Make Your Body Sing • Let's Get Intimate • Slow Is The Way

ISLEY, JASPER, ISLEY   '85

Trio consisting of Ernie Isley, Chris Jasper, Marvin Isley. All were members of **The Isley Brothers** from 1973-84.

12/22/84+	28	20	1	Broadway's Closer To Sunset Blvd.	135	$8	CBS Associated 39873
11/2/85	3	32	2	Caravan Of Love	77	$8	CBS Associated 40118

Dancin' Around The World • **Insatiable Woman** [13] • I Can Hardly Wait • Liberation • **Caravan Of Love** [1] • If You Believe In Love • High Heel Syndrome

6/6/87	40	19	3	Different Drummer		$8	CBS Associated 40409

J

JACKSON, Chuck   '66

Born on 7/22/37 in Latta, South Carolina; raised in Pittsburgh.

8/6/66	21	3	1	A Tribute To Rhythm And Blues		$30	Wand 673
5/25/68	48	3	2	Chuck Jackson Arrives!		$25	Motown 667

★52★   **JACKSON, Freddie**   '86

Born on 10/2/56 in Harlem, New York. Singer/songwriter.

5/25/85	❶¹⁴	63	▲ 1	Rock Me Tonight	10	$8	Capitol 12404

He'll Never Love You (Like I Do) [8] • Love Is Just A Touch Away [9] • I Wanna Say I Love You • **You Are My Lady** [1] • Rock Me Tonight (For Old Times' Sake) [1] • Sing A Song Of Love • Calling • Good Morning Heartache

11/8/86	❶²⁶	69	▲ 2	Just Like The First Time	23	$8	Capitol 12495

Tasty Love [1] • Have You Ever Loved Somebody [1] • Look Around [69] • **Jam Tonight** [1] • Just Like The First Time • I Can't Let You Go • **I Don't Want To Lose Your Love** [2] • Janay • Still Waiting • You Are My Love

8/13/88	❶¹	50	● 3	Don't Let Love Slip Away	48	$8	Capitol 48987

Nice 'N' Slow [1] • Hey Lover [1] • Don't Let Love Slip Away • **Crazy (For Me)** [17] • One Heart Too Many • If You Don't Know Me By Now • **You And I Got A Thang** [5] • Special Lady • Yes, I Need You • It's Gonna Take A Long, Long Time

12/1/90+	❶²	46	● 4	Do Me Again	59	$8	Capitol 92217

Don't It Feel Good • **Love Me Down** [1] • **Main Course** [2] • It Takes Two • I'll Be Waiting For You • Don't Say You Love Me • Do Me Again [1] • Live For The Moment • **Second Time For Love** [81] • I Can't Take It • **All Over You** [4]

8/29/92	7	28	5	Time For Love	83	$8	Capitol 96859

I Could Use A Little Love (Right Now) [2] • Time For Love Tonight • Chivalry • Trouble • **Can I Touch You** [30] • All I'll Ever Ask • Will You Be There • Come With Me Tonight • Can We Try • **Me And Mrs. Jones** [32] • Live My Life Without You

2/5/94	11	15	6	Here It Is	66	$8	Orpheus 66318
2/12/94	45	10	7	The Greatest Hits of Freddie Jackson		$8	[G] Capitol 27641
12/17/94	65	4	8	At Christmas		$8	[X] RCA 66451
3/18/95	28	14	9	Private Party	187	$8	Street Life 75457

JACKSON, Jackie   '89

Born Sigmund Jackson on 5/4/51 in Gary, Indiana. The eldest son of **The Jacksons** family group.

4/15/89	84	7		Be The One		$8	Polydor 837766

★67★   **JACKSON, Janet**   '86

Born on 5/16/66 in Gary, Indiana. Sister of **The Jacksons**. Singer/songwriter/actress. Acted in the TV shows *Good Times*, *Diff'rent Strokes* and *Fame*. Married James DeBarge of **DeBarge** in August 1984; marriage annulled in March 1985. Starred in the 1993 movie *Poetic Justice*.

11/6/82+	6	45	1	Janet Jackson	63	$10	A&M 4907

Say You Do [15] • You'll Never Find (A Love Like Mine) • Young Love [6] • Love And My Best Friend • Don't Mess Up This Good Thing • Forever Yours • The Magic Is Working • **Come Give Your Love To Me** [17]

9/22/84	19	15	2	Dream Street	147	$10	A&M 4962
3/1/86	❶⁸	91	▲⁵ 3	Control	1²	$8	A&M 5106

Control [1] • Nasty [1] • What Have You Done For Me Lately [1] • You Can Be Mine • The Pleasure Principle [1] • When I Think Of You [3] • He Doesn't Know I'm Alive • **Let's Wait Awhile** [1] • Funny How Time Flies (When You're Having Fun)

10/7/89	❶³	86	▲⁶ 4	Janet Jackson's Rhythm Nation 1814	1⁴	$8	A&M 3920

Rhythm Nation [1] • State Of The World • The Knowledge • Miss You Much [1] • Love Will Never Do (Without You) [3] • Livin' In A World (They Didn't Make) • **Alright** [2] • Escapade [1] • Black Cat [10] • Lonely • **Come Back To Me** [2] • Someday Is Tonight

6/5/93	❶³	97	▲⁶ 5	janet.	1⁶	$8	Virgin 87825

That's The Way Love Goes [1] • You Want This [9] • If [3] • This Time • Throb • What'll I Do • Funky Big Band • New Agenda • Because Of Love [9] • Again [7] • Where Are You Now • The Body That Loves You • **Any Time, Any Place** [1] • Are You Still Up

10/28/95	4	25	▲² 6	Design Of A Decade 1986/1996	3	$8	[G] A&M 0399

Runaway [6] • What Have You Done For Me Lately [1] • Nasty [1] • When I Think Of You [3] • Escapade [1] • Miss You Much [1] • Love Will Never Do (Without You) [3] • Alright [2] • Control [1] • The Pleasure Principle [1] • Black Cat [10] • Rhythm Nation [1] • That's The Way Love Goes [1] • Come Back To Me [2] • Let's Wait Awhile [1] • Twenty Foreplay

10/25/97	2¹	76	▲³ 7	The Velvet Rope	1¹	$8	Virgin 44762

JANET

Velvet Rope • You • Got 'Til It's Gone • My Need • Go Deep • Free Xone • **Together Again** [8] • Empty • What About • Every Time • Tonight's The Night • **I Get Lonely** [1] • Rope Burn • Anything • Special

DEBUT	PEAK	WKS	Gold	Album Title	Pop #	$	Label & Number

★78★ **JACKSON, Jermaine**   **'80**

Born on 12/11/54 in Gary, Indiana. Fourth eldest of **The Jacksons**. Member of The Jackson 5 until group left Motown in 1976. Married Hazel Joy Gordy, daughter of Motown founder Berry Gordy, on 12/15/73; later divorced. Rejoined The Jacksons in 1984 for the group's *Victory* album and tour.

1)*Let's Get Serious*   2)*Jermaine Jackson*   3)*Jermaine*

DEBUT	PEAK	WKS	Gold	Album Title	Pop #	$	Label & Number
8/12/72	6	29		1 **Jermaine**	27	$10	Motown 752

That's How Love Goes [23] • I'm In A Different World • Homeward Bound • Take Me In Your Arms (Rock Me For A Little While) • I Only Have Eyes For You • I Let Love Pass Me By • Live It Up • If You Were My Woman • Ain't That Peculiar • **Daddy's Home** [3]

6/30/73	30	6		2 **Come Into My Life**	152	$10	Motown 775
9/25/76	29	9		3 **My Name Is Jermaine**	164	$10	Motown 842
8/13/77	36	6		4 **Feel The Fire**	174	$10	Motown 888
4/12/80	❶⁵	29	●	5 **Let's Get Serious**	6	$10	Motown 928

Let's Get Serious [1] • Where Are You Now • You Got To Hurry Girl • We Can Put It Back Together • Burnin' Hot • **You're Supposed To Keep Your Love For Me** [32] • Feelin' Free

12/13/80+	17	31		6 **Jermaine**	27	$10	Motown 948
9/26/81	31	21		7 **I Like Your Style**	86	$10	Motown 952
8/14/82	9	22		8 **Let Me Tickle Your Fancy**	46	$10	Motown 6017

Let Me Tickle Your Fancy [5] • Very Special Part [54] • Uh, Uh, I Didn't Do It • You Belong To Me • You Moved A Mountain • Running • Messing Around • This Time • There's A Better Way • I Like Your Style

5/19/84	❶¹	48	●	9 **Jermaine Jackson**	19	$8	Arista 8203

Dynamite [8] • Sweetest Sweetest • Tell Me I'm Not Dreamin' (Too Good To Be True) • Escape From The Planet Of The Ant Men • Come To Me (One Way Or Another) • **Do What You Do** [14] • Take Good Care Of My Heart • Some Things Are Private • Oh Mother

3/22/86	25	26		10 **Precious Moments**	46	$8	Arista 8277
11/11/89+	18	35		11 **Don't Take It Personal**	115	$8	Arista 8493
11/30/91+	39	17		12 **You Said**		$8	LaFace 26001

JACKSON, J.J.   **'67**

Born on Jerome Louis Jackson on 4/8/41 in Brooklyn, New York. Not to be confused with the former MTV VJ.

2/4/67	24	2		**But It's Alright/I Dig Girls**		$20	Calla 1101

JACKSON, LaToya   **'80**

Born on 5/29/56 in Gary, Indiana. Sister of **The Jacksons**.

10/11/80	26	20		1 **LaToya Jackson**	116	$10	Polydor 6291
7/7/84	65	3		2 **Heart Don't Lie**	149	$8	Private I 39361

JACKSON, Marlon   **'87**

Born on 3/12/57 in Gary, Indiana. Member of **The Jacksons**.

10/24/87	22	22		**Baby Tonight**	175	$8	Capitol 46942

JACKSON, Michael   ★15★   **'83**

Born on 8/29/58 in Gary, Indiana. Became lead singer of **The Jackson 5** at age five. Played "The Scarecrow" in the 1978 movie musical *The Wiz*. Starred in the 15-minute movie *Captain Eo*, which was shown exclusively at Disneyland and Disneyworld. His 1988 autobiography, *Moonwalker*, became a movie the same year. Won Grammy's Living Legends Award in 1993. Married to Elvis Presley's daughter, Lisa Marie, from 1994-96.

1)*Thriller*   2)*Bad*   3)*Off The Wall*

DEBUT	PEAK	WKS	Gold	Album Title	Pop #	$	Label & Number
2/19/72	3	24		1 **Got To Be There**	14	$15	Motown 747

Ain't No Sunshine • **I Wanna Be Where You Are** [2] • Girl Don't Take Your Love From Me • In Our Small Way • Got To Be There [4] • Rockin' Robin [2] • Wings Of My Love • Maria (You Were The Only One) • Love Is Here And Now You're Gone • You've Got A Friend

10/14/72	4	22		2 **Ben**	5	$15	Motown 755

Ben [5] • Greatest Show On Earth • People Make The World Go Round • We've Got A Good Thing Going • Everybody's Somebody's Fool • My Girl • What Goes Around Comes Around • In Our Small Way • Shoo Be Doo Be Doo Da Day • You Can Cry On My Shoulder

5/5/73	24	10		3 **Music & Me**	92	$15	Motown 767
2/8/75	10	12		4 **Forever, Michael**	101	$12	Motown 825

We're Almost There [7] • Take Me Back • One Day In Your Life [42] • Cinderella Stay Awhile • We've Got Forever • **Just A Little Bit Of You** [4] • You Are There • Dapper-Dan • Dear Michael • I'll Come Home To You

10/11/75	44	5		5 **The Best Of Michael Jackson**	[G]	156	$12	Motown 851
9/1/79	❶¹⁶	61	▲⁷	6 **Off The Wall**	3	$8	Epic 35745

Don't Stop 'Til You Get Enough [1] • Rock With You [1] • Working Day And Night • Get On The Floor • Off The Wall [5] • Girlfriend • She's Out Of My Life [43] • I Can't Help It • It's The Falling In Love • Burn This Disco Out

5/2/81	41	10		7 **One Day In Your Life**	[E]	144	$8	Motown 956

recordings from 1973-75

12/25/82+	❶³⁷	101	▲²⁵	8 **Thriller**	1³⁷	$8	Epic 38112

Wanna Be Startin' Somethin' [5] • Baby Be Mine • The Girl Is Mine [1] • Thriller [3] • Beat It [1] • Billie Jean [1] • Human Nature [27] • P.Y.T. (Pretty Young Thing) [46] • The Lady In My Life

6/9/84	31	15		9 **Farewell My Summer Love 1984**	[E]	46	$8	Motown 6101

recordings from 1973

9/26/87	❶¹⁸	77	▲⁸	10 **Bad**	1⁶	$8	Epic 40600

Bad [1] • The Way You Make Me Feel [1] • Speed Demon • Liberian Girl • Just Good Friends • Another Part Of Me [1] • Man In The Mirror [1] • I Just Can't Stop Loving You [1] • Dirty Diana [5] • Smooth Criminal

12/14/91+	❶¹²	112	▲⁶	11 **Dangerous**	1⁴	$8	Epic 45400

Jam [3] • Why You Wanna Trip On Me • In The Closet [1] • She Drives Me Wild • Remember The Time [1] • Can't Let Her Get Away • Heal The World [62] • Black Or White [3] • Who Is It [6] • Give In To Me • Will You Be There [53] • Keep The Faith • Gone Too Soon • Dangerous

DEBUT	PEAK	WKS	Gold	Album Title	Pop #	$	Label & Number

JACKSON, Michael — Cont'd

| 7/8/95 | ❶² | 37 | ▲⁶ | 12 **HIStory: Past, Present And Future - Book I** .... [G] | 1² | $15 | Epic 59000 [2] |

disc 1: greatest hits; disc 2: new recordings
Billie Jean *[1]* • The Way You Make Me Feel *[1]* • Black Or White *[3]* • Rock With You *[1]* • She's Out Of My Life *[43]* • Bad *[1]* • I Just Can't Stop Loving You *[1]* • Man In The Mirror *[1]* • Thriller *[3]* • Beat It *[1]* • The Girl Is Mine *[1]* • Remember The Time *[1]* • Don't Stop 'Til You Get Enough *[1]* • Wanna Be Startin' Somethin' *[5]* • Heal The World *[62]* • Scream *[2]* • They Don't Care About Us *[10]* • Stranger In Moscow • This Time Around • Earth Song • D.S. • Money • Come Together • You Are Not Alone *[1]* • Childhood • Tabloid Junkie • 2 Bad • HIStory • Little Susie • Smile

| 6/7/97 | 12 | 10 | ● | 13 **Blood On The Dance Floor: HIStory In The Mix** .... | 24 | $8 | MJJ Music 68000 |

contains remixes from album #12 above

JACKSON, Millie ★62★   '77

Born on 7/15/44 in Thompson, Georgia; raised in Newark, New Jersey. Singer/songwriter.
1)Feelin' Bitchy 2)Caught Up 3)Live And Outrageous (Rated XXX)

| 9/29/73 | 13 | 14 | | 1 **It Hurts So Good** .... | 175 | $12 | Spring 5706 |
| 11/30/74+ | 4 | 16 | ● | 2 **Caught Up** .... | 21 | $10 | Spring 6703 |

If Loving You Is Wrong I Don't Want To Be Right *[flip]* • The Rap *[42]* • All I Want Is A Fighting Chance • I'm Tired Of Hiding • It's All Over But The Shouting • It's Easy Going • I'm Through Trying To Prove My Love To You *[58]* • Summer (The First Time)

8/2/75	27	15		3 **Still Caught Up**	112	$10	Spring 6708
5/8/76	17	11		4 **Free And In Love**		$10	Spring 6709
1/22/77	44	5		5 **Lovingly Yours**	175	$10	Spring 6712
9/10/77	4	38	●	6 **Feelin' Bitchy**	34	$10	Spring 6715

All The Way Lover *[12]* • Lovin' Your Good Thing Away • Angel In Your Arms • A Little Taste Of Outside Love • You Created A Monster • Cheatin' Is • If You're Not Back In Love By Monday *[5]* • Feelin' Like A Woman

7/22/78	14	19	●	7 **Get It Out'cha System**	55	$10	Spring 6719
5/5/79	47	11		8 **A Moment's Pleasure**	144	$10	Spring 6722
10/27/79	17	24		9 **Royal Rappin's**	80	$10	Polydor 6229

MILLIE JACKSON & ISAAC HAYES

| 12/15/79+ | 22 | 27 | | 10 **Live & Uncensored** .... [L] | 94 | $12 | Spring 6725 [2] |

recorded at The Roxy in Los Angeles

6/28/80	23	15		11 **For Men Only**	100	$10	Spring 6727
1/10/81	25	23		12 **I Had To Say It**	137	$10	Spring 6730
8/15/81	43	7		13 **Just A Lil' Bit Country**	201	$10	Spring 6732
3/13/82	11	22		14 **Live And Outrageous (Rated XXX)** .... [L]	113	$10	Spring 6735

recorded at Mr. Vees Figure 8 in Atlanta

11/20/82	29	16		15 **Hard Times**	201	$10	Spring 6737
10/22/83	40	18		16 **E.S.P. (Extra Sexual Persuasion)**		$10	Spring 6740
11/15/86+	16	32		17 **An Imitation Of Love**	119	$8	Jive 1016
7/1/89	79	12		18 **Back To The S--t!**		$8	Jive 1186

JACKSON, Paul Jr.   '93

Singer/songwriter/multi-instrumentalist.

| 5/8/93 | 83 | 4 | | **A River In The Desert** .... | | $8 | Atlantic 82441 |

JACKSON, Rebbie   '84

Born Maureen Jackson on 5/29/50 in Gary, Indiana. Sister of **The Jacksons**.

10/20/84	13	22		1 **Centipede**	63	$8	Columbia 39238
10/25/86	54	5		2 **Reaction**		$8	Columbia 40364
3/12/88	58	7		3 **R U Tuff Enuff**		$8	Columbia 40896

JACKSON, Walter   '76

Born on 3/19/38 in Pensacola, Florida. Died of a cerebral hemorrhage on 6/20/83 (age 45).

5/13/67	26	6		1 **Speak Her Name**	194	$25	Okeh 12120
10/2/76	14	23		2 **Feeling Good**	113	$12	Chi-Sound 656
4/16/77	25	10		3 **I Want To Come Back As A Song**	141	$12	Chi-Sound 733
3/4/78	51	5		4 **Good To See You**		$12	Chi-Sound 844
8/25/79	68	4		5 **Send In The Clowns**		$10	20th Century 586
6/6/81	45	10		6 **Tell Me Where It Hurts**	206	$10	Columbia 37132

JACKSON, Willis   '75

Born on 4/25/32 in Miami. Died of heart failure on 10/25/87 (age 55). Jazz tenor saxophonist. Formerly married to **Ruth Brown**.

| 8/23/75 | 50 | 4 | | **The Way We Were** .... | 182 | $12 | Atlantic 18145 |

JACKSON 5/JACKSONS ★16★   '70

Group of brothers formed and managed by their father beginning in 1966 in Gary, Indiana. Consisted of **Jackie Jackson**, Tito Jackson, **Jermaine Jackson**, **Marlon Jacckson** and lead singer **Michael Jackson**. First recorded for Steeltown in 1968. Known as **The Jackson 5** from 1968-75. Jermaine replaced by Randy in 1976. Jermaine rejoined the group group for 1984's highly publicized *Victory* album and tour. Marlon left for a solo career in 1987. Their sisters **Rebbie Jackon**, **La Toya Jackson** and **Janet Jackson** backed the group; each had solo hits. Michael and Janet emerged with superstar solo careers in the '80s. Group lineup since 1989: Jackie, Tito, Jermaine and Randy Jackson. Group inducted into the Rock and Roll Hall of Fame in 1997.

1)ABC 2)Third Album 3)Diana Ross Presents The Jackson 5

THE JACKSON 5:

| 1/17/70 | ❶⁹ | 33 | | 1 **Diana Ross Presents The Jackson 5** | 5 | $25 | Motown 700 |

Zip-A-Dee-Doo-Dah • Nobody • I Want You Back *[1]* • Can You Remember • Standing In The Shadows Of Love • You've Changed • My Cherie Amour • Who's Loving You *[flip]* • Chained • (I Know) I'm Losing You • Stand • Born To Love You

| 6/6/70 | ❶¹² | 25 | | 2 **ABC** | 4 | $25 | Motown 709 |

The Love You Save *[1]* • One More Chance • ABC *[1]* • 2-4-6-8 • (Come Round Here) I'm The One You Need • Don't Know Why I Love You • Never Had A Dream Come True • True Love Can Be Beautiful • La-La Means I Love You • I'll Bet You • I Found That Girl *[flip]* • The Young Folks

98

DEBUT	PEAK	WKS	Gold	Album Title	Pop #	$	Label & Number
				JACKSON 5 — Cont'd			
10/3/70	❶¹⁰	35		**3 Third Album**	4	$15	Motown 718
				I'll Be There *[1]* • Ready Or Not Here I Come (Can't Hide From Love) • Oh How Happy • Bridge Over Troubled Water • Can I See You In The Morning • Goin' Back To Indiana • How Funky Is Your Chicken • **Mama's Pearl** *[2]* • Reach In • The Love I Saw In You Was Just A Mirage • Darling Dear			
5/1/71	❶⁶	38		**4 Maybe Tomorrow**	11	$15	Motown 735
				Maybe Tomorrow *[3]* • She's Good • **Never Can Say Goodbye** *[1]* • The Wall • Petals • Sixteen Candles • (We've Got) Blue Skies • My Little Baby • It's Great To Be Here • Honey Chile • I Will Find A Way			
10/16/71	5	19		**5 Goin' Back To Indiana** [TV]	16	$15	Motown 742
				I Want You Back • Maybe Tomorrow • The Day Basketball Was Saved • Stand • I Want To Take You Higher • Feeling Alright • Medley: Walk On/The Love You Save • Goin' Back To Indiana			
1/8/72	2⁵	29		**6 Jackson 5 Greatest Hits** [G]	12	$15	Motown 741
				I Want You Back *[1]* • ABC *[1]* • Never Can Say Goodbye *[1]* • Sugar Daddy *[3]* • I'll Be There *[1]* • Maybe Tomorrow *[3]* • The Love You Save *[1]* • **Who's Loving You** *[flip]* • **Mama's Pearl** *[2]* • Goin' Back To Indiana • I Found That Girl *[flip]*			
6/10/72	3	22		**7 Lookin' Through The Windows**	7	$15	Motown 750
				Ain't Nothing Like The Real Thing • **Lookin' Through The Windows** *[5]* • Don't Let Your Baby Catch You • To Know • Doctor My Eyes • **Little Bitty Pretty One** *[8]* • E-Ne-Me-Ni-Ne-Moe (The Choice Is Yours To Pull) • If I Have To Move A Mountain • Don't Want To See Tomorrow • Children Of The Light • I Can Only Give You Love			
4/28/73	15	13		**8 Skywriter**	44	$12	Motown 761
9/29/73	4	19		**9 Get It Together**	100	$12	Motown 783
				Get It Together *[2]* • Don't Say Good Bye Again • Reflections • Hum Along And Dance • Mama I Gotta Brand New Thing (Don't Say No) • It's Too Late To Change The Time • You Need Love Like I Do (Don't You?) • **Dancing Machine** *[1]*			
6/14/75	6	17		**10 Moving Violation**	36	$12	Motown 829
				Forever Came Today *[6]* • Moving Violation • (You Were Made) Especially For Me • Honey Love • Body Language (Do The Love Dance) • All I Do Is Think Of You *[50]* • Breezy • Call Of The Wild • Time Explosion			
7/10/76	32	5		**11 Jackson Five Anthology** .... [G]	84	$20	Motown 868 [3]
				THE JACKSONS:			
12/4/76+	6	27	●	**12 The Jacksons**	36	$10	Epic 34229
				Enjoy Yourself *[2]* • Think Happy • Good Times • Keep On Dancing • Blues Away • **Show You The Way To Go** *[6]* • Living Together • Strength Of One Man • Dreamer • Style Of Life			
11/5/77	11	13		**13 Goin' Places**	63	$10	Epic 34835
12/9/78+	3	45	▲	**14 Destiny**	11	$10	Epic 35552
				Blame It On The Boogie *[3]* • Push Me Away • Things I Do For You • **Shake Your Body (Down To The Ground)** *[3]* • Destiny • Bless His Soul • All Night Dancin' • That's What You Get (For Being Polite)			
10/18/80	❶²	39	▲	**15 Triumph**	10	$10	Epic 36424
				Can You Feel It *[30]* • Lovely One *[2]* • Your Ways • Everybody • **Heartbreak Hotel** *[2]* • Time Waits For No One • **Walk Right Now** *[50]* • Give It Up • Wondering Who			
11/28/81+	10	22	●	**16 Jacksons Live** [L]	30	$12	Epic 37545 [2]
				Can You Feel It • Things I Do For You • Off The Wall • Ben • Heartbreak Hotel • She's Out Of My Life • Medley: I Want You Back/ABC/The Love You Save • I'll Be There • Rock With You • Lovely One • Working Day And Night • Don't Stop 'Til You Get Enough • Shake Your Body (Down To The Ground)			
7/28/84	3	28	▲²	**17 Victory**	4	$8	Epic 38946
				Torture *[12]* • Wait • One More Chance • Be Not Always • State Of Shock *[4]* • We Can Change The World • The Hurt • Body *[39]*			
6/17/89	14	23		**18 2300 Jackson Street**	59	$8	Epic 40911
				title refers to their previous address in Gary, Indiana			
				JADE '94			
				Female vocal trio: Joi Marshall and Tonya Kelly (from Chicago), with Diana Reed (from Houston).			
12/5/92+	19	63	▲	**1 JADE To The Max**	56	$8	Giant 24466
9/18/93	67	14		**2 BET's Listening Party Starring Jade**		$8	Giant 24520
10/15/94	16	28	●	**3 Mind, Body & Song**	80	$8	Giant 24558
				JAGGED EDGE '98			
				Male vocal group from Atlanta: twin brothers Brasco and Case Dinero, with Wingo Dollar and Quick.			
3/7/98	19	57	●	**A Jagged Era**	104	$8	So So Def 68181
				JAKE THE FLAKE & THE FLINT THUGS '98			
				Male rapper from Flint, Michigan. The Flint Thugs: Shoestring, DFC and Bone Skanless.			
2/28/98	98	1		**Jake The Flake & The Flint Thugs**		$8	Power 5298
				JAKES, T.D. '98			
				Born in West Virginia. Male gospel singer.			
11/28/98	75	1		**Live From The Potter's House** .... [L]		$8	Integrity 69542
				T.D. JAKES With The Potter's House Mass Choir			
				JAMAICA BOYS, The '90			
				Trio from Queens, New York: Mark Stevens (vocals), **Marcus Miller** (guitar, bass) and Lenny White (drums). Stevens is the brother of **Chaka Khan**.			
5/5/90	26	20		**J Boys**		$8	Reprise 26076
				JAMAL '95			
				Male rapper Jamal Phillips. One-half of the **Illegal** duo.			
11/25/95	37	15		**Last Chance, No Breaks**	198	$8	Rowdy 37008
				JAMAL, Ahmad '74			
				Born Fritz Jones on 7/2/30 in Pittsburgh. Jazz pianist.			
3/23/74	29	9		**1 Jamalca** .... [I]	201	$12	20th Century 432
1/11/75	41	5		**2 Jamal Plays Jamal** .... [I]	203	$12	20th Century 459
2/9/80	53	10		**3 Genetic Walk** .... [I-K]	173	$10	20th Century 600
12/6/80	64	3		**4 Intervals** .... [I]		$10	20th Century 622

★153★ JAMES, Bob '76

Born on 12/25/39 in Marshall, Missouri. Jazz fusion keyboardist. Formed the Tappan Zee record label. Member of **Fourplay**.

1)Double Vision 2)Three 3)One On One

DEBUT	PEAK	WKS	Gold	#	Album Title		Pop #	$	Label & Number
8/3/74	48	4		1	One	[I]	85	$12	CTI 6043
4/26/75	28	14		2	Two	[I]	75	$12	CTI 6057
7/4/76	23	14		3	Three	[I]	49	$12	CTI 6063
5/28/77	33	5		4	BJ4	[I]	38	$12	CTI 7074
1/5/80	26	20	●	5	One On One		23	$10	Tappan Zee 36241
					BOB JAMES AND EARL KLUGH				
9/26/81	27	11		6	Sign Of The Times	[I]	56	$10	Tappan Zee 37495
11/20/82+	23	26		7	Two Of A Kind		44	$8	Capitol 12244
					EARL KLUGH & BOB JAMES				
6/25/83	43	6		8	The Genie (Themes & Variations From The TV Series "Taxi")	[I]	77	$8	Columbia 38678
10/22/83	45	8		9	Foxie	[I]	106	$8	Tappan Zee 38801
12/1/84	67	3		10	12	[I]	136	$8	Tappan Zee 39580
7/5/86	16	39	▲	11	Double Vision	[I]	50	$8	Warner 25393
					BOB JAMES/DAVID SANBORN				
11/22/86	49	19		12	Obsession	[I]	142	$8	Warner 25495
10/22/88	99	1		13	Ivory Coast	[I]	196	$8	Warner 25757
12/5/92	88	7		14	Cool	[I]	170	$8	Warner 26939
					BOB JAMES/EARL KLUGH				

JAMES, Etta '68

Born Jamesetta Hawkins on 1/25/38 in Los Angeles. Nicknamed "Miss Peaches." Inducted into the Rock and Roll Hall of Fame in 1993.

DEBUT	PEAK	WKS	Gold	#	Album Title	Pop #	$	Label & Number
3/16/68	21	11		1	Tell Mama	82	$20	Cadet 802
9/8/73	41	9		2	Etta James	154	$15	Chess 50042
6/22/74	47	3		3	Come A Little Closer		$15	Chess 60029

JAMES, Rick ★34★ '81

Born James Johnson on 2/1/52 in Buffalo. Funk-rock singer/songwriter/guitarist. In Mynah Birds band with Neil Young in the late '60s. To London; formed the band Main Line. Returned to the U.S. and formed **Stone City Band**; produced **Teena Marie**, **Mary Jane Girls**, **Eddie Murphy** and others. In mid-1994, sentenced to five years in prison for assaults on two women; released from prison in August 1996.

1)Street Songs 2)Cold Blooded 3)Throwin' Down

DEBUT	PEAK	WKS	Gold	#	Album Title		Pop #	$	Label & Number
5/27/78	3	47	●	1	Come Get It!		13	$10	Gordy 981
					Stone City Band • **You And I** [1] • Sexy Lady • Dream Maker • Be My Lady • **Mary Jane** [3] • Hollywood				
2/10/79	2[6]	34		2	Bustin' Out Of L Seven		16	$10	Gordy 984
					Bustin' Out [8] • High On Your Love Suite [12] • Spacey Love • Cop 'N' Blow • Jefferson Ball • **Fool On The Street** [35]				
11/3/79	5	29		3	Fire It Up		34	$10	Gordy 990
					Fire It Up • Love Gun [13] • Lovin' You Is A Pleasure • Love In The Night • **Come Into My Life** [26] • Stormy Love • When Love Is Gone				
8/9/80	17	15		4	Garden Of Love		83	$10	Gordy 995
5/2/81	❶[20]	78	▲	5	Street Songs		3	$8	Gordy 1002
					Give It To Me Baby [1] • **Ghetto Life** [38] • Make Love To Me • Mr. Policeman • Super Freak [3] • Fire And Desire • Call Me Up • Below The Funk (Pass The J)				
6/5/82	2[10]	39	●	6	Throwin' Down		13	$8	Gordy 6005
					Dance Wit' Me [3] • Money Talks • Teardrops • Throwdown • **Standing On The Top** [6] • **Hard To Get** [15] • Happy • She Blew My Mind (69 Times) [62] • My Love				
9/3/83	❶[10]	33	●	7	Cold Blooded		16	$8	Gordy 6043
					U Bring The Freak Out [16] • **Cold Blooded** [1] • Ebony Eyes [22] • 1,2,3 (U, Her And Me) • Doin' It • New York Town • P.I.M.P. The S.I.M.P. • Tell Me (What You Want) • Unity				
9/1/84	10	23		8	Reflections	[G]	41	$8	Gordy 6095
					17 [6] • Oh What A Night (4 Luv) • **You Turn Me On** [31] • Fire And Desire • **Bustin' Out** [8] • **You And I** [1] • Mary Jane [3] • Dance Wit' Me [3] • Give It To Me Baby [1] • Super Freak [3]				
5/18/85	7	29		9	Glow		50	$8	Gordy 6135
					Can't Stop [10] • **Spend The Night With Me** [41] • Melody Make Me Dance • Somebody (The Girl's Got) • **Glow** [5] • Moonchild • Sha La La La La (Come Back Home) • Rock And Roll Control				
6/21/86	16	17		10	The Flag		95	$8	Gordy 6185
7/23/88	12	19		11	Wonderful		148	$8	Reprise 25659
11/1/97	31	10		12	Urban Rapsody		170	$8	Private I 417070

JANKEL, Chas '82

Born on 4/16/52. Former keyboardist/guitarist with Ian Dury & The Blockheads.

DEBUT	PEAK	WKS	Gold	Album Title	Pop #	$	Label & Number
3/13/82	42	13		Questionnaire	126	$8	A&M 4885

★79★ JARREAU, Al '81

Born on 3/12/40 in Milwaukee. Has master's degree in psychology from the University of Iowa.

1)Breakin' Away 2)Jarreau 3)This Time

DEBUT	PEAK	WKS	Gold	#	Album Title		Pop #	$	Label & Number
8/21/76	30	8		1	Glow		132	$10	Reprise 2248
6/25/77	19	27		2	Look To The Rainbow/Live In Europe	[L]	49	$12	Warner 3052 [2]
11/4/78	27	19		3	All Fly Home		78	$10	Warner 3229
6/21/80	6	39	●	4	This Time		27	$8	Warner 3434
					Never Givin' Up [26] • Gimme What You Got [63] • Love Is Real • Alonzo • (If I Could Only) Change Your Mind • Spain (I Can Recall) • Distracted [61] • Your Sweet Love • (Rhyme) This Time				

DEBUT	PEAK	WKS	Gold	Album Title	Pop #	$	Label & Number

JARREAU, Al — Cont'd

| 8/22/81 | ❶² | 77 | ▲ | 5 Breakin' Away | 9 | $8 | Warner 3576 |

Closer To Your Love • My Old Friend • **We're In This Love Together** [6] • Easy • Our Love • **Breakin' Away** [25] • Roof Garden • (Round, Round, Round) Blue Rondo A La Turk • **Teach Me Tonight** [51]

| 4/16/83 | 4 | 43 | ● | 6 Jarreau | 13 | $8 | Warner 23801 |

Mornin' [6] • **Boogie Down** [9] • I Will Be Here For You (Nitakungodea Milele) • Save Me • Step By Step • Black And Blues • Trouble In Paradise [66] • Not Like This • Love Is Waiting

| 11/24/84 | 12 | 33 | | 7 High Crime | 49 | $8 | Warner 25106 |
| 10/5/85 | 55 | 9 | | 8 Al Jarreau In London [L] | 125 | $8 | Warner 25331 |

recorded November 1984 at Wembley Arena in London

10/18/86	30	23	●	9 L Is For Lover	81	$8	Warner 25477
12/10/88+	11	27	●	10 Heart's Horizon	75	$8	Reprise 25778
7/11/92	30	19		11 Heaven And Earth	105	$8	Reprise 26849
6/11/94	25	15		12 Tenderness	114	$8	Reprise 45422

JASPER, Chris   '88
Member of **The Isley Brothers** from 1969-84. Formed **Isley Jasper Isley** with cousins Ernie and Marvin Isley.

| 2/13/88 | 31 | 17 | | 1 Superbad | 182 | $8 | CBS Associated 44053 |
| 9/9/89 | 99 | 2 | | 2 Time Bomb | | $8 | Gold City 45169 |

JAYE, Miles   '89
Born Miles Davis in Brooklyn, New York. Singer/songwriter. Member of the **Village People** from 1982-85.

10/31/87	18	37		1 Miles	125	$8	Island 90615
5/27/89	16	38		2 Irresistible	160	$8	Island 91235
7/13/91	54	14		3 Strong		$8	Island 848422

JAY-Z   '98
Born Shawn Carter in New York City. Male rapper. Founded the Roc-A-Fella record label.

| 7/6/96 | 3 | 55 | ● | 1 Reasonable Doubt | 23 | $8 | Roc-A-Fella 50592 |

Can't Knock The Hustle [35] • Politics As Usual • Brooklyn's Finest • **Dead Presidents** [74] • **Feelin' It** [46] • D'Evils • 22 Two's • Can I Live • **Ain't No Nigga** [17] • Friend Or Foe • Coming Of Age • Cashmere Thoughts • Bring It On • Regrets

| 11/15/97 | 2¹ | 70 | ▲ | 2 In My Lifetime, Vol. 1 | 3 | $8 | Roc-A-Fella 536392 |

A Million And One Questions [49] • **The City Is Mine** [37] • I Know What Girls Like • Imaginary Player • Streets Is Watching • Friend Or Foe '98 • Lucky Me • **Sunshine** [37] • **Who You Wit** [25] • Face Off • Real Niggaz • Rap Game - Crack Game • Where I'm From • You Must Love Me

| 10/10/98 | ❶⁶ | 43↑ | ▲⁴ | 3 Vol. 2...Hard Knock Life | 1⁵ | $8 | Roc-A-Fella 558902 |

Hand It Down • **Hard Knock Life (Ghetto Anthem)** [10] • If I Should Die • Ride Or Die • **Jigga What?** [35] • Money, Cash, Hoes [36] • A Week Ago • Coming Of Age (Da Sequel) • **Can I Get A...** [6] • Paper Chase • Reservoir Dogs • It's Like That • **It's Alright** [32] • Money Ain't A Thang [10]

JAZ   '89
Born Jonathan Burks in Brooklyn, New York. Male rapper.

| 6/17/89 | 88 | 9 | | Word To The Jaz | | $8 | EMI 91170 |

JAZZMASTERS, The   '95
Studio group featuring multi-instrumentalist **Paul Hardcastle** and singer Helen Rogers.

| 8/12/95 | 35 | 13 | | The Jazzmasters II | 132 | $8 | JVC 2049 |

J.B.'s — see WESLEY, Fred

JEAN, Wyclef   '97
Born in 1970 in Haiti. Member of **The Fugees**.

| 7/12/97 | 4 | 63 | ▲² | Wyclef Jean Presents The Carnival Featuring Refugee Allstars | 16 | $8 | Ruffhouse 67974 |

Apocalypse • Guantanamera • Bubblegoose • **Cheated (To All The Girls)** [53] • Anything Can Happen • **Gone Till November** [9] • Year Of The Dragon • Sang Fézi • Mona Lisa • Street Jeopardy • **We Trying To Stay Alive** [14] • Gunpowder • Jaspora • Yelé • Carnival

JEFFRIES, Michael   '90
Born in Memphis; raised in San Francisco. Lead singer of **Tower Of Power** from 1977-79.

| 2/3/90 | 71 | 6 | | Michael Jeffries | | $8 | Warner 25925 |

JERKY BOYS, The   '94
Prank telephone callers from New York City: John Brennan and Kamal Ahmed. Duo starred in the 1995 movie The Jerky Boys.

| 9/10/94 | 16 | 28 | ▲ | The Jerky Boys 2 [C] | 12 | $8 | Select 92411 |

JERU THE DAMAJA   '96
Born Kendrick Jeru Davis in Brooklyn, New York. Male rapper.

| 6/4/94 | 5 | 17 | | 1 The Sun Rises In The East | 36 | $8 | Payday 124001 |

D. Original [74] • Brooklyn Took It • Mental Stamina • Da Bichez • You Can't Stop The Prophet • Ain't The Devil Happy • My Mind Spray • **Come Clean** [53] • Jungle Music • Statik

| 10/26/96 | 3 | 16 | | 2 Wrath Of The Math | 35 | $8 | Payday 124119 |

Wrath Of The Math • Frustrated Nigga • Black Cowboys • Tha Bullshit • Whatever • Physical Stamina • One Day • Revenge Of The Prophet (Part 5) • Scientifical Madness • Not The Average • **Me Or The Papes** [78] • Now I'm Livin' • Too Perverted • **Ya Playin' Yaself** [57] • Invasion

JESSE   '95
Born Jesse Campbell in Maywood, Illinois.

| 4/22/95 | 53 | 12 | | Never Let You Go | | $8 | Underworld 29476 |

JETS, The   '86
Family group from Minneapolis, consisting of eight brothers and sisters: Leroy, Eddie, Eugene, Haini, Rudy, Kathi, Elizabeth and Moana Wolfgramm. Their parents are from the South Pacific country of Tonga. All members play at least two instruments. Eugene left group and formed duo Boys Club in 1988.

11/23/85+	16	62	▲	1 The Jets	21	$8	MCA 5667
11/14/87+	26	38	●	2 Magic	35	$8	MCA 42085
9/9/89	74	4		3 Believe	107	$8	MCA 6313

DEBUT	PEAK	WKS	Gold	Album Title	Pop #	$	Label & Number
				JIBRI WISE ONE '91			
				Born in Cincinnati. Male rapper.			
9/14/91	34	31		Jibri Wise One..		$8	Ear Candy 31000
				J.J. FAD '88			
				Female rap trio from Los Angeles: Juana Burns, Dania Birks and Michelle Franklin. J.J. Fad stands for Just Jammin' Fresh And Def.			
7/30/88	20	30	●	Supersonic - The Album.....................................	49	$8	Ruthless 90959
				produced by Dr. Dre			
				J-MACK '96			
				Born in San Francisco. Male rapper.			
5/4/96	85	1		Crime Rate...		$8	Priority 50572
				JODECI '91			
				Pronounced: joe-deh-see. Two pairs of brothers from Tiny Grove, North Carolina: Joel "JoJo" and Cedric "K-Ci" Hailey, with Dalvin and Donald "DeVante Swing" DeGrate. The Haileys later recorded as K-Ci & JoJo.			
6/29/91	❶²	102	▲³	1 Forever My Lady	18	$8	Uptown/MCA 10198
				Stay [1] • Come & Talk To Me [1] • Forever My Lady [1] • I'm Still Waiting [10] • U & I • My Phone • Gotta Love [79] • Play Thang • It's Alright • Treat U • Times We Share			
1/8/94	❶²	44	▲²	2 Diary Of A Mad Band	3	$8	Uptown/MCA 10915
				My Heart Belongs To U • Cry For You [1] • Feenin' [2] • What About Us [14] • Ride & Slide • Alone • You Got It • Won't Waste You • In The Meanwhile • Gimme All You Got • Sweaty • Jodecidal Hotline • Success			
8/5/95	❶¹	63	▲	3 The Show - The After-Party - The Hotel	2¹	$8	Uptown/MCA 11258
				The Show • Bring On Da' Funk • Room 723 • Fun 2Nite • Room 577 • S-More • The After-Party • Get On Up [4] • Room 499 • Can We Flo? • Zipper • Let's Do It All • P.I.B. 4Play • Pump It Back • D.J. Don Jeremy • Freek'n You [3] • Time & Place • Fallin' • Love U 4 Life [8] • 4 U • Good Luv			
				JOE '97			
				Born Joseph Thomas in Cuthbert, Georgia. Singer/songwriter/guitarist.			
9/4/93	16	44		1 Everything..	105	$8	Mercury 518016
8/16/97	4	58	▲	2 All That I Am	13	$8	Jive 41603
				All The Things (Your Man Won't Do) [2] • The Love Scene • Don't Wanna Be A Player [5] • Good Girls • How Soon • Sanctified Girl (Can't Fight This Feeling) • All That I Am • No One Else Comes Close • Come Around • U Shoulda Told Me (U Had A Man) • Love Don't Make No Sense			
				JOE PUBLIC '92			
				Vocal group from Buffalo, New York: Kevin Scott, Joe Carter, Joseph Sayles and Dwight Wyatt.			
3/14/92	23	32		Joe Public...	111	$8	Columbia 48628
				JOHN, Elton '79			
				Born Reginald Kenneth Dwight on 3/25/47 in Pinner, Middlesex, England. Singer/songwriter/pianist. Charted 36 pop albums from 1970-97. Inducted into the Rock and Roll Hall of Fame in 1994.			
7/21/79	71	4		The Thom Bell Sessions................................[M]	51	$10	MCA 13921
				JOHNNY P '98			
				Born Orville Morgan in New York City. Male rapper.			
5/9/98	64	4		The Next..		$8	Rap-A-Lot 45628
				JOHNSON, Al '80			
				Born in 1948 in Newport News, Virginia. Former lead singer of The Unifics.			
4/26/80	48	8		Back For More..		$10	Columbia 36266
				JOHNSON, Alphonso '76			
				Born in 1951 in Philadelphia. Jazz bassist.			
5/8/76	47	3		Moonshadows...		$10	Epic 34118
				JOHNSON, Howard '82			
				Born in Miami. Former member of Niteflyte.			
7/31/82	10	21		1 Keepin' Love New	122	$8	A&M 4895
				So Fine [6] • Take Me Through The Night • This Is Heaven • Jam Song • Keepin' Love New [47] • So Glad You're My Lady • Say You Wanna • Forever Falling In Love			
2/11/84	61	6		2 Doin' It My Way..		$8	A&M 4961
9/14/85	46	10		3 The Vision...		$8	A&M 4982
				JOHNSON, Jesse '85			
				Born on 5/29/60 in Rock Island, Illinois. Lead guitarist of The Time.			
3/16/85	8	48	●	1 Jesse Johnson's Revue	43	$8	A&M 5024
				Be Your Man [4] • I Want My Girl [7] • She Won't Let Go • Just Too Much • Let's Have Some Fun [87] • Can You Help Me [3] • Special Love • She's A Doll			
10/25/86	15	23		2 Shockadelica..	70	$8	A&M 5122
4/30/88	26	22		3 Every Shade Of Love......................................	79	$8	A&M 5188
				JOHNSON, Puff '96			
				Born in 1973 in Detroit; raised in Los Angeles. Female singer.			
6/15/96	61	12		Miracle...		$8	Work 53022
				JOHNSON, Syl '74			
				Born Sylvester Thompson on 7/1/39 in Holly Springs, Mississippi. Singer/guitarist.			
1/12/74	19	13		1 Back For A Taste Of Your Love............................		$12	Hi 32081
3/20/76	56	2		2 Total Explosion..		$12	Hi 32096
				JOHNSON, Troy '89			
				Born in California. Singer/songwriter/producer.			
8/26/89	87	5		The Way It Is...		$8	RCA 9690
				JOLI, France '79			
				Born in 1963 in Montreal. Female dance singer.			
10/6/79	25	10		France Joli...	26	$10	Prelude 12170

DEBUT	PEAK	WKS	Gold	Album Title	Pop #	$	Label & Number

JON B '98
Born Jonathan Buck in Rhode Island. Male singer/songwriter.

DEBUT	PEAK	WKS	Gold	Album Title	Pop #	$	Label & Number
6/10/95	24	32	●	1 Bonafide	79	$8	Yab Yum 66436
10/4/97+	5	76	▲	2 Cool Relax	107	$8	Yab Yum 67805

Shine • Bad Girl • Don't Say [34] • They Don't Know [2] • Can't Help It • Cool Relax • Are U Still Down [9] • Pride & Joy • I Do (Whatcha Say Boo) [18] • Let Me Know • I Ain't Going Out • Let's Go • Can We Get Down • Love Hurts • Tu Amor

JONES, Donell '96
Born in Chicago. Male singer/songwriter.

| 6/22/96 | 30 | 45 | | My Heart | 180 | $8 | LaFace 26025 |

JONES, Glenn '87
Born in 1961 in Jacksonville, Florida. Singer/actor. Appeared in the Broadway musical *Sing Mahalia, Sing*.

10/20/84	18	42		1 Finesse		$8	RCA Victor 8036
9/20/86	44	9		2 Take It From Me		$8	RCA Victor 5807
10/10/87	16	23		3 Glenn Jones	94	$8	Jive 1062
6/23/90	27	20		4 All For You		$8	Jive 1181
2/29/92	22	40		5 Here I Go Again		$8	Atlantic 82352
4/16/94	39	12		6 Here I Am		$8	Atlantic 82513

JONES, Grace '81
Born on 5/19/52 in Spanishtown, Jamaica; raised in Syracuse, New York. Singer/model/actress. Acted in several movies.

12/3/77	52	4		1 Portfolio	109	$10	Island 9470
8/5/78	57	3		2 Fame	97	$10	Island 9525
5/23/81	9	20		3 Nightclubbing	32	$10	Island 9624

Walking In The Rain • Pull Up To The Bumper [5] • Use Me • Nightclubbing • Art Groupie • I've Seen That Face Before (Libertango) • Feel Up • Demolition Man • I've Done It Again

12/11/82+	19	27		4 Living My Life	86	$10	Island 90018
11/30/85+	25	23		5 Slave To The Rhythm	73	$8	Manhattan 53021
12/20/86+	26	14		6 Inside Story	81	$8	Manhattan 53038

JONES, Howard '85
Born on 2/23/55 in Southampton, England. Pop singer/songwriter/keyboardist.

| 6/15/85 | 65 | 9 | ▲ | Dream Into Action | 10 | $8 | Elektra 60390 |

JONES, Joe '71
Jazz guitarist. Nicknamed: "Boogaloo Joe."

| 1/16/71 | 49 | 2 | | Right On Brother | [I] | $15 | Prestige 7766 |

JONES, Linda '67
Born on 1/14/44 in Newark, New Jersey. Died of diabetes on 3/14/72 (age 28).

| 10/28/67 | 26 | 3 | | 1 Hypnotized | | $30 | Loma 5907 |
| 6/10/72 | 35 | 6 | | 2 Your Precious Love | | $15 | Turbo 7007 |

JONES, Oran "Juice" '86
Born in 1959 in Houston; raised in Harlem. Male singer/rapper.

| 8/9/86 | 3 | 27 | | 1 Oran "Juice" Jones | 44 | $8 | Def Jam 40367 |

The Rain [1] • You Can't Hide From Love [75] • Here I Go Again [45] • Curiosity [45] • Your Song • Love Will Find A Way • It's Yours • 1.2.1 • Two Faces

| 11/21/87 | 36 | 9 | | 2 G.T.O. Gangsters Takin' Over | | $8 | Def Jam 40955 |

JONES, Quincy ★45★ '90
Born Quincy Delight Jones, Jr. on 3/14/33 in Chicago; raised in Seattle. Songwriter/producer. Began as a jazz trumpeter with Lionel Hampton from 1950-53. Music director for Mercury Records in 1961, then vice president in 1964. Wrote scores for many movies from 1965-73. Established own Qwest label in 1981. Married to actress Peggy Lipton (TV's *Mod Squad*) from 1974-89.

1)Back On The Block 2)Body Heat 3)The Dude

12/13/69+	6	27		1 Walking In Space	[I]	56	$12	A&M 3023
8/29/70	16	15		2 Gula Matari	[I]	63	$12	A&M 3030
10/23/71	11	27		3 Smackwater Jack	[I]	56	$12	A&M 3037
6/16/73	14	26		4 You've Got It Bad Girl		94	$12	A&M 3041
6/8/74	❶¹	40	●	5 Body Heat		6	$10	A&M 3617

Body Heat [85] • Soul Saga (Song Of The Buffalo Soldier) • Everything Must Change • Boogie Joe, The Grinder [70] • One Track Mind • Just A Man • Along Came Betty • If I Ever Lose This Heaven [71]

| 8/30/75 | 3 | 14 | | 6 Mellow Madness | | 16 | $10 | A&M 4526 |

Is It Love That We're Missin' [18] • Paranoid • Mellow Madness [82] • Beautiful Black Girl • Listen (What It Is) • Just A Little Taste Of Me • My Cherie Amour • Tryin' To Find Out About You • Cry Baby • Bluesette

| 10/2/76 | 16 | 17 | | 7 I Heard That!! | [K] | 43 | $12 | A&M 3705 |
| 2/26/77 | 6 | 11 | ● | 8 Roots | [TV] | 21 | $10 | A&M 4626 |

"Roots" Medley [32] • Mama Aifambeni • Behold, The Only Thing Greater Than Yourself (Birth) • Oluwa (Many Rains Ago) • Boyhood To Manhood • The Toubob Is Here! (The Capture) • Middle Passage (Slaveship Crossing) • You In Americuh Now, African • Ole Fiddler • Jumpin' De Broom (Marriage Ceremony) • What Shall I Do? (Hush, Hush, Somebody's Calling My Name) • Oh Lord, Come By Here • Free At Last? (The Civil War)

| 6/24/78 | 4 | 23 | ▲ | 9 Sounds...And Stuff Like That!! | | 15 | $10 | A&M 4685 |

Stuff Like That [1] • I'm Gonna Miss You In The Morning • Love, I Never Had It So Good [60] • Tell Me A Bedtime Story • Love Me By Name • Superwoman (Where Were You When I Needed You) • Takin' It To The Streets

DEBUT	PEAK	WKS	Gold	Album Title	Pop #	$	Label & Number

JONES, Quincy — Cont'd

DEBUT	PEAK	WKS		Album Title	Pop #	$	Label & Number
4/4/81	3	81	▲ 10	The Dude	10	$8	A&M 3721

Ai No Corrida *[10]* • The Dude • Just Once *[11]* • Betcha' Wouldn't Hurt Me • Somethin' Special • **Razzamatazz** *[17]* • One Hundred Ways *[10]* • Velas • Turn On The Action

| 7/10/82 | 45 | 6 | 11 | The Best | [G] | 122 | $8 | A&M 3200 |
| 12/16/89+ | ❶ 12 | 39 | ▲ 12 | Back On The Block | | 9 | $8 | Qwest 26020 |

Back On The Block • I Don't Go For That *[15]* • I'll Be Good To You • The Verb To Be • **Wee B. Dooinit** *[83]* • The Places You Find Love *[39]* • Jazz Corner Of The Word • Birdland • Setembro (Brazilian Wedding Song) • One Man Woman • **Tomorrow (A Better You, Better Me)** *[1]* • The Secret Garden (Sweet Seduction Suite) *[1]*

| 8/28/93 | 86 | 3 | | 13 Live At Montreux | [I-L] | | $8 | Warner 45221 |

MILES DAVIS & QUINCY JONES
recorded on July 8, 1991 at the Montreaux Jazz Festival in Switzerland

| 11/25/95 | 6 | 48 | ▲ 14 | Q's Jook Joint | 32 | $8 | Qwest 45875 |

Let The Good Times Roll • Cool Joe, Mean Joe (Killer Joe) • **You Put A Move On My Heart** *[16]* • Rock With You • Moody's Mood For Love • Stomp • Do Nothin' Till You Hear From Me • Is It Love That We're Missin' • Heaven's Girl • Stuff Like That • **Slow Jams** *[19]* • At The End Of The Day (Grace)

JONES, Shirley   **'86**
Born in Detroit. Lead singer of **The Jones Girls**.

| 8/2/86 | 8 | 35 | | Always In The Mood | 128 | $8 | Philadelphia I. 53031 |

Do You Get Enough Love *[1]* • Breaking Up • **Last Night I Needed Somebody** *[36]* • She Knew About Me *[80]* • Always In The Mood • I'll Do Anything For You • Surrender • Caught Me With My Guard Down

JONES, Tamiko   **'75**
Born Barbara Tamiko Ferguson in 1945 in Kyle, West Virginia; raised in Detroit. Female singer.

| 5/24/75 | 40 | 5 | | Love Trip | 204 | $12 | Arista 4040 |

JONES, Tom   **'70**
Born Thomas Jones Woodward on 6/7/40 in Pontypridd, South Wales. Pop singer. Won the 1965 Best New Artist Grammy Award. Host of his own TV show from 1969-71.

| 8/2/69 | 45 | 3 | ● | 1 This Is Tom Jones | 4 | $20 | Parrot 71028 |
| 11/22/69+ | 5 | 19 | ● | 2 Tom Jones Live In Las Vegas | [L] | 3 | $20 | Parrot 71031 |

recorded at The Flamingo Hotel
Turn On Your Love Light • Bright Lights And You Girl • I Can't Stop Loving You • Hard To Handle • Delilah • Danny Boy • I'll Never Fall In Love Again • Help Yourself • Yesterday • Hey Jude • Love Me Tonight • It's Not Unusual • Twist And Shout

| 12/5/70 | 26 | 10 | ● | 3 I (Who Have Nothing) | 23 | $20 | Parrot 71039 |

JONESES, The   **'75**
Vocal group from Pittsburgh: brothers Reggie and Wendall Noble, Harold Taylor, Sam White and Glenn Dorsey.

| 12/21/74+ | 51 | 5 | | Keepin' Up With The Joneses | 202 | $12 | Mercury 1021 |

JONES GIRLS, The   **'81**
Vocal trio from Detroit: sisters Brenda, Valorie and **Shirley Jones**.

| 5/19/79 | 8 | 22 | | 1 The Jones Girls | 50 | $10 | Philadelphia I. 35757 |

This Feeling's Killing Me • You Made Me Love You • Show Love Today • **You Gonna Make Me Love Somebody Else** *[5]* • Life Goes On • Who Can I Run To • **We're A Melody** *[78]* • I'm At Your Mercy *[77]*

| 10/25/80+ | 7 | 27 | | 2 At Peace With Woman | 96 | $10 | Philadelphia I. 36767 |

Children Of The Night • Let's Celebrate (Sittin' On Top Of The World) • **Dance Turned Into A Romance** *[22]* • I Close My Eyes • At Peace With Woman • When I'm Gone • **I Just Love The Man** *[9]* • Back In The Day

| 12/12/81+ | 25 | 21 | | 3 Get As Much Love As You Can | 155 | $10 | Philadelphia I. 37627 |
| 11/19/83 | 59 | 12 | | 4 On Target | | | $8 | RCA Victor 4817 |

JONZUN CREW, The   **'83**
Funk electronic group from Boston: brothers Michael (lead vocals) and Soni Johnson, with Steve Thorpe and Gordy Worthy.

| 5/14/83 | 17 | 23 | | Lost In Space | 66 | $8 | Tommy Boy 1001 |

JOPLIN, Janis   **'71**
Born on 1/19/43 in Port Arthur, Texas. Died of a heroin overdose in Hollywood on 10/4/70 (age 27). White blues-rock singer. Nicknamed "Pearl." To San Francisco in 1966, joined **Big Brother & The Holding Company**. Left band to go solo in 1968. The Bette Midler movie *The Rose* was inspired by Joplin's life. Inducted into the Rock and Roll Hall of Fame in 1995.

| 10/18/69 | 23 | 14 | ● | 1 I Got Dem Ol' Kozmic Blues Again Mama! | 5 | $20 | Columbia 9913 |
| 2/20/71 | 13 | 21 | ▲³ | 2 Pearl | 1⁹ | $15 | Columbia 30322 |

JORDAN, Montell   **'95**
Born on 12/3/68 in Los Angeles. Male singer/songwriter.

| 4/22/95 | 4 | 33 | ▲ | 1 This Is How We Do It | 12 | $8 | Def Jam 527179 |

Somethin' 4 Da Honeyz *[18]* • This Is How We Do It *[1]* • Payback • I'll Do Anything • Don't Keep Me Waiting • Comin' Home • It's Over • I Wanna • Down On My Knees • Gotta Get My Roll On • Close The Door • **Daddy's Home** *[74]*

| 9/14/96+ | 14 | 44 | ● | 2 More... | 47 | $8 | Def Jam 533191 |
| 4/18/98 | 8 | 29 | ● | 3 Let's Ride | 20 | $8 | Def Jam 536987 |

When You Get Home *[74]* • Don't Call Me • **Let's Ride** *[1]* • I Can Do That *[4]* • Midnight Rain • One Last Chance • Anything And Everything • Body Ah • Irresistible • Can I? • Missing You • The Longest Night • 4 You • I Say Yes

JORDAN, Ronny   **'93**
Born in London. Jazz guitarist.

10/17/92	70	7		1 The Antidote	[I]		$8	4th & B'way 444047
11/13/93	70	13		2 Quiet Revolution	[I]		$8	4th & B'way 444060
8/31/96	87	3		3 Light To Dark	[I]		$8	4th & B'way 531060

JORDAN, Stanley   **'85**
Born in Palo Alto, California. Jazz guitarist.

6/1/85	31	61		1 Magic Touch	[I]	64	$8	Blue Note 85101
2/7/87	52	10		2 Standards, Volume 1	[I]	116	$8	Blue Note 85130
11/5/88	83	9		3 Flying Home	[I]	131	$8	EMI 48682

DEBUT	PEAK	WKS	Gold	Album Title	Pop #	$	Label & Number

JOSEPH, Margie   '71
Born in 1950 in Gautier, Mississippi.

| 2/13/71 | 7 | 15 | | 1 Margie Joseph Makes A New Impression | 67 | $30 | Volt 6012 |

Stop! In The Name Of Love *[38]* • Punish Me • Medicine Bend • Come Tomorrow • Sweeter Tomorrow • Same Thing • How Beautiful The Rain • I'm Fed Up • Make Me Believe You'll Stay • Temptation's About To Take Your Love

2/17/73	21	9		2 Margie Joseph		$15	Atlantic 7248
4/13/74	56	3		3 Sweet Surrender	165	$15	Atlantic 7277
5/24/75	53	4		4 Margie		$15	Atlantic 18126
7/24/76	38	5		5 Hear The Words, Feel The Feeling		$12	Cotillion 9906
3/12/83	34	11		6 Knockout!		$10	HCRC 20009

JT THE BIGGA FIGGA   '95
Born in San Francisco. Male rapper.

| 3/19/94 | 91 | 2 | | 1 Playaz N The Game | | $8 | Getlow 1 |
| 10/28/95 | 24 | 5 | | 2 Dwellin' In Tha Labb | 168 | $8 | Getlow 53981 |

JUICY   '86
Brother-and-sister duo of Jerry and Katreese Barnes.

| 4/2/83 | 57 | 3 | | 1 Juicy | | $10 | Arista 9582 |
| 3/1/86 | 32 | 17 | | 2 It Takes Two | | $8 | Private I 40098 |

JUNGLE BROTHERS   '97
Rap trio from Brooklyn, New York: Nathaniel Hall, Michael Small and Sammy Burwell.

9/3/88	39	12		1 Straight Out The Jungle		$10	Idlers 2704
12/16/89+	46	19		2 Done By The Forces Of Nature		$8	Warner 26072
7/10/93	52	3		3 J. Beez Wit The Remedy		$8	Warner 26679
6/21/97	37	4		4 Raw Deluxe		$8	Gee Street 27001

JUNIOR   '82
Born Junior Giscombe in London. Funk singer/songwriter.

5/8/82	15	23		1 "Ji"	71	$8	Mercury 4043
7/30/83	54	5		2 Inside Lookin' Out	177	$8	Mercury 812325
5/3/86	34	19		3 Acquired Taste		$8	Mercury 828001
5/21/88	56	7		4 Sophisticated Street		$8	London 828083

JUNIOR M.A.F.I.A.   '95
Gathering of four rap acts: Lil' Kim, Klepto, Snakes (Trife & Larceny) and The Sixes (Little Caesar, Chico & Nino Brown). Proteges of **The Notorious B.I.G.** M.A.F.I.A.: Masters At Finding Intelligent Attitudes.

| 9/9/95 | 2[2] | 43 | ● | Conspiracy | 8 | $8 | Undeas/Big Beat 92614 |

White Chalk • Excuse Me... • Realms Of Junior M.A.F.I.A. • **Player's Anthem** *[7]* • **I Need You Tonight** *[43]* • **Get Money** *[4]* • I've Been... • Crazaay • Back Stabbers • Shot! • Lyrical Wizardry • Oh My Lord • Murder Onze

JUNK YARD BAND   '96

| 6/22/96 | 98 | 1 | | Reunion | | $8 | Street 2040 |

JUST-ICE   '88
Born Joseph Williams in the Bronx, New York. Male rapper.

11/22/86	67	2		1 Back To The Old School		$8	Fresh 1
1/23/88	14	21		2 Kool & Deadly (Justicizms)		$8	Fresh 5
4/1/89	19	16		3 The Desolate One		$8	Fresh 82010
6/30/90	73	6		4 Masterpiece		$8	Fresh 82016
4/10/93	67	1		5 Gun Talk		$8	Savage 50211

JUVENILE   '99
Born Terius Gray in 1975 in New Orleans. Male rapper. Member of **Hot Boy$**.

| 5/17/97 | 55 | 4 | | 1 Solja Rags | | $8 | Cash Money 9612 |
| 11/21/98+ | 4 | 37↑ | ▲ | 2 400 Degreez | 16 | $8 | Cash Money 53162 |

Ha *[16]* • Gone Ride With Me • Flossin Season • Ghetto Children • Cash Money Concert • Welcome 2 Tha Nolia • U.P.T. • Run For It • Rich Niggaz • Back That Azz Up • Off Top • After Cash Money Concert • 400 Degreez • Juvenile On Fire • Solja Rag

K

KAI   '98
Male vocal group from San Francisco: Andrey Silva, Errol Viray, Andrew Gapuz, A.C. Lorenzo and Leo Chan.

| 7/4/98 | 57 | 3 | | Kai | | $8 | Geffen 25205 |

KALYAN   '77
Disco-reggae group from Trinidad led by singer Olsop David.

| 5/7/77 | 55 | 3 | | Kalyan | 173 | $12 | MCA 2245 |

KAM   '93
Born Craig Miller in Los Angeles. Male rapper.

| 3/6/93 | 18 | 26 | | 1 Neva Again | 110 | $8 | Street Know. 92208 |
| 4/1/95 | 20 | 7 | | 2 Made In America | 158 | $8 | EastWest 61754 |

KAMOZE, Ini   '95
First name pronounced: I-nee. Born in Kingston, Jamaica. Male dancehall reggae singer.

| 5/6/95 | 81 | 4 | | 1 Here Comes The Hotstepper | | $8 | Columbia 67056 |
| 8/19/95 | 58 | 5 | | 2 Lyrical Gangsta | | $8 | EastWest 61764 |

KANE, Big Daddy   '89
Born Antonio Hardy on 9/10/68 in Brooklyn, New York. Male rapper. Kane is an acronym for King Asiatic Nobody's Equal. Appeared in the movies *The Meteor Man* and *Posse*.

7/16/88	5	38	●	1 Long Live The Kane	116	$8	Cold Chillin' 25731

Long Live The Kane • Raw • Set It Off • The Day You're Mine • On The Bugged Tip • Ain't No Half-Steppin' [53] • I'll Take You There [73] • Just Rhymin' With Biz • Mister Cee's Master Plan • Word To The Mother(Land)

10/7/89	4	33	●	2 It's A Big Daddy Thing	33	$8	Cold Chillin' 25941

It's A Big Daddy Thing • Another Victory • Mortal Combat • Children R The Future • Young, Gifted And Black • **Smooth Operator** [11] • Calling Mr. Welfare • **I Get The Job Done** [27] • Ain't No Stoppin' Us Now • Pimpin' Ain't Easy • Big Daddy's Theme • To Be Your Man • The House That Cee Built • On The Move • Warm It Up, Kane

11/24/90+	10	27		3 Taste Of Chocolate	37	$8	Cold Chillin' 26303

Taste Of Chocolate • **Cause I Can Do It Right** [22] • It's Hard Being The Kane [91] • Who Am I • Dance With The Devil • No Damn Good • **All Of Me** [14] • Keep 'Em On The Floor • Mr. Pitiful • Put Your Weight On It • Big Daddy Vs. Dolemite • Down The Line

11/23/91	25	26		4 Prince Of Darkness	57	$8	Cold Chillin' 26715
6/12/93	9	17		5 Looks Like A Job For...	52	$8	Cold Chillin' 45128

Looks Like A Job For... • How U Get A Record Deal [86] • Chocolate City • The Beef Is On • Stop Shammin' • Brother Man, Brother Man • Rest In Peace • **Very Special** [23] • Here Comes Kane, Scoob And Scrap • Niggaz Never Learn • Give It To Me • 'Nuff Respect

10/1/94	26	5		6 Daddy's Home	155	$8	MCA 11102
11/14/98	62	2		7 Veteranz Day		$8	Mercury 371801

KANE, General   '86
Born Mitchell McDowell in New York City. Male rapper.

11/15/86	46	9		1 In Full Chill		$8	Gordy 6216
9/12/87	57	7		2 Wide Open		$8	Motown 6238

KANE & ABEL   '98
Male rap duo from Oakland: twin brothers David and Daniel Garcia.

10/26/96	29	19		1 The 7 Sins	179	$8	No Limit 50634
7/18/98	❶¹	19	●	2 Am I My Brothers Keeper	5	$8	No Limit 50720

Time After Time • This Is For The Smokers • Tryin 2 Have Sumthin' • Soldier Story • Throw Them Thangs • Out Of Town B's • Ghetto Day • Stress • We Don't Care • The Game • Watch Me • Only God Knows • Call Me When You Need Some • No Limit Nigga's • Bout That Combat • No Turnin Back • Betta Kill Me • My Hood To Yo Hood • Am I My Brothers Keeper • Gangstafied Forever • Let's Go Get Em • Greens, Cornbread & Cabbage • I Ain't Runnin

KANO   '81
Disoc studio group from Italy.

1/24/81	26	13		1 Kano		$10	Emergency 7505
12/26/81+	53	8		2 New York Cake	189	$10	Mirage 19327

KAOS & MYSTRO   '90
Rap duo: Don Rico Brent ("Kaos") and Jason Wilson ("Mystro").

5/12/90	99	5		Outcast Vol. I		$8	World One 500

KaSANDRA   '68
Born John Anderson on 7/30/36 in Panama City, Florida. Singer/songwriter.

11/23/68	26	18		1 John W. Anderson Presents KaSandra	142	$15	Capitol 2957
3/29/69	45	2		2 A Higher Plateau		$15	Capitol 157

KASHIF   '84
Born Michael Jones in 1959 in Brooklyn, New York. Techno-funk singer/musician. Member of **B.T. Express** from 1976-79.

4/9/83	10	46		1 Kashif	54	$8	Arista 9620

Don't Stop My Love • Stone Love [22] • I Just Gotta Have You (Lover Turn Me On) [5] • Help Yourself To My Love [28] • Rumors • Say Something Love • The Mood • All

7/14/84	4	37		2 Send Me Your Love	51	$8	Arista 8205

Baby Don't Break Your Baby's Heart [6] • Ooh Love [75] • Are You The Woman [25] • Love Has No End • Call Me Tonight • Send Me Your Love • I've Been Missin' You • Edgartown Groove • That's How It Goes

12/14/85	32	19		3 Condition Of The Heart	144	$8	Arista 8385
12/5/87+	17	32		4 Love Changes	118	$8	Arista 8447
11/4/89	29	20		5 Kashif		$8	Arista 8595

KAUSION   '95
Rap trio from Los Angeles: Gonzoe, Cel and Kaydo.

10/28/95	37	9		South Central Los Skanless		$8	Lench Mob 2002

produced by Ice Cube

KC AND THE SUNSHINE BAND   '75
Disco group from Hialeah, Florida. Formed by Harry "KC" Casey (vocals, keyboards) and Richard Finch (bass). Other members included Jerome Smith (guitar), Fermin Coytisolo (congas), Robert Johnson (drums), and Ronnie Smith, Denvil Liptrot, James Weaver, and Charles Williams (horn section).

8/16/75	❶¹	31		1 KC And The Sunshine Band	4	$10	TK 603

Let It Go • **That's The Way (I Like It)** [1] • Get Down Tonight [1] • Boogie Shoes [29] • Ain't Nothin' Wrong • I'm So Crazy ('Bout You) • What Makes You Happy • I Get Lifted

10/11/75	24	8		2 The Sound Of Sunshine	131	$10	TK 604

THE SUNSHINE BAND

10/30/76	5	50		3 Part 3	13	$10	TK 605

Baby I Love You (Yes, I Do) • **Wrap Your Arms Around Me** [24] • I Like To Do It [4] • (Shake, Shake, Shake) Shake Your Booty [1] • Let's Go Party • Come On In • **I'm Your Boogie Man** [3] • Keep It Comin' Love [1]

8/26/78	25	11		4 Who Do Ya (Love)	36	$10	TK 607
6/30/79	19	36		5 Do You Wanna Go Party	50	$10	TK 611
4/5/80	62	3		6 Greatest Hits	[G] 132	$10	TK 612

DEBUT	PEAK	WKS	Gold	Album Title	Pop #	$	Label & Number

K-CI & JOJO   **'98**
Brothers Cedric "K-Ci" and Joel "JoJo" Hailey from Charlotte, North Carolina. K-Ci was born on 9/2/69; JoJo was born on 6/10/71. Both were founding members of **Jodeci**.

| 7/5/97+ | 2² | 91 | ▲³ | **Love Always** | 6 | $8 | MCA 11613 |

HBI • Last Night's Letter [15] • Baby Come Back • Just For Your Love • Now And Forever • Don't Rush (Take Love Slowly) [24] • You Bring Me Up [7] • Still Waiting • Love Ballad • How Many Times (Will You Let Him Break Your Heart) • All My Life [1] • How Could You [16]

K-DEE   **'95**
Born Darrell Johnson in Los Angeles. Male rapper.

| 11/19/94+ | 33 | 22 | | **Ass, Gas or Cash (No one rides for free)** | | $8 | Lench Mob 1002 |

produced by Ice Cube

KELLIS, Rick   **'89**
Born in New York City. Saxophonist.

| 1/28/89 | 58 | 12 | | **Manhattan Suite** ....[I] | | $8 | Sedona 7502 |

KELLY, Paul   **'73**
Born on 6/19/40 in Miami. Singer/songwriter.

| 4/21/73 | 44 | 2 | | 1 **Don't Burn Me** | | $12 | Warner 2689 |
| 9/21/74 | 55 | 4 | | 2 **Hooked, Hogtied & Collared** | | $12 | Warner 2812 |

| ★122★ | | | | **KELLY, R.** | | | **'94** |

Born Robert Kelly on 1/8/69 in Chicago. Singer/producer/multi-instrumentalist. Also see **Public Announcement**.

| 2/15/92 | 3 | 74 | ▲ | 1 **Born Into The 90's** | 42 | $8 | Jive 41469 |

R. KELLY and Public Announcement
She's Loving Me • She's Got That Vibe [7] • Definition Of A Hotti • I Know What You Need • Keep It Street • Born Into The 90's • Slow Dance (Hey Mr. DJ) [1] • Dedicated [9] • Honey Love [1] • Hangin' Out • Hey Love (Can I Have A Word) [15]

| 11/27/93+ | ❶⁹ | 101 | ▲⁵ | 2 **12 Play** | 2¹ | $8 | Jive 41527 |

Your Body's Callin' [2] • Bump N' Grind [1] • Homie Lover Friend • It Seems Like You're Ready • Freak Dat Body • I Like The Crotch On You • Summer Bunnies [20] • For You • Back To The Hood Of Things • Sadie • Sex Me [8]

| 12/2/95 | ❶² | 76 | ▲⁵ | 3 **R. Kelly** | 1¹ | $8 | Jive 41579 |

Hump Bounce • Not Gonna Hold On • You Remind Me Of Something [1] • Step In My Room • Baby, Baby, Baby, Baby... • (You To Be) Be Happy • Down Low (Nobody Has To Know) [1] • I Can't Sleep Baby (If I) [1] • Thank God It's Friday • Love Is On The Way • Heaven If You Hear Me • Religious Love • Tempo Slow • As I Look Into My Life • Trade In My Life

| 11/28/98 | ❶¹ | 36↑ | ▲⁴ | 4 **R.** | 2¹ | $12 | Jive 41625 [2] |

Home Alone [22] • Spendin' Money [84] • If I'm Wit You • Half On A Baby [61] • When A Woman's Fed Up [5] • Get Up On A Room • One Man • We Ride • The Opera • The Interview • Only The Loot Can Make Me Happy • Don't Put Me Out • Suicide • Etcetera • If I Could Turn Back The Hands Of Time • What I Feel • The Chase • V.I.P. • Did You Ever Think [8] • Dollar Bill • Reality • 2nd Kelly • Ghetto Queen • Down Low Double Life • Looking For Love • Dancing With A Rich Man • I'm Your Angel [5] • Money Makes The World Go Round • I Believe I Can Fly [1]

KEMP, Johnny   **'88**
Born in Nassau, Bahamas; raised in Harlem, New York. Singer/dancer/actor/songwriter.

| 6/7/86 | 36 | 15 | | 1 **Johnny Kemp** | | $8 | Columbia 40192 |
| 5/28/88 | 4 | 28 | | 2 **Secrets Of Flying** | 68 | $8 | Columbia 40770 |

Just Got Paid [1] • One Thing Led To Another [40] • My Only Want Is You • Dancin' With Myself [5] • Urban Times Medley: Inner City Blues (Make Me Wanna Holler)/Mercy Mercy Me (The Ecology) • Feeling Without Touching • Just Like Flyin'

KEMP, Tara   **'91**
Born in San Francisco. Female singer/songwriter/pianist.

| 2/23/91 | 34 | 18 | | **Tara Kemp** | 109 | $8 | Giant 24408 |

| ★84★ | | | | **KENDRICKS, Eddie** | | | **'74** |

Born on 12/17/39 in Union Springs, Alabama; raised in Birmingham. Died of cancer on 10/5/92 (age 52). Joined group the Primes in Detroit in the late '50s. Group later evolved into **The Temptations**; Kendricks sang lead from 1960-71. Kendricks later dropped letter "s" from his last name. Also see **Daryl Hall & John Oates**.

1)Boogie Down! 2)He's A Friend 3)Eddie Kendricks

| 5/15/71 | 6 | 44 | | 1 **All By Myself** | 80 | $12 | Tamla 309 |

Let's Go Back To Day One • This Used To Be The Home Of Johnnie Mae • I Did It All For You • It's So Hard For Me To Say Good-Bye [37] • Something's Burning • Can I [37] • Didn't We

| 6/10/72 | 13 | 26 | | 2 **People...Hold On** | 131 | $12 | Tamla 315 |
| 6/23/73 | 5 | 26 | | 3 **Eddie Kendricks** | 18 | $12 | Tamla 327 |

Only Room For Two • Darling Come Back Home [26] • Each Day I Cry A Little • Can't Help What I Am • Keep On Truckin' [1] • Any Day Now • Not On The Outside • Where Do You Go (Baby)

| 3/16/74 | ❶¹ | 16 | | 4 **Boogie Down!** | 30 | $12 | Tamla 330 |

The Thin Man • Tell Her Love Has Felt The Need [8] • Son Of Sagittarius [5] • Boogie Down [1] • Hooked On Your Love • Honey Brown • You Are The Melody Of My Life • Trust Your Heart • Girl Of My Dreams • Loving You The Second Time Around

| 12/21/74+ | 8 | 28 | | 5 **For You** | 108 | $12 | Tamla 335 |

Please Don't Go Away • One Tear [8] • Shoeshine Boy [1] • Deep And Quiet Love • Let Yourself Go • If • If You Think (You Can) • Time In A Bottle

| 7/19/75 | 9 | 12 | | 6 **The Hit Man** | 63 | $12 | Tamla 338 |

If Anyone Can • Happy [8] • Get The Cream Off The Top [7] • Body Talk • Fortune Teller • Skippin' Work Today • You Loved Me Then • I've Got To Be

| 2/7/76 | 3 | 18 | | 7 **He's A Friend** | 38 | $12 | Tamla 343 |

He's A Friend [2] • A Part Of Me • I Won't Take No • Never Gonna Leave You • Get It While It's Hot [24] • Chains • The Sweeter You Treat Her • It's Not What You Got • On My Way Home • All Of My Love

10/9/76	22	7		8 **Goin' Up In Smoke**	144	$12	Tamla 346
10/8/77	47	12		9 **Slick**		$12	Tamla 356
3/11/78	48	8		10 **At His Best** ....[G]		$12	Tamla 354
3/25/78	33	21		11 **Vintage '78**	180	$10	Arista 4170
1/12/80	69	4		12 **Something More**		$10	Arista 4250
8/15/81	62	3		13 **Love Keys**	207	$10	Atlantic 19294
12/26/87+	60	5		14 **Ruffin & Kendrick**		$8	RCA Victor 6765

DAVID RUFFIN & EDDIE KENDRICK

KENNEDY, Joyce '84
Born in Chicago. Former lead singer of **Mother's Finest**.

| 9/1/84 | 17 | 25 | | Lookin' For Trouble .... | 79 | $8 | A&M 4996 |

★71★ **KENNY G** '94
Born Kenny Gorelick on 7/6/56 in Seattle. Fusion saxophonist. Joined **Love Unlimited Orchestra** in 1973. With **Jeff Lorber**'s fusion group from 1979-81.

| 2/25/84 | 17 | 27 | ▲ | 1 G Force .... | 62 | $8 | Arista 8192 |
| 6/1/85 | 37 | 12 | ▲ | 2 Gravity .... | 97 | $8 | Arista 8282 |

KENNY G & G FORCE

| 9/13/86+ | 8 | 86 | ▲⁵ | 3 Duotones .... | 6 | $8 | Arista 8427 |

What Does It Take (To Win Your Love) [15] • Midnight Motion • **Don't Make Me Wait For Love** [17] • Sade • Champagne • Slip Of The Tongue • You Make Me Believe • **Songbird** [23] • Three Of A Kind • Esther

| 10/29/88+ | 10 | 38 | ▲⁴ | 4 Silhouette .... | [I] | 8 | $8 | Arista 8457 |

Silhouette [35] • Tradewinds • I'll Be Alright • **Against Doctor's Orders** [65] • Pastel • **We've Saved The Best For Last** [18] • All In One Night • Summer Song • Let Go • Home

| 12/23/89+ | 15 | 27 | ▲⁴ | 5 Live .... | [L] | 16 | $10 | Arista 8613 [2] |

recorded August 26-27, 1989 in Seattle

| 12/5/92+ | 2¹ | 185 | ▲¹² | 6 Breathless .... | [I] | 2¹¹ | $8 | Arista 18646 |

The Joy Of Life • **Forever In Love** [73] • In The Rain • Sentimental • **By The Time This Night Is Over** [37] • End Of The Night • Alone • Morning • Even If My Heart Would Break • G-Bop • Sister Rose • A Year Ago • Homeland • The Wedding Song

| 12/3/94 | ❶³ | 8 | ▲⁸ | 7 Miracles - The Holiday Album .... | [X-I] | 1³ | $8 | Arista 18767 |

Winter Wonderland • White Christmas • Have Yourself A Merry Little Christmas • Silent Night • Greensleeves • Miracles • Little Drummer Boy • The Chanukah Song • Silver Bells • Away In A Manger • Brahms Lullaby

| 10/19/96 | 9 | 48 | ▲⁴ | 8 The Moment .... | [I] | 2¹ | $8 | Arista 18935 |

The Moment [62] • Passages • Havana • Always • That Somebody Was You • The Champion's Theme • Eastside Jam • Moonlight • Gettin' On The Step • Everytime I Close My Eyes • Northern Lights • Innocence

| 12/6/97+ | 15 | 34 | ▲² | 9 Greatest Hits .... | [G-I] | 19 | $8 | Arista 18991 |

KERR, George '71

| 10/30/71 | 31 | 7 | | If This World Were Mine .... | | $20 | All Platinum 3004 |

★106★ **KHAN, Chaka** '78
Born Yvette Marie Stevens on 3/23/53 in Great Lakes, Illinois. Became lead singer of **Rufus** in 1972. Recorded solo and with Rufus since 1978. Sister of vocalists **Taka Boom** and Mark Stevens (**Jamaica Boys**).
1)Chaka 2)What Cha' Gonna Do For Me 3)I Feel For You

| 11/11/78 | 2⁵ | 22 | ● | 1 Chaka .... | 12 | $10 | Warner 3245 |

I'm Every Woman [1] • Love Has Fallen On Me • Roll Me Through The Rushes • Sleep On It • **Life Is A Dance** [40] • We Got The Love • Some Love • A Woman In A Man's World • The Message In The Middle Of The Bottom • I Was Made To Love Him

| 6/21/80 | 6 | 23 | | 2 Naughty .... | 43 | $10 | Warner 3385 |

Clouds [10] • Get Ready, Get Set [48] • Move Me No Mountain • Nothing's Gonna Take You Away • So Naughty • Too Much Love • All Night's All Right • What You Did • **Papillon (aka Hot Butterfly)** [22] • Our Love's In Danger

| 5/9/81 | 3 | 23 | ● | 3 What Cha' Gonna Do For Me .... | 17 | $10 | Warner 3526 |

We Can Work It Out [34] • What Cha' Gonna Do For Me [1] • I Know You, I Love You • **Any Old Sunday** [68] • We Got Each Other • And The Melody Still Lingers On (Night In Tunisia) • Night Moods • Heed The Warning • Father He Said • Fate

| 12/25/82+ | 5 | 24 | | 4 Chaka Khan .... | 52 | $8 | Warner 23729 |

Tearin' It Up [48] • Slow Dancin' • Best In The West • **Got To Be There** [5] • Be Bop Medley: Hot House/East Of Suez (Cone On Sailor)/Epistrophy (I Want To Play)/Yardbird Suite/Con Alma/Giant Steps • Twisted • So Not To Worry • Pass It On (A Sure Thing) (Pasa Lo Esta Seguro)

| 10/27/84 | 4 | 47 | ▲ | 5 I Feel For You .... | 14 | $8 | Warner 25162 |

This Is My Night [11] • Stronger Than Before • My Love Is Alive • Eye To Eye • La Flamme • **I Feel For You** [1] • Hold Her Through The Fire [15] • Caught In The Act • Chinatown

8/30/86	24	17		6 Destiny	67	$8	Warner 25425
12/17/88+	17	28		7 C.K.	125	$8	Warner 25707
5/2/92	9	31		8 The Woman I Am	92	$8	Warner 26296

Everything Changes • Give Me All • Telephone • Keep Givin' Me Lovin' • Facts Of Love • **Love You All My Lifetime** [2] • I Want [62] • **You Can Make The Story Right** [8] • Be My Eyes • This Time • The Woman I Am • Love With No Strings • Don't Look At Me That Way

| 11/30/96 | 22 | 21 | | 9 Epiphany: The Best Of Chaka Khan Volume One .... | [G] | 84 | $8 | Reprise 45865 |
| 10/17/98+ | 49 | 15 | | 10 Come 2 My House .... | | $8 | NPG 9281 |

KHAYREE '97

| 8/9/97 | 73 | 3 | | Khayree Brings You The Blackalation (The World Is Yours) .... | | $8 | Young Black Br. 4884 |

KIARA '89
Duo from Detroit: Gregory Charley (vocals, bass) and John Winston (guitar, backing vocals). Kiara (pronounced: kee-air-a) is Swahili for change.

| 9/24/88+ | 23 | 44 | | 1 To Change And/Or Make A Difference .... | | $8 | Arista 8533 |
| 9/22/90 | 53 | 20 | | 2 Civilized Rogue .... | | $8 | Arista 8617 |

KID CAPRI '98
Born David Love in 1968 in the Bronx, New York. DJ/rapper.

| 3/23/91 | 87 | 6 | | 1 The Tape .... | | $8 | Cold Chillin' 26474 |
| 12/5/98 | 25 | 11 | | 2 Soundtrack To The Streets .... | 135 | $8 | Track Masters 68781 |

KID CREOLE AND THE COCONUTS '82
Kid Creole was born Thomas Augustus Darnell Browder on 8/12/50 in Montreal, Canada. Singer/songwriter/producer. Member of **Dr. Buzzard's Original "Savannah" Band** during the mid-1970s. Formed The Coconuts with his wife, Adriana "Addy" Kaegi, and Andy "Coati Mundi" Hernandez.

| 7/3/82 | 43 | 19 | | Wise Guy .... | 145 | $8 | Sire 3681 |

DEBUT	PEAK	WKS	Gold	Album Title	Pop #	$	Label & Number

KIDDO '83
Funk group from Long Beach, California: Donnie Sterling (vocals), Michael Hampton (guitar), Willie Jenkins (percussion), Leroy Davis (sax), Fred Johnson (bass) and Leon Goodin (drums).

| 4/2/83 | 29 | 12 | | Kiddo | 206 | $10 | A&M 4924 |

KID FROST '95
Born Arturo Molina on 5/31/64 in East Los Angeles. Male rapper. Later shortened name to **Frost**.

8/18/90	45	12		1 Hispanic Causing Panic	67	$8	Virgin 91377
5/23/92	54	15		2 East Side Story	73	$8	Virgin 92097
11/11/95	36	21		3 Smile Now, Die Later	119	$8	Ruthless 1504
7/19/97	64	4		4 When HELL.A. Freezes Over	154	$8	Ruthless 1578

FROST (above 2)

KID 'N PLAY '89
Rap duo from Queens, New York: Christopher "Kid" Reid and Christopher "Play" Martin. Starred in the *House Party* movies.

| 11/26/88+ | 9 | 50 | ● | 1 2 Hype | 96 | $8 | Select 21628 |

Rollin' With Kid 'N Play [11] • Brother Man Get Hip • **Gittin' Funky [53]** • Soul Man • Damn That DJ (The Wizard M.E.) • Last Night • **2 Hype [46]** • Can You Dig That • Undercover • The Kid 'N Play Kick Step • Do This My Way

| 3/31/90 | 11 | 24 | ● | 2 Kid 'N Play's Funhouse | 58 | $8 | Select 21638 |
| 10/19/91 | 27 | 20 | | 3 Face The Nation | 144 | $8 | Select 61206 |

KID SENSATION '90
Born Steven Spence in Seattle. DJ/keyboardist.

| 7/28/90 | 48 | 20 | | 1 Rollin' With Number One | 175 | $8 | Nastymix 70180 |
| 3/28/92 | 62 | 19 | | 2 The Power Of Rhyme | | $8 | Nastymix 7101 |

KILLAFORNIA ORGANIZATION '96

| 11/2/96 | 88 | 2 | | Killafornia Organization | | $8 | Killa Cali/Thug 3003 |

KILLAFORNIA ORGANIZATION FEATURING COMPTONS MOST WANTED

KILLAH PRIEST '98
Born William Reed in New York City. Male rapper. Member of **Sunz Of Man**.

| 3/28/98 | 4 | 9 | | Heavy Mental | 24 | $8 | Geffen 24971 |

One Step [84] • Blessed Are Those • From Then Till Now • Cross My Heart • Fake MC's • It's Over • Crusaids • Tai Chi • Heavy Mental • If You Don't Know • Atoms To Adam • High Explosives • Wisdom • Basic Instructions Before Leaving Earth • Mystic City • Information • Science Project • Almost There • The Professional

KILLARMY '97
Male rap group from New York City: Killa Sin, Shogun Assassin, Ninth Prince, Baretta Nine, Islord and Dom Pachino.

| 8/23/97 | 10 | 12 | | 1 Silent Weapons For Quiet Wars | 34 | $8 | Wu-Tang 50633 |

Dress To Kill • Clash Of The Titans • Burning Season • Blood For Blood • Seems It Never Fails • Universal Soldiers • Love, Hell Or Right • **Wake Up [89]** • Fair, Love & War • **Wu-Renegades [69]** • Full Moon • Under Siege • Shelter • Camouflage Ninjas • Swinging Swords • War Face • 5 Stars

| 8/29/98 | 13 | 7 | | 2 Dirty Weaponry | 40 | $8 | Wu-Tang 50014 |

KILLA TAY '98
Born in Sacramento, California. Male rapper.

| 10/24/98 | 69 | 1 | | Mr. Mafioso | | $8 | AWOL 46597 |

KILO '97
Born Kilo Ali in Atlanta. Male rapper.

5/30/92	67	17		1 A-Town Rush		$8	Wrap 8110
9/9/95+	57	18		2 Get This Party Started		$8	Wrap 8147
8/16/97	44	9		3 Organized Bass	173	$8	Death Row 90128

KILO ALI

KINFOLK '96

| 7/6/96 | 89 | 1 | | Each & Every Day | | $8 | Wild West 43061 |

KINFUSION '97

| 12/27/97 | 89 | 1 | | Da Unhatched Breed | | $8 | Before Dawn 2017 |

KING, Albert '72
Born Albert Nelson on 4/25/23 in Indianola, Mississippi. Died of a heart attack on 12/21/92 (age 69). Blues singer/guitarist.

| 11/16/68 | 40 | 5 | | 1 Live Wire/Blues Power | 150 | $20 | Stax 2003 |

recorded at the Fillmore in San Francisco

| 5/31/69+ | 46 | 13 | | 2 Years Gone By | 133 | $25 | Stax 2010 |
| 7/19/69 | 23 | 4 | | 3 Jammed Together | 171 | $25 | Stax 2020 | [I]

ALBERT KING/STEVE CROPPER/POP STAPLES

7/3/71	29	14		4 Lovejoy	188	$20	Stax 2040
10/14/72	11	18		5 I'll Play The Blues For You	140	$20	Stax 3009
5/11/74	37	18		6 I Wanna Get Funky		$15	Stax 5505
3/13/76	26	10		7 Truckload Of Lovin'	166	$12	Utopia 1387
9/25/76	54	2		8 Albert		$12	Utopia 1731
3/17/79	74	3		9 New Orleans Heat		$12	Tomato 7022

KING, B.B. ★26★   '71

Born Riley King on 9/16/25 in Itta Bena, Mississippi. Legendary blues singer/guitarist. Moved to Memphis in 1946. Own radio show on WDIA-Memphis, 1949-50, where he was dubbed "The Beale Street Blues Boy," later shortened to "Blues Boy," then simply "B.B." First recorded for Bullet in 1949. Inducted into the Rock and Roll Hall of Fame in 1987. Won Grammy's Lifetime Achievement Award in 1987.

1)Live In Cook County Jail 2)Together For The First Time...Live 3)Completely Well
4)Live At The Regal 5)Indianola Mississippi Seeds

DEBUT	PEAK	WKS		#	Album Title		Pop #	$	Label & Number
5/1/65	6	5		1	**B.B. King: Live At The Regal** [L]			$40	ABC-Paramount 509
					recorded on November 21, 1964 in Chicago				
					Every Day I Have The Blues • Sweet Little Angel • It's My Own Fault • How Blue Can You Get? • Please Love Me • You Upset Me Baby • Worry, Worry • Woke Up This Morning • You Done Lost Your Good Thing Now • Help The Poor				
8/24/68	46	3		2	Blues On Top Of Blues			$25	BluesWay 6011
6/28/69	11	29		3	Live & Well [L]		56	$20	BluesWay 6031
					side 1: live; side 2: studio				
12/27/69+	5	30		4	**Completely Well**		38	$20	BluesWay 6037
					So Excited [14] • No Good • You're Losin' Me • What Happened • Confessin' The Blues • Key To My Kingdom • Cryin' Won't Help You Now • You're Mean • **The Thrill Is Gone** [3]				
10/24/70	8	31		5	**Indianola Mississippi Seeds**		26	$12	ABC 713
					Nobody Loves Me But My Mother • You're Still My Woman • **Ask Me No Questions** [18] • Until I'm Dead And Cold • King's Special • Ain't Gonna Worry My Life Anymore • **Chains And Things** [6] • Go Underground • **Hummingbird** [25]				
3/6/71	❶³	31		6	Live In Cook County Jail [L]		25	$12	ABC 723
					Every Day I Have The Blues • How Blue Can You Get • Worry, Worry, Worry • Medley: 3 O'Clock Blues/Darlin' You Know I Love You • Sweet Sixteen • The Thrill Is Gone • Please Accept My Love				
10/23/71	15	17		7	B.B. King In London		57	$12	ABC 730
3/4/72	14	25		8	L.A. Midnight		53	$12	ABC 743
10/14/72	21	16		9	Guess Who		65	$12	ABC 759
3/31/73	28	6		10	The Best Of B.B. King [G]		101	$12	ABC 767
9/15/73	13	33		11	To Know You Is To Love You		71	$12	ABC 794
8/24/74	27	14		12	Friends		153	$12	ABC 825
10/26/74+	2¹	16	●	13	Together For The First Time...Live [L]		43	$15	Dunhill/ABC 50190 [2]
					B.B. KING & BOBBY BLAND				
					3 O'Clock Blues • It's My Own Fault • Driftin' Blues • That's The Way Love Is • I'm Sorry • I'll Take Care Of You • Don't Cry No More • Don't Answer The Door • Medley: Good To Be Back Home/Driving Wheel/Rock Me Baby/Black Night/Cherry Red/It's My Own Fault/3 O'Clock Blues/Worried Life Blues/Chains Of Love/Gonna Get Me An Old Woman • Why I Sing The Blues • Goin' Down Slow • I Like To Live The Love				
11/15/75+	25	10		14	Lucille Talks Back		140	$12	ABC 898
7/17/76	9	15		15	Together Again...Live [L]		73	$12	ABC/Impulse 9317
					BOBBY BLAND & B.B. KING				
					Let The Good Times Roll [20] • Medley: Stormy Monday Blues/Strange Things Happen • Feel So Bad • Medley: Mother-In-Law Blues/Mean Old World • Everyday (I Have The Blues) • Medley: The Thrill Is Gone/I Ain't Gonna Be The First To Cry				
2/19/77	34	6		16	King Size		154	$12	ABC 977
5/13/78	27	26		17	Midnight Believer		124	$12	ABC 1061
8/25/79	22	22		18	Take It Home		112	$10	MCA 3151
4/26/80	45	11		19	"Now Appearing" at Ole Miss		162	$12	MCA 8016 [2]
					recorded at the University of Mississippi				
2/28/81	26	19		20	There Must Be A Better World Somewhere		131	$8	MCA 5162
5/1/82	45	23		21	Love Me Tender		179	$8	MCA 5307
7/2/83	38	20		22	Blues 'N' Jazz		172	$8	MCA 5413
10/19/85	31	20		23	Six Silver Strings			$8	MCA 5616
2/29/92	76	13		24	There Is Always One More Time			$8	MCA 10295
7/10/93	64	14		25	Blues Summit		182	$8	MCA 10710

KING, Ben E.   '75

Born Benjamin Earl Nelson on 9/23/38 in Henderson, North Carolina; raised in New York City. Former lead singer of **The Drifters**.

DEBUT	PEAK	WKS		#	Album Title		Pop #	$	Label & Number
5/3/75	13	10		1	Supernatural		39	$12	Atlantic 18132
7/30/77	14	19		2	Benny And Us		33	$12	Atlantic 19105
					AVERAGE WHITE BAND & BEN E. KING				
6/7/80	73	2		3	Music Trance			$10	Atlantic 19269
5/2/92	82	10		4	What's Important To Me			$8	Ichiban 1133

KING, Diana   '95

Born on 11/8/70 in St. Catherine, Jamaica. Reggae singer.

DEBUT	PEAK	WKS			Album Title		Pop #	$	Label & Number
7/1/95	85	8	●		Tougher Than Love		179	$8	Work 64189

KING, Evelyn "Champagne"   '82   ★124★

Born on 6/29/60 in the Bronx, New York; raised in Philadelphia. Disco singer.

DEBUT	PEAK	WKS		#	Album Title		Pop #	$	Label & Number
5/27/78	8	51	●	1	Smooth Talk		14	$10	RCA Victor 2466
					Smooth Talk • I Don't Know If It's Right [7] • Til I Come Off The Road • Dancin', Dancin', Dancin' • **Shame** [7] • Nobody Knows • We're Going To A Party • The Show Is Over				
4/14/79	12	21	●	2	Music Box		35	$10	RCA Victor 3033
10/11/80	58	7		3	Call On Me		124	$10	RCA Victor 3543
7/18/81	6	28	●	4	I'm In Love		28	$10	RCA Victor 3962
					I'm In Love [1] • If You Want My Lovin' • **Don't Hide Our Love** [28] • What Are You Waiting For • **Spirit Of The Dancer** [51] • The Other Side Of Love • I Can't Take It • The Best Is Yet To Come				

DEBUT	PEAK	WKS	Gold	Album Title	Pop #	$	Label & Number
				KING, Evelyn "Champagne" — Cont'd			
9/11/82	❶²	38	●	5 Get Loose	27	$10	RCA Victor 4337
				EVELYN KING (above 2)			
				Love Come Down [1] • I Can't Stand It • Betcha She Don't Love You [2] • Get Loose [61] • Back To Love • Stop That • Get Up Off Your Love • I'm Just Warmin' Up			
1/7/84	24	36		6 Face To Face	91	$10	RCA Victor 4725
11/10/84	38	18		7 So Romantic	203	$10	RCA Victor 5308
12/28/85+	38	22		8 A Long Time Coming (A Change Is Gonna Come)		$10	RCA Victor 7015
5/28/88	20	40		9 Flirt	192	$8	EMI-Manhattan 46968
				KING, Freddie '75			
				Born Freddie Christian on 9/3/34 in Gilmer, Texas. Died of a heart attack on 12/28/76 (age 42). Blues singer/guitarist.			
8/25/73	54	2		1 Woman Across The River	158	$15	Shelter 8919
1/18/75	53	3		2 Burglar		$12	RSO 4803
				KING, Rev. Martin Luther '68			
				Born on 1/15/29 in Atlanta. Assassinated on 4/4/68 (age 39) in Memphis. Civil rights leader.			
5/4/68	10	10		1 I Have A Dream [T]	69	$20	Creed 3201
				speeches from the March on Washington (August 28, 1963)			
5/11/68	20	7		2 The Great March To Freedom [T]	141	$50	Gordy 906
				speech at Detroit's Freedom Rally (June 23, 1963); album first released in 1963			
6/1/68	32	2		3 Dr. Martin Luther King; Funeral Services; Ebenezer Baptist Church; 04-09-68 [T]		$20	Brotherhood 2001
6/1/68	37	4		4 In Search Of Freedom [T]	150	$20	Mercury 61170
				various speeches from 1964-68			
7/6/68	48	3		5 ...Free At Last [T]		$30	Gordy 929
5/12/73	46	2		6 Keep The Dream Alive [T]		$15	RCA Victor 6093
				KING CURTIS '71			
				Born Curtis Ousley on 2/7/34 in Fort Worth, Texas. Stabbed to death on 8/13/71 (age 37) in New York City. Legendary saxophonist.			
6/3/67	11	11		1 The Great Memphis Hits [I]	185	$20	Atco 211
12/23/67+	25	4		2 King Size Soul [I]	168	$20	Atco 231
8/10/68	47	2		3 Sweet Soul [I]	198	$20	Atco 247
12/7/68	40	4		4 The Best of King Curtis [G-I]	190	$20	Atco 266
8/16/69	40	3		5 Instant Groove [I]	160	$20	Atco 293
8/15/70	37	8		6 Get Ready [I]	198	$20	Atco 338
8/14/71	9	15		7 Live At Fillmore West [I-L]	54	$20	Atco 359
				Memphis Soul Stew • A Whiter Shade Of Pale • Whole Lotta Love • I Stand Accused • Changes • Ode To Billie Joe • Mr. Bojangles • Signed Sealed Delivered I'm Yours • Soul Serenade			
3/25/72	48	2		8 Everybody's Talkin' [I]	189	$20	Atco 385
				KING HARVEST '73			
				Six-man, Pop-rock group based in Olcott, New York. Formed by Ronny Altback (piano), Rod Novak (sax), Eddie Tulya (guitar) and Doc Robinson (bass).			
2/10/73	50	2		Dancing In The Moonlight	136	$12	Perception 36
				KING JUST '95			
				Born Adrian Angevin in Staten Island, New York. Male rapper.			
6/3/95	33	8		Mystics Of The God		$8	Black Fist 23001
				KING PIN SKINNY PIMP '96			
				Male rapper from Memphis.			
4/20/96	56	3		King Of Da Playaz Ball		$8	Prophet 4403
				KINGS OF PRESSURE '89			
				Rap group from Long Island, New York.			
7/29/89	89	6		Slang Teacher		$8	Next Plateau 1017
				KING SUN '91			
				Born Todd Turnbow on 2/23/67 in Paterson, New Jersey. Male rapper.			
12/22/90+	54	18		Righteous But Ruthless		$8	Profile 1299
				KING TEE '93			
				Born Roger McBride in Los Angeles. Male rapper.			
12/24/88+	35	27		1 Act A Fool	125	$8	Capitol 90544
10/27/90	35	20		2 At Your Own Risk	175	$8	Capitol 92359
2/13/93	17	13		3 Tha Triflin' Album	95	$8	Capitol 99354
4/15/95	23	6		4 IV Life	171	$8	MCA 11146
				KINSMAN DAZZ — see DAZZ BAND			
				KLEEER '81			
				Group from New York City: Paul Crutchfield (vocals), Richard Lee (guitar), Norman Durham (bass) and Woody Cunningham (drums).			
7/14/79	53	4		1 I Love To Dance	208	$10	Atlantic 19237
3/1/80	24	22		2 Winners	140	$10	Atlantic 19262
2/28/81	13	24		3 License To Dream	81	$8	Atlantic 19288
2/20/82	31	15		4 Taste The Music	139	$8	Atlantic 19334
4/14/84	49	27		5 Intimate Connection		$8	Atlantic 80145
				KLEMMER, John '69			
				Born on 7/3/46 in Chicago. Jazz saxophonist/flutist.			
9/27/69	46	3		1 Blowin' Gold [I]	176	$20	Cadet Concept 321
7/30/77	49	5		2 LifeStyle (Living & Loving) [I]	51	$10	ABC 1007
8/1/81	53	5		3 Hush [I]	99	$8	Elektra 527

KLIQUE '83

Pronounced: click. Vocal trio: **Howard Huntsberry**, Isaac Suthers and his sister Deborah Hunter.

7/4/81	40	12		1 It's Winning Time		$10	MCA 5198
10/1/83	11	20		2 Try It Out	70	$10	MCA 39008
5/11/85	25	17		3 Love Cycles		$10	MCA 5532

KLUGH, Earl ★96★ '81

Born on 9/16/53 in Detroit. Jazz acoustic guitarist/pianist.
1)Crazy For You 2)Wishful Thinking 3)Dream Come True

12/11/76	58	2		1 Living Inside Your Love [I]	188	$10	Blue Note 667
7/16/77	31	13		2 Finger Paintings [I]	84	$10	Blue Note 737
5/19/79	32	20		3 Heart String [I]	49	$10	United Artists 942
1/5/80	26	20	●	4 One On One [I]	23	$10	Tappan Zee 36241
				BOB JAMES AND EARL KLUGH			
4/26/80	22	13		5 Dream Come True [I]	42	$10	United Artists 1026
12/27/80+	40	18		6 Late Night Guitar [I]	98	$8	Liberty 1079
11/7/81	14	26		7 Crazy For You [I]	53	$8	Liberty 51113
11/20/82+	23	26		8 Two Of A Kind	44	$8	Capitol 12244
				EARL KLUGH & BOB JAMES			
5/14/83	27	23		9 Low Ride [I]	38	$8	Capitol 12253
3/31/84	18	27		10 Wishful Thinking [I]	69	$8	Capitol 12323
11/3/84	42	13		11 Nightsongs [I]	107	$8	Capitol 12372
5/18/85	23	21		12 Soda Fountain Shuffle [I]	110	$8	Warner 25262
9/13/86	61	11		13 Life Stories [I]	143	$8	Warner 25478
7/11/87	28	22	●	14 Collaboration [I]	59	$8	Warner 25580
				GEORGE BENSON/EARL KLUGH			
5/4/91	96	2		15 Midnight In San Juan [I]	189	$8	Warner 26293
12/5/92	88	7		16 Cool [I]	170	$8	Warner 26939
				BOB JAMES/EARL KLUGH			

KLYMAXX '85

Female group formed in Los Angeles by drummer/producer Bernadette Cooper. Consisted of **Joyce "Fenderella" Irby**, Lorena Shelby, Cheryl Cooley, Robin Grider and Lynn Malsby. In 1987, Cooper founded and produced **Madame X**. Re-organized as a trio in 1990 with Shelby, Cooley and Grider. Shelby married to William Shelby of the group **Dynasty**.

1/19/85	9	65	●	1 Meeting In The Ladies Room	18	$8	Constellation 5529

The Men All Pause *[5]* • Lock And Key *[47]* • I Miss You *[11]* • Just Our Luck • **Meeting In The Ladies Room** *[4]* • Video Kid • Ask Me No Questions • Love Bandit • I Betcha

12/6/86+	25	47		2 Klymaxx	98	$8	Constellation 5832
6/16/90	32	11		3 The Maxx Is Back	168	$8	MCA 6376

KMC '91

Rap trio from Los Angeles: Rocc, Tee and Poison Ivey. KMC stands for Kaotic Minds Corruptin'.

5/25/91	83	9		Three Men With The Power Of Ten		$8	Priority 57122

K.M.D. '91

Rap trio from Brooklyn, New York: Onyx, Subroc and Zevlove X.

6/8/91	67	10		Mr. Hood		$8	Elektra 60977

KNIGHT, Frederick '74

Born on 8/15/44 in Alabama. Singer/songwriter/producer.

2/16/74	58	3		I've Been Lonely For So Long		$12	Stax 3011

KNIGHT, Gladys, & The Pips ★8★ '73

Family vocal group from Atlanta: Gladys (b: 5/28/44), her brother Merald "Bubba" Knight and sister Brenda, and cousins William and Eleanor Guest. Named "Pips" for their manager, cousin James "Pip" Woods. First recorded for Brunswick in 1958. Brenda and Eleanor replaced by cousins Edward Patten and Langston George in 1959. Langston left group in 1962 and group has remained a quartet with the same members ever since. Hosted their own TV show in July 1975. Due to legal problems, Gladys could not record with the Pips from 1977-80. Gladys was a cast member of the 1985 TV series *Charlie & Co.* Group inducted into the Rock and Roll Hall of Fame in 1996.

1)Imagination 2)All Our Love 3)Neither One Of Us 4)Good Woman 5)I Feel A Song

10/28/67+	12	26		1 Everybody Needs Love	60	$25	Soul 706
5/25/68	12	21		2 Feelin' Bluesy	158	$25	Soul 707
1/4/69	11	24		3 Silk N' Soul	136	$25	Soul 711
10/25/69+	11	21		4 Nitty Gritty	81	$25	Soul 713
4/4/70	5	20		5 Gladys Knight & The Pips Greatest Hits [G]	55	$15	Soul 723

Every Beat Of My Heart *[1]* • Letter Full Of Tears *[3]* • Giving Up *[38]* • Everybody Needs Love *[3]* • I Heard It Through The Grapevine *[1]* • The End Of Our Road *[5]* • I Wish It Would Rain *[15]* • Didn't You Know (You'd Have To Cry Sometime) *[11]* • You Need Love Like I Do (Don't You) *[3]* • Friendship Train *[2]* • The Nitty Gritty *[2]* • It Should Have Been Me *[9]*

5/22/71	4	25		6 If I Were Your Woman	35	$15	Soul 731

If I Were Your Woman *[1]* • Feeling Alright • One Less Bell To Answer • Let It Be • **I Don't Want To Do Wrong** *[2]* • One Step Away • Here I Am Again • How Can You Say That Ain't Love • Is There A Place (In His Heart For Me) • Everybody Is A Star • Signed Gladys • Your Love's Been Good For Me

1/22/72	11	22		7 Standing Ovation	60	$15	Soul 736
3/17/73	❶²	32		8 Neither One Of Us	9	$15	Soul 737

Neither One Of Us (Wants To Be The First To Say Goodbye) *[1]* • It's Gotta Be That Way • For Once In My Life • This Child Needs Its Father • Who Is She (And What Is She To You) • And This Is Love • **Daddy Could Swear, I Declare** *[2]* • Can't Give It Up No More • Don't It Make You Feel Guilty

7/7/73	14	23		9 All I Need Is Time	70	$15	Soul 739

KNIGHT, Gladys, & The Pips — Cont'd

DEBUT	PEAK	WKS	Gold	Album Title	Pop #	$	Label & Number
11/3/73	❶⁷	53	●	10 Imagination	9	$12	Buddah 5141

Midnight Train To Georgia [1] • I've Got To Use My Imagination [1] • Storms Of Troubled Times • **Best Thing That Ever Happened To Me** [1] • Once In A Lifetime Thing • **Where Peaceful Waters Flow** [6] • I Can See Clearly Now • Perfect Love • Window Raisin' Granny

| 3/23/74 | 29 | 11 | | 11 Knight Time | 139 | $12 | Soul 741 |
| 5/4/74 | ❶¹ | 34 | ● | 12 Claudine [S] | 35 | $12 | Buddah 5602 |

Mr. Welfare Man • To Be Invisible • **On And On** [2] • The Makings Of You • Claudine Theme • Hold On • **Make Yours A Happy Home** [13]

| 5/4/74 | 10 | 16 | | 13 Anthology [G] | 77 | $15 | Motown 792 [2] |

Every Beat Of My Heart [1] • Letter Full Of Tears [3] • Giving Up [38] • Just Walk In My Shoes • Take Me In Your Arms And Love Me • Everybody Needs Love [3] • I Heard It Through The Grapevine [1] • The End Of Our Road [5] • It Should Have Been Me [9] • I Wish It Would Rain [15] • Didn't You Know (You'd Have To Cry Sometime) [11] • The Nitty Gritty [2] • Friendship Train [2] • The Tracks Of My Tears • You Need Love Like I Do (Don't You?) • Every Little Bit Hurts • If I Were Your Woman [1] • I Don't Want To Do Wrong [2] • Make Me The Woman You Go Home To • **Help Me Make It Through The Night** [13] • For Once In My Life • Neither One Of Us (Wants To Be The First To Say Goodbye) [1] • Daddy Could Swear, I Declare [2]

| 11/23/74 | ❶¹ | 34 | ● | 14 I Feel A Song | 17 | $12 | Buddah 5612 |

I Feel A Song (In My Heart) [1] • Love Finds It's Own Way [3] • Seconds • The Going Ups And The Coming Downs • The Way We Were/Try To Remember [6] • Better You Go Your Way • Don't Burn Down The Bridge • The Need To Be • Tenderness Is His Way

| 5/10/75 | 32 | 4 | | 15 A Little Knight Music [K] | 164 | $12 | Soul 744 |
| 11/1/75 | 4 | 15 | ● | 16 2nd Anniversary | 24 | $12 | Buddah 5639 |

Money [4] • Street Brother • **Part Time Love** [4] • At Every End There's A Beginning • Georgia On My Mind • You And Me Against The World • Where Do I Put His Memory • Summer Sun • Feel Like Makin' Love

| 2/7/76 | 8 | 16 | ● | 17 The Best Of Gladys Knight & The Pips [G] | 36 | $12 | Buddah 5653 |

Make Yours A Happy Home [13] • Best Thing That Ever Happened To Me [1] • I Feel A Song (In My Heart) [1] • The Going Ups And The Coming Downs • Midnight Train To Georgia [1] • On And On [2] • Where Peaceful Waters Flow [6] • I've Got To Use My Imagination [1] • I Can See Clearly Now • The Way We Were/Try To Remember [6]

11/27/76+	16	12		18 Pipe Dreams [S]	94	$12	Buddah 5676
4/16/77	18	14		19 Still Together	51	$12	Buddah 5689
9/2/78	30	7		20 The One And Only	145	$12	Buddah 5701
11/25/78	57	5		21 Miss Gladys Knight		$12	Buddah 5714
3/31/79	71	3		22 Gladys Knight	201	$10	Columbia 35704
				GLADYS KNIGHT (above 2)			
5/31/80	5	23		23 About Love	48	$10	Columbia 36387

Landlord [3] • Taste Of Bitter Love [38] • Still Such A Thing • Get The Love • Add It Up • **Bourgie, Bourgie** [45] • Friendly Persuasion • We Need Hearts

| 9/5/81 | 22 | 39 | | 24 Touch | 109 | $10 | Columbia 37086 |
| 5/21/83 | 3 | 53 | ● | 25 Visions | 34 | $10 | Columbia 38205 |

When You're Far Away [42] • Just Be My Lover • **Save The Overtime (For Me)** [1] • Heaven Sent • Don't Make Me Run Away • Ain't No Greater Love • Seconds • **You're Number One (In My Book)** [5] • Oh La De Da • Hero [64]

| 3/30/85 | 31 | 22 | | 26 Life | 126 | $10 | Columbia 39423 |
| 12/12/87+ | ❶² | 34 | ● | 27 All Our Love | 39 | $8 | MCA 42004 |

Love Overboard [1] • Lovin' On Next To Nothin' [3] • Thief In Paradise • You • Let Me Be The One • Complete Recovery • Say What You Mean • **It's Gonna Take All Our Love** [29] • Love Is Fire (Love Is Ice) • Point Of View • Overnight Success

| 7/27/91 | ❶¹ | 41 | | 28 Good Woman | 45 | $8 | MCA 10329 |

Men [2] • Meet Me In The Middle [78] • This Is Love • **Where Would I Be** [66] • Superwoman • Give Me A Chance • Good Woman • If You Only Knew • Mr. Love • Waiting On You • In This Life

| 10/1/94 | 6 | 55 | ● | 29 Just For You | 53 | $8 | MCA 10946 |
| | | | | GLADYS KNIGHT (above 2) | | | |

Next Time [30] • I Don't Want To Know [32] • I'll Fall In Love If You Hang Around • Our Love • Home Alone • Choice Of Colors • Guilty • Somehow He Loves Me • **End Of The Road Medley** [76]

KNIGHT, Jean   '71
Born on 1/26/43 in New Orleans. Female singer.

| 8/21/71 | 8 | 15 | | **Mr. Big Stuff** | 60 | $25 | Stax 2045 |

Mr. Big Stuff [1] • A Little Bit Of Something (Is Better Than All Of Nothing) • Don't Talk About Jody • Think It Over • Take Him (You Can Have My Man) • You City Slicker • Why I Keep Living These Memories • Call Me Your Fool (If You Want To) • One-Way Ticket To Nowhere (It's The End Of The Ride) • Your Six-Bit Change

KNIGHT, Jerry   '81
Born in Los Angeles. Singer/bassist. Former member of Raydio.

| 5/31/80 | 51 | 12 | | 1 Jerry Knight | 165 | $10 | A&M 4788 |
| 3/28/81 | 30 | 14 | | 2 Perfect Fit | 146 | $10 | A&M 4843 |

K-9 POSSE   '89
Rap duo from Teaneck, New Jersey: Vernon Lynch and Wardell Mahone.

| 3/4/89 | 28 | 18 | | 1 K-9 Posse | 98 | $8 | Arista 8569 |
| 4/20/91 | 66 | 12 | | 2 On A Different Tip | | $8 | Arista 8665 |

KNUCKLES, Frankie   '91
Born in the Bronx, New York. Moved to Chicago in 1977; worked at Chicago's Warehouse club. Dubbed the "Godfather of House" music.

| 10/5/91 | 54 | 10 | | Beyond The Mix | | $8 | Virgin 91618 |

KOKANE   '94
Male rapper.

| 4/30/94 | 56 | 9 | | Funk Upon A Rhyme | | $8 | Ruthless 5512 |

KOKOMO   '75
British jazz-rock group.

| 5/31/75 | 34 | 11 | | Kokomo | 159 | $12 | Columbia 33442 |

KOOL & THE GANG ★22★   '79

Group from Jersey City, New Jersey. Core members: Robert "Kool" Bell (bass) and his brother Ronald Bell (sax), Claydes Smith (guitar), Rick Westfield (keyboards), Dennis Thomas (sax), Robert Mickens (trumpet) and George Brown (drums). Added lead singer **James "J.T."** **Taylor** in 1978. Westfield left in 1978; replaced by Earl Toon. In 1987, Curtis "Fitz" Williams replaced Toon. Taylor left group in 1988; replaced by lead singers: Gary Brown, Odeen Mays and Skip Martin (**Dazz Band**). Brown left by 1990.

1)Ladies' Night   2)Something Special   3)Celebrate!   4)Emergency   5)In The Heart

DEBUT	PEAK	WKS	Gold	#	Album Title	Pop #	$	Label & Number
1/10/70	43	8		1	Kool & The Gang .... [I]		$25	De-Lite 2003
2/13/71	6	33		2	**Live At The Sex Machine**	[I-L]	122	$12	De-Lite 2008
					Medley: What Would The World Be Like Without Music/Let The Music Take Your Mind • Walk On By • Chocolate Buttermilk • Trying To Make A Fool Of Me • Who's Gonna Take The Weight • Pneumonia • Wichita Lineman • **I Want To Take You Higher** *[35]* • Funky Man • The Touch Of You			
9/25/71	32	12		3	The Best Of Kool And The Gang .... [G]	157	$12	De-Lite 2009
12/25/71+	24	11		4	Live At P.J.'s .... [I-L]	171	$12	De-Lite 2010
					recorded on May 29, 1971 in Hollywood			
8/5/72	25	13		5	Music Is The Message		$12	De-Lite 2011
3/24/73	34	6		6	Good Times	142	$12	De-Lite 2012
10/13/73+	6	36	●	7	**Wild And Peaceful**	33	$10	De-Lite 2013
					Funky Stuff *[5]* • More Funky Stuff • **Jungle Boogie** *[2]* • Heaven At Once • **Hollywood Swinging** *[1]* • This Is You, This Is Me • Life Is What You Make It • Wild And Peaceful			
3/9/74	26	9		8	Kool Jazz .... [I-K]	187	$10	De-Lite 4001
10/19/74	16	15	●	9	Light Of Worlds	63	$10	De-Lite 2014
3/22/75	21	6	●	10	Kool & The Gang Greatest Hits! .... [G]	81	$10	De-Lite 2015
9/6/75	5	13		11	**Spirit Of The Boogie**	48	$10	De-Lite 2016
					Spirit Of The Boogie *[1]* • Ride The Rhythm • Jungle Jazz • Sunshine And Love • Ancestral Ceremony • Mother Earth • Winter Sadness • **Caribbean Festival** *[6]*			
3/27/76	9	23		12	**Love & Understanding**	68	$10	De-Lite 2018
					Love And Understanding (Come Together) *[8]* • Sugar • Do It Right Now • Cosmic Energy • Hollywood Swinging • **Summer Madness** *[36]* • Universal Sound *[71]* • Come Together			
11/20/76	9	20		13	**Open Sesame**	110	$10	De-Lite 2023
					Open Sesame *[6]* • Gift Of Love • Little Children • All Night Long • Whisper Softly • **Super Band** *[17]* • L-O-V-E • Sunshine			
1/21/78	33	9		14	The Force	142	$10	De-Lite 9501
11/25/78	71	2		15	Everybody's Dancin'	207	$10	De-Lite 9509
9/22/79	❶²	44	▲	16	**Ladies' Night**	13	$10	De-Lite 9513
					Ladies Night *[1]* • Got You Into My Life • If You Feel Like Dancin' • **Hangin' Out** *[36]* • Tonight's The Night • **Too Hot** *[3]*			
10/25/80+	2⁴	42	▲	17	**Celebrate!**	10	$10	De-Lite 9518
					Celebration *[1]* • Jones Vs. Jones *[33]* • Take It To The Top *[11]* • Morning Star • Love Festival • Just Friends • Night People • Love Affair			
10/24/81	❶¹	57	▲	18	**Something Special**	12	$8	De-Lite 8502
					Steppin' Out *[12]* • Good Time Tonight • **Take My Heart (You Can Have It If You Want It)** *[1]* • Be My Lady • **Get Down On It** *[4]* • Pass It On • Stand Up And Sing • No Show			
10/9/82	5	28	●	19	**As One**	29	$8	De-Lite 8505
					Street Kids *[78]* • Big Fun *[6]* • As One • Hi De Hi, Hi De Ho • **Let's Go Dancin' (Ooh La La, La)** *[7]* • Pretty Baby • Think It Over			
12/10/83+	5	38	●	20	**In The Heart**	29	$8	De-Lite 8508
					In The Heart • **Joanna** *[1]* • **Tonight** *[7]* • Rollin' • Place For Us • **Straight Ahead** *[49]* • Home Is Where The Heart Is • You Can Do It • September Love			
12/15/84+	3	70	▲²	21	**Emergency**	13	$8	De-Lite 822943
					Emergency *[7]* • **Fresh** *[1]* • **Misled** *[3]* • **Cherish** *[1]* • Surrender • Bad Woman • You Are The One			
12/6/86+	9	42	●	22	**Forever**	25	$8	Mercury 830398
					Victory *[2]* • I.B.M.C. • **Stone Love** *[4]* • Forever • **Holiday** *[9]* • Peace Maker • Broadway • Special Way • God's Country			
9/3/88	58	10		23	Everything's Kool & The Gang: Greatest Hits & More .... [G]	109	$8	Mercury 834780
7/29/89	52	14		24	Sweat		$8	Mercury 838233

KOOL G RAP & D.J. POLO   '95

Rap duo from Queens, New York: Nathaniel "Kool Genius of Rap" Wilson (b: 7/20/68) and DJ Polo.

DEBUT	PEAK	WKS	Gold	#	Album Title	Pop #	$	Label & Number
4/8/89	26	22		1	Road To The Riches		$8	Cold Chillin' 25820
9/15/90	34	14		2	Wanted: Dead Or Alive		$8	Cold Chillin' 26165
12/5/92	18	20		3	Live And Let Die	185	$8	Cold Chillin' 5001
4/2/94	92	3		4	Killer Kuts		$8	Cold Chillin' 5002
10/7/95	❶¹	19		5	4,5,6	24	$8	Cold Chillin' 57808
					4,5,6 • It's A Shame • Take 'Em To War • Executioner Style • For Da Brothaz • Blowin' Up In The World • **Fast Life** *[42]* • Ghetto Knows • Money On My Brain			
11/14/98	43	6		6	Roots Of Evil		$8	Illstreet 6001
					KOOL G RAP (above 2)			

KOOL MOE DEE '89
Born Mohanndas DeWese on 8/8/67 in Harlem, New York. Male rapper. Formerly with the Treacherous Three.

DEBUT	PEAK	WKS	Gold	Album Title	Pop #	$	Label & Number
4/4/87	20	26		1 Kool Moe Dee	83	$8	Jive 1025
11/28/87+	4	50	▲	2 How Ya Like Me Now	35	$8	Jive 1079

How Ya Like Me Now [22] • Wild, Wild West [4] • Way Way Back • 50 Ways • No Respect • Don't Dance • I'm A Player • Suckers • Stupid • Rock You • Get Paid

| 6/17/89 | 2² | 34 | ● | 3 Knowledge Is King | 25 | $8 | Jive 1182 |

They Want Money [3] • The Avenue • I Go To Work [13] • All Night Long [70] • Knowledge Is King • I'm Hittin' Hard • Get The Picture • I'm Blowin' Up • The Don • Pump Your Fist

| 7/6/91 | 19 | 18 | | 4 Funke Funke Wisdom | 72 | $8 | Jive 1388 |

KRAFTWERK '81
Techno group from Dusseldorf, Germany. Formed by Ralf Hutter and Florian Schneider. Kraftwerk is German for power station.

| 7/25/81 | 32 | 34 | | Computer-World | [l] 72 | $8 | Warner 3549 |

KRIS KROSS '92
Male rap duo from Atlanta: Chris "Mack Daddy" Kelly and Chris "Daddy Mack" Smith.

| 4/18/92 | ❶⁶ | 55 | ▲⁴ | 1 Totally Krossed Out | 1² | $8 | Ruffhouse 48710 |

Jump [2] • Lil' Boys In Da Hood • Warm It Up [3] • The Way Of Rhyme • Party • We're In Da House • A Real Bad Dream • It's A Shame [55] • Can't Stop The Bum Rush • You Can't Get With This • I Missed The Bus [29]

| 8/21/93 | 2² | 36 | ▲ | 2 Da Bomb | 13 | $8 | Ruffhouse 57278 |

Da Bomb [74] • Sound Of My Hood • It Don't Stop • Alright [8] • I'm Real [45] • 2 Da Beat Ch'yall • Freak Da Funk • A Lot 2 Live 4 • Take Um Out

| 1/27/96 | 2¹ | 24 | ● | 3 Young, Rich & Dangerous | 15 | $8 | Ruffhouse 67441 |

Some Cut Up • When The Homies Show Up • Tonite's Tha Night [6] • Young, Rich And Dangerous • Live And Die For Hip Hop [36] • Money, Power And Fame • It's A Group Thang • Mackin' Ain't Easy • Da Streets Ain't Right • Hey Sexy

KRS-ONE '95
Born Lawrence Parker in 1966 in the Bronx, New York. Male rapper. Co-founder of Boogie Down Productions.

| 10/16/93 | 5 | 32 | | 1 Return Of The Boom Bap | 37 | $8 | Jive 41517 |

KRS-ONE Attacks • Outta Here [61] • Black Cop • Mortal Thought • I Can't Wake Up • Slap Them Up • Sound Of Da Police [79] • Mad Crew • Uh Oh • Brown Skin Woman • Return Of The Boom Bap • "P" Is Still Free • Stop Frontin' • Higher Level

| 10/28/95 | 2¹ | 19 | | 2 KRS One | 19 | $8 | Jive 41570 |

Rappaz R. N. Dainja • De Automatic • MC's Act Like They Don't Know [35] • Ah-Yeah • R.E.A.L.I.T.Y. • Free Mumia • Hold • Wannabemceez • Represent The Real Hip Hop • The Truth • Build Ya Skillz • Out For Fame • Squash All Beef • Health, Wealth, Self

| 6/7/97 | 2¹ | 18 | ● | 3 I Got Next | 3 | $8 | Jive 41601 |

The MC [67] • Medley: I Got Next/Neva Hadda Gun • Heartbeat • Step Into A World (Rapture's Delight) [22] • A Friend [70] • Hip Hop • Halftime • Klassicks • Blowe • Real Hip-Hop • Come To Da Party • Can't Stop, Won't Stop • Over Ya Head • Just To Prove A Point

KRYSTOL '86
Female vocal trio: Tina Scott, Robbie Danzie and Robyrda Stiger. Stiger was with Alton McClain & Destiny.

| 9/27/86 | 55 | 4 | | Passion From A Woman | | $8 | Epic 40362 |

K7 '94
Born Louis Sharpe in New York City. Male rapper. Former member of TKA.

| 11/27/93+ | 54 | 32 | ● | Swing Batta Swing | 96 | $8 | Tommy Boy 1071 |

K-SOLO '92
Born Kevin Madison in Central Islip, New York. Male rapper. K-Solo stands for Kevin Self Organization Left Others.

| 7/14/90 | 45 | 32 | | 1 Tell The World My Name | | $8 | Atlantic 82108 |
| 6/20/92 | 36 | 16 | | 2 Times Up | 135 | $8 | Atlantic 82388 |

K-STONE '92
Born Kevin Bailey in Detroit. Male rapper.

| 9/19/92 | 70 | 11 | | 6.0.1. | | $8 | Bryant 4127 |

KURIOUS '94
Born Jorge Antonio Alvarez in Manhattan, New York. Male rapper.

| 2/5/94 | 68 | 3 | | A Constipated Monkey | | $8 | Columbia 53223 |

KURUPT '98
Born Ricardo Brown in Los Angeles. Member of Tha Dogg Pound.

| 10/24/98 | 4 | 10 | | Kuruption! | 8 | $12 | A&M 540963 [2] |

This One's For U • Make Some Noize • Put That On Something • Play My Cards • We Can Freak It [89] • Fresh • C-Walk • Ho's A Housewife • Can't Let That Slide • That's Gangsta • Another Day • Ask Yourself A Question • It's A Set Up • Light Shit Up • Game • Gimmewhutchagot • If You See Me • The Life • No Feelings • It's Time • I Wanna... • Who Do U Be • We Can Freak It (Out)

KUT KLOSE '95
Female vocal trio: Tabitha Duncan, Athena Cage and LaVonn Battle.

| 4/1/95 | 12 | 28 | | Surrender | 66 | $8 | Keia 61668 |

KWAMÉ AND A NEW BEGINNING '89
Born Kwamé Holland in Queens, New York. Male rapper.

4/15/89	13	30		1 The Boy Genius featuring A New Beginning	114	$8	Atlantic 81941
6/23/90	34	21		2 "A Day In The Life" A Pokadelick Adventure	113	$8	Atlantic 82100
7/4/92	56	10		3 Nastee		$8	Atlantic 82356

KWICK '80
Vocal group from Memphis: Terry Bartlett, Bertram Brown, William Sullivan and Vince Williams.

| 5/24/80 | 53 | 8 | | Kwick | 197 | $10 | EMI America 17025 |

KYPER '90
Born Randall Kyper in Baton Rouge, Louisiana. Male rapper.

| 8/25/90 | 79 | 7 | | Tic Tac Toe | 82 | $8 | Atlantic 82116 |

L

LaBELLE, Patti/LaBELLE ★29★   '86

Born Patricia Holt on 5/24/44 in Philadelphia. Began singing career as leader of the Ordettes which evolved into **The Blue Belles**. The quartet, formed in Philadelphia in 1962, included **Nona Hendryx**, Sarah Dash and Cindy Birdsong. Birdsong left in 1967 to join **The Supremes**. Group continued as a trio. In 1971, group shortened its name to **LaBelle**. In 1977, group disbanded and Patti recorded solo.

1)Winner In You 2)I'm In Love Again 3)Nightbirds 4)Gems 5)Burnin'

PATTI LaBELLE & THE BLUE BELLES:

DEBUT	PEAK	WKS	Gold	Album Title	Pop #	$	Label & Number
5/28/66	20	2		1 Over The Rainbow		$30	Atlantic 8119
				LaBELLE:			
2/15/75	4	25	●	2 Nightbirds	7	$12	Epic 33075

Lady Marmalade *[1]* • Somebody Somewhere • Are You Lonely? • It Took A Long Time • Don't Bring Me Down • **What Can I Do For You?** *[8]* • Nightbird • Space Children • All Girl Band • You Turn Me On

DEBUT	PEAK	WKS	Gold	Album Title	Pop #	$	Label & Number
5/31/75	42	3		3 Moon Shadow		$15	Warner 2618

released in 1972

DEBUT	PEAK	WKS	Gold	Album Title	Pop #	$	Label & Number
9/20/75	10	10		4 Phoenix	44	$12	Epic 33579

Phoenix (The Amazing Flight Of A Lone Star) • Slow Burn • Black Holes In The Sky • Good Intentions • **Far As We Felt Like Goin'** *[99]* • **Messin' With My Mind** *[19]* • Chances Go Round • Cosmic Dancer • Take The Night Off • Action Time

DEBUT	PEAK	WKS	Gold	Album Title	Pop #	$	Label & Number
9/18/76	21	25		5 Chameleon	94	$10	Epic 34189
				PATTI LaBELLE:			
9/17/77	16	22		6 Patti LaBelle	62	$10	Epic 34847
6/17/78	39	8		7 Tasty	129	$10	Epic 35335
3/31/79	33	17		8 It's Alright With Me	145	$10	Epic 35772
4/12/80	21	22		9 Released	114	$10	Epic 36381
9/26/81	43	9		10 The Spirit's In It	156	$10	Philadelphia I. 37380
2/13/82	61	4		11 Best Of Patti LaBelle .... [G]		$10	Epic 36997
1/7/84	4	46	●	12 I'm In Love Again	40	$10	Philadelphia I. 38539

I'm In Love Again • Lover Man (Oh, Where Can You Be?) • **Love, Need And Want You** *[10]* • If Only You Knew *[1]* • Body Language • I'll Never, Never Give Up • Love Bankrupt • When Am I Gonna Find True Love

DEBUT	PEAK	WKS	Gold	Album Title	Pop #	$	Label & Number
8/17/85	13	41		13 Patti	72	$10	Philadelphia I. 40020
5/24/86	❶[8]	42	▲	14 Winner In You	1[1]	$8	MCA 5737

Oh, People *[7]* • On My Own *[1]* • Something Special (Is Gonna Happen Tonight) *[50]* • Kiss Away The Pain *[13]* • Twisted • You're Mine Tonight • Finally We're Back Together Again • Beat My Heart Like A Drum • Sleep With Me Tonight • There's A Winner In You

DEBUT	PEAK	WKS	Gold	Album Title	Pop #	$	Label & Number
7/22/89	14	39		15 Be Yourself	86	$8	MCA 6292
10/26/91+	9	51	●	16 Burnin'	71	$8	MCA 10439

Feels Like Another One *[3]* • Somebody Loves You Baby (You Know Who It Is) *[2]* • When You Love Somebody (I'm Saving My Love For You) *[70]* • I Don't Do Duets • Temptation • When You've Been Blessed (Feels Like Heaven) *[4]* • Burnin' (The Fire Is Still) Burnin' For You • I Hear Your Voice • We're Not Makin' Love Anymore • Release Yourself • Love Never Dies • Crazy Love

DEBUT	PEAK	WKS	Gold	Album Title	Pop #	$	Label & Number
12/5/92	18	24		17 Live! .... [L]	135	$8	MCA 10691

recorded at the Apollo Theatre in New York City

DEBUT	PEAK	WKS	Gold	Album Title	Pop #	$	Label & Number
6/25/94	7	38	●	18 Gems	48	$8	MCA 10870

I'm In Love • **All This Love** *[42]* • **The Right Kinda Lover** *[8]* • This Word Is All • Too Good To Be Through • **I Never Stopped Loving You** *[67]* • Stay In My Corner • If I Didn't Have You • I Can't Tell My Heart What To Do • Time Will Tell • Our World • Come As You Are

DEBUT	PEAK	WKS	Gold	Album Title	Pop #	$	Label & Number
12/21/96	58	12		19 Greatest Hits .... [G]		$8	MCA 11567
7/12/97	10	50	●	20 Flame	39	$8	MCA 11642

Someone Like You • I Like The Way It Feels • You Are My Solid Ground • Flame • Let Me Be Your Lady • Does He Love You • Shoe Was On The Other Foot • Addicted To You • **When You Talk About Love** *[12]* • Love Is Just A Whisper Away • If By Chance • Let Me Be There For You • You Saved My Life • Don't Block The Blessings

DEBUT	PEAK	WKS	Gold	Album Title	Pop #	$	Label & Number
10/10/98	51	3		21 Live! One Night Only .... [L]	182	$12	MCA 11814 [2]

recorded at the Hammerstein Ballroom in New York City

L.A. BOPPERS   '80

Group from Los Angeles: Vance Tennort (vocals, drums), Kenny Styles (guitar), Stan Martin (trumpet) and Ed Reddick (bass).

DEBUT	PEAK	WKS	Gold	Album Title	Pop #	$	Label & Number
2/23/80	25	15		L.A. Boppers	85	$10	Mercury 3816

LACE   '87

Female vocal trio from Washington DC: Kathy Merrick, Vivian Ross and Lisa Frazier.

DEBUT	PEAK	WKS	Gold	Album Title	Pop #	$	Label & Number
10/31/87	52	10		Shades Of Lace	187	$8	Wing 833451

L.A. DREAM TEAM   '86

Rap group led by Rudy Pardee (from Cleveland) and Chris Wilson (from Los Angeles).

DEBUT	PEAK	WKS	Gold	Album Title	Pop #	$	Label & Number
8/30/86	27	14		Kings Of The West Coast	138	$8	MCA 5779

LADY OF RAGE, The   '97

Born Robin Allen in Farmville, Virginia. Female rapper.

DEBUT	PEAK	WKS	Gold	Album Title	Pop #	$	Label & Number
7/12/97	7	12		Necessary Roughness	32	$8	Death Row 90109

Necessary Roughness • Big Bad Lady • Sho Shot • No Shorts • Get With Da Wickedness (Flow Like That) • Raw Deal • Breakdown • Rough, Rugged & Raw • Super Supreme • Some Shit • Microphone Pon Cok • Confessions

LADY RED   '96

DEBUT	PEAK	WKS	Gold	Album Title	Pop #	$	Label & Number
5/4/96	62	2		Lady Red		$8	Hi-Powered 1430

DEBUT	PEAK	WKS	Gold	Album Title	Pop #	$	Label & Number
				LAID BACK '84			
				Vocal/instrumental duo from Denmark: Tim Stahl (keyboards) and John Guldberg (guitar).			
4/7/84	22	16		...Keep Smiling	67	$8	Sire 25058
	★154★			**LAKESIDE** '81			
				Funk group from Dayton, Ohio: Tiemeyer McCain, Thomas Oliver Shelby, Otis Stokes and Mark Wood (vocals), Steve Shockley (guitar), Fred Lewis (percussion), Norman Beavers (keyboards), Marvin Craig (bass) and Fred Alexander (drums).			
12/9/78+	10	23	1	Shot Of Love	74	$10	Solar 2937
				Shot Of Love • Hold On Tight • One Minute After Midnight • Time • Given In To Love [73] • It's All The Way Live [4] • Visions Of My Mind			
10/27/79	21	24	2	Rough Riders	141	$10	Solar 3490
11/29/80+	2³	39	● 3	Fantastic Voyage	16	$10	Solar 3720
				Fantastic Voyage [1] • Your Love Is On The One [14] • I Need You • Strung Out • Say Yes • Eveready Man • I Love Everything You Do			
12/12/81+	32	15	4	Keep On Moving Straight Ahead	109	$10	Solar 3974
12/26/81+	9	34	5	Your Wish Is My Command	58	$10	Solar 26
				Your Wish Is My Command [25] • Something About That Woman • I Want To Hold Your Hand [5] • Special • Magic Moments • The Urban Man • I'll Be Standing By • The Songwriter			
5/14/83	10	35	6	Untouchables	42	$8	Solar 60204
				Raid [8] • Turn The Music Up [38] • So Let's Love • Real Love [17] • Alibi • Untouchable • Tinsel Town Theory			
7/28/84	11	25	7	Outrageous	68	$8	Solar 60355
5/2/87	35	27	8	Power		$8	Solar 72553
				LA LA '87			
				Born LaForrest Cope in Queens, New York. Female singer/songwriter.			
7/4/87	57	5		La La		$8	Arista 8403
				LAND OF THE HEARTLESS '98			
4/18/98	89	1		Sabotage		$8	Fully Loaded 8001
				LANIER & CO. '83			
				Group led by singer Farris Lanier.			
3/5/83	47	10		Lanier & Co.		$10	Larc 8012
				LARR, Larry '91			
				Born Lawrence Hill in Logan, Pennsylvania. Male rapper.			
8/31/91	67	10		Da Wizzard Of Odds		$8	Ruffhouse 47119
	★168★			**LaSALLE, Denise** '83			
				Born Denise Allen on 7/16/39 in Belzoni, Mississippi; raised in Chicago. Singer/songwriter.			
				1)A Lady In The Street 2)Still Trapped 3)Right Place, Right Time			
1/22/72	38	6	1	Trapped By A Thing Called Love	120	$15	Westbound 2012
4/28/73	46	2	2	On The Loose		$15	Westbound 2016
1/7/78	47	15	3	The Bitch Is Bad		$12	ABC 1027
9/23/78	58	2	4	Under The Influence		$12	ABC 1087
6/2/79	46	8	5	Unwrapped	205	$10	MCA 3098
4/30/83	23	31	6	A Lady In The Street		$10	Malaco 7412
4/21/84	38	25	7	Right Place, Right Time	204	$10	Malaco 7417
6/8/85	67	9	8	Love Talkin'		$10	Malaco 7422
6/21/86	48	14	9	Rain And Fire		$10	Malaco 7434
1/14/89	61	14	10	Hittin Where It Hurts		$10	Malaco 7447
7/28/90	27	33	11	Still Trapped		$8	Malaco 7454
7/18/92	73	20	12	Love Me Right		$8	Malaco 7464
4/5/97	69	10	13	Smokin' In Bed		$8	Malaco 7479
				LAST POETS, The '70			
				Protest group from Harlem, New York: Abiodun Oyewole, Alafia Pudim, Omar Ben Hassen, Nilaja, David Nelson, Felipe Luciano and Gylan Kain. Nelson, Luciano and Kain split from the others to record as **The Original Last Poets**.			
6/27/70	3	35	1	The Last Poets	29	$20	Douglas 3
				Run Nigger • On The Subway • Scared Of Revolution • Black Thighs • Gashman • Wake Up Niggers • New York, New York • Jones Comin' Down • When The Revolution Comes • Just Because • Black Wish • Two Little Boys • Surprises			
2/13/71	43	7	2	Right On! [S]	106	$20	Juggernaut 8802
				THE ORIGINAL LAST POETS			
4/3/71	14	16	3	This Is Madness	104	$20	Douglas 30583
				LA THE DARKMAN '98			
				Born Lawrence Jackson in New York City. Male rapper.			
12/5/98	37	6		Heist Of The Century		$8	Wu-Tang 30072
				LATIMORE '74			
				Born Benjamin Latimore on 9/7/39 in Charleston, Tennessee. Singer/songwriter.			
8/17/74	13	23	1	More, More, More		$12	Glades 6503
6/28/75	49	3	2	Latimore II		$12	Glades 7505
1/15/77	47	4	3	It Ain't Where You Been	181	$12	Glades 7509
12/2/78+	51	10	4	Dig A Little Deeper		$12	Glades 7515
10/9/82	61	3	5	Singing In The Key Of Love		$10	Malaco 7409
12/17/83	66	8	6	I'll Do Anything For You		$10	Malaco 7414
4/20/91	34	16	7	The Only Way Is Up		$8	Malaco 7456
				LATIN ALLIANCE '91			
				Latin rap group with members from Los Angeles and New York City.			
9/7/91	83	6		Latin Alliance	133	$8	Virgin 91625

LATTIMORE, Kenny   '98
Born in Washington DC. Singer/songwriter/producer.

6/1/96+	19	89	●	1 Kenny Lattimore	140	$8	Columbia 67125
11/7/98	15	31		2 From The Soul Of Man	71	$8	Columbia 68854

★175★   LATTISAW, Stacy   '81
Born on 11/25/66 in Washington DC. Female singer.

6/7/80	9	35	1 Let Me Be Your Angel	44	$10	Cotillion 5219

Jump To The Beat • **Dynamite!** *[8]* • You Don't Love Me Anymore • Dreaming • **Let Me Be Your Angel** *[8]* • Don't You Want To Feel It (For Yourself) • You Know I Like It • My Love

7/18/81	8	18	2 With You	46	$10	Cotillion 16049

Feel My Love Tonight *[71]* • Screamin' Off The Top • **It Was So Easy** *[61]* • Baby I Love You • **Love On A Two Way Street** *[2]* • With You • Young Girl • Spotlight • You Take Me To Heaven

8/28/82	11	23	3 Sneakin' Out	55	$10	Cotillion 90002
8/6/83	26	16	4 Sixteen	160	$10	Cotillion 90106
3/17/84	27	25	5 Perfect Combination	139	$10	Cotillion 90136
			STACY LATTISAW & JOHNNY GILL			
10/18/86	36	26	6 Take Me All The Way	131	$8	Motown 6212
2/27/88	24	28	7 Personal Attention	153	$8	Motown 6247
11/18/89+	16	30	8 What You Need		$8	Motown 6280

LAURNEÁ   '97
Born Laurneá Wilkinson in Omaha, Nebraska; raised in Los Angeles. Female singer.

8/30/97	80	3	Betta Listen	$8	Yab Yum 67508

LaVETTE, Bettye   '82
Born Betty Haskin in 1946 in Muskegon, Michigan. Singer/actress. Appeared in the Broadway musical *Bubbling Brown Sugar*.

2/20/82	48	5	Tell Me A Lie	207	$10	Motown 6000

LAWRENCE, Billy   '97
Born in St. Louis. Female singer/songwriter.

7/12/97	57	1	Paradise	$8	EastWest 61945

LAWRENCE, Martin   '93
Born on 4/16/65 in Frankfurt, Germany; raised in New York City. Actor/comedian. Starred in own TV series and several movies.

10/9/93	10	33	1 Talkin' Shit [C]		$8	EastWest 92289

Boxin' • Eddie's House • Worrying About Your Weight • Michael Jackson • Ilado • White Kids - Black Kids • Smokin' Weed • Drivin' Cross Country • I Love Sex • Braggin' On Their Dicks • Talking During Sex • Head • Fartin' & Shitin'

10/14/95	35	5	2 Funk It! [C]		$8	EastWest 61749

LAWS, Debra   '81
Born in Houston. Sister of **Eloise Laws**, **Hubert Laws** and **Ronnie Laws**.

3/28/81	13	37	Very Special	70	$10	Elektra 300

LAWS, Eloise   '78
Born in Houston. Sister of **Debra Laws**, **Hubert Laws** and **Ronnie Laws**.

2/18/78	49	7	1 Eloise	156	$10	ABC 1022
2/21/81	51	12	2 Eloise Laws	175	$10	Liberty 1063

LAWS, Hubert   '75
Born in 1939 in Houston. Brother of **Ronnie Laws**, **Eloise Laws** and **Debra Laws**. Jazz flutist.

9/13/75	18	9	1 The Chicago Theme [I]	42	$12	CTI 6058
11/20/76	33	6	2 Romeo & Juliet [I]	139	$12	Columbia 34330
4/28/79	48	4	3 Land Of Passion	93	$10	Columbia 35708

★178★   LAWS, Ronnie   '80
Born on 10/3/50 in Houston. Jazz saxophonist. Brother of **Debra Laws**, **Eloise Laws** and **Hubert Laws**. Member of **Earth, Wind & Fire** from 1972-73. Formed **Pressure** in 1979.

9/27/75	25	10		1 Pressure Sensitive [I]	73	$12	Blue Note 452
6/12/76	13	17		2 Fever [I]	46	$12	Blue Note 628
5/7/77	13	31	●	3 Friends And Strangers [I]	37	$10	Blue Note 730
11/11/78	16	22		4 Flame	51	$10	United Artists 881
2/16/80	4	19		5 Every Generation	24	$10	United Artists 1001

Young Child • Never Get Back To Houston • **Every Generation** *[12]* • Tomorrow • O.T.B.A. Law (Outta Be A Law) • Love's Victory • Thoughts & Memories • As One

10/10/81	17	25	6 Solid Ground	51	$10	Liberty 51087
8/6/83	24	16	7 Mr. Nice Guy	98	$10	Capitol 12261
1/12/85	33	18	8 Classic Masters [K]	201	$10	Capitol 12375
6/1/91	80	8	9 Identity		$8	ATA 75753

LEADERS OF THE NEW SCHOOL   '93
Rap group from Uniondale, New York: **Busta Rhymes**, Charlie Brown, Dinco D and Cut Monitor Milo.

7/27/91	53	13	1 A Future Without A Past...	128	$8	Elektra 60976
10/30/93	15	10	2 T.I.M.E. - The Inner Mind's Eye - The Endless Dispute With Reality	66	$8	Elektra 61382

LED ZEPPELIN   '70
British heavy-metal rock group: Robert Plant (vocals), Jimmy Page (guitar), John Paul Jones (bass, keyboards) and John Bonham (drums). Bonham died of asphyxiation on 9/25/80 (age 33). Group disbanded in December 1980. Plant and Page formed **The Honeydrippers** in 1984. Group inducted into the Rock and Roll Hall of Fame in 1995.

1/3/70	32	11	▲[11]	1 Led Zeppelin II	1[7]	$20	Atlantic 8236
11/7/70	30	14	▲[6]	2 Led Zeppelin III	1[4]	$15	Atlantic 7201

DEBUT	PEAK	WKS	Gold Album Title	Pop #	$	Label & Number

LEE, Jackie   '66
Born Earl Nelson on 9/8/28 in Lake Charles, Louisiana. Male singer/songwriter.

| 2/26/66 | 8 | 4 | The Duck | 85 | $25 | Mirwood 7000 |

The Duck [4] • Hully Gully • The Shotgun And The Duck • Do The Temptation Walk • The Neighborhood • Land Of A Thousand Dances • Dancin' In The Street • The Bounce • Do You Love Me • Everybody Jerk • Harlem Shuffle

LEE, Laura   '72
Born Laure Lee Rundless on 3/9/45 in Chicago. Singer/songwriter.

| 1/22/72 | 12 | 13 | Women's Love Rights | 117 | $15 | Hot Wax 708 |

LEE, Tracey   '97
Born in Philadelphia. Male rapper.

| 4/26/97 | 23 | 12 | Many Facez | 111 | $8 | Universal 53036 |

LEGENDARY BLUES BAND   '89
Blues group from Chicago: Smokey Smothers (vocals), Billy Flynn (guitar), Madison Slim (harmonica), Calvin Jones (bass) and Willie Smith (drums).

| 5/13/89 | 68 | 7 | Woke Up With The Blues | | $10 | Ichiban 1039 |

LeMANS, Tony   '89
Born in Santa Monica, California. Died in a car crash on 6/24/92 (age 29). Singer/songwriter.

| 11/18/89 | 58 | 5 | Tony LeMans | | $8 | Paisley Park 25995 |

LEOTIS   '89
Born Leotis Clyburn in Brooklyn, New York. Male singer.

| 7/1/89 | 96 | 1 | On A Mission | | $8 | Mercury 838188 |

LE PAMPLEMOUSSE   '78
Disco studio group led by producers Lauren Rinder and W. Michael Lewis. Group name is French for The Grapefruit.

| 2/18/78 | 47 | 8 | Le Spank | 116 | $10 | AVI 6032 |

LES NUBIANS   '99
Vocal duo of sisters from Bordeaux, France: Helene and Celia Faussart.

| 12/19/98+ | 25 | 29↑ | Princesses Nubiennes | | $8 | OmTown 45997 |

LEVEL 42   '86
Pop-rock group from Manchester, England: Mark King (vocals, bass), brothers Boon (guitar) and Phil (drums) Gould, and Mike Lindup (keyboards).

| 6/21/86 | 64 | 3 | World Machine | 18 | $8 | Polydor 827487 |

★163★   **LEVERT**   '87
Vocal/instrumental trio from Cleveland: brothers **Gerald Levert** and **Sean Levert**, with Marc Gordon. The Leverts are the sons of Eddie Levert (of The O'Jays).

| 8/23/86 | 8 | 36 | 1 Bloodline | 192 | $8 | Atlantic 81669 |

(Pop, Pop, Pop, Pop) Goes My Mind [1] • **Fascination** [26] • Pose • I Start You Up, You Turn Me On • Kiss And Make Up • **Let's Go Out Tonight** [14] • Grip • Looking For Love

| 8/22/87 | 3 | 43 | ● 2 The Big Throwdown | 32 | $8 | Atlantic 81773 |

Casanova [1] • Good Stuff • Don't U Think It's Time • **My Forever Love** [2] • Love The Way U Love Me • **Sweet Sensation** [4] • In N Out • Temptation • Throwdown

| 11/26/88+ | 6 | 50 | ● 3 Just Coolin' | 79 | $8 | Atlantic 81926 |

Pull Over [2] • Just Coolin' [1] • Gotta Get The Money [4] • Take Your Time • Join In The Fun • Let's Get Romantic • Feel Real • **Smilin'** [16] • Start Me Up Again • Loveable

| 12/1/90+ | 9 | 58 | ● 4 Rope A Dope Style | 122 | $8 | Atlantic 82164 |

Now You Know • **Rope A Dope Style** [7] • Absolutely Positive • **All Season** [4] • Rain • Nobody Does It Better • I've Been Waiting • Baby I'm Ready [1] • Hey Girl • Give A Little Love [63]

| 4/10/93 | 5 | 36 | ● 5 For Real Tho' | 35 | $8 | Atlantic 82462 |

Me 'N' You • Clap Your Hands • Tribute Song • **Good Ol' Days** [12] • She's All That (I've Been Looking For) • For Real Tho' • Quiet Storm • **Do The Thangs** [41] • My Place (Your Place) • Say You Will • **abc-123** [5]

| 3/29/97 | 10 | 18 | 6 The Whole Scenario | 49 | $8 | Atlantic 82986 |

Whole Scenario • Do It Right Here • You Keep Me Comin' • **Tru Dat** [52] • **Sorry Is** [33] • Swing My Way • Like Water • Keys To My House • Playground • I'll Get It Done • Ain't No Thang • Mama's House

| **★181★** | | | **LEVERT, Gerald**   '92 | | | |

Born on 7/13/66 in Cleveland. Member of **Levert**.

| 11/9/91+ | ❶² | 62 | ● 1 Private Line | 48 | $8 | EastWest 91777 |

Private Line [1] • School Me [3] • Baby Hold On To Me [1] • Can You Handle It [9] • Shootin' The Breeze • I Wanna Be Bad • Just A Little Something • Hurting For You • Just Because I'm Wrong • Hugs & Kisses • You Oughta Be With Me

| 9/24/94 | 2¹ | 56 | ▲ 2 Groove On | 18 | $8 | EastWest 92416 |

Groove On • Rock Me (All Nite Long) • Let The Juices Flow • **I'd Give Anything** [4] • Answering Service [12] • Someone • **How Many Times** [56] • **Can't Help Myself** [15] • Have Mercy • Same Place, Same Time • Nice & Wet • Love Street

| 10/14/95 | 2¹ | 47 | ● 3 Father And Son | 20 | $8 | EastWest 61859 |

GERALD LEVERT & EDDIE LEVERT, SR.
For The Love • I Got Your Back • **Already Missing You** [7] • **Wind Beneath My Wings** [30] • I Got You • **Get Your Thing Off** [59] • You Need Love • Don't Make Me Beg • You're Hurting Me • I'm Savin' Your Place • You Got Your Hooks In Me • The Apple Don't Fall

| 8/8/98 | 2¹ | 42 | ● 4 Love & Consequences | 17 | $8 | EastWest 62261 |

No Sense • **Thinkin' Bout It** [2] • Point The Finger • Breaking My Heart • That's The Way I Feel About You • It's Your Turn • No I'm Not The Blame • No Man's Land • Men Like Us • **Taking Everything** [3] • What About Me • Definition Of A Man • Humble Me

LEVERT, Sean   '95
Born on 9/28/68 in Cleveland. Member of **Levert**.

| 7/8/95 | 22 | 14 | The Other Side | 146 | $8 | Atlantic 82663 |

119

LEWIS, Barbara '65
Born on 2/9/43 in South Lyon, Michigan. Singer/songwriter/multi-instrumentalist.

DEBUT	PEAK	WKS		Album Title	Pop #	$	Label & Number
10/2/65	7	5		1 **Baby, I'm Yours**	118	$40	Atlantic 8110

Baby, I'm Yours [5] • My Heart Went Do Da Dat • Come Home • Think A Little Sugar • If You Love Her • Stop That Girl • **Puppy Love** [38] • **Hello Stranger** [1] • Someday We're Gonna Love Again • **Snap Your Fingers** [71] • How Can I Say Goodbye • Straighten Up Your Heart

| 3/28/70 | 46 | 4 | | 2 The Many Grooves of Barbara Lewis | | $25 | Enterprise 1006 |

LEWIS, Linda '75
Born in London. Singer/actress. Appeared in the movies *Taste Of Honey* and *A Hard Day's Night*.

| 10/18/75 | 58 | 2 | | Not A Little Girl Anymore | 204 | $10 | Arista 4047 |

LEWIS, Marcus '89

| 3/25/89 | 66 | 13 | | Sing Me A Song | | $10 | Aegis 45055 |

LEWIS, Ramsey ★31★ '65
Born on 5/27/35 in Chicago. Male jazz pianist. Formed the Gentlemen Of Swing, a jazz-oriented trio, in 1956 in Chicago. Consisted of Ramsey, Eldee Young (bass) and Isaac "Red" Holt (drums). All had been in The Clefs in the early '50s. First recorded for Chess/Argo in 1956. Disbanded in 1965. Young and Holt then formed **The Young-Holt Trio**. Lewis re-formed his trio with Cleveland Eaton (bass) and **Maurice White** (later with Earth, Wind & Fire; drums). Reunited with Young and Holt in 1983.

1)The In Crowd 2)Sun Goddess 3)Wade In The Water 4)Hang On Ramsey! 5)Don't It Feel Good

RAMSEY LEWIS TRIO:

DEBUT	PEAK	WKS		Album Title	Pop #	$	Label & Number
8/14/65	❶12	19		1 The In Crowd [I-L]	2¹	$40	Argo 757

recorded May 13-15, 1965 at The Bohemian Caverns in Washington DC
The "In" Crowd [2] • Since I Fell For You • Tennessee Waltz • You Been Talkin' 'Bout Me Baby • Love Theme From Spartacus • Felicidade (Happiness) • Come Sunday • The In Crowd • Sloopy Downtown

| 11/6/65 | 9 | 2 | | 2 Choice! The Best Of The Ramsey Lewis Trio   [G-I] | 54 | $20 | Cadet 755 |

Something You Got [63] • Little Liza Jane • Memphis In June • Travel On • Delilah • C C Rider • Lonely Avenue • Look-A-Here • My Bucket's Got A Hole In It • Hello, Cello! • Blue Spring • Carmen • Blues For The Night Owls

| 2/19/66 | 4 | 14 | | 3 Hang On Ramsey!   [I-L] | 15 | $20 | Cadet 761 |

recorded October 14-17, 1965 at The Lighthouse in Hermosa Beach, California
A Hard Day's Night [29] • All My Love Belongs To You • He's A Real Gone Guy • And I Love Her • Movin' Easy • Medley: Billy Boy/Hi-Heel Sneakers • The More I See You • Satin Doll • **Hang On Sloopy** [6]

RAMSEY LEWIS:

| 9/3/66 | 2² | 22 | | 4 Wade In The Water   [I] | 16 | $20 | Cadet 774 |

Wade In The Water [3] • Ain't That Peculiar • Tobacco Road • Money In The Pocket • Message To Michael • Up Tight [30] • Hold It Right There • Day Tripper • Mi Compasion • Hurt So Bad

DEBUT	PEAK	WKS		Album Title	Pop #	$	Label & Number
3/18/67	16	8		5 Goin' Latin [I]	95	$20	Cadet 790
11/18/67	16	10		6 Dancing In The Street [I-L]	59	$20	Cadet 794
4/20/68	25	22		7 Up Pops Ramsey Lewis [I]	52	$20	Cadet 799
8/3/68	14	25		8 Maiden Voyage [I]	55	$15	Cadet 811
3/8/69	10	30		9 Mother Nature's Son [I]	156	$15	Cadet 821

Mother Nature's Son • Rocky Raccoon • **Julia** [37] • Back In The USSR • Dear Prudence • Cry Baby Cry • Good Night • Everybody's Got Something To Hide Except Me And My Monkey • Sexy Sadie • Black Bird

| 9/20/69 | 34 | 12 | | 10 Another Voyage   [I] | 139 | $15 | Cadet 827 |
| 10/17/70+ | 34 | 15 | | 11 Them Changes   [I-L] | 177 | $15 | Cadet 844 |

recorded May 8-9, 1970 at The Depot in Minneapolis

| 6/5/71 | 25 | 11 | | 12 Back To The Roots   [I] | 163 | $15 | Cadet 6001 |
| 7/8/72 | 9 | 12 | | 13 Upendo Ni Pamoja   [I] | 79 | $12 | Columbia 31096 |

Slippin' Into Darkness [44] • People Make The World Go Round • Please Send Me Someone To Love • Got To Be There • Concierto De Aranjuez • Upendo Ni Pamoja (Love Is Together) • Trilogy Medley: Morning/The Nite Before/Eternal Peace • Put Your Hand In The Hand • Collage

| 10/27/73 | 50 | 4 | | 14 Ramsey Lewis' Newly Recorded All-Time, Non-Stop Golden Hits   [I] | 198 | $12 | Columbia 32490 |
| 1/4/75 | ❶¹ | 33 | ● | 15 Sun Goddess   [I] | 12 | $10 | Columbia 33194 |

Sun Goddess [20] • Living For The City • Love Song • Jungle Strut • **Hot Dawgit** [61] • Tambura • Gemini Rising

| 10/11/75 | 5 | 11 | | 16 Don't It Feel Good   [I] | 46 | $10 | Columbia 33800 |

Don't It Feel Good [99] • Juaacklyn • What's The Name Of This Funk (Spider Man) [50] • Something About You • That's The Way Of The World • Fish Bite • I Dig You • Can't Function

DEBUT	PEAK	WKS		Album Title	Pop #	$	Label & Number
5/22/76	17	10		17 Salongo [I]	77	$10	Columbia 34173
5/28/77	31	5		18 Love Notes [I]	79	$10	Columbia 34696
8/30/80	51	7		19 Routes [I]	173	$10	Columbia 36423
7/4/81	52	5		20 Three Piece Suite [I]	152	$10	Columbia 37153
3/13/82	50	8		21 Live At The Savoy [I-L]	202	$10	Columbia 37687

recorded at The Savoy Theater in New York City

| 9/1/84 | 42 | 12 | | 22 The Two Of Us | 144 | $10 | Columbia 39326 |

RAMSEY LEWIS & NANCY WILSON

LEWIS, Webster '80
Born in Baltimore. Male keyboardist.

| 1/26/80 | 21 | 21 | | 1 8 For The 80's | 114 | $8 | Epic 36197 |
| 5/16/81 | 49 | 11 | | 2 Let Me Be The One | | $8 | Epic 36878 |

LIFESTYLE '77
Disco group from Rochester, New York.

| 5/7/77 | 41 | 4 | | Lifestyle | | $10 | MCA 2246 |

DEBUT	PEAK	WKS	Gold	Album Title	Pop #	$	Label & Number
				LIGHTER SHADE OF BROWN '94			
				Hispanic rap duo from Riverside, California: Robert Gutierrez and Robert Ramirez.			
12/26/92+	87	4		1 Hip Hop Locos		$8	Pump 19114
8/13/94	54	4		2 Layin' In The Cut	169	$8	Mercury 522479
				LIL1/2DEAD '94			
				Born Donald Smith in 1972 in Long Beach, California. Male rapper. Cousin of **Nate Dogg**.			
11/12/94	39	18		1 The Dead Has Arisen		$8	Priority 53937
6/8/96	47	3		2 Steel On A Mission		$8	Priority 53984
				LIL' KEKE '98			
				Born Marcus Edwards in Los Angeles. Male rapper.			
7/19/97	43	11		1 Don't Mess Wit Texas		$8	Jam Down 1005
4/11/98	37	8		2 The Commission	176	$8	Jam Down 481000
				LIL' KIM '96			
				Born Kimberly Jones in Brooklyn, New York. Female rapper. Member of **Junior M.A.F.I.A.**			
11/23/96	3	69	▲	Hard Core	11	$8	Undeas/Big Beat 92733
				Big Momma Thang • **No Time [9]** • Spend A Little Doe • Take It! • Crush On You • Drugs • Scheamin' • Queen Bitch • Dreams • M.A.F.I.A. Land • We Don't Need It • **Not Tonight [3]** • Player Haters • Fuck You			
				LINK '98			
				Born Lincoln Browder in Dallas. Male rapper.			
7/18/98	46	27		Sex Down	187	$8	Relativity 1645
				LINX '81			
				Funk group from London: David Grant (vocals), Bob Carter (keyboards), Peter Martin (bass) and Andy Duncan (drums).			
5/23/81	39	11		Intuition	175	$10	Chrysalis 1332
				LIPPS, INC. '80			
				Pronounced: lip-synch. Funk group from Minneapolis formed by producer/songwriter/multi-instrumentalist Steven Greenberg. Vocals by Cynthia Johnson.			
3/29/80	5	26	●	1 Mouth To Mouth	5	$10	Casablanca 7197
				Funkytown [2] • All Night Dancing • **Rock It [85]** • Power			
10/11/80	37	12		2 Pucker Up	63	$10	Casablanca 7242
				LISA LISA AND CULT JAM '87			
				Trio from Harlem, New York: Lisa Velez (vocals), Alex Moseley (guitar) and Mike Hughes (drums).			
9/7/85+	16	61	▲	1 Lisa Lisa & Cult Jam with Full Force	52	$8	Columbia 40135
5/16/87	7	54	▲	2 Spanish Fly	7	$8	Columbia 40477
				Everything Will B-Fine [9] • **Head To Toe [1]** • A Face In The Crowd • **Someone To Love Me For Me [7]** • Talking Nonsense • I Promise You • A Fool Is Born Everyday • **Lost In Emotion [1]** • Playing With Fire			
5/20/89	18	20		3 Straight To The Sky	77	$8	Columbia 44378
9/14/91	29	12		4 Straight Outta Hell's Kitchen	133	$8	Columbia 46035
				LITTLE, J. '95			
				Born in Cleveland. Male rapper. Former member of the **Rude Boys**.			
12/3/94+	64	14		Puttin' It Down		$8	Atlantic 82705
				LITTLE ANTHONY AND THE IMPERIALS '65			
				Vocal group from Brooklyn, New York: Anthony Gourdine (b: 1/8/40), Ernest Wright, Tracy Lord, Glouster Rogers, Sammy Strain and Clarence Collins. Strain later joined **The O'Jays**.			
2/13/65	5	9		1 Goin' Out Of My Head	74	$30	DCP 6808
				Goin' Out Of My Head [22] • What A Difference A Day Made • Reputation • Hurt • It's Just A Matter Of Time • Never Again • **Hurt So Bad [3]** • Where Are You • **Take Me Back [15]** • Who's Sorry Now? • **I Miss You [23]** • Get Out Of My Life			
3/5/66	9	3		2 The Best Of Little Anthony & The Imperials [G]	97	$30	DCP 6809
				Goin' Out Of My Head [22] • **Take Me Back [15]** • Shimmy Shimmy Ko-Ko Bop • **Hurt So Bad [3]** • Tears On My Pillow • **I Miss You [23]** • I'm On The Outside (Looking In) [15] • Hurt • Reputation • Our Song • Never Again • Get Out Of My Life			
				LITTLE BRUCE '94			
7/2/94	60	4		Exxxtra Manish		$8	Sick Wid' It 1723
	★180★			**LITTLE MILTON** '65			
				Born Milton Campbell on 9/7/34 in Inverness, Mississippi. Blues singer/guitarist.			
				1)We're Gonna Make It 2)If Walls Could Talk 3)Waiting For Little Milton			
5/29/65	3	11		1 We're Gonna Make It	101	$70	Checker 2995
				We're Gonna Make It [1] • You're Welcome To The Club • I'm Gonna Move To The Outskirts Of Town • Blues In The Night • Country Style • **Who's Cheating Who? [4]** • **Blind Man [86]** • Can't Hold Back The Tears • Believe In Me • Stand By Me • Life Is Like That • Ain't No Big Deal On You			
7/26/69	41	3		2 Grits Ain't Groceries	159	$25	Checker 3011
3/14/70	23	11		3 If Walls Could Talk	197	$25	Checker 3012
7/14/73	39	15		4 Waiting For Little Milton		$20	Stax 3012
8/10/74	45	8		5 Blues 'N Soul		$20	Stax 5514
10/23/76	50	2		6 Friend Of Mine		$12	Glades 7508
6/11/83	53	8		7 Age Ain't Nothin' But A Number		$10	MCA 5414
8/11/84	55	18		8 Playing For Keeps		$10	Malaco 7419
1/21/89	73	17		9 Back To Back		$10	Malaco 7448
3/31/90	40	29		10 Too Much Pain		$8	Malaco 7453
8/10/91	57	16		11 Reality		$8	Malaco 7462
10/17/92	63	7		12 Strugglin' Lady		$8	Malaco 7465
				LITTLE RICHARD '67			
				Born Richard Wayne Penniman on 12/5/32 in Macon, Georgia. Legendary rock-and-roll singer/pianist. One of the key figures in the transition from R&B to rock and roll. Inducted into the Rock and Roll Hall of Fame in 1986. Won Grammy's Lifetime Achievement Award in 1993.			
8/12/67	29	3		Little Richard's Greatest Hits [L]	184	$25	Okeh 14121

DEBUT	PEAK	WKS	Gold	Album Title	Pop #	$	Label & Number

LITTLE ROYAL   '73
Singer/songwriter Royal Torrence.

| 1/27/73 | 47 | 4 | | Jealous | | $15 | Tri-Us 1145 |

LITTLE SONNY   '74
Harmonica player from Detroit. Known as "The King of the Blues Harmonica."

| 1/19/74 | 42 | 9 | | Hard Goin' Up | | $12 | Enterprise 1036 |

★66★   **LL COOL J**   '87
Born James Todd Smith on 8/16/68 in Queens, New York. Male rapper. Stage name is abbreviation for Ladies Love Cool James. Appeared in the movies *Krush Groove*, *The Hard Way* and *Toys*. Starred on TV's *In The House*.

| 12/28/85+ | 6 | 47 | ▲ | 1 Radio | 46 | $8 | Columbia 40239 |

I Can't Live Without My Radio [15] • You Can't Dance • Dear Yvette • I Can Give You More • Dangerous • **Rock The Bells** [17] • I Need A Beat • That's A Lie • **You'll Rock** [59] • I Want You

| 6/20/87 | ❶[11] | 47 | ▲[2] | 2 Bigger And Deffer | 3 | $8 | Def Jam 40793 |

I'm Bad [4] • Kanday • Get Down • The Bristol Hotel • My Rhyme Ain't Done • .357 - Break It On Down • Go Cut Creator Go • The Breakthrough • **I Need Love** [1] • Ahh, Let's Get Ill • The Do Wop • On The Ill Tip

| 7/1/89 | ❶[5] | 24 | ▲ | 3 Walking With A Panther | 6 | $8 | Def Jam 45172 |

Droppin' Em • Smokin' Dopin' • Fast Peg • Clap Your Hands • Nitro • You're My Heart • **I'm That Type Of Guy** [7] • Why Do You Think They Call It Dope? • It Gets No Rougher • **Big Ole Butt** [57] • **One Shot At Love** [68] • 1-900 L.L. Cool J • Two Different Worlds • Jealous • **Jingling Baby** [32] • Def Jam In The Motherland

| 10/6/90 | 2[6] | 53 | ▲[2] | 4 Mama Said Knock You Out | 16 | $8 | Def Jam 46888 |

The Boomin' System [6] • **Around The Way Girl** [5] • Eat Em Up L Chill • Mr. Good Bar • Murdergram • Cheesy Rat Blues • Farmers Blvd. (Our Anthem) • **Mama Said Knock You Out** [12] • Milky Cereal • **Jingling Baby** [32] • To Da Break Of Dawn • 6 Minutes Of Pleasure [26] • Illegal Search • The Power Of God

| 4/10/93 | ❶[2] | 30 | ● | 5 14 Shots To The Dome | 5 | $8 | Def Jam 53325 |

How I'm Comin' [28] • Buckin' Em Down • **Stand By Your Man** [67] • A Little Somethin' • **Pink Cookies In A Plastic Bag Getting Crushed By Buildings** [34] • Straight From Queens • Funkadelic Relic • All We Got Left Is The Beat • No Frontin' Allowed • **Back Seat (Of My Jeep)** [24] • Soul Survivor • Ain't No Stoppin' This • Diggy Down • Crossroads

| 12/9/95 | 4 | 56 | ▲[2] | 6 Mr. Smith | 20 | $8 | Def Jam 529583 |

Make It Hot • Hip Hop • **Hey Lover** [3] • **Doin It** [7] • Life As... • I Shot Ya • Mr. Smith • No Airplay • **Loungin** [4] • Hollis To Hollywood • God Bless • Get Da Drop On 'Em

| 11/23/96 | 21 | 28 | ● | 7 All World | [G] | 29 | $8 | Def Jam 534125 |
| 11/1/97 | 4 | 26 | ▲ | 8 Phenomenon | 7 | $8 | Def Jam 539186 |

Phenomenon [16] • Candy • Starsky And Hutch • Another Dollar • Nobody Can Freak You • Hot, Hot, Hot • **4, 3, 2, 1** [24] • Wanna Get Paid • **Father** [12] • Don't Be Late, Don't Come Too Soon

LLOYD, Charles   '69
Born on 3/15/38 in Memphis. Jazz tenor saxophonist.

| 4/26/69 | 39 | 3 | | Soundtrack | | $15 | Atlantic 1519 |

LOCKSMITH   '80
Instrumental group: Richard Steacker (guitar), James Simmons (keyboards), John Blake (violin), Leonard Gibbs (percussion), Tyrone Brown (bass) and Millard Yinson (drums).

| 9/13/80 | 59 | 6 | | Unlock The Funk | [I] | $10 | Arista 4274 |

LO-KEY?   '92
Funk group from Minneapolis: Prof T. and Dre (vocals), Lance Alexander (keyboards), T-Bone (bass) and "D" (drums).

| 10/31/92 | 18 | 34 | | 1 Where Dey At? | 121 | $8 | Perspective 1003 |
| 11/5/94 | 64 | 10 | | 2 Back 2 Da Howse | | $8 | Perspective 9010 |

LONDONBEAT   '91
Group based in England. Vocal trio of Americans Jimmy Helms and George Chandler, with Trinidad native Jimmy Chambers. Backed by British producer/multi-instrumentalist Willy M.

| 4/27/91 | 83 | 9 | ● | In The Blood | 21 | $8 | Radioactive 10192 |

LONGMIRE, Wilbert   '79
Born in Cincinnati. Singer/guitarist.

| 4/28/79 | 69 | 2 | | 1 Champagne | | $10 | Tappan Zee 35754 |
| 3/15/80 | 71 | 2 | | 2 With All My Love | | $10 | Tappan Zee 36342 |

LOOSE ENDS   '85
Trio from London: Carl McIntosh (lead vocals, guitar), Steve Nichol and Jane Eugene. Nichol and Eugene left in 1990; replaced by Sunay Suleyman and Linda Carriere.

| 6/1/85 | 5 | 28 | | 1 A Little Spice | 46 | $8 | MCA 5588 |

Hangin' On A String (Contemplating) [1] • Choose Me [47] • Music Takes Me Higher • Dial 999 • Tell Me What You Want • A Little Spice • So Much Love • Let's Rock

| 10/25/86+ | 7 | 55 | | 2 Zagora | 59 | $8 | MCA 5745 |

Stay A Little While, Child [18] • **Slow Down** [1] • I Can't Wait (Another Minute) • Sweetest Pain • Ooh, You Make Me Feel • Who Are You? • **You Can't Stop The Rain** [32] • Be Thankful (Mama's Song) • **Nights Of Pleasure** [58] • Let's Get Back To Love

| 7/16/88 | 16 | 28 | | 3 The Real Chuckeeboo | 80 | $8 | MCA 42196 |
| 12/1/90+ | 28 | 30 | | 4 Look How Long | 124 | $8 | MCA 10044 |

LORBER, Jeff   '86
Born in Philadelphia. Jazz fusion keyboardist. His fusion group included **Kenny G** (flute), Danny Wilson (bass) and Dennis Bradford (drums).

| 5/2/81 | 45 | 6 | | 1 Galaxian | 77 | $8 | Arista 9545 |

THE JEFF LORBER FUSION

4/3/82	44	10		2 It's A Fact	73	$8	Arista 9583
3/31/84	44	11		3 In The Heat Of The Night	106	$8	Arista 8025
3/16/85	33	20		4 Step By Step	90	$8	Arista 8269
11/15/86	29	20		5 Private Passion	68	$8	Warner 25492
5/8/93	71	10		6 Worth Waiting For	[I]	$8	Verve Forecast 517998

LORD FINESSE   '96
Born Robert Hall in the Bronx, New York. Male rapper.

DEBUT	PEAK	WKS	Gold	Album Title	Pop #	$	Label & Number
4/21/90	93	7		1 Funky Technician		$8	Wild Pitch 2003

LORD FINESSE & DJ MIKE SMOOTH

3/28/92	95	4		2 Return Of The Funky Man		$8	Giant 24437
3/9/96	36	9		3 The Awakening		$8	Penalty 3035

LORDS OF THE UNDERGROUND   '93
Rap trio from Raleigh, North Carolina: Mr. Funke, DoltAll and Lord Jazz.

4/17/93	13	45		1 Here Come The Lords	66	$8	Pendulum 61415
11/19/94	16	15		2 Keepers Of The Funk	57	$8	Pendulum 30710

LORD TARIQ & PETER GUNZ   '98
Rap duo from New York City: Sean Hamilton ("Lord Tariq") and Peter Panky ("Peter Gunz").

6/20/98	8	15		Make It Reign	38	$8	Columbia 69010

Make It Reign • We Will Ball • Massive Heat • One Life To Live • Fiesta • Startin' Somethin' • A Night In The Bronx With Lord & Gunz • Who Am I • **Deja Vu (Uptown Baby)** *[4]* • Keep On • Worldwide • Streets To Da Stage • Cross Bronx Expressway • My Time To Go

LORENZ, Trey   '92
Born on 1/19/69 in Florence, South Carolina. Male singer.

10/24/92	32	21		Trey Lorenz	111	$8	Epic 47840

LORENZO   '92
Born Lorenzo Smith in Miami. Male singer.

8/8/92	24	48		1 Lorenzo		$8	Alpha Int'l. 781000
5/13/95	41	12		2 Love On My Mind		$8	Luke 214

LOST BOYZ   '96
Rap group from Queens, New York: Spigg Nice, Mr. Cheeks, Freekie Tah and Pretty Lou. Freekie Tah (real name: Raymond Rogers) was shot to death on 3/29/99 (age 28).

6/15/96	❶[1]	45	●	1 Legal Drug Money	6	$8	Universal 53010

The Yearn • **Music Makes Me High** *[28]* • Jeeps, Lex Coups, Bimaz & Benz *[63]* • Lifestyles Of The Rich And Shameless *[60]* • **Renee** *[13]* • All Right • Legal Drug Money • **Get Up** *[31]* • Is This Da Part • Straight From Da Ghetto • Keep It Real • Channel Zero • Da Game • 1, 2, 3

7/5/97	2[1]	22	●	2 Love, Peace And Nappiness	9	$8	Universal 53080

Summer Time • **Me And My Crazy World** *[23]* • Beasts From The East • Love, Peace & Nappiness • So Love • My Crew • What's Wrong • Certain Things We Do • Games • Get Your Hustle • Tight Situations • Day 1 • Why • From My Family To Yours (Dedication)

LOVE, Le Juan   '88
Born Le Juan Biggers in Newport News, Virginia. Male rapper.

9/3/88	59	9		I Still Feel Good		$10	Luke Skyywalker 104

LOVE, Monie   '91
Born Simone Johnson on 7/2/70 in London; raised in Brooklyn, New York. Female rapper.

11/24/90+	26	38		1 Down To Earth	109	$8	Warner 26358
4/10/93	75	1		2 In A Word Or 2		$8	Warner 45054

LOVE AND KISSES   '77
Disco studio group assembled by European producer Alec Costandinos. Singers included Don Daniels, Elaine Hill, Dianne Brooks and Jean Graham.

8/27/77	54	6		1 Love And Kisses	135	$10	Casablanca 7063
5/27/78	58	2		2 How Much, How Much I Love You	85	$10	Casablanca 7091

LOVE DE-LUXE   '79
Disco studio group assembled by Alan Hawkshaw.

9/8/79	68	3		Here Comes That Sound		$10	Warner 3342

LOVE DE-LUXE With Hawkshaw's Discophonia

LOVE UNLIMITED   '74
Female vocal trio from San Pedro, California: sisters Glodean and Linda James, with Diane Taylor. **Barry White**, who married Glodean on 7/4/74, was their manager and producer.

4/22/72	19	13		1 Love Unlimited	151	$15	Uni 73131
9/1/73+	3	38	●	2 Under The Influence Of...	3	$12	20th Century 414

Love's Theme • **Under The Influence Of Love** *[70]* • Lovin' You, That's All I'm After • **Oh Love, Well We Finally Made It** *[70]* • Say It Again • Someone Really Cares For You • **It May Be Winter Outside, (But In My Heart It's Spring)** *[35]* • Yes, We Finally Made It

10/26/74	15	26		3 In Heat	85	$12	20th Century 443
3/26/77	51	9		4 He's All I've Got	192	$10	Unlimited Gold 101
12/22/79	70	3		5 Love Is Back		$10	Unlimited Gold 36130

LOVE UNLIMITED ORCHESTRA   '74
Forty-piece studio orchestra conducted and arranged by **Barry White**. Formed to back **Love Unlimited**; also heard on some of White's solo hits. Kenny G was a member at age 17.

2/16/74	2[1]	20	●	1 Rhapsody In White [I]	8	$12	20th Century 433

Barry's Theme • **Rhapsody In White** *[48]* • Midnight And You • I Feel Love Coming On • Baby Blues • Don't Take It Away From Me • What A Groove • **Love's Theme** *[10]*

10/12/74	33	6		2 Together Brothers [I-S]	96	$10	20th Century 101
11/23/74+	10	25	●	3 White Gold [I]	28	$12	20th Century 458

Barry's Love • **Satin Soul** *[23]* • Always Thinking Of You • Power Of Love • Spanish Lei • You Make Me Feel Like This (When You Touch Me) • Only You Can Make Me Blue • Dreaming • Just Living It Up • Just Like A Baby

1/10/76	14	11		4 Music Maestro Please [I]	92	$12	20th Century 480
10/30/76	35	8		5 My Sweet Summer Suite [I]	123	$12	20th Century 517
3/25/78	53	3		6 My Musical Bouquet [I]	201	$12	20th Century 554

LOW PROFILE '90
Rap duo from Los Angeles: WC and Aladdin. WC went on to form **WC & The Maad Circle**.

3/17/90	66	14		We're In This Together		$8	Priority 57116

LOX, The '98
Male rap trio from New York City: David Styles, Sean Jacobs and Jason Phillips.

1/24/98	❶[1]	28	●	Money, Power & Respect	3	$8	Bad Boy 73015

Livin' The Life • If You Think I'm Jiggy [21] • Money, Power & Respect [8] • Get This Money • Let's Start Rap Over • I Wanna Thank You • Goin' Be Some Shit • The Heist • Not To Be Fucked With • Bitches From Eastwick • Can't Stop, Won't Stop • All For The Love • So Right • Everybody Wanna Ratt • We'll Always Love Big Poppa

LSG '97
All-star trio: Gerald Levert, Keith Sweat and Johnny Gill.

11/29/97	2[3]	50	▲	Levert - Sweat - Gill	4	$8	EastWest 62125

Door #1 • Round & Round • You Got Me • Where Did I Go Wrong • **My Body [1]** • All The Times • My Side Of The Bed • Curious • Let A Playa Get His Freak On • Love Hurts • Drove Me To Tears • Where Would We Go

★126★ L.T.D. '77
Group from Greensboro, North Carolina: **Jeffrey Osborne** (vocals, drums), John McGhee (guitar), Abraham Miller and Lorenzo Carnegie (saxophones), Billy Osborne and Jimmie Davis (keyboards), Carle Vickers (trumpet), Jake Riley (trombone), Henry Davis (bass) and Alvino Bennett (drums). The Osborne brothers left in 1980. Leslie Wilson and Andre Ray joined as vocalists. L.T.D. stands for Love, Togetherness and Devotion.

3/16/74	54	4	1	Love, Togetherness & Devotion		$12	A&M 3602
1/25/75	40	6	2	Gittin' Down		$12	A&M 3668
7/31/76	7	30	3	Love To The World	52	$10	A&M 4589

Love To The World [27] • Time For Pleasure • **Love Ballad [1]** • Get Your It Together • Let The Music Keep Playing • The Word • Love To The World Prayer

7/30/77	❶[1]	40	●	4 Something To Love	21	$10	A&M 4646

Age Of The Showdown • (Won't Cha) Stay With Me • **(Every Time I Turn Around) Back In Love Again [1]** • You Come First At Last • We Party Hearty • If You're In Need • **Never Get Enough Of Your Love [8]** • Make Someone Smile, Today! • Material Things

6/17/78	3	36	▲	5 Togetherness	18	$10	A&M 4705

Holding On (When Love Is Gone) [1] • We Both Deserve Each Other's Love [19] • Jam • You Must Have Known I Needed Love • Don't Stop Loving Me Now • It's Time To Be Real • Concentrate On You • You Fooled Me • Together Forever • Let's All Live And Give Together

7/7/79	5	36	●	6 Devotion	29	$10	A&M 4771

One On One • **Share My Love [69]** • Stand Up L.T.D. • Say That You'll Be Mine • **Dance "N" Sing "N" [15]** • Sometimes • Promise You'll Stay • **Stranger [14]** • Feel It

9/6/80	6	32		7 Shine On	28	$10	A&M 4819

You Gave Me Love • **Where Did We Go Wrong [7]** • Getaway • Will Love Grow • Love Is What You Need • Shine On [19] • Lovers Everywhere • Lady Love • Don'tcha Know

11/28/81+	21	31		8 Love Magic	83	$10	A&M 4881
7/30/83	66	13		9 For You		$10	Montage 105

L'TRIMM '88
Female rap duo: Tigra (from New York) and Bunny D (from Chicago).

9/3/88	55	26		1 Grab It!	132	$8	Atlantic 81925
				originally released on Time-X 3307			
10/28/89	93	3		2 Drop That Bottom		$8	Atlantic 82026

LUCAS, Carrie '82
Born in Los Angeles. Former session singer.

5/19/79	37	10		1 Carrie Lucas In Danceland	119	$10	Solar 3219
12/27/80+	57	14		2 Portrait Of Carrie	185	$10	Solar 3579
7/24/82	33	10		3 Still In Love	180	$10	Solar 60008
8/10/85	40	10		4 Horsin' Around		$8	Constellation 5513

LUCIEN, Jon '91
Born in St. Thomas, Virgin Islands. Former jingle singer.

10/18/75	51	3		1 Song For My Lady	203	$12	Columbia 33544
5/18/91	43	19		2 Listen Love		$8	Mercury 848532

★64★ LUKE/2 LIVE CREW '89
Rap group from Miami: Luther "Luke" Campbell, David "Mr. Mixx" Hobbs, Chris "Fresh Kid Ice" Wong Won and Mark "Brother Marquis" Ross. Group's obscenity arrests sparked national censorship controversy in 1990. By 1994, group consisted of Campbell, Won and Larry "Verb" Dobson; changed name to The New 2 Live Crew. Campbell split from the group in early 1996.

1)As Nasty As They Wanna Be 2)Uncle Luke 3)In The Nude

THE 2 LIVE CREW:

3/7/87	24	29	●	1 The 2 Live Crew "is what we are"	128	$10	Luke Skyywalker 100
5/28/88	20	59	●	2 Move Somethin'	68	$10	Luke Skyywalker 101
7/29/89	3	72	▲	3 As Nasty As They Wanna Be	29	$12	Luke Skyywalker 107 [2]

Me So Horny [34] • Put Her In The Buck • Dick Almighty • C'mon Babe • Dirty Nursery Rhymes • Break It On Down • 2 Live Blues • I Ain't Bullshittin' • Get Loose Now • The Fuck Shop • If You Believe In Having Sex • My Seven Bizzos • Get The Fuck Out Of My House • Reggae Joint • Fraternity Record • Bad Ass Bitch • Mega Mixx III • Coolin'

8/11/90	10	24	●	4 Banned In The U.S.A.	21	$8	Luke 91424

LUKE Featuring THE 2 LIVE CREW
Banned In The U.S.A. [13] • Man, Not A Myth • Fuck Martinez • Strip Club • Do The Bart [76] • Face Down Ass Up • Bass 9-1-7 • So Funky • Mamolapenga • I Ain't Bullshittin' II • This Is To Luke From The Posse • Fuck A Gang • Arrest In Effect • Mega Mixx IV

1/19/91	46	20		5 Live In Concert .... [L]	92	$8	Effect 3003
11/2/91	19	24	●	6 Sports Weekend (As Nasty As They Wanna Be Part II)	22	$8	Luke 91720

LUKE:

2/29/92	20	40		7 I Got Shit On My Mind	52	$8	Luke 91830

DEBUT	PEAK	WKS	Gold Album Title	Pop #	$	Label & Number

LUKE — Cont'd

DEBUT	PEAK	WKS	Album Title	Pop #	$	Label & Number
11/7/92	62	13	8 The 2 Live Crew's Greatest Hits ....[G]		$8	Luke 122
			THE 2 LIVE CREW			
7/3/93	8	17	9 In The Nude	54	$8	Luke 200

Do You Hear The Lambs Calling • **Work It Out** *[58]* • Bad Land Boogie • Tell Me What You Know • Dre's Momma Needs A Haircut • **Cowards In Compton** *[93]* • Head, Head & More Head • Menage A Tois • The Hero • Whatever • The Hop • L.L.O.L.M. • Freestyle Joint • $100 Bet • Bust A Nut • Wear A Rubber • Take It Off • Headbanger

DEBUT	PEAK	WKS	Album Title	Pop #	$	Label & Number
2/26/94	9	19	10 Back At Your Ass For The Nine-4	52	$8	Luke 207
			THE NEW 2 LIVE CREW			

Dem A Talk • **Yeah, Yeah** *[93]* • Pussy And Dick Thing • **You Go Girl** *[88]* • 2 Live Freestyle • We Want Some Pussy Too • The Initiation • Fuck Nigga • Suck My Dick • Fuck 'Em • Work That Pussy • Captain Dick And Dolemite • The Trick • Mega Mix

DEBUT	PEAK	WKS	Album Title	Pop #	$	Label & Number
7/30/94	24	11	11 Freak For Life 6996	174	$8	Luke 6996
6/1/96	8	22	12 Uncle Luke	51	$8	Luther Campbell 161000

Scarred *[31]* • **Bounce To Da Beat** *[96]* • Never Forget From Whence You Came • Freaky Bitches • Luke Mega Mix • Asshole Naked • Do It Do It • Work It Baby • Bone • Are You Ready • Ol' G • Off Da Hook • Straight Beef

DEBUT	PEAK	WKS	Album Title	Pop #	$	Label & Number
8/24/96	33	8	13 Shake A Lil' Somethin'...	145	$8	Lil' Joe 215
			THE 2 LIVE CREW			
11/29/97	49	19	14 Changin' The Game		$8	Luke 524446
4/25/98	59	24	15 The Real One		$8	Lil' Joe 231
			THE 2 LIVE CREW			

LUNASICC   '98
Born in Sacramento, California. Male rapper.

DEBUT	PEAK	WKS	Album Title	Pop #	$	Label & Number
10/4/97	92	2	1 Mr. Lunasicc		$8	AWOL 20619
6/20/98	88	2	2 A Million Words, A Million Dollars		$8	AWOL 45804

LUNIZ   '95
Rap duo from Oakland: Jerold Ellis and Garrick Husband.

DEBUT	PEAK	WKS	Album Title	Pop #	$	Label & Number
7/22/95	❶²	37	● 1 Operation Stackola	20	$8	Noo Trybe 40523

Put The Lead On Ya • **I Got 5 On It** *[4]* • Broke Hos • Pimps, Playas & Hustlas • **Playa Hata** *[51]* • Broke Niggaz • Operation Stackola • 5150 • 900 Blame A Nigga • Yellow Brick Road • So Much Drama • She's Just A Freak • Plead Guilty

DEBUT	PEAK	WKS	Album Title	Pop #	$	Label & Number
11/29/97	8	19	2 Lunitik Musik	34	$8	Noo Trybe 44966

Highest Niggaz In The Industry • Funkin Over Nuthin' • In My Nature • Jus Mee & U • Game • My Baby Mamma • Is It Kool? • Sad Millionaire • Killaz On The Payroll • Phillies • Mobb Shit • Y Do Thugz Die • Hypnotize • Handcuff Your Hoes • 20 Bluntz A Day

LUSHUS DAIM & THE PRETTY VAIN   '86
Born in Los Angeles. Female singer.

DEBUT	PEAK	WKS	Album Title	Pop #	$	Label & Number
12/7/85+	52	18	More Than You Can Handle		$10	Motown 6150

LUV, Ray   '95
Born in San Francisco. Male rapper.

DEBUT	PEAK	WKS	Album Title	Pop #	$	Label & Number
8/19/95	39	9	Forever Hustlin'		$8	Atlantic 82775

L.V.   '96
Born Larry Sanders in Los Angeles. Former member of **South Central Cartel**. L.V. stands for Large Variety.

DEBUT	PEAK	WKS	Album Title	Pop #	$	Label & Number
5/25/96	100	1	I Am L.V.		$8	Tommy Boy 1140

LYNN, Cheryl   '79
Born on 3/11/57 in Los Angeles. Female dance singer.

DEBUT	PEAK	WKS	Album Title	Pop #	$	Label & Number
11/11/78+	5	28	● 1 Cheryl Lynn	23	$10	Columbia 35486

Got To Be Real *[1]* • All My Lovin' • **Star Love** *[16]* • Come In From The Rain • You Saved My Day • Give My Love To You • Nothing To Say • You're The One • Daybreak (Storybook Children)

DEBUT	PEAK	WKS	Album Title	Pop #	$	Label & Number
1/12/80	47	8	2 In Love	167	$10	Columbia 36145
7/18/81	14	16	3 In The Night	104	$10	Columbia 37034
7/17/82	7	37	4 Instant Love	133	$10	Columbia 38057

Instant Love *[16]* • Sleep Walkin' • Day After Day • **Look Before You Leap** *[77]* • Say You'll Be Mine • I Just Wanna Be Your Fantasy • Believe In Me • **If This World Were Mine** *[4]*

DEBUT	PEAK	WKS	Album Title	Pop #	$	Label & Number
1/7/84	8	24	5 Preppie	161	$10	Columbia 38961

Encore *[1]* • Fix It • Fool A Fool • **This Time** *[49]* • Change The Channel • **Preppie** *[85]* • Love Rush • No One Else Will Do • Free • Life's Too Short

DEBUT	PEAK	WKS	Album Title	Pop #	$	Label & Number
8/17/85	56	7	6 It's Gonna Be Right	202	$10	Columbia 40024
4/25/87	55	12	7 Start Over		$8	Manhattan 53035
10/21/89	42	18	8 Whatever It Takes		$8	Virgin 91254

LYNN, Trudy   '89
Born in Houston.

DEBUT	PEAK	WKS	Album Title	Pop #	$	Label & Number
10/7/89	76	5	1 Trudy Sings The Blues		$8	Ichiban 1043
11/10/90	76	5	2 Come To Mama		$8	Ichiban 1063

LYNNE, Gloria   '65
Born on 11/23/31 in New York City. Jazz-styled vocalist.

DEBUT	PEAK	WKS	Album Title	Pop #	$	Label & Number
6/5/65	7	4	1 Soul Serenade	82	$25	Fontana 27541

Soul Serenade • That's My Desire • Baby Won't You Please Come Home • If I Loved You • Don't Go To Strangers • **Watermelon Man** *[8]* • Teach Me Tonight • People Will Say We're In Love • All Alone • I'll Be Around • Joey, Joey, Joey • It Could Happen To You

DEBUT	PEAK	WKS	Album Title	Pop #	$	Label & Number
8/1/70	29	16	2 Happy And In Love		$15	Canyon 7709
3/27/76	47	9	3 I Don't Know How To Love Him		$12	ABC/Impulse 9311

LYTLE, Johnny   '66
Born on 10/13/32 in Springfield, Ohio. Died of kidney failure on 12/15/95 (age 63). Jazz vibraphonist.

DEBUT	PEAK	WKS	Album Title	Pop #	$	Label & Number
3/12/66	18	1	The Village Caller! ....[I]	141	$25	Riverside 480

M

MABLEY, Moms '66
Born Loretta Mary Aiken on 3/19/1894 in Brevard, North Carolina. Died on 5/23/75 (age 81). Female comedian.

11/5/66	24	2	1 Moms Mabley At The White House .... [C]	$25	Mercury 21090
4/20/68	28	3	2 Best Of Moms Mabley .... [C-K]	$25	Mercury 21139
4/12/69	46	3	3 Her Young Thing .... [C]	$15	Mercury 61205
5/9/70	50	2	4 Live At Sing Sing .... [C]	$15	Mercury 61263

MAC '98
Male rapper from New Orleans.

8/8/98	4	17	**Shell Shocked**	11	$8	No Limit 50727

Boss Chick • Be All You Can Be • Soldier Party • Murda, Murda, Kill, Kill • Tank Dogs • Slow Ya Roll • We Don't Love 'Em • Wooo • Can I Ball • Money Gets • The Game • Callin' Me • Memories • Meet Me At The Hotel • Shell Shocked • Paranoid • Nobody Make A Sound • Beef • Camouflage Love • Empire • My Brother

MAC BAND '88
Group from Flint, Michigan. brothers Charles, Derrick, Kelvin and Ray McCampbell (vocals), Mark Harper (guitar), Rodney Frazier (keyboards), Ray Flippin (bass) and Slye Fuller (drums).

7/9/88	22	21	1 Mac Band	109	$8	MCA 42090
2/1/92	78	9	2 The Real Deal		$8	Ultrax 020393

MacDONALD, Ralph '84
Born in 1944 in Harlem, New York. Session percussionist/bandleader.

10/9/76	43	9	1 Sound Of A Drum .... [I]	114	$12	Marlin 2202
9/22/84	26	17	2 Universal Rhythm	108	$10	Polydor 823323

MAC DRE '98
Born in Vallejo, California. Male rapper.

6/5/93	93	1	1 Young Black Brother - The Album		$8	Stirctly Busin. 2029
12/28/96+	82	5	2 Mac Dre Presents: The Rompalation		$8	Romp 1049
5/2/98	60	2	3 Stupid Doo Doo Dumb		$8	Romp 1050

MACEO '71
Born Maceo Parker on 2/14/43 in Kinston, North Carolina. Saxophonist for **James Brown**.

4/17/71	32	4	1 **Doin' Their Own Thing**		$20	House Of Fox 1
			MACEO AND ALL THE KING'S MEN			
7/6/74	42	6	2 Us .... [I]		$15	People 6601
			MACEO AND THE MACKS			

MACK, Craig '94
Born in Long Island, New York. Male rapper.

10/8/94	6	33	●	1 **Project: Funk Da World**	21	$8	Bad Boy 73001

Funk Da World • **Get Down** [17] • Making Moves • That Y'all • **Flava In Ya Ear** [4] • Funk Wit Da Style • Judgement Day • Real Raw • Mainline • When God Comes • Welcome To 1994

7/12/97	17	10	2 Operation: Get Down	46	$8	Street Life 75521

MACK 10 '95
Born David Rolison on 8/9/71 in Inglewood, California. Male rapper. Member of **Westside Connection**.

7/1/95	2²	26	●	1 **Mack 10**	33	$8	Priority 53938

Foe Life [42] • Wanted Dead • **On Them Thangs** [74] • Pigeon Coup • Chicken Hawk • Here Comes The G • Westside Slaughterhouse • Niggaz Dog Scraping • Armed & Dangerous • H-O-E-K • 10 Million Ways • Mozi-Wozi • Mack 10's The Name

10/4/97	5	28	●	2 **Based On A True Story**	14	$8	Priority 50675

Chicken Hawk II • Mack 10, Mack 10 • **Backyard Boogie** [23] • Can't Stop • Tonight's The Night • The Guppies • Inglewood Swangin' • Dopeman • What You Need? • Only In California • Westside Foe Life • Based On A True Story

10/24/98	6	15	●	3 **The Recipe**	15	$8	Hoo Bangin' 53512

The Recipe • You Ain't Seen Nothin • Made Niggaz • Get Yo Ride On • **Money's Just A Touch Away** [31] • Get A Lil Head • For The Money • Ghetto Horror Show • LBC And The ING • Let The Games Begin • #1 Crew In The Area • Gangsta Shit's Like A Drug • The Letter • Should I Stay Or Should I Go

MAC MALL '96
Born Jamal Darocker in Vallejo, California. Male rapper.

10/16/93+	71	20	1 **Illegal Business?**		$8	Young Black Br. 2022
5/11/96	6	17	2 **Untouchable**	35	$8	Relativity 1505

Let's Get A Telly • Straight Lace • Servin Game • Young Nigga • Dopefiends Lullaby • Ghetto Stardom • Get Right • Playas Wit Da Choppas • Get Away • Pimp Or Die • Untouchable • Opening Doors • Playa Tip • Crestside

MADAME X '87
Female vocal trio: Iris Parker, Valerie Victoria and Alisa Randolph.

9/19/87	29	13	Madame X	162	$8	Atlantic 81774

MAD CJ MAC '95
Rap duo: CJ Mac and Mad Mac.

6/10/95	41	12	True Game		$8	Rap-A-Lot 40485

MAD COBRA '92
Born Ewart Everton Brown on 3/31/68 in Kingston, Jamaica. Reggae rapper.

9/26/92	17	27	Hard To Wet, Easy To Dry	125	$8	Columbia 52751

MAD DOG CLIQUE '97

5/3/97	75	1	Just Mad Dog'n It		$8	Crosstown 1001

MADHOUSE '87
Jazz-fusion group from Minneapolis. Led by saxophonist Eric Leeds.

2/28/87	25	12	8 .... [I]	107	$8	Paisley Park 25545

DEBUT	PEAK	WKS	Gold	Album Title	Pop #	$	Label & Number

MAD LADS, The '66
Vocal group from Detroit: Julius Green, Sam Nelson, Quincy Billops and Robert Phillips.

| 7/23/66 | 17 | 5 | | 1 The Mad Lads In Action | | $30 | Volt 414 |
| 7/12/69 | 46 | 5 | | 2 The Mad, Mad, Mad, Mad, Mad Lads | 180 | $30 | Volt 6005 |

MAD LION '95
Born in London; raised in Brooklyn, New York. Male rapper.

| 5/27/95 | 20 | 12 | | 1 Real Ting | 114 | $8 | Weeded 2006 |
| 7/12/97 | 96 | 1 | | 2 Ghetto Gold & Platinum Respect | | $8 | Weeded 20210 |

MADONNA '85
Born Madonna Louise Ciccone on 8/16/58 in Bay City, Michigan. Singer/songwriter/actress. Married to actor Sean Penn from 1985-89. Acted in several movies. One of the top female pop artists of the past fifteen years.

| 10/8/83+ | 20 | 78 | ▲4 | 1 Madonna | 8 | $8 | Sire 23867 |
| 12/22/84+ | 10 | 48 | ▲10 | 2 Like A Virgin | 1³ | $8 | Sire 25157 |

Material Girl [49] • Angel [71] • Like A Virgin [9] • Over And Over • Love Don't Live Here Anymore • **Dress You Up** [64] • Shoo-Bee-Doo • Pretender • Stay

9/20/86	47	10	▲7	3 True Blue	1⁵	$8	Sire 25442
4/15/89	55	12	▲4	4 Like A Prayer	1⁶	$8	Sire 25844
1/19/91	81	6	▲6	5 The Immaculate Collection [G]	2²	$8	Sire 26440

MAD SKILLZ '96
Born David Lewis in Richmond, Virginia. Male rapper.

| 3/2/96 | 18 | 9 | | From Where??? | 154 | $8 | Big Beat 92623 |

MAGGOTRON '89
Bass group from Miami led by Dee X. Jay.

| 5/13/89 | 65 | 11 | | 1 The Invasion Will Not Be Televised (Cos' We Don't Have A Video) | | $8 | Jamarc 9001 |
| 3/2/91 | 68 | 6 | | 2 Bass Planet Paranoia | | $8 | Jamarc 9003 |

MAGIC '98
Born Atwood Johnson in New Orleans. Male rapper.

| 10/3/98 | 3 | 9 | | Skys The Limit | 15 | $8 | No Limit 50017 |

Ghetto Godzilla • Did What I Had 2 • Depend On Me • 9th Ward • No Hope • Take It To Da Streets • Ball 'Til We Fall • I Got Love 4 Ya • I Never • Money Don't Make Me • Sky's The Limit • No Limit • New Generation • What I Gotta • Hard Times • Life Is A Bitch • Gimpin' • Special Forces • When Drama Came • Mobb 4 Ever • Chastity

MAGNIFICENT MEN, The '67
Group from Harrisburg, Pennsylvania: David Bupp (vocals), Terry Crousore (guitar), Tommy Hoover (organ), Tom Pane (sax), Buddy King (trumpet), Jimmy Seville (bass) and Bob Angelucci (drums).

| 9/9/67 | 18 | 3 | | The Magnificent Men "Live!" [L] | 89 | $20 | Capitol 2775 |

MAGOO — see TIMBALAND

MAHAL, Taj '75
Born Henry Fredericks on 5/17/40 in New York City. Blues singer/guitarist.

3/22/69	47	5		1 The Natch'l Blues	160	$15	Columbia 9698
10/18/75	40	5		2 Music Keeps Me Together	155	$12	Columbia 33801
5/15/76	54	3		3 Satisfied 'N Tickled Too	201	$12	Columbia 34103

MAHOANEY, Skip, & The Casuals '75
Vocal group from Washington DC: Skip Mahoaney, Tracy Reid, Julius Jerome Rogers and Elwood Morgan.

| 1/25/75 | 56 | 4 | | Your Funny Moods | | $12 | D.C. Int'l. 3001 |

MAIN INGREDIENT, The ★151★ '75
Vocal trio from New York City: Donald McPherson, Luther Simmons and Tony Sylvester. McPherson died of leukemia on 7/4/71; replaced by Cuba Gooding in 1971. Gooding's son, Cuba Jr., is a prominent movie actor.
1)Rolling Down A Mountainside 2)Euphrates River 3)Bitter Sweet

3/13/71	26	19		1 Tasteful Soul	146	$12	RCA Victor 4412
9/25/71	35	4		2 Black Seeds	176	$12	RCA Victor 4483
6/17/72	10	33		3 Bitter Sweet	79	$12	RCA Victor 4677

Traveling • Where Are You? • **You've Got To Take It (If You Want It)** [18] • Everybody Plays The Fool [2] • Whirl-Wind • Fly Baby Fly • I Can't See Me Without You • Where Do Broken Hearted Lovers Go? • Who Can I Turn To (When Nobody Needs Me) • No Tears (In The End)

4/28/73	16	14		4 Afrodisiac	132	$12	RCA Victor 4834
10/20/73+	32	15		5 Greatest Hits [G]	205	$12	RCA Victor 0314
3/2/74	8	29		6 Euphrates River	52	$12	RCA Victor 0335

Euphrates • Have You Ever Tried It • Summer Breeze • **California My Way** [48] • Happiness Is Just Around The Bend [7] • Looks Like Rain • Don't You Worry 'Bout A Thing • **Just Don't Want To Be Lonely** [8]

| 5/10/75 | 3 | 14 | | 7 Rolling Down A Mountainside | 90 | $12 | RCA Victor 0644 |

Rolling Down A Mountainside [7] • Of This I'm Sure • **The Good Old Days** [45] • I Want To Make You Glad • Thanks For The Laughs • You And Me - Me And You • Family Man • A Broken Heart Don't Really Break • That Ain't My Style

12/6/75+	27	10		8 Shame On The World	158	$12	RCA Victor 1003
8/7/76	46	4		9 Super Hits [G]	201	$12	RCA Victor 1858
9/13/80	69	5		10 Ready For Love	207	$10	RCA Victor 3641

THE MAIN INGREDIENT Featuring Cuba Gooding

| 12/9/89+ | 59 | 21 | | 11 I Just Wanna Love You | | $8 | Polydor 841249 |

MAIN SOURCE '91
Rap trio from New York City: William Mitchell, with brothers Kevin and Shawn McKenzie.

| 2/23/91 | 40 | 30 | | Breaking Atoms | | $8 | Wild Pitch 2004 |

MAKAVELI — see 2 PAC

MAKEBA, Miriam　　　　'68
Born Zensi Miriam Makeba on 3/4/32 in Johannesburg, South Africa. Folk singer. Married to **Hugh Masekela** from 1964-66.

| 12/9/67+ | 10 | 16 | | Pata Pata | 74 | $15 | Reprise 6274 |

Pata Pata [7] • Ha Po Zamani • What Is Love • Maria Fulo • Yetentu Tizaleny • Click Song #1 • Ring Bell, Ring Bell • Jol'inkomo • West Wind • Saduva • A Piece Of Ground

MALEMEN, The　　　　'91
Vocal group from South Carolina: Greg Jones, Gerald Massengill, Darrell Kelly, Dennis Montford and Michael Hale.

| 2/23/91 | 73 | 13 | | 1st Class Male | | $8 | Muscle Shoals 2207 |

MALO　　　　'72
Latin-rock group. Core members: Arcelio Garcia (vocals), **Jorge Santana** (guitar; brother of **Carlos Santana**), Richard Kermode (keyboards) and Pablo Tellez (bass). Malo is Spanish for Bad.

| 3/4/72 | 10 | 25 | | 1 Malo | 14 | $12 | Warner 2584 |

Pana • Just Say Goodbye • Cafe • Nena • Suavecito • Peace

| 11/25/72+ | 13 | 17 | | 2 Dos | 62 | $12 | Warner 2652 |
| 5/26/73 | 39 | 8 | | 3 Evolution | 101 | $12 | Warner 2702 |

MAMADO & SHE　　　　'89
Mamado is female singer Willetta Smith from Florida. She consisted of Joan York, Talien Richardson, Gary Chisholm, Victor Blanco, Nancy Jones, Sonya Lindsey and Gino Williams.

| 7/8/89 | 53 | 10 | | Wild | | $8 | WTG 45205 |

MANCHILD　　　　'77
Group from Indianapolis: Flash Ferrell (vocals), Kenneth Edmonds (guitar), Reggie Griffin (reeds), Daryl Simmons (percussion), Chuckie Bush (keyboards), Anthony Johnson (bass) and Robert Parson (drums). Edmonds later formed **The Deele** and recorded solo as **Babyface**.

| 10/1/77 | 29 | 6 | | Power And Love | 154 | $12 | Chi-Sound 765 |

MANDRÉ　　　　'79
Disco-funk artist Andre Lewis; formerly with **Maxayn**, **Buddy Miles** and Frank Zappa.

| 4/21/79 | 74 | 2 | | M3000 | 209 | $10 | Motown 917 |

★165★　MANDRILL　　　　'73
Latin jazz-rock-funk group from Brooklyn, New York: brothers Louis (trumpet), Richard (sax) and Carlos (flute) Wilson, Omar Mesa (guitar), Claude Cave (keyboards), Fudgie Kae (bass) and Charlie Pardo (drums).
　　　　1)Just Outside Of Town 2)Composite Truth 3)Solid

4/24/71	27	13		1 Mandrill	48	$12	Polydor 4050
6/17/72	24	10		2 Mandrill Is	56	$12	Polydor 5025
2/24/73	8	33		3 Composite Truth	28	$12	Polydor 5043

Hang Loose [25] • Fencewalk [19] • Hagalo • Don't Mess With People • Polk Street Carnival • Golden Stone • Out With The Boys • Moroccan Nights

| 10/13/73 | 6 | 17 | | 4 Just Outside Of Town | 82 | $12 | Polydor 5059 |

Mango Meat [40] • Never Die • Love Song [65] • Fat City Strut • Two Sisters Of Mystery • Afrikus Retrospectus • She Ain't Lookin' Too Tough • Aspiration Flame

10/12/74	28	6		5 Mandrilland		$15	Polydor 9002 [2]
5/3/75	18	11		6 Solid	92	$12	United Artists 408
7/19/75	51	5		7 The Best Of Mandrill	[G] 194	$12	Polydor 6047
2/14/76	28	8		8 Beast From The East	143	$12	United Artists 577
11/19/77	26	12		9 We Are One	124	$10	Arista 4144
12/2/78+	30	14		10 New Worlds	154	$10	Arista 4195
4/5/80	68	3		11 Getting In The Mood		$10	Arista 9527

MANGIONE, Chuck　　　　'80
Born on 11/29/40 in Rochester, New York. Flugelhorn player/bandleader/composer.

10/28/78	37	8	●	1 Children of Sanchez	[I-S] 14	$12	A&M 6700 [2]
2/23/80	13	17	●	2 Fun and Games	[I] 8	$10	A&M 3715
6/27/81	51	4		3 Tarantella	[I-L] 55	$12	A&M 6513 [2]

benefit concert for Italy's earthquake victims

| 7/24/82 | 53 | 4 | | 4 Love Notes | [I] 83 | $10 | Columbia 38101 |

★101★　MANHATTANS, The　　　　'80
Vocal group from Jersey City, New Jersey: George Smith, Winfred Lovett, Edward Bivins, Kenneth Kelly and Richard Taylor. Smith died on 12/16/70; replaced by **Gerald Alston**. Taylor left in 1976; died on 12/7/87 (age 47).
　　　　1)After Midnight 2)The Manhattans 3)It Feels So Good

3/26/66	19	2		1 Dedicated To You		$200	Carnival 201
11/4/72+	35	15		2 A Million To One		$25	Deluxe 12004
8/4/73	19	16		3 There's No Me Without You	150	$15	Columbia 32444
11/23/74	59	2		4 That's How Much I Love You	160	$15	Columbia 33064
5/8/76	6	21	●	5 The Manhattans	16	$12	Columbia 33820

Searching For Love • We'll Have Forever To Love • Take It Or Leave It • Reasons • How Can Anything So Good Be So Bad For You? • Hurt [10] • Wonderful World Of Love • If You're Ever Gonna Love Me • La La La Wish Upon A Star • Kiss And Say Goodbye [1]

2/26/77	12	25	●	6 It Feels So Good	68	$12	Columbia 34450
3/4/78	18	15		7 There's No Good In Goodbye	78	$12	Columbia 35252
4/7/79	20	32		8 Love Talk	141	$12	Columbia 35693
4/19/80	4	33	●	9 After Midnight	24	$12	Columbia 36411

Shining Star [4] • It's Not The Same • Girl Of My Dream [30] • Cloudy, With A Chance Of Tears • The Closer You Are • Medley: If My Heart Could Speak/One Life To Live • Just As Long As I Have You • It Couldn't Hurt • Tired Of The Single Life • I'll Never Run Away From Love Again

12/20/80+	18	17		10 Manhattans Greatest Hits	[G] 87	$12	Columbia 36861
8/15/81	21	14		11 Black Tie	86	$10	Columbia 37156
8/6/83	17	19		12 Forever By Your Side	104	$10	Columbia 38600
4/13/85	44	12		13 Too Hot To Stop It	171	$10	Columbia 39277

DEBUT	PEAK	WKS	Gold	Album Title	Pop #	$	Label & Number
				MANHATTAN TRANSFER, The '83			
				Vocal group from New York City: Tim Hauser, Alan Paul, Janis Siegel and Laurel Masse.			
10/15/83	38	13		Bodies And Souls	52	$10	Atlantic 80104
	★184★			**MANN, Herbie** '69			
				Born Herbert Jay Solomon on 4/16/30 in Brooklyn, New York. Jazz flutist.			
				1)Memphis Underground 2)Discotheque 3)Push Push			
10/22/66	24	2		1 Our Mann Flute ....[I]	139	$20	Atlantic 1464
5/24/69	2²	47		2 Memphis Underground ....[I]	20	$12	Atlantic 1522
				Memphis Underground [42] • New Orleans • Hold On, I'm Comin' • Chain Of Fools • Battle Hymn Of The Republic			
11/22/69+	32	12		3 Live At The Whisky A Go Go ....[I-L]	139	$12	Atlantic 1536
4/3/71	41	2		4 Memphis Two-Step ....[I]	137	$12	Embryo 531
11/27/71	21	11		5 Push Push ....[I]	119	$12	Embryo 532
3/29/75	19	14		6 Discotheque ....[I]	27	$12	Atlantic 1670
9/27/75	21	8		7 Waterbed	75	$12	Atlantic 1676
5/22/76	56	2		8 Surprises	178	$12	Atlantic 1682
2/19/77	46	3		9 Bird In A Silver Cage ....[I]	132	$10	Atlantic 18209
2/24/79	38	11		10 Super Mann	77	$10	Atlantic 19221
				MANTRONIX '88			
				Rap duo from New York City: Curtis "Mantronik" Kahleel and M.C. Tee. Bryce Wilson replaced Tee in 1989. Wilson later formed **Groove Theory**.			
3/8/86	47	15		1 The Album		$10	Sleeping Bag 6
1/24/87	27	29		2 Music Madness		$10	Sleeping Bag 8
4/9/88	18	13		3 In Full Effect	108	$8	Capitol 48336
3/17/90	61	9		4 This Should Move Ya	161	$8	Capitol 91119
	★112★			**MARIE, Teena** '81			
				Born Mary Christine Brockert on 3/5/56 in Santa Monica, California. White funk singer/songwriter/guitarist.			
5/5/79	18	26		1 Wild and Peaceful	94	$10	Gordy 986
3/8/80	18	26		2 Lady T	45	$10	Gordy 992
9/13/80	9	42		3 Irons In The Fire	38	$10	Gordy 997
				I Need Your Lovin' [9] • Young Love [41] • First Class Love • Irons In The Fire • Chains • You Make Love Like Springtime • Tune In Tomorrow			
6/20/81	2⁸	33	●	4 It Must Be Magic	23	$10	Gordy 1004
				It Must Be Magic [30] • Revolution • Where's California • 365 • Opus III (Does Anybody Care) • Square Biz [3] • The Ballad Of Cradle Rob And Me • Portuguese Love [54] • Yes Indeed			
11/12/83+	13	39		5 Robbery	119	$8	Epic 38882
12/15/84+	9	41	●	6 Starchild	31	$8	Epic 39528
				Lovergirl [9] • Help Youngblood Get To The Freaky Party • Out On A Limb [56] • Alibi • Jammin [45] • Starchild • We've Got To Stop (Meeting Like This) • My Dear Mr. Gaye • Light			
7/12/86	20	12		7 Emerald City	81	$8	Epic 40318
4/16/88	15	26		8 Naked To The World	65	$8	Epic 40872
10/20/90	27	29		9 Ivory	132	$8	Epic 45101
				MAR-KEYS '69			
				Instrumental group from Memphis: Steve Cropper and Charlie Freeman (guitars), Jerry Lee Smith (piano), Charles Axton, Wayne Jackson and Don Nix (horns), Donald "Duck" Dunn (bass) and Terry Johnson (drums). Staff musicians at Stax/Volt. Cropper and Dunn later joined **Booker T. & The MG's**. Jackson joined **The Memphis Horns**. Axton later joined **The Packers**.			
7/12/69	34	5		Damifiknew		$20	Stax 2025
				MARK IV '73			
				Vocal group from New York City: Jimmy Ponder, Lawrence Jones, Candido Antomade and Walter Moreland.			
4/14/73	48	2		Mark IV		$12	Mercury 651
				MARKHAM, Pigmeat '68			
				Born Dewey Markham on 4/18/06 in Durham, North Carolina. Died on 12/13/81 (age 75). Stage and TV comedian.			
4/20/68	41	2		1 Backstage ....[C]		$20	Chess 1521
7/27/68	40	8		2 Here Come The Judge ....[C]	109	$20	Chess 1523
				MARKY MARK And The Funky Bunch '93			
				Born Mark Wahlberg on 6/5/71 in Boston. Singer/rapper/actor. The younger brother of Donnie Wahlberg of **New Kids On The Block**. Acted in several movies.			
12/26/92+	66	3		You Gotta Believe	67	$8	Interscope 92203
	★128★			**MARLEY, Bob, & The Wailers** '76			
				Born on 2/6/45 in Rhoden Hall, Jamaica. Died of cancer on 5/11/81 (age 36). Legendary reggae singer/guitarist. Father of **Ziggy Marley**. The Wailers included Marley's wife Rita, **Peter Tosh**, Bunny Wailer, Judy Mowatt and Marcia Griffiths. Tosh was murdered on 9/11/87 (age 42). Bob Marley was inducted into the Rock and Roll Hall of Fame in 1994.			
				1)Rastaman Vibration 2)Exodus 3)Songs Of Freedom			
4/5/75	44	7		1 Natty Dread	92	$15	Island 9281
7/26/75	41	5	●	2 Burnin'	151	$15	Island 9256
				THE WAILERS			
11/22/75	51	4	●	3 Catch A Fire	171	$15	Island 9241
5/22/76	11	16	●	4 Rastaman Vibration	8	$12	Island 9383
9/11/76	59	2		5 The Birth Of A Legend ....[E]		$15	Calla 1240 [2]
11/13/76	47	2	●	6 Live! ....[L]	90	$12	Island 9376
				recorded on July 18, 1975 at the Lyceum in London			
6/25/77	15	17	●	7 Exodus	20	$12	Island 9498
5/27/78	50	3	●	8 Kaya	50	$12	Island 9517
1/13/79	58	5		9 Babylon By Bus ....[L]	102	$15	Island 11 [2]
11/17/79	32	15		10 Survival	70	$12	Island 9542

DEBUT	PEAK	WKS	Gold	Album Title	Pop #	$	Label & Number
				MARLEY, Bob, & The Wailers — Cont'd			
8/9/80	41	17	●	11 Uprising	45	$12	Island 9596
10/31/81	32	8		12 Chances Are.................... [E]	117	$10	Cotillion 5228
				BOB MARLEY recordings from 1968-72			
6/18/83	31	16	●	13 Confrontation	55	$10	Island 90085
9/1/84	34	15	▲10	14 Legend .... [K]	54	$10	Island 90169
				recordings from 1972-1981			
4/29/89	95	2		15 Bob Marley .... [K]		$10	Urban-Tek 3002
				previously unreleased tracks from 1968-72			
12/5/92	24	14	▲2	16 Songs Of Freedom .... [K]	86	$30	Tuff Gong 512280 [4]
				BOB MARLEY (above 2)			
				MARLEY, Ziggy, And The Melody Makers '88			
				Family reggae group from Kingston, Jamaica: David "Ziggy" (vocals, guitar), Stephen, Sharon and Cedella Marley. Children of **Bob Marley**.			
5/21/88	26	36	▲	1 Conscious Party	23	$8	Virgin 90878
8/26/89	43	15	●	2 One Bright Day	26	$8	Virgin 91256
7/17/93	75	7		3 Joy And Blues	178	$8	Virgin 87961
				MARLEY MARL '88			
				Born Marlon Williams on 9/30/62 in Queens, New York. Rap producer.			
10/1/88	25	24		1 In Control, Volume 1	163	$8	Cold Chillin' 25783
10/26/91	46	10		2 In Control Volume II - For Your Steering Pleasure	152	$8	Cold Chillin' 26257
				MARSALIS, Branford '90			
				Born on 8/26/60 in New Orleans. Jazz saxophonist. Brother of **Wynton Marsalis**. Leader of TV's *Tonight Show* band from 1992-95. Formed **Buckshot LeFonque**. His quartet included **Terence Blanchard** (trumpet), Kenny Kirkland (piano), Robert Hurst (bass) and Jeff Watts (drums).			
9/1/90	21	18		Mo' Better Blues .... [S]	63	$8	Columbia 46792
				THE BRANFORD MARSALIS QUARTET FEATURING TERENCE BLANCHARD			
				MARSALIS, Wynton '84			
				Born on 10/18/61 in New Orleans. Jazz trumpeter. Brother of **Branford Marsalis**. Member of **Fuse One**.			
11/24/84	53	25	●	Hot House Flowers .... [I]	90	$10	Columbia 39530
				MARTHA & THE VANDELLAS '66			
				Vocal trio from Detroit: Martha Reeves (b: 7/18/41), Annette Beard and Rosalind Ashford. Beard left in 1964, replaced by Betty Kelly. Group disbanded from 1969-71; re-formed with Martha and her sister Lois Reeves, and Sandra Tilley in 1971. Martha Reeves went solo in 1972. Group inducted into the Rock and Roll Hall of Fame in 1995.			
				MARTHA & THE VANDELLAS:			
6/11/66	6	13		1 Greatest Hits [G]	50	$30	Gordy 917
				My Baby Loves Me [3] • Come And Get These Memories [6] • Heat Wave [1] • Dancing In The Street [2] • Quicksand [8] • Live Wire [42] • You've Been In Love Too Long [25] • In My Lonely Room [44] • Love (Makes Me Do Foolish Things) [22] • A Love Like Yours (Don't Come Knocking Everyday) • Nowhere To Run [5] • Wild One [34]			
1/14/67	14	10		2 Watchout!	116	$30	Gordy 920
				MARTHA REEVES & THE VANDELLAS:			
6/1/68	13	11		3 Ridin' High	167	$20	Gordy 926
4/1/72	30	7		4 Black Magic	146	$20	Gordy 958
				MARTHA REEVES:			
7/6/74	54	5		5 Martha Reeves		$15	MCA 414
				MARTIN, Keith '95			
				Born in Washington DC. Male singer/rapper.			
5/6/95	82	3		It's Long Overdue		$8	Ruffhouse 67024
				MARVALESS '98			
				Born in Sacramento, California. Female rapper.			
5/14/94	100	1		1 Ghetto Blues		$8	AWOL 7194
1/28/95	71	1		2 Just Marvaless		$8	AWOL 7198
9/7/96	48	6		3 Wiccked		$8	AWOL 7200
5/9/98	43	3		4 Fearless		$8	AWOL 45675
				MARVELETTES, The '66			
				Female vocal group from Inkster, Michigan: Gladys Horton, Georgeanna Tillman, Wanda Young, Katherine Anderson and Juanita Cowart. Young and Horton both sang lead. Cowart left in 1962. Gordon left in 1965; died on 1/6/80. Horton left in 1967, replaced by Anne Bogan (later of **The New Birth**).			
3/19/66	4	11		1 Greatest Hits [G]	84	$25	Tamla 253
				Don't Mess With Bill [3] • You're My Remedy [48] • Locking Up My Heart [25] • As Long As I Know He's Mine [47] • Too Many Fish In The Sea [15] • Danger Heartbreak Dead Ahead [11] • Please Mr. Postman [1] • Playboy [4] • Strange I Know [10] • Forever [24] • Twistin' Postman [13] • Beechwood 4-5789 [7]			
4/8/67	13	10		2 The Marvelettes	129	$25	Tamla 274
9/28/68	41	9		3 Sophisticated Soul		$25	Tamla 286
11/14/70	50	2		4 The Return Of The Marvelettes		$20	Tamla 305
				MARY JANE GIRLS '85			
				Female vocal group: Joanne McDuffie, Candice Ghant, Kim Wuletich and Yvette Marina. Formed and produced by **Rick James**.			
5/14/83	6	47	●	1 Mary Jane Girls	56	$10	Gordy 6040
				Candy Man [23] • Boys [29] • Prove It • Jealousy [84] • You Are My Heaven • On The Inside • All Night Long [11] • Musical Love			
3/23/85	5	47	●	2 Only Four You	18	$10	Gordy 6092
				In My House [3] • Break It Up [79] • Shadow Lover Interlude • Shadow Lover • Lonely For You • Wild And Crazy Love [10] • Girlfriend • I Betcha • Leather Queen			

MASE '97
Born Mason Betha in 1977 in Jacksonville, Florida; raised in Harlem, New York. Male rapper.

11/8/97	❶¹	52	▲³	**Harlem World**	1²	$8	Bad Boy 73017

Do You Wanna Get Money? • Take What's Yours • Will They Die 4 You? • **Lookin' At Me** *[8]* • Love U So • The Player Way • Niggaz Wanna Act • **Feel So Good** *[5]* • **What You Want** *[3]* • Cheat On You • 24 Hrs. To Live • I Need To Be • Wanna Hurt Mase? • Jealous Guy

MASEKELA, Hugh '68
Born on 4/4/39 in Wilbank, South Africa. Trumpeter/bandleader/arranger. Married to **Miriam Makeba** from 1964-66.

4/15/67	24	9	1	Emancipation Of Hugh Masakela		$20	Chisa 101
1/27/68	7	7	2	Hugh Masekela Is Alive And Well At The Whiskey [L]	90	$15	Uni 73015

MRA (Christopher Columbus) • Little Miss Sweetness • A Whiter Shade Of Pale • **Up-Up And Away** *[47]* • Son Of Ice Bag • Senor Coraza • Coincidence • Ha Lese Le Di Khanna

6/8/68	2¹	27	3	The Promise of a Future	17	$15	Uni 73028

Ain't No Mountain High Enough • Madonna • No Face, No Name And No Number • Almost Seedless • Stop • **Grazing In The Grass** *[1]* • Vuca (Wake Up) • Bajabula Bonke (The Healing Song) • There Are Seeds To Sow

1/25/69	45	2	4	Masekela	195	$15	Uni 73041
8/3/74	35	12	5	I Am Not Afraid	149	$12	Blue Thumb 6015
8/2/75	18	12	6	The Boy's Doin' It	132	$10	Casablanca 7017
3/27/76	42	6	7	Colonial Man		$10	Casablanca 7023
1/15/77	55	1	8	Melody Maker		$10	Casablanca 7036

MASKMAN & THE AGENTS, The '69
Group consisted of Harmon "Maskman" Bethea (vocals), Tyrone Gray, Paul Williams and Johnny Hood.

5/10/69	32	7		One Eye Open		$20	Dynamo 8004

MASON, Barbara '73
Born on 8/9/47 in Philadelphia. Singer/songwriter.

5/18/68	42	2	1	Oh How It Hurts		$30	Arctic 1004
2/3/73	17	14	2	Give Me Your Love	95	$12	Buddah 5117
1/19/74	29	10	3	Lady Love		$12	Buddah 5140
3/8/75	42	4	4	Love's The Thing	187	$12	Buddah 5628

MASON, Harvey '78
Born on 2/22/47 in Atlantic City, New Jersey. Singer/songwriter/drummer. Member of **Fourplay**.

1/24/76	45	8	1	Marching In The Street		$10	Arista 4054
3/25/78	37	10	2	Funk In A Mason Jar		$10	Arista 4157
5/5/79	48	11	3	Groovin' You	149	$10	Arista 4227
6/20/81	62	3	4	M.V.P.	186	$10	Arista 4283

MASON, Vaughan, And Crew '80
Disco group from New York City led by multi-instrumentalist Vaughan Mason.

6/21/80	25	16		Bounce, Rock, Skate, Roll		$10	Brunswick 754221

MASQUERADERS, The '75
Group from Texas: Lee Hatim, Robert Wrightsil, David Sanders, Harold Thomas and Sammy Hutchinson.

11/1/75	57	3		Everybody Wanna Live On		$12	ABC 921

produced by Isaac Hayes

MASS PRODUCTION '79
Disco-funk group from Richmond, Virginia: Agnes Kelly (female vocals), Larry Marshall (male vocals), LeCoy Bryant (guitar), James Drumgole (trumpet), Greg McCoy (sax), Tyrone Williams (keyboards), Emanuel Redding (percussion), Kevin Douglas (bass) and Ricardo Williams (drums).

1/8/77	35	13	1	Welcome To Our World	142	$10	Cotillion 9910
8/27/77	38	11	2	Believe	83	$10	Cotillion 9918
7/8/78	50	3	3	Three Miles High	207	$10	Cotillion 5205
4/14/79	10	39	4	In The Purest Form	43	$10	Cotillion 5211

Firecracker *[4]* • With Pleasure • Our Thought (Purity) • **Can't You See I'm Fired Up** *[43]* • Eyeballin' • Next Year • Strollin'

3/29/80	24	19	5	Massterpiece	133	$10	Cotillion 5218
5/2/81	42	13	6	Turn Up The Music	166	$10	Cotillion 5226
4/10/82	46	7	7	In A City Groove	203	$10	Cotillion 5233

MASTA ACE INCORPORATED '95
Masta Ace is a rapper from Brownsville, New York. His posse includes Lord Digga and rap trio Eyceurokk (Master Eyce, Uneek and Diesalrokk).

9/1/90	38	12	1	Take A Look Around		$8	Cold Chillin' 26179
				MASTER ACE			
5/22/93	32	20	2	SlaughtaHouse	134	$8	Delicious Vinyl 92249
5/20/95	19	23	3	Sittin' On Chrome	69	$8	Delicious Vinyl 32873

MASTERFLEET '74

7/20/74	54	4		High On The Seas		$12	Sussex 8023

MASTER P '98
★173★
Born Percy Miller on 4/29/70 in New Orleans. Male rapper. Member of **Tru**. Founder of the No Limit record label. Played professional basketball for the CBA's Fort Wayne Fury in 1998. Brother of **Silkk The Shocker**.

3/25/95	41	6	1	99 Ways To Die		$8	No Limit 9901
5/4/96	3	98	●	2 Ice Cream Man	26	$8	No Limit 53978

Mr. Ice Cream Man *[55]* • Time For A 187 • 1/2 On A Bag Of Dank • Break 'Em Off Somethin' • How G's Ride • **No More Tears** *[78]* • The Ghetto Won't Change • Playa From Around The Way • Sellin' Ice Cream • Time To Check My Crackhouse • Bout It, Bout It • Back Up Off Me • Never Ending Game • Watch Dees Hoes • Bout That Drama • Killer Pussy • Things Ain't What They Used To Be • My Ghetto Heroes

DEBUT	PEAK	WKS	Gold Album Title	Pop #	$	Label & Number

MASTER P — Cont'd

DEBUT	PEAK	WKS	Gold Album Title	Pop #	$	Label & Number
9/13/97	❶²	97	▲² 3 **Ghetto D**	1¹	$8	No Limit 50659

Ghetto D • Let's Get 'Em • **I Miss My Homies** *[16]* • We Riders • Throw 'Em Up • Tryin 2 Do Something • Plan B • Weed & Money • Captain Kirk • Stop Hatin • Eyes On Your Enemies • **Make Em' Say Uhh!** *[18]* • Going Through Somethangs • Only Time Will Tell • After Dollars, No Cents • Gangstas Need Love • Pass Me Da Green • Come And Get Some • Burbons And Lacs

6/13/98	❶⁴	48	▲⁴ 4 **MP Da Last Don**	1²	$12	No Limit 53538 [2]

Da Last Don • Till We Dead And Gone • Thinkin' Bout U • Soldiers, Riders, And G's • The Ghetto's Got Me Trapped • Get Your Paper • Ride • Thug Girl • These Streets Keep Me Rollin' • Black And White • War Wounds • Dear Mr. President • Mama Raised Me • Let Me 9 Get Em' • More 2 Life • Ghetto Life • Gangsta B.... • So Many Souls Deceased • Rock-A-Bye Haters • Snitches • Family Business • Let's Get Em' • **Goodbye To My Homies** *[38]* • Welcome To My City • Ghetto Love • Make Em' Say Uhh! #2 • **Hot Boys And Girls** *[87]* • Reverse The Game • Eternity

MASTERS OF CEREMONY '88
Rap group from New York City: **Grand Puba**, Don Barron, Dr. Who and D.J. Shabazz.

9/17/88	91	4	**Dynamite**		$8	4th & B'way 444010

MATHIS, Johnny '69
Born on 9/30/35 in San Francisco. Male singer. Charted 69 pop albums from 1957-97.

12/30/67+	19	4	1 **Up, Up And Away**	60	$15	Columbia 9526
7/6/68	44	6	2 **Love Is Blue**	26	$15	Columbia 9637
12/28/68+	2²	4	3 **Those Were The Days**	60	$15	Columbia 9705

Those Were The Days • Little Green Apples • The End Of The World • This Guy's In Love With You • The 59th Street Bridge Song (Feelin' Groovy) • Light My Fire • Every Time I Dream Of You • The World I Used To Know • You Make Me Think About You • Turn Around Look At Me

4/15/78	4	18	▲ 4 **You Light Up My Life**	9	$10	Columbia 35259

You Light Up My Life • Emotion • All I Ever Need • Where Or When • If You Believe • **Too Much, Too Little, Too Late** *[1]* • How Deep Is Your Love • Till Love Touches Your Life • I Wrote A Symphony On My Guitar • It Was Almost Like A Song

7/29/78	14	11	● 5 **That's What Friends Are For**	19	$10	Columbia 35435

JOHNNY MATHIS & DENIECE WILLIAMS

10/20/79	68	2	6 **Mathis Magic**		$10	Columbia 36216
6/12/82	61	3	7 **Friends In Love**	147	$10	Columbia 37748
3/24/84	60	5	8 **A Special Part Of Me**	157	$10	Columbia 38718

MATTHEWS, David '77
Born on 4/3/42 in Sonora, Kentucky. Jazz arranger/songwriter/pianist.

9/17/77	54	2	**Dune**	[I]	169	$12	CTI 5005

MAXAYN '73
Group consisted of Maxayn Lewis (female vocals), Marlo Henderson (guitar), André Lewis (keyboards, bass) and Emilio Thomas (drums). Lewis later recorded as **Mandré**.

5/19/73	43	6	**Mindful**	206	$12	Capricorn 0110

MAXWELL '98
Born in 1974 in Brooklyn, New York. Singer/songwriter/producer.

4/20/96	8	103	▲ 1 **Maxwell's Urban Hang Suite**	45	$8	Columbia 66434

The Urban Theme • Welcome • **Sumthin' Sumthin'** *[23]* • **Ascension (Don't Ever Wonder)** *[8]* • Dancewitme • **...Til The Cops Come Knockin'** *[79]* • Whenever Wherever Whatever • Lonely's The Only Company • Reunion • Suitelady (The Proposal Jam) • The Suite Theme

8/2/97	15	35	2 **MTV Unplugged**	[L-M]	53	$6	Columbia 68515
7/18/98	2²	55↑	▲ 3 **Embrya**		3	$8	Columbia 68968

Gestation: Mythos • Everwanting: To Want You To Want • I'm You: You Are Me And We Are You • Luxury: Cococure • Drowndeep: Hula • **Matrimony: Maybe You** *[79]* • Arroz Con Pollo • Know These Things: Shouldn't You • Submerge: Til We Become The Sun • Gravity: Pushing To Pull • EachHourEachSecondEachMinuteEachDay: Of My Life • Embrya

MAYFIELD, Curtis ★33★ '72
Born on 6/3/42 in Chicago. Singer/songwriter/guitarist/producer. Member of **The Impressions** from 1957-70. Started own Curtom record label in 1968. Paralyzed from the chest down when a stage lighting tower fell on him before a concert on 8/13/90. Won Grammy's Lifetime Achievement Award in 1995. Inducted into the Rock and Roll Hall of Fame in 1999.

1)Superfly 2)Curtis 3)Back To The World 4)Sweet Exorcist 5)Curtis/Live!

10/10/70+	❶⁵	43	● 1 **Curtis**	19	$15	Curtom 8005

(Don't Worry) If There's A Hell Below We're All Going To Go *[3]* • The Other Side Of Town • The Makings Of You • We The People Who Are Darker Than Blue • Move On Up • Miss Black America • Wild And Free • Give It Up

5/29/71	3	31	2 **Curtis/Live!**	[L]	21	$20	Curtom 8008 [2]

Mighty Mighty (Spade And Whitey) • I Plan To Stay A Believer • We're A Winner • We've Only Just Begun • People Get Ready • Stare And Stare • Check Out Your Mind • Gypsy Woman • The Makings Of You • We The People Who Are Darker Than Blue • (Don't Worry) If There's A Hell Below We're All Going To Go • Stone Junkie

11/20/71	6	18	3 **Roots**	40	$15	Curtom 8009

Get Down *[13]* • Keep On Keeping On • Underground • **We Got To Have Peace** *[32]* • Beautiful Brother Of Mine *[45]* • Now You're Gone • Love To Keep You In My Mind

8/12/72	❶⁶	36	● 4 **Superfly**	[S]	1⁴	$15	Curtom 8014

also see #18 below

Little Child Runnin' Wild • Pusherman • **Freddie's Dead (Theme From "Superfly")** *[2]* • Junkie Chase • Give Me Your Love (Love Song) • Eddie You Should Know Better • No Thing On Me (Cocaine Song) • Think • Superfly *[5]*

6/9/73	❶²	25	● 5 **Back To The World**	16	$15	Curtom 8015

Back To The World • Future Shock *[11]* • Right On For The Darkness • If I Were Only A Child Again *[22]* • Can't Say Nothin' *[16]* • Keep On Trippin' • Future Song (Love A Good Woman, Love A Good Man)

6/1/74	2¹	27	6 **Sweet Exorcist**	39	$12	Curtom 8601

Sweet Exorcist *[32]* • To Be Invisible • Power To The People • Kung Fu *[3]* • Suffer • Make Me Believe In You

DEBUT	PEAK	WKS	Gold	Album Title	Pop #	$	Label & Number

MAYFIELD, Curtis — Cont'd

DEBUT	PEAK	WKS		Album Title	Pop #	$	Label & Number
11/30/74	17	12		7 Got To Find A Way	76	$12	Curtom 8604
6/21/75	13	17		8 There's no place like America Today	120	$12	Curtom 5001
7/4/76	16	15		9 Give, Get, Take And Have	171	$12	Curtom 5007
3/26/77	32	8		10 Never Say You Can't Survive	173	$12	Curtom 5013
11/19/77	59	3		11 Short Eyes [S]		$12	Curtom 5017
9/2/78	52	6		12 Do It All Night		$12	Curtom 5022
7/28/79	19	25		13 Heartbeat	42	$10	RSO 3053
7/5/80	53	4		14 The Right Combination	180	$10	RSO 3084

LINDA CLIFFORD/CURTIS MAYFIELD

DEBUT	PEAK	WKS		Album Title	Pop #	$	Label & Number
7/26/80	33	15		15 Something To Believe In	128	$10	RSO 3077
10/10/81	39	24		16 Love Is The Place		$10	Boardwalk 33239
10/9/82	49	10		17 Honesty		$10	Boardwalk 33256
9/10/88	88	8		18 Superfly [R-S]		$8	Curtom 2002

reissue of #4 above

DEBUT	PEAK	WKS		Album Title	Pop #	$	Label & Number
3/24/90	59	17		19 Take It To The Street		$8	Curtom 2008
10/19/96	24	50		20 New World Order	137	$8	Warner 46348
3/22/97	91	3		21 The Very Best Of Curtis Mayfield [G]		$8	Rhino 72584

MAY MAY '92

Born May May Ali in Chicago. Female rapper. Daughter of boxer Muhammed Ali.

DEBUT	PEAK	WKS		Album Title	Pop #	$	Label & Number
5/2/92	87	4		The Introduction		$8	Scotti Brothers 75233

MAYSA '95

Born Maysa Leak in London. Female singer.

DEBUT	PEAK	WKS		Album Title	Pop #	$	Label & Number
9/30/95	64	4		Maysa		$8	Blue Thumb/GRP 7001

MAZARATI '86

Funk-rock group from Minneapolis: Sir Casey Terry (vocals), Craig Powell and Tony Christian (guitars), Aaron Paul Keith and Mark Starr (keyboards), Romeo (bass) and Kevin Patricks (drums).

DEBUT	PEAK	WKS		Album Title	Pop #	$	Label & Number
4/19/86	49	21		Mazarati	133	$8	Paisley Park 25368

MAZE Featuring Frankie Beverly ★58★ '85

Group from Philadelphia. Core members: Frankie Beverly (vocals, guitar), Wayne Thomas (guitar), Sam Porter (keyboards), Roame Lowry (percussion), Robin Duhe (bass) and Michael White (drums).
1)Can't Stop The Love 2)Silky Soul 3)Back To Basics

DEBUT	PEAK	WKS	Gold	Album Title	Pop #	$	Label & Number
3/12/77	6	41	●	1 Maze featuring Frankie Beverly	52	$10	Capitol 11607

Time Is On My Side • Happy Feelin's • Color Blind • Lady Of Magic [13] • While I'm Alone [21] • You • Look At California

| 2/11/78 | 9 | 23 | ● | 2 Golden Time Of Day | 27 | $10 | Capitol 11710 |

Travelin' Man [flip] • Song For My Mother • You're Not The Same • Workin' Together [9] • Golden Time Of Day [39] • I Wish You Well [61] • I Need You

| 4/14/79 | 5 | 26 | ● | 3 Inspiration | 33 | $10 | Capitol 11912 |

Lovely Inspiration • Feel That You're Feelin' [7] • Call On Me • Timin' [55] • Welcome Home • Woman Is A Wonder • Ain't It Strange • Lovely Inspiration

| 8/2/80 | 5 | 34 | ● | 4 Joy And Pain | 31 | $10 | Capitol 12087 |

Changing Times • The Look In Your Eyes [29] • Family • Roots • Joy And Pain • Southern Girl [9] • Happiness

| 7/4/81 | 3 | 39 | ● | 5 Live In New Orleans | 34 | $12 | Capitol 12156 [2] |

You • Changing Times • Joy And Pain • Happy Feelin's • Southern Girl • Look At California • Feel That You're Feelin' • The Look In Your Eyes • Running Away [7] • Before I Let Go [13] • We Need Love To Live [29] • Reason

| 5/28/83 | 5 | 48 | | 6 We Are One | 25 | $8 | Capitol 12262 |

Love Is The Key [5] • Right On Time • Your Own Kind Of Way • I Wanna Thank You [59] • We Are One [47] • Never Let You Down [26] • I Love You Too Much • Metropolis

| 3/30/85 | ❶¹ | 47 | ● | 7 Can't Stop The Love | 45 | $8 | Capitol 12377 |

Back In Stride [1] • Can't Stop The Love • Reaching Down Inside • Too Many Games [5] • I Want To Feel I'm Wanted [28] • Magic • A Place In My Heart

| 9/27/86 | 12 | 26 | | 8 Live In Los Angeles [L] | 92 | $10 | Capitol 12479 [2] |

sides 1-3: live; side 4: new studio recordings

| 9/23/89 | ❶¹ | 38 | ● | 9 Silky Soul | 37 | $8 | Warner 25802 |

Silky Soul [4] • Can't Get Over You [1] • Just Us • Somebody Else's Arms • Love's On The Run [13] • Change Our Ways • Songs Of Love [37] • Mandela

| 12/9/89 | 57 | 13 | | 10 Lifelines Volume I [G] | | $8 | Capitol 92810 |
| 9/11/93 | 3 | 50 | ● | 11 Back To Basics | 37 | $8 | Warner 45297 |

Nobody Knows What You Feel Inside • Love Is • The Morning After [19] • Laid Back Girl [15] • What Goes Up [32] • In Time • All Night Long • Don't Wanna Lose Your Love • Twilight

| 2/10/96 | 57 | 24 | | 12 Anthology [G] | | $12 | Right Stuff 35885 [2] |

MC/M.C.:

M.C. ADE '90

Born Adrian Hines on 7/14/67 in Miami. Male rapper.

DEBUT	PEAK	WKS		Album Title	Pop #	$	Label & Number
11/18/89+	66	22		How Much Can You Take		$10	4-Sight 5526

MC BRAINS '92

Born James Davis in Cleveland. Male rapper.

DEBUT	PEAK	WKS		Album Title	Pop #	$	Label & Number
4/11/92	31	26		Lovers Lane	47	$8	Motown 6342

M.C. BREED '94

Born Eric Breed in Flint, Michigan. Male rapper.

DEBUT	PEAK	WKS		Album Title	Pop #	$	Label & Number
4/13/91	38	52		1 M.C. Breed & DFC	142	$8	S.D.E.G. 4103
5/23/92	40	28		2 20 Below	155	$8	Wrap 8109
5/15/93	16	34		3 The New Breed	156	$8	Wrap 8120

DEBUT	PEAK	WKS	Gold Album Title	Pop #	$	Label & Number

M.C. BREED — Cont'd

| 6/25/94 | 9 | 18 | 4 Funkafied | 106 | $8 | Wrap 8133 |

Underground Address • What You Want • Smokin' • Late Nite Creep (Booty Call) • Teach My Kids • This Is How We Do It • One Time • Seven Years • The Deal Is Da Funk • Shootin' From The Hip • Break Yourself • Back Up In Ya! • Flava Uv Phony • B.R. Double E.D. • Ol' School

7/8/95	17	7	5 Big Baller	143	$8	Wrap 8148
10/21/95	66	4	6 The Best Of MC Breed ....[G]		$8	Wrap 8150
6/1/96	34	7	7 To Da Beat Ch'all		$8	Wrap 8154
10/11/97	48	3	8 Flatline		$8	Wrap 8159

MC EIHT   '94

Born Aaron Tyler in Los Angeles. Male rapper. Leader of **Compton's Most Wanted.**

| 8/6/94 | ❶5 | 25 | ● 1 We Come Strapped | 5 | $8 | Epic Street 57696 |

Niggaz That Kill • Def Wish III • Take 2 With Me • All For The Money • Compton Cyco • Niggaz Make The Hood Go Round • Nuthin' But High • We Come Strapped • Can I Still Kill It • Goin' Out Like Geez • Nuthin' But The Gangsta • Hard Times • Compton Bomb • 2 Tha Westside

| 4/27/96 | 3 | 19 | 2 Death Threatz | 16 | $8 | Epic Street 67139 |

MC EIHT Featuring CMW (above 2)
Def Wish IV (Tap That Azz) • Ain't Nuthin 2 It • Killin Nigguz • Run 4 Your Life • Endoness • Thuggin It Up • Love 4 Tha Hood • Fuck Em All • Late Nite Hype • Set Trippin • Collect My Stripez • Fuck Your Hood • You Can't See Me • Drugs & Killin • Killin Season

| 11/29/97 | 13 | 14 | 3 Last Man Standing | 64 | $8 | Epic Street 68041 |

MC5   '69

Hard-rock group from Detroit: Rob Tyner (vocals), Wayne Kramer and Fred "Sonic" Smith (guitars), Michael Davis (bass) and Dennis Thompson (drums). Tyner died of a heart attack on 9/17/91 (age 46). Smith died of a heart attack on 11/4/94 (age 45). MC5 is short for Motor City Five.

| 4/12/69 | 45 | 2 | Kick Out The Jams ....[L] | 30 | $50 | Elektra 74042 |

recorded October 30-31, 1968 at the Grande Ballroom in Detroit

| | ★86★ | | **M.C. HAMMER**   '90 | | | |

Born Stanley Kirk Burrell on 3/30/63 in Oakland. Male rapper. Billed as **Hammer** from 1991-94.

| 11/5/88+ | ❶1 | 73 | ▲2 1 Let's Get It Started | 30 | $8 | Capitol 90924 |

Turn This Mutha Out [12] • Let's Get It Started • Ring 'Em • Cold Go M.C. Hammer • You're Being Served • It's Gone • (Hammer Hammer) They Put Me In The Mix [40] • Son Of The King • That's What I Said • Feel My Power • Pump It Up [46]

| 3/17/90 | ❶29 | 68 | ▲10 2 Please Hammer Don't Hurt 'Em | 1²1 | $8 | Capitol 92857 |

Here Comes The Hammer [15] • U Can't Touch This [1] • Have You Seen Her [4] • Yo!! Sweetness • **Help The Children** [12] • On Your Face • Dancin' Machine • Pray [4] • Crime Story • She's Soft And Wet • Black Is Black • Lets Go Deeper • Work This

| 11/16/91+ | 3 | 42 | ▲3 3 Too Legit To Quit | 2² | $8 | Capitol 98151 |

This Is The Way We Roll [20] • Brothers Hang On • **2 Legit 2 Quit** [3] • Living In A World Like This • Tell Me (Why Can't We Live Together) • Releasing Some Pressure • Find Yourself A Friend • Count It Off • Good To Go • Lovehold • Street Soldiers • **Do Not Pass Me By** [15] • Gaining Momentum

| 3/19/94 | 2¹ | 28 | ▲ 4 The Funky Headhunter | 12 | $8 | Giant 24545 |

HAMMER (above 2)
Oaktown • It's All Good [14] • Somethin' For The O.G.'s • **Don't Stop** [63] • Pumps And A Bump [21] • One Mo' Time • Clap Yo' Hands • Break 'Em Off Somethin' Proper • Don't Fight The Feelin' • Somethin' 'Bout The Goldie In Me • Sleepin' On A Master Plan • It's All That • The Funky Headhunter • Help Lord (Won't You Come)

| 9/30/95 | 23 | 12 | 5 V Inside Out | 119 | $8 | Giant 24637 |

MC LYTE   '89

Born Lana Moorer on 10/11/71 in Queens, New York. Female rapper.

| 5/28/88 | 50 | 16 | 1 Lyte As A Rock | | $8 | First Priority 90905 |
| 10/7/89 | 6 | 30 | 2 Eyes On This | 86 | $8 | First Priority 91304 |

Cha Cha Cha [35] • Slave 2 The Rhythm • Cappucino • Stop, Look, Listen • Throwin' Words At U • Not Wit' A Dealer • Survival Of The Fittest • Shut The Eff Up! (Hoe) • I Am The Lyte • Rhyme Hangover • Funky Song • Please Understand • K-Rocks Housin'

10/12/91	14	33	3 Act Like You Know	102	$8	First Priority 91731
7/10/93	16	25	4 Ain't No Other	90	$8	First Priority 92230
9/14/96	11	25	5 Bad As I Wanna B	59	$8	EastWest 61781
9/5/98	71	1	6 Seven & Seven		$8	EastWest 62198

M.C. MADNESS — see D.J. Magic Mike

MC NAS-D & DJ FRED   '92

Rap duo from Tampa, Florida: Darnell Williams (b: 8/15/71) and Frederick Gray (b: 7/28/67).

| 12/5/92 | 68 | 2 | It's My Cadillac (Got That Bass) | | $8 | Pandisc 8822 |

M.C. POOH   '92

Born Lawrence Thomas in Los Angeles. Male rapper.

| 5/4/91 | 39 | 27 | 1 Life Of A Criminal | | $8 | In-A-Minute 187 |
| 4/4/92 | 38 | 17 | 2 Funky As I Wanna Be | 158 | $8 | Jive 41476 |

POOH-MAN (MC POOH)

| 8/14/93 | 57 | 11 | 3 Judgement Day | | $8 | Righteous 3001 |
| 9/3/94 | 85 | 5 | 4 Ain't No Love | | $8 | In-A-Minute 8600 |

MC REN   '93

Born Lorenzo Patterson in Los Angeles. Male rapper. Former member of **N.W.A.**

| 7/18/92 | 10 | 25 | ▲ 1 Kizz My Black Azz | 12 | $8 | Ruthless 53802 |

Check It Out Y'all • Behind The Scenes • The Final Frontier [80] • Right Up My Alley • Hound Dogz • Kizz My Black Azz

| 11/27/93 | ❶1 | 24 | 2 Shock Of The Hour | 22 | $8 | Ruthless 5505 |

11:55 • **Same Ol' Shit** [62] • Fuck What Ya Heard • All Bullshit Aside • One False Move • You Wanna Fuck Her • Mayday On The Front Line • Attack On Babylon • Do You Believe • Mr. Fuck Up • Shock Of The Hour

| 4/27/96 | 7 | 10 | 3 The Villain In Black | 31 | $8 | Ruthless 5544 |

Bitch Made Nigga Killa • Keep It Real • It's Like That • Mad Scientist • Live From Compton 'Saturday Night' • Still The Same Nigga • I Don't Give A Damn • Mind Blown • Great Elephant • Muhammad Speaks • Bring It On

DEBUT	PEAK	WKS	Gold	Album Title	Pop #	$	Label & Number
				MC REN — Cont'd			
7/18/98	14	9		4 Ruthless For Life	100	$8	Ruthless 69313
				MC SERCH '92			
				Born Michael Berrin in Queens, New York. White rapper. Former member of 3rd Bass.			
9/19/92	28	18		Return Of The Product	103	$8	Def Jam 52964
				M.C. SHAN '87			
				Born Shawn Moltke in Queens, New York. Male rapper.			
8/1/87	40	15		1 Down By Law		$8	Cold Chillin' 500
11/12/88	48	15		2 Born To Be Wild		$8	Cold Chillin' 25797
5/19/90	40	12		3 Play It Again, Shan		$8	Cold Chillin' 26155
				MC SHY D '88			
				Born Peter Jones in the Bronx, New York. Male rapper.			
5/30/87	41	23		1 Got To Be Tough	197	$10	Luke Skyywalker 1004
8/6/88	35	23		2 Comin' Correct In 88		$10	Luke Skyywalker 1005
4/21/90	80	10		3 Don't Sweat Me		$8	Benz 9003
				MC SMOOTH '90			
				Born in Los Angeles. Female rapper.			
8/18/90	72	16		Smooth & Legit		$8	Crush 254
				M.C. TROUBLE '90			
				Born LaTasha Rogers in Westlake, California. Died of heart failure on 6/4/91 (age 20). Female rapper.			
9/15/90	94	2		Gotta Get A Grip		$8	Motown 6303
				M.C. TWIST '89			
				Born in Los Angeles. Male rapper.			
3/25/89	35	17		1 Comin' Thru Like Warriors		$8	Luke Skyywalker 106
				M.C. TWIST & THE DEF SQUAD			
2/16/91	66	15		2 Bad Influence		$8	Lethal Beat 104

Mc:

DEBUT	PEAK	WKS	Gold	Album Title	Pop #	$	Label & Number
				McBRIDE, Geoff '90			
				Born in Lexington, North Carolina.			
8/18/90	55	23		Do You Still Remember Love		$8	Arista 8543
				McCANN, Les '70			
				Born on 9/23/35 in Lexington, Kentucky. Jazz keyboardist/singer.			
3/22/69	32	4		1 Much Les ....[I]	169	$15	Atlantic 1516
12/13/69+	2³	33		2 Swiss Movement [I-L]	29	$15	Atlantic 1537
				LES McCANN & EDDIE HARRIS			
				recorded June 1969 at the Montreaux Jazz Festival in Switzerland			
				Compared To What [35] • Cold Duck [44] • Kathleen's Theme • You Got It In Your Soulness • The Generation Gap			
4/25/70	48	6		3 Comment		$15	Atlantic 1547
6/12/71	14	18		4 Second Movement ....[I]	41	$15	Atlantic 1583
				EDDIE HARRIS & LES McCANN			
11/29/75+	36	8		5 Hustle To Survive	161	$12	Atlantic 1679
				McCARTNEY, Paul '82			
				Born on 6/18/42 in Liverpool, England. Founding member/bass guitarist of The Beatles. Won Grammy's Lifetime Achievement Award in 1990. Inducted into the Rock and Roll Hall of Fame in 1999. Charted 28 pop albums from 1970-97.			
5/15/82	11	19	▲	1 Tug Of War	1³	$10	Columbia 37462
1/21/84	49	10	▲	2 Pipes Of Peace	15	$10	Columbia 39149
				McCLAIN, Alton, & Destiny '79			
				Female vocal trio: Alton McClain, Robyrda Stiger and Delores Warren. Stiger went on to join Krystol. Warren died in a car crash on 2/22/85 (age 32).			
4/7/79	27	12		Alton McClain & Destiny	88	$10	Polydor 6163
				McCOO, Marilyn, & Billy Davis, Jr. '77			
				Husband/wife vocal duo. McCoo was born on 9/30/43 in Jersey City, New Jersey. Davis was born on 6/26/39 in St. Louis. Both were members of The 5th Dimension. Married in 1969. McCoo co-hosted TV's Solid Gold from 1981-84.			
9/18/76+	7	26	●	1 I Hope We Get To Love In Time	30	$12	ABC 952
				You Don't Have To Be A Star (To Be In My Show) [1] • Your Love [9] • I Still Will Be With You • Never Gonna Let You Go • Nothing Can Stop Me • You Can't Change My Heart • I Hope We Get To Love In Time [37] • My Love For You (Will Always Be The Same) • Easy Way Out • We've Got To Get It On Again			
8/20/77	26	13		2 The Two Of Us	57	$12	ABC 1026
10/14/78	59	1		3 Marilyn & Billy	146	$10	Columbia 35603
				McCOY, Van '75			
				Born on 1/6/44 in Washington DC. Died of a heart attack on 7/6/79 (age 35). Disco songwriter/producer.			
5/3/75	❶¹	20		1 Disco Baby	12	$12	Avco 69006
				VAN McCOY & The Soul City Symphony			
				Disco Baby • Fire • The Hustle [1] • Get Dancin' • Doctor's Orders • Turn This Mother Out • Shakey Ground • Spanish Boogie • Pick Up The Pieces • Hey Girl, Come And Get It			
9/27/75	41	7		2 From Disco To Love ....[E]	181	$12	Buddah 5648
				released in 1972			
11/1/75	18	6		3 The Disco Kid	80	$12	Avco 69009
5/15/76	22	10		4 The Real McCoy	106	$12	H&L 69012
10/16/76	44	3		5 Rhythms Of The World	202	$12	H&L 69014

McCRAE, George '74
Born on 10/19/44 in West Palm Beach, Florida. Disco singer. Married to **Gwen McCrae**.

8/24/74	7	16		1 Rock Your Baby	38	$12	TK 501

Rock Your Baby *[1]* • **I Can't Leave You Alone** *[10]* • You Got My Heart • You Can Have It All • **Look At You** *[31]* • Make It Right • I Need Somebody Like You • **I Get Lifted** *[8]*

| 7/19/75 | 24 | 7 | | 2 George McCrae | 152 | $12 | TK 602 |
| 1/3/76 | 33 | 8 | | 3 Together | | $12 | Cat 2606 |

GEORGE & GWEN McCRAE

McCRAE, Gwen '75
Born on 12/21/43 in Pensacola, Florida. Disco singer. Married to **George McCrae**.

| 6/28/75 | 18 | 9 | | 1 Rockin' Chair | 121 | $12 | Cat 2605 |
| 1/3/76 | 33 | 8 | | 2 Together | | $12 | Cat 2606 |

GEORGE & GWEN McCRAE

| 11/14/81 | 38 | 13 | | 3 Gwen McCrae | | $10 | Atlantic 19308 |

McCRARYS, The '78
Vocal group consisting of siblings Linda, Charity, Alfred and Sam McCrary.

| 8/26/78 | 32 | 11 | | Loving Is Living | 138 | $10 | Portrait 34764 |

McDANIEL, Chris '90
Born in Memphis. Male singer.

| 2/10/90 | 74 | 11 | | A Woman's Touch | | $8 | Megajam 1000 |

McDONALD, Michael '82
Born on 12/2/52 in St. Louis. Singer/songwriter/keyboardist. Former member of **The Doobie Brothers**.

| 9/4/82 | 10 | 25 | ● | If That's What It Takes | 6 | $10 | Warner 23703 |

Playin' By The Rules • **I Keep Forgettin'** **(Every Time You're Near)** *[7]* • Love Lies • I Gotta Try • I Can Let Go Now • That's Why • If That's What It Takes • No Such Luck • Losin' End • Believe In It

McDUFF, Brother Jack '66
Born Eugene McDuffy on 9/17/26 in Champaign, Illinois. Jazz organist.

| 8/20/66 | 10 | 17 | | 1 A Change Is Gonna Come [I] | | $20 | Atlantic 1463 |

Down In The Valley • A Change Is Gonna Come • What'd I Say • Gonna Hang Me Up A Sign • Hotcha • No Tears • Minha Saudade • Same Old Same Old • Can't Find The Keyhole Blues

2/18/67	20	8		2 Tobacco Road [I]		$20	Atlantic 1472
4/6/68	32	6		3 Double-Barrelled Soul [I]		$20	Atlantic 1498
12/13/69+	20	17		4 Down Home Style [I]	192	$15	Blue Note 84322
8/22/70	42	4		5 Moon Rappin' [I]		$15	Blue Note 84334

McFADDEN & WHITEHEAD '79
Duo of Gene McFadden and John Whitehead from Philadelphia. Wrote and produced songs for many Philadelphia soul acts; defined "The Sound Of Philadelphia." Whitehead is the father of Kenny and Johnny Whitehead (**Whitehead Bros.**).

| 5/19/79 | 5 | 22 | ● | 1 McFadden & Whitehead | 23 | $10 | Philadelphia I. 35800 |

Ain't No Stoppin' Us Now *[1]* • **I've Been Pushed Aside** *[73]* • Mr. Music • Just Wanna Love You Baby • Got To Change • You're My Someone To Love • I Got The Love • Do You Want To Dance

| 10/4/80 | 29 | 8 | | 2 I Heard It In A Love Song | 153 | $10 | TSOP 36773 |

McFERRIN, Bobby '88
Born on 3/11/50 in New York City. Unaccompanied, jazz-styled improvisation vocalist.

| 5/2/87 | 62 | 13 | | 1 Spontaneous Inventions | 103 | $10 | Blue Note 85110 |
| 4/30/88 | 12 | 41 | ▲ | 2 Simple Pleasures | 5 | $8 | EMI-Manhattan 48059 |

McGHEE, Jacci '93
Born in the Bronx, New York. Female singer.

| 1/30/93 | 54 | 11 | | Jacci McGhee | | $8 | MCA 10291 |

McGRIFF, Jimmy '69
Born on 4/3/36 in Philadelphia. Jazz organist.

| 12/28/68+ | 10 | 24 | | 1 The Worm [I] | 161 | $20 | Solid State 18045 |

The Worm *[28]* • Keep Loose • Heavyweight • Think • Lock It Up • Girl Talk • Blue Juice • Take The "A" Train

| 6/26/76 | 43 | 5 | | 2 The Mean Machine [I] | 208 | $12 | Groove Merchant 3311 |

McGRUFF '98
Male rapper from New York City.

| 7/4/98 | 19 | 6 | | Destined To Be | 169 | $8 | Uptown 53126 |

McKNIGHT, Brian '98
Born on 6/5/69 in Buffalo, New York. Brother of Claude McKnight of **Take 6**.

| 7/25/92+ | 17 | 99 | ▲ | 1 Brian McKnight | 149 | $8 | Mercury 848605 |
| 8/26/95 | 4 | 49 | ● | 2 I Remember You | 22 | $8 | Mercury 528280 |

On The Down Low *[12]* • On The Floor • Your Love Is Ooh • Up Around My Way • Anyway • **Still In Love** *[24]* • Every Beat Of My Heart • I Remember You • Must Be Love • **Crazy Love** *[10]* • Marilie • Kiss Your Love Goodbye • You • The Day The Earth Stood Still • Niko's Lullaby

| 10/11/97+ | ❶³ | 76 | ▲² | 3 Anytime | 13 | $8 | Mercury 536215 |

Anytime • Could • **You Should Be Mine (Don't Waste Your Time)** *[4]* • Show Me The Way Back To Your Heart • Everytime We Say Goodbye • You Got The Bomb • **Hold Me** *[12]* • The Only One For Me • Til I Get Over You • I Belong To You • Jam Knock • When The Chariot Comes

| 12/12/98+ | 33 | 5 | | 4 Bethlehem [X] | 95 | $8 | Motown 0944 |

McLAREN, Malcolm '84
Born on 1/22/46 in London. British entrepeneur. Former manager of the Sex Pistols.

| 1/21/84 | 43 | 16 | | D'ya Like Scratchin' [M] | 173 | $8 | Island 90124 |

with The World Famous Supreme Team

DEBUT	PEAK	WKS	Gold	Album Title	Pop #	$	Label & Number

McLEAN, Penny   '76
Born in Klagenforn, West Germany. Member of **Silver Convention**.

| 4/17/76 | 59 | 2 | | Lady Bump | | $10 | Atco 130 |

McNEIR, Ronnie   '76
Born in Camden, Alabama; raised in Pontiac, Michigan. Male singer/keyboardist.

| 1/17/76 | 58 | 2 | | Ronnie McNeir | | $10 | Prodigal 10007 |

McRAE, Carmen   '75
Born on 4/8/20 in New York City. Died of a stroke on 11/10/94 (age 74). Jazz singer/pianist.

| 9/13/75 | 56 | 2 | | I Am Music | | $12 | Blue Note 462 |

MEADOWS, Marion   '94
Born in West Virginia; raised in Connecticut. Male saxophonist.

2/9/91	59	18		1 For Lovers Only	[I]	$8	Novus 3097
4/2/94	52	12		2 Forbidden Fruit	[I]	$8	RCA 63167
8/12/95	81	2		3 Body Rhythm	[I]	$8	RCA 66623

MECO   '77
Born Domenico Monardo on 11/29/39 in Johnsonburg, Pennsylvania. Disco producer.

| 9/17/77 | 8 | 15 | ▲ | 1 **Star Wars And Other Galactic Funk** | [I] | 13 | $10 | Milennium 8001 |

     Star Wars Theme/Cantina Band [8] • Imperial Attack • The Desert And The Robot Auction • The Princess Appears • The Land Of The Sand People • Princess Leia's Theme • Cantina Band • The Last Battle • The Throne Room And End Title • Other • Galactic • Funk

| 1/21/78 | 35 | 6 | | 2 Encounters Of Every Kind | [I] | 62 | $10 | Milennium 8004 |
| 10/7/78 | 49 | 5 | | 3 The Wizard Of Oz | [I] | 68 | $10 | Milennium 8009 |

MEDEIROS, Glenn   '90
Born on 6/24/70 in Hawaii. Male singer/songwriter.

| 6/30/90 | 93 | 3 | | Glenn Medeiros | | 82 | $8 | MCA 6399 |

MEL AND TIM   '73
Vocal duo from Holly Springs, Mississippi: cousins Mel Hardin and Tim McPherson.

| 1/13/73 | 39 | 10 | | 1 Starting All Over Again | | 175 | $20 | Stax 3007 |
| 3/30/74 | 58 | 3 | | 2 Mel And Tim | | | $20 | Stax 5501 |

MELENDEZ, Lisette   '94
Born in Harlem, New York. Female dance singer.

| 2/5/94 | 100 | 1 | | True To Life | | | $8 | Fever 53453 |

MELLOW MAN ACE   '90
Born Ulpiano Sergio Reyez on 4/12/67 in Cuba; raised in Southgate, California. Male rapper. His brother Senen is a member of **Cypress Hill**.

| 9/30/89+ | 47 | 29 | | Escape From Havana | | 69 | $8 | Capitol 91295 |

MELVIN, Harold, And The Blue Notes   '76
   ★123★
Vocal group from Philadelphia: Harold Melvin, **Teddy Pendergrass**, Lawrence Brown, Jerry Cummings and Bernard Wilson. Pendergrass left in 1976, replaced by David Ebo. Melvin died of a stroke on 3/24/97 (age 57).

| 10/14/72 | 4 | 22 | | 1 Harold Melvin & The Blue Notes | | 53 | $12 | Philadelphia I. 31648 |

     I Miss You [7] • Ebony Woman • Yesterday I Had The Blues [12] • If You Don't Know Me By Now [1] • Be For Real • Let Me Into Your World • Let It Be You

| 9/29/73+ | 5 | 32 | | 2 Black & Blue | | 57 | $12 | Philadelphia I. 32407 |

     Cabaret • The Love I Lost [1] • It All Depends On You • Concentrate On Me • Satisfaction Guaranteed (Or Take Your Love Back) [6] • Is There A Place For Me • I'm Weak For You [87] • I'm Comin' Home Tomorrow

| 3/1/75 | ❶¹ | 33 | ● | 3 To Be True | | 26 | $12 | Philadelphia I. 33148 |

     Where Are All My Friends [8] • To Be True • Pretty Flower • Hope That We Can Be Together Soon [1] • Nobody Could Take Your Place • Somewhere Down The Line • Bad Luck [4] • It's All Because Of A Woman

| 12/6/75+ | ❶² | 28 | ● | 4 <u>Wake Up Everybody</u> | | 9 | $12 | Philadelphia I. 33808 |

     Wake Up Everybody [1] • Keep On Lovin' You • You Know How To Make Me Feel So Good • Don't Leave Me This Way • Tell The World How I Feel About 'Cha Baby [7] • To Be Free To Be Who We Are • I'm Searching For A Love

7/4/76	23	9		5 All Their Greatest Hits!	[G]	51	$12	Philadelphia I. 34232
2/12/77	15	11		6 Reaching For The World		56	$10	ABC 969
12/24/77	50	7		7 Now Is The Time			$10	ABC 1041
3/22/80	15	29		8 The Blue Album		95	$10	Source 3197
10/31/81	47	7		9 All Things Happen In Time			$10	MCA 5261

MEMBERS ONLY   '87
Instrumental group: Billy Masters and Jimi Tunnell (guitars), Michael Brecker (sax; **The Brecker Brothers**), Nelson Rangell (flute), Lou Solof (trumpet), Andy Marvel and Haim Cotton (keyboards), Bashiri Johnson (percussion), Yossi Fine (bass) and Chris Hills (drums).

| 10/10/87 | 60 | 3 | | Members Only | [I] | | $8 | Muse 5332 |

MEMPHIS HORNS, The   '77
Studio group from Memphis: Wayne Jackson (trumpet), Andrew Love (tenor sax), James Mitchell (baritone sax), Lewis Collins (soprano sax) and Jack Hale (trombone). Jackson was a member of the **Mar-Keys**.

11/12/77	32	10		1 Get Up & Dance		201	$10	RCA Victor 2198
7/8/78	48	3		2 Band II		163	$10	RCA Victor 2643
10/27/90	89	5	●	3 Midnight Stroll		51	$8	Mercury 846652

     THE ROBERT CRAY BAND FEATURING THE MEMPHIS HORNS

MEN AT LARGE   '94
Vocal duo from Cleveland: David Tolliver and Jason Champion.

| 6/27/92 | 24 | 56 | | 1 Men At Large | | 122 | $8 | EastWest 92159 |
| 11/5/94 | 17 | 22 | | 2 One Size Fits All | | 151 | $8 | EastWest 92459 |

MEN AT WORK '83
Pop-rock group from Melbourne, Australia: Colin Hay (vocals, guitar), Ron Strykert (guitar), Greg Ham (sax, keyboards), John Rees (bass) and Jerry Speiser (drums). Won the 1982 Best New Artist Grammy Award.

1/29/83	29	41	▲6	Business As Usual	1 15	$10	Columbia 37978

MENACE '90
Male singer/guitarist.

2/10/90	79	5		Doghouse		$8	Jump Street 2001

MENACE CLAN '95
Male rap duo from Houston: Walter Adams and Dante Miller.

10/28/95	44	4		Da Hood		$8	Rap-A-Lot 40710

MENDES, Sergio, & Brasil '66 '69
Mendes was born on 2/11/41 in Niteroi, Brazil. Pianist/leader of Latin-styled group originating from Brazil. Member Lani Hall (vocals) married Herb Alpert.

6/1/68	16	34	● 1	Look Around	5	$15	A&M 4137
12/7/68+	10	25	● 2	Fool On The Hill	3	$15	A&M 4160

Fool On The Hill • Festa • Casa Forte • Canto Triste • Upa, Neguinho • Lapinha • Scarborough Fair • When Summer Turns To Snow • Laia Ladaia (Reza)

5/21/83	22	23	3	Sergio Mendes	27	$8	A&M 4937

MEN OF VIZION '96
Vocal group from Brooklyn, New York: George Spencer, Corley Randolph, Spanky Williams, Brian Deramus and Desmond Greggs.

7/6/96	29	10		Personal	186	$8	MJJ Music 66947

ME PHI ME '92
Born Laron Wilburn in Flint, Michigan. Male rapper. Me Phi Me is Greek for Fraternity Of One.

8/8/92	71	11		One		$8	RCA 61036

METERS, The '69
Instrumental group from New Orleans: Art Neville (keyboards; brother of Aaron Neville), Leo Nocentelli (guitar), George Porter (bass) and Joe Modeliste (drums).

6/21/69	23	19	1	The Meters [I]	108	$60	Josie 4010
2/7/70	23	15	2	Look-Ka Py Py [I]	198	$60	Josie 4011
6/27/70	32	12	3	Struttin'	200	$60	Josie 4012
7/1/72	48	5	4	Cabbage Alley		$20	Reprise 2076
9/6/75	41	5	5	Fire On The Bayou	179	$20	Reprise 2228

METHENY, Pat '82
Born on 8/12/55 in Kansas City, Missouri. Jazz guitarist.

6/5/82	43	19		Offramp [I]	50	$10	ECM 1216

PAT METHENY GROUP

METHOD MAN '94
Born Clifford Smith in Staten Island, New York. Male rapper. Member of the Wu-Tang Clan.

12/3/94	❶1	78	▲ 1	Tical	4	$8	Def Jam 523839

Tical • Biscuits • Bring The Pain [30] • I'll Be There For You/You're All I Need To Get By [1] • What The Blood Clot • Meth Vs. Chef • Sub Crazy • Release Yo' Delf • P.L.O. Style • I Get My Thang In Action • Mr. Sandman • Stimulation • Method Man

11/28/98	❶1	28	▲ 2	Tical 2000: Judgement Day	2 1	$8	Def Jam 558920

Perfect World • Cradle Rock • Dangerous Grounds [42] • Sweet Love • Torture • Suspect Chin Music • Retro Godfather • Spazzola • You Play Too Much • Party Crasher • Grid Iron Rap • Step By Step • Play IV Keeps • Elements • Killin' Fields • Big Dogs • Break Ups 2 Make Ups [29] • Judgement Day [48]

MFSB '74
Group of studio musicians from Philadelphia. Produced by Kenny Gamble and Leon Huff for their own label, Philadelphia International. Name means "Mother, Father, Sister, Brother."

4/7/73	20	16	1	MFSB [I]	131	$10	Philadelphia I. 32046
1/26/74	❶6	30	● 2	Love Is The Message [I]	4	$10	Philadelphia I. 32707

Love Is The Message [42] • Cheaper To Keep Her • My One And Only Love • TSOP (The Sound Of Philadelphia) [1] • Medley: Zack's Fanfare (I Hear Music)/Touch Me In The Morning • Bitter Sweet

6/28/75	2 1	15	3	Universal Love [I]	44	$10	Philadelphia I. 33158

Sexy [2] • MFSB • Human Machine • Love Has No Time Or Place • T.L.C. (Tender Lovin' Care) [54] • Let's Go Disco • K-Jee • My Mood

11/29/75+	14	11	4	Philadelphia Freedom [I]	39	$10	Philadelphia I. 33845
7/4/76	18	11	5	Summertime	106	$10	Philadelphia I. 34238
2/7/81	54	6	6	Mysteries Of The World [I]		$10	TSOP 36405

MIAMI '76
Disco group from Miami: Robert Moore (vocals), Freddie Scott, Warren Thompson, Bobby Williams and Willie Jackson.

9/4/76	57	3		Notorious Miami		$12	Drive 102

MIAMI BOYZ '89
Rap duo from Miami.

3/18/89	57	24		Getting Off		$10	On Top 9001

MIAMI SOUND MACHINE — see ESTEFAN, Gloria

MIA X '97
Born Mia Young in Mississippi. Female rapper. Member of the group Tru.

7/5/97	2 1	34	● 1	Unlady Like	21	$8	No Limit 50705

You Don't Wanna Go 2 War • The Party Don't Stop • I Pitty U • Who Got Tha Clout • Ain't 2 Be Played Wit • Unladylike • I'll Take Ya Man • Let's Get It Straight • Forever Tru • Bring Da Drama • All N's • Mama's Family • I Don't Know Why • Hoodlum Poetry • Rainy Dayz • Mommie's Angels • You & Me • R.I.P. Jill • Thank You

11/21/98	3	18	2	Mama Drama	7	$8	No Limit 53502

Bring It On • Whatcha Wanna Do? [32] • Don't Start No Shit • Mama Drama • Imma Shine • I Think Somebody • Mama's Tribute • What's Ya Point • Thugs Like Me • Ride Or Run • TRU Bitches • Puttin' It Down • Ghetto Livin' • Play Wit Pussy • Don't Blame Me • Daddy • Like Dat • Sex Ed. • Flip 2 Rip • Fallen Angels (Dear Jill)

MICHAEL, George   '88

Born Georgios Kyriacos Panayiotou on 6/25/63 in Bushey, England. Singer/songwriter. Formed **Wham!** duo with Andrew Ridgeley.

2/9/85	20	36	▲⁶	1 Make It Big	1³	$8	Columbia 39595
				WHAM!			
12/5/87+	**❶**⁶	61	▲¹⁰	2 Faith	1¹²	$8	Columbia 40867

Faith • **Father Figure** *[6]* • **I Want Your Sex** *[43]* • **One More Try** *[1]* • **Hard Day** *[21]* • Hand To Mouth • Look At Your Hands • **Monkey** *[8]* • **Kissing A Fool** *[33]*

| 10/20/90 | 61 | 15 | ▲² | 3 Listen Without Prejudice .... | 2¹ | $8 | Columbia 46898 |

MICHEL, Pras   '98

Born Prakazrel Michel in 1972 in New York City. Member of **The Fugees**.

| 11/14/98 | 35 | 3 | | Ghetto Supastar | 55 | $8 | Ruffhouse 69516 |

MICHELE, Yvette   '97

Born in New York City. Female singer/rapper.

| 11/1/97 | 46 | 3 | | My Dream .... | | $8 | Loud/RCA 67487 |

MICHEL'LE   '90

Born Michel'le (pronounced: mee-shell-LAY) Toussant in Los Angeles. Female singer.

| 1/6/90 | 5 | 78 | ● | 1 Michel'le .... | 35 | $8 | Ruthless 91282 |

No More Lies *[2]* • Nicety *[5]* • If? *[22]* • Keep Watchin *[65]* • Something In My Heart *[2]* • 100% Woman • Silly Love Song • Never Been In Love • Close To Me • Special Thanks

| 9/12/98 | 56 | 3 | | 2 Hung Jury .... | | $8 | Death Row 53530 |

MIDNIGHT STAR   '83

★171★

Funk group from Louisville, Kentucky: Belinda Lipscomb (vocals), brothers Reginald and Vincent Calloway (horns), Jeffrey Cooper (guitar), Kenneth Gant (keyboards), Melvin Gentry (bass) and Bill Simmons (drums). In 1988, Bobby Lovelace joined when the Calloway brothers left to form own duo **Calloway**.

9/19/81	54	5		1 Standing Together		$10	Solar 19
9/11/82	58	11		2 Victory	205	$10	Solar 60145
7/9/83	2¹⁰	80	▲²	3 No Parking On The Dance Floor	27	$10	Solar 60241

Electricity • Night Rider • Feels So Good • **Wet My Whistle** *[8]* • No Parking (On The Dance Floor) *[43]* • Freak-A-Zoid *[2]* • Slow Jam • Playmates

| 12/15/84+ | 7 | 36 | ● | 4 Planetary Invasion .... | 32 | $10 | Solar 60384 |

Body Snatchers *[31]* • **Scientific Love** *[16]* • Let's Celebrate • Curious • Planetary Invasion • **Operator** *[1]* • Today My Love • Can You Stay With Me

| 6/7/86 | 7 | 33 | ● | 5 Headlines .... | 56 | $10 | Solar 60454 |

Headlines *[3]* • **Midas Touch** *[7]* • Stay Here By My Side • Close To Midnight • Get Dressed • **Engine No. 9** *[11]* • Close Encounter • Dead End • Searching For Love

| 10/29/88 | 14 | 29 | | 6 Midnight Star .... | 96 | $8 | Solar 72564 |
| 6/16/90 | 41 | 20 | | 7 Work It Out .... | | $8 | Solar 75316 |

MIGHTY CLOUDS OF JOY   '76

Gospel vocal group from Los Angeles: Willie Joe Ligon, Johnny Martin, Elmo Franklin, Richard Wallace, Leon Polk and David Walker.

| 10/5/74 | 58 | 4 | | 1 It's Time .... | 165 | $12 | Dunhill/ABC 50177 |
| 12/20/75+ | 34 | 8 | | 2 Kickin' .... | 168 | $12 | ABC 899 |

MiiLKBONE   '95

Born in Orange, New Jersey. White male rapper.

| 7/8/95 | 81 | 1 | | Da' Miilkrate .... | | $8 | Capitol 30697 |

MILES, Buddy   '72

★190★

Born George Miles on 9/5/46 in Omaha. Singer/drummer. With **Jimi Hendrix**'s Band Of Gypsys from 1969-70. Later became lead voice for **The California Raisins**.

7/25/70+	14	44		1 Them Changes	35	$15	Mercury 61280
11/28/70	14	25		2 We Got To Live Together	53	$15	Mercury 61313
4/17/71	12	21		3 A Message To The People	60	$15	Mercury 608
10/16/71	10	22		4 Buddy Miles Live [L]	50	$20	Mercury 7500 [2]

Take It Off Him And Put It On Me • Down By The River • Wrap It Up • Place Over There • **Them Changes** *[36]* • We Got To Live Together

| 7/22/72 | 6 | 12 | ▲ | 5 Carlos Santana & Buddy Miles! Live!   [L] | 8 | $12 | Columbia 31308 |

recorded at Hawaii's Diamond Head volcano crater
Marbles • Lava • Evil Ways • Them Changes • Free Form Funkafide Filth

4/7/73	36	3		6 Chapter VII	123	$12	Columbia 32048
				THE BUDDY MILES BAND			
12/15/73	47	5		7 Booger Bear	194	$12	Columbia 32694
				BUDDY MILES EXPRESS			
8/9/75	27	11		8 More Miles Per Gallon	68	$10	Casablanca 7019

MILIRA   '90

Born Milira Jones in Manhattan, New York. Female singer.

| 6/16/90 | 29 | 42 | | 1 Milira .... | | $8 | Motown 6297 |
| 7/25/92 | 81 | 10 | | 2 Milira, Back Again!!! .... | | $8 | Motown 6328 |

MILITIA   '98

Duo of rap producers Emanuel Dean and Shawn Billups. Featuring rappers Diz and Devious.

| 3/14/98 | 97 | 1 | | Militia .... | | $8 | Red Ant 111003 |

MILLER, Marcus   '94

Born on 6/14/59 in Brooklyn, New York. Bassist/guitarist. Former member of **The Jamaica Boys**.

| 4/16/94 | 93 | 4 | | Sun Don't Lie .... | | $8 | PRA 60201 |

MILLER, Steve, Band '77

Born on 10/5/43 in Milwaukee; raised in Dallas. Blues-rock singer/songwriter/guitarist. Charted 19 pop albums from 1968-93.

4/2/77	19	8	▲⁴ 1	Fly Like An Eagle..	3	$10	Capitol 11497
10/16/82	40	8	▲ 2	Abracadabra..	3	$10	Capitol 12216

MILLI VANILLI '89

Europop act formed in Germany by producer Frank Farian. Originally thought to be Rob Pilatus (from Germany) and Fabrice Morvan (from France). Duo was stripped of its 1989 Best New Artist Grammy Award when it was revealed that they didn't sing on their debut album. Actual vocalists are Charles Shaw, John Davis and Brad Howe. Milli Vanilli is Turkish for positive energy. Pilatus died of a drug overdose on 4/2/98 (age 32).

3/25/89	8	61	▲⁶ 1	Girl You Know It's True	1⁸	$8	Arista 8592

Girl You Know It's True [3] • Baby Don't Forget My Number [9] • More Than You'll Ever Know • Blame It On The Rain [14] • Take It As It Comes • It's Your Thing • Dreams To Remember • All Or Nothing [54] • Girl I'm Gonna Miss You [20]

6/23/90	80	8	● 2	The Remix Album	[K] 32	$8	Arista 8622

★70★ MILLS, Stephanie '87

Born on 3/26/56 in Brooklyn, New York. Singer/actress. Played "Dorothy" in Broadway's *The Wiz*. Briefly married to Jeffrey Daniels of Shalamar in 1980.

1)If I Were Your Woman 2)Sweet Sensation 3)Stephanie

5/12/79	12	43	● 1	Whatcha Gonna Do...With My Lovin'?	22	$10	20th Century 583
5/3/80	3	52	● 2	Sweet Sensation	16	$10	20th Century 603

Sweet Sensation [3] • Try My Love • I Just Wanna Say • Wish That You Were Mine • D-A-N-C-I-N' • Still Mine • Never Knew Love Like This Before [12] • Mixture Of Love

5/23/81	3	27	● 3	Stephanie	30	$10	20th Century 700

Winner • Two Hearts [3] • Don't Stop Doin' What 'Cha Do • Top Of My List • I Believe In Love Songs • Night Games [33] • My Love's Been Good To You • Magic

8/14/82	10	33		4	Tantalizingly Hot	48	$10	Casablanca 7265

Last Night [14] • Still Lovin' You • Keep Away Girls [13] • You Can't Run From My Love [59] • True Love Don't Come Easy • 'Ole Love • Your Love Is Always New • I Can't Give Back The Love I Feel For You

9/10/83	12	29		5	Merciless	104	$10	Casablanca 811364
10/27/84	10	22		6	I've Got The Cure	73	$10	Casablanca 822421

The Medicine Song [8] • Edge Of The Razor [47] • In My Life • Give It Half A Chance • Outrageous • You Just Might Need A Friend • Everlasting Love • Rough Trade • Undercover

1/18/86	4	39		7	Stephanie Mills	47	$8	MCA 5669

Stand Back [15] • Automatic Passion • Rising Desire [11] • Time Of Your Life • Hold On To Midnight • Just You • I Have Learned To Respect The Power Of Love [1] • Under Pressure

6/27/87	❶¹	50	● 8	If I Were Your Woman	30	$8	MCA 5996

I Feel Good All Over [1] • If I Were Your Woman [19] • (You're Puttin') A Rush On Me [1] • Jesse • Secret Lady [7] • Touch Me Now • Running For Your Love • Can't Change My Ways

7/22/89	5	49	● 9	Home	82	$8	MCA 6312

Something In The Way (You Make Me Feel) [1] • Real Love [53] • Home [1] • So Good, So Right • Comfort Of A Man [8] • I Come To You • Good Girl Gone Bad • Ain't No Cookin' • Fast Talk

12/12/92	22	23		10	Something Real		$8	MCA 10690

MINT CONDITION '96

Funk group from Minneapolis: Stokley Williams (vocals, drums), Homer O'Dell (guitar), Larry Weddell and Keri Lewis (keyboards), Jeff Allen (sax) and Ricky Kinchen (bass).

1/25/92	13	35		1	Meant To Be Mint..	63	$8	Perspective 1001
10/23/93+	18	42		2	From The Mint Factory	104	$8	Perspective 9005
10/12/96	13	42	● 3	Definition Of A Band	76	$8	Perspective 9028
6/27/98	78	2		4	The Collection (1991-1998) .... [G]		$8	Perspective 9039

MIRACLES, The ★24★ '66

Vocal group from Detroit: Smokey Robinson, Bobby Rogers, Ronnie White and Warren "Pete" Moore. Robinson went solo in 1972, replaced by Billy Griffin. White died of leukemia on 8/26/95 (age 57).

1)Going To A Go-Go 2)Special Occasion 3)Greatest Hits From The Beginning 4)Make It Happen 5)Away We Go-Go

THE MIRACLES:

4/17/65	2⁹	24		1	Greatest Hits From The Beginning	[G] 21	$50	Tamla 254 [2]

Got A Job • I Cry • Mama Done Told Me • (I Need Some) Money • Bad Girl • I Love Your Baby • I Need A Change • All I Want Is You • (You Can) Depend On Me • Who's Lovin' You • That's What Love Is Made Of [35] • Mickey's Monkey [3] • I Gotta Dance To Keep From Crying [35] • You've Really Got A Hold On Me [1] • I Like It Like That [27] • A Love She Can Count On [21] • Shop Around [1] • Way Over There • I've Been Good To You • Would I Love You • I'll Try Something New [11] • What's So Good About Good-by [16]

SMOKEY ROBINSON & THE MIRACLES:

12/4/65+	❶⁵	28		2	Going To A Go-Go	8	$30	Tamla 267

The Tracks Of My Tears [2] • Going To A Go-Go [2] • Ooo Baby Baby [4] • My Girl Has Gone [3] • In Case You Need Love • Choosey Beggar [35] • Since You Won My Heart • From Head To Toe • All That's Good • My Baby Changes Like The Weather • Let Me Have Some • A Fork In The Road

12/17/66+	3	19		3	Away We A Go-Go	41	$25	Tamla 271

Whole Lot Of Shakin' In My Heart (Since I Met You) [20] • You Don't Have To Say You Love Me • (Come 'Round Here) I'm The One You Need [4] • Save Me • Oh Be My Love • Can You Love A Poor Boy • Beauty Is Only Skin Deep • I Just Don't Know What To Do With Myself • Baby, Baby • Walk On By • Swept For You Baby • More, More, More Of Your Love

DEBUT	PEAK	WKS	Gold Album Title	Pop #	$	Label & Number
			MIRACLES, The — Cont'd			
9/30/67	**3**	23	4 **Make It Happen**	28	$25	Tamla 276
			also see #11 below			
			The Soulful Shack • **The Love I Saw In You Was Just A Mirage** *[10]* • My Love For You • I'm On The Outside (Looking In) • Don't Think It's Me • My Love Is Your Love (Forever) • **More Love** *[5]* • After You Put Back The Pieces (I'll Still Have A Broken Heart) • It's A Good Feeling • You Must Be Love • Dancing's Alright • **The Tears Of A Clown** *[1]*			
2/24/68	**2**¹	48	5 **Greatest Hits, Vol. 2** [G]	7	$25	Tamla 280
			Going To A Go-Go *[2]* • **The Tracks Of My Tears** *[2]* • **I Second That Emotion** *[1]* • **Ooo Baby Baby** *[4]* • **My Girl Has Gone** *[3]* • Come On Do The Jerk *[50]* • Whole Lot Of Shakin' In My Heart (Since I Met You) *[20]* • The Love I Saw In You Was Just A Mirage *[10]* • (Come 'Round Here) I'm The One You Need *[4]* • **More Love** *[5]* • Choosey Beggar *[35]* • Save Me			
9/28/68	**❶**²	30	6 **Special Occasion**	42	$20	Tamla 290
			Yester Love *[9]* • **If You Can Want** *[3]* • **Special Occasion** *[4]* • Everybody Needs Love • Just Losing You • Give Her Up • I Heard It Through The Grapevine • Yesterday • Your Mother's Only Daughter • Much Better Off • You Only Build Me Up To Tear Me Down			
2/15/69	**6**	17	7 **Live!** [L]	71	$20	Tamla 289
			Medley: Once In A Lifetime/You And The Night And The Music • I Second That Emotion • The Tracks Of My Tears • Poinciana • Up, Up And Away • Valley Of The Dolls, Theme From • Yester Love • Walk On By • Yesterday • If You Can Want • Mickey's Monkey • Ooo Baby Baby • Going To A Go-Go			
12/6/69+	**3**	19	8 **Four In Blue**	78	$20	Tamla 297
			You Send Me (With Your Good Lovin') • Dreams, Dreams • Tomorrow Is Another Day • Hey Jude • California Soul • A Legend In Its Own Time • You've Lost That Lovin' Feelin' • We Can Make It We Can • When Nobody Cares • Don't Say You Love Me • Wish I Knew • My World Is Empty Without You			
6/6/70	**9**	16	9 **What Love Has...Joined Together**	97	$15	Tamla 301
			What Love Has Joined Together • My Cherie Amour • If This World Were Mine • You've Made Me So Very Happy • This Guy's In Love With You • And I Love Her			
10/31/70	**10**	17	10 **A Pocket Full Of Miracles**	56	$15	Tamla 306
			Flower Girl • **Who's Gonna Take The Blame** *[9]* • Darling Dear • You've Got The Love I Need • Get Ready • Bridge Over Troubled Water • Medley: Something/Something You Got • **Point It Out** *[4]* • Don't Take It So Hard • Backfire • The Reel Of Time • Wishful Thinking			
1/9/71	**30**	13	11 **The Tears Of A Clown** .... [R]	143	$15	Tamla 246
			reissue (new title) of #4 above			
9/25/71	**17**	15	12 **One Dozen Roses**	92	$15	Tamla 312
10/14/72	**31**	7	13 **Flying High Together**	46	$15	Tamla 318
1/13/73	**14**	15	14 **1957-1972** .... [L]	75	$20	Tamla 320 [2]
			recorded July 14-16, 1972 at the Carter Barron Ampitheatre in Washington D.C.			
			THE MIRACLES:			
6/9/73	**33**	5	15 **Renaissance**	174	$15	Tamla 325
5/4/74	**19**	13	16 **Smokey Robinson & The Miracles' Anthology** ....[G]	97	$30	Motown 793 [3]
11/2/74	**4**	18	17 **Do It Baby**	41	$15	Tamla 334
			Do It Baby *[4]* • Up Again • Where Are You Going To My Love • What Is A Heart Good For • **Give Me Just Another Day** *[47]* • We Feel The Same • Calling Out Your Name • A Foolish Thing To Say • Can't Get Ready For Losing You			
2/15/75	**7**	11	18 **Don't Cha Love It**	96	$15	Tamla 336
			Keep On Keepin' On (Doin' What You Do) • Sweet Sweet Lovin' • A Little Piece Of Heaven • **Don't Cha Love It** *[4]* • Got Me Goin' (Again) • **Gemini** *[43]* • Brokenhearted Girl-Brokenhearted Boy • Take It All • Gonna Tell The World (Wedding Song) • You Are Love			
10/25/75	**29**	8	19 **City Of Angels**	33	$15	Tamla 339
10/16/76	**35**	3	20 **The Power Of Music**	178	$15	Tamla 344
3/19/77	**31**	6	21 **Love Crazy**	117	$12	Columbia 34460
			MISSION '87			
			Funk group from Philadelphia: Curt Campbell and Bobby Lovett (vocals), Randy Bowland (guitar), Curt Dowd and Sid Weston (keyboards), John Martin (bass) and Russ Weekley (drums).			
11/14/87	**62**	5	**Search**		$8	Columbia 40759
			MISS JONES '98			
			Born Tarsha Jones in New York City. Female hip-hop singer.			
7/11/98	**51**	6	**The Other Woman**		$8	Motown 0949
			MISTA '96			
			Male vocal group: Darryl Allen, Bobby Wilson, Brandon Brown and Byron Reeder.			
8/17/96	**37**	10	**Mista**	183	$8	EastWest 61912
			MR. FINGERS '92			
			Born Lawrence Heard in Chicago. Dance producer/songwriter.			
8/1/92	**67**	13	**Introduction**		$8	MCA 10571
			MR. ILL '96			
			Born in Los Angeles. Male rapper.			
10/12/96	**76**	2	**The Rebirth**		$8	Cell Block 50638
			MR. KING GEORGE '97			
			Born in San Leandro, California. Male rapper.			
6/15/96	**82**	3	1 **Life Of A Kingpin**		$8	Me & Mine 2001
			KING GEORGE			
8/2/97	**80**	3	2 **Tru Player**		$8	Wrap 8157
			MR. LEE '90			
			Born Leroy Haggard in Chicago. Producer/remixer/multi-instrumentalist.			
5/19/90	**65**	13	**Get Busy**		$8	Jive 1273
			MR. MIKE '96			
			Born Michael Walls in Corpus Christi, Texas. Male rapper. Leader of **South Circle**.			
8/17/96	**5**	14	**Wicked Wayz**	29	$8	Suave House 1519
			Southwest • G's Perspective • **Where Ya Love At** *[87]* • Total Shock • Untouchable • Can You Feel Me • Wicked Wayz • Da Boogie Man • Dope Fiction • Game Affiliation • In The Midst Of Smoke • Life On Tha Line • Stop Lying			

MR. SERV-ON '97
Born Edward Smith in Washington DC. Male rapper.

| 8/16/97 | 5 | 22 | | Life Insurance | 23 | $8 | No Limit 50717 |

Let's Get It Started • My Best Friend • Head & Shoulders • Heaven Is So Close • It's Real • P Dreams • Die Rich • Who Raised Me • You Know I Would • Hustlin • Cemetery Made • 5 Hollow Points • Tryin' To Make It Out Da Ghetto • Time To Check My Fetty • Affiliated • We Ain't The Same • Throw Ya City Up • Last Wordz

MISTRESS & D.J. MADAME E, The '89
Female rap duo.

| 8/5/89 | 98 | 2 | | Leather & Lace | | $10 | Techno Kut 2001 |

MITCHELL, Billy '87
Born on 11/3/26 in Kansas City, Missouri. Jazz keyboardist.

| 7/18/87 | 38 | 11 | 1 | Faces | [I] | $10 | Vista 2501 |
| 3/18/89 | 70 | 8 | 2 | In Focus | [I] | $10 | Optimism 2502 |

MITCHELL, Blue '76
Born Richard Mitchell in 1930 in Miami. Died on 5/21/79 (age 49). Jazz trumpeter.

| 1/3/76 | 57 | 2 | | Stratosonic Nuances | | $12 | RCA Victor 1109 |

MITCHELL, Willie '68
Born on 1/3/28 in Ashland, Mississippi; raised in Memphis. Trumpeter/keyboardist/arranger/producer. Led house band and later became president of Hi record label.

| 5/4/68 | 22 | 8 | 1 | Soul Serenade | [I] | 151 | $25 | Hi 32039 |
| 3/1/69 | 28 | 11 | 2 | On Top | [I] | | $25 | Hi 32048 |

MIZELLE, Cindy '94
Born in New York City. Former session singer.

| 10/15/94 | 99 | 1 | | Cindy Mizelle | | $8 | EastWest 92255 |

MOBB DEEP '96
Rap duo from Queens, New York: Havoc and Prodigy.

| 5/13/95 | 3 | 34 | ● | 1 The Infamous... | 18 | $8 | Loud/RCA 66480 |

The Start Of Your Ending (41st Side) • Survival Of The Fittest [60] • Eye For An Eye (Your Beef Is Mines) • Give Up The Goods (Just Step) • Temperature's Rising • Up North Trip • Trife Life • Hectic • Right Back At You • Cradle To The Grave • Drink Away The Pain (Situations) • Shook Ones [52] • Party Over

| 12/7/96 | ❶[1] | 28 | ● | 2 Hell On Earth | 6 | $8 | Loud/RCA 66992 |

Animal Instinct • Drop A Gem On 'Em • Bloodsport • Extortion • More Trife Life • Man Down • Can't Get Enough Of It • Nighttime Vultures • G.O.D. [64] • Get Dealt With • Front Lines (Hell On Earth) [57] • Give It Up Fast • Still Shinin' • Apostle's Warning

MOKENSTEF '95
Female vocal trio from Los Angeles: Monifa, Kenya and Stephanie.

| 7/8/95 | 24 | 19 | | Azz Izz | 117 | $8 | OutBurst 527364 |

★118★ MOMENTS, The '80
Vocal trio from Hackensack, New Jersey: Harry Ray, Al Goodman and Billy Brown. Changed group name to Ray, Goodman & Brown in 1978. Harry Ray left in 1982, replaced by Kevin "Ray" Owens. Harry Ray died of a stroke on 10/1/92 (age 45).
1)Ray, Goodman & Brown 2)Not On The Outside, But On The Inside, Strong! 3)Look At Me

| 8/23/69+ | 8 | 22 | | 1 Not On The Outside, But On The Inside, Strong! | | $30 | Stang 1001 |

Not On The Outside [13] • I Won't Do Anything • Hurts On Me Baby • I'm So Lost [43] • Somebody Loves You, Baby • Sunday [13] • Love On A Two-Way Street [1] • Pocketful Of Heartbreak • Understanding • You Make Me Feel Good

11/21/70	36	7		2 A Moment With The Moments		$30	Stang 1003
3/13/71	24	11		3 Moments Greatest Hits	[G]	184	$20	Stang 1004
5/22/71	25	6		4 The Moments Live at the New York State Womans Prison	[L]	147	$20	Stang 1006
4/6/74	23	11		5 The Best Of The Moments	[G]		$15	Stang 1019
7/12/75	13	9		6 Look At Me		132	$15	Stang 1026
1/22/77	40	7		7 Moments With You			$15	Stang 1030

RAY, GOODMAN & BROWN:

| 1/5/80 | 2[2] | 29 | ● | 8 Ray, Goodman & Brown | 17 | $10 | Polydor 6240 |

Inside Of You [14] • Special Lady [1] • Slipped Away • The Way It Should Be • Treat Her Right • Medley: Thrill/Friends • Deja Vu • Another Day

10/11/80	16	21		9 Ray, Goodman & Brown II	84	$10	Polydor 6299
1/16/82	33	18		10 Stay	151	$10	Polydor 6341
12/27/86+	24	29		11 Take It To The Limit		$8	EMI America 17235
1/21/89	66	15		12 Mood For Lovin'		$8	EMI-Manhattan 90037

MONA LISA '96
Born on 11/20/79 in New York City. Female hip-hop singer.

| 6/29/96 | 38 | 8 | | "11-20-79" | | $8 | Island 524244 |

MJG — see EIGHTBALL & MJG

MONICA '98
Born Monica Arnold on 10/24/80 in Atlanta. Female hip-hop singer.

| 8/5/95+ | 7 | 79 | ▲[2] | 1 Miss Thang | 36 | $8 | Rowdy 37006 |

Miss Thang • Don't Take It Personal (just one of dem days) [1] • Like This And Like That [4] • Get Down • With You • Skate • Angel • Woman In Me • Tell Me If You Still Care • Let's Straighten It Out • Before You Walk Out Of My Life [1] • Now I'm Gone • Why I Love You So Much [3] • Never Can Say Goodbye • Forever Always

| 8/1/98 | 2[1] | 53↑ | ▲[2] | 2 The Boy Is Mine | 8 | $8 | Arista 19011 |

Street Symphony • The Boy Is Mine [1] • Ring Da Bell • The First Night [1] • Misty Blue • Angel Of Mine [2] • Gone Be Fine • Inside • Take Him Back • Right Here Waiting • 'Cross The Room • I Keep It To Myself • For You I Will [2]

MONIFAH　　　　　　　　　　　　　　　　　　　　　　　　　**'96**
Born Monifah Carter in New York City. Female singer/actress.

| 6/8/96 | 4 | 39 | | 1 Moods...Moments | 42 | $8 | Uptown 53004 |

You [11] • It's Alright • **You Don't Have To Love Me** [36] • Nobody's Body • Don't Waste My Time • Lay With You • **I Miss You (Come Back Home)** [16] • All I Want • You've Got My Heart • Everything You Do • You Should Have Told Me • Jesus Is Love

| 9/12/98 | 42 | 32 | | 2 Mo'Hogany | 96 | $8 | Uptown 53155 |

MONK, T.S.　　　　　　　　　　　　　　　　　　　　　　　　**'81**
Singer/drummer Thelonious Monk Jr. (son of the legendary jazz pianist), with sister Boo Boo, and Yvonne Fletcher.

| 1/24/81 | 13 | 25 | | 1 House Of Music | 64 | $10 | Mirage 19291 |
| 1/16/82 | 60 | 3 | | 2 More Of The Good Life | 176 | $10 | Mirage 19324 |

★121★　**MONTGOMERY, Wes**　　　　　　　　　　　　　**'67**
Born John Leslie Montgomery on 3/6/25 in Indianapolis. Died on 6/15/68 (age 43). Jazz guitarist.

| 3/26/66 | 7 | 23 | | 1 Goin' Out Of My Head | [I] | | $20 | Verve 8642 |

Goin' Out Of My Head • O Morro Nao Tem Vez • Boss City • Chim Chim Cheree • Naptown Blues • Twisted Blues • End Of A Love Affair • It Was A Very Good Year • Golden Earrings

| 8/27/66 | 4 | 32 | | 2 Tequila | [I] | 51 | $20 | Verve 8653 |

Tequila • Little Child (Daddy Dear) • What The World Needs Now Is Love • The Big Hurt • Bumpin' On Sunset • How Insensitive • The Thumb • Midnight Mood

| 3/11/67 | 4 | 29 | | 3 California Dreaming | [I] | 65 | $20 | Verve 8672 |

Sun Down • Oh You Crazy Moon • More, More, Amor • Without You • Winds Of Barcelona • Sunny • Green Peppers • Mr. Walker • South Of The Border (Down Mexico Way)

| 5/27/67 | 10 | 12 | | 4 Jimmy & Wes The Dynamic Duo | [I] | 129 | $20 | Verve 8678 |

JIMMY SMITH & WES MONTGOMERY
Down By The Riverside • Night Train • James And Wes • 13 (Death March) • Baby, It's Cold Outside

| 10/28/67 | 2² | 63 | ● | 5 A Day In The Life | [I] | 13 | $15 | A&M 3001 |

A Day In The Life • Watch What Happens • When A Man Loves A Woman • California Nights • Angel • Eleanor Rigby • Willow Weep For Me • **Windy** [48] • Trust In Me • The Joker

| 12/30/67+ | 17 | 5 | | 6 The Best Of Wes Montgomery | [I-K] | 56 | $15 | Verve 8714 |
| 5/11/68 | 4 | 30 | | 7 Down Here On The Ground | [I] | 38 | $15 | A&M 3006 |

Wind Song • Georgia On My Mind • The Other Man's Grass Is Always Greener • Down Here On The Ground • Up And At It • Goin' On To Detroit • I Say A Little Prayer • When I Look In Your Eyes • Know It All • Theme From The Fox

| 11/16/68 | 39 | 10 | | 8 Road Song | [I] | 94 | $15 | A&M 3012 |
| 4/18/70 | 46 | 4 | | 9 Greatest Hits | [I-K] | 175 | $15 | A&M 4247 |

MOORE, Chanté　　　　　　　　　　　　　　　　　　　　　**'94**
Born in San Francisco. Female singer.

| 10/24/92+ | 20 | 61 | ● | 1 Precious | 101 | $8 | Silas/MCA 10605 |
| 12/3/94 | 11 | 42 | | 2 A Love Supreme | 64 | $8 | Silas/MCA 11157 |

MOORE, Dorothy　　　　　　　　　　　　　　　　　　　　　**'76**
Born in 1946 in Jackson, Mississippi. Female singer.

| 5/29/76 | 10 | 18 | | 1 Misty Blue | 29 | $12 | Malaco 6351 |

The Only Time You Ever Say You Love Me • Dark End Of The Street • Funny How Time Slips Away [7] • Laugh It Off • **Misty Blue** [2] • Enough Woman Left (To Be Your Lady) • I Don't Want To Be With Nobody But You • Ain't That A Mother's Luck • Too Much Love • It's So Good

| 8/6/77 | 26 | 18 | | 2 Dorothy Moore | 120 | $12 | Malaco 6353 |
| 2/9/91 | 49 | 15 | | 3 Feel The Love | | $8 | Malaco 7455 |

MOORE, Jackie　　　　　　　　　　　　　　　　　　　　　　**'74**
Born in Jacksonville, Florida. Female singer.

| 1/12/74 | 45 | 9 | | 1 Sweet Charlie Babe | | $15 | Atlantic 7285 |
| 8/18/79 | 45 | 7 | | 2 I'm On My Way | | $10 | Columbia 35991 |

★116★　**MOORE, Melba**　　　　　　　　　　　　　　　　　**'87**
Born Melba Hill on 10/29/45 in New York City. Singer/actress. Appeared in the Broadway and movie productions of *Hair*; Tony Award-winning performer as "Lutiebelle" in the musical *Purlie*. In the movie *Def By Temptation*. Daughter of '40s singer Bonnie Davis.
　　1)*A Lot Of Love*　2)*Never Say Never*　3)*The Other Side Of The Rainbow*

2/27/71	43	4		1 Look What You're Doing To The Man	157	$15	Mercury 61321
5/3/75	49	5		2 Peach Melba	176	$12	Buddah 5629
4/24/76	32	10		3 This Is It	145	$12	Buddah 5657
12/25/76+	30	9		4 Melba	177	$12	Buddah 5677
11/4/78+	35	19		5 Melba	114	$10	Epic 35507
10/20/79	71	2		6 Burn		$10	Epic 36128
11/7/81	46	14		7 What A Woman Needs	201	$10	EMI America 17060
11/6/82	18	34		8 The Other Side Of The Rainbow	152	$8	Capitol 12243
12/24/83+	9	35		9 Never Say Never	147	$8	Capitol 12305

Love Me Right [15] • Keepin' My Lover Satisfied [14] • Got To Have Your Love • **Livin' For Your Love** [6] • It's Really Love • Never Say Never • Lovin' Touch • Lean On Me

| 4/27/85 | 24 | 34 | | 10 Read My Lips | 130 | $8 | Capitol 12382 |
| 8/30/86+ | 7 | 59 | | 11 A Lot Of Love | 91 | $8 | Capitol 12471 |

There I Go Falling In Love Again • **It's Been So Long** [6] • I'm Not Gonna Let You Go [26] • Love The One I'm With (A Lot Of Love) [5] • You Trip Me Out • A Little Bit More [1] • Falling [1] • Stay • When We Touch (It's Like Fire) • Don't Go Away

| 7/9/88 | 45 | 22 | | 12 I'm In Love | | $8 | Capitol 46944 |
| 4/28/90 | 52 | 26 | | 13 Soul Exposed | | $8 | Capitol 92355 |

MOORE, René　　　　　　　　　　　　　　　　　　　　　　**'89**
Half of the Rene & Angela duo. Male singer/songwriter. Brother of Bobby Watson of **Rufus**.

| 12/3/88+ | 59 | 26 | | Destination Love | | $8 | Polydor 837556 |

MOORE, Rudy Ray　　　'70
Born in New York City. X-rated comedian.

8/8/70	24	10		1 Eat Out More Often .... [C]		$20	Kent 001
11/7/70	49	2		2 This Pussy Belongs To Me .... [C]		$20	Kent 002

MOORE, Tina　　　'95
Born in Milwaukee. Female singer.

7/29/95	90	1		Tina Moore		$8	Street Life 75454

M.O.P.　　　'96
Rap duo from New York City: Lil' Fame and Billy Danzenie. Group name is short for Mashed Out Posse.

4/30/94	68	2		1 To The Death		$8	Select 21648
11/9/96	12	8		2 Firing Squad	94	$8	Relativity 1555
8/29/98	14	8		3 First Family 4 Life	80	$8	Relativity 1618

MORGAN, Denroy　　　'82
Born in Jamaica. Male singer.

1/16/82	52	7		I'll Do Anything For You		$10	Becket 015

MORGAN, Lee　　　'65
Born on 7/10/38 in Philadelphia. Fatally shot on 2/19/72 (age 33). Jazz trumpeter.

1/30/65	10	1		1 The Sidewinder .... [I]	25	$25	Blue Note 84157
				The Sidewinder [81] • Totem Pole • Gary's Notebook • Boy, What A Night • Hocus-Pocus			
9/17/66	16	6		2 Search For The New Land .... [I]	143	$25	Blue Note 84169
3/8/69	42	7		3 Caramba! .... [I]	190	$25	Blue Note 84289

MORGAN, Meli'sa　　　'86
Pronounced: me-lee-say. Born in Queens, New York. Female session singer. Former member of **High Fashion**.

2/15/86	4	44		1 Do Me Baby	41	$8	Capitol 12434
				Fool's Paradise [24] • Heart Breaking Decision • Do You Still Love Me? [5] • I'll Give It When I Want It • Do Me Baby [1] • Getting To Know You Better • Now Or Never • Lies			
12/19/87+	11	24		2 Good Love	108	$8	Capitol 46943
5/9/92	38	23		3 Still In Love With You		$8	Pendulum 61273

MORNING, NOON & NIGHT　　　'77
Disco group from Detroit.

5/14/77	56	6		Morning, Noon & Night		$12	Roadshow 6712

MORRISON, Mark　　　'97
Born in Hanover, Germany; raised in Leicester, England. Moved to Florida at age 14. Moved back to England in 1993.

3/29/97	30	25		Return Of The Mack	76	$8	Atlantic 82963

MOSSIE, The　　　'97

10/18/97	62	3		Have Heart Have Money		$8	Sick Wid' It 45008

MOST REQUESTED RHYTHM BAND　　　'78

12/10/77+	50	8		Got To Give It Up		$12	Magic Disc 114

MOTHER NIGHT　　　'72
Group from New York City: Ronnie Pace (vocals), Eddie Martinez (guitar), Skip McPhee (organ), Sonny McPhee, Ronnie Taylor, Bill O'Hashi and Gary Pribek (horns), Val Burke (bass) and Arnold Ramsey (drums).

6/3/72	49	2		Mother Night		$15	Columbia 31304

MOTHER'S FINEST　　　'79
Group from Dayton, Ohio: Glenn Murdoch, **Joyce Kennedy** (husband-and-wife), Gary "Mo" Moore (guitar), Michael Keck (keyboards), Jerry "Wizard" Seay (bass) and Barry "B.B." Borden (drums). Disbanded in early 1980s. Kennedy recorded solo. In 1989, Murdoch, Kennedy, Moore and Seay regrouped with drummer Dion Derek.

9/30/78+	22	26		1 Mother Factor	123	$10	Epic 35546
11/3/79	32	6		2 Mother's Finest Live .... [L]	203	$10	Epic 35976
11/4/89	84	2		3 Looks Could Kill		$8	Capitol 48988

MO THUGS FAMILY　　　'96
Gathering of rap acts from Cleveland. Assembled by **Bone Thugs-N-Harmony**. Acts include Tre, Graveyard Shift, Souljah Boy, Ken Dawg and II Tru.

11/23/96	2[1]	22	▲	1 Family Scriptures	2[1]	$8	Mo Thugs 1561
				Searchin' 4 Peace • Ghetto Bluez • Killing Fields • Mo' Murder • Ain't No Reason • Take Your Time • Welcome To My World • Thug Devotion • Here With Me • Playa In Me • No Pretender • Rumors & War • II Tru • Low Down • Family Scriptures			
6/13/98	8	33	●	2 Family Scriptures Chapter II: Family Reunion	25	$8	Mo Thugs 1632
				Mighty Mighty Warrior • Mighty Mo Thug • Heart Of It • The Queen • Riot • All Good • **Ghetto Cowboy** [14] • Believe • Urban Souljah • Ain't Said No Names • Mo Thuggin' • U Don't Own Me • Ride With A Playa • Pimpin' Ain't Easy • Otherside			

MOUZON, Alphonse　　　'83
Born on 11/21/48 in Charleston, South Carolina. Singer/pianist/drummer.

11/6/82+	24	18		1 Distant Lover	146	$10	Highrise 100
4/25/87	50	8		2 Love, Fantasy .... [I]		$10	MPC 6001
4/2/88	47	8		3 Early Spring .... [I]		$10	Optimism 6002

MOVEMENT EX　　　'91
Rap duo: Lord Mustafa Hasan Ma'd and DJ King Born Khaaliq.

12/22/90+	72	17		Movement Ex		$8	Columbia 46894

MS. TEE　　　'96

5/18/96	87	5		Female Baller		$8	Cash Money 9608

DEBUT	PEAK	WKS	Gold	Album Title	Pop #	$	Label & Number

MTUME   **'83**
Progressive-funk band led by James Mtume (pronounced: Em-too-may; vocals, percussion). Mtume had been a percussionist with **Miles Davis** in the early '70s. Included Tawatha Agee (vocals), Phil Fields (keyboards) and Raymond Johnson (bass). Agee also backed Roxy Music; recorded solo in 1987 as **Tawatha**.

10/4/80	30	12		1 In Search Of The Rainbow Seekers	119	$10	Epic 36017
5/21/83	3	30		2 Juicy Fruit	26	$8	Epic 38588

Green Light [66] • Juicy Fruit [1] • Hips • Would You Like To (Fool Around) [11] • Your Love's Too Good (To Spread Around) • Hip Dip Skippedabeat • Ready For Your Love

9/1/84	5	32		3 You, Me And He	77	$8	Epic 39473

C.O.D. (I'll Deliver) [20] • You Are My Sunshine • You, Me And He [2] • I Simply Like • Prime Time • Tie Me Up • Sweet For You And Me (Monogamy Mix) • To Be Or Not To Bop That Is The Question (Whether We Funk Or Not)

7/5/86	23	19		4 Theater Of The Mind	135	$8	Epic 40262

MUHAMMAD, Idris   **'77**
Born Leo Morris in 1939 in New Orleans. Prolific session drummer.

2/28/76	51	3		1 House Of The Rising Sun ...... [I]		$12	Kudu 27
6/4/77	16	24		2 Turn This Mutha Out ...... [I]	127	$12	Kudu 34
5/20/78	45	7		3 Boogie To The Top ...... [I]		$12	Kudu 38

MURDER SQUAD   **'95**
Project of rapper/producer Prodeje (of **South Central Cartel**).

3/4/95	12	14		S.C.C. Presents Murder Squad Nationwide	106	$8	DJ West 124040

MURDOCK, Shirley   **'87**
Born in Toledo, Ohio. Former gospel singer.

4/5/86+	9	63	●	1 Shirley Murdock!	44	$8	Elektra 60443

Be Free [86] • No More [24] • Go On Without You [5] • Truth Or Dare • Danger Zone • Teaser • **As We Lay** [5] • The One I Need • Tribute

7/16/88	19	33		2 A Woman's Point Of View	137	$8	Elektra 60791
7/13/91	22	22		3 Let There Be Love!		$8	Elektra 60951

MURPHY, Eddie   **'84**
Born on 4/3/61 in Hempstead, New York. Comedian/actor. Former cast member of TV's *Saturday Night Live*. Starred in several movies.

9/4/82	26	11	▲	1 Eddie Murphy ...... [C]	52	$10	Columbia 38180
11/26/83+	10	32	▲²	2 Eddie Murphy: Comedian ...... [C]	35	$10	Columbia 39005

Faggots Revisited • Sexual Crime • Singers • Ice Cream Man • Shoe Throwin' Mothers • Modern Women • The Barbecue • The Fart Game • Politics • Racism • Languages • TV

10/26/85+	17	25		3 How Could It Be	26	$8	Columbia 39952
8/26/89	22	14		4 So Happy	70	$8	Columbia 40970
3/13/93	80	2		5 Love's Alright		$8	Motown 6354

MURRAY, Keith   **'94**
Born in 1972 in Long Island, New York. Male singer/rapper.

11/26/94	5	32	●	1 The Most Beautifullest Thing In This World	34	$8	Jive 41555

Live From New York • Sychosymatic • Dip Dip Di • **The Most Beautifullest Thing In This World** [19] • Herb Is Pumpin' • Sychoward • Straight Loonie • Danger • **Get Lifted** [33] • How's That • The Chase • Take It To The Streetz • Bom Bom Zee • Countdown • Escapism

12/14/96	6	17		2 Enigma	39	$8	Jive 41595

Call My Name • Manifique (Original Rules) • Whut's Happnin' • **The Rhyme** [59] • Dangerous Ground • Rhymin' Wit Kel • What A Feelin' • Hot To Def • Yeah • Love L.O.D. • To My Mans • World Be Free

MUSCLE SHOALS HORNS   **'76**
Studio group from Muscle Shoals, Alabama: Harrison Calloway (vocals, trumpet), Ronnie Eades (sax), Charles Rose (trombone) and Harvey Thompson (flute).

6/5/76	26	14		Born To Get Down	154	$15	Bang 403

MUSICAL YOUTH   **'83**
Five schoolboys (ages 11 to 16 in 1983) from Birmingham, England: Dennis Seaton (vocals), with brothers Kelvin (guitar) and Michael (keyboards) Grant, and Patrick (bass) and Junior (drums) Waite. Patrick Waite died in February 1993 (age 24).

1/8/83	11	25		1 The Youth Of Today	23	$8	MCA 5389
1/28/84	50	10		2 Different Style!	144	$8	MCA 5454

MYA   **'98**
Born Mya Harrison in Washington DC. Female singer.

5/9/98	13	54	▲	Mya	29	$8	University 90166

MYCHALS, Robbie   **'90**
Born in Richmond, Virginia. Male singer.

10/27/90	71	4		Robbie Mychals		$8	Alpha Int'l. 70952

MYERS, Alicia   **'84**
Former lead singer of **One Way**.

4/18/81	41	25		1 Alicia		$10	MCA 5181
10/2/82	27	19		2 I Fooled You This Time		$10	MCA 5361
9/1/84	12	28		3 I Appreciate	186	$10	MCA 5485

MYRON   **'98**
Born Myron Davis in Cleveland. Male singer.

8/15/98	38	7		Destiny	156	$8	Island 524479

MYSTIKAL   **'97**
Born Michael Tyler in New Orleans. Male rapper.

2/18/95	14	86		1 Mystikal	103	$8	Big Boy 12
11/22/97	❶¹	61	▲	2 Unpredictable	3	$8	No Limit 41620

Born 2 Be A Soldier • Murder 2 • 13 Years • Unpredictable • **Ain't No Limit** [63] • Ghetto Child • Did I Do It • Here We Go • We Got The Clout • Still Smokin' • U Can't Handle This • The Man Right Chea • Dick On The Track • Sleepin' With Me • It Yearns • Gangstas • Shine

MYSTIKAL — Cont'd

| 12/26/98+ | ❶¹ | 32↑ | ▲ | 3 Ghetto Fabulous | 5 | $8 | No Limit 41655 |

Round Out The Tank • There He Go • Keep It Hype • **That's The Rapper** *[60]* • Ghetto Fabulous • Life Ain't Cool • I'm On Fire • Whacha Want, Whacha Need • The Stick Up • I Smell Smoke • Respect My Mind • Stack Yo Chips • Dirty South, Dirty Jerz • Yaah! • Let's Go Do It • What's Your Alias?

N

NAJEE   '87
Born in Manhattan; raised in Queens, New York. Male jazz saxophonist.

12/27/86+	12	68	●	1 Najee's Theme .... [I]	56	$8	EMI America 17241
7/16/88	23	46		2 Day By Day	76	$8	EMI-Manhattan 90096
4/28/90	17	42		3 Tokyo Blue .... [I]	63	$8	EMI 92248
7/25/92	25	44	●	4 Just An Illusion .... [I]	107	$8	EMI 99400
10/22/94	23	22		5 Share My World .... [I]	163	$8	EMI 30789
12/2/95	67	9		6 Najee Plays Songs From The Key Of Life - A Tribute To Stevie Wonder .... [I]		$8	EMI 35704
11/21/98	65	10		7 Morning Tenderness .... [I]		$8	Verve Forecast 559062

NAS   '96
Born Nasir Jones in Long Island, New York. Male rapper.

| 5/7/94 | 2¹ | 28 | ● | 1 Illmatic | 12 | $8 | Columbia 57684 |

The Genesis • N.Y. State Of Mind • Life's A Bitch • **The World Is Yours** *[67]* • Halftime • Memory Lane (Sittin' In Da Park) • One Love • One Time 4 Your Mind • Represent • **It Ain't Hard To Tell** *[57]*

| 7/13/96 | ❶⁷ | 41 | ▲² | 2 It Was Written | 1⁴ | $8 | Columbia 67015 |

The Message • **Street Dreams** *[18]* • I Gave You Power • Watch Dem Niggas • Take It In Blood • Nas Is Coming • Affirmative Action • The Set Up • Black Girl Lost • Suspect • Shootouts • Live Nigga Rap • **If I Ruled The World** *[17]*

NASH, Johnny   '72
Born on 8/19/40 in Houston. Singer/guitarist/actor. Acted in the 1959 movie *Take A Giant Step*.

| 12/7/68+ | 23 | 13 | | 1 Hold Me Tight .... | 109 | $25 | JAD 1207 |
| 10/14/72 | 10 | 28 | | 2 I Can See Clearly Now .... | 23 | $15 | Epic 31607 |

Stir It Up • That's The Way We Get By • Guava Jelly • (It Was) So Nice While It Lasted • Ooh Baby You've Been Good To Me • You Poured Sugar On Me • **I Can See Clearly Now** *[38]* • Comma Comma • We're All Alike • How Good It Is • Cream Puff • There Are More Questions Than Answers

| 7/7/73 | 49 | 6 | | 3 My Merry-Go-Round .... | 169 | $15 | Epic 32158 |

NATE DOGG   '98
Born Nathan Hale in Los Angeles. Male rapper. Former partner of **Warren G**. Cousin of **Snoop Dogg**.

| 8/8/98 | 20 | 7 | | G-Funk Classics Vol. 1 & 2 .... | 58 | $12 | Breakaway 3000 [2] |

NATURAL FOUR   '74
Vocal group from San Francisco: Chris James, Darryl Canady, Steve Striplin and Delmos Whitley.

| 5/11/74 | 36 | 12 | | 1 Natural Four .... | 207 | $20 | Curtom 8600 |
| 7/12/75 | 49 | 5 | | 2 Heaven Right Here On Earth .... | 182 | $20 | Curtom 5004 |

NATURE'S DIVINE   '79
Group from Detroit: Lynn Smith (female vocals), Robert Carter (male vocals), Duane Mitchell (guitar), Charles Woods and Marvin Jones (keyboards), Charles Green and Opelton Parker (horns), Robert Johnson (percussion), Keith Fondren (bass) and Mark Mitchell (drums).

| 10/20/79 | 17 | 12 | | In The Beginning .... | 91 | $10 | Infinity 9013 |

NAUGHTY BY NATURE   '93
Rap trio from East Orange, New Jersey: Anthony Criss, Vincent Brown and Kier Gist.

| 9/21/91 | 10 | 42 | ▲ | 1 Naughty By Nature | 16 | $8 | Tommy Boy 1044 |

Yoke The Joker • Wickedest Man Alive • **O.P.P.** *[5]* • Ghetto Bastard • Let The Ho's Go • Everyday All Day • Guard Your Grill • Pin The Tail On The Donkey • 1,2,3 • Strike A Nerve • Rhyme'll Shine On • Thankx For Sleepwalking

| 3/6/93 | ❶² | 36 | ▲ | 2 19 Naughty III | 3 | $8 | Tommy Boy 1069 |

19 Naughty III • **Hip Hop Hooray** *[1]* • Ready For Dem • Take It To Ya Face • Daddy Was A Street Corner • The Hood Comes First • The Only Ones • **It's On** *[43]* • Cruddy Clique • Knock Em Out Da Box • Hot Potato • Sleepin' On Jersey • **Written On Ya Kitten** *[53]* • Sleepwalkin' II

| 6/10/95 | ❶³ | 22 | ● | 3 Poverty's Paradise | 3 | $8 | Tommy Boy 1111 |

Poverty's Paradise • **Clap Yo Hands** *[70]* • City Of Ci-Lo • Hang Out And Hustle • It's Workin' • Holdin' Fort • Chain Remains • **Feel Me Flow** *[17]* • **Craziest** *[27]* • Sunshine • Respect Due • World Go Round • Klickow-Klickow • Slang Bang • Connections

NAYOBE   '90
Born Nayobe Catalina Gomez in Brooklyn, New York. Female singer/actress.

| 9/15/90 | 86 | 7 | | Promise Me .... | | $8 | WTG 45163 |

NDEGÉOCELLO, Me'Shell   '96
Pronounced: Nuh-DAY-gay-O-CHEL-lo. Born on 8/29/69 in Berlin, Maryland; raised in Oxon Hill, Maryland. Female singer/bassist. Last name means "free like a bird" in Swahili.

| 1/22/94 | 35 | 30 | | 1 Plantation Lullabies .... | 166 | $8 | Maverick 45333 |
| 7/13/96 | 15 | 23 | | 2 Peace Beyond Passion .... | 63 | $8 | Maverick 46033 |

NEMESIS   '93
Rap group from Dallas: The Snake, M.C. Azim and Big Al. By 1993, group consisted of Big Al, **Ron "C"**, Devo X and M.C. Joe Macc.

1/20/90	97	3		1 To Hell And Back		$8	Profile 1283
7/6/91	52	35		2 Munchies For Your Bass	183	$8	Profile 1411
7/17/93	49	8		3 Temple Of Boom	159	$8	Profile 1441
5/20/95	74	4		4 Tha People Want Bass		$8	Profile 1461

NESBY, Ann   '96
Born in Joliet, Illinois. Lead singer of **Sounds Of Blackness**.

| 6/8/96 | 27 | 60 | | I'm Here For You | 157 | $8 | Perspective 9022 |

NEVIL, Robbie   '87
Born on 10/2/60 in Los Angeles. Pop singer/songwriter/guitarist.

| 1/17/87 | 32 | 12 | | Robbie Nevil | 37 | $8 | Manhattan 53006 |

NEVILLE, Aaron   '95
Born on 1/24/41 in New Orleans. Member of The Neville Brothers. Brother Art was keyboardist of **The Meters**.

7/13/91	62	13	▲	1 Warm Your Heart	44	$8	A&M 5354
5/6/95	50	14	●	2 The Tattooed Heart	64	$8	A&M 0349
11/1/97	73	3		3 ...To Make Who I Am	188	$8	A&M 0784

★174★   NEW BIRTH, The   '73
Vocal group from Louisville, Kentucky: Londee Loren, Bobby Downs, Melvin Wilson, Leslie Wilson, Ann Bogan and Alan Frye, with instrumental backing by **The Nite-Liters**. Bogan was a member of **The Marvelettes**.

12/4/71	50	2		1 Ain't No Big Thing, But It's Growing	189	$15	RCA Victor 4526
6/17/72	40	4		2 Coming Together		$15	RCA Victor 4697
3/24/73	❶¹	29		3 Birth Day	31	$12	RCA Victor 4797

I Can Understand It [4] • Until It's Time For You To Go [21] • Got To Get A Knutt • Theme From Buck & The Preacher • Stop, Look, Listen (To Your Heart) • Easy, Evil • You Are What I'm All About

| 10/20/73+ | 7 | 44 | ● | 4 It's Been A Long Time | 50 | $12 | RCA Victor 0285 |

It's Been A Long Time [9] • Keep On Doin' It • Wildflower [17] • Ain't No Change • I'd Spend My Whole Life Loving You • Pains Of Love • Heaven Says • Come On And Dream Some Paradise

8/24/74	20	18		5 Comin' From All Ends	56	$12	RCA Victor 0494
5/31/75	17	15		6 Blind Baby	57	$12	Buddah 5636
7/26/75	45	5		7 The Best Of The New Birth	[G] 175	$12	RCA Victor 1021
7/24/76	22	12		8 Love Potion	168	$10	Warner 2953
11/5/77	28	12		9 Behold The Mighty Army	164	$10	Warner 3071

NEWCLEUS   '84
Rap group from Brooklyn, New York: brother-and-sister Ben and Yvette Cenad, with brother-and-sister Bob and Monique Crafton.

| 7/7/84 | 15 | 34 | | 1 Jam On Revenge | 74 | $10 | Sunnyview 4901 |
| 8/24/85 | 43 | 8 | | 2 Space Is The Place | | $10 | Sunnyview 4903 |

★99★   NEW EDITION   '85
Vocal group from Boston: Ralph Tresvant, Ronald DeVoe, Michael Bivins, **Bobby Brown** and Ricky Bell. Brown left in 1986; replaced by Johnny Gill in 1988. Bell, Bivins and DeVoe recorded as **Bell Biv DeVoe** in 1990. All six members reunited in 1996.

| 8/13/83 | 14 | 43 | | 1 Candy Girl | 90 | $10 | Streetwise 3301 |
| 10/13/84+ | ❶⁵ | 57 | ▲² | 2 New Edition | 6 | $8 | MCA 5515 |

Cool It Now [1] • Mr. Telephone Man [1] • I'm Leaving You Again • Baby Love • Delicious • My Secret (Didja Gitit Yet?) [27] • Hide And Seek • **Lost In Love** [6] • Kinda Girls We Like [87] • Maryann

| 11/30/85+ | 3 | 50 | ▲ | 3 All For Love | 32 | $8 | MCA 5679 |

Count Me Out [2] • A Little Bit Of Love (Is All It Takes) [3] • Sweet Thing • With You All The Way [7] • Let's Be Friends • Kickback • Tonight's Your Night • Whispers In Bed • Who Do You Trust • School • All For Love

12/21/85	45	5		4 Christmas All Over The World	[X]	$8	MCA 4987
12/20/86+	11	21	●	5 Under The Blue Moon	43	$8	MCA 5912
7/16/88	3	63	▲²	6 Heart Break	12	$8	MCA 42207

That's The Way We're Livin' • Where It All Started • If It Isn't Love [2] • N.E. Heart Break [13] • Crucial [4] • You're Not My Kind Of Girl [3] • Can You Stand The Rain [1] • Competition • I'm Comin' Home • Boys To Men

| 11/9/91 | 78 | 8 | | 7 New Edition's Greatest Hits, Volume One | [G] 99 | $8 | MCA 10434 |
| 9/28/96 | ❶¹ | 39 | ▲² | 8 Home Again | 1¹ | $8 | MCA 11480 |

Oh Yeah, It Feels So Good • Hit Me Off [1] • You Don't Have To Worry [10] • Tighten It Up • Shop Around • Hear Me Out • Something About You • Try Again • How Do You Like Your Love Served • One More Day [22] • I'm Still In Love With You [7] • Thank You • Home Again

NEW HORIZONS   '83
Family funk group from Dayton, Ohio: brothers Art (vocals), Varges (keyboards), Bart (bass) and Mark (drums) Thomas, with cousin Timothy Abrams (guitar).

| 7/30/83 | 51 | 8 | | Something New | 210 | $10 | Columbia 38709 |

NEW KIDS ON THE BLOCK   '94
Vocal group from Boston: Joe McIntyre, Donnie Wahlberg, Danny Wood, and brothers Jordan and Jon Knight. Shortened group name to NKOTB in 1992.

10/29/88+	46	68	▲⁸	1 Hangin' Tough	1²	$8	Columbia 40985
11/11/89+	67	11	▲²	2 Merry, Merry Christmas	[X] 9	$8	Columbia 45280
6/30/90	62	8	▲³	3 Step By Step	1¹	$8	Columbia 45129
2/12/94	24	4		4 Face The Music	37	$8	Columbia 52969

NKOTB

NEWMAN, David   '68
Born in Dallas. Saxophonist. Nicknamed "Fathead."

11/2/68	42	8		1 Bigger & Better	[I]	$15	Atlantic 1505
4/1/72	45	2		2 Lonely Avenue	[I]	$15	Atlantic 1600
5/1/76	53	4		3 Mr. Fathead	[I]	$12	Warner 2917

NEWTON-JOHN, Olivia   '82
Born on 9/26/48 in Cambridge, England; raised in Australia. Pop singer/actress. Co-starred in the movies *Grease*, *Xanadu* and *Two Of A Kind*. Charted 18 pop albums from 1971-98.

| 2/13/82 | 32 | 10 | ▲² | Physical | 6 | $10 | MCA 5229 |

NEW YORK CITY '73
Vocal group from New York City: Tim McQueen, John Brown, Ed Shell and Claude Johnston.

DEBUT	PEAK	WKS		Album Title	Pop #	$	Label & Number
6/23/73	35	8	1	I'm Doin' Fine Now	122	$15	Chelsea 0198
10/26/74	50	9	2	Soulful Road		$15	Chelsea 500

NEXT '98
Vocal trio from Minneapolis: R.L., Tweety and T-Low.

10/18/97+	13	73	▲	Rated Next	86	$8	Arista 18973

NICE & SMOOTH '94
Rap duo from New York City: Gregg "Nice" Mays and Darryl "Smooth" Barnes.

12/23/89+	26	34	1	Nice & Smooth		$8	Fresh 82013
10/12/91	29	46	2	Ain't A Damn Thing Changed	141	$8	RAL 47373
7/16/94	13	9	3	Jewel Of The Nile	66	$8	RAL 523336
11/15/97	75	1	4	IV: Blazing Hot		$8	Street Life 75534

NICOLE '98
Born Nicole Wray in Salinas, California; raised in Portsmouth, Virginia.

9/12/98	19	13		Make It Hot	42	$8	EastWest 62209

NIGHTINGALE, Maxine '79
Born on 11/2/52 in Wembley, England. Singer/actress.

6/12/76	38	3	1	Right Back Where We Started From	65	$12	United Artists 626
8/11/79	35	10	2	Lead Me On	45	$10	Windsong 3404
12/25/82+	35	10	3	It's A Beautiful Thing	176	$10	Highrise 101

NIKKI D '91
Born Nichelle Strong on 9/10/68 in Los Angeles. Female hip-hop singer.

9/28/91	54	8		Daddy's Little Girl		$8	Def Jam 44031

NINE '95
Born on 9/19/69 in New York City. Male rapper.

3/25/95	16	16	1	Nine Livez	90	$8	Profile 1460
8/24/96	45	6	2	Cloud 9		$8	Profile 1469

9.9 '85
Female vocal trio from Boston: Margo Thunder, Leslie Jones and Wanda Perry.

8/24/85	15	31		9.9	79	$8	RCA Victor 8049

98° '98
White vocal group from Cincinnati: brothers Nick and Drew Lachey, with Jeff Timmons and Justin Jeffre.

9/6/97	88	4	1	98°	145	$8	Motown 0796
11/14/98+	34	38↑	▲ 2	98° And Rising	14	$8	Motown 0956

95 SOUTH '93
Rap group from Miami: Natahaniel Orange, Church's, Black, Bootyman and K-Knock. By 1995, group reduced to duo of A.B. and Black. Orange formed **Quad City DJ's**.

4/3/93	20	34	1	Quad City Knock	71	$8	Toy 8117
1/28/95	29	24	2	One Mo' 'Gen	158	$8	Rip-It 9501

NITEFLYTE '79
Disco group led by **Howard Johnson** and Sandy Torano.

6/30/79	59	8		Niteflyte		$10	Ariola America 50060

NITE-LITERS, The '71
Instrumental group from Louisville, Kentucky. Provided instrumental backing for **The New Birth**.

7/31/71	31	12	1	Morning, Noon & The Nite-Liters [I]	167	$15	RCA Victor 4493
4/22/72	41	3	2	Instrumental Directions [I]	198	$15	RCA Victor 4580
11/17/73	34	8	3	Anal-Y-Sis [I]		$15	RCA Victor 0211

NO FACE '90
Rap duo from Queens, New York: Mark Skeete and Shawn Tyrone.

10/20/90	73	6		Wake Your Daughter Up		$8	No Face 46837

NO I.D. '97
Born in Chicago. Male rapper.

10/11/97	94	1		Accept Your Own & Be Yourself (The Black Album)		$8	Relativity 1227

NONCHALANT '96
Born Tanya Pointer in Washington DC. Female singer/rapper.

5/11/96	20	11		Until The Day	94	$8	MCA 11265

NORMA JEAN '78
Born Norma Jean Wright in Elyria, Ohio. Former member of **Chic** and **State Of Art**.

8/26/78	57	5		Norma Jean	134	$10	Bearsville 6983

NORTH, Freddie '72
Born in Nashville. Male singer/songwriter.

1/29/72	41	4		Friend	179	$15	Mankind 204

DEBUT	PEAK	WKS	Gold	Album Title	Pop #	$	Label & Number

NOTORIOUS B.I.G., The   **'97**
Born Christopher Wallace on 5/21/72 in Brooklyn, New York. Shot to death on 3/9/97 (age 24). Male rapper. Also known as Biggy Smallz. Married singer **Faith Evans**.

| 10/1/94 | 3 | 88 | ▲3 | 1 Ready To Die | 15 | $8 | Bad Boy 73000 |

Things Done Changed • Gimme The Loot • Machine Gun Funk • **Warning** *[flip]* • Ready To Die • **One More Chance/Stay With Me** *[1]* • **The What** *[flip]* • **Juicy** *[14]* • Everyday Struggle • Me & My Bitch • **Big Poppa** *[4]* • Respect • Friend Of Mine • Unbelievable *[flip]* • Suicidal Thoughts

| 4/5/97 | ❶4 | 90 | ▲8 | 2 Life After Death | 14 | $12 | Bad Boy 73011 [2] |

Somebody's Gotta Die • **Hypnotize** *[1]* • Kick In The Door • Fuck You Tonight • Last Day • I Love The Dough • What's Beef? • **Mo Money Mo Problems** *[2]* • Niggas Bleed • I Got A Story To Tell • Notorious Thugs • Miss U • Another • Going Back To Cali *[31]* • Ten Crack Commandments • Playa Hater • Nasty Boy • **Sky's The Limit** *[34]* • The World Is Filled... • My Downfall • Long Kiss Goodnight • You're Nobody (Til Somebody Kills You)

N-PHASE   **'94**
Vocal group from Rock Hill, South Carolina: Melvin Baxter, Al Boyd, Tevlin Williamson, Donnie Mayes and Marlon Davis.

| 11/12/94 | 58 | 4 | | N-Phase | | $8 | Maverick 45607 |

N2DEEP   **'92**
White rap duo from Vallejo, California: Jay Trujillo and T.L. Lyon.

| 7/11/92 | 29 | 43 | ● | Back To The Hotel | 58 | $8 | Profile 1427 |

NIIU   **'95**
Vocal group from New Jersey: Chuckie Howard, Chris Herbert, Don Carlis and Craig Hill.

| 1/28/95 | 90 | 3 | | NIIU | | $8 | Arista 18751 |

NUNN, Bobby   **'82**
Born in Buffalo, New York. Singer/songwriter/keyboardist.

| 10/9/82 | 14 | 26 | | 1 Second To Nunn | 148 | $10 | Motown 6022 |
| 10/8/83 | 41 | 22 | | 2 Private Party | | $10 | Motown 6051 |

NU SHOOZ   **'86**
Husband-and-wife duo from Portland, Oregon: John Smith and Valerie Day.

| 6/7/86 | 18 | 23 | ● | 1 Poolside | 27 | $8 | Atlantic 81647 |
| 6/11/88 | 49 | 7 | | 2 Told U So | 93 | $8 | Atlantic 81804 |

NUTTIN' NYCE   **'95**
Female vocal trio from California: Eboni Foster, Onnie Ponder and Teece Wallace.

| 7/15/95 | 34 | 7 | | Down 4 Whateva... | | $8 | Pocketown 41525 |

NUYORICAN SOUL   **'97**
Group is actually duo of dance producers Louie Vega and Kenny Gonzalez (known as Masters At Work).

| 4/19/97 | 58 | 13 | | Nuyorican Soul | [I] | $8 | Giant Step 1130 |

N.W.A.   **'91**
Rap group from Los Angeles: Eric **"Eazy-E"** Wright, Lorenzo **"MC Ren"** Patterson, Andre **"Dr. Dre"** Young, O'Shea **"Ice Cube"** Jackson and Antoine **"Yella"** Carraby. Dr. Dre was also a member of **World Class Wreckin Cru** and is a top record producer. Eazy-E died of AIDS on 3/26/95 (age 31). N.W.A.: Niggas With Attitude.

| 7/30/88 | 39 | 32 | ● | 1 N.W.A. And The Posse | | $10 | Macola 1057 |
| 3/4/89 | 9 | 48 | ▲2 | 2 Straight Outta Compton | 37 | $8 | Ruthless 57102 |

Straight Outta Compton • Fuck Tha Police • **Gangsta Gangsta** *[91]* • If It Ain't Ruff • Parental Discretion Iz Advised • **Express Yourself** *[45]* • Compton's N The House • I Ain't Tha 1 • Dopeman • Quiet On Tha Set

| 9/8/90 | 10 | 26 | ▲ | 3 100 Miles And Runnin' | [M] | 27 | $6 | Ruthless 7224 |

100 Miles And Runnin' *[51]* • Just Don't Bite It • Sa Prize • Real Niggaz • Kamurshol

| 6/15/91 | 2¹ | 35 | ▲ | 4 EFIL4ZAGGIN | 1¹ | $8 | Ruthless 57126 |

title actually appears as an inverse image of NIGGAZ4LIFE

Prelude • Real Niggaz Don't Die • Niggaz 4 Life • Protest • Appetite For Destruction • Don't Drink That Wine • Alwayz Into Somethin' • Message To B.A. • Real Niggaz • To Kill A Hooker • One Less Bitch • Findum, Fuckum & Flee • Automobile • She Swallowed It • I'd Rather Fuck You • Approach To Danger • 1-900-2-COMPTON • The Dayz Of Wayback

| 7/20/96 | 20 | 15 | | 5 Greatest Hits | [G] | 48 | $8 | Ruthless 50561 |

NYRO, Laura   **'72**
Born Laura Nigro on 10/18/47 in the Bronx, New York. Died of cancer on 4/8/97 (age 49). White singer/songwriter.

| 1/15/72 | 41 | 7 | | Gonna Take A Miracle | 46 | $15 | Columbia 30987 |

O

OAKTOWN'S 3.5.7   **'89**
Female rap group from Oakland: Djuana Johnican, Tabatha King, Vicious C and Sweet Pea. By 1991, reduced to a duo of Johnican and King.

| 4/29/89 | 24 | 39 | | 1 Wild & Loose | 126 | $8 | Capitol 90926 |
| 8/31/91 | 31 | 35 | | 2 Fully Loaded | | $8 | Capitol 92996 |

O'BRYAN   **'84**
Born O'Bryan Burnett in 1961 in Sneads Ferry, North Carolina. Male singer.

| 4/3/82 | 10 | 20 | | 1 Doin' Alright | 80 | $8 | Capitol 12192 |

Right From The Start • Love Has Found It's Way • **The Gigolo** *[5]* • It's Over • Doin' Alright • Can't Live Without Your Love • Mother Nature's Callin' • **Still Water (Love)** *[23]*

| 3/12/83 | 13 | 34 | | 2 You And I | 87 | $8 | Capitol 12256 |
| 5/26/84 | 3 | 37 | | 3 Be My Lover | 64 | $8 | Capitol 12332 |

Lovelite *[1]* • Be My Lover • You Gotta Use It • **Go On And Cry** *[62]* • **Breakin' Together** *[32]* • You're Always On My Mind • Too Hot • Lady I Love You

DEBUT	PEAK	WKS	Gold	Album Title	Pop #	$	Label & Number

O'BRYAN — Cont'd

| 12/27/86+ | 67 | 14 | | 4 Surrender | | $8 | Capitol 12520 |

O.C. '97
Born Omar Credle. Male rapper.

| 11/5/94 | 34 | 6 | | 1 Word...Life | | $8 | Wild Pitch 30928 |
| 9/6/97 | 16 | 9 | | 2 Jewelz | 90 | $8 | Payday 524399 |

OCEAN, Billy '86
Born Leslie Sebastian Charles on 1/21/50 in Trinidad; raised in England. Singer/songwriter.

7/11/81	27	13		1 Nights (Feel Like Getting Down)	152	$10	Epic 37406
7/31/82	53	5		2 Inner Feelings		$10	Epic 38129
8/11/84	3	70	▲²	3 Suddenly	9	$8	Jive 8213

Caribbean Queen (No More Love On The Run) [1] • Mystery Lady [10] • Syncopation • The Long And Winding Road • Loverboy [20] • Lucky Man • Dancefloor • If I Should Lose You • Suddenly [5]

| 5/24/86 | ❶¹ | 43 | ▲² | 4 Love Zone | 6 | $8 | Jive 8409 |

When The Going Gets Tough, The Tough Get Going [6] • Love Zone [1] • Without You • There'll Be Sad Songs (To Make You Cry) [1] • Bitter Sweet • It's Never Too Late To Try • Showdown • Promise Me • Love Is Forever [10]

| 3/26/88 | 7 | 35 | ▲ | 5 Tear Down These Walls | 18 | $8 | Jive 8495 |

Tear Down These Walls [27] • Gun For Hire • Stand And Deliver • The Colour Of Love [10] • Calypso Crazy • Get Outta My Dreams, Get Into My Car [1] • Soon As You're Ready • Pleasure • Because Of You • Here's To You

| 11/18/89 | 65 | 15 | ▲ | 6 Greatest Hits | [G] | 77 | $8 | Jive 1271 |

ODD SQUAD '94
Rap trio from Houston: The Fat Square Twista, Jugg Mugg and Rob Quest.

| 2/26/94 | 66 | 4 | | Fadanuf Fa Erybody!! | | $8 | Rap-A-Lot 53866 |

ODYSSEY '77
Vocal trio from New York City: Tony Reynolds, with sisters Lillian and Louise Lopez.

10/15/77	16	25		1 Odyssey	36	$10	RCA Victor 2204
12/2/78	72	2		2 Hollywood Party Tonight	123	$10	RCA Victor 3031
5/31/80	66	5		3 Hang Together	181	$10	RCA Victor 3526
7/11/81	62	7		4 I Got The Melody	175	$10	RCA Victor 3910
7/3/82	23	18		5 Happy Together		$10	RCA Victor 4240

O.G. STYLE '91
Rap duo. O.G. stands for Original Gangster.

| 5/11/91 | 69 | 11 | | I Know How To Play 'Em | | $8 | Rap-A-Lot 57151 |

OHIO PLAYERS ★32★ '74
Funk group from Dayton, Ohio: Clarence Satchell (vocals, sax), Leroy Bonner (vocals, guitar), Billy Beck (keyboards), Marvin Pierce and Ralph Middlebrook (trumpets), Marshall Jones (bass) and Jimmy Williams (drums).

1)Skin Tight 2)Fire 3)Honey

| 2/19/72 | 21 | 25 | | 1 Pain | 177 | $20 | Westbound 2015 |
| 12/30/72+ | 4 | 31 | | 2 Pleasure | 63 | $20 | Westbound 2017 |

Pleasure [45] • Laid It • Pride And Vanity • Walt's First Trip • Varee Is Love • Walked Away From You • Paint Me • Funky Worm [1] • Our Love Has Died

| 10/6/73+ | 19 | 19 | | 3 Ecstasy | 70 | $20 | Westbound 2021 |
| 5/4/74 | ❶⁶ | 46 | ● | 4 Skin Tight | 11 | $12 | Mercury 705 |

Skin Tight [2] • Streakin' Cheek To Cheek • Medley: It's Your Night/Words Of Love • Jive Turkey [6] • Heaven Must Be Like This • Is Anybody Gonna Be Saved?

| 5/18/74 | 32 | 5 | | 5 The Ohio Players | [E] | | $12 | Capitol 11291 |

first released in 1969 as Observations In Time on Capitol 192 ($50)

| 11/2/74 | 24 | 11 | | 6 Climax | [K] | 102 | $15 | Westbound 1003 |
| 11/30/74+ | ❶⁵ | 29 | ● | 7 Fire | 1¹ | $12 | Mercury 1013 |

Fire [1] • Together • Runnin' From The Devil • I Want To Be Free [6] • Smoke • It's All Over • What The Hell • Medley: Together/Feelings

| 3/1/75 | 22 | 6 | | 8 Ohio Players Greatest Hits | [G] | 92 | $15 | Westbound 1005 |
| 8/23/75 | ❶³ | 32 | ● | 9 Honey | 2¹ | $12 | Mercury 1038 |

Honey • Fopp [9] • Let's Love • Ain't Givin' Up No Ground • Sweet Sticky Thing [1] • Love Rollercoaster [1] • Alone

| 12/20/75+ | 8 | 14 | | 10 Rattlesnake | [K] | 61 | $15 | Westbound 211 |

recordings from 1972-73
Rattlesnake [69] • Introducing The Players • What It Is • Rooster Poot • Gone Forever • Hustle Bird • Spinning • Hollywood Hump • Laid It • Varee (Is Love) • She Locked It

| 6/12/76 | ❶¹ | 22 | ● | 11 Contradiction | 12 | $12 | Mercury 1088 |

Contradiction • Precious Love • Little Lady Maria • Far East Mississippi [26] • Who'd She Coo? [1] • My Life • Tell The Truth • My Ladies Run Me Crazy • Bi-Centennial

| 11/13/76 | 10 | 13 | ● | 12 Ohio Players Gold | [G] | 31 | $12 | Mercury 1122 |

Feel The Beat (Everybody Disco) [31] • Love Rollercoaster [1] • I Want To Be Free [6] • Fopp [9] • Far East Mississippi [26] • Skin Tight [2] • Fire [1] • Sweet Sticky Thing [1] • Jive Turkey [6] • Only A Child Can Love • Who'd She Coo? [1]

| 4/2/77 | 9 | 31 | | 13 Angel | 41 | $10 | Mercury 3701 |

Angel • Merry Go Round [77] • Glad To Know You're Mine • Don't Fight My Love • Body Vibes [19] • Can You Still Love Me • O-H-I-O [9] • Faith

| 7/16/77 | 58 | 1 | | 14 The Best Of The Early Years | [G] | | $15 | Westbound 304 |

DEBUT	PEAK	WKS	Gold	Album Title	Pop #	$	Label & Number

OHIO PLAYERS — Cont'd

1/7/78	11	16		15 Mr. Mean	68	$12	Mercury 13707
8/19/78	15	13		16 Jass-Ay-Lay-Dee	69	$12	Mercury 3730
4/21/79	19	20		17 Everybody Up	80	$10	Arista 4226
4/4/81	49	10		18 Tenderness	165	$10	Boardwalk 37090
9/3/88	55	12		19 Back		$10	Track 58810

O'JAYS, The ★17★ '74

Vocal group from Canton, Ohio: Eddie Levert, Walter Williams and William Powell. Named after Cleveland DJ, Eddie O'Jay (d: 4/10/98). Powell retired from touring due to illness in late 1975 (d: 5/26/77); replaced by Sammy Strain, formerly with **Little Anthony & The Imperials**. Strain returned to his former group by 1993; replaced by Nathaniel Best. Levert's sons Gerald Levert and Sean Levert are members of the trio **Levert**.

1)Ship Ahoy 2)So Full Of Love 3)Survival 4)Family Reunion 5)Emotionally Yours

| 10/14/72 | 3 | 39 | ● | 1 Back Stabbers | 10 | $12 | Philadelphia I. 31712 |

When The World's At Peace • Back Stabbers [1] • Who Am I • (They Call Me) Mr. Lucky • Time To Get Down [2] • 992 Arguments [13] • Listen To The Clock On The Wall • Shiftless, Shady, Jealous Kind Of People • Sunshine • Love Train [1]

| 5/5/73 | 37 | 7 | | 2 The O'Jays In Philadelphia ...... [E] | 156 | $12 | Philadelphia I. 32120 |

first released in 1969 on Neptune 202 ($30)

| 11/17/73+ | ❶⁵ | 47 | ▲ | 3 Ship Ahoy | 11 | $12 | Philadelphia I. 32480 |

Put Your Hands Together [2] • Ship Ahoy • This Air I Breathe • You Got Your Hooks In Me • For The Love Of Money [3] • Now That We Found Love • Don't Call Me Brother • People Keep Tellin' Me

| 7/6/74 | 2² | 27 | ● | 4 The O'Jays Live In London | [L] | 17 | $12 | Philadelphia I. 32953 |

recorded December 1973 at the Hammersmith Odeon in London
Put Your Hands Together • When The World Is At Peace • Wildflower • Back Stabbers • Sunshine [17] • Love Train

| 2/8/75 | 52 | 6 | | 5 The O'Jays ...... [E] | | $12 | Bell 6082 |

recordings from 1967-68

| 5/3/75 | ❶² | 23 | ● | 6 Survival | 11 | $12 | Philadelphia I. 33150 |

Give The People What They Want [1] • Let Me Make Love To You [10] • Survival [flip] • Where Did We Go Wrong • Rich Get Richer • How Time Flies • What Am I Waiting For • Never Break Us Up

| 11/29/75 | ❶¹ | 29 | ▲ | 7 Family Reunion | 7 | $12 | Philadelphia I. 33807 |

Unity • Family Reunion [45] • You And Me • She's Only A Woman • Livin' For The Weekend [1] • Stairway To Heaven [flip] • I Love Music [1]

| 10/2/76 | 3 | 26 | ● | 8 Message In The Music | 20 | $12 | Philadelphia I. 34245 |

Message In Our Music [1] • A Prayer • Paradise • Make A Joyful Noise • Desire Me • Darlin' Darlin' Baby (Sweet, Tender, Love) [1] • I Swear, I Love No One But You • Let Life Flow

| 5/28/77 | 6 | 26 | ● | 9 Travelin' At The Speed Of Thought | 27 | $12 | Philadelphia I. 34684 |

Travelin' At The Speed Of Thought • We're All In This Thing Together • So Glad I Got You, Girl • Stand Up • Those Lies (Done Caught Up With You This Time) • Feelings • Work On Me [7] • Let's Spend Some Time Together

| 4/29/78 | ❶³ | 29 | ▲ | 10 So Full Of Love | 6 | $12 | Philadelphia I. 35355 |

Sing My Heart Out • Use Ta Be My Girl [1] • Cry Together • This Time Baby • Brandy [21] • Take Me To The Stars • Help (Somebody Please) • Strokety Stroke

| 9/15/79 | 3 | 30 | ▲ | 11 Identify Yourself | 16 | $12 | Philadelphia I. 36027 |

Sing A Happy Song [7] • Get On Out And Party • Identify • So Nice I Tried It Twice • Hurry Up & Come Back • Forever Mine [4] • I Want You Here With Me [49] • One In A Million (Girl)

| 8/30/80 | 6 | 20 | | 12 The Year 2000 | 36 | $10 | TSOP 36416 |

The Year 2000 • To Prove I Love You • You'll Never Know (All There Is To Know 'Bout My Love) • You're The Girl Of My Dreams (Sho Nuff Real) • You Won't Fail • Girl, Don't Let It Get You Down [3] • The Answer's In You • Once Is Not Enough [44]

| 5/15/82 | 7 | 29 | | 13 My Favorite Person | 49 | $10 | Philadelphia I. 37999 |

I Just Want To Satisfy [15] • Your Body's Here With Me (But Your Mind's On The Other Side Of Town) [13] • My Favorite Person • One On One • I Like To See Us Get Down • Your True Heart (And Shining Star) • Out In The Real World • Don't Walk Away Mad

7/2/83	19	20		14 When Will I See You Again	142	$10	Epic 38518
6/9/84	35	17		15 Love And More		$10	Philadelphia I. 39367
9/21/85	20	25		16 Love Fever	121	$10	Philadelphia I. 53015
6/20/87	3	50		17 Let Me Touch You	66	$8	EMI-Manhattan 53036

Don't Take Your Love Away [60] • Lovin' You [1] • True Love Never Dies • Still Missing • I Just Want Somebody To Love Me • Let Me Touch You [5] • Undercover Lover • No Lies To Cloud My Eyes • Don't Let The Dream Get Away • Cause I Want You Back Again

| 5/27/89 | 4 | 48 | | 18 Serious | 114 | $8 | EMI 90921 |

Out Of My Mind [11] • Leave It Alone • Have You Had Your Love Today [1] • Serious Hold On Me [9] • Friend Of A Friend [55] • Never Been Better • Rainbow • Fading • Pot Can't Call The Kettle Black

| 2/16/91 | 2¹ | 48 | ● | 19 Emotionally Yours | 73 | $8 | EMI 93390 |

Don't Let Me Down [2] • Something For Nothing • Emotionally Yours [5] • Respect • Keep On Lovin' Me [4] • Love & Trust • Don't You Know True Love • That's How Love Is • Closer To You • If I Find Love Again • Keep On Pleasin' Me • Lies • Make It Feel Good

| 12/21/91+ | 78 | 5 | | 20 Home For Christmas ...... [X] | | $8 | EMI 96420 |
| 8/14/93 | 7 | 22 | | 21 Heartbreaker | 75 | $8 | EMI 89740 |

Cryin' The Blues • One Wonderful Girl • Somebody Else Will [27] • Show Me The Right Way • Trouble • Can't Let You Go • Decisions • No Can Do • Heartbreaker [66] • He Loves You

| 8/2/97 | 14 | 18 | | 22 Love You To Tears | 75 | $8 | Global Soul 31149 |

O'KAYSIONS, The '68

Group from Wilson, North Carolina: Donny Weaver, Ron Turner, Jim Spidel, Wayne Pittman, Jimmy Hennant and Bruce Joyner.

| 11/23/68 | 49 | 2 | | Girl Watcher | 153 | $40 | ABC 664 |

DEBUT	PEAK	WKS	Gold	Album Title	Pop #	$	Label & Number

OL DIRTY BASTARD   '95
Born Russell Jones on 11/15/68 in Brooklyn, New York. Male rapper. Member of **Wu-Tang Clan**.

4/15/95	2²	33	●	**Return To The 36 Chambers: The Dirty Version**	7	$8	Elektra 61659

Shimmy Shimmy Ya [47] • Baby C'mon • **Brooklyn Zoo** [40] • Hippa To Da Hoppa • Raw Hide • Damage • Don't U Know • The Stomp • Goin' Down • Drunk Game (Sweet Sugar Pie) • Snakes • Tiger Crane • The Zoo • Cuttin' Headz • Dirty Dancin' • Harlem World

OLIVER, David   '78
Born in Florida. Singer/songwriter.

4/29/78	18	14		1 David Oliver	128	$10	Mercury 1183
2/24/79	51	9		2 Mind Magic		$10	Mercury 3747
10/20/79	52	3		3 Rain Fire		$10	Mercury 3784

OL SKOOL   '98
Group from St. Louis: Pookie (vocals), Tony Love (guitar), Curtis Jefferson (bass) and Bobby Crawford (drums).

3/14/98	10	16		Ol Skool	49	$8	Universal 53104

Set You Free [94] • Come With Me • Slip Away • Still Here 4 U • Without You • Just Between You And Me • It Won't Let Go • Don't Be Afraid • Am I Dreaming [5] • Touch You

OLYMPIC RUNNERS   '75
British group: George Chandler (vocals), Joe Jammer (guitar), Pete Wingfield (keyboards), DeLisle Harper (bass) and Glen LeFleur (drums).

8/16/75	49	3		Out In Front		$15	London 658

★191★   **O'NEAL, Alexander**   '87
Born on 11/15/53 in Natchez, Mississippi. Former lead singer of Flyte Tyme which included Jimmy "Jam" Harris, Terry Lewis and Monte Moir and later evolved into **The Time**. Went solo in 1980.

4/13/85	21	74		1 Alexander O'Neal	92	$8	Tabu 39331
8/22/87	2²	44	●	2 Hearsay	29	$8	Tabu 40320

(What Can I Say) To Make You Love Me [68] • Hearsay • The Lovers [41] • Fake [1] • Criticize [4] • Never Knew Love Like This [2] • Sunshine • Crying Overtime • When The Party's Over

12/17/88+	54	5		3 My Gift To You .... [X]	149	$8	Tabu 45016
2/25/89	67	7		4 All Mixed Up .... [K]	185	$8	Tabu 44492

contains remixes of his previous hits

2/23/91	3	29	●	5 All True Man	49	$8	Tabu 45349

Time Is Running Out • The Yoke (G.U.O.T.R.) [73] • Every Time I Get Up • Somebody (Changed Your Mind) • Midnight Run • Used • All True Man [5] • Sentimental • What Is This Thing Called Love? [21] • The Morning After • Hang On • Shame On Me

2/27/93	18	21		6 Love Makes No Sense	89	$8	Tabu 9501
4/24/93	89	3		7 The Greatest Hits Of Alexander O'Neal - This Thing Called Love ..... [G]		$8	Tabu/Epic 53833
11/4/95	76	2		8 The Best Of Alexander O'Neal .... [G]		$8	Tabu/Motown 0591

O'NEAL, Shaquille   '98
Born on 3/6/72 in Newark, New Jersey. Male rapper/actor. Professional basketball player with the NBA's Orlando Magic and Los Angeles Lakers. Starred in the movies *Blue Chips*, *Kazaam* and *Steel*.

11/13/93	10	30	▲	1 Shaq Diesel	25	$8	Jive 41529

(I Know I Got) Skillz [20] • I'm Outstanding [29] • Where Ya At? • I Hate 2 Brag • Let Me In, Let Me In • Shoot Pass Slam • Boom! • Are You A Roughneck • Giggin' On Em • What's Up Doc? (Can We Rock?) [56] • Game Over

11/26/94	19	16	●	2 Shaq-Fu: da Return	67	$8	Jive 41550
12/7/96	21	33		3 You Can't Stop The Reign	82	$8	Trauma 90087
10/3/98	8	10		4 Respect	58	$8	A&M 540947

Fiend '98 • The Way It's Goin' Down • Voices • Fly Like An Eagle • Got To Let Me Know • Heat It Up • Pool Jam • Make This A Night To Remember • Blaq Supaman • Deeper • The Bomb Baby • Three Times Dope • Like What • The Buzzer

ONE CAUSE ONE EFFECT   '91
Male-female rap duo from Mississippi: Terrence Davis and Treasure Shields Redmond.

3/16/91	51	15		Drop The Axxe		$8	Capitol 94847

187 FAC   '97

9/13/97	81	2		Fac Not Fiction		$8	Penalty 3045

100 PROOF AGED IN SOUL   '71
Vocal trio from Detroit: Clyde Wilson, Joe Stubbs and Eddie Anderson. Stubbs is the brother of Levi Stubbs of the **Four Tops**.

12/12/70+	31	7		1 Somebody's Been Sleeping In My Bed	151	$15	Hot Wax 704
3/3/73	40	5		2 100 Proof Aged In Soul		$15	Hot Wax 712

101 NORTH   '88
Instrumental group: Josie James, Carl Carwell, Ellis Hall and Byron Miller.

9/3/88	76	11		101 North .... [I]		$8	Capitol 90911

112   '96
Group from Atlanta: Daron (keyboards), Marvin (strings), Mike (keyboards) and Q (drums). All share lead vocals.

9/14/96	5	62	▲	1 112	37	$8	Bad Boy 73009

Now That We're Done • Pleasure & Pain • Cupid [2] • Call My Name • Come See Me [15] • Can I Touch You • I Can't Believe • Only You [3] • I Will Be There • In Love With You • Just A Little While • Why Does • This Is Your Day • Throw It All Away

11/28/98	6	36↑	▲	2 Room 112	20	$8	Bad Boy 73021

Be With You • Love Me [8] • The Only One • Anywhere [5] • Love You Like I Did • For Awhile • Stay With Me • Whatcha Gonna Do • Crazy Over You • Funny Feelings • Never Mind • Someone To Hold • All My Love • Your Letter

★100★   **ONE WAY**   '84
Group from Detroit. Core members: Al Hudson (male vocals), **Alicia Myers** (female vocals), Dave Roberson (guitar), Kevin McCord (bass) and Gregory Green (drums). Myers left in 1980, replaced by Candyce Edwards.
1)*Lady* 2)*Who's Foolin' Who* 3)*Fancy Dancer*

9/8/79	30	9		1 Happy Feet		$10	MCA 1087
10/27/79+	43	23		2 One Way featuring Al Hudson	181	$10	MCA 3178
6/28/80	25	25		3 One Way Featuring Al Hudson	128	$10	MCA 5127
3/7/81	18	28		4 Love Is...One Way	157	$10	MCA 5163

DEBUT	PEAK	WKS	Gold	Album Title	Pop #	$	Label & Number
				ONE WAY — Cont'd			
10/3/81	**11**	22		5 Fancy Dancer	79	$10	MCA 5247
3/27/82	**8**	33		6 Who's Foolin' Who	51	$10	MCA 5279
				Cutie Pie [4] • Sweet Lady • You • You're So Very Special • **Who's Foolin' Who [34]** • Age Ain't Nothing But A Number • Give Me One More Chance • **Runnin' Away [83]**			
10/30/82	**16**	30		7 Wild Night		$10	MCA 5369
7/30/83	**27**	20		8 Shine On Me	164	$10	MCA 5428
4/28/84	**❶**[1]	37		9 Lady	58	$10	MCA 5470
				Lady You Are [5] • I'll Make It Up To You • If Only You Knew • **Don't Stop [51]** • Mr. Groove [8] • Smile • Dynomite • Can't Get Enough Of Your Love			
8/10/85	**28**	19		10 Wrap Your Body	156	$10	MCA 5552
11/15/86	**27**	38		11 One Way IX		$10	MCA 5823
				ONYX '95			
				Rap group from Jamaica, New York: Sticky Fingaz, Big D.S., Fredro Star and Suave Sonny Caesar. Big D.S. left in 1995. Fredro Star went on to act in several movies.			
4/17/93	**8**	47	▲	1 Bacdafucup	17	$8	JMJ/RAL 53302
				Bacdafucup • Bichasniguz • **Throw Ya Gunz [61]** • Here 'N' Now • Bust Dat Ass • Atak Of Da Bal-Hedz • Da Mad Face Invasion • Blac Vagina Finda • Da Bounca Nigga • Nigga Bridges • Onyx Is Here • **Slam [11]** • Stik 'N' Muve • Bichasbootleguz • **Shifftee [52]** • Phat ('N' All Dat) • Da Nex Niguz • Getdafucout			
11/11/95	**2**[1]	19		2 All We Got Iz Us	22	$8	JMJ/RAL 529265
				Last Dayz [61] • All We Got Iz Us (Evil Streets) • Purse Snatchaz • Shout • Betta Off Dead • Live Niguz • Punkmotherfukaz • Most Def • Getto Mentalitee • 2 Wrongs • Walk In New York			
6/20/98	**3**	14		3 Shut 'Em Down	10	$8	Def Jam 536988
				Raze It Up • Street Niguz • **Shut 'Em Down [61]** • Broke Willies • Rob & Vic • Face Down • Conspiracy • Black Dust • **React [62]** • Veronica • Fuck Dat • Ghetto Starz • Take That • **The Worst [64]**			
				ORGANIZED KONFUSION '94			
				Male rap duo: Pharoahe Monch and Prince Poetry.			
9/3/94	**28**	6		1 Stress: The Extinction Agenda	187	$8	Hollywood 61406
10/11/97	**29**	5		2 The Equinox	141	$8	Priority 50560
				ORIGINAL FLAVOR '94			
				Rap trio: David Willis, Antonio Hooker and Willie Sanchez.			
4/9/94	**85**	3		Beyond Flavor		$8	Atlantic 82508
				ORIGINALS, The '70			
				Vocal group from Detroit: Freddie Gorman, Crathman Spencer, Henry Dixon and Walter Gaines.			
11/22/69+	**18**	21		1 Baby, I'm For Real	174	$25	Soul 716
7/18/70	**47**	4		2 Portrait Of The Originals	198	$25	Soul 724
11/21/70	**44**	2		3 Naturally Together		$25	Soul 729
6/14/75	**51**	4		4 California Sunset		$15	Motown 826
				ORIGINOO GUNN CLAPPAZ '96			
				Male rap trio: Starang Wondah, Louieville Sluggah and Top Dog.			
11/9/96	**10**	21		Da Storm	47	$8	Duck Down 50577
				Calm Before Da Storm • NoFear [63] • Boom...Boom...Prick • Gunn Clapp • Emergency Broadcast System • Hurricane Starang • Danjer • Elements Of Da Storm • Da Storm • Wild Cowboys In Bucktown • God Don't Like Ugly • X-Unknown • Elite Fleet • Flappin			
★141★				**OSBORNE, Jeffrey** '83			
				Born on 3/9/48 in Providence, Rhode Island. Singer/songwriter/drummer. Former lead singer of L.T.D.			
6/19/82	**3**	48		1 Jeffrey Osborne	49	$8	A&M 4896
				New Love • Eenie Meenie • **I Really Don't Need No Light [3]** • **On The Wings Of Love [13]** • Ready For Your Love • Who You Talkin' To? • You Were Made To Love • Ain't Nothin' Missin' • Baby • Congratulations			
8/13/83	**3**	74	●	2 Stay With Me Tonight	25	$8	A&M 4940
				Don't You Get So Mad [3] • We're Going All The Way [16] • Stay With Me Tonight [4] • Greatest Love Affair • **Plane Love [10]** • Other Side Of The Coin • I'll Make Believe • When Are You Coming Back? • Forever Mine • Two Wrongs Don't Make A Right			
10/27/84	**7**	38	●	3 Don't Stop	39	$8	A&M 5017
				Don't Stop [6] • Let Me Know [44] • The Borderlines [7] • The Power • Is It Right • You Can't Be Serious • Crazy 'Bout Cha • Hot Coals • Live For Today			
7/5/86	**5**	29	●	4 Emotional	26	$8	A&M 5103
				We Belong To Love • **You Should Be Mine (The Woo Woo Song) [2]** • Soweto [18] • **In Your Eyes [82]** • Room With A View [29] • Emotional • A Second Chance • Love's Not Ready • Who Would Have Guessed • Come Midnight			
8/27/88	**12**	28		5 One Love-One Dream	86	$8	A&M 5205
12/15/90+	**9**	36		6 Only Human	95	$8	Arista 8620
				If My Brother's In Trouble [11] • Only Human [3] • Good Things Come To Those Who Wait • **The Morning After I Made Love To You [24]** • Lay Your Head • Baby Wait A Minute • Sending You A Love Song • Feel Like Making Love • Back In Your Arms • Nitetime • Getting Better All The Time			
12/27/97	**86**	1		7 Something Warm For Christmas .... [X]		$8	Modern 61346
				OSBORNE & GILES '85			
				Duo of Billy Osborne and Attala Zane Giles.			
10/5/85	**40**	14		Stranger In The Night		$10	Red Label 73103
				OSIBISA '71			
				Group from Ghana, West Africa: Kofi Ayivor (vocals, congas), Teddy Osei (sax), Mac Tontoh (trumpet), Jean Dikoto Mandengue (bass) and Sol Amarfio (drums).			
7/10/71	**11**	16		1 Osibisa	55	$15	Decca 75285
2/26/72	**50**	4		2 Wcyaya	66	$15	Decca 75327
10/21/72	**26**	18		3 Heads	125	$15	Decca 75368
7/7/73	**41**	10		4 Superfly T.N.T. .... [S]	159	$12	Buddah 5136
5/8/76	**58**	3		5 Welcome Home	200	$12	Island 9355

OSKAR, Lee '76
Born on 3/24/48 in Copenhagen, Denmark. Harmonica player. Member of **War**.

4/24/76	10	20		1 Lee Oskar	[I]	29	$12	United Artists 594

The Journey • The Immigrant • The Promised Land • Blisters • BLT [23] • Sunshine Keri [85] • Down The Nile • Starkite

10/7/78	29	15		2 Before The Rain	86	$10	Elektra 150
8/22/81	47	5		3 My Road Our Road	162	$10	Elektra 526

OSMONDS, The '71
Family group from Ogden, Utah: Alan, Wayne, Merrill, Jay and Donny Osmond. Charted 12 pop albums from 1971-78.

2/13/71	13	13	●	Osmonds	14	$12	MGM 4724

OUTKAST '96
Male rap duo from Atlanta: Andre Benjamin and Antoine Patton.

5/14/94	3	50	▲	1 Southernplayalisticadillacmuzik	20	$8	LaFace 26010

Myintrotoletuknow • Ain't No Thang • **Southernplayalisticadillacmuzik** [41] • Call Of Da Wild • **Player's Ball** [12] • Claimin' True • Funky Ride • Git Up, Git Out [59] • Crumblin' Erb • Hootie Hoo • Deep

9/7/96	❶²	40	▲	2 ATLiens	2¹	$8	LaFace 26029

Two Dope Boyz (In A Cadillac) • **ATLiens** [23] • **Wheelz Of Steel** [flip] • **Jazzy Belle** [25] • **Elevators (me & you)** [5] • Ova Da Wudz • Babylon • Wailin' • Mainstream • Decatur Psalm • Millennium • Extraterrestrial • 13th Floor (Growing Old)

10/17/98	2¹	42↑	▲	3 Aquemini	2¹	$8	LaFace 26053

Hold On, Be Strong • Return Of The "G" • **Rosa Parks** [19] • Skew It On The Bar-B • Aquemini • Synthesizer • Slump • West Savannah • **Da Art Of Storytellin'** [67] • Mamacita • SpottieOttieDopaliscious • Y'All Scared • Nathaniel • Liberation • Chonkfire

OZONE '82
Funk group from Nashville: Benny Wallace (vocals), Herman Brown (guitar), James Stewart (keyboards), Thomas Bumpass, William White and Ray Woodard (horns), Charles Glenn (bass) and Paul Hines (drums).

12/26/81+	61	6		1 Send It		$10	Motown 962
9/4/82	45	8		2 Li'l Suzy	152	$10	Motown 6011
5/7/83	50	11		3 Glasses	201	$10	Motown 6037

P

PACKERS, The '66
Instrumental group formed by Charles "Packy" Axton (tenor sax). Axton, son of Estelle Axton, co-owner of Stax/Volt, had been in the **Mar-Keys**.

2/12/66	7	3		Hole In The Wall	[I]		$20	Pure Soul 1001

Hole In The Wall [5] • There's No Tomorrow • Pure Soul • Goodness, Goodness • Headin' Home • Sweet Grapes • Hollywood Baby • Go Head On • Hoppin' John • I'm Converted • Cherio O

PAGAN, Ralfi '71

8/21/71	50	2		With Love		$15	Fania 397

PAGE, Gene '75
Born in 1940 in Los Angeles. Died on 8/24/98 (age 58). Keyboardist/arranger/conductor.

2/15/75	41	5		1 Hot City	[I]	156	$12	Atlantic 18111
2/14/76	45	4		2 Lovelock!	[I]		$12	Atlantic 18161

P.A. (PARENTAL ADVISORY) '98
Male rap trio from Atlanta: James Hollins, Kawan Prather and Maurice Sinclair.

8/1/98	90	1		Straight No Chase		$8	DreamWorks 50028

PAPERBOY '93
Born in Los Angeles. Male rapper.

2/13/93	26	28	●	The Nine Yards	48	$8	Next Plateau 1012

PARIS '94
Born Oscar Jackson on 10/29/67 in San Francisco. Male rapper.

12/8/90+	41	16		1 The Devil Made Me Do It	158	$8	Tommy Boy 1030
12/12/92	23	15		2 Sleeping With The Enemy	182	$8	Scarface 100
10/22/94	20	9		3 Guerrilla Funk	128	$8	Priority 53882

PARIS, Mica '89
Pronounced: MEE-sha. Born Michelle Wallen on 4/27/69 in London. Female singer.

5/27/89	29	24		1 So Good	86	$8	Island 90970
3/30/91	58	15		2 Contribution		$8	Island 846814
6/26/93	99	1		3 Whisper A Prayer		$8	Island 514776

★98★ PARKER, Ray Jr./Raydio '82
Born on 5/1/54 in Detroit. Singer/songwriter/guitarist. Formed **Raydio** in 1977 with Arnell Carmichael, **Jerry Knight**, Larry Tolbert, Darren Carmichael and Charles Fearing. Parker went solo in 1982. Knight later recorded in duo Ollie & Jerry.
1)A Woman Needs Love 2)The Other Woman 3)Rock On

RAYDIO:

3/4/78	8	24	●	1 Raydio	27	$10	Arista 4163

Is This A Love Thing [20] • You Need This (To Satisfy That) • Betcha You Can't Love Me Just Once • Honey I'm Rich [43] • Jack And Jill [5] • Me • Let's Go All The Way • Get Down

4/21/79	4	32	●	2 Rock On	45	$10	Arista 4212

What You Waitin' For • Hot Stuff • You Can't Change That [3] • Rock On • More Than One Way To Love A Woman [25] • When You're In Need Of Love • Goin' Thru School And Love • Honey I'm A Star

RAY PARKER JR. & RAYDIO:

DEBUT	PEAK	WKS	Gold	Album Title	Pop #	$	Label & Number
4/19/80	6	26	●	3 Two Places At The Same Time	33	$10	Arista 9515

It's Time To Party Now • Until The Morning Comes • **Two Places At The Same Time** *[6]* • Tonight's The Night • A Little Bit Of You • Everybody Makes Mistakes • **Can't Keep From Cryin'** *[57]* • For Those Who Like To Groove *[14]*

| 4/18/81 | ❶² | 29 | ● | 4 A Woman Needs Love | 13 | $10 | Arista 9543 |

A Woman Needs Love (Just Like You Do) *[1]* • **It's Your Night** *[73]* • That Old Song • All In The Way You Get Down • You Can't Fight What You Feel • Old Pro • Still In The Groove • So Into You

RAY PARKER JR.:

| 5/8/82 | ❶¹ | 28 | ● | 5 The Other Woman | 11 | $8 | Arista 9590 |

The Other Woman *[2]* • Streetlove • Stay The Night • **It's Our Own Affair** *[44]* • Let Me Go *[3]* • Let's Get Off • Stop, Look Before You Love • Just Havin' Fun

12/18/82+	17	25		6 Greatest Hits ....[G]	51	$8	Arista 9612
12/3/83	18	24		7 Woman Out Of Control	45	$8	Arista 8087
12/22/84+	36	12	●	8 Chartbusters ....[G]	60	$8	Arista 8266
11/9/85	48	12		9 Sex And The Single Man	65	$8	Arista 8280
10/17/87	27	24		10 After Dark	86	$8	Geffen 24124
8/24/91	97	3		11 I Love You Like You Are		$8	MCA 10327

PARKER, Robert　'66
Born on 10/14/30 in Crescent City, Louisiana. Singer/saxophonist.

| 8/13/66 | 16 | 9 | | Barefootin' .... | | $30 | Nola 1001 |

PARLET　'78
Female vocal trio portion of **George Clinton**'s organization: Janice Evans, Jeanette Washington and Shirley Hayden.

| 5/6/78 | 55 | 3 | | 1 Pleasure Principle | | $12 | Casablanca 7094 |
| 6/16/79 | 73 | 3 | | 2 Invasion Of The Booty Snatchers .... | | $12 | Casablanca 7146 |

★93★　**PARLIAMENT**　'79
Ensemble of nearly 40 musicians assembled by **George Clinton** that also recorded as **Funkadelic**. Members included brothers Phelps and **William "Bootsy" Collins**, Eddie Hazel, Clarence "Fuzzy" Haskins, Bernie Worrell and Frank Waddy. Parliament/Funkadelic inducted into the Rock and Roll Hall of Fame in 1997.
1)*Motor-Booty Affair* 2)*Funkentelechy Vs. The Placebo Syndrome* 3)*The Clones Of Dr. Funkenstein*

8/24/74	17	10		1 Up For The Down Stroke	201	$40	Casablanca 7002
5/3/75	18	14		2 Chocolate City	91	$40	Casablanca 7014
2/14/76	4	33	▲	3 Mothership Connection	13	$30	Casablanca 7022

P. Funk (Wants To Get Funked Up) *[33]* • **Star Child (Mothership Connection)** *[26]* • Unfunky UFO • Supergroovalisticprosifunkstication (The Thumps Bump) • Handcuffs • **Tear The Roof Off The Sucker (Give Up The Funk)** *[15]* • Night Of The Thumpasorus Peoples

| 10/23/76 | 3 | 24 | ● | 4 The Clones Of Dr. Funkenstein | 20 | $30 | Casablanca 7034 |

Gamin' On Ya • **Dr. Funkenstein** *[43]* • Children Of Production • Gettin' To Know You • **Do That Stuff** *[22]* • Everything Is On The One • I've Been Watching You (Move Your Sexy Body) • Funkin' For Fun

| 5/7/77 | 6 | 21 | | 5 Parliament Live/P. Funk Earth Tour　[L] | 29 | $40 | Casablanca 7053 [2] |

P. Funk (Wants To Get Funked Up) • Dr. Funkenstein's Supergroovalisticprosifunkstication Medley: Let's Take It To The Stage/Take Your Dead Ass Home (Say Som'n Nasty) • Do That Stuff • The Landing (Of The Holy Mothership) • The Undisco Kidd (The Girl Is Bad!) • Children Of Production • Star Child (Mothership Connection) • Swing Down, Sweet Chariot • This Is The Way We Funk With You • Dr. Funkenstein • Gamin' On Ya! • Medley: Tear The Roof Off The Sucker (Give Up The Funk)/Get Off Your Ass And Jam • Night Of The Thumpasorus Peoples • Fantasy Is Reality

| 12/24/77+ | 2³ | 33 | ▲ | 6 Funkentelechy Vs. The Placebo Syndrome | 13 | $30 | Casablanca 7084 |

Bop Gun (Endangered Species) *[14]* • Sir Nose D'Voidoffunk (Pay Attention - B3M) • Wizard Of Finance • **Funkentelechy** *[27]* • Placebo Syndrome • **Flash Light** *[1]*

| 12/16/78+ | 2⁷ | 22 | ● | 7 Motor-Booty Affair | 23 | $30 | Casablanca 7125 |

Mr. Wiggles • **Rumpofsteelskin** *[63]* • (You're A Fish And I'm A) Water Sign • **Aqua Boogie (A Psychoalphadiscobetabioaquadoloop)** *[1]* • One Of Those Funky Things • Liquid Sunshine • The Motor-Booty Affair • Deep

| 12/22/79+ | 3 | 23 | ● | 8 Gloryhallastoopid (Or Pin The Tale On The Funky) | 44 | $30 | Casablanca 7195 |

(Gloryhallastoopid) Pin The Tale On The Funky • **Party People** *[39]* • **The Big Bang Theory** *[50]* • The Freeze (Sizzaleenmean) • Colour Me Funky • **Theme From The Black Hole** *[8]* • May We Bang You?

| 12/27/80+ | 16 | 14 | | 9 Trombipulation | 61 | $30 | Casablanca 7249 |
| 6/5/93 | 79 | 3 | | 10 Tear The Roof Off - 1974-1980 ....[G] | | $12 | Casablanca 514417 [2] |

PARRISH, Man　'83
Mysterious techno performer.

| 2/12/83 | 43 | 13 | | Man Parrish | | $10 | Importe/12 320 |

PARTNERS-N-CRIME　'98
Male rap duo: Meanor and Kangol.

| 11/25/95 | 98 | 1 | | 1 Pump Tha Party (Puttin' In Work) .... | | $8 | Big Boy 11 |
| 2/14/98 | 73 | 5 | | 2 What'cha Wanna Do? .... | | $8 | Upper Level 0006 |

PASADENAS, The　'89
British vocal group: brothers Michael and David Milliner, with Jeff Brown, John Banfield and Hammish Seelochan. Banfield is the brother of Susan Banfield of **The Cookie Crew**.

| 3/25/89 | 49 | 13 | | To Whom It May Concern .... | 89 | $8 | Columbia 45065 |

PASSION　'96
Born in 1974 in Oakland. Female rapper.

| 9/14/96 | 85 | 1 | | Baller's Lady .... | | $8 | MCA 11338 |

PATRA　'94
Born Dorothy Smith on 11/22/72 in Kingston, Jamaica. Female dance-reggae singer.

| 10/23/93+ | 15 | 51 | ● | 1 Queen Of The Pack .... | 103 | $8 | Epic 53763 |
| 9/2/95 | 28 | 9 | | 2 Scent Of Attraction .... | 151 | $8 | 550 Music/Epic 67094 |

PATTERSON, Kellee   '77
Born in Gary, Indiana. Singer/actress.

| 10/22/77 | 38 | 12 | | Be Happy | 201 | $10 | Shadybrook 007 |

PATTERSON, Rahsaan   '97
Born in New York City. Male singer/songwriter.

| 2/15/97 | 48 | 40 | | Rahsaan Patterson | | $8 | MCA 11559 |

★134★   **PAUL, Billy**   '73
Born Paul Williams on 12/1/34 in Philadelphia. Singer/songwriter.
1)360 Degrees Of Billy Paul 2)Live In Europe 3)War Of The Gods

8/1/70	12	15		1 Ebony Woman	183	$20	Neptune 201
				also see #4 below			
10/9/71+	42	17		2 Going East	197	$12	Philadelphia I. 30580
11/25/72+	❶²	29	●	3 360 Degrees Of Billy Paul	17	$12	Philadelphia I. 31793
				Brown Baby • I'm Just A Prisoner • It's Too Late • Me And Mrs. Jones [1] • Am I Black Enough For You [29] • Let's Stay Together • Your Song • I'm Gonna Make It This Time			
5/12/73	43	4		4 Ebony Woman [R]	186	$12	Philadelphia I. 32118
				reissue of #1 above			
11/24/73+	12	35		5 War Of The Gods	110	$12	Philadelphia I. 32409
7/6/74	10	12		6 Live In Europe [L]	187	$10	Philadelphia I. 32952
				Medley: Introduction/War Of The Gods/Brown Baby • Thanks For Saving My Life • Me And Mrs. Jones • Your Song			
3/1/75	20	10		7 Got My Head On Straight	140	$10	Philadelphia I. 33157
12/13/75+	17	17		8 When Love Is New	139	$10	Philadelphia I. 33843
1/22/77	27	17		9 Let 'Em In	88	$10	Philadelphia I. 34389
1/7/78	36	5		10 Only The Strong Survive	152	$10	Philadelphia I. 34923
7/16/88	61	7		11 Wide Open		$10	Ichiban 1025

PAYNE, Freda   '71
Born on 9/19/45 in Detroit. Female singer.

8/15/70	17	13		1 Band Of Gold	60	$20	Invictus 7301
6/19/71	12	14		2 Contact	76	$20	Invictus 7307
4/8/72	44	12		3 The Best Of Freda Payne [G]	152	$20	Invictus 9804
8/17/74	55	5		4 Payne & Pleasure		$15	Dunhill/ABC 50176

★185★   **PEACHES & HERB**   '79
Vocal duo from Washington DC: Herb Fame (b: Herbert Feemster in 1942) and Francine Barker (b: Francine Hurd in 1947). Marlene Mack filled in for Barker from 1968-69. Re-formed with Fame and Linda Green in 1977.

3/18/67	4	26		1 Let's Fall In Love	30	$25	Date 4004
				Let's Fall In Love [11] • Just One Look • I'm In The Mood For Love • Because Of You • Time After Time • Will You Love Me Tomorrow • Close Your Eyes [4] • True Love • We Belong Together • When I Fall In Love • I Will Watch Over You			
9/9/67	12	10		2 For Your Love	135	$25	Date 4005
2/10/68	28	3		3 Golden Duets		$25	Date 4007
9/28/68	48	2		4 Peaches & Herb's Greatest Hits [G]	187	$25	Date 4012
11/25/78+	❶⁸	44	▲	5 2 Hot!	2⁶	$10	Polydor 6172
				We've Got Love [25] • Shake Your Groove Thing [4] • Reunited [1] • All Your Love (Give It Here) • Love It Up Tonight • Four's A Traffic Jam • The Star Of My Life • Easy As Pie			
11/17/79	18	21	●	6 Twice The Fire	31	$10	Polydor 6239
10/18/80	51	10		7 Worth The Wait	120	$10	Polydor 6298

PEARSON, Dunn Jr.   '90
Born in Los Angeles. Singer/songwriter/keyboardist.

| 3/31/90 | 72 | 7 | | Color Tapestry | | $8 | Compose 9904 |

PEARSON, Mr. Danny   '79
Born in Racine, Wisconsin. Singer/songwriter.

| 2/17/79 | 72 | 4 | | Barry White Presents Danny Pearson | | $10 | Unlimited Gold 35633 |

PEASTON, David   '89
Born in St. Louis. Singer/songwriter. Nephew of **Fontella Bass**.

7/15/89	7	46		1 Introducing...David Peaston	113	$8	Geffen 24228
				Two Wrongs (Don't Make It Right) [3] • God Bless The Child • Take Me Now [77] • Tonight • We're All In This Together [11] • Can I? [14] • Eyes Of Love • Don't Say No • Thank You For The Moment			
11/30/91	80	16		2 Mixed Emotions		$8	MCA 10383

PEBBLES   '88
Born Perri Alette McKissack on 8/29/65 in Oakland. Nicknamed "Pebbles" by her family for her resemblance to cartoon character Pebbles Flintstone. Married singer/songwriter/producer L.A. Reid of **The Deele** in 1989; later divorced. Cousin of **Cherrelle**. Put together/managed TLC.

1/16/88	5	42	▲	1 Pebbles	14	$8	MCA 42094
				Girlfriend [1] • Two Hearts • First Step (In The Right Direction) • Take Your Time [3] • Slip Away • Mercedes Boy [1] • Do Me Right [67] • Love/Hate • Baby Love • Give Me Your Love			
10/6/90	12	52	●	2 Always	37	$8	MCA 10025
9/30/95	43	3		3 Straight From My Heart		$8	MCA 11190

PEDICIN, Michael Jr.   '88
Born in Philadelphia. Male saxophonist. His father recorded in the late 1950s.

| 3/5/88 | 70 | 6 | | City Song [I] | | $10 | Optimism 3106 |

PEEBLES, Ann   '74
Born on 4/27/47 in St. Louis. Female singer.

2/20/71	40	4		1 Part Time Love		$20	Hi 32059
5/13/72	42	5		2 Straight From The Heart	188	$20	Hi 32065
4/13/74	25	11		3 I Can't Stand The Rain	155	$20	Hi 32079

DEBUT	PEAK	WKS	Gold	Album Title	Pop #	$	Label & Number

PEEBLES, Ann — Cont'd

| 12/20/75+ | **41** | 6 | | 4 Tellin' It .... | | $20 | Hi 32091 |

PENDERGRASS, Teddy ★27★   **'79**
Born on 3/26/50 in Philadelphia. Lead singer for **Harold Melvin & The Blue Notes** from 1970-76. Acted in the 1982 movie *Soup For One*. Auto accident on 3/18/82 left him partially paralyzed.

    1)Teddy 2)Life Is A Song Worth Singing 3)Joy

3/19/77	**5**	33	▲	1 **Teddy Pendergrass**	17	$10	Philadelphia I. 34390
				You Can't Hide From Yourself • Somebody Told Me • Be Sure • And If I Had • **I Don't Love You Anymore** *[5]* • The Whole Town's Laughing At Me *[16]* • Easy, Easy, Got To Take It Easy • The More I Get, The More I Want			
6/24/78	**❶²**	38	▲	2 **Life Is A Song Worth Singing**	11	$10	Philadelphia I. 35095
				Life Is A Song Worth Singing • **Only You** *[22]* • Cold, Cold World • Get Up, Get Down, Get Funky, Get Loose • **Close The Door** *[1]* • It Don't Hurt Now • When Somebody Loves You Back			
6/30/79	**❶⁸**	34	▲	3 **Teddy**	5	$10	Philadelphia I. 36003
				Come Go With Me *[14]* • **Turn Off The Lights** *[2]* • I'll Never See Heaven Again • All I Need Is You • If You Know Like I Know • Do Me • Set Me Free • Life Is A Circle			
12/22/79+	**5**	20	●	4 **Teddy Live! Coast To Coast** [L]	33	$12	Philadelphia I. 36294 [2]
				Life Is A Song Worth Singing • Only You • Medley: If You Don't Know Me By Now/The Love I Lost/Bad Luck/Wake Up Everybody • When Somebody Loves You Back • Get Up, Get Down, Get Funky, Get Loose • Come Go With Me • Close The Door • Turn Off The Lights • Do Me • Where Did All The Lovin' Go • **It's You I Love** *[44]* • **Shout And Scream** *[21]*			
8/16/80	**3**	39	▲	5 **TP**	14	$10	Philadelphia I. 36745
				Is It Still Good To Ya • Take Me In Your Arms Tonight • I Just Called To Say • **Can't We Try** *[3]* • Feel The Fire • Girl You Know • **Love T.K.O.** *[2]* • Let Me Love You			
10/3/81	**6**	40	●	6 **It's Time For Love**	19	$10	Philadelphia I. 37491
				I Can't Live Without Your Love *[10]* • **You're My Latest, My Greatest Inspiration** *[4]* • Nine Times Out Of Ten *[flip]* • Keep On Lovin' Me • It's Time For Love • She's Over Me • I Can't Leave Your Love Alone • You Must Live On			
8/21/82	**6**	27		7 **This One's For You**	59	$10	Philadelphia I. 38118
				I Can't Win For Losing *[32]* • This One's For You • Loving You Was Good • **This Gift Of Life** *[31]* • Now Tell Me That You Love Me • It's Up To You (What You Do With Your Life) • Don't Leave Me Out Along The Road • Only To You			
11/26/83	**9**	22		8 **Heaven Only Knows**	123	$10	Philadelphia I. 38646
				Crazy About Your Love • Judge For Yourself • **I Want My Baby Back** *[61]* • Life Is For Living • You And Me For Right Now • Just Because You're Mine • Heaven Only Knows • Don't Ever Stop (Giving Your Love To Me)			
6/23/84	**4**	39	●	9 **Love Language**	38	$8	Asylum 60317
				In My Time • So Sad The Song • Hot Love • Stay With Me • **Hold Me** *[5]* • **You're My Choice Tonight (Choose Me)** *[15]* • Love • This Time Is Ours			
1/5/85	**68**	3		10 **Greatest Hits** [G]		$8	Philadelphia I. 39252
11/16/85+	**6**	43		11 **Workin' It Back**	96	$8	Asylum 60447
				Love 4/2 *[6]* • One Of Us Fell In Love • **Never Felt Like Dancin'** *[21]* • **Let Me Be Closer** *[67]* • Lonely Color Blue • Want You Back In My Life • Workin' It Back • Love Emergency			
5/28/88	**2¹**	41	●	12 **Joy**	54	$8	Elektra 60775
				Joy *[1]* • 2 A.M. *[3]* • Good To You • I'm Ready • **Love Is The Power** *[57]* • This Is The Last Time • Through The Falling Rain (Love Story) • Can We Be Lovers			
3/30/91	**4**	26		13 **Truly Blessed**	49	$8	Elektra 60891
				She Knocks Me Off My Feet • **It Should've Been You** *[1]* • Don't You Ever Stop • It's Over • **Glad To Be Alive** *[31]* • How Can You Mend A Broken Heart • **I Find Everything In You** *[31]* • Spend The Night • With You • We Can't Keep Going On (Like This) • Truly Blessed			
10/23/93	**13**	42		14 **A Little More Magic**	92	$8	Elektra 61497
5/3/97	**24**	24		15 **You And I**	137	$8	Surefire 13045
4/18/98	**65**	14		16 **Greatest Hits** .... [G]		$8	Right Stuff 36994
12/26/98	**83**	2		17 **This Christmas (I'd Rather Have Love)** .... [X]		$8	Surefire 13048

PENISTON, Ce Ce   **'92**
Born on 9/6/69 in Dayton, Ohio; raised in Phoenix. Female singer.

3/7/92	**13**	52	●	1 **Finally**	70	$8	A&M 5381
2/12/94	**20**	34		2 **Thought 'Ya Knew**	96	$8	A&M 0138
9/28/96	**48**	4		3 **I'm Movin' On**		$8	A&M 0562

PENN, Dawn   **'94**
Born in Kingston, Jamaica. Reggae singer/songwriter.

| 5/21/94 | **83** | 3 | | **No, No, No** .... | | $8 | Big Beat 92365 |

PENTHOUSE PLAYERS CLIQUE   **'92**
Male rap duo: Playa Hamm and Tweed Cadillac.

| 5/16/92 | **28** | 19 | | **Paid The Cost** .... | 76 | $8 | Ruthless 57181 |

PEOPLE'S CHOICE   **'75**
Group from Philadelphia: Frankie Brunson (vocals), Guy Fiske and Donell Jordan (guitars), Donald Ford (keyboards), Roger Andrews (bass) and David Thompson (drums).

9/20/75	**7**	11		1 **Boogie Down U.S.A.**	56	$12	TSOP 33154
				Do It Any Way You Wanna *[1]* • Are You Sure • Mickey D's • I'm Leaving You • The Sooner You Get Here • Boogie Down U.S.A. • Nursery Rhymes *[22]* • Party Is A Groovy Thing *[45]* • If You Want Me Back • Don't Send Me Away			
6/26/76	**38**	6		2 **We Got The Rhythm**	174	$12	TSOP 34124

PERFECT GENTLEMEN '90
Vocal trio from Boston: Corey Blakely, Maurice Starr Jr. and Tyrone Sutton. Starr's father managed and produced **New Edition** and **New Kids On The Block.**

					Pop #	$	Label & Number
6/9/90	39	16		Rated PG	72	$8	Columbia 46070

PERRI '90
Vocal group consisting of sisters Carolyn, Darlene, Lori and Sharon Perry.

6/10/89	81	9		1 The Flight		$8	Zebra/MCA 42017
9/1/90	58	7		2 Tradewinds		$8	MCA 6386

PERRY, Phil '91
Born on 1/1/52 in Springfield, Illinois. Former session singer.

3/30/91	17	35		1 The Heart Of The Man	191	$8	Capitol 92115
10/15/94+	50	47		2 Pure Pleasure		$8	GRP 4026
2/28/98	67	17		3 One Heart One Love		$8	Private Music 82163

PERSON, Houston '70
Born on 11/10/34 in Florence, South Carolina. Tenor saxophonist.

3/14/70	32	12		1 Goodness	[I]	$15	Prestige 7678
1/24/76	33	7		2 Get Out'a My Way!	[I]	$12	20th Century 219

PERSUADERS, The '72
Vocal group from New York City: Douglas Scott, Willie Holland, James Barnes and Charles Stodghill. New lineup in 1974 consisted of Thomas Lee Hill, Douglas Scott, Richard Gant and Willie Coleman.

3/25/72	35	7		1 Thin Line Between Love And Hate	141	$25	Win Or Lose 387
4/7/73	39	5		2 The Persuaders	178	$20	Atco 7021
6/15/74	36	10		3 Best Thing That Ever Happened To Me		$20	Atco 7046

PERSUASIONS, The '72
Vocal group from New York City: Jerry Lawson, Joseph Russell, Jayotis Washington, Herbert Rhoad and Jimmy Hayes. Rhoad died of a stroke on 12/8/88 (age 44).

8/7/71	32	10		1 We Came To Play	189	$25	Capitol 791
2/12/72	16	16		2 Street Corner Symphony	88	$25	Capitol 872
10/14/72	40	6		3 Spread The Word		$25	Capitol 11101
6/16/73	49	2		4 We Still Ain't Got No Band	178	$20	MCA 326
6/15/74	52	4		5 More Than Before	207	$15	A&M 3635

PET SHOP BOYS '86
British duo: Neil Tennant (vocals) and Christopher Lowe (keyboards).

5/24/86	34	16	▲	Please	7	$8	EMI America 17193

PETTUS, Giorge '87
Born in Long Island, New York. Male singer.

11/21/87	74	1		Giorge Pettus		$8	MCA 5826

P. FUNK ALL-STARS '96
Funk group led by **George Clinton**, containing members of **Funkadelic** and **Parliament.**

1/14/84	48	15		1 Urban Dancefloor Guerillas		$10	CBS Associated 39168
6/29/96	27	9		2 T.A.P.O.A.F.O.M. - The Awesome Power Of A Fully-Operational Mothership **GEORGE CLINTON & THE P-FUNK ALLSTARS**	121	$8	550 Music/Epic 67144

PHAJJA '97
Female vocal trio from Chicago: sisters Kena and Nakia Epps, with Karen Johnson.

7/12/97	79	1		Seize The Moment		$8	Warner 46319

PHARCYDE, The '95
Male rap group from Los Angeles: Tre Hardson, Imani Wilcox, Romye Robinson and Derrick Stewart.

12/12/92+	23	40	●	1 Bizarre Ride II The Pharcyde	75	$8	Delicious Vinyl 92222
12/2/95	17	21		2 Labcabincalifornia	37	$8	Delicious Vinyl 35102

PHILLIP & LLOYD '76
Vocal duo of Phillip James and Lloyd Campbell.

1/24/76	58	3		The Blues Busters		$12	Scepter 5121

PHILLIPS, Esther '71
Born Esther Mae Jones on 12/23/35 in Galveston, Texas; raised in Los Angeles. Died of liver failure on 8/7/84 (age 49). Singer/multi-instrumentalist. Discovered by Johnny Otis. Toured and recorded with Otis as "Little Esther." Assumed name "Esther Phillips" in 1962. Bouts with drug addiction frequently interrupted her career and eventually led to her death.

11/14/70+	7	24		1 Burnin'	[L]	115	$25	Atlantic 1565

recorded at Freddie Jett's Pied Piper Club in Los Angeles
Don't Let Me Lose This Dream • And I Love Him • Cry Me A River Blues • I'm Gettin' 'Long Alright • Release Me • Makin' Whoopee • If It's The Last Thing I Do • Shangri-La • Please Send Me Someone To Love

2/26/72	16	17		2 From A Whisper To A Scream	137	$15	Kudu 05
12/16/72+	26	16		3 Alone Again, Naturally	177	$15	Kudu 09
1/19/74	17	9		4 Black-Eyed Blues	205	$15	Kudu 14
9/14/74	46	8		5 Performance		$15	Kudu 18
8/16/75	13	13		6 What A Diff'rence A Day Makes	32	$15	Kudu 23
1/31/76	35	7		7 Confessin' The Blues	[L]	170	$15	Atlantic 1680

side 2: recorded at Freddie Jett's Pied Piper Club in Los Angeles

3/13/76	33	9		8 For All We Know		$15	Kudu 28
1/8/77	40	5		9 Capricorn Princess	150	$15	Kudu 31

DEBUT	PEAK	WKS	Gold	Album Title		Pop #	$	Label & Number

★63★

PICKETT, Wilson '66
Born on 3/18/41 in Prattville, Alabama. Singer/songwriter. Sang in local gospel groups. To Detroit in 1955. With The Falcons from 1961-63. Career took off after recording in Memphis with guitarist/producer Steve Cropper. Inducted into the Rock and Roll Hall of Fame in 1991.
1)The Exciting Wilson Pickett 2)In The Midnight Hour 3)The Wicked Pickett

DEBUT	PEAK	WKS		Album	Pop #	$	Label & Number
10/30/65	3	7	1	**In The Midnight Hour**	107	$50	Atlantic 8114

In The Midnight Hour [1] • Teardrops Will Fall • Take A Little Love • For Better Or Worse • **I Found A Love** [6] • That's A Man's Way • I'm Gonna Cry • **Don't Fight It** [4] • Take This Love I've Got • Come Home Baby • I'm Not Tired • Let's Kiss And Make Up

8/27/66	3	27	2	The Exciting Wilson Pickett	21	$40	Atlantic 8129

Land Of 1000 Dances [1] • Something You Got • **634-5789 (Soulsville, U.S.A.)** [1] • Barefootin' • Mercy, Mercy • You're So Fine • In The Midnight Hour [1] • **Ninety-Nine And A Half (Won't Do)** [13] • Danger Zone • I'm Drifting • It's All Over • She's So Good To Me

1/14/67	5	21	3	The Wicked Pickett	42	$40	Atlantic 8138

Mustang Sally [6] • New Orleans • Sunny • **Everybody Needs Somebody To Love** [19] • Ooh Poo Pah Doo • She Ain't Gonna Do Right • Knock On Wood • Time Is On My Side • Up Tight Good Woman • You Left The Water Running • Three Time Loser • Nothing You Can Do

8/12/67	7	8	4	The Sound Of Wilson Pickett	54	$40	Atlantic 8145

Soul Dance Number Three [10] • **Funky Broadway** [1] • I Need A Lot Of Loving Every Day • **I Found A Love** [6] • You Can't Stand Alone [26] • Mojo Mamma • I Found The One • Something Within Me • I'm Sorry About That • Love Is A Beautiful Thing

11/18/67	9	28	5	The Best Of Wilson Pickett [G]	35	$30	Atlantic 8151

In The Midnight Hour [1] • I Found A Love [6] • 634-5789 (Soulsville, U.S.A.) [1] • If You Need Me [30] • Mustang Sally [6] • **Don't Fight It** [4] • Everybody Needs Somebody To Love [19] • It's Too Late [7] • Ninety-Nine And A Half (Won't Do) [13] • Funky Broadway [1] • Soul Dance Number Three [10] • Land Of 1000 Dances [1] • I Found A True Love [11]

2/17/68	9	16	6	I'm In Love	70	$25	Atlantic 8175

Jealous Love [18] • Stag-O-Lee [13] • That Kind Of Love • I'm In Love [4] • Hello Sunshine • Don't Cry No More • We've Got To Have Love • Bring It On Home To Me • **She's Lookin' Good** [7] • I've Come A Long Way [46]

7/20/68	10	10	7	The Midnight Mover	91	$25	Atlantic 8183

I'm A Midnight Mover [6] • It's A Groove • Remember, I Been Good To You • I'm Gonna Cry • Deborah • **I Found A True Love** [11] • Down By The Sea • Trust Me • Let's Get An Understanding • For Better Or Worse

2/22/69	15	18	8	Hey Jude	97	$20	Atlantic 8215
3/21/70	36	13	9	Right On	197	$20	Atlantic 8250
9/19/70	12	32	10	Wilson Pickett In Philadelphia	64	$15	Atlantic 8270
5/22/71	8	16	11	The Best Of Wilson Pickett, Vol. II [G]	73	$15	Atlantic 8290

Don't Let The Green Grass Fool You [2] • Sugar Sugar [4] • Engine Number 9 [3] • I'm A Midnight Mover [6] • A Man And A Half • Born To Be Wild [41] • She's Lookin' Good • I'm In Love [4] • Hey Joe [29] • Cole, Cooke & Redding [11] • Hey Jude [13] • You Keep Me Hangin' On [16] • I Found A True Love [11]

1/1/72	23	10	12	Don't Knock My Love	132	$15	Atlantic 8300
2/17/73	33	8	13	Wilson Pickett's Greatest Hits [G]	178	$20	Atlantic 501 [2]
4/7/73	30	7	14	Mr. Magic Man	187	$15	RCA Victor 4858
9/22/73	34	9	15	Miz Lena's Boy	212	$12	RCA Victor 0312
12/1/79+	69	13	16	I Want You	205	$10	EMI America 17019
10/17/87	75	1	17	American Soul Man		$8	Motown 6244

PIECES OF A DREAM '84
Jazz trio from Philadelphia: James Lloyd (keyboards), Cedric Napoleon (bass) and Curtis Harmon (drums).

10/10/81	38	14	1	Pieces Of A Dream	170	$8	Elektra 350
7/17/82	22	32	2	We Are One	114	$8	Elektra 60142
12/17/83+	16	40	3	Imagine This	90	$8	Elektra 60270
7/26/86	18	22	4	Joyride	102	$8	Manhattan 53023
7/9/88	62	13	5	Makes You Wanna		$8	EMI-Manhattan 48740
10/7/89+	56	17	6	'Bout Dat Time		$8	EMI 92050
6/26/93	81	7	7	In Flight		$8	Manhattan 81496

PIPER, Wardell '79
Born in Philadelphia. Female disco singer.

8/18/79	70	4		Wardell Piper	203	$10	Midsong Int'l. 009

P.K.O. '94

3/19/94	74	5		Thagood, The Bad, The Mafia		$8	Youngsta 2470

PLANET PATROL '83
Vocal group from Boston: Rodney Butler, Melvin Franklin, Herb Jackson, Michael Anthony Jones and Joe Lites.

12/3/83	64	7		Planet Patrol		$10	Tommy Boy 1002

PLATTERS, The '66
Vocal group formed in Los Angeles: Sonny Turner, David Lynch, Nate Nelson, Herb Reed and Sandra Dawn. Lynch died of cancer on 1/2/81 (age 61). Group inducted into the Rock and Roll Hall of Fame in 1990.

6/25/66	12	17		I Love You 1,000 Times	100	$20	Musicor 3091

PLAYA '98
Vocal trio from Louisville, Kentucky: Ben Bush, John Peacock and Stephen Garrett.

4/11/98	19	17		Cheers 2 U	86	$8	Def Jam 536386

PLAYA FLY '98

7/4/98	90	1		Movin' On		$8	Super Sigg 0020

PLAYAZ TRYNA STRIVE '96

11/30/96	100	1		All Frames Of The Game		$8	Sick Wid' It 45007

PLAYER '78
Pop-rock group from Los Angeles: Peter Becket (vocals, guitar), John Crowley (guitar), Wayne Cooke (keyboards), Ronn Moss (bass) and John Friesen (drums). Moss plays "Ridge Forrester" on TV's *The Bold & The Beautiful*.

2/4/78	32	8	●	Player	26	$10	RSO 3026

DEBUT	PEAK	WKS	Gold	Album Title	Pop #	$	Label & Number

PLAYERS, The   '67
Vocal trio: Herbert Butler, Otha Lee Givens and Tony Lee Johnson.

| 11/19/66+ | 10 | 14 | | **He'll Be Back** | | $20 | Minit 40006 |

Get Hep To Love • **He'll Be Back** *[24]* • I Love You A Thousand Times • I Wanna Be Free • **I'm Glad I Waited** *[32]* • Peace Of Mind • Since I Don't Have You • Sunny • There's Got To Be A Way • When A Man Loves A Woman • Why Did I Lie • Why Do I Love You

PLAYERS ASSOCIATION, The   '77
Jazz trio: Chris Hills (vocals, guitar, drums), Joe Farrell (tenor sax) and Jon Faddis (trumpet).

| 4/30/77 | 30 | 8 | | 1 **The Players Association** | | $12 | Vanguard 79384 |
| 2/4/78 | 57 | 3 | | 2 **Born To Dance** | | $12 | Vanguard 79398 |

PLEASURE   '79
Group from Portland, Oregon: Sherman Davis (vocals), Marlon McClain (guitar), brothers Donald and Michael Hepburn (keyboards), Bruce Smith (percussion), Dennis Springer (sax), Nathaniel Phillips (bass) and Bruce Carter (drums).

6/7/75	54	7		1 **Dust Yourself Off**		$10	Fantasy 9473
6/5/76	32	21		2 **Accept No Substitutes**	162	$10	Fantasy 9506
4/9/77	34	15		3 **Joyous**	113	$10	Fantasy 9526
5/13/78	42	6		4 **Get To The Feeling**	119	$10	Fantasy 9550
8/11/79	13	32		5 **Future Now**	67	$10	Fantasy 9578
7/19/80	27	16		6 **Special Things**	97	$10	Fantasy 9600
4/24/82	30	13		7 **Give It Up**	164	$8	RCA Victor 4209

PMD   '94
Born Parrish Smith on 5/13/68 in Smithtown, New York. Male rapper. One-half of **EPMD** duo.

| 10/15/94 | 12 | 6 | | 1 **Shade Business** | 65 | $8 | RCA 66475 |
| 11/9/96 | 29 | 4 | | 2 **Bu$ine$$ I$ Bu$ine$$** | 180 | $8 | Relativity 1569 |

PM DAWN   '93
Rap duo from Jersey City, New Jersey: brothers Attrell and Jarrett Cordes.

| 11/9/91 | 29 | 26 | ● | 1 **Of The Heart, Of The Soul And Of The Cross:** **The Utopian Experience** | 48 | $8 | Gee Street 510276 |
| 4/10/93 | 23 | 25 | ● | 2 **The Bliss Album...?** | 30 | $8 | Gee Street 514517 |

PO' BROKE 'N LONELY?   '95
Vocal trio from Los Angeles: Christopher Taylor, Mike Lynn and Ruben Cruz.

| 9/2/95 | 99 | 1 | | **Forbidden Vibe** | | $8 | Big Beat 92533 |

POCKETS   '77
Group from Baltimore: Larry Jacobs (vocals), Jacob Sheffer (guitar), Al McKinney (keyboards), Charles Williams, Irving Madison and Kevin Barnes (horns), Gary Grainger (bass) and George Gray (drums).

10/15/77	17	24		1 **Come Go With Us**	57	$10	Columbia 34879
10/14/78	22	10		2 **Take It On Up**	85	$10	Columbia 35384
9/29/79	43	6		3 **So Delicious**	209	$10	Columbia 36001

POETIC HUSTLA'Z   '97
Male rap trio from Cleveland: Mo Hart, Tony Tone and Boogy Nikke.

| 11/29/97 | 96 | 1 | | **Trials & Tribulations** | | $8 | Mo Thugs 1581 |

POINT BLANK   '97

| 6/7/97 | 73 | 1 | | **N-Tha-Do'** | | $8 | Priority 50701 |

POINTER, Bonnie   '79
Born on 7/11/50 in Oakland. Member of the **Pointer Sisters** from 1971-78.

| 12/16/78+ | 34 | 15 | | 1 **Bonnie Pointer** | 96 | $10 | Motown 911 |
| 12/22/79+ | 40 | 14 | | 2 **Bonnie Pointer** | 63 | $10 | Motown 929 |

above 2 are different albums

POINTER, June   '83
Born on 11/30/54 in Oakland. Youngest member of the **Pointer Sisters**.

| 7/30/83 | 65 | 2 | | **Baby Sister** | 202 | $10 | Planet 4508 |

POINTER, Noel   '77
Born in Brooklyn, New York. Died of a stroke on 12/19/94 (age 39). Jazz-fusion violin player.

6/18/77	45	3		1 **Phantazia**	[I]	144	$12	Blue Note 736
10/13/79	59	6		2 **Feel It**	[I]	138	$10	United Artists 973
5/9/81	53	8		3 **All My Reasons**	201	$10	Liberty 1094

★77★   **POINTER SISTERS**   '73
Vocal group from Oakland: sisters Ruth, Anita, **Bonnie Pointer** and **June Pointer**. Sang in nostalgic 1940s style from 1973-77. Appeared in the 1976 movie *Car Wash*. Bonnie went solo in 1978, group continued as trio in a more contemporary style.
1)The Pointer Sisters 2)Steppin 3)Break Out

| 7/21/73 | 3 | 23 | ● | 1 **The Pointer Sisters** | 13 | $12 | Blue Thumb 48 |

Yes We Can Can *[12]* • Cloudburst • Jada • River Boulevard • Old Songs • That's How I Feel • Sugar • Pains And Tears • Naked Foot • Wang Dang Doodle *[24]*

| 4/6/74 | 33 | 6 | ● | 2 **That's A Plenty** | 82 | $12 | Blue Thumb 6009 |
| 9/28/74 | 29 | 8 | | 3 **Live At The Opera House** | [L] | 96 | $15 | Blue Thumb 8002 [2] |

recorded on April 21, 1974 in San Francisco

| 7/12/75 | 3 | 20 | | 4 **Steppin** | 22 | $12 | Blue Thumb 6021 |

How Long (Betcha' Got A Chick On The Side) *[1]* • Sleeping Alone • Easy Days • Chainey Do • I Ain't Got Nothin' But The Blues Medley: I Ain't Got Nothin' But The Blues/Rocks In My Bed/Creole Love Song/Satin Doll/I Got It Bad (And That Ain't Good)/Mood Indigo • Save The Bones For Henry Jones • Wanting Things • **Going Down Slowly** *[16]*

| 1/8/77 | 33 | 4 | | 5 **The Best Of The Pointer Sisters** | [G] | 164 | $15 | Blue Thumb 6026 [2] |
| 11/26/77 | 51 | 4 | | 6 **Having A Party** | 176 | $12 | Blue Thumb 6023 |

POINTER SISTERS — Cont'd

DEBUT	PEAK	WKS	Gold	Album Title	Pop #	$	Label & Number
11/25/78+	9	19	●	7 Energy	13	$10	Planet 1

Lay It On The Line • Dirty Work • Hypnotized • As I Come Of Age • Come And Get Your Love • **Happiness** [20] • **Fire** [14] • Angry Eyes • Echoes Of Love • Everybody Is A Star

DEBUT	PEAK	WKS	Gold	Album Title	Pop #	$	Label & Number
10/6/79	44	6		8 Priority	72	$10	Planet 9003
8/23/80	19	28		9 Special Things	34	$10	Planet 9
7/4/81	9	25	●	10 Black & White	12	$10	Planet 18

Sweet Lover Man • Someday We'll Be Together • Take My Heart, Take My Soul • **Slow Hand** [7] • We're Gonna Make It • **What A Surprise** [52] • Got To Find Love • Fall In Love Again • Should I Do It

DEBUT	PEAK	WKS	Gold	Album Title	Pop #	$	Label & Number
7/24/82	24	22		11 So Excited!	59	$10	Planet 4355
11/26/83+	6	58	▲2	12 Break Out	8	$10	Planet 4705

Jump (For My Love) [3] • Automatic [2] • I'm So Excited • **I Need You** [13] • **Neutron Dance** [13] • Dance Electric • Easy Persuasion • Baby Come And Get It [24] • Telegraph Your Love • Operator

DEBUT	PEAK	WKS	Gold	Album Title	Pop #	$	Label & Number
8/17/85	11	36	▲	13 Contact	24	$8	RCA Victor 5487
12/6/86	39	13		14 Hot Together	48	$8	RCA Victor 5609

POISON CLAN '93
Rap duo from Florida: Debonaire and Jeff Tompkins. Debonaire later formed **Home Team**.

DEBUT	PEAK	WKS	Gold	Album Title	Pop #	$	Label & Number
1/26/91	42	23		1 2 Low Life Muthas		$8	Effect 3001

POISON CLAN (The Baby 2 Live Crew)

DEBUT	PEAK	WKS	Gold	Album Title	Pop #	$	Label & Number
4/18/92	62	33		2 Poisonous Mentality		$8	Effect 3006
9/11/93	12	11		3 Ruff Town Behavior	97	$8	Luke 202
12/9/95	80	3		4 Strait Zooism		$8	Warlock 2763

PONTY, Jean-Luc '82
Born on 9/29/42 in Normandy, France. Classically-trained, jazz-rock violinist.

DEBUT	PEAK	WKS	Gold	Album Title	Pop #	$	Label & Number
3/27/82	43	7		Mystical Adventures [I]	44	$10	Atlantic 19333

POOR RIGHTEOUS TEACHERS '90
Rap trio from Trenton, New Jersey: Wise Intelligent, Culture Freedom and Father Shaheed.

DEBUT	PEAK	WKS	Gold	Album Title	Pop #	$	Label & Number
5/19/90	17	34		1 Holy Intellect	142	$8	Profile 1289
9/21/91	23	35		2 Pure Poverty	155	$8	Profile 1415
10/2/93	29	7		3 Black Business	167	$8	Profile 1443
11/2/96	57	4		4 The New World Order		$8	Profile 1471

POPPA LQ '95
Born Kenneth Green in Houston. Male rapper.

DEBUT	PEAK	WKS	Gold	Album Title	Pop #	$	Label & Number
8/19/95	82	1		Your Entertainment, My Reality		$8	Rap-A-Lot 40607

PORTER, Art '92
Born in Little Rock, Arkansas. Died in a boating accident on 11/23/96 (age 35). Alto saxophonist.

DEBUT	PEAK	WKS	Gold	Album Title	Pop #	$	Label & Number
9/12/92	50	12		1 Pocket City [I]		$8	Verve Forecast 511877
7/10/93	75	9		2 Straight To The Point [I]		$8	Verve Forecast 517997

PORTER, David '70
Born on 11/21/41 in Memphis. Prolific songwriter, often teamed with **Isaac Hayes**.

DEBUT	PEAK	WKS	Gold	Album Title	Pop #	$	Label & Number
3/21/70	4	20		1 Gritty, Groovy, & Gettin' It	163	$20	Enterprise 1009

I Only Have Eyes For You • Guess Who • I'm A-Tellin' You • Just Be True • The Way You Do The Things You Do • **Can't See You When I Want To** [29] • One Part - Two Parts • I Don't Know Why I Love You

DEBUT	PEAK	WKS	Gold	Album Title	Pop #	$	Label & Number
11/21/70+	9	22		2 David Porter...Into A Real Thing	104	$20	Enterprise 1012

Hang On Sloopy • Ooo-Wee Girl • Too Real To Live A Lie • Grocery Man • I Don't Want To Cry • Thirty Days

DEBUT	PEAK	WKS	Gold	Album Title	Pop #	$	Label & Number
10/30/71	46	4		3 Victim Of The Joke?		$20	Enterprise 1019
12/8/73	50	3		4 Sweat And Love		$20	Enterprise 1026

PORTRAIT '93
Male vocal group: Eric Kirkland and Michael Saulsberry (both from Los Angeles), Irving Washington (from Providence, Rhode Island) and Phillip Johnson (from Tulsa, Oklahoma).

DEBUT	PEAK	WKS	Gold	Album Title	Pop #	$	Label & Number
11/21/92+	16	32		1 Portrait	70	$8	Capitol 93496
3/25/95	26	16		2 All That Matters	131	$8	Capitol 28709

POSITIVE K '93
Born Darryl Gibson in the Bronx, New York. Male rapper.

DEBUT	PEAK	WKS	Gold	Album Title	Pop #	$	Label & Number
12/5/92+	50	23		The Skills Dat Pay Da Bills	168	$8	Island 514057

POWELL, Adam Clayton '67
Born on 11/29/08 in New Haven, Connecticut. Died on 4/4/72 (age 63). Congressman from New York City (1944-70).

DEBUT	PEAK	WKS	Gold	Album Title	Pop #	$	Label & Number
3/4/67	13	5		Keep The Faith, Baby! [T]	112	$15	Jubilee 2062

POWELL, Doc '96

DEBUT	PEAK	WKS	Gold	Album Title	Pop #	$	Label & Number
5/25/96	89	3		Laid Back		$8	Discovery 77037

POWELL, Jesse '99
Born in Gary, Indiana. Singer/songwriter.

DEBUT	PEAK	WKS	Gold	Album Title	Pop #	$	Label & Number
3/30/96	35	16		1 Jesse Powell		$8	Silas 11287
9/26/98+	15	34↑	●	2 'Bout It	63	$8	Silas 11789

PRESIDENTS, The '71
Vocal trio from Washington DC: Archie Powell, Bill Shorter and Tony Boyd.

DEBUT	PEAK	WKS	Gold	Album Title	Pop #	$	Label & Number
1/2/71	15	13		5-10-15-20-25-30 years of love	158	$25	Sussex 7005

PRESSHA '98
Born David Jones in Atlanta. Male rapper.

DEBUT	PEAK	WKS	Gold	Album Title	Pop #	$	Label & Number
8/29/98	98	1		Don't Get It Twisted		$8	Tony Mercedes 26051

PRESSURE   '80
Group formed in Los Angeles: Melvin Robinson (vocals), Pat Kelly (guitar), **Ronnie Laws** (sax), Barnaby Finch (keyboards), Bobby Vega (bass) and Art Rodriguez (drums).

| 2/2/80 | 72 | 7 | | Pressure .... | 207 | $10 | L.A. 3195 |

★147★ PRESTON, Billy   '73
Born on 9/9/46 in Houston; raised in Los Angeles. Singer/songwriter/keyboardist.
1)Everybody Likes Some Kind Of Music 2)The Most Exciting Organ Ever 3)Music Is My Life

| 6/26/65 | 5 | 7 | | 1 The Most Exciting Organ Ever | [I] 143 | $50 | Vee-Jay 1123 |

If I Had A Hammer • Low Down • Slippin' And Slidin' • Drown In My Tears • I Am Coming Through • The Octopus • Don't Let The Sun Catch You Crying • Soul Meetin' • Let Me Know • Billy's Bag • The Masquerade Is Over • Steady Gettin' It

| 7/2/66 | 9 | 8 | | 2 Wildest Organ In Town! | [I] 118 | $40 | Capitol 2532 |

In The Midnight Hour • Uptight (Everything's Alright) • A Hard Day's Night • Ain't Got No Time To Play • Love Makes Me Do Foolish Things • The Duck • Advice • (I Can't Get No) Satisfaction • I Got You (I Feel Good) • It's Got To Happen • Free Funk • The "In" Crowd

| 3/6/71 | 50 | 2 | | 3 Encouraging Words .... | | $20 | Apple 3370 |
| 4/15/72 | 9 | 22 | | 4 I Wrote A Simple Song | 32 | $12 | A&M 3507 |

Should've Known Better • I Wrote A Simple Song • John Henry • Without A Song • **The Bus** *[43]* • **Outa-Space** *[1]* • The Looner Tune • You Done Got Older • Swing Down Chariot • God Is Great • My Country 'Tis Of Thee

| 12/23/72+ | 7 | 33 | | 5 Music Is My Life | 32 | $12 | A&M 3516 |

We're Gonna Make It • One Time Or Another • Blackbird • I Wonder Why • **Will It Go Round In Circles** *[10]* • Ain't That Nothin' • God Loves You • Make The Devil Mad (Turn On To Jesus) • Nigger Charlie • Heart Full Of Sorrow • Music's My Life

| 10/27/73 | 3 | 17 | | 6 Everybody Likes Some Kind Of Music | 52 | $12 | A&M 3526 |

Everybody Likes Some Kind Of Music • **You're So Unique** *[11]* • How Long Has The Train Been Gone • My Soul Is A Witness • Sunday Morning • You've Got Me For Company • Listen To The Wind • **Space Race** *[1]* • Do You Love Me? • I'm So Tired • It's Alright Ma (I'm Only Bleeding) • Minuet For Me

| 10/12/74 | 8 | 18 | | 7 The Kids & Me | 17 | $12 | A&M 3645 |

Tell Me You Need My Loving • **Nothing From Nothing** *[8]* • **Struttin'** *[11]* • Sister Sugar • Sad Sad Song • You Are So Beautiful • Sometimes I Love You • St. Elmo • John The Baptist • Little Black Boys And Girls • Creature Feature

7/26/75	18	9		8 It's My Pleasure	43	$12	A&M 4532
12/17/77	49	4		9 A Whole New Thing		$12	A&M 4656
11/3/79	73	2		10 Late At Night	49	$10	Motown 925
8/22/81	48	5		11 Billy Preston & Syreeta	127	$10	Motown 958

PRICE, Kelly   '98
Born in New York City. Female singer/rapper.

| 8/29/98 | 2[1] | 49↑ | ▲ | Soul Of A Woman | 15 | $8 | Island 524516 |

Friend of Mine *[1]* • Secret Love *[34]* • Don't Say Goodbye • Kiss Test • Soul Of A Woman • You Complete Me • Her • Your Love • Take Me To A Dream • Lord Of All

PRIEST, Maxi   '90
Born Max Elliott on 6/10/60 in London to Jamaican parents. Dancehall reggae singer.

9/22/90	16	29	●	1 Bonafide	47	$8	Charisma 91384
1/4/92	45	12		2 Best Of Me	[G] 189	$8	Charisma 91804
11/21/92	46	14		3 fe Real	191	$8	Charisma 86500
7/27/96	43	11		4 Man With The Fun	108	$8	Virgin 41612

PRIME MINISTER PETE NICE & DADDY RICH '93
Former members of **3rd Bass**: rapper Pete Nash and DJ Richard Lawson.

| 7/31/93 | 50 | 3 | | Dust To Dust | 171 | $8 | Def Jam 53454 |

PRIME SUSPECTS   '98
Male rap trio from New Orleans: E, Gangsta T and Skinow.

| 10/24/98 | 14 | 6 | | Guilty Til Proven Innocent .... | 36 | $8 | No Limit 50728 |

PRINCE ♀ ★9★   '84
Born Prince Roger Nelson on 6/7/58 in Minneapolis. Singer/songwriter/producer/multi-instrumentalist. Starred in the movies *Purple Rain*, *Under The Cherry Moon*, *Sign 'O' The Times* and *Graffiti Bridge*. Founded the Paisley Park record label. The Revolution featured Lisa Coleman (keyboards), Wendy Melvoin (guitar), Matt Fink (keyboards), Eric Leeds (sax), Brownmark (bass) and Bobby Z (drums). Brownmark formed **Mazarati** in 1986. Leeds formed **Madhouse** in 1987. Coleman and Melvoin formed duo **Wendy and Lisa** in 1987. Sheila E. (drums) joined Prince's band in 1986. Prince formed new band, New Power Generation, in 1990, featuring **Rosie Gaines** (vocals), Levi Seacer (guitar), Tommy Barbarella (keyboards), Sonny T. (bass) and Michael Bland (drums). Prince changed his name on 6/7/93 to a combination male/female symbol. By 1994 referred to as "The Artist Formerly Known As Prince" or "The Artist."

1)Purple Rain 2)Diamonds And Pearls 3)Parade 4)The Gold Experience 5)Come

| 7/22/78 | 21 | 23 | | 1 For You .... | 163 | $15 | Warner 3150 |
| 11/17/79 | 3 | 31 | ▲ | 2 Prince | 22 | $12 | Warner 3366 |

I Wanna Be Your Lover *[1]* • Why You Wanna Treat Me So Bad? *[13]* • Sexy Dancer • When We're Dancing Close And Slow • With You • Bambi • Still Waiting *[65]* • I Feel For You • It's Gonna Be Lonely

| 11/8/80 | 7 | 32 | ● | 3 Dirty Mind | 45 | $12 | Warner 3478 |

Dirty Mind *[65]* • When You Were Mine • Do It All Night • Gotta Broken Heart Again • Uptown *[5]* • Head • Sister • Partyup

| 11/7/81 | 3 | 35 | ▲ | 4 Controversy | 21 | $12 | Warner 3601 |

Controversy *[3]* • Sexuality • Do Me, Baby • Private Joy • Ronnie, Talk To Russia • **Let's Work** *[9]* • Annie Christian • Jack U Off

| 11/20/82 | 4 | 93 | ▲4 | 5 Prince **1999** | 9 | $15 | Warner 23720 [2] |

1999 *[4]* • Little Red Corvette *[15]* • Delirious *[18]* • Let's Pretend We're Married *[55]* • D.M.S.R. • Automatic • Something In The Water (Does Not Compute) • Free • Lady Cab Driver • All The Critics Love U In New York • International Lover

| 7/14/84 | ❶19 | 48 | ▲13 | 6 Purple Rain | 1[24] | $10 | Warner 25110 |

Let's Go Crazy *[1]* • Take Me With U *[40]* • The Beautiful Ones • Computer Blue • Darling Nikki • When Doves Cry *[1]* • I Would Die 4 U *[11]* • Baby I'm A Star • Purple Rain *[4]*

DEBUT	PEAK	WKS	Gold	Album Title	Pop #	$	Label & Number

PRINCE — Cont'd

DEBUT	PEAK	WKS	Gold	#	Album Title	Pop #	$	Label & Number
5/11/85	4	43	▲²	7	**Around the World in a Day**	1³	$10	Paisley Park 25286

Around The World In A Day • Paisley Park • Condition Of The Heart • **Raspberry Beret** *[3]* • Tamborine • America *[35]* • **Pop Life** *[8]* • The Ladder • Temptation

| 4/26/86 | 2³ | 26 | ▲ | 8 | **Parade** | 3 | $10 | Paisley Park 25395 |

music from the movie *Under The Cherry Moon*
PRINCE and the REVOLUTION (above 3)
Christopher Tracy's Parade • New Position • I Wonder U • Under The Cherry Moon • Girls & Boys • Life Can Be So Nice • Venus De Milo • **Mountains** *[15]* • Do U Lie? • **Kiss** *[1]* • **Anotherloverholenyohead** *[18]* • Sometimes It Snows In April

| 5/2/87 | 4 | 48 | ▲ | 9 | **Sign "O" The Times** | 6 | $12 | Paisley Park 25577 [2] |

Sign 'O' The Times *[1]* • Play In The Sunshine • Housequake • The Ballad Of Dorothy Parker • It • Starfish And Coffee • Slow Love • **Hot Thing** *[14]* • Forever In My Life • **U Got The Look** *[11]* • **If I Was Your Girlfriend** *[12]* • Strange Relationship • I Could Never Take The Place Of Your Man • The Cross • It's Gonna Be A Beautiful Night • Adore

| 5/28/88 | 5 | 17 | ● | 10 | **Lovesexy** | 11 | $10 | Paisley Park 25720 |

I No • **Alphabet St.** *[3]* • **Glam Slam** *[44]* • Anna Stesia • Dance On • Lovesexy • When 2 R In Love • **I Wish U Heaven** *[18]* • Positivity

| 7/15/89 | 5 | 29 | ▲² | 11 | **Batman** | 1⁶ | $10 | Warner 25936 |

The Future • Electric Chair • The Arms Of Orion • **Partyman** *[5]* • Vicki Waiting • Trust • Lemon Crush • **Scandalous!** *[5]* • **Batdance** *[1]*

| 9/15/90 | 6 | 21 | ● | 12 | **Graffiti Bridge** | 6 | $8 | Paisley Park 27493 |

Can't Stop This Feeling I Got • **New Power Generation** *[27]* • Release It *[Time]* • The Question Of U • Elephants & Flowers • **Round And Round** *[Tevin Campbell]* *[3]* • We Can Funk *[George Clinton]* • Joy In Repetition • Love Machine *[Time]* • Tick, Tick, Bang • Shake! *[Time]* • **Thieves In The Temple** *[1]* • The Latest Fashion *[Time]* • Melody Cool *[Mavis Staples]* • Still Would Stand All Time • Graffiti Bridge

| 10/19/91 | ❶¹ | 42 | ▲² | 13 | **Diamonds And Pearls** | 3 | $8 | Paisley Park 25379 |

Thunder • Daddy Pop • **Diamonds And Pearls** *[1]* • Cream • Strollin' • Willing And Able • **Gett Off** *[6]* • Walk Don't Walk • Jughead • **Money Don't Matter 2 Night** *[14]* • Push • **Insatiable** *[3]* • Live 4 Love

| 10/31/92 | 8 | 35 | ▲ | 14 | **⚥ (untitled)** | 5 | $8 | Paisley Park 45037 |

PRINCE & THE NEW POWER GENERATION (above 2)
My Name Is Prince *[25]* • **Sexy MF** *[76]* • Love 2 The 9's • **The Morning Papers** *[68]* • The Max • Blue Light • I Wanna Melt With U • Sweet Baby • The Continental • **Damn U** *[32]* • Arrogance • The Flow • 7 • And God Created Woman • 3 Chains O' Gold • The Sacrifice Of Victor

| 10/2/93 | 6 | 20 | ▲ | 15 | **The Hits/The B-Sides** [G] | 19 | $25 | Paisley Park 45440 [3] |

When Doves Cry *[1]* • Pop Life *[8]* • Soft And Wet *[12]* • I Feel For You • Why You Wanna Treat Me So Bad? *[13]* • When You Were Mine • Uptown *[5]* • Let's Go Crazy *[1]* • 1999 *[45]* • I Could Never Take The Place Of Your Man • **Nothing Compares 2 U** *[62]* • Adore • Pink Cashmere *[14]* • Alphabet St. *[3]* • Sign 'O' The Times *[1]* • Thieves In The Temple *[1]* • Diamonds And Pearls *[1]* • 7 *[61]* • Controversy *[3]* • Dirty Mind *[65]* • I Wanna Be Your Lover *[1]* • Head • Do Me, Baby • Delirious *[18]* • Little Red Corvette *[15]* • I Would Die 4 U *[11]* • Raspberry Beret *[3]* • If I Was Your Girlfriend *[12]* • Kiss *[1]* • Peach • U Got The Look *[11]* • Sexy MF *[76]* • Gett Off *[6]* • Cream • Pope • Purple Rain *[4]* • Hello • 200 Balloons • Escape • Gotta Stop (Messin' About) • Horny Toad • Feel U Up • Girl • I Love U In Me • Erotic City • Shockadelica • Irresistible Bitch *[flip]* • Scarlet Pussy • La, La, La, He, He, Hee • She's Always In My Hair • 17 Days • How Come U Don't Call Me Anymore • Another Lonely Christmas • God • 4 The Tears In Your Eyes • Power Fantastic

| 10/2/93 | 14 | 21 | ▲ | 16 | **The Hits 1** [G] | 46 | $8 | Paisley Park 45431 |

disc one of *The Hits/The B-Sides*

| 10/2/93 | 23 | 21 | ▲ | 17 | **The Hits 2** [G] | 54 | $8 | Paisley Park 45435 |

disc two of *The Hits/The B-Sides*

| 6/4/94 | 29 | 12 | | 18 | **The Beautiful Experience** ⚥ [M] | 92 | $6 | NPG 71003 |

| 9/3/94 | 2¹ | 13 | ● | 19 | **Come** | 15 | $8 | Warner 45700 |

PRINCE (1958-1993)
Come • **Space** *[71]* • Pheromone • Loose! • Papa • Race • Dark • Solo • **Letitgo** *[10]* • Orgasm

| 12/10/94 | 18 | 13 | | 20 | **The Black Album** [E] | 6 | $8 | Warner 45793 |

recorded in 1987

| 10/14/95 | 2¹ | 17 | ● | 21 | **The Gold Experience** ⚥ | 6 | $8 | Warner 45999 |

P Control • Endorphinmachine • Shhh • We March • **The Most Beautiful Girl In The World** *[2]* • Dolphin • Now • 319 • Shy • Billy Jack Bitch • **I Hate U** *[3]* • **Gold** *[92]*

| 4/6/96 | 15 | 9 | | 22 | **Girl 6** [S] | 75 | $8 | Warner 46239 |

PRINCE and The New Power Generation

| 12/7/96 | 6 | 26 | ▲² | 23 | **Emancipation** ⚥ | 11 | $20 | NPG 54982 [3] |

Jam Of The Year • Right Back Here In My Arms • Somebody's Somebody • Get Yo Groove On • Courtin' Time • Betcha By Golly Wow! • White Mansion • Damned If I Do • I Can't Make U Love Me • Mr. Happy • In This Bed I Scream • Sex In The Summer • One Kiss At A Time • Soul Sanctuary • Emale • Curious Child • Dreamin' About U • Joint 2 Joint • The Holy River • Let's Have A Baby • Saviour • The Plan • Friend, Lover, Sister, Mother, Wife • Slave • New World • The Human Body • Face Down • La, La, La Means I Love You • Style • Sleep Around • Da, Da, Da • My Computer • One Of Us • The Love We Make • Emancipation

| 3/14/98 | 59 | 4 | | 24 | **Crystal Ball** ⚥ [K] | 62 | $30 | NPG 9871 [4] |

packaged in a special clear-plastic ball

| 7/18/98 | 9 | 11 | | 25 | **Newpower Soul** ⚥ | 22 | $8 | NPG 9872 |

⚥ & NEW POWER GENERATION
Newpower Soul • Mad Sex • Until U're In My Arms Again • When U Love Somebody • Shoo-Bed-Ooh • Push It Up! • Freaks On This Side • Come On • The One • (I Like) Funky Music

PRINCE MARKIE DEE   '92

Born Mark Morales on 2/19/60 in Brooklyn, New York. Former member of the **Fat Boys**.

| 10/24/92 | 47 | 24 | | 1 | **Free** | | $8 | Columbia 48686 |

PRINCE MARKIE DEE AND THE SOUL CONVENTION

| 8/26/95 | 91 | 1 | | 2 | **Love Daddy** | | $8 | Motown 0555 |

163

DEBUT	PEAK	WKS	Gold	Album Title	Pop #	$	Label & Number
				PROFESSOR GRIFF '90			
				Born Richard Griffin in Long Island, New York. Male rapper. Former member of **Public Enemy**.			
4/7/90	24	16		1 Pawns In The Game	127	$8	Luke Skyywalker 111
				PROFESSOR GRIFF and THE LAST ASIATIC DISCIPLES			
9/14/91	70	7		2 Kao's II Wiz *7* Dome		$8	Luke 91721
				PROFESSOR X '91			
				Born Lumumba Carson in Brooklyn, New York. Male rapper. Member of **X-Clan**.			
3/16/91	97	4		Years Of The 9, On The Blackhand Side		$8	4th & B'way 444033
				PROPHET POSSE '98			
				Rap group: Indo G, **Gangsta Boo**, Paul, Juicy J, M-Child, Scarecrow, Crunchy Black, The Kaze and Droopy Drew Dog.			
3/7/98	54	4		Body Parts	168	$8	Prophet 4406
	★72★			**PRYOR, Richard** '74			
				Born on 12/1/40 in Peoria, Illinois. Legendary comedian/actor. Appeared in several movies.			
				1)That Nigger's Crazy 2)Is It Something I Said? 3)Wanted			
11/24/73+	41	9		1 Richard Pryor ....[C-E]		$12	Reprise 6325
				first released in 1968 on Dove 6325 ($20)			
6/22/74	❶⁴	49	●	2 That Nigger's Crazy [C]	29	$12	Partee 2404
				I Hope I'm Funny • Nigger With A Seizure • Have Your Ass Home By 11:00 • Black & White Life Styles • Exorcist • Wino Dealing With Dracula • Flying Saucers • The Back Down • Black Man/White Woman • Niggers Vs. Police • Wino & Junkie			
8/30/75	❶²	16	▲	3 Is It Something I Said? [C]	12	$12	Reprise 2227
				Eulogy • Shortage Of White People • New Niggers • Cocaine • Just Us • Mudbone • Little Feets • When Your Woman Leaves You • The Good Night Kiss • Women Are Beautiful • Our Text For Today			
9/13/75	56	2		4 Down 'N' Dirty ....[C]		$12	Laff 184
10/9/76	4	17	●	5 Bicentennial Nigger [C]	22	$12	Warner 2960
				Hillbilly • Black & White Women • Our Gang • Bicentennial Prayer • Black Hollywood • Mudbone Goes To Hollywood • Chinese Restaurant • Acid • Bicentennial Nigger			
5/21/77	12	12		6 Are You Serious??? ....[C-E]	58	$12	Laff 196
6/11/77	41	4		7 L.A. Jail ....[C-E]	114	$12	Tiger Lily 14023
6/25/77	7	7	▲	8 Richard Pryor's Greatest Hits [C-K]	68	$10	Warner 3057
				Ali • Exorcist • My Father • Nigger With A Seizure • My Neighborhood • Have Your Ass Home By 11:00 • Wino • Craps • Cocaine • When Your Woman Leaves You • Mudbone • Little Feets			
1/6/79	4	19	●	9 Wanted [C]	32	$12	Warner 3364 [2]
				New Year's Eve • White And Black People • Black Funerals • Discipline • Heart Attacks • Ali • Keeping In Shape • Leon Spinks • Dogs And Horses • Jim Brown • Monkeys • Kids • Nature • Things In The Woods • Deer Hunter • Chinese Food • Being Sensitive			
9/1/79	41	13		10 Outrageous ....[C-E]	176	$10	Laff 206
4/12/80	58	6		11 Insane ....[C-E]		$10	Laff 209
10/25/80	37	17		12 Holy Smoke! ....[C-E]		$10	Laff 212
7/25/81	44	9		13 Reverend Du Rite ....[C-E]		$10	Laff 216
4/17/82	13	17		14 Richard Pryor Live On The Sunset Strip ....[C-S]	21	$10	Warner 3660
11/12/83	22	15		15 Richard Pryor: Here And Now ....[C-S]	71	$10	Warner 23981
				PRYSOCK, Arthur '65			
				Born on 1/2/29 in Spartanburg, South Carolina. Died on 6/14/97 (age 68).			
9/4/65	10	10		1 A Double Header with Arthur Prysock	116	$25	Old Town 2009
				All Or Nothing At All • Let It Be Me • There Goes My Heart • A Hard Day's Night • They Say You're Laughing At Me • The Sun, The Sand And The Sea • You're Nothing But A Girl • Let Me Call You Sweetheart • Open Up Your Heart • Who Can I Turn To (When Nobody Needs Me) • I Live My Love • Goodnight My Love (Pleasant Dreams)			
3/26/66	20	1		2 Arthur Prysock/Count Basie	107	$20	Verve 8646
2/4/67	15	8		3 Art and Soul		$20	Verve 5009
11/16/74	57	2		4 Love Makes It Right		$12	Old Town 12-002
2/5/77	36	7		5 All My Life	153	$12	Old Town 12-004
				PSYCHO REALM, The '97			
				Rap trio: brothers Jacken and Mr. Duke, with **Cypress Hill** member Louis Freese.			
11/15/97	68	2		The Psycho Realm	183	$8	Ruffhouse 68153
				PUBLIC ANNOUNCEMENT '98			
				Vocal group from Chicago: Earl Robinson, Felony Davis, Euclid Gray and Glen Wright. Former backing group for **R. Kelly**.			
4/11/98	14	32		All Work, No Play	81	$8	A&M 540882
	★131★			**PUBLIC ENEMY** '88			
				Rap group from Long Island, New York: Carlton Ridenhauer (**"Chuck D"**), William Drayton (**"Flavor Flav"**), Norman Rogers (**"Terminator X"**) and Richard Griffin (**"Professor Griff"**). Griffin left in 1989, returned in 1997.			
5/9/87+	28	53	●	1 Yo! Bum Rush The Show	125	$8	Def Jam 40658
7/23/88	❶¹	49	▲	2 It Takes A Nation Of Millions To Hold Us Back	42	$8	Def Jam 44303
				Countdown To Armageddon • **Bring The Noise [56]** • Don't Believe The Hype [18] • Cold Lampin' With Flavor • Terminator X To The Edge Of Panic • Mind Terrorist • Louder Than A Bomb • Caught, Can We Get A Witness? • Show 'Em Whatcha Got • She Watch Channel Zero?! • **Night Of The Living Baseheads [62]** • Black Steel In The Hour Of Chaos [86] • Security Of The First World • Rebel Without A Pause • Prophets Of Rage • Party For Your Right To Fight			
4/28/90	3	41	▲	3 Fear Of A Black Planet	10	$8	Def Jam 45413
				Contract On The World Love Jam • **Brothers Gonna Work It Out [20]** • 911 Is A Joke [15] • Incident At 66.6 FM • Welcome To The Terrordome [15] • Meet The G That Killed Me • Pollywanacraka • Anti-Nigger Machine • Burn Hollywood Burn • Power To The People • Who Stole The Soul? • Fear Of A Black Planet • Revolutionary Generation • Can't Do Nuttin' For Ya Man • Reggie Jax • Leave This Off Your Fuckin Charts • B. Side Wins Again • War At 33 1/3 • Final Count Of The Collision Between Us And The Damned • **Fight The Power [20]**			
10/19/91	❶¹	32	▲	4 Apocalypse 91...The Enemy Strikes Black	4	$8	Def Jam 47374
				Lost At Birth • Rebirth • Nighttrain • **Can't Truss It [9]** • I Don't Wanna Be Called Yo Niga • How To Kill A Radio Consultant • By The Time I Get To Arizona • Move! • 1 Million Bottlebags • More News At 11 • **Shut Em Down [26]** • A Letter To The NY Post • Get The Fuck Outta Dodge • Bring Tha Noize			

DEBUT	PEAK	WKS	Gold	Album Title	Pop #	$	Label & Number

PUBLIC ENEMY — Cont'd

| 10/3/92 | **10** | 19 | ● | 5 **Greatest Misses** [K] | 13 | $8 | Def Jam 53014 |

Tie Goes To The Runner • Hit Da Road Jack • Gett Off My Back • Gotta Do What I Gotta Do • Air Hoodlum • **Hazy Shade Of Criminal** *[58]* • Megablast • Louder Than A Bomb • You're Gonna Get Yours • How To Kill A Radio Consultant • Who Stole The Soul? • Party For Your Right To Fight • Shut Em Down

| 9/10/94 | **4** | 10 | ● | 6 **Muse Sick-N-Hour Mess Age** | 14 | $8 | Def Jam 523362 |

Whole Lotta Love Goin On In The Middle Of Hell • Theatrical Parts • **Give It Up** *[30]* • What Side You On? • Bedlam 13:13 • Stop In The Name... • What Kind Of Power We Got? • So Whatcha Gone Do Now? • White Heaven/Black Hell • Race Against Time • They Used To Call It Dope • Aintnuttin Buttersong • Live And Undrugged • Thin Line Between Law & Rape • I Ain't Mad At All • Death Of A Carjacka • I Stand Accused • Godd Complexx • Hitler Day • Harry Allen's Interactive Superhighway Phone Call To Chuck D • Living In A Zoo

| 5/16/98 | **10** | 10 | | 7 **He Got Game** [S] | 26 | $8 | Def Jam 558130 |

Resurrection • **He Got Game** *[78]* • Unstoppable • Shake Your Booty • Is Your God A Dog • House Of The Rising Sun • Revelation 33 1/3 Revolutions • Game Face • Politics Of The Sneaker Pimps • What You Need Is Jesus • Super Agent • Go Cat Go • Sudden Death

PUFF DADDY **'97**
Born Sean Combs in 1970 in Harlem, New York. Songwriter/producer/rapper. Founded the Bad Boy record label.

| 8/2/97 | **❶**[5] | 58 | ▲[6] | **No Way Out** | 1[4] | $8 | Bad Boy 73012 |

PUFF DADDY & THE FAMILY
No Way Out • **Victory** *[13]* • **Been Around The World** *[11]* • What You Gonna Do? • Don't Stop What You're Doing • If I Should Die Tonight • Do You Know? • Young G's • I Love You Baby • **It's All About The Benjamins** *[7]* • Pain • Is This The End? • I Got The Power • Friend • Senorita • **I'll Be Missing You** *[1]* • **Can't Nobody Hold Me Down** *[1]*

PURE SOUL **'95**
Female vocal group from Washington DC: Shawn Allen, Heather Perkins, Keitha Shepherd and Kirstin Hall.

| 10/21/95 | 33 | 25 | | **Pure Soul** | 173 | $8 | Step Sun 92638 |

PURIM, Flora **'76**
Born on 3/6/42 in Rio de Janeiro. Female singer.

| 5/8/76 | 38 | 4 | | **Open Your Eyes You Can Fly** | 59 | $12 | Milestone 9065 |

Q

QUAD CITY DJ'S **'96**
Studio dance group from Orlando, Florida: Nathaniel Orange, Johnny McGowan and Lana LeFleur. Orange was a member of **95 South**.

| 7/13/96 | 23 | 35 | ▲ | **Get On Up And Dance** | 31 | $8 | Big Beat 82905 |

QUAD FORCE **'92**

| 8/29/92 | 47 | 12 | | **Feel The Real Bass** | | $8 | Attitude 14002 |

QUAZAR **'78**
Funk group from New Jersey: Peachena (female vocals), Kevin Goins (male vocals, guitar), Harvey Banks (guitar), Monica Peters (trumpet), Darryl Dixon (sax), Greg Fitz and Rich Banks (keyboards), Darryl Deliberto (percussion), Eugene Jackson (bass) and Jeff Adams (drums).

| 11/18/78 | 21 | 13 | | **Quazar** | 121 | $10 | Arista 4187 |

QUEEN **'80**
Rock group from England: Freddie Mercury (vocals), Brian May (guitar), John Deacon (bass) and Roger Taylor (drums). Mercury died of AIDS on 11/24/91 (age 45).

| 9/20/80 | 8 | 15 | ▲ | 1 **The Game** | 1[5] | $12 | Elektra 513 |

Play The Game • Dragon Attack • **Another One Bites The Dust** *[2]* • Need Your Loving Tonight • Crazy Little Thing Called Love • Rock It (Prime Jive) • Don't Try Suicide • Sail Away Sweet Sister • Coming Soon • Save Me

| 7/3/82 | 40 | 5 | ● | 2 **Hot Space** | 22 | $12 | Elektra 60128 |

QUEEN LATIFAH **'90**
Born Dana Owens on 3/18/70 in Newark, New Jersey. Female rapper/actress. Appeared in several movies. Cast member of TV series *Living Single*. Latifah is Arabic for delicate and sensitive.

| 11/25/89+ | 6 | 32 | | 1 **All Hail The Queen** | 124 | $8 | Tommy Boy 1022 |

Dance For Me • Mama Gave Birth To The Soul Children • **Come Into My House** *[81]* • Latifah's Law • Wrath Of My Madness • The Pros • **Ladies First** *[64]* • A King And Queen Creation • Queen Of Royal Badness • Evil That Men Do • Princess Of The Posse • Inside Out

9/28/91+	32	32		2 **Nature Of A Sista'**	117	$8	Tommy Boy 1035
12/4/93+	15	44	●	3 **Black Reign**	60	$8	Motown 6370
7/4/98	16	11		4 **Order In The Court**	95	$8	Motown 0895

QUEEN PEN **'98**
Born Lynise Walters in New York City. Female rapper.

| 1/3/98 | 13 | 29 | | **My Melody** | 78 | $8 | Lil' Man 90151 |

QUESTIONMARK ASYLUM **'95**
Rap group: Kenny Jones, Marcell Gadson, Dominick Warren and Douglas Francis.

| 6/10/95 | 50 | 8 | | **The Album** | | $8 | RCA 66560 |

QUINDON **'96**
Born Quindon Tarver in 1983 in Plano, Texas. Male singer.

| 6/29/96 | 79 | 2 | | **Quindon** | | $8 | Virgin 41500 |

R

RAab   '94
Male singer from Florida.

| 12/25/93+ | 67 | 12 | | You're The One | | $8 | Rip-It 1002 |

RADICE, Mark   '76
Born on 11/23/57 in Newark, New Jersey. Singer/songwriter/pianist.

| 9/4/76 | 56 | 3 | | Ain't Nothin' But A Party | | $10 | United Artists 629 |

RAEKWON   '95
Born Corey Woods in New York City. Male rapper. Member of **Wu-Tang Clan**.

| 8/19/95 | 2² | 44 | ● | **Only Built 4 Cuban Linx...** | 4 | $8 | Loud/RCA 66663 |

Striving For Perfection • Knuckleheadz • Knowledge God • Criminology *[32]* • **Incarcerated Scarfaces** *[73]* • Rainy Dayz • Guillotine (Swordz) • Can It Be All So Simple • Shark Niggas (Biters) • Ice Water • **Glaciers Of Ice** *[flip]* • Verbal Intercourse • Wisdom Body • Spot Rusherz • **Ice Cream** *[37]* • Wu-Gambinos • Heaven & Hell • North Star (Jewels)

RAHEEM   '88
Born Oscar Seres on 7/6/71 in Houston. At age 15 was an original member of **The Geto Boys**.

9/10/88	67	10		1 **The Vigilante**		$8	A&M 5212
7/11/92	71	9		2 **The Invincible**		$8	Rap-A-Lot 57180
4/12/97	83	4		3 **Greatest Hits 1986-1997** [G]		$8	Tight 2 Def 4497
4/25/98	69	2		4 **Tight 4 Life**		$8	Breakaway 481001

RAKIM — see ERIC B. & RAKIM

RAMPAGE   '97
Born in New York City. Male rapper.

| 8/16/97 | 15 | 9 | | **Scouts Honor...By Way Of Blood** | 65 | $8 | Violator 62022 |

RANDOLPH, Boots   '67
Born Homer Louis Randolph on 6/3/27 in Paducah, Kentucky. Session saxophonist.

| 4/15/67 | 21 | 17 | ● | **Boots with Strings** [I] | 36 | $20 | Monument 18066 |

RANKS, Shabba   '91
Born Rawlston Fernando Gordon on 1/17/66 in Sturgetown, Jamaica. Male reggae singer.

| 6/22/91 | ❶¹ | 60 | ● | 1 **As Raw As Ever** | 89 | $8 | Epic 47310 |

Trailor Load A Girls • Where Does Slackness Come From • Woman Tangle • Gun Pon Me • Gone Up • **Housecall (Your Body Can't Lie To Me)** *[4]* • Flesh Axe • A Mi Di Girls Dem Love • Fist-A-Ris • **The Jam** *[52]* • Ambi Get Scarce • Park Yu Benz

7/6/91	75	10		2 **Rappin' With The Ladies**		$8	Pow Wow 7417
5/30/92	56	12		3 **Mr. Maximum**		$8	Pow Wow 7423
8/8/92	24	14		4 **Rough & Ready - Vol. 1**	78	$8	Epic 52443
10/17/92	11	36	●	5 **X-tra Naked**	64	$8	Epic 52464
11/13/93	84	2		6 **Rough & Ready - Volume II**		$8	Epic 57203
7/1/95	25	9		7 **A Mi Shabba**	133	$8	Epic 57801

RAPPIN' 4-TAY   '96
Born Anthony Forté in 1969 in San Francisco. Male rapper.

| 8/6/94 | 52 | 30 | | 1 **Don't Fight The Feelin' - She's A Sell Out** | 174 | $8 | Rag Top 30889 |
| 4/6/96 | 10 | 11 | | 2 **Off Parole** | 38 | $8 | Rag Top 35509 |

I Paid My Dues • New Trump • **A Lil Some'Em Some'Em** *[74]* • Check Ya Self • **Ain't No Playa Like...** *[55]* • Never Talk Down • 25-2-Life • Boogie Bang Bang • Comin' Back • Hala At A Playa • Game On The Shelf • Off Parole • Where's The Party • Phat Like That • Still Phuckin' Wit My Folks

| 11/8/97 | 46 | 3 | | 3 **4 Tha Hard Way** | 169 | $8 | Noo Trybe 57117 |

RAPPIN' RON & ANT DIDDLEY DOG   '95
Rap duo: Ron Royster and Anthony Nelson.

| 3/25/95 | 83 | 1 | | **Bad N-Fluenz** | | $8 | Cell Block 4002 |

RARE EARTH   '70
Rock group from Detroit: Gil Bridges (vocals, saxophone), Rod Richards (guitar), Mark Olson (keyboards), Ed Guzman (percussion), John Persh (bass) and Pete Rivera (drums). Numerous personnel changes through the years. Persh died in 1979 of a staph virus. Olson died of alcohol-related complications in 1982. Guzman died on 7/29/93 (age 49).

| 1/24/70 | 4 | 40 | | 1 **Get Ready** | 12 | $15 | Rare Earth 507 |

Magic Key • Tobacco Road • Feeling Alright • In Bed • Train To Nowhere • **Get Ready** *[20]*

| 7/18/70 | 4 | 30 | | 2 **Ecology** | 15 | $15 | Rare Earth 514 |

Born To Wander *[48]* • Long Time Leavin' • **(I Know) I'm Losing You** *[20]* • Satisfaction Guaranteed • Nice Place To Visit • No. 1 Man • Eleanor Rigby

7/31/71	12	15		3 **One World**	28	$15	Rare Earth 520
1/29/72	19	16		4 **Rare Earth In Concert** [L]	29	$20	Rare Earth 534 [2]
2/10/73	46	6		5 **Willie Remembers..**	90	$15	Rare Earth 543
6/23/73	12	27		6 **Ma**	65	$15	Rare Earth 546

RARE ESSENCE   '95
Funk group from Washington DC: James Thomas (vocals), Andre Johnson (guitar), Mark Larson (keyboards), Benny Harley (trumpet), John Jones (trombone), Rory Felton (sax), David Green (timbales), Tyrone (congas), Michael Neal (bass) and Quentin Davidson (drums).

3/18/95	53	11		1 **Get Your Freak On**		$8	Snd. Of Capitol 315
9/28/96	60	3		2 **Body Snatchers**		$8	Snd. Of Capitol 900
6/13/98	81	1		3 **We Go On And On**		$8	Rare One 2000

DEBUT	PEAK	WKS	Gold	Album Title	Pop #	$	Label & Number

RASCALS, The   '68

White group from New York City: Felix Cavaliere (vocals, organ), Gene Cornish (vocals, guitar), Eddie Brigati (vocals, percussion) and Dino Danelli (drums). Inducted into the Rock and Roll Hall of Fame in 1997.

| 3/11/67 | 5 | 25 | ● | 1 **Collections** | 14 | $25 | Atlantic 8134 |

What Is The Reason • Since I Fell For You • **I've Been Lonely Too Long** *[33]* • No Love To Give • Medley: Mickey's Monkey/Love Lights • Come On Up • Too Many Fish In The Sea • More • Nineteen Fifty-Six • Love Is A Beautiful Thing • Land Of 1000 Dances

| 8/19/67 | 7 | 19 | ● | 2 **Groovin'** | 5 | $25 | Atlantic 8148 |

THE YOUNG RASCALS (above 2)
A Girl Like You • Find Somebody • I'm So Happy Now • Sueno • How Can I Be Sure • **Groovin'** *[3]* • If You Knew • I Don't Love You Anymore • You Better Run • A Place In The Sun • It's Love

| 3/16/68 | 7 | 22 | | 3 **Once Upon A Dream** | 9 | $20 | Atlantic 8169 |

Easy Rollin' • Rainy Day • Please Love Me • Sound Effect • It's Wonderful • I'm Gonna Love You • Dave & Eddie • My Hawaii • My World • Silly Girl • Singin' The Blues Too Long • Bells • Sattva • Once Upon A Dream

| 7/13/68 | 4 | 33 | ● | 4 **Time Peace/The Rascals' Greatest Hits** [G] | 1¹ | $20 | Atlantic 8190 |

I Ain't Gonna Eat Out My Heart Anymore • Good Lovin' • You Better Run • Come On Up • Mustang Sally • Love Is A Beautiful Thing • In The Midnight Hour • **I've Been Lonely Too Long** *[33]* • **Groovin'** *[3]* • A Girl Like You • How Can I Be Sure • It's Wonderful • Easy Rollin' • **A Beautiful Morning** *[36]*

| 4/12/69 | 40 | 2 | ● | 5 **Freedom Suite** | 17 | $20 | Atlantic 901 [2] |

RAS KASS   '98

Born John Austin in Carson, California. Male rapper.

| 10/19/96 | 35 | 4 | | 1 **Soul On Ice** | 169 | $8 | Priority 50529 |
| 10/10/98 | 11 | 7 | | 2 **Rasassination** | 63 | $8 | Priority 50739 |

RAW FUSION   '94

Rap duo from Oakland: Ron Brooks and DJ Fuze. Brooks was a member of **Digital Underground**.

| 5/14/94 | 71 | 2 | | **Hoochiefied Funk** | | $8 | Hollywood 61452 |

RAWLS, Lou ★19★   '66

Born on 12/1/35 in Chicago. Singer/actor. With several gospel groups before siging with Capitol in 1961. Hosted own TV variety show in 1969. Acted in the movies *Angel Angel, Down We Go* and *Believe In Me*. Voice of many Budweiser beer ads.

1)Lou Rawls Live! 2)Lou Rawls Soulin' 3)All Things In Time 4)Lou Rawls Carryin' On 5)Too Much!

| 4/30/66 | ❶¹² | 63 | ● | 1 **Lou Rawls Live!** [L] | 4 | $20 | Capitol 2459 |

Stormy Monday • Southside Blues • Tobacco Road • St. James Infirmary • The Shadow Of Your Smile • I'd Rather Drink Muddy Water • Goin' To Chicago Blues • In The Evening When The Sun Goes Down • The Girl From Ipanema • I Got It Bad And That Ain't Good • Street Corner Hustlers' Blues • World Of Trouble

| 9/3/66 | ❶⁹ | 44 | ● | 2 **Lou Rawls Soulin'** | 7 | $20 | Capitol 2566 |

A Whole Lotta Woman • **Love Is A Hurtin' Thing** *[1]* • So Hard To Laugh, So Easy To Cry • You're The One • Don't Explain • What Now My Love • Memory Lane • Old Man's Memories • It Was A Very Good Year • Growing Old Gracefully • Old Folks • Autumn Leaves • On A Clear Day (You Can See Forever) • Breaking My Back (Instead Of Using My Mind)

| 1/28/67 | 2³ | 28 | | 3 **Lou Rawls Carryin' On!** | 20 | $20 | Capitol 2632 |

Mean Black Snake • Walking Proud • The Devil In Your Eyes • Find Out What's Happening • **You Can Bring Me All Your Heartaches** *[35]* • A Woman Who's A Woman • The Life That I Lead • Yesterday • Trouble Down Here Below • You're Gonna Hear From Me • Something Stirring In My Soul • On Broadway

| 5/20/67 | 2² | 18 | | 4 **Too Much!** | 18 | $20 | Capitol 2713 |

Yes It Hurts (Doesn't It?) • It's An Uphill Climb To The Bottom • I Just Want To Make Love To You • You're Takin' My Bag • Then You Can Tell Me Goodbye • **Dead End Street** *[3]* • Twelfth Of Never • Righteous Woman • I Wanna Little Girl • Why (Do I Love You So) • I'll Take Time • You're Always On My Mind

| 8/26/67 | 5 | 11 | | 5 **That's Lou** | 29 | $20 | Capitol 2756 |

When Love Goes Wrong • Problems • Reminiscing • They Don't Give Medals (To Yesterday's Heroes) • Ear Bender • What Are You Doing About Today • **Show Business** *[25]* • Please Give Me Someone To Love • Hard To Get Thing Called Love • (How Do You Say) I Don't Love You Anymore • Street Of Dreams • The Love That I Give

| 3/9/68 | 10 | 18 | | 6 **Feelin' Good** | 103 | $20 | Capitol 2864 |

The Letter • My Ancestors • For What It's Worth • Even When You Cry • Hang-Ups • Evil Woman • My Son • Feelin' Good • Encore • I'm Gonna Use What I Got (To Get What I Need) • Gotta Find A Way

8/3/68	23	5		7 **You're Good For Me**	165	$20	Capitol 2927
8/17/68	19	16		8 **The Best Of Lou Rawls** [G]	103	$20	Capitol 2948
6/7/69	6	34		9 **The way it was - The way it is**	71	$15	Capitol 215

Fa Fa Fa Fa Fa (Sad Song) • Trying Just As Hard As I Can • **Your Good Thing (Is About To End)** *[3]* • I Love You Yes I Do • When A Man Loves A Woman • Season Of The Witch • Gentle On My Mind • I Wonder • I Want To Be Loved (But Only By You) • It's You

| 7/26/69 | 47 | 7 | | 10 **Close-Up** [E] | 191 | $20 | Capitol 261 [2] |

reissue of *Black And Blue* and *Tobacco Road* albums

11/29/69	24	9		11 **Your Good Thing**	200	$15	Capitol 325
4/11/70	47	3		12 **You've Made Me So Very Happy**	172	$15	Capitol 427
9/11/71	27	19		13 **Natural Man**	68	$12	MGM 4771
3/4/72	32	4		14 **Silk & Soul**	186	$15	MGM 4809 [2]
1/18/75	52	5		15 **She's Gone**		$12	Bell 1318
6/12/76	❶¹	28	▲	16 **All Things In Time**	7	$10	Philadelphia I. 33957

You're The One • **You'll Never Find Another Love Like Mine** *[1]* • Time • **Groovy People** *[19]* • Need You Forever • From Now On • Pure Imagination • **This Song Will Last Forever** *[74]* • Let's Fall In Love All Over Again

| 11/27/76 | 56 | 3 | | 17 **Naturally** | | $10 | Polydor 6086 |
| 4/16/77 | 14 | 21 | ● | 18 **Unmistakably Lou** | 41 | $10 | Philadelphia I. 34488 |

DEBUT	PEAK	WKS	Gold	Album Title	Pop #	$	Label & Number

RAWLS, Lou — Cont'd

DEBUT	PEAK	WKS		Album Title	Pop #	$	Label & Number
12/17/77+	13	31	●	19 When You Hear Lou, You've Heard It All	41	$10	Philadelphia I. 35036
11/25/78	42	11		20 Lou Rawls Live [L]	108	$10	Philadelphia I. 35517 [2]
				recorded at the Mack Hellinger Theater in New York City			
6/9/79	13	18		21 Let Me Be Good To You	49	$10	Philadelphia I. 36006
1/12/80	19	25		22 Sit Down And Talk To Me	81	$10	Philadelphia I. 36304
1/17/81	34	11		23 Shades Of Blue	110	$10	Philadelphia I. 36774
8/21/82	45	9		24 Now Is The Time	201	$10	Epic 37488
2/13/88	73	1		25 Family Reunion		$10	Gamble & Huff 100
10/14/89	96	4		26 At Last		$8	Blue Note 91937
12/1/90	92	6		27 It's Supposed To Be Fun		$8	Blue Note 93841

RAY, Harry   **'83**
Born on 12/15/46 in Hackensack, New Jersey. Died of a stroke on 10/1/92 (age 45). Member of **The Moments**.

| 1/29/83 | 55 | 6 | | It's Good To Be Home | | $10 | Sugar Hill 269 |

RAYDIO — see PARKER, Ray

RAY, GOODMAN & BROWN — see MOMENTS

RAY J   **'97**
Born Willie Ray Norwood in 1981 in McComb, Mississippi; raised in California. Brother of **Brandy**. Acted on TV's *The Sinbad Show* and in the movie *Steel*.

| 4/12/97 | 56 | 7 | | Everything You Want | | $8 | EastWest 62017 |

R.B.L. POSSE   **'97**
Rap duo from San Francisco: Christian Mathews and Kyle Church. R.B.L stands for Ruthless By Law.

12/19/92+	60	29		1 A Lesson To Be Learned		$8	In-A-Minute 8000
11/19/94	23	28		2 Ruthless By Law	197	$8	In-A-Minute 8700
10/18/97	14	6		3 An Eye For An Eye	70	$8	Big Beat 92771

R.B.L. POSSE'S HITMAN   **'95**

| 11/4/95 | 91 | 2 | | Solo Creep | | $8 | Right Way 9500 |

RBX   **'95**
Born in Long Beach, California. Male rapper.

| 10/14/95 | 12 | 7 | | The RBX Files | 62 | $8 | Premeditated 45866 |

READY FOR THE WORLD   **'85**
Group from Flint, Michigan: **Melvin Riley** (vocals), Gordon Strozier (guitar), Greg Potts (keyboards), Willie Triplett (percussion), John Eaton (bass) and Gerald Valentine (drums).

6/1/85	3	51	▲	1 **Ready For The World**	17	$8	MCA 5594
				Tonight [6] • Digital Display [4] • Ceramic Girl [82] • Deep Inside Your Love [6] • Oh Sheila [1] • Human Toy • **Slide Over** [57] • Out Of Town Lover • I'm The One Who Loves You			
11/29/86+	5	27	●	2 **Long Time Coming**	32	$8	MCA 5829
				Love You Down [1] • Baby (Let Me Love You) • Long Time Coming [54] • So In Love • In My Room • **Mary Goes 'Round** [23] • Some People Don't Care • Here I Am • It's All A Game • Do You Get Enough			
10/15/88	17	23		3 Ruff 'N' Ready	65	$8	MCA 42198
7/20/91+	43	35		4 Straight Down To Business		$8	MCA 10224

REAL LIVE   **'96**
Rap duo from New Jersey: Larry-O and K-Def.

| 10/19/96 | 57 | 2 | | The Turnaround: A Long Awaited Drama | | $8 | Big Beat 92668 |

REAL ROXANNE, The   **'88**
Born Joanne Martinez in New York City. Female rapper.

| 11/26/88 | 30 | 22 | | The Real Roxanne | | $10 | Select 21627 |

REDD, Jeff   **'90**
Born in Mt. Vernon, New York. Singer/songwriter.

| 3/24/90 | 40 | 24 | | A Quiet Storm | | $8 | MCA 42299 |

REDDING, Gene   **'74**
Born in 1945 in Anderson, Indiana. No relation to Otis Redding.

| 6/15/74 | 45 | 5 | | Blood Brother | 208 | $12 | Haven 9200 |

REDDING, Otis ★47★   **'68**
Born on 9/9/41 in Dawson, Georgia. Killed in a plane crash on 12/10/67 (age 26) in Lake Monona in Madison, Wisconsin. Singer/songwriter/producer/pianist. Recorded as a duo with **Carla Thomas**. Plane crash also killed four members of the **Bar-Kays**. Otis's sons formed **The Reddings**. Inducted into the Rock and Roll Hall of Fame in 1989.

1)The Dock Of The Bay 2)History Of Otis Redding 3)Otis Blue/Otis Redding Sings Soul

4/10/65	3	14		1 **The Great Otis Redding Sings Soul Ballads**	147	$80	Volt 411
				That's How Strong My Love Is [18] • Chained And Bound [70] • Woman, Lover, A Friend • Your One And Only Man • Nothing Can Change This Love • It's Too Late • For Your Precious Love • I Want To Thank You • **Come To Me** [69] • Home In Your Heart • Keep Your Arms Around Me • **Mr. Pitiful** [10]			
10/2/65	❶¹	13		2 **Otis Blue/Otis Redding Sings Soul**	75	$40	Volt 412
				Ole Man Trouble • Respect [4] • Change Is Gonna Come • Down In The Valley • **I've Been Loving You Too Long (To Stop Now)** [2] • Shake [16] • My Girl • Wonderful World • Rock Me Baby • Satisfaction [4] • You Don't Miss Your Water			

DEBUT	PEAK	WKS	Gold	Album Title	Pop #	$	Label & Number
				REDDING, Otis — Cont'd			
5/7/66	**3**	28		3 The Soul Album	54	$40	Volt 413
				Just One More Day [15] • It's Growing • Cigarettes And Coffee • Chain Gang • Nobody Knows You (When You're Down And Out) • Good To Me • Scratch My Back • Treat Her Right • Everybody Makes A Mistake • Any Ole Way • 634-5789 (Soulsville, U.S.A.)			
11/19/66+	**5**	22		4 Complete & Unbelievable....The Otis Redding Dictionary Of Soul	73	$40	Volt 415
				Fa-Fa-Fa-Fa-Fa (Sad Song) [12] • I'm Sick Y'all • Tennessee Waltz • Sweet Lorene • Try A Little Tenderness [4] • Day Tripper • My Lover's Prayer • She Put The Hurt On Me • Ton Of Joy • You're Still My Baby • Hawg For You • Love Have Mercy			
4/15/67	**5**	25		5 King & Queen	36	$40	Stax 716
				OTIS REDDING & CARLA THOMAS			
				Knock On Wood [8] • Let Me Be Good To You • **Tramp** [2] • Tell It Like It Is • When Something Is Wrong With My Baby • **Lovey Dovey** [21] • New Year's Resolution • It Takes Two • Are You Lonely For Me Baby • Bring It On Home To Me • Ooh Carla, Ooh Otis			
8/12/67	**8**	20		6 Otis Redding Live In Europe	[L] 32	$30	Volt 416
				Respect • I Can't Turn You Loose • I've Been Loving You Too Long (To Stop Now) • My Girl • Shake • Satisfaction • Fa-Fa-Fa-Fa-Fa (Sad Song) • These Arms Of Mine • Day Tripper • Try A Little Tenderness			
1/6/68	**❶**[1]	48		7 History Of Otis Redding	[G] 9	$30	Volt 418
				I've Been Loving You Too Long (To Stop Now) [2] • Try A Little Tenderness [4] • These Arms Of Mine [20] • Pain In My Heart [61] • My Lover's Prayer [10] • Fa-Fa-Fa-Fa-Fa (Sad Song) [12] • Respect [4] • Satisfaction [4] • Mr. Pitiful [10] • Security [97] • I Can't Turn You Loose [11] • Shake [16]			
3/23/68	**❶**[3]	37		8 The Dock Of The Bay	4	$30	Volt 419
				(Sittin' On) The Dock Of The Bay [1] • I Love You More Than Words Can Say [30] • Let Me Come On Home • Open The Door • Don't Mess With Cupid • Glory Of Love [19] • I'm Coming Home • Tramp [2] • The Huckle-Buck • Nobody Knows You (When You're Down And Out) • Ole Man Trouble			
7/13/68	**3**	28		9 The Immortal Otis Redding	58	$20	Atco 252
				I've Got Dreams To Remember [6] • You Made A Man Out Of Me • Nobody's Fault But Mine • Hard To Handle [38] • Thousand Miles Away • The Happy Song (Dum-Dum) [10] • Think About It • A Waste Of Time • Champagne And Wine • A Fool For You • Amen [15]			
12/7/68+	**7**	18		10 Otis Redding In Person At The Whiskey A Go Go	[L] 82	$20	Atco 265
				I Can't Turn You Loose • Pain In My Heart • Just One More Day • Mr. Pitiful • Satisfaction • I'm Depending On You • Any Ole Way • These Arms Of Mine • Papa's Got A Brand New Bag [10] • Respect			
7/26/69	**8**	20		11 Love Man	[K] 46	$20	Atco 289
				I'm A Changed Man • (Your Love Has Lifted Me) Higher And Higher • That's A Good Idea • I'll Let Nothing Separate Us • Direct Me • Love Man [17] • Groovin' Time • Your Feeling Is Mine • Got To Get Myself Together • Free Me [30] • A Lover's Question [20] • Look At That Girl			
8/1/70	**26**	10		12 Tell The Truth	[K] 200	$15	Atco 333
10/3/70	**15**	9	●	13 Monterey International Pop Festival	[L-S] 16	$20	Reprise 2029
				THE JIMI HENDRIX EXPERIENCE/OTIS REDDING			
				recorded June 1967 and featured in the movie *Monterey Pop*; side 1: Hendrix; side 2: Redding			
10/14/72	**34**	12		14 The Best Of Otis Redding	[G] 76	$20	Atco 801 [2]
				REDDINGS, The '82			
				Consisted of **Otis Redding**'s sons Dexter (vocals, bass) and Otis III (guitar), and cousin Mark Locket (vocals, drums, keyboards).			
11/22/80+	**21**	16		1 The Awakening	174	$10	Believe 36875
8/1/81	**40**	10		2 Class	106	$10	Believe 37175
6/5/82	**19**	14		3 Steamin' Hot	153	$10	Believe 37974
8/27/83	**50**	7		4 Back To Basics		$10	Believe 38690
5/25/85	**24**	14		5 If Looks Could Kill		$8	Polydor 823324
11/19/88	**88**	3		6 The Reddings		$8	Polydor 835292
				REDHEAD KINGPIN AND THE FBI '89			
				Born David Guppy in Englewood, New Jersey. Male rapper. The FBI included D.J. Wildstyle, Bo Roc, Lt. Squeak, Buzz and Poochie.			
8/26/89	**47**	40		1 A Shade Of Red		$8	Virgin 91269
4/27/91	**51**	13		2 The Album With No Name	182	$8	Virgin 91608
				REDMAN '96			
				Born Reggie Noble in Newark, New Jersey. Male rapper.			
10/24/92	**5**	48	●	1 Whut? Thee Album	49	$8	RAL 52967
				Psycho Ward • Time 4 Sum Aksion [63] • Da Funk • News Break • So Ruff • Rated "R" • Watch Yo Nuggets • Psycho Dub • Jam 4 U • Blow Your Mind [33] • Hardcore • Funky Uncles • Redman Meets Reggie Noble • Tonight's Da Night [78] • I'm A Bad • Sessed One Night • How To Roll A Blunt • A Day Of Sooperman Lover • Encore			
12/10/94	**❶**[1]	25	●	2 Dare Iz A Darkside	13	$8	RAL 523846
				Dr. Trevis • Bobyahed2dis • Journey Throo Da Darkside • Da Journee • A Million And 1 Buddah Spots • Noorotic • Boodah Session • Cosmic Slop • Rockafella [62] • Green Island • Basically • Can't Wait [61] • Winicumuhround • Wuditlooklike • Slide And Rock On • Sooperman Luva II • We Run N.Y.			
12/28/96	**❶**[1]	32	●	3 Muddy Waters	12	$8	Def Jam 533470
				Iz He 4 Real • Rock Da Spot • Case Closed • Pick It Up [69] • Smoke Buddah • Whateva Man [18] • On Fire • Do What Ya Feel • Creepin' • It's Like That (My Big Brother) [40] • Da Bump • Yesh Yesh Ya'll • What U Lookin' 4 • Soopaman Luva 3 • Rollin' • Da III Out			
12/26/98	**❶**[1]	27	▲	4 Doc's Da Name 2000	11	$8	Def Jam 558945
				Welcome 2 Da Bricks • Let Da Monkey Out [99] • I'll Bee Dat [50] • Get It Live • Jersey Yo! • Close Ya Doorz • I Don't Kare • Boodah Break • Keep On '99 • Well All Rite Cha • Da Goodness [50] • My Zone! • Da Da Da • Down South Funk • Dogs • Beet Drop • Brick City Mashin'! • Soopaman Luva IV • I Got A Secret			
				REED, Jimmy '74			
				Born Mathis James Reed on 9/6/25 in Dunleith, Mississippi. Died from an epileptic seizure on 8/29/76 (age 50). Blues singer/guitarist. Inducted into the Rock and Roll Hall of Fame in 1991.			
1/5/74	**54**	6		The History Of Jimmy Reed	[K]	$20	Trip 9515 [2]

REESE, Della   '66
Born Delloreese Patricia Early on 7/6/31 in Detroit. Singer/actress. Appeared in many movies and TV shows.

10/29/66	21	3		1 Della Reese Live ....[L]	149	$20	ABC 569
4/25/70	44	2		2 Black Is Beautiful...		$15	Avco Embassy 33004

REEVES, Dianne   '90
Born in 1956 in Detroit; raised in Denver. Jazz singer. Niece of jazz bassist Charles Burrell.

2/20/88	28	35		1 Dianne Reeves..	172	$8	Blue Note 46906
3/3/90	14	31		2 Never Too Far	81	$8	EMI 92401
3/12/94	93	3		3 Art And Survival		$8	EMI 28494

REEVES, Martha — see MARTHA & THE VANDELLAS

REFLECTIONS, The   '76
Vocal group from New York City: Herman Edwards, Josh Pridgen, with brothers John and Ed Simmons. John Simmons died on 3/16/89.

1/3/76	54	4		Love On Delivery		$12	Capitol 11460

RENÉ AND ANGELA   '86
Duo of René Moore and Angela Winbush.

8/8/81	15	18		1 Wall To Wall	100	$10	Capitol 12161
8/13/83	33	29		2 Rise		$10	Capitol 12267
6/29/85+	5	76	●	3 Street Called Desire	64	$8	Mercury 824607

Save Your Love (For #1) [1] • I'll Be Good [4] • No How - No Way [29] • You Don't Have To Cry [2] • Street Called Desire • Your Smile [1] • Who's Foolin' Who • Drive My Love

RENTIE, Damon   '86
Fusion singer/saxophonist/flutist.

3/8/86	52	11		Designated Hitter...		$10	TBA 212

RETURN TO FOREVER   '76
Jazz-rock group: Al Di Meola (guitar), Chick Corea (keyboards), Stanley Clarke (bass) and Lenny White (drums; Twennynine).

4/17/76	23	8	●	Romantic Warrior ....[I]	35	$10	Columbia 34076

REYNOLDS, Jeannie   '76
Sister of L. J. Reynolds. Committed suicide in July 1980, after taking the lives of her two children.

10/2/76	59	2		Cherries, Bananas & Other Fine Things		$12	Casablanca 7029

REYNOLDS, L.J.   '84
Singer/songwriter/producer Larry J. Reynolds. Brother of Jeannie Reynolds. Member of The Dramatics from 1973-79.

7/11/81	54	19		1 L. J. Reynolds		$10	Capitol 12127
10/23/82	53	7		2 Travelin'		$10	Capitol 12223
6/9/84	52	8		3 Lovin' Man		$8	Mercury 818479

RHYTHM HERITAGE   '76
Studio group assembled by producers Steve Barri and Michael Omartian. Vocals by Oren and Luther Waters.

3/13/76	20	13		1 Disco-Fied ....[I]	40	$10	ABC 934
3/19/77	60	2		2 Last Night On Earth	138	$10	ABC 987
2/25/78	56	6		3 Sky's The Limit	202	$10	ABC 1037

RICE, Gene   '91
Born in Maryland. Singer/songwriter.

7/6/91	26	34		1 Just For You..		$8	RCA 3159
2/27/93	93	1		2 Gene Rice		$8	RCA 66053

RICH, Tony, Project   '96
Born in Detroit. Singer/songwriter/keyboardist.

2/3/96	18	47	▲	1 'Words'	31	$8	LaFace 26022
8/29/98	66	2		2 Birdseye		$8	LaFace 26042

★88★   **RICHIE, Lionel**   '83
Born on 6/20/49 in Tuskegee, Alabama. Singer/songwriter/pianist. Former lead singer of the Commodores.

10/30/82	❶[1]	83	▲[4]	1 Lionel Richie	3	$8	Motown 6007

Serves You Right • Wandering Stranger • Tell Me • My Love [6] • Round And Round • Truly [2] • You Are [2] • You Mean More To Me • Just Put Some Love In Your Heart

11/12/83	❶[23]	91	▲[10]	<u>2 Can't Slow Down</u>	1[3]	$8	Motown 6059

Can't Slow Down • All Night Long (All Night) [1] • Penny Lover [8] • Stuck On You [8] • Love Will Find A Way • The Only One • Running With The Night [6] • Hello [1]

9/13/86	3	50	▲[4]	3 Dancing On The Ceiling	1[2]	$8	Motown 6158

Dancing On The Ceiling [6] • Se La [12] • Ballerina Girl [5] • Don't Stop • Deep River Woman • Love Will Conquer All [2] • Tonight Will Be Alright • Say You, Say Me [1]

5/23/92	7	35	▲	4 Back To Front ....[G]	19	$8	Motown 6338

Do It To Me [1] • My Destiny [56] • Love, Oh Love • All Night Long (All Night) [1] • Easy [1] • Still [1] • Endless Love [1] • Running With The Night [6] • Sail On [8] • Hello [1] • Truly [2] • Penny Lover [8] • Say You, Say Me [1] • Three Times A Lady [1]

5/4/96	15	19	●	5 Louder Than Words	28	$8	Mercury 532240
7/11/98	77	3		6 Time	152	$8	Mercury 558518

RICHIE RICH   '96
Born Richard Serrell in Oakland. Male rapper. Member of 415.

2/24/96	57	8		1 Half Thang		$8	Shot 8000
11/23/96	11	28		2 Seasoned Veteran	35	$8	Def Jam 533471

RIFF   '91
Vocal group from Paterson, New Jersey : Kenny Kelly, Steven Capers, Anthony Fuller, Dwayne Jones and Michael Best.

4/13/91	41	31		Riff...	177	$8	SBK 95828

RIGHTEOUS BROTHERS, The '65
Vocal duo: Bill Medley (b: 9/19/40 in Santa Ana, California) and Bobby Hatfield (b: 8/10/40 in Beaver Dam, Wisconsin).

1/30/65	3	6		1 You've Lost That Lovin' Feelin'	4	$40	Philles 4007

You've Lost That Lovin' Feelin' [3] • Ko Ko Mo • Ol' Man River • Look At Me • What'd I Say • The Angels Listened In • Sick And Tired • Summertime • Over And Over • Soul City • There's A Woman

1/30/65	8	1		2 Right Now! [E]	11	$40	Moonglow 1001

Let The Good Times Roll • My Babe • Bye Bye Love • B-Flat Blues • Little Latin Lupe Lu • My Prayer • In That Great Gettin' Up Mornin' • Georgia On My Mind • Koko Joe • I'm So Lonely • Love Or Magic • Fee-Fi-Fidily-I-Oh

8/14/65	8	4		3 Just Once In My Life...	9	$40	Philles 4008

Just Once In My Life [26] • Big Boy Pete • Unchained Melody [6] • You Are My Sunshine • The Great Pretender • Sticks And Stones • See That Girl • Ooh Poo Pah Doo • You'll Never Walk Alone • Guess Who • The Blues

5/7/66	18	5	●	4 Soul & Inspiration	7	$25	Verve 5001

RILEY, Cheryl Pepsii '88
Born in Brooklyn, New York. Female dance singer.

10/15/88	9	29		1 Me, Myself And I	128	$8	Columbia 44409

Sister Knows What She Wants • Thanks For My Child [1] • Falling From The Floor • Every Little Thing About You • Me, Myself And I [18] • He Said - She Said • Sisters • Seein' Is Believin' • Life Goes On

6/29/91	62	15		2 Chapters		$8	Columbia 45452

RILEY, Melvin '94
Born in Flint, Michigan. Former lead singer of Ready For The World.

7/9/94	23	21		Ghetto Love	155	$8	MCA 11016

RIMSHOTS '76
Funk group.

9/4/76	41	3		Down To Earth		$15	Stang 1028

RIPERTON, Minnie '75
Born on 11/8/47 in Chicago. Died of cancer on 7/12/79 (age 31). Lead singer of Rotary Connection from 1967-70.

8/10/74+	❶³	26	●	1 Perfect Angel	4	$12	Epic 32561

Reasons • It's So Nice (To See Old Friends) • Take A Little Trip • Seeing You This Way • The Edge Of A Dream • Perfect Angel • Every Time He Comes Around • Lovin' You [3] • Our Lives

6/7/75	5	14		2 Adventures In Paradise	18	$12	Epic 33454

Baby, This Love I Have • Feelin' That Your Feelin's Right • When It Comes Down To It • Minnie's Lament • Love And Its Glory • Adventures In Paradise [72] • Inside My Love [26] • Alone In Brewster Bay • Simple Things [70] • Don't Let Anyone Bring You Down

3/19/77	19	11		3 Stay In Love	71	$12	Epic 34191
5/19/79	5	31		4 Minnie	29	$10	Capitol 11936

Memory Lane [16] • Lover And Friend [20] • Return To Forever • Dancin' & Actin' Crazy • Love Hurts • Never Existed Before • I'm A Woman • Light My Fire

9/6/80	11	17		5 Love Lives Forever	35	$10	Capitol 12097
1/9/82	59	4		6 The Best Of Minnie Riperton [G]	203	$10	Capitol 12189

RIPPINGTONS, The — see FREEMAN, Russ

RITCHIE FAMILY, The '76
Female disco trio from Philadelphia: Cheryl Jackson, Cassandra Wooten and Gwen Oliver. The 1982 trio consisted of Vera Brown, Jacqui Smith-Lee and Dodie Draher.

10/25/75	26	7		1 Brazil	53	$12	20th Century 498
8/7/76	23	15		2 Arabian Nights	30	$12	Marlin 2201
9/3/77	57	2		3 African Queens	164	$12	Marlin 2206
6/12/82	36	14		4 I'll Do My Best	203	$10	RCA Victor 4323

RITENOUR, Lee '81
Born on 1/11/52 in Los Angeles. Guitarist/composer/arranger. Nicknamed "Captain Fingers." Member of Fourplay.

5/23/81	20	20		1 "Rit"	26	$10	Elektra 331
12/25/82+	53	9		2 Rit/2	99	$10	Elektra 60186
10/28/89	62	1		3 Color Rit		$8	GRP 9594
5/29/93	54	8		4 Wes Bound		$8	GRP 9697

R.J.'S LATEST ARRIVAL '87
Seven-member group led by keyboardist Ralph James Rice from Detroit.

8/10/85	57	6		1 R.J.'s Latest Arrival		$8	Atlantic 81260
9/27/86+	40	45		2 Hold On		$8	Manhattan 53037
7/9/88	42	16		3 Truly Yours		$8	EMI-Manhattan 48090

ROB BASE & D.J. E-Z ROCK '88
Rap duo from Harlem, New York: Robert Ginyard and DJ Rodney "E-Z Rock" Bryce.

10/8/88	4	58	▲	1 It Takes Two	31	$8	Profile 1267

It Takes Two [17] • Joy And Pain [11] • Don't Sleep On It • Check This Out • Crush • Get On The Dance Floor [11] • Times Are Gettin' Ill • Keep It Going Now • Make It Hot • Creativity

12/9/89+	20	27	●	2 The Incredible Base	50	$8	Profile 1285

ROB BASE

ROBBINS, Rockie '80
Born Edward Robbins in Minneapolis. Singer/songwriter.

5/31/80	19	21		1 You And Me	71	$10	A&M 4805
9/19/81	47	15		2 I Believe In Love	147	$10	A&M 4869
3/30/85	60	5		3 Rockie Robbins		$8	MCA 5526

ROBIN S '93
Born Robin Stone in Queens, New York. Female dance singer.

7/24/93	37	19		1 Show Me Love	110	$8	Big Beat 82509
6/21/97	79	2		2 From Now On		$8	Big Beat 92716

DEBUT	PEAK	WKS	Gold	Album Title		Pop #	$	Label & Number
				ROBINSON, Bert '87				
				Born in Detroit.				
10/17/87	35	18		No More Cold Nights			$8	Capitol 46921
				ROBINSON, Freddy '70				
				Born in 1939 in Memphis. Blues guitarist.				
10/17/70	42	4		The Coming Atlantis .... [I]		133	$15	Pacific Jazz 20162
				ROBINSON, Keith '89				
				Born in Moss Point, Mississippi. Singer/guitarist.				
11/18/89	72	9		Perfect Love			$8	Orpheus 75611

ROBINSON, Smokey ★39★ '81

Born William Robinson on 2/19/40 in Detroit. Formed **The Miracles** (then called the Matadors) at Northern High School in 1955. First recorded for End in 1958. Married Miracles' member Claudette Rogers in 1963; later divorced. Left The Miracles on 1/29/72. Wrote dozens of hit songs for Motown artists. Vice President of Motown Records, 1985-1988. Inducted into the Rock and Roll Hall of Fame in 1987. Won Grammy's Living Legends Award in 1989.

1)Being With You 2)One Heartbeat 3)Warm Thoughts

DEBUT	PEAK	WKS	Gold	Album Title		Pop #	$	Label & Number
7/28/73	10	21		1 **Smokey**		70	$12	Tamla 328
				Holly • Medley: Never My Love/Never Can Say Goodbye • A Silent Partner In A Three-Way Love Affair • Just My Soul Responding • **Sweet Harmony** [31] • Will You Love Me Tomorrow? • Wanna Know My Mind • The Family Song • **Baby Come Close** [7]				
4/27/74	12	24		2 Pure Smokey		99	$12	Tamla 331
5/3/75	7	16		3 **A Quiet Storm**		36	$12	Tamla 337
				Quiet Storm [25] • **The Agony And The Ecstasy** [7] • **Baby That's Backatcha** [1] • Wedding Song • Happy • Love Letters • Coincidentally				
3/13/76	9	16		4 **Smokey's Family Robinson**		57	$12	Tamla 341
				When You Came • Get Out Of Town • Do Like I Do • **Open** [10] • So In Love • Like Nobody Can • Castles Made Of Sand				
2/26/77	16	15		5 Deep In My Soul		47	$12	Tamla 350
8/13/77	39	12		6 Big Time .... [S]			$12	Tamla 355
3/25/78	19	21		7 Love Breeze		75	$12	Tamla 359
12/9/78	70	2		8 Smokin' .... [L]		165	$15	Tamla 363 [2]
6/23/79+	8	51		9 **Where There's Smoke..**		17	$10	Tamla 366
				It's A Good Night • I Love The Nearness Of You • The Hurt's On You • Ever Had A Dream • **Get Ready** [82] • Share It • **Cruisin'** [4]				
3/15/80	4	23		10 **Warm Thoughts**		14	$10	Tamla 367
				Let Me Be The Clock [4] • **Heavy On Pride (Light On Love)** [34] • Into Each Rain Some Life Must Fall • Wine, Women And Song • Melody Man • What's In Your Life For Me • I Want To Be Your Love • Travelin' Through				
3/14/81	**❶**[5]	30	●	11 **Being With You**		10	$10	Tamla 375
				Being With You [1] • Food For Thought • If You Wanna Make Love (Come 'Round Here) • **Who's Sad** [62] • Can't Fight Love • You Are Forever [31] • As You Do • I Hear The Children Singing				
2/20/82	6	28		12 **Yes It's You Lady**		33	$10	Tamla 6001
				Tell Me Tomorrow [3] • Yes It's You Lady • **Old Fashioned Love** [17] • Are You Still Here • The Only Game In Town • International Baby • Merry-Go-Ride • I'll Try Something New • Destiny				
2/5/83	8	22		13 **Touch The Sky**		50	$10	Tamla 6030
				Touch The Sky [68] • Even Tho' • Gone Again • All My Life's A Lie • Sad Time • Dynamite • **I've Made Love To You A Thousand Times** [8]				
9/3/83	28	13		14 **Blame It On Love & All The Great Hits** .... [G]		124	$10	Tamla 6064
6/23/84	35	22		15 Essar		141	$10	Tamla 6098
				title is Robinson's initials (S.R.) spelled out				
2/15/86	23	18		16 Smoke Signals		104	$10	Tamla 6156
3/28/87	**❶**[1]	61	●	17 **One Heartbeat**		26	$8	Motown 6226
				Just To See Her [2] • **One Heartbeat** [3] • It's Time To Stop Shoppin' Around • Why Do Happy Memories Hurt So Bad • You Don't Know What It's Like • **What's Too Much** [16] • Love Brought Us Here Tonight • **Love Don't Give No Reason** [31] • Keep Me				
3/17/90	23	19		18 Love, Smokey		112	$8	Motown 6268
11/23/91	64	8		19 Double Good Everything			$8	SBK 97968
				ROBINSON, Vicki Sue '76				
				Born in 1955 in Philadelphia. Disco singer/actress. In the Broadway productions of *Hair* and *Jesus Christ Superstar*.				
5/29/76	51	4		1 **Never Gonna Let You Go**		49	$12	RCA Victor 1256
10/16/76	39	4		2 Vicki Sue Robinson		45	$12	RCA Victor 1829
3/25/78	56	2		3 Half And Half		110	$12	RCA Victor 2294
				ROBINSON, Wanda '71				
				Born on 11/18/49 in Baltimore. Female poet.				
9/11/71	29	20		Black Ivory .... [T]		186	$12	Perception 18
				ROBYN '98				
				Born Robyn Carlsson on 6/12/79 in Stockholm, Sweden. Female dance singer.				
7/12/97+	51	18	▲	Robyn Is Here		68	$8	RCA 67477
				ROCK, Chris '97				
				Born in 1967 in New York City. Actor/comedian. Regular on TV's *Saturday Night Live* from 1989-91. Acted in several movies.				
4/26/97	41	14		Roll With The New .... [C]		93	$8	DreamWorks 50008

DEBUT	PEAK	WKS	Gold	Album Title	Pop #	$	Label & Number

ROCK, Pete, & C.L. Smooth   '92
Rap duo from Mt. Vernon, New York: Peter "Pete Rock" Phillips and Corey "C.L. Smooth" Penn.

| 10/19/91+ | 53 | 25 | | 1 All Souled Out .... [M] | | $6 | Elektra 61175 |
| 6/27/92 | 7 | 45 | | 2 Mecca And The Soul Brother | 43 | $8 | Elektra 60948 |

Return Of The Mecca • For Pete's Sake • Ghettos Of The Mind • **Lots Of Lovin** *[66]* • Act Like You Know • **Straighten It Out** *[61]* • Soul Brother #1 • Wig Out • Anger In The Nation • **They Reminisce Over You (T.R.O.Y.)** *[10]* • On And On • It's Like That • Can't Front On Me • The Basement • If It Ain't Rough, It Ain't Right • Skinz

| 11/26/94 | 9 | 17 | | 3 The Main Ingredient | 51 | $8 | Elektra 61661 |

In The House • Carmel City • I Get Physical • Sun Won't Come Out • **I Got A Love** *[69]* • Escape • The Main Ingredient • Worldwide • All The Places • Tell Me • **Take You There** *[67]* • Searching • Check It Out • In The Flesh • It's On You • Get On The Mic

| 11/28/98 | 7 | 14 | | 4 Soul Survivor | 39 | $8 | Loud/RCA 67616 |

PETE ROCK
Tru Master *[68]* • Half Man Half Amazin' • Respect Mine • Tha Game • #1 Soul Brother • Rock Steady • Truly Yours • It's About That Time • One Life To Live • **Take Your Time** *[80]* • Mind Blowin' • Soul Survivor • Da Two • Verbal Murder • Strange Fruit • Massive (Hold Tight)

ROCKWELL   '84
Born Kennedy Gordy on 3/15/64 in Detroit. Son of Motown owner Berry Gordy.

| 2/18/84 | 5 | 29 | ● | 1 Somebody's Watching Me | 15 | $8 | Motown 6052 |

Somebody's Watching Me *[1]* • Obscene Phone Caller *[9]* • Taxman • Change Your Ways • Runaway • Wasting Away • Knife • Foreign Country

| 3/9/85 | 52 | 8 | | 2 Captured .... | 120 | $8 | Motown 6122 |
| 7/19/86 | 59 | 6 | | 3 The Genie .... | | $8 | Motown 6178 |

RODNEY O & JOE COOLEY   '89
Rap trio from Los Angeles: Rodney Oliver, Joe Cooley and Jeff Page.

12/3/88+	26	34		1 Me And Joe	187	$8	Egyptian Empire 00777
3/31/90	71	10		2 Three The Hard Way	128	$8	Atlantic 82082
5/25/91	51	20		3 Get Ready To Roll		$8	Nastymix 70300
11/21/92+	50	18		4 F__k New York		$8	Psychotic 1101

★198★ **ROGER**   '81
Born Roger Troutman on 11/29/51 in Hamilton, Ohio. Shot to death by his brother Larry in a murder-suicide on 4/25/99. Roger was age 47 and Larry was age 54. Leader of family group **Zapp**.

| 10/3/81 | ❶¹ | 32 | ● | 1 The Many Facets Of Roger | 26 | $10 | Warner 3594 |

I Heard It Through The Grapevine *[1]* • So Ruff, So Tuff • A Chunk Of Sugar • **Do It Roger** *[24]* • Maxx Axe • Blue (A Tribute To The Blues)

| 6/9/84 | 13 | 22 | | 2 The Saga Continues... .... | 64 | $10 | Warner 23975 |
| 12/5/87+ | 4 | 26 | ● | 3 Unlimited! | 35 | $8 | Reprise 25496 |

I Want To Be Your Man *[1]* • Night And Day • Been This Way Before • Composition To Commemorate (May 30, 1918) • Papa's Got A Brand New Bag • **Thrill Seekers** *[27]* • Tender Moments • If You're Serious • Private Lover • I Really Want To Be Your Man

| 11/23/91 | 45 | 18 | | 4 Bridging The Gap .... | | $8 | Reprise 26524 |
| 11/13/93 | 9 | 103 | ▲ | 5 All The Greatest Hits [G] | 39 | $8 | Reprise 45143 |

ZAPP & ROGER
More Bounce To The Ounce *[2]* • Be Alright *[26]* • I Heard It Through The Grapevine *[1]* • So Ruff, So Tuff • **Do It Roger** *[24]* • Dance Floor *[1]* • Doo Wa Ditty (Blow That Thing) *[10]* • **I Can Make You Dance** *[4]* • Heartbreaker *[15]* • In The Mix *[10]* • Midnight Hour '93 • Computer Love *[65]* • Night And Day '93 • **I Want To Be Your Man** *[1]* • Curiosity '93 • Slow And Easy *[18]* • Mega Medley *[30]*

| 12/7/96 | 93 | 3 | | 6 The Compilation: Greatest Hits II And More .... [G] | | $8 | Reprise 46243 |

ROGER & ZAPP

ROGERS, D.J.   '76
Born DeWayne Julius Rogers in Los Angeles. Singer/songwriter/keyboardist.

4/17/76	36	8		1 It's Good To Be Alive		$12	RCA Victor 1099
9/25/76	49	3		2 On The Road Again	175	$12	RCA Victor 1697
8/26/78	54	9		3 Love Brought Me Back		$10	Columbia 35393

ROLLING STONES, The   '70
R&B-influenced rock group from London: Mick Jagger (vocals), Keith Richards and Mick Taylor (guitars), Bill Wyman (bass) and Charlie Watts (drums). Ron Wood replaced Taylor in 1975. Group won Grammy's Lifetime Achievement Award in 1986. Inducted into the Rock and Roll Hall of Fame in 1989.

1/24/70	19	10	▲²	1 Let It Bleed	3	$15	London 4
8/12/78	46	4	▲⁴	2 Some Girls	1²	$10	Rolling Stones 39108
8/30/80	35	12	▲	3 Emotional Rescue	1⁷	$10	Rolling Stones 16015

ROLLINS, Sonny   '66
Born on 9/7/30 in New York City. Tenor jazz saxophonist.

| 10/29/66 | 17 | 5 | | Alfie .... [I] | | $15 | Impulse 9111 |

ROME   '97
Born in Benton Harbor, Michigan. Male singer.

| 5/3/97 | 7 | 44 | ● | Rome | 30 | $8 | RCA 67441 |

I Belong To You (Every Time I See Your Face) *[2]* • Do You Like This *[10]* • Crazy Love • Just Once, Once More, Three Times • I Gotta Be Down • Do Me Right • That's The Way I Feel About 'Cha • Real Love • Feelin' Kinda Good • Let Me Come Home • Never Find Another Love Like Mine • Real Joy • Heaven

RON "C"   '90
Born Ron Carey in Oakland. Male rapper. Member of **Nemesis**.

3/10/90	39	25		1 "C" Ya	170	$8	Profile 1284
8/1/92	58	11		2 Back On The Street	183	$8	Profile 1431
10/8/94	69	5		3 The "C" Theory		$8	Profile 1454

DEBUT	PEAK	WKS	Gold	Album Title	Pop #	$	Label & Number

RONETTES, The '92

Vocal group from New York City: Veronica "Ronnie" Bennett Spector, sister Estelle Bennett Vann and cousin Nedra Talley Ross. Ronnie was married to producer Phil Spector from 1968-74.

12/19/92	91	1		The Best Of The Ronettes ...... [G]		$8	Phil Spector 72122

ROOTS, The '96

Hip-hop group from Philadelphia: Tariq Trotter, Ahmir-Khalib Thompson, Malik Abdul-Basit and Leonard Hubbard.

2/4/95	22	22		1 Do You Want More?!!!??!	104	$8	DGC 24708
10/12/96	4	27		2 illadelph halflife	21	$8	DGC 24972

Respond/React • Section • Panic!!!!! • It Just Don't Stop • Episodes • Push Up Ya Lighter • **What They Do** [21] • ? vs. Scratch • Concerto Of The Desperado • **Clones** [62] • UNIverse at War • No Alibi • Dave vs. US • No Great Pretender • The Hypnotic • Ital (The Universal Side) • One Shine • The Adventures In Wonderland

10/25/97	93	1		3 Organix		$8	Cargo/MCA 81100

ROSE BROTHERS, The '86

Vocal group: brothers Bobby, Greg, Kenny and Larry Rose.

4/5/86	32	17		The Rose Brothers		$10	Muscle Shoals 2201

★172★ ROSE ROYCE '77

Group from Los Angeles: Gwen Dickey (vocals), Kenji Brown (guitar), Victor Nix (keyboards), Kenny Copeland, Freddie Dunn and Michael Moore (horns), Terral Santiel (percussion), Lequient Jobe (bass) and Henry Garner (drums). Dickey left after first album, replaced by Rose Norwalt. Dickey then returned from 1978 until 1980 when she was replaced by Ricci Benson. Nix left after first album, replaced by Michael Nash. Brown left in 1980, replaced by Walter McKinney.

10/16/76+	2[4]	35	●	1 Car Wash [S]	14	$12	MCA 6000 [2]

Car Wash [1] • 6 O'Clock DJ (Let's Rock) • **I Wanna Get Next To You** [3] • Put Your Money Where Your Mouth Is • Zig Zag • You're On My Mind • Mid Day DJ Theme • Born To Love You • Daddy Rich • You Gotta Believe • **I'm Going Down** [10] • Yo Yo • Sunrise • Righteous Rhythm • Water • Crying • Doin' What Comes Naturally • Keep On Keepin' On

8/27/77	❶[3]	36	▲	2 Rose Royce II/In Full Bloom	9	$10	Whitfield 3074

Wishing On A Star [52] • You Can't Please Everybody • **Ooh Boy** [3] • Do Your Dance [4] • You're My World Girl • Love, More Love • Funk Factory • It Makes You Feel Like Dancin'

9/9/78	4	29	●	3 Rose Royce III/Strikes Again!	28	$10	Whitfield 3227

Get Up Off Your Fat • Do It, Do It • **I'm In Love (And I Love The Feeling)** [5] • First Come, First Serve [65] • Love Don't Live Here Anymore [5] • Angel In The Sky • Help • Let Me Be The First To Know • That's What's Wrong With Me

9/15/79	22	11		4 Rose Royce IV/Rainbow Connection	74	$10	Whitfield 3387
2/14/81	30	20		5 Golden Touch	160	$10	Whitfield 3512
6/12/82	50	9		6 Stronger Than Ever	210	$10	Epic 37939
2/21/87	50	11		7 Fresh Cut		$10	Omni 90557

ROSS, Diana ★11★ '80

Born Diane Earle on 3/26/44 in Detroit. Lead singer of The Supremes from 1961-69. Acted in the movies *Lady Sings The Blues, Mahogany* and *The Wiz*.

1)Diana 2)Touch Me In The Morning 3)Diana Ross 4)Lady Sings The Blues 5)Diana!

7/18/70	❶[2]	22		1 Diana Ross	19	$15	Motown 711

Reach Out And Touch (Somebody's Hand) [7] • Now That There's You • You're All I Need To Get By • These Things Will Keep Me Loving You • **Ain't No Mountain High Enough** [1] • Something On My Mind • I Wouldn't Change The Man He Is • Keep An Eye • Where There Was Darkness • Can't It Wait Until Tomorrow • Dark Side Of The World

11/28/70	5	17		2 Everything Is Everything	42	$15	Motown 724

My Place • Ain't No Sad Song • Everything Is Everything • Baby It's Love • **I'm Still Waiting** [40] • Doobedood'ndoobe, Doobedood'ndoobe, Doobedood'ndoo • Come Together • The Long And Winding Road • I Love You (Call Me) • How About You • (They Long To Be) Close To You

4/24/71	3	16		3 Diana! [TV]	46	$15	Motown 719

Don't Rain On My Parade • Medley: Mama's Pearl/Walk On By/The Love You Save • (They Long To Be) Close To You • Love Story • Remember Me • Medley: I'll Be There/Feelin' Alright • Ain't No Mountain High Enough • I Love You (Call Me)

8/7/71	10	17		4 Surrender	56	$15	Motown 723

Surrender [16] • I Can't Give Back The Love I Feel For You • **Remember Me** [10] • And If You See Him • **Reach Out I'll Be There** [17] • Didn't You Know (You'd Have To Cry Sometime) • A Simple Thing Like Cry • Did You Read The Morning Paper? • I'll Settle For You • I'm A Winner • All The Befores

12/9/72+	2[3]	32		5 Lady Sings The Blues [S]	1[2]	$20	Motown 758 [2]

The Arrest • Lady Sings The Blues • Baltimore Brothel • Billie Sneaks Into Dean & Dean's • T'Ain't Nobody's Bizness If I Do • Big Ben • All Of Me • The Man I Love • Them There Eyes • Gardenias From Louis • Cafe Manhattan • Country Tune • I Cried For You • Billie & Harry • Mean To Me • Fine And Mellow • What A Little Moonlight Can Do • Louis Visits Billie On Tour • Cafe Manhattan Party • T'Ain't Nobody's Bizness If I Do • Agent's Office • Love Is Here To Stay • Fine And Mellow • Lover Man (Oh Where Can You Be?) • You've Changed • Gimme A Pigfoot And A Bottle Of Beer • **Good Morning Heartache** [20] • All Of Me • Love Theme • My Man • Don't Explain • I Cried For You • Strange Fruit • God Bless The Child • Closing Theme

7/14/73	❶[2]	23		6 Touch Me In The Morning	5	$15	Motown 772

Touch Me In The Morning [5] • All Of My Life • We Need You • Leave A Little Room • I Won't Last A Day Without You • Little Girl Blue • My Baby (My Baby My Own) • Imagine • Medley: Brown Baby/Save The Children

11/17/73+	7	27		7 Diana & Marvin	26	$15	Motown 803

DIANA ROSS & MARVIN GAYE
You Are Everything • Love Twins • **Don't Knock My Love** [25] • You're A Special Part Of Me [4] • Pledging My Love • Just Say, Just Say • Stop, Look, Listen (To Your Heart) • I'm Falling In Love With You • **My Mistake (Was To Love You)** [15] • Include Me In Your Life

12/29/73+	12	18		8 Last Time I Saw Him	52	$12	Motown 812
6/22/74	15	12		9 Diana Ross Live At Caesars Palace [L]	64	$12	Motown 801

DEBUT	PEAK	WKS	Gold	Album Title	Pop #	$	Label & Number

ROSS, Diana — Cont'd

DEBUT	PEAK	WKS	Album Title	Pop #	$	Label & Number
3/6/76	4	24	10 **Diana Ross**	5	$12	Motown 861

Theme From Mahogany (Do You Know Where You're Going To) [14] • I Thought It Took A Little Time (But Today I Fell In Love) [61] • Love Hangover [1] • Kiss Me Now • You're Good My Child • One Love In My Lifetime [10] • Ain't Nothin' But A Maybe • After You • Smile

| 8/14/76 | 10 | 12 | 11 **Diana Ross' Greatest Hits** | 13 | $12 | Motown 869 |

Touch Me In The Morning [5] • Love Hangover [1] • Last Time I Saw Him [15] • I Thought It Took A Little Time (But Today I Fell In Love) [61] • Theme From Mahogany (Do You Know Where You're Going To) [14] • Ain't No Mountain High Enough [1] • Remember Me [10] • One Love In My Lifetime [10] • Reach Out And Touch (Somebody's Hand) [7] • Good Morning Heartache [20]

| 2/19/77 | 14 | 8 | 12 An Evening With Diana Ross ....[L] | 29 | $15 | Motown 877 |

recorded at the Ahmanson Theatre in Los Angeles

| 10/8/77 | 7 | 17 | 13 **Baby It's Me** | 18 | $12 | Motown 890 |

Gettin' Ready For Love [16] • **You Got It** [39] • Baby It's Me • Too Shy To Say • **Your Love Is So Good For Me** [16] • Top Of The World • All Night Lover • Confide In Me • The Same Love That Made Me Laugh • Come In From The Rain

| 10/21/78 | 32 | 7 | 14 Ross .... | 49 | $12 | Motown 907 |
| 6/23/79 | 10 | 38 | ● 15 **The Boss** | 14 | $10 | Motown 923 |

No One Gets The Prize • I Ain't Been Licked • All For One • **The Boss** [12] • Once In The Morning • **It's My House** [27] • Sparkle • I'm In The World

| 6/21/80 | ❶[8] | 48 | ▲ 16 **Diana** | 2[2] | $10 | Motown 936 |

Upside Down [1] • Tenderness • Friend To Friend • **I'm Coming Out** [6] • Have Fun (Again) • My Old Piano • Now That You're Gone • Give Up

3/14/81	16	16	17 To Love Again ....[K]	32	$10	Motown 951
10/24/81	14	25	18 All The Great Hits ....[G]	37	$12	Motown 960 [2]
11/14/81+	4	33	▲ 19 **Why Do Fools Fall In Love**	15	$10	RCA Victor 4153

Why Do Fools Fall In Love [6] • Sweet Surrender • **Mirror, Mirror** [2] • Endless Love [1] • It's Never Too Late • Think I'm In Love • Sweet Nothings • Two Can Make It • **Work That Body** [34]

| 10/23/82 | 5 | 28 | ● 20 **Silk Electric** | 27 | $10 | RCA Victor 4384 |

Muscles [4] • So Close [76] • Still In Love • Fool For Your Love • Turn Me Over • Who • Love Lies • In Your Arms • Anywhere You Run To • I Am Me

6/11/83	44	10	21 Diana Ross Anthology ....[G]	63	$15	Motown 6049 [2]
7/30/83	14	15	22 Ross	32	$8	RCA Victor 4677
10/6/84	7	48	● 23 **Swept Away**	26	$8	RCA Victor 5009

Missing You [1] • Touch By Touch • Rescue Me • It's Your Move • Swept Away [3] • Telephone [13] • Nobody Makes Me Crazy Like You Do • All Of You [38] • We Are The Children Of The World • Forever Young

10/19/85	27	21	24 Eaten Alive	45	$8	RCA Victor 5422
6/13/87	39	9	25 Red Hot Rhythm & Blues	73	$8	RCA Victor 6388
6/24/89	34	19	26 Workin' Overtime	116	$8	Motown 6274
10/19/91	66	6	27 The Force Behind The Power	102	$8	Motown 6316
5/8/93	73	2	28 Diana Ross Live - Stolen Moments ....[L]		$8	Motown 6340

recorded on December 4, 1992 at the Ritz Theatre in New York City

| 11/13/93+ | 88 | 3 | 29 Forever Diana ....[K] | | $30 | Motown 6357 [4] |

includes a 92 page booklet

| 4/30/94 | 68 | 4 | 30 Diana Extended/The Remixes ....[K] | | $8 | Motown 6377 |
| 10/14/95 | 38 | 5 | 31 Take Me Higher .... | 114 | $8 | Motown 0586 |

ROTTIN RAZKALS   '95

Rap trio from East Orange, New Jersey: Jeff Ray, Chap and Fam.

| 4/8/95 | 28 | 8 | Rottin Ta Da Core .... | 190 | $8 | Illtown 0461 |

ROYAL FLUSH   '89

Rap group from Houston.

| 4/29/89 | 91 | 2 | Uh Oh! .... | | $8 | Rap-A-Lot 101 |

ROYAL FLUSH   '97

Born Ramel Govantes in Cuba; raised in Queens, New York. Male rapper.

| 9/6/97 | 48 | 6 | Ghetto Millionaire .... | | $8 | Blunt/TVT 6610 |

ROY "C"   '73

Born Roy Charles Hammond in 1943 in New York City.

| 10/27/73 | 56 | 2 | Sex And Soul .... | | $15 | Mercury 678 |

RUDE BOYS   '91

Vocal group from Cleveland: Larry Marcus, Melvin Sephus, and brothers Edward Lee Banks and J. Little.

| 12/8/90+ | 11 | 39 | 1 Rude Awakenings .... | 68 | $8 | Atlantic 82121 |
| 8/15/92 | 33 | 20 | 2 Rude House .... | | $8 | Atlantic 82401 |

| ★143★ | | | **RUFFIN, David**   '69 | | | |

Born Davis Eli Ruffin on 1/18/41 in Meridian, Mississippi. Died of a drug overdose on 6/1/91 (age 50). Brother of **Jimmy Ruffin**. Co-lead singer of **The Temptations** from 1963-68. Also see **Daryl Hall & John Oates**.

1)My Whole World Ended 2)Who I Am 3)Feelin' Good

| 6/21/69 | ❶[2] | 22 | 1 **My Whole World Ended** | 31 | $20 | Motown 685 |

My Whole World Ended (The Moment You Left Me) [2] • Pieces Of A Man • Somebody Stole My Dream • I've Lost Everything I've Ever Loved [11] • Everlasting Love • I've Got To Find Myself A Brand New Baby • The Double Cross • Message From Maria • World Of Darkness • We'll Have A Good Thing Going On • My Love Is Growing Stronger • Flower Child

| 1/3/70 | 9 | 19 | 2 **Feelin' Good** | 148 | $15 | Motown 696 |

Loving You (Is Hurting Me) • Put A Little Love In Your Heart • **I'm So Glad I Fell For You** [18] • Feeling Alright • I Could Never Be President • I Pray Everyday You Won't Regret Loving Me • What You Gave Me • One More Hurt • I Let Love Slip Away • I Don't Know Why I Love You • The Forgotten Man • The Letter

| 10/17/70 | 15 | 12 | 3 I Am My Brother's Keeper .... | 178 | $20 | Soul 728 |

THE RUFFIN BROTHERS (Jimmy & David)

| 3/24/73 | 34 | 6 | 4 David Ruffin .... | 160 | $12 | Motown 762 |
| 12/21/74+ | 37 | 7 | 5 Me 'N Rock 'N Roll Are Here To Stay .... | 201 | $12 | Motown 818 |

RUFFIN, David — Cont'd

DEBUT	PEAK	WKS		Album Title	Pop #	$	Label & Number
11/15/75+	5	23		6 Who I Am	31	$12	Motown 849

Who I Am • It Takes All Kinds Of People To Make A World • Walk Away From Love [1] • I've Got Nothing But Time • The Finger Pointers • Wild Honey • **Heavy Love [8]** • Statue Of A Fool • Love Can Be Hazardous To Your Health

5/29/76	16	12		7 Everything's Coming Up Love	51	$12	Motown 866
6/18/77	36	8		8 In My Stride		$12	Motown 885
10/6/79	19	14		9 So Soon We Change	206	$10	Warner 3306
9/13/80	66	3		10 Gentleman Ruffin		$10	Warner 3416
12/26/87+	60	5		11 Ruffin & Kendrick		$8	RCA Victor 6765

DAVID RUFFIN & EDDIE KENDRICK

RUFFIN, Jimmy   '70

Born on 5/7/39 in Collinsville, Mississippi. Brother of **David Ruffin**.

6/7/69	50	2		1 Ruff'N Ready	196	$30	Soul 708
10/17/70	15	12		2 I Am My Brother's Keeper	178	$20	Soul 728

THE RUFFIN BROTHERS (Jimmy & David)

★60★   RUFUS Featuring Chaka Khan   '76

Group from Chicago that evolved from members of the rock quartet American Breed. First known as Smoke, then Ask Rufus. Group included **Chaka Khan** (vocals), Al Ciner (guitar), Ron Stockert and Kevin Murphy (keyboards), Dennis Belfield (bass) and Andre Fischer (drums). Khan stepped out as a solo singer in 1978. By 1979, group included Tony Maiden (vocals, guitar), David Wolinski and Kevin Murphy (keyboards), Bobby Watson (bass) and John Robinson (drums). Khan reunited with group for several albums since her 1978 departure.

1)Rufus featuring Chaka Khan 2)Ask Rufus 3)Masterjam

7/7/73	44	10		1 Rufus	175	$12	ABC 783
6/15/74	4	37	●	2 Rags To Rufus	4	$12	ABC 809

RUFUS (above 2)
You Got The Love [1] • I Got The Right Street (But The Wrong Direction) • Walkin' In The Sun • Rags To Rufus • Swing Down Chariot • Sideways • Ain't Nothin' But A Maybe • **Tell Me Something Good [3]** • Look Through My Eyes • In Love We Grow • Smokin' Room

1/4/75	2²	30	●	3 Rufusized	7	$12	ABC 837

Once You Get Started [4] • Somebody's Watching You • Pack'd My Bags • Your Smile • Rufusized • I'm A Woman (I'm A Backbone) • Right Is Right • Half Moon • **Please Pardon Me (You Remind Me Of A Friend) [6]** • Stop On By

11/29/75+	❶⁶	31	●	4 Rufus featuring Chaka Khan	7	$12	ABC 909

Fool's Paradise • Have A Good Time • Ooh I Like Your Loving • Everybody Has An Aura • Circles • **Sweet Thing [1]** • Dance Wit Me [5] • Little Boy Blue • On Time • Jive Talkin' [35]

2/5/77	❶³	27	▲	5 Ask Rufus	12	$12	ABC 975

At Midnight (My Love Will Lift You Up) [1] • Close The Door • Medley: Slow Screw Against The Wall/Flat Fry • Earth Song • **Everlasting Love [17]** • Hollywood [3] • Magic In Your Eyes • Better Days • Egyptian Song

2/18/78	❶¹	27	●	6 Street Player	14	$12	ABC 1049

Street Player • **Stay [3]** • Turn • Best Of Your Heart • **Blue Love [34]** • Stranger To Love • Take Time • Destiny • Change Your Ways

2/17/79	15	10		7 Numbers	81	$12	ABC 1098

RUFUS

11/17/79	❶²	28	●	8 Masterjam	14	$10	MCA 5103

Do You Love What You Feel [1] • Any Love [24] • Heaven Bound • Walk The Rockway • Live In Me • Body Heat • **I'm Dancing For Your Love [43]** • What Am I Missing? • Masterjam

3/28/81	24	18		9 Party 'Til You're Broke	73	$10	MCA 5159

RUFUS

11/7/81	15	16		10 Camouflage	98	$10	MCA 5270
3/12/83	49	7		11 Seal In Red		$10	Warner 23753

RUFUS

9/17/83	4	31		12 Live-Stompin' At The Savoy	[L] 50	$12	Warner 23679 [2]

recorded February 1982 at the Savoy Theatre in New York City; side 4: newly-recorded studio cuts
You Got The Love • Once You Get Started • Dance Wit Me • Sweet Thing • Tell Me Something Good • Stop On By • Pack'd My Bags • I'm A Woman (I'm A Backbone) • At Midnight (My Love Will Lift You Up) • Ain't That Peculiar • Stay • What Cha' Gonna Do For Me • Do You Love What You Feel • **Ain't Nobody [1]** • One Million Kisses [37] • Try A Little Understanding • Don't Go To Strangers

★114★   RUN-D.M.C.   '86

Rap trio from Queens, New York: rappers Joseph Simmons (Run) and Darryl McDaniels (DMC) with DJ Jason Mizell (Jam-Master Jay). Group appeared in the movies Krush Groove and Tougher Than Leather.

5/12/84	14	55	●	1 Run-D.M.C.	53	$8	Profile 1202
2/23/85	12	65	▲	2 King Of Rock	52	$8	Profile 1205
6/14/86	❶⁷	60	▲³	3 Raising Hell	3	$8	Profile 1217

Peter Piper • It's Tricky [21] • My Adidas [5] • Walk This Way [8] • Is It Live • Perfection • Hit It Run • Raising Hell • **You Be Illin' [12]** • Dumb Girl • Son Of Byford • Proud To Be Black

6/4/88	2⁵	26	▲	4 Tougher Than Leather	9	$8	Profile 1265

Run's House [10] • Mary, Mary [29] • They Call Us Run-D.M.C. • Beats To The Rhyme • Radio Station • Papa Crazy • Tougher Than Leather • **I'm Not Going Out Like That [40]** • How'd Ya Do It Dee • Miss Elaine • Soul To Rock And Roll • Ragtime

12/8/90+	16	26		5 Back From Hell	81	$8	Profile 1401
11/30/91	75	9		6 Greatest Hits 1983-1991	[G] 199	$8	Profile 1419
5/22/93	❶¹	19		7 Down With The King	7	$8	Profile 1440

Down With The King [9] • Come On Everybody • Can I Get It, Yo • Hit 'Em Hard • To The Maker • 3 In The Head • **Ooh, Whatcha Gonna Do [78]** • Big Willie • Three Little Indians • In The House • Can I Get A Witness • Get Open • What's Next • Wreck Shop • For 10 Years

RUSH, Bobby   '91

Born Emmett Ellis on 11/10/40 in Homer, Louisiana. Singer/songwriter/multi-instrumentalist.

11/2/91	69	24		I Ain't Studdin' You		$8	Urgent! 4117

DEBUT	PEAK	WKS	Gold	Album Title	Pop #	$	Label & Number

RUSHEN, Patrice   '82
Born on 9/30/54 in Los Angeles. Singer/songwriter/keyboardist.

2/28/76	48	6		1 Before The Dawn		$12	Prestige 10098
2/17/79	27	10		2 Patrice	98	$10	Elektra 160
11/17/79+	11	23		3 Pizzazz	39	$10	Elektra 243
11/29/80	23	21		4 Posh	71	$10	Elektra 302
4/24/82	4	29		5 Straight From The Heart	14	$10	Elektra 60015

Forget Me Nots [4] • I Was Tired Of Being Alone (Glad I Got Cha) [79] • All We Need • Number One • Where There Is Love • Breakout! [46] • If Only • Remind Me • (She Will) Take You Down To Love

| 6/23/84 | 7 | 26 | | 6 Now | 40 | $10 | Elektra 60360 |

Feels So Real (Won't Let Go) [3] • Gone With The Night • Gotta Find It • Superstar • Heartache Heartbreak • Get Off (You Fascinate Me) [26] • My Love's Not Going Anywhere • Perfect Love • High In Me • To Each His Own

| 4/4/87 | 19 | 20 | | 7 Watch Out! | 77 | $8 | Arista 8401 |

RUSSELL, Brenda   '88
Born Brenda Gordon in Brooklyn, New York. Singer/songwriter/keyboardist. Co-hosted the Canadian TV series *Music Machine*.

9/22/79	26	24		1 Brenda Russell	65	$10	Horizon 739
4/11/81	42	10		2 Love Life	107	$10	A&M 4811
4/2/88	20	25		3 Get Here	49	$8	A&M 5178
9/22/90	65	9		4 Kiss Me With The Wind		$8	A&M 5271

RYDER, Mitch   '67
Born William Levise on 2/26/45 in Detroit. Leader of white soul-rock group The Detroit Wheels.

| 4/15/67 | 24 | 7 | | Sock It To Me! | 34 | $25 | New Voice 2003 |

         MITCH RYDER AND THE DETROIT WHEELS

RZA   '98
Pronounced: Riz-ah. Born Robert Diggs in New York City. Rapper/producer. Member of **Wu-Tang Clan** and **Gravediggaz**.

| 12/12/98 | 3 | 17 | ● | RZA As Bobby Digital In Stereo | 16 | $8 | Gee Street 32521 |

B.O.B.B.Y. [92] • Unspoken Word • Airwaves • Love Jones • N.Y.C. Everything • Mantis • Holocaust (Silkworm) • Terrorist • Bobby Did It (Spanish Fly) • Handwriting On The Wall • Kiss Of A Black Widow • My Lovin' Is Digi • Domestic Violence • Project Talk • Lab Drunk • Fuck What You Think • Daily Routine

S

SADANE   '81
Born Marcus Sadane in Savannah, Georgia. Singer/dancer.

| 4/11/81 | 50 | 8 | | One-Way Love Affair | | $10 | Warner 3503 |

SADAT X   '96
Born Derek Murphy on 12/29/68 in New York City. Former member of rap group **Brand Nubian**.

| 8/3/96 | 13 | 9 | | Wild Cowboys | 83 | $8 | Loud/RCA 66922 |

SADE   ★92★   '86
Pronounced: SHAH-day. Born Helen Folasade Adu on 1/16/59 in Ibadan, Nigeria; raised in London. Appeared in the 1986 movie *Absolute Beginners*. Won the 1985 Best New Artist Grammy Award. Also see **Sweetback**.

| 2/23/85 | 3 | 76 | ▲4 | 1 Diamond Life | 5 | $8 | Portrait 39581 |

Smooth Operator [5] • Your Love Is King [35] • Hang On To Your Love [14] • Frankie's First Affair • When Am I Going To Make A Living • Cherry Pie • Sally • I Will Be Your Friend • Why Can't We Live Together

| 12/14/85+ | ❶11 | 45 | ▲4 | 2 Promise | 1² | $8 | Portrait 40263 |

Is It A Crime [55] • The Sweetest Taboo [3] • War Of The Hearts • Jezebel • Mr. Wrong • Never As Good As The First Time [8] • Fear • Tar Baby • Maureen

| 6/4/88 | 3 | 44 | ▲3 | 3 Stronger Than Pride | 7 | $8 | Epic 44210 |

Love Is Stronger Than Pride • Paradise [1] • Nothing Can Come Between Us [3] • Haunt Me • Turn My Back On You [12] • Keep Looking • Clean Heart • Give It Up • I Never Thought I'd See The Day • Siempre Hay Esperanza

| 11/21/92 | 2¹ | 105 | ▲4 | 4 Love Deluxe | 3 | $8 | Epic 53178 |

No Ordinary Love [9] • Feel No Pain [59] • I Couldn't Love You More • Like A Tattoo • Kiss Of Life [10] • Cherish The Day [45] • Pearls • Bullet Proof Soul • Mermaid

| 11/26/94 | 7 | 111 | ▲4 | 5 Best Of Sade | [G] | 9 | $8 | Epic 66686 |

Your Love Is King [35] • Hang On To Your Love [14] • Smooth Operator [5] • Jezebel • The Sweetest Taboo [3] • Is It A Crime [55] • Never As Good As The First Time [8] • Love Is Stronger Than Pride • Paradise [1] • Nothing Can Come Between Us [3] • No Ordinary Love [9] • Like A Tattoo • Kiss Of Life [10] • Please Send Me Someone To Love • Cherish The Day [45] • Pearls

SA-DEUCE   '96
Female duo from Queens, New York: Asiah and Janai.

| 4/13/96 | 79 | 4 | | Sa-Deuce | | $8 | EastWest 61891 |

SA-FIRE   '88
Born Wilma Cosme in New York City. Female dance singer.

| 10/29/88 | 84 | 12 | | Sa-Fire | 79 | $8 | Cutting 834922 |

SAIN, Oliver   '75
Born on 3/1/32 in Dundee, Mississippi. Bandleader/saxophonist/drummer.

| 2/15/75 | 45 | 6 | | 1 Bus Stop | [I] | $12 | Abet 406 |
| 2/14/76 | 48 | 4 | | 2 Blue Max | [I] | $12 | Abet 407 |

SAINT TROPEZ   '82
Pronounced: san tro-pay. Female disco trio: Phyllis Rhodes, Lyndie White and Mona Young.

| 5/22/82 | 51 | 9 | | Hot And Nasty | | $10 | Destiny 10004 |

SALSOUL ORCHESTRA '76
Disco orchestra conducted by Philadelphia producer/arranger Vincent Montana. Vocalists included Phyllis Rhodes, Ronni Tyson, Carl Helm, Philip Hurt and Jocelyn Brown.

DEBUT	PEAK	WKS	Gold	Album Title	Pop #	$	Label & Number
12/13/75+	20	20		1 The Salsoul Orchestra [I]	14	$12	Salsoul 5501
10/9/76	23	11		2 Nice 'N' Naasty	61	$12	Salsoul 5502
12/25/76+	38	4		3 Christmas Jollies [X]	48	$12	Salsoul 5507
7/2/77	51	5		4 Magic Journey	61	$12	Salsoul 5515
5/6/78	52	3		5 Up The Yellow Brick Road	117	$12	Salsoul 8500

SALTER, Sam '97
Born in 1978 in Los Angeles. Male singer.

10/18/97	41	20		It's On Tonight	199	$8	LaFace 26040

★193★ SALT-N-PEPA '94
Female rap trio from Queens, New York: Cheryl "Salt" James, Sandra "Pepa" Denton and Dee Dee "Spinderella" Roper.

4/4/87+	7	64	▲	1 Hot, Cool & Vicious	26	$8	Next Plateau 1007

Beauty And The Beat • Tramp [21] • I'll Take Your Man • It's All Right • Chick On The Side [55] • I Desire • The Showstopper • My Mike Sounds Nice [41]

8/20/88	8	39	●	2 A Salt With A Deadly Pepa	38	$8	Next Plateau 1011

A Salt With A Deadly Pepa • I Like It Like That • Solo Power (Let's Get Paid) • Shake Your Thang [4] • I Gotcha • Let The Rhythm Run • Everybody Get Up • Spinderella's Not A Fella (But A Girl DJ) • Solo Power (Syncopated Soul) • Twist And Shout [45] • Hyped On The Mic

4/14/90	15	23	▲	3 Blacks' Magic	38	$8	Next Plateau 1019
1/5/91	63	10		4 A Blitz Of Salt-N-Pepa Hits: The Hits Remixed [K]		$8	Next Plateau 1025
10/30/93+	6	75	▲5	5 Very Necessary	4	$8	London 828392

Groove • No One Does It Better • Somebody's Gettin' On My Nerves • Whatta Man [3] • None Of Your Business [57] • Step • Shoop [3] • Heaven Or Hell • Big Shot • Sexy Noises Turn Me On • Somma Time Man • Break Of Dawn • I've Got AIDS

11/8/97	16	22	●	6 Brand New	37	$8	London 828959

SAM & DAVE '66
Vocal duo: Samuel Moore (b: 10/12/35 in Miami) and David Prater (b: 5/9/37 in Ocilla, Georgia). Prater was killed in a car crash on 4/9/88 (age 50). Duo inducted into the Rock and Roll Hall of Fame in 1992.

7/30/66	❶1	19		1 Hold On, I'm Comin'	45	$40	Stax 708

Hold On, I'm Comin' [1] • If You Got The Loving • I Take What I Want • Ease Me • I Got Everything I Need • Don't Make It So Hard On Me • It's A Wonder • Don't Help Me Out • Just Me • You Got It Made • You Don't Know Like I Know [7] • Blame Me (Don't Blame My Heart)

1/7/67	7	15		2 Double Dynamite	118	$30	Stax 712

You Got Me Hummin' [7] • Said I Wasn't Gonna Tell Nobody [8] • That's The Way It's Gotta Be • When Something Is Wrong With My Baby [2] • Soothe Me [16] • Just Can't Get Enough • Sweet Pains • I'm Your Puppet • Sleep Good Tonight • I Don't Need Nobody (To Tell Me 'Bout My Baby) • Home At Last • Use Me

11/18/67	5	14		3 Soul Men	62	$30	Stax 725

Soul Man [1] • May I Baby • Broke Down Piece Of Man • Let It Be Me • Hold It Baby • I'm With You • Don't Knock It • Just Keep Holding On • The Good Runs The Bad Away • Rich Kind Of Poverty • I've Seen What Loneliness Can Do

12/7/68	38	8		4 I Thank You		$25	Atlantic 8205
3/1/69	24	13		5 The Best Of Sam & Dave [G]	87	$20	Atlantic 8218

SAMPLE, Joe '79
Born on 2/1/39 in Houston. Jazz keyboardist. Founding member of The Crusaders.

2/17/79	25	9		1 Carmel [I]	56	$10	ABC 1126
2/7/81	29	15		2 Voices In The Rain [I]	65	$10	MCA 5172
4/16/83	44	16		3 The Hunter [I]	125	$10	MCA 5397
5/13/89	53	15		4 Spellbound [I]	129	$8	Warner 25781
11/24/90	85	19		5 Ashes To Ashes [I]		$8	Warner 26318
4/10/93	43	15		6 Invitation [I]	194	$8	Warner 45209

SAMUELLE '90
Male singer Samuelle Prater. Former member of Club Nouveau.

9/29/90	37	25		Living In Black Paradise		$8	Atlantic 82130

★149★ SANBORN, David '86
Born on 7/30/45 in Tampa, Florida; raised in St. Louis. Alto saxophonist.
1)Double Vision 2)Voyeur 3)Backstreet

9/25/76	55	2		1 Sanborn [I]	125	$10	Warner 2957
4/5/80	33	14	●	2 Hideaway [I]	63	$10	Warner 3379
4/25/81	18	21	●	3 Voyeur [I]	45	$10	Warner 3546
7/17/82	32	22		4 As We Speak [I]	70	$8	Warner 23650
11/26/83+	21	47		5 Backstreet [I]	81	$8	Warner 23906
2/9/85	31	20	●	6 Straight To The Heart [I-L]	64	$8	Warner 25150

featuring live studio cuts of his well known compositions

7/5/86	16	39	▲	7 Double Vision [I]	50	$8	Warner 25393

BOB JAMES/DAVID SANBORN

3/14/87	43	32	●	8 A Change Of Heart [I]	74	$8	Warner 25479
7/23/88	38	19	●	9 Close-Up [I]	59	$8	Reprise 25715
5/30/92	60	24	●	10 Upfront [I]	107	$8	Elektra 61272
6/25/94	39	10		11 Hearsay [I]	116	$8	Elektra 61620

SANDERS, Deion '95
Born on 8/9/67 in Ft. Myers, Florida. Professional baseball/football player.

1/28/95	70	7		Prime Time		$8	Bust It 2421

DEBUT	PEAK	WKS	Gold	Album Title	Pop #	$	Label & Number
				SANDERS, Pharoah '78			
				Born Farrel Sanders on 10/13/40 in Little Rock, Arkansas. Jazz tenor saxophonist.			
10/11/69	47	8		1 Karma ....[I]	188	$20	Impulse 9181
5/2/70	46	2		2 Jewels Of Thought ....[I]		$20	Impulse 9190
4/1/78	41	10		3 Love Will Find A Way ....[I]	163	$12	Arista 4161
				SAN QUINN '96			
				Born in Oakland. Male rapper.			
8/31/96	48	2		The Hustle Continues		$8	Priority 50573
				SANTA ESMERALDA '78			
				Disco studio group assembled by producers Nicolas Skorsky and Jean-Manuel de Scarano. Lead vocals by Leroy Gomez and Jimmy Goings.			
12/3/77+	23	17	●	1 Don't Let Me Be Misunderstood	25	$12	Casablanca 7080
4/1/78	51	4		2 The House Of The Rising Sun	41	$12	Casablanca 7088
				SANTAMARIA, Mongo '69			
				Born Ramon Santamaria on 4/7/22 in Havana, Cuba. Bandleader/conga player.			
7/30/66	19	2		1 Hey! Let's Party ....[I]	135	$15	Columbia 2473
6/8/68	31	12		2 Soul Bag ....[I]	171	$15	Columbia 9653
3/8/69	6	23		3 Stone Soul ....[I]	62	$15	Columbia 9780
				See-Saw • Son-Of-A-Preacher-Man • Love Child • Where We Are • Hitchcock Railway • Stoned Soul Picnic • Who's Making Love • The Now Generation • Little Green Apples • Cloud Nine [33]			
12/20/69+	43	3		4 Workin' On A Groovy Thing ....[I]	193	$15	Columbia 9937
3/21/70	49	2		5 Feelin' Alright ....[I]	171	$12	Atlantic 8252
6/5/71	46	5		6 Mongo's Way ....[I]		$12	Atlantic 1581
★85★				**SANTANA** '71			
				Latin-rock group formed in San Francisco by singer/guitarist **Carlos Santana** (b: 7/20/47 in Autlan de Navarro, Mexico). Various members over the years included Alex Ligertwood (vocals), Neal Schon (guitar), Gregg Rolie (keyboards) and Michael Shrieve (drums). Schon and Rolie went on to form the rock group, Journey.			
				1)Abraxas 2)Santana III 3)Caravanserai			
12/20/69+	13	26	▲²	1 Santana	4	$12	Columbia 9781
10/17/70+	3	42	▲⁴	2 Abraxas	1⁶	$12	Columbia 30130
				Singing Winds, Crying Beasts • Medley: Black Magic Woman/Gypsy Queen • **Oye Como Va** [32] • Incident At Neshabur • Se A Cabo • Mother's Daughter • Samba Pa Ti • Hope You're Feeling Better • El Nicoya			
10/30/71	5	31	▲²	3 Santana III	4	$12	Columbia 30595
				Batuka • No One To Depend On • Taboo • Toussaint L'Overture • **Everybody's Everything** [39] • Guajira • Jungle Strut • Everything's Coming Our Way • Para Los Rumberos			
7/22/72	6	12	▲	4 Carlos Santana & Buddy Miles! Live! [L]	8	$12	Columbia 31308
				recorded at Hawaii's Diamond Head volcano crater			
				Marbles • Lava • Evil Ways • Them Changes • Free Form Funkafide Filth			
11/11/72	6	20	▲	5 Caravanserai	8	$12	Columbia 31610
				Eternal Caravan Of Reincarnation • Waves Within • Look Up (To See What's Coming Down) • Just In Time To See The Sun • Song Of The Wind • All The Love Of The Universe • Future Primitive • Stone Flower • La Fuente Del Ritmo • Every Step Of The Way			
8/17/74	27	10	▲²	6 Santana's Greatest Hits ....[G]	17	$12	Columbia 33050
11/9/74	33	7		7 Illuminations ....[I]	79	$12	Columbia 32900
				TURIYA ALICE COLTRANE/DEVADIP CARLOS SANTANA			
11/16/74	18	14	●	8 Borboletta	20	$12	Columbia 33135
4/17/76	8	16	●	9 Amigos	10	$12	Columbia 33576
				Dance Sister Dance (Baila Mi Hermana) • Take Me With You • Let Me • Gitano • Tell Me Are You Tired • Europa (Earth's Cry Heaven's Smile) • **Let It Shine** [78] • Caramba			
2/12/77	29	6	●	10 Festival	27	$12	Columbia 34423
11/11/78	36	7	●	11 Inner Secrets	27	$12	Columbia 35600
10/27/79	39	19	●	12 Marathon	25	$12	Columbia 36154
4/25/81	36	8	●	13 Zebop!	9	$12	Columbia 37158
5/28/83	55	6		14 Havana Moon	31	$12	Columbia 38642
				CARLOS SANTANA			
				SANTANA, Jorge '78			
				Born on 6/13/54 in Jalisco, Mexico. Former member of **Malo**. Younger brother of **Carlos Santana**.			
10/28/78	54	2		Jorge Santana	202	$12	Tomato 7020
				SATURDAY NIGHT BAND '78			
				Disco studio group assembled by producers Jesse Boyce and Moses Dillard.			
7/15/78	57	2		Come On Dance, Dance	125	$10	Prelude 12155
				SAVAGE, Chantay '96			
				Born in Chicago. Female singer/songwriter.			
3/30/96	14	15		I Will Survive {Doin' It My Way}	106	$8	RCA 66775
				SCAGGS, Boz '76			
				Born William Royce Scaggs on 6/8/44 in Ohio; raised in Texas. Singer/songwriter. Member of **Steve Miller**'s band (1959, 1967-69).			
8/21/76	6	22	▲⁵	1 Silk Degrees	2⁵	$12	Columbia 33920
				What Can I Say [68] • Georgia • Jump Street • What Do You Want The Girl To Do • Harbor Lights • Lowdown [5] • It's Over • Love Me Tomorrow • Lido Shuffle • We're All Alone			
7/12/80	36	14	▲	2 Middle Man	8	$10	Columbia 36106

DEBUT	PEAK	WKS	Gold	Album Title	Pop #	$	Label & Number
	★152★			**SCARFACE** '93 Born Brad Jordan on 11/9/69 in Houston. Male rapper. Member of **The Geto Boys**.			
10/26/91	13	38	●	1 **Mr. Scarface Is Back**	51	$8	Rap-A-Lot 57167
8/28/93	❶²	44	●	2 **The World Is Yours**	7	$8	Rap-A-Lot 53861
				Lettin' Em Know • Comin' Agg • The Wall • **Let Me Roll** *[50]* • You Don't Hear Me Doe • One Time • Dying With Your Boots On • I Need A Favor • Still That Aggin • Strictly For The Funk Lovers • **Now I Feel Ya** *[79]* • Funky Lil Aggin • Mr Scarface: Part III The Final Chapter • He's Dead • I'm Black			
11/5/94	2³	49	▲	3 **The Diary**	2¹	$8	Rap-A-Lot 39946
				The White Sheet • No Tears • Jesse James • G's • **I Never Seen A Man Cry (aka I Seen A Man Die)** *[15]* • One • Goin' Down • One Time • **People Don't Believe (a.k.a. Hand Of The Dead Body)** *[39]* • Mind Playin' Tricks 94 • The Diary			
3/22/97	❶²	37	▲	4 **The Untouchable**	1¹	$8	Rap-A-Lot 42799
				The Untouchable • No Warning • Southside • Sunshine • Money Makes The World Go Round • For Real • Ya Money Or Ya Life • Mary Jane • **Smile** *[4]* • Smartz • Faith • Game Over			
3/14/98	❶²	30	▲	5 **My Homies**	4	$12	Rap-A-Lot 45471 [2]
				Ma Homiez • Hustler • Do What You Do • Southside: Houston, Texas • Don't Testify • Homies & Thuggs • The Geto • Fuck Faces • What's Goin On • 2 Real • Rules 4 Real Niggas • Win Lose Or Draw • Overnight • Small Time • Krunch Time • City Under Siege • Do What You Want • Dog These Ho's • Boo Boo'n • You Owe Me • In My Blood • Sleepin In My Nikes • Greed • Who Run This • Cocaine • All Night Long • Use Them Ho's • Menace Niggas Never Die • Warriors			
				SCHIFRIN, Lalo '76 Born Boris Schifrin on 6/21/32 in Buenos Aires, Argentina. Pianist/conductor/composer. Scored several movies.			
9/4/76	59	2		**Black Widow** [I]	202	$12	CTI 5000
				SCHOOLLY D '88 Born Jesse Weaver on 6/22/66 in Philadelphia. Male rapper.			
11/7/87	59	10		1 **Saturday Night! - The Album**		$8	Jive 1066
8/27/88	50	9		2 **Smoke Some Kill**	180	$8	Jive 1101
				SCOTT, Freddie '67 Born on 4/24/33 in Providence, Rhode Island.			
3/25/67	21	6		**Are You Lonely For Me**		$20	Shout 501
				SCOTT, Kimberly '98 Born in 1985 in Baltimore. Female singer.			
3/14/98	95	2		**Kimberly Scott**		$8	Columbia 67837
				SCOTT, Millie '87 Born in Savannah, Georgia. Female singer.			
4/11/87	57	6		**Love Me Right**		$8	4th & B'way 444004
				SCOTT, Rena '89 Born in Detroit. Female singer/actress.			
8/12/89	70	10		**Love Zone**		$8	Sedona 7511
				SCOTT, Tom '76 Born on 5/19/48 in Los Angeles. Pop-jazz-fusion saxophonist. Composed several movie and TV scores. Led the house band for TV's *Pat Sajak Show*.			
3/29/75	18	17		1 **Tom Cat** [I] TOM SCOTT & THE L.A. EXPRESS	18	$10	Ode 77029
12/27/75+	15	16		2 **New York Connection** [I]	42	$10	Ode 77033
9/24/77	39	5		3 **Blow It Out** [I]	87	$10	Ode 34966
2/26/94	100	1		4 **Reed My Lips** [I]		$8	GRP 9752
				SCOTT-ADAMS, Peggy '97 Born in Opp, Alabama; raised in Pensacola, Florida. Recorded in the male-female duo **Peggy Scott & Jo Jo Benson**.			
3/1/69	36	7		1 **Soulshake** PEGGY SCOTT & JO JO BENSON	196	$25	SSS Int'l. 1
1/25/97	9	44		2 **Help Yourself**	72	$8	Miss Butch 4003
				Bill *[50]* • **Help Yourself** *[76]* • I'll Take Care Of You • You, Her And His • Cleaning House • I'm Getting What I Want • Slow Drag • I Don't Wanna Steal It • Burning • Part Time Lover, Full Time Fool			
11/22/97+	48	34		3 **Contagious**		$8	Miss Butch 4005
	★199★			**SCOTT-HERON, Gil, And Brian Jackson** '75 Gil Scott-Heron was born on 4/1/49 in Chicago. Met Brian Jackson while attending Lincoln University in Pennsylvania. Both are singers/songwriters/keyboardists. Duo was together from 1974-80. Scott-Heron then went solo. 1)The First Minute Of A New Day 2)Secrets 3)Reflections			
2/8/75	8	14		1 **The First Minute Of A New Day**	30	$10	Arista 4030
				Offering • The Liberation Song (Red, Black And Green) • Must Be Something • Ain't No Such Thing As Superman • Pardon Our Analysis (We Beg Your Pardon) • Guerilla • Winter In America • Western Sunrise • Alluswe			
11/15/75	28	8		2 **From South Africa To South Carolina**	103	$10	Arista 4044
11/6/76	34	6		3 **It's Your World** recorded July 1-2, 1976 at Paul's Mall in Boston	168	$12	Arista 5001 [2]
9/9/78	10	27		4 **Secrets**	61	$10	Arista 4189
				Angel Dust *[15]* • Madison Avenue • Cane • Third World Revolution • Better Days Ahead • Three Miles Down • Angola, Louisiana • Show Bizness *[83]* • Medley: Prayer For Everybody/To Be Free			
3/8/80	22	13		5 **1980**	82	$10	Arista 9514
				GIL SCOTT-HERON:			
2/14/81	63	4		6 **Real Eyes**	63	$10	Arista 9540
10/10/81+	21	27		7 **Reflections**	106	$10	Arista 9566
9/25/82	33	10		8 **Moving Target**	123	$10	Arista 9606
9/29/84	45	8		9 **The Best Of Gil Scott-Heron** [G]		$10	Arista 8248
6/11/94	84	6		10 **Spirits**		$8	TVT 4310

DEBUT	PEAK	WKS	Gold	Album Title	Pop #	$	Label & Number
				SEAGRAM **'94**			
				Born in 1972 in Oakland. Male rapper.			
2/20/93	74	2		1 The Dark Roads		$8	Rap-A-Lot 57192
6/18/94	53	7		2 Reality Check		$8	Rap-A-Lot 53908
8/30/97	66	2		3 Souls On Ice		$8	Rap-A-Lot 44566
				SEASE, Marvin **'87**			
				Born on 2/16/46 in Blackville, South Carolina. Singer/songwriter/producer.			
4/11/87	14	46		1 Marvin Sease	114	$8	London 830794
7/2/88	72	2		2 Breakfast		$8	London 834633
11/11/89	61	35		3 The Real Deal		$8	London 838593
11/30/91	72	13		4 Show Me What You Got		$8	Mercury 510494
5/15/93	55	13		5 The Housekeeper		$8	Jive 41512
11/12/94	69	5		6 Do You Need A Licker?		$8	Jive 41549
5/4/96	54	16		7 Please Take Me		$8	Jive 41585
11/15/97	64	15		8 The Bitch Git It All		$8	Jive 41619
				SEAWIND **'80**			
				Jazz-pop group from Hawaii: husband-and-wife Pauline (vocals) and Bob (drums) Wilson, Bud Nuanez (guitar), Larry Williams (keyboards), Kim Hutchcroft (sax), Jerry Hey (trumpet) and Ken Wild (bass).			
4/16/77	51	7		1 Seawind	188	$12	CTI 5002
2/25/78	55	2		2 Window Of A Child	122	$12	CTI 5007
10/25/80	20	21		3 Seawind	83	$10	A&M 4824
				2ND II NONE **'92**			
				Rap duo from Compton, California: cousins Tha D and KK.			
11/9/91+	26	45		2nd II None	83	$8	Profile 1416
				SECTION 8 MOB **'94**			
				Rap group from New York City.			
6/25/94	98	1		Controlled Dangerous Substance		$8	Dark City 72595
				SEDUCTION **'90**			
				Female vocal trio from New York City: Idalis Leon, April Harris and Michelle Visage. Idalis was later a VJ for MTV.			
1/20/90	28	17	●	Nothing Matters Without Love	36	$8	A&M 5280
				SEFF THE GEFFLA **'95**			
				Male rapper.			
3/4/95	64	1		Livin Kind Of Lavish		$8	Getlow 9240
				SEMBELLO, Michael **'83**			
				Born on 4/17/54 in Philadelphia. Singer/songwriter/guitarist. Guitarist on **Stevie Wonder**'s albums from 1974-79.			
10/15/83	53	6		Bossa Nova Hotel	80	$10	Warner 23920
				SEQUENCE, The **'82**			
				Female funk trio from Columbia, South Carolina: Gwendolyn Chisolm, Angie Stone and Cheryl Cook. Stone was later a member of **Vertical Hold**.			
1/23/82	60	5		1 The Sequence		$10	Sugar Hill 250
8/7/82	51	5		2 The Sequence	207	$10	Sugar Hill 267
				above 2 are different albums			
				SERMON, Erick **'93**			
				Born on 11/25/68 in Bayshore, New York. Male rapper. One-half of **EPMD** duo.			
11/6/93	2[1]	26		1 No Pressure	16	$8	Def Jam 57460
				Payback II • **Stay Real** [52] • Imma Gitz Mine • Hostile • Do It Up • Safe Sex • Hittin' Switches • Erick Sermon • The Hype • Lil Crazy • The Ill Shit • Swing It Over Here • All In The Mind • Female Species			
11/18/95	6	21		2 Double Or Nothing	35	$8	Def Jam 529286
				Bomdigi [39] • Freak Out • In The Heat • Tell 'Em • Boy Meets World • **Welcome** [41] • Set It Off • Focus • Move On • Do Your Thing • Man Above • Open Fire			
				7A3, The **'89**			
				Rap trio from Brooklyn, New York: brothers Brett B and Sean B, with DJ Grandmixer Muggs (later joined **Cypress Hill**). #7A is the apartment where Brett and Sean were raised.			
12/10/88+	47	20		Coolin' In Cali		$8	Geffen 24209
				7 MILE **'98**			
				Vocal group from Detroit: Deion Lucas, Seantezz Robinson, Luther Jackson and Glynis Martin.			
5/16/98	64	10		7 Mile		$8	Crave 68043
				702 **'97**			
				Female vocal trio from Las Vegas: Kameelah Williams and sisters Irish and Lemisha Grinstead. Group named after the Las Vegas area code.			
10/26/96+	24	50	●	No Doubt	82	$8	Biv 10 0738
				7TH WONDER **'80**			
				Funk group from Tuskegee, Alabama: Wilbert Cox, Allen Williams, and Deborah Matthews (vocals), Marvin Patton (guitar), William Butler (trumpet) and Lloyd Obie (trombone), Julius Chislom (keyboards), Jerome Thornton (bass) and Johnnie Hammon (drums).			
10/4/80	74	3		Thunder		$10	Chocolate City 2012
				SEXY C **'91**			
				Born Cynthia Powell in Fort Myers, Florida. Female rapper.			
11/9/91	90	4		Queen Of The Villains		$8	Joey Boy 3002
				SHABAZZ, Lakim **'91**			
3/2/91	78	7		The Lost Tribe Of Shabazz		$8	Tuff City 0571
				SHADZ OF LINGO **'94**			
				Rap trio from Richmond, Virginia: Lingo, Kolorado and Rocco.			
2/26/94	51	4		A View To A Kill		$8	EMI 80919

SHAGGY '95
Born Orville Richard Burrell on 10/22/68 in Kingston, Jamaica. Reggae singer.

7/29/95	11	38	▲	1 Boombastic	34	$8	Virgin 40158
9/13/97	82	4		2 Midnite Lover		$8	Virgin 44487

SHAI '93
Pronounced: shy. Vocal group from Washington DC: Garfield Bright, Marc Gay, Carl Martin and Darnell Van Rensalier.

1/9/93	3	54	▲²	1 ...If I Ever Fall In Love	6	$8	Gasoline Alley 10762

Comforter [4] • If I Ever Fall In Love [2] • Sexual • Together Forever [89] • Flava • Baby I'm Yours [19] • Waiting For The Day • Changes • Don't Wanna Play • Lord I've Come

12/25/93+	42	11		2 Right Back At Cha	[K]	127	$8	Gasoline Alley 10945

contains remixes and new versions of songs from #1 above

11/4/95	15	17		3 Blackface	42	$8	Gasoline Alley 11176

SHAKATAK '82
Jazz group from London: Jill Saward (vocals), Keith Winter (guitar), Bill Sharpe (keyboards), George Anderson (bass) and Roger Odell (drums).

11/13/82	55	5		Night Birds	202	$10	Polydor 6354

SHALAMAR ★113★ '82
Vocal trio formed in 1978 by Don Cornelius, the producer/host of TV's *Soul Train*. Consisted of **Jody Watley**, Jeffrey Daniels and Gerald Brown. **Howard Hewett** replaced Brown in early 1979. Watley and Daniels (former husband of **Stephanie Mills**) pursued solo careers in 1984; replaced by Delisa Davis (former Miss Teenage Georgia and Miss Tennessee State) and Micki Free. Hewett left in 1985, replaced by Sydney Justin (former football defensive back with the Los Angeles Rams).
1)Friends 2)Big Fun 3)Three For Love

5/28/77	22	8		1 Uptown Festival	48	$12	Soul Train 2289
11/18/78+	52	14		2 Disco Gardens	171	$10	Solar 2895
10/20/79+	4	41	●	3 Big Fun	23	$10	Solar 3479

The Right Time For Us • Take Me To The River • **Right In The Socket [22]** • The Second Time Around [1] • I Owe You One [60] • Let's Find The Time For Love • Girl

1/10/81	8	54	●	4 Three For Love	40	$10	Solar 3577

Full Of Fire [24] • Attention To My Baby • Somewhere There's A Love • Some Things Never Change • **Make That Move [6]** • This Is For The Lover In You [17] • Work It Out • Pop Along Kid

10/31/81	18	19		5 Go For It	115	$10	Solar 3984
2/20/82	❶²	39	●	6 Friends	35	$10	Solar 28

A Night To Remember [8] • Don't Try To Change Me • Help Me • On Top Of The World • I Don't Wanna Be The Last To Know • Friends • Playing To Win • I Just Stopped By Because I Had To • There It Is • **I Can Make You Feel Good [33]**

7/31/82	48	7		7 Greatest Hits	[G]		$10	Solar 4262
8/13/83	13	35		8 The Look	38	$8	Solar 60239
12/15/84+	32	25		9 Heart Break	90	$8	Solar 60385
8/1/87	29	28		10 Circumstantial Evidence		$8	Solar 72556

SHAMUS '97

6/21/97	65	3		Serving Life	[M]		$6	Raw Track 1298

SHANICE '92
Born Shanice Wilson on 5/14/73 in Pittsburgh; raised in Los Angeles. Female singer.

11/7/87	38	27		1 Discovery	149	$8	A&M 5128

SHANICE WILSON

12/7/91+	13	46	●	2 Inner Child	83	$8	Motown 6319
7/9/94	46	12		3 21...Ways To Grow	184	$8	Motown 0302

SHANNON '84
Born Brenda Shannon Greene in Washington DC. Female dance singer.

2/25/84	11	33	●	1 Let The Music Play	32	$10	Mirage 90134
5/25/85	39	25		2 Do You Wanna Get Away	92	$10	Mirage 90267

SHANTÉ, Roxanne '90
Born Lolita Gooden on 3/8/70 in Long Island, New York. Female rapper.

10/12/85	61	6		1 Def Mix Vol. I		$10	Pop Art 4450
12/2/89+	52	11		2 Bad Sister		$8	Cold Chillin' 25809
11/14/92	82	3		3 The Bitch Is Back		$8	Livin' Large 3001

SHARP, Dee Dee '76
Born Dione LaRue on 9/9/45 in Philadelphia. Married record producer Kenny Gamble in 1967. Also recorded as **Dee Dee Sharp Gamble**.

5/8/76	48	4		1 Happy 'Bout The Whole Thing		$12	Philadelphia I. 33839
2/21/81	59	5		2 Dee Dee	204	$10	Philadelphia I. 36370

DEE DEE SHARP GAMBLE

SHAW, Marlena '77
Born Marlena Burgess in 1944 in New Rochelle, New York. Female singer.

4/5/75	47	3		1 Who Is This Bitch, Anyway?	159	$15	Blue Note 397
3/19/77	14	18		2 Sweet Beginnings	62	$12	Columbia 34458

SHEILA E. '84
Born Sheila Escovedo on 12/12/59 in San Francisco. Singer/percussionist. With father Pete Escovedo in the band **Azteca** in the mid-1970s. Toured with **Lionel Richie** and **Prince**. Her brother Peto was in **Con Funk Shun**. Her uncle **Coke Escovedo** was a noted percussionist.

6/30/84	7	42	●	1 Sheila E. in The Glamorous Life	28	$8	Warner 25107

The Belle Of St. Mark [68] • Shortberry Strawcake • Noon Rendezvous • Oliver's House • Next Time Wipe The Lipstick Off Your Collar • The Glamorous Life [9]

9/21/85	12	33	●	2 Sheila E. In Romance 1600	50	$8	Paisley Park 25317
3/28/87	24	12		3 Sheila E.	56	$8	Paisley Park 25498
4/20/91	56	14		4 Sex Cymbal	146	$8	Warner 26255

DEBUT	PEAK	WKS	Gold	Album Title	Pop #	$	Label & Number

SHERRICK '87
Born in 1962 in Austin, Texas. Male singer/songwriter/multi-instrumentalist.

DEBUT	PEAK	WKS	Album Title	Pop #	$	Label & Number
10/3/87	44	12	Sherrick		$8	Warner 25576

SHINEHEAD '90
Born Edmund Carl Aiken on 4/10/62 in London; raised in Jamaica and the Bronx, New York. Reggae rapper.

DEBUT	PEAK	WKS	Album Title	Pop #	$	Label & Number
11/19/88+	86	13	1 Unity	185	$8	Elektra 60802
7/28/90	79	5	2 The Real Rock	155	$8	Elektra 60890
10/31/92	94	4	3 Sidewalk University		$8	Elektra 61139

SHIRLEY AND COMPANY '75
Disco group: Shirley Goodman (female vocals), Jesus Alvarez (male vocals), Walter Morris (guitar), Bernadette Randle (keyboards), Seldon Powell (sax), Jonathan Williams (bass) and Clarence Oliver (drums). Goodman recorded in Shirley & Lee duo with Leonard Lee ("Let The Good Times Roll").

DEBUT	PEAK	WKS	Album Title	Pop #	$	Label & Number
7/26/75	47	4	Shame Shame Shame	169	$12	Vibration 128

SHOCK '82
Funk group from Portland, Oregon: Malcolm Noble (vocals), Scott Boyd (guitar), brothers Roger and Steve Sause (keyboards), Steve Liddle, Ricky Ollison and Steve Snyder (horns), Joe Plass (bass) and Johnny Riley (drums).

DEBUT	PEAK	WKS	Album Title	Pop #	$	Label & Number
2/13/82	61	5	1 Shock		$10	Fantasy 9613
7/10/82	58	3	2 Waves		$10	Fantasy 9619

SHOCKY SHAY '89
Female rapper.

DEBUT	PEAK	WKS	Album Title	Pop #	$	Label & Number
6/3/89	70	10	No Joke		$8	Orpheus 75608

SHOMARI '92
Male vocal trio from New Haven, Connecticut: brothers N'namdi and Rahsaan Langley with their cousin Troy Frost.

DEBUT	PEAK	WKS	Album Title	Pop #	$	Label & Number
8/1/92	77	6	Every Day Has A Sun		$8	Mercury 848896

SHORTER, Wayne '75
Born on 8/25/33 in Newark, New Jersey. Jazz saxophonist. Member of **Weather Report**.

DEBUT	PEAK	WKS	Album Title	Pop #	$	Label & Number
6/14/75	53	5	Native Dancer	183	$12	Columbia 33418

SHOTGUN '77
Funk group from Detroit: Billy Talbert (vocals, guitar), Ernest Lattimore (guitar), William Gentry (trumpet), Greg Ingram (sax), Larry Austin (bass) and Tyrone Steels (drums).

DEBUT	PEAK	WKS	Album Title	Pop #	$	Label & Number
7/9/77	42	13	1 Shotgun	202	$12	ABC 979
5/20/78	57	2	2 Good, Bad & Funky	172	$12	ABC 1060
3/31/79	62	4	3 Shotgun III	163	$10	MCA 1118
2/23/80	51	4	4 Shotgun IV	206	$10	MCA 3201

SHOWBIZ & A.G. '95
Rap duo from the Bronx, New York: Rodney "Showbiz" Lemay and Andre "A.G." Barnes.

DEBUT	PEAK	WKS	Album Title	Pop #	$	Label & Number
7/4/92	78	7	1 Showbiz & A.G.		$8	London 828309
10/31/92	78	5	2 Runaway Slave		$8	London 828334
6/17/95	23	10	3 Goodfellas		$8	Payday 124007
			SHOW & A.G.			

SHYHEIM '94
Born Shyheim Franklin in Staten Island, New York. Male rapper.

DEBUT	PEAK	WKS	Album Title	Pop #	$	Label & Number
5/7/94	7	10	1 AKA The Rugged Child	52	$8	Virgin 39385

Here Come The Hits • **On And On** *[58]* • Pass It Off • Never Say Never • One's 4 Da Money • Here I Am • Move It Over Here • Buckwylyn • You The Man • Napsack • The Rugged Onez • Little Rascals • 4 The Headpiece • Party's Goin' On

DEBUT	PEAK	WKS	Album Title	Pop #	$	Label & Number
6/15/96	10	12	2 The Lost Generation	63	$8	Noo Trybe 41583

This Iz Real *[84]* • Dear God • Jiggy Comin' • 5 Elements • Shaolin Style • Real Bad Boys • What Makes The World Go Round • Can You Feel It • Life As A Shorty • Don't Front/Let's Chill • Things Happen • See What I See • Still There • Young Gods

SIDE EFFECT '77
Vocal group from Los Angeles: Augie Johnson, Sylvia St. James, Louis Patton and Gregory Matta. Nabors was replaced by Helen Lowe, who was replaced by Sylvia St. James in 1977. **Miki Howard** replaced St. James in late 1979.

DEBUT	PEAK	WKS	Album Title	Pop #	$	Label & Number
1/8/77	26	27	1 What You Need	115	$12	Fantasy 9513
1/14/78	53	5	2 Goin' Bananas	86	$12	Fantasy 9537
1/13/79	57	10	3 Rainbow Visions	135	$12	Fantasy 9569
5/10/80	70	5	4 After The Rain	208	$10	Elektra 261
6/13/81	52	6	5 Portraits		$10	Elektra 335

SIGLER, Bunny '78
Born Walter Sigler on 3/27/41 in Philadelphia. Male singer/songwriter/multi-instrumentalist.

DEBUT	PEAK	WKS	Album Title	Pop #	$	Label & Number
5/25/74	27	9	1 That's How Long I'll Be Loving You		$15	Philadelphia I. 32859
2/11/78	18	15	2 Let Me Party With You	77	$12	Gold Mind 7502
3/31/79	49	9	3 I've Always Wanted To Sing...Not Just Write Songs	119	$12	Gold Mind 9503

SILK '93
Vocal group from Atlanta: Timothy Cameron, Jimmy Gates, Jonathan Rasboro, Gary Jenkins and Gary Glenn.

DEBUT	PEAK	WKS	Gold	Album Title	Pop #	$	Label & Number
12/5/92+	❶[1]	67	▲[2]	1 Lose Control	7	$8	Elektra 61394

Happy Days *[13]* • Don't Keep Me Waiting • **Girl U For Me** *[6]* • **Freak Me** *[1]* • When I Think About You • Baby It's You • Lose Control *[4]* • It Had To Be You *[45]* • I Gave To You

DEBUT	PEAK	WKS	Gold	Album Title	Pop #	$	Label & Number
12/2/95	10	29	●	2 Silk	46	$8	Elektra 61849

Hooked On You *[12]* • Because Of Your Love • It's So Good • **Don't Rush** *[39]* • I Can Go Deep *[22]* • What Kind Of Love Is This • Don't Go To Bed Mad • Don't Cry For Me • Now That I've Lost You • How Could You Say You Love Me • Remember Me

SILKK THE SHOCKER '98
Born Zyshonne Miller in New Orleans. Male rapper. Brother of **Master P**. Member of the group **Tru**.

9/7/96	6	44		1 **The Shocker**	49	$8	No Limit 50591

Murder • I Ain't Takin No Shorts • I Represent • The Shocker • No Limit Party • Free Loaders • 1 Morning • How We Mobb • It's On • Ain't Nothing • Ghetto Tears • Mr. • It's Time To Ride • If My 9 Could Talk • Got Em Fiending • My Car • Ghetto 211 • Why My Homie

2/28/98	❶²	56	▲	2 **Charge It 2 Da Game**	3	$8	No Limit 50716

I'm A Soldier • Give Me The World • Throw Yo Hood Up • **Just Be Straight With Me** *[36]* • If I Don't Gotta • Spotaggin • We Can Dance • Mama Always Told Me • You Ain't Gotta Lie To Kick It • Thug 'N' Me • All Night • Who Can I Trust • **It Ain't My Fault** *[5]* • What Gangstas Do • Ummm • Let Me Hit It • How Many... • Who I Be • Tell Me • Me And You

SILK TYMES LEATHER '90
Female rap trio from Atlanta: Vicki "Silk" Jordan, Dyonna "Diamond X" Lewis and Jocelyn "Leather" Rabon.

6/30/90	73	15		It Ain't Where Ya From...It's Where Ya At		$8	Geffen 24289

SILLS, Dwight '90
Born in Raleigh, North Carolina. Jazz guitarist.

9/29/90	79	8		Dwight Sills	[I]	$8	Columbia 46089

SILVER, Horace, Quintet '65
Born on 9/2/28 in Norwalk, Connecticut. Jazz pianist.

6/5/65	8	3		1 **Song For My Father (Cantiga Para Meu Pai)**	[I] 95	$20	Blue Note 84185

Song For My Father • The Natives Are Restless Tonight • Calcutta Cutie • Que Pasa • The Kicker • Lonely Woman

7/20/68	41	5		2 Serenade To A Soul Sister	[I]	$20	Blue Note 84277

THE HORACE SILVER QUINTET Featuring Stanley Turrentine

SILVER CONVENTION '75
Disco studio group from Germany. Vocals by **Penny McLean**, Ramona Wolf and Linda Thompson.

9/20/75	❶¹	21	●	1 **Save Me**	10	$12	Midland Int'l. 1129

Save Me • I Like It • Fly, Robin, Fly *[1]* • Another Girl • Heart Of Stone • Chains Of Love • Son Of A Gun • Tiger Baby • Please Don't Change

4/10/76	9	14		2 **Silver Convention**	13	$12	Midland Int'l. 1369

Get Up And Boogie (That's Right) *[5]* • No, No, Joe *[34]* • San Francisco Hustle • Play Me Like A Yo-Yo • You've Got What It Takes (To Please Your Woman) • Old Wine In New Bottles • You Turned Me On, But You Can't Turn Me Off • The Boy With The Ohh-La-La • Thank You Mr. D.J.

12/18/76+	47	5		3 Madhouse	65	$12	Midland Int'l. 1824

SIMMONS, Aleese '89
Born in California. Female singer.

1/21/89	51	17		I Want It		$8	Orpheus 75601

SIMON, Joe '71
★120★
Born on 9/2/43 in Simmesport, Louisiana. Male singer.
1)The Sounds Of Simon 2)Get Down 3)Drowning In The Sea Of Love

4/20/68	22	6		1 No Sad Songs		$40	Sound Stage 7 15004
4/19/69	41	6		2 Simon Sings		$40	Sound Stage 7 15005
6/14/69	18	15		3 The Chokin' Kind	81	$30	Sound Stage 7 15006
3/20/71	9	15		4 **The Sounds Of Simon**	153	$25	Spring 4701

To Lay Down Beside You *[flip]* • I Can't See Nobody • Most Of All • No More Me • **Your Time To Cry** *[3]* • Help Me Make It Through The Night *[13]* • My Woman, My Woman, My Wife • I Love You More (Than Anything) • **Georgia Blues** *[19]* • All My Hard Times *[26]*

3/25/72	11	19		5 Drowning In The Sea Of Love	71	$25	Spring 5702
12/23/72+	20	8		6 Joe Simon's Greatest Hits Featuring Misty Blue	[G]	$25	Sound Stage 7 31916
2/24/73	15	13		7 The Power Of Joe Simon	97	$25	Spring 5704
10/13/73	57	1		8 Simon County	207	$15	Spring 5705
8/31/74	44	7		9 Mood, Heart And Soul		$15	Spring 6702
7/26/75	10	15		10 **Get Down**	129	$15	Spring 6706

Get Down, Get Down (Get On The Floor) *[1]* • Fire Burning • It Be's That Way Sometimes • **Music In My Bones** *[7]* • You Don't Want To Believe It (My Man) • In My Baby's Arms • Still At The Mercy Of Your Love • It's Crying Time In Memphis

7/10/76	35	8		11 Joe Simon Today		$15	Spring 6710
3/26/77	56	3		12 Easy To Love		$15	Spring 6713
1/20/79	34	10		13 Love Vibrations		$15	Spring 6720
4/18/81	49	12		14 Glad You Came My Way		$12	Posse 10002

SIMON & GARFUNKEL '68
Folk-rock duo from New York City: Paul Simon (b: 10/13/41 in Newark, New Jersey) and Art Garfunkel (b: 11/5/41 in Forest Hills, New York). Duo inducted into the Rock and Roll Hall of Fame in 1990.

5/18/68	32	15	●	The Graduate	[S] 1⁹	$15	Columbia 3180

SIMONE, Nina '65
Born Eunice Waymon on 2/21/33 in Tryon, South Carolina. Jazz-influenced singer/songwriter/pianist.

10/16/65	8	7		1 **Pastel Blues**	139	$20	Philips 187

Be My Husband • Nobody Knows You When You're Down And Out • End Of The Line • Trouble In Mind • Tell Me More And More And Then Some • Chilly Winds Don't Blow • Ain't No Use • Strange Fruit • Sinnerman

4/9/66	19	3		2 Let It All Out		$20	Philips 202
9/10/66	12	19		3 Wild Is The Wind	110	$20	Philips 207
4/29/67	29	2		4 The High Priestess Of Soul		$20	Philips 219
7/29/67	29	2		5 Nina Simone Sings The Blues		$15	RCA Victor 3789
11/18/67	24	10		6 Silk & Soul	158	$15	RCA Victor 3837
2/8/69	44	6		7 'Nuff Said!		$15	RCA Victor 4065
3/7/70	21	18		8 Black Gold	149	$15	RCA Victor 4248
1/5/74	40	7		9 Portrait Of Nina		$12	Trip 9521

DEBUT	PEAK	WKS	Gold	Album Title	Pop #	$	Label & Number
				SIMPLE E '94			
				Born Erica Williams in Oakland. Female rapper.			
10/29/94	88	1		Colouz Uv Sound		$8	Fox 11021
				SIMPLY RED '86			
				Group from Manchester, England: Mick "Red" Hucknall (vocals), Sylvan Richardson (guitar), Fritz McIntyre and Tim Kellett (keyboards), Tony Bowers (bass) and Chris Joyce (drums).			
5/24/86	26	21	▲	1 Picture Book	16	$8	Elektra 60452
4/8/89	62	23	●	2 A New Flame	22	$8	Elektra 60828
				SIMPSON, Valerie '71			
				Born on 8/26/46 in New York City. Half of husband-and-wife duo **Ashford & Simpson**.			
7/24/71	30	11		1 Valerie Simpson Exposed	159	$15	Tamla 311
8/19/72	50	1		2 Valerie Simpson	162	$15	Tamla 317
				SIMS, Joyce '88			
				Born in Rochester, New York. Dance singer.			
12/26/87+	22	27		1 Come Into My Life		$10	Sleeping Bag 10
1/27/90	65	10		2 All About Love		$8	Sleeping Bag 52017
				SINGLETON, Charlie '85			
				Born in Louisiana. Funk singer/guitarist. Former member of **Cameo**.			
10/12/85	37	11		Nothing Ventured, Nothing Gained		$8	Arista 8389
				CHARLIE SINGLETON & MODERN MAN			
				SINISTER '94			
				Born in Los Angeles. Male rapper.			
8/20/94	83	1		Mobbin' 4 Life		$8	Interscope 92401
				SIR MIX-A-LOT '92			
				Born Anthony Ray on 8/12/63 in Seattle. Male rapper. Appeared as the host of the anthology TV series *The Watcher*.			
5/28/88	20	62	▲	1 Swass	82	$8	Nastymix 70123
11/11/89	25	60	●	2 Seminar	67	$8	Nastymix 70150
2/22/92	19	56	▲	3 Mack Daddy	9	$8	Def American 26765
8/6/94	28	10		4 Chief Boot Knocka	69	$8	Rhyme Cartel 45540
9/14/96	55	4		5 Return Of The Bumpasaurus	123	$8	Rhyme Cartel 43081
★192★				**SISTER SLEDGE** '79			
				Vocal group of sisters from Philadelphia: Debra, Joni, Kim and **Kathy Sledge**.			
3/8/75	56	3		1 Circle Of Love		$20	Atco 105
2/24/79	❶[7]	34	▲	2 We Are Family	3	$10	Cotillion 5209
				He's The Greatest Dancer [1] • Lost In Music [35] • Somebody Loves Me • Thinking Of You • We Are Family [1] • Easier To Love • You're A Friend To Me • One More Time			
3/8/80	7	19		3 Love Somebody Today	31	$10	Cotillion 16012
				Got To Love Somebody [6] • You Fooled Around • I'm A Good Girl • Easy Street • Reach Your Peak [21] • Pretty Baby • How To Love • Let's Go On Vacation [63]			
2/28/81	13	25		4 All American Girls	42	$10	Cotillion 16027
2/20/82	17	16		5 The Sisters	69	$10	Cotillion 5231
5/21/83	35	17		6 Bet Cha Say That To All The Girls	169	$10	Cotillion 90069
7/13/85	52	6		7 When The Boys Meet The Girls		$8	Atlantic 81255
				SISTER SOULJAH '92			
				Born Lisa Williamson in the Bronx, New York. Female rapper. Gained fame when then-candidate Bill Clinton denounced her political views.			
4/25/92	72	13		360 Degrees Of Power		$8	Epic 48713
				69 BOYZ '94			
				Rap group from Jacksonville, Florida: Thrill Van, Fast, Slow and Rottweiler Mike Mike. All members were born in 1969.			
6/18/94	13	68	▲	1 Nineteen Ninety Quad	59	$8	Downlow 6901
8/1/98	39	4		2 The Wait Is Over	114	$8	QuadraSound 83031
				SKEE-LO '95			
				Born Antoine Roundtree in Riverside, California. Male rapper.			
7/15/95	37	14	●	I Wish	53	$8	Sunshine 75486
				SKILLET & LEROY '70			
4/18/70	48	2		1 1-2-3 Times A Day .... [C]		$15	Laff 131
5/9/70	44	2		2 Burglar In The Bedroom .... [C]		$15	Laff 141
				SKINNY BOYS '87			
				Rap trio from Bridgeport, Connecticut: brothers Shaun and James Harrison, with cousin Jacque Harrison.			
12/5/87	71	2		Skinny & Proud		$8	Jive 1077
				SKULL DUGGERY '98			
				Born in New Orleans. Male rapper.			
10/19/96	29	5		1 Hoodlum Fo' Life		$8	No Limit 50543
				SKULL DUGREY			
9/26/98	4	9		2 These Wicked Streets	21	$8	Penalty 3082
				Where You From • If It Don't Make $$$... • The Set Up • Testimony • Satisfied • Mistakes In The Game • My Regiment • Shakin In The Streets • I'm Not A Victim • It's No Limit • Pain • Murder Crime • If U Feel • Drama • What What • These Wicked Streets • For The Fans • Ghetto Niggas			
★150★				**SKYY** '82			
				Funk group from Brooklyn, New York: sisters Denise, Delores and Bonnie Dunning (vocals), Solomon Roberts (vocals, guitar), Anibal Sierra (guitar), Larry Greenberg (keyboards), Gerald LaBon (bass) and Tommy McConnell (drums).			
4/21/79	40	24		1 Skyy	117	$10	Salsoul 8517
3/8/80	17	26		2 Skyway	61	$10	Salsoul 8532
12/13/80+	16	31		3 Skyyport	85	$10	Salsoul 8537

DEBUT	PEAK	WKS	Gold	Album Title	Pop #	$	Label & Number
				SKYY — Cont'd			
11/21/81+	❶⁴	43	●	4 Skyy Line	18	$10	Salsoul 8548

Let's Celebrate [16] • **Call Me** [1] • Girl In Blue • Jam The Box • **When You Touch Me** [43] • Gonna Get It On • Get Into The Beat

11/27/82	22	19		5 Skyyjammer	81	$10	Salsoul 8555
8/6/83	44	13		6 Skyylight	183	$10	Salsoul 8562
6/28/86	33	15		7 From The Left Side		$8	Capitol 12448
4/1/89	16	37		8 Start Of A Romance	155	$8	Atlantic 81853
4/4/92	52	9		9 Nearer To You		$8	Atlantic 82328
	★135★			**SLAVE**			**'81**

Funk group from Dayton, Ohio: Mike Williamson (vocals), Danny Webster (guitar), Steve Washington and Floyd Miller (horns), Mark Hicks (keyboards), Mark Adams (bass) and Rodger Parker (drums). Numerous personnel changes. **Steve Arrington** was lead singer from 1979-82.
1)Stone Jam 2)Slave 3)Show Time

4/2/77	6	31	●	1 Slave	22	$10	Cotillion 9914

Slide [1] • Screw Your Wig On Tite • Party Hardy • Son Of Slide • You And Me • Love Me • The Happiest Days • Separated

12/24/77+	31	13		2 The Hardness Of The World	67	$10	Cotillion 5201
8/19/78	11	11		3 The Concept	78	$10	Cotillion 5206
12/1/79+	11	23		4 Just a Touch of Love	92	$10	Cotillion 5217
10/25/80+	5	43	●	5 Stone Jam	53	$10	Cotillion 5224

Let's Spend Some Time • **Feel My Love** [62] • Starting Over • **Sizzlin' Hot** [57] • **Watching You** [6] • Dreamin' • Never Get Away • Stone Jam

10/10/81	7	30		6 Show Time	46	$10	Cotillion 5227

Snap Shot [6] • Party Lites • Spice Of Life (Oh Yes, You're The Best) • Smokin • **Wait For Me** [20] • Steal Your Heart • For The Love Of U • Funken Town

12/25/82+	46	11		7 Visions Of The Lite	177	$10	Cotillion 90024
10/8/83	30	8		8 Bad Enuff	168	$10	Cotillion 90118
5/10/86	56	6		9 Unchained At Last		$8	Ichiban 1002
8/8/87	44	13		10 Make Believe		$8	Ichiban 1009
3/12/94	44	13		11 Stellar Fungk: The Best Of [G]		$8	Rhino 71592
				SLEDGE, Kathy			**'92**

Born in 1959 in Philadelphia. Member of **Sister Sledge**.

5/16/92	86	9		Heart		$8	Epic 46851
				SLEDGE, Percy			**'66**

Born on 11/25/40 in Leighton, Alabama. Male singer.

6/4/66	2²	12		1 When A Man Loves A Woman	37	$50	Atlantic 8125

When A Man Loves A Woman [1] • My Adorable One • Put A Little Lovin' On Me • Love Me All The Way • When She Touches Me (Nothing Else Matters) • You're Pouring Water On A Drowning Man • Thief In The Night • You Fooled Me • Love Makes The World Go Round • Success • Love Me Like You Mean It

11/19/66+	9	17		2 Warm & Tender Soul	136	$50	Atlantic 8132

It Tears Me Up [7] • I'm Hanging Up My Heart For You • You've Really Got A Hold On Me • That's How Strong My Love Is • A Sweet Woman Like You • **Love Me Tender** [35] • **Warm And Tender Love** [5] • Try A Little Tenderness • So Much Love • I Stand Accused • Heart Of A Child • Oh How Happy

5/25/68	27	10		3 Take Time To Know Her	148	$50	Atlantic 8180
3/8/69	27	10		4 The Best Of Percy Sledge [G]	133	$25	Atlantic 8210
2/15/75	48	6		5 I'll Be Your Everything		$15	Capricorn 0147
				SLICK RICK			**'89**

Born Ricky Walters on 1/14/65 in London. Moved to New York City in 1979. Male rapper. Former member of **Doug E. Fresh And The Get Fresh Crew**.

1/7/89	❶⁴	46	▲	1 The Great Adventures Of Slick Rick	31	$8	Def Jam 40513

Treat Her Like A Prostitute • The Ruler's Back • **Children's Story** [5] • The Moment I Feared • Let's Get Crazy • Indian Girl (An Adult Story) • **Teenage Love** [16] • Mona Lisa • Kit (What's The Scoop) • **Hey Young World** [42] • Teacher, Teacher • Lick The Balls

7/27/91	18	16		2 The Ruler's Back	29	$8	Def Jam 47372
12/10/94	11	22		3 Behind Bars	51	$8	Def Jam 523847
				SLY AND ROBBIE			**'90**

Duo of Sly Dunbar and Robbie Shakespeare. Prominent reggae multi-instrumentalists/producers.

11/25/89+	71	13		Silent Assassin		$8	Island 91277
	★103★			**SLY & THE FAMILY STONE**			**'73**

Funk group formed in San Francisco by singer/keyboardist Sylvester "Sly Stone" Stewart (b: 3/15/44 in Dallas). The Family Stone consisted of Freddie Stone (guitar), Cynthia Robinson (trumpet), Jerry Martini (sax), Sly's sister Rose Stone Banks (piano, vocals), Sly's cousin **Larry Graham** (bass) and Gregg Errico (drums). Group inducted into the Rock and Roll Hall of Fame in 1993.

4/27/68	11	10		1 Dance To The Music	142	$15	Epic 26371
5/3/69	3	82	▲	2 Stand!	13	$15	Epic 26456

Stand! [14] • Don't Call Me Nigger, Whitey • **I Want To Take You Higher** [24] • Somebody's Watching You • **Sing A Simple Song** [28] • **Everyday People** [1] • Sex Machine • You Can Make It If You Try

11/21/70	❶¹	48	▲³	3 Greatest Hits [G]	2¹	$12	Epic 30325

I Want To Take You Higher [24] • Everybody Is A Star • **Stand!** [14] • Life • Fun • You Can Make It If You Try • **Dance To The Music** [9] • **Everyday People** [1] • Hot Fun In The Summertime [3] • M'Lady • Sing A Simple Song [28] • **Thank You (Falettinme Be Mice Elf Agin)** [1]

11/20/71+	❶²	29	●	4 There's A Riot Goin' On	1²	$12	Epic 30986

Luv N' Haight • Just Like A Baby • Poet • **Family Affair** [1] • Africa Talks To You "The Asphalt Jungle" • There's A Riot Goin' On • Brave & Strong • **Smilin'** [21] • Time • Spaced Cowboy • **Runnin' Away** [15] • Thank You For Talkin' To Me Africa

6/30/73	❶³	25	●	5 Fresh	7	$12	Epic 32134

In Time • **If You Want Me To Stay** [3] • Let Me Have It All • **Frisky** [28] • Thankful N' Thoughtful • Skin I'm In • I Don't Know (Satisfaction) • Keep On Dancin' • Que Sera, Sera (Whatever Will Be, Will Be) • **If It Were Left Up To Me** [57] • Babies Makin' Babies

DEBUT	PEAK	WKS	Gold	Album Title	Pop #	$	Label & Number
				SLY & THE FAMILY STONE — Cont'd			
11/8/75	11	7		6 High On You	45	$10	Epic 33835
				SLY STONE			
12/18/76	33	5		7 Heard Ya Missed Me, Well I'm Back		$10	Epic 34348
11/3/79	31	7		8 Back On The Right Track	152	$10	Warner 3303
11/17/79	62	2		9 Ten Years Too Soon		$10	Epic 35974
				SLY STONE			
				SLY FOX ·'86			
				Duo of Gary "Mudbone" Cooper (of **Parliament**) and Michael Camacho.			
4/19/86	34	11		Let's Go All The Way	31	$8	Capitol 12367
				SMALL CHANGE '91			
				Vocal group: Tamika Jarmon, Lakuana Brockington, Neamen Howard and Kairi Guinn-Styles.			
7/20/91	69	15		Small Change		$8	Mercury 848367
				SMILEY '90			
				Female rapper.			
9/22/90	56	10		The Smile Gets Wild		$8	Bryant 20010
				SMITH, Frankie '81			
				Born in Philadelphia. Singer/songwriter/producer.			
8/1/81	12	14		Children Of Tomorrow	54	$10	WMOT 37391
★105★				**SMITH, Jimmy** '66			
				Born on 12/8/25 in Norristown, Pennsylvania. Jazz organist.			
				1)Got My Mojo Workin' 2)Organ Grinder Swing 3)Respect			
5/8/65	5	5		1 Monster .... [I]	35	$25	Verve 8618
				Goldfinger • St. James Infirmary • Gloomy Sunday • Theme From Bewitched • Theme From The Munsters • Theme From The Man With The Golden Arm • The Creeper • Monlope			
9/18/65	2²	11		2 Organ Grinder Swing .... [I]	15	$25	Verve 8626
				The Organ Grinder's Swing • Oh, No, Babe • Blues For J • Greensleeves • I'll Close My Eyes • Satin Doll			
3/12/66	❶²	22		3 Got My Mojo Workin' .... [I]	28	$25	Verve 8641
				High Heel Sneakers • (I Can't Get No) Satisfaction • 1-2-3 • Mustard Greens • Got My Mojo Working [17] • Johnny Come Lately • C Jam Blues • Hobson's Hop			
8/27/66	7	10		4 Hoochie Cooche Man .... [I]	77	$25	Verve 8667
				I'm Your Hoochie Cooche Man [49] • One Mint Julep • Ain't That Just Like A Woman • Boom Boom • Blues And The Abstract Truth • TNT			
12/3/66+	12	10		5 "Bucket"! .... [E-I]	121	$25	Blue Note 84235
5/27/67	10	12		6 Jimmy & Wes The Dynamic Duo .... [I]	129	$20	Verve 8678
				JIMMY SMITH & WES MONTGOMERY			
				Down By The Riverside • Night Train • James And Wes • 13 (Death March) • Baby, It's Cold Outside			
10/21/67	3	26		7 Respect .... [I]	60	$20	Verve 8705
				Mercy, Mercy, Mercy • Respect • Funky Broadway • T-Bone Steak • Get Out Of My Life			
6/8/68	29	8		8 Jimmy Smith's Greatest Hits! .... [G-I]	128	$25	Blue Note 89901
6/29/68	40	3		9 Stay Loose...Jimmy Smith Sings Again		$20	Verve 8745
10/26/68	41	8		10 Livin' It Up! .... [I]	169	$20	Verve 8750
7/26/69	48	2		11 The Boss .... [I]	144	$20	Verve 8770
2/12/77	51	5		12 Sit On It .... [I]		$12	Mercury 1127
				SMITH, Lonnie '70			
				Jazz organist.			
3/15/69	46	4		1 Think! .... [I]		$20	Blue Note 84290
3/7/70	24	16		2 Move Your Hand .... [I-L]	186	$15	Blue Note 84326
				recorded on August 9, 1969 at Club Harlem in Atlantic City			
2/27/71	44	2		3 Drives .... [I]		$15	Blue Note 84351
11/29/75	53	5		4 Afro-Desia .... [I]		$12	Groove Merchant 3308
★179★				**SMITH, Lonnie Liston** '75			
				Born on 12/28/40 in Richmond, Virginia. Keyboardist/trumpeter. Formed own group, The Cosmic Echoes.			
				1)Visions Of A New World 2)Reflections Of A Golden Dream 3)Expansions			
				LONNIE LISTON SMITH & THE COSMIC ECHOES:			
5/24/75	27	13		1 Expansions	85	$12	Flying Dutchman 0934
10/11/75	14	18		2 Visions Of A New World	74	$12	Flying Dutchman 1196
4/10/76	18	9		3 Reflections Of A Golden Dream	75	$12	Flying Dutchman 1460
12/25/76+	49	6		4 Renaissance	73	$10	RCA Victor 1822
				LONNIE LISTON SMITH:			
7/30/77	33	14		5 Live! .... [I-L]	58	$10	RCA Victor 2433
				recorded May 19-21, 1977 at Smucker's Cabaret in New York City			
5/6/78	37	11		6 Loveland	120	$10	Columbia 35332
2/24/79	50	6		7 Exotic Mysteries	123	$10	Columbia 35654
9/29/79	57	6		8 A Song For The Children	208	$10	Columbia 36141
4/26/80	51	8		9 Love Is The Answer	202	$10	Columbia 36373
5/21/83	46	6		10 Dreams Of Tomorrow	193	$10	Doctor Jazz 38447
4/21/90	40	26		11 Love Goddess		$8	Startrak 4021
12/7/91+	75	15		12 Magic Lady		$8	Startrak 1000

DEBUT	PEAK	WKS	Gold	Album Title	Pop #	$	Label & Number

SMITH, O.C.   **'68**
Born Ocie Lee Smith on 6/21/36 in Mansfield, Louisiana; raised in Los Angeles. Male singer.

7/6/68	❶¹	48		1 Hickory Holler Revisited	19	$15	Columbia 9680

The Son Of Hickory Holler's Tramp *[32]* • (Sittin' On) The Dock Of The Bay • Main Street Mission • By The Time I Get To Phoenix • Long Black Limousine • The House Next Door • **Little Green Apples** *[2]* • Take Time To Know Her • **Honey (I Miss You)** *[44]* • The Best Man • Seven Days

3/22/69	8	18		2 For Once In My Life	50	$15	Columbia 9756

Isn't It Lonely Together *[40]* • For Once In My Life • Hey Jude • Wichita Lineman • Promises • I Ain't The Worryin' Kind • Melodee • Stormy • Cycles • Keep On Keepin' On • Sounds Of Goodbye

10/18/69	7	20		3 O.C. Smith At Home	58	$15	Columbia 9908

Daddy's Little Man *[9]* • **Friend, Lover, Woman, Wife** *[25]* • Color Him Father • Clean Up Your Own Back Yard • If I Leave You Now • My Cherie Amour • The Learning Tree • Didn't We • Sweet Changes • San Francisco Is A Lonely Town • Can't Take My Eyes Off You

10/23/71	49	2		4 Help Me Make It Through The Night	159	$15	Columbia 30664
6/26/82	61	5		5 Love Changes		$10	Motown 6019

SMITH, Sylvia   **'75**

6/7/75	59	2		Woman Of The World		$12	ABC 876

SMITH, Will   **'98**
Born on 9/25/68 in Philadelphia. Rapper/actor. One-half of **D.J. Jazzy Jeff & The Fresh Prince** duo from 1986-93. Starred on TV's *Fresh Prince of Bel Air* and in several movies. Married actress Jada Pinkett on 12/31/97.

12/13/97+	9	85	▲⁶	Big Willie Style	10	$8	Columbia 68683

Y'All Know • **Gettin' Jiggy Wit It** *[6]* • Candy • Chasing Forever • Don't Say Nothin' • **Miami** *[73]* • Yes Yes Y'All • I Loved You • It's All Good • **Just The Two Of Us** *[17]* • Big Willie Style • Men In Black

SMOOTH   **'95**
Female rapper.

9/11/93	77	9		1 You Been Played		$8	TNT/Jive 41523
8/19/95	35	7		2 Smooth		$8	TNT/Jive 41556
3/28/98	48	6		3 Reality		$8	Perspective 9033

SMOOTHEDAHUSTLER   **'96**
Born in Brooklyn, New York. Male rapper.

5/4/96	11	11		Once Upon A Time In America	93	$8	Profile 1467

SMOOTH, Tim   **'94**
Born in Houston. Male rapper.

5/14/94	66	4		Straight Up Drivin' Em		$8	Rap-A-Lot 53891

SNAP!   **'90**
Studio group assembled by producers Michael Muenzing and Luca Anzilotti. Features a revolving lineup of lead singers including Durron Butler, Jackie Harris, **Pennye Ford**, Thea Austin, Niki Harris and Paula Brown.

6/16/90	13	41	●	1 World Power	30	$8	Arista 8536
12/5/92	56	1		2 The Madman's Return	121	$8	Arista 18693

SNOOP DOGGY DOGG   ★194★   **'93**
Born Calvin Broadus on 10/20/72 in Long Beach, California. Male rapper.

12/11/93	❶⁵	102	▲⁴	1 Doggy Style	1³	$8	Death Row 92279

Bathtub • **Gin & Juice** *[13]* • Tha Shiznit • Lodi Dodi • Murder Was The Case • Serial Killa • **What's My Name?** *[8]* • For All My Niggaz & Bitches • Ain't No Fun (If The Homies Can't Have None) • Doggy Dogg World • Gz And Hustlas • Gz Up, Hoes Down • Next Episode

11/23/96	❶¹	40	▲²	2 Tha Doggfather	1¹	$8	Death Row 90038

Doggfather • Up Jump The Boogie • Freestyle Conversation • Snoop Bounce • Gold Rush • (Tear 'Em Off) Me & My Doggz • You Thought • Vapors • Groupie • 2001 • Sixx Minutes • (D.J.) Wake Up • Snoop's Upside Ya Head • Blueberry • Doggyland • Downtown Assassins

8/15/98	❶³	37	▲²	3 Da Game Is To Be Sold, Not To Be Told	1²	$8	No Limit 50000

Snoop World • Slow Down • **Woof** *[31]* • Gin & Juice II • Show Me Love • Hustle & Ball • Don't Let Go • Tru Tank Dogs • Whatcha Gon Do? • **Still A G Thang** *[16]* • 20 Dollars To My Name • D.O.G.'s Get Lonely 2 • Ain't Nut'in Personal • DP Gangsta • Game Of Life • See Ya When I Get There • Pay For P... • Picture This • Doggz Gonna Get Ya • Hoes, Money & Clout • Get Bout It & Rowdy

SNOW   **'93**
Born Darrin O'Brien on 10/30/69 in Toronto. White reggae singer.

2/6/93	12	32	▲	12 Inches Of Snow	5	$8	EastWest 92207

SNOW, Phoebe   **'75**
Born Phoebe Laub on 7/17/52 in New York City; raised in New Jersey. Singer/songwriter/guitarist.

5/31/75	22	9	●	1 Phoebe Snow	4	$12	Shelter 2109
3/13/76	33	5	●	2 Second Childhood	13	$10	Columbia 33952
11/12/77	36	16		3 Never Letting Go	73	$10	Columbia 34875

SOCCIO, Gino   **'81**
Born in 1955 in Montreal. Techno-disco singer/multi-instrumentalist.

4/7/79	34	11		1 Outline	79	$10	RFC 3309
5/23/81	26	17		2 Closer	96	$10	Atlantic 16042
7/24/82	45	7		3 Face To Face		$10	Atlantic 19358

SOCIETY OF SOUL   **'96**
Vocal group from Atlanta: Roni, Pat Brown, Rico, Ray and Big Rube.

5/18/96	93	1		Brainchild		$8	LaFace 26023

SOFT CELL   **'82**
Electro-rock duo from England: Marc Almond (vocals) and David Ball (synthesizer).

2/27/82	55	10		Non-Stop Erotic Cabaret	22	$10	Sire 3647

DEBUT	PEAK	WKS	Gold	Album Title	Pop #	$	Label & Number

SOLO   '96
Vocal group from New York City: Eunique Mack, Darnell Chavis, Daniele Stokes and Robert Anderson.

| 9/30/95+ | 8 | 57 | ● | 1 Solo | 52 | $8 | Perspective 9017 |

What A Wonderful World • Back 2 Da Street • Blowin' My Mind • Cupid • **Heaven** [7] • Xxtra • It's Such A Shame • **He's Not Good Enough** [50] • Medley: Another Saturday Night/Everybody Loves To Cha Cha Cha • **Where Do U Want Me To Put It** [8] • Keep It Right Here • I'm Sorry • Under The Boardwalk • In Bed • (Last Night I Made Love) Like Never Before • Prince Street • Holdin' On • A Change Is Gonna Come

| 10/10/98 | 25 | 7 | | 2 4 Bruthas & A Bass | 123 | $8 | Perspective 9040 |

SOMETHIN' FOR THE PEOPLE   '97
Vocal trio from Oakland: Jeff Young, Curtis Wilson and Rochad Holiday.

| 7/13/96 | 66 | 11 | | 1 Somethin' For The People | | $8 | Warner 46060 |
| 10/11/97 | 33 | 26 | | 2 This Time It's Personal | 154 | $8 | Warner 46753 |

SOMETHING SPECIAL   '90
Vocal trio from Richmond, Virginia: Bobby Foster, Martin Radden and Danny Thomas.

| 7/7/90 | 89 | 8 | | Something Special | | $8 | Epic/Associated 45302 |

SONS OF FUNK   '98
Rap group from Richmond, California: brothers G-Smooth and Dez with thier cousins Renzo and Rico.

| 5/9/98 | 14 | 14 | | The Game Of Funk | 44 | $8 | No Limit 50725 |

S.O.S. BAND, The   ★156★   '80
Funk group from Atlanta: **Mary Davis** (vocals, keyboards), Bruno Speight (guitar), Willie Killebrew (sax), Billy Ellis (flute), Jason Bryant (keyboards), John Simpson (bass) and James Earl Jones III (drums). Numerous personnel changes. **Pennye Ford** was lead singer from 1987-89.

| 6/28/80 | 2³ | 26 | ● | 1 S.O.S. | 12 | $10 | Tabu 36332 |

S.O.S. (Dit Dit Dit Dash Dash Dash Dit Dit Dit) [20] • What's Wrong With Our Love Affair? [87] • Open Letter • Love Won't Wait For Love • Take Your Time (Do It Right) [1] • I'm In Love • Take Love Where You Find It

8/22/81	30	11		2 Too	117	$10	Tabu 37449
12/4/82	27	24		3 S.O.S. III	172	$10	Tabu 38352
8/6/83	7	36	●	4 On The Rise	47	$10	Tabu 38697

Tell Me If You Still Care [5] • Just Be Good To Me [2] • For Your Love [34] • I'm Not Runnin' • If You Want My Love • On The Rise • Who's Making Love • Steppin' The Stones

| 9/1/84 | 6 | 37 | | 5 Just The Way You Like It | 60 | $10 | Tabu 39332 |

No One's Gonna Love You [15] • Weekend Girl [40] • Just The Way You Like It [6] • Break Up • Feeling • I Don't Want Nobody Else • Body Break

| 5/17/86 | 4 | 31 | ● | 6 Sands Of Time | 44 | $8 | Tabu 40279 |

Even When You Sleep [34] • Sands Of Time • Borrowed Love [14] • Nothing But The Best • The Finest [2] • No Lies [43] • Two Time Lover • Do You Still Want To?

| 10/28/89 | 43 | 10 | | 7 Diamonds In The Raw | 194 | $8 | Tabu 44147 |
| 11/4/95 | 27 | 44 | | 8 The Best Of The S.O.S. Band [G] | 185 | $8 | Tabu/Motown 0594 |

SOUL CHILDREN, The   '69
Vocal group: Anita Louis, Shelbra Bennett, John Colbert and Norman West. Colbert later recorded as J. Blackfoot.

| 10/11/69 | 9 | 16 | | 1 Soul Children | 154 | $30 | Stax 2018 |

I'll Understand [29] • Move Over • When Tomorrow Comes • The Sweeter He Is [7] • Tighten Up My Thang [49] • Give 'Em Love [40] • Doin' Our Thang • Take Up The Slack • Super Soul • My Baby Specializes

7/31/71	20	11		2 Best Of Two Worlds	203	$30	Stax 2043
4/8/72	36	18		3 Genesis	159	$30	Stax 3003
5/25/74	38	14		4 Friction		$30	Stax 5507
4/10/76	54	2		5 Finders Keepers		$15	Epic 33902

SOUL FOR REAL   '95
Vocal group from Long Island, New York: brothers Chris, Andre, Brian and Jason Dalyrimple.

| 4/15/95 | 5 | 31 | ▲ | 1 Candy Rain | 23 | $8 | Uptown/MCA 11125 |

Candy Rain [1] • Every Little Thing I Do [11] • All In My Mind • If You Want It [53] • I Wanna Be Your Friend • Ain't No Sunshine • Spend The Night • I Don't Know • If Only You Knew • Thinking Of You

| 10/12/96 | 29 | 8 | | 2 For Life... | 119 | $8 | Uptown 53012 |

SOULFUL STRINGS, The   '68
Instrumental group from Chicago: Philip Upchurch and Ron Steel (guitars), Lennie Druss (oboe, flute) and Bobby Christian (vibes).

| 7/1/67 | 25 | 6 | | 1 Paint It Black [I] | 166 | $10 | Cadet 776 |
| 12/2/67+ | 6 | 31 | | 2 Groovin' With The Soulful Strings [I] | 59 | $10 | Cadet 796 |

Burning Spear [36] • All Blues • What Now My Love • Within You Without You • Our Day Will Come • Soul Prelude • Groovin' • Alfie • Comin' Home Baby • (I Know) I'm Losing You

| 8/3/68 | 43 | 3 | | 3 Another Exposure [I] | 189 | $10 | Cadet 805 |
| 5/31/69 | 47 | 3 | | 4 In Concert/Back By Demand [I-L] | 125 | $10 | Cadet 820 |

recorded November 6-7, 1968 at The London House in Chicago

SOULJA SLIM   '98
Born James Smith in New Orleans. Male rapper.

| 5/23/98 | 4 | 18 | | Give It 2 'Em Raw | 13 | $8 | No Limit 53547 |

From What I Was Told • Street Life • Wright Me • At The Same Time • Only Real N... • Pray For Your Baby • Head Buster • Me And My Cousin • You Got It (II) • You Ain't Never Seen • Anything • Imagine • Takin' Hits • Wootay • Get High With Me • Law Brekaz • What's Up, What's Happening • Hustlin' Is A Habit • Getting Real • N.L. Party

SOULS OF MISCHIEF   '93
Rap group from Oakland: Tajai Massey, Opio Lindsey, Damani Thompson and Adam Carter.

| 10/16/93 | 17 | 21 | | 1 93 'Til Infinity | 85 | $8 | Jive 41514 |
| 10/28/95 | 27 | 4 | | 2 No Man's Land | 111 | $8 | Jive 41551 |

DEBUT	PEAK	WKS	Gold	Album Title	Pop #	$	Label & Number

SOUL SURVIVORS   '68

Group from New York City: brothers Charles and Richard Ingui (vocals), Kenneth Jeremiah (vocals), Edward Leonetti (guitar), Paul Venturini (organ) and Joey Forigone (drums).

1/13/68	25	4		When The Whistle Blows Anything Goes	123	$50	Crimson 502

SOUL II SOUL   '89

Group from London led by the duo Beresford Romeo and Nellee Hooper. Features female vocalists **Caron Wheeler**, Do'Reen Marcia Lewis and Rose Windross, and musical backing by the Reggae Philharmonic Orchestra. Wheeler left in 1990.

7/8/89	❶[1]	51	▲[2]	1 **Keep On Movin'**	14	$8	Virgin 91267

Keep On Movin' [1] • Fairplay • Holdin' On • Feeling Free • African Dance • Dance • Feel Free • Happiness • **Back To Life (However Do You Want Me)** [1] • Jazzie's Groove [6]

6/23/90	14	22	●	2 Vol II - 1990 - A New Decade	21	$8	Virgin 91367
5/23/92	32	21		3 Volume III Just Right	88	$8	Virgin 91771
10/14/95	67	3		4 Volume V Believe		$8	Virgin 40628

SOUL TRAIN GANG, The   '76

Studio singers from the syndicated TV show *Soul Train*.

12/20/75+	31	8		Don Cornelius Presents The Soul Train Gang		$12	Soul Train 1278

SOUND EXPERIENCE   '74

Funk group from Baltimore.

11/16/74	57	4		Don't Fight The Feeling		$12	Soulville 1650

SOUNDS OF BLACKNESS   '91

Gospel group from Minneapolis. Featured vocalist is **Ann Nesby**.

6/8/91	4	50	●	1 **The Evolution Of Gospel**	176	$8	Perspective 1000

Chains • **Optimistic** [3] • Ah Been Workin' • **The Pressure** [16] • **Testify** [12] • Gonna Be Free One Day • Stand • Your Wish Is My Command • Hallelujah Lord! • We Give You Thanks • He Holds The Future • What Shall I Call Him? • Better Watch Your Behavior • Please Take My Hand • I'll Fly Away • Harambee

12/5/92+	19	6		2 The Night Before Christmas - A Musical Fantasy [X]	129	$8	Perspective 9000
12/25/93+	54	3		3 The Night Before Christmas - A Musical Fantasy [X-R]		$8	Perspective 9000
5/7/94	15	56	●	4 Africa To America: The Journey Of The Drum	109	$8	Perspective 9006
5/24/97	24	47		5 Time For Healing	144	$8	Perspective 9029

SOUTH CENTRAL CARTEL   '94

Rap group from Los Angeles: Larry "L.V." Sanders, Havoc da Mouthpiece, Prodeje, Havikk da Rymeson, Kaos #1 and Gripp.

3/14/92	51	26		1 South Central Madness		$8	Pump 15189
5/28/94	4	20		2 **'N Gatz We Truss**	32	$8	GWK 57294

Bring It On • Drive Bye Homicide • Servin' 'Em Heat • **Gang Stories** [63] • Seventeen Switches • U Couldn't Deal Wit Dis • Do It SC Style • Dick Suckin' Contest • Had To Be Loc'd • Lil Knucklehead • It's A S.C.C. Thang • Stay Out Da Hood • Rollin' Down Da Block • Get 'Em • Gangsta Team • Shot Outz • Marinate • Hoo Ridin' In Da Central

6/21/97	35	5		3 All Day Everyday	178	$8	Def Jam 531159

SOUTH CIRCLE   '95

Rap trio from Houston: Suave House, Michael "Mr. Mike" Walls and Rex Robinson.

7/22/95	8	25		**Anotha Day Anotha Balla**	63	$8	Suave 1518

Geto Madness • It's Going Down • New Day • Unsolved Mysteries • Pimp Thang • Anotha Day Anotha Balla • Attitudes • Final Call • No Escape • Neva Take Me Alive • Mental Murder • Gotta Maintain • Everyday Allday

SOUTH SHORE COMMISSION   '76

Funk group from Washington DC. Lead vocals by Frank McCurry and Sheryl Henry.

12/6/75+	37	9		South Shore Commission	205	$12	Wand 6100

SOUTH SIDE MOVEMENT, The   '73

Group from Chicago.

8/4/73	52	5		The South Side Movement	207	$15	Wand 695

SPARKLE   '98

Born in New York City. Female singer.

5/30/98	2[2]	23		**Sparkle**	3	$8	Rock Land 90149

Good Life • Time To Move On • Lean On Me • I'm Gone • Turn Away • What About • Be Careful • Nothing Can Compare • Quiet Place • Lovin' You • Straight Up • Vegas • No Greater • Play On • Plenty Good Lovin'

SPEAKS, Michael   '95

Born in Benton Harbor, Michigan. Singer/songwriter.

8/19/95	59	8		No Equal		$8	EastWest 61770

SPECIAL DELIVERY   '76

Vocal group featuring lead singer Terry Huff.

7/4/76	34	5		The Lonely One		$12	Mainstream 420

SPECIAL ED   '89

Born Edward Archer in Brooklyn, New York. Male rapper.

4/29/89	8	38		1 **Youngest In Charge**	73	$8	Profile 1280

Taxing • I Got It Made [18] • I'm The Magnificent [37] • Club Scene • Hoedown • Think About It [68] • Ak-Shun • Monster Jam • The Bush • Fly M.C. • Heds And Dreds

8/18/90	15	32		2 Legal	84	$8	Profile 1297
7/15/95	12	9		3 Revelations	107	$8	Profile 1463

SPECIAL GENERATION   '91

Vocal group from St. Petersburg, Florida: Charles Salter, Maurice Dowdell, Maquet Robinson, Chip Carter and Kendrick Washington.

11/24/90+	17	35		1 Take It To The Floor		$8	Capitol 94846
11/21/92	81	2		2 Butterflies		$8	Capitol 71220

SPENCER, J.   '95

Born in Oakland. Male soprano saxophonist.

11/13/93	100	2		1 Chimera [I]		$8	MoJazz 7004
9/9/95	49	11		2 Blue Moon [I]		$8	MoJazz 0551

DEBUT	PEAK	WKS	Gold	Album Title	Pop #	$	Label & Number

SPENCER, Tracie   '91
Born on 7/12/76 in Waterloo, Iowa. Female singer.

| 7/9/88 | 57 | 36 | | 1 Tracie Spencer | 146 | $8 | Capitol 48186 |
| 10/6/90+ | 38 | 92 | | 2 Make The Difference | 107 | $8 | Capitol 92153 |

★164★   **SPICE 1**   '93
Born in Bryan, Texas; raised in Hayward, California. Male rapper.

8/10/91	69	15		1 Let It Be Known		$8	Triad 8701
5/9/92	14	69	●	2 Spice 1	82	$8	Jive 41481
10/9/93	❶²	37	●	3 187 He Wrote	10	$8	Jive 41513

I'm The Fuckin' Murderer • **Dumpin' 'Em In Ditches** [79] • Gas Chamber • 187 He Wrote • Don't Ring The Alarm (The Heist) • Clip & The Trigga • Smoke 'Em Like A Blunt • The Murda Show • 380 On That Ass • Mo' Mail • Runnin' Out Da Crackhouse • **Trigga Gots No Heart** [71] • Trigga Happy • RIP • All He Wrote

| 12/3/94 | 2¹ | 33 | ● | 4 AmeriKKKa's Nightmare | 22 | $8 | Jive 41547 |

D-Boyz Got Love For Me • Face Of A Desperate Man • **Strap On The Side** [74] • Jealous Got Me Strapped • Tell Me What That Mail Like • Doncha Runaway • Hard To Kill • Nigga Sings The Blues • You Can Get The Gat For That • Busta's Can't See Me • Murder Ain't Crazy • Stickin' To The "G" Code • Give The "G" A Gat • Three Strikes • You Done Fucked Up

| 12/23/95 | 3 | 16 | | 5 1990-Sick | 30 | $8 | Jive 41583 |

1990-Sick (Kill 'Em All) [91] • Dirty Bay • Mind Of A Sick Nigga • Drama • Mobbin' • Survival • Tales Of The Niggas Who Got Crept On • Sucka Ass Niggas • Faces Of Death • 1-800 (Straight From The Pen) • Ain't No Love • Funky Chickens • Snitch Killas • Can U Feel It

| 11/15/97 | 5 | 13 | | 6 The Black Bossalini (aka Dr. Bomb From Da Bay) | 28 | $8 | Jive 41596 |

The Thug In Me • I'm High • Recognize Game • Playa Man • Caught Up In My Gunplay • Ballin' • Tha Boss Mobsta • 510,213 • Kill Street Blues • Fetty Chico And The Mack • Wanna Be A G • Diamonds • Down Payment On Heaven • 2 Hands And A Razor

| 11/28/98 | 82 | 1 | | 7 Hits | | $8 | Jive 41656 |

[G]

SPINNERS ★46★   '73
Vocal group from Detroit: G.C. Cameron, Bobbie Smith, Pervis Jackson, Henry Fambrough and Billy Henderson. **Philippé Wynne** replaced Cameron in 1972. John Edwards replaced Wynne in 1977. Wynne died of a heart attack on 7/13/84 (age 43).

1)Spinners 2)Mighty Love 3)New And Improved

| 11/7/70 | 46 | 3 | | 1 2nd Time Around | 199 | $40 | V.I.P. 405 |
| 4/21/73 | ❶³ | 25 | ● | 2 Spinners | 14 | $12 | Atlantic 7256 |

Just Can't Get You Out Of My Mind • Just You And Me Baby • Don't Let The Green Grass Fool You • I Could Never (Repay Your Love) • **I'll Be Around** [1] • One Of A Kind (Love Affair) [1] • We Belong Together • **Ghetto Child** [4] • How Could I Let You Get Away [14] • Could It Be I'm Falling In Love [1]

| 5/19/73 | 37 | 5 | | 3 The Best of The Spinners | 124 | $15 | Motown 769 |

[G]

| 3/30/74 | ❶¹ | 49 | ● | 4 Mighty Love | 16 | $12 | Atlantic 7296 |

Since I Been Gone • Ain't No Price On Happiness • I'm Glad You Walked Into My Life • **I'm Coming Home** [3] • He'll Never Love You Like I Do • Love Has Gone Away • **Love Don't Love Nobody** [4] • **Mighty Love** [1]

| 12/28/74+ | ❶¹ | 32 | ● | 5 New And Improved | 9 | $12 | Atlantic 18118 |

Sittin' On Top Of The World • Smile, We Have Each Other • **Then Came You** [2] • There's No One Like You • **Living A Little, Laughing A Little** [7] • **Sadie** [7] • Lazy Susan • I've Got To Make It On My Own

| 8/9/75 | 2² | 26 | ● | 6 Pick Of The Litter | 8 | $12 | Atlantic 18141 |

Honest I Do • I Don't Want To Lose You • **Love Or Leave** [8] • Sweet Love Of Mine • All That Glitters Ain't Gold • You Made A Promise To Me • **"They Just Can't Stop It" the (Games People Play)** [1] • Just As Long As We Have Love

| 12/20/75+ | 4 | 17 | | 7 Spinners Live! | 20 | $15 | Atlantic 910 [2] |

[L] Fascinating Rhythm • I've Got To Make It On My Own • Living A Little, Laughing A Little • One Of A Kind (Love Affair) • Then Came You • Sadie • How Could I Let You Get Away • Could It Be I'm Falling In Love • Superstar Medley: It's Not Unusual/Don't Mess With Bill/Paper Doll/Stop! In The Name Of Love/If I Didn't Care/Hound Dog/Hello Dolly • Love Don't Love Nobody • Mighty Love

| 7/31/76 | 5 | 28 | ● | 8 Happiness Is Being With The Spinners | 25 | $12 | Atlantic 18181 |

Now That We're Together • You're All I Need In Life • If You Can't Be In Love • **The Rubberband Man** [1] • Toni My Love • Four Hands In The Fire • The Clown • **Wake Up Susan** [11]

4/2/77	11	14		9 Yesterday, Today & Tomorrow	26	$12	Atlantic 19100
12/17/77+	34	10		10 Spinners/8	57	$12	Atlantic 19146
6/3/78	56	2		11 The Best of The Spinners	115	$12	Atlantic 19179
5/19/79	61	3		12 From Here To Eternally	165	$12	Atlantic 19219
11/17/79+	11	29		13 Dancin' And Lovin'	32	$10	Atlantic 19256
6/21/80	16	31		14 Love Trippin'	53	$10	Atlantic 19270
4/4/81	40	11		15 Labor Of Love	128	$10	Atlantic 16032
12/12/81+	34	10		16 Can't Shake This Feelin'	196	$10	Atlantic 19318
11/6/82	43	7		17 Grand Slam	167	$10	Atlantic 80020
4/28/84	47	9		18 Cross Fire	201	$10	Atlantic 80150

SPLIT IMAGE   '89

| 12/24/88+ | 64 | 11 | | Life In The City | | $8 | Bentley 8500 |

SPORTY THIEVZ   '98
Rap trio from New York City: Marlon Brando, King Kirk and Big Dubez.

| 9/5/98 | 66 | 7 | | Street Cinema | | $8 | Roc-A-Blok 69159 |

re-issued with additional tracks on Roc-A-Blok/Ruffhouse 63647 and re-entered on 7/3/99

SPYRO GYRA   '80

Jazz-pop group formed in Buffalo, New York. Led by saxophonist Jay Beckenstein (b: 5/14/51). Numerous personnel changes. **The Brecker Brothers** (Michael and Randy) were longtime members.

DEBUT	PEAK	WKS	Gold	Album Title	Pop #	$	Label & Number
5/27/78	48	8		1 Spyro Gyra .... [I]	99	$12	Amherst 1014
4/14/79	33	33	▲	2 Morning Dance .... [I]	27	$10	Infinity 9004
3/29/80	23	18	●	3 Catching The Sun .... [I]	19	$8	MCA 5108
11/8/80	24	23		4 Carnaval .... [I]	49	$8	MCA 5149
9/26/81	29	13		5 Freetime .... [I]	41	$8	MCA 5238
11/6/82	39	18		6 Incognito .... [I]	46	$8	MCA 5368
7/21/84	41	13		7 Access All Areas .... [I-L]	59	$10	MCA 6893 [2]
				recorded November 17-19, 1983 in Florida			
8/3/85	41	12		8 Alternating Currents .... [I]	66	$8	MCA 5606
10/17/87	67	2		9 Stories Without Words .... [I]	84	$8	MCA 42046

S.S.O.   '76

Disco group featuring Douglas Lucas and the Sugar Sisters.

DEBUT	PEAK	WKS	Gold	Album Title	Pop #	$	Label & Number
1/24/76	48	6		Tonight's The Night		$12	Shadybrook 33001

STACEY Q   '86

Born Stacey Swain in Los Angeles. Female dance singer.

DEBUT	PEAK	WKS	Gold	Album Title	Pop #	$	Label & Number
10/18/86	46	6		Better Than Heaven	59	$8	Atlantic 81676

STANLEY, Chuck   '87

Born in Queens, New York.

DEBUT	PEAK	WKS	Gold	Album Title	Pop #	$	Label & Number
4/18/87	49	16		The Finer Things In Life		$8	Def Jam 40514

STANSFIELD, Lisa   '90

Born on 4/11/66 in Rochdale, England. Dance singer.

DEBUT	PEAK	WKS	Gold	Album Title	Pop #	$	Label & Number
3/17/90	5	37	▲	1 Affection	9	$8	Arista 8554

All Around The World [1] • Mighty Love • **This Is The Right Time** [13] • **You Can't Deny It** [1] • What Did I Do To You? • Affection • Live Together • Sincerity • The Love In Me • Poison • When Are You Coming Back? • Wake Up Baby • The Way You Want It

DEBUT	PEAK	WKS	Gold	Album Title	Pop #	$	Label & Number
12/7/91+	6	47	●	2 Real Love	43	$8	Arista 18679

Change [12] • Time To Make You Mine • Symptoms Of Loneliness & Heartache • **All Woman** [1] • Soul Deep • **A Little More Love** [30] • Make Love To Ya • Set Your Loving Free • First Joy • Real Love • Tenderly • It's Got To Be Real • I Will Be Waiting

DEBUT	PEAK	WKS	Gold	Album Title	Pop #	$	Label & Number
8/16/97	30	14		3 Lisa Stansfield	65	$8	Arista 18738
6/20/98	82	4		4 The #1 Remixes .... [M]		$6	Arista 19012

STAPLES, Mavis   '70

Born in 1940 in Chicago. Member of **The Staple Singers**. Appeared in the 1990 movie *Graffiti Bridge*.

DEBUT	PEAK	WKS	Gold	Album Title	Pop #	$	Label & Number
9/19/70	45	10		1 Only For The Lonely	188	$20	Volt 6010
11/12/77	51	5		2 A Piece Of The Action		$12	Curtom 5019

STAPLES, Pop — see KING, Albert

STAPLE SINGERS, The   ★160★   '75

Family group consisting of Roebuck "Pop" Staples (b: 12/28/15, Winoma, Mississippi), with his son Pervis (who left in 1971) and daughters Cleotha, Yvonne and **Mavis Staples**. Roebuck was a blues guitarist in his teens, later with the Golden Trumpets gospel group. Moved to Chicago in 1935.

DEBUT	PEAK	WKS	Gold	Album Title	Pop #	$	Label & Number
3/27/71	9	18		1 The Staple Swingers	117	$20	Stax 2034

This Is A Perfect World • What's Your Thing • **You've Got To Earn It** [11] • You're Gonna Make Me Cry • Little Boy • How Do You Move A Mountain • Almost • I'm A Lover • **Love Is Plentiful** [31] • **Heavy Makes You Happy (Sha-Na-Boom Boom)** [6] • I Like The Things About You • Give A Hand - Take A Hand

DEBUT	PEAK	WKS	Gold	Album Title	Pop #	$	Label & Number
3/11/72	3	26		2 Bealtitude: Respect Yourself	19	$15	Stax 3002

This World [6] • **Respect Yourself** [2] • Name The Missing Word • **I'll Take You There** [1] • This Old Town • We The People • Are You Sure • Who Do You Think You Are (Jesus Christ Superstar)? • I'm Just Another Soldier • Who

DEBUT	PEAK	WKS	Gold	Album Title	Pop #	$	Label & Number
8/25/73+	13	24		3 Be What You Are	102	$15	Stax 3015
9/7/74	13	15		4 City In The Sky	125	$15	Stax 5515
10/11/75	❶²	23		5 Let's Do It Again .... [S]	20	$12	Curtom 5005

Let's Do It Again [1] • Funky Love • A Whole Lot Of Love • **New Orleans** [4] • I Want To Thank You • Big Mac • After Sex • Chase

DEBUT	PEAK	WKS	Gold	Album Title	Pop #	$	Label & Number
9/18/76	20	11		6 Pass It On	155	$12	Warner 2945
10/8/77	58	4		7 Family Tree		$12	Warner 3064
10/14/78	34	17		8 Unlock Your Mind		$12	Warner 3192
				THE STAPLES (above 3)			
10/20/84	43	9		9 Turning Point		$10	Private I 39460

STARGARD   '78

Disco trio: Rochelle Runnells, Debra Anderson and Janice Williams. Appeared as "The Diamonds" in the 1978 movie *Sgt. Pepper's Lonely Hearts Club Band*.

DEBUT	PEAK	WKS	Gold	Album Title	Pop #	$	Label & Number
3/11/78	12	12		1 Stargard	26	$10	MCA 2321
11/18/78	50	6		2 What You Waitin' For	206	$10	MCA 3064
11/24/79	57	3		3 The Changing Of The Gard		$10	Warner 3386

STARPOINT   '86

Dance group from Maryland: brothers Ernesto, George, Orlando and Gregory Phillips, with Renee Diggs and Kayode Adeyemo.

DEBUT	PEAK	WKS	Gold	Album Title	Pop #	$	Label & Number
8/23/80	62	7		1 Starpoint		$10	Chocolate City 2013
4/25/81	31	15		2 Keep On It	138	$10	Chocolate City 2018
9/11/82	52	4		3 All Night Long	208	$10	Chocolate City 2022
7/2/83	32	8		4 It's So Delicious		$10	Boardwalk 33266
4/7/84	40	9		5 It's All Yours		$8	Elektra 60353
8/24/85+	14	54	●	6 Restless	60	$8	Elektra 60424
4/18/87	29	17		7 Sensational	95	$8	Elektra 60722
12/3/88	75	6		8 Hot To The Touch		$8	Elektra 60810

DEBUT	PEAK	WKS	Gold	Album Title	Pop #	$	Label & Number

STARR, Edwin   '70
Born Charles Hatcher on 1/21/42 in Nashville; raised in Cleveland. Singer/songwriter.

| 5/17/69 | 9 | 10 | | **1 25 Miles** | 73 | $25 | Gordy 940 |

Twenty-Five Miles *[6]* • I'm Still A Struggling Man *[27]* • Backyard Lovin' Man • He Who Picks A Rose • Soul City (Open Your Arms To Me) • You Beat Me To The Punch • Gonna Keep On Tryin' Till I Win Your Love • Pretty Little Angel • If My Heart Could Tell The Story • Who Cares If You're Happy Or Not (I Do) • 24 Hours (To Find My Baby) • Mighty Good Lovin'

| 9/5/70 | 9 | 10 | | **2 War & Peace** | 52 | $20 | Gordy 948 |

War *[3]* • Running Back And Forth • Adios Senorita • All Around The World • I Can't Escape Your Memory • At Last (I Found A Love) • I Just Wanted To Cry • Raindrops Keep Fallin' On My Head • Time *[39]* • California Soul • I Can't Replace My Old Love • She Should Have Been Home

8/28/71	45	2		3 Involved	178	$15	Gordy 956
11/22/75	43	11		4 Free To Be Myself	210	$12	Granite 1005
12/23/78+	22	16		5 Clean	80	$10	20th Century 559
7/28/79	44	8		6 Happy Radio	115	$10	20th Century 591

STARS ON   '81
Studio group assembled by Dutch producer Jaap Eggermont.

| 7/4/81 | 30 | 9 | ● | 1 Stars On Long Play | 9 | $10 | Radio 16044 |
| 5/15/82 | 53 | 4 | | 2 Stars On Long Play III | 163 | $10 | Radio 19349 |

STATE OF ART   '92
Duo of **Chic** members Raymond Jones (from New York) and **Norma Jean** Wright (from Ohio).

| 2/29/92 | 100 | 2 | | Community | | $8 | Columbia 47968 |

STATON, Candi   '71
Born Canzata Staton on 5/13/40 in Hanceville, Alabama. Female singer. Formerly married to **Clarence Carter**.

5/23/70	37	10		1 I'm Just A Prisoner		$20	Fame 4201
1/9/71	12	12		2 Stand By Your Man	188	$20	Fame 4202
12/28/74+	54	5		3 Candi		$12	Warner 2830
6/26/76	14	13		4 Young Hearts Run Free	129	$12	Warner 2948
8/6/77	46	7		5 Music Speaks Louder Than Words		$12	Warner 3040
7/29/78	19	28		6 House Of Love		$12	Warner 3207
7/14/79	23	14		7 Chance	129	$12	Warner 3333
7/26/80	70	3		8 Candi Staton		$12	Warner 3428

STEADY B   '87
Born Warren McGlone in Philadelphia. Male rapper.

3/14/87	44	18		1 Bring The Beat Back		$8	Jive 1020
10/24/87	49	19		2 What's My Name	149	$8	Jive 1060
10/22/88	56	11		3 Let The Hustlers Play	193	$8	Jive 1122
11/25/89+	51	15		4 Going Steady		$8	Jive 1284

STEADY MOBB'N   '97
Male rap duo from Oakland.

| 5/17/97 | 6 | 16 | | **1 Pre-Meditated Drama** | 29 | $8 | No Limit 50704 |

Strong Heart • It's On • Animosity • Trouble • West To South • Puff Puff Pass • Check Ya Nuts • Trying To Get Mine • Blood Money • Lil N • Up To No Good • Block Monsters • 4 Corners • If I Could Change

| 12/12/98 | 19 | 8 | | 2 Black Mafia | 82 | $8 | No Limit 50026 |

STEELE, Terry   '90
Born in Los Angeles. Male singer/songwriter/pianist.

| 9/22/90 | 60 | 10 | | King Of Hearts | | $8 | SBK 94101 |

STEEL PULSE   '82
Reggae group from Birmingham, England: David Hinds, Selwyn Brown, Alphonso Martin, Steve Nesbitt and Alvin Ewen.

| 9/18/82 | 62 | 5 | | True Democracy | 120 | $10 | Elektra 60113 |

STEELY DAN   '81
Pop/jazz-styled duo from Los Angeles: Donald Fagen and Walter Becker. Charted 10 pop albums from 1972-95.

| 1/31/81 | 19 | 14 | ▲ | Gaucho | 9 | $10 | MCA 6102 |

STERLING, Michael   '90

| 10/6/90 | 86 | 8 | | Trouble | | $8 | New 1060 |

STETSASONIC   '88
Rap group from Brooklyn, New York: Glenn "Daddy-O" Bolton, Marvin Wright, Arnold Hamilton, Leonardo Roman, Martin Nemley and Paul Huston. Hamilton and Huston later formed **Gravediggaz**.

5/30/87	32	15		1 On Fire		$10	Tommy Boy 1012
7/30/88	20	28		2 In Full Gear		$10	Tommy Boy 1017
3/2/91	75	6		3 Blood, Sweat & No Tears		$8	Tommy Boy 1024

STEVIE B   '88
Born Steven Hill in Miami.

9/3/88	63	12	●	1 Party Your Body	78	$8	LMR 5500
3/18/89	75	19	●	2 In My Eyes	77	$8	LMR 5531
8/18/90	81	7	●	3 Love & Emotion	54	$8	LMR 2307

STEWART, Amii   '79
Born in 1956 in Washington DC. Disco singer/dancer/actress. In the Broadway musical *Bubbling Brown Sugar*.

| 3/10/79 | 9 | 21 | ● | **Knock On Wood** | 19 | $10 | Ariola 50054 |

Knock On Wood *[6]* • You Really Touched My Heart • **Light My Fire/137 Disco Heaven** *[36]* • Bring It On Back To Me • Closest Thing To Heaven • Am I Losing You • Get Your Love Back • Only A Child In Your Eyes

DEBUT	PEAK	WKS	Gold	Album Title	Pop #	$	Label & Number

STEWART, Billy   '65
Born on 3/24/37 in Washington DC. Died in a car crash on 1/17/70 (age 32). Singer/keyboardist. Nicknamed "Fat Boy."

| 7/3/65 | 2² | 11 | | 1 **I Do Love You** | 97 | $40 | Chess 1496 |

I Do Love You *[6]* • Strange Feeling *[25]* • I'm No Romeo • Oh My! What Can The Matter Be • Fat Boy • Once Again • **Sitting In The Park** *[4]* • Sweet Senorita • Count Me Out • **Reap What You Sow** *[18]* • A Fat Boy Can Cry • Keep Lovin'

| 3/26/66 | 7 | 18 | | 2 **Unbelievable** | 138 | $40 | Chess 1499 |

Summertime *[7]* • Foggy Day • Teach Me Tonight • Canadian Sunset • Time After Time • Misty • Moon River • My Funny Valentine • Love Is Here To Stay • That Old Black Magic • Almost Like Being In Love • Over The Rainbow

STEWART, Jermaine   '85
Born in Ohio. Male singer/dancer.

11/24/84+	30	24		1 The Word Is Out	90	$8	Arista 8261
3/15/86	31	22		2 Frantic Romantic	32	$8	Arista 8395
4/30/88	45	11		3 Say It Again	98	$8	Arista 8455

STEZO   '89
Born in New Haven, Connecticut. Male rapper.

| 7/1/89 | 37 | 29 | | Crazy Noise | | $10 | Fresh 82011 |

STING   '85
Born Gordon Sumner on 10/2/51 in Wallsend, England. Lead singer/bass guitarist of The Police. Acted in several movies.

| 8/10/85 | 35 | 15 | ▲³ | 1 The Dream Of The Blue Turtles | 2⁶ | $8 | A&M 3750 |
| 11/28/87 | 52 | 10 | ▲² | 2 ...Nothing Like The Sun | 9 | $10 | A&M 6402 [2] |

STONE CITY BAND   '80
Funk group: Levi Ruffin (vocals), Tom McDermott (guitar), OBX and Erskine Williams (keyboards), Oscar Alston (bass) and Lanise Hughes (drums). Backing group for **Rick James.**

3/15/80	30	11		1 In 'N' Out	122	$10	Gordy 991
				RICK JAMES presents the STONE CITY BAND			
3/7/81	53	6		2 The Boys Are Back	205	$10	Gordy 1001
8/27/83	56	11		3 Out From The Shadow		$10	Gordy 6042

STREET CORNER SYMPHONY   '76
Vocal group from Atlanta: Milton Hayes, Maurice Chessnut, Luigi Smith, Jesse Harris and Lawrence Miller.

| 2/28/76 | 51 | 3 | | Harmony Grits | | $12 | Bang 406 |

STRIKERS, The   '81
Funk group from New York City: Ruben Faison (vocals), Robert Gilliom and Robert Rodriguez (guitars), Darryl Gibbs (sax), Howie Young (keyboards), Willie Slaughter (bass) and Milton Brown (drums).

| 8/1/81 | 33 | 11 | | The Strikers | 174 | $10 | Prelude 14100 |

STRONG, Barrett   '75
Born on 2/5/41 in Mississippi. Singer/songwriter.

| 5/17/75 | 47 | 6 | | Stronghold | | $12 | Capitol 11376 |

STUFF   '77
Group of New York's top session musicians: Cornell Dupree and **Eric Gale** (guitars), Richard Tee (keyboards), Gordon Edwards (bass), and Christopher Parker and Stephen Gadd (drums). Tee died of cancer on 7/21/93 (age 49). Gale died of cancer on 5/25/94 (age 55).

| 12/11/76 | 53 | 3 | | 1 Stuff | [I] | 163 | $12 | Warner 2968 |
| 8/20/77 | 43 | 7 | | 2 More Stuff | [I] | 61 | $12 | Warner 3061 |

STYLISTICS, The   ★73★   '72
Vocal group from Philadelphia: Russell Thompkins, Airrion Love, James Smith, James Dunn and Herbie Murrell.
1)The Stylistics 2)Round Two: The Stylistics 3)Let's Put It All Together

| 12/4/71+ | 3 | 40 | ● | 1 The Stylistics | 23 | $20 | Avco 33023 |

Stop, Look, Listen (To Your Heart) *[6]* • Point Of No Return • **Betcha By Golly, Wow** *[2]* • Country Living • You're A Big Girl Now *[7]* • **You Are Everything** *[10]* • People Make The World Go Round *[6]* • Ebony Eyes • If I Love You

| 11/4/72 | 3 | 37 | ● | 2 Round 2: The Stylistics | 32 | $20 | Avco 11006 |

I'm Stone In Love With You *[4]* • If You Don't Watch Out • You And Me • It's Too Late • Children Of The Night • **You'll Never Get To Heaven (If You Break My Heart)** *[8]* • Break Up To Make Up *[5]* • Peek-A-Boo • You're As Right As Rain • Pieces

| 11/24/73+ | 5 | 25 | | 3 Rockin' Roll Baby | 66 | $20 | Avco 11010 |

Only For The Children • Could This Be The End • Let Them Work It Out • Make It Last • Pay Back Is A Dog • Love Comes Easy • There's No Reason • **Rockin' Roll Baby** *[3]* • **You Make Me Feel Brand New** *[5]* • I Won't Give You Up

| 6/8/74 | 4 | 30 | ● | 4 Let's Put It All Together | 14 | $15 | Avco 69001 |

Let's Put It All Together *[8]* • I Got A Letter • We Can Make It Happen Again • Keeping My Fingers Crossed • **You Make Me Feel Brand New** *[5]* • I Got Time On My Hands • Doin' The Streets • I Take It Out On You • Love Is The Answer

| 11/23/74 | 8 | 14 | | 5 Heavy | 43 | $15 | Avco 69004 |

The Miracle • She Did A Number On Me • **Star On A TV Show** *[13]* • **Heavy Fallin' Out** *[4]* • What's Happenin', Baby? • Go Now • Don't Put It Down Til You Been There • Hey Girl, Come And Get It • From The Mountain

| 3/8/75 | 13 | 11 | | 6 The Best of The Stylistics | [G] | 41 | $15 | Avco 69005 |
| 6/21/75 | 9 | 12 | | 7 Thank You Baby | 72 | $15 | Avco 69008 |

Thank You Baby *[7]* • **Can't Give You Anything (But My Love)** *[18]* • What Goes Around Comes Around • I'd Rather Be Hurt By You (Than Be Loved By Somebody Else) • Disco Baby • Tears And Souvenirs • A Honky Tonk Cafe • I'm Gonna Win • Stay • Sing Baby Sing

11/8/75	12	11		8 You Are Beautiful	99	$15	Avco 69010
6/12/76	32	4		9 Fabulous	117	$12	H&L 69013
1/8/77	45	4		10 Once Upon A Jukebox	209	$12	H&L 69015
8/5/78	43	7		11 In Fashion		$12	Mercury 3727
10/11/80	11	26		12 Hurry Up This Way Again	127	$10	TSOP 36470
9/19/81	44	7		13 Closer Than Close	210	$10	TSOP 37458
12/22/84+	63	8		14 Some Things Never Change		$10	Streetwise 3304
10/26/91	65	8		15 Love Talk		$8	Amherst 54404

DEBUT	PEAK	WKS	Gold	Album Title	Pop #	$	Label & Number
				SUAVE' **'88**			
				Born on 2/22/66 in Los Angeles. Son of Waymond Anderson (of **GQ**).			
4/23/88	26	21		I'm Your Playmate	101	$8	Capitol 48686
				SUBWAY **'95**			
				Vocal group from Chicago: Eric McNeal, Roy Jones, Keith Thomas and Trerail Puckett.			
2/11/95	23	26		Good Times	101	$8	Biv 10 0354
				SUCCESS-N-EFFECT **'89**			
				Rap group from Atlanta: Eric Bridges, Jevon Moore, Torriano Hardnett and John Battle.			
7/29/89	42	36		1 In Tha Hood		$10	On Top 9002
5/4/91	73	14		2 Back-N-Effect		$8	Wrap 1108
10/24/92	51	6		3 Drive-By Of Uh Revolutionist		$8	Wrap 8113
				SUGA FREE **'97**			
				Born in Oakland; raised in Compton, California. Male rapper.			
7/12/97	37	17		Street Gospel		$8	Island 524385
				SUGARHILL GANG **'82**			
				Rap trio from Harlem, New York: Michael Wright, Guy O'Brien and Henry Jackson. The first commercially successful rap group.			
4/19/80	32	12		1 Sugarhill Gang		$12	Sugar Hill 245
1/16/82	15	20		2 8th Wonder	50	$12	Sugar Hill 249
				SUGA T **'96**			
				Born in San Francisco. Female rapper. Member of **The Click**. Sister of **E-40**.			
5/1/93	88	2		1 It's All Good		$8	Sick Wid' It 713
3/16/96	28	4		2 Paper Chasin' (4eva Hustlin')	193	$8	Jive 41578
	★59★			**SUMMER, Donna** **'79**			
				Born Adrian Donna Gaines on 12/31/48 in Boston. Singer/actress. In European productions of *Hair, Godspell, The Me Nobody Knows* and *Porgy And Bess*. In the 1978 movie *Thank God It's Friday*. Dubbed "The Queen of Disco."			
				1)Bad Girls 2)Live And More 3)On The Radio-Greatest Hits-Volumes I & II			
10/18/75	6	25	●	1 Love To Love You Baby	11	$12	Oasis 5003
				Love To Love You Baby *[3]* • Full Of Emptiness • Need-A-Man Blues • Whispering Waves • Pandora's Box			
4/3/76	16	22	●	2 A Love Trilogy	21	$12	Oasis 5004
11/13/76	13	20	●	3 Four Seasons Of Love	29	$10	Casablanca 7038
6/11/77	11	28	●	4 I Remember Yesterday	18	$10	Casablanca 7056
11/26/77	13	26	●	5 Once Upon A Time	26	$12	Casablanca 7078 [2]
9/23/78	4	42	▲	6 Live And More	1[1]	$12	Casablanca 7119 [2]
				Once Upon A Time • Fairy Tale High • Faster And Faster To Nowhere • Spring Affair • Rumour Has It • I Love You • Only One Man • I Remember Yesterday • Love's Unkind • My Man Medley: The Man I Love/I Got It Bad And That Ain't Good/Some Of These Days • The Way We Were • Mimi's Song • Try Me, I Know We Can Make It • Love To Love You Baby • I Feel Love • Last Dance • MacArthur Park *[8]* • One Of A Kind • Heaven Knows *[10]*			
5/19/79	❶[3]	45	▲[2]	7 Bad Girls	1[6]	$12	Casablanca 7150
				Hot Stuff *[3]* • Bad Girls *[1]* • Love Will Always Find You • Walk Away *[35]* • Dim All The Lights *[13]* • Journey To The Centre Of Your Heart • One Night In A Lifetime • Can't Get To Sleep At Night • On My Honor • There Will Always Be A You • All Through The Night • My Baby Understands • Our Love • Lucky • Sunset People			
11/10/79	4	30	▲[2]	8 On The Radio-Greatest Hits-Volumes I & II [G]	1[1]	$12	Casablanca 7191 [2]
				On The Radio *[9]* • Love To Love You Baby *[3]* • Try Me, I Know We Can Make It *[35]* • I Feel Love *[9]* • Our Love • I Remember Yesterday • I Love You *[28]* • Heaven Knows *[10]* • Last Dance *[5]* • MacArthur Park *[8]* • Hot Stuff *[3]* • Bad Girls *[1]* • Dim All The Lights *[13]* • Sunset People • No More Tears (Enough Is Enough) *[20]* • On The Radio *[9]*			
10/18/80	54	6		9 Walk Away - Collector's Edition (The Best Of 1977-1980) ....[G]	50	$10	Casablanca 7244
11/8/80	12	15	●	10 The Wanderer	13	$10	Geffen 2000
8/14/82	6	38	●	11 Donna Summer	20	$10	Geffen 2005
				Love Is In Control (Finger On The Trigger) *[4]* • Mystery Of Love • The Woman In Me *[30]* • State Of Independence *[31]* • Livin' In America • Protection • (If It) Hurts Just A Little • Love Is Just A Breath Away • Lush Life			
7/16/83	5	33	●	12 She Works Hard For The Money	9	$10	Mercury 812265
				She Works Hard For The Money *[1]* • Stop, Look And Listen • He's A Rebel • Woman • Unconditional Love *[9]* • Love Has A Mind Of Its Own *[35]* • Tokyo • People, People • I Do Believe (I Fell In Love)			
10/6/84	24	13		13 Cats Without Claws	40	$10	Geffen 24040
10/24/87	53	5		14 All Systems Go	122	$10	Geffen 24102
5/27/89	71	9		15 Another Place And Time	53	$8	Atlantic 81987
10/5/91	97	2		16 Mistaken Identity		$8	Atlantic 82285
				SUMMERS, Bill, & Summers Heat **'82**			
				Percussionist Summers was formerly with **Herbie Hancock**'s group.			
4/4/81	19	24		1 Call It What You Want	129	$10	MCA 5176
12/12/81+	15	27		2 Jam The Box!	92	$10	MCA 5266
11/13/82	31	10		3 Seventeen		$10	MCA 5367
				SUN **'79**			
				Funk group from Dayton, Ohio: Byron Byrd (vocals), Sheldon Reynolds and Anthony Thompson (guitars), Dean Francis (keyboards), Ernie Knisley (percussion), Robert Arnold, Gary King and Larry Hatchet (horns), Don Taylor (bass) and Kym Yancey (drums).			
5/1/76	54	5		1 Live On, Dream On		$10	Capitol 11461
5/14/77	39	3		2 Sun-Power		$10	Capitol 11609
4/15/78	21	27	●	3 Sunburn	69	$10	Capitol 11723
7/14/79	17	13		4 Destination: Sun	85	$10	Capitol 11941
5/2/81	52	4		5 Sun: Force Of Nature	205	$10	Capitol 12142
				SUNRIZE **'82**			
				Funk group: Ronnie Scruggs (vocals), Dave Townsend (guitar), Kevin Jones (congas), Tony Herbert (bass) and Everett Collins (drums).			
10/9/82	29	8		Sunrize	206	$10	Boardwalk 33257

SUNZ OF MAN '98
Rap group from New York City: **Killah Priest**, 60 Second Assassin, Prodigal Sunn and Hell Razah.

| 8/8/98 | 7 | 10 | | The Last Shall Be First | | 20 | $8 | Red Ant 12305 |

Cold • Natural High • Flaming Swords • Illusions • Israeli News • Tribulations • The Plan • Collaboration '98 • Inmates To The Fire • Not Promised Tomorrow • Medley: For The Lust Of Money/The Grandz • Can I See You • The Battle • Next Up • Intellectuals • Five Arch Angels

SUPER CAT '92
Born William Maragh on 6/25/63 in Kingston, Jamaica. Reggae singer/rapper.

| 6/6/92 | 37 | 43 | | 1 Don Dada | | 21 | $8 | Columbia 52435 |
| 9/2/95 | 60 | 6 | | 2 The Struggle Continues | | | $8 | Columbia 64197 |

SUPER LOVER CEE & CASANOVA RUD '88
Rap duo from New York City: Calente Fredericks ("Super Lover Cee") and Erik Rudnicki ("Casanova Rud").

| 11/5/88 | 39 | 15 | | Girls I Got 'Em Locked | | | $8 | Elektra 60807 |

SUPREMES, The ★5★ '67
Vocal trio from Detroit: **Diana Ross, Mary Wilson** and Florence Ballard. Ballard left in 1967, replaced by Cindy Birdsong (formerly with **Patti LaBelle's Blue Belles**). Ross left in 1969, replaced by Jean Terrell. Birdsong left in 1972, replaced by Lynda Lawrence. Terrell and Lawrence left in 1973. Mary Wilson re-formed group with Scherrie Payne (sister of **Freda Payne**) and Cindy Birdsong. Birdsong left again in 1976, replaced by Susaye Greene. Ballard died of heart failure on 2/22/76 (age 32). Group inducted into the Rock and Roll Hall of Fame in 1988.

1)Diana Ross and the Supremes Greatest Hits 2)TCB 3)The Supremes A' Go-Go
4)Diana Ross & the Supremes Join the Temptations 5)The Supremes sing Holland-Dozier-Holland

| 1/30/65 | ❶[1] | 10 | | 1 Where Did Our Love Go | | 2[4] | $40 | Motown 621 |

Where Did Our Love Go [1] • Run, Run, Run [93] • Baby Love [1] • When The Lovelight Starts Shining Through His Eyes [23] • Come See About Me [3] • Long Gone Lover • I'm Giving You, Your Freedom • A Breath Taking Guy • He Means The World To Me • Standing At The Crossroads Of Love • Your Kiss Of Fire • Ask Any Girl

| 1/30/65 | 5 | 5 | | 2 A Bit Of Liverpool | | 21 | $40 | Motown 623 |

How Do You Do It • A World Without Love • House Of The Rising Sun • Hard Day's Night • Because • You've Really Got A Hold On Me • You Can't Do That • Do You Love Me • Can't Buy Me Love • I Want To Hold Your Hand • Bits And Pieces

| 5/22/65 | 5 | 6 | | 3 We Remember Sam Cooke | | 75 | $30 | Motown 629 |

You Send Me • Nothing Can Change This Love • Cupid • Chain Gang • Bring It On Home To Me • Only Sixteen • Havin' A Party • Shake • Wonderful World • A Change Is Gonna Come • Ain't That Good News

| 8/21/65 | 2[6] | 19 | | 4 More Hits By The Supremes | | 6 | $30 | Motown 627 |

Ask Any Girl • **Nothing But Heartaches** [6] • Mother Dear • **Stop! In The Name Of Love** [2] • Honey Boy • **Back In My Arms Again** [1] • Whisper You Love Me Boy • The Only Time I'm Happy • He Holds His Own • Who Could Ever Doubt My Love • (I'm So Glad) Heartaches Don't Last Always • I'm In Love Again

| 12/4/65+ | 2[1] | 20 | | 5 The Supremes at the Copa | [L] | 11 | $30 | Motown 636 |

Put On A Happy Face • I Am Woman • Baby Love • Stop! In The Name Of Love • The Boy From Ipanema • Make Someone Happy • Come See About Me • Rock-A-Bye Your Baby With A Dixie Melody • Queen Of The House • Somewhere • Back In My Arms Again • Sam Cooke Medley: You Send Me/(I Love You) For Sentimental Reasons/Cupid/Chain Gang/Bring It On Home To Me/Shake • You're Nobody 'Til Somebody Loves You

| 3/19/66 | ❶[1] | 19 | | 6 I Hear A Symphony | | 8 | $25 | Motown 643 |

Stranger In Paradise • Yesterday • **I Hear A Symphony** [2] • Unchained Melody • With A Song In My Heart • Without A Song • **My World Is Empty Without You** [10] • A Lover's Concerto • Any Girl In Love (Knows What I'm Going Through) • Wonderful, Wonderful • Everything Is Good About You • He's All I Got

| 9/24/66 | ❶[4] | 35 | | 7 The Supremes A' Go-Go | | 1[2] | $25 | Motown 649 |

Love Is Like An Itching In My Heart [7] • This Old Heart Of Mine (Is Weak For You) • **You Can't Hurry Love** [1] • Shake Me, Wake Me (When It's Over) • Baby I Need Your Loving • These Boots Are Made For Walking • I Can't Help Myself • Get Ready • Put Yourself In My Place • Money (That's What I Want) • Come And Get These Memories • Hang On Sloopy

| 2/18/67 | ❶[3] | 24 | | 8 The Supremes sing Holland-Dozier-Holland | | 6 | $25 | Motown 650 |

Funny How Time Slips Away • My Heart Can't Take It No More • It Makes No Difference Now • You Didn't Care • Tears In Vain • I'll Turn To Stone • Tumbling Tumbleweeds • Lazybones • You Need Me • Baby Doll • Sunset • (The Man With The) Rock And Roll Banjo Band

| 6/17/67 | 3 | 18 | | 9 The Supremes Sing Rodgers & Hart | | 20 | $25 | Motown 659 |

The Lady Is A Tramp • Mountain Greenery • This Can't Be Love • Where Or When • Lover • My Funny Valentine • My Romance • My Heart Stood Still • Falling In Love With Love • Thou Swell • Dancing On The Ceiling • Blue Moon

DIANA ROSS & THE SUPREMES:

| 9/30/67 | ❶[12] | 58 | | 10 Diana Ross and the Supremes Greatest Hits | | 1[5] | $30 | Motown 663 [2] |

When The Lovelight Starts Shining Through His Eyes [23] • Where Did Our Love Go [1] • Ask Any Girl • Baby Love [1] • Run, Run, Run [93] • Stop! In The Name Of Love [2] • Back In My Arms Again [1] • Come See About Me [3] • Nothing But Heartaches [6] • Everything Is Good About You • I Hear A Symphony [2] • Love Is Here And Now You're Gone [1] • My World Is Empty Without You [10] • Whisper You Love Me Boy • The Happening [12] • You Keep Me Hangin' On [1] • You Can't Hurry Love [1] • Standing At The Crossroads Of Love • Love Is Like An Itching In My Heart [7] • There's No Stopping Us Now

| 5/4/68 | 3 | 28 | | 11 Reflections | | 18 | $25 | Motown 665 |

Reflections [4] • I'm Gonna Make It (I Will Wait For You) • Forever Came Today [17] • I Can't Make It Alone • In And Out Of Love [16] • Bah-Bah-Bah • What The World Needs Now Is Love • Up, Up And Away • Love (Makes Me Do Foolish Things) • Then • Misery Makes Its Home In My Heart • Ode To Billie Joe

10/5/68	22	20		12 Live at London's Talk Of The Town	[L]	57	$25	Motown 676
11/9/68	45	6		13 Funny Girl		150	$25	Motown 672
12/7/68	❶[4]	32		14 Diana Ross & the Supremes Join the Temptations		2[1]	$25	Motown 679

DIANA ROSS & THE SUPREMES with THE TEMPTATIONS
Try It Baby • I Second That Emotion • Ain't No Mountain High Enough • **I'm Gonna Make You Love Me** [2] • This Guy's In Love With You • Funky Broadway • **I'll Try Something New** [8] • A Place In The Sun • Sweet Inspiration • Then • The Impossible Dream

DEBUT	PEAK	WKS	Gold	Album Title	Pop #	$	Label & Number

SUPREMES, The — Cont'd

12/7/68	3	24		15 Love Child	14	$25	Motown 670

Love Child [2] • Keep An Eye • How Long Has That Evening Train Been Gone • Does Your Mama Know About Me • Honey Bee (Keep On Stinging Me) • Some Things You Never Get Used To [43] • He's My Sunny Boy • You've Been So Wonderful To Me • (Don't Break These) Chains Of Love • You Ain't Livin' Till You're Lovin' • I'll Set You Free • Can't Shake It Loose

| 1/4/69 | ❶⁶ | 28 | | 16 TCB | 1¹ | $25 | Motown 682 |

DIANA ROSS & THE SUPREMES with THE TEMPTATIONS [TV]

T.C.B. • Stop! In The Name Of Love • You Keep Me Hangin' On • Get Ready • The Way You Do The Things You Do • Medley: A Taste Of Honey/Eleanor Rigby/Do You Know The Way To San Jose/Mrs. Robinson • Respect • Somewhere • Ain't Too Proud To Beg • Hello, Young Lovers • For Once In My Life • (I Know) I'm Losing You • Medley: With A Song In My Heart/Without A Song • Medley: Come See About Me/My World Is Empty Without You/Baby Love • I Hear A Symphony • The Impossible Dream

| 6/28/69 | 7 | 17 | | 17 Let The Sunshine In | 24 | $25 | Motown 689 |

The Composer [21] • Everyday People • No Matter What Sign You Are [17] • Hey Western Union Man • What Becomes Of The Brokenhearted • I'm Livin' In Shame [8] • Aquarius/Let The Sunshine In (The Flesh Failures) • Let The Music Play • With A Child's Heart • Discover Me (And You'll Discover Love) • Will This Be The Day • I'm So Glad I Got Somebody (Like You Around)

| 10/25/69 | 6 | 21 | | 18 Together | 28 | $25 | Motown 692 |

DIANA ROSS & THE SUPREMES with THE TEMPTATIONS

Stubborn Kind Of Fellow • I'll Be Doggone • The Weight [33] • Ain't Nothing Like The Real Thing • Uptight (Everything's Alright) • Sing A Simple Song • Medley: My Girl/My Guy • For Better Or Worse • Can't Take My Eyes Off You • Why (Must We Fall In Love)

| 11/29/69 | 3 | 27 | | 19 Cream Of The Crop | 33 | $25 | Motown 694 |

Someday We'll Be Together [1] • Can't You See It's Me • You Gave Me Love • Hey Jude • The Young Folks • Shadows Of Society • Loving You Is Better Than Ever • When It's To The Top (Still I Won't Stop Giving You Love) • Till Johnny Comes • Blowin' In The Wind • The Beginning Of The End

| 12/13/69 | 4 | 15 | | 20 On Broadway [TV] | 38 | $25 | Motown 699 |

DIANA ROSS & THE SUPREMES with THE TEMPTATIONS

G.I.T. On Broadway • Broadway Medley • Malteds Over Manhattan • Medley: Leading Lady/Doin' What Comes Natur'lly/I'm Gonna Wash That Man Right Outa My Hair/Wouldn't It Be Loverly/People/Everything's Coming Up Roses/Mame • Fiddler On The Roof • Student Mountie • The Rhythm Of Life • Medley: Let The Sunshine In/Funky Broadway/G.I.T. On Broadway

| 1/17/70 | 5 | 21 | | 21 Diana Ross & The Supremes Greatest Hits, Volume 3 [G] | 31 | $20 | Motown 702 |

Reflections [4] • Love Is Here And Now You're Gone [1] • Someday We'll Be Together [1] • Love Child [2] • Some Things You Never Get Used To [43] • Forever Came Today [17] • In And Out Of Love [16] • The Happening [12] • I'm Livin' In Shame [8] • No Matter What Sign You Are [17] • The Composer [21]

| 5/23/70 | 31 | 15 | | 22 Farewell [L] | 46 | $25 | Motown 708 |

recorded on January 14, 1970 at the Frontier Hotel in Las Vegas

THE SUPREMES:

| 6/6/70 | 4 | 21 | | 23 Right On | 25 | $20 | Motown 705 |

Up The Ladder To The Roof [5] • Then We Can Try Again • Everybody's Got The Right To Love [11] • Wait A Minute Before You Leave Me • You Move Me • But I Love You More • I Got Hurt (Trying To Be The Only Girl In Your Life) • Baby Baby • Take A Closer Look At Me • Then I Met You • Bill, When Are You Coming Back • The Loving Country

10/31/70	12	20		24 New Ways But Love Stays	68	$20	Motown 720
10/31/70	18	19		25 The Magnificent 7	113	$20	Motown 717

SUPREMES & FOUR TOPS

| 6/26/71 | 6 | 13 | | 26 Touch | 85 | $20 | Motown 737 |

This Is The Story • Nathan Jones [8] • Here Comes The Sunrise • Love It Came To Me This Time • Johnny Raven • Have I Lost You • Time And Love • Touch • Happy (Is A Bumpy Road) • It's So Hard For Me To Say Good-Bye

| 6/26/71 | 18 | 6 | | 27 The Return Of The Magnificent Seven | 154 | $20 | Motown 736 |

SUPREMES & FOUR TOPS

| 2/5/72 | 21 | 4 | | 28 Dynamite | 160 | $20 | Motown 745 |

SUPREMES & FOUR TOPS

6/3/72	12	12		29 Floy Joy	54	$15	Motown 751
12/2/72+	27	13		30 The Supremes	129	$15	Motown 756
7/13/74	24	8	●	31 Anthology (1962-1969)	66	$25	Motown 794 [3]

DIANA ROSS & THE SUPREMES

6/21/75	25	9		32 The Supremes	152	$15	Motown 828
5/15/76	24	12		33 High Energy	42	$15	Motown 863
5/31/86	61	16		34 25th Anniversary [K]	112	$20	Motown 5381 [3]

DIANA ROSS & THE SUPREMES

SURFACE '89

Trio from New Jersey: Bernard Jackson (vocals, bass), David Townsend (guitar, keyboards) and David Conley (sax, drums).

4/4/87	11	35		1 Surface	55	$8	Columbia 40374
11/12/88+	5	71	▲	2 2nd Wave	56	$8	Columbia 44284

Shower Me With Your Love [1] • Closer Than Friends [1] • Can We Spend Some Time [5] • You Are My Everything [1] • I Missed [3] • Black Shades • Hold On To Love • Where's That Girl

| 12/1/90+ | 19 | 37 | ● | 3 3 Deep | 65 | $8 | Columbia 46772 |

SVENSSON, Bo '88

Male tenor saxophonist.

| 4/23/88 | 69 | 4 | | Living On The Edge | | $10 | Golden Boy 4001 |

SWANN, Bettye '69

Born Betty Jean Champion on 10/24/44 in Shreveport, Louisiana. Female singer.

| 6/14/69 | 48 | 3 | | The Soul View Now! | | $15 | Capitol 190 |

DEBUT	PEAK	WKS	Gold	Album Title	Pop #	$	Label & Number

| DEBUT | PEAK | WKS | Gold | Album Title | Pop # | $ | Label & Number |

★80★   SWEAT, Keith   '88
Born on 7/22/61 in New York City. Singer/songwriter.

| 12/26/87+ | ❶³ | 78 | ▲³ | 1 Make It Last Forever | 15 | $8 | Vintertainment 60763 |

Something Just Ain't Right [3] • Right And A Wrong Way • Tell Me It's Me You Want • I Want Her [1] • Make It Last Forever [2] • In The Rain • How Deep Is Your Love • Don't Stop Your Love [9]

| 6/30/90 | ❶¹ | 60 | ▲² | 2 I'll Give All My Love To You | 6 | $8 | Vintertainment 60861 |

Make You Sweat [1] • Come Back • Merry Go Round [2] • Your Love [4] • Just One Of Them Thangs • I Knew That You Were Cheatin' • Love To Love You • I'll Give All My Love To You [1]

| 12/14/91+ | ❶³ | 67 | ▲ | 3 Keep It Comin' | 19 | $8 | Elektra 61216 |

Keep It Comin' [1] • Spend A Little Time • Why Me Baby? [2] • I Really Love You • Let Me Love You • I Want To Love You Down [20] • I'm Going For Mine • (There You Go) Tellin' Me No Again • Give Me What I Want • Ten Commandments Of Love

| 7/16/94 | ❶² | 37 | ▲ | 4 Get Up On It | 8 | $8 | Elektra 61550 |

How Do You Like It? [9] • It Gets Better • Get Up On It [12] • Feels So Good • My Whole World • Grind On You • When I Give My Love [21] • Put Your Lovin' Through The Test • Telephone Love • Come Into My Bedroom • For You (You Got Everything)

| 7/13/96 | ❶¹ | 63 | ▲³ | 5 Keith Sweat | 5 | $8 | Elektra 61707 |

Twisted [1] • Funky Dope Lovin' • Yumi • Whatever You Want • Just A Touch • Freak With Me • Nature's Rising • Come With Me [27] • In The Mood • Show Me The Way • Nobody [1] • Chocolate Girl

| 10/10/98 | 2¹ | 34 | ▲ | 6 Still In The Game | 6 | $8 | Elektra 62262 |

Come And Get With Me [6] • Rumors • Can We Make Love • Let Me Have My Way • What Goes Around • Love Jones • Too Hot • I'm Not Ready [12] • Show U What Love Is • Just Another Day • You Know I Like • In Your Eyes

SWEAT BAND   '81
Spin-off of George Clinton's corporation. Core members: William "Bootsy" Collins, Fred Wesley, Maceo Parker, Bernie Worrell, Joel Johnson and Carl Smalls.

| 11/29/80+ | 22 | 16 | | Sweat Band | 150 | $10 | Uncle Jam 36857 |

SWEETBACK   '97
Trio consisting of the musicians from Sade's band: Stuart Matthewman (guitar, sax), Andrew Hale (keyboards) and Paul Denman (bass).

| 11/2/96+ | 46 | 21 | | Sweetback | [I] 169 | $8 | Epic 67492 |

SWEET INSPIRATIONS, The   '68
Vocal group: Cissy Houston (mother of Whitney Houston), Estelle Brown, Sylvia Shemwell and Myrna Smith. Houston left in 1970.

| 4/6/68 | 12 | 14 | | 1 The Sweet Inspirations | 90 | $20 | Atlantic 8155 |
| 9/22/73 | 60 | 2 | | 2 Estelle, Myrna & Sylvia | | $20 | Stax 3017 |

SWEET OBSESSION   '89
Vocal trio from Detroit: sisters Keena, Kimmla and Michelle Green.

| 11/5/88+ | 45 | 33 | | Sweet Obsession | | $8 | Epic 44419 |

SWEET SABLE   '94
Born Ceybil Jeffries in Brooklyn, New York. Female singer.

| 7/16/94 | 70 | 3 | | Old Times' Sake | | $8 | Street Life 75448 |

SWEET TEE   '89
Born Toi Jackson from Queens, New York. Female rapper.

| 12/3/88+ | 31 | 25 | | It's Tee Time | 169 | $8 | Profile 1269 |

SWEET THUNDER   '78
Group from Youngstown, Ohio: Booker Newberry (vocals, keyboards), Charles Buie (guitar), Rudell Alexander (bass) and John Aaron (drums).

| 6/24/78 | 43 | 10 | | Sweet Thunder | 125 | $10 | Fantasy 9547 |

SWITCH   '78
Funk group from Mansfield, Ohio: Phillip Ingram (vocals), brothers Bobby (keyboards) and Tommy (bass) DeBarge, Greg Williams and Eddie Fluellen (horns) and Jody Sims (drums). Bobby DeBarge died of AIDS on 8/16/95 (age 36).

| 9/2/78 | 6 | 37 | | 1 Switch | 37 | $10 | Gordy 980 |

I Wanna Be With You • There'll Never Be [6] • I Wanna Be Closer [22] • We Like To Party...Come On • Fever • You Pulled A Switch • It's So Real • Somebody's Watchin' You

| 5/26/79 | 8 | 43 | | 2 Switch II | 37 | $10 | Gordy 988 |

You're The One For Me • Next To You • Best Beat In Town [16] • Calling On All Girls • Go On Doin' What You Feel • Fallin' • I Call Your Name [10]

4/12/80	23	17		3 Reaching For Tomorrow	57	$10	Gordy 993
11/22/80	21	27		4 This Is My Dream	85	$10	Gordy 999
11/21/81	48	8		5 Switch V	174	$10	Gordy 1007

SWOOP G   '98

| 1/3/98 | 99 | 1 | | Undisputed | | $8 | Handle Bar 6620 |

SWV (Sisters With Voices)   '93
Female vocal trio from New York City: Cheryl Gamble, Tamara Johnson and Leanne Lyons.

| 11/14/92+ | 2⁴ | 84 | ▲³ | 1 It's About Time | 8 | $8 | RCA 66074 |

Anything [4] • I'm So Into You [2] • Right Here [13] • Weak [1] • Always On My Mind [8] • Downtown [flip] • Coming Home • Give It To Me • Blak Pudd'n • It's About Time • Think You're Gonna Like It • That's What I Need • SWV (In The House)

| 5/28/94 | 9 | 14 | ● | 2 The Remixes | [K-M] 92 | $6 | RCA 66401 |

Anything • Right Here/Human Nature [1] • I'm So Into You • Weak • Downtown • Always On My Mind

| 5/11/96 | 3 | 48 | ▲ | 3 New Beginning | 9 | $8 | RCA 66487 |

You're The One [1] • Whatcha Need • On & On • It's All About U [32] • Use Your Heart • Fine Time • Love Is So Amazin' • You Are My Love • I'm So In Love • When This Feeling • What's It Gonna Be • That's What I'm Here For • Don't Waste Your Time

| 8/30/97 | 5 | 39 | ● | 4 Release Some Tension | 24 | $8 | RCA 67525 |

Someone [5] • Release Some Tension • Lose My Cool • Love Like This • Can We [31] • Rain [7] • Give It Up • Come And Get Some • When U Cry • Lose Myself • Here For You • Gettin' Funky

| 12/27/97 | 85 | 2 | | 5 A Special Christmas | [X] | $8 | RCA 67539 |

DEBUT	PEAK	WKS	Gold	Album Title		Pop #	$	Label & Number
				SYBIL	**'89**			
				Born Sybil Lynch from Paterson, New Jersey.				
10/7/89	12	39		1 Sybil		75	$8	Next Plateau 1018
12/15/90+	70	8		2 Sybilization			$8	Next Plateau 1024
				SYLK-E. FYNE	**'98**			
				Female rapper from Los Angeles.				
4/11/98	47	12		Raw Sylk		121	$8	RCA 67551
				SYLVERS, Foster	**'73**			
				Born on 2/25/62 in Memphis. Singer/songwriter/producer. Youngest member of **The Sylvers**.				
7/7/73	31	9		Foster Sylvers		159	$12	Pride 0027
				SYLVERS, The	**'76**			
				Family group from Memphis: Olympia-Ann, Leon, Charmaine, James, Edmund, Ricky, Angelia, Pat, Jonathon and **Foster Sylvers**.				
1/20/73	15	12		1 The Sylvers		180	$12	Pride 0007
7/21/73	37	14		2 The Sylvers II		164	$12	Pride 0026
1/10/76	23	17		3 Showcase		58	$10	Capitol 11465
11/20/76	13	22		4 Something Special		80	$10	Capitol 11580
11/26/77	43	14		5 New Horizons		134	$10	Capitol 11705
9/16/78	40	8		6 Forever Yours		132	$10	Casablanca 7103
				SYLVESTER	**'78**			
				Born Sylvester James on 9/6/47 in Los Angeles. Died of AIDS on 12/16/88 (age 41). Male disco singer.				
7/22/78	7	40	●	1 Step II		28	$10	Fantasy 9556
				You Make Me Feel (Mighty Real) [20] • Dance (Disco Heat) [4] • Grateful • I Took My Strength From You • Was It Something That I Said • Just You And Me Forever				
5/5/79	27	13		2 Stars		63	$10	Fantasy 9579
12/1/79	45	26		3 Living Proof [L]		123	$12	Fantasy 79010 [2]
				recorded on March 11, 1979 in San Francisco				
9/27/80	44	7		4 Sell My Soul		147	$10	Fantasy 9601
7/11/81	51	5		5 Too Hot Too Sleep		156	$10	Fantasy 9607
1/29/83	35	17		6 All I Need		168	$10	Megaton 1005
2/7/87	46	8		7 Mutual Attraction		164	$8	Warner 25527
				SYLVIA	**'73**			
				Born Sylvia Vanderpool on 5/6/36 in New York City. Singer/songwriter/producer. Half of Mickey & Sylvia duo ("Love Is Strange"). Married Joe Robinson, owner of All-Platinum/Vibration Records (later known as Sugar Hill). Their son Joey was leader of **West Street Mob**.				
5/26/73	16	11		Pillow Talk		70	$15	Vibration 126
				SYREETA	**'72**			
				Born Rita Wright in 1946 in Pittsburgh. Singer/songwriter. Married to **Stevie Wonder** from 1972-74.				
7/29/72	38	4		1 Syreeta		185	$15	Mowest 113
10/19/74	53	3		2 Stevie Wonder presents Syreeta		116	$12	Motown 808
				above 2 produced by Stevie Wonder				
5/17/80	39	14		3 Syreeta		73	$10	Tamla 372
1/16/82	40	10		4 Set My Love In Motion		189	$10	Tamla 376
				SYSTEM, The	**'87**			
				Techno-funk duo from New York City: Mic Murphy (vocals, guitar) and David Frank (keyboards).				
2/26/83	14	27		1 Sweat		94	$10	Mirage 90062
4/7/84	56	7		2 X-Periment		182	$10	Mirage 90146
8/10/85	40	29		3 The Pleasure Seekers			$10	Mirage 90281
3/14/87	13	33		4 Don't Disturb This Groove		62	$8	Atlantic 81691
7/8/89	85	7		5 Rhythm And Romance			$8	Atlantic 81896
				SZABO, Gabor	**'67**			
				Born on 3/8/36 in Budapest, Hungary. Died on 2/26/82 (age 45). Jazz guitarist.				
12/31/66+	16	11		Spellbinder [I]		140	$20	Impulse 9123

T

DEBUT	PEAK	WKS	Gold	Album Title		Pop #	$	Label & Number
				TAG TEAM	**'93**			
				Rap duo from Atlanta: Cecil Glenn and Steve Gibson.				
8/7/93	28	25	●	Whoomp! (There It Is)		39	$8	Life 78000
				TAKE 6	**'94**			
				Vocal group from Huntsville, Alabama: Claude McKnight (brother of **Brian McKnight**), Mark Kibble, Mervyn Warren, Cedric Dent, David Thomas and Alvin Chea.				
3/18/89	41	22	▲	1 Take 6		71	$8	Reprise 25670
10/6/90	22	24		2 So Much 2 Say		72	$8	Reprise 25892
12/12/92	84	1		3 He Is Christmas [X]		100	$8	Reprise 26665
7/16/94	17	17	●	4 Join The Band		86	$8	Reprise 45497
11/16/96	71	3		5 Brothers			$8	Reprise 46235
11/14/98	92	1		6 So Cool			$8	Reprise 46795

DEBUT	PEAK	WKS	Gold	Album Title	Pop #	$	Label & Number

TALKING HEADS   **'83**
Group from New York City: David Byrne (vocals, guitar), Jerry Harrison (keyboards, guitar), Tina Weymouth (bass) and husband Chris Frantz (drums). Weymouth and Frantz also formed the **Tom Tom Club**.

| 9/10/83 | 55 | 12 | ▲ | Speaking In Tongues | 15 | $10 | Sire 23883 |

TA MARA & THE SEEN   **'85**
Dance group from Minneapolis: Margaret "Ta Mara" Cox (vocals), Oliver Leiber (guitar), Gina Fellicetta (keyboards), Keith Woodson (bass) and Jamie Chez (drums). Leiber is the son of songwriter Jerry Leiber (of Leiber & Stoller).

| 11/2/85 | 20 | 28 | | Ta Mara & The Seen | 54 | $8 | A&M 5078 |

TAMIA   **'98**
Born in Windsor, Ontario, Canada. Female singer.

| 5/2/98 | 18 | 38 | | Tamia | 67 | $8 | Qwest 46213 |

TASTE OF HONEY, A   **'78**
Disco group from Los Angeles: Janice Johnson (vocals, guitar), Hazel Payne (vocals, bass), Perry Kibble (keyboards) and Donald Johnson (drums). Group later reduced to a duo of Johnson and Payne.

| 6/17/78 | 2⁶ | 27 | ▲ | 1 A Taste of Honey | 6 | $10 | Capitol 11754 |

Boogie Oogie Oogie [1] • This Love Of Ours • Distant • World Spin • **Disco Dancin'** [69] • You • If We Loved • Sky High • You're In Good Hands

7/28/79	26	13		2 Another Taste	59	$10	Capitol 11951
8/9/80+	12	32		3 Twice As Sweet	36	$8	Capitol 12089
5/1/82	14	15		4 Ladies Of The Eighties	73	$8	Capitol 12173

| | ★138★ | | | **TAVARES**   **'75** | | | |

Family vocal group from New Bedford, Massachusetts: brothers Ralph, Antone, Feliciano, Arthur and Perry Lee Tavares. Feliciano was formerly married to Lola Falana.

1)In The City 2)Hard Core Poetry 3)Madam Butterfly

2/2/74	20	13		1 Check It Out	160	$12	Capitol 11258
9/7/74	11	36		2 Hard Core Poetry	121	$12	Capitol 11316
8/9/75	8	15		3 In The City	26	$12	Capitol 11396

It Only Takes A Minute [1] • Fool's Hall Of Fame • **The Love I Never Had** [11] • Nothing You Can Do • In The Eyes Of Love • Ready, Willing And Able • We Fit To A Tee • **Free Ride** [8] • I Hope She Chooses Me • In The City

6/12/76	20	29		4 Sky High!	24	$12	Capitol 11533
4/30/77	15	18		5 Love Storm	59	$12	Capitol 11628
11/5/77	42	11		6 The Best Of Tavares .... [G]	72	$12	Capitol 11701
5/13/78	55	5		7 Future Bound	115	$12	Capitol 11719
2/10/79	13	16		8 Madam Butterfly	92	$10	Capitol 11874
3/1/80	20	11		9 Supercharged	75	$10	Capitol 12026
9/18/82	30	30		10 New Directions	137	$10	RCA Victor 4357
10/1/83	48	11		11 Words And Music	208	$10	RCA Victor 4700

TAWATHA   **'87**
Born Tawatha Agee in Philadelphia. Female singer.

| 7/11/87 | 34 | 14 | | Welcome To My Dream | | $8 | Epic 40355 |

TAYLOR, Bobby, And The Vancouvers   **'68**
Interracial group from Vancouver, Canada: Bobby Taylor (vocals), Tommy Chong (of Cheech & Chong) and Edward Patterson (guitars), Robbie King (keyboards), Wes Henderson (bass) and Ted Lewis (drums).

| 9/21/68 | 20 | 10 | | Bobby Taylor And The Vancouvers | | $60 | Gordy 930 |

TAYLOR, Gary   **'88**
Born in Los Angeles. Singer/songwriter.

9/3/88	75	7		1 Compassion		$8	Virgin 90902
1/18/92	79	8		2 Take Control		$8	Valley Vue 21191
9/2/95	80	3		3 The Mood Of Moonlight		$8	Morning Crew 1853

TAYLOR, James "J.T."   **'91**
Born 8/16/53 in South Carolina. Lead singer of **Kool & The Gang** from 1979-88.

| 12/2/89 | 77 | 8 | | 1 Master Of The Game | | $8 | MCA 6347 |
| 9/14/91 | 57 | 9 | | 2 Feel The Need | | $8 | MCA 10304 |

J.T. TAYLOR

TAYLOR, Johnnie ★36★   **'76**
Born on 5/5/38 in Crawfordsville, Arkansas. Former gospel singer. Nicknamed "The Soul Philosopher."

1)Eargasm 2)Taylored in Silk 3)Who's Making Love 4)One Step Beyond 5)Rated Extraordinaire

| 4/22/67 | 26 | 4 | | 1 Wanted: One Soul Singer | | $50 | Stax 715 |
| 1/25/69 | 5 | 33 | | 2 Who's Making Love... | 42 | $25 | Stax 2005 |

Who's Making Love [1] • I'm Not The Same Person • Hold On This Time • Woman Across The River • Can't Trust Your Neighbor • **Take Care Of Your Homework** [2] • I'm Trying • Poor Make Believer • Payback Hurts • Mr. Nobody Is Somebody Now • I'd Rather Drink Muddy Water

5/10/69	24	11		3 Raw Blues	126	$25	Stax 2008
7/5/69+	25	12		4 The Johnnie Taylor Philosophy Continues	109	$25	Stax 2023
7/26/69	33	4		5 Rare Stamps		$25	Stax 2012
12/5/70+	26	17		6 Johnnie Taylor's Greatest Hits .... [G]	141	$25	Stax 2032

DEBUT	PEAK	WKS	Gold	Album Title	Pop #	$	Label & Number
				TAYLOR, Johnnie — Cont'd			
3/27/71	**6**	19		7 **One Step Beyond**	112	$25	Stax 2030
				Time After Time • Party Life • Will You Love Me Forever • **I Am Somebody** *[4]* • **I Don't Wanna Lose You** *[13]* • Don't Take My Sunshine • **Jody's Got Your Girl And Gone** *[1]* • A Fool Like Me			
7/7/73	**3**	21		8 **Taylored in Silk**	54	$20	Stax 3014
				We're Getting Careless With Our Love *[5]* • Starting All Over Again • **Cheaper To Keep Her** *[2]* • Talk To Me • **I Believe In You (You Believe In Me)** *[1]* • One Thing Wronmg With My Woman • I Can Read Between The Lines • This Bitter Earth			
5/25/74	**10**	14		9 **Super Taylor**	182	$20	Stax 5509
				It's September *[26]* • Darling I Love You • **Try Me Tonight** *[51]* • Free • **I've Been Born Again** *[13]* • At Night Time (My Pillow Tells A Tale On Me) • It Don't Pay To Get Up In The Morning • Just One Moment			
3/20/76	**❶**²	26	●	10 **Eargasm**	5	$12	Columbia 33951
				Disco Lady *[1]* • Please Don't Stop (That Song From Playing) • Don't Touch Her Body (If You Can't Touch Her Mind) • I'm Gonna Keep On Loving You • You're The Best In The World • Running Out Of Lies • **Somebody's Gettin' It** *[5]* • It Don't Hurt Me Like It Used To • Pick Up The Pieces			
3/12/77	**6**	18		11 **Rated Extraordinaire**	51	$12	Columbia 34401
				Your Love Is Rated X *[17]* • Stormy • Here I Go (Through These Changes Again) • Did He Make Love To You • And I Panicked • **Love Is Better In The A.M.** *[3]* • It Ain't What You Do (It's How You Do It) • Not Just Another Booty Song • I'm Just A Shoulder To Cry On • Stop Giving People Hard Luck Stories			
4/29/78	35	7		12 **Ever Ready**	164	$12	Columbia 35340
10/27/79	53	8		13 **She's Killing Me**		$12	Columbia 36061
8/30/80	75	2		14 **A New Day**		$12	Columbia 36548
10/30/82	19	31		15 **Just Ain't Good Enough**		$12	Beverly Glen 10001
1/19/85	55	18		16 **This Is Your Night**		$10	Malaco 7421
2/1/86	46	33		17 **Wall To Wall**		$10	Malaco 7431
9/3/88	43	29		18 **In Control**		$10	Malaco 7446
1/20/90	47	27		19 **Crazy 'Bout You**		$8	Malaco 7452
11/9/91+	59	36		20 **(I Know It's Wrong, But I...) Just Can't Do Right**		$8	Malaco 7460
10/17/92	84	6		21 **The Best Of Johnnie Taylor...on Malaco Vol. 1** [G]		$8	Malaco 7463
3/12/94	76	5		22 **Real Love**		$8	Malaco 7472
6/29/96	15	60		23 **Good Love**	108	$8	Malaco 7480
4/25/98	44	18		24 **Taylored To Please**		$8	Malaco 7488
				TAYLOR, Little Johnny **'88**			
				Born Johnny Young on 2/11/43 in Memphis. Blues singer/harmonica player.			
5/7/88	62	10		1 **Stuck In The Mud**		$10	Ichiban 1022
8/26/89	63	9		2 **Ugly Man**		$10	Ichiban 1042
				TAYLOR, Ted **'66**			
				Born Austin Taylor on 2/16/37 in Okmulgee, Oklahoma. Died in a car crash on 10/22/87 (age 50).			
3/12/66	14	2		**Ted Taylor's Greatest Hits** [G]		$40	Okeh 12113
				T-CONNECTION **'79**			
				Disco group from Nassau, Bahamas: brothers Theophilus (vocals, keyboards) and Kirkwood (bass) Coakley, with David Mackey (guitar) and Anthony Flowers (drums).			
5/14/77	32	11		1 **Magic**	109	$10	Dash 30004
2/4/78	40	4		2 **On Fire**	139	$10	Dash 30008
1/6/79	20	26		3 **T-Connection**	51	$10	Dash 30009
10/27/79	38	9		4 **Totally Connected**	188	$10	Dash 30014
3/14/81	31	15		5 **Everything Is Cool**	138	$8	Capitol 12128
3/6/82	31	20		6 **Pure & Natural**	123	$8	Capitol 12191
5/5/84	59	7		7 **Take It To The Limit**		$8	Capitol 12333
				TEARS FOR FEARS **'85**			
				British duo: Roland Orzabal (vocals, guitar, keyboards) and Curt Smith (vocals, bass).			
9/21/85	38	14	▲⁵	**Songs From The Big Chair**	1⁵	$8	Mercury 824300
				TEASE **'86**			
				Group from Los Angeles: brothers Thomas (guitar) and Derek (drums) Organ, with Kipper Jones (vocals) and Jay Shanklin (bass).			
5/10/86	32	19		**Tease**		$8	Epic 40091
				TECHMASTER P.E.B. **'93**			
				Male techno-bass artist from Florida.			
2/1/92	83	17		1 **Bass Computer**	132	$8	Newtown 2208
8/21/93	81	3		2 **It Came From Outer Bass II** [I]	186	$8	Newtown 2211
				TECHNOTRONIC **'90**			
				Dance studio group created by Belgian DJ/producer Thomas DeQuincey (real name: Jo Bogaert) and female rapper Ya Kid K (of Hi Tek 3). Non-vocalist Felly, a model from Zaire, fronted the group for videos.			
12/23/89+	23	30	▲	**Pump Up The Jam - The Album**	10	$8	SBK 93422
				TELA **'98**			
				Pronounced: Tee-la. Male rapper from Memphis.			
11/23/96+	17	42		1 **Piece Of Mind**	70	$8	Suave House 1553
10/24/98	13	21		2 **Now Or Never**	49	$8	Rap-A-Lot 46588
				TEMPREES, The **'74**			
				Vocal trio: William Johnson, Jasper Phillips and Harold Scott.			
10/14/72	30	10		1 **Lovemen**		$12	We Produce 1901
1/12/74	29	14		2 **Love's Maze**		$12	We Produce 1903

TEMPTATIONS, The ★1★   '65

Vocal group from Detroit: **Eddie Kendricks**, **David Ruffin**, Paul Williams, Melvin Franklin and Otis Williams. Ruffin left in 1968, replaced by **Dennis Edwards**. Kendricks and Paul Williams left in 1971, replaced by Damon Harris and Richard Street. Harris left in 1975, replaced by Glenn Leonard. Louis Price replaced Edwards from 1977-79. Ali-Ollie Woodson replaced Edwards from 1984-87. Paul Williams died of a self-inflicted gunshot on 8/17/73 (age 34). Ruffin died of a drug overdose on 6/1/91 (age 50). Kendricks died of cancer on 10/5/92 (age 52). Franklin died of heart failure on 2/23/95 (age 52). Billed as the "Emperors Of Soul." Inducted into the Rock and Roll Hall of Fame in 1989.

1)The Temptations Sing Smokey 2)Puzzle People 3)Temptin' Temptations 4)Cloud Nine
5)The Temptations Greatest Hits

| 3/27/65 | ❶18 | 29 | 1 **The Temptations Sing Smokey** • | 35 | $30 | Gordy 912 |

The Way You Do The Things You Do [11] • Baby, Baby I Need You • **My Girl** [1] • What Love Has Joined Together • You'll Lose A Precious Love • It's Growing [3] • Who's Lovin' You • What's So Good About Good Bye • You Beat Me To The Punch • Way Over There • You've Really Got A Hold On Me • (You Can) Depend On Me

| 12/4/65 | ❶14 | 34 | 2 **Temptin' Temptations** | 11 | $30 | Gordy 914 |

Since I Lost My Baby [4] • The Girl's Alright With Me • Just Another Lonely Night • **My Baby** [4] • You've Got To Earn It [22] • Everybody Needs Love • **Girl (Why You Wanna Make Me Blue)** [26] • Don't Look Back [15] • I Gotta Know Now • Born To Love You • I'll Be In Trouble [33] • You're The One I Need

| 7/9/66 | ❶6 | 31 | 3 **Gettin' Ready** | 12 | $30 | Gordy 918 |

Say You • Little Miss Sweetness • **Ain't Too Proud To Beg** [1] • **Get Ready** [1] • Lonely, Lonely Man Am I • Too Busy Thinking About My Baby • I've Been Good To You • It's A Lonely World Without Your Love • Fading Away • Who You Gonna Run To • You're Not An Ordinary Girl • Not Now, I'll Tell You Later

| 12/17/66 | ❶9 | 114 | 4 **The Temptations Greatest Hits** | [G] | 5 | $25 | Gordy 919 |

The Way You Do The Things You Do [11] • **My Girl** [1] • **Ain't Too Proud To Beg** [1] • Don't Look Back [15] • **Get Ready** [1] • Beauty Is Only Skin Deep [1] • Since I Lost My Baby [4] • The Girl's Alright With Me • **My Baby** [4] • It's Growing [3] • I'll Be In Trouble [33] • Girl (Why You Wanna Make Me Blue) [26]

| 4/1/67 | ❶3 | 26 | 5 **Temptations Live!** | [L] | 10 | $25 | Gordy 921 |

Medley: Girl (Why You Wanna Make Me Blue)/The Girl's Alright With Me/I'll Be In Trouble/I Want A Love I Can See • What Love Has Joined Together • My Girl • Medley: Yesterday/What Now My Love • Beauty Is Only Skin Deep • I Wish You Love • Ain't Too Proud To Beg • Ol' Man River • Get Ready • Fading Away • My Baby • You'll Lose A Precious Love • Baby, Baby I Need You • Don't Look Back

| 8/12/67 | ❶1 | 30 | 6 **With A Lot O' Soul** | 7 | $25 | Gordy 922 |

(I Know) I'm Losing You [1] • Ain't No Sun Since You've Been Gone • All I Need [2] • (Loneliness Made Me Realize) It's You That I Need [3] • No More Water In The Well • Save My Love For A Rainy Day • Just One Last Look • Sorry Is A Sorry Word • You're My Everything [3] • Now That You've Won Me • Two Sides To Love • Don't Send Me Away

| 12/23/67+ | ❶7 | 58 | 7 **The Temptations in a Mellow Mood** | 13 | $25 | Gordy 924 |

Hello Young Lovers • A Taste Of Honey • For Once In My Life • Somewhere • Ol' Man River • I'm Ready For Love • Try To Remember • Who Can I Turn To (When Nobody Needs Me) • What Now My Love • That's Life • With These Hands • The Impossible Dream

| 5/25/68 | ❶3 | 41 | 8 **Wish It Would Rain** | 13 | $25 | Gordy 927 |

I Could Never Love Another (After Loving You) [1] • Cindy • **I Wish It Would Rain** [1] • Please Return Your Love To Me [4] • Fan The Flame • He Who Picks A Rose • Why Did You Leave Me Darling • I Truly, Truly Believe [41] • This Is My Beloved • Gonna Give Her All The Love I've Got • I've Passed This Way Before • No Man Can Love Her Like I Do

| 12/7/68 | ❶4 | 32 | 9 **Diana Ross & the Supremes Join the Temptations** | 2¹ | $25 | Motown 679 |

Try It Baby • I Second That Emotion • Ain't No Mountain High Enough • **I'm Gonna Make You Love Me** [2] • This Guy's In Love With You • Funky Broadway • I'll Try Something New [8] • A Place In The Sun • Sweet Inspiration • Then • The Impossible Dream

| 1/4/69 | ❶6 | 28 | 10 **TCB** | [TV] | 1¹ | $25 | Motown 682 |

DIANA ROSS & THE SUPREMES with THE TEMPTATIONS (above 2)
T.C.B. • Stop! In The Name Of Love • You Keep Me Hangin' On • Get Ready • The Way You Do The Things You Do • Medley: A Taste Of Honey/Eleanor Rigby/Do You Know The Way To San Jose/Mrs. Robinson • Respect • Somewhere • Ain't Too Proud To Beg • Hello, Young Lovers • For Once In My Life • (I Know) I'm Losing You • Medley: With A Song In My Heart/Without A Song • Medley: Come See About Me/My World Is Empty Without You/Baby Love • I Hear A Symphony • The Impossible Dream

| 1/4/69 | 2¹ | 29 | 11 **Live At The Copa** | [L] | 15 | $25 | Gordy 938 |

Get Ready • You're My Everything • I Truly, Truly Believe • I Wish It Would Rain • For Once In My Life • I Could Never Love Another (After Loving You) • Hello Young Lovers • With These Hands • Swanee • The Impossible Dream • Please Return Your Love To Me • (I Know) I'm Losing You

| 3/15/69 | ❶13 | 49 | 12 **Cloud Nine** | 4 | $25 | Gordy 939 |

Cloud Nine [2] • I Heard It Through The Grapevine • **Run Away Child, Running Wild** • Love Is A Hurtin' Thing • Hey Girl • Why Did She Have To Leave Me (Why Did She Have To Go) • I Need Your Lovin' • Don't Let Him Take Your Love From Me • I Gotta Find A Way (To Get You Back) • Gonna Keep On Tryin' Till I Win Your Love

| 8/9/69 | 2³ | 20 | 13 **The Temptations Show** | [TV] | 24 | $25 | Gordy 933 |

Get Ready • Medley: Girl (Why You Wanna Make Me Blue)/Beauty Is Only Skin Deep/You're My Everything/My Girl/Ain't Too Proud To Beg • I've Got To Be Me • Cloud Nine • For Once In My Life • Try It Baby • When I Lay My Burdens Down • Medley: The Best Things In Life Are Free/Life • Medley: Old Man River/Swanee/Old Folks • Medley: Hello Young Lovers/Cloud Nine/If I Didn't Care • Run Away Child, Running Wild • Somebody's Keepin' Score

| 10/11/69 | ❶15 | 35 | 14 **Puzzle People** | 5 | $25 | Gordy 949 |

I Can't Get Next To You [1] • Hey Jude • **Don't Let The Joneses Get You Down** [2] • Message From A Black Man • It's Your Thing • Little Green Apples • You Don't Love Me No More • Since I've Lost You • Running Away (Ain't Gonna Help You) • That's The Way Love Is • Slave

| 10/25/69 | 6 | 21 | 15 **Together** | 28 | $25 | Motown 692 |

Stubborn Kind Of Fellow • I'll Be Doggone • **The Weight** [33] • Ain't Nothing Like The Real Thing • Uptight (Everything's Alright) • Sing A Simple Song • Medley: My Girl/My Guy • For Better Or Worse • Can't Take My Eyes Off You • Why (Must We Fall In Love)

| 12/13/69 | 4 | 15 | 16 **On Broadway** | [TV] | 38 | $25 | Motown 699 |

DIANA ROSS & THE SUPREMES with THE TEMPTATIONS (above 2)
G.I.T. On Broadway • Broadway Medley • Malteds Over Manhattan • Medley: Leading Lady/Doin' What Comes Natur'lly/I'm Gonna Wash That Man Right Outa My Hair/Wouldn't It Be Lovely/People/Everything's Coming Up Roses/Mame • Fiddler On The Roof • Student Mountie • The Rhythm Of Life • Medley: Let The Sunshine In/Funky Broadway/G.I.T. On Broadway

| 4/4/70 | ❶4 | 28 | 17 **Psychedelic Shack** | 9 | $20 | Gordy 947 |

Psychedelic Shack [2] • You Make Your Own Heaven And Hell Right Here On Earth • Hum Along And Dance • Take A Stroll Thru Your Mind • **It's Summer** [29] • War • You Need Love Like I Do (Don't You) • Friendship Train

DEBUT	PEAK	WKS	Gold	Album Title		Pop #	$	Label & Number

TEMPTATIONS, The — Cont'd

DEBUT	PEAK	WKS	Album Title	Pop #	$	Label & Number
8/22/70	5	14	18 **Live at London's Talk of The Town** [L]	21	$20	Gordy 953

Medley: Get Ready/Girl (Why You Wanna Make Me Blue)/Beauty Is Only Skin Deep/You're My Everything/My Girl/Ain't Too Proud To Beg • I'm Gonna Make You Love Me • The Impossible Dream • Runaway Child, Running Wild • Don't Let The Joneses Get You Down • Love Theme From Romeo & Juliet (A Time For Us) • I Can't Get Next To You • This Guy's In Love With You • I've Gotta Be Me • (I Know) I'm Losing You • Cloud Nine • Everything Is Going To Be Alright

| 10/3/70 | 2³ | 45 | 19 **Temptations Greatest Hits II** [G] | 15 | $20 | Gordy 954 |

Cloud Nine [2] • I Wish It Would Rain [1] • Ball Of Confusion (That's What The World Is Today) [2] • (I Know) I'm Losing You [1] • I Can't Get Next To You [1] • You're My Everything [3] • Psychedelic Shack [2] • Please Return Your Love To Me [4] • Run Away Child, Running Wild [1] • I Could Never Love Another (After Loving You) [1] • Don't Let The Joneses Get You Down [2] • (Loneliness Made Me Realize) It's You That I Need [3]

| 5/22/71 | 2⁴ | 33 | 20 **Sky's The Limit** | 16 | $20 | Gordy 957 |

Gonna Keep On Tryin' Till I Win Your Love • Just My Imagination (Running Away With Me) [1] • I'm The Exception To The Rule • Smiling Faces Sometimes • Man • Throw A Farewell Kiss • Ungena Za Ulimwengu (Unite The World) [8] • Love Can Be Anything (Can't Nothing Be Love But Love)

| 1/29/72 | ❶² | 27 | 21 **Solid Rock** | 24 | $20 | Gordy 961 |

Take A Look Around [10] • Ain't No Sunshine • Stop The War Now • What It Is? • Smooth Sailing (From Now On) • Superstar (Remember How You Got Where You Are) [8] • It's Summer [29] • The End Of Our Road

| 10/14/72 | ❶¹ | 33 | 22 **All Directions** | 2² | $20 | Gordy 962 |

Funky Music Sho Nuff Turns Me On [27] • Run Charlie Run • Papa Was A Rollin' Stone [5] • Love Woke Me Up This Morning • I Ain't Got Nothin' • The First Time Ever (I Saw Your Face) • Mother Nature [flip] • Do Your Thing

| 3/17/73 | ❶² | 27 | 23 **Masterpiece** | 7 | $20 | Gordy 965 |

Hey Girl (I Like Your Style) [2] • Masterpiece [1] • Ma • Law Of The Land • The Plastic Man [8] • Hurry Tomorrow

| 9/8/73 | 5 | 17 | 24 **Anthology** [G] | 65 | $30 | Motown 782 [3] |

The Way You Do The Things You Do [11] • I'll Be In Trouble [33] • The Girl's Alright With Me • Girl (Why You Wanna Make Me Blue) [26] • My Girl [1] • It's Growing [3] • Since I Lost My Baby [4] • Don't Look Back [15] • Get Ready [1] • Ain't Too Proud To Beg [1] • Beauty Is Only Skin Deep [1] • (I Know) I'm Losing You [1] • All I Need [2] • You're My Everything [3] • (Loneliness Made Me Realize) It's You That I Need [3] • I Wish It Would Rain [1] • I Truly, Truly Believe [41] • I Could Never Love Another (After Loving You) [1] • Please Return Your Love To Me [4] • Cloud Nine [2] • Run Away Child, Running Wild [1] • Don't Let The Joneses Get You Down [2] • I Can't Get Next To You [1] • Psychedelic Shack [2] • Ball Of Confusion (That's What The World Is Today) [2] • Funky Music Sho Nuff Turns Me On [27] • I Ain't Got Nothin' • Ol' Man River • Try To Remember • The Impossible Dream • I'm Gonna Make You Love Me [2] • Just My Imagination (Running Away With Me) [1] • Superstar (Remember How You Got Where You Are) [8] • Mother Nature [flip] • Love Woke Me Up This Morning • Papa Was A Rollin' Stone [5]

| 12/29/73+ | 2¹ | 30 | 25 **1990** | 19 | $15 | Gordy 966 |

Let Your Hair Down [1] • I Need You • Heavenly [8] • You've Got My Soul On Fire [8] • Ain't No Justice • 1990 • Zoom

| 2/8/75 | ❶¹ | 36 | 26 **A Song For You** | 13 | $15 | Gordy 969 |

Happy People [1] • Glasshouse [9] • Shakey Ground [1] • The Prophet • A Song For You • Memories • I'm A Bachelor • Firefly

| 12/6/75+ | 11 | 11 | 27 **House Party** | 40 | $15 | Gordy 973 |
| 4/3/76 | 3 | 16 | 28 **Wings Of Love** | 29 | $15 | Gordy 971 |

Sweet Gypsy Jane • Sweetness In The Dark • Up The Creek (Without A Paddle) [21] • China Doll • Mary Ann • Dream World (Wings Of Love) • Paradise

| 9/11/76 | 10 | 12 | 29 **The Temptations Do The Temptations** | 53 | $15 | Gordy 975 |

Why Can't You And Me Get Together • Who Are You [22] • I'm On Fire (Body Song) • Put Your Trust In Me, Baby • There's No Stopping (Til We Set The Whole World Rockin') • Let Me Count The Ways (I Love You) • Is There Anybody Else • I'll Take You

12/10/77	38	10	30 **Hear To Tempt You**	113	$12	Atlantic 19143
10/21/78	46	4	31 **Bare Back**	205	$12	Atlantic 19188
5/10/80	13	22	32 **Power**	45	$12	Gordy 994
9/5/81	36	11	33 **The Temptations**	119	$12	Gordy 1006
5/1/82	2⁵	24	34 **Reunion**	37	$12	Gordy 6008

Standing On The Top [6] • You Better Beware • Lock It In The Pocket • I've Never Been To Me • Backstage • More On The Inside [82] • Money's Hard To Get

3/26/83	19	18	35 **Surface Thrills**	159	$12	Gordy 6032
11/5/83+	30	30	36 **Back To Basics**	152	$12	Gordy 6085
11/17/84+	3	38	37 **Truly For You**	55	$12	Gordy 6119

Running • Treat Her Like A Lady [2] • How Can You Say That It's Over [81] • My Love Is True (Truly For You) [14] • Memories • Just To Keep You In My Life • Set Your Love Right • I'll Keep My Light In My Window

12/21/85+	20	24	38 **Touch Me**	146	$12	Gordy 6164
5/31/86	55	17	39 **25th Anniversary** [K]	140	$15	Motown 5389 [2]
7/26/86	4	42	40 **To Be Continued...**	74	$25	Gordy 6207

Lady Soul [4] • Message To The World • To Be Continued... [25] • Put Us Together Again • Someone [45] • Girls (They Like It) • More Love, Your Love • A Fine Mess [63] • You're The One • Love Me Right

10/24/87	12	28	41 **Together Again**	112	$12	Motown 6246
9/16/89	25	44	42 **Special**		$12	Motown 6275
12/21/91+	88	12	43 **Milestone**		$8	Motown 6331
10/14/95	43	26	44 **For Lovers Only**		$8	Motown 0568
9/5/98	8	48↑ ●	45 **Phoenix Rising**	44	$8	Motown 0937

Hereafter • Stay • False Faces • How Could He Hurt You [61] • I'm Calling You • This Is My Promise [54] • My Love • Tempt Me • If I Give You My Heart • Take Me In Your Arms • That's What Friends Are For • Just Like I Told You

| 11/21/98 | 60 | 6 | 46 **The Ultimate Collection** [G] | 137 | $8 | Motown 0562 |

TEN CITY   **'89**

Dance trio from Chicago: Byron Stingily (vocals), Herb Lawson (guitar) and Byron Burke (keyboards).

| 3/4/89 | 49 | 16 | **Foundation** | | $8 | Atlantic 81939 |

10db   **'89**

Dance duo: Audrey Hollis and Stanley Thermond. "db" is shorthand for decibels.

| 6/24/89 | 57 | 12 | **Steppin' Out** | | $10 | Crush 224 |

TERMINATOR X '91
Born Norman Lee Rogers on 8/25/66 in New York City. Male rapper. Member of **Public Enemy**.

| 6/1/91 | 19 | 18 | | 1 Terminator X & The Valley Of The Jeep Beets | 97 | $8 | P.R.O. Div. 46896 |
| 7/9/94 | 38 | 4 | | 2 Super Bad | 189 | $8 | P.R.O. Div. 523343 |

TERMINATOR X AND THE GODFATHERS OF THREATT

TERRELL, Tammi '69
Born Tammy Montgomery on 1/24/46 in Philadelphia. Died of a brain tumor on 3/16/70 (age 24). Female singer.

| 10/7/67 | 7 | 22 | | 1 United | 69 | $30 | Tamla 277 |

Ain't No Mountain High Enough [3] • You Got What It Takes • **If I Could Build My Whole World Around You** [2] • Somethin' Stupid • **Your Precious Love** [2] • Hold Me Oh My Darling • Two Can Have A Party • Little Ole Boy, Little Ole Girl • **If This World Were Mine** [27] • Sad Wedding • Give A Little Love • Oh How I'd Miss You

| 9/21/68 | 4 | 19 | | 2 You're All I Need | 60 | $30 | Tamla 284 |

MARVIN GAYE & TAMMI TERRELL (above 2)
Ain't Nothing Like The Real Thing [1] • **Keep On Lovin' Me Honey** [11] • **You're All I Need To Get By** [1] • Baby Don'tcha Worry • You Ain't Livin' Till You're Lovin' • Give In, You Just Can't Win • When Love Comes Knocking At My Heart • Come On And See Me • I Can't Help But Love You • That's How It Is (Since You've Been Gone) • I'll Never Stop Loving You Baby • Memory Chest

| 3/8/69 | 39 | 4 | | 3 Irresistible Tammi | | $50 | Motown 652 |
| 6/13/70 | 17 | 8 | | 4 Marvin Gaye & Tammi Terrell Greatest Hits ... [G] | 171 | $20 | Tamla 302 |

TERROR FABULOUS '94
Born Cecil Campbell in Kingston, Jamaica. Reggae rapper.

| 7/9/94 | 51 | 18 | | Yaga Yaga | | $8 | EastWest 92327 |

TERRY, Todd '89
Born in 1967 in Brooklyn, New York. Rap producer.

| 12/10/88+ | 56 | 10 | | To The Batmobile Let's Go | | $10 | Fresh 82009 |

THE TODD TERRY PROJECT

TERRY, Tony '88
Born on 3/12/64 in Pinehurst, North Carolina; raised in Washington DC. Singer/actor. Appeared in the Broadway musicals *Black Nativity* and *Mama, I Want To Sing*.

12/5/87+	27	40		1 Forever Yours	151	$8	Epic 40890
2/2/91	35	68		2 Tony Terry	184	$8	Epic 45015
10/22/94	47	9		3 Heart Of A Man		$8	Virgin 39861

TEX, Joe ★157★ '65
Born Joseph Arrington on 8/8/33 in Rogers, Texas. Died of a heart attack on 8/13/82 (age 49). Former gospel singer. Converted to the Muslim faith, changed name to "Joseph Hazziez" in July 1972.
1)Hold What You've Got 2)The New Boss 3)The Love You Save

| 1/30/65 | 2[2] | 6 | | 1 Hold What You've Got | 124 | $40 | Atlantic 8106 |

You Got What It Takes [10] • Tell Me Right Now • One Monkey Don't Stop No Show [20] • Hold What You've Got [2] • I'm Not Going To Work Today • Are We Ready • You Better Get It [15] • Heep See Few Know • Fresh Out Of Tears • You Can Stay • There Is A Girl • Together We Stand

| 11/20/65 | 3 | 13 | | 2 The New Boss | 142 | $40 | Atlantic 8115 |

C C Rider • Stop Look And Listen • For Your Love • A Woman Can Change A Man [12] • What In The World • You Got What It Takes [10] • Don't Make Your Children Pay • King Of The Road • Detroit City • Any Little Bit • Hold What You've Got [2] • I Want To (Do Everything For You) [1]

| 5/7/66 | 3 | 11 | | 3 The Love You Save | 108 | $40 | Atlantic 8124 |

The Love You Save (May Be Your Own) [2] • Live For Yourself • Build Your Love (On A Solid Foundation) • I Don't Trust Myself Around You • Funny Bone • A Sweet Woman Like You [1] • I'm A Man • You Better Believe It, Baby • Close The Door • If Sugar Was As Sweet As You • Heartbreak Hotel • Don't Let Your Left Hand Know

1/21/67	24	2		4 I've Got To Do A Little Bit Better		$40	Atlantic 8133
8/19/67	23	4		5 The Best Of Joe Tex ... [G]	168	$20	Atlantic 8144
2/17/68	13	14		6 Live and Lively ... [L]	84	$20	Atlantic 8156
8/31/68	45	5		7 Soul Country	154	$20	Atlantic 8187
4/29/72	5	17		8 I Gotcha	17	$15	Dial 6002

I Gotcha [1] • Give The Baby Anything The Baby Wants [20] • Takin' A Chance • Baby Let Me Steal You • It Ain't Gonna Work Baby • God Of Love • You Said A Bad Word [12] • Bad Feet • The Woman Cares • Love Me Right Girl • For My Woman • You're In Too Deep

| 2/3/73 | 42 | 9 | | 9 Joe Tex Spills The Beans | | $15 | Dial 6004 |
| 5/7/77 | 32 | 10 | | 10 Bumps & Bruises | 108 | $12 | Epic 34666 |

THERESA '87
Duo of Theresa King and Victor Porter.

| 10/3/87 | 62 | 3 | | Broken Puzzle | | $8 | RCA Victor 6488 |

3RD BASS '90
White rap duo from Queens, New York: Pete Nash and Michael **"MC Serch"** Berrin. Supported by black DJ Richard Lawson. Nash and Lawson recorded as **Prime Minister Pete Nice & DJ Daddy Rich**.

| 12/9/89+ | 5 | 41 | ● | 1 The Cactus Album | 55 | $8 | Def Jam 45415 |

Stymie's Theme • Sons Of 3rd Bass • Russell Rush • **The Gas Face** [29] • Monte Hall • Oval Office • Hoods • Soul In The Hole • Triple Stage Darkness • M.C. Disagree • Wordz Of Wizdom • Product Of The Environment • Desert Boots • The Cactus • Jim Backus • Flippin' Off The Wall Like Lucy Ball • **Brooklyn - Queens** [82] • **Steppin' To The A.M.** [54] • Episode #3 • Who's On Third

| 7/13/91 | 10 | 22 | ● | 2 Derelicts Of Dialect | 19 | $8 | Def Jam 47369 |

The Merchant Of Grooves • Derelicts Of Dialect • Ace In The Hole • French Toast • **Portrait Of The Artist As A Hood** [67] • **Pop Goes The Weasel** [26] • Sea Vessel Soliloquy • Daddy Rich In The Land Of 1210 • Word To The Third • Herbalz In Your Mouth • Al'za-B-Cee'z • No Master Plan No Master Race • Come In • No Static At All • Eye Jammie • Microphone Techniques • Problem Child • 3 Strikes 5000 • Kick Em In The Grill • Green Eggs And Swine • M.C. Disagree And The Re-animator

DEBUT	PEAK	WKS	Gold	Album Title	Pop #	$	Label & Number

THIRD WORLD   **'79**
Reggae fusion group from Jamaica: William Clarke (vocals), Stephen Coore (guitar), Michael Cooper (keyboards), Irvin Jarrett (percussion), Richard Daley (bass) and Willie Stewart (drums). Jarrett left by 1989.

11/25/78+	14	21		1 Journey To Addis	55	$12	Island 9554
8/23/80	59	3		2 Third World, Prisoner in The Street ....[L-S]	186	$12	Island 9616
8/15/81	50	5		3 Rock The World	186	$10	Columbia 37402
3/20/82	20	21		4 You've Got The Power	63	$10	Columbia 37744
10/8/83	50	11		5 All The Way Strong	137	$10	Columbia 38687
4/20/85	42	22		6 Sense Of Purpose	119	$10	Columbia 39877
6/24/89	30	23		7 Serious Business	107	$8	Mercury 836952
8/15/92	51	11		8 Committed		$8	Mercury 510279

THOMAS, Carla   **'67**
Born on 12/21/42 in Memphis. Daughter of **Rufus Thomas** and sister of **Vaneese Thomas**.

3/12/66	11	10		1 Comfort Me	134	$40	Stax 706
10/22/66	7	16		2 Carla	130	$40	Stax 709

B-A-B-Y [3] • Red Rooster • **Let Me Be Good To You** [11] • I Got You, Boy • Medley: Baby What You Want Me To Do/For Your Love • What Have You Got To Offer Me • I'm So Lonesome I Could Cry • I Fall To Pieces • You Don't Have To Say You Love Me • Fate • Looking Back

4/15/67	5	25		3 King & Queen	36	$40	Stax 716

OTIS REDDING & CARLA THOMAS
Knock On Wood [8] • Let Me Be Good To You • **Tramp** [2] • Tell It Like It Is • When Something Is Wrong With My Baby • Lovey Dovey [21] • New Year's Resolution • It Takes Two • Are You Lonely For Me Baby • Bring It On Home To Me • Ooh Carla, Ooh Otis

7/1/67	16	8		4 The Queen Alone	133	$40	Stax 718
6/28/69	26	8		5 Memphis Queen	151	$40	Stax 2019
9/4/71	42	3		6 Love Means...	213	$40	Stax 2044

THOMAS, Joe   **'76**
Male saxophonist.

3/20/76	52	4		Masada ....[I]		$12	Groove Merchant 3310

THOMAS, Leon   **'74**
Born in 1938 in New York City. Died of leukemia on 5/8/99 (age 61). Jazz singer. Known for unique yodeling style vocals.

3/9/74	54	4		Full Circle		$12	Flying Dutchman 10167

THOMAS, Lillo   **'84**
Born in Brooklyn, New York. Male singer.

9/17/83	23	22		1 Let Me Be Yours	201	$10	Capitol 12290
8/25/84	9	33		2 All Of You	186	$8	Capitol 12346

Your Love's Got A Hold On Me [11] • Holding On • Show Me • **Settle Down** [60] • **(Can't Take Half)** All Of You [28] • My Girl • Never Give You Up • I Like Your Style

4/25/87	10	51		3 Lillo		$8	Capitol 12450

I'm In Love [2] • Her Love • Sweet Surrender • That Guy (Could Have Been Me) • **Sexy Girl** [9] • **Wanna Make Love (All Night Long)** [7] • I've Been Loving You Too Long (To Stop Now) • **Downtown** [11] • Put Your Foot Down

THOMAS, Philip Michael   **'88**
Born on 5/26/49 in Columbus, Ohio. Played "Ricardo Tubbs" on TV's *Miami Vice*.

10/8/88	98	1		Somebody		$8	Atlantic 90960

THOMAS, Rufus   **'71**
Born on 3/26/17 in Cayce, Mississippi. Singer/songwriter/choreographer. Father of singers **Carla Thomas** and **Vaneese Thomas**. Worked as a DJ at WDIA in Memphis.

5/9/70	32	5		1 Do The Funky Chicken		$25	Stax 2028
3/13/71	19	13		2 Rufus Thomas Live/Doing The Push & Pull At P.J.'s ....[L]	147	$25	Stax 2039
12/1/73	42	5		3 Crown Prince Of Dance		$25	Stax 3008

THOMAS, Timmy   **'73**
Born on 11/13/44 in Evansville, Indiana. Singer/songwriter/keyboardist.

1/20/73	10	15		Why Can't We Live Together	53	$15	Glades 6501

Why Can't We Live Together [1] • Rainbow Power • Take Care Of Home • The First Time Ever I Saw Your Face • The Coldest Days Of My Life • In The Beginning • Cold Cold People • Opportunity • Dizzy Dizzy World • Funky Me

THOMAS, Vaneese   **'87**
Daughter of **Rufus Thomas** and sister of **Carla Thomas**.

8/8/87	45	22		Vaneese		$8	Geffen 24141

THOMPSON, Gina   **'96**
Born in 1974 in Vineland, New Jersey. Female singer.

8/31/96	36	10		Nobody Does It Better		$8	Mercury 532060

THOMPSON, Tony   **'95**
Born in Waco, Texas; raised in Oklahoma City. Lead singer of **Hi-Five**.

7/15/95	17	16		Sexsational	99	$8	Giant 24596

THORNTON, Fonzi   **'83**
Born Alfonzo Thornton in Harlem, New York. Male singer/songwriter.

5/28/83	50	9		The Leader		$10	RCA Victor 4433

THP ORCHESTRA   **'78**
Disco studio group from Canada assembled by producer W. Michael Lewis. Lead vocals by Barbara Fry.

4/8/78	57	2		Two Hot For Love!	65	$10	Butterfly 005

THREAT   **'93**
Born in Hawthorne, California. Male rapper.

8/21/93	73	6		Sickinnahead		$8	Mercury 518017

DEBUG	PEAK	WKS	Gold	Album Title	Pop #	$	Label & Number
				THREE DEGREES, The '70			
				Female vocal trio from Philadelphia: Sheila Ferguson, Valerie Holiday and Fayette Pinkney.			
8/8/70	16	13		1 "Maybe"	139	$40	Roulette 42050
2/22/75	33	7		2 The Three Degrees	28	$12	Philadelphia I. 32406
3/22/75	56	3		3 So Much In Love		$15	Roulette 3015
6/28/75	31	4		4 International	99	$12	Philadelphia I. 33162
12/27/75+	34	5		5 The Three Degrees Live ....[L]	199	$12	Philadelphia I. 33840
				recorded at Bailey's in London			
7/29/89	76	4		6 ...And Holding		$10	Ichiban 1041
				THREE SHADES BROWN '92			
				Female vocal trio: Kim Cage, Leah Johnson and Christi Thornton.			
6/20/92	98	2		Stronger Than Strong		$8	Interscope 92106
				THREE 6 MAFIA '97			
				Rap group: female **Gangsta Boo** with males Jordan Houston, Crunchy Black, Paul Beauregard, Koopsta Knicca and Lord Infamous.			
5/27/95	59	2		1 Mystic Stylez		$8	Prophet 4401
3/29/97	42	11		2 The End	126	$8	Prophet 4405
11/22/97	18	40	●	3 Chpt. 2: "World Domination"	40	$8	Relativity 1644
				3T '96			
				Vocal trio from Los Angeles: brothers Taryll, T.J. and Taj Jackson. Sons of Tito Jackson (of **The Jacksons**).			
11/25/95+	65	22		Brotherhood	127	$8	MJJ Music 57450
				THREE TIMES DOPE '89			
				Rap trio from Philadelphia: Duerwood Beale, Walter Griggs and Robert Waller.			
4/8/89	18	31		1 Original Stylin'	122	$8	Arista 8571
8/11/90	30	21		2 Live From Acknickulous Land		$8	Arista 8615
				3XKRAZY '97			
				Rap trio from Oakland: Bart, Keek Tha Sneek and Agerman.			
4/26/97	28	13		Stackin Chips	136	$8	Noo Trybe 42961
				3-2 '96			
				Born in Louisiana; raised in Houston. Male rapper.			
10/5/96	28	6		The Wicked Buddah Baby		$8	Rap-A-Lot 42087
				THUG LIFE '94			
				Rap group: **2 Pac**, Syke, Macadoshis, Mopreme and The Rated R. 2 Pac died on 9/13/96 of wounds suffered on 9/7/96 in a shooting in Las Vegas.			
10/29/94	6	65	●	Volume 1	42	$8	Interscope 92360
				Bury Me A G • Don't Get It Twisted • Shit Don't Stop • Pour Out A Little Liquor • Stay True • How Long Will They Mourn Me? • Under Pressure • Street Fame • Cradle To The Grave [91] • Str8 Ballin'			
				THURSTON, Bobby '80			
				Born in 1954 in Washington DC. Singer/percussionist.			
4/12/80	74	2		You Got What It Takes		$10	Prelude 12174
				TIERRA '81			
				Latin group from Los Angeles: brothers Steve (vocals, trombone) and Rudy (guitar) Salas, Joey Guerra (keyboards), Bobby Navarrete (reeds), Andre Baeza (congas), Steve Falomir (bass) and Phil Madayag (drums). The Salas brothers and Baeza were formerly with El Chicano.			
1/31/81	15	13		City Nights	38	$10	Boardwalk 36995
				TIMBALAND AND MAGOO '97			
				Timbaland is male rapper/producer Timothy Mosley. Magoo is a male rapper. Both were born in Norfolk, Virginia.			
11/29/97	9	38	▲	1 Welcome To Our World	33	$8	Blackground 92772
				Beep Beep • Feel It • Up Jumps Da Boogie [4] • Clock Strikes [24] • 15 After Da Hour • Luv 2 Luv U • Smoke In Da Air • Peepin' My Style • Writin' Rhymes • Deep In Your Memory • Man Undercover • Joy			
12/12/98	11	19		2 Tim's Bio	41	$8	Blackground 92813
				TIMBALAND			
				TIME, The '82			
				Funk group from Minneapolis: **Morris Day** (vocals), **Jesse Johnson** (guitar), Jimmy "Jam" Harris and Monte Moir (keyboards), Terry Lewis (bass) and Jellybean Johnson (drums). Lewis, Harris and Moir left before band's featured role in movie Purple Rain. Paul Peterson (keyboards) and Jerome Benton (dancer) joined in 1984; group disbanded later that year. Lewis and Harris became highly successful songwriting/producing team. Lewis married **Karyn White**. Original lineup (and Benton) regrouped in 1990.			
8/29/81	7	45	●	1 The Time	50	$10	Warner 3598
				Get It Up [6] • Girl [49] • After Hi School • Cool [7] • Oh, Baby • The Stick [flip]			
9/18/82	2³	38	●	2 What Time Is It?	26	$10	Warner 23701
				Wild And Loose • 777-9311 [2] • One Day I'm Gonna Be Somebody • The Walk [24] • Gigolos Get Lonely Too [77] • I Don't Wanna Leave You			
7/28/84	3	46	▲	3 Ice Cream Castle	24	$10	Warner 25109
				Ice Cream Castles [11] • My Drawers • Chili Sauce • Jungle Love [6] • If The Kid Can't Make You Come • The Bird [33]			
8/4/90	9	22	●	4 Pandemonium	18	$8	Paisley Park 27490
				Dreamland • Pandemonium • Sexy Socialites • Jerk-Out [1] • Yount • Blondie • Donald Trump (Black Version) • Chocolate [44] • Cooking Class • Skillet • It's Your World • Sometimes I Get Lonely • Data Bank • My Summertime Thang • Pretty Little Women			
				TIMEX SOCIAL CLUB '87			
				Rap trio from Berkeley, California: Michael Marshall, Marcus Thompson and Alex Hill.			
12/6/86+	29	45		Vicious Rumors		$10	Danya 9645
				TISDALE, Wayman '95			
				Born on 6/9/64 in Tulsa, Oklahoma. Jazz bassist. Pro basketball player with the NBA's Phoenix Suns.			
7/22/95	48	17		1 Power Forward ....[I]		$8	MoJazz 0552
9/7/96	66	6		2 In The Zone		$8	MoJazz 0696

DEBUT	PEAK	WKS	Gold	Album Title	Pop #	$	Label & Number

TJADER, Cal   '65
Born Callen Tjader on 7/16/25 in St. Louis. Died on 5/5/82 (age 56). Latin jazz vibraphonist.

| 4/17/65 | 8 | 7 | | 1 **Soul Sauce**   [I] | 52 | $25 | Verve 8614 |

Soul Sauce (Guacha Guaro) • Afro-Blue • Pantano • Somewhere In The Night • Maramoor • Tanya • Leyte • Spring Is Here • Joao

| 4/24/71 | 34 | 6 | | 2 Tjader ....[I] | | $15 | Fantasy 8406 |

T LA ROCK   '87
Born in the Bronx, New York. Male rapper.

| 6/6/87 | 64 | 11 | | Lryical King (From The Boogie Down Bronx) .... | | $10 | Fresh 2 |

TLC   '94
Female vocal trio from Atlanta: Tionne "T-Boz" Watkins, Lisa "Left Eye" Lopes and Rozonda "Chilli" Thomas. Founded and managed by Pebbles.

| 3/21/92 | 3 | 68 | ▲⁴ | 1 **Ooooooohhh...On The TLC Tip** | 14 | $8 | LaFace 26003 |

Ain't 2 Proud 2 Beg [2] • Shock Dat Monkey • Hat 2 Da Back [14] • Das Da Way We Like 'Em • **What About Your Friends** [2] • His Story • Bad By Myself • Somethin' You Wanna Know • Baby-Baby-Baby [1] • This Is How It Should Be Done • Depend On Myself

| 12/3/94 | 2⁵ | 89 | ▲¹⁰ | 2 **CrazySexyCool** | 3 | $8 | LaFace 26009 |

Creep [1] • Kick Your Game • **Diggin' On You** [7] • Case Of The Fake People • Red Light Special [3] • Waterfalls [4] • Let's Do It Again • If I Was Your Girlfriend • Take Your Time • Switch • Sumthin' Wicked This Way Comes

TODAY   '89
Vocal group from Englewood, New Jersey: Frederick Lee Drakeford, Larry McCain, Wesley Adams and Larry Singletary. Drakeford later recorded solo as **Big Bub**.

| 12/10/88+ | 11 | 43 | | 1 Today | 86 | $8 | Motown 6261 |
| 10/13/90 | 19 | 27 | | 2 The New Formula | 132 | $8 | Motown 6309 |

TOMS, Gary, Empire   '75
Disco group from New York City: Gary Toms (keyboards), Helen Jacobs (vocals), Rick Kenny (guitar), Eric Oliver (trumpet), Les Rose (sax), Warren Tesoro (percussion), John Freeman (bass) and Rick Murray (drums).

| 8/23/75 | 33 | 9 | | 7-6-5-4-3-2-1 Blow Your Whistle .... | 178 | $12 | PIP 6814 |

TOM TOM CLUB   '83
Studio funk project formed by **Talking Heads** members/husband-and-wife Chris Frantz and Tina Weymouth.

| 8/27/83 | 49 | 6 | | Close To The Bone .... | 73 | $10 | Sire 23916 |

TONE LOC   '89
Born Anthony Smith on 3/3/66 in Los Angeles. Male rapper/actor. Appeared in several movies.

| 2/25/89 | 3 | 28 | ▲² | 1 **Loc-Ed After Dark** | 1¹ | $8 | Delicious Vinyl 3000 |

On Fire • **Wild Thing** [3] • I Got It Goin' On [59] • Cutting Rhythms • **Funky Cold Medina** [7] • Next Episode • Cheeba Cheeba • Don't Get Close • Loc'in On The Shaw • The Homies

| 12/21/91+ | 46 | 15 | | 2 Cool Hand Loc .... | | $8 | Delicious Vinyl 510609 |

TONEY, Oscar Jr.   '67
Born on 5/26/39 in Selma, Alabama; raised in Columbus, Georgia. Own gospel group, Sensational Melodies Of Joy, while in high school. Own group, the Searchers, first recorded for Max in 1957. Recorded solo for King in 1958. Oscar's three sisters sang as the Tonettes.

| 8/5/67 | 27 | 2 | | For Your Precious Love .... | 192 | $25 | Bell 6006 |

TONY D   '91
Born Tony Dofat in Trenton, New Jersey. White rap producer.

| 5/4/91 | 71 | 11 | | Droppin' Funky Verses .... | | $8 | 4th & B'way 444025 |

TONY M.F. ROCK   '90
Born in Atlanta. Male rapper.

| 12/23/89+ | 86 | 12 | | Let Me Take You To The Rock House .... | | $8 | Effect 3000 |

★200★ TONY! TONI! TONÉ!   '93
Trio from Oakland: brothers Raphael Saadiq (vocals, bass, keyboards) and D'wayne Wiggins (vocals, guitar), with cousin Timothy Christian Riley (drums). Trio appeared in the movie *House Party 2*.

| 5/14/88 | 14 | 66 | ● | 1 Who? | 69 | $8 | Wing 835549 |
| 5/26/90 | 4 | 66 | ▲ | 2 The Revival | 34 | $8 | Wing 841902 |

Feels Good [1] • All The Way • Oakland Stroke • **The Blues** [1] • Let's Have A Good Time • It Never Rains (In Southern California) [1] • **Whatever You Want** [1] • I Care • Sky's The Limit • All My Love • Don't Talk About Me • Skin Tight • Jo-Jo • Those Were The Days

| 7/10/93 | 3 | 56 | ▲² | 3 **Sons Of Soul** | 24 | $8 | Wing 514933 |

If I Had No Loot [8] • What Goes Around Comes Around • My Ex-Girlfriend • Tell Me Mama • Leavin' [41] • Slow Wine [21] • (Lay Your Head On My) Pillow [4] • I Couldn't Keep It To Myself • Gangsta Groove • Tonyies! In The Wrong Key • Dance Hall • Fun • **Anniversary** [2] • Castleers

| 12/7/96 | 10 | 44 | ▲ | 4 **House Of Music** | 32 | $8 | Mercury 534250 |

Thinking Of You [5] • Top Notch • **Let's Get Down** [flip] • Til Last Summer • Lovin' You • Still A Man • Don't Fall In Love • Holy Smokes & Gee Whiz • Annie May • Let Me Know • Tossin' & Turnin' • Wild Child • Party Don't Cry

| 11/22/97 | 54 | 6 | | 5 Hits ....[G] | | $8 | Mercury 536368 |

TOO MUCH TROUBLE   '92
Rap group from Houston: Tracy Howze, Marvin Randolph, Dwayne Barard and Johnny VanBibber.

| 4/4/92 | 54 | 11 | | 1 Bringing Hell On Earth | | $8 | Rap-A-Lot 57174 |

TOO MUCH TROUBLE (The Baby Geto Boys)

| 6/5/93 | 55 | 11 | | 2 Player's Choice .... | | $8 | Rap-A-Lot 57186 |
| 9/27/97 | 75 | 1 | | 3 Too Much Weight .... | | $8 | Rap-A-Lot 44699 |

DEBUT	PEAK	WKS	Gold	Album Title	Pop #	$	Label & Number

★115★ TOO $HORT '93
Born Todd Shaw on 4/28/66 in Los Angeles. Male rapper.

DEBUT	PEAK	WKS	Gold	Album Title	Pop #	$	Label & Number
5/28/88	50	13	●	1 Born To Mack..		$8	Jive 1100
2/25/89	9	41	▲²	2 Life Is...Too Short	37	$8	Jive 1149

Life Is...Too Short [43] • Rhymes • I Ain't Trippin' • Nobody Does It Better • Don't Fight The Feelin' • CussWords • City Of Dope • Pimp The Ho

DEBUT	PEAK	WKS	Gold	Album Title	Pop #	$	Label & Number
9/29/90	3	39	▲	3 Short Dog's In The House	20	$8	Jive 1348

Short Dog's In The House • It's Your Life • The Ghetto [12] • Short But Funky [36] • In The Oaktown • Dead Or Alive • Punk Bitch • Ain't Nothin' But A Word To Me • Hard On The Boulevard • Pimpology • Paula & Janet • Rap Like Me

DEBUT	PEAK	WKS	Gold	Album Title	Pop #	$	Label & Number
8/1/92	11	40	▲	4 Shorty The Pimp..	6	$8	Jive 41467
11/13/93	❶²	47	▲	5 Get In Where You Fit In	4	$8	Jive 41526

I'm A Player [39] • Just Another Day • Gotta Get Some Lovin' • Money In The Ghetto [64] • Blowjob Betty • All My Bitches Are Gone • The Dangerous Crew • Get In Where You Fit In • Playboy $hort • Way Too Real • It's All Good • Oakland Style

DEBUT	PEAK	WKS	Gold	Album Title	Pop #	$	Label & Number
2/11/95	❶²	29	▲	6 Cocktails	6	$8	Jive 41553

Ain't Nothing Like Pimpin' • Cocktales [43] • Can I Get A Bitch • Coming Up $hort • Thangs Change • Paystyle • Giving Up The Funk • Top Down • We Do This • Game • Sample The Funk • Don't Fuck For Free

DEBUT	PEAK	WKS	Gold	Album Title	Pop #	$	Label & Number
6/8/96	❶²	27	▲	7 Gettin' It (Album Number Ten)	3	$8	Jive 41584

Gettin' It [49] • Survivin' The Game • That's Why • Bad Ways • Fuck My Car • Take My Bitch • Buy You Some • Pimp Me • Baby D • Nasty Rhymes • Never Talk Down • I Must Confess • So Watcha Sayin' • I've Been Watching You (Move Your Sexy Body)

TOP AUTHORITY '95
Rap duo of cousins from Flint, Michigan: Dia Kanyama Peacock and Diallo Sekou Peacock.

DEBUT	PEAK	WKS	Gold	Album Title	Pop #	$	Label & Number
2/12/94	21	38		1 Somethin' To Blaze To...		$8	Trak 72576
11/25/95	16	20		2 Rated G...	144	$8	Trak 72668
11/8/97	21	12		3 Uncut - The New Yea...	192	$8	Wrap 8160

TOP QUALITY '94
Born in White Plains, New York. Male rapper.

DEBUT	PEAK	WKS	Gold	Album Title	Pop #	$	Label & Number
6/11/94	95	1		Magnum Opus...		$8	RCA 66328

TOSH, Peter '81
Born Winston Hubert MacIntosh on 10/9/44 in Westmoreland, Jamaica. Fatally shot on 9/11/87 (age 42) during a robbery at his home in Jamaica. Former member of Bob Marley's Wailers.

DEBUT	PEAK	WKS	Gold	Album Title	Pop #	$	Label & Number
7/11/81	40	11		1 Wanted Dread & Alive...	91	$10	EMI America 17055
6/25/83	49	10		2 Mama Africa..	59	$10	EMI America 17095

TOTAL '96
Female vocal trio from New York City: Kima Raynor, Keisha Spivey and Pam Long.

DEBUT	PEAK	WKS	Gold	Album Title	Pop #	$	Label & Number
3/2/96	4	38	●	1 Total	23	$8	Bad Boy 73006

Do You Know • No One Else [54] • Kissin' You [6] • Do You Think About Us [20] • Can't You See [3] • Someone Like You • Tell Me • Love Is All We Need • Don't Ever Change • Spend Some Time • When Boy Meets Girl [28]

DEBUT	PEAK	WKS	Gold	Album Title	Pop #	$	Label & Number
11/21/98	9	35	●	2 Kima, Keisha & Pam	39	$8	Bad Boy 73120

Trippin' [3] • I Tried • Rock Track • If You Want Me • Press Rewind • Sitting Home [10] • What About Us [4] • Do Something • Rain • The Most Beautiful... • I Don't Wanna • Move Too Fast • Bet She Can't • I Don't Wanna Smile

TOTAL CONTRAST '86
Male techno-soul duo from England: Robin Achampong and Delroy Murray.

DEBUT	PEAK	WKS	Gold	Album Title	Pop #	$	Label & Number
4/5/86	49	16		Total Contrast		$8	London 828002

TOTAL DEVASTATION '93
Rap trio from San Francisco: Tuff Cut Tim, Tone and Freakin' Puertrican B-Fresh.

DEBUT	PEAK	WKS	Gold	Album Title	Pop #	$	Label & Number
12/25/93	82	3		Legalize It!..		$8	Arista 18734

TOTALLY INSANE '92
Rap duo from Oakland: Phillip Allen and Adam Hicks.

DEBUT	PEAK	WKS	Gold	Album Title	Pop #	$	Label & Number
8/22/92	61	15		1 Direct From The Backstreet		$8	In-A-Minute 7700
10/30/93	87	4		2 Goin Insane		$8	In-A-Minute 8500
8/5/95	48	7		3 Back Street Life		$8	In-A-Minute 8900

★189★ TOWER OF POWER '73
Interracial funk group from Oakland. Varying lineup included Greg Adams (trumpet), Mic Gillette (trombone), Steve Kupka, Emilio Castillo and Lenny Pickett (saxophones), Chester Thompson (keyboards) and Francis Prestia (bass). Vocalists included Lenny Williams, Rufus Miller, Edward McGhee and Michael Jeffries.
1)Tower of Power 2)Back to Oakland 3)Bump City

DEBUT	PEAK	WKS	Gold	Album Title	Pop #	$	Label & Number
7/22/72	16	19		1 Bump City	85	$15	Warner 2616
6/16/73	11	19	●	2 Tower Of Power	15	$15	Warner 2681
4/27/74	13	14		3 Back to Oakland	26	$15	Warner 2749
2/1/75	19	18		4 Urban Renewal	22	$15	Warner 2834
10/18/75	29	7		5 In The Slot	67	$15	Warner 2880
5/29/76	29	6		6 Live And In Living Color ....[L]	99	$15	Warner 2924
9/18/76	25	9		7 Ain't Nothin' Stoppin' Us Now	42	$10	Columbia 34302
4/22/78	33	6		8 We Came To Play!	89	$10	Columbia 34906
8/18/79	28	13		9 Back On The Streets	106	$10	Columbia 35784
5/8/93	92	1		10 T.O.P.		$8	Epic 52805

TOWNS, Eddie '86

DEBUT	PEAK	WKS	Gold	Album Title	Pop #	$	Label & Number
7/12/86	59	5		Best Friends...		$8	Total Exp. 5717

ET (EDDIE TOWNS)

TOYS, The '66
Female vocal trio from Queens, New York: Barbara Harris, June Montiero and Barbara Parritt.

DEBUT	PEAK	WKS	Gold	Album Title	Pop #	$	Label & Number
2/12/66	9	1		The Toys sing "A Lover's Concerto" and "Attack!"	92	$50	DynoVoice 9002

Can't Get Enough Of You Baby • Deserted • See How They Run • Hallelujah • I Got A Man • A Lover's Concerto [4] • What's Wrong With Me Baby • Yesterday • Baby's Gone • This Night • Back Street • Attack

				TQ **'98**			
				Born Terrance Quaites in Mobile, Alabama; raised in Los Angeles. Former member of **Coming Of Age**.			
11/28/98	28	18		They Never Saw Me Coming	122	$8	ClockWork 69431
				TRAMAINE **'86**			
				Born Tramaine Hawkins. Female gospel singer.			
3/29/86	33	14		The Search Is Over		$8	A&M 5110
				TRAMMPS, The **'76**			
				Vocal group from Philadelphia: Jimmy Ellis, Earl Young, brothers Harold and Stanley Wade, and Robert Upchurch.			
5/10/75	30	9		1 Trammps	159	$12	Golden Fleece 33163
5/22/76	13	13		2 Where The Happy People Go	50	$10	Atlantic 18172
1/29/77	16	23	●	3 Disco Inferno	46	$10	Atlantic 18211
12/10/77	27	10		4 The Trammps III	85	$10	Atlantic 19148
9/23/78	57	2		5 The Best Of The Trammps ....[G]	139	$10	Atlantic 19194
				TRAPP **'97**			
				Born John Parker in Atlanta. Male rapper/producer.			
5/10/97	45	6		Stop The Gunfight	123	$8	Deff Trapp 9268
				TRE 8 **'95**			
				Born in Los Angeles. Male rapper.			
11/18/95	84	3		Ghetto Stories		$8	No Limit 50537
				TRESVANT, Ralph **'91**			
				Born on 5/16/68 in Roxbury, Massachusetts. Member of **New Edition**. Appeared in the movie *House Party 2*.			
12/8/90+	❶²	41	▲	1 Ralph Tresvant	17	$8	MCA 10116
				Rated R [69] • Sensitivity [1] • She's My Love Thang • Stone Cold Gentleman [3] • Do What I Gotta Do [2] • Love Hurts • Girl I Can't Control It • Love Takes Time • Public Figure (Ordinary Guy) • Last Night • I Love You (Just For You) • Alright Now			
1/8/94	24	12		2 It's Goin' Down	131	$8	MCA 10889
				TRIBE **'74**			
				Group from Los Angeles: Edward Romias (vocals, guitar), Earl Foster (keyboards), Donald Eubank (percussion), Robert Apodaca (bass) and Benton Miles Little (drums).			
4/13/74	48	8		1 Ethnic Stew		$12	ABC 807
4/12/75	56	3		2 Tribal Bumpin		$12	ABC 859
	★187★			**TRIBE CALLED QUEST, A** **'93**			
				Rap trio from Queens, New York: Jonathan Davis, Ali Shaheed Muhammad and Malik Taylor.			
4/28/90	23	44	●	1 People's Instinctive Travels And The Paths Of Rhythm	91	$8	Jive 1331
10/19/91	13	46	▲	2 The Low End Theory	45	$8	Jive 1418
11/27/93	❶¹	42	▲	3 Midnight Marauders	8	$8	Jive 41490
				Midnight Marauders Tour Guide • Steve Biko (Stir It Up) • Award Tour [27] • 8 Million Stories • Sucka Nigga • Midnight • We Can Get Down • Electric Relaxation (Relax Yourself Girl) [38] • Clap Your Hands • Oh My God [69] • Keep It Rollin' • The Chase • Lyrics To Go • God Lives Through			
8/17/96	❶¹	25	▲	4 Beats, Rhymes And Life	1¹	$8	Jive 41587
				Phony Rappers • Get A Hold • Motivators • Jam • Crew • The Pressure • 1nce Again • Mind Power • The Hop • Keeping It Moving • Baby Phife's Return • Separate/Together • What Really Goes On • Word Play • Stressed Out [56]			
10/10/98	3	19	●	5 The Love Movement	3	$8	Jive 41638
				Start It Up • Find A Way [29] • Da Booty • Steppin' It Up • Like It Like That • Common Ground (Get It Goin' On) • 4 Moms • His Name Is Mutty Ranks • Give Me • Pad & Pen • Busta's Lament • Hot 4 U • Against The World • The Love • Rock Rock Y'all • Scenario • Money Maker • Hot Sex • Oh My God • Jazz (We've Got) • One Two Shit			
				TRICK DADDY DOLLARS **'98**			
				Born in Miami. Male rapper/producer.			
10/25/97+	59	15		1 Based On A True Story		$8	Slip-N-Slide 2790
10/10/98+	7	43↑		2 www.thug.com		$8	Slip-N-Slide 2802
				TRICK DADDY			
				Log On • For The Thugs • Back In The Days • So What • Tater Head • Nann [20] • Hold On • Call From Dante • Change My Life • I'll Be Your Other Man • Suckin' Fuckin' • Stroke It Gently • Run Nigga • Living In A World • I'll Be Your Player • Log Off			
				TRINERE **'89**			
				Born Trinere Veronica Farrington in Miami. Female dance singer.			
8/12/89	61	12		1 Greatest Hits ....[K]	196	$8	Pandisc 8804
				TRINERE & FRIENDS			
1/5/91	68	8		2 Forever Yours		$8	Pandisc 8812
				TRIN-I-TEE 5:7 **'98**			
				Female vocal trio from New Orleans: Terri Brown, Chanelle Hayes and Angel Taylor.			
8/1/98	20	49		Trin-I-Tee 5:7	139	$8	B-Rite 90094
				TRINITY GARDEN CARTEL **'94**			
				Rap trio from Houston: Lil' D, Gangsta G and Herb Man. Group named after a Houston ghetto.			
5/7/94	75	2		Don't Blame It On Da Music		$8	Rap-A-Lot 53890
				TROOP **'90**			
				Group from Pasadena, California: lead singers Steve Russell and Allen McNeil, with Rodney Benford, John Harreld and Reggie Warren. Troop stands for Total Respect Of Other People.			
7/9/88	19	39		1 Troop	133	$8	Atlantic 81851
11/18/89+	5	59	●	2 Attitude	73	$8	Atlantic 82035
				My Music • That's My Attitude [14] • I'm Not Souped [19] • My Love • Spread My Wings [1] • All I Do Is Think Of You [1] • I Will Always Love You [31] • Another Lover • For You • Souped Mix			
6/20/92	21	25		3 Deepa	78	$8	Atlantic 82393
9/10/94	80	3		4 A Lil' Sumpin' Sumpin'		$8	Bust It 72983
7/11/98	99	1		5 Mayday		$8	Warrior 8007

DEBUG	PEAK	WKS	Gold	Album Title	Pop #	$	Label & Number
				TROPEA '76			
				Born John Tropea in Florida. Guitarist.			
4/10/76	42	8		1 Tropea .... [I]	138	$12	Marlin 2200
6/4/77	43	3		2 Short Trip To Space .... [I]	149	$12	Marlin 2204
				TROUBLE FUNK '82			
				Funk group from Washington DC: Robert Reed (vocals), Tony Fisher, James Avery, Taylor Reed, Timothy David, Mack Carey, Emmett Nixon, Alonzo Robinson, Dean Harris, David Rudd and Chester Davis.			
5/8/82	38	16		Drop The Bomb	121	$10	Sugar Hill 266
				TRU '97			
				Rap group from Los Angeles: brothers **Master P**, **Silkk The Shocker** and C-Murder, with **Mia X** and Mo B Dick. TRU stands for The Real Untouchables.			
8/12/95	25	57		1 True		$8	No Limit 53983
3/8/97	2³	87	▲²	2 Tru 2 Da Game	8	$12	No Limit 50660 [2]
				No Limit Soldiers • I Always Feel Like (Somebody's Watching Me) [42] • There Dey Go • I Got Candy • Ghetto Thang • Fedz • What They Call Us? • Smoking Green • Gangstas Make The World • Swamp Aggin • Ghetto Cheeze • Heaven 4 A Gangsta • Tru 2 Da Game • Freak Hoes • Tru Questions • 1nce Upon A Time • Pop Goes My 9 • It's My Time • Torcher Chamber • They Can't Stop Us! • The Lord Is Testin Me • Final Ride			
				TRUE, Andrea, Connection '76			
				Born in Nashville. Female disco singer/actress. Appeared in several X-rated movies in the 1970s.			
6/19/76	49	11		More, More, More	47	$10	Buddah 5670
				TRUE LOVE '88			
				Born Terrance Reed in Trenton, New Jersey.			
7/23/88	54	8		I'm Bustin' Out		$8	Critique 90940
				TRUTH!, Tha '97			
				Female vocal trio from Houston: Cindy Goodson, Teresa Seymore and Jamie Williams.			
3/29/97	93	1		Makin' Moves...Everyday		$8	Priority 50553
				TRUTH INC. '92			
				Group led by singer Jimmy Demers.			
8/29/92	85	6		Truth Inc.		$8	Interscope 91763
				TUFF CREW '89			
				Rap duo from Philadelphia: Smooth K and Icedog.			
9/9/89	74	7		Back To Wreck Shop		$8	Warlock 2712
	★125★			**TURNER, Ike & Tina** '71			
				Husband-and-wife duo: guitarist Ike Turner (b: Izear Luster Turner on 11/5/31 in Clarksdale, Mississippi) and singer **Tina Turner** (b: Anna Mae Bullock on 11/26/38 in Brownsville, Tennessee). Married from 1958-76. Inducted into the Rock and Roll Hall of Fame in 1991.			
				1)Workin' Together 2)Live At Carnegie Hall 3)Live! The Ike & Tina Turner Show			
2/6/65	8	3		1 Live! The Ike & Tina Turner Show [L]	126	$30	Warner 1579
				Finger Poppin' • Down In The Valley • Good Times • You Are My Sunshine • Good Time Tonight • Twist And Shout • Something's Got A Hold On Me • I Know (You Don't Want Me No More) • High Heel Sneakers (Tight Pants) • My Man, He's A Lovin' Man • I Can't Stop Loving You • Tell The Truth			
6/21/69	43	7		2 Outta Season	91	$20	Blue Thumb 5
8/9/69	19	11		3 In Person .... [L]	142	$20	Minit 24018
				recorded at the Basin Street West in San Francisco			
10/4/69	28	14		4 River Deep-Mountain High	102	$20	A&M 4178
1/31/70	49	2		5 The Hunter	176	$15	Blue Thumb 11
5/16/70	13	20		6 Come Together	130	$15	Liberty 7637
11/28/70+	3	47		7 Workin' Together	25	$15	Liberty 7650
				Workin' Together [41] • (As Long As I Can) Get You When I Want You • Get Back • The Way You Love Me • You Can Have It • Game Of Love • Funkier Than A Mosquita's Tweeter • Ooh Poo Pah Doo [31] • Proud Mary [5] • Goodbye, So Long • Let It Be			
7/17/71	7	22	●	8 Live At Carnegie Hall/What You Hear Is What You Get [L]	25	$15	United Artists 9953 [2]
				Piece Of My Heart • Everyday People • Doin' The Tina Turner • Sweet Soul Music • Ooh Poo Pah Doo • Honky Tonk Women • A Love Like Yours (Don't Come Knockin' Everyday) • Proud Mary • I Smell Trouble • Ike's Tune • I Want To Take You Higher • I've Been Loving You Too Long • Respect			
11/27/71+	21	9		9 'Nuff Said	108	$12	United Artists 5530
8/5/72	28	4		10 Feel Good	160	$12	United Artists 5598
10/6/73	47	6		11 The World Of Ike & Tina .... [L]	211	$15	United Artists 064 [2]
				recorded on their European tour			
12/15/73+	21	14		12 Nutbush City Limits	163	$12	United Artists 180
				TURNER, Ruby '90			
				Born in Jamaica; raised in Birmingham, England. Former session singer.			
2/10/90	39	23		Paradise	194	$8	Jive 1298
				TURNER, Spyder '67			
				Born Dwight Turner in 1947 in Beckley, West Virginia; raised in Detroit. Male singer/songwriter.			
4/8/67	14	4		Stand By Me	158	$30	MGM 4450
	★188★			**TURNER, Tina** '84			
				Born Anna Mae Bullock on 11/26/38 in Brownsville, Tennessee. Singer/actress. In successful recording duo with husband **Ike Turner**, from 1958-74; divorced in 1976. Acted in the movies *Tommy* (1975) and *Mad Max-Beyond Thunderdome* (1985). Her autobiography, *What's Love Got To Do With It*, was made into a movie in 1993.			
10/4/75	39	5		1 Acid Queen	155	$12	United Artists 495
6/23/84	❶³	84	▲⁵	2 Private Dancer	3	$8	Capitol 12330
				I Might Have Been Queen (Soul Survivor) • What's Love Got To Do With It [2] • Show Some Respect [50] • I Can't Stand The Rain • Better Be Good To Me [6] • Let's Stay Together [3] • 1984 • Steel Claw • Private Dancer [3]			
10/11/86	7	32	▲	3 Break Every Rule	4	$8	Capitol 12530
				Typical Male [3] • What You Get Is What You See • Two People [18] • Till The Right Man Comes Along • Afterglow • Girls • Back Where You Started • Break Every Rule • Overnight Sensation • Paradise Is Here • I'll Be Thunder			

DEBUT	PEAK	WKS	Gold	Album Title	Pop #	$	Label & Number
				TURNER, Tina — Cont'd			
10/21/89	83	4	●	4 Foreign Affair	31	$8	Capitol 91873
7/3/93	8	41	▲	5 What's Love Got To Do With It [S]	6	$8	Virgin 88189
				I Don't Wanna Fight *[51]* • Rock Me Baby • Disco Inferno • Why Must We Wait Until Tonight? • Nutbush City Limits • (Darlin') You Know I Love You • Proud Mary • A Fool In Love • It's Gonna Work Out Fine • Stay Awhile • I Might Have Been Queen (Soul Survivor) • What's Love Got To Do With It			
7/24/93	99	2	▲	6 Simply The Best [G]	113	$8	Capitol 97152
9/21/96	26	36		7 Wildest Dreams	61	$8	Virgin 41920
★133★				**TURRENTINE, Stanley** '75			
				Born on 4/5/34 in Pittsburgh. Jazz tenor saxophonist.			
				1)In The Pocket 2)Pieces Of Dreams 3)The Baddest Turrentine			
12/31/66+	20	3		1 Rough 'N Tumble [I]	149	$20	Blue Note 84240
7/20/68	41	5		2 Serenade To A Soul Sister [I]		$20	Blue Note 84277
				THE HORACE SILVER QUINTET Featuring Stanley Turrentine			
8/31/68	38	4		3 The Look Of Love [I]	193	$20	Blue Note 84286
1/30/71	29	17		4 Sugar [I]	182	$12	CTI 6005
12/18/71	47	2		5 Salt Song [I]		$12	CTI 6010
11/23/74+	14	28		6 Pieces Of Dreams [I]	69	$12	Fantasy 9465
12/14/74+	18	11		7 The Baddest Turrentine [I-K]	185	$12	CTI 6048
3/22/75	21	11		8 The Sugar Man [I-K]	110	$12	CTI 6052
5/10/75	9	13		9 In The Pocket [I]	65	$10	Fantasy 9478
				Have It Your Way, Sandy • You Are The Melody Of My Life • Over To Where You Are • Naked As The Day I Was Born • In The Pocket • Spaced • You're My Baby • Black Lassie • Loving You Is Sweeter Than Ever			
11/8/75	27	8		10 Have You Ever Seen The Rain [I]	76	$10	Fantasy 9493
6/26/76	29	7		11 Everybody Come On Out [I]	100	$10	Fantasy 9508
11/27/76	32	7		12 The Man With The Sad Face [I]	96	$10	Fantasy 9519
11/19/77	47	5		13 Nightwings [I]	84	$10	Fantasy 9534
7/5/80	65	3		14 Inflation [I]	209	$10	Elektra 269
				TWELVE A.M. '97			
				Vocal group: Marcus Phillips, Tracy Johnson, Earnest Riggs, Victor Johnson and Gerald Williams.			
11/16/96+	27	7		The Time Has Come		$8	ALV 5001
				12 GAUGE '94			
				Born Isiah Pinkney in Augusta, Georgia. Male rapper.			
4/2/94	44	12		12 Gauge	141	$8	Street Life 75439
				TWENNYNINE FEATURING LENNY WHITE '80			
				Funk group from New York City: Lenny White (drums; **Return To Forever**), Donald Blackman (vocals), Eddie Martinez and Nick Moroch (guitars), Denzil Miller (keyboards) and Barry Johnson (bass).			
10/13/79+	15	20		1 Best of Friends	54	$10	Elektra 223
11/8/80	22	19		2 Twennynine with Lenny White	106	$10	Elektra 304
12/12/81+	41	14		3 Just Like Dreamin'	162	$10	Elektra 551
				20-2-LIFE '96			
7/27/96	55	5		Twenty-Two-Life		$8	Inmate 1
				TWIN HYPE '89			
				Rap duo from New Jersey: twin brothers Glennis and Lennis Brown.			
7/29/89	44	19		1 Twin Hype	140	$8	Profile 1281
6/22/91	75	6		2 Double Barrel		$8	Profile 3408
				TWINZ '95			
				Rap duo from Long Beach, California: twin brothers Deon and DeWayne Williams.			
9/9/95	8	12		Conversation	36	$8	G Funk/RAL 527883
				Round & Round *[60]* • Good Times • 4 Eyes 2 Heads • Jump Ta This • **Eastside LB** *[58]* • Sorry I Kept You • Journey Wit Me • Hollywood • 1st Round Draft Pick • Don't Get It Twisted • Pass It On			
				TWISTA '98			
				Born in Chicago. Male rapper.			
7/12/97	13	44		1 Adrenaline Rush	77	$8	Creator's Way 92757
10/24/98	9	11		2 Mobstability	34	$8	Creator's Way 83142
				TWISTA & THE SPEEDKNOT MOBSTAZ			
				Crook County • Mob Up • Front Porch • **In Your World** *[63]* • Legit Ballers • Mobstability • Party Hoes • Warm Embrace • Smoke Wit You • Loyalty • Motive 4 Murder • Dreams • Rock Y'all Spot			
				2-BIGG MC '90			
				Born Kevin Wilson in Oakland. Male rapper.			
12/15/90	90	5		He's King Of The Hype!		$8	Crush 550
				II D EXTREME '93			
				Vocal trio from Washington DC: D'Extra Wiley, Randy Gill (brother of **Johnny Gill**) and Jermaine Mickey.			
11/27/93	22	17		II D Extreme	115	$8	Gasoline Alley 10958
				2 IN A ROOM '91			
				Dance duo from Washington Heights, New York: rapper Rafael Vargas and remixer Roger Pauletta.			
2/2/91	58	8		Wiggle It	151	$8	Cutting 91594
				2 LOW '94			
				Born Cedric White in Houston. Male rapper.			
2/5/94	25	16		Funky Lil Brotha	176	$8	Rap-A-Lot 53884

DEBUT	PEAK	WKS	Gold	Album Title	Pop #	$	Label & Number

2 PAC   **★54★**   '96

Born Tupac Amaru Shakur on 6/16/71 in New York City. Died on 9/13/96 of wounds suffered on 9/7/96 in a shooting in Las Vegas. Male rapper/actor. Member of **Digital Underground** in 1991 and founder of **Thug Life**. Appeared in the movies *Nothing But Trouble*, *Juice* and *Poetic Justice*.

2/1/92	13	34	●	1 2Pacalypse Now	64	$8	Interscope 91767
3/6/93	4	67	▲	2 Strictly 4 My N.I.G.G.A.Z...	24	$8	Interscope 92209

Holler If Ya Hear Me • Point The Finga • Last Wordz • Souljah's Revenge • Peep Game • Strugglin' • Guess Who's Back • Representin' 93 • **Keep Ya Head Up** *[7]* • Strictly 4 My N.I.G.G.A.Z... • The Streetz R Deathrow • **I Get Around** *[5]* • Papa'z Song *[82]* • 5 Deadly Venomz

4/1/95	❶⁴	97	▲²	3 Me Against The World	1⁴	$8	Interscope 92399

If I Die 2Nite • Me Against The World • **So Many Tears** *[21]* • Temptations *[35]* • Young Niggaz • Heavy In The Game • Lord Knows • **Dear Mama** *[3]* • It Ain't Easy • Can U Get Away • Old School • Fuck The World • Death Around The Corner • Outlaw

2/24/96	❶³	105	▲⁹	4 All Eyez On Me	1²	$12	Death Row 524204 [2]

Ambitionz Az A Ridah • All About U • Skandalouz • Got My Mind Made Up • **How Do U Want It** • 2 Of Amerikaz Most Wanted • No More Pain • Heartz Of Men • Life Goes On • Only God Can Judge Me • Tradin War Stories • **California Love** *[flip]* • I Ain't Mad At Cha • What'z Ya Phone # • Can't C Me • Shorty Wanna Be A Thug • Holla At Me • Wonda Why They Call U Bytch • When We Ride • Thug Passion • Picture Me Rollin' • Check Out Time • Ratha Be Ya Nigga • All Eyez On Me • Run Tha Streetz • Ain't Hard 2 Find • Heaven Ain't Hard 2 Find

11/16/96	❶⁶	103	▲⁴	5 The Don Killuminati - The 7 Day Theory	1¹	$8	Death Row 90039

MAKAVELI

Bomb First (My Second Reply) • Hail Mary • Toss It Up • To Live & Die In L.A. • Blasphemy • Life Of An Outlaw • Just Like Daddy • Krazy • White Man'z World • Me And My Girlfriend • Hold Ya Head • Against All Odds

12/6/97	❶²	33	▲⁴	6 R U Still Down? [Remember Me]	2¹	$12	Amaru 41628 [2]

Redemption • Open Fire • R U Still Down? [Remember Me] • Hellrazor • Thug Style • **I Wonder If Heaven Got A Ghetto** *[14]* • Nothing To Lose • I'm Gettin Money • Lie To Kick It • Fuck All Y'all • Let Them Thangs Go • Definition Of A Thug Nigga • Ready 4 Whatever • When I Get Free • Hold On Be Strong • I'm Losin It • Fake Ass Bitches • **Do For Love** *[10]* • Enemies With Me • Nothin But Love • 16 On Death Row • When I Get Free II • Only Fear Of Death

8/8/98	43	11		7 In His Own Words	112	$8	Mecca 8807
12/12/98	❶²	34↑	▲⁵	8 Greatest Hits	[G] 3	$8	Amaru 90301 [2]

Keep Ya Head Up *[7]* • 2 Of Amerikaz Most Wanted • Temptations *[35]* • God Bless The Dead • Hail Mary • Me Against The World • **How Do U Want It** *[1]* • So Many Tears *[21]* • Unconditional Love • Trapped • Life Goes On • Hit 'Em Up • Troublesome '96 • **Brenda's Got A Baby** *[23]* • I Ain't Mad At Cha • I Get Around *[5]* • Changes *[12]* • California Love *[flip]* • Picture Me Rollin' • How Long Will They Mourn Me? • Toss It Up • Dear Mama *[3]* • All About U • 2 Live & Die In L.A. • Heartz Of Men

II TRU   '97

Female rap duo from Cleveland: Jhaz and Brina. Part of the **Mo Thugs Family**.

10/18/97	49	4		A New Breed Of Female	194	$8	Mo Thugs 1582

TWO TONS O' FUN   '80

Vocal duo of **Martha Wash** and Izora Rhodes. Later recorded as The Weather Girls.

4/5/80	28	18		Two Tons Of Fun	91	$10	Honey 9584

TYMES, The   '76

Vocal group from Philadelphia: George Williams, Albert Berry, Charles Nixon, Donald Banks and Norman Burnett. Nixon left in 1975, replaced by Wade Davis and Jerry Ferguson.

12/21/74+	46	6		1 Trustmaker	205	$12	RCA Victor 0727
2/14/76	40	6		2 Tymes Up	202	$12	RCA Victor 1072

TYNER, McCoy   '76

Born on 12/11/38 in Philadelphia. Jazz pianist.

7/4/76	55	4		1 Fly With The Wind	[I] 128	$12	Milestone 9067
9/18/82	61	3		2 Looking Out	[I] 207	$10	Columbia 38053

TYRESE   '99

Born in 1979 in Los Angeles. Male singer/actor.

10/17/98+	6	42↑	▲	Tyrese	17	$8	RCA 66901

Nobody Else *[12]* • Tell Me, Tell Me • Promises • **Sweet Lady** *[9]* • Lately • Give Love A Try • Ain't Nothin' Like A Jones • You Get Yours • Do You Need • Taste My Love • I Can't Go On • Stay In Touch

TYZIK   '84

Jazz trumpeter Jeff Tyzik (pronounced: Tie-zik).

7/7/84	35	17		Jammin' In Manhattan	172	$8	Polydor 821605

U

UBC, The   '90

Rap group from Hempstead, New York: Torey Thorpe, Daryl Monroe, Michael Dolvin, Ian Richmond and Keith Griffin. UBC: United Brothers Coalition.

8/11/90	92	3		2 All Serious Thinkers		$8	EMI 93919

UGK — see UNDERGROUND KINGZ

ULTRAMAGNETIC MC'S   '93

Rap group from the Bronx, New York: Cedric Miller, Keith Thornton, Maurice Smith and Trevor Randolph.

12/3/88+	57	12		1 Critical Beatdown		$8	Next Plateau 1013
9/11/93	55	4		2 The Four Horsemen		$8	Wild Pitch 89917

U.M.C.'S, The   '92

Male rap duo from Staten Island, New York: Kool Kim and Hass G.

11/30/91+	32	33		1 Fruits Of Nature		$8	Wild Pitch 97544
2/12/94	63	2		2 Unleashed		$8	Wild Pitch 27340

UNCLE SAM   '98
Born Sam Turner in Detroit. Male singer.

11/1/97+	24	35	●	Uncle Sam		68	$8	Stonecreek/Epic 67731

UNDERGROUND KINGZ   '96
Male rap duo: Pimp C and Bun B.

| 12/5/92 | 37 | 44 | | 1 Too Hard To Swallow | | | $8 | Jive 41502 |
| 9/17/94 | 9 | 31 | | 2 Super Tight... | | 95 | $8 | Jive 41524 |

Return • Underground • It's Supposed To Bubble • I Left It Wet For You • Feds In Town • Pocket Full Of Stones • Front, Back & Side To Side • Protect & Serve • Stoned Junkee • Pussy Got Me Dizzy • Three Sixteens

| 8/17/96 | 2¹ | 31 | ● | 3 Ridin' Dirty | | 15 | $8 | Jive 41586 |

UGK

One Day • Murder • Pinky Ring • Diamonds & Wood • 3 In The Mornin' • Touched • Fuck My Car • That's Why I Carry • Hi Life • Good Stuff • Ridin' Dirty

UNDISPUTED TRUTH, The   '71
Vocal group from Detroit: Joe Harris, Billie Calvin and Brenda Evans. Personnel changed in 1973 to Harris, Tyrone Berkeley, Tyrone Douglas, Calvin Stevens and Virginia McDonald. **Taka Boom** replaced Douglas and McDonald in 1976.

| 7/24/71 | 7 | 22 | | 1 The Undisputed Truth | | 43 | $25 | Gordy 955 |

You Got The Love I Need • **Save My Love For A Rainy Day [43]** • California Soul • Aquarius • Ball Of Confusion (That's What The World Is Today) • **Smiling Faces Sometimes [2]** • We've Got A Way Out Love • Since I've Lost You • Ain't No Sun Since You've Been Gone • I Heard It Through The Grapevine • Like A Rolling Stone

2/12/72	16	11		2 Face To Face With The Truth		114	$20	Gordy 959
7/28/73	52	5		3 Law Of The Land		191	$20	Gordy 963
9/7/74	35	10		4 Down To Earth		208	$20	Gordy 968
4/5/75	42	7		5 Cosmic Truth		186	$20	Gordy 970
11/1/75	52	4		6 Higher Than High		173	$20	Gordy 972
1/29/77	19	14		7 Method To The Madness		66	$12	Whitfield 2967

UNIFICS, The   '69
Vocal group from Washington DC: Al Johnson, Hal Worthington, Michael Ward and Greg Cook. Worthington was shot to death on 2/20/90 (age 42).

| 2/1/69 | 38 | 7 | | Sittin' In At The Court Of Love | | | $25 | Kapp 3582 |

UNLIMITED TOUCH   '81
Group from Brooklyn, New York: **Audrey Wheeler** and Stephanie James (vocals), Philip Hamilton (guitar), Galen Underwood (keyboards), Samuel Anderson (bass) and Tony Cintron (drums).

| 6/13/81 | 35 | 13 | | Unlimited Touch | | 142 | $10 | Prelude 12184 |

U.N.L.V.   '96

| 9/14/96 | 86 | 4 | | Uptown 4 Life | | | $8 | Cash Money 9609 |

UNV   '93
Vocal group from Detroit: brothers John and Shawn Powe, John Clay and Demetrius Peete. UNV: Universal Nubian Voices.

| 7/17/93 | 7 | 20 | | 1 Something's Goin' On | | 59 | $8 | Maverick 45287 |

UNV Thang • When Will I Know • Who Will It Be? • **Close Tonight [87]** • Gonna Give U What U Want • Tempted • **Something's Goin' On [3]** • 2 B Or Not 2 B • **Straight From My Heart [36]** • Hold On • No One Compares To You

| 7/15/95 | 39 | 8 | | 2 Universal Nubian Voices | | 161 | $8 | Maverick 45839 |

USA FOR AFRICA   '85
A gathering of major artists formed to help the suffering people of Africa and America.

| 4/20/85 | 6 | 17 | ▲³ | We Are The World | | 1³ | $8 | Columbia 40043 |

We Are The World [1] • If Only For The Moment, Girl [Steve Perry] • Just A Little Closer [Pointer Sisters] • Trapped [Bruce Springsteen] • Tears Are Not Enough [Northern Lights] • 4 The Tears In Your Eyes [Prince] • Good For Nothing [Chicago] • Total Control [Tina Turner] • Little More Love [Kenny Rogers] • Trouble In Paradise [Huey Lewis & The News]

USHER   '98
Born Usher Raymond on 10/14/78 in Chattanooga, Tennessee. Male singer/actor.

| 9/17/94 | 25 | 51 | | 1 Usher | | 167 | $8 | LaFace 26008 |
| 10/4/97+ | ❶³ | 75 | ▲⁵ | 2 My Way | | 4 | $8 | LaFace 26043 |

You Make Me Wanna... [1] • Just Like Me • **Nice & Slow [1]** • Slow Jam • **My Way [4]** • Come Back • I Will • Bedtime • One Day You'll Be Mine

US3   '94
Pronounced: us three. Jazz/rap collaboration by London producers Mel Simpson (keyboards) and Geoff Wilkinson (samples).

| 12/18/93+ | 21 | 33 | ▲ | 1 Hand On The Torch | | 31 | $8 | Blue Note 80883 |
| 4/26/97 | 90 | 2 | | 2 Broadway & 52nd | | | $8 | Blue Note 30027 |

UTFO   '87
Rap group from Brooklyn, New York: Shawn Fequiere, Fred Reeves, Jeffrey Campbell and Maurice Bailey. UTFO: Untouchable Force Organization.

6/15/85	11	24		1 UTFO		80	$10	Select 21614
8/2/86	14	27		2 Skeezer Pleezer		142	$10	Select 21616
8/29/87	2²	34		3 Lethal		67	$10	Select 21619

Mo' Bass • Ya Cold Wanna Be With Me [43] • Lethal • Diss • S.W.A.T. (Get Down) • The Ride • Ask Yo Mama • Let's Get It On • So Be It • Burning Bed • Master - Baby

| 6/3/89 | 30 | 18 | | 4 Doin' It! | | 143 | $10 | Select 21629 |

UZI $ BROS.   '90
Rap trio from Palo Alto, California: Will Griffin, Bob Robertson and Kenny Strong.

| 11/3/90 | 84 | 4 | | Kick That Thang! | | | $8 | Original Sound 8890 |

V

VALENTI, John   **'76**
Born in Chicago. Singer/songwriter.

| 10/30/76 | 51 | 3 | | Anything You Want .... | | | $12 | Ariola America 50012 |

VALENTINE BROTHERS, The   **'84**
Vocal duo from Columbus, Ohio: brothers John and Billy Valentine.

| 8/21/82 | 46 | 11 | | 1 First Take... | | | $10 | Bridge 01936 |
| 8/11/84 | 40 | 14 | | 2 Have A Good Time .... | | | $8 | A&M 4989 |

VANDROSS, Luther ★18★   **'85**
Born on 4/20/51 in New York City. Singer/songwriter/producer. Commercial jingle singer, then a prolific session singer/arranger. Sang with the studio group, **Change.** Much songwriting and production work for other artists. Appeared in the movie *The Meteor Man.*

1)The Night I Fell In Love 2)Power Of Love 3)Forever, For Always, For Love

| 9/19/81 | ❶¹ | 86 | ▲² | 1 **Never Too Much** | | 19 | $10 | Epic 37451 |

Never Too Much *[1]* • Sugar And Spice (I Found Me A Girl) *[72]* • Don't You Know That? *[10]* • I've Been Working • How Deep Is Your Love • She's A Super Lady • You Stopped Loving Me • A House Is Not A Home

| 10/16/82 | ❶³ | 43 | ▲ | 2 **Forever, For Always, For Love** | | 20 | $10 | Epic 38235 |

Bad Boy/Having A Party *[3]* • You're The Sweetest One • Since I Lost My Baby *[17]* • Forever, For Always, For Love • Better Love • Promise Me *[72]* • She Loves Me Back • Once You Know How

| 12/24/83+ | ❶² | 47 | ▲ | 3 **Busy Body** | | 32 | $10 | Epic 39196 |

I Wanted Your Love • Busy Body • I'll Let You Slide *[9]* • Make Me A Believer *[48]* • For The Sweetness Of Your Love • How Many Times Can We Say Goodbye *[7]* • Superstar/Until You Come Back To Me (That's What I'm Gonna Do) *[5]*

| 4/6/85 | ❶⁷ | 80 | ▲² | 4 <u>**The Night I Fell In Love**</u> | | 19 | $8 | Epic 39882 |

'Til My Baby Comes Home *[4]* • The Night I Fell In Love • If Only For One Night *[59]* • Creepin' • It's Over Now *[4]* • Wait For Love *[11]* • My Sensitivity (Gets In The Way) • Other Side Of The World

| 10/25/86 | ❶² | 64 | ▲² | 5 **Give Me The Reason** | | 14 | $8 | Epic 40415 |

Stop To Love *[1]* • See Me • I Gave It Up (When I Fell In Love) • So Amazing *[94]* • Give Me The Reason *[3]* • There's Nothing Better Than Love *[1]* • I Really Didn't Mean It *[6]* • Because It's Really Love • Anyone Who Had A Heart

| 10/22/88 | ❶² | 43 | ▲ | 6 **Any Love** | | 9 | $8 | Epic 44308 |

I Wonder • She Won't Talk To Me *[3]* • I Know You Want To • Come Back • Any Love *[1]* • Love Won't Let Me Wait • Are You Gonna Love Me • For You To Love *[3]* • The Second Time Around

| 11/4/89+ | 2² | 51 | ▲³ | 7 **The Best Of Luther Vandross...The Best Of Love** | [G] | 26 | $10 | Epic 45320 [2] |

Searching *[23]* • The Glow Of Love *[49]* • Never Too Much *[1]* • If This World Were Mine *[4]* • A House Is Not A Home • **Bad Boy/Having A Party** *[3]* • Since I Lost My Baby *[17]* • Promise Me *[72]* • 'Til My Baby Comes Home *[4]* • Medley: If Only For One Night/Creepin' • Superstar/Until You Come Back To Me (That's What I'm Gonna Do) *[5]* • Stop To Love *[1]* • So Amazing *[94]* • There's Nothing Better Than Love *[1]* • Give Me The Reason *[3]* • Any Love *[1]* • I Really Didn't Mean It *[6]* • Love Won't Let Me Wait • Treat You Right *[5]* • Here And Now *[1]*

| 5/25/91 | ❶⁵ | 62 | ▲² | 8 **Power Of Love** | | 7 | $8 | Epic 46789 |

She Doesn't Mind • Power Of Love/Love Power *[1]* • I'm Gonna Start Today • The Rush *[6]* • I Want The Night To Stay • **Don't Want To Be A Fool** *[4]* • I Can Tell You That • Sometimes It's Only Love *[9]* • Emotional Love • I Who Have Nothing

| 6/19/93 | 3 | 42 | ▲ | 9 **Never Let Me Go** | | 6 | $8 | LV/Epic 53231 |

Little Miracles (Happen Every Day) *[10]* • Heaven Knows *[24]* • Love Me Again • Can't Be Doin' That Now • Too Far Down • Love Is On The Way (Real Love) • Hustle • Emotion Eyes • Lady, Lady • How Deep Is Your Love • Love Don't Love Nobody • **Never Let Me Go** *[31]*

| 10/8/94 | 2² | 43 | ▲² | 10 **Songs** | | 5 | $8 | LV/Epic 57775 |

Love The One You're With *[flip]* • Killing Me Softly • **Endless Love** *[7]* • Evergreen • Reflections • Hello • Ain't No Stoppin' Us Now • **Always And Forever** *[16]* • Going In Circles *[28]* • Since You've Been Gone • All The Woman I Need • What The World Needs Now • The Impossible Dream

| 11/25/95 | 4 | 8 | ● | 11 **This Is Christmas** | [X] | 28 | $8 | LV/Epic 75595 |

With A Christmas Heart • This Is Christmas • The MistleTOE JAM (Everybody Kiss Somebody) • Every Year, Every Christmas • My Favorite Things • Have Yourself A Merry Little Christmas • I Listen To The Bells • Please Come Home For Christmas • A Kiss For Christmas • O' Come All Ye Faithful

| 10/19/96 | 2¹ | 42 | ▲ | 12 **Your Secret Love** | | 9 | $8 | LV/Epic 67553 |

Your Secret Love *[5]* • Love Don't Love You Anymore • It's Hard For Me To Say • Crazy Love • **I Can Make It Better** *[15]* • Too Proud To Beg • I Can't Wait No Longer (Let's Do This) • Nobody To Love • Whether Or Not The World Gets Better • This Time I'm Right • Knocks Me Off My Feet • Goin' Out Of My Head

| 10/18/97 | 17 | 36 | ● | 13 **One Night With You - The Best Of Love Volume 2** .... | [G] | 44 | $8 | LV/Epic 68220 |
| 8/29/98 | 9 | 36 | ● | 14 **I Know** | | 26 | $8 | Virgin 46089 |

Keeping My Faith In You • Isn't There Someone • Religion • Get It Right • I Know • **I'm Only Human** *[57]* • Nights In Harlem • Dream Lover • When I Need You • Are You Using Me? • Are You Mad At Me? • Now That I Have You

| 10/10/98 | 85 | 3 | | 15 **Always & Forever - The Classics** .... | [G] | | $8 | LV/Epic 69591 |

VANILLA FUDGE   **'68**
Psychedelic-rock group from New York City: Mark Stein (vocals, keyboards), Vinnie Martell (guitar), Tim Bogert (bass) and Carmine Appice (drums).

| 3/9/68 | 11 | 12 | | 1 **The Beat Goes On** .... | | 17 | $20 | Atco 237 |
| 12/21/68 | 46 | 2 | | 2 **Vanilla Fudge** .... | | 6 | $20 | Atco 224 |

VANILLA ICE '90
Born Robert Van Winkle on 10/31/68 in Miami Lakes, Florida. White rapper. Starred in the movie *Cool As Ice*.

8/25/90	6	39	▲⁷	To The Extreme	1¹⁶	$8	SBK 95325

Ice Ice Baby *[6]* • Yo Vanilla • Stop That Train • Hooked • Ice Is Workin' It • Life Is A Fantasy • **Play That Funky Music** *[22]* • Dancin' • Go III • It's A Party • Juice To Get Loose Boy • Ice Cold • Rasta Man • I Love You • Havin' A Roni

VANITY '82
Born Denise Mathews on 1/3/63 in Niagara, Canada. Singer/actress. Lead singer of **Vanity 6** (which included Susan Moonsie and Brenda Bennett). Acted in several movies. Also see **Apollonia 6**.

10/2/82	6	36		1 Vanity 6	45	$10	Warner 23716

Nasty Girl *[7]* • Wet Dream • Drive Me Wild • He's So Dull • If A Girl Answers (Don't Hang Up) • Make-Up • Bite The Beat

10/6/84	14	26		2 Wild Animal	62	$8	Motown 6102
3/15/86	18	20		3 Skin On Skin	66	$8	Motown 6167

VANNELLI, Gino '78
Born on 6/16/52 in Montreal. Pop singer/songwriter.

9/13/75	35	6		1 Storm at Sunup	66	$10	A&M 4533
9/4/76	35	8		2 The Gist of The Gemini	32	$10	A&M 4596
11/11/78	12	16	▲	3 Brother To Brother	13	$10	A&M 4722
4/18/81	22	17		4 Nightwalker	15	$8	Arista 9539

VAN PEEBLES, Melvin '69
Born on 8/21/32 in Chicago. Movie actor/director. Father of actor Mario Van Peebles.

3/8/69	43	3		1 Br'er Soul		$15	A&M 4161
4/20/74	53	4		2 What The .... You Mean I Can't Sing?		$12	Atlantic 7295

VEGA, Tata '79
Born Carmen Rosa Vega on 10/7/51 in Queens, New York. Female singer.

4/14/79	63	12		Try My Love	170	$10	Tamla 360

VERTICAL HOLD '93
Vocal trio: Willie Bruno, David Bright and Angie Stone (former member of **The Sequence**).

7/10/93	33	12		1 A Matter Of Time		$8	A&M 0010
6/24/95	67	3		2 Head First		$8	A&M 0333

VESTA '91
Born **Vesta Williams** in Coshocton, Ohio; raised in Los Angeles. Female singer.

11/22/86+	43	31		1 Vesta		$8	A&M 5118
11/12/88+	26	55		2 Vesta 4 U	131	$8	A&M 5223

VESTA WILLIAMS (above 2)

8/10/91	15	26		3 Special		$8	A&M 5347
9/4/93	65	6		4 Everything-N-More		$8	A&M 0114
10/3/98	55	4		5 Relationships		$8	I.E. Music 557615

VICIOUS '95
Born in Brooklyn, New York. Male rapper.

11/19/94+	37	21		Destination Brooklyn		$8	Epic Street 57857

VICIOUS BASE '91
Rap duo: D.J. Lace and M.C. Madness.

1/5/91	51	27	●	Back To Haunt You!	153	$8	Cheetah 9404

VICIOUS BASE Featuring D.J. MAGIC MIKE!

VILLAGE PEOPLE '79
Disco vocal group from New York City: Victor Willis (Policeman), Randy Jones (Cowboy), David Hodo (Construction Worker), Felipe Rose (Indian), Alexander Briley (G.I.) and Glenn Hughes (Leatherman). Group appeared in the 1980 movie *Can't Stop The Music*.

10/29/77	36	8	●	1 Village People	54	$10	Casablanca 7064
4/1/78	31	32	▲	2 Macho Man	24	$10	Casablanca 7096
10/28/78+	5	29	▲	3 Cruisin'	3	$10	Casablanca 7118

Y.M.C.A. *[32]* • Medley: The Women/I'm A Cruiser • Hot Cop • My Roomate • Ups And Downs

4/21/79	14	12	▲	4 Go West	8	$10	Casablanca 7144
11/24/79	57	3		5 Live and Sleazy [L]	32	$12	Casablanca 7183 [2]

record 1: live; record 2: studio

VOICES '92
Female vocal group from Los Angeles: sisters LaToya and LaPetra McMoore, with Monique Wilson and Arike Rice.

11/21/92	66	3		Just The Beginning...		$8	Zoo 11039

VOICES OF EAST HARLEM, The '70
20-member choir from Harlem, New York.

10/24/70	40	4		Right On Be Free	191	$15	Elektra 74080

VOICES OF THEORY '99
Male vocal group from Philadelphia: James Cartagena, Mechi Cebollero, David Cordoba, Hector Ramos and Eric Serrano.

6/6/98+	56	8		Voices Of Theory		$8	H.O.L.A. 341016

VOLUME 10 '94
Born Dino Hawkins in Los Angeles. Male rapper.

5/14/94	66	2		Hip-Hopera		$8	Immortal 66276

VOYAGE '78
European disco group: Sylvia Mason (vocals), Slim Pezin (guitar), Marc Chantereau (keyboards), Sauver Mallin (bass) and Pierre-Alain Dahan (drums).

6/3/78	57	2		Voyage	40	$12	Marlin 2213

VYBE '95
Female vocal group from Los Angeles: Pam, Tanya, Debbie and Dove.

6/10/95	63	3		Vybe		$8	Island 527067

WALDEN, Narada Michael   '80
Born Michael Walden on 4/23/52 in Kalamazoo, Michigan. Singer/songwriter/drummer/producer.

DEBUT	PEAK	WKS		Album Title	Pop #	$	Label & Number
3/3/79	15	19		1 Awakening	103	$10	Atlantic 19222
12/22/79+	9	24		2 The Dance Of Life	74	$10	Atlantic 19259

You're Soo Good • **I Shoulda Loved Ya** *[4]* • Lovin' You Madly • Crazy For Ya • **Tonight I'm Alright** *[35]* • Why Did You Turn Me On • Carry On • The Dance Of Life

10/18/80	21	17		3 Victory	103	$10	Atlantic 19279
6/5/82	30	11		4 Confidence	135	$10	Atlantic 19351
5/21/83	51	9		5 Looking At You, Looking At Me		$10	Atlantic 80058
6/11/88	67	4		6 Divine Emotion		$8	Reprise 25694

NARADA

WALKER, Chris   '91
Born in Houston. Male singer/bassist.

11/9/91	32	40		1 First Time		$8	Pendulum 61136
12/4/93+	69	11		2 Sincerely Yours		$8	Pendulum 27720

WALKER, David T.   '74
Born in Detroit. Top session guitarist. Member of **Paul Humphrey's Cool Aid Chemists** and **Afrique**.

2/28/70	48	2		1 Going Up		$15	Revue 7211
2/6/71	49	3		2 Plum Happy		$15	Zea 1000
5/27/72	50	2		3 David T. Walker		$12	Ode 77011
12/29/73+	23	16		4 Press On [I]	187	$12	Ode 77020
9/11/76	56	3		5 On Love	166	$12	Ode 77035

WALKER, Jimmie   '75
Born on 6/25/49 in New York City. Actor/comedian. Played "J.J. Evans" on TV's *Good Times*.

6/7/75	29	6		Dyn-O-Mite [C]	130	$12	Buddah 5635

| | ★102★ | | | **WALKER, Jr., & The All Stars**   '65 | | | |

Born Autry DeWalt Walker on 6/14/31 in Blythesville, Arkansas. Died of cancer on 11/23/95 (age 64). Singer/saxophonist. The All Stars: Willie Woods (guitar), Vic Thomas (keyboards) and James Graves (drums). Woods died on 5/27/97 (age 60).

1)Shotgun 2)Road Runner 3)Soul Session

7/3/65	❶[1]	22		1 Shotgun	108	$30	Soul 701

Cleo's Mood *[14]* • Do The Boomerang *[10]* • Shotgun *[1]* • (I'm A) Road Runner *[4]* • Shake And Fingerpop *[7]* • Shoot Your Shot *[33]* • Tune Up • Hot Cha • Monkey Jump • Tally Ho • **Cleo's Back** *[7]* • Ain't That The Truth

4/2/66	7	10		2 Soul Session [I]	130	$30	Soul 702

Good Rockin' • Hewbie Steps Out • Shake Everything • Everybody Get Together • Mark Anthony (Speaks) • Us • Moonlight In Vermont • Decidedly • Eight Hour Drag • Brainwasher • Three Four Three • Satan's Blues

8/27/66	6	18		3 Road Runner	64	$30	Soul 703

(I'm A) Road Runner *[4]* • How Sweet It Is (To Be Loved By You) *[3]* • Pucker Up Buttercup *[11]* • Money (That's What I Want) *[35]* • Last Call • Anyway You Wannta' • Baby You Know You Ain't Right • Ame' Cherie (Soul Darling) • Twist Lackawanna • San-Ho-Zay • Mutiny

10/7/67	22	6		4 "Live!" [L]	119	$30	Soul 705
2/15/69	26	8		5 Home Cookin'	172	$20	Soul 710
7/5/69	19	23		6 Greatest Hits [G]	43	$20	Soul 718
12/27/69+	12	21		7 What Does It Take To Win Your Love	92	$20	Soul 721
5/23/70	22	15		8 Jr. Walker & The All Stars Live [L]		$20	Soul 725
10/10/70	28	9		9 A Gasssss	110	$20	Soul 726
7/31/71	12	17		10 Rainbow Funk	91	$15	Soul 732
1/22/72	22	20		11 Moody Jr.	142	$15	Soul 733
5/26/73	47	5		12 Peace & Understanding Is Hard To Find	202	$15	Soul 738
2/21/76	45	4		13 Hot Shot		$12	Soul 745

WALTER & SCOTTY   '93
Twin brothers Walter and Wallace "Scotty" Scott. Born on 9/3/43 in Fort Worth, Texas; raised in Los Angeles. Members of **The Whispers**.

5/22/93	14	21		My Brother's Keeper	151	$8	Capitol 92958

WANSEL, Dexter   '78
Born in Philadelphia. Keyboardist/producer/arranger.

8/14/76	44	4		1 Life On Mars		$10	Philadelphia I. 34079
5/21/77	45	2		2 What The World Is Coming To	168	$10	Philadelphia I. 34487
4/8/78	37	5		3 Voyager	139	$10	Philadelphia I. 34985
10/13/79	58	4		4 Time Is Slipping Away		$10	Philadelphia I. 36024

WAR ★42★ '73

Latin group from Long Beach, California: Howard Scott (guitar), **Lee Oskar** (harmonica), Lonnie Jordan (keyboards), Charles Miller (saxophone; fatally shot by robber in 1980), Thomas Allen (percussion; died on 8/30/88), Morris Dickerson (bass) and Harold Brown (drums). All share vocals. **Eric Burdon**'s backup band until 1971. Alice Tweed Smyth (vocals) added in 1978. Dickerson left in 1979, replaced by Luther Rabb (bass), Pat Rizzo (horns) and Ron Hammond (percussion). Smyth left group in 1982. Lineup by 1994: Jordan, Scott, Brown and Hammond, with Charles Green (flute), Kerry Campbell (sax), Tetsuya Nakamura (harmonica) and Sal Rodriguez (drums).

1)The World Is A Ghetto 2)War Live! 3)Deliver The Word

9/12/70	47	5		1 Eric Burdon Declares "War"	18	$15	MGM 4663
1/9/71	39	5		2 The Black-Man's Burdon	82	$20	MGM 4710 [2]
				ERIC BURDON AND WAR (above 2)			
4/3/71	42	5		3 War	190	$15	United Artists 5508
11/27/71+	**6**	39	●	4 All Day Music	16	$15	United Artists 5546

All Day Music *[18]* • Get Down • That's What Love Will Do • There Must Be A Reason • Nappy Head • **Slippin' Into Darkness** *[12]* • Baby Brother

11/18/72+	❶[7]	48	●	5 The World Is A Ghetto	1[2]	$12	United Artists 5652

The Cisco Kid *[5]* • Where Was You At • City, Country, City • Four Cornered Room • **The World Is A Ghetto** *[3]* • Beetles In The Bog

9/1/73	❶[1]	27	●	6 Deliver The Word	6	$12	United Artists 128

H Overture • In Your Eyes • **Gypsy Man** *[6]* • **Me And Baby Brother** *[18]* • Deliver The Word • Southern Part Of Texas • Blisters

3/30/74	❶[2]	21	●	7 War Live!	[L]	$15	United Artists 193 [2]

Sun Oh Son • The Cisco Kid • Slippin' Into Darkness • All Day Music • **Ballero** *[17]* • Lonely Feelin' • Get Down

7/12/75	❶[1]	23	●	8 Why Can't We Be Friends?	8	$10	United Artists 441

Don't Let No One Get You Down • Lotus Blossom • Medley: Heartbeat/Leroy's Latin Lament • Lonnie Dreams • The Way We Feel • La Fiesta • Lament • Smile Happy • So • **Low Rider** *[1]* • In Mazatlan • **Why Can't We Be Friends?** *[9]*

9/25/76	12	10	▲	9 Greatest Hits [G]	6	$10	United Artists 648
7/23/77	6	19	●	10 Platinum Jazz	23	$12	Blue Note 690 [2]

War Is Coming! War Is Coming • Slowly We Walk Together • Platinum Jazz • I Got You • **L.A. Sunshine** *[2]* • River Niger • H Overture • City, Country, City • Smile Happy • Deliver The Word • Nappy Head (Theme from Ghetto Man) • Four Cornered Room

12/10/77+	6	21	●	11 Galaxy	15	$10	MCA 3030

Galaxy *[5]* • Baby Face (She Said Do Do Do Do) • Sweet Fighting Lady • **Hey Senorita** *[70]* • The Seven Tin Soldiers

8/12/78	40	6		12 Youngblood	69	$10	United Artists 904
4/14/79	11	19	●	13 The Music Band	41	$10	MCA 3085
12/15/79+	34	16		14 The Music Band 2	111	$10	MCA 3193
3/20/82	15	33		15 Outlaw	48	$10	RCA Victor 4208
7/23/83	36	10		16 Life (Is So Strange)	164	$10	RCA Victor 4598
6/25/94	52	9		17 Peace Sign	200	$8	Avenue 71706

WARD, Anita '79

Born on 12/20/57 in Memphis. Disco singer.

5/19/79	2[3]	19		Songs Of Love	8	$12	Juana 200,004

Make Believe Lovers • If I Could Feel That Old Feeling Again • Spoiled By Your Love • I Won't Stop Loving You • **Ring My Bell** *[1]* • Sweet Splendor • There's No Doubt About It • You Lied

WARE, Leon '79

Born in Detroit. Singer/songwriter/producer.

12/8/79	62	3		Inside Is Love		$10	Fabulous 8500

WARREN G '94

Born Warren Griffin in Long Beach, California. Male rapper.

6/25/94	❶[3]	40	▲[3]	1 Regulate...G Funk Era	2[1]	$8	Violator 523364

Regulate *[7]* • **Do You See** *[45]* • Gangsta Sermon • Recognize • Super Soul Sis • '94 Ho Draft • So Many Ways • **This DJ** *[14]* • This Is The Shack • What's Next • And Ya Don't Stop • Runnin' Wit No Breaks

4/12/97	4	15	●	2 Take A Look Over Your Shoulder (Reality)	11	$8	Def Jam 537254

Annie Mae • **Smokin' Me Out** *[20]* • Ricky In Church • Reality • Ricky & G-Child • Young Fun • What We Go Through • We Brings Heat • Transformers • Relax Ya Mind • To All D.J.'s • Back Up • Can You Feel It • **I Shot The Sheriff** *[16]*

WARWICK, Dee Dee '69

Born in 1945 in East Orange, New Jersey. Younger sister of **Dionne Warwick**; cousin of **Whitney Houston**.

6/21/69	30	5		1 Foolish Fool		$25	Mercury 61221
9/12/70	36	3		2 Turning Around		$25	Atco 337

WARWICK, Dionne ★14★ '67

Born Marie Dionne Warwick on 12/12/40 in East Orange, New Jersey. Sister of **Dee Dee Warwick**; cousin of **Whitney Houston**. Added an "e" to her last name from 1972-75. Co-hosted TV's *Solid Gold* from 1980-81 and 1985-86. Later hosted TV infomercials for the Psychic Friends Network.

1)Here Where There Is Love 2)Valley Of The Dolls 3)Soulful 4)Dionne Warwick's Golden Hits, Part One 5)Here I Am

2/6/65	10	1		1 Make Way For Dionne Warwick	68	$20	Scepter 523

A House Is Not A Home *[71]* • People • They Long To Be Close To You • The Last One To Be Loved • Land Of Make Believe • **Reach Out For Me** *[20]* • You'll Never Get To Heaven (If You Break My Heart) *[34]* • **Walk On By** *[6]* • Wishin' And Hopin' • I Smiled Yesterday • Get Rid Of Him • Make The Night A Little Longer

DEBUT	PEAK	WKS	Gold	Album Title	Pop #	$	Label & Number
				WARWICK, Dionne — Cont'd			
1/1/66	3	12		2 Here I Am	45	$15	Scepter 531
				In Between Heartaches • Here I Am • If I Ever Make You Cry • **Looking With My Eyes** *[38]* • Once In A Lifetime • This Little Light • Don't Go Breaking My Heart • Window Wishing • Long Day, Short Night • **Are You There (With Another Girl)** *[35]* • How Can I Hurt You • I Loves You, Porgy			
4/23/66	3	11		3 Dionne Warwick in Paris	[L] 76	$15	Scepter 534
				recorded on January 18, 1966 at the Olympia Theater			
				I Love Paris • C'est Si Bon • Message To Michael • A House Is Not A Home • Walk On By • I've Got You Under My Skin • Begin The Beguine • It's All Right With Me • Anything Goes • All Of You • I Concentrate On You • Just One Of Those Things • Night And Day • Oh Yeah Yeah Yeah • The Good Life • La Vie En Rose • You'll Never Get To Heaven (If You Break My Heart) • What'd I Say			
2/25/67	❶²	49	●	4 Here Where There is Love	18	$15	Scepter 555
				Go With Love • What The World Needs Now Is Love • **I Just Don't Know What To Do With Myself** *[20]* • Here Where There Is Love • **Trains And Boats And Planes** *[49]* • **Alfie** *[5]* • As Long As He Needs Me • I Wish You Love • (I Never Knew) What You Were Up To • Blowing In The Wind			
4/15/67	11	12		5 On Stage and in The Movies	169	$15	Scepter 559
9/16/67	11	22		6 The Windows of The World	22	$15	Scepter 563
11/18/67+	3	58		7 Dionne Warwick's Golden Hits, Part One	[G] 10	$15	Scepter 565
				Don't Make Me Over *[5]* • Anyone Who Had A Heart *[8]* • Make It Easy On Yourself *[26]* • I Smiled Yesterday • Wishin' And Hopin' • Walk On By *[6]* • Reach Out For Me *[20]* • You'll Never Get To Heaven (If You Break My Heart) *[34]* • **This Empty Place** *[26]* • It's Love That Really Counts • (There's) Always Something There To Remind Me • Any Old Time Of Day • Somewhere			
3/9/68	2³	37	●	8 Valley of the Dolls	6	$15	Scepter 568
				As Long As There's An Apple Tree • Up, Up And Away • You're My World • **(Theme From) Valley Of The Dolls** *[13]* • Silent Voices • **Do You Know The Way To San Jose** *[23]* • For The Rest Of My Life • Let Me Be Lonely • Where Would I Go • Walking Backwards Down The Road			
8/17/68	49	2		9 The Magic Of Believing		$15	Scepter 567
				inspirational songs			
12/28/68+	7	29		10 Promises, Promises	18	$15	Scepter 571
				Promises, Promises *[47]* • This Girl's In Love With You *[7]* • Little Green Apples • Where Is Love • **Who Is Gonna Love Me?** *[43]* • Whoever You Are, I Love You • Where Am I Going • Wanting Things • Lonely In My Heart • Yesterday I Heard The Rain			
4/5/69	2²	25		11 Soulful	11	$15	Scepter 573
				You've Lost That Lovin' Feelin' *[13]* • I'm Your Puppet • People Got To Be Free • You're All I Need To Get By • We Can Work It Out • A Hard Day's Night • Do Right Woman - Do Right Man • I've Been Loving You Too Long • People Get Ready • Hey Jude			
8/16/69	10	23	●	12 Dionne Warwick's Greatest Motion Picture Hits	[K] 31	$15	Scepter 575
				The Look Of Love • Alfie *[5]* • (Theme From) Valley Of The Dolls *[13]* • People • **A House Is Not A Home** *[71]* • Wives And Lovers • **The April Fools** *[33]* • Slaves • One Hand, One Heart • With These Hands • Here I Am • As Long As He Needs Me • Somewhere			
11/1/69	9	27		13 Dionne Warwick's Golden Hits, Part 2	[G] 28	$15	Scepter 577
				What The World Needs Now Is Love • Message To Michael *[5]* • Are You There (With Another Girl) *[35]* • I Just Don't Know What To Do With Myself *[20]* • Do You Know The Way To San Jose? *[23]* • I Say A Little Prayer *[8]* • Who Can I Turn To *[36]* • Unchained Melody • Forever My Love • Trains And Boats And Planes *[49]* • In Between Heartaches • **The Windows Of The World** *[27]*			
5/2/70	7	26		14 I'll Never Fall In Love Again	23	$15	Scepter 581
				The Wine Is Young • I'll Never Fall In Love Again *[17]* • Raindrops Keep Fallin' On My Head • Loneliness Remembers What Happiness Forgets • Something • Paper Mache • Knowing When To Leave • **Let Me Go To Him** *[45]* • Didn't We • My Way			
12/12/70+	8	26		15 Very Dionne	37	$15	Scepter 587
				Check Out Time • Yesterday • We've Only Just Begun • Here's That Rainy Day • The Green Grass Starts To Grow • They Don't Give Medals To Yesterday's Heroes • Walk The Way You Talk • **Make It Easy On Yourself** *[26]* • Going Out Of My Head • I Got Love			
11/13/71	16	13	●	16 The Dionne Warwicke Story	[L] 48	$20	Scepter 596 [2]
2/19/72	22	8		17 Dionne	54	$12	Warner 2585
3/15/75	35	6		18 Then Came You	167	$12	Warner 2846
				DIONNE WARWICKE (above 3)			
12/6/75+	15	14		19 Track of the Cat	137	$12	Warner 2893
2/26/77	20	11		20 A Man And A Woman	[L] 49	$12	HBS 996 [2]
				ISAAC HAYES & DIONNE WARWICK			
6/23/79	10	44	▲	21 Dionne	12	$10	Arista 4230
				Who, What, When, Where, Why • **After You** *[33]* • The Letter • I'll Never Love This Way Again *[18]* • **Deja Vu** *[25]* • Feeling Old Feelings • In Your Eyes • My Everlasting Love • Out Of My Hands • All The Time			
8/16/80	22	25		22 No Night So Long	23	$10	Arista 9526
6/20/81	35	15		23 Hot! Live And Otherwise	[L] 72	$12	Arista 8605 [2]
				3 of 4 sides are live			
5/8/82	33	15		24 Friends In Love	83	$10	Arista 9585
10/30/82	13	30	●	25 Heartbreaker	25	$10	Arista 9609
11/5/83	19	19		26 How Many Times Can We Say Goodbye	57	$10	Arista 8104
3/16/85	50	10		27 Finder Of Lost Loves	106	$8	Arista 8262
12/21/85+	8	24	●	28 Friends	12	$8	Arista 8398
				That's What Friends Are For *[1]* • Whisper In The Dark *[49]* • Remember Your Heart • Love At Second Sight • Moments Aren't Moments • Stronger Than Before • Stay Devoted • No One There (To Sing Me A Love Song) • How Long? • Extravagant Gestures			
8/29/87	32	31		29 Reservations For Two	56	$8	Arista 8446
2/13/93	84	2		30 Friends Can Be Lovers		$8	Arista 18682
				WASH, Martha '93			
				Born in San Francisco. Former member of **Two Tons O' Fun**. Uncredited vocalist on hits by **Black Box**, **C & C Music Factory** and **Seduction**.			
3/13/93	42	10		Martha Wash	169	$8	RCA 66052
				WASHINGTON, Deborah '78			
				Born on 3/16/54 in Philadelphia. Singer/actress.			
9/30/78	52	4		Any Way You Want It	205	$10	Ariola America 50040

WASHINGTON, Donna   **'81**
Born in Los Angeles. Female singer.

| 6/13/81 | 53 | 11 | | Going For The Glow.. | | | $10 | Capitol 12147 |

WASHINGTON, Grover Jr. ★37★   **'75**
Born on 12/12/43 in Buffalo, New York. Male saxophonist/pianist/bassist.

1)*Mister Magic* 2)*Feels So Good* 3)*Winelight*

12/18/71+	8	35		1 **Inner City Blues**	[I]	62	$12	Kudu 03
				Inner City Blues *[42]* • Georgia On My Mind • Mercy Mercy Me (The Ecology) • Medley: Ain't No Sunshine/Man And Boy (Better Days) • Until It's Time For You To Go • I Loves You, Porgy				
10/14/72	20	11		2 **All The King's Horses**...[I]		111	$12	Kudu 07
7/21/73	26	18		3 **Soul Box**...[I]		100	$15	Kudu 1213 [2]
3/22/75	❶¹	34		4 **Mister Magic**	[I]	10	$12	Kudu 20
				Earth Tones • Passion Flower • **Mister Magic** *[16]* • Black Frost				
11/22/75	❶¹	30		5 **Feels So Good**	[I]	10	$12	Kudu 24
				The Sea Lion • Moonstreams • Knucklehead • It Feels So Good • Hydra				
1/8/77	7	16		6 **A Secret Place**	[I]	31	$12	Kudu 32
				A Secret Place • Dolphin Dance • Not Yet • Love Makes It Better				
1/21/78	4	24		7 **Live At The Bijou**	[I-L]	11	$15	Kudu 3637 [2]
				recorded May 1977 at the Bijou Cafe in Philadelphia				
				On The Cusp • You Make Me Dance • Lock It In The Pocket • Medley: Days In Our Lives/Mr. Magic • Summer Song *[57]* • Juffure • Sausalito • Funkfoot				
10/21/78	7	23		8 **Reed Seed**	[I]	35	$10	Motown 910
				Do Dat *[75]* • Step'N' Thru • Reed Seed (Trio Tune) • Maracas Beach • Santa Cruzin • Just The Way You Are • Loran's Dance				
4/28/79	15	21		9 **Paradise**..[I]		24	$10	Elektra 182
3/8/80	8	25		10 **Skylarkin'**...[I]		24	$10	Motown 933
				Easy Loving You • Bright Moments • **Snake Eyes** *[88]* • I Can't Help It • Love • Open Up Your Mind (Wide)				
9/13/80	40	11		11 **Baddest**..[I-K]		96	$12	Motown 940 [2]
11/22/80+	2⁴	49	▲	12 **Winelight**	[I]	5	$10	Elektra 305
				Winelight • **Let It Flow ("For Dr. J")** *[62]* • In The Name Of Love • Take Me There • **Just The Two Of Us** *[3]* • Make Me A Memory (Sad Samba)				
11/7/81	44	8		13 **Anthology**..[I-K]		149	$12	Motown 961 [2]
12/18/82+	8	33		14 **The Best Is Yet To Come**		50	$10	Elektra 60215
				Can You Dig It • **The Best Is Yet To Come** *[14]* • More Than Meets The Eye • Things Are Getting Better • Mixty Motions • Brazilian Memories • I'll Be With You • Cassie's Theme				
10/27/84	21	26		15 **Inside Moves**		79	$10	Elektra 60318
8/22/87	29	20		16 **Strawberry Moon**...		66	$8	Columbia 40510
3/3/90	60	13		17 **Time Out Of Mind**..[I]			$8	Columbia 45253
5/30/92	26	21		18 **Next Exit**..		149	$8	Columbia 48530
10/5/96	45	15		19 **Soulful Strut** ....[I]		187	$8	Columbia 57505

WASHINGTON, Keith   **'91**
Born in Detroit. Former session singer.

5/4/91	❶²	51	●	1 **Make Time For Love**		48	$8	Qwest 26528
				All Night • **Make Time For Love** *[22]* • Kissing You *[1]* • Are You Still In Love With Me *[15]* • When You Love Somebody *[26]* • Ready, Willing And Able • I'll Be There • When It Comes To You • Lovers After All • Closer				
10/9/93	15	34		2 **You Make It Easy**		100	$8	Qwest 45336
3/28/98	27	28		3 **KW**		125	$8	Silas 11744

WATANABE, Sadao   **'84**
Pronounced: sah-day-o wah-tah-nob-bee. Born in 1933 in Utsunomiya, Japan. Male saxophonist.

| 9/15/84 | 37 | 13 | | **Rendezvous** ....[I] | | | $8 | Elektra 60371 |

WATAZ   **'98**
Male rap duo from New York City: Chris Stokes and Claudio Cueni.

| 3/28/98 | 68 | 2 | | **Natural High** .... | | | $8 | Fully Loaded 2041 |

WATERS, Crystal   **'91**
Born in 1964 in Philadelphia. Female dance singer.

| 7/20/91 | 65 | 16 | | 1 **Surprise** .... | | 197 | $8 | Mercury 848894 |
| 6/4/94 | 73 | 6 | ● | 2 **Storyteller** .... | | 199 | $8 | Mercury 522105 |

WATERS, Kim   **'90**
Born in Baltimore. Male saxophonist.

| 2/17/90 | 56 | 14 | | 1 **Sweet And Saxy** ....[I] | | | $8 | Warlock 2713 |
| 5/22/93 | 80 | 3 | | 2 **Peaceful Journey** ....[I] | | | $8 | Warlock 2737 |

WATLEY, Jody   **'87**
Born on 1/30/59 in Chicago. Female vocalist of **Shalamar** (1977-84) and former dancer on TV's *Soul Train*. Goddaughter of **Jackie Wilson**. Won the 1987 Best New Artist Grammy Award.

| 3/28/87 | ❶³ | 68 | ▲ | 1 **Jody Watley** | | 10 | $8 | MCA 5898 |
| | | | | Looking For A New Love *[1]* • Still A Thrill *[3]* • Some Kind Of Lover *[3]* • For The Girls • Love Injection • **Don't You Want Me** *[3]* • Do It To The Beat • Most Of All *[11]* • Learn To Say No | | | | |

WATLEY, Jody — Cont'd

| 4/22/89 | 5 | 37 | ● | 2 Larger Than Life | 16 | $8 | MCA 6276 |

Real Love [1] • Friends [3] • Everything [3] • What 'Cha Gonna Do For Me • L.O.V.E.R. • For Love's Sake • Lifestyle • Precious Love [51] • Something New • Once You Leave • Come Into My Life • Only You

| 12/9/89 | 48 | 12 | | 3 You Wanna Dance With Me? ....[K] | 86 | $8 | MCA 6343 |

contains remixes of her hits

1/4/92	21	29		4 Affairs Of The Heart........	124	$8	MCA 10355
11/27/93	38	22		5 Intimacy	164	$8	MCA 10947
7/29/95	59	7		6 Affection		$8	Avitone 73007

★130★ WATSON, Johnny "Guitar" '77

Born on 2/3/35 in Houston. Died of a heart attack on 5/17/96 (age 61). Singer/songwriter/guitarist.

1)A Real Mother For Ya 2)Ain't That A Bitch 3)Funk Beyond The Call Of Duty

| 8/30/75 | 40 | 7 | | 1 I Don't Want To Be Alone, Stranger........ | 201 | $12 | Fantasy 9484 |
| 7/10/76 | 4 | 36 | ● | 2 Ain't That A Bitch .... | 52 | $10 | DJM 3 |

I Need It [40] • I Want To Ta-Ta You Baby • Superman Lover [19] • Ain't That A Bitch • Since I Met You Baby • We're No Exception • Won't You Forgive Me Baby

| 4/23/77 | 3 | 31 | ● | 3 A Real Mother For Ya .... | 20 | $10 | DJM 7 |

A Real Mother For Ya [5] • Nothing Left To Be Desired • Your Love Is My Love • The Real Deal • Tarzan • I Wanna Thank You • Lover Jones [34]

| 12/24/77+ | 10 | 20 | | 4 Funk Beyond The Call Of Duty .... | 84 | $10 | DJM 714 |

Funk Beyond The Call Of Duty • It's About The Dollar Bill • Give Me My Love • It's A Damn Shame • I'm Gonna Get You Baby • Barn Door • Love That Will Not Die [59]

| 4/8/78 | 39 | 5 | | 5 Master Funk .... | 154 | $10 | DJM 13 |

WATSONIAN INSTITUTE

10/21/78	20	15		6 Giant	157	$10	DJM 19
6/30/79	35	9		7 What The Hell Is This	204	$10	DJM 24
6/14/80	20	23		8 Love Jones	115	$10	DJM 31
6/13/81	49	5		9 Johnny "Guitar" Watson And The Family Clone........	177	$10	DJM 501
12/19/81+	50	9		10 That's What Time It Is		$10	A&M 4880
10/15/94+	48	39		11 Bow Wow		$8	Wilma 71007

WATSON, Kino '96

Born in Dallas, North Carolina. Male singer/songwriter.

| 8/10/96 | 92 | 1 | | True 2 The Game .... | | $8 | Columbia 67696 |

WATTS, Ernie '82

Born on 10/23/45 in Norfolk, Virginia. Male saxophonist.

| 2/27/82 | 46 | 10 | | Chariots Of Fire ....[I] | 161 | $10 | Qwest 3637 |

WC AND THE MAAD CIRCLE '98

Born in Los Angeles. Male rapper. Member of Low Profile and Westside Connection. The MAAD Circle: Coolio, Big Gee and D.J. Crazy Toones. Coolio left in 1994.

11/2/91	52	27		1 Ain't A Damn Thang Changed........		$8	Priority 57156
10/21/95	15	10		2 Curb Servin'........	85	$8	London 828650
5/16/98	2[1]	16		3 The Shadiest One	19	$8	Red Ant 828957

WC

Hog • Where Y'all From • Fuckin' Wit Uh House Party • The Shadiest One • Can't Hold Back • Keep Hustlin' • Just Clownin' [18] • The Autobiography • Worldwide Gunnin' • Like That • Call It What You Want • Rich Rollin' • Cheddar • Bank Lick • It's All Bad • Better Days [33] • The Outcome

WEATHER REPORT '75

Jazz-fusion group formed by Austrian-born Josef Zawinul (keyboards) and Wayne Shorter (sax). Zawinul was a member of Cannonball Adderley's group for nine years; formed the Zawinul Syndicate in 1988.

6/23/73	41	4		1 Sweetnighter........[I]	85	$12	Columbia 32210
7/13/74	31	10		2 Mysterious Traveller........[I]	46	$10	Columbia 32494
6/21/75	12	10		3 Tale Spinnin'........[I]	31	$10	Columbia 33417
5/1/76	20	7		4 Black Market ....[I]	42	$10	Columbia 34099
5/28/77	33	3	▲	5 Heavy Weather ....[I]	30	$10	Columbia 34418
4/9/83	46	6		6 Procession ....[I]	96	$8	Columbia 38427

WEATHERS, Barbara '90

Born on 12/7/63 in Greensboro, North Carolina. Lead singer of Atlantic Starr from 1984-89.

| 8/11/90 | 79 | 6 | | Barbara Weathers .... | | $8 | Reprise 26166 |

WEAVER, Jason '95

Born in 1980 in Chicago. Singer/actor. Played the young Michael Jackson in the TV movie The Jacksons: An American Dream.

| 9/2/95 | 69 | 5 | | Love Ambition .... | | $8 | Motown 0322 |

WEE PAPA GIRLS, The '89

Rap duo from Acton, England: sisters Sandra and Timmy Lawrence.

| 3/18/89 | 96 | 2 | | The Beat, The Rhyme, The Noise........ | | $8 | Jive 1172 |

WELDON, Maxine '74

Born in California. Female singer.

| 3/16/74 | 48 | 4 | | Some Singin'........ | | $12 | Monument 32588 |

WELLS, Brandi '82

Born in Philadelphia. Female singer.

| 1/30/82 | 37 | 16 | | Watch Out........ | 202 | $10 | WMOT 37668 |

WENDY and LISA '89

Duo of Wendy Melvoin (guitar, vocals) and Lisa Coleman (keyboards). Formerly with Prince's band The Revolution. Wendy is the sister of Susannah Melvoin (of The Family).

| 4/8/89 | 71 | 8 | | Fruit At The Bottom .... | 119 | $8 | Columbia 44341 |

WESLEY, Fred, & The J.B.'s '73
James Brown's super-funk backup band led by trombonist/keyboardist **Fred Wesley**. He and other JB members were members of the **Parliament/Funkadelic** organization.

DEBUT	PEAK	WKS		Album Title	Pop #	$	Label & Number
8/5/72	34	3		1 Food For Thought		$30	People 5601
8/4/73	7	14		2 Doing It To Death	77	$30	People 5603

THE JB's
Doing It To Death [1] • You Can Have Watergate Just Gimme Some Bucks And I'll Be Straight • More Peas • La Di Da La Di Day • Sucker

6/8/74	20	10		3 Damn Right I Am Somebody	197	$20	People 6602
2/1/75	36	5		4 Breakin' Bread		$20	People 6604
4/30/77	31	10		5 A Blow For Me, A Toot For You	181	$15	Atlantic 18214

FRED WESLEY & THE HORNY HORNS

WEST COAST RAP ALL-STARS, The '90
Rap benefit for inner city youth: Above The Law, Body & Soul, Def Jef, Digital Underground, Eazy-E, Ice-T, J.J. Fad, King Tee, M.C. Hammer, Michel'le, N.W.A., Oaktown's 3-5-7, Tone Loc and Young MC.

| 7/7/90 | 15 | 16 | | We're All In The Same Gang | 60 | $8 | Warner 26241 |

WESTSIDE CONNECTION '96
Collaboration of rap stars **Ice Cube**, **Mack 10** and **WC** (of WC and The MAAD Circle).

| 11/9/96 | ❶[1] | 46 | ▲ | Bow Down | 2[1] | $8 | Priority 50583 |

World Domination • Bow Down [19] • Gangstas Make The World Go Round [30] • All The Critics In New York • Do You Like Criminals? • Gangstas Don't Dance • The Gangsta, The Killa And The Dope Dealer • Cross 'Em Out And Put A 'K • King Of The Hill • 3 Time Felons • Westward Ho • The Pledge • Hoo-Bangin'

WEST STREET MOB '81
Dance trio from Englewood, New Jersey: Joey Robinson, Warren Moore and Sebrina Gillison. Robinson is the son of **Sylvia**.

| 12/19/81 | 56 | 13 | | West Street Mob | | $10 | Sugar Hill 263 |

WHALUM, Kirk '93
Born in Memphis. Jazz tenor saxophonist.

| 3/6/93 | 42 | 21 | | Cache [I] | | $8 | Columbia 46931 |

WHAM! — see MICHAEL, George

WHATNAUTS '71
Vocal trio from Baltimore: Billy Herndon, Garnet Jones and Gerald Pinkney.

| 5/8/71 | 29 | 4 | | Introducing The Whatnauts | | $15 | Stang 1005 |

WHEELER, Audrey '92
Born in Queens, New York. Former session singer.

| 12/21/91+ | 57 | 18 | | I'm Yours Tonight | | $8 | Ear Candy 31002 |

WHEELER, Caron '90
Born on 1/19/63 in London. Featured female vocalist with Soul II Soul.

| 10/27/90 | 30 | 30 | | 1 UK Blak | 133 | $8 | EMI 93497 |
| 3/13/93 | 81 | 5 | | 2 Beach Of The War Goddess | | $8 | EMI 97879 |

WHISPERS, The ★25★ '80
Vocal group from Los Angeles: Gordy Harmon, twin brothers Walter and Wallace "Scotty" Scott, Marcus Hutson and Nicholas Caldwell. Harmon left in 1973, replaced by Leaveil Degree replaced Harmon in 1973. The Scotts recorded as **Walter & Scotty**.

1)The Whispers 2)Love Is Where You Find It 3)Love For Love 4)Just Gets Better With Time 5)Imagination

4/22/72	34	9		1 The Whispers' Love Story	186	$40	Janus 3041
12/23/72+	44	12		2 Life And Breath		$40	Janus 3046
10/20/73	48	4		3 Planets Of Life		$40	Janus 3055
6/22/74	40	11		4 Bingo		$40	Janus 7006
3/15/75	48	5		5 Greatest Hits [G]		$30	Janus 7013
7/17/76	40	13		6 One For The Money	189	$15	Soul Train 1450
7/23/77	23	17		7 Open Up Your Love	65	$15	Soul Train 2270
6/3/78	22	37		8 Headlights	77	$12	Solar 2774
4/14/79	28	16		9 Whisper In Your Ear	146	$12	Solar 3105
11/24/79	50	11		10 Happy Holidays To You [X]	201	$12	Solar 3489
1/5/80	❶[8]	34	▲	11 The Whispers	6	$12	Solar 3521

A Song For Donny [21] • My Girl • Lady [3] • Can You Do The Boogie • And The Beat Goes On [1] • I Love You • Out The Box • Welcome Into My Dream

| 1/17/81 | 3 | 31 | ● | 12 Imagination | 23 | $12 | Solar 3578 |

Imagination • It's A Love Thing [2] • Say You (Would Love For Me Too) • Continental Shuffle • I Can Make It Better [40] • Girl I Need You • Up On Soul Train • Fantasy

9/26/81	15	26		13 This Kind Of Lovin'	100	$12	Solar 3976
1/16/82	58	2		14 Happy Holidays To You [X-R]		$10	Solar 3489
1/30/82	❶[1]	33	●	15 Love Is Where You Find It	35	$10	Solar 27

In The Raw [8] • Turn Me Out • Cruisin' In • Emergency [22] • Say Yes • Love Is Where You Find It • Only You • Small Talkin'

| 4/2/83 | 2[4] | 40 | | 16 Love For Love | 37 | $10 | Solar 60216 |

Tonight [4] • Keep On Lovin' Me [4] • Love For Love • This Time [32] • Had It Not Been For You • Try It Again • Do They Turn You On • Keep Your Love Around • Lay It On Me

DEBUT	PEAK	WKS	Gold	Album Title	Pop #	$	Label & Number

WHISPERS, The — Cont'd

DEBUT	PEAK	WKS	Gold	Album Title	Pop #	$	Label & Number
12/15/84+	8	32		17 **So Good**	88	$10	Solar 60356

Some Kinda Lover [17] • **Contagious** [10] • Sweet Sensation • On Impact • Suddenly • **Don't Keep Me Waiting** [60] • Are You Going My Way • Never Too Late • So Good

| 5/30/87 | 3 | 47 | ▲ | 18 **Just Gets Better With Time** | 22 | $8 | Solar 72554 |

I Want You • Special F/X • **Rock Steady** [1] • No Pain, No Gain [74] • In The Mood [16] • **Just Gets Better With Time** [12] • Love's Calling • Give It To Me

| 8/18/90 | 8 | 49 | ● | 19 **More Of The Night** | 83 | $8 | Capitol 92957 |

More Of The Night • **My Heart Your Heart** [4] • Mind Blowing • Don't Be Late For Love • You Are The One • **Is It Good To You** [7] • **Innocent** [3] • Girl Don't Make Me Wait • Misunderstanding • Forever Lover • Babes • **I Want 2B The 14U** [58] • Help Them See The Light

| 12/17/94+ | 42 | 4 | | 20 **Christmas Moments** ....[X] | | $8 | Capitol 89070 |
| 4/8/95 | 8 | 29 | | 21 **Toast To The Ladies** | 92 | $8 | Capitol 30270 |

Make Sweet Love To Me [41] • Every Little Thing You Do • Heaven • Crowd Of 1 • Whisperin • **Come On Home** [60] • Better Watch Your Heart • Toast To The Ladies • You're Driving Me Crazy • Pissed Off (Baby Come Back) • You're So Good To Me • My Funny Valentine

6/29/96	87	3		22 **Greatest Slow James Volume One** ....[G]		$8	Solar 52273
6/21/97	89	2		23 **Greatest Hits** ....[G]		$8	Solar 57604
12/13/97	27	19		24 **Song Book Volume One - The Songs Of Babyface**		$8	Interscope 90111

WHISTLE   '86

Group from Brooklyn, New York: Garvin Dublin, Brian Faust and Rickford Bennett. By late 1988, Kerry Hodge was added and Dublin left, replaced by Tarek Stevens.

DEBUT	PEAK	WKS	Gold	Album Title	Pop #	$	Label & Number
10/18/86	24	17		1 **Whistle**		$8	Select 21615
4/30/88	42	13		2 **Transformation**		$8	Select 21625
4/28/90	34	16		3 **Always And Forever**		$8	Select 21635
3/14/92	75	7		4 **Get The Love**		$8	Select 61252

WHITE, Artie "Blues Boy"   '90

Born in Vicksburg, Mississippi. Blues singer/guitarist.

DEBUT	PEAK	WKS	Gold	Album Title	Pop #	$	Label & Number
9/15/90	74	7		1 **Tired Of Sneaking Around**		$8	Ichiban 1061
10/26/91	95	3		2 **Dark End Of The Street**		$8	Ichiban 1117

WHITE, Barry ★21★   '77

Born on 9/12/44 in Galveston, Texas; raised in Los Angeles. Singer/songwriter/keyboardist/producer. At age 11, played piano on Jesse Belvin's hit "Goodnight My Love." Formed female vocal trio Love Unlimited, which included future wife Glodean James. Leader of 40-piece Love Unlimited Orchestra.

1)Barry White Sings For Someone You Love 2)Barry White The Man 3)I've Got So Much To Give
4)Can't Get Enough 5)Stone Gon'

DEBUT	PEAK	WKS	Gold	Album Title	Pop #	$	Label & Number
4/28/73	❶²	54	●	1 **I've Got So Much To Give**	16	$10	20th Century 407

Standing In The Shadows Of Love • Bring Back My Yesterday • I've Found Someone • **I've Got So Much To Give** [5] • I'm Gonna Love You Just A Little More Baby [1]

| 12/1/73+ | ❶² | 32 | ● | 2 **Stone Gon'** | 20 | $10 | 20th Century 423 |

Girl It's True, Yes I'll Always Love You • **Honey Please, Can't Ya See** [6] • You're My Baby • Hard To Believe That I Found You • Never, Never Gonna Give Ya Up [2]

| 9/14/74 | ❶² | 37 | ● | 3 **Can't Get Enough** | 1¹ | $10 | 20th Century 444 |

Mellow Mood • **You're The First, The Last, My Everything** [1] • I Can't Believe You Love Me • **Can't Get Enough Of Your Love, Babe** [1] • Oh Love, Well You Finally Made It • I Love You More Than Anything (In This World Girl)

| 4/19/75 | ❶¹ | 16 | ● | 4 **Just Another Way To Say I Love You** | 17 | $10 | 20th Century 466 |

Heavenly, That's What You Are To Me • **I'll Do For You Anything You Want Me To** [4] • All Because Of You • Love Serenade • What Am I Gonna Do With You [1] • Let Me Live My Life Lovin' You Babe

| 11/15/75 | 15 | 9 | ▲ | 5 **Barry White's Greatest Hits** ....[G] | 23 | $10 | 20th Century 493 |
| 2/7/76 | 8 | 18 | | 6 **Let The Music Play** | 42 | $10 | 20th Century 502 |

I Don't Know Where Love Has Gone • If You Know, Won't You Tell Me • I'm So Blue And You Are Too • **Baby, We Better Try To Get It Together** [29] • You See The Trouble With Me [14] • Let The Music Play [4]

| 11/13/76 | 25 | 11 | | 7 **Is This Whatcha Wont?** | 125 | $10 | 20th Century 516 |
| 9/24/77 | ❶⁵ | 34 | ▲ | 8 **Barry White Sings For Someone You Love** | 8 | $10 | 20th Century 543 |

Playing Your Game, Baby [8] • It's Ecstasy When You Lay Down Next To Me [1] • You're So Good You're Bad • I Never Thought I'd Fall In Love With You • You Turned My Whole World Around • Oh What A Night For Dancing [13] • Of All The Guys In The World

| 10/21/78 | ❶³ | 30 | ▲ | 9 **Barry White The Man** | 36 | $10 | 20th Century 571 |

Look At Her • **Your Sweetness Is My Weakness** [2] • Sha La La Means I Love You • September When I First Met You • It's Only Love Doing Its Thing • **Just The Way You Are** [45] • Early Years

4/21/79	14	18	●	10 **The Message Is Love**	67	$10	Unlimited Gold 35763
8/25/79	40	7		11 **I Love To Sing The Songs I Sing**	132	$10	20th Century 590
7/12/80	19	18		12 **Barry White's Sheet Music**	85	$10	Unlimited Gold 36208
5/16/81	44	8		13 **Barry & Glodean**	201	$10	Unlimited Gold 37054

BARRY WHITE & GLODEAN WHITE

10/24/81	40	20		14 **Beware!**	207	$10	Unlimited Gold 37176
9/11/82	19	15		15 **Change**	148	$10	Unlimited Gold 38048
11/7/87	28	24		16 **The Right Night & Barry White**	159	$8	A&M 5154
11/11/89+	22	47		17 **The Man Is Back!**	143	$8	A&M 5256
11/2/91	8	28		18 **Put Me In Your Mix**	96	$8	A&M 5377

Let's Get Busy • Love Is Good With You • For Real Chill • Break It Down With You • Volare • **Put Me In Your Mix** [2] • Who You Giving Your Love To • Love Will Find Us • We're Gonna Have It All • Dark And Lovely (you over there) [29]

DEBUT	PEAK	WKS	Gold	Album Title	Pop #	$	Label & Number

WHITE, Barry — Cont'd

DEBUT	PEAK	WKS		Album Title	Pop #	$	Label & Number
6/25/94+	70	64	● 19	All-Time Greatest Hits ....[G]		$8	Mercury 522459
10/22/94	❶¹	58	▲² 20	The Icon Is Love	20	$8	A&M 0115

Practice What You Preach [1] • There It Is [54] • I Only Want To Be With You • The Time Is Right • Baby's Home • **Come On** [12] • Love Is The Icon • Sexy Undercover • Don't You Want To Know? • Whatever We Had, We Had

WHITE, Karyn   **'89**
Born on 10/14/65 in Los Angeles. Former session singer. Married to producer Terry Lewis (of **The Time**).

| 10/1/88+ | ❶⁷ | 57 | ▲ 1 | Karyn White | 19 | $8 | Warner 25637 |

The Way You Love Me [1] • Secret Rendezvous [4] • Slow Down [36] • Superwoman [1] • Family Man • Love Saw It [1] • Don't Mess With Me • Tell Me Tomorrow • One Wish

| 10/5/91 | 7 | 32 | ● 2 | Ritual Of Love | 53 | $8 | Warner 26320 |

Romantic [1] • Ritual Of Love • **The Way I Feel About You** [5] • Hooked On You • Walkin' The Dog [34] • Love That's Mine • How I Want You • One Heart • Tears Of Joy • Beside You • Do Unto Me [24] • Hard To Say Goodbye

| 10/15/94 | 22 | 47 | 3 | Make Him Do Right .... | 99 | $8 | Warner 45400 |

WHITE, Lynn   **'90**
Born in Memphis. Female singer.

| 7/21/90 | 67 | 14 | | The New Me .... | | $8 | Chelsea Avenue 7003 |

WHITE, Maurice   **'85**
Born on 12/19/41 in Memphis. Percussionist with **Ramsey Lewis** from 1966-71. Founder and co-lead vocalist of **Earth, Wind & Fire**.

| 10/5/85 | 12 | 29 | | Maurice White .... | 61 | $8 | Columbia 39883 |

WHITE, Tony Joe   **'69**
Born on 7/23/43 in Goodwill, Louisiana. Singer/songwriter.

| 8/9/69 | 29 | 16 | | Black And White .... | 51 | $15 | Monument 18114 |

WHITEHEAD BROS.   **'94**
Duo of Kenny and Johnny Whitehead; sons of prolific songwriter John Whitehead of **McFadden & Whitehead**.

| 9/10/94 | 35 | 23 | | Serious .... | | $8 | Motown 0346 |

WHITFIELD, Robert "Goodie"   **'82**
Born in Dallas. Singer/keyboardist.

| 9/11/82 | 31 | 10 | | Call Me Goodie .... | 207 | $10 | Total Exp. 3002 |

WHODINI   **'86**
Rap trio from New York City. Began as a duo of Jalil "Whodini" Hutchins and John "Ecstacy" Fletcher. Grandmaster Dee joined in 1986.

| 11/17/84+ | 5 | 48 | ▲ 1 | Escape | 35 | | Jive 8251 |

Five Minutes Of Funk [flip] • Freaks Come Out At Night [43] • Featuring Grandmaster Dee • Big Mouth [64] • Escape (I Need A Break) • Friends [4] • Out Of Control • We Are Whodini

| 5/24/86 | 4 | 40 | ● 2 | **Back In Black** | 35 | | Jive 8407 |

Funky Beat [19] • One Love [10] • Growing Up [58] • I'm A Ho • Fugitive • Echo Scratch • Last Night (I Had A Long Talk With Myself) • The Good Part

| 10/24/87 | 8 | 25 | ● 3 | **Open Sesame** | 30 | $8 | Jive 8494 |

Rock You Again (Again & Again) • Be Yourself [20] • Cash Money • Hooked On You • Early Mother's Day Card • Life Is Like A Dance • You Brought It On Yourself • I'm Def (Jump Back And Kiss Myself) • Remember Where You Came From • For The Body • You Take My Breath Away

| 4/13/91 | 48 | 14 | 4 | Bag-A-Trix .... | | $8 | MCA 10201 |
| 10/5/96 | 55 | 4 | 5 | Six .... | | $8 | So So Def 66948 |

WHORIDAS, The   **'98**
Rap duo from Oakland: Mr. Taylor and King Sann.

| 12/13/97+ | 39 | 9 | | Whoridin' .... | | $8 | Southpaw 71800 |

WILD CHERRY   **'76**
White funk group from Steubenville, Ohio: Robert Parissi (vocals, guitar), Bryan Bassett (guitar), Mark Avsec (keyboards), Allen Wentz (bass) and Ron Beitle (drums).

| 7/24/76 | ❶¹ | 20 | ▲ 1 | Wild Cherry | 5 | $10 | Sweet City 34195 |

Play That Funky Music [1] • The Lady Wants Your Money • 99 1/2 • Don't Go Near The Water • Nowhere To Run • I Feel Sanctified • Hold On • Get It Up • What In The Funk Do You See

| 4/2/77 | 33 | 5 | 2 | Electrified Funk .... | 51 | $10 | Sweet City 34462 |
| 3/18/78 | 54 | 3 | 3 | I Love My Music .... | 84 | $10 | Sweet City 35011 |

WILDE, Eugene   **'85**
Born Ronald Broomfield in Miami. Singer/songwriter.

| 12/15/84+ | 14 | 33 | 1 | Eugene Wilde .... | 97 | $8 | Philly World 90239 |
| 12/14/85+ | 17 | 26 | 2 | Serenade .... | | $8 | Philly World 90490 |

WILD MAN STEVE   **'70**
Born Steven Gallon in Boston. Comedian/DJ for WILD radio in Boston.

| 12/20/69+ | 28 | 29 | | My Man! Wild Man! ....[C] | 185 | $15 | Raw 7000 |

WILD ORCHID   **'97**
Female vocal trio from Los Angeles: Stacy Ferguson, Stefanie Ridel and Renee Sandstrom. Both Ferguson (1984-89) and Sandstrom (1984-87) were regulars on the TV show *Kids Incorporated*.

| 4/12/97 | 84 | 2 | | Wild Orchid .... | 153 | $8 | RCA 66894 |

WILLIAMS, Alyson   **'90**
Born in Harlem, New York. Female singer.

| 4/1/89+ | 25 | 69 | 1 | Raw .... | | $8 | Def Jam 40515 |
| 4/25/92 | 31 | 24 | 2 | Alyson Williams .... | | $8 | Columbia 45417 |

WILLIAMS, Beau   **'86**
Born in Houston. Male singer.

| 9/8/84 | 56 | 14 | 1 | Bodacious! .... | | $8 | Capitol 12344 |
| 10/11/86 | 48 | 10 | 2 | No More Tears .... | | $8 | Capitol 12486 |

DEBUT	PEAK	WKS	Gold	Album Title	Pop #	$	Label & Number

WILLIAMS, Christopher   '93
Born in Harlem, New York. Nephew of Ella Fitzgerald.

DEBUT	PEAK	WKS			Pop #	$	Label & Number
8/19/89	23	46		1 Adventures In Paradise	63	$8	Geffen 24220
1/16/93	12	39		2 Changes	63	$8	Uptown/MCA 10751
3/18/95	13	15		3 Not A Perfect Man	104	$8	Giant 24564

★110★   **WILLIAMS, Deniece**   '77
Born Deniece Chandler on 6/3/51 in Gary, Indiana. Singer/songwriter. Member of Wonderlove, **Stevie Wonder**'s backup group, from 1972-75.
     1)This Is Niecy   2)Niecy   3)Let's Hear It For The Boy

10/9/76+	3	33	●	1 This is Niecy	33	$10	Columbia 34242

It's Important To Me • That's What Friends Are For [65] • How'd I Know That Love Would Slip Away • **Cause You Love Me Baby** [74] • Free [2] • Watching Over • If You Don't Believe

| 11/26/77+ | 23 | 18 | | 2 Song Bird | 66 | $10 | Columbia 34911 |
| 7/29/78 | 14 | 11 | ● | 3 That's What Friends Are For | 19 | $10 | Columbia 35435 |

    JOHNNY MATHIS & DENIECE WILLIAMS

7/21/79	27	23		4 When Love Comes Calling	96	$8	ARC 35568
4/4/81	13	36		5 My Melody	74	$8	ARC 37048
4/17/82	5	29		6 Niecy	20	$8	ARC 37952

Waiting By The Hotline [29] • It's Gonna Take A Miracle [1] • Love Notes • I Believe In Miracles • How Does It Feel • Waiting [72] • Now Is The Time For Love • A Part Of Love

| 6/4/83 | 10 | 25 | | 7 I'm So Proud | 54 | $8 | Columbia 38622 |

Do What You Feel [9] • I'm So Proud [28] • So Deep In Love • I'm Glad It's You • Heaven In Your Eyes • They Say • Love, Peace And Unity • It's Okay

| 6/9/84 | 10 | 27 | | 8 Let's Hear It For The Boy | 26 | $8 | Columbia 39366 |

Let's Hear It For The Boy [1] • I Want You • Picking Up The Pieces • Black Butterfly [22] • Next Love [22] • Haunting Me • Don't Tell Me We Have Nothing • Blind Dating • Wrapped Up • Whiter Than Snow

9/27/86	58	7		9 Hot On The Trail		$8	Columbia 40084
5/23/87	39	11		10 Water Under The Bridge		$8	Columbia 40486
10/29/88	48	18		11 As Good As It Gets		$8	Columbia 44322
3/30/96	85	1		12 Gonna Take A Miracle: The Best Of Deniece Williams ...... [G]		$8	Legacy 64839

WILLIAMS, James (D-Train)   '82
Born in Brooklyn, New York. Singer/songwriter.

| 4/24/82 | 16 | 34 | | 1 "D" Train | 128 | $10 | Prelude 14105 |
| 6/4/83 | 31 | 15 | | 2 Music | | $10 | Prelude 14109 |

    "D" TRAIN (above 2)

| 10/18/86+ | 51 | 21 | | 3 Miracles Of The Heart | | $8 | Columbia 40465 |
| 8/13/88 | 46 | 11 | | 4 In Your Eyes | | $8 | Columbia 40914 |

WILLIAMS, Lenny   '78
Born in 1945 in Pine Bluff, Arkansas; raised in Oakland. Lead singer of **Tower Of Power** from 1972-75.

7/30/77	25	23		1 Choosing You	99	$10	ABC 1023
7/22/78	17	32	●	2 Spark of Love	87	$10	ABC 1073
7/14/79	24	15		3 Love Current	108	$10	MCA 3155
11/1/80	57	15		4 Let's Do It Today	185	$10	MCA 5147
5/26/84	51	6		5 Changing		$10	Rocshire 9513
4/7/90	46	21		6 Layin' In Wait		$8	Crush 230

WILLIAMS, Vanessa   '92
Born on 3/18/63 in Tarrytown, New York. Singer/actress. In 1983, became the first black woman to win the Miss America pageant; relinquished crown after Penthouse magazine scandal. Appeared in the Broadway production Kiss Of The Spider Woman. Appeared in the movie Harley Davidson & The Marlboro Man and the TV mini-series The Jacksons: An American Dream.

| 7/2/88 | 18 | 63 | ● | 1 The Right Stuff | 38 | $8 | Wing 835694 |
| 9/14/91+ | ❶¹ | 91 | ▲³ | 2 The Comfort Zone | 17 | $8 | Wing 843522 |

The Comfort Zone [2] • Running Back To You [1] • Work To Do [3] • You Gotta Go • Still In Love • **Save The Best For Last** [1] • What Will I Tell My Heart • Strangers Eyes • 2 Of A Kind • Freedom Dance (Get Free!) • **Just For Tonight** [11] • One Reason • Better Off Now • Goodbye

12/24/94	25	37	▲	3 The Sweetest Days	57	$8	Wing 526172
11/23/96	24	8	●	4 Star Bright .... [X]	36	$8	Mercury 532827
9/13/97	28	11		5 Next	53	$8	Mercury 536060

WILLIAMS, Vesta — see VESTA

WILLIE D   '92
Born Willie James Dennis on 11/1/66 in Houston. Male rapper. Member of **The Geto Boys**.

| 3/31/90 | 53 | 23 | | 1 Controversy | | $8 | Rap-A-Lot 104 |

    WILLIE DEE

| 10/3/92 | 27 | 20 | | 2 I'm Goin' Out Lika Soldier | 88 | $8 | Rap-A-Lot 57188 |
| 11/12/94 | 31 | 9 | | 3 Play Witcha Mama | | $8 | Wize Up 8141 |

WILLIS, Bruce   '87
Born on 3/19/55 in Penns Grove, New Jersey. Actor/singer. Played "David Addison" on TV's Moonlighting. Starred in several movies. Married actress Demi Moore on 11/21/87.

| 2/28/87 | 27 | 13 | ● | The Return Of Bruno | 14 | $8 | Motown 6222 |

WILSON, Al   '74
Born on 6/19/39 in Meridian, Mississippi. Singer/drummer.

| 12/29/73+ | 9 | 19 | | 1 Show And Tell | 70 | $15 | Rocky Road 3601 |

Show And Tell [10] • I'm Out To Get You • Queen Of The Ghetto • Touch And Go [23] • My Song • Broken Home • What You See • Love Me Gentle, Love Me Blind • Moonlightin' • For Cryin' Out Loud • A Song For You

| 10/26/74 | 35 | 11 | | 2 La La Peace Song | 171 | $15 | Rocky Road 3700 |
| 6/19/76 | 43 | 6 | | 3 I've Got A Feeling | 185 | $12 | Playboy 410 |

DEBUT	PEAK	WKS	Gold	Album Title		Pop #	$	Label & Number
				WILSON, Charlie '92				
				Born in Tulsa, Oklahoma. Lead singer of **The Gap Band**.				
8/22/92	42	13		You Turn My Life Around			$8	MCA 10587
				WILSON, Flip '68				
				Born Clerow Wilson on 12/8/33 in Jersey City, New Jersey. Died of cancer on 11/25/98 (age 64). Comedian. Host of own TV variety show from 1970-74.				
8/26/67+	14	28		1 Cowboys & Colored People	[C]	34	$15	Atlantic 8149
6/1/68	18	15		2 You Devil You	[C]	147	$15	Atlantic 8179
2/28/70	24	28	●	3 "The Devil made me buy this dress"	[C]	17	$12	Little David 1000
1/9/71	16	9		4 "Flip" - The Flip Wilson Show	[C]	45	$12	Little David 2000
				WILSON, Gerald '67				
				Born on 9/4/18 in Shelby, Mississippi. Jazz trumpeter.				
12/31/66+	18	4		Golden Sword			$15	Pacific Jazz 10111
				WILSON, Jackie '67				
				Born on 6/9/34 in Detroit. Died on 1/21/84 (age 49). Male singer. Godfather of **Jody Watley**. On 9/25/75, Wilson collapsed from a heart attack, on stage, at the Latin Casino in Cherry Hill, New Jersey; spent rest of his life comatose in nursing homes. Inducted into the Rock and Roll Hall of Fame in 1987.				
12/31/66+	15	10		1 Whispers		108	$30	Brunswick 754122
12/2/67	28	3		2 Higher And Higher		163	$30	Brunswick 754130
5/18/68	18	5		3 Manufacturers of Soul		195	$20	Brunswick 754134
				JACKIE WILSON/COUNT BASIE				
4/19/69	43	2		4 Jackie Wilson's Greatest Hits	[G]		$20	Brunswick 754140
1/3/70	50	2		5 Do Your Thing			$20	Brunswick 754154
				WILSON, Mary '79				
				Born on 3/6/44 in Mississippi; raised in Detroit. Founding member of **The Supremes**.				
10/13/79	73	2		Mary Wilson		208	$10	Motown 927

WILSON, Nancy ★30★   '65

Born on 2/20/37 in Chillicothe, Ohio; raised in Columbus, Ohio. Jazz stylist with **Rusty Bryant**'s Carolyn Club Band In Columbus. First recorded for Dot in 1956. Moved to New York City in 1959.

1)Today-My Way 2)Tender Loving Care 3)Nancy-Naturally

DEBUT	PEAK	WKS	Album Title		Pop #	$	Label & Number
2/6/65	4	10	1 The Nancy Wilson Show!	[L]	29	$20	Capitol 2136
			recorded at the Cocoanut Grove in Los Angeles				
			Fireworks • Don't Take Your Love From Me • Don't Talk, Just Sing • Guess Who I Saw Today • Ten Good Years • The Saga Of Bill Bailey • The Music That Makes Me Dance • I'm Beginning To See The Light • You Can Have Him				
6/19/65	2[1]	11	2 Today-My Way		7	$20	Capitol 2321
			Reach Out For Me • Welcome, Welcome • My Love, Forgive Me (Amore, Scusami) • Dear Heart • Don't Come Running Back To Me • And Satisfy • You've Lost That Lovin' Feelin' • Love Has Many Faces • Take What I Have • I'm All Smiles • If I Ruled The World				
9/18/65	7	6	3 Gentle Is My Love		17	$20	Capitol 2351
			Who Can I Turn To (When Nobody Needs Me) • There Will Never Be Another You • If Love Is Good To Me • My One And Only Love • Funnier Than Funny • More • Gentle Is My Love • At Long Last Love • Time After Time • If Ever I Would Leave You • When He Makes Music				
5/28/66	4	18	4 A Touch Of Today		15	$20	Capitol 2495
			You've Got Your Troubles [48] • And I Love Him • Uptight (Everything's Alright) • Have A Heart • Before The Rain • Shadow Of Your Smile • Call Me • Yesterday • Wasn't It Wonderful • You're Gonna Hear From Me • No One Else But You • Goin' Out Of My Head				
8/27/66	3	19	5 Tender Loving Care		35	$20	Capitol 2555
			Don't Go To Strangers • Gee Baby, Ain't I Good To You • Your Name Is Love • Too Late Now • Like Someone In Love • Tender Loving Care • As You Desire Me • I Want To Talk About You • Love-Wise • Try A Little Tenderness • Close Your Eyes				
2/4/67	4	20	6 Nancy-Naturally		35	$20	Capitol 2634
			In The Dark • Ten Years Of Tears • Since I Fell For You • Willow Weep For Me • My Babe • Just For A Thrill • Alright, Okay, You Win • I Wish I Didn't Love You So • Watch What Happens • Ain't That Lovin' You				
6/3/67	8	12	7 Just For Now		40	$20	Capitol 2712
			Born Free • That's Life • What Now My Love • Rain Sometimes • Alfie • Mercy, Mercy, Mercy • Winchester Cathedral • If He Walked Into My Life • Love Can Do Anything • Just For Now • I'll Make A Man Of The Man				
9/16/67	8	9	8 Lush Life		46	$20	Capitol 2757
			Free Again • Midnight Sun • Only The Young • (Ah, The Apple Trees) When The World Was Young • The Right To Love (Reflections) • Lush Life • Over The Weekend • You've Changed • River Shallow • Sunny • (I Stayed) Too Long At The Fair				
3/30/68	26	8	9 Welcome To My Love		115	$15	Capitol 2844
6/1/68	5	25	10 Easy		51	$15	Capitol 2909
			Wave • Make Me A Present Of You • Gentle On My Mind • When I Look In Your Eyes • Love Is Blue • Walk Away • **Face It Girl, It's Over** [15] • The Look Of Love • One Like You • Make Me Rainbows • How Insensitive				
8/31/68	23	14	11 The Best Of Nancy Wilson	[G]	145	$15	Capitol 2947
10/12/68	20	7	12 The Sound Of Nancy Wilson		122	$15	Capitol 2970
2/22/69	38	11	13 Nancy		117	$15	Capitol 148
7/5/69	20	23	14 Son of a Preacher Man		122	$15	Capitol 234
12/13/69+	19	14	15 Hurt So Bad		92	$15	Capitol 353
3/21/70	38	6	16 Can't Take My Eyes Off You		155	$15	Capitol 429

WILSON, Nancy — Cont'd

DEBUT	PEAK	WKS		Album Title	Pop #	$	Label & Number
12/19/70+	5	23		17 Now I'm A Woman	54	$15	Capitol 541

Now I'm A Woman *[41]* • Joe • (They Long To Be) Close To You • The Long And Winding Road • Bridge Over Troubled Water • Let's Fall In Love All Over • Lonely, Lonely • How Many Broken Wings • The Real Me • Make It With You

12/7/74+	11	16		18 All In Love Is Fair	97	$12	Capitol 11317
7/19/75	14	13		19 Come Get To This	119	$12	Capitol 11386
5/8/76	26	14		20 This Mother's Daughter	126	$12	Capitol 11518
7/23/77	42	9		21 I've Never Been To Me	198	$12	Capitol 11659
9/1/84	42	12		22 The Two Of Us	144	$10	Columbia 39326

RAMSEY LEWIS & NANCY WILSON

4/14/90	68	17		23 A Lady With A Song		$8	Columbia 45378
5/21/94	63	12		24 Love, Nancy		$8	Columbia 57425

WILSON, Shanice — see SHANICE

WILSON-JAMES, Victoria   **'91**
Born in Indianapolis. Later moved to England. Female singer/songwriter.

5/4/91	55	16		Perseverance		$8	Epic 46853

★169★   **WINANS, BeBe & CeCe**   **'91**
Younger brother and sister of the Detroit gospel-singing family, **The Winans**: Benjamin "BeBe" and Priscilla "CeCe." They are the seventh and eighth children in a 10-sibling family.

8/8/87	49	17		1 BeBe & CeCe Winans		$8	Capitol 12573
1/14/89	10	47	●	2 Heaven	95	$8	Capitol 90959

Heaven *[12]* • Celebrate New Life *[25]* • Lost Without You *[8]* • You • Wanna Be More • Hold Up The Light • Meantime • Don't Cry • Trust Him • Bridge Over Troubled Water

7/27/91	❶²	56	▲	3 Different Lifestyles	74	$8	Capitol 92078

Depend On You *[24]* • Addictive Love *[1]* • It's O.K. *[6]* • The Blood *[78]* • Two Different Lifestyles • Supposed To Be • I'll Take You There *[1]* • You Know And I Know • Searching For Love (It's Real) • Better Place • Can't Take This Away

12/11/93+	17	5		4 First Christmas	[X]	163	$8	Capitol 89757
10/8/94	19	28	●	5 Relationships	111	$8	Capitol 28216
11/16/96	80	9		6 Greatest Hits	[G]	$8	Sparrow 37048
11/15/97	36	27		7 BeBe Winans	125	$8	Atlantic 83041
4/4/98	35	27		8 Everlasting Love	107	$8	Pioneer 92793

CeCe WINANS

WINANS, The   **'90**
Family gospel group from Detroit: brothers Michael, Ronald, Marvin and Carvin Winans (Marvin and Carvin are twins). Brothers of **BeBe & CeCe Winans**.

1/11/86	57	19		1 Let My People Go		$8	Qwest 25344
9/26/87	30	21		2 Decisions	109	$8	Qwest 25510
5/19/90	12	42	●	3 Return	90	$8	Qwest 26161
9/11/93	41	9		4 All Out		$8	Qwest 45213

WINBUSH, Angela   **'87**
Born in St. Louis. Singer/songwriter. In **Rene & Angela** duo with **Rene Moore** from 1980-86. Married Ronald Isley of **The Isley Brothers** on 6/26/93.

10/24/87	7	51		1 Sharp	81	$8	Mercury 832733

Sharp • Sensual Lover • **Run To Me** *[4]* • Imagination Of The Heart • C'est Toi (It's You) *[47]* • Angel *[1]* • Hello Beloved *[26]* • You Had A Good Girl • No One Has Ever Cared (Like You)

11/4/89	12	47		2 The Real Thing	113	$8	Mercury 838866
4/2/94	11	25		3 Angela Winbush	96	$8	Elektra 61591

WINDJAMMER   **'84**
Group from New Orleans: Carl Dennis (vocals), Roy Paul Joseph and Kevin McLin (guitars), Fred McCray (keyboards), Chris Severin (bass) and Darrell Winchester (drums).

6/16/84	53	8		Windjammer II		$8	MCA 39021

WING AND A PRAYER FIFE AND DRUM CORPS., The   **'76**
Studio group from New York City; vocals by Linda November, Vivian Cherry, Arlene Martell and Helen Miles.

2/28/76	19	7		Babyface	47	$12	Wing & A Prayer 3025

WINSTONS, The   **'69**
Vocal group from Washington, DC: Richard Spencer, Ray Maritano, Quincy Mattison, Phil Tolotta, Sonny Peckrol and G.C. Coleman.

8/9/69	12	16		Color Him Father	78	$60	Metromedia 1010

WINTERS, Robert, & Fall   **'81**
Born in Detroit. Singer/keyboardist. Stricken with polio at age five; confined to a wheelchair. Own group, Fall, features singer Walter Turner.

4/18/81	27	14		1 Magic Man	71	$10	Buddah 5732
1/15/83	54	5		2 L-O-V-E		$10	Casablanca 7275

WINWOOD, Steve   **'86**
Born on 5/12/48 in Birmingham, England. Rock singer/keyboardist. Lead singer of Spencer Davis Group, **Blind Faith** and Traffic.

9/6/86	46	12	▲³	1 Back in the High Life	3	$8	Island 25448
9/3/88	93	1	▲²	2 Roll With It	1¹	$8	Virgin 90946

WITCHDOCTOR   **'98**
Born in Atlanta. Male rapper.

5/9/98	37	5		...A S.W.A.T. Healin' Ritual	157	$8	Organized N. 90146

DEBUT	PEAK	WKS		Album Title	Pop #	$	Label & Number
	★104★			**WITHERS, Bill** '72			
				Born on 7/4/38 in Slab Fork, West Virginia. Singer/songwriter/guitarist.			
				1)Still Bill 2)Just As I Am 3)Bill Withers Live At Carnegie Hall			
6/12/71	5	38		1 **Just As I Am**	39	$15	Sussex 7006
				Harlem • **Ain't No Sunshine** *[6]* • **Grandma's Hands** *[18]* • Sweet Wanomi • Everybody's Talkin' • Do It Good • Hope She'll Be Happier • Let It Be • I'm Her Daddy • In My Heart • Moanin' And Groanin' • Better Off Dead			
5/20/72	❶⁶	38	●	2 **Still Bill**	4	$15	Sussex 7014
				Lonely Town, Lonely Street • Let Me In Your Life • Who Is He And What Is He To You? • **Use Me** *[2]* • **Lean On Me** *[1]* • Kissing My Love *[12]* • I Don't Know • Another Day To Run • I Don't Want You On My Mind • Take It All In And Check It All Out			
4/21/73	6	20		3 **Bill Withers Live At Carnegie Hall** [L]	63	$20	Sussex 7025 [2]
				Use Me • Friend Of Mine • Ain't No Sunshine • Grandma's Hands • World Keeps Going Around • Let Me In Your Life • Better Off Dead • For My Friend • I Can't Write Left Handed • Lean On Me • Lonely Town Lonely Street • Hope She'll Be Happier • Let Us Love • Medley: Harlem/Cold Baloney			
4/13/74	7	34		4 **+'Justments**	67	$15	Sussex 8032
				You *[15]* • **The Same Love That Made Me Laugh** *[10]* • Stories • Green Grass • Ruby Lee • **Heartbreak Road** *[13]* • Can We Pretend • Liza • Make A Smile For Me • Railroad Man			
5/24/75	33	5		5 **The Best Of Bill Withers** [G]	182	$15	Sussex 8037
11/8/75+	7	19		6 **Making Music**	81	$12	Columbia 33704
				I Wish You Well *[54]* • The Best You Can • **Make Love To Your Mind** *[10]* • I Love You Dawn • She's Lonely • Sometimes A Song • Paint Your Pretty Picture • Family Table • Don't You Want To Stay? • Hello Like Before			
10/30/76	41	4		7 **Naked & Warm**	169	$12	Columbia 34327
11/5/77+	16	23	●	8 **Menagerie**	39	$12	Columbia 34903
3/10/79	50	5		9 **'Bout Love**	134	$10	Columbia 35596
7/18/81	58	2		10 **Bill Withers' Greatest Hits** [G]	183	$10	Columbia 37199
5/18/85	42	25		11 **Watching You Watching Me**	143	$8	Columbia 39887
				WITHERSPOON, Jimmy '75			
				Born on 8/8/23 in Gurdon, Arkansas. Died on 9/18/97 (age 74). Blues singer/bassist.			
2/15/75	26	6		1 **Love Is A Five Letter Word**	176	$12	Capitol 11360
2/21/76	57	3		2 **Spoonful**		$12	Blue Note 534
				WOLFER, Bill '83			
				Born in Cheyenne, Wyoming. Singer/songwriter/keyboardist.			
1/15/83	50	11		**Wolf**		$10	Constellation 60187
	★53★			**WOMACK, Bobby** '82			
				Born on 3/4/44 in Cleveland. Singer/songwriter/guitarist. Toured as guitarist with **Sam Cooke**. Married for a time to Cooke's widow, Barbara. Bobby's brother, Cecil and Sam Cooke's daughter, Linda recorded as **Womack & Womack**. Nicknamed "The Preacher."			
				1)The Poet 2)The Poet II 3)So Many Rivers			
1/18/69	34	7		1 **Fly Me To The Moon**	174	$30	Minit 24014
5/9/70	44	3		2 **My Prescription**		$30	Minit 24027
3/13/71	13	16		3 **The Womack "Live"** [L]	188	$15	Liberty 7645
11/20/71+	7	40		4 **Communication**	83	$12	United Artists 5539
				Communication *[40]* • Come L'Amore • Fire And Rain • (If You Don't Want My Love) Give It Back • (They Long To Be) Close To You • Everything Is Beautiful • **That's The Way I Feel About Cha** *[2]* • Yield Not To Temptation			
7/1/72	7	42		5 **Understanding**	43	$12	United Artists 5577
				I Can Understand It • **Woman's Gotta Have It** *[1]* • And I Love Her • Got To Get You Back • Simple Man • Ruby Dean • Thing Called Love • **Sweet Caroline (Good Times Never Seemed So Good)** *[16]* • Harry Hippie *[8]*			
2/3/73	6	20		6 **Across 110th Street** [S]	50	$12	United Artists 5525
				Across 110th Street *[19]* • Harlem Clavinette • If You Don't Want My Love • Hang On In There • Quicksand • Harlem Love Theme • Do It Right • Hang On In There • If You Don't Want My Love			
7/14/73	6	21		7 **Facts Of Life**	37	$12	United Artists 043
				Nobody Wants You When You're Down And Out *[2]* • **I'm Through Trying To Prove My Love To You** *[80]* • If You Can't Give Her Love Give Her Up • That's Heaven To Me • Medley: Holdin' On To My Baby's Love/Nobody • Medley: Fact Of Life/He'll Be There When The Sun Goes Down • Can't Stop A Man In Love • The Look Of Love • Natural Man • All Along The Watchtower			
2/9/74	5	26		8 **Lookin' For A Love Again**	85	$12	United Artists 199
				Lookin' For A Love *[1]* • I Don't Wanna Be Hurt By Ya Love Again • Doing It My Way • Let It Hang Out • Point Of No Return • **You're Welcome, Stop On By** *[5]* • You're Messing Up A Good Thing • Don't Let Me Down • Copper Kettle • There's One Thing That Beats Failing			
12/21/74+	30	8		9 **Bobby Womack's Greatest Hits** [G]	142	$12	United Artists 346
5/10/75	20	6		10 **I Don't Know What The World Is Coming To**	126	$12	United Artists 353
11/29/75+	40	15		11 **Safety Zone**	147	$12	United Artists 544
7/14/79	55	7		12 **Roads Of Life**	206	$10	Arista 4222
11/14/81+	❶⁵	37		13 **The Poet**	29	$10	Beverly Glen 10000
				So Many Sides Of You • Lay Some Lovin' On Me • **Secrets** *[55]* • Just My Imagination • Stand Up • Games • If You Think You're Lonely Now *[3]* • Where Do We Go From Here *[26]*			
3/31/84	5	29		14 **The Poet II**	60	$10	Beverly Glen 10003
				Love Has Finally Come At Last *[3]* • It Takes A Lot Of Strength To Say Goodbye *[76]* • Through The Eyes Of A Child • Surprise Surprise • Tryin' To Get Over You • **Tell Me Why** *[54]* • Who's Foolin' Who • I Wish I Had Someone To Go Home To • American Dream			
6/1/85	59	5		15 **Someday We'll All Be Free**	207	$10	Beverly Glen 10006
9/21/85	5	26		16 **So Many Rivers**	66	$8	MCA 5617
				I Wish He Didn't Trust Me So Much *[2]* • So Baby, Don't Leave Home Without It • So Many Rivers • Got To Be With You Tonight • Gypsy Woman • Whatever Happened To The Times? • **Let Me Kiss It Where It Hurts** *[50]* • Only Survivor • That's Where It's At • Check It Out			
2/7/87	68	4		17 **Womagic**		$8	MCA 5899
10/1/94	91	4		18 **Resurrection**		$8	Continuum 19401

DEBUT	PEAK	WKS	Gold	Album Title	Pop #	$	Label & Number

WOMACK & WOMACK   '84

Duo of husband-and-wife Linda and Cecil Womack. Linda (daughter of **Sam Cooke**) was born in 1952 in Chicago. Cecil (brother of **Bobby Womack**) was born in 1947 in Cleveland.

3/10/84	34	26		1 Love Wars		$8	Elektra 60293
7/13/85	51	6		2 Radio M.U.S.C. Man..		$8	Elektra 60406
9/3/88	74	7		3 Conscience		$8	Island 90915

WONDER, Stevie ★4★   '76

Born Steveland Morris on 5/13/50 in Saginaw, Michigan. Singer/songwriter/multi-instrumentalist. Blind since birth. Signed to Motown in 1960, did backup work. First recorded in 1962, named "**Little Stevie Wonder**" by Berry Gordy. Married to **Syreeta** Wright from 1970-72. Near-fatal auto accident on 8/16/73. Appeared in the movies *Bikini Beach* and *Muscle Beach Party*. Inducted into the Rock and Roll Hall of Fame in 1989. Won Grammy's Lifetime Achievement Award in 1996.

1)*Songs In The Key Of Life* 2)*Hotter Than July* 3)*In Square Circle* 4)*Fulfillingness' First Finale* 5)*Characters*

| 5/28/66 | **2**[1] | 24 | | 1 **Up-Tight Everything's Alright** | 33 | $30 | Tamla 268 |

Love A Go Go • Hold Me • **Blowin In The Wind** *[1]* • **Nothing's Too Good For My Baby** *[4]* • Teach Me Tonight • **Uptight (Everything's Alright)** *[1]* • Ain't That Asking For Trouble • I Want My Baby Back • Pretty Little Angel • Music Talk • Contract On Love • **With A Child's Heart** *[8]*

| 1/21/67 | **8** | 12 | | 2 **Down To Earth** | 92 | $25 | Tamla 272 |

A Place In The Sun *[3]* • Bang Bang • Down To Earth • Thank You Love • Be Cool, Be Calm (And Keep Yourself Together) • Sylvia • My World Is Empty Without You • The Lonesome Road • Angel Baby (Don't You Ever Leave Me) • Mr. Tambourine Man • Sixteen Tons • **Hey Love** *[9]*

| 9/30/67 | **7** | 13 | | 3 **I Was Made To Love Her** | 45 | $25 | Tamla 279 |

I Was Made To Love Her *[1]* • Send Me Some Lovin' • I'd Cry • Everybody Needs Somebody (I Need You) • Respect • My Girl • Baby Don't You Do It • A Fool For You • Can I Get A Witness • I Pity The Fool • Please, Please, Please • Every Time I See You I Go Wild

| 5/4/68 | **6** | 37 | | 4 **Greatest Hits** | [G] | 37 | $20 | Tamla 282 |

Uptight (Everything's Alright) *[1]* • I'm Wondering *[4]* • I Was Made To Love Her *[1]* • Hey Love *[9]* • Blowin In The Wind *[1]* • A Place In The Sun *[3]* • Contract On Love • Workout Stevie, Workout *[33]* • Fingertips *[1]* • Castles In The Sand *[52]* • Hey Harmonica Man *[29]* • Nothing's Too Good For My Baby *[4]*

| 1/11/69 | **4** | 19 | | 5 **For Once In My Life** | 50 | $20 | Tamla 291 |

For Once In My Life *[2]* • Shoo-Be-Doo-Be-Doo-Da-Day *[1]* • You Met Your Match *[2]* • I Wanna Make Her Love Me • I'm More Than Happy (I'm Satisfied) • I Don't Know Why • Sunny • I'd Be A Fool Right Now • Ain't No Lovin' • God Bless The Child • Do I Love Her • The House On The Hill

| 1/25/69 | **37** | 2 | | 6 **Eivets Rednow** | [I] | $30 | Gordy 932 |
| 10/11/69 | **3** | 26 | | 7 **My Cherie Amour** | 34 | $20 | Tamla 296 |

My Cherie Amour *[4]* • Hello Young Lovers • At Last • Light My Fire • The Shadow Of Your Smile • You And Me • Pearl • Somebody Knows, Somebody Cares • **Yester-Me, Yester-You, Yesterday** *[5]* • Angie Girl • Give Your Love • I've Got You

| 4/11/70 | **16** | 14 | | 8 **Stevie Wonder Live** | [L] | 81 | $20 | Tamla 298 |
| 9/5/70 | **7** | 23 | | 9 **Signed Sealed & Delivered** | 25 | $20 | Tamla 304 |

Never Had A Dream Come True *[11]* • We Can Work It Out *[3]* • Signed, Sealed, Delivered I'm Yours *[1]* • Heaven Help Us All *[2]* • You Can't Judge A Book By It's Cover • Sugar • Don't Wonder Why • Anything You Want Me To Do • I Can't Let My Heaven Walk Away • Joy (Takes Over Me) • I Gotta Have A Song • Something To Say

| 5/8/71 | **7** | 28 | | 10 **Where I'm Coming From** | 62 | $20 | Tamla 308 |

Look Around • Do Yourself A Favor • Think Of Me As Your Soldier • Something Out Of The Blue • If You Really Love Me *[4]* • I Wanna Talk To You • Take Up A Course In Happiness • Never Dreamed You'd Leave In Summer • Sunshine In Their Eyes

| 11/27/71 | **10** | 12 | | 11 **Stevie Wonder's Greatest Hits, Vol. 2** | [G] | 69 | $20 | Tamla 313 |

Shoo-Be-Doo-Be-Doo-Da-Day *[1]* • Signed, Sealed, Delivered I'm Yours *[1]* • If You Really Love Me *[4]* • For Once In My Life *[2]* • We Can Work It Out *[3]* • You Met Your Match *[2]* • Never Had A Dream Come True *[11]* • Yester-Me, Yester-You, Yesterday *[5]* • My Cherie Amour *[4]* • Never Dreamed You'd Leave In Summer • **Travlin Man** *[31]* • Heaven Help Us All *[2]*

| 4/1/72 | **6** | 31 | | 12 **Music Of My Mind** | 21 | $20 | Tamla 314 |

Love Having You Around • **Superwoman (Where Were You When I Needed You)** *[13]* • I Love Every Little Thing About You • Sweet Little Girl • Happier Than The Morning Sun • Girl Blue • Seems So Long • **Keep On Running** *[36]* • Evil

| 11/25/72+ | **❶**[3] | 40 | | 13 **Talking Book** | 3 | $15 | Tamla 319 |

You Are The Sunshine Of My Life *[3]* • Maybe Your Baby • You And I • Tuesday Heartbreak • You've Got It Bad Girl • **Superstition** *[1]* • Big Brother • Blame It On The Sun • Lookin' For Another Pure Love • I Believe (When I Fall In Love It Will Be Forever)

| 8/18/73 | **❶**[2] | 51 | | 14 **Innervisions** | 4 | $15 | Tamla 326 |

Too High • Visions • **Living For The City** *[1]* • Golden Lady • Higher Ground *[1]* • Jesus Children Of America • All In Love Is Fair • **Don't You Worry 'Bout A Thing** *[2]* • He's Misstra Know-It-All

| 8/10/74 | **❶**[8] | 39 | | 15 **Fulfillingness' First Finale** | 1[2] | $15 | Tamla 332 |

Smile Please • Heaven Is 10 Zillion Light Years Away • Too Shy To Say • **Boogie On Reggae Woman** *[1]* • Creepin' • You Haven't Done Nothin *[1]* • It Ain't No Use • They Won't Go When I Go • Bird Of Beauty • Please Don't Go

| 10/16/76 | **❶**[20] | 48 | | 16 **Songs In The Key Of Life** | 1[14] | $20 | Tamla 340 [2] |

Love's In Need Of Love Today • Have A Talk With God • Village Ghetto Land • Contusion • **Sir Duke** *[1]* • **I Wish** *[1]* • Knocks Me Off My Feet • Pastime Paradise • Summer Soft • Ordinary Pain • Isn't She Lovely • Joy Inside My Tears • Black Man • Ngiculela-Es Una Historia - I Am Singing • If It's Magic • **As** *[36]* • **Another Star** *[18]*

| 1/7/78 | **15** | 10 | | 17 **Looking Back** | [K] | 34 | $25 | Motown 804 [3] |
| 12/1/79 | **4** | 19 | | 18 **Journey Through The Secret Life Of Plants** | 4 | $15 | Tamla 371 [2] |

Earth's Creation • The First Garden • Voyage To India • Same Old Story • Venus' Flytrap And The Bug • Ai No, Sono • Seasons • Power Flower • **Send One Your Love** *[5]* • Race Babbling *[56]* • Black Orchid • Ecclesiastes • Kesse Ye Lolo De Ye • Come Back As A Flower • Medley: A Seed's A Star/Tree • The Secret Life Of Plants • Tree

| 11/15/80 | **❶**[13] | 44 | ▲ | 19 **Hotter Than July** | 3 | $12 | Tamla 373 |

Did I Hear You Say You Love Me *[74]* • All I Do • Rocket Love • **I Ain't Gonna Stand For It** *[4]* • As If You Read My Mind • **Master Blaster (Jammin')** *[1]* • Do Like You • Cash In Your Face • **Lately** *[29]* • Happy Birthday *[70]*

DEBUT	PEAK	WKS	Gold	Album Title	Pop #	$	Label & Number

WONDER, Stevie — Cont'd

DEBUT	PEAK	WKS	Gold	Album Title	Pop #	$	Label & Number
5/29/82	❶³	38	●	20 Stevie Wonder's Original Musiquarium I	4	$15	Tamla 6002 [2]

Superstition [1] • You Haven't Done Nothin [1] • Living For The City [1] • Front Line • Superwoman (Where Were You When I Needed You) [13] • Send One Your Love [5] • You Are The Sunshine Of My Life [1] • Ribbon In The Sky [10] • Higher Ground [1] • Sir Duke [!1] • Master Blaster (Jammin') [1] • Boogie On Reggae Woman [1] • That Girl [1] • I Wish [1] • Isn't She Lovely • Do I Do [2]

| 9/29/84 | ❶⁴ | 38 | ▲ | 21 The Woman in Red [S] | 4 | $10 | Motown 6108 |

The Woman In Red • It's You • It's More Than You • I Just Called To Say I Love You [1] • Love Light In Flight [4] • Moments Aren't Moments • Weakness • Don't Drive Drunk

| 10/19/85 | ❶¹² | 52 | ▲² | 22 In Square Circle | 5 | $10 | Tamla 6134 |

Part-Time Lover [1] • I Love You Too Much • Whereabouts • Stranger On The Shore Of Love • Never In Your Sun • Spiritual Walkers • Land Of La La [19] • Go Home [2] • Overjoyed [8] • It's Wrong (Apartheid)

| 12/12/87 | ❶⁷ | 48 | ▲ | 23 Characters | 17 | $8 | Motown 6248 |

You Will Know [1] • Dark 'N' Lovely • In Your Corner • With Each Beat Of My Heart [28] • One Of A Kind • Skeletons [1] • Get It [4] • Galaxy Paradise • Cryin' Through The Night • Free

| 6/22/91 | ❶² | 41 | ● | 24 Music From The Movie Jungle Fever [S] | 24 | $8 | Motown 6291 |

Fun Day [6] • Queen In The Black • These Three Words [7] • Each Other's Throat • If She Breaks Your Heart • Gotta Have You [3] • Make Sure You're Sure • Jungle Fever • I Go Sailing • Chemical Love • Lighting Up The Candles

| 4/8/95 | 2¹ | 20 | ● | 25 Conversation Peace | 16 | $8 | Motown 0238 |

Rain Your Love Down • Edge Of Eternity • Taboo To Love • Take The Time Out • I'm New • My Love Is With You • Treat Myself [92] • Tomorrow Robins Will Sing [60] • Sensuous Whisper • For Your Love [11] • Cold Chill • Sorry • Conversation Peace

| 12/9/95+ | 88 | 2 | | 26 Natural Wonder ....[L] | | $8 | Motown 0546 |

recorded in Osaka, Japan and Tel Aviv, Israel

| 1/4/97 | 100 | 1 | | 27 Song Review - A Greatest Hits Collection ....[G] | | $12 | Motown 0767 [2] |

WOODS, Rev. Maceo   '70

Born in Chicago. Choir director/pianist for the Christian Tabernacle Baptist Church in Chicago.

| 1/10/70 | 45 | 3 | | Hello Sunshine | | $15 | Volt 6004 |

WOODS, Stevie   '82

Born in Columbus, Ohio. Male singer/songwriter. Son of Rusty Bryant.

| 12/12/81+ | 44 | 9 | | Take Me To Your Heaven .... | 153 | $10 | Cotillion 5229 |

WORLD CLASS WRECKIN CRU, The   '88

Rap/funk group from Los Angeles: Alonzo Williams, Andre "Dr. Dre" Young, Antoine "Yella" Carraby, Shakespeare and Michelle "Michel'le" Toussant.

| 5/21/88 | 26 | 19 | | 1 Turn Off The Lights in the Fast Lane .... | | $10 | Techno Kut 1001 |

LONZO & THE WORLD CLASS WRECKIN KRU

| 12/15/90+ | 77 | 13 | | 2 Phases In Life .... | | $8 | SOH 7004 |

WORRELL, Bernie   '79

Born on 4/19/44 in Long Branch, New Jersey. Singer/keyboardist. Member of Parliament.

| 3/10/79 | 59 | 4 | | All The Woo In The World .... | | $10 | Arista 4209 |

WRECKX-N-EFFECT   '92

Male rap trio: Aqil Davidson, Markell Riley and Brandon Mitchell. Riley is brother of Guy member/prolific producer Teddy Riley. Mitchell was shot to death in 1990.

| 9/30/89+ | 16 | 32 | | 1 Wrecks-N-Effect .... | 103 | $8 | Motown 6281 |
| 12/12/92 | 6 | 30 | ▲ | 2 Hard Or Smooth | 9 | $8 | MCA 10566 |

Rump Shaker [3] • New Jack Swing II • Wreckx Shop [46] • Knock-N-Boots [71] • Here We Come • Tell Me How You Feel • My Cutie [75] • Wreckx-N-Effect • Ez Come Ez Go (What Goes Up Must Come Down) • Hard (Short) • Smooth (Short)

WRIGHT, Bernard   '81

Born in 1965 in New York City. Singer/keyboardist.

3/21/81	23	24		1 'Nard	116	$10	GRP 5011
12/3/83	58	5		2 Funky Beat		$10	Arista 8103
11/30/85	25	27		3 Mr. Wright		$10	Manhattan 53014

WRIGHT, Betty   '78

Born on 12/21/53 in Miami. Female singer.

3/11/72	32	5		1 I Love The Way You Love	123	$15	Alston 388
8/11/73	54	3		2 Hard To Stop		$15	Alston 7026
6/17/78	6	40		3 Betty Wright Live [L]	26	$12	Alston 4408

Lovin' Is Really My Game • Tonight Is The Night [11] • A Song For You • Medley: Clean Up Woman/Pillow Talk/You Got The Love/Mr. Melody/Midnight At The Oasis/Me And Mrs. Jones/(You Are My) Sunshine/Let's Get Married Today • You Can't See For Lookin' • Where Is The Love

6/2/79	48	17		4 Betty Travelin' In The Wright Circle	138	$12	Alston 4410
7/18/81	54	5		5 Betty Wright		$10	Epic 36879
4/23/83	41	8		6 Wright Back At You		$10	Epic 38558
5/7/88	28	30		7 Mother Wit	127	$10	Ms. B 3301
3/18/89	51	10		8 4U2NJOY		$10	Ms. B 3308

WRIGHT, Charles, And The Watts 103rd Street Rhythm Band   '70

Born in 1942 in Clarksdale, Mississippi. Singer/songwriter/pianist/guitarist.

| 5/3/69 | 40 | 6 | | 1 Together .... | 140 | $15 | Warner 1761 |
| 10/18/69 | 42 | 5 | | 2 In The Jungle, Babe .... | 145 | $15 | Warner 1801 |

THE WATTS 103RD STREET RHYTHM BAND (above 2)

7/4/70	27	20		3 Express Yourself	182	$12	Warner 1864
6/12/71	39	5		4 You're So Beautiful	147	$12	Warner 1904
1/5/74	45	9		5 Doin' What Comes Naturally		$12	Dunhill/ABC 50162

DEBUT	PEAK	WKS	Gold	Album Title	Pop #	$	Label & Number

WRIGHT, O.V.   **'65**
Born Overton Vertis Wright on 10/9/39 in Leno, Tennessee. Died of heart failure on 11/16/80 (age 41). Male singer.

| 7/24/65 | 10 | 2 | | 1 **(If It Is) Only For Tonight** | | $100 | Back Beat 61 |

(If It Is) Only For Tonight • Why Don't You Believe Me • Can't Find True Love • Motherless Child • You've Been Crying • I Could Write A Book (About Heartache) • **You're Gonna Make Me Cry** *[6]* • Wish I Were That Boy • Monkey Dog • Don't Want To Sit Down • Everybody Knows (The River Song) • I Can't Believe (You've Got The Nerve To Cry)

| 8/13/77 | 40 | 14 | | 2 Into Something (Can't Shake Loose) | | $25 | Hi 6001 |

WU-TANG CLAN   **'97**
Rap group from Staten Island, New York: Gary Grice (**"Genius/GZA"**), Clifford Smith (**"Method Man"**), Russell Jones (**"Ol Dirty Bastard"**), Corey Woods (**"Raekwon"**), Jason Hunter (**"Inspectah Deck"**), Dennis Coles (**"Ghostface Killah"**), Lamont Hawkins (**"U-God"**), Robert Diggs (**"RZA"**) and Elgin Turner (**"Masta Killa"**). Diggs was also a member of **Gravediggaz**.

| 11/27/93+ | 8 | 140 | ▲ | 1 **Enter The Wu-Tang (36 Chambers)** | 41 | $8 | Loud/RCA 66336 |

Bring Da Ruckus • Shame On A Nigga • Clan In Da Front • Wu-Tang: 7th Chamber • **Can It Be All So Simple** *[82]* • Da Mystery Of Chessboxin' • Wu-Tang Clan Ain't Nuthing Ta F' Wit • **C.R.E.A.M. (Cash Rules Everything Around Me)** *[32]* • **Method Man** *[40]* • **Protect Ya Neck** *[86]* • Tearz

| 6/21/97 | ❶² | 43 | ▲⁴ | 2 **Wu-Tang Forever** | 1¹ | $12 | Loud/RCA 66905 [2] |

Wu-Revolution • Reunited • For Heavens Sake • Medley: Cash Still Rules/Scary Hours • Visionz • As High As Wu-Tang Get • Severe Punishment • Older Gods • Maria • A Better Tomorrow • **It's Yourz** *[75]* • Triumph • Impossible • Little Ghetto Boys • Deadly Melody • The City • The Projects • Bells Of War • The M.G.M. • Dog Shit • Duck Seazon • Hellz Wind Staff • Heaterz • Black Shampoo • Second Coming

WU-TANG KILLA BEES   **'98**
Rap group from New York City. Features **Wu-Tang Clan** members **RZA**, **Method Man**, **Ghostface Killah**, **Raekwon**, Inspectah Deck and Masta Killa, with **Cappadonna**, **Killarmy** and **Sunz Of Man**.

| 8/8/98 | 3 | 11 | ● | **The Swarm** | 4 | $8 | Wu-Tang 50013 |

The Legacy • Concrete Jungle • Co-Defendant • S.O.S. • Execute Them • Bronx War Stories • And Justice For All • Punishment • Bastards • On The Strength • Cobra Clutch • Never Again • Where Was Heaven • '97 Mentality • Fatal Sting

WYCOFF, Michael   **'82**
Born in Torrance, California. Singer/keyboardist.

| 3/27/82 | 54 | 13 | | 1 **Love Conquers All** | | $10 | RCA Victor 8004 |
| 10/22/83 | 54 | 6 | | 2 On The Line | | $10 | RCA Victor 4563 |

WYNNE, Philippé   **'77**
Born on 4/3/41 in Cincinnati. Died of a heart attack on 7/13/84 (age 43). Lead singer of the **Spinners** from 1971-77.

| 11/12/77 | 58 | 3 | | **Starting All Over** | | $12 | Cotillion 9920 |

X

XAVIER   **'82**
Eight-member group. Lead vocals by Xavier Smith and Ayanna Little.

| 4/10/82 | 16 | 14 | | **Point Of Pleasure** | 129 | $8 | Liberty 51116 |

X-CLAN   **'90**
Rap group from Brooklyn, New York: Lumumba Carson (**"Professor X"**), Jason Hunter (**"Brother J"**), Sugar Shaft and Paradise. Sugar Shaft died of AIDS on 9/1/95 (age 25).

| 5/19/90 | 11 | 40 | | 1 **To The East, Blackwards** | 97 | $8 | 4th & B'way 444019 |
| 6/6/92 | 11 | 22 | | 2 Xodus-The New Testament | 31 | $8 | Polydor 513225 |

XSCAPE   **'95**
Female vocal group from Atlanta: sisters LaTocha and Tamika Scott, with Kandi Burruss and Tameka Cottle.

| 10/30/93 | 3 | 42 | ▲ | 1 **Hummin' Comin' At 'Cha** | 17 | $8 | So So Def 57107 |

Hummin' Comin' At 'Cha • **Just Kickin' It** *[1]* • Pumpin' • Let Me Know • **Understanding** *[1]* • W.S.S. Deez Nuts • With You • Is My Living In Vain • **Love On My Mind** *[16]* • Tonight *[59]*

| 8/5/95 | 3 | 53 | ▲ | 2 **Off The Hook** | 23 | $8 | So So Def 67022 |

Do Your Thang • **Feels So Good** *[8]* • Hard To Say Goodbye • **Can't Hang** *[16]* • **Who Can I Run To?** *[1]* • Hip Hop Barber Shop Request Line • **Do You Want To** *[9]* • What Can I Do • Do Like Lovers Do • Work Me Slow • Love's A Funny Thing • Keep It On The Real

| 5/30/98 | 6 | 50 | ▲ | 3 **Traces Of My Lipstick** | 28 | $8 | So So Def 68042 |

All About Me • **My Little Secret** *[2]* • **Softest Place On Earth** *[28]* • Do You Know • One Of Those Love Songs • **The Arms Of The One Who Loves You** *[4]* • I Will • Your Eyes • All I Need • Am I Dreamin' • The Runaround • Hold On

XZIBIT   **'98**
Born in Detroit; raised in New Mexico. Male rapper.

| 11/2/96 | 22 | 16 | | 1 At The Speed Of Life | 74 | $8 | Loud/RCA 66816 |
| 9/12/98 | 14 | 8 | | 2 40 Dayz & 40 Nightz | 58 | $8 | Loud/RCA 67578 |

Y

YANKOVIC, "Weird Al"   **'84**
Born on 10/24/59 in Lynwood, California. Novelty singer/accordionist. Specializes in song parodies. Starred in the movie *UHF*.

| 4/14/84 | 46 | 6 | ▲ | **"Weird Al" Yankovic In 3-D** | [N] 17 | $8 | Rock 'n' Roll 39221 |

YARBROUGH & PEOPLES   '81
Male-female vocal duo from Dallas: Cavin Yarbrough and Alisa Peoples.

| 12/27/80+ | ❶² | 30 | ● | 1 The Two Of Us | 16 | $10 | Mercury 3834 |

Don't Stop The Music [1] • Crazy • **Third Degree** [74] • Easy Tonight • I Want You Back Again • Come To Me • You're My Song • Two Of Us • I Believe I'm Falling In Love

| 3/12/83 | 25 | 12 | | 2 Heartbeats .... | | $8 | Total Exp. 3003 |
| 4/14/84 | 6 | 31 | | 3 Be A Winner | 90 | $8 | Total Exp. 5700 |

Don't Waste Your Time [1] • I'm Ready To Jam • I'll Be There • I Only Love You • **Be A Winner** [20] • The Power • Who Said That • Let Me Have It (From The Start) • I Gave My All (To You)

| 1/25/86 | 13 | 34 | | 4 Guilty .... | | $8 | Total Exp. 5715 |

YAZOO   '82
British electronic pop duo: Alison Moyet (vocals) and Vince Clarke (keyboards).

| 10/2/82 | 37 | 10 | ▲ | Upstairs At Eric's .... | 92 | $8 | Sire 23737 |

YELLA   '96
Born Antoine Carraby in Compton, California. Male rapper. Member of **N.W.A.**

| 4/13/96 | 23 | 6 | | One Mo Nigga Ta Go.. | 82 | $8 | Street Life 75488 |

YELLOW MAGIC ORCHESTRA   '80
Electronic trio from Japan: Ryuichi Sakamoto, Yukihiro Takahashi and Haruomi Hosono.

| 1/19/80 | 37 | 22 | | Yellow Magic Orchestra .... | 81 | $8 | Horizon 736 |

Y?N-VEE   '94
Pronounced: why envy. Female vocal group: Natasha Walker, Tescia Harris, Nicole Chaney and Yenan Ragsdale. Group appeared in the movie *Phat Beach*.

| 11/5/94 | 75 | 3 | | Y?N-Vee .... | | $8 | PMP/RAL 523585 |

YOUNG, Val   '86
Born in Detroit. Female singer.

| 11/16/85+ | 39 | 27 | | Seduction .... | | $8 | Gordy 6147 |

YOUNG AND COMPANY   '81
Group from New Jersey: brothers William, Michael and Kenny Young (vocals), with Jackie Thomas (guitar), Buddy Hank (bass) and Dave Reyes (drums).

| 2/21/81 | 58 | 8 | | I Like What You're Doing To Me .... | | $10 | Brunswick 754224 |

YOUNG & RESTLESS   '90
Male rap duo from Miami: Charles Trahan and Leonerist Johnson.

| 3/24/90 | 28 | 22 | | Something To Get You Hyped .... | 104 | $8 | Pandisc 8809 |

YOUNG BLACK TEENAGERS   '93
White rap group from New York City: Firstborn, Kamron, A.T.A. and DJ Skribble.

| 2/20/93 | 56 | 14 | | Dead Enz Kidz Doin' Lifetime Bidz .... | 158 | $8 | Soul 10733 |

YOUNG BLEED   '98
Born in New Orleans. Male rapper. Member of **Concentration Camp II.**

| 2/7/98 | ❶¹ | 26 | ● | All I Have In This World, Are...My Balls And My Word | 10 | $8 | No Limit 50738 |

Keep It Real • Bring The Noise • An Offer U Can't Refuse • The Day They Make Me Boss • Mo Money • Pull It Off • Times So Hard • How Ya Do Dat • Better Than Last Time • Lil Poppa Got A Brand New Bag • Confedi • Da Last Outlaw • Ghostrider • We Don't Stop

YOUNGBLOOD, Sydney   '90
Born Sydney Ford in San Antonio, Texas.

| 11/10/90 | 72 | 5 | | Sydney Youngblood .... | 185 | $8 | Arista 8651 |

YOUNG HEARTS   '69
Vocal group from Los Angeles: Ronald Preyer, Charles Ingersoll, Earl Carter and James Moore.

| 5/31/69 | 13 | 11 | | 1 Sweet Soul Shakin .... | | $20 | Minit 24016 |
| 2/16/74 | 42 | 11 | | 2 Do You Have The Time .... | | $12 | 20th Century 427 |

YOUNG-HOLT UNLIMITED   '69
Instrumental trio from Chicago: Eldee Young (bass), Isaac Holt (drums; both of the **Ramsey Lewis Trio**) and Don Walker (piano). Walker left in 1968.

| 1/14/67 | 10 | 10 | | 1 Wack Wack | [I] 132 | $20 | Brunswick 754121 |

YOUNG-HOLT TRIO
Monday, Monday • Strangers In The Night • Song For My Father • Girl Talk • **Wack Wack** [12] • Sunny • Red Sails In The Sunset • You Know That I Love You • Yesterday • This Little Light Of Mine

| 1/4/69 | 2² | 27 | | 2 Soulful Strut | [I] 9 | $15 | Brunswick 754144 |

Who's Making Love • Please Sunrise, Please • Be By My Side • What Now My Love • Baby Your Light Is Out • **Soulful Strut** [3] • Just Ain't No Love • Little Green Apples • Funky Is As Funky Does • Love Makes A Woman • Ain't There Something Money Can't Buy

YOUNG LAY   '96
Born Lathan Williams in 1975 in San Leandro, California. Male rapper.

| 6/22/96 | 42 | 4 | | Black 'N Dangerous .... | | $8 | Atlantic 82843 |

YOUNG MC   '89
Born Marvin Young on 5/10/67 in London; raised in Queens, New York. Male rapper.

| 9/30/89 | 8 | 37 | ▲ | 1 Stone Cold Rhymin' | 9 | $8 | Delicious Vinyl 91309 |

I Come Off [52] • **Principal's Office** [51] • Bust A Move [9] • Non Stop • Fastest Rhyme • My Name Is Young • Know How • Roll With The Punches • I Let 'Em Know • Pick Up The Pace • Got More Rhymes • Stone Cold Buggin' • Just Say No

| 9/7/91 | 61 | 9 | ● | 2 Brainstorm .... | 66 | $8 | Capitol 96337 |

YOUNG RASCALS — see RASCALS

YOURS TRULY   '91
Male vocal trio: Jerry Brinson, Ricky Jones and Terence.

| 9/21/91 | 91 | 5 | | Truly Yours .... | | $8 | Motown 6323 |

DEBUT	PEAK	WKS	Gold	Album Title	Pop #	$	Label & Number

YO-YO   '91
Born Yolanda Whitaker on 8/4/71 in Los Angeles. Female rapper.

4/20/91	5	28		1 **Make Way For The Motherlode**	74	$8	EastWest 91605

Stand Up For Your Rights • Stompin' Tha 90's • **You Can't Play With My Yo-Yo** [11] • Cube Gets Played • Put A Lid On It • What Can I Do? • Dedication • Sisterland • The I.B.W.C. National Anthem • Make Way For The Motherlode • Tonight's The Night • I Got Played • Girl, Don't Be No Fool • **Ain't Nobody Better** [30] • More Of What Can I Do

7/11/92	32	14		2 Black Pearl	145	$8	EastWest 92120
7/10/93	21	20		3 You Better Ask Somebody	107	$8	EastWest 92252
11/16/96	46	3		4 Total Control		$8	EastWest 61898

YZ   '90
Born Anthony Hill in Paterson, New Jersey. Male rapper.

6/16/90	47	15		1 Sons Of The Father		$8	Tuff City 0569
4/27/91	81	6		2 EP [M]		$6	Tuff City 8065
11/27/93	78	2		3 The Ghetto's Been Good To Me		$8	Livin' Large 3017

Z

ZAGER, Michael, Band   '78
Born in 1943 in Jersey City, New Jersey. Keyboardist/producer.

5/6/78	56	2		Let's All Chant	120	$10	Private Stock 7013

★146★   **ZAPP**   '80
Funk group from Dayton, Ohio: brothers **Roger** (vocals, guitar), Larry (percussion), Tony (bass) and Lester (drums) Troutman. Roger was shot to death by Larry in a murder-suicide on 4/25/99. Roger was age 47 and Larry was age 54.

9/20/80	❶²	30	●	1 **Zapp**	19	$10	Warner 3463

More Bounce To The Ounce [2] • Freedom • Brand New Player • Funky Bounce • Be Alright [26] • Coming Home

8/7/82	2⁴	36	●	2 **Zapp II**	25	$8	Warner 23583

Dance Floor [1] • Playin' Kinda Ruff • **Doo Wa Ditty (Blow That Thing)** [10] • Do You Really Want An Answer? • Come On • A Touch Of Jazz

9/3/83	9	31		3 **Zapp III**	39	$8	Warner 23875

Heartbreaker [15] • **I Can Make You Dance** [4] • Play Some Blues • **Spend My Whole Life** [77] • We Need The Buck • Tut-Tut (Jazz) • Doo Wa Ditty (Blow That Thing)

11/16/85+	8	33	●	4 **The New Zapp IV U**	110	$8	Warner 25327

It Doesn't Really Matter [41] • Computer Love [8] • Itchin' For Your Twitchin' [81] • Radio People • I Only Have Eyes For You • Rock 'N' Roll • Cas-Ta-Spellome • Make Me Feel Good • Ja Ready To Rock

10/7/89	34	15		5 Zapp V	154	$8	Reprise 25807
11/13/93	9	103	▲	6 **All The Greatest Hits** [G]	39	$8	Reprise 45143

ZAPP & ROGER
More Bounce To The Ounce [2] • Be Alright [26] • I Heard It Through The Grapevine [1] • So Ruff, So Tuff • Do It Roger [24] • Dance Floor [1] • Doo Wa Ditty (Blow That Thing) [10] • I Can Make You Dance [4] • Heartbreaker [15] • In The Mix [10] • Midnight Hour • Computer Love [8] • Night And Day • I Want To Be Your Man [1] • Curiosity • Slow And Easy [18] • Mega Medley [30]

12/7/96	93	3		7 The Compilation: Greatest Hits II And More [G]		$8	Reprise 46243

ROGER & ZAPP

ZHANÉ   '94
Pronounced: Jah-Nay. Female vocal duo from Philadelphia: Reneé Neufville and Jean Norris.

2/26/94	8	40	▲	1 **Pronounced Jah-Nay**	37	$8	Motown 6369

Hey Mr. D.J. [3] • Vibe [33] • **Sending My Love** [5] • Sweet Taste Of Love • Changes • **You're Sorry Now** [38] • Love Me Today • Off My Mind • La, La, La • Groove Thang [2] • For A Reason

5/10/97	8	21		2 **Saturday Night**	41	$8	Motown 0751

Request Line [9] • Saturday Night • So Badd • **Crush** [24] • This Song Is For You • Just Like That • Last Dance • Good Times • For The Longest Time • Rendez-vous • My Word Is Bond • Kindness For Granted • Temporary Thing • Confusion • Color • Piece It Together

ZHIGGE   '92
Pronounced: shiggy. Rap group from New York City: Kazo, Face, Prancer, Sound and Tonga.

9/26/92	55	9		Zhigge		$8	Polydor 513241

Z'LOOKE   '89
Funk group from Los Angeles: Arthur Zamora, Michael Carpenter, Wayne Cockerham and Eric Strickland.

1/7/89	37	23		Take U Back To My Place		$8	Orpheus 75600

ZOOM   '82
Group from Los Angeles: Norman Semien (vocals), Floyd Bonner (guitar), Marcus Robinson and Todd Duncan (keyboards), Henry Prejean and Darryl Williams (horns), John Haynes (bass) and George Mitchell (drums).

1/30/82	44	19		Saturday, Saturday Night		$10	Polydor 6343

ZULEMA   '75
Born Zulema Cusseaux on 1/3/47 in Tampa, Florida. Female singer/songwriter/multi-instrumentalist.

8/19/72	48	1		1 Zulema		$15	Sussex 7015
2/16/74	48	4		2 Zulema		$15	Sussex 8029
2/22/75	43	3		3 Zulema		$12	RCA Victor 0819

above 3 are different albums

DEBUT	PEAK	WKS	Gold	Album Title	Pop #	$	Label & Number

SOUNDTRACKS

Each movie's stars are listed after the title. Also shown are the Composer (cp), Conductor (cd), and Songwriter [music & lyrics] (sw). The following symbols are also used in this section: [I] Instrumental, [M] Musical, [O] Oldies and [V] Various Artists.

4/9/94 ❶¹⁰ 40 ◢² 1 **Above The Rim** .... [V] 2¹ $8 Death Row 92359
Duane Martin/Leon/**2 Pac**/Marlon Wayans/David Bailey/Bernie Mac
Anything [SWV] [4] • **Old Time's Sake** [Sweet Sable] [15] • **Part Time Lover** [H-Town] [9] • Big Pimpin' [Dogg Pound] • Didn't Mean To Turn You On [2nd II None] • Doggie Style [D.J. Rogers] • **Regulate** [Warren G. & Nate Dogg] [7] • Pour Out A Little Liquor [Thug Life] • Gonna Give It To Ya [Jewell & Aaron Hall] • **Afro Puffs** [Lady Of Rage] [31] • Jus So Ya No [CPO-Boss Hog] • Hoochies Need Love Too [Paradise] • **I'm Still In Love With You** [Al B. Sure!] [62] • Crack 'Em [O.F.T.B.] • U Bring Da Dog Out [Rhythm & Knowledge] • It's Not Deep Enough [Jewell] • Blowed Away [B Rezell] • Dogg Pound 4 Life [Dogg Pound]

Across 110th Street - see WOMACK, Bobby
Anthony Quinn/Yaphet Kotto/Anthony Franciosa/Antonio Fargas

12/18/93 98 1 2 **Addams Family Values** .... [V] $8 Atlas 521502
Anjelica Huston/Raul Julia/Christopher Lloyd/Joan Cusack

5/5/84 50 5 ● 3 **Against All Odds** .... [I+V] 12 $10 Atlantic 80152
Rachel Ward/Jeff Bridges/James Woods/Alex Karras; cp/cd: Larry Carlton and Michel Colombier

4/5/80 63 3 4 **All That Jazz** .... [M] 36 $12 Casablanca 7198
Roy Scheider/Jessica Lange/Ann Reinking/Ben Vereen; cd: Ralph Burns

4/8/95 13 17 ● 5 **Bad Boys** .... [V] 26 $8 Work 67009
Martin Lawrence/Will Smith/Téa Leoni/Theresa Randall

Batman - see PRINCE
Jack Nicholson/Michael Keaton/Kim Basinger/Robert Wuhl/Pat Hingle

6/9/84 10 23 ● 6 **Beat Street, Volume 1** .... [V] 14 $10 Atlantic 80154
Rae Dawn Chong/Guy Davis/John Chardiet/Leon W. Grant
Beat Street Breakdown [Grandmaster Melle Mel & The Furious Five] [8] • Baptize The Beat [System] • Strangers In A Strange World [Jenny Burton & Patrick Jude] • Frantic Situation [Afrika Bambaataa & The Soul Sonic Force] • **Beat Street Strut** [Juicy] • Us Girls [Sharon Green, Lisa Counts & Debbie D.] • This Could Be The Night [Cindy Mizelle] • Breaker's Revenge [Arthur Baker] • Tu Carino/Carmen's Theme [Ruben Blades]

10/20/84 47 5 7 **Beat Street, Volume 2** .... [V] 137 $10 Atlantic 80158
more songs from the movie

11/21/98 2¹ 35↑ ● 8 **Belly** .... [V] 5 $8 Def Jam 558925
Nas/DMX/Method Man/Taral Hicks
No Way In, No Way Out [Lady] • Devil's Pie [D'Angelo] • **The Grand Finale** [DMX/Method Man/Nas/Ja Rule] [63] • Never Dreamed You'd Leave In Summer [Jerome] • What About [Sparkle] • Two Sides [Hot Totti] • Movin' Out [Mya] • Top Shotter [DMX/Sean Paul/Mr. Vegas] • Story To Tell [Ja Rule] • Crew Love [Jay-Z] • Sometimes [Noreaga] • We All Can Get It On [Drag-On] • Militia [Gang Starr] • Windpipe [Wu-Tang Clan] • Pre-Game [Sauce Money] • Tommy's Theme [Made Men] • Some Niggaz [Half-A-Mil] • I Wanna Live [Braveheart]

2/9/85 6 32 ◢² 9 **Beverly Hills Cop** .... [V] 1² $10 MCA 5547
Eddie Murphy/Judge Reinhold/Lisa Eilbacher/John Ashton
New Attitude [Patti LaBelle] [3] • **Don't Get Stopped In Beverly Hills** [Shalamar] [79] • Do You Really (Want My Love?) [Junior] • BHC (I Can't Stop) [Rick James] • **Neutron Dance** [Pointer Sisters] [13] • The Heat Is On [Glenn Frey] • Gratitude [Danny Elfman] • **Stir It Up** [Patti LaBelle] [5] • Rock 'N Roll Me Again [System] • **Axel F** [Harold Faltermeyer] [13] • All Revved Up [Jermaine Jackson]

7/11/87 36 13 ▲ 10 **Beverly Hills Cop II** .... [V] 8 $10 MCA 6207
Eddie Murphy/Judge Reinhold/Brigitte Nielsen/Ronny Cox

5/28/94 66 6 11 **Beverly Hills Cop III** .... [V] 158 $8 MCA 11021
Eddie Murphy/Judge Reinhold/Hector Elizondo/Theresa Randle

11/26/83 40 20 ◢² 12 **Big Chill, The** .... [O-V] 17 $10 Motown 6062
William Hurt/Glenn Close/Jobeth Williams/Jeff Goldblum/Kevin Kline

Bill Cosby "Himself" - see COSBY, Bill
concert movie

Black Caesar - see BROWN, James
Fred Williamson/Art Lund/Julius W. Harris/Gloria Hendry

9/5/98 28 16 ● 13 **Blade** .... [V] 36 $8 TVT Soundtrax 8210
Wesley Snipes/Stephen Dorff/Kris Kristofferson/Udo Kier

Bodyguard, The - see HOUSTON, Whitney
Kevin Costner/**Whitney Houston**/Gary Kemp/Ralph Waite/Bill Cobbs

7/18/92 ❶⁸ 59 ◢³ 14 **Boomerang** .... [V] 4 $8 LaFace 26006
Eddie Murphy/Halle Berry/Robin Givens/David Alan Grier
Give U My Heart [Babyface] [2] • It's Gonna Be Alright [Aaron Hall] • Tonight Is Right [Keith Washington] • **I'd Die Without You** [PM Dawn] [16] • 7 Day Weekend [Grace Jones] • **End Of The Road** [Boyz II Men] [1] • Reversal Of A Dog [LaFace Cartel] • **Love Shoulda Brought You Home** [Toni Braxton] [2] • There U Go [Johnny Gill] • Don't Wanna Love You [Shanice] • Feels Like Heaven [Kenny Vaughan & The Art Of Love] • Hot Sex [Tribe Called Quest]

3/15/97 4 34 ▲ 15 **Booty Call** .... [V] 24 $8 Jive 41604
Jamie Foxx/Tommy Davidson/Vivica A. Fox/Tamala Jones
Can We [SWV] [31] • **Don't Wanna Be A Player** [Joe] [5] • Baby, Baby, Baby, Baby, Baby... [R. Kelly] • Fire & Desire [Johnny Gill & Coko] • **Call Me** [Too $hort & Lil' Kim] [30] • Don't Stop, Don't Quit [1 Accord] • Feel Good [Silk] • Don't Blame It On Me [E-40 & B-Legit] • Hold That Thought [Gerald Levert] • If You Stay [Backstreet Boys] • Let Me See You Squirrel [Squirrel] • (I'll Be Yo') Huckleberry [D-Shot] • Plan Up Your Family [KRS-One] • Chocolate [L.a. Ganz] • Looking For Love [Whitey Don] • When I Rise [Crooked]

7/27/91 ❶⁴ 20 ● 16 **Boyz N The Hood** .... [V] 12 $8 Qwest 26643
Laurence Fishburne/**Ice Cube**/Cuba Gooding Jr./Nia Long
How To Survive In South Central [Ice Cube] • **Just Ask Me To** [Tevin Campbell] [9] • Mama Don't Take No Mess [Yo-Yo] • Growin' Up In The Hood [Comptons Most Wanted] • Just A Friendly Game Of Baseball [Main Source] • Me And You [Tony! Toni! Toné!] • Work It Out [Monie Love] • Every Single Weekend [KAM] • Too Young [Hi-Five] • Hangin' Out [2 Live Crew] • It's Your Life [Too $hort] • Spirit (Does Anybody Care?) [Force One Network] • Setembro [Quincy Jones] • Black On Black Crime [Stanley Clarke]

6/9/84 2² 22 ▲ 17 **Breakin'** .... [V] 8 $10 Polydor 821919
Lucinda Dickey/Adolfo Quinones/Michael Chambers/**Ice-T**
Breakin'...There's No Stopping Us [Ollie & Jerry] [3] • **Freakshow On The Dance Floor** [Bar-Kays] [2] • Body Work [Hot Streak] • 99 1/2 [Carol Lynn Townes] [22] • Showdown [Ollie & Jerry] • Heart Of The Beat [3-V] • Street People [Fire Fox] • Cut-It [Re-Flex] • **Ain't Nobody** [Rufus & Chaka Khan] [1] • Reckless [Chris Taylor, David Storrs & Ice-T]

1/19/85 25 11 18 **Breakin' 2 Electric Boogaloo** .... [V] 52 $10 Polydor 823696
Lucinda Dickey/Adolfo Quinones/Michael Chambers/Susie Bono

9/21/96 37 10 19 **Bulletproof** .... [V] 85 $8 MCA 11498
Adam Sandler/Damon Wayans/James Caan/James Farentino

| --- | --- | --- | --- | --- | --- | --- | --- |

SOUNDTRACKS — Cont'd

| 5/2/98 | 4 | 24 | ● | 20 **Bulworth** .... [V] | 10 | $8 | Interscope 90160 |

Warren Beatty/Halle Berry/Don Cheadle/Oliver Platt/Paul Sorvino
Zoom *[Dr. Dre & LL Cool J]* • **Ghetto Supastar (That Is What You Are)** *[Pras Michel] [8]* • How Come *[Canibus & Youssou N'Dour]* • Bulworth (They Talk About It While We Live It) *[Method Man]* • Holiday/12 Scanner *[Witchdoctor]* • The Chase *[RZA]* • Eve Of Destruction *[Eve]* • Maniac In The Brainiac *[Mack 10 & Ice Cube]* • Freak Out *[Nutta Butta]* • Joints & Jams *[Black Eyed Peas]* • Run *[Cappadonna]* • Lunatics In The Grass *[B Real]* • Kill Em Live *[Public Enemy]* • Bitches Are Hustlers Too *[D-Fyne]*

Bustin' Loose - see FLACK, Roberta
Richard Pryor/Cicely Tyson/Robert Christian/Janet Wong
Car Wash - see ROSE ROYCE
Richard Pryor/Franklin Ajaye/Ivan Dixon/George Carlin

| 3/14/98 | 6 | 7 | | 21 **Caught Up** .... [V] | 30 | $8 | Noo Trybe 45451 |

Bokeem Woodbine/Cynda Williams/Tony Todd/**Snoop Doggy Dogg**
Ride On (Caught Up)! *[Snoop Doggy Dogg & Kurupt]* • Work *[Gang Starr]* • U Should Know Me *[Joe]* • You Don't Want None *[Mack 10 & Road Dawgs]* • All In The Club *[Do Or Die]* • Ordinary Guy *[Lost Boyz]* • My Buddy *[Luniz]* • Cross My Heart *[Killah Priest]* • Ey-Yo! (The Reggae Virus) *[KRS-One/Mad Lion/Shaggy]* • Rock Me *[AZ]* • R.U. Down *[Somethin' For The People]* • I Like *[Shiro]* • Girl *[Luniz]* • Made Man *[O]*

| 3/20/93 | 13 | 15 | | 22 **CB4** .... [V] | 41 | $8 | MCA 10803 |

Chris Rock/Allen Payne/Phil Hartman/Chris Elliott
Children of Sanchez - see MANGIONE, Chuck
Anthony Quinn/Dolores Del Rio/Melanie Farrar/Lucia Mendez
Claudine - see KNIGHT, Gladys
Diahann Carroll/James Earl Jones/Lawrence Hilton-Jacobs/Tamu

| 8/11/73 | 13 | 17 | | 23 **Cleopatra Jones** .... [I+V] | 109 | $15 | Warner 2718 |

Tamara Dobson/Bernie Casey/Shelley Winters/Antonio Fargas; cp/cd: J.J. Johnson

| 9/23/95 | 54 | 5 | | 24 **Clockers** .... [V] | | $8 | MCA 11304 |

Harvey Keitel/John Turturro/Delroy Lindo/Mekhi Phifer/Keith David

| 3/8/86 | 33 | 12 | | 25 **Color Purple, The** .... [I+V] | 79 | $12 | Qwest 25389 [2] |

Whoopi Goldberg/Danny Glover/Margaret Avery/Oprah Winfrey; cp/cd: **Quincy Jones**

| 5/21/88 | 13 | 16 | ● | 26 **Colors** .... [V] | 31 | $10 | Warner 25713 |

Sean Penn/Robert Duvall/Maria Conchita Alonso/Randy Brooks

| 9/10/88 | 91 | 1 | | 27 **Coming To America** .... [V] | 177 | $8 | Atco 90958 |

Eddie Murphy/Arsenio Hall/James Earl Jones/John Amos

| 10/18/75 | 45 | 5 | | 28 **Cooley High** .... [V] | | $12 | Motown 840 |

Glynn Turman/Lawrence-Hilton Jacobs/Garrett Morris/Corin Rogers
Cornbread, Earl and Me - see BLACKBYRDS, The
Moses Gunn/Bernie Casey/Rosalind Cash/Madge Sinclair

| 5/28/94 | 10 | 11 | | 29 **Crooklyn** .... [V] | 59 | $8 | MCA 11036 |

Alfre Woodard/Delroy Lindo/David Patrick Kelly/Zelda Harris
Crooklyn *[Crooklyn Dodgers] [32]* • Respect Yourself *[Staple Singers] [2]* • **Everyday People** *[Sly & The Family Stone] [1]* • Pusher Man *[Curtis Mayfield]* • Thin Line Between Love And Hate *[Persuaders] [1]* • El Pito (I'll Never Go Back To Georgia) *[Joe Cuba]* • ABC *[Jackson 5] [1]* • Oh Girl *[Chi-Lites] [1]* • **Mighty Love** *[Spinners] [1]* • **Mr. Big Stuff** *[Jean Knight] [1]* • Ooh Child *[Five Stairsteps] [14]* • Pass The Peas *[JB's] [29]* • Time Has Come Today *[Chambers Brothers] [65]* • **People Make The World Go Round** *[Marc Dorsey] [65]*

| 3/1/97 | 3 | 11 | | 30 **Dangerous Ground** .... [V] | 20 | $8 | Jive 41590 |

Ice Cube/Elizabeth Hurley/Ving Rhames/Sechaba Morajele
The World Is Mine *[Ice Cube] [55]* • You're Only A Customer *[Jay-Z]* • Only Way *[Celly Cel]* • Keep On Pushin' *[MC Lyte/Bahamadia/Nonchalant/Yo-Yo]* • Dangerous Ground *[Keith Murray]* • Mr. Shit Talker *[Mystikal]* • Buddup Bap *[Whitey Don]* • Fa-Sho *[K-Dee]* • Ghetto Smile *[B-Legit]* • Perhaps She'll Die *[KRS-One]* • It's Alright *[Too $hort]* • Struggled & Strived *[Click]* • 2 Hands And A Razor *[Spice 1]* • Murder *[Crooked]* • Count On Me *[L.A. Ganz]* • Chocolate Chips *[Lil Doe Doe]*

| 8/12/95 | 2[1] | 42 | ▲[3] | 31 **Dangerous Minds** .... [V] | 1[4] | $8 | MCA 11228 |

Michelle Pfeiffer/George Dzundza/Courtney B. Vance/Robin Bartlett
Gangsta's Paradise *[Coolio] [2]* • **Curiosity** *[Aaron Hall] [36]* • Havin Thangs *[Big Mike]* • Problems *[Rappin' 4-Tay]* • True O.G. *[Mr. Dalvin & Static]* • Put Ya Back Into It *[Tre Black]* • Don't Go There *[24-K]* • Feel The Funk *[Immature] [15]* • It's Alright *[Sista]* • Message For Your Mind *[Rappin' 4-Tay]* • Gin & Juice *[DeVante]* • This Is The Life *[Wendy & Lisa]*

| 2/11/84 | 56 | 7 | | 32 **D.C. Cab** .... | 181 | $10 | MCA 6128 |

Adam Baldwin/**Irene Cara**/Max Gail/Gary Busey/Mr. T

| 10/14/95 | ❶[2] | 45 | ● | 33 **Dead Presidents** .... [O-V] | 14 | $8 | Underworld 32438 |

Larenz Tate/Keith David/Chris Tucker/N'Bushe Wright/Rose Jackson
If You Want Me To Stay *[Sly & The Family Stone] [3]* • Walk On By *[Isaac Hayes] [13]* • The Payback *[James Brown] [1]* • I'll Be Around *[Spinners] [1]* • Never, Never Gonna Give Ya Up *[Barry White] [2]* • I Miss You *[Harold Melvin & The Blue Notes] [7]* • Get Up And Get Down *[Dramatics] [16]* • (Don't Worry) If There's A Hell Below We're All Going To Go *[Curtis Mayfield] [3]* • Do Right Woman-Do Right Man *[Aretha Franklin] [37]* • Where Is The Love *[Jesse & Trina] [40]* • Tired Of Being Alone *[Al Green] [7]* • Love Train *[O'Jays] [1]* • The Look Of Love *[Isaac Hayes]* • Dead Presidents Theme *[Danny Elfman]*

| 4/20/96 | 45 | 17 | | 34 **Dead Presidents Volume II** .... [O-V] | | $8 | Underworld 35818 |

more songs from the movie
Death Wish - see HANCOCK, Herbie
Charles Bronson/Hope Lange/Vincent Gardenia/Olympia Dukakis

| 5/9/92 | 9 | 24 | | 35 **Deep Cover** .... [V] | 166 | $8 | Solar 75330 |

Laurence Fishburne/Jeff Goldblum/Gregory Sierra/Victoria Dillard
Deep Cover *[Dr. Dre] [46]* • Love Or Lust *[Jewell]* • Down With My Nigga *[Paradise]* • Sex Is On *[Po', Broke & Lonely?]* • Way (Is In The House) *[Calloway]* • Minute You Fall In Love *[3rd Avenue]* • John And Betty's Theme *[Michel Colombier]* • **Mr. Loverman** *[Shabba Ranks] [2]* • I See Ya Jay *[Ragtime]* • Nickel Slick Nigga *[Ko-Kane]* • Typical Relationship *[Times 3]* • Digits *[Deele]* • Sound Of One Hand Clapping *[Calloway]* • Why You Frontin' On Me *[Emmage]*

| 5/19/90 | 85 | 9 | | 36 **Def By Temptation** .... [V] | | $8 | Orpheus 75625 |

James Bond III/Kadeem Hardison/Bill Nunn/Samuel L. Jackson

| 8/23/97 | 2[1] | 13 | ● | 37 **Def Jam's How To Be A Player** .... [V] | 7 | $8 | Def Jam 537973 |

Bill Bellamy/Natalie Desselle/Lark Voorhies/Gilbert Gottfried
Big Bad Mamma *[Foxy Brown] [10]* • Hard To Get (Revisited) *[Rick James & Richie Rich]* • I Gotta Know *[Playa]* • Young Casanovas *[Junior M.A.F.I.A.]* • Down Wit Us *[Redman]* • The Usual Suspects *[Mic Geronimo]* • How To Be A Playa *[Master P]* • It's A Cold Day *[Too $hort]* • Street 2 Street *[Jayo Felony]* • In The Wind *[Eightball & MJG]* • Never Seen Before *[EPMD]* • Never Wanna Let You Go *[Absolute]* • When The Playas Live *[Crucial Conflict]* • Troublesome *[2 Pac]* • Say What *[Dymon]* • If U Stay Ready *[Suga Free]* • Don't Ever *[Black Azz Chill]*

| 10/3/87 | 69 | 3 | | 38 **Disorderlies** .... [V] | 99 | $8 | Polydor 833274 |

The Fat Boys/Ralph Bellamy/Tony Plana/Anthony Geary/Troy Beyer

DEBUT	PEAK	WKS	Gold	Album Title		Pop #	$	Label & Number
				SOUNDTRACKS — Cont'd				
7/8/89	11	24		39 **Do The Right Thing**...................	[V]	68	$8	Motown 6272
				Danny Aiello/Ossie Davis/Ruby Dee/Spike Lee/John Turturro				
1/27/96	3	22	●	40 **Don't Be A Menace To South Central While Drinking Your Juice In The Hood**	[V]	18	$8	Island 524146
				Shawn Wayans/Marlon Wayans/Chris Spencer/Omar Epps/LaWanda Page **Winter Warz** [Ghostface Killah] • **Renee** [Lost Boyz] **[13]** • Funky Sounds [Lil Bud & Tizone] • **Can't Be Wasting My Time** [Mona Lisa] **[20]** • Time To Shine [Lil Kim] • Maintain [Erick Sermon] • We Got More [Shock G] • **Let's Lay Together** [Isley Brothers] **[24]** • All The Things (Your Man Won't Do) [Joe] **[2]** • Tempo Slow [R. Kelly] • Live Wires Connect [UGK] • Up North Trip [Mobb Deep] • Freak It Out! [Doug E. Fresh] • Suga Daddy [Suga-T] • It's Time [Blue Raspberry] • **Don't Give Up** [Island Inspirational All-Stars] **[28]**				
12/26/98+	86	7		41 **Down In The Delta**...................	[V]		$8	Virgin 46914
				Alfre Woodard/Esther Rolle/Wesley Snipes/Loretta Devine				
7/4/98	4	34	▲2	42 **Dr. Dolittle**...................	[V]	4	$8	Blackground 83113
				Eddie Murphy/Ossie Davis/Oliver Platt/Peter Boyle That's Why I Lie [Ray J.] • **Let's Ride** [Montell Jordan] **[1]** • Are You That Somebody? [Aaliyah] • Same Ol' G [Ginuwine] • Lady Marmalade [All Saints] • Da Funk [Timbaland] • Do Little Things [Changing Faces] • Your Dress [Playa] • **Woof Woof** [69 Boyz] **[24]** • Rock Steady [Dawn Robinson] • **In Your World** [Twista & The Speed Knot Mobsters] **[63]** • Lovin' You So [Jody Watley] • Dance [Robin S] • Push 'Em Up [Eddie Kane & DeVille] • Ain't Nothin' But A Party [Sugarhill Gang]				
6/15/96	44	12		43 **Eddie**...................	[V]	119	$8	Island 524243
				Whoopi Goldberg/Frank Langella/Dennis Farina/Richard Jenkins				
8/1/81	9	21	●	44 **Endless Love**...................	[I+V]	9	$10	Mercury 2001
				Brooke Shields/Martin Hewitt/Shirley Knight/Don Murray; sp: Jonathan Tunick/**Lionel Richie** **Endless Love** [Diana Ross & Lionel Richie] **[1]** • Dreaming Of You [Diana Ross & Lionel Richie] • I Was Made For Lovin' You [Kiss] • Dreaming [Cliff Richard] • Dreaming Of You • Heart Song • David Goes To Jade's House • Ann Sees David And Jade Making Love • David At The Institution				
8/23/80	21	15	▲	45 **Fame**...................	[M]	7	$12	RSO 3080
				Irene Cara/Eddie Barth/Maureen Teefy/Lee Curreri/Laura Dean				
8/23/97	67	2		46 **5th Ward**...................	[V]		$8	Fish Bowl 7001
				Nestor Gregory Carter				
10/5/96	61	5		47 **First Wives Club, The**...................	[V]	90	$8	Work 67814
				Bette Midler/Goldie Hawn/Diane Keaton/Maggie Smith/Dan Hedaya				
4/27/91	10	20		48 **Five Heartbeats, The**...................	[V]	58	$8	Virgin 91609
				Robert Townsend/Michael Wright/Leon/Harry J. Lennix/Tico Wells **A Heart Is A House For Love** [Dells] **[13]** • We Haven't Finished Yet [Patti LaBelle] • **Nights Like This** [After 7] **[7]** • Bring Back The Days [U.S. Male] • Baby Stop Running Around [Bird & The Midnight Falcons] • In The Middle [Flash & The Five Heartbeats] • Nothing But Love [Five Heartbeats] • Are You Ready For Me [Flash & The Ebony Sparks] • Stay In My Corner [Dells] • I Feel Like Going On [Eddie, Baby Doll and The L.A. Mass Choir]				
5/7/83	6	43	▲6	49 **Flashdance**...................	[V]	1²	$8	Casablanca 811492
				Jennifer Beals/Michael Nouri/Lilia Skala/Cynthia Rhodes **Flashdance...What A Feeling** [Irene Cara] **[2]** • He's A Dream [Shandi] • Love Theme From Flashdance [Helen St. John] • Manhunt [Karen Kamon] • Lady, Lady, Lady [Joe "Bean" Esposito] • Imagination [Laura Branigan] • Romeo [Donna Summer] • Seduce Me Tonight [Cycle V] • I'll Be Here Where The Heart Is [Kim Carnes] • Maniac [Michael Sembello]				
8/3/96	60	3		50 **Fled**...................	[V]		$8	Rowdy 37012
				Laurence Fishburne/Stephen Baldwin/Will Patton/Salma Hayek				
4/21/84	16	21	▲8	51 **Footloose**...................	[V]	1¹⁰	$8	Columbia 39242
				Kevin Bacon/Lori Singer/John Lithgow/Dianne Wiest/Christopher Penn				
9/14/68	28	3		52 **For Love Of Ivy**...................	[I+V]	192	$25	ABC 7
				Sidney Poitier/Abbey Lincoln/Beau Bridges/Carroll O'Connor; cp/cd: **Quincy Jones**				
				Foxy Brown - see HUTCH, Willie Pam Grier/Peter Brown/Terry Carter/Kathryn Loder				
7/31/93	49	20	●	53 **Free Willy**...................	[V]	47	$8	MJJ Music 57280
				Jason James Richter/Lori Petty/Jayne Atkinson/Michael Madsen				
9/17/94	34	4		54 **Fresh**...................	[V]		$8	Loud/RCA 66478
				Sean Nelson/Giancarlo Esposito/N'Bushe Wright/Samuel L. Jackson				
4/29/95	❶6	64	▲2	55 **Friday**...................	[V]	1²	$8	Priority 53959
				Ice Cube/Chris Tucker/Nia Long/Tiny Lister/Regina King Friday [Ice Cube] • **Keep Their Heads Ringin'** [Dr. Dre] **[10]** • Friday Night [Scarface] • Lettin' Niggas Know [Threat] • Roll It Up, Light It Up, Smoke It Up [Cypress Hill] • Take A Hit [Mack 10] • Tryin' To See Another Day [Isley Brothers] • You Got Me Wide Open [Funkdoobiest] • **Mary Jane** [Rick James] **[3]** • **I Wanna Get Next To You** [Rose Royce] **[3]** • Superhoes [Funkdoobiest] • Coast II Coast [Alkaholiks] • Blast If I Have To [E-A-Ski] • Hoochie Mama [2 Live Crew] • **I Heard It Through The Grapevine** [Roger] **[1]**				
5/20/95	57	5		56 **Friday, Old School**...................	[O-V]		$8	Priority 57194
				more music from the movie				
10/18/97	❶2	24	▲2	57 **Gang Related**...................	[V]	2¹	$12	Death Row 53509 [2]
				James Belushi/2 Pac/Lela Rochon/Dennis Quaid/James Earl Jones Way Too Major [Daz Dillinger] • Life's So Hard [2Pac] • Greed [Ice Cube] • Get Yo Bang On [Mack 10] • These Days [Nate Dogg] • Mash For Our Dreams [Storm] • Free 'Em All [J-Flexx] • Staring Through My Rearview [2Pac] • Devotion [Paradise] • I Can't Fix It [Jackers] • Questions [Tech9ne] • Hollywood Bank Robbery [Gang] • Made Niggaz [2Pac] • Loc'd Out Hood [Kurupt] • Gang Related [WC, CJ Mac, Daz Dillinger, Tray Deee] • Keep Your Eyes Open [O.F.T.B.] • Lady [6 Feet] • Take A Nigga Like Me [Young Soldierz] • What Have You Done? [B.G.O.T.I.] • What's Ya Fantasy [Outlawz & Daz Dillinger] • Change To Come [J-Flexx] • Freak Somethin' [Roland] • Feelin A Good Thang [2DV] • Lost Souls [2Pac]				
10/26/96	38	6		58 **Get On The Bus**...................	[V]	184	$8	Interscope 90089
				Ossie Davis/Charles S. Dutton/Andre Braugher/Albert Hall				
7/14/84	8	10	▲	59 **Ghostbusters**...................	[V]	6	$8	Arista 8246
				Bill Murray/Dan Aykroyd/Sigourney Weaver/Harold Ramis/Rick Moranis **Ghostbusters** [Ray Parker, Jr.] **[1]** • Cleanin' Up The Town [Bus Boys] • Savin' The Day [Alessi] • In The Name Of Love [Thompson Twins] • I Can Wait Forever [Air Supply] • Hot Night [Laura Branigan] • Magic [Mick Smiley] • Ghostbusters Main Title Theme [Elmer Bernstein] • Dana's Theme [Elmer Bernstein]				
7/8/89	24	13	●	60 **Ghostbusters II**...................	[V]	14	$8	MCA 6306
				Bill Murray/Dan Aykroyd/Sigourney Weaver/Harold Ramis/Rick Moranis				
				Girl 6 - see PRINCE Theresa Randle/Isaiah Washington/Spike Lee/Jennifer Lewis				
8/9/97	65	4		61 **Good Burger**...................	[V]	101	$8	Capitol 57955
				Kel Mitchell/Kenan Thompson/Abe Vigoda/Dan Schneider/Sinbad				

DEBUT	PEAK	WKS	Gold	Album Title		Pop #	$	Label & Number
				SOUNDTRACKS — Cont'd				
4/6/68	10	21		62 **Good, The Bad And The Ugly, The**	[I]	4	$15	United Artists 5172

Clint Eastwood/Lee Van Cleef/Eli Wallach/Rada Rassimov; cp/cd: Ennio Morricone
The Good, The Bad And The Ugly • The Sundown • The Strong • The Desert • The Carriage Of The Spirits • Marcia • The Story Of A Soldier • Marcia Without Hope • The Death Of A Soldier • The Ecstasy Of Gold • The Trio

Graduate, The - see SIMON & GARFUNKEL
Anne Bancroft/Dustin Hoffman/Katharine Ross/Murray Hamilton

Graffiti Bridge - see PRINCE
Prince/Morris Day/Jill Jones/Mavis Staples/George Clinton

5/18/96	27	11		63 **Great White Hype, The**	[V]	93	$8	Hudlin Bros. 67636

Samuel L. Jackson/Jeff Goldblum/Peter Berg/Jon Lovitz/Jamie Foxx

7/9/77	40	16		64 **Greatest, The**	[I+V]	166	$12	Arista 7000

Muhammad Ali/Ernest Borgnine/Robert Duvall/James Earl Jones; cp: Michael Masser

2/15/97	❶²	16	●	65 **Gridlock'd**	[V]	1¹	$8	Death Row 90114

2 Pac/Tim Roth/Thandie Newton/Charles Fleischer/Tom Towles
Wanted Dead Or Alive [2Pac & Snoop Doggy Dogg] • Sho Shot [Lady Of Rage] • It's Over Now [Danny Boy] • Don't Try To Play Me Homey [Dat Nigga Daz] • Never Had A Friend Like Me [2Pac] • Why [Nate Dogg] • Out The Moon (Boom, Boom, Boom) [Snoop Doggy Dogg] • I Can't Get Enough [Danny Boy] • Tonight It's On [BGOTI] • Off The Hook [Snoop Doggy Dogg] • Lady Heroin [J. Flex] • Will I Rize [Storm] • Body And Soul [O.F.T.B.] • Life Is A Traffic Jam [Eight Mile Road] • Deliberation [Anonymous]

7/4/98	6	10		66 **HavPlenty**	[V]	39	$8	Yab Yum 69356

Christopher Scott Cherot/Chenoa Maxwell/Hill Harper/Betty Vaughn
Fire [Babyface & Des'ree] • Heat [Absolute] • Keep It Real [Jon B. & Coko] • I Can't Help It [Shya] • I Can't Get You (Out Of My Mind) [BLACKstreet] • Tears Away [Faith Evans] • What The Hell Do You Want [Az Yet] • Rock The Body [Queen Pen & Tracey Lee] • I Wanna Be Where You Are [SWV] • Whatcha Gonna Do [Jayo Felony] • Any Other Night [Chico DeBarge] • What I've Been Missin' [Changing Faces] • Ye Yo [Erykah Badu]

He Got Game - see PUBLIC ENEMY
Denzel Washington/Ray Allen/Milla Jovovich/Ned Beatty/Jim Brown

9/28/96	4	18	●	67 **High School High**	[V]	20	$8	Big Beat 92709

Jon Lovitz/Tia Carrere/Louise Fletcher/Mekhi Pfifer/John Neville
So Many Ways [Braxtons] [22] • **I Got Somebody Else** [Changing Faces] [49] • Wu-Wear: The Garment Renaissance [RZA] [40] • Get Down For Mine [Real Live] • I Just Can't [Faith Evans] • Your Precious Love [D'Angelo & Erykah Badu] • Rap World [Large Professor & Pete Rock] • Queen Bitch [Lil' Kim] • Why You Wanna Funk? [Spice 1 & The Click] • I Can't Call It [De La Soul] • **Bohemian Rhapsody** [Braids] [45] • High School Rock [KRS-One] • Peace, Prosperity & Paper [Tribe Called Quest] • Wild Side [Jodeci] • Ultimate (You Know The Time) [Artifacts] • Next Spot [Sadat X & Grand Puba] • Skrilla [Scarface] • Semi-Automatic: Full Rap Metal Jacket [Inspectah Deck & U-God] • Good, The Bad And The Desolate [Roots] • C'mon N' Ride It (The Train) [Quad City DJ's]

1/28/95	9	22		68 **Higher Learning**	[V]	39	$8	550 Music/Epic 66944

Omar Epps/Kristy Swanson/Laurence Fishburne/Ice Cube
Higher [Ice Cube] • Something To Think About [Ice Cube] • Soul Searchin' (I Wanna Know If It's Mine) [Me'Shell Ndegéocello] • Situation: Grimm [Mista Grimm] • Ask Of You [Raphael Saadiq] [2] • Losing My Religion [Tori Amos] • Phobia [OutKast] • My New Friend [Cole Hauser & Michael Rapaport] • Year Of The Boomerang [Rage Against The Machine] • Higher Learning/Time For Change [Brand New Heavies] • Don't Have Time [Liz Phair] • Butterfly [Tori Amos] • By Your Side [Zhané] • Eye [Eve's Plum] • Learning Curve [Stanley Clarke]

8/30/97	23	11		69 **Hoodlum**	[V]	94	$8	Loud/Interscope 90131

Laurence Fishburne/Tim Roth/Andy Garcia/Cicely Tyson

4/7/90	20	19		70 **House Party**	[V]	104	$8	Motown 6296

Kid 'N Play/Robin Harris/Martin Lawrence/Tisha Campbell

11/23/91	23	16		71 **House Party 2**	[V]	55	$8	MCA 10397

Kid 'N Play/Eugene Allen/Tisha Campbell/Iman/Martin Lawrence

2/5/94	55	9		72 **House Party 3**	[V]		$8	Select 21647

Kid 'N Play/David Edwards/Tisha Campbell/Gilbert Gottfried

8/29/98	3	31	●	73 **How Stella Got Her Groove Back**	[V]	8	$8	Flyte Tyme 11806

Angela Bassett/Taye Diggs/Regina King/Whoopi Goldberg
Jazzie B. [Jazzie B.] • Mastablasta '98 [Stevie Wonder & Wyclef Jean] • Luv Me, Luv Me [Shaggy] • Beautiful [Mary J. Blige] • Never Say Never Again [K-Ci & JoJo] • Makes Me Sweat [Big Punisher & Beenie Man] • Your Home Is In My Heart (Stella's Love Theme) [Boyz II Men] • Free Again [Soul II Soul] • Make My Body Hot [Diana King] • Art Of Seduction [Maxi Priest] • Let Me Have You [Me'Shell Ndegéocello] • Dance For Me [Kevin Ford] • Escape To Jamaica [Lady Saw] • Jazzie's Groove [Jazzie B.]

4/18/98	❶³	20	▲	74 **I Got The Hook-Up!**	[V]	3	$8	No Limit 50745

Master P/A.J. Johnson/Gretchen Palmer/Tiny Lister
Hook It Up [Master P] • Ghetto Vet [Ice Cube] • What The Game Made Me [Jay-Z/Sauce Money/Memphis Bleek] • From What I Was Told [Soulja Slim] • Let's Ride [Eight-Ball & MJG] • **I Got The Hook-Up!** [Master P/Sons Of Funk] [11] • Hooked [Snoop Doggy Dogg] • Down With You • Shake Somethin' [Mystikal/Mia X] • I Don't Want To Go [Mo B. Dick] • Would You Hesitate [C-Murder] • Itch Or Scratch [Master P] • Keep It Real [Mechalie Jamison] • Who Rock This [Ol' Dirty Bastard/Mystikal] • Bump And Grill [U.G.K.] • Tell Me What You're Lookin' For [Kane & Abel/Gotti/Full Blooded] • Call It What You Want [Steady Mobbin'] • What You Need [Commission] • Drama [Skull Dugrey] • We Got It [Mr. Serv-On/Big Ed/Magic/Fiend] • Bang Or Ball [Mack 10]

6/7/97	❶¹	53	●	75 **I'm Bout It**	[V]	4	$8	No Limit 50643

Master P/Anthony Boswell/Moon Jones/Tracy Philpott/Mack 10
Meal Ticket [Master P] • Situation On Dirty [Brotha Lynch Hung] • What Cha Think [Mystickal] • Come On [E-40 & B-Legit] • How Ya Do Dat [Master P] • Don't Mess Around [Fiend] • If I Could Change [Master P/Steady Mobb'n] • Faces Of Death [E-A-Ski] • Down & Dirty [Tru] • Much Love [Mia X] • Pushin' Inside You [Sons Of Funk] • Before I Die [Mr. Serv-On] • For Realz [Kane & Abel] • Lock Down [Mac] • Heat [Skull Drugery] • Murder Murder [Ghetto Twins] • Ride 4U [Mr. Jinks] • That Thing Is On [Mo B. Dick] • Who's Who [C-Loc] • Cops Runnin' After Ya [Prime Suspects] • Game Tight [J.T. The Bigga Figga & The Fast One] • Why They Wanna See Me Dead [Gambino Family]

1/21/89	53	11		76 **I'm Gonna Git You Sucka**	[V]		$8	Arista 8574

Keenen Ivory Wayans/Isaac Hayes/Jim Brown/Bernie Casey

4/6/85	35	12		77 **Into The Night**	[V]	118	$10	MCA 5561

Jeff Goldblum/Michelle Pfeiffer/Richard Farnsworth/Dan Aykroyd

1/10/98	28	8		78 **Jackie Brown**	[O-V]	73	$8	Maverick 46841

Pam Grier/Samuel L. Jackson/Robert Forster/Bridget Fonda

10/15/94	❶¹	41	▲	79 **Jason's Lyric**	[V]	17	$8	Mercury 522915

Forest Whitaker/Allen Payne/Jada Pinkett/Bokeem Woodbine
U Will Know [B.M.U. (Black Men United)] [5] • **Forget I Was A G** [Whitehead Brothers] [32] • Candyman [LL Cool J] • If Trouble Was Money [Mint Condition] • Just Like My Papa [Tony Toni Toné] • **If You Think You're Lonely Now** [K-Ci Hailey] [11] • Rodeo Style [Jamecia] • Up And Down [J. Quest] • Walk Away [Five Footer Crew] • Love Is The Key [LSD] • No More Love [DRS] • Crazy Love [Brian McKnight] [10] • That's How It Is [Ahmad] • First Round Draft Pick [Twinz] • Brothers And Sistas [Jayo Felony] • This City Needs Help [Buddy Guy] • Nigga Sings The Blues [Spice 1] • Jesse James [Scarface] • Love Is Still Enough [Savory] • Many Rivers To Cross [Oleta Adams]

236

SOUNDTRACKS — Cont'd

DEBUT	PEAK	WKS	Gold	Album Title	Pop #	$	Label & Number
2/1/86	39	9		80 **Jewel Of The Nile, The** .... [V]	55	$10	Jive 8406

Michael Douglas/Kathleen Turner/Danny DeVito/Spiros Focas

| 1/18/92 | 3 | 27 | ● | 81 **Juice** [V] | 17 | $8 | MCA 10462 |

Omar Epps/Jermaine Hopkins/Khalil Kain/**2 Pac**/Samuel L. Jackson

Uptown Anthem [Naughty By Nature] [58] • **Juice (know the ledge)** [Eric B. & Rakim] [38] • Is It Good To You [Teddy Riley] • Sex, Money & Murder [M.C. Pooh] • Nuff Respect [Big Daddy Kane] • So You Want To Be A Gangster [Too Short] • It's Going Down [EPMD] • **Don't Be Afraid** [Aaron Hall] [1] • He's Gamin' On Ya [Salt-N-Pepa] • Shoot 'Em Up [Cypress Hill Crew] • Flipside [Juvenile Committee] • What Could Be Better Bitch [Son Of Bazerk] • Does Your Man Know About Me [Rahiem] • People Get Ready [Brand New Heavies]

Jungle Fever - see WONDER, Stevie
Wesley Snipes/Annabella Sciorra/Spike Lee/Ossie Davis/Ruby Dee

| 11/2/85 | 14 | 22 | | 82 **Krush Groove** [V] | 79 | $10 | Warner 25295 |

Sheila E./Run-DMC/The Fat Boys/Kurtis Blow
Lady Sings The Blues - see ROSS, Diana
Diana Ross/Billy Dee Williams/**Richard Pryor**/James Callahan

| 4/6/85 | 29 | 15 | | 83 **Last Dragon, The** [V] | 58 | $8 | Motown 6128 |

Taimak/Julius J. Carry III/Chris Murney/Leo O'Brien/**Vanity**

| 1/9/93 | 71 | 5 | | 84 **Leap Of Faith** [V] | | $8 | MCA 10671 |

Steve Martin/Debra Winger/Lolita Davidovich/Liam Neeson/Lukas Haas

| 1/23/88 | 22 | 14 | ● | 85 **Less Than Zero** [V] | 31 | $8 | Def Jam 44042 |

Andrew McCarthy/Jami Gertz/Robert Downey Jr./James Spader
Let's Do It Again - see STAPLE SINGERS, The
Sidney Poitier/**Bill Cosby**/Jimmie Walker/John Amos

| 3/29/97 | 3 | 38 | ● | 86 **Love Jones** [V] | 16 | $8 | Columbia 67917 |

Larenz Tate/Nia Long/Isaiah Washington/Bill Bellamy/Khalil Kain

Hopeless [Dionne Farris] • The Sweetest Thing [Refugee Camp All-Stars] • I Got A Love Jones For You [Refugee Camp All-Stars] • **Sumthin' Sumthin'** [Maxwell] [23] • Never Enough [Groove Theory] • Inside My Love [Trina Broussard] • In The Rain [Xscape] • You Move Me [Cassandra Wilson] • Rush Over [Marcus Miller & Me'Shell Ndegéocello] • I Like It [Brand New Heavies] • Girl [Cassie] • Can't Get Enough [Kenny Lattimore] • Jelly, Jelly [Lincoln Center Jazz Orch.] • In A Sentimental Mood [Duke Ellington & John Coltrane]

| 11/26/94 | 14 | 17 | ● | 87 **Low Down Dirty Shame, A** [V] | 70 | $8 | Jive 41536 |

Keenan Ivory Wayans/Charles S. Dutton/Jada Pinkett/Salli Richardson
Mack, The - see HUTCH, Willie
Max Julien/Don Gordon/**Richard Pryor**/Carol Speed
Mad Dogs & Englishmen - see COCKER, Joe
concert movie

| 9/7/85 | 47 | 8 | | 88 **Mad Max Beyond Thunderdome** [I] | 39 | $8 | Capitol 12429 |

Mel Gibson/**Tina Turner**/Angelo Rossitto/Helen Buday/Rod Zuanic; cp/cd: Maurice Jarre

| 11/15/75 | 15 | 14 | | 89 **Mahogany** [I] | 19 | $12 | Motown 858 |

Diana Ross/Billy Dee Williams/Anthony Perkins; cp/cd: Lee Holdridge

| 12/5/92 | 23 | 10 | | 90 **Malcolm X** [V] | 130 | $8 | Qwest 45130 |

Denzel Washington/Angela Bassett/Albert Hall/Spike Lee; also see **Terence Blanchard**

| 7/19/97 | 2[2] | 31 | ▲[3] | 91 **Men In Black** [V] | 1[2] | $8 | Columbia 68169 |

Tommy Lee Jones/**Will Smith**/Linda Fiorentino/Vincent D'Onofrio

Men In Black [Will Smith] • We Just Wanna Party With You [Snoop Doggy Dogg] • I'm Feelin' You [Ginuwine] • Dah Dee Dah (Sexy Thing) [Alicia Keys] • Just Cruisin' [Will Smith] • The 'Notic [Roots] • Make You Happy [Trey Lorenz] • Escobar '97 [Nas] • Erotik City [Emoja] • Same Ol' Thing [Tribe Called Quest] • Killing Time [Destiny's Child] • Waiting For Love [37] • Chanel No. Fever [De La Soul] • Some Cow Fonque (More Tea, Vicar?) [Buckshot LeFonque] • Men In Black Main Theme [Danny Elfman] • Men In Black Closing Theme [Danny Elfman]

| 6/12/93 | ❶[6] | 51 | ▲ | 92 **Menace II Society** [V] | 23 | $8 | Jive 41509 |

Tyrin Turner/Larenz Tate/Jada Pinkett/Samuel L. Jackson

Trigga Gots No Heart [Spice 1] [71] • **Streiht Up Menace** [MC Eiht] [46] • Packin' A Gun [Ant Banks] • Top Of The World [Kenya Gruv] • Only The Strong Survive [Too $hort] • All Over A Ho [Mz. Kilo] • Guerillas Aint Gangstas [Da Lench Mob] • **You Been Played** [Smooth] [54] • Lick Dem Muthaphuckas [Brand Nubian] • Death Becomes You [Pete Rock & C.L. Smooth] • **Unconditional Love** [Hi-Five] [21] • "P" Is Still Free [Boogie Down Productions] • Stop Lookin' At Me [Cutthroats] • Pocket Full Of Stone [U.G.K.] • Can't Fuck Wit A Nigga [DJ Quik]

| 4/2/94 | 70 | 5 | | 93 **Mi Vida Loca** [V] | | $8 | Mercury 518882 |

Angel Aviles/Seidy Lopez/Jacob Vargas/Marlo Marron/Salma Hayek
Mo' Better Blues - see BLANCHARD, Terence / MARSALIS, Branford
Denzel Washington/Spike Lee/Wesley Snipes/John Turturro

| 7/11/92 | 2[5] | 21 | ▲ | 94 **Mo' Money** [V] | 6 | $8 | Perspective 1004 |

Damon Wayans/Marlon Wayans/Stacey Dash/Joe Santos/John Diehl

Mo' Money Groove [Mo' Money Allstars] • **The Best Things In Life Are Free** [Luther Vandross & Janet Jackson] [1] • Ice Cream Dream [Mo C Lyte] • Let's Just Run Away [Johnny Gill] • I Adore You [Caron Wheeler] • Get Off My Back [Public Enemy] • Forever Love [Color Me Badd] • **Money Can't Buy You Love** [Ralph Tresvant] [2] • Let's Get Together (So Groovy Now) [Krush] • Joy [Sounds Of Blackness] • A New Style [Jam & Lewis] • A Job Ain't Nuthin' But Work [Big Daddy Kane] • My Dear [Mint Condition] • Brother Will [Harlem Yacht Club]

| 9/6/97 | 6 | 33 | ● | 95 **Money Talks** [V] | 37 | $8 | Arista 18975 |

Chris Tucker/Charlie Sheen/Heather Locklear/Paul Sorvino

Avenues [Refugee Camp All Stars] [28] • My Everything [Barry White & Faith Evans] • No Way Out [Puff Daddy] • A Dream [Mary J. Blige] • Money Talks [Lil' Kim] • Penetration [Next & Naughty By Nature] • Tell Me How You Want It [SWV] • Everyday [Angie Stone & Devox] • Keep It Bubblin' [Brand Nubian] • The Teaching [Me'Shell Ndegéocello] • **Feel So Good** [Mase] [5] • **Things Just Ain't The Same** [Deborah Cox] [22] • Back In You Again [Rick James] • Real Thing [Lisa Stansfield] • You're The First, The Last, My Everything [Barry White]

Monterey International Pop Festival - see HENDRIX, Jimi / REDDING, Otis
concert movie

| 11/5/94 | ❶[3] | 46 | ▲[2] | 96 **Murder Was The Case** [V] | 1[2] | $8 | Death Row 92484 |

Snoop Doggy Dogg/Charlie Murphy/C Style/Freeze Luv

Murder Was The Case [Snoop Doggy Dogg] • **Natural Born Killaz** [Dr. Dre & Ice Cube] [16] • What Would U Do? [Tha Dogg Pound] • 21 Jumpstreet [Snoop Doggy Dogg & Tray Deee] • One More Day [Nate Dogg] • Harvest For The World [Jewell] • Who Got Some Gangsta Shit? [Snoop Doggy Dogg] • Come When I Call [Danny Boy] • **U Better Recognize** [Sam Sneed] [48] • Come Up To My Room [Jodeci] • Woman To Woman [Jewell] [16] • Dollars & Sense [D.J. Quik] • The Eulogy [Slip Capone & CPO] • Horny [B-Rezell] • Eastside-Westside [Young Soldierz]

DEBUT	PEAK	WKS	Gold	Album Title		Pop #	$	Label & Number
				SOUNDTRACKS — Cont'd				
3/30/91	❶[8]	31	▲ 97	**New Jack City**	[V]	2[1]	$8	Giant 24409

Wesley Snipes/Ice-T/Chris Rock/Mario Van Peebles/Judd Nelson
New Jack Hustler (Nino's Theme) *[Ice-T]* [49] • I'm Dreamin' *[Christopher Williams]* [1] • New Jack City *[Guy]* • I'm Still Waiting *[Johnny Gill]* [27] • (There You Go) Tellin' Me No Again *[Keith Sweat]* • Facts Of Life *[Danny Madden]* • For The Love Of Money/Living For The City *[Troop & Levert]* [12] • I Wanna Sex You Up *[Color Me Badd]* [1] • Lyrics 2 The Rhythm *[Essence]* • Get It Together (Black Is A Force) *[F.S. Effect]* • In The Dust *[2 Live Crew]*

| 4/15/95 | 3 | 19 | ● 98 | **New Jersey Drive Vol. 1** | [V] | 22 | $8 | Tommy Boy 1114 |

Sharron Corley/Gabriel Casseus/Saul Stein/Gwen McGee/Andre Moore
Don't Shut Down On A Player *[Ill Al Skratch]* • Where Am I? *[Redman]* • Do What U Want *[Blak Panta]* [78] • Old Thing *[Sabelle]* • All About My Fetti *[Young Lay]* • Can't You See *[Total]* [3] • Burn Rubber *[Lords Of The Underground]* • 21 In The Ghetto *[Poets Of Darkness]* • Love Slave *[Undacova]* • Benz Or Beamer *[Outkast]* • Check It Out *[Heavy D]* • Jersey *[Queen Latifah]* • East Left *[Keith Murray]* • Ain't Nuttin' But Killin *[MC Eiht]* • Thru The Window *[Coolio]* • Before I Let Go *[Maze]* • One And Only *[Smooth]*

| 4/29/95 | 9 | 7 | 99 | **New Jersey Drive Vol. 2** | [V] | 58 | $8 | Tommy Boy 1130 |

more songs from the movie
Funky Piano *[E. Bros.]* • Headz Ain't Ready *[Black Moon & Smif 'N' Wessun]* • Connections *[Naughty By Nature]* • Nobody Beats The Biz *[Biz Markie]* • Invasion *[Jeru The Damaja]* • Own Destiny *[Mad Lion]* • You Won't Go Far *[O.C. & Organized Konfusion]* • Flip Squad's In Da House *[Flip Squad All-Stars]*

| 7/19/97 | 5 | 12 | ● 100 | **Nothing To Lose** | [V] | 12 | $8 | Tommy Boy 1169 |

Martin Lawrence/Tim Robbins/John C. McGinley/Kelly Preston
Nothin' To Lose *[Naughty By Nature]* • Not Tonight *[Lil' Kim]* [6] • C U When U Get There *[Coolio]* [12] • Put The Monkey In It *[Dat Nigga Daz & Soopafly]* • Thug Paradise *[Capone-N-Noreaga]* • Way 2 Saucy *[Mac & A.K.]* • Get Down With Me *[Amani]* • Poppin' That Fly *[Oran "Juice" Jones]* • Hit 'Em Up *[Master P]* • Everlasting *[OutKast]* • In A Magazine *[911]* • Not Tonight *[Eightball & MJG]* • It's Alright *[Queen Latifah]* • What's Going On *[Black Caesar]* • Go Stetsa I *[Stetsasonic]* • Crazy Maze *[Des'ree]* • Route 69 *[Quad City DJ's]*

| 6/22/96 | ❶[1] | 25 | ▲ 101 | **Nutty Professor, The** | [V] | 8 | $8 | Def Jam 531911 |

Eddie Murphy/Jada Pinkett/James Coburn/Dave Chappelle
Touch Me Tease Me *[Case]* [14] • I Like *[Montell Jordan]* [28] • My Crew Can't Go For That *[Trigger Tha Gambler]* • Ain't Nobody *[Monica]* • Pillow *[Richie Rich]* • Last Night *[Az Yet]* [9] • Come Around *[Dos Of Soul]* • We Want Yo Hands Up *[Warren G]* • Ain't No Nigga *[Jay Z]* [50] • Breaker 1, Breaker 2 *[Def Squad]* • Doin It Again *[L.L. Cool J]* • Nasty Immigrants *[12 O'Clock]* • Love You Down *[Da Bassment]*

| 5/18/96 | 8 | 10 | 102 | **Original Gangstas** | [V] | 41 | $8 | Noo Trybe 41533 |

Fred Williamson/Jim Brown/Pam Grier/Paul Winfield/Isabel Sanford
Inner City Blues *[Ideal]* • World Is A Ghetto *[Geto Boys]* [82] • X.O. *[Luniz]* • On The Grind *[Click]* • White Chalk *[Junior M.A.F.I.A.]* • How Many *[N.O. Joe]* • Flowamatic 9 *[3X Crazy]* • Ain't No Fun *[Dino]* • Rivals *[Facemob]* • War's On *[Almighty RSO]* • Who Wanna Be The Villain *[MC Ren]* • Slugs *[Spice 1]* • How Does It Feel *[Ice T]* • Good Stuff *[Dino]*

| 5/20/95 | 5 | 11 | ● 103 | **Panther** | [V] | 37 | $8 | Mercury 525479 |

Kadeem Hardison/Bokeem Woodbine/Tyrin Turner/Joe Don Baker
Freedom (Theme from Panther) *[Various Artists]* [18] • Express Yourself *[Joe]* • We'll Meet Again *[BLACKstreet]* • Black People *[Funkadelic]* • Let's Straighten It Out *[Monica & Usher]* • The Points *[Various Artists]* [80] • Slick Partner *[Bobby Brown]* • Stand (You Got To) *[Aaron Hall]* • World Is A Ghetto *[Da Lench Mob]* • If I Were Your Woman *[Shanice]* • We Shall Not Be Moved *[Sounds Of Blackness]* • Natural Woman *[Female]* • Head Nod *[Hodge]* • Stand *[Tony Toni Toné]* • Don't Give Me No Broccoli And Tell Me It's Greens *[Last Poets]* • Star Spangled Banner *[Brian McKnight]* • Ultimate Sacrifice *[William Kidd]*

| 8/3/85 | 68 | 2 | 104 | **Perfect** .... | [V] | 45 | $8 | Arista 8278 |

John Travolta/Jamie Lee Curtis/Marilu Henner/Laraine Newman

| 8/17/96 | 40 | 4 | 105 | **Phat Beach** | [V] | | $8 | TVT Soundtrax 8020 |

Jermaine Hopkins/Brian Hooks/Tiny Lister/**Coolio**/Alma Collins

Pipe Dreams - see KNIGHT, Gladys
Gladys Knight/Barry Hankerson/Bruce French/Sally Kirkland

| 4/4/98 | 2[3] | 31 | ▲ 106 | **Players Club, The** | [V] | 10 | $8 | A&M 540886 |

Bernie Mac/Monica Calhoun/Lisa Raye/**Ice Cube**/Jamie Foxx
We Be Clubbin' *[Ice Cube]* • Who Are You Lovin' *[Ice Cube]* • Same Tempo *[Changing Faces]* • Under Pressure *[Kurupt]* • You Know I'm A Ho *[Master P & Ice Cube]* • Splackavellie *[Pressha]* [14] • You Delinquent *[Mack 10 & Scarface]* • From Marcy To Hollywood *[Jay-Z]* • Don't Play Me Wrong *[Brownstone]* • Shake Whatcha Mama Gave Ya (But Make Sho Your Niggas Pay Ya) *[Mia X]* • What A Woman Feels *[Public Announcement]* • Don't Worry (My Shorty) *[Rufus Blaq]* • My Loved One *[Ice Cube]* • Get Mine *[Mr. Dalvin]* • Dreamin' *[Emmage]*

| 7/17/93 | 3 | 19 | ● 107 | **Poetic Justice** | [V] | 23 | $8 | Epic 57131 |

Janet Jackson/2 Pac/Tyra Farrell/Regina King/Joe Torry
Get It Up *[TLC]* [15] • Indo Smoke *[Mista Grimm]* [63] • Well Alright *[Babyface]* • Call Me A Mack *[Usher Raymond]* • Waiting For You *[Tony! Toni! Toné!]* • One In A Million *[Pete Rock & C.L. Smooth]* • Nite & Day *[Cultural Revolution]* • Poor Man's Poetry *[Naughty By Nature]* • I've Been Waiting *[Terri & Monica]* • Niggas Don't Give A Fuck *[Dogg Pound]* • Definition Of A Thug Nigga *[2 Pac]* • I Wanna Be Your Man *[Chaka Demus & Pliers]* • Cash In My Hands *[Nice & Smooth]* • Never Dreamed You'd Leave In Summer *[Stevie Wonder]* • Justice's Groove *[Stanley Clarke]*

| 5/29/93 | 46 | 4 | 108 | **Posse** .... | [V] | 178 | $8 | A&M 0081 |

Mario Van Peebles/Tone Loc/Big Daddy Kane/Blair Underwood

Preacher's Wife, The - see HOUSTON, Whitney
Denzel Washington/Whitney Houston/Gregory Hines/Courtney B. Vance

| 12/26/98+ | 32 | 11 | ● 109 | **Prince Of Egypt - Inspirational, The** .... | [V] | 73 | $8 | DreamWorks 50050 |

animated movie; voices by: Val Kilmer/Ralph Fiennes/Michelle Pfeiffer/Sandra Bullock/Jeff Goldblum; this album contains songs inspired by the movie

Purple Rain - see PRINCE
Prince/Apollonia/Morris Day/Clarence Williams III

| 9/22/90 | 72 | 9 | 110 | **Return Of Superfly** .... | [V] | | $8 | Capitol 94244 |

Nathan Purdee/Margaret Avery/Leonard Thomas/David Groh

| 2/1/97 | ❶[1] | 17 | ● 111 | **Rhyme & Reason** .... | [V] | 16 | $8 | Priority 50635 |

concert movie
Nothin' But The Cavi Hit *[Mack 10 & Tha Dogg Pound]* • Wild Hot *[Busta Rhymes & A Tribe Called Quest]* • Reason For Rhyme *[Eight Ball & MJG]* • Uni-4-Orm *[Ras Kass, Heltah Skeltah & Cannibus]* • Bogus Mayn *[Crucial Conflict]* • Every Year *[E-40]* • Tragedy *[RZA]* • Represent *[MC Eiht]* • Niggaz Don't Want It *[Lost Boyz]* • Bring It Back *[KRS-ONE]* • Is There A Heaven 4 A Gangsta? *[Master P]* • Liquor Store Run *[Volume 10]* • The Way It Iz *[Guru, Kai Bee & Lil' Dap]* • Business First *[Nyoo & DeCoca]* • No Identity *[Delinquent Habits]*

Richard Pryor Live On The Sunset Strip - see PRYOR, Richard
concert movie

Richard Pryor: Here And Now - see PRYOR, Richard
concert movie

DEBUT	PEAK	WKS	Gold	Album Title	Pop #	$	Label & Number

3/7/98 | **13** | 10 | | **112 Ride** .... [V] | 54 | $8 | Tommy Boy 1227
Malik Yoba/Melissa De Sousa/John Witherspoon/Fredro Starr

Right On! - see LAST POETS, The
David Nelson/Felipe Luciano/Gylan Kain

5/7/77 | **32** | 6 | ▲ | **113 Rocky** .... [I] | 4 | $10 | United Artists 693
Sylvester Stallone/Talia Shire/Carl Weathers/Burgess Meredith; cp/cd: Bill Conti

8/30/86 | **38** | 7 | | **114 Running Scared** .... [V] | 43 | $8 | MCA 6169
Gregory Hines/Billy Crystal/Steven Bauer/Dan Hedaya/Jimmy Smits

10/3/98 | **2**¹ | 32 | ▲ | **115 Rush Hour** .... [V] | 5 | $8 | Def Jam 558663
Jackie Chan/Chris Tucker/Tom Wilkinson/Chris Penn/Elizabeth Peña
How Deep Is Your Love [Dru Hill] [1] • Faded Pictures [Case & Joe] • **Can I Get A...** [Jay-Z] [6] • And You Don't Stop [Wu-Tang Clan] • Bitch Betta Have My Money [Ja Rule] • Disco [Grenique] • Impress The Kid [Slick Rick] • If I Die Tonight [Montell Jordan] • Glad That We Loved [Jon B.] • Terror Squadians [Terror Squad] • Way Too Crazy [Tray Dee] • N.B.C. [Charli Baltimore] • You'll Never Miss Me 'Til I'm Gone [Terry Dexter] • Nasty Girl [Kasino] • No Love [Imajin] • Tell The Feds [Too $hort] • Rush Hour Title Theme [Lalo Schifrin]

8/16/86 | **50** | 8 | ● | **116 Ruthless People** .... [V] | 20 | $8 | Epic 40398
Danny Devito/Bette Midler/Judge Reinhold/Helen Slater/Anita Morris

Saturday Night Fever - see BEE GEES
John Travolta/Karen Lynn Gorney/Donna Pescow/Barry Miller

4/2/88 | **14** | 15 | | **117 School Daze** .... [V] | 81 | $8 | EMI-Manhattan 48680
Laurence Fishburne/Giancarlo Esposito/Tisha Campbell/Spike Lee

10/12/96 | **3** | 41 | ▲ | **118 Set It Off** .... [V] | 4 | $8 | EastWest 61951
Jada Pinkett/**Queen Latifah**/Vivica A. Fox/Kimberly Elise
Set It Off [Organized Noize] • **Missing You** [Brandy, Tamia, Gladys Knight & Chaka Khan] [25] • **Don't Let Go (Love)** [En Vogue] [2] • Days Of Our Livez [Bone Thugs-N-Harmony] • Live To Regret [Busta Rhymes] • Sex Is On My Mind [Blulight] • Angel [Simply Red] • Name Callin' [Queen Latifah] • Angelic Wars [Goodie Mob] • Come On [Billy Lawrence] • Let It Go [Ray J.] • Hey Joe [Seal] • The Heist [Da 5 Footaz] • From Yo Blind Side [X-Man]

Shaft - see HAYES, Isaac
Richard Roundtree/Moses Gunn/Charles Cioffi/Antonio Fargas

7/7/73 | **27** | 12 | | **119 Shaft in Africa** .... [I] | 147 | $20 | ABC 793
Richard Roundtree/Vonetta McGee/Frank Finlay/Neda Arneric; cp/cd: Johnny Pate

Short Eyes - see MAYFIELD, Curtis
Bruce Davison/Jose Perez/Nathan George/Don Blakely

8/26/95 | **❶**⁶ | 30 | ▲ | **120 Show, The** .... [V] | 4 | $8 | Def Jam 529021
concert movie
Hip Hop Is... [Kid Creole, Kid Capri, Ecstasy] • **Live!!!** [Onyx] [81] • Move On... [Slick Rick] • My Block [2Pac] • **What's Up Star?** [Suga] [72] • Headbanger Boogie [Method Man] • **How High** [Redman/Method Man] [10] • It's Entertainment... [Dr. Dre] • Everyday Thang [Bone Thugs-N-Harmony] • Everyday It Rains [Mary J. Blige] • It's All I Had [Notorious B.I.G.] • **Ol' Skool** [Isaac 2 Isaac] [52] • Domino's In The House [Domino] • **Summertime In The LBC** [Dove Shack] [37] • West Coast... [Treach] • Sowhatusayin [South Central Cartel Productions] • Zoom Zooms And Wam Wam [Jayo Felony] • Droppin Bombz [Tray D] • Save Yourself [Snoop Doggy Dogg] • Still Can't Fade It [Warren G] • Papa Luv It [L.L. Cool J] • Glamour And Glitz [Tribe Called Quest] • Nuttin' But A Drumbeat... [Russell Simmons] • Kill Dem All [Kali Ranks] • Me And My Bitch (Live From Philly) [Notorious B.I.G.] • It's What I Feel Inside... [Kid Creole & Ecstasy] • The Show Theme [Stanley Clarke]

12/25/93+ | **40** | 15 | ● | **121 Sister Act 2: Back In The Habit** .... [V] | 74 | $8 | Hollywood 61562
Whoopi Goldberg/Kathy Najimy/James Coburn/Maggie Smith/Mary Wickes

5/3/97 | **33** | 8 | | **122 6th Man, The** .... [V] | | $8 | Hollywood 62097
Marlon Wayans/Kadeem Hardison/Kevin Dunn/David Paymer/Gary Jones

10/31/98 | **24** | 5 | | **123 Slam** .... [V] | 84 | $8 | Immortal 69587
Saul Williams/Sonja Sohn/Bonz Malone/Beau Sia/Lawrence Wilson

Slaughter's Big Rip-Off - see BROWN, James
Jim Brown/Ed McMahon/Brock Peters/Don Stroud/Art Metrano

10/4/97 | **❶**¹ | 38 | ▲² | **124 Soul Food** .... [V] | 4 | $8 | LaFace 26041
Vanessa Williams/Vivica A. Fox/Nia Long/Mekhi Phifer
A Song For Mama [Boyz II Men] [1] • Call Me [BLACKstreet] • I Care 'Bout You [Milestone] [10] • **What About Us** [Total] [4] • Don't Stop What You're Doing [Puff Daddy] • We're Not Making Love No More [Dru Hill] • Baby I [Tenderoni] • Let's Do It Again [Xscape] • In Due Time [OutKast] • Slow Jam [Monica & Usher] • Boys And Girls [Tony Toni Toné] • You Are The Man [En Vogue] • September [Earth, Wind & Fire] [1]

10/4/97 | **13** | 9 | | **125 Soul In The Hole** .... [V] | 73 | $8 | Loud/RCA 67531
concert movie

10/2/71 | **10** | 14 | | **126 Soul To Soul** .... [V] | 112 | $15 | Atlantic 7207
concert movie
Soul To Soul [Ike & Tina Turner] • Run Shaker Life [Voices Of East Harlem] • Heyjorler [Eddie Harris & Les McCann] • Freedom Song [Roberta Flack] • Tryin' Times [Roberta Flack] • Medley: Are You Sure/He's Alright [Staple Singers] • I Smell Trouble [Ike & Tina Turner] • Funky Broadway [Wilson Pickett] • Land Of 1000 Dances [Wilson Pickett]

6/12/82 | **42** | 8 | | **127 Soup For One** .... [V] | 168 | $10 | Mirage 19353
Saul Rubinek/Marcia Strassman/Gerrit Graham; sw: Bernard Edwards and Nile Rodgers (Chic)

11/30/96+ | **5** | 60 | ▲⁵ | **128 Space Jam** .... [V] | 5 | $8 | Warner Sunset 82961
Michael Jordan/Wayne Knight/Theresa Randle/Bill Murray
Fly Like An Eagle [Seal] [44] • The Winner [Coolio] • Space Jam [Quad City DJ's] [49] • **I Believe I Can Fly** [R. Kelly] [1] • Hit 'Em High [B Real/Busta Rhymes/Coolio/LL Cool J/Method Man] • I Found My Smile Again [D'Angelo] • **For You I Will** [Monica] [2] • Upside Down ('Round-N-'Round) [Salt-N-Pepa] • Givin' U All That I've Got [Robin S.] • Basketball Jones [Barry White & Chris Rock] • I Turn To You [All-4-One] • All Of My Days [R. Kelly] • That's The Way (I Like It) [Spin Doctors] • Buggin' [Bugs Bunny]

Sparkle - see FRANKLIN, Aretha
Philip Michael Thomas/Irene Cara/Dorian Harewood

5/17/97 | **9** | 16 | | **129 Sprung** .... [V] | 89 | $8 | Qwest 46541
Tisha Campbell/Rusty Cundieff/Paula Jai Parker/Joe Torry
Who You Wit [Jay-Z] [25] • Let Me Know [Keystone] • Group Home Family [Canibus] • I Don't Know [Next Level] • Move On (I'm Leaving) [Forte] • If It Ain't Love [Keystone] • One In A Million [Aaliyah] • I Still Love You [Monifah] • Since You've Gone Away (The Lockdown Anthem) [Bonnie & Clyde] • 2 Nite's The Nite [Mr. Dalvin] • Goal Tendin' [E-40] • Freak [Money Boss Players] • Let's Get It Started [G-Ratz] • Bounce [Noggin Nodders] • Don't Ask My Neighbor [Tisha Campbell & Tichina Arnold] • Secret Garden [Quincy Jones] • I Want Your Love [Stanley Clarke]

8/30/97 | **26** | 7 | | **130 Steel** .... [V] | 185 | $8 | Qwest 46678
Shaquille O'Neal/Annabeth Gish/Richard Roundtree/Judd Nelson

12/24/94+ | **34** | 10 | | **131 Street Fighter** .... [V] | 135 | $8 | Priority 53948
Jean-Claude Van Damme/Raul Julia/Kylie Minogue/Wes Studi

SOUNDTRACKS — Cont'd

DEBUT	PEAK	WKS	Gold	#	Album Title		Pop #	$	Label & Number
5/30/98	3	20		132	**Streets Is Watching**	[V]	27	$8	Roc-A-Fella 558132

Jay-Z/Dame Dash/Kareem Burke
It's Alright [Memphis Bleek & Jay-Z] [32] • Love For Free [Rell] [28] • Only A Customer [Jay-Z] • Pimp This Love [Christion] • Murdergram [Murder, Inc.] • The Doe [Diamonds In Da Rough] • Crazy [Usual Suspects] • In My Lifetime [Jay-Z] • Your Love [Christion] • Thugs R Us [DJ Clue] • My Nigga Hill Figga [M.O.P.] • Celebration [Team Roc]

DEBUT	PEAK	WKS	Gold	#	Album Title		Pop #	$	Label & Number
11/30/91+	64	11		133	Strictly Business	[V]		$8	Uptown/MCA 10428

Tommy Davidson/Joseph C. Phillips/Anne Marie Johnson/Halle Berry

DEBUT	PEAK	WKS	Gold	#	Album Title		Pop #	$	Label & Number
4/27/96	18	11		134	Substitute, The	[V]	90	$8	Priority 50576

Tom Berenger/Ernie Hudson/Diane Venora/Glenn Plummer

DEBUT	PEAK	WKS	Gold	#	Album Title		Pop #	$	Label & Number
3/5/94	34	13		135	Sugar Hill	[V]	169	$8	Beacon 11016

Wesley Snipes/Michael Wright/Theresa Randle/Clarence Williams III

DEBUT	PEAK	WKS	Gold	#	Album Title		Pop #	$	Label & Number
5/4/96	❶[1]	17	▲	136	**Sunset Park**	[V]	4	$8	Flavor Unit 61904

Rhea Perlman/Fredro Starr/Carol Kane/Camille Saviola
High 'Til I Die [2Pac] • Motherless Child [Ghostface Killer] • Just Doggin' [Dogg Pound] • Back At You [Mobb Deep] • Are You Ready [Aaliyah] • It's Alright [Groove Theory] • Elements I'm Among [Queen Latifah] • **Keep On, Keepin' On** [MC Lyte] [3] • **Hoop N Yo Face** [69 Boyz] [62] • For The Funk [Adina Howard] • We Don't Need It [Junior M.A.F.I.A.] • All Uv It [Big Mike] • Thangz Changed [Onyx] • Shorty's Game [Miles Goodman]

Superfly - see MAYFIELD, Curtis
Ron O'Neal/Carl Lee/Sheila Frazier/Julius W. Harris

Superfly T.N.T. - see OSIBISA
Ron O'Neal/Roscoe Lee Browne/Sheila Frazier/Robert Guillaume

DEBUT	PEAK	WKS	Gold	#	Album Title		Pop #	$	Label & Number
6/12/71	13	23		137	Sweet Sweetback's Baadasssss Song	[I]	139	$20	Stax 3001

Melvin Van Peebles/Rhetta Hughes/Simon Chuckster/John Amos

DEBUT	PEAK	WKS	Gold	#	Album Title		Pop #	$	Label & Number
5/27/95	❶[1]	14	●	138	**Tales From The Hood**	[V]	16	$8	MCA 11243

Corbin Bernsen/David Alan Grier/Wings Hauser/Clarence Williams III
Let Me At Them [Wu-Tang Clan] • Face Mob [Face Mob] • **Tales From The Hood** [Domino] [51] • Born II Die [Spice 1] • Ol' Dirty's Back [Ol Dirty Bastard] • I'm Talkin' To Myself [NME & Grench The Mean 1] • The Hood Got Me Feelin' The Pain [Havoc & Prodeje] • One Less Nigga [MC Eiht] • From The Dark Side [Gravediggaz] • Death Represents My Hood [Bokie Loc] • Hot Ones Echo Thru The Ghetto [Click] • The Grave [N.G.N.]

DEBUT	PEAK	WKS	Gold	#	Album Title		Pop #	$	Label & Number
3/11/89	87	7		139	Tap	[V]	166	$8	Epic 45084

Gregory Hines/Suzzanne Douglas/Joe Morton/Sammy Davis Jr.

DEBUT	PEAK	WKS	Gold	#	Album Title		Pop #	$	Label & Number
5/26/90	35	10	▲	140	Teenage Mutant Ninja Turtles	[V]	13	$8	SBK 91066

Judith Hoag/Elias Koteas

DEBUT	PEAK	WKS	Gold	#	Album Title		Pop #	$	Label & Number
5/13/78	6	17	▲	141	**Thank God It's Friday**	[V]	10	$20	Casablanca 7099 [2]

Donna Summer/Valerie Landsburg/Jeff Goldblum/Debra Winger
Thank God It's Friday [Love And Kisses] [23] • After Dark [Pattie Brooks] • With Your Love [Donna Summer] • **Last Dance** [Donna Summer] [5] • Disco Queen [Paul Jabara] • Find My Way [Cameo] • **Too Hot Ta Trot** [Commodores] [1] • Leatherman's Theme [Wright Bros. Flying Machine] • I Wanna Dance [Marathon] • Take It To The Zoo [Sunshine] • Sevilla Nights [Santa Esmeralda] • You're The Most Precious Thing In My Life [Love And Kisses] • Do You Want The Real Thing [D.C. Larue] • Trapped In A Stairway [Paul Jabara] • Floyd's Theme [Natural Juices] • Lovin', Livin' And Givin' [Diana Ross] • Love Masterpiece [Thelma Houston] • Je T'Aime (Moi Non Plus) [Donna Summer]

That's The Way Of The World - see EARTH, WIND & FIRE
Harvey Keitel/Ed Nelson/Cynthia Bostick/Bert Parks/Jimmy Boyd

DEBUT	PEAK	WKS	Gold	#	Album Title		Pop #	$	Label & Number
3/2/96	5	31	●	142	**Thin Line Between Love & Hate, A**	[V]	22	$8	Warner 46134

Martin Lawrence/Lynn Whitfield/Regina King/**Della Reese**
Beware Of My Crew [L.B.C. Crew] • **A Thin Line Between Love & Hate** [H-Town] [6] • Damned If I Do [Somethin' For The People] • Freak Tonight [R. Kelly] • I Don't Hang [Soopafly] • Love Got My Mind Trippin' [Ganjah K] • Ring My Bell [Luniz] • Playa Fo Real [Dru Down] • Chocolate City [Roger Troutman] • Thin Line [Drawz] • It's Ladies Night At Chocolate City [Dark Complexion] • Knocks Me Off My Feet [Tevin Campbell] • **Let's Stay Together** [Eric Benet] [45] • Come Over [Sandra St. Victor] • Way Back When [Smooth]

Three The Hard Way - see IMPRESSIONS, The
Jim Brown/Fred Williamson/Jim Kelly/Alex Rocco/Corbin Bernsen

DEBUT	PEAK	WKS	Gold	#	Album Title		Pop #	$	Label & Number
11/18/67	8	10		143	To Sir, With Love	[I+V]	16	$25	Fontana 67569

Sidney Poitier/Judy Geeson/Christian Roberts/Lulu; cp/cd: Ron Grainer
To Sir With Love [Lulu] [9] • Stealing My Love From Me [Lulu] • Thackeray Meets Faculty, Then Alone • Off And Running [Mindbenders] • Thackeray Loses Temper, Gets An Idea • Museum Outings Montage "To Sir, With Love" • Classical Lesson • Perhaps I Could Tidy Your Desk • Potter's Loss Of Temper In Gym • Thackeray Reads Letter About Job • Thackeray And Denham Box In Gym • The Funeral • It's Getting Harder All The Time [Mindbenders]

Together Brothers - see LOVE UNLIMITED ORCHESTRA
Glynn Turman/Anthony Wilson/Ahmad Nurradin/Richard Yniguez

DEBUT	PEAK	WKS	Gold	#	Album Title		Pop #	$	Label & Number
12/12/92	16	12		144	Trespass	[V]	82	$8	Sire 26978

Bill Paxton/William Sadler/Ice Cube/Ice-T/Glenn Plummer

Trouble Man - see GAYE, Marvin
Robert Hooks/Paul Winfield/Ralph Waite/Paula Kelly

Truck Turner - see HAYES, Isaac
Isaac Hayes/Yaphet Kotto/Alan Weeks/Sam Laws

Under The Cherry Moon - see PRINCE
Prince/Jerome Benton/Kristin Scott Thomas/Steven Berkoff

Uptight - see BOOKER T. & THE MG'S
Raymond St. Jacques/Ruby Dee/Frank Silvera/Roscoe Lee Browne

DEBUT	PEAK	WKS	Gold	#	Album Title		Pop #	$	Label & Number
12/2/95	❶[10]	70	▲[7]	145	**Waiting To Exhale**	[V]	1[5]	$8	Arista 18796

Whitney Houston/Angela Bassett/Lela Rochon/Loretta Devine
Exhale (Shoop Shoop) [Whitney Houston] [1] • Why Does It Hurt So Bad [Whitney Houston] [22] • Let It Flow [Toni Braxton] [flip] • It Hurts Like Hell [Aretha Franklin] [51] • Sittin' Up In My Room [Brandy] [2] • This Is How It Works [TLC] • Not Gon' Cry [Mary J. Blige] [1] • My Funny Valentine [Chaka Khan] • And I Gave My Love To You [Sonja Marie] • All Night Long [SWV] • Wey U [Chanté Moore] • My Love, Sweet Love [Patti LaBelle] • Kissing You [Faith Evans] [flip] • Love Will Be Waiting At Home [For Real] • How Could You Call Her Baby [Shanna] • Count On Me [Whitney Houston & CeCe Winans] [7]

DEBUT	PEAK	WKS	Gold	#	Album Title		Pop #	$	Label & Number
2/17/73	❶[2]	19		146	**Wattstax: The Living Word**	[V]	28	$20	Stax 3010 [2]

concert movie
Medley: Oh La De Da/I Like The Things About Me/Respect Yourself/I'll Take You There [Staple Singers] • Medley: Knock On Wood/Lay Your Loving On Me [Eddie Floyd] • Medley: I Like What You're Doing (To Me)/Gee Whiz/I Have A Good Who Leaves [Carla Thomas] • Medley: The Breakdown/Do The Funky Chicken/Do The Funky Penguin [Rufus Thomas] • Medley: Son Of Shaft/Feel It/I Can't Turn You Loose [Bar-Kays] • Medley: Killing Floor/I'll Play The Blues For You/Angel Of Mercy [Albert King] • Medley: I Don't Know What This World Is Coming To/Hearsay [Soul Children] • Ain't No Sunshine [Isaac Hayes]

DEBUT	PEAK	WKS	Gold	#	Album Title		Pop #	$	Label & Number
9/15/73	30	5		147	Wattstax 2: The Living Word	[V]	157	$20	Stax 3018 [2]

more music from the movie

DEBUT	PEAK	WKS	Gold	Album Title	Pop #	$	Label & Number

SOUNDTRACKS — Cont'd

What's Love Got To Do With It - see TURNER, Tina
Angela Bassett/Laurence Fishburne/Vanessa Bell Calloway

DEBUT	PEAK	WKS		Album Title	Pop #	$	Label & Number
3/1/97	64	3	148	**When We Were Kings** .... [V]		$8	Mercury 534462

documentary about Muhammad Ali and George Foreman

| 5/2/92 | 48 | 9 | 149 | **White Men Can't Jump** .... [V] | 92 | $8 | EMI 98414 |

Wesley Snipes/Woody Harrelson/Rosie Perez/Kadeem Hardison

| 5/9/92 | 79 | 5 | 150 | **White Men Can't Rap** .... [V] | | $8 | EMI 99087 |

Wesley Snipes/Woody Harrelson/Rosie Perez; more music from the movie *White Men Can't Jump*

| 5/8/93 | 8 | 13 | 151 | **Who's The Man?** .... [V] | 32 | $8 | Uptown/MCA 10794 |

Doctor Dre & Ed Lover/Badja Djola/Denis Leary
Part And Bullshit *[Big]* • **Let's Go Through The Motions** *[Jodeci]* **[31]** • What's Next On The Menu? *[Pete Rock & C.L. Smooth]* • **You Don't Have To Worry** *[Mary J. Blige]* **[11]** • Hittin' Switches *[Erick Sermon]* • Hotness *[Heavy D & Buju Banton]* • **Who's The Man?** *[House Of Pain]* **[77]** • Lovin' You *[Crystal J. Johnson]* • Pimp Or Die *[Father M.C.]* • Hello, It's Me *[Spark 950 & Timbo King]* • Ease Up *[3rd Eye & The Group Home]*

| 9/26/98 | 15 | 6 | 152 | **Why Do Fools Fall In Love** .... [V] | 55 | $8 | EastWest 62265 |

Halle Berry/Vivica A. Fox/Lela Rochon/Larenz Tate/**Little Richard**

| 3/23/74 | 52 | 5 | 153 | **Willie Dynamite** .... [V] | | $12 | MCA 393 |

Roscoe Orman/Diana Sands/Thalmus Rasulala/Roger Robinson

| 10/21/78 | 33 | 8 | ● 154 | **Wiz, The** .... [M] | 40 | $15 | MCA 14000 [2] |

Diana Ross/Michael Jackson/Richard Pryor/Nipsey Russell; sw: Charlie Smalls; cd: Quincy Jones; also see **Original Casts**

Woman in Red, The - see WONDER, Stevie
Gene Wilder/Kelly LeBrock/Gilda Radner/Charles Grodin

| 5/23/98 | 8 | 19 | 155 | **Woo** .... [V] | 52 | $8 | Untertainment 69364 |

Jada Pinkett Smith/Tommy Davidson/Dave Chappelle/**LL Cool J**
Woo Woo (Freak Out) *[M.C. Lyte]* • **Money** *[Charli Baltimore]* **[59]** • Bouncin' *[Lost Boyz]* • **Nobody Does It Better** *[Nate Dogg]* **[18]** • Get'n It On *[Mona Lisa]* • If You Love Me *[Stokley]* • T Shirt & Panties *[Adina Howard]* • Niggas Dun Started Sumthin' *[DMX, The Lox, Mase]* • **And I Telling You I'm Not Going** *[Jane Blaze]* • 357 *[Cam'ron]* **[88]** • Let It Be *[Allure]* • Take A Ride *[Heavy D]* • I Will *[Simone Hines]* • Superman *[Chico DeBarge]* • Searching (For Your Love) *[Brownstone]* • Drama In My Life *[Eightball]* • I Know You Love Her *[Too $hort]*

| 5/30/98 | 89 | 1 | 156 | **Woo - The DJ's Choice From The Motion Picture Soundtrack** .... [V] | | $12 | Untertainment 78941 [2] |

more music from the movie; available only on vinyl

| 6/20/70 | 19 | 19 | 157 | **Woodstock** .... [V] | 1⁴ | $20 | Cotillion 500 [3] |

concert movie

ORIGINAL CASTS

The original cast stars are listed below the title. Also shown are the Lyricist (ly), Music Writer (mu) and Songwriter (sw).

| 5/22/82 | 4 | 26 | ● 1 | **Dreamgirls** | 11 | $10 | Geffen 2007 |

Jennifer Holliday/Loretta Devine/Cleavant Derricks; mu: Henry Krieger; ly: Tom Eyen
Move (You're Steppin' On My Heart) • Fake Your Way To The Top • Cadillac Car • Steppin' To The Bad Side • Family • Dreamgirls • Press Conference • **And I Am Telling You I'm Not Going** *[Jennifer Holliday]* **[1]** • Ain't No Party • When I First Saw You • **I Am Changing** *[Jennifer Holliday]* **[29]** • I Meant You No Harm • The Rap • Firing Of Jimmy • I Miss You Old Friend • One Night Only • Hard To Say Goodbye, My Love

| 5/10/75 | 30 | 14 | ● 2 | **Wiz, The** | 43 | $12 | Atlantic 18137 |

Stephanie Mills/Tiger Haynes/Ted Ross/Hinton Battle; sw: Charlie Smalls; also see **Soundtracks**

TELEVISION ALBUMS

The stars of the show are listed directly below the title.

| 1/11/97 | 77 | 4 | 1 | **All That - The Album** .... [V] | 134 | $8 | Loud/RCA 67423 |

Kel Mitchell/Kenan Thompson

| 3/8/86 | 52 | 10 | 2 | **Cosby Show, Music From The - A House Full Of Love** ....[I] | 125 | $8 | Columbia 40270 |

Bill Cosby/Phylicia Rashad; sw: Bill Cosby/Stu Gardner; pf: Grover Washington Jr.

| 11/28/92 | 41 | 8 | 3 | **Jacksons: An American Dream, The** .... [V] | 137 | $8 | Motown 6356 |

Lawrence Hilton-Jacobs/Lynn Whitfield/**Vanessa Williams**

| 10/19/85 | 9 | 24 | ▲⁴ 4 | **Miami Vice** .... [V] | 1¹¹ | $10 | MCA 6150 |

Don Johnson/**Philip Michael Thomas**
The Original Miami Vice Theme *[Jan Hammer]* • Smuggler's Blues *[Glenn Frey]* • Own The Night *[Chaka Khan]* **[66]** • You Belong To The City *[Glenn Frey]* • In The Air Tonight *[Phil Collins]* • **Miami Vice Theme** *[Jan Hammer]* **[10]** • Vice *[Grandmaster Melle Mel]* • **Better Be Good To Me** *[Tina Turner]* **[6]** • Flashback *[Jan Hammer]* • Chase *[Jan Hammer]* • Evan *[Jan Hammer]*

| 10/7/95 | 12 | 12 | 5 | **New York Undercover** .... [V] | 73 | $8 | Uptown/MCA 11342 |

Michael DeLorenzo/Malik Yoba/Patti D'Arbanville-Quinn

| 2/14/98 | 75 | 3 | 6 | **New York Undercover - A Night At Natalies** .... [V] | | $8 | MCA 11549 |

more songs from the TV show

ESPN

A sampling of artists featured on each album is listed directly below the title.

| 8/26/95 | 33 | 71 | ▲² 1 | **ESPN Presents Jock Jams Volume 1** .... | 30 | $8 | Tommy Boy 1137 |

Black Box, C & C Music Factory, Naughty By Nature, 69 Boyz, Technotronic, Village People

| 9/12/98 | 43 | 18 | ● 2 | **ESPN Presents Jock Jams Volume 4** .... | 20 | $8 | Tommy Boy 1266 |

Amber, Luke, Notorious B.I.G., Salt-N-Pepa, Will Smith, and others

MTV

A sampling of artists featured on each album is listed directly below the title.

| 6/29/91 | 91 | 3 | ● 1 | **Club MTV Party To Go - Volume One** .... | 38 | $8 | Tommy Boy 1037 |

Paula Abdul, Bell Biv DeVoe, Candyman, Digital Underground, M.C. Hammer, and others

| 8/1/98 | 91 | 2 | 2 | **MTV Jams** .... | | $8 | Kedar/Universal 53103 |

Busta Rhymes, Montell Jordan, R. Kelly, SWV, and others

| 12/13/97 | 46 | 11 | ● 3 | **MTV: Party To Go '98** .... | 50 | $8 | Tommy Boy 1234 |

Aaliyah, Foxy Brown, Lil' Kim, Mark Morrison, and others

| 12/12/98+ | 38 | 12 | ● 4 | **MTV: Party To Go '99** .... | 60 | $8 | Tommy Boy 1268 |

Big Punisher, Busta Rhymes, Missy Elliott, Next, and others

| 12/5/92+ | 67 | 11 | ▲ 5 | **MTV: Party To Go Volume 2** .... | 19 | $8 | Tommy Boy 1053 |

Another Bad Creation, Boyz II Men, Color Me Badd, Naughty By Nature, PM Dawn, and others

DEBUT	PEAK	WKS	Gold	Album Title	Pop #	$	Label & Number
				TELEVISION ALBUMS — Cont'd			
8/14/93	45	10	●	6 MTV: Party To Go Volume 3	29	$8	Tommy Boy 1074
				Mary J. Blige, Boyz II Men, House Of Pain, Jodeci, Shabba Ranks, and others			
8/14/93	48	9	●	7 MTV: Party To Go Volume 4	35	$8	Tommy Boy 1075
				Das EFX, En Vogue, Kris Kross, Naughty By Nature, TLC, and others			
6/18/94	42	10	●	8 MTV: Party To Go Volume 5	36	$8	Tommy Boy 1097
				Dr. Dre, H-Town, Onyx, 2 Pac, Zhané, and others			
12/10/94+	41	13	●	9 MTV: Party To Go Volume 6	54	$8	Tommy Boy 1109
				Aaliyah, Tevin Campbell, Coolio, Domino, R. Kelly, and others			
11/18/95	55	11	●	10 MTV: Party To Go Volume 7	54	$8	Tommy Boy 1138
				Bone Thugs-N-Harmony, Brandy, Adina Howard, Madonna, Total, and others			
12/9/95+	46	18	●	11 MTV: Party To Go Volume 8	47	$8	Tommy Boy 1139
				Brownstone, Coolio, Method Man, Naughty By Nature, Notorious B.I.G., and others			
7/27/96	31	10	●	12 MTV: Party To Go Volume 9	28	$8	Tommy Boy 1164
				Brandy, Coolio, Jodeci, R. Kelly, LL Cool J, Notorious B.I.G., and others			
11/16/96	50	12	●	13 MTV: Party To Go Volume 10	40	$8	Tommy Boy 1168
				Bone Thugs-N-Harmony, La Bouche, SWV, 2 Pac, and others			
3/14/98	75	2		14 MTV Presents: Hip Hop Back In The Day	152	$8	Priority 51070
				Kurtis Blow, Heavy D. & The Boyz, LL Cool J, M.C. Shan, Tone Loc, and others			
6/19/93	17	18		15 Uptown MTV Unplugged [L]	71	$8	Uptown/MCA 10858
				Mary J. Blige, Heavy D & The Boyz, Jodeci, and others			
7/12/97	42	7		16 Yo! MTV Raps	88	$8	Def Jam 534746
				Bone Thugs-N-Harmony, Foxy Brown, Lil' Kim, 2 Pac, Wu-Tang Clan, and others			

VARIOUS ARTIST COMPILATIONS

A sampling of artists featured on each album is listed directly below the title.

DEBUT	PEAK	WKS	Gold	Album Title	Pop #	$	Label & Number
7/13/96	12	10		1 America Is Dying Slowly	51	$8	Red Hot 61925
				Coolio, Domino, Goodie Mob, Spice 1, Wu-Tang Clan, and others			
5/17/97	53	16		2 ...And Then There Was Bass	198	$8	Tony Mercedes 26038
				B-Rock & The Bizz, A Few Good Men, Luke, and others			
10/31/98	17	16	●	3 Bad Boy Greatest Hits Volume 1	51	$8	Bad Boy 73022
				Faith Evans, The Lox, Mase, The Notorious B.I.G., 112, Puff Daddy, and others			
3/13/93	95	2		4 Bam Bam It's Murder		$8	Mango 9923
				Chaka Demus & Pliers, Brent Dowe, Nardo Ranks, Skullman, Taxi Gang, and others			
9/17/88	57	14		5 Bass That Ate Miami, The		$8	Pandisc 8801
				Maggatron Crushing Crew, Maggazulu Too, Palmerforce Two, and others			
12/23/95	44	9		6 Bay Area Playaz		$8	Anonymous 1002
				Deliquents, J.T. The Bigga Figga, R.B.L. Posse, Totally Insane, and others			
5/31/97	60	3		7 Best Of Black Market Records, The		$8	Black Market 50697
				Brotha Lynch Hung, Doomsday, Homicide, Lunasicc, and others			
11/9/91	82	4		8 Best Of Electric Slide, The		$8	SOH 7010
				Chill Rob G, Grandmaster Slice & Izzy Chill, World Class Wreckin Cru, Young & Restless, and others			
3/5/88	43	12		9 Best Of House Music		$12	Profile 1248 [2]
				Exit, Jeanne Harris, Hercules, Pleasure Pump, and others			
1/21/89	68	11		10 Best Of House Music Volume 2 - Gotta Have House		$12	Profile 1273 [2]
				Black Riot, Blaze, Natalie Cole, Kechia Jenkins, and others			
2/19/94	76	10		11 Big Blunts		$8	Tommy Boy 1077
				Lone Ranger, Rita Marley, Mighty Diamonds, Wayne Smith, and others			
5/17/97	53	2		12 Big Boy Presents: The Compilation Album		$8	Big Boy 0024
				Boot Camp Click, Ghetto Slaves, Ice Mike, Mystikal, and others			
9/16/95	90	2		13 Big Phat Ones Of Hip-Hop Volume I		$8	Boxtunes 444068
				Coolio, R. Kelly, Craig Mack, Method Man, Notorious B.I.G., and others			
4/26/75	54	2		14 Black Caucus Concert, The [L]		$12	Chess 60037
				Gladys Knight & The Pips, Kool & The Gang, Curtis Mayfield, War, and others			
10/12/91	76	6		15 Blues From The Montreux Jazz Festival [L]		$8	Malaco 2008
				Bobby Bland, Denise LaSalle, Mosley & Johnson and Johnnie Taylor			
3/8/97	99	1		16 Blunt Special Blends		$8	Blunt/TVT 1010
				Bounty Killer, Mic Geronimo, Royal Flush, and others			
11/21/98	100	1		17 Bootleg Booty! 2		$8	Intersound 9536
				Disco & The City Boyz, DJ Nasty Knock, MC Shy D, Sir Mix-A-Lot, and others			
4/19/97	49	16		18 Booty Mix 2	93	$8	Intersound 9510
				Luke, 95 South, 69 Boyz, and others			
4/18/98	98	1		19 Booty Mix 3 - Wiggle Patrol	182	$12	Intersound 9526 [2]
				Freak Nasty, Kilo, 12 Gauge, and others			
4/29/95	15	21		20 Boss Ballin	137	$8	Shot 7000
				C-Bo, D-Shot, R.B.L. Posse, and others			
6/27/98	48	6		21 Boss Ballin 2		$8	Shot 9000
				The Click, E-40, Luniz, Redman, Too $hort, and others			
8/16/69	46	5		22 Boy Meets Girl		$20	Stax 2024
				William Bell, Eddie Floyd, Johnnie Taylor, Carla Thomas, and others			
11/6/82	32	27		23 Casino Lights [L]	63	$10	Warner 23718
				Randy Crawford, Al Jarreau, David Sanborn, and others			
4/13/96	12	13		24 Cell Block Compilation	121	$8	Cell Bl./Pri. 50556
				The Delinquents, Devin, Father Dom, Richie Rich, Too $hort, and others			
7/18/98	52	6		25 Cellblock Compilation II - Face/Off		$12	Cellblock 0557 [2]
				Junior M.A.F.I.A., MC Breed, Too $hort, 2 Pac, and others			
12/21/96+	30	4		26 Christmas On Death Row [X]	155	$8	Death Row 90108
				Danny Boy, Michel'le, Snoop Doggy Dogg, and others			
12/12/87	30	6		27 Christmas Rap [X]	130	$10	Profile 1247
				Dana Dane, Derek B, Run-D.M.C., and others			
8/31/91	86	8		28 Cut It Up Def		$8	Pandisc 0101
				Dynamix 1+1, Jock D., Kooley C., Latin & Lethal, and others			

DEBUT	PEAK	WKS	Gold	Album Title	Pop #	$	Label & Number
				VARIOUS ARTIST COMPILATIONS — Cont'd			
12/14/96	**15**	31		29 Death Row - Greatest Hits	35	$12	Death Row 50677 [2]
				Dr. Dre, Ice Cube, The Lady Of Rage, Snoop Doggy Dogg, and others			
11/14/98	**22**	6		30 Def Jam Survival Of The Illest: Live From 125 N.Y.C.	84	$8	Def Jam 538176
				Foxy Brown, Def Squad, DMX, Method Man, Onyx, and others			
2/14/76	**53**	3		31 Disco-Trek		$12	Atlantic 18158
				Blue Magic, Jackie Moore, Sister Sledge, and others			
2/14/76	**48**	4		32 Discotech #3		$12	Motown 853
				Commodores, The Jackson 5, Eddie Kendricks, Smokey Robinson, and others			
4/11/98	**57**	5		33 D.J. Magic Mike Presents Bootyz In Motion	130	$8	Interscope 90188
				Bone Thugs-N-Harmony, Duice, Sir Mix-A-Lot, 69 Boyz, 2 Live Crew, and others			
12/6/97	**76**	3		34 DJ Skribble's Traffic Jams		$8	Warlock 2791
				Big Punisher, Mary J. Blige, Wyclef Jean, LL Cool J, and others			
11/18/95	**13**	42	●	35 Down South Hustlers Bouncin' And Swingin' Tha Value Pack Compilation	139	$12	No Limit 53993 [2]
				Eightball & MJG, Gangsta T, Master P, and others			
12/14/96	**3**	17	▲	36 Dr. Dre Presents...The Aftermath	6	$8	Aftermath 90044
				East Coast/West Coast Killas [Group Therapy] • Sh**tin' On The World [Mel-Man] • Blunt Time [RBX] • Been There Done That [Dr. Dre] • Choices [Kim Summerson] • As The World Keeps Turning [Miscellaneous] • Got Me Open [Hands-On] • Str-8 Gone [King T] • Please [Maurice Wilcher] • Do 4 Love [Jheryl Lockhart] • Sexy Dance [RC] • No Second Chance [Whoz Who] • L.A.W. (Lyrical Assault Weapon) [Sharief] • Nationowl [NOWL] • Fame [RC]			
2/6/82	**38**	9		37 Echoes Of An Era	105	$10	Elektra 60021
				Chick Corea, Joe Henderson, Freddie Hubbard, Chaka Khan and Lenny White			
1/12/91	**77**	10		38 Explicit Rap		$8	Priority 7993
				N.W.A., Too $hort, 2 Live Crew, and others			
12/1/73	**42**	7		39 Fillet Of Soul		$15	Stax 3021
				The Dramatics, Isaac Hayes, Mel and Tim, Johnnie Taylor, Rufus Thomas, and others			
11/25/95+	**15**	31		40 Funkmaster Flex: The Mix Tape Volume I	108	$8	Loud/RCA 66805
				Yvette Michelle, Keith Murray, Redman, Erick Sermon, and others			
3/1/97	**2**[1]	21	●	41 Funkmaster Flex: The Mix Tape Volume II	19	$8	Loud/RCA 67472
				Everyday & Everynight [Yvette Michelle] • Get Up [Masters At Work] • Keith Murray & Redman - Freestyle • Zulu War Chant [Time Zone] • Loud Hangover [Akinyele & Sadat] • 20 Minute Workout [DJ Kool] • Award Tour [Tribe Called Quest] • Erick Sermon - Freestyle • Medley: Shook Ones Pt. II [Mobb Deep]/Wu-Tang Clan Ain't Nothing Ta F' Wit [Wu-Tang Clan] • Incarcerated Scarfaces [Raekwon] • Fugees - Freestyle • I-ight [Doug E. Fresh] • Fat Joe & Punisher - Freestyle • Let's Be Specific [Cool Whip] • Hey Girlfriend Promo • 900 Number [Mark The 45 King] • All For One [Brand Nubian] • Party Groove [Showbiz] • Busta Rhymes - Freestyle • Give Up The Goods (Just Step) [Mobb Deep] • Puff Daddy Promo • Rasta T - Freestyle • Q-Tip - Freestyle • Puerto Rico [Frankie Cutlass] • Redman & Method Man - Freestyle • Peter Piper [Run-DMC] • Eric B. Is President [Eric B. & Rakim] • Make The Music With Your Mouth [Biz Markie] • Nobody Beats The Biz [Biz Markie] • I Got It Made [Special Ed] • Rock The Bells [L.L. Cool J] • Droppin' Science [Marley Marl] • Kaotic Style - Freestyle • KRS-One Speech • Cormega - Freestyle • Clear My Throat [DJ Kool] • Sucker MC's [Run-D.M.C.] • Back To Life (However Do You Want Me) [Soul II Soul] • Here We Go [Run-D.M.C.] • Mona Lisa [Slick Rick] • Flex Outro			
8/29/98	**2**[1]	11	●	42 Funkmaster Flex: The Mix Tape Volume III	4	$8	Loud/RCA 67647
				Freestyle Over Chic "Good Times" & "Take Me To The Mardi Gras" [Busy Bee] • Here We Go [Khadejia] • Freestyle Over Mobb Deep "Give Up The Goods (Just Step)" [DMX] • Freestyle Over Raekwon "Incarcerated Scarfaces" [Charlie Baltimore & Cam'Ron] • Ain't No Nigga (VA: Funkmaster Flex: The Mix Tape V. III) [Jay Z] • Freestyle Over Instrumental [KRS-One] • Wild For The Night [Rampage] • Thug Brothers [Big Punisher & Noreaga] • Freestyle Over Instrumental [Mos Def] • Prime Time [Alkaholiks & Xzibit] • Freestyle Over Xzibit "Los Angeles Times" [Common] • Freestyle Over Raekwon "Ice Cream" [Canibus] • Freestyle Over Wu-Tang Clan "Triumph" [Missy Elliott] • Freestyle Over "Mona Lisa" [Slick Rick] • Show Down [Buckshot & Q-Tip] • Do That [Cocoa Brovas] • Freestyle Over Mobb Deep "Shook Ones Pt. II" [Mariah Carey] • Freestyle Over Wu-Tang Clan "It's Yourz" [King Sun] • Freestyle Over Instrumental [Gang Starr] • Shake Whatcha Mama Gave Ya [Lyve-N- Dyrect] • Get Money [Junior M.A.F.I.A.] • Wu-Tang Cream Team Line-Up [Wu-Tang Clan] • Freestyle Over Tha Alkaholiks "Next Level" [Peter Gunz & Lord Tariq] • Freestyle Over Raekwon "Glaciers Of Ice" [Mobb Deep] • That Shit [Tribe Called Quest & JD] • Freestyle Over Mobb Deep "Hell On Earth" [Erykah Badu] • Freestyle Over Xzibit "At The Speed Of Life" [Big Punisher/Fat Joe/Terror Squad] • Shimmy Shimmy Ya [Ol Dirty Bastard] • Put Your Hammer Down [Wu-Tang Clan] • Jump Around [House Of Pain] • OPP [Naughty By Nature] • Whoop Whoop [DJ Pooh] • Freestyle Over Instrumental [Eightball] • Freestyle Over Mobb Deep "Drop A Gem On Em" [EPMD] • Freestyle Over Sadat X "Lump Lump" [Keith Murray] • Show Me Love [24/7] • Freestyle Over Instrumental [Busta Rhymes] • 10% DIS [Foxy Brown] • Freestyle Over Instrumental [Shaquille O'Neill & Sonja Blade]			
3/28/98	**54**	5		43 Ghetto Politix		$8	Thump 1100
				Big Dappa Don, Cold Blue, Dove Shack, Jayo Felony, and others			
1/31/87	**61**	5		44 Gift Rapping - The Select Best		$10	Select 21617
				The Real Roxanne, UTFO, Whistle, and others			
5/3/97	**71**	3		45 Gimmie Dat Beat - The Best Of D.C. Go Go Volume 2		$8	Liaison 1227
				Chuck Brown & The Soul Searchers, DJ Kool, Rare Essence, and others			
12/5/92	**11**	8		46 Handel's Messiah - A Soulful Celebration	82	$8	Reprise 26980
				Tevin Campbell, Chaka Khan, Gladys Knight, Johnny Mathis, Stevie Wonder, and others			
4/16/88	**48**	6		47 Hard As Hell!		$8	Profile 1251
				Demon Boyz, Derek B, DJ Hanway, Lady Sugar Sweet, and others			
12/3/88	**93**	2		48 Hard As Hell! Volume 2		$8	Profile 1264
				Derek B, D.J. Daddy, Hijack, M.C. Duke, and others			
9/13/97	**42**	7		49 Heat	161	$8	Boss/Swerve 70012
				Celly Cell, Dru Down, Snoop Doggy Dogg, 2 Pac, and others			
4/6/68	**35**	2		50 History of Rhythm & Blues, volume 3/Rock & Roll 1956-57	189	$20	Atlantic 8163
				LaVern Baker, The Clovers, The Drifters, Joe Turner, Chuck Willis, and others			
12/5/92+	**59**	6	●	51 Hitsville USA - The Motown Singles Collection 1959-1971		$30	Motown 6312 [4]
				The Four Tops, Marvin Gaye, The Supremes, The Temptations, Stevie Wonder, and others			
12/6/97	**4**	20	●	52 In Tha Beginning...There Was Rap	15	$8	Priority 50639
				Sucker MC's [Wu-Tang Clan] • Fuck Tha Police [Bone Thugs-N-Harmony] • Big Ole Butt [Sean "Puffy" Combs] • 6 'N Tha Mornin' [Master P] • Freaky Tales [Snoop Doggy Dogg] • Knick Knack Patty Wack [Dogg Pound] • Rapper's Delight [Erick Sermon/Keith Murray/Redman] • I'm Still #1 [Cypress Hill] • I Need A Freak [Too $hort] • Dopeman [Mack 10] • Money (Dollar Bill Y'all) [Coolio] • The Show [Roots]			
11/4/95	**48**	4		53 Inner City Blues - The Music Of Marvin Gaye	106	$8	Motown 0452
				Boyz II Men, Nona Gaye, Madonna, Stevie Wonder, and others			
5/11/96	**10**	9		54 Insomnia - The Erick Sermon Compilation Album	53	$8	Interscope 90060
				Funkorama [Redman] • The Vibe [Xross-Breed] • As The... [Passion] • Beez Like That (Sometimes) [Jamal & Calif] • It's That Hit [Keith Murray] • Up Jump The Boogie [Wixtons] • I Feel It [L.O.D.] • On The Regular [Duo] • Fear [Tommy Gunn] • Ready For War [Domo] • Reign [Erick Sermon]			

DEBUT	PEAK	WKS	Gold	Album Title	Pop #	$	Label & Number
				VARIOUS ARTIST COMPILATIONS — Cont'd			
1/5/91	63	11		55 Jam Harder - The A&M Underground Dance Compilation	131	$8	A&M 5339
				Certain Ratio, D.N.A., New Life, **Seduction**, and others			
12/26/98+	57	3		56 Jermaine Dupri Presents 12 Soulful Nights Of Christmas ...[X]		$8	So So Def 69674
				K-Ci & JoJo, Chaka Khan, Gerald Levert, Brian McKnight, and others			
12/11/93+	22	5		57 LaFace Family Christmas, A ...[X]	186	$8	LaFace 26011
				Toni Braxton, Outkast, TLC, Usher, and others			
10/4/97	43	4		58 Lawhouse Experience Volume One, The	169	$8	Street Life 75525
				Coolio, Eightball & MJG, Ice Cube, Ice-T, and others			
8/6/77	17	10		59 Let's Clean Up The Ghetto	121	$12	Philadelphia I. 34659
				Harold Melvin & The Blue Notes, The O'Jays, Billy Paul, Lou Rawls, and others			
11/15/69	34	7		60 Live At Yankee Stadium ...[L]	169	$25	T-Neck 3004 [2]
				The Five Stairsteps, Edwin Hawkins' Singers, The Isley Brothers, and others			
1/21/95	55	6		61 Loud '95 Nudder Budders E.P. ...[M]		$6	Loud/RCA 66543
				Tha Alkaholiks, Cella Dwellas, Mobb Deep, and others			
2/15/97	90	4		62 Luke's Hall Of Fame		$8	Lil' Joe 221
				Luke, Poison Clan, 2 Live Crew, and others			
10/31/98	59	8		63 Luke's Hall Of Fame Volume 3		$8	Lil' Joe 234
				Home Team, H-Town, Luke, Poison Clan, 2 Live Crew, and others			
12/20/97	88	2		64 Luke's Peep Show		$8	Priority 50681
				Father, Luke, No Good But So Good, Underground, and others			
5/23/98	52	8		65 Lyricist Lounge Volume One ...[L]	167	$12	Open Mic 1129 [2]
				Black Star, Natural Elements, Prime, Problemz, Mike Zoot, and toerhs			
12/14/96	64	5		66 MCA Master Mix Non-Stop Dance		$8	Thump 9954
				Bell Biv DeVoe, Bobby Brown, Pebbles, Jody Watley, and others			
10/17/98	6	11	●	67 Mean Green - Major Players Compilation	9	$8	No Limit 53505
				We... [Fiend & Mac] • Tossed Up [UGK] • Devil's Playground [Commission] • Major Players [Master P/Mia X/Silkk The Shocker/Porsha] • Better Player [Too $hort] • Dying In My City [C-Murder/Snoop Dogg/Magic] • M G There [Steady Mobb'n] • Sucka Repellent [E-40 & Suga T] • Ashes And Dust [Gambino Family] • Close 2 You [Lil' Soldiers] • Luv 4 Me [Mr. Serv-On & Full Blooded] • That's The Nigga [Mystikal] • Mirror Don't Lie [2 For 1] • For Ya Troubles [Prime Suspects] • Don't Be Mad [Passion] • Bigga Than... [B-Legit & C-Murder] • Tell Me When [Mo B. Dick] • Gotta Have Cash [Mack 10 & The Comrads]			
2/3/90	65	9		68 Miami Bass Express		$8	Pandisc 8806
				DJ Fingerz, Maggotron Crushing Crew, Maggozulu Too, Smokey Dee, and others			
9/16/89	79	7		69 Miami Bass Machine		$8	Jamarc 9002
				Bassadelic, DXJ, The Rapp Mechanix, The Third Degree, and others			
2/4/89	47	14		70 Miami Bass Wars, The		$8	Pandisc 8802
				DXJ & The Miami Bass, The Rock Rangers, We Down Express, and others			
3/23/91	64	14		71 Miami Bass Wars II: Battle Of The Boom		$8	Pandisc 8813
				DXJ & The Miami Bass Mob, The Rapp Mechanix, Sonarphonics, and others			
5/6/89	52	13		72 Miami Bass Waves Volume II		$12	Luke Skyywalker 5001 [2]
				Anquette, Gucci Crew II, MC Shy D, 2 Live Crew, and others			
12/5/98	67	2		73 Midwest Funk Volume 2		$8	Ratti 2526
				Angel Dust, Catfish, Money Train, Unusual Suspect, and others			
8/1/98	86	4		74 Millennium Funk Party	124	$8	Rhino 75467
				Brick, Commodores, Gap Band, Parliament, Wild Cherry, and others			
9/27/97	78	2		75 Million Dollar Dream		$12	Dogday 3700 [2]
				Dru Down, Mad Dog Clique, Seff Tha Geffla, and others			
10/26/96	61	3		76 Mobbin' Thru The Bay!		$8	Swerve 70002
				11/5, Mac Mall, N2Deep, Young Lay, and others			
4/11/70	36	5		77 Motown at the Hollywood Palace ...[L]	105	$15	Motown 703
				The Jackson 5, Gladys Knight & The Pips, The Supremes, Stevie Wonder, and others			
12/30/95	99	1		78 Motown Christmas Carol, A ...[X]		$8	Motown 0433
				The Jackson 5, The Miracles, The Temptations, Stevie Wonder, and others			
4/29/95	81	1		79 Motown Comes Home		$8	Motown 0400
				Boyz II Men, Johnny Gill, Smokey Robinson, The Temptations, and others			
3/7/98	38	5		80 Motown 40 Forever	65	$12	Motown 0849 [2]
				Boyz II Men, Marvin Gaye, The Jackson 5, Diana Ross, The Temptations, Stevie Wonder, and others			
3/1/69	41	7		81 Motown Winners' Circle/No. 1 Hits, Vol. 2	135	$15	Gordy 936
				The Four Tops, Martha & The Vandellas, The Supremes, Stevie Wonder, and others			
2/14/87	43	11		82 Mr. Magic's Rap Attack, Volume 2		$12	Profile 1227 [2]
				Dana Dane, D.J. Jazzy Jeff & The Fresh Prince, Eric B., Run-D.M.C., and others			
1/9/88	50	11		83 Mr. Magic's Rap Attack, Volume 3		$12	Profile 1249 [2]
				Dana Dane, Derek B, Eric B. & Rakim, Run-D.M.C., and others			
12/24/88+	76	7		84 Mr. Magic's Rap Attack, Volume 4		$12	Profile 1268 [2]
				De La Soul, EPMD, Kool Moe Dee, Public Enemy, and others			
10/28/89	59	16		85 Nasty Blues		$8	Ichiban 1048
				Clarence Carter, Gary B.B. Coleman, Trudy Lynn, Little Johnny Taylor, Artie White, and others			
12/15/90+	77	6		86 Nasty Blues 2		$8	Ichiban 1066
				Nappy Brown, Clarence Carter, Legendary Blues Band, Artie White, and others			
8/4/79	37	15	●	87 Night At Studio 54, A	21	$15	Casablanca 7161 [2]
				Chic, GQ, Instant Funk, Donna Summer, Village People, and others			
10/8/88	96	2	●	88 1988 Summer Olympics Album/One Moment In Time	31	$8	Arista 8551
				Bee Gees, The Four Tops, Jennifer Holliday, Whitney Houston, and others			
12/26/98	2[1]	18		89 No Limit Soldier Compilation - We Can't Be Stopped	19	$8	No Limit 50724
				No Limit Soldiers II [Master P/C-Murder/Fiend/Magic/Mr. Serv-On/Mia X/Mystikal] • I Ain't Playin' [Mystikal] • Gangsta Move [Snoop Dogg] • Girl Power [Mia X] • Break Something [Fiend] • Real Niggaz Gon Ride [C-Murder & Magic] • Ghost In Da Dark II [Ghetto Commission] • Red Rum [Steady Mobb'n] • Heaven 4 A Thug [Magic & Mac] • Hound Out [Full Blooded and the hounds] • It's A Riot [Kane & Abel] • Straight From Da Heart [Prime Suspects] • My City [Mr Serv-On] • New Orleans Threats [Gotti/Q.B./Pheno] • Assassin [Big Ed] • Where Da Lil Soldiers At? [Lil' Soldiers] • Bring My Burners [Freedom]			
3/1/97	89	3		90 Notorious Pimps, Playas & Hustlas		$8	Loc-N-Load 6666
				The Delinquents, Dru Down, Mac Mall, Spice 1, and others			
12/19/98	31	6		91 N.W.A. - Straight Outta Compton - 10th Anniversary Tribute	142	$8	Priority 53532
				Big Punisher, Bone Thugs-N-Harmony, Fat Joe, Snoop Doggy Dogg, and others			

DEBUT	PEAK	WKS	Gold	Album Title	Pop #	$	Label & Number
				VARIOUS ARTIST COMPILATIONS — Cont'd			
1/8/94	35	51	●	92 Old School	123	$8	Thump 4010
				The Gap Band, Mary Jane Girls, Parliament, Whodini, and others			
6/18/94	35	18		93 Old School Volume 2	147	$8	Thump 4020
				James Brown, Dazz Band, Ohio Players, Salt-N-Pepa, and others			
10/15/94	76	5		94 Old School Volume 3		$8	Thump 4030
				Cameo, Rick James, Kool & The Gang, Ohio Players, and others			
3/15/97	46	9		95 Old School Funk		$8	Thump 9956
				The Deele, Lakeside, Midnight Star, Tavares, and others			
2/21/98	42	11		96 Old School Funk II		$8	Thump 9960
				Al Green, Midnight Star, The O'Jays, Shalamar, and others			
9/12/98	66	5		97 Old School Jams		$8	Thump 4200
				Five Special, Chaka Khan, Starpoint, The Time, Zapp, and others			
2/18/95	52	11		98 Old School Love Songs		$8	Thump 4710
				Gregory Abbott, Blue Magic, Marvin Gaye, Tower Of Power, and others			
6/10/95	63	8		99 Old School Love Songs Volume 2		$8	Thump 4720
				Bloodstone, Earth, Wind & Fire, Ohio Players, Rose Royce, and others			
6/7/97	59	8		100 Old School Love Songs Volume 4		$8	Thump 4740
				The Floaters, The O'Jays, Billy Paul, Barry White, Bill Withers, and others			
9/13/97	40	7		101 Old School Mixx		$8	Thump 4100
				Cameo, Carl Carlton, Kool & The Gang, Ohio Players, Slave, and others			
9/24/94	81	3		102 Old School Rap Volume 1		$8	Thump 4510
				Kurtis Blow, Kool Moe Dee, Sugarhill Gang, Whodini, and others			
8/13/94	45	9		103 1-800-NEW-FUNK		$8	NPG 71006
				George Clinton, Nona Gaye, Madhouse, Prince, Mavis Staples, and others			
11/25/95	36	14		104 One Million Strong		$8	Mergela 72667
				Dr. Dre, Ice Cube, Snoop Doggy Dogg, 2 Pac, and others			
12/24/94	89	3		105 Original Soul Christmas, The [X]		$8	Rhino 71788
				William Bell, Ray Charles, King Curtis, Otis Redding, Joe Tex, and others			
2/21/98	60	5		106 Party Over Here 98	105	$8	Elektra 62088
				Blackstreet, Busta Rhymes, En Vogue, Keith Sweat, and others			
4/21/90	74	7		107 Peters Posse		$8	Peters 1001
				Captain Sky, Kenny B. Devine, Money D. & Wayne, Northside Alliance, and others			
9/3/94	91	1		108 Phat Trax: The Best Of Old School, Vol. 1		$8	Rhino 71752
				Brass Construction, Brick, Fatback, Funkadelic, Mass Production, and others			
4/15/95	41	11		109 Pump Ya Fist - Hip Hop Inspired By The Black Panthers		$8	Avatar 4048
				Fugees, Grand Puba, Jeru The Damaja, KRS-One, 2 Pac, and others			
5/23/98	56	18	●	110 Pure Funk [O]	51	$8	Polygram 558299
				Commodores, Earth, Wind & Fire, Kool & The Gang, Curtis Mayfield, Parliament, and others			
6/21/97	35	8		111 Pure Soul	124	$8	Polygram 553641
				Boyz II Men, Goodfellaz, Jodeci, Barry White, and others			
9/29/90	59	10		112 Rap Miami Style		$8	Pandisc 8811
				Clay D, D.J. Magic Mike, The Get Fresh Girls, and others			
10/3/87	54	5		113 Rap Pak, The		$10	Fresh 3
				Kenny Beck, Just-Ice, M.C. Tee, T La Rock, and others			
12/20/86	62	5	●	114 Rap's Greatest Hits	114	$10	Priority 9466
				The Boogie Boys, Fat Boys, Run-D.M.C., Timex Social Club, and others			
12/7/96	48	8		115 Rap-A-Lot Records - 10th Anniversary		$8	Rap-A-Lot 42510
				Big Mike, Geto Boys, Scarface, Willie D, and others			
10/12/74	37	5		116 Recorded Live At Newport In New York [L]		$12	Buddah 5616
				Ray Charles, Aretha Franklin, Donny Hathaway, Stevie Wonder, and others			
4/16/94	89	4		117 Red Alert - DJ Red Alert's Propmaster Dancehall Show		$8	Epic Street 57135
				Patra, Shabba Ranks, Shaggy, and others			
3/14/98	91	4		118 Rhythm & Quad 166 Vol. 1		$8	EastWest 62150
				DJ Smurf, Emperor Searcy, K.P. & Envyi, Sammy Sam, and others			
3/19/94	15	21	▲	119 Rhythm Country And Blues	18	$8	MCA 10965
				Al Green, B.B. King, Gladys Knight, Aaron Neville, and others			
6/8/96	58	10		120 Rhythm Of The Games - 1996 Olympic Games Album	138	$8	LaFace 26026
				Mary J. Blige, Boyz II Men, Tevin Campbell, Brian McKnight, and others			
6/5/93	29	13		121 Roll Wit Tha Flava	135	$8	Flavor Unit 53615
				Apache, Naughty By Nature, Queen Latifah, Zhané, and others			
4/11/98	44	3		122 Ruthless Records Tenth Anniversary Compilation - Decade Of Game	119	$12	Ruthless/Epic 68766 [2]
				Above The Law, Eazy-E, J.J. Fad, N.W.A., and others			
5/18/74	38	8		123 Save The Children		$15	Motown 800 [2]
				Roberta Flack, Marvin Gaye, Curtis Mayfield, The Temptations, and others			
2/28/98	57	2		124 17 Reasons		$8	Black-N-Brown 1415
				B-Legit, 11/5, Mac Dre, Marvaless, and others			
6/6/98	7	19	●	125 $hort Records - Nationwide - Independence Day: The Compilation	38	$12	$hort/Jive 46100 [2]
				$hort Dog - Hit 'Em Up [Too $hort] • Independence Day [Too $hort] • Get Your Hustle On [Baby D] • Spread Your Love [Murda One] • Abstract Hustle [38 Deep & Kat] • When You See Me [G-Side] • All About It [Too $hort & Pimp C] • Time After Time [Casual & Dollar Will] • Are You Ready For This [Badwayz] • Lady Luv [Zu] • Wreckognize [Mddl Fngz] • Paper Chase [Al Block] • Playa Hatin' Hoes [Playa Playa] • Pimpin' Ain't Easy [Polyester Playas] • Couldn't Be A Better Player [Lil' Jon & The Eastside Boyz] • Don't Stop [Lyrical Giants] • Get All Your Change [Too $hort] • Whatever Man [Redman] • I Ain't Gonna Forget This [Badwayz] • If I Wasn't High [Studd] • Hellbound [Slink Capone] • Who Loves Ya [Jay-O Felony] • Same Old Song [Father Dom] • Keep It Real [Sylk-E. Fyne] • Killa Team [Joe Riz]			
12/9/95	36	7		126 Sick Wid' It Records Compilation - The Hogg In Me		$8	Sick Wid' It 45005
				B-Legit, Celly Cell, Suga T, Young Dog, and others			
11/19/66	15	6		127 16 Original Big Hits, Volume 5	57	$20	Motown 651
				The Contours, Marvin Gaye, Brenda Holloway, Stevie Wonder, and others			
4/29/67	27	3		128 16 Original Big Hits, Volume 6	95	$20	Motown 655
				Four Tops, The Isley Brothers, The Miracles, The Supremes, and others			
10/21/67	27	2		129 16 Original Big Hits, Volume 7	81	$20	Motown 661
				Marvin Gaye, Shorty Long, The Marvelettes, Jr. Walker & The All Stars, and others			

VARIOUS ARTIST COMPILATIONS — Cont'd

DEBUT	PEAK	WKS		Album Title	Pop #	$	Label & Number
12/30/67+	**13**	7	130	**16 Original Big Hits, Volume 8** .... Four Tops, Gladys Knight & The Pips, Jimmy Ruffin, The Supremes, and others	163	$20	Motown 666
1/25/69	**46**	2	131	**16 Original Big Hits, Volume 9** .... Four Tops, Marvin Gaye, Martha & The Vandellas, Stevie Wonder, and others	173	$20	Motown 668
5/17/69	**34**	8	132	**16 Original Big Hits, Volume 10** .... Gladys Knight & The Pips, Spinners, Edwin Starr, The Supremes, and others		$20	Motown 684
3/12/88	**42**	11	133	**Sleeping Bag's Greatest Mixers Collection II** ....[G] Dhar Braxton, Hanson & Davis, Nocera, Joyce Sims, and others		$10	Sleeping Bag 42012
12/14/96+	**44**	5	134	**Slow Jams Christmas Volume 1** ....[X] Charles Brown, Nat "King" Cole, The Emotions, Donny Hathaway, The Stylistics and others		$8	Right Stuff 53041
6/17/95	**100**	1	135	**Slow Jams: The 70s Volume 4** .... Bloodstone, Commodores, Billy Paul, Minnie Riperton, Tavares, and others		$8	Right Stuff 30576
8/27/94	**52**	24	136	**Slow Jams: The Timeless Collection Volume 1** .... Cameo, Chapter 8, The Isley Brothers, Rose Royce, and others		$8	Right Stuff 29139
8/27/94	**74**	7	137	**Slow Jams: The Timeless Collection Volume 2** .... Shirley Brown, Con Funk Shun, Enchantment, Patti LaBelle, The O'Jays, and others		$8	Right Stuff 29140
6/17/95	**79**	2	138	**Slow Jams: The Timeless Collection Volume 3** .... Shirley Murdock, Smokey Robinson, Tavares, Lillo Thomas, and others		$8	Right Stuff 31973
6/17/95	**64**	2	139	**Slow Jams: The Timeless Collection Volume 4** .... Con Funk Shun, The Dramatics, Enchantment, Alicia Myers, Sun, and others		$8	Right Stuff 31974
2/24/96	**86**	2	140	**Slow Jams: The Timeless Collection Volume 5** ....[O] Rick James, The Manhattans, Teddy Pendergrass, Skyy, and others		$8	Right Stuff 36995
3/4/95	**33**	43	141	**Smooth Grooves: A Sensual Collection Volume 1** .... Average White Band, Champaign, Earth, Wind & Fire, Heatwave, Deniece Williams, and others		$8	Rhino 71859
3/4/95	**34**	31	142	**Smooth Grooves: A Sensual Collection Volume 2** .... Atlantic Starr, Bobby Caldwell, Larry Graham, Stacy Lattisaw, Teddy Pendergrass, and others		$8	Rhino 71860
3/4/95	**38**	20	143	**Smooth Grooves: A Sensual Collection Volume 3** .... Blue Magic, Norman Connors, Aretha Franklin, The Isley Brothers, Tower Of Power, and others		$8	Rhino 71861
3/4/95	**39**	22	144	**Smooth Grooves: A Sensual Collection Volume 4** .... The Gap Band, Marvin Gaye, Evelyn King, Mtume, Patrice Rushen, and others		$8	Rhino 71862
2/10/96	**45**	9	145	**Smooth Grooves: A Sensual Collection Volume 5** ....[O] Earth, Wind & Fire, GQ, One Way, Skyy, Spinners, and others		$8	Rhino 71863
2/10/96	**71**	5	146	**Smooth Grooves: A Sensual Collection Volume 6** .... Blue Magic, The Dramatics, Debra Laws, Shirley Murdock, and others		$8	Rhino 71864
2/10/96	**43**	8	147	**Smooth Grooves: A Sensual Collection Volume 7** .... Anquette, Champaign, Klymaxx, Stacy Lattisaw, Ready For The World, and others		$8	Rhino 71865
10/5/96	**64**	2	148	**Smooth Grooves: A Sensual Collection Volume 8** .... Atlantic Starr, Miki Howard, The Jones Girls, Levert, and others		$8	Rhino 72510
10/5/96	**84**	1	149	**Smooth Grooves: A Sensual Collection Volume 9** .... Delegation, Rose Royce, Patrice Rushen, Tavares, Zapp, and others		$8	Rhino 72511
6/22/96	**9**	39	● 150	**So So Def Bass All-Stars** My Boo [Ghost Town DJ's] [18] • Thyow [Zoe] • Whatz Up, Whatz Up [Playa Poncho & LA Sno] • Shakedown [Trigga Man] • So So Def Bass Contest [Raheem The Dream] • Koochie Kuterz [Playa Poncho] • City Boy Bounce [City Boyz] • Body Hop (Oh My Goodness) [T'Baby] • Sexiest [Don Yute] • Mega Mix [Bass Allstars] • Let It Burn [Edward J] • Es Verano [Corina]	32	$8	So So Def 67532
7/12/97	**26**	30	151	**So So Def Bass All-Stars Vol. II** .... Corina, Ghostown DJ's, Inoj, Luke, and others	71	$8	So So Def 67998
10/24/98	**58**	4	152	**So So Def Bass All-Stars Volume III** .... Ricky Bell, Butter, Inoj, Katrina, Lathun, and others	129	$8	So So Def 69346
4/23/66	**7**	9	153	**Solid Gold Soul** .... Got To Get You Off My Mind [Solomon Burke] [1] • Don't Fight It [Wilson Pickett] [4] • I Want To (Do Everything For You) [Joe Tex] [1] • Seesaw [Don Covay] [5] • Don't Play That Song (You Lied) [Ben E. King] [2] • Mr. Pitiful [Otis Redding] [10] • In The Midnight Hour [Wilson Pickett] [1] • Hold What You've Got [Joe Tex] [2] • Mercy, Mercy [Don Covay] [35] • I've Been Loving You Too Long (To Stop Now) [Otis Redding] [2] • Just Out Of Reach (Of My Two Open Arms) [Solomon Burke] [7] • Stand By Me [Ben E. King] [1]	107	$20	Atlantic 8116
3/22/97	**6**	13	154	**Soul Assassins - Chapter I** .... Puppet Master [Dr. Dre & B Real] • Decisions, Decisions [Goodie Mob] • Third World [RZA & GZA/Genius] • Battle Of 2001 [Cypress Hill] • Devil In A Blue Dress [LA The Darkman] • Heavy Weights [MC Eiht] • Move Ahead [KRS-One] • It Could Happen To You [Mobb Deep] • Life Is Tragic [Infamous Mobb] • New York Undercover [Call O' Da Wild] • John 3:16 [Wyclef Jean]	20	$8	Columbia 66820
5/10/69	**36**	3	155	**Soul Explosion** .... Booker T. & The MG's, Eddie Floyd, Albert King, Johnnie Taylor, Carla Thomas, and others	172	$20	Stax 2007 [2]
12/20/97+	**35**	4	156	**Soul Train Christmas Starfest Album, The** ....[X] Boyz II Men, Natalie Cole, En Vogue, New Edition, Luther Vandross, and others		$8	Epic 68679
10/20/73	**55**	3	157	**Soul Years 1948-73, The** .... Brook Benton, Ray Charles, Clarence Carter, Aretha Franklin, Otis Redding, and others		$40	Atlantic 504 [2]
12/23/95	**71**	3	158	**Soulful Christmas From WDAS 105.3 FM, A** ....[X]		$8	Collectables 5679
1/3/98	**25**	20	159	**Source Presents Hip Hop Hits - Volume 1, The** .... Bone Thugs-N-Harmony, EPMD, Puff Daddy, Redman, Scarface, Wu-Tang Clan, and others	38	$8	Polygram 536204
11/28/98	**29**	20	● 160	**Source Presents Hip Hop Hits - Volume 2, The** .... Busta Rhymes, Cam'ron, DMX, Master P, Noreaga, Snoop Doggy Dogg, and others	46	$8	Polygram 565668
9/13/97	**2**[1]	10	161	**Southwest Riders** .... Represent [A-1] • Walk With Me [W.C.] • Get Cha Mind Right [Mystikal] • Big Bank [Mr. Malik] • Paystyle [918] • Call The Coroner [3X Krazy] • Cop Stories [Graveyard Shift] • Capable [Luniz] • Flashin' [Cydal] • Ain't Fuckin' Around [SKA-Face Al Kapone] • Respect It [Celly Cel] • On Top Of The World [Comrads] • Bad Bitches [Suga T.] • Playa Haters [San Quinn & Messy Marv] • Mean Green [E-40 & B-Legit/Richie Rich] • Dis Year [Tela] • Yay Deep [UGK] • About My Money [Calvin-T] • Evil Ways [Komacauszy] • Niggas Talk Shit [Eight Ball & MJG] • After Dollars No Cents [Master P] • Y'All My Nugz [Twista] • Tremendous [Brotha Lynch Hung] • Who Do I Trust [D-Shot] • Threesixafix [Three 6 Mafia] • Load Unload [Chilla] • Getto Tales [Coughnut & Baldhead]	23	$12	Sick Wid' It 45009 [2]
12/21/96+	**66**	3	162	**Special Gift** ....[X] Tanya Blount, Kurtis Blow, Dru Hill, The Isley Brothers, and others		$8	Island 524307
6/14/97	**42**	7	163	**Spread Yo' Hustle** .... B-Legit, Brotha Lynch Hung, Mac Dre, N2Deep, and others		$8	Swerve 70011
9/2/67	**30**	1	164	**Stax/Volt Revue - Live In London, The** ....[L] Booker T. & The MG's, Eddie Floyd, Sam & Dave, Carla Thomas, and others	145	$25	Stax 721

DEBUT	PEAK	WKS	Gold	Album Title	Pop #	$	Label & Number
				VARIOUS ARTIST COMPILATIONS — Cont'd			
11/12/94	92	1		165 Stolen Moments Red Hot + Cool		$12	GRP 9794 [2]
				Donald Byrd, Digable Planets, Herbie Hancock, The Pharcyde, The Roots, and others			
2/19/94	58	4		166 Straight From Da Streets volume 1	129	$8	Priority 53885
				George Clinton, Ice Cube, Public Enemy, Sir Mix-A-Lot, 2 Pac, and others			
9/21/91	62	7		167 Straight From The Hood	95	$8	Priority 7063
				Eazy-E, EPMD, Geto Boys, Ice Cube, WC & The Maad Circle, and others			
9/15/84	68	3		168 Street Beats		$15	Sugar Hill 9228 [2]
				Grandmaster Flash, Sugarhill Gang, West Street Mob, and others			
8/16/97	4	14		169 Suave House	26	$8	Suave House 1585
				Rider [Tela] • Heat Of The Night [Fedz] • Trapped [NOLA] • Just Like Candy [8-Ball & MJG] • Questions [Thorough Of South Circle] • Starships And Rockets [Eightball] • Life Is Crying [NOLA] • Getto Madness [South Circle] • Death Notes [Fedz] • Dusk Til Dawn [Fedz]			
8/24/91	92	4		170 Super Bass		$8	Record Guys 1000
				Gucci Crew II, L'Trimm, Sir Mix-A-Lot, 2 Live Crew, and others			
8/19/67	6	21		171 Super Hits, The	12	$20	Atlantic 501
				Hold On, I'm Comin' [Sam & Dave] [1] • Mustang Sally [Wilson Pickett] [6] • Respect [Aretha Franklin] [1] • Knock On Wood [Eddie Floyd] [1] • When A Man Loves A Woman [Percy Sledge] [1] • Good Lovin' [Young Rascals] • In The Midnight Hour [Wilson Pickett] [1] • Baby, I'm Yours [Barbara Lewis] [5] • Hip Hug-Her [Booker T. & The MG's] [6] • B-A-B-Y [Carla Thomas] [3] • Philly Dog [Mar-Keys] [19] • S.Y.S.L.J.F.M. (The Letter Song) [Joe Tex] [9]			
12/21/68+	43	9		172 Super Hits, Vol. 2, The	76	$20	Atlantic 8188
				Bar-Kays, Aretha Franklin, Otis Redding, Sam & Dave, and others			
12/28/68+	16	8		173 Super Hits, Vol. 3, The	68	$20	Atlantic 8203
				Archie Bell & The Drells, Arthur Conley, Cream, Wilson Pickett, and others			
12/29/73+	38	7		174 Sound Of Philadelphia '73, The		$12	Philadelphia I. 32713
				The Ebonys, The O'Jays, Billy Paul, Bunny Sigler, and others			
6/3/89	68	18		175 This Is Bass		$10	Hot Productions 3312
				Gucci Crew II, L'Trimm, MC A.D.E., 2 Live Crew, and others			
3/30/68	22	9		176 This Is Soul	146	$20	Atlantic 8170
				Solomon Burke, Arthur Conley, The Drifters, Percy Sledge, Joe Tex, and others			
6/6/98	76	2		177 3 Beam Circus		$8	Swerve 54262
				Latino Velvet Click, Mac Dre, N2Deep, R.B.L. Posse, and others			
3/23/85	39	9		178 Tommy Boy Greatest Beats		$15	Tommy Boy 1005 [2]
				Afrika Bambaataa, Force M.D.'S, The Jonzun Crew, Pressure Drop, and others			
12/9/95	23	22		179 Too $hort Presents The Dangerous Crew - Don't Try This At Home......	191	$8	Dangerous 41573
				MC Breed, Shorty B, Spice 1, Too $hort, and others			
3/12/94	17	23		180 Tribute To Curtis Mayfield, A	56	$8	Warner 45500
				Aretha Franklin, Whitney Houston, The Isley Brothers, Gladys Knight, Stevie Wonder, and others			
12/21/96+	56	4		181 12 Soulful Nights Of Christmas - Part 1 ....[X]		$8	So So Def 67755
				Faith Evans, Trey Lorenz, Brian McKnight, Xscape, and others			
6/11/83	32	13	●	182 25 #1 Hits From 25 Years	42	$15	Motown 5308 [2]
				Four Tops, Rick James, Thelma Houston, The Supremes, Stevie Wonder, and others			
6/11/83	45	8		183 25 Years Of Grammy Greats	107	$12	Motown 5309
				Dazz Band, Thelma Houston, Jermaine Jackson, Eddie Kendricks, The Temptations, and others			
9/13/97	32	22	●	184 Ultimate Hip Hop Party 1998	46	$8	Arista 18977
				Brandy, Faith Evans, R. Kelly, Lil' Kim, LL Cool J, Wu-Tang Clan, and others			
12/31/94	93	1		185 Ultimate R&B Christmas Volume 2, The ....[X]		$8	Right Stuff 29230
				Brook Benton, Al Green, Isaac Hayes, Lou Rawls, The Temptations, and others			
7/4/98	58	3		186 U-N-I VS. ALL featuring The Universal Emcees		$8	Universal 53138
				A+, Canibus, Crucial Conflict, Tracey Lee, McGruff, and others			
3/21/87	69	9		187 Uptown Is Kickin' It		$10	MCA 5815
				Finesse & Synquis, Heavy D & The Boyz, Marley Marl, and others			
12/27/97	99	1		188 WDAS 105.3 FM Classic Soul Hits Volume Two		$8	Collectables 5895
9/10/94	29	15		189 West Coast Bad Boyz		$8	No Limit 7187
				C-Bo, J.T. The Bigga Figga, Rappin' 4-Tay, Totally Insane, and others			
2/15/97	2[1]	31		190 West Coast Bad Boyz II	8	$8	No Limit 50658
				R.I.P. Tupac [Master P] • Bangin' [Westside Connection] • Survival 1st [C-BO, Lunasice & Marvaless] • Tryin 2 Make Ends [11/5] • Datz What I Said [Brotha Lynch Hung] • Got Tha Best Hand [Comrads & Allfrumthai] • Up's And Down's [Rappin' 4-Tay] • Bad Boyz On A Mission [Tru] • Call It What You Want [RBL Posse] • IMG [E-A-Ski] • Roll Yo Voges [Cellski] • What Cha Like [Mac Dre] • Mr. Dayton [Homicide] • Hands On My Four 5 [Shocker] • Unexpected [GLP] • Dead Man (Commercial) [Mr. Serv-On] • Paper Chasing [MC Eiht] • Breaking' Skrill [Delinquents] • Steady Mobbin' [C-Murder]			
2/14/98	46	4		191 Westcoast Trippin' - AWOL Killa Compilation		$8	AWOL 45440
				C-Bo, Lunasicc, Marvaless, and others			
9/14/96	81	4		192 Young Southern Playaz Vol. 1		$8	Priority 50590
				Gangsta Pat, Indo G, Three 6 Mafia, and others			

Lists, alphabetically, all tracks that appeared on every Top 10 album.

Below are some guidelines:

The year the track debuted on a Top 10-charted album, from January 30, 1965 through December 26, 1998, is listed to the left.

The artist name is listed in italics to the right.

This index differs from the title indexes of our books based on the singles charts, in that tracks with identical titles are listed together even if they are different compositions. Listed below the track title in chronological order are the artists' names.

Letter symbols in parentheses next to the artist name identify tracks from special album categories. The following symbols designate these categories:

> **OC**: Original Casts
> **St**: Soundtracks
> **TV**: Television Shows/Mini Series
> **VA**: Various Artist Compilations

The name of the various artists album is listed to the right of the letter code for all of these special album categories.

Abbreviated titles such as "F.B.I." and "L.A. Sunshine" are listed at the beginning of their respective first letters. ("F.B.I." appears at the beginning of the F's.) Conversely, abbreviated titles which spell out a word, such as "C.R.E.A.M." and "D.A.I.S.Y." are sorted together with the regular spellings of these words.

Titles which are <u>identical</u> except for an apostrophized word in one of the titles are shown together. ("Dancin' Machine" and "Dancing Machine" are grouped together.) The same is true for titles with nearly identical pronunciations but slightly different spellings. ("Do U Believe" and "Do You Believe" are listed together as are "It's All Right With Me" and "It's Alright With Me.") All artists are shown under the title that was recorded by more than one artist. If each was recorded by the same number of artists, then all artists are listed under the earliest title.

If either of the articles "A," "An," or "The" is the first word of a title, it is not shown. However, if a title is made up of only one other word, then it is shown, as in the case below.

> 90 Bomb, The   *Ice Cube*

However, if more than one artist recorded such a track and one of the recordings does not have an article at the beginning of the title, then the article is not shown. In the example below, Montell Jordan's recording is simply titled "Payback" and the recording by James Brown is titled "The Payback."

> Payback
> 73 *James Brown*
> 95 *Montell Jordan*

Tracks that begin with "Theme From," "Love Theme From," etc. are alphabetized under the subsequent part of the title. For example, "Theme From The Bodyguard" appears as "Bodyguard, Theme From."

The title of a medley does not appear in the track titles index if the album lists the individual songs that make up the medley. For example, The Supremes' "Sam Cooke Medley" is not listed as such in the index since the titles of its six tracks are listed on the album: "You Send Me," "(I Love You) For Sentimental Reasons," "Cupid," "Chain Gang," "Bring It On Home To Me," and "Shake." See example below:

> Cupid
> 65 *Sam Cooke*
> 65 *Supremes (medley)*
> 95 *Solo*
> 96 *112*

If a song from the medley, is the only song with that title in the Tracks Titles Index, then "(medley)" appears in parentheses immediately following, as the example below shows.

> Love Lights (medley)
> 67 *Rascals*

Two-word titles which have the <u>exact</u> spelling as one-word titles are listed together. ("Dream Lover" and "Dreamlover" appear together.)

Titles beginning with a contraction follow titles that begin with a similar non-contracted word. (Can't follows Can.)

A

ABC
70 *Jackson 5*
91 *Another Bad Creation*
94 *Jackson 5 (St: Crooklyn)*
93 **abc-123** *Levert*
96 **Abandon Ship** *Busta Rhymes*
97 **About My Money** *Calvin-T (VA: Southwest Riders)*
98 **Above The Clouds** *Gang Starr*
93 **Above The Rim** *Bell Biv DeVoe*
90 **Absolutely Positive** *Levert*
98 **Abstract Hustle** *38 Deep & Kat (VA: $hort Records - Nationwide)*
83 **Accept Me (I'm Not A Girl Anymore)** *Angela Bofill*
91 **Ace In The Hole** *3rd Bass*
73 **Across 110th Street** *Bobby Womack*
92 **Act Like You Know** *Pete Rock & C.L. Smooth*
95 **Actin' Bad** *Click*
75 **Action Time** *LaBelle*
74 **Actual Proof** *Herbie Hancock*
80 **Add It Up** *Gladys Knight & The Pips*
93 **Addicted To Danger** *Ice-T*
97 **Addicted To You** *Patti LaBelle*
85 **Addiction** [medley] *Morris Day*
91 **Addictive Love** *BeBe & CeCe Winans*
70 **Adios Senorita** *Edwin Starr*
87 **Adore** *Prince*
75 **Adventures In Paradise** *Minnie Riperton*
96 **Adventures In Wonderland** *Roots*
66 **Advice** *Billy Preston*
90 **Affection** *Lisa Stansfield*
97 **Affiliated** *Mr. Serv-On*
76 **Affirmation** *George Benson*
96 **Affirmative Action** *Nas*
88 **Africa (Goin' Back Home)** *Doug E. Fresh & The Get Fresh Crew*
71 **Africa Talks To You "The Asphalt Jungle"** *Sly & The Family Stone*
89 **African Dance** *Soul II Soul*
75 **Africano** *Earth, Wind & Fire*
73 **Afrikus Retrospectus** *Mandrill*
97 **Afro** *Erykah Badu*
65 **Afro-Blue** *Cal Tjader*
94 **Afro Puffs** *Lady Of Rage (St: Above The Rim)*
70 **Afro-Spanish Omelet** *"Cannonball" Adderley*
76 **Afro Wiggle** *John Handy*
98 **After Cash Money Concert** *Juvenile*
78 **After Dark** *Pattie Brooks (St: Thank God It's Friday)*
After Dollars, No Cents
97 *Master P*
97 *Master P (VA: Southwest Riders)*
81 **After Hi School** *Time*
82 **After I Put My Lovin' On You** *Richard "Dimples" Fields*
95 **After-Party** *Jodeci*
75 **After Sex** *Staple Singers*
76 **After The Dance** *Marvin Gaye*
79 **After The Love Has Gone** *Earth, Wind & Fire*
96 **After The Smoke Is Clear** *Ghostface Killah*
90 **After We Make Love** *Whitney Houston*
After You
76 *Diana Ross*
78 *Roberta Flack*
79 *Dionne Warwick*
70 **After You Done It** *James Brown*
67 **After You Put Back The Pieces (I'll Still Have A Broken Heart)** *Miracles*
65 **After You're Through** *James Brown*
86 **Afterglow** *Tina Turner*
93 **Again** *Janet Jackson*
96 **Against All Odds** *Makaveli*
88 **Against Doctor's Orders** *Kenny G*
98 **Against The World** *Tribe Called Quest*
69 **Agatha Van Thurgood** *Dells*
Age Ain't Nothing But A Number
82 *One Way*
94 *Aaliyah*
77 **Age Of The Showdown** *L.T.D.*
72 **Agent's Office** *Diana Ross*
75 **Agony And The Ecstasy** *Smokey Robinson*
91 **Ah Been Workin'** *Sounds Of Blackness*
67 **(Ah, The Apple Trees) When The World Was Young** *Nancy Wilson*
95 **Ah-Yeah** *KRS One*
87 **Ahh, Let's Get Ill** *LL Cool J*
77 **Ahh...The Name Is Bootsy, Baby!** *William "Bootsy" Collins*
81 **Ai No Corrida** *Quincy Jones*
79 **Ai No, Sono** *Stevie Wonder*
94 **Aiiight Chill...** *Gang Starr*
93 **Ain't A Damn Thing Changed** *Ice-T*
97 **Ain't Fuckin' Around** *SKA-Face Al Kapone (VA: Southwest Riders)*
75 **Ain't Givin' Up No Ground** *Ohio Players*
78 **Ain't Givin' Up No Love** *Isley Brothers*
73 **Ain't Gon' Change A Thang** *Crusaders*
77 **Ain't Gonna' Hurt Nobody** *Brick*
70 **Ain't Gonna Worry My Life Anymore** *B.B. King*
92 **Ain't Got No Class** *Da Lench Mob*
66 **Ain't Got No Time To Play** *Billy Preston*
96 **Ain't Hard 2 Find** *2 Pac*
74 **Ain't I Been Good To You** *Isley Brothers*
72 **Ain't It A Groove** *James Brown*
78 **Ain't It A Shame** *Ashford & Simpson*
70 **Ain't It Funky Now** *James Brown*
85 **Ain't It Funny (How Things Turn Around)** *Marvin Gaye*
79 **Ain't It Strange** *Maze Featuring Frankie Beverly*
65 **Ain't No Big Deal On You** *Little Milton*
73 **Ain't No Change** *New Birth*
89 **Ain't No Cookin'** *Stephanie Mills*
96 **Ain't No Fun** *Dino (St: Original Gangstas)*
93 **Ain't No Fun (If The Homies Can't Have None)** *Snoop Doggy Dogg*
83 **Ain't No Greater Love** *Gladys Knight & The Pips*
Ain't No Half Steppin'
77 *Heatwave*
88 *Big Daddy Kane*
73 **Ain't No Justice** *Temptations*
97 **Ain't No Limit** *Mystikal*
95 **Ain't No Love** *Spice 1*
74 **Ain't No Love In The Heart Of The City** *Bobby Bland*
77 **Ain't No Love Left (In My Heart For You)** *High Inergy*
69 **Ain't No Lovin'** *Stevie Wonder*
Ain't No Mountain High Enough
67 *Marvin Gaye & Tammi Terrell*
68 *Hugh Masekela*
68 *Supremes with The Temptations*
70 *Diana Ross*
77 *Marvin Gaye [medley]*
93 **Ain't No Mystery** *Brand Nubian*
Ain't No Nigga
96 *Jay-Z*
96 *Jay Z (St: The Nutty Professor)*
97 *Jay Z (VA: Funkmaster Flex Vol. III)*
82 **Ain't No Party** *OC: Dreamgirls*
96 **Ain't No Playa Like...** *Rappin' 4-Tay*
74 **Ain't No Price On Happiness** *Spinners*
96 **Ain't No Reason** *Mo Thugs Family*
70 **Ain't No Sad Song** *Diana Ross*
93 **Ain't No Stoppin' This** *LL Cool J*
Ain't No Stoppin' Us Now
79 *McFadden & Whitehead*
89 *Big Daddy Kane*
94 *Luther Vandross*
75 **Ain't No Such Thing As Superman** *Gil Scott-Heron & Brian Jackson*
Ain't No Sun Since You've Been Gone
67 *Temptations*
71 *Undisputed Truth*
Ain't No Sunshine
71 *Grover Washington, Jr. [medley]*
71 *Bill Withers*
72 *Michael Jackson*
72 *Temptations*
73 *Dells*
73 *Isaac Hayes [medley]*
73 *Isaac Hayes (St: Wattstax: The Living Word)*
95 *C-BO*
95 *Soul For Real*
68 **Ain't No Telling** *Jimi Hendrix*
Ain't No Thang
94 *Da Brat*
94 *OutKast*
97 *Levert*
Ain't No Use
65 *Gene Chandler*
65 *Nina Simone*
68 **Ain't No Way** *Aretha Franklin*
72 **Ain't No Woman (Like The One I've Got)** *Four Tops*
Ain't Nobody
83 *Rufus Featuring Chaka Khan*
84 *Rufus Featuring Chaka Khan (St: Breakin')*
95 *Faith Evans*
96 *Monica (St: The Nutty Professor)*
82 **Ain't Nobody, Baby** *Con Funk Shun*
91 **Ain't Nobody Better** *Yo-Yo*
85 **Ain't Nobody Ever Loved You** *Aretha Franklin*
67 **Ain't Nobody (Gonna Turn Me Around)** *Aretha Franklin*
92 **Ain't Nobody Like You** *Miki Howard*
Ain't Nothin' But A Maybe
74 *Rufus*
76 *Diana Ross*
98 **Ain't Nothin' But A Party** *Sugarhill Gang (St: Dr. Dolittle)*
90 **Ain't Nothin' But A Word To Me** *Too $hort*
97 **Ain't Nothin Changed** *Bone Thugs-N-Harmony*
98 **Ain't Nothin' Like A Jones** *Tyrese*
82 **Ain't Nothin' Missin'** *Jeffrey Osborne*
75 **Ain't Nothin' Wrong** *KC & The Sunshine Band*
96 **Ain't Nothing** *Silkk The Shocker*
79 **Ain't Nothing I Can Do** *Tyrone Davis*
95 **Ain't Nothing Like Pimpin'** *Too $hort*
Ain't Nothing Like The Real Thing
68 *Marvin Gaye & Tammi Terrell*
69 *Supremes with The Temptations*
72 *Jackson 5*
74 *Aretha Franklin*
77 *Marvin Gaye [medley]*
83 *Angela Bofill*
90 **Ain't Nut'in' Changed!** *Bell Biv DeVoe*
98 **Ain't Nut'in Personal** *Snoop Doggy Dogg*
89 **Ain't Nuthin' In The World** *Miki Howard*
96 **Ain't Nuthin 2 It** *MC Eiht/CMW*
95 **Ain't Nuttin' But Killin** *MC Eiht (St: New Jersey Drive Vol. 1)*
98 **Ain't Said No Names** *Mo Thugs Family*
76 **Ain't That A Bitch** *Johnny "Guitar" Watson*
67 **Ain't That A Groove** *James Brown*
76 **Ain't That A Mother's Luck** *Dorothy Moore*
66 **Ain't That Asking For Trouble** *Stevie Wonder*
65 **Ain't That Good News** *Supremes*
66 **Ain't That Just Like A Woman** *Jimmy Smith*
67 **Ain't That Lovin' You** *Nancy Wilson*
72 **Ain't That Nothin'** *Billy Preston*
Ain't That Peculiar
66 *Marvin Gaye*
66 *Ramsey Lewis*
69 *Delfonics*
72 *Jermaine Jackson*
83 *Rufus Featuring Chaka Khan*
65 **Ain't That The Truth** *Jr. Walker & The All Stars*
94 **Ain't The Devil Happy** *Jeru The Damaja*
69 **Ain't There Something Money Can't Buy** *Young-Holt Unlimited*
97 **Ain't 2 Be Played Wit** *Mia X*
72 **Ain't Too Much Of Nothin'** *Chi-Lites*
Ain't Too Proud To Beg
66 *Temptations*
92 *TLC*
78 **Ain't We Funkin' Now** *Brothers Johnson*
91 **Ain't With Being Broke** *Geto Boys*
94 **Aintnuttin Buttersong** *Public Enemy*
92 **Air Hoodlum** *Public Enemy*
98 **Airplane** *Crucial Conflict*
98 **Airwaves** *RZA*
89 **Ak-Shun** *Special Ed*
98 **Akickdoe!** *C-Murder*
91 **Al'za-B-Cee'z** *3rd Bass*
Alfie
67 *Soulful Strings*
67 *Dionne Warwick*
67 *Nancy Wilson*
Alibi
83 *Lakeside*
84 *Teena Marie*
91 **Alive On Arrival** *Ice Cube*
83 **All** *Kashif*
97 **All A Dream** *Big Mike*
98 **All About It** *Too $hort & Pimp C (VA: $hort Records - Nationwide)*
All About Love
75 *Earth, Wind & Fire*
92 *After 7*
98 **All About Me** *Xscape*
95 **All About My Fetti** *Young Lay (St: New Jersey Drive Vol. 1)*
80 **All About The Heaven** *Brothers Johnson*
96 **All About U** *2 Pac*
All Alone
65 *Gloria Lynne*
96 *Dru Hill*
All Along The Watchtower
68 *Jimi Hendrix*
73 *Bobby Womack*
All Around The World
70 *Edwin Starr*
90 *Lisa Stansfield*
94 *Boyz II Men*
85 **All At Once** *Whitney Houston*
75 **All Because Of You** *Barry White*
67 **All Blues** *Soulful Strings*
93 **All Bullshit Aside** *MC Ren*
All Day All Night
88 *Bobby Brown*
97 *Changing Faces*
71 **All Day Music** *War*
96 **All Day Thinkin'** *Babyface*
96 **All Eyez On Me** *2 Pac*
All For Love
85 *New Edition*
91 *Color Me Badd*
All For One
75 *James Brown*
79 *Diana Ross*
97 *Brand Nubian (VA: Funkmaster Flex Vol. II)*
98 **All For The Love** *Lox*
94 **All For The Money** *MC Eiht*
67 **All For You** *Ray Charles*
98 **All 4 Nuthin'** *Eightball & MJG*
75 **All Girl Band** *LaBelle*
98 **All Good** *Mo Thugs Family*
93 **All He Wrote** *Spice 1*
75 **All I Ask** *Blackbyrds*
All I Do
80 *Stevie Wonder*
81 *Four Tops*
All I Do Is Think Of You
75 *Jackson 5*
89 *Troop*
78 **All I Ever Need** *Johnny Mathis*
98 **All I Ever Wanted** *C-BO*
98 **All I Know** *Fiend*
All I Need
67 *Temptations*
98 *Xscape*
79 **All I Need Is You** *Teddy Pendergrass*
96 **All I Want** *Monifah*
94 **All I Want For Christmas Is You** *Mariah Carey*
80 **All I Want In This World (Is To Find That Girl)** *Kurtis Blow*
74 **All I Want Is A Fighting Chance** *Millie Jackson*
65 **All I Want Is You** *Miracles*
92 **All I'll Ever Ask** *Freddie Jackson with Najee*
93 **All I've Ever Wanted** *Mariah Carey*
98 **All In A Week** *Fiend*
73 **All In Love Is Fair** *Stevie Wonder*
82 **All In My Lover's Eyes** *Isley Brothers*
All In My Mind
95 *Eightball & MJG*
95 *Soul For Real*
88 **All In One Night** *Kenny G*
All In The Club
98 *Do Or Die*
98 *Do Or Die (St: Caught Up)*
93 **All In The Mind** *Erick Sermon*
87 **All In The Name Of Love** *Atlantic Starr*
81 **All In The Way You Get Down** *Ray Parker Jr.*
90 **All In Your Mind** *Mariah Carey*
94 **All Is Not Gone** *Changing Faces*
93 **All My Bitches Are Gone** *Too $hort*
71 **All My Hard Times** *Joe Simon*
97 **All My Life** *K-Ci & JoJo*
83 **All My Life's A Lie** *Smokey Robinson*
All My Love
90 *Tony! Toni! Toné!*
98 *112*
66 **All My Love Belongs To You** *Ramsey Lewis*
78 **All My Lovin'** *Cheryl Lynn*
97 **All N's** *Mia X*
All Night
91 *Keith Washington*
97 *Erykah Badu [medley]*
98 *Silkk The Shocker*
78 **All Night Dancin'** *Jacksons*
80 **All Night Dancing** *Lipps, Inc.*
All Night Long
76 *Kool & The Gang*
83 *Mary Jane Girls*
89 *Kool Moe Dee*
93 *Maze Featuring Frankie Beverly*
95 *SWV (St: Waiting To Exhale)*
97 *Boyz II Men*
98 *Faith Evans*
98 *Scarface*
83 **All Night Long (All Night)** *Lionel Richie*
77 **All Night Lover** *Diana Ross*
80 **All Night's All Right** *Chaka Khan*
All Of Me
72 *Diana Ross*
90 *Big Daddy Kane*
96 **All Of My Days** *R. Kelly (St: Space Jam)*
73 **All Of My Life** *Diana Ross*
76 **All Of My Love** *Eddie Kendricks*
97 **All Of My Own** *Changing Faces*

93	**Blue Funk** *Heavy D & The Boyz*
68	**Blue Juice** *Jimmy McGriff*
92	**Blue Light** *Prince*
78	**Blue Love** *Rufus Featuring Chaka Khan*
67	**Blue Moon** *Supremes*
65	**Blue Spring** *Ramsey Lewis*
96	**Blueberry** *Snoop Doggy Dogg*
89	**Blueprint** *Boogie Down Productions*

Blues
- 8 *Righteous Brothers*
- 90 *Tony! Toni! Toné!*

71 **Blues & Pants** *James Brown*
66 **Blues And The Abstract Truth** *Jimmy Smith*
76 **Blues Away** *Jacksons*
65 **Blues For J** *Jimmy Smith*
76 **Blues For Louis Jordan** *John Handy*
65 **Blues For The Night Owls** *Ramsey Lewis*
66 **Blues For Yna Yna** *Richard "Groove" Holmes*
92 **Blues Happy** *Arrested Development*
69 **Blues In The Gutter** *Booker T. & The MG's*
65 **Blues In The Night** *Little Milton*

Bluesette
- 66 *Four Tops*
- 75 *Quincy Jones*

96 **Blunt Time** *RBX (VA: Dr. Dre Presents...The Aftermath)*
89 **Bo! Bo! Bo!** *Boogie Down Productions*
73 **Bo Diddley** [medley] *Bloodstone*
68 **Bobbie's Blues (Who Do You Think Of?)** *5th Dimension*
98 **B.O.B.B.Y.** *RZA*
98 **Bobby Did It (Spanish Fly)** *RZA*
98 **Bobo On The Corner** *Beastie Boys*
94 **Bobyahed2dis** *Redman*
94 **Bodhisattva Vow** *Beastie Boys*
84 **Body** *Jacksons*
98 **Body Ah** *Montell Jordan*
91 **Body And Mind** *Heavy D & The Boyz*

Body & Soul
- 94 *Anita Baker*
- 97 *O.F.T.B. (St: Gridlock'd)*

84 **Body Break** *S.O.S. Band*
91 **Body Count** *Ice-T*
80 **Body Fever** *Bar-Kays*

Body Heat
- 74 *Quincy Jones*
- 79 *Rufus Featuring Chaka Khan*

96 **Body Hop (Oh My Goodness)** *T'Baby (VA: So So Def Bass All-Stars)*
98 **Body In The Trunk** *Capone-N-Noreaga*

Body Language
- 75 *Isaac Hayes*
- 84 *Patti LaBelle*

75 **Body Language (Do The Love Dance)** *Jackson 5*
97 **Body Rock** *Busta Rhymes*
97 **Body Rott** *Bone Thugs-N-Harmony*
84 **Body Snatchers** *Midnight Star*

Body Talk
- 75 *Eddie Kendricks*
- 83 *Deele*

93 **Body That Loves You** *Janet Jackson*
77 **Body Vibes** *Ohio Players*
84 **Body Work** *Hot Streak (St: Breakin')*
97 **Bogus Mayn** *Crucial Conflict (St: Rhyme & Reason)*
96 **Bohemian Rhapsody** *Braids (St: High School High)*
68 **Bold As Love** *Jimi Hendrix*
90 **Bom Bom Zee** *Keith Murray*
90 **Bomb, The** *Ice Cube*
98 **Bomb Baby** *Shaquille O'Neal*
96 **Bomb First (My Second Reply)** *Makaveli*
96 **Bomdigi** *Erick Sermon*
96 **Bone** *Luke*
93 **Bonnie & Clyde** *D.R.S.*
73 **Boo Boo'n** *Scarface*
96 **Boo Yow!** *C-BO*
94 **Boodah Break** *Redman*
96 **Boodah Session** *Redman*
96 **Boogie Bang Bang** *Rappin' 4-Tay*
80 **Boogie Body Land** *Bar-Kays*

Boogie Down
- 74 *Eddie Kendricks*
- 83 *Al Jarreau*

75 **Boogie Down U.S.A.** *People's Choice*
72 **Boogie Joe, The Grinder** *Quincy Jones*

Boogie Nights
- 77 *Heatwave*
- 97 *Erykah Badu* [medley]

74 **Boogie On Reggae Woman** *Stevie Wonder*

Boogie Oogie Oogie
- 78 *Taste Of Honey*
- 79 *GQ*

Boogie Shoes
- 75 *KC & The Sunshine Band*
- 78 *K.C. & The Sunshine Band (see Bee Gees LP #3)*

93 **Boogie Wonderland** *Earth, Wind & Fire*
67 **Booker's Notion** *Booker T. & The MG's*
93 **Boom!** *Shaquille O'Neal*
95 **Boom Biddy Bye Bye** *Cypress Hill*
66 **Boom Boom** *Jimmy Smith*
96 **Boom...Boom...Prick** *Originoo Gunn Clappaz*
94 **Boomerang** *Big Punisher*
90 **Boomin' System** *LL Cool J*
84 **Boon Dox** *EPMD*
94 **Booti Call** *BLACKstreet*
95 **Bootsee** *E-40*
92 **Bootsy Get Live** *William "Bootsy" Collins*
78 **Bootsy? (What's The Name Of This Town)** *William "Bootsy" Collins*
78 **Bootzilla** *William "Bootsy" Collins*
77 **Bop Gun (Endangered Species)** *Parliament*
93 **Bop Gun (One Nation)** *Ice Cube*
94 **Border Song (Holy Moses)** *Aretha Franklin*
84 **Borderlines** *Jeffrey Osborne*
91 **Born And Raised In Compton** *DJ Quik*
67 **Born Free** *Nancy Wilson*
93 **Born Gangsta** *Boss*
92 **Born Into The 90's** *R. Kelly*
72 **Born Loser** *Ray Charles*
75 **Born On Halloween** *Blue Magic*
97 **Born 2 Be A Soldier** *Mystikal*
71 **Born To Be Wild** *Wilson Pickett*
83 **Born II Die** *Spice 1 (St: Tales From The Hood)*
91 **Born To Get Busy** *Cypress Hill*
83 **Born To Love** *Peabo Bryson/Roberta Flack*

Born To Love You
- 65 *Temptations*
- 70 *Jackson 5*
- 76 *Rose Royce*

70 **Born To Wander** *Rare Earth*
86 **Borrowed Love** *S.O.S. Band*

Boss
- 73 *James Brown*
- 79 *Diana Ross*

93 **Boss Baller** *Click*
98 **Boss Chick** *Mac*
66 **Boss City** *Wes Montgomery*

Bounce
- 66 *Jackie Lee*
- 97 *Noggin Nodders (St: Sprung)*

96 **Bounce To Da Beat** *Luke*
98 **Bounce Wit Me** *Eightball & MJG*
98 **Bouncin'** *Lost Boyz (St: Woo)*

Bourgie Bourgie
- 77 *Ashford & Simpson*
- 80 *Gladys Knight & The Pips*

98 **Bout It, Bout It** *Master P*
98 **Bout That Combat** *Kane & Abel*
98 **Bout That Drama** *Master P*
96 **Bow Down** *Westside Connection*
96 **Box In Hand** *Ghostface Killah*
98 **Boxin'** *Martin Lawrence*
65 **Boy From Ipanema** *Supremes*

Boy Is Mine
- 98 *Brandy*
- 98 *Monica*

95 **Boy Meets World** *Erick Sermon*
65 **Boy, What A Night** *Lee Morgan*
76 **Boy With The Ohh-La-La** *Silver Convention*
77 **Boyhood To Manhood** *Quincy Jones*
83 **Boys** *Mary Jane Girls*
97 **Boys And Girls** *Tony Toni Toné (St: Soul Food)*
79 **Boys Are Back In Town** *Gap Band*
88 **Boys To Men** *New Edition*
87 **Boys Will Be Boys** *Fat Boys*
91 **Boyz N Tha Hood** *Eazy-E*
93 **Braggin' On Their Dicks** *Martin Lawrence*
94 **Brahms Lullaby** *Kenny G*
98 **Brain On Drugs** *Bizzy Bone*
94 **Brainstorm** *Gang Starr*
94 **Brainwasher** *Jr. Walker & The All Stars*
96 **Brakes** *De La Soul*
94 **Brand New Formula** *D.O.C.*
88 **Brand New Funk** *D.J. Jazzy Jeff & The Fresh Prince*

Brand New Me
- 69 *Jerry Butler*
- 71 *Isaac Hayes*
- 72 *Aretha Franklin*

80 **Brand New Player** *Zapp*
93 **Brand Nubian Rock The Set** *Brand Nubian*
78 **Brandy** *O'Jays*
86 **Brass Monkey** *Beastie Boys*

71 **Brave & Strong** *Sly & The Family Stone*
82 **Brazilian Memories** *Grover Washington, Jr.*
85 **Break Dancer** *Boogie Boys*
93 **Break 'Em Off Some** *Cypress Hill*
94 **Break 'Em Off Somethin'** *Master P*
94 **Break 'Em Off Somethin' Proper** *M.C. Hammer*
86 **Break Every Rule** *Tina Turner*
72 **Break In (Police Shoot Big)** *Marvin Gaye*
91 **Break It Down With You** *Barry White*
89 **Break It On Down** *Luke*
77 **Break It To Me Gently** *Aretha Franklin*

Break It Up
- 85 *Mary Jane Girls*
- 91 *Cypress Hill*

93 **Break Of Dawn** *Salt-N-Pepa*
94 **Break Something** *Fiend (VA: No Limit Soldier Compilation)*
84 **Break Up** *S.O.S. Band*

Break Up To Make Up
- 72 *Stylistics*
- 86 *Jean Carn*
- 97 *Mariah Carey*
- 97 *Lady Of Rage*

96 **Breaker 1, Breaker 2** *Def Squad (St: The Nutty Professor)*
84 **Breaker's Revenge** *Arthur Baker (St: Beat Street, Volume 1)*
81 **Breakin' Away** *Al Jarreau*
97 **Breakin' Skrill** *Delinquents (VA: West Coast Bad Boyz II)*
84 **Breakin'...There's No Stopping Us** *Ollie & Jerry (St: Breakin')*
84 **Breakin' Together** *O'Bryan*
66 **Breaking My Back (Instead Of Using My Mind)** *Lou Rawls*
66 **Breaking My Heart** *Gerald Levert*
86 **Breaking Up** *Shirley Jones*
94 **Breakout!** *Patrice Rushen*
80 **Breaks** *Kurtis Blow*
87 **Breakthrough** *LL Cool J*
89 **Breath Control** *Boogie Down Productions*
90 **Breath Control II** *Boogie Down Productions*
65 **Breath Taking Guy** *Supremes*
94 **Breathe Again** *Toni Braxton*
76 **Breezin'** *George Benson*
75 **Breezy** *Jackson 5*
72 **Brenda** *Four Tops*
98 **Brenda's Got A Baby** *2Pac*
98 **Brick City** *Brick*
98 **Brick City Mashin'!** *Redman*
77 **Brick House** *Commodores*

Bridge Over Troubled Water
- 70 *Jackson 5*
- 70 *Miracles*
- 70 *Nancy Wilson*
- 71 *Roberta Flack*
- 71 *Aretha Franklin*
- 89 *BeBe & CeCe Winans*

Bright Lights & You Girl
- 68 *Ray Charles*
- 78 *Tom Jones*

80 **Bright Moments** *Grover Washington, Jr.*
93 **Bring Back My Yesterday** *Barry White*
94 **Bring Back Somethin Fo Da Hood** *Coolio*
91 **Bring Back Tha Days** *U.S. Male (St: Five Heartbeats)*
97 **Bring Da Drama** *Mia X*
93 **Bring Da Ruckus** *Wu-Tang Clan*
97 **Bring It Back** *KRS-One (St: Rhyme & Reason)*

Bring It On
- 93 *Geto Boys*
- 94 *South Central Cartel*
- 96 *Johnny Gill*
- 96 *Jay-Z*
- 96 *MC Ren*
- 96 *Mia X*

79 **Bring It On Back To Me** *Amii Stewart*

Bring It On Home To Me
- 65 *Sam Cooke*
- 65 *Supremes*
- 68 *Otis Redding & Carla Thomas*
- 68 *Wilson Pickett*

70 **Bring It Up** *James Brown*
70 **Bring Me Together** *Four Tops*
98 **Bring My Burners** *Freedom (VA: No Limit Soldier Compilation)*
95 **Bring On Da' Funk** *Jodeci*

Bring The Noise
- 88 *Public Enemy*
- 94 *Young Bleed*

94 **Bring The Pain** *Method Man*
81 **Bristol Hotel** *LL Cool J*
86 **Broadway** *Kool & The Gang*
86 **Broadway Gypsy Lady** *Linda Clifford*
69 **Broadway Medley** *Supremes & The Temptations*
96 **Broccoli** *E-40*
96 **Broke Down Piece Of Man** *Sam & Dave*
95 **Broke Hos** *Luniz*
95 **Broke Niggaz** *Luniz*
96 **Broke Willies** *Onyx*
75 **Broken Heart Don't Really Break** *Main Ingredient*
73 **Broken Home** *Al Wilson*
94 **Broken Wing Bird** *5th Dimension*
94 **Brokenhearted** *Brandy*
96 **Brokenhearted Girl-Brokenhearted Boy** *Miracles*
96 **Bronx Keeps Creating It** *Fat Joe*
95 **Bronx Tale** *Fat Joe*
98 **Bronx War Stories** *Wu-Tang Killa Bees*
89 **Brooklyn - Queens** *3rd Bass*
95 **Brooklyn To T-Neck** *DAS EFX*
94 **Brooklyn Took It** *Jeru The Damaja*
95 **Brooklyn Zoo** *Ol Dirty Bastard*
96 **Brooklyn's Finest** *Jay-Z*
95 **Brother, Brother** *Isley Brothers*
77 **Brother Man** *Brothers Johnson*
77 **Brother Man, Brother Man** *Big Daddy Kane*
88 **Brother Man Get Hip** *Kid 'N Play*
70 **Brother Rapp** *James Brown*
92 **Brother Will** *Harlem Yacht Club (St: Mo' Money)*
94 **Brothers And Sistas** *Jayo Felony (St: Jason's Lyric)*
90 **Brothers Gonna Work It Out** *Public Enemy*
91 **Brothers Hang On** *Hammer*
91 **Brothers On My Jock** *EPMD*

Brown Baby
- 72 *Billy Paul*
- 73 *Diana Ross* [medley]

Brown Eyed Girl
- 74 *Isley Brothers*
- 93 *Tevin Campbell*

94 **Brown Skin Woman** *KRS-One*
95 **Brown Sugar** *D'Angelo*
91 **Brownsville II Long Beach** *Heltah Skeltah*
97 **Bubblegoose** *Wyclef Jean*

Bubbles
- 75 *Herbie Hancock*
- 76 *Norman Connors*

95 **Buck-Buck** *DAS EFX*
98 **Buck 'Em** *Big Ed*
92 **Buck Tha Devil** *Da Lench Mob*
91 **Buckin' Em Down** *LL Cool J*
95 **Buckingham Palace** *Canibus*
95 **Bucktown** *Cocoa Brovaz*
91 **Bucktown USA** *Cocoa Brovaz*
94 **Buckwylyn** *Shyheim*
92 **Buddah Lovaz** *Bone Thugs-N-Harmony*
91 **Buddup Bap** *Whitey Don (St: Dangerous Ground)*
89 **Buddy** *De La Soul*
95 **Budsmokers Only** *Bone Thugs-N-Harmony*
96 **Buggin'** *Bugs Bunny (St: Space Jam)*
92 **Bugs** *Bobbie Gentry*
95 **Build & Destroy** *Channel Live*
95 **Build Ya Skillz** *KRS-One*
66 **Build Your Love (On A Solid Foundation)** *Joe Tex*
73 **Build Your Nest** *Earth, Wind & Fire*
92 **Bullet Proof Soul** *Sade*
98 **Bulworth (They Talk About It While We Live It)** *Method Man (St: Bulworth)*
75 **Bump** *Commodores*
98 **Bump And Grill** *U.G.K. (St: I Got The Hook-Up!)*
93 **Bump N' Grind** *R. Kelly*
98 **Bumpin' Bullet Loco** *Jayo Felony*
86 **Bumpin' Gum People** *Gap Band*
96 **Bumpin' On Sunset** *Wes Montgomery*
75 **Bumpy's Blues** *Isaac Hayes*
93 **Buncha Niggas** *Heavy D & The Boyz*
97 **'Burban & Impalas** *Big Mike*
97 **Burbons And Lacs** *Master P*
90 **Burn Hollywood Burn** *Public Enemy*
96 **Burn Rubber** *Lords Of The Underground (St: New Jersey Drive Vol. 1)*
81 **Burn Rubber (Why You Wanna Hurt Me)** *Gap Band*
79 **Burn This Disco Out** *Michael Jackson*
76 **Burnin' Bush** *Earth, Wind & Fire*

266

273

76 Like Nobody Can *Smokey Robinson*
98 Like Some Ho's *Geto Boys*
66 Like Someone In Love *Nancy Wilson*
98 Like That *WC & The MAAD Circle*
98 Like This *Crucial Conflict*
95 Like This And Like That *Monica*
97 Like Water *Levert*
98 Like What *Shaquille O'Neal*
97 Likkle Youth Man Dem *Boot Camp Clik*
96 Lil Advice *Crucial Conflict*
93 Lil Ass Gee *Ice Cube*
92 Lil' Boys In Da Hood *Kris Kross*
91 Lil' Brother *Tevin Campbell*
93 Lil Crazy *Erick Sermon*
93 Lil' Ghetto Boy *Dr. Dre*
94 Lil Knucklehead *South Central Cartel*
97 Lil N *Steady Mobb'n*
98 Lil Poppa Got A Brand New Bag
  Young Bleed
93 Lil' Putos *Cypress Hill*
96 Lil Some'Em Some'Em *Rappin' 4-Tay*
98 Lil Sum Sum *Do Or Die*
74 Lilies Of The Nile *Crusaders*
96 Limos, Demos & Bimbos *Ice Cube*
79 Liquid Love *Isley Brothers*
78 Liquid Sunshine *Parliament*
95 Liquid Swords *Genius/GZA*
97 Liquor Store Run
  Volume 10 (St: Rhyme & Reason)
68 Listen Here *Eddie Harris*
72 Listen To The Clock On The Wall *O'Jays*
73 Listen To The Music *Isley Brothers*
73 Listen To The Wind *Billy Preston*
75 Listen (What It Is) *Quincy Jones*
86 Little Bit More
  Melba Moore & Freddie Jackson
85 Little Bit Of Love (Is All It Takes)
  New Edition
82 Little Bit Of Loving (Goes A Long Way)
  Tyrone Davis
Little Bit Of Soap
70 *Brook Benton*
89 *De La Soul*
71 Little Bit Of Something (Is Better Than
  All Of Nothing) *Jean Knight*
80 Little Bit Of You *Ray Parker Jr.*
92 Little Bit Older Now *Hi-Five*
72 Little Bitty Pretty One *Jackson 5*
74 Little Black Boys And Girls *Billy Preston*
71 Little Boy *Staple Singers*
75 Little Boy Blue
  Rufus Featuring Chaka Khan
85 Little Boys - Dangerous Toys *Cameo*
68 Little Brown Boy *Impressions*
66 Little Child (Daddy Dear)
  Wes Montgomery
72 Little Child Runnin' Wild *Curtis Mayfield*
76 Little Children *Kool & The Gang*
66 Little Darling, I Need You *Marvin Gaye*
94 Little Drummer Boy *Kenny G*
72 Little Ghetto Boy *Donny Hathaway*
97 Little Ghetto Boys *Wu-Tang Clan*
71 Little Girl *Donny Hathaway*
73 Little Girl Blue *Diana Ross*
Little Green Apples
68 *Johnny Mathis*
68 *O.C. Smith*
68 *Dionne Warwick*
69 *Mongo Santamaria*
69 *Temptations*
69 *Young-Holt Unlimited*
68 Little Groove Maker Me *James Brown*
76 Little Lady Maria *Ohio Players*
65 Little Latin Lupe Lu *Righteous Brothers*
65 Little Liza Jane *Ramsey Lewis*
93 Little Miracles (Happen Every Day)
  Luther Vandross
68 Little Miss Lover *Jimi Hendrix*
68 Little Miss Strange *Jimi Hendrix*
Little Miss Sweetness
66 *Temptations*
66 *Hugh Masekela*
Little More Love
85 *Kenny Rogers (see USA for Africa)*
91 *Lisa Stansfield*
95 Little Of This *Grand Puba*
67 Little Ole Boy, Little Ole Girl
  Marvin Gaye & Tammi Terrell
75 Little Piece Of Heaven *Miracles*
94 Little Rascals *Shyheim*
82 Little Red Corvette *Prince*
65 Little Red Rooster *Sam Cooke*
88 Little Romance *Boys*
91 Little Soldiers *Another Bad Creation*
93 Little Somethin' *LL Cool J*
68 Little Soul Sister *Ray Bryant*
85 Little Spice *Loose Ends*
95 Little Susie *Michael Jackson*
77 Little Taste Of Outside Love
  Millie Jackson

76 Little Things *Boyz II Men*
69 Little Understanding *Dells*
88 Little Wing *Jimi Hendrix*
65 Little Young Lover *Impressions*
95 Live!!! *Onyx (St: The Show)*
96 Live And Die For Hip Hop *Kris Kross*
94 Live And Undrugged *Public Enemy*
98 Live At The O.M.N.I. *Goodie Mob*
88 Live At Union Square, November 1986
  D.J. Jazzy Jeff & The Fresh Prince
91 Live 4 Love *Prince*
84 Live For The Moment *Freddie Jackson*
80 Live For Today *Jeffrey Osborne*
66 Live For Yourself *Joe Tex*
96 Live From Compton 'Saturday Night'
  MC Ren
79 Live From New York *Keith Murray*
79 Live In Me *Rufus Featuring Chaka Khan*
Live It Up
72 *Jermaine Jackson*
74 *Isley Brothers*
75 *Da Brat*
98 Live Me Long *Fiend*
92 Live My Life Without You
  Freddie Jackson with D'Atra Hicks
96 Live Niggaz Rap *Nas*
97 Live On Live Long *Capone-N-Noreaga*
94 Live Right Now *Eddie Harris*
96 Live Soil *Flesh-N-Bone*
96 Live To Regret
  Busta Rhymes (St: Set It Off)
92 Live Together *Lisa Stansfield*
66 Live Wire *Martha & The Vandellas*
96 Live Wires Connect
  UGK (St: Don't Be A Menace...)
98 Livin' 4 The Moment *Geto Boys*
75 Livin' For The Weekend *O'Jays*
73 Livin' For You *Al Green*
83 Livin' For Your Love *Melba Moore*
79 Livin' In A World (They Didn't Make)
  Janet Jackson
82 Livin' In America *Donna Summer*
77 Livin' In The Life *Isley Brothers*
79 Livin' Inside Your Love *George Benson*
93 Livin' Loc'd *Boss*
93 Livin' The Life *Lox*
74 Living A Little, Laughing A Little
  Spinners
Living For The City
73 *Stevie Wonder*
75 *Ramsey Lewis*
77 Living From The Mind *Brick*
98 Living In A World *Trick Daddy*
98 Living In A World Like This *Hammer*
94 Living In A Zoo *Public Enemy*
91 Living In Confusion *Phyllis Hyman*
72 Living In The Footsteps Of Another Man
  Chi-Lites
81 Living In The Streets *Aretha Franklin*
95 Living In The World Today *Genius/GZA*
66 Living Soul *Richard "Groove" Holmes*
Living Together
76 *Jacksons*
74 *Bee Gees*
97 Liza *Bill Withers*
97 Load Unload
  Chilla (VA: Southwest Riders)
97 Loc'd Out Hood
  Kurupt (St: Gang Related)
93 Loc'ed After Dark *Tone Loc*
98 Loc'in On The Shaw *Tone Loc*
97 Lock And Key *Klymaxx*
97 Lock Down *Mac (St: I'm Bout It)*
Lock It In The Pocket
78 *Grover Washington, Jr.*
82 *Temptations*
Lock It Up
68 *Jimmy McGriff*
95 *Channel Live*
66 Locking Up My Heart *Marvelettes*
95 Locotes *Cypress Hill*
95 Lodi Dodi *Snoop Doggy Dogg*
98 Loe Is Gone *Billy Eckstine*
98 Log Off *Trick Daddy*
98 Log On *Trick Daddy*
98 Loked Out Hood *DJ Quik*
72 London Berry Blues *Chuck Berry*
75 Loneliest House On The Block
  Blue Magic
67 (Loneliness Made Me Realize) It's You
  That I Need *Temptations*
70 Loneliness Remembers What
  Happiness Forgets *Dionne Warwick*
Lonely
89 *Janet Jackson*
90 *Anita Baker*
65 Lonely Avenue *Ramsey Lewis*
65 Lonely Color Blue *Teddy Pendergrass*
74 Lonely Feelin' *War*

85 Lonely For You *Mary Jane Girls*
91 Lonely Heart *Boyz II Men*
68 Lonely In My Heart *Dionne Warwick*
82 Lonely Like Me *Gap Band*
70 Lonely, Lonely *Nancy Wilson*
66 Lonely, Lonely Man Am I *Temptations*
Lonely Man
65 *Impressions*
72 *Chi-Lites*
72 Lonely Town, Lonely Street *Bill Withers*
65 Lonely Woman *Horace Silver Quintet*
95 Lonely's The Only Company *Maxwell*
76 Lonesome Cowboy *Roy Ayers*
69 Lonesome Mood *Friends Of Distinction*
67 Lonesome Road *Stevie Wonder*
95 Long Ago *Mariah Carey*
Long And Winding Road
70 *Diana Ross*
70 *Nancy Wilson*
72 *Aretha Franklin*
84 *Billy Ocean*
93 Long Beach Thang *Domino*
68 Long Black Limousine *O.C. Smith*
66 Long Day, Short Night *Dionne Warwick*
90 Long Gone *Guy*
65 Long Gone Lover *Supremes*
68 Long Hot Summer Night *Jimi Hendrix*
96 Long Island Degrees *De La Soul*
93 Long Island Wildin' *De La Soul*
97 Long Kiss Goodnight *Notorious B.I.G.*
88 Long Live The Kane *Big Daddy Kane*
70 Long Lonely Nights *Dells*
65 Long Long Winter *Impressions*
70 Long Time Comin' My Way
  Friends Of Distinction
86 Long Time Coming *Ready For The World*
70 Long Time Leavin' *Rare Earth*
93 Long Way From Home *Johnny Gill*
Long Way To Go
77 *Emotions*
94 *Gang Starr*
92 Longest Night *Montell Jordan*
75 Lonnie Dreams *War*
66 Look-A-Here *Ramsey Lewis*
Look Around
71 *Stevie Wonder*
86 *Freddie Jackson*
77 Look At California
  Maze Featuring Frankie Beverly
78 Look At Her *Barry White*
66 Look At Me *Righteous Brothers*
69 Look At That Girl *Otis Redding*
74 Look At You *George McCrae*
67 Look At Your Hands *George Michael*
82 Look Before You Leap *Cheryl Lynn*
73 Look Beyond The Hill *Crusaders*
80 Look In Your Eyes
  Maze Featuring Frankie Beverly
97 Look Into My Eyes
  Bone Thugs-N-Harmony
67 Look Into Your Heart *Aretha Franklin*
74 Look Me Up *Blue Magic*
Look Of Love
68 *Nancy Wilson*
69 *Dionne Warwick*
70 *Isaac Hayes*
73 *Bobby Womack*
94 *Anita Baker*
95 *Isaac Hayes (St: Dead Presidents)*
71 Look Over Yonder *Jimi Hendrix*
74 Look Through My Eyes *Rufus*
98 Look Thru My Eyes *DMX*
80 Look To The Rainbow *Aretha Franklin*
72 Look Up (To See What's Coming Down)
  Santana
91 Look What We'd Have (If You Were
  Mine) *Tevin Campbell*
72 Look What You Done For Me *Al Green*
75 Look What You've Done To Me
  Commodores
91 Look Who's Burnin' *Ice Cube*
77 Lookin' Ahead *Blackbyrds*
97 Lookin' At Me *Mase*
74 Lookin' For A Love *Bobby Womack*
72 Lookin' For Another Pure Love
  Stevie Wonder
72 Lookin' Through The Windows
  Jackson 5
66 Looking Back *Carla Thomas*
87 Looking For A New Love *Jody Watley*
Looking For Love
86 *Levert*
97 *Whitey Don (St: Booty Call)*
98 *R. Kelly*
91 Looking In *Mariah Carey*
66 Looking With My Eyes *Dionne Warwick*
93 Looks Like A Job For... *Big Daddy Kane*
74 Looks Like Rain *Main Ingredient*
72 Looner Tune *Billy Preston*
82 Loopzilla [medley] *George Clinton*

94 Loose! *Prince*
84 Loose Talk *Bar-Kays*
92 Looseys *DAS EFX*
94 Loot *Ant Banks*
78 Loran's Dance *Grover Washington, Jr.*
92 Lord Have Mercy *Da Lench Mob*
93 Lord I've Come *Shai*
96 Lord Is My Shepherd *Whitney Houston*
96 Lord Is Real (Time Will Reveal)
  BLACKstreet
97 Lord Is Testin Me *Tru*
92 Lord Knows *2 Pac*
98 Lord Of All *Kelly Price*
83 Lord's Prayer *Heavy D & The Boyz*
92 Lose Control *Silk*
97 Lose My Cool *SWV (Sisters With Voices)*
97 Lose Myself *SWV*
82 Losin' End *Michael McDonald*
91 Losing My Faith *Gambino Family*
95 Losing My Religion
  Tori Amos (St: Higher Learning)
Lost
69 *Jerry Butler*
98 *Eightball & MJG*
91 Lost At Birth *Public Enemy*
87 Lost In Emotion *Lisa Lisa & Cult Jam*
84 Lost In Love *New Edition*
79 Lost In Music *Sister Sledge*
92 Lost In Tha System *Da Lench Mob*
93 Lost In The Moment *Bell Biv DeVoe*
91 Lost In The Night *Peabo Bryson*
98 Lost Ones *Lauryn Hill*
66 Lost Someone *James Brown*
97 Lost Souls *2Pac (St: Gang Related)*
89 Lost Without Her Love *El DeBarge*
95 Lost Without You *BeBe & CeCe Winans*
92 Lot 2 Live 4 *Kris Kross*
92 Lots Of Lovin *Pete Rock & C.L. Smooth*
75 Lotus Blossom *War*
97 Loud Hangover *Akinyele & Sadat (VA:
  Funkmaster Flex Vol. II)*
88 Louder Than A Bomb *Public Enemy*
81 Louie Louie *Stanley Clarke/George Duke*
92 Louis Visits Billie On Tour *Diana Ross*
95 Loungin *LL Cool J*
L-O-V-E
65 *Nat "King" Cole*
76 *Brass Construction*
76 *Graham Central Station*
76 *Kool & The Gang*
80 *Grover Washington, Jr.*
84 *Teddy Pendergrass*
85 *Morris Day [medley]*
91 *Natalie Cole*
97 *God's Property*
98 *Kirk Franklin*
98 *Tribe Called Quest*
66 Love A Go Go *Stevie Wonder*
93 Love Across The Wire *Earth, Wind & Fire*
Love Affair
81 *Kool & The Gang*
93 *Toni Braxton*
72 Love Ain't Gonna Run Me Away
  Luther Ingram
81 Love All The Hurt Away *Aretha Franklin*
86 Love Always *El DeBarge*
72 Love And Happiness *Al Green*
75 Love And Its Glory *Minnie Riperton*
82 Love And My Best Friend *Janet Jackson*
69 Love And Peace *Quincy Jones*
91 Love & Trust *O'Jays*
76 Love And Understanding (Come
  Together) *Kool & The Gang*
87 Love At First Sight *Dana Dane*
85 Love At Second Sight *Dionne Warwick*
Love Ballad
76 *L.T.D.*
79 *George Benson*
87 *K-Ci & JoJo*
85 Love Bandit *Klymaxx*
84 Love Bankrupt *Patti LaBelle*
70 Love Bones *Tyrone Davis*
87 Love Brought Us Here Tonight
  Smokey Robinson
92 Love By Day, Love By Night *After 7*
71 Love Can Be Anything (Can't Nothing
  Be Love But Love) *Temptations*
75 Love Can Be Hazardous To Your Health
  David Ruffin
67 Love Can Do Anything *Nancy Wilson*
73 Love Can Make It Easier *Dells*
Love Child
68 *Supremes*
69 *Booker T. & The MG's*
69 *Mongo Santamaria*
82 Love Come Down
  Evelyn "Champagne" King
79 Love Comes And Goes *Isley Brothers*
73 Love Comes Easy *Stylistics*
73 Love Comes In All Sizes *Chi-Lites*

281

282

287

79 **One More Time** *Sister Sledge*
87 **One More Try** *George Michael*
96 **1 Morning** *Silkk The Shocker*
78 **One Nation Under A Groove** *Funkadelic*
89 **One Night** *After 7*
79 **One Night In A Lifetime** *Donna Summer*
82 **One Night Only** *OC: Dreamgirls*
97 **1-900 Get Da Boot** *Boot Camp Clik*
89 **1-900 L.L. Cool J** *LL Cool J*
96 **1-900-Off-Your Square** *Crucial Conflict*
91 **1-900-2-COMPTON** *N.W.A.*
74 **One Nite Stand** *Al Green*
One Of A Kind
78 *Donna Summer*
87 *Stevie Wonder*
89 *Isley Brothers*
73 **One Of A Kind (Love Affair)** *Spinners*
65 **One Of These Days** *Marvin Gaye*
72 **One Of These Good Old Days** *Al Green*
78 **One Of Those Funky Things** *Parliament*
98 **One Of Those Love Songs** *Xscape*
94 **One Of Those Things** *Changing Faces*
96 **One Of Us** *Prince*
85 **One Of Us Fell In Love**
Teddy Pendergrass
One On One
79 *L.T.D.*
82 *O'Jays*
83 *Daryl Hall & John Oates*
88 **One Or The Other** *Paula Abdul*
70 **One Part - Two Parts** *David Porter*
68 **One Rainy Wish** *Jimi Hendrix*
91 **One Reason** *Vanessa Williams*
65 **One Room Paradise** *Aretha Franklin*
96 **One Shine** *Roots*
89 **One Shot At Love** *LL Cool J*
91 **One Song** *Tevin Campbell*
98 **One Step** *Killah Priest*
67 **One Step Ahead** *Aretha Franklin*
71 **One Step Away** *Gladys Knight & The Pips*
95 **One Sweet Day**
Mariah Carey & Boyz II Men
74 **One Tear** *Eddie Kendricks*
88 **One Thing Led To Another** *Johnny Kemp*
73 **One Thing Wronmg With My Woman**
Johnnie Taylor
One Time
93 *Scarface*
94 *MC Breed*
94 **One Time 4 Your Mind** *Nas*
72 **One Time Or Another** *Billy Preston*
78 **One To One** *Michael Henderson*
74 **One Track Mind** *Quincy Jones*
86 **1.2.1** *Oran "Juice" Jones*
98 **One Two Shit** *Tribe Called Quest*
1-2-3
66 *Jimmy Smith*
91 *Naughty By Nature*
96 *Lost Boyz*
83 **1,2,3 (U, Her And Me)** *Rick James*
98 **One Voice** *Brandy*
70 **One Way Ticket** *Aretha Franklin*
71 **One-Way Ticket To Nowhere (It's The End Of The Ride)** *Jean Knight*
88 **One Wish** *Karyn White*
One Woman
69 *Isaac Hayes*
73 *Al Green*
One Woman Man
70 *Jerry Butler*
73 *Four Tops*
93 **One Wonderful Girl** *O'Jays*
94 **One's 4 Da Money** *Shyheim*
76 **Only A Child Can Love** *Ohio Players*
79 **Only A Child In Your Eyes** *Amii Stewart*
98 **Only A Customer**
Jay-Z (St: Streets Is Watching)
98 **Only A Few** *Fiend*
69 **Only A Lonely Man Would Know**
Marvin Gaye
97 **Only Fear Of Death** *2 Pac*
94 **Only For A While** *Anita Baker*
73 **Only For The Children** *Stylistics*
98 **Only For U** *Daz Dillinger*
98 **Only G's Ride** *Gambino Family*
82 **Only Game In Town** *Smokey Robinson*
96 **Only God Can Judge Me** *2 Pac*
Only God Knows
95 *Bushwick Bill*
98 *Kane & Abel*
Only Heaven Can Wait (For Love)
80 *Roberta Flack*
80 *Roberta Flack & Peabo Bryson [medley]*
90 **Only Human** *Jeffrey Osborne*
97 **Only In California** *Mack 10*
Only One
83 *Lionel Richie*
98 *112*
97 **Only One For Me** *Brian McKnight*
78 **Only One Man** *Donna Summer*
93 **Only Ones** *Naughty By Nature*
98 **Only Real N...** *Soulja Slim*
73 **Only Room For Two** *Eddie Kendricks*
Only Sixteen
65 *Sam Cooke*
65 *Supremes*
85 **Only Survivor** *Bobby Womack*
98 **Only The Loot Can Make Me Happy**
R. Kelly
Only The Strong Survive
69 *Jerry Butler*
93 *Too $hort (St: Menace II Society)*
98 *C-Murder*
67 **Only The Young** *Nancy Wilson*
65 **Only Time I'm Happy** *Supremes*
97 **Only Time Will Tell** *Master P*
76 **Only Time You Ever Say You Love Me**
Dorothy Moore
82 **Only To You** *Teddy Pendergrass*
97 **Only Way**
Celly Cel (St: Dangerous Ground)
Only You
67 *James Brown*
78 *Teddy Pendergrass*
82 *Whispers*
89 *Jody Watley*
96 *112*
74 **Only You Can Make Me Blue**
Love Unlimited Orchestra
93 **Onyx Is Here** *Onyx*
72 **Ooh Baby You've Been Good To Me**
Johnny Nash
77 **Ooh Boy** *Rose Royce*
67 **Ooh Carla, Ooh Otis**
Otis Redding & Carla Thomas
94 **Ooh Child** *Five Stairsteps (St: Crooklyn)*
92 **Ooh 4 You Girl** *Al B. Sure!*
75 **Ooh I Like Your Loving**
Rufus Featuring Chaka Khan
84 **Ooh Love** *Kashif*
Ooh Poo Pah Doo
65 *Righteous Brothers*
67 *Wilson Pickett*
70 *Ike & Tina Turner*
90 **Ooh This Jazz Is So** *Al B. Sure!*
86 **Ooh, What A Feeling** *Gap Band*
93 **Ooh, Whatcha Gonna Do** *Run-D.M.C.*
86 **Ooh, You Make Me Feel** *Loose Ends*
Ooo ..also see: Ooh
65 **Ooo Baby Baby** *Miracles*
70 **Ooo-Wee Girl** *David Porter*
67 **Oooh, Baby Baby** *Five Stairsteps*
88 **Oooh This Love Is So** *Al B. Sure!*
76 **Open** *Smokey Robinson*
83 **Open All Night** *Daryl Hall & John Oates*
95 **Open Arms** *Mariah Carey*
Open Fire
95 *Erick Sermon*
97 *2 Pac*
80 **Open Letter** *S.O.S. Band*
96 **Open Minded** *Geto Boys*
74 **Open Our Eyes** *Earth, Wind & Fire*
Open Sesame
76 *Kool & The Gang*
78 *Kool & The Gang (see Bee Gees LP #3)*
68 **Open The Door** *Otis Redding*
Open Up
80 *Chic*
93 *Aaron Hall*
70 **Open Up My Heart** *Dells*
65 **Open Up Your Heart** *Arthur Prysock*
Open Up Your Mind (Wide)
79 *Gap Band*
80 *Grover Washington, Jr.*
80 **Open Your Heart** *Bar-Kays*
96 **Opening Doors** *Mac Mall*
98 **Opera** *R. Kelly*
96 **Operation Lock Down** *Heltah Skeltah*
95 **Operation Stackola** *Luniz*
Operator
83 *Pointer Sisters*
84 *Midnight Star*
73 **Opportunity** *Timmy Thomas*
88 **Opposites Attract** *Paula Abdul*
91 **Optimistic** *Sounds Of Blackness*
81 **Opus III (Does Anybody Care)**
Teena Marie
91 **Orange Colored Sky** *Natalie Cole*
98 **Ordinary Guy** *Lost Boyz (St: Caught Up)*
70 **Ordinary Joe** *Jerry Butler*
76 **Ordinary Pain** *Stevie Wonder*
65 **Organ Grinder's Swing** *Jimmy Smith*
94 **Orgasm** *Prince*
90 **Original Lyrics** *Boogie Down Productions*
85 **Original Miami Vice Theme**
Jan Hammer (TV: Miami Vice)
77 **Other** *Meco*
91 **Other Level** *Geto Boys*
68 **Other Man's Grass Is Always Greener**
Wes Montgomery
96 **Other Side** *Facemob*
81 **Other Side Of Love**
Evelyn "Champagne" King
83 **Other Side Of The Coin** *Jeffrey Osborne*
85 **Other Side Of The World** *Luther Vandross*
70 **Other Side Of Town** *Curtis Mayfield*
82 **Other Woman** *Ray Parker Jr.*
98 **Otherside** *Mo Thugs Family*
97 **Otherside Of The Game** *Erykah Badu*
70 **Our Ages Or Our Hearts** *Roberta Flack*
98 **Our Daily Bread** *Daz Dillinger*
Our Day Will Come
66 *Fontella Bass*
67 *Soulful Strings*
70 *Isaac Hayes*
74 **Our Lives** *Minnie Riperton*
Our Love
77 *Natalie Cole*
79 *Donna Summer*
81 *Al Jarreau*
94 *Gladys Knight*
97 *Mary J. Blige*
72 **Our Love Has Died** *Ohio Players*
91 **Our Love Is Here To Stay** *Natalie Cole*
81 **Our Love Keeps Growing Strong**
Larry Graham
80 **Our Love's In Danger** *Chaka Khan*
Our Song
66 *Little Anthony & The Imperials*
87 *Herb Alpert*
79 **Our Thought (Purity)** *Mass Production*
94 **Our World** *Patti LaBelle*
95 **Out For Fame** *KRS One*
70 **Out In The Country** *Friends Of Distinction*
82 **Out In The Real World** *O'Jays*
95 **Out My Body** *Click*
84 **Out Of Control** *Whodini*
79 **Out Of My Hands** *Dionne Warwick*
89 **Out Of My Mind** *O'Jays*
65 **Out Of Sight** *James Brown*
98 **Out Of Town B's** *Kane & Abel*
85 **Out Of Town Lover** *Ready For The World*
84 **Out On A Limb** *Teena Marie*
80 **Out The Box** *Whispers*
97 **Out The Moon (Boom, Boom, Boom)**
Snoop Doggy Dogg (St: Gridlock'd)
73 **Out With The Boys** *Mandrill*
72 **Outa-Space** *Billy Preston*
98 **Outcome** *WC*
95 **Outlaw** *2 Pac*
98 **Outlaws** *Fatal*
84 **Outrageous** *Stephanie Mills*
97 **Outside** *Mariah Carey*
79 **Outside My Window** *Stevie Wonder*
73 **Outside Woman** *Bloodstone*
82 **Outstanding** *Gap Band*
95 **Outta Bounds** *E-40*
93 **Outta Here** *KRS-One*
84 **Outta The World** *Ashford & Simpson*
96 **Ova Da Wudz** *OutKast*
89 **Oval Office** *3rd Bass*
Over And Over
65 *Righteous Brothers*
70 *Delfonics*
84 *Madonna*
Over The Rainbow
66 *Richard "Groove" Holmes*
66 *Billy Stewart*
91 **Over The Rainbow And On To The Sun**
Tevin Campbell
67 **Over The Weekend** *Nancy Wilson*
75 **Over To Where You Are**
Stanley Turrentine
97 **Over Ya Head** *KRS-One*
82 **Overdue** *Tyrone Davis*
85 **Overjoyed** *Stevie Wonder*
98 **Overnight** *Scarface*
86 **Overnight Sensation** *Tina Turner*
87 **Overnight Success**
Gladys Knight & The Pips
87 **Overweight Lovers In The House**
Heavy D & The Boyz
87 **Overweighter** *Heavy D & The Boyz*
95 **Own Destiny** *Mad Lion (St: New Jersey Drive Vol. 2)*
85 **Own The Night**
Chaka Khan (TV: Miami Vice)
70 **Oye Como Va** *Santana*

P

95 **P Control** *Prince*
97 **P Dreams** *Mr. Serv-On*
"P" Is Still Free
93 *KRS-One*
93 *Boogie Down Productions (St: Menace II Society)*
76 **P. Funk (Wants To Get Funked Up)**
Parliament
78 **P.E. Squad (Doo Doo Chasers)**
Funkadelic
94 **P.L.O. Style** *Method Man*
82 **P.Y.T. (Pretty Young Thing)**
Michael Jackson
93 **Pacifics** *Digable Planets*
75 **Pack'd My Bags**
Rufus Featuring Chaka Khan
90 **Packet Man** *Digital Underground*
94 **Packin' A Gat** *Ant Banks*
93 **Packin' A Gun**
Ant Banks (St: Menace II Society)
98 **Pad & Pen** *Tribe Called Quest*
87 **Paid In Full** *Eric B. & Rakim*
Pain
97 *Puff Daddy*
98 *Skull Duggery*
68 **Pain In My Heart** *Otis Redding*
73 **Pains And Tears** *Pointer Sisters*
73 **Pains Of Love** *New Birth*
72 **Paint Me** *Ohio Players*
75 **Paint Your Pretty Picture** *Bill Withers*
85 **Paisley Park** *Prince*
71 **Pali Gap** *Jimi Hendrix*
74 **Palm Grease** *Herbie Hancock*
72 **Pana** *Malo*
90 **Pandemonium** *Time*
75 **Pandora's Box** *Donna Summer*
96 **Panic!!!!! Roots**
65 **Pantano** *Cal Tjader*
94 **Papa** *Prince*
88 **Papa Crazy** *Run-D.M.C.*
74 **Papa Don't Take No Mess** *James Brown*
95 **Papa Luv It** *L.L. Cool J (St: The Show)*
72 **Papa Was A Rollin' Stone** *Temptations*
67 **Papa, Won't You Let Me Go To Town With You** *Bobbie Gentry*
Papa's Got A Brand New Bag
65 *James Brown*
68 *Otis Redding*
87 *Roger*
93 **Papa'z Song** *2 Pac*
Paper Chase
98 *Jay-Z*
98 *Al Block (VA: $hort Records - Nationwide)*
97 **Paper Chasing** *MC Eiht (VA: West Coast Bad Boyz II)*
70 **Paper Cup** *5th Dimension*
75 **Paper Doll** [medley] *Spinners*
70 **Paper Mache** *Dionne Warwick*
91 **Paper Moon** *Natalie Cole*
96 **Paperchase** *Do Or Die*
92 **Papes In The End** *Al B. Sure!*
80 **Papillon (aka Hot Butterfly)** *Chaka Khan*
71 **Para Los Rumberos** *Santana*
Paradise
76 *O'Jays*
76 *Temptations*
81 *Change*
88 *Sade*
86 **Paradise Is Here** *Tina Turner*
Paranoid
75 *Quincy Jones*
98 *Mac*
75 **Pardon Our Analysis (We Beg Your Pardon)** *Gil Scott-Heron & Brian Jackson*
98 **Parental Discretion** *Big Punisher*
89 **Parental Discretion Iz Advised** *N.W.A.*
91 **Parents** *Another Bad Creation*
88 **Parents Just Don't Understand**
D.J. Jazzy Jeff & The Fresh Prince
93 **Paris** *Tevin Campbell*
97 **Park Joint** *Camp Lo*
91 **Park Yu Benz** *Shabba Ranks*
94 **Parlayin'** *Ant Banks*
97 **Parole Violators** *Capone-N-Noreaga*
95 **Part Deux** *Fat Joe*
82 **Part Of Love** *Deniece Williams*
Part Of Me
76 *Eddie Kendricks*
90 *En Vogue*
Part-Time Love
71 *Isaac Hayes*
75 *Gladys Knight & The Pips*
Part-Time Lover
85 *Stevie Wonder*
94 *H-Town (St: Above The Rim)*
97 **Part Time Lover, Full Time Fool**
Peggy Scott-Adams
Party
90 *En Vogue*
92 *Kris Kross*
93 **Party And Bullshit**
Big (St: Who's The Man?)
83 **Party Animal** *James Ingram*
85 **Party Asteroid** *Boogie Boys*
98 **Party Continues** *Jermaine Dupri*
98 **Party Crasher** *Method Man*
96 **Party Don't Cry** *Tony Toni Toné*
97 **Party Don't Stop** *Mia X*

77 **River Rat** *Crusaders*
67 **River Shallow** *Nancy Wilson*
98 **Riverside** *Kirk Franklin*
93 **Roach, The** *Dr. Dre*
98 **Rob & Vic** *Onyx*
94 **Robbin' Hood (Cause It Ain't All Good)** *Ice Cube*
98 **Robbin Hood Theory** *Gang Starr*
91 **Robin Lench** *Ice Cube*
79 **Rock** *Cameo*
98 **Rock-A-Bye Haters** *Master P*
Rock-A-Bye Your Baby With A Dixie Melody
65 *Supremes*
67 *Aretha Franklin*
86 **Rock-A-Lott** *Aretha Franklin*
75 **Rock And Roll Again** *Donald Byrd*
85 **Rock And Roll Control** *Rick James*
93 **Rock Bottom** *Babyface*
75 **Rock Creek Park** *Blackbyrds*
96 **Rock Da Spot** *Redman*
80 **Rock It** *Lipps, Inc.*
85 **Rock It All Night** *Con Funk Shun*
80 **Rock It (Prime Jive)** *Queen*
98 **Rock Me** *AZ (St: Caught Up)*
94 **Rock Me (All Nite Long)** *Gerald Levert*
Rock Me Baby
65 *Otis Redding*
73 *Isaac Hayes*
74 *B.B. King & Bobby Bland [medley]*
93 *Tina Turner*
85 **Rock Me Tonight (For Old Times Sake)** *Freddie Jackson*
85 **Rock 'N' Roll** *Zapp*
85 **Rock 'N Roll Me Again** *System (St: Beverly Hills Cop)*
79 **Rock On** *Ray Parker Jr.*
75 **Rock Orchestra** [medley] *Stanley Clarke*
98 **Rock Rock Y'all** *Tribe Called Quest*
87 **Rock Ruling** *Fat Boys*
Rock Steady
72 *Aretha Franklin*
87 *Whispers*
98 *Pete Rock & C.L. Smooth*
98 *Dawn Robinson (St: Dr. Dolittle)*
79 **Rock That!** *Earth, Wind & Fire*
87 **Rock The Bass** *Heavy D & The Boyz*
Rock The Bells
85 *LL Cool J*
97 *L.L. Cool J (VA: Funkmaster Flex Vol. II)*
98 **Rock The Body** *Queen Pen & Tracey Lee (St: HavPlenty)*
98 **Rock Track** *Total*
95 **Rock Up My Birdie** *Click*
88 **Rock Wit'cha** *Bobby Brown*
76 **Rock With Me** *Aretha Franklin*
Rock With You
79 *Michael Jackson*
81 *Jacksons*
95 *Quincy Jones*
98 **Rock Y'all Spot** *Twista*
87 **Rock You** *Kool Moe Dee*
87 **Rock You Again (Again & Again)** *Whodini*
83 **Rock You Good** *Isley Brothers*
74 **Rock Your Baby** *George McCrae*
94 **Rockafella** *Redman*
80 **Rocket Love** *Stevie Wonder*
87 **Rocket To The Moon** *Herb Alpert*
82 **Rockin' After Midnight** *Marvin Gaye*
98 **Rockin' And Rollin'** *Cam'ron*
97 **Rockin' It** *Camp Lo*
72 **Rockin' Robin** *Michael Jackson*
73 **Rockin' Roll Baby** *Stylistics*
78 **Rockin' With Fire** *Isley Brothers*
83 **Rockit** *Herbie Hancock*
75 **Rocks In My Bed** [medley] *Pointer Sisters*
69 **Rocky Raccoon** *Ramsey Lewis*
98 **Rodeo** *Big Ed*
79 **Rodeo Drive (High Steppin')** *Crusaders*
94 **Rodeo Style** *Jamecia (St: Jason's Lyric)*
98 **Roll Call** *Bizzy Bone*
95 **Roll It Up, Light It Up, Smoke It Up** *Cypress Hill (St: Friday)*
78 **Roll Me Through The Rushes** *Chaka Khan*
98 **Roll Somethin** *Crucial Conflict*
91 **Roll The Dice** *Color Me Badd*
94 **Roll With The Clan** *DFC*
89 **Roll With The Punches** *Young M.C.*
97 **Roll Yo Voges** *Cellski (VA: West Coast Bad Boyz II)*
80 **Roller Skates** *Cameo*
Rollin'
83 *Kool & The Gang*
96 *Redman*
94 **Rollin' Down Da Block** *South Central Cartel*
90 **Rollin' Wit The Lench Mob** *Ice Cube*
88 **Rollin' With Kid 'N Play** *Kid 'N Play*
75 **Rolling Down A Mountainside** *Main Ingredient*
68 **Romancing To The Folk Song** *Impressions*
91 **Romantic** *Karyn White*
83 **Romeo** *Donna Summer (St: Flashdance)*
68 **Romeo And Juliet** *Chambers Brothers*
88 **Roni** *Bobby Brown*
81 **Ronnie, Talk To Russia** *Prince*
97 **Roof** *Mariah Carey*
81 **Roof Garden** *Al Jarreau*
98 **(Roof Is) On Fire** *Bizzy Bone*
95 **Room 577** *Jodeci*
95 **Room 499** *Jodeci*
71 **Room Full Of Mirrors** *Jimi Hendrix*
95 **Room 723** *Jodeci*
86 **Room With A View** *Jeffrey Osborne*
75 **Rooster Poot** *Ohio Players*
94 **Root Down** *Beastie Boys*
80 **Roots** *Maze Featuring Frankie Beverly*
77 **"Roots" Medley** *Quincy Jones*
90 **Rope A Dope Style** *Levert*
97 **Rope Burn** *Janet Jackson*
98 **Rosa Parks** *OutKast*
98 **Rose Is Still A Rose** *Aretha Franklin*
67 **Rosecrans Blvd.** *5th Dimension*
79 **Rotation** *Herb Alpert*
78 **Roto-Rooter** *William "Bootsy" Collins*
83 **Rough** *Herbie Hancock*
97 **Rough, Rugged & Raw** *Lady Of Rage*
84 **Rough Trade** *Stephanie Mills*
Round And Round
82 *Lionel Richie*
90 *Tevin Campbell (see Prince LP #12)*
91 *Tevin Campbell*
95 *Twinz*
97 *Mary J. Blige*
97 *LSG*
88 **'Round And 'Round (Merry Go 'Round Of Love)** *Guy*
98 **Round Out The Tank** *Mystikal*
81 **(Round, Round, Round) Blue Rondo A La Turk** *Al Jarreau*
96 **Round 2** *Celly Cell*
97 **Route 69** *Quad City DJ's (St: Nothing To Lose)*
91 **Route 66** *Natalie Cole*
98 **Royalty** *Gang Starr*
90 **Rub You The Right Way** *Johnny Gill*
77 **Rubber Duckie** *William "Bootsy" Collins*
76 **Rubberband Man** *Spinners*
72 **Ruby Dean** *Bobby Womack*
74 **Ruby Lee** *Bill Withers*
98 **Ruff Ryders' Anthem** *DMX*
75 **Rufusized** *Rufus Featuring Chaka Khan*
94 **Rugged Onez** *Shyheim*
97 **Rugged Terrain** *Boot Camp Clik*
89 **Ruler's Back** *Slick Rick*
88 **Rules** *Anita Baker*
98 **Rules 4 Real Niggas** *Scarface*
Rumors
83 *Kashif*
98 *Keith Sweat*
96 **Rumors & War** *Mo Thugs Family*
78 **Rumour Has It** *Donna Summer*
92 **Rump Shaker** *Wreckx-N-Effect*
78 **Rumpofsteelskin** *Parliament*
Run
98 *Cappadonna*
98 *Cappadonna (St: Bulworth)*
69 **Run Away Child, Running Wild** *Temptations*
72 **Run Charlie Run** *Temptations*
Run For Cover
68 *Dells*
90 *Eric B. & Rakim*
98 *Flipmode Squad*
98 **Run For It** *Juvenile*
96 **Run 4 Your Life** *MC Eiht/CMW*
98 **Run Nigga** *Trick Daddy*
70 **Run Nigger** *Last Poets*
65 **Run, Run, Run** *Supremes*
71 **Run Shaker Life** *Voices Of East Harlem (St: Soul To Soul)*
69 **Run Tank Run** *Booker T. & The MG's*
96 **Run Tha Streetz** *2 Pac*
87 **Run To Me** *Angela Winbush*
92 **Run To You** *Whitney Houston*
88 **Run's House** *Run-D.M.C.*
98 **Runaround** *Xscape*
Runaway
84 *Rockwell*
95 *Janet Jackson*
78 **Runaway Love** *Linda Clifford*
77 **Runnin** *Earth, Wind & Fire*
Runnin' Away
71 *Sly & The Family Stone*
82 *One Way*
77 **Runnin' For Your Lovin'** *Brothers Johnson*
74 **Runnin' From The Devil** *Ohio Players*
85 **Runnin' From Your Love** *Boogie Boys*
93 **Runnin' Out Da Crackhouse** *Spice 1*
Runnin' Out Of Fools
65 *Aretha Franklin*
70 *Isaac Hayes*
94 **Runnin' Wit No Breaks** *Warren G*
Running
82 *Jermaine Jackson*
84 *Temptations*
Running Away
77 *Roy Ayers*
81 *Maze Featuring Frankie Beverly*
69 **Running Away (Ain't Gonna Help You)** *Temptations*
70 **Running Back And Forth** *Edwin Starr*
91 **Running Back To You** *Vanessa Williams*
87 **Running For Your Love** *Stephanie Mills*
79 **Running In And Out Of My Life** *Bar-Kays*
76 **Running Out Of Lies** *Johnnie Taylor*
83 **Running With The Night** *Lionel Richie*
91 **Rush** *Luther Vandross*
98 **Rush Hour Main Title Theme** *Lalo Schifrin (St: Rush Hour)*
97 **Rush Over** *Marcus Miller & Me'Shell Ndegéocello (St: Love Jones)*
80 **Rushing To** *Ashford & Simpson*
89 **Russell Rush** *3rd Bass*

S

95 **S-More** *Jodeci*
80 **S.O.S. (Dit Dit Dit Dash Dash Dash Dit Dit Dit)** *S.O.S. Band*
92 **SWV (In The House)** *SWV (Sisters With Voices)*
67 **S.Y.S.L.J.F.M. (The Letter Song)** *Joe Tex (VA: The Super Hits)*
90 **Sa Prize** *N.W.A.*
94 **Sabotage** *Beastie Boys*
94 **Sabrosa** *Beastie Boys*
67 **Sack O'Woe** *"Cannonball" Adderley*
92 **Sacrifice Of Victor** *Prince*
68 **Sad Gypsy** *Jose Feliciano*
97 **Sad Millionaire** *Luniz*
65 **Sad Mood** *Sam Cooke*
65 **Sad, Sad Girl And Boy** *Impressions*
74 **Sad Sad Song** *Billy Preston*
65 **Sad Souvenirs** *Four Tops*
83 **Sad Time** *Smokey Robinson*
67 **Sad Wedding** *Marvin Gaye & Tammi Terrell*
86 **Sade** *Kenny G*
Sadie
74 *Spinners*
93 *R. Kelly*
67 **Saduva** *Miriam Makeba*
95 **Safe + Sound** *DJ Quik*
93 **Safe Sex** *Erick Sermon*
97 **Saga Begins** *Eric B. & Rakim*
65 **Saga Of Bill Bailey** *Nancy Wilson*
67 **Said I Wasn't Gonna Tell Nobody** *Sam & Dave*
80 **Sail Away Sweet Sister** *Queen*
79 **Sail On** *Commodores*
80 **Sailaway** *Earth, Wind & Fire*
68 **Sailboat Song** *5th Dimension*
Sally
73 *Chi-Lites*
85 *Sade*
88 *Morris Day*
78 **Salsation** *David Shire (see Bee Gees LP #3)*
88 **Salt With A Deadly Pepa** *Salt-N-Pepa*
70 **Samba Pa Ti** *Santana*
76 **Sambo (Progression)** *Brass Construction*
Same Love That Made Me Laugh
74 *Bill Withers*
77 *Diana Ross*
98 **Same Ol' G** *Ginuwine (St: Dr. Dolittle)*
93 **Same Ol' Shit** *MC Ren*
97 **Same Ol' Thing** *Tribe Called Quest (St: Men In Black)*
66 **Same Old Same Old** *Brother Jack McDuff*
98 **Same Old Song** *Father Dom (VA: $hort Records - Nationwide)*
79 **Same Old Story** *Stevie Wonder*
86 **Same Ole Love (365 Days A Year)** *Anita Baker*
94 **Same Place, Same Time** *Gerald Levert*
91 **Same Song** *Digital Underground*
98 **Same Tempo** *Changing Faces (St: The Players Club)*
71 **Same Thing** *Margie Joseph*
95 **Sample The Funk** *Too $hort*
76 **San Francisco Hustle** *Silver Convention*
69 **San Francisco Is A Lonely Town** *O.C. Smith*
74 **San Francisco Lights** *Bobbi Humphrey*
66 **San-Ho-Zay** *Jr. Walker & The All Stars*
77 **Sanctified Feeling** *Roy Ayers*
97 **Sanctified Girl (Can't Fight This Feeling)** *Joe*
85 **Sanctified Lady** *Marvin Gaye*
70 **Sanctuary** *Miles Davis*
86 **Sands Of Time** *S.O.S. Band*
97 **Sang Fézi** *Wyclef Jean*
76 **Sansho Shima** *Herbie Hancock*
94 **Santa Claus Is Comin' To Town** *Mariah Carey*
78 **Santa Cruzin** *Grover Washington, Jr.*
66 **Satan's Blues** *Jr. Walker & The All Stars*
Satin Doll
65 *Jimmy Smith*
66 *Ramsey Lewis*
74 *Bobbi Humphrey*
75 *Pointer Sisters [medley]*
74 **Satin Soul** *Love Unlimited Orchestra*
65 **Satisfaction** *Otis Redding*
70 **Satisfaction Guaranteed** *Rare Earth*
73 **Satisfaction Guaranteed (Or Take Your Love Back)** *Harold Melvin & The Blue Notes*
Satisfied
96 *Dru Hill*
98 *Skull Duggery*
68 **Sattva** *Rascals*
93 **Saturday** *Babyface*
85 **Saturday Love** *Cherrelle*
Saturday Night
81 *Commodores*
97 *Zhané*
76 **Saturday Nite** *Earth, Wind & Fire*
78 **Sausalito** *Grover Washington, Jr.*
85 **Savage In The Sack** *Marvin Gaye*
77 **Save It For A Rainy Day** *High Inergy*
95 **Save It Up** *After 7*
Save Me
66 *Miracles*
67 *Aretha Franklin*
69 *Isley Brothers*
75 *Silver Convention*
76 *Graham Central Station*
80 *Queen*
83 *Al Jarreau*
91 *Lisa Fischer*
Save My Love For A Rainy Day
67 *Temptations*
71 *Undisputed Truth*
91 **Save The Best For Last** *Vanessa Williams*
75 **Save The Bones For Henry Jones** *Pointer Sisters*
Save The Children
71 *Marvin Gaye*
73 *Diana Ross [medley]*
89 *Regina Belle [medley]*
70 **Save The Country** *5th Dimension*
83 **Save The Overtime (For Me)** *Gladys Knight & The Pips*
85 **Save Your Love (For #1)** *René & Angela*
95 **Save Yourself** *Snoop Doggy Dogg (St: The Show)*
84 **Savin' The Day** *Alessi (St: Ghostbusters)*
85 **Saving All My Love For You** *Whitney Houston*
76 **Saving My Love For You** *Tyrone Davis*
96 **Savior More Than Life** *Kirk Franklin*
96 **Saviour** *Prince*
78 **Savoir Faire** *Chic*
92 **Say Hi To The Bad Guy** *Ice Cube*
73 **Say It Again** *Love Unlimited*
69 **Say It Loud - I'm Black And I'm Proud** *James Brown*
80 **Say It Through Love** *Bar-Kays*
89 **Say No Go** *De La Soul*
83 **Say Something Love** *Kashif*
79 **Say That You'll Be Mine** *L.T.D.*
97 **Say What** *Dymon (St: Def Jam's How To Be A Player)*
87 **Say What You Mean** *Gladys Knight & The Pips*
Say Word
95 *Fat Joe*
97 *Camp Lo*
98 *Def Squad*
78 **Say Yeah** *Commodores*
Say Yes
80 *Lakeside*
82 *Whispers*
66 **Say You** *Temptations*
82 **Say You Do** *Janet Jackson*
86 **Say You, Say Me** *Lionel Richie*
82 **Say You Wanna** *Howard Johnson*
Say You Will
80 *Isley Brothers*
86 *Gregory Abbott*
93 *Levert*
81 **Say You (Would Love For Me Too)** *Whispers*

86 **She's Mine** *Cameo*
90 **She's My Love Thang** *Ralph Tresvant*
75 **She's Not Blind** *Roberta Flack*
89 **She's Not Just Another Woman (Monique)** *Biz Markie*
75 **She's Only A Woman** *O'Jays*
She's Out Of My Life
79   *Michael Jackson*
81   *Jacksons*
81 **She's Over Me** *Teddy Pendergrass*
92 **She's Playing Hard To Get** *Hi-Five*
68 **She's So Fine** *Jimi Hendrix*
66 **She's So Good To Me** *Wilson Pickett*
90 **She's Soft And Wet** *M.C. Hammer*
84 **She's Strange** *Cameo*
68 **She's Too Good To Me** *Jose Feliciano*
79 **Shejam (Almost Bootsy Show)** *William "Bootsy" Collins*
98 **Shell Shocked** *Mac*
97 **Shelter** *Killarmy*
Shhh
93   *Tevin Campbell*
95   *Prince*
68 **Shhhhhhh (For A Little While)** *James Brown*
84 **Shifftee** *Onyx*
72 **Shiftless, Shady, Jealous Kind Of People** *O'Jays*
66 **Shimmy Shimmy Ko-Ko Bop** *Little Anthony & The Imperials*
Shimmy Shimmy Ya
95   *Ol Dirty Bastard*
98   *Ol Dirty Bastard (VA: Funkmaster Flex Vol. III)*
Shine
97   *Jon B*
97   *Mystikal*
98   *DAS EFX*
83 **Shine A Light** *Jennifer Holliday*
97 **Shine And Recline** *Eightball & MJG*
80 **Shine On** *L.T.D.*
95 **Shinin...Next Shit** *Cocoa Brovaz*
Shining Star
75   *Earth, Wind & Fire*
80   *Manhattans*
92 **Shining Through** *Miki Howard*
73 **Ship Ahoy** *O'Jays*
93 **Shit, Damn, Motherfucker** *D'Angelo*
94 **Shit Don't Stop** *Thug Life*
93 **Shit Hit The Fan** *Ice-T*
95 **Shit Is Real** *Fat Joe*
96 **Sh**tin' On The World** *Mel-Man (VA: Dr. Dre Presents...The Aftermath)*
Sho Shot
97   *Lady Of Rage*
97   *Lady Of Rage (St: Gridlock'd)*
77 **Sho'nuff Must Be Luv** *Heatwave*
92 **Shock Dat Monkey** *TLC*
93 **Shock Of The Hour** *MC Ren*
93 **Shockadelica** *Prince*
96 **Shocker** *Silkk The Shocker*
83 **Shoe Throwin' Mothers** *Eddie Murphy*
97 **Shoe Was On The Other Foot** *Patti LaBelle*
96 **Shoeshine Boy** *Eddie Kendricks*
Shoo-Be-Doo-Be-Doo-Da-Day
69   *Stevie Wonder*
72   *Michael Jackson*
98 **Shoo-Bed-Ooh** *Prince*
84 **Shoo-Bee-Doo** *Madonna*
Shook Ones
95   *Mobb Deep*
97   *Mobb Deep (VA: Funkmaster Flex: The Mix Tape V. II) [medley]*
93 **Shoop** *Salt-N-Pepa*
65 **Shoop Shoop Song (It's In His Kiss)** *Aretha Franklin*
92 **Shoot 'Em Up** *Cypress Hill Crew (St: Juice)*
93 **Shoot Pass Slam** *Shaquille O'Neal*
Shoot Your Shot
65   *Jr. Walker & The All Stars*
73   *James Brown*
87 **Shoot 'em Up Movies** *Deele*
94 **Shootin' From The Hip** *MC Breed*
91 **Shootin' The Breeze** *Gerald Levert*
96 **Shootouts** *Nas*
Shop Around
65   *Miracles*
94   *New Edition*
90 **Short But Funky** *Too $hort*
98 **Short Dog - Hit 'Em Up** *Too $hort (VA: $hort Records - Nationwide)*
90 **Short Dog's In The House** *Too $hort*
94 **Shortberry Strawcake** *Sheila E.*
96 **Shorty Wanna Be A Thug** *2PAC*
96 **Shorty's Game** *Miles Goodman (St: Sunset Park)*

Shot
93   *Ice Cube*
95   *Junior M.A.F.I.A.*
78 **Shot Of Love** *Lakeside*
94 **Shot Outz** *South Central Cartel*
65 **Shotgun** *Jr. Walker & The All Stars*
66 **Shotgun And The Duck** *Jackie Lee*
95 **Shotz To Tha Double Glock** *Bone Thugs-N-Harmony*
81 **Should I Do It** *Pointer Sisters*
81 **Should I Stay Or Should I Go** *Mack 10*
72 **Should've Known Better** *Billy Preston*
95 **Shout** *Onyx*
79 **Shout And Scream** *Teddy Pendergrass*
Show
93   *Jodeci*
97   *Roots (VA: In Tha Beginning...There Was Rap)*
73 **Show And Tell** *Al Wilson*
78 **Show Bizness** *Gil Scott-Heron & Brian Jackson*
67 **Show Business** *Lou Rawls*
98 **Show Down** *Buckshot & Q-Tip (VA: Funkmaster Flex Vol. III)*
88 **Show 'Em Whatcha Got** *Public Enemy*
78 **Show Is Over** *Evelyn "Champagne" King*
79 **Show Love Today** *Jones Girls*
Show Me
68   *Dells*
84   *Lillo Thomas*
90   *Howard Hewett*
Show Me Love
97   *Eric B. & Rakim*
98   *Snoop Doggy Dogg*
98   *24/7 (VA: Funkmaster Flex Vol. III)*
98 **Show Me Luv** *C-Murder*
93 **Show Me The Right Way** *O'Jays*
Show Me The Way
93   *Bell Biv DeVoe*
96   *Keith Sweat*
97 **Show Me The Way Back To Your Heart** *Brian McKnight*
84 **Show Some Respect** *Tina Turner*
95 **Show Theme** *Stanley Clarke (St: The Show)*
98 **Show U What Love Is** *Keith Sweat*
76 **Show You The Way To Go** *Jacksons*
84 **Show You The Way To Love** *Philip Bailey*
Showdown
78   *Isley Brothers*
84   *Ollie & Jerry (St: Breakin')*
81   *Billy Ocean*
96   *Crucial Conflict*
91 **Shower Me With Your Love** *Surface*
91 **Shower You With Love** *Peabo Bryson*
87 **Showstopper** *Salt-N-Pepa*
Shut Em Down
91   *Public Enemy*
96   *Do Or Die*
96   *Onyx*
89 **Shut The Eff Up! (Hoe)** *MC Lyte*
77 **Shut The Funk Up** *Bar-Kays*
96 **Shy** *Prince*
97 **Sicc Made House** *Brotha Lynch Hung*
65 **Sick And Tired** *Righteous Brothers*
93 **Sickness** *D.R.S.*
76 **Side By Side** *Earth, Wind & Fire*
74 **Sideshow** *Blue Magic*
Sideways
74   *Rufus*
95   *E-40*
Sidewinder
65   *James Brown*
66   *Lee Morgan*
88 **Siempre Hay Esperanza** *Sade*
87 **Sign 'O' The Times** *Prince*
71 **Signed Gladys** *Gladys Knight & The Pips*
Signed, Sealed, Delivered I'm Yours
70   *Stevie Wonder*
71   *King Curtis*
96 **Silence Isn't Over** *Flesh-N-Bone*
Silent Night
93   *Boyz II Men*
94   *Mariah Carey*
94   *Kenny G*
73 **Silent Partner In A Three-Way Love Affair** *Smokey Robinson*
68 **Silent Voices** *Dionne Warwick*
68 **Silhouette** *Kenny G*
93 **Silky** *Heavy D & The Boyz*
89 **Silky Soul** *Maze Featuring Frankie Beverly*
68 **Silly Girl** *Rascals*
Silly Love Song
68   *Enchantment*
90   *Michel'le*
98 **Silly Putty** *Stanley Clarke*
94 **Silver & Gold** *Kirk Franklin*
94 **Silver Bells** *Kenny G*
85 **Silver Shadow** *Atlantic Starr*

96 **Simple Days** *Babyface*
72 **Simple Man** *Bobby Womack*
71 **Simple Thing Like Cry** *Diana Ross*
75 **Simple Things** *Minnie Riperton*
72 **Simply Beautiful** *Al Green*
95 **Simply Say I Love U** *Johnny Gill*
74 **Since I Been Gone** *Spinners*
Since I Don't Have You
75   *Players*
70   *Eddie Holman*
Since I Fell For You
65   *Ramsey Lewis*
66   *Fontella Bass*
67   *Rascals*
67   *Nancy Wilson*
76   *Dells*
76 **Since I Had You** *Marvin Gaye*
Since I Lost My Baby
65   *Temptations*
82   *Luther Vandross*
74 **Since I Lost You Lady** *Jerry Butler*
76 **Since I Met You Baby** *Johnny "Guitar" Watson*
Since I've Lost You
69   *Temptations*
71   *Undisputed Truth*
70 **Since My Love Has Gone** *Eddie Holman*
65 **Since You Won My Heart** *Miracles*
Since You've Been Gone
94   *Four Tops*
94   *Luther Vandross*
97 **Since You've Gone Away (The Lockdown Anthem)** *Bonnie & Clyde (St: Sprung)*
82 **Sincerely** *Richard "Dimples" Fields*
90 **Sincerity** *Lisa Stansfield*
90 **Sing A Happy Song** *O'Jays*
74 **Sing A Love Song** *William DeVaughn*
75 **Sing A Message To You** *Earth, Wind & Fire*
Sing A Simple Song
69   *Booker T. & The MG's*
69   *Sly & The Family Stone*
69   *Supremes with The Temptations*
75 **Sing A Song** *Earth, Wind & Fire*
83 **Sing A Song Of Love** *Freddie Jackson*
75 **Sing Baby Sing** *Stylistics*
74 **Sing It Again - Say It Again** *Aretha Franklin*
78 **Sing My Heart Out** *O'Jays*
71 **Singer** *5th Dimension*
82 **Singer's Become A Dancer** *Peter Brown*
83 **Singers** *Eddie Murphy*
85 **Singin' The Blues Too Long** *Rascals*
76 **Singing Winds, Crying Beasts** *Santana*
85 **Single Heart** *DeBarge*
85 **Single Life** *Cameo*
96 **Sinnerman** *Nina Simone*
96 **Sippin On A 40** *Eazy-E*
99 **Sir Duke** *Stevie Wonder*
77 **Sir Nose D'Voidoffunk (Pay Attention - B3M)** *Parliament*
80 **Sister** *Prince*
73 **Sister From Texas** *Aretha Franklin*
88 **Sister Knows What She Wants** *Cheryl Pepsii Riley*
74 **Sister Love** *Donald Byrd*
91 **Sister Rose** *Kenny G*
91 **Sister Sister** *Heavy D & The Boyz*
76 **Sister Sugar** *Billy Preston*
76 **Sister Twister** *Brick*
91 **Sisterland** *Yo-Yo*
88 **Sisters** *Cheryl Pepsii Riley & Lisa Lisa*
85 **Sisters Are Doin' It For Themselves** *Eurythmics & Aretha Franklin*
70 **Sit Down And Cry** *Aretha Franklin*
(Sittin' On) The Dock Of The Bay
68   *Otis Redding*
68   *O.C. Smith*
Sittin' On Top Of The World
96   *Spinners*
96   *Da Brat*
95 **Sittin' Up In My Room** *Brandy (St: Waiting To Exhale)*
97 **Sitting By Heaven's Door** *En Vogue*
98 **Sitting Home** *Total*
Sitting In The Park
68   *Billy Stewart*
80   *GQ*
Situation
93   *Bell Biv DeVoe*
93   *Brotha Lynch Hung*
95 **Situation: Grimm** *Mista Grimm (St: Higher Learning)*
86 **Situation #9** *Club Nouveau*
93 **Situation On Dirty** *Brotha Lynch Hung (St: I'm Bout It)*
Six Feet Deep
93   *Geto Boys*
94   *Gravediggaz*

96 **6 Million** *Do Or Die*
97 **6 Minutes Of Pleasure** *LL Cool J*
97 **6 'N Tha Mornin'** *Master P (VA: In Tha Beginning...There Was Rap)*
76 **6 O'Clock DJ (Let's Rock)** *Rose Royce*
634-5789 (Soulsville, U.S.A.)
66   *Wilson Pickett*
66   *Otis Redding*
76 **Six To Four** *George Benson*
73 **Sixteen Candles** *Jackson 5*
97 **16 On Death Row** *2 Pac*
67 **Sixteen Tons** *Stevie Wonder*
96 **Sixx Minutes** *Snoop Doggy Dogg*
80 **Sizzlin' Hot** *Slave*
96 **Skandalouz** *2 Pac*
91 **Skanless** *DJ Quik*
95 **Skanlezz Azz Butchez** *Celly Cell*
95 **Skanlezz Call** *Celly Cell*
95 **Skate** *Monica*
87 **Skeletons** *Stevie Wonder*
98 **Skew It On The Bar-B** *OutKast*
90 **Skillet** *Time*
Skin I'm In
73   *Sly & The Family Stone*
88   *Cameo*
Skin Tight
74   *Ohio Players*
90   *Tony! Toni! Toné!*
69 **Skinny Man** *5th Dimension*
92 **Skinz** *Pete Rock & C.L. Smooth*
75 **Skippin' Work Today** *Eddie Kendricks*
95 **Skoundrels Get Lonely** *D.R.S.*
96 **Skrilla** *Scarface (St: High School High)*
Sky High
73   *Donald Byrd*
78   *Taste Of Honey*
Sky's The Limit
90   *Tony! Toni! Toné!*
97   *Notorious B.I.G.*
98   *Magic*
93 **Slam** *Onyx*
95 **Slang Bang** *Naughty By Nature*
98 **Slang Editorial** *Cappadonna*
91 **Slangin'** *Fiend*
93 **Slap Them Up** *KRS-One*
Slave
69   *Temptations*
96   *Prince*
89 **Slave 2 The Rhythm** *MC Lyte*
69 **Slaves** *Dionne Warwick*
90 **Sleep Around** *Prince*
67 **Sleep Good Tonight** *Sam & Dave*
98 **Sleep Late, My Lady Friend** *Jose Feliciano*
78 **Sleep On It** *Chaka Khan*
82 **Sleep Walkin'** *Cheryl Lynn*
86 **Sleep With Me Tonight** *Patti LaBelle*
95 **Sleepin In My Nikes** *Scarface*
94 **Sleepin' On A Master Plan** *M.C. Hammer*
93 **Sleepin' On Jersey** *Naughty By Nature*
97 **Sleepin' With Me** *Mystikal*
95 **Sleeping Alone** *Pointer Sisters*
93 **Sleepwalkin' II** *Naughty By Nature*
95 **Slick Partner** *Bobby Brown (St: Panther)*
77 **Slide** *Slave*
94 **Slide And Rock On** *Redman*
86 **Slide Over** *Ready For The World*
67 **Slim Jenkins' Joint** *Booker T. & The MG's*
Slip Away
88   *Pebbles*
98   *Ol Skool*
Slip Of The Tongue
85   *Commodores*
66   *Kenny G*
80 **Slipped Away** *Moments*
95 **Slippery When Wet** *Commodores*
97 **Slippin'** *Eightball & MJG*
65 **Slippin' And Slidin'** *Billy Preston*
Slippin' Into Darkness
71   *War*
72   *Ramsey Lewis*
65 **Sloopy Downtown** *Ramsey Lewis*
93 **Slop Jar Blues** *Donald Byrd*
93 **Slow And Easy** *Zapp & Roger*
96 **Slow And Low** *Beastie Boys*
75 **Slow Burn** *LaBelle*
92 **Slow Dance (Hey Mr. DJ)** *R. Kelly*
82 **Slow Dancin'** *Chaka Khan*
Slow Down
86   *Loose Ends*
88   *Karyn White*
84   *Mary J. Blige*
93   *Heavy D & The Boyz*
98   *Snoop Doggy Dogg*
83 **Slow Down Children** *Isley Brothers*
97 **Slow Drag** *Peggy Scott-Adams*
81 **Slow Hand** *Pointer Sisters*
96 **Slow Is The Way** *Isley Brothers*

297

305

THE TOP ARTISTS

This section includes the rankings of the Top 200 album artists from 1965-1998.

To the right of each name is an accumulated point total. The point system used to create this total is explained on the next page. This ranking includes all titles that peaked <u>prior</u> to 1999.

Headings And Special Symbols:

Rank: Artist ranking in *Top R&B Albums 1965-1998*

● **Deceased Solo Artist or Group Leader**

■ **Deceased Group Member**

★ **Hot Artist**
Artist who charted a Top 10 album in the past 3 years (1996-1998)

+   Subject to change since an album is still charted as of the July 31, 1999 cut-off date.

POINT SYSTEM

Points are awarded according to the following formula:

1. Each artist's charted albums are given points based on their highest charted position:

#1	=	100 points for its first week at #1, plus 10 points for each additional week at #1
#2	=	90 points for its first week at #2, plus 5 points for each additional week at #2
#3	=	80 points for its first week at #3, plus 3 points for each additional week at #3
#4-5	=	70 points
#6-10	=	60 points
#11-15	=	55 points
#16-20	=	50 points
#21-30	=	45 points
#31-40	=	40 points
#41-50	=	35 points
#51-60	=	30 points
#61-70	=	25 points
#71-80	=	20 points
#81-90	=	15 points
#91-100	=	10 points

2. Total weeks charted are added in.

In the case of a tie, the artist listed first is determined by the following tie-breaker rules:

1) Most charted albums
2) Most Top 40 albums
3) Most Top 10 albums

When two artists combine for a hit album, such as Roberta Flack and Donny Hathaway, the full point value is given to both artists. Duos, such as Ashford & Simpson, are considered a regular recording team, and their points are not shared by either artist individually.

TOP 200 ARTISTS (#1-100)

Rank		Points	Rank		Points
★1.	The Temptations ■ ■ ■	5,749 +	51.	Peabo Bryson	1,312
★2.	Aretha Franklin	4,555	52.	Freddie Jackson	1,309
3.	James Brown	3,867	53.	Bobby Womack	1,266
4.	Stevie Wonder	3,371	★54.	2 Pac ●	1,264 +
5.	The Supremes ■	3,205	55.	Ashford & Simpson	1,248
6.	Marvin Gaye ●	2,881	56.	Tyrone Davis	1,239
7.	The Isley Brothers ■	2,786	★57.	Whitney Houston	1,230 +
8.	Gladys Knight & The Pips	2,644	58.	Maze Featuring Frankie Beverly	1,226
★9.	Prince	2,575	59.	Donna Summer	1,214
10.	Isaac Hayes	2,469	60.	Rufus Featuring Chaka Khan	1,212
11.	Diana Ross	2,445	61.	Bar-Kays ■ ■ ■	1,202
12.	Earth, Wind & Fire	2,419	62.	Millie Jackson	1,170
13.	Four Tops ■	2,417	63.	Wilson Pickett	1,151
14.	Dionne Warwick	2,360	★64.	Luke/2 Live Crew	1,129
15.	Michael Jackson	2,225	65.	Jerry Butler	1,127
16.	Jackson 5/Jacksons	2,182	★66.	LL Cool J	1,121
17.	The O'Jays ■	2,176	★67.	Janet Jackson	1,115
★18.	Luther Vandross	2,103	68.	Herbie Hancock	1,108
19.	Lou Rawls	2,047	69.	Funkadelic	1,095
20.	Al Green	1,945	70.	Stephanie Mills	1,063
21.	Barry White	1,943	★71.	Kenny G	1,055
22.	Kool & The Gang	1,934	72.	Richard Pryor	1,047
23.	Commodores	1,837	73.	The Stylistics	1,036
24.	The Miracles ■	1,786	★74.	Mariah Carey	1,021
25.	The Whispers	1,776	75.	Roy Ayers	1,012
26.	B.B. King	1,720	76.	The Dramatics	1,010
27.	Teddy Pendergrass	1,634	77.	Pointer Sisters	995
28.	George Benson	1,631	78.	Jermaine Jackson	994
★29.	Patti LaBelle/LaBelle	1,628	79.	Al Jarreau	994
30.	Nancy Wilson	1,627	★80.	Keith Sweat	979
31.	Ramsey Lewis	1,602	81.	George Duke	969
32.	Ohio Players	1,596	82.	The Chi-Lites	958
33.	Curtis Mayfield	1,580	★83.	Ice Cube	954
34.	Rick James	1,571	84.	Eddie Kendricks ●	950
35.	Cameo	1,558	85.	Santana	942
36.	Johnnie Taylor	1,549	86.	M.C. Hammer	924
37.	Grover Washington, Jr.	1,533	87.	Con Funk Shun	920
38.	Natalie Cole	1,514	88.	Lionel Richie	916
39.	Smokey Robinson	1,512	89.	Jimi Hendrix ●	914
40.	The Crusaders	1,465	90.	The 5th Dimension	910
41.	Bobby Bland	1,448	91.	Anita Baker	894
42.	War ■	1,391	92.	Sade	891
43.	The Dells	1,370	93.	Parliament	889
44.	Roberta Flack	1,363	94.	Bill Cosby	886
45.	Quincy Jones	1,363	95.	Atlantic Starr	885
46.	Spinners ■	1,346	96.	Earl Klugh	874
47.	Otis Redding ●	1,339	97.	Booker T. & The MG's ■	869
48.	Ray Charles	1,332	98.	Ray Parker Jr./Raydio	869
49.	The Gap Band	1,326	★99.	New Edition	866
★50.	The Impressions	1,312	100.	One Way	859

313

Rank		Points
101.	The Manhattans ■■	858
102.	Jr. Walker & The All Stars ●■	853
103.	Sly & The Family Stone	852
104.	Bill Withers	838
105.	Jimmy Smith	837
106.	Chaka Khan	835
★107.	Mary J. Blige	833
108.	Eddie Harris ●	831
109.	Average White Band ■	830
110.	Deniece Williams	829
111.	The Brothers Johnson	828
112.	Teena Marie	824
113.	Shalamar	810
114.	Run-D.M.C.	810
★115.	Too $hort	808
116.	Melba Moore	803
117.	Larry Graham	801
118.	The Moments ■	770
119.	Clarence Carter	763
120.	Joe Simon	758
121.	Wes Montgomery ●	758
★122.	R. Kelly	757 +
123.	Harold Melvin & The Blue Notes ●	753
124.	Evelyn "Champagne" King	751
125.	Ike & Tina Turner	749
126.	L.T.D.	747
127.	Phyllis Hyman ●	746
128.	Bob Marley & The Wailers ●■	738
129.	Fatback	737
130.	Johnny "Guitar" Watson ●	737
★131.	Public Enemy	735
★132.	Boyz II Men	734
133.	Stanley Turrentine	729
134.	Billy Paul	728
135.	Slave	722
★136.	Heavy D & The Boys ■	721
★137.	Bone Thugs-N-Harmony	716
138.	Tavares	715
139.	Chic ■	714
140.	George Howard ●	713
141.	Jeffrey Osborne	704
142.	Bobby Brown	703
143.	David Ruffin ●	701
144.	Brass Construction	701
145.	Dazz Band	697
146.	Zapp ■■	696
147.	Billy Preston	692
★148.	Babyface	691
149.	David Sanborn	690
150.	Skyy	687

Rank		Points
151.	The Main Ingredient ■	684
152.	Scarface	683
153.	Bob James	682
154.	Lakeside	682
155.	The Emotions	681
156.	The S.O.S. Band	679
157.	Joe Tex ●	677
157.	Donald Byrd	673
★159.	The Geto Boys	670
160.	The Staple Singers	668
161.	William "Bootsy" Collins	636
162.	The Blackbyrds	635
★163.	Levert	631
★164.	Spice 1	629
165.	Mandrill	627
166.	Angela Bofill	625
★167.	EPMD	625
168.	Denise LaSalle	624
169.	BeBe & CeCe Winans	621
170.	Norman Connors	620
171.	Midnight Star	619
172.	Rose Royce	606
★173.	Master P	604
174.	The New Birth	601
175.	Stacy Lattisaw	601
176.	Cypress Hill	597
177.	Freddie Hubbard	596
178.	Ronnie Laws	596
179.	Lonnie Liston Smith	593
180.	Little Milton	590
★181.	Gerald Levert	587
182.	Stanley Clarke	586
183.	Michael Henderson	583
184.	Herbie Mann	572
185.	Peaches & Herb	571
186.	Randy Crawford	561
★187.	A Tribe Called Quest	556
188.	Tina Turner	554
189.	Tower Of Power	552
190.	Buddy Miles	548
191.	Alexander O'Neal	548
192.	Sister Sledge	545
193.	Salt-N-Pepa	543
★194.	Snoop Doggy Dogg	539
195.	Cannonball Adderley ●	538
★196.	Johnny Gill	538
197.	B.T. Express	535
198.	Roger ●	534
199.	Gil Scott-Heron & Brian Jackson	533
★200.	Tony! Toni! Toné!	533

A-Z — TOP 200 ARTISTS

TOP 25 ARTISTS OF EACH DECADE

SIXTIES ('65-'69)

		Points
1.	The Temptations	2,980
2.	The Supremes	2,316
3.	Aretha Franklin	1,877
4.	James Brown	1,654
5.	Dionne Warwick	1,241
6.	Lou Rawls	1,203
7.	Otis Redding	1,168
8.	Nancy Wilson	1,056
9.	Four Tops	1,003
10.	Ramsey Lewis	899
11.	The Miracles	882
12.	The Impressions	847
13.	Jimmy Smith	802
14.	Marvin Gaye	752
15.	Bill Cosby	730
16.	Wes Montgomery	719
17.	Wilson Pickett	672
18.	Ray Charles	621
19.	Stevie Wonder	602
20.	Joe Tex	496
21.	Booker T. & The MG's	457
22.	Jr. Walker & The All Stars	447
23.	Sam Cooke	429
24.	The Rascals	401
25.	The Dells	401

SEVENTIES

		Points
1.	Isaac Hayes	2,034
2.	James Brown	1,973
3.	Jackson 5/Jacksons	1,759
4.	Gladys Knight & The Pips	1,612
5.	The Temptations	1,601
6.	Al Green	1,592
7.	Aretha Franklin	1,575
8.	Ohio Players	1,509
9.	Earth, Wind & Fire	1,508
10.	Marvin Gaye	1,505
11.	Stevie Wonder	1,420
12.	The Isley Brothers	1,366
13.	Diana Ross	1,338
14.	The O'Jays	1,239
15.	Barry White	1,211
16.	Curtis Mayfield	1,204
17.	Commodores	1,189
18.	B.B. King	1,173
19.	War	1,158
20.	Four Tops	1,125
21.	Kool & The Gang	1,085
22.	The Crusaders	1,048
23.	Funkadelic	1,012
24.	Spinners	994
25.	Rufus Featuring Chaka Khan	935

EIGHTIES

		Points
1.	Prince	1,259
2.	Rick James	1,143
3.	The Gap Band	1,115
4.	Cameo	1,091
5.	Luther Vandross	1,073
6.	Stevie Wonder	1,060
7.	Michael Jackson	1,008
8.	Diana Ross	962
9.	The Temptations	934
10.	The Whispers	910
11.	Stephanie Mills	897
12.	Smokey Robinson	888
13.	Peabo Bryson	864
14.	Freddie Jackson	862
15.	Teddy Pendergrass	861
16.	Aretha Franklin	858
17.	Kool & The Gang	849
18.	The Isley Brothers	847
19.	One Way	805
20.	Maze Feat. Frankie Beverly	762
21.	Lionel Richie	724
22.	Shalamar	713
23.	New Edition	699
24.	Earl Klugh	695
25.	Atlantic Starr	694

NINETIES ('90-'98)

		Points
1.	2 Pac	1,264 +
2.	Prince	1,125
3.	Luther Vandross	1,030
4.	Mariah Carey	1,021
5.	Ice Cube	954
6.	Mary J. Blige	833
7.	Luke/2 Live Crew	791
8.	Keith Sweat	781
9.	Whitney Houston	769 +
10.	R. Kelly	757 +
11.	M.C. Hammer	751
12.	Boyz II Men	734
13.	Bone Thugs-N-Harmony	716
14.	Scarface	683
15.	Kenny G	682
16.	The Geto Boys	670
17.	Too $hort	659
18.	Spice 1	629
19.	Master P	604
20.	LL Cool J	603
21.	Cypress Hill	597
22.	Gerald Levert	587
23.	A Tribe Called Quest	556
24.	Snoop Doggy Dogg	539
25.	Michael Jackson	534

TOP ARTIST ACHIEVEMENTS

MOST CHARTED ALBUMS

1. James Brown 52
2. The Temptations 46
3. Aretha Franklin 40
4. The Supremes 34
5. Marvin Gaye 32
6. Four Tops 32
7. Diana Ross 31
8. Dionne Warwick 30
9. The Isley Brothers................. 29
10. Gladys Knight & The Pips 29
11. Stevie Wonder........................ 27
12. Lou Rawls.............................. 27
13. Prince.................................... 25
14. B.B. King 25
15. Kool & The Gang.................... 24
16. The Whispers 24
17. Nancy Wilson 24
18. Johnnie Taylor 24
19. Isaac Hayes 23
20. Bobby Bland........................... 23
21. Ray Charles 23
22. Earth, Wind & Fire 22
23. The O'Jays............................. 22
24. Ramsey Lewis 22
25. The Dells 22
26. Al Green................................. 21
27. The Miracles 21
28. Patti LaBelle/LaBelle.............. 21
29. Curtis Mayfield 21
30. The Crusaders........................ 21
31. Tyrone Davis 21

MOST TOP 40 ALBUMS

1. James Brown 47
2. The Temptations 41
3. Aretha Franklin 39
4. The Supremes........................32
5. Gladys Knight & The Pips 27
6. Dionne Warwick 27
7. Marvin Gaye 26
8. The Isley Brothers 26
9. Diana Ross 26
10. Four Tops...............................26
11. Stevie Wonder........................25
12. Prince 24
13. The Miracles...........................21
14. Isaac Hayes 20
15. The O'Jays.............................20
16. Kool & The Gang....................20
17. B.B. King 20
18. Nancy Wilson 20
19. Earth, Wind & Fire..................19
20. Jackson 5/Jacksons 18
21. Lou Rawls...............................18
22. Barry White 18
23. The Crusaders........................18
24. The Impressions 18
25. Ramsey Lewis 17
26. Smokey Robinson 17
27. Ray Charles 17

MOST TOP 10 ALBUMS

1. The Temptations.....................32
2. Aretha Franklin 30
3. James Brown 25
4. Stevie Wonder........................22
5. The Supremes.........................21
6. Marvin Gaye 18
7. Prince 18
8. The Isley Brothers 17
9. Diana Ross 15
10. The O'Jays..............................15
11. Gladys Knight & The Pips.......14
12. Earth, Wind & Fire..................14
13. Dionne Warwick......................14
14. Jackson 5/Jacksons 14
15. Luther Vandross 13
16. Four Tops...............................12
17. Kool & The Gang 12
18. The Miracles...........................12
19. Teddy Pendergrass 12
20. Otis Redding 11
21. Commodores 10
22. Nancy Wilson 10
23. Roberta Flack.........................10
24. Isaac Hayes............................9
25. Barry White 9
26. Cameo 9
27. Grover Washington, Jr. 9
28. Smokey Robinson 9
29. Maze Feat. Frankie Beverly 9

MOST #1 ALBUMS

1. The Temptations 17
2. Aretha Franklin 10
3. Stevie Wonder........................ 10
4. The Supremes 7
5. Marvin Gaye 7
6. The Isley Brothers................... 7
7. Isaac Hayes 7
8. Luther Vandross 7
9. Barry White............................. 7
10. Gladys Knight & The Pips 6
11. Earth, Wind & Fire 6
12. Al Green................................. 6
13. Michael Jackson 5
14. Jackson 5/Jacksons 5
15. Commodores........................... 5
16. 2 Pac 5
17. Keith Sweat 5

MOST WEEKS AT THE #1 POSITION

1. The Temptations....................109
2. Michael Jackson 85
3. Aretha Franklin 74
4. Stevie Wonder........................74
5. Isaac Hayes 53
6. Freddie Jackson 43
7. Jackson 5/Jacksons 39
8. Marvin Gaye 35
9. Earth, Wind & Fire..................33
10. The Supremes........................31
11. Rick James.............................30
12. M.C. Hammer.........................30
13. Commodores..........................28
14. Whitney Houston 24
15. Lionel Richie 24
16. Luther Vandross 22
17. Lou Rawls...............................22

MOST GOLD & PLATINUM ALBUMS

1. Prince 19
2. Luther Vandross 14
3. Earth, Wind & Fire 13
4. Aretha Franklin 12
5. Santana 12
6. Donna Summer 11
7. The Isley Brothers 10
8. The O'Jays 10
9. Barry White 10
10. Kool & The Gang 10
11. Natalie Cole 10
12. Jimi Hendrix 10
13. George Benson 9
14. War 9
15. Kenny G..................................9
16. Bob Marley & The Wailers........9

Ties are broken according to rank in the *Top 200 Artists* section.

MOST CONSECUTIVE #1 ALBUMS

1. 13 **The Temptations** (1965-1970)
2. 7 **Luther Vandross** (1981-1991)
3. 6 **Aretha Franklin** (1967-1969)
4. 6 **Isaac Hayes** (1969-1973)
5. 6 **Al Green** (1972-1975)
6. 6 **Stevie Wonder** (1980-1991)
7. 5 **Marvin Gaye** (1971-1977)
8. 5 **The Isley Brothers** (1974-1978)
9. 5 **Michael Jackson** (1979-1995)
10. 5 **Keith Sweat** (1988-1996)

Excludes any albums marked with a special symbol (ex: [K]), duos and/or inspirational albums (unless they add to the streak).

LONGEST ALBUM CHART CAREERS

Dates	Artist (Years/Months/Weeks)
3/27/65 - 7/31/99 +	**The Temptations** (34/4/1)
1/30/65 - 9/5/98	**Aretha Franklin** (33/7/1)
5/28/66 - 10/24/98	**Patti LaBelle/LaBelle** (32/5/0)
4/22/67 - 9/19/98	**Johnnie Taylor** (31/5/0)
7/16/66 - 10/4/97	**The Isley Brothers** (31/2/3)
5/28/66 - 1/4/97	**Stevie Wonder** (30/7/1)
3/15/69 - 6/19/99	**Tyrone Davis** (30/3/1)
4/26/69 - 11/14/98	**George Benson** (29/6/3)
2/6/65 - 8/6/94	**Nancy Wilson** (29/6/0)
3/1/69 - 8/8/98	**Peggy Scott-Adams** (29/5/1)
5/1/65 - 10/9/93	**B.B. King** (28/5/1)
4/3/65 - 7/10/93	**Ray Charles** (28/3/1)
2/6/65 - 2/20/93	**Dionne Warwick** (28/0/2)
4/17/65 - 4/3/93	**James Brown** (27/11/2)
5/29/65 - 11/28/92	**Little Milton** (27/6/0)

+ still charted

#1 R&B ALBUMS ARTIST

THE TEMPTATIONS

THE TOP ALBUMS

This section lists, in rank order, the biggest #1 albums from 1965 through 1998.

The ranking is based on the most weeks an album held the #1 position. Ties are broken according to this order: total weeks in the Top 10, total weeks in the Top 40; and, finally, total weeks charted.

The Top 40 album covers are shown first, followed by a complete listing of the Top 100 albums.

> **The total weeks at No. 1 is shown below each album's cover photo, along with the year the album peaked.**

1. Thriller...*Michael Jackson*
37 / 1983

2. Please Hammer Don't Hurt 'Em...*M.C. Hammer*
29 / 1990

3. Just Like The First Time...*Freddie Jackson*
26 / 1986

4. Can't Slow Down...*Lionel Richie*
23 / 1983

5. Songs In The Key Of Life...*Stevie Wonder*
20 / 1976

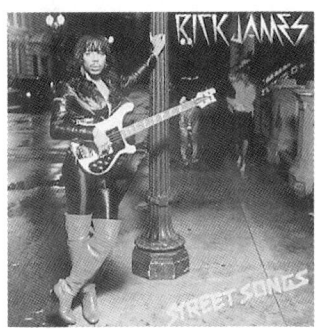

6. Street Songs
Rick James
20 / 1981

7. Purple Rain
Prince And The Revolution/Soundtrack
19 / 1984

8. Bad
Michael Jackson
18 / 1987

9. The Temptations Sing Smokey
The Temptations
18 / 1965

10. Aretha Now
Aretha Franklin
17 / 1968

11. Off The Wall
Michael Jackson
16 / 1979

12. Aretha: Lady Soul
Aretha Franklin
16 / 1968

13. Puzzle People
The Temptations
15 / 1969

14. Rock Me Tonight
Freddie Jackson
14 / 1985

15. Temptin' Temptations
The Temptations
14 / 1965

16. I Never Loved A Man The Way I Love You
Aretha Franklin
14 / 1967

17. Shaft
Isaac Hayes/Soundtrack
14 / 1971

18. Cloud Nine
The Temptations
13 / 1969

19. Hotter Than July
Stevie Wonder
13 / 1980

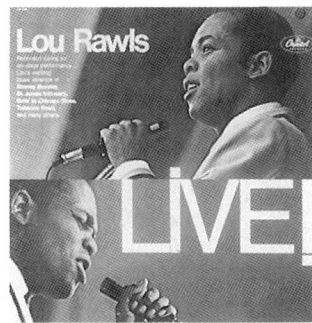

20. Lou Rawls Live!
Lou Rawls
12 / 1966

21. Dangerous
Michael Jackson
12 / 1992

22. Diana Ross and the Supremes Greatest Hits
Diana Ross & The Supremes
12 / 1967

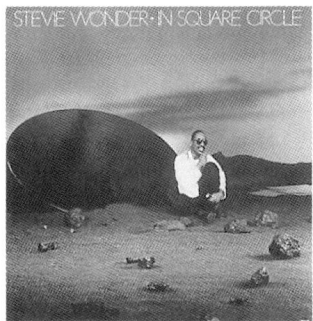

23. In Square Circle
Stevie Wonder
12 / 1985

24. Back On The Block
Quincy Jones
12 / 1990

25. ABC
Jackson 5
12 / 1970

26. The In Crowd
Ramsey Lewis Trio
12 / 1965

27. Don't Be Cruel
Bobby Brown
11 / 1988

28. Tender Lover
Babyface
11 / 1989

29. Promise
Sade
11 / 1986

30. To Be Continued
Isaac Hayes
11 / 1970

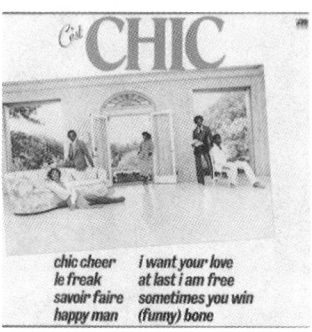

31. C'est Chic
Chic
11 / 1978

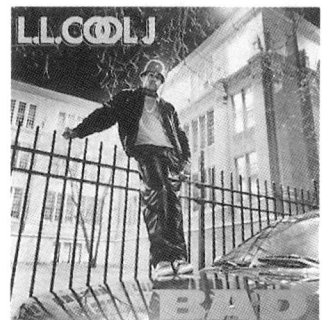

32. Bigger And Deffer
LL Cool J
11 / 1987

33. Let's Get It On
Marvin Gaye
11 / 1973

34. Raise!
Earth, Wind & Fire
11 / 1981

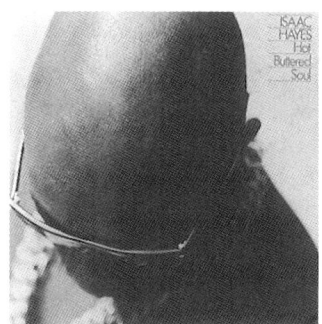

35. Hot Buttered Soul
Isaac Hayes
10 / 1969

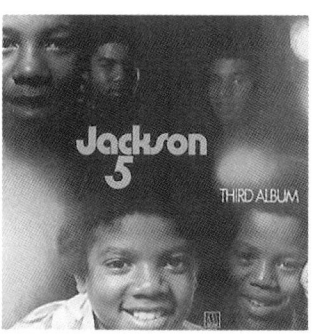

36. Third Album
Jackson 5
10 / 1970

37. Waiting To Exhale
Soundtrack
10 / 1995

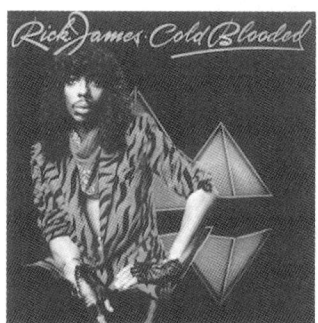

38. Cold Blooded
Rick James
10 / 1983

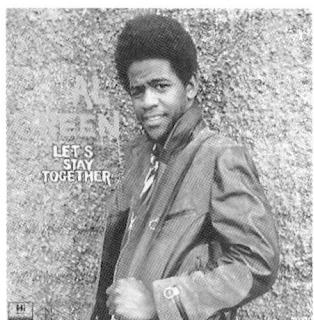

39. Let's Stay Together
Al Green
10 / 1972

40. Above The Rim
Soundtrack
10 / 1994

ALL-TIME TOP 100 ALBUMS
1965-1998

PK YR	WKS CHR	WKS T40	WKS T10	WKS @ #1	RANK	TITLE	ARTIST
83	101	90	76	37	1.	Thriller	Michael Jackson
90	68	60	48	29	2.	Please Hammer Don't Hurt 'Em	M.C. Hammer
86	69	55	44	26	3.	Just Like The First Time	Freddie Jackson
83	91	79	58	23	4.	Can't Slow Down	Lionel Richie
76	48	44	32	20	5.	Songs In The Key Of Life	Stevie Wonder
81	78	49	27	20	6.	Street Songs	Rick James
84	48	40	31	19	7.	Purple Rain	Prince And The Revolution/Soundtrack
87	77	52	38	18	8.	Bad	Michael Jackson
65	29	29	29	18	9.	The Temptations Sing Smokey	The Temptations
68	35	35	26	17	10.	Aretha Now	Aretha Franklin
79	61	51	36	16	11.	Off The Wall	Michael Jackson
68	53	51	32	16	12.	Aretha: Lady Soul	Aretha Franklin
69	35	34	25	15	13.	Puzzle People	The Temptations
85	63	60	41	14	14.	Rock Me Tonight	Freddie Jackson
65	34	34	30	14	15.	Temptin' Temptations	The Temptations
67	66	52	28	14	16.	I Never Loved A Man The Way I Love You	Aretha Franklin
71	68	55	27	14	17.	Shaft	Isaac Hayes/Soundtrack
69	49	48	30	13	18.	Cloud Nine	The Temptations
80	44	36	26	13	19.	Hotter Than July	Stevie Wonder
66	63	63	45	12	20.	Lou Rawls Live!	Lou Rawls
92	112	67	29	12	21.	Dangerous	Michael Jackson
67	58	52	27	12	22.	Diana Ross and the Supremes Greatest Hits	Diana Ross & The Supremes
85	52	44	25	12	23.	In Square Circle	Stevie Wonder
90	39	33	21	12	24.	Back On The Block	Quincy Jones
70	25	23	20	12	25.	ABC	Jackson 5
65	19	19	19	12	26.	The In Crowd	Ramsey Lewis Trio
88	80	72	51	11	27.	Don't Be Cruel	Bobby Brown
89	66	58	37	11	28.	Tender Lover	Babyface
86	45	38	24	11	29.	Promise	Sade
70	46	45	23	11	30.	To Be Continued	Isaac Hayes
78	38	24	20	11	31.	C'est Chic	Chic
87	47	26	18	11	32.	Bigger And Deffer	LL Cool J
73	46	40	17	11	33.	Let's Get It On	Marvin Gaye
81	29	22	17	11	34.	Raise!	Earth, Wind & Fire
69	68	62	42	10	35.	Hot Buttered Soul	Isaac Hayes
70	35	35	26	10	36.	Third Album	Jackson 5
95	70	33	24	10	37.	Waiting To Exhale	Soundtrack
83	33	26	19	10	38.	Cold Blooded	Rick James
72	38	34	18	10	39.	Let's Stay Together	Al Green
94	40	24	17	10	40.	Above The Rim	Soundtrack
66	114	108	42	9	41.	The Temptations Greatest Hits	The Temptations
94	101	51	38	9	42.	12 Play	R. Kelly
71	53	52	34	9	43.	What's Going On	Marvin Gaye
66	44	44	29	9	44.	Lou Rawls Soulin'	Lou Rawls
82	55	50	25	9	45.	Gap Band IV	The Gap Band
70	33	31	20	9	46.	Diana Ross Presents The Jackson 5	Jackson 5
77	36	28	20	9	47.	All 'N All	Earth, Wind & Fire
86	91	84	56	8	48.	Control	Janet Jackson
93	105	66	33	8	49.	The Chronic	Dr. Dre
90	53	49	32	8	50.	I'm Your Baby Tonight	Whitney Houston

PK YR: Peak Year **WKS CHR:** Weeks Charted **WKS T40:** Weeks in Top 40 **WKS T10:** Weeks in Top 10 **WKS @ #1:** Weeks at #1

PK YR	WKS CHR	WKS T40	WKS T10	WKS @ #1	RANK	TITLE	ARTIST
77	44	36	29	8	51.	Commodores	Commodores
92	122	75	28	8	52.	The Bodyguard	Whitney Houston/Soundtrack
94	85	45	27	8	53.	My Life	Mary J. Blige
96	63	36	27	8	54.	The Score	Fugees
92	59	38	25	8	55.	Boomerang	Soundtrack
79	44	33	23	8	56.	2 Hot!	Peaches & Herb
88	46	37	21	8	57.	Giving You The Best That I Got	Anita Baker
80	48	35	21	8	58.	Diana	Diana Ross
74	39	35	21	8	59.	Fulfillingness' First Finale	Stevie Wonder
82	43	29	21	8	60.	Midnight Love	Marvin Gaye
86	42	32	18	8	61.	Winner In You	Patti LaBelle
78	32	27	18	8	62.	Natural High	Commodores
80	34	28	17	8	63.	The Whispers	The Whispers
79	34	23	17	8	64.	Teddy	Teddy Pendergrass
91	31	22	15	8	65.	New Jack City	Soundtrack
89	57	46	32	7	66.	Karyn White	Karyn White
70	53	44	29	7	67.	The Isaac Hayes Movement	Isaac Hayes
92	64	48	27	7	68.	What's The 411?	Mary J. Blige
88	57	46	27	7	69.	In Effect Mode	Al B. Sure!
85	80	51	26	7	70.	The Night I Fell In Love	Luther Vandross
86	60	49	25	7	71.	Raising Hell	Run-D.M.C.
73	48	38	24	7	72.	The World Is A Ghetto	War
68	58	53	20	7	73.	The Temptations in a Mellow Mood	The Temptations
87	48	31	20	7	74.	Characters	Stevie Wonder
73	53	46	19	7	75.	Imagination	Gladys Knight & The Pips
77	32	31	19	7	76.	Rejoice	Emotions
72	40	36	17	7	77.	Black Moses	Isaac Hayes
79	34	28	17	7	78.	We Are Family	Sister Sledge
82	38	23	14	7	79.	Jump To It	Aretha Franklin
78	26	22	13	7	80.	Blam!!	The Brothers Johnson
96	41	19	12	7	81.	It Was Written	Nas
85	116	86	64	6	82.	Whitney Houston	Whitney Houston
98	47 +	47 +	33	6	83.	The Miseducation Of Lauryn Hill	Lauryn Hill
66	31	31	27	6	84.	Getting' Ready	The Temptations
96	103	37	24	6	85.	The Don Killuminati – The 7 Day Theory	Makaveli
78	38	35	23	6	86.	Saturday Night Fever	Bee Gees/Soundtrack
88	61	46	22	6	87.	Faith	George Michael
92	55	44	22	6	88.	Totally Krossed Out	Kris Kross
76	46	31	22	6	89.	Breezin'	George Benson
76	31	30	22	6	90.	Rufus featuring Chaka Khan	Rufus featuring Chaka Khan
74	46	44	21	6	91.	Skin Tight	Ohio Players
76	29	27	21	6	92.	Gratitude	Earth, Wind & Fire
98	43 +	38	19	6	93.	Vol. 2...Hard Knock Life	Jay-Z
72	38	37	19	6	94.	Still Bill	Bill Withers
81	37	32	19	6	95.	The Gap Band III	The Gap Band
76	31	30	19	6	96.	Hot On The Tracks	Commodores
69	28	28	19	6	97.	TCB	Diana Ross & The Supremes With The Temptations
71	38	36	18	6	98.	Maybe Tomorrow	Jackson 5
93	51	21	14	6	99.	Menace II Society	Soundtrack
72	36	35	12	6	100.	Superfly	Curtis Mayfield/Soundtrack

+ still charted as of the 7/31/99 cut-off date

TOP 40 ALBUMS BY DECADE
1965-1969

PK YR	WKS CHR	WKS T40	WKS T10	WKS @ #1	RANK	TITLE	ARTIST
65	29	29	29	18	1.	The Temptations Sing Smokey	The Temptations
68	35	35	26	17	2.	Aretha Now	Aretha Franklin
68	53	51	32	16	3.	Aretha: Lady Soul	Aretha Franklin
69	35	34	25	15	4.	Puzzle People	The Temptations
65	34	34	30	14	5.	Temptin' Temptations	The Temptations
67	66	52	28	14	6.	I Never Loved A Man The Way I Love You	Aretha Franklin
69	49	48	30	13	7.	Cloud Nine	The Temptations
66	63	63	45	12	8.	Lou Rawls Live!	Lou Rawls
67	58	52	27	12	9.	Diana Ross and the Supremes Greatest Hits ...Diana Ross & The Supremes	
65	19	19	19	12	10.	The In Crowd	Ramsey Lewis Trio
69	68	62	42	10	11.	Hot Buttered Soul	Isaac Hayes
66	114	108	42	9	12.	The Temptations Greatest Hits	The Temptations
66	44	44	29	9	13.	Lou Rawls Soulin'	Lou Rawls
68	58	53	20	7	14.	The Temptations in a Mellow Mood	The Temptations
66	31	31	27	6	15.	Gettin' Ready	The Temptations
69	28	28	19	6	16.	TCB	Diana Ross & The Supremes With The Temptations
67	28	28	26	5	17.	Aretha Arrives	Aretha Franklin
66	28	28	24	5	18.	Going To A Go-Go	Smokey Robinson & The Miracles
66	35	35	24	4	19.	The Supremes A' Go-Go	The Supremes
69	36	35	18	4	20.	Aretha's Gold	Aretha Franklin
69	32	31	18	4	21.	Aretha Franklin: Soul '69	Aretha Franklin
68	32	26	17	4	22.	Diana Ross & the Supremes Join the Temptations ...Diana Ross & The Supremes & The Temptations	
65	15	15	15	4	23.	Shake	Sam Cooke
65	27	27	26	3	24.	Sam Cooke At The Copa	Sam Cooke
68	41	36	22	3	25.	Wish It Would Rain	The Temptations
67	26	26	22	3	26.	Temptations Live!	The Temptations
68	37	35	19	3	27.	The Dock Of The Bay	Otis Redding
65	18	18	18	3	28.	Four Tops	Four Tops
67	24	24	14	3	29.	The Supremes sing Holland-Dozier-Holland	The Supremes
66	22	22	16	2	30.	Got My Mojo Workin'	Jimmy Smith
67	49	49	13	2	31.	Here Where There is Love	Dionne Warwick
65	13	13	13	2	32.	People Get Ready	The Impressions
67	23	23	12	2	33.	Revenge	Bill Cosby
68	30	29	11	2	34.	Special Occasion	Smokey Robinson & The Miracles
69	22	22	8	2	35.	My Whole World Ended	David Ruffin
69	32	28	7	2	36.	M.P.G.	Marvin Gaye
66	29	29	24	1	37.	Crying Time	Ray Charles
68	48	46	23	1	38.	Hickory Holler Revisited	O.C. Smith
65	22	22	22	1	39.	Shotgun	Jr. Walker & The All Stars
67	33	33	19	1	40.	Four Tops Live!	Four Tops

PK YR	WKS CHR	WKS T40	WKS T10	WKS @ #1	RANK	TITLE	ARTIST
76	48	44	32	20	1.	Songs In The Key Of Life	Stevie Wonder
79	61	51	36	16	2.	Off The Wall	Michael Jackson
71	68	55	27	14	3.	Shaft	Isaac Hayes/Soundtrack
70	25	23	20	12	4.	ABC	Jackson 5
70	46	45	23	11	5.	To Be Continued	Isaac Hayes
78	38	24	20	11	6.	C'est Chic	Chic
73	46	40	17	11	7.	Let's Get It On	Marvin Gaye
70	35	35	26	10	8.	Third Album	Jackson 5
72	38	34	18	10	9.	Let's Stay Together	Al Green
71	53	52	34	9	10.	What's Going On	Marvin Gaye
70	33	31	20	9	11.	Diana Ross Presents The Jackson 5	Jackson 5
77	36	28	20	9	12.	All 'N All	Earth, Wind & Fire
77	44	36	29	8	13.	Commodores	Commodores
79	44	33	23	8	14.	2 Hot!	Peaches & Herb
74	39	35	21	8	15.	Fulfillingness' First Finale	Stevie Wonder
78	32	27	18	8	16.	Natural High	Commodores
79	34	23	17	8	17.	Teddy	Teddy Pendergrass
70	53	44	29	7	18.	The Isaac Hayes Movement	Isaac Hayes
73	48	38	24	7	19.	The World Is A Ghetto	War
73	53	46	19	7	20.	Imagination	Gladys Knight & The Pips
77	32	31	19	7	21.	Rejoice	Emotions
72	40	36	17	7	22.	Black Moses	Isaac Hayes
79	34	28	17	7	23.	We Are Family	Sister Sledge
78	26	22	13	7	24.	Blam!!	The Brothers Johnson
78	38	35	23	6	25.	Saturday Night Fever	Bee Gees/Soundtrack
76	46	31	22	6	26.	Breezin'	George Benson
76	31	30	22	6	27.	Rufus featuring Chaka Khan	Rufus featuring Chaka Khan
74	46	44	21	6	28.	Skin Tight	Ohio Players
76	29	27	21	6	29.	Gratitude	Earth, Wind & Fire
72	38	37	19	6	30.	Still Bill	Bill Withers
76	31	30	19	6	31.	Hot On The Tracks	Commodores
71	38	36	18	6	32.	Maybe Tomorrow	Jackson 5
72	36	35	12	6	33.	Superfly	Curtis Mayfield/Soundtrack
74	30	25	11	6	34.	Love Is The Message	MFSB
71	43	41	32	5	35.	Curtis	Curtis Mayfield
72	53	52	30	5	36.	I'm Still In Love With You	Al Green
74	47	44	28	5	37.	Ship Ahoy	The O'Jays
71	37	36	23	5	38.	Aretha Live At Fillmore West	Aretha Franklin
75	33	33	23	5	39.	That's The Way Of The World	Earth, Wind & Fire/Soundtrack
75	29	28	22	5	40.	Fire	Ohio Players

PK YR	WKS CHR	WKS T40	WKS T10	WKS @ #1	RANK	TITLE	ARTIST
83	101	90	76	37	1.	Thriller	Michael Jackson
86	69	55	44	26	2.	Just Like The First Time	Freddie Jackson
83	91	79	58	23	3.	Can't Slow Down	Lionel Richie
81	78	49	27	20	4.	Street Songs	Rick James
84	48	40	31	19	5.	Purple Rain	Prince And The Revolution/Soundtrack
87	77	52	38	18	6.	Bad	Michael Jackson
85	63	60	41	14	7.	Rock Me Tonight	Freddie Jackson
80	44	36	26	13	8.	Hotter Than July	Stevie Wonder
85	52	44	25	12	9.	In Square Circle	Stevie Wonder
88	80	72	51	11	10.	Don't Be Cruel	Bobby Brown
89	66	58	37	11	11.	Tender Lover	Babyface
86	45	38	24	11	12.	Promise	Sade
87	47	26	18	11	13.	Bigger And Deffer	LL Cool J
81	29	22	17	11	14.	Raise!	Earth, Wind & Fire
83	33	26	19	10	15.	Cold Blooded	Rick James
82	55	50	25	9	16.	Gap Band IV	The Gap Band
86	91	84	56	8	17.	Control	Janet Jackson
88	46	37	21	8	18.	Giving You The Best That I Got	Anita Baker
80	48	35	21	8	19.	Diana	Diana Ross
82	43	29	21	8	20.	Midnight Love	Marvin Gaye
86	42	32	18	8	21.	Winner In You	Patti LaBelle
80	34	28	17	8	22.	The Whispers	The Whispers
89	57	46	32	7	23.	Karyn White	Karyn White
88	57	46	27	7	24.	In Effect Mode	Al B. Sure!
85	80	51	26	7	25.	The Night I Fell In Love	Luther Vandross
86	60	49	25	7	26.	Raising Hell	Run-D.M.C.
87	48	31	20	7	27.	Characters	Stevie Wonder
82	38	23	14	7	28.	Jump To It	Aretha Franklin
85	116	86	64	6	29.	Whitney Houston	Whitney Houston
88	61	46	22	6	30.	Faith	George Michael
81	37	32	19	6	31.	The Gap Band III	The Gap Band
89	73	65	41	5	32.	Guy	Guy
86	52	44	37	5	33.	Word Up!	Cameo
85	57	44	29	5	34.	New Edition	New Edition
80	29	24	15	5	35.	Let's Get Serious	Jermaine Jackson
82	37	29	14	5	36.	The Poet	Bobby Womack
81	30	25	13	5	37.	Being With You	Smokey Robinson
80	27	21	13	5	38.	Go All The Way	The Isley Brothers
89	36	22	12	5	39.	3 Feet High And Rising	De La Soul
89	24	19	12	5	40.	Walking With A Panther	LL Cool J

PK YR	WKS CHR	WKS T40	WKS T10	WKS @ #1	RANK	TITLE	ARTIST
90	68	60	48	29	1.	Please Hammer Don't Hurt 'Em	M.C. Hammer
92	112	67	29	12	2.	Dangerous	Michael Jackson
90	39	33	21	12	3.	Back On The Block	Quincy Jones
95	70	33	24	10	4.	Waiting To Exhale	Soundtrack
94	40	24	17	10	5.	Above The Rim	Soundtrack
94	101	51	38	9	6.	12 Play	R. Kelly
93	105	66	33	8	7.	The Chronic	Dr. Dre
90	53	49	32	8	8.	I'm Your Baby Tonight	Whitney Houston
92	122	75	28	8	9.	The Bodyguard	Whitney Houston/Soundtrack
94	85	45	27	8	10.	My Life	Mary J. Blige
96	63	36	27	8	11.	The Score	Fugees
92	59	38	25	8	12.	Boomerang	Soundtrack
91	31	22	15	8	13.	New Jack City	Soundtrack
92	64	48	27	7	14.	What's The 411?	Mary J. Blige
96	41	19	12	7	15.	It Was Written	Nas
98	47 +	47 +	33	6	16.	The Miseducation Of Lauryn Hill	Lauryn Hill
96	103	37	24	6	17.	The Don Killuminati – The 7 Day Theory	Makaveli
92	55	44	22	6	18.	Totally Krossed Out	Kris Kross
98	43 +	38	19	6	19.	Vol. 2...Hard Knock Life	Jay-Z
93	51	21	14	6	20.	Menace II Society	Soundtrack
95	64	22	12	6	21.	Friday	Soundtrack
95	30	14	10	6	22.	The Show	Soundtrack
96	68	46	30	5	23.	Another Level	Blackstreet
93	102	43	28	5	24.	Doggy Style	Snoop Doggy Dogg
91	62	52	19	5	25.	Power Of Love	Luther Vandross
97	58	39	19	5	26.	No Way Out	Puff Daddy & The Family
97	77	43	17	5	27.	God's Property	God's Property
92	46	29	17	5	28.	Dead Serious	DAS EFX
94	25	15	9	5	29.	We Come Strapped	MC Eiht Featuring CMW
97	75	55	25	4	30.	Share My World	Mary J. Blige
97	64	41	21	4	31.	Baduizm	Erykah Badu
95	97	41	20	4	32.	Me Against The World	2 Pac
97	90	39	18	4	33.	Life After Death	The Notorious B.I.G.
94	53	36	12	4	34.	Rhythm Of Love	Anita Baker
93	43	27	10	4	35.	Black Sunday	Cypress Hill
91	20	15	10	4	36.	Boyz N The Hood	Soundtrack
98	48	19	7	4	37.	MP Da Last Don	Master P
93	105	69	49	3	38.	Toni Braxton	Toni Braxton
93	97	66	27	3	39.	janet.	Janet Jackson
96	105	69	26	3	40.	All Eyez On Me	2 Pac

+ still charted as of the 7/31/99 cut-off date

MOST VALUABLE ALBUMS

Following is a list of all albums in this book valued at $50 or more.

Year	Value	Title	Artist...Label & Number
66	$200	1. Dedicated To You	The Manhattans.....Carnival 201
67	$150	2. You Got My Mind Messed Up	James Carr.....Goldway 3001
66	$100	3. The Soul Of The Man	Bobby Bland.....Duke 79
65	$100	4. (If It Is) Only For Tonight	O.V. Wright.....Back Beat 61
66	$80	5. The 'New' Look	Fontella Bass.....Checker 2997
67	$80	6. Live At The Garden	James Brown.....King 1018
74	$80	7. Hell	James Brown.....Polydor 9001
68	$80	8. La La Means I Love You	The Delfonics.....Philly Groove 1150
69	$80	9. Sound Of Sexy Soul	The Delfonics.....Philly Groove 1151
65	$80	10. The Great Otis Redding Sings Soul Ballads	Otis Redding.....Volt 411
68	$70	11. Live At The Apollo, Volume II	James Brown.....King 1022
65	$70	12. We're Gonna Make It	Little Milton.....Checker 2995
66	$60	13. And Now...Booker T. & The MG's	Booker T. & The MG's.....Stax 711
71	$60	14. Revolution Of The Mind	James Brown.....Polydor 3003
72	$60	15. Get On The Good Foot	James Brown.....Polydor 3004
72	$60	16. America Eats Its Young	Funkadelic.....Westbound 2020
69	$60	17. The Meters	The Meters.....Josie 4010
70	$60	18. Look-Ka Py Py	The Meters.....Josie 4011
70	$60	19. Struttin'	The Meters.....Josie 4012
68	$60	20. Bobby Taylor And The Vancouvers	Bobby Taylor & The Vancouvers.....Gordy 930
69	$60	21. Color Him Father	The Winstons.....Metromedia 1010
67	$50	22. Hip Hug-Her	Booker T. & The MG's.....Stax 717
68	$50	23. Doin' Our Thing	Booker T. & The MG's.....Stax 724
66	$50	24. I Got You (I Feel Good)	James Brown.....King 946
66	$50	25. It's A Man's Man's Man's World	James Brown.....King 985
67	$50	26. Raw Soul	James Brown.....King 1016
67	$50	27. Cold Sweat	James Brown.....King 1020
68	$50	28. James Brown Presents His Show Of Tomorrow	James Brown.....King 1024
68	$50	29. I Can't Stand Myself (When You Touch Me)	James Brown.....King 1030
68	$50	30. I Got The Feelin'	James Brown.....King 1031
68	$50	31. James Brown Plays Nothing But Soul	James Brown.....King 1034
69	$50	32. Say It Loud-I'm Black And I'm Proud	James Brown.....King 1047
69	$50	33. Gettin' Down To It	James Brown.....King 1051
70	$50	34. Sex Machine	James Brown.....King 1115
73	$50	35. The Payback	James Brown.....Polydor 3007
73	$50	36. Black Caesar	James Brown.....Polydor 6014
73	$50	37. Slaughter's Big Rip-Off	James Brown.....Polydor 6015
65	$50	38. Gene Chandler – Live On Stage In '65	Gene Chandler.....Constellation 1425
70	$50	39. Funkadelic	Funkadelic.....Westbound 2000
70	$50	40. Free Your Mind...And Your Ass Will Follow	Funkadelic.....Westbound 2001
71	$50	41. Maggot Brain	Funkadelic.....Westbound 2007
73	$50	42. Cosmic Slop	Funkadelic.....Westbound 2022
74	$50	43. Standing On The Verge Of Getting It On	Funkadelic.....Westbound 1001
75	$50	44. Funkadelic's Greatest Hits	Funkadelic.....Westbound 1004
75	$50	45. Let's Take It To The Stage	Funkadelic.....Westbound 215
76	$50	46. Tales Of Kidd Funkadelic	Funkadelic.....Westbound 227
66	$50	47. Soul Cargo	Leon Haywood.....Fat Fish 2525
67	$50	48. Are You Experienced?	Jimi Hendrix.....Reprise 6261
68	$50	49. The Great March To Freedom	Rev. Martin Luther King.....Gordy 906
69	$50	50. Kick Out The Jams	MC5.....Elektra 74042
65	$50	51. Greatest Hits From The Beginning	The Miracles.....Tamla 254
65	$50	52. In The Midnight Hour	Wilson Pickett.....Atlantic 8114
65	$50	53. The Most Exciting Organ Ever	Billy Preston.....Vee-Jay 1123
66	$50	54. When A Man Loves A Woman	Percy Sledge.....Atlantic 8125
66	$50	55. Warm & Tender Soul	Percy Sledge.....Atlantic 8132
68	$50	56. Take Time To Know Her	Percy Sledge.....Atlantic 8180
68	$50	57. When The Whistle Blows Anything Goes	Soul Survivors.....Crimson 502
67	$50	58. Wanted: One Soul Singer	Johnnie Taylor.....Stax 715
69	$50	59. Irresistible Tammi	Tammi Terrell.....Motown 652
66	$50	60. The Toys sing "A Lover's Concerto" and "Attack!"	The Toys.....DynoVoice 9002

ALBUMS OF LONGEVITY

Albums with 85 or more total weeks charted.

PK YR	PK WKS	PK POS	WKS CHR	RANK	TITLE	ARTIST
93	1	2	185	1. Breathless	Kenny G
94	2	8	140	2. Enter The Wu-Tang (36 Chambers)	Wu-Tang Clan
94	2	25	124	3. Rachelle Ferrell	Rachelle Ferrell
92	8	1	122	4. The Bodyguard	Whitney Houston/Soundtrack
91	2	1	122	5. Cooleyhighharmony	Boyz II Men
94	2	2	119	6. Creepin On Ah Come Up	Bone Thugs-N-Harmony
85	6	1	116	7. Whitney Houston	Whitney Houston
66	9	1	114	8. The Temptations Greatest Hits	The Temptations
92	12	1	112	9. Dangerous	Michael Jackson
94	1	7	111	10. Best Of Sade	Sade
86	3	1	108	11. Rapture	Anita Baker
95	1	6	108	12. Kirk Franklin and the family	Kirk Franklin and the family
93	8	1	105	13. The Chronic	Dr. Dre
93	3	1	105	14. Toni Braxton	Toni Braxton
96	3	1	105	15. All Eyez On Me	2 Pac
95	3	1	105	16. E. 1999 Eternal	Bone Thugs-N-Harmony
92	1	2	105	17. Love Deluxe	Sade
96	6	1	103	18. The Don Killuminati – The 7 Day Theory	Makaveli
96	4	8	103	19. Maxwell's Urban Hang Suite	Maxwell
93	1	9	103	20. All The Greatest Hits	Zapp & Roger
93	5	1	102	21. Doggy Style	Snoop Doggy Dogg
91	2	1	102	22. Forever My Lady	Jodeci
92	4	4	102	23. Cypress Hill	Cypress Hill
83	37	1	101	24. Thriller	Michael Jackson
94	9	1	101	25. 12 Play	R. Kelly
93	2	17	99	26. Brian McKnight	Brian McKnight
96	1	3	98	27. Ice Cream Man	Master P
95	4	1	97	28. Me Against The World	2 Pac
93	3	1	97	29. janet.	Janet Jackson
97	2	1	97	30. Ghetto D	Master P
89	1	10	97	31. Forever Your Girl	Paula Abdul
95	1	34	97	32. Al Green/Greatest Hits	Al Green
82	10	4	93	33. Prince **1999**	Prince
82	3	17	93	34. Down Home	Z.Z. Hill
96	1	1	92	35. Secrets	Toni Braxton
91	1	38	92	36. Make The Difference	Tracie Spencer
83	23	1	91	37. Can't Slow Down	Lionel Richie
86	8	1	91	38. Control	Janet Jackson
92	1	1	91	39. The Comfort Zone	Vanessa Williams
98	2	2	91	40. Love Always	K-Ci & JoJo
97	4	1	90	41. Life After Death	The Notorious B.I.G.
94	2	1	89	42. II	Boyz II Men
94	5	2	89	43. CrazySexyCool	TLC
97	3	19	89	44. Kenny Lattimore	Kenny Lattimore
94	1	3	88	45. Ready To Die	The Notorious B.I.G.
97	3	2	87	46. Tru 2 Da Game	Tru
93	2	2	87	47. For The Cool In You	Babyface
95	3	6	87	48. Brandy	Brandy
89	3	1	86	49. Janet Jackson's Rhythm Nation 1814	Janet Jackson
93	2	1	86	50. Music Box	Mariah Carey
81	1	1	86	51. Never Too Much	Luther Vandross
87	4	8	86	52. Duotones	Kenny G
95	1	14	86	53. Mystikal	Mystikal
94	8	1	85	54. My Life	Mary J. Blige
98	1	9	85	55. Big Willie Style	Will Smith

1945-1964
R&B
ALBUMS

This section lists, alpabetically by artist, R&B albums that charted on *Billboard's* Pop Albums charts, from the debut of that chart on March 24, 1945 through December 26, 1964. Prior to *Billboard's* debut of the R&B Albums chart on January 30, 1965, popular R&B albums made *Billboard's* Pop Albums charts. These included albums by R&B stars, such as Louis Armstrong, Ray Charles, and The Miracles. Had there been an R&B Albums chart back to 1945, many of the albums on the following pages surely would have made a big impact on that chart.

All albums are listed chronologically below each artist.

The year of the album's debut on the Pop Albums chart is listed to the far left of the title.

The album's record label and number follows to the right of the title.

ADDERLEY, Cannonball

'62	30	Nancy Wilson/Cannonball Adderley...*Capitol 1657*
'63	11	Jazz Workshop Revisited...*Riverside 444*

AMMONS, Gene

'62	53	Bad! Bossa Nova...*Prestige 7257*

ANDERSON, Ernestine

'58	15	Hot Cargo!...*Mercury 20354*

ARMSTRONG, Louis

'51	14	Louis Armstrong All-Stars...*RCA Victor 14*
'51	10	Satchmo At Symphony Hall...*Decca 8037*
'52	9	Satchmo At Pasadena, Vol. 1...*Decca 336*
'55	10	Satch Plays Fats...*Columbia 708*
'56	12	Ella And Louis...*Verve 4003*
'64	1 [6]	Hello, Dolly!...*Kapp 3364*

BASIE, Count

'63	5	Sinatra-Basie...*Reprise 1008*
'63	19	This Time By Basie! Hits of the 50's And 60's... *Reprise 6070*
'63	123	Li'l Ol' Groovemaker...Basie!...*Verve 8549*
'63	69	Ella And Basie!...*Verve 4061*
'64	150	More Hits Of The 50's And 60's...*Verve 8563*
'64	13	It Might As Well Be Swing...*Reprise 1012*

BENTON, Brook

'61	82	Golden Hits...*Mercury 60607*
'61	70	The Boll Weevil Song And 11 Other Great Hits... *Mercury 60641*
'62	77	If You Believe...*Mercury 60619*
'62	40	Singing The Blues – Lie To Me...*Mercury 60740*
'63	82	Golden Hits, Volume 2...*Mercury 60774*

BERRY, Chuck

'63	29	Chuck Berry On Stage...*Chess 1480*
'64	34	Chuck Berry's Greatest Hits...*Chess 1485*
'64	124	St. Louis To Liverpool...*Chess 1488*

BLACK('S), Bill, Combo

'60	23	Solid And Raunchy...*Hi 12003*

BLAND, Bobby

'62	53	Here's The Man!!!...*Duke 75*
'63	11	Call On Me/That's The Way Love Is...*Duke 77*
'64	119	Ain't Nothing You Can Do...*Duke 78*

BONDS, Gary (U.S.)

'61	6	Dance 'til Quarter To Three...*Legrand 3001*

BOOKER T. & THE MG'S

'62	33	Green Onions...*Stax 701*

BROWN, James

'63	2 [2]	Live At The Apollo...*King 826*
'63	73	Prisoner Of Love...*King 851*
'64	10	Pure Dynamite! Live At The Royal...*King 883*
'64	61	Showtime...*Smash 67054*

BURRELL, Kenny

'63	108	Blue Bash!...*Verve 8553*

BUTLER, Jerry

'64	102	Delicious Together...*Vee-Jay 1099*

BYRD, Donald

'64	110	A New Perspective...*Blue Note 84124*

CAMBRIDGE, Godfrey

'64	42	Ready Or Not...Here's Godfrey Cambridge... *Epic 13101*

CANNON, Ace

'62	44	"Tuff"-Sax...*Hi 32007*

CHANDLER, Gene

'62	69	The Duke Of Earl...*Vee-Jay 1040*

CHARLES, Ray

'60	17	The Genius Of Ray Charles...*Atlantic 1312*
'60	13	Ray Charles In Person...*Atlantic 8039*
'60	9	The Genius Hits The Road...*ABC-Paramount 335*
'61	11	Dedicated To You...*ABC-Paramount 355*
'61	4	Genius + Soul = Jazz...*Impulse! 2*
'61	20	What'd I Say...*Atlantic 8029*
'61	49	The Genius After Hours...*Atlantic 1369*
'61	52	Ray Charles & Betty Carter...*ABC-Paramount 385*
'61	73	The Genius Sings The Blues...*Atlantic 8052*
'61	11	Do The Twist!...*Atlantic 8054*
'62	1 [14]	Modern Sounds In Country And Western Music... *ABC-Paramount 410*
'62	14	The Ray Charles Story...*Atlantic 900*
'62	5	Ray Charles' Greatest Hits...*ABC-Paramount 415*
'62	2 [2]	Modern Sounds In Country And Western Music (Volume Two)...*ABC-Paramount 435*
'63	2 [2]	Ingredients In A Recipe For Soul...*ABC-Paramount 465*
'64	9	Sweet & Sour Tears...*ABC-Paramount 480*
'64	36	Have A Smile With Me...*ABC-Paramount 495*

CHECKER, Chubby

'60	3	Twist With Chubby Checker...*Parkway 7001*
'61	110	It's Pony Time...*Parkway 7003*
'61	11	Let's Twist Again...*Parkway 7004*
'61	8	For Twisters Only...*Parkway 7002*
'61	2 [6]	Your Twist Party...*Parkway 7007*
'61	7	Bobby Rydell/Chubby Checker...*Cameo 1013*
'62	17	For Teen Twisters Only...*Parkway 7009*
'62	54	Twistin' Round The World...*Parkway 7008*
'62	29	Don't Knock The Twist...*Parkway 7011*
'62	23	All The Hits (For Your Dancin' Party)...*Parkway 7014*
'62	117	Down To Earth...*Cameo 1029*
'62	11	Limbo Party...*Parkway 7020*
'62	27	Chubby Checker's Biggest Hits...*Parkway 7022*
'63	87	Let's Limbo Some More...*Parkway 7027*
'63	90	Beach Party...*Parkway 7030*
'63	104	Chubby Checker In Person...*Parkway 7026*

CLAY, Cassius

'63	61	I Am The Greatest!...*Columbia 2093*

COLE, Nat "King"

'45	1 [12]	The King Cole Trio...*Capitol 8*
'46	1 [4]	King Cole Trio – Vol. 2...*Capitol 29*
'48	4	King Cole Trio – Volume 3...*Capitol 59*
'49	10	King Cole Trio – Volume 4...*Capitol 139*
'52	10	Penthouse Serenade...*Capitol 332*
'53	6	Two In Love...*Capitol 420*
'53	10	Unforgettable...*Capitol 357*
'54	7	10th Anniversary...*Capitol 514*
'56	16	Ballads Of The Day...*Capitol 680*
'57	13	After Midnight...*Capitol 782*
'57	1 [8]	Love Is The Thing...*Capitol 824*
'57	18	This Is Nat "King" Cole...*Capitol 870*
'57	18	Just One Of Those Things...*Capitol 903*
'58	18	St. Louis Blues...*Capitol 993*
'58	12	Cole Espanol...*Capitol 1031*
'58	17	The Very Thought Of You...*Capitol 1084*
'59	45	To Whom It May Concern...*Capitol 1190*
'60	33	Tell Me All About Yourself...*Capitol 1331*
'60	4	Wild Is Love...*Capitol 1392*
'61	79	The Touch Of Your Lips...*Capitol 1574*
'62	27	Nat King Cole sings/George Shearing plays...*Capitol 1675*
'62	3	Ramblin' Rose...*Capitol 1793*
'62	24	Dear Lonely Hearts...*Capitol 1838*
'63	68	Where Did Everyone Go?...*Capitol 1859*
'63	14	Those Lazy-Hazy-Crazy Days Of Summer...*Capitol 1932*
'64	18	I Don't Want To Be Hurt Anymore...*Capitol 2118*
'64	74	My Fair Lady...*Capitol 2117*

COOKE, Sam

'58	16	Sam Cooke...*Keen 2001*
'62	72	Twistin' The Night Away...*RCA Victor 2555*
'62	22	The Best Of Sam Cooke...*RCA Victor 2625*
'63	94	Mr. Soul...*RCA Victor 2673*
'63	62	Night Beat...*RCA Victor 2709*
'64	34	Ain't That Good News...*RCA Victor 2899*
'64	29	Sam Cooke At The Copa...*RCA Victor 2970*

CORTEZ, Dave "Baby"

'62	107	Rinky Dink...*Chess 1473*

COSBY, Bill

'64	21	Bill Cosby Is A Very Funny Fellow, Right!...*Warner 1518*
'64	32	I Started Out As A Child...*Warner 1567*

CRAWFORD, Hank

'64	143	True Blue...*Atlantic 1423*

DAVIS, Miles

'61	68	Miles Davis In Person (Friday & Saturday Nights At The Blackhawk, San Francisco)...*Columbia 8494*
'62	116	Someday My Prince Will Come...*Columbia 8456*
'62	59	Miles Davis At Carnegie Hall...*Columbia 8612*
'63	62	Seven Steps To Heaven...*Columbia 8851*
'64	93	Quiet Nights...*Columbia 8906*
'64	116	Miles Davis In Europe...*Columbia 8983*

DIDDLEY, Bo

'62	117	Bo Diddley...*Checker 2984*

DOMINO, Fats

'56	18	Fats Domino – Rock And Rollin'...*Imperial 9009*
'57	19	This Is Fats Domino!...*Imperial 9028*
'57	17	Rock And Rollin' With Fats Domino...*Imperial 9004*
'62	113	Million Sellers By Fats...*Imperial 9195*
'63	130	Here Comes...Fats Domino...*ABC-Paramount 455*

DONALDSON, Lou

'63	141	The Natural Soul...*Blue Note 84108*

DRIFTERS, The

'63	110	Up On The Roof – The Best Of The Drifters...*Atlantic 8073*
'64	40	Under The Boardwalk...*Atlantic 8099*

ECKSTINE, Billy

'50	4	Songs By Billy Eckstine...*MGM 48*
'62	92	Don't Worry 'Bout Me...*Mercury 60736*

ELLINGTON, Duke

'48	11	Mood Ellington...*Columbia 164*
'57	14	Ellington At Newport...*Columbia 934*
'64	133	Ellington '65: Hits of the 60's/This Time By Ellington...*Reprise 6122*

ESSEX, The

'63	119	Easier Said Than Done...*Roulette 25234*

FITZGERALD, Ella

'55	7	Songs from Pete Kelly's Blues...*Decca 8166*
'56	15	Ella Fitzgerald sings the Cole Porter Song Book...*Verve 4001*
'56	12	Ella And Louis...*Verve 4003*
'57	11	Ella Fitzgerald sings the Rodgers and Hart Song Book...*Verve 4002*
'60	11	Mack The Knife – Ella In Berlin...*Verve 4041*
'61	35	Ella In Hollywood...*Verve 4052*
'63	69	Ella And Basie!...*Verve 4061*
'64	111	Ella Fitzgerald sings the George and Ira Gershwin Song Books...*Verve V-29-5*
'64	146	Hello, Dolly!...*Verve 4064*

FRANKLIN, Aretha

'62	69	The Tender, The Moving, The Swinging Aretha Franklin...*Columbia 8676*
'64	84	Runnin' Out Of Fools...*Columbia 9081*

GARNER, Erroll

'57	16	Other Voices...*Columbia 1014*
'58	12	Concert By The Sea...*Columbia 883*
'61	35	Dreamstreet...*ABC-Paramount 365*
'63	94	One World Concert...*Reprise 6080*

GAYE, Marvin
'64	42	Together...*Motown 613*
'64	72	Marvin Gaye/Greatest Hits...*Tamla 252*

GRANT, Earl
'61	7	Ebb Tide...*Decca 74165*
'62	17	Beyond The Reef...*Decca 74231*
'62	92	Earl Grant At Basin Street East...*Decca 74299*
'64	139	Fly Me To The Moon...*Decca 74454*
'64	149	Just For A Thrill...*Decca 74506*

GREGORY, Dick
'61	23	In Living Black & White...*Colpix 417*

HAMILTON, Chico
'64	145	Man From Two Worlds...*Impulse! 59*

HAMPTON, Lionel
'52	10	Gene Norman Presents Just Jazz...*Decca 154*

HARRIS, Eddie
'61	2 [1]	Exodus To Jazz...*Vee-Jay 3016*

HENDERSON, Joe
'62	93	Snap Your Fingers...*Todd 2701*

HIBBLER, Al
'56	20	Starring Al Hibbler...*Decca 8328*

HORNE, Lena
'57	24	Lena Horne at the Waldorf Astoria...*RCA Victor 1028*
'58	20	Give The Lady What She Wants...*RCA Victor 1879*
'59	13	Porgy & Bess...*RCA Victor 1507*
'62	102	Lena On The Blue Side...*RCA Victor 2465*
'63	102	Lena...Lovely And Alive...*RCA Victor 2587*

IMPRESSIONS, The
'63	43	The Impressions...*ABC-Paramount 450*
'64	52	The Never Ending Impressions...*ABC-Paramount 468*
'64	8	Keep On Pushing...*ABC-Paramount 493*

INK SPOTS
'46	1 [7]	Ink Spots...*Decca 477*
'48	11	Ink Spots, Volume 3...*Decca 667*

ISLEY BROTHERS, The
'62	61	Twist & Shout...*Wand 653*

JACKSON, Mahalia
'62	130	Sweet Little Jesus Boy...*Columbia 702*

JAMAL, Ahmad
'58	3	But Not For Me/Ahmad Jamal at the Pershing...*Argo 628*
'58	11	Ahmad Jamal, Volume IV...*Argo 636*
'60	32	Jamal At The Penthouse...*Argo 646*

JAMES, Etta
'61	68	At Last!...*Argo 4003*
'63	117	Etta James Top Ten...*Argo 4025*
'64	96	Etta James Rocks The House...*Argo 4032*

JOHNSON, Pete, And Albert Ammons
'45	2 [1]	8 To The Bar (Two Piano Boogie Woogie For Dancing)...*RCA Victor 69*

JONES, Jonah
'58	7	Muted Jazz...*Capitol 839*
'58	7	Swingin' On Broadway...*Capitol 963*
'58	14	Jumpin' With Jonah...*Capitol 1039*

JONES, Quincy
'62	112	Big Band Bossa Nova...*Mercury 60751*

KING, Ben E.
'61	57	Spanish Harlem...*Atco 133*

KING, Rev. Martin Luther
'63	141	The Great March To Freedom...*Gordy 906*
'63	102	The March On Washington...*Mr. Maestro 1000*
'63	119	Freedom March On Washington...*20th Century 3110*

KING CURTIS
'64	103	Soul Serenade...*Capitol 2095*

KITT, Eartha
'53	1 [1]	RCA Victor Presents Eartha Kitt...*RCA Victor 3062*
'54	5	That Bad Eartha...*RCA Victor 3187*

LANCE, Major
'63	113	The Monkey Time...*Okeh 12105*
'64	100	Um, Um, Um, Um, Um, Um/The Best Of Major Lance...*Okeh 12106*

LESTER, Ketty
'62	53	Love Letters...*Era 108*

LEWIS, Ramsey
'62	129	Sound Of Christmas...*Argo 687*
'64	125	Bach To The Blues...*Argo 732*
'64	103	The Ramsey Lewis Trio At The Bohemian Caverns...*Argo 741*

LITTLE EVA
'62	97	Llllloco-Motion...*Dimension 6000*

LITTLE RICHARD
'57	13	Here's Little Richard...*Specialty 2100*

LUTCHER, Nellie
'48	4	Nellie Lutcher...*Capitol 70*

LYMON, Frankie, and The Teenagers
'57	19	The Teenagers featuring Frankie Lymon...*Gee 701*

LYNNE, Gloria
'61	51	I'm Glad There Is You...*Everest 5126*
'61	101	He Needs Me...*Everest 5128*
'61	57	This Little Boy Of Mine...*Everest 5131*
'62	58	Gloria Lynne at Basin Street East...*Everest 5137*
'63	39	Gloria Lynne at the Las Vegas Thunderbird...*Everest 5208*
'63	27	Gloria, Marty & Strings...*Everest 5220*
'64	43	I Wish You Love...*Everest 5226*

MABLEY, Moms
'61	16	Moms Mabley At The "UN"...*Chess 1452*
'61	121	Moms Mabley Onstage...*Chess 1447*
'61	39	Moms Mabley at The Playboy Club...*Chess 1460*
'62	28	Moms Mabley At Geneva Conference...*Chess 1463*
'62	27	Moms Mabley Breaks It Up...*Chess 1472*
'63	19	Young Men, Si – Old Men, No...*Chess 1477*
'63	41	I Got Somethin' To Tell You!...*Chess 1479*
'64	134	The Funny Sides Of Moms Mabley...*Chess 1482*
'64	48	Out On A Limb...*Mercury 60889*
'64	118	Moms Wows...*Chess 1486*
'64	128	Moms The Word...*Mercury 60907*

MAKEBA, Miriam
'63	86	The World Of Miriam Makeba...*RCA Victor 2750*
'64	122	The Voice Of Africa...*RCA Victor 2845*

MANN, Herbie
'62	30	Herbie Mann at the Village Gate...*Atlantic 1380*
'62	100	Right Now...*Atlantic 1384*
'63	86	Do The Bossa Nova With Herbie Mann...*Atlantic 1397*
'63	104	Herbie Mann Live At Newport...*Atlantic 1413*

MARTHA & THE VANDELLAS
'63	125	Heat Wave...*Gordy 907*

McDUFF, Brother Jack
'63	101	Screamin'...*Prestige 7259*
'63	81	Live!...*Prestige 7274*

McGRIFF, Jimmy
'62	22	I've Got A Woman...*Sue 1012*
'64	146	Topkapi...*Sue 1033*

MILLS BROTHERS, The
'46	3	Famous Barber Shop Ballads, Volume One...*Decca 476*
'49	9	Mills Brothers Souvenir Album...*Decca 668*
'50	8	Famous Barber Shop Ballads, Volume Two...*Decca 5051*

MIMMS, Garnet, & The Enchanters
'63	91	Cry Baby And 11 Other Hits...*United Artists 3305*

MIRACLES, The
'63	118	The Fabulous Miracles...*Tamla 238*
'63	139	The Miracles On Stage...*Tamla 241*
'64	113	doin' Mickey's Monkey...*Tamla 245*

MONK, Thelonious
'63	127	Criss-Cross...*Columbia 8838*

MORGAN, Lee
'64	25	The Sidewinder...*Blue Note 84157*

ORLONS, The
'62	80	The Wah-Watusi...*Cameo 1020*
'63	123	South Street...*Cameo 1041*

PARKER, Charlie
'50	9	Charlie Parker With Strings...*Mercury 101*

PETERSON, Oscar, Trio
'63	145	Bursting Out With The All Star Big Band!...*Verve 8476*
'63	127	Affinity...*Verve 8516*
'64	81	Oscar Peterson Trio + One...*Mercury 60975*

PHILLIPS, Esther
'63	46	Release Me!...*Lenox 227*

PLATTERS, The
'56	7	The Platters...*Mercury 20146*
'57	12	The Platters, Volume Two...*Mercury 20216*
'59	15	Remember When?...*Mercury 20410*
'60	6	Encore Of Golden Hits...*Mercury 20472*
'60	20	More Encore Of Golden Hits...*Mercury 20591*

PRYSOCK, Arthur
'63	138	Coast To Coast...*Old Town 2005*
'63	97	A Portrait Of Arthur Prysock...*Old Town 2006*
'64	131	Everlasting Songs For Everlasting Lovers...*Old Town 2007*

RAWLS, Lou
'63	130	Black And Blue...*Capitol 1824*

REDDING, Otis
'64	103	Pain In My Heart...*Atco 161*

REED, Jimmy
'61	46	Jimmy Reed at Carnegie Hall...*Vee-Jay 1035*
'62	103	Just Jimmy Reed...*Vee-Jay 1050*

REESE, Della
'60	35	Della...*RCA Victor 2157*
'61	113	Special Delivery...*RCA Victor 2391*
'62	94	The Classic Della...*RCA Victor 2419*

RONETTES, The
'64	96	...presenting the fabulous Ronettes featuring Veronica...*Philles 4006*

RUBY AND THE ROMANTICS
'63	120	Our Day Will Come...*Kapp 3323*

SANTAMARIA, Mongo
'63	42	Watermelon Man!...*Battle 96120*

SHARP, Dee Dee
'62   44   It's Mashed Potato Time...*Cameo 1018*
'62   117   Down To Earth...*Cameo 1029*

SHIRELLES, The
'62   59   Baby It's You...*Scepter 504*
'63   19   The Shirelles Greatest Hits...*Scepter 507*
'63   68   Foolish Little Girl...*Scepter 511*

SIMONE, Nina
'61   23   Nina At Newport...*Colpix 412*
'64   102   Nina Simone In Concert...*Philips 135*

SLACK, Freddie
'45   1 [5]   Boogie Woogie...*Capitol 12*
'48   6   Boogie-Woogie, Vol. 2...*Capitol 83*

SMALL, Millie
'64   132   My Boy Lollipop...*Smash 67055*

SMITH, Jimmy
'62   28   Midnight Special...*Blue Note 84078*
'62   10   Bashin'...*Verve 8474*
'63   14   Back At The Chicken Shack...*Blue Note 84117*
'63   11   Hobo Flats...*Verve 8544*
'63   25   Any Number Can Win...*Verve 8552*
'63   64   Rockin' The Boat...*Blue Note 84141*
'63   108   Blue Bash!...*Verve 8553*
'64   16   Who's Afraid Of Virginia Woolf?...*Verve 8583*
'64   86   Prayer Meetin'...*Blue Note 84164*
'64   12   The Cat...*Verve 8587*

STATON, Dakota
'58   4   The Late, Late Show...*Capitol 876*
'58   22   Dynamic!...*Capitol 1054*
'59   23   Crazy He Calls Me...*Capitol 1170*
'59   47   Time To Swing...*Capitol 1241*

SUNNY & THE SUNLINERS
'63   142   Talk To Me...*Tear Drop 2000*

SUPREMES, The
'64   2 [4]   Where Did Our Love Go...*Motown 621*
'64   21   A Bit Of Liverpool...*Motown 623*

TAYLOR, Little Johnny
'63   140   Little Johnny Taylor...*Galaxy 203*

TEMPTATIONS, The
'64   95   Meet The Temptations...*Gordy 911*

THOMAS, Irma
'64   104   Wish Someone Would Care...*Imperial 12266*

THOMAS, Rufus
'63   138   Walking The Dog...*Stax 704*

TYMES, The
'63   15   So Much In Love...*Parkway 7032*
'63   117   The Sound Of The Wonderful Tymes...*Parkway 7038*
'64   122   Somewhere...*Parkway 7039*

VAUGHAN, Sarah
'56   20   Linger Awhile...*Columbia 914*
'56   21   Sassy...*EmArcy 36089*
'57   14   Great Songs From Hit Shows...*Mercury 100*
'57   14   Sarah Vaughan sings George Gershwin...*Mercury 101*

WARWICK, Dionne
'64   68   Make Way For Dionne Warwick...*Scepter 523*

WASHINGTON, Dinah
'60   34   What a diff'rence a day makes!...*Mercury 20479*
'61   10   Unforgettable...*Mercury 20572*
'61   56   September In The Rain...*Mercury 20638*
'62   33   Dinah '62...*Roulette 25170*
'62   78   Drinking Again...*Roulette 25183*
'62   131   I Wanna Be Loved...*Mercury 20729*
'63   61   Back To The Blues...*Roulette 25189*
'64   130   A Stranger On Earth...*Roulette 25253*

WELCH, Lenny
'64   73   Since I Fell For You...*Cadence 3068*

WELLS, Mary
'63   49   Two Lovers and other great hits...*Motown 607*
'64   42   Together...*Motown 613*
'64   18   Greatest Hits...*Motown 616*
'64   111   Mary Wells Sings My Guy...*Motown 617*

WILSON, Jackie
'62   137   Jackie Wilson At The Copa...*Brunswick 754108*
'63   36   Baby Workout...*Brunswick 754110*

WILSON, Nancy
'62   30   Nancy Wilson/Cannonball Adderley...*Capitol 1657*
'62   49   Hello Young Lovers...*Capitol 1767*
'63   18   Broadway-My Way...*Capitol 1828*
'63   11   Hollywood-My Way...*Capitol 1934*
'64   4   Yesterday's Love Songs/Today's Blues...*Capitol 2012*
'64   10   Today, Tomorrow, Forever...*Capitol 2082*
'64   4   How Glad I Am...*Capitol 2155*

WONDER, Stevie
'63   1 [1]   Little Stevie Wonder/The 12 Year Old Genius...
      Tamla 240

YURO, Timi
'61   51   Timi Yuro...*Liberty 3208*

SOUNDTRACKS
'64   110   Lilies Of The Field...*Epic 26094*
'59   8   Porgy and Bess...*Columbia 2016*

VARIOUS ARTISTS

'62	99	Alan Freed's Memory Lane...*End 314*
'64	43	Apollo Saturday Night...*Atco 159*
'49	9	Giants Of Jazz...*Capitol 106*
'63	97	Golden Goodies, Vol. 1...*Roulette 25207*
'63	89	Golden Goodies, Vol. 2...*Roulette 25210*
'63	112	Golden Goodies, Vol. 3...*Roulette 25218*
'63	124	Golden Goodies, Vol. 5...*Roulette 25215*
'63	86	Golden Goodies, Vol. 6...*Roulette 25216*
'55	5	I Like Jazz!...*Columbia 1*
'48	7	Jazz At The Philharmonic, Vol. 8...*Mercury 8*
'49	4	Jazz At The Philharmonic, Vol. 9...*Mercury 9*
'49	5	Jazz At The Philharmonic, Vol. 10...*Mercury 10*
'59	12	Oldies But Goodies...*Original Sound 5001*
'61	12	Oldies But Goodies, Vol. 3...*Original Sound 5004*
'62	15	Oldies But Goodies, Vol. 4...*Original Sound 5005*
'63	16	Oldies But Goodies, Vol. 5...*Original Sound 5007*
'64	31	Oldies But Goodies, Vol. 6...*Original Sound 5011*
'63	47	Motor-Town Review, Vol. 1, The...*Motown 609*
'64	102	Motor-Town Review, Vol. 2, The...*Motown 615*
'61	63	Murray the "K's" Sing Along with the Original Golden Gassers ...*Roulette 25159*
'61	26	Murray the K's Blasts From The Past...*Chess 1461*
'62	124	Murray the K's Gassers For Submarine Race Watchers...*Chess 1470*
'63	69	Murray the K's Nineteen-Sixty Two Boss Golden Gassers...*Scepter 510*
'64	95	Saturday Night At The Uptown...*Atlantic 8101*
'64	84	16 Original Big Hits...*Motown 614*
'61	19	12 + 3 = 15 Hits...*End 310*

LABEL ABBREVIATIONS

Alpha Int'l.	Alpha International
Believe In A D.	Believe In A Dream
Cell Bl./Pri.	Cell Block/Priority
D.C. Int'l.	D.C. International
Midland Int'l.	Midland International
Midsong Int'l.	Midsong International
Neighborhood W.	Neighborhood Watch
Organized N.	Organized Noize
P.R.O. Div.	P.R.O. Division
Philadelphia I.	Philadelphia International
Snd. Of Capitol	Sound Of Capitol
Sound Of N.Y.	Sound Of New York
Street Know.	Street Knowledge
Strictly Busin.	Strictly Business
Total Exp.	Total Experience
Young Black Br.	Young Black Brotha

#1 ALBUMS

This section lists in chronological order, by peak date, all of the 448 albums which hit the #1 position on *Billboard's Top R&B Albums* chart from 1965 through 1998.

Billboard has not published an issue for the last week of the year since 1976. For the years 1976 through 1991, *Billboard* considered the charts listed in the last published issue of the year to be "frozen" and all chart positions remained the same for the unpublished week. This frozen chart data is included in our tabulations. Since 1992, *Billboard* has compiled the *Top R&B Albums* chart for the last week of the year, even though an issue is not published. This chart is only available through *Billboard's* computerized information network or by mail. Our tabulations include this unpublished chart data.

See the introduction pages of this book for more details on researching the *Top R&B Albums* charts.

DATE: Date album first peaked at the #1 position

WKS: Total weeks album held the #1 position

↕: Indicates album hit #1, dropped down, and then returned to the #1 spot

❶: Indicates album debuted at the #1 position

> Each year's top #1 album(s) is boxed out for quick reference. The top albums are determined by the most weeks at the #1 position.

#1 ALBUMS

1965

	DATE	WKS	
1.	1/30	1	**Where Did Our Love Go** *The Supremes*
2.	2/6	3	**Sam Cooke At The Copa** *Sam Cooke*
3.	2/27	4	**Shake** *Sam Cooke*
4.	3/27	2	**People Get Ready** *The Impressions*
5.	4/10	18↕	**The Temptations Sing Smokey** *The Temptations*
6.	7/3	3	**Four Tops** *Four Tops*
7.	7/24	1	**Shotgun** *Jr. Walker & The All Stars*
8.	9/11	12↕	**The In Crowd** *Ramsey Lewis Trio*
9.	10/30	1	**Otis Blue/Otis Redding Sings Soul** *Otis Redding*
10.	12/11	14↕	**Temptin' Temptations** *The Temptations*

1966

	DATE	WKS	
1.	1/15	5↕	**Going To A Go-Go** *Smokey Robinson & The Miracles*
2.	4/23	1	**I Hear A Symphony** *The Supremes*
3.	4/30	2	**Got My Mojo Workin'** *Jimmy Smith*
4.	5/14	1	**Crying Time** *Ray Charles*
5.	5/21	12↕	**Lou Rawls Live!** *Lou Rawls*
6.	7/30	6↕	**Gettin' Ready** *The Temptations*
7.	8/20	1	**Hold On, I'm Comin'** *Sam & Dave*
8.	10/1	9↕	**Lou Rawls Soulin'** *Lou Rawls*
9.	10/22	4	**The Supremes A' Go-Go** *The Supremes*
10.	12/31	9↕	**The Temptations Greatest Hits** *The Temptations*

1967

	DATE	WKS	
1.	2/4	1	**Four Tops Live!** *Four Tops*
2.	3/11	3	**The Supremes sing Holland-Dozier-Holland** *The Supremes*
3.	4/1	1	**Mercy, Mercy, Mercy!** *"Cannonball" Adderley*
4.	4/8	3	**Temptations Live!** *The Temptations*
5.	4/29	14↕	**I Never Loved A Man The Way I Love You** *Aretha Franklin*
6.	7/15	2	**Revenge** *Bill Cosby*
7.	7/29	2	**Here Where There is Love** *Dionne Warwick*
8.	9/2	1	**With A Lot O' Soul** *The Temptations*
9.	9/9	5	**Aretha Arrives** *Aretha Franklin*
10.	10/14	12	**Diana Ross and the Supremes Greatest Hits** *Diana Ross & The Supremes*

1968

	DATE	WKS	
1.	1/6	7	**The Temptations in a Mellow Mood** *The Temptations*
2.	2/24	1	**History Of Otis Redding** *Otis Redding*
3.	3/2	16↕	**Aretha: Lady Soul** *Aretha Franklin*
4.	4/20	3↕	**The Dock Of The Bay** *Otis Redding*
5.	6/22	3↕	**Wish It Would Rain** *The Temptations*
6.	7/27	17↕	**Aretha Now** *Aretha Franklin*
7.	11/23	1	**Hickory Holler Revisited** *O.C. Smith*

1968 (Cont'd)

	DATE	WKS	
8.	12/7	2	**Special Occasion** *Smokey Robinson & The Miracles*
9.	12/21	4	**Diana Ross & the Supremes Join the Temptations** *Diana Ross & The Supremes & The Temptations*

1969

	DATE	WKS	
1.	1/18	6	**TCB** *Diana Ross & The Supremes With The Temptations*
2.	3/1	4	**Aretha Franklin: Soul '69** *Aretha Franklin*
3.	3/29	13↕	**Cloud Nine** *The Temptations*
4.	6/21	2	**M.P.G.** *Marvin Gaye*
5.	7/12	2	**My Whole World Ended** *David Ruffin*
6.	7/26	4	**Aretha's Gold** *Aretha Franklin*
7.	8/23	10	**Hot Buttered Soul** *Isaac Hayes*
8.	11/1	15	**Puzzle People** *The Temptations*

1970

	DATE	WKS	
1.	2/14	9	**Diana Ross Presents The Jackson 5** *Jackson 5*
2.	4/18	4	**Psychedelic Shack** *The Temptations*
3.	5/16	7↕	**The Isaac Hayes Movement** *Isaac Hayes*
4.	6/20	12↕	**ABC** *Jackson 5*
5.	9/26	2	**Diana Ross** *Diana Ross*
6.	10/10	10	**Third Album** *Jackson 5*
7.	12/19	1	**Greatest Hits** *Sly & The Family Stone*
8.	12/26	11↕	**To Be Continued** *Isaac Hayes*

1971

	DATE	WKS	
1.	2/6	5↕	**Curtis** *Curtis Mayfield*
2.	4/10	3	**Live In Cook County Jail** *B.B. King*
3.	5/8	6	**Maybe Tomorrow** *Jackson 5*
4.	6/19	5	**Aretha Live At Fillmore West** *Aretha Franklin*
5.	7/24	9	**What's Going On** *Marvin Gaye*
6.	9/25	14	**Shaft** *Isaac Hayes/Soundtrack*

1972

	DATE	WKS	
1.	1/1	2	**There's A Riot Goin' On** *Sly & The Family Stone*
2.	1/15	7	**Black Moses** *Isaac Hayes*
3.	3/4	2	**Solid Rock** *The Temptations*
4.	3/18	10	**Let's Stay Together** *Al Green*
5.	5/27	2	**First Take** *Roberta Flack*
6.	6/10	5	**A Lonely Man** *The Chi-Lites*
7.	7/15	6	**Still Bill** *Bill Withers*

> **Billboard did not publish a *Best Selling Soul LP's* chart from 8/26/72 to 10/7/72.**

	DATE	WKS	
8.	10/14	6	**Superfly** *Curtis Mayfield/Soundtrack*
9.	11/25	1	**All Directions** *The Temptations*
10.	12/2	5	**I'm Still In Love With You** *Al Green*

#1 ALBUMS

1973

	DATE	WKS		
1.	1/6	2	**360 Degrees Of Billy Paul**	*Billy Paul*
2.	1/20	3	**Talking Book**	*Stevie Wonder*
3.	2/10	7	**The World Is A Ghetto**	*War*
4.	3/31	2	**Wattstax: The Living Word**	*Soundtrack*
5.	4/14	2	**Neither One Of Us**	*Gladys Knight & The Pips*
6.	4/28	2	**Masterpiece**	*The Temptations*
7.	5/12	3	**Spinners**	*Spinners*
8.	6/2	1	**Birth Day**	*The New Birth*
9.	6/9	2	**Call Me**	*Al Green*
10.	6/23	2	**Live At The Sahara Tahoe**	*Isaac Hayes*
11.	7/7	2	**I've Got So Much To Give**	*Barry White*
12.	7/21	2	**Back To The World**	*Curtis Mayfield*
13.	8/4	3	**Fresh**	*Sly & The Family Stone*
14.	8/25	2	**Touch Me In The Morning**	*Diana Ross*
15.	9/8	2	**Innervisions**	*Stevie Wonder*
16.	9/22	1	**Deliver The Word**	*War*
17.	9/29	11	**Let's Get It On** *Marvin Gaye*	
18.	12/15	7	**Imagination**	*Gladys Knight & The Pips*

1974

	DATE	WKS		
1.	2/2	2	**Stone Gon'**	*Barry White*
2.	2/16	5↕	**Ship Ahoy**	*The O'Jays*
3.	2/23	1	**Livin' For You**	*Al Green*
4.	3/16	6	**Love Is The Message**	*MFSB*
5.	4/27	1	**Boogie Down!**	*Eddie Kendricks*
6.	5/4	2	**The Payback**	*James Brown*
7.	5/18	1	**Let Me In Your Life**	*Aretha Franklin*
8.	5/25	1	**Open Our Eyes**	*Earth, Wind & Fire*
9.	6/1	1	**Mighty Love**	*Spinners*
10.	6/22	2	**War Live!**	*War*
11.	7/6	1	**Body Heat**	*Quincy Jones*
12.	7/13	1	**Claudine**	*Gladys Knight & The Pips*
13.	7/20	6	**Skin Tight**	*Ohio Players*
14.	8/31	2↕	**Marvin Gaye Live!**	*Marvin Gaye*
15.	9/7	4	**That Nigger's Crazy**	*Richard Pryor*
16.	10/5	8↕	**Fulfillingness' First Finale** *Stevie Wonder*	
17.	11/16	1	**Live It Up**	*The Isley Brothers*
18.	11/23	2	**Can't Get Enough**	*Barry White*
19.	12/28	1	**I Feel A Song**	*Gladys Knight & The Pips*

1975

	DATE	WKS		
1.	1/4	5	**Fire** *Ohio Players*	
2.	2/8	1	**Kung Fu Fighting And Other Great Love Songs**	*Carl Douglas*
3.	2/15	1	**New And Improved**	*Spinners*
4.	2/22	1	**Do It ('Til You're Satisfied)**	*B.T. Express*
5.	3/1	3	**AWB**	*Average White Band*
6.	3/22	1	**Al Green Explores Your Mind**	*Al Green*
7.	3/29	3	**Perfect Angel**	*Minnie Riperton*
8.	4/19	5↕	**That's The Way Of The World** *Earth, Wind & Fire/Soundtrack*	
9.	5/3	1	**A Song For You**	*The Temptations*
10.	5/10	1	**To Be True**	*Harold Melvin & The Blue Notes*
11.	5/17	1	**Mister Magic**	*Grover Washington, Jr.*
12.	5/24	1	**Sun Goddess**	*Ramsey Lewis*
13.	5/31	1	**Just Another Way To Say I Love You** *Barry White*	

1975 (Cont'd)

	DATE	WKS		
14.	6/7	2	**Survival**	*The O'Jays*
15.	7/12	1	**Disco Baby**	*Van McCoy*
16.	7/19	4↕	**The Heat Is On**	*The Isley Brothers*
17.	8/9	2	**Chocolate Chip**	*Isaac Hayes*
18.	8/23	1	**Cut The Cake**	*Average White Band*
19.	8/30	1	**Why Can't We Be Friends?**	*War*
20.	9/6	2	**Non-Stop**	*B.T. Express*
21.	9/27	3↕	**Honey**	*Ohio Players*
22.	10/11	2	**Is It Something I Said?**	*Richard Pryor*
23.	11/1	2	**Al Green Is Love**	*Al Green*
24.	11/15	1	**KC And The Sunshine Band** *KC And The Sunshine Band*	
25.	11/22	1	**Inseparable**	*Natalie Cole*
26.	11/29	1	**Save Me**	*Silver Convention*
27.	12/6	2	**Let's Do It Again**	*The Staple Singers*
28.	12/20	1	**Feels So Good**	*Grover Washington, Jr.*
29.	12/27	1	**Family Reunion**	*The O'Jays*

1976

	DATE	WKS		
1.	1/3	6↕	**Gratitude**	*Earth, Wind & Fire*
2.	1/24	2	**Wake Up Everybody** *Harold Melvin & The Blue Notes*	
3.	2/28	6	**Rufus featuring Chaka Khan** *Rufus featuring Chaka Khan*	
4.	4/10	2	**Eargasm**	*Johnnie Taylor*
5.	4/24	3	**Brass Construction**	*Brass Construction*
6.	5/15	1	**I Want You**	*Marvin Gaye*
7.	5/22	6↕	**Breezin'**	*George Benson*
8.	5/29	4	**Look Out For #1**	*The Brothers Johnson*
9.	6/26	1	**Harvest For The World**	*The Isley Brothers*
10.	7/24	1	**Contradiction**	*Ohio Players*
11.	7/31	1	**Sparkle**	*Aretha Franklin*
12.	8/21	1	**All Things In Time**	*Lou Rawls*
13.	8/28	6↕	**Hot On The Tracks**	*Commodores*
14.	9/11	1	**Wild Cherry**	*Wild Cherry*
15.	10/16	20↕	**Songs In The Key Of Life** *Stevie Wonder*	

1977

	DATE	WKS		
1.	1/8	1	**Good High**	*Brick*
2.	3/12	3	**Ask Rufus**	*Rufus Featuring Chaka Khan*
3.	4/2	3	**Unpredictable**	*Natalie Cole*
4.	4/23	1	**Ahh...The Name Is Bootsy, Baby!** *Bootsy's Rubber Band*	
5.	4/30	2	**Marvin Gaye Live At The London Palladium** *Marvin Gaye*	
6.	5/14	2↕	**Go For Your Guns**	*The Isley Brothers*
7.	5/21	8↕	**Commodores**	*Commodores*
8.	7/23	7↕	**Rejoice**	*Emotions*
9.	8/6	3	**The Floaters**	*The Floaters*
10.	10/1	3↕	**Rose Royce II/In Full Bloom**	*Rose Royce*
11.	10/8	1	**Something To Love**	*L.T.D.*
12.	10/15	5↕	**Barry White Sings For Someone You Love** *Barry White*	
13.	11/12	2	**Brick**	*Brick*
14.	12/17	9	**All 'N All** *Earth, Wind & Fire*	

#1 ALBUMS

1978

	DATE	WKS	
1.	2/18	6↕	**Saturday Night Fever**
			Bee Gees/Soundtrack
2.	3/25	3	**Bootsy? Player Of The Year**
			Bootsy's Rubber Band
3.	4/15	1	**Street Player** *Rufus/Chaka Khan*
4.	4/29	2	**Weekend In L.A.** *George Benson*
5.	5/13	3	**Showdown** *The Isley Brothers*
6.	6/3	3	**So Full Of Love** *The O'Jays*
7.	6/24	8↕	**Natural High** *Commodores*
8.	8/12	2	**Life Is A Song Worth Singing**
			Teddy Pendergrass
9.	9/2	7	**Blam!!** *The Brothers Johnson*
10.	10/21	1	**Is It Still Good To Ya** *Ashford & Simpson*
11.	10/28	4	**One Nation Under A Groove** *Funkadelic*
12.	11/25	3	**Barry White The Man** *Barry White*
13.	12/16	11	**C'est Chic** *Chic*

1979

	DATE	WKS	
1.	3/3	8↕	**2 Hot!** *Peaches & Herb*
2.	3/31	1	**Instant Funk** *Instant Funk*
3.	4/7	7↕	**We Are Family** *Sister Sledge*
4.	6/23	3	**Bad Girls** *Donna Summer*
5.	7/14	1	**I Am** *Earth, Wind & Fire*
6.	7/21	8	**Teddy** *Teddy Pendergrass*
7.	9/15	1	**Midnight Magic** *Commodores*
8.	10/6	16↕	**Off The Wall** *Michael Jackson*
9.	10/27	2	**Ladies' Night** *Kool & The Gang*
10.	12/22	2	**Masterjam** *Rufus & Chaka*

1980

	DATE	WKS	
1.	2/23	8	**The Whispers** *The Whispers*
2.	4/19	2	**Light Up The Night** *The Brothers Johnson*
3.	5/3	5	**Go All The Way** *The Isley Brothers*
4.	6/7	5	**Let's Get Serious** *Jermaine Jackson*
5.	7/12	2	**Cameosis** *Cameo*
6.	7/26	8	**Diana** *Diana Ross*
7.	9/20	4	**Give Me The Night** *George Benson*
8.	10/18	1	**Love Approach** *Tom Browne*
9.	10/25	2	**Zapp** *Zapp*
10.	11/8	2	**Triumph** *Jacksons*
11.	11/22	13	**Hotter Than July** *Stevie Wonder*

1981

	DATE	WKS	
1.	2/21	6↕	**The Gap Band III** *The Gap Band*
2.	3/7	2	**The Two Of Us** *Yarbrough & Peoples*
3.	4/18	5	**Being With You** *Smokey Robinson*
4.	5/23	2	**A Woman Needs Love** *Ray Parker Jr.*
5.	6/6	20	**Street Songs** *Rick James*
6.	10/24	2	**Breakin' Away** *Al Jarreau*
7.	11/7	1	**The Many Facets Of Roger** *Roger*
8.	11/14	1	**Never Too Much** *Luther Vandross*
9.	11/21	1	**Something Special** *Kool & The Gang*
10.	11/28	11	**Raise!** *Earth, Wind & Fire*

1982

	DATE	WKS	
1.	2/13	4↕	**Skyy Line** *Skyy*
2.	2/20	5	**The Poet** *Bobby Womack*
3.	4/17	1	**Love Is Where You Find It** *The Whispers*
4.	4/24	2	**Friends** *Shalamar*
5.	5/8	3	**Brilliance** *Atlantic Starr*
6.	5/29	1	**The Other Woman** *Ray Parker Jr.*
7.	6/5	3↕	**Stevie Wonder's Original Musiquarium**
			I *Stevie Wonder*
8.	6/19	1	**Keep It Live** *Dazz Band*
9.	7/3	9	**Gap Band IV** *The Gap Band*
10.	9/4	7	**Jump To It** *Aretha Franklin*
11.	10/23	2	**Get Loose** *Evelyn "Champagne" King*
12.	11/6	3	**Forever, For Always, For Love**
			Luther Vandross
13.	11/27	1	**Lionel Richie** *Lionel Richie*
14.	12/4	8	**Midnight Love** *Marvin Gaye*

1983

	DATE	WKS	
1.	1/29	37↕	**Thriller** *Michael Jackson*
2.	7/23	1	**Between The Sheets** *The Isley Brothers*
3.	9/17	10	**Cold Blooded** *Rick James*
4.	11/26	23↕	**Can't Slow Down** *Lionel Richie*

1984

	DATE	WKS	
1.	4/14	2	**Busy Body** *Luther Vandross*
2.	4/28	2	**She's Strange** *Cameo*
3.	7/7	1	**Jermaine Jackson** *Jermaine Jackson*
4.	7/14	1	**Lady** *One Way*
5.	7/21	3↕	**Private Dancer** *Tina Turner*
6.	7/28	19	**Purple Rain**
			Prince And The Revolution/Soundtrack
7.	12/8	4	**The Woman in Red**
			Stevie Wonder/Soundtrack

1985

	DATE	WKS	
1.	1/5	5	**New Edition** *New Edition*
2.	2/9	4	**Solid** *Ashford & Simpson*
3.	3/9	2	**Gap Band VI** *The Gap Band*
4.	4/6	3	**Nightshift** *Commodores*
5.	4/27	1	**Can't Stop The Love**
			Maze Featuring Frankie Beverly
6.	5/4	7	**The Night I Fell In Love** *Luther Vandross*
7.	6/22	6↕	**Whitney Houston** *Whitney Houston*
8.	6/29	14↕	**Rock Me Tonight** *Freddie Jackson*
9.	11/9	12	**In Square Circle** *Stevie Wonder*

#1 ALBUMS

#1 ALBUMS

1993

	DATE	WKS		
1.	2/6	8↕	**The Chronic**	*Dr. Dre*
2.	3/13	2	**19 Naughty III**	*Naughty By Nature*
3.	3/27	2	❶ **Till Death Do Us Part**	*The Geto Boys*
4.	4/10	1	**Lose Control**	*Silk*
5.	4/17	2	**14 Shots To The Dome**	*LL Cool J*
6.	5/22	1	❶ **Down With The King**	*Run-D.M.C.*
7.	5/29	1	**Fever For Da Flavor**	*H-Town*
8.	6/5	3	❶ **janet.**	*Janet Jackson*
9.	6/26	6	**Menace II Society**	*Soundtrack*
10.	8/7	4	❶ **Black Sunday**	*Cypress Hill*
11.	9/4	2	**The World Is Yours**	*Scarface*
12.	9/18	2	❶ **Music Box**	*Mariah Carey*
13.	10/2	3↕	**Toni Braxton**	*Toni Braxton*
14.	10/16	2	**187 He Wrote**	*Spice 1*
15.	11/6	1	**It's On (Dr. Dre) 187um Killa**	*Eazy E*
16.	11/13	2	❶ **Get In Where You Fit In**	*Too $hort*
17.	11/27	1	❶ **Midnight Marauders**	*A Tribe Called Quest*
18.	12/4	1	**Shock Of The Hour**	*MC Ren*
19.	12/11	5↕	❶ **Doggy Style**	*Snoop Doggy Dogg*
20.	12/25	1	**Lethal Injection**	*Ice Cube*

1994

	DATE	WKS		
1.	1/22	2	**Diary Of A Mad Band**	*Jodeci*
2.	2/5	9	**12 Play**	*R. Kelly*
3.	4/9	10↕	❶ **Above The Rim**	*Soundtrack*
4.	6/11	1	❶ **Nuttin' But Love**	*Heavy D & The Boyz*
5.	6/25	3	❶ **Regulate...G Funk Era**	*Warren G*
6.	7/16	2	❶ **Get Up On It**	*Keith Sweat*
7.	7/30	1	**Funkdafied**	*Da Brat*
8.	8/6	5	❶ **We Come Strapped**	
			MC Eiht Featuring CMW	
9.	9/10	1	❶ **Changing Faces**	*Changing Faces*
10.	9/17	2	❶ **II**	*Boyz II Men*
11.	10/1	4	❶ **Rhythm Of Love**	*Anita Baker*
12.	10/29	1	**Jason's Lyric**	*Soundtrack*
13.	11/5	3	❶ **Murder Was The Case**	*Soundtrack*
14.	11/26	1	**The Icon Is Love**	*Barry White*
15.	12/3	1	❶ **Tical**	*Method Man*
16.	12/10	1	❶ **Dare Iz A Darkside**	*Redman*
17.	12/17	8↕	❶ **My Life**	*Mary J. Blige*
18.	12/24	3	**Miracles - The Holiday Album**	*Kenny G*

1995

	DATE	WKS		
1.	2/11	2	❶ **Cocktails**	*Too $hort*
2.	3/11	2	❶ **Safe + Sound**	*DJ Quik*
3.	4/1	4	❶ **Me Against The World**	*2 Pac*
4.	4/29	6	❶ **Friday**	*Soundtrack*
5.	6/10	1	**Tales From The Hood**	*Soundtrack*
6.	6/17	3	**Poverty's Paradise**	*Naughty By Nature*
7.	7/8	2	❶ **HIStory: Past, Present And Future -**	
			Book I *Michael Jackson*	
8.	7/22	2	❶ **Operation Stackola**	*Luniz*
9.	8/5	1	❶ **The Show - The After-Party - The Hotel**	
			Jodeci	
10.	8/12	3	**E. 1999 Eternal**	*Bone Thugs-N-Harmony*
11.	9/2	6	**The Show**	*Soundtrack*

1995 (Cont'd)

	DATE	WKS		
12.	10/14	1	**4,5,6**	*Kool G Rap*
13.	10/21	1	❶ **Daydream**	*Mariah Carey*
14.	10/28	1	❶ **Doe Or Die**	*AZ*
15.	11/4	2	**Dead Presidents**	*Soundtrack*
16.	11/18	2	**Dogg Food**	*Tha Dogg Pound*
17.	12/2	2	❶ **R. Kelly**	*R. Kelly*
18.	12/16	10↕	**Waiting To Exhale**	*Soundtrack*

1996

	DATE	WKS		
1.	2/17	1	❶ **Str8 Off Tha Streetz Of Muthaphukkin**	
			Compton *Eazy-E*	
2.	3/2	3	**All Eyez On Me**	*2Pac*
3.	3/23	8↕	**The Score**	*Fugees*
4.	4/13	1	❶ **The Coming**	*Busta Rhymes*
5.	4/20	1	**The Resurrection**	*The Geto Boys*
6.	5/11	1	**Sunset Park**	*Soundtrack*
7.	6/8	2	❶ **Gettin' It (Album Number Ten)**	*Too $hort*
8.	6/22	1	**Legal Drug Money**	*Lost Boyz*
9.	6/29	1	**The Nutty Professor**	*Soundtrack*
10.	7/6	1	❶ **Secrets**	*Toni Braxton*
11.	7/13	1	❶ **Keith Sweat**	*Keith Sweat*
12.	7/20	7↕	**It Was Written**	*Nas*
13.	8/17	1	❶ **Beats, Rhymes And Life**	
			A Tribe Called Quest	
14.	9/14	2	**ATLiens**	*OutKast*
15.	9/28	1	❶ **Home Again**	*New Edition*
16.	10/5	5	**Another Level**	*BLACKstreet*
17.	11/9	1	❶ **Bow Down**	*Westside Connection*
18.	11/16	1	❶ **Ironman**	*Ghostface Killah*
19.	11/23	6↕	**The Don Killuminati - The 7 Day**	
			Theory *Makaveli*	
20.	11/30	1	**Tha Doggfather**	*Snoop Doggy Dogg*
21.	12/7	1	❶ **Hell On Earth**	*Mobb Deep*
22.	12/28	1	❶ **Muddy Waters**	*Redman*

1997

	DATE	WKS		
1.	1/4	2	**The Preacher's Wife**	
			Whitney Houston/Soundtrack	
2.	2/1	1	❶ **Rhyme & Reason**	*Soundtrack*
3.	2/15	2	❶ **Gridlock'd**	*Soundtrack*
4.	3/1	4	❶ **Baduizm**	*Erykah Badu*
5.	3/29	2	**The Untouchable**	*Scarface*
6.	4/12	4	**Life After Death**	*The Notorious B.I.G.*
7.	5/10	4	**Share My World**	*Mary J. Blige*
8.	6/7	1	❶ **I'm Bout It**	*Soundtrack*
9.	6/14	5↕	**God's Property**	*God's Property*
10.	6/21	2	❶ **Wu-Tang Forever**	*Wu-Tang Clan*
11.	8/2	1	**Supa Dupa Fly**	*Missy "Misdemeanor" Elliott*
12.	8/9	5↕	**No Way Out**	*Puff Daddy & The Family*
13.	9/6	1	❶ **The Art Of War**	*Bone thugs-n-harmony*
14.	9/20	2	**Ghetto D**	*Master P*
15.	10/4	1	**When Disaster Strikes...**	*Busta Rhymes*
16.	10/11	1	❶ **Evolution**	*Boyz II Men*
17.	10/18	1	**Soul Food**	*Soundtrack*
18.	10/25	2	**Gang Related**	*Soundtrack*
19.	11/8	1	**The Firm - The Album**	*The Firm*

#1 ALBUMS

1997 (Cont'd)

20.	11/15	1	**Harlem World**	*Mase*
21.	11/22	1	**The 18th Letter**	*Rakim*
22.	11/29	1	**Unpredictable**	*Mystikal*
23.	12/6	3↕	**Live**	*Erykah Badu*
24.	12/13	2	**R U Still Down? [Remember Me]**	*2 Pac*

1998

	DATE	WKS		
1.	1/10	3	**My Way**	*Usher*
2.	1/31	1	**Money, Power & Respect**	*The Lox*
3.	2/7	1 ❶	**All I Have In This World, Are...My Balls And My Word**	*Young Bleed*
4.	2/14	3	**Anytime**	*Brian McKnight*
5.	3/7	2	**Charge It 2 Da Game**	*Silkk The Shocker*
6.	3/21	2	**My Homies**	*Scarface*
7.	4/4	1	**Life Or Death**	*C-Murder*
8.	4/11	1	**The Pillage**	*Cappadonna*
9.	4/18	1	**Moment Of Truth**	*Gang Starr*
10.	4/25	3	**I Got The Hook-Up!**	*Soundtrack*
11.	5/16	2↕	**Capital Punishment**	*Big Punisher*
12.	5/23	1	**There's One In Every Family**	*Fiend*
13.	6/6	2 ❶	**It's Dark And Hell Is Hot**	*DMX*
14.	6/20	4	**MP Da Last Don**	*Master P*
15.	7/18	1 ❶	**El Niño**	*Def Squad*
16.	7/25	1	**Am I My Brothers Keeper**	*Kane & Abel*
17.	8/1	1	**N.O.R.E.**	*Noreaga*
18.	8/8	2	**Jermaine Dupri Presents Life In 1472 - The Original Soundtrack**	*Jermaine Dupri*
19.	8/22	3	**Da Game Is To Be Sold, Not To Be Told**	*Snoop Dogg*
20.	9/12	6↕ ❶	**The Miseducation Of Lauryn Hill**	*Lauryn Hill*
21.	10/17	6	**Vol. 2...Hard Knock Life**	*Jay-Z*
22.	11/28	1 ❶	**R.**	*R. Kelly*
23.	12/5	1	**Tical 2000: Judgement Day**	*Method Man*
24.	12/12	2 ❶	**Greatest Hits**	*2 Pac*
25.	12/26	1 ❶	**Doc's Da Name 2000**	*Redman*

THE CHARTS FROM

Only Joel Whitburn's Record Research Books List Every

When the talk turns to music, more people turn to Joel Whitburn's Record Research Collection than to any other reference source.

That's because these are the **only** books that get right to the bottom of *Billboard's* major charts, with **complete, fully accurate chart data on every record ever charted**. So they're quoted with confidence by DJ's, music show hosts, program directors, collectors and other music enthusiasts worldwide.

Each book lists every record's significant chart data, such as peak position, debut date, peak date, weeks charted, label, record number and much more, all conveniently arranged for fast, easy reference. Most books also feature artist biographies, record notes, RIAA Platinum/Gold Record certifications, top artist and record achievements, all-time artist and record rankings, a chronological listing of all #1 hits, and additional in-depth chart information.

TOP POP SINGLES 1955-1996
Over 22,000 pop singles — every "Hot 100" hit — arranged by artist. Features thousands of artist biographies and countless titles notes. Also, for the first time, includes the B-side title of every "Hot 100" hit, doubling the number of titles listed in any previous edition. 912 pages. $79.95 Hardcover / $69.95 Softcover.

POP ANNUAL 1955-1994
A year-by-year ranking, based on chart performance, of over 20,000 pop hits. 880 pages. $69.95 Hardcover / $59.95 Softcover.

POP HITS 1940-1954
Compiled strictly from *Billboard* and divided into two easy-to-use sections — one lists all the hits artist-by-artist and the other year-by-year. Filled with artist bios, title notes, and many special sections. 414 pages. Hardcover. $44.95.

POP MEMORIES 1890-1954
Unprecedented in depth and dimension. An artist-by-artist, title-by-title chronicle of the 65 formative years of recorded popular music. Fascinating facts and statistics on over 1,600 artists and 12,000 recordings, compiled directly from America's popular music charts, surveys and record listings. 660 pages. Hardcover. $59.95.

TOP POP ALBUMS 1955-1996
An artist-by-artist history of the over 18,300 albums that ever appeared on *Billboard's* pop albums charts, with a complete A-Z listing below each artist of <u>every</u> track from <u>every</u> charted album by that artist. 1,056 pages. Hardcover. $89.95.

TOP POP ALBUM TRACKS 1955-1992
An all-inclusive, alphabetical index of every song track from every charted music album, with the artist's name and the album's chart debut year. 544 pages. Hardcover. $34.95.

TOP POP ALBUM TRACKS 1993-1996
A 3 1/2-year supplement to the above Tracks book — alphabetically indexes over 21,000 tracks from the more than 1,600 albums that have appeared on *The Billboard 200* pop albums charts since 1992. 88 pages. Softcover. $14.95.

BILLBOARD HOT 100/POP SINGLES CHARTS:

THE EIGHTIES 1980-1989
THE SEVENTIES 1970-1979
THE SIXTIES 1960-1969
Three complete collections of the actual weekly "Hot 100" charts from each decade; black-and-white reproductions at 70% of original size. Over 550 pages each. Deluxe Hardcover. $79.95 each.

POP CHARTS 1955-1959
Reproductions of every weekly pop singles chart *Billboard* published from 1955 through 1959 ("Best Sellers," "Jockeys," "Juke Box," "Top 100" and "Hot 100"). 496 pages. Deluxe Hardcover. $59.95.

BILLBOARD POP ALBUM CHARTS 1965-1969
The greatest of all album eras...straight off the pages of *Billboard*! Every weekly *Billboard* pop albums chart, shown in its entirety, from 1965 through 1969. Black-and-white reproductions at 70% of original size. 496 pages. Deluxe Hardcover. $59.95.

TOP COUNTRY SINGLES 1944-1997
The complete history of the most genuine of American musical genres, with an artist-by-artist listing of every "Country" single ever charted. 544 pages. Hardcover. $64.95.

COUNTRY ANNUAL 1944-1997
A year-by-year ranking, based on chart performance, of over 16,000 Country hits. 704 pages. Hardcover. $64.95.

TOP TO BOTTOM!

Record To Ever Appear On Every Major Billboard Chart.

TOP COUNTRY ALBUMS 1964-1997
First edition! A music industry first and a Record Research exclusive — features an artist-by-artist listing of every album to appear on *Billboard's* Top Country Albums chart from its first appearance in 1964 through September, 1997. Includes complete listings of all tracks from every Top 10 Country album. 304 pages. Hardcover. $49.95.

TOP R&B SINGLES 1942-1995
Revised edition of our R&B bestseller — loaded with new features! Every "Soul," "Black," "Urban Contemporary" and "Rhythm & Blues" charted single, listed by artist. 704 pages. Hardcover. $64.95.

TOP R&B ALBUMS 1965-1998
First edition! An artist-by-artist listing of each of the 2,177 artists and 6,940 albums to appear on Billboard's "Top R&B Albums" chart. Includes complete listings of all tracks from every Top 10 R&B album. 360 pages. Hardcover. $49.95.

TOP ADULT CONTEMPORARY 1961-1993
America's leading listener format is covered hit by hit in this fact-packed volume. Lists, artist by artist, the complete history of *Billboard's* "Easy Listening" and "Adult Contemporary" charts. 368 pages. Hardcover. $39.95.

ROCK TRACKS
Two artist-by-artist listings of the over 3,700 titles that appeared on *Billboard's* "Album Rock Tracks" chart from March, 1981 through August, 1995 and the over 1,200 titles that appeared on *Billboard's* "Modern Rock Tracks" chart from September, 1988 through August, 1995. 288 pages. Softcover. $34.95.

BUBBLING UNDER SINGLES AND ALBUMS 1998 Edition
All "Bubbling Under The Hot 100" (1959-1997) and "Bubbling Under The Top Pop Albums" (1970-1985) charts covered in full and organized artist by artist. Also features a photo section of every EP that hit *Billboard's* "Best Selling Pop EP's" chart (1957-1960). 416 pages. Softcover. $49.95.

BILLBOARD TOP 10 CHARTS 1958-1997
A complete listing of each weekly Top 10 chart, along with each week's "Highest Debut" and "Biggest Mover" from the entire "Hot 100" chart, and more! 780 pages. Hardcover. $39.95.

BILLBOARD TOP 10 ALBUM CHARTS 1963-1998
This books contains more than 1,800 individual Top 10 charts from over 35 years of *Billboard's* weekly Top Albums chart (currently titled The Billboard 200). Each chart shows each album's current and previous week's positions, total weeks charted on the entire Top Albums chart, original label & number, and more. 536 pages. Hardcover. $39.95.

BILLBOARD TOP 1000 x 5 1996 Edition
Includes five complete <u>separate</u> rankings — from #1 through #1000 — of the all-time top charted hits of Pop & Hot 100 Singles 1955-1996, Pop Singles 1940-1954, Adult Contemporary Singles 1961-1996, R&B Singles 1942-1996, and Country Singles 1944-1996. 288 pages. Softcover. $29.95.

DAILY #1 HITS 1940-1992
A desktop calendar of a half-century of #1 pop records. Lists one day of the year per page of every record that held the #1 position on the pop singles charts on that day for each of the past 53+ years. 392 pages. Spiral-bound softcover. $24.95.

MUSIC YEARBOOKS 1998/1997/1996/1995/1994/1993/1992/1991/1990
A complete review of each year's charted music — as well as a superb supplemental update of our Record Research Pop Singles and Albums, Country Singles, R&B Singles, Adult Contemporary Singles, and Bubbling Under Singles books. Various page lengths. Softcover. 1995 thru 1998 editions $34.95 each / 1990 thru 1994 editions $29.95 each.

For complete book descriptions and ordering information, call, write, fax or e-mail today.

RECORD RESEARCH INC.
P.O. Box 200
Menomonee Falls, WI 53052-0200   U.S.A.

Phone: 414-251-5408
Fax: 414-251-9452
E-mail: record@execpc.com

We're On The Internet — If you'd like to place an order electronically, simply use the convenient order form on our Web Site: **http://www.recordresearch.com**.

The *RECORD RESEARCH* Collection

Book Title	Quantity	Price	Total
1. Billboard Pop Charts 1955-1959 (hardcover)		$59.95	
2. Billboard Hot 100 Charts - The Sixties (hardcover)		$79.95	
3. Billboard Hot 100 Charts - The Seventies (hardcover)		$79.95	
4. Billboard Hot 100 Charts - The Eighties (hardcover)		$79.95	
5. Billboard Pop Album Charts 1965-1969 (hardcover)		$59.95	
6. Top Pop Albums 1955-1996 (hardcover)		$89.95	
7. Top Pop Album Tracks 1955-1992 (hardcover)		$34.95	
8. Top Pop Album Tracks 1993-1996 (softcover)		$14.95	
9. Top Pop Singles 1955-1996 (hardcover)		$79.95	
10. Top Pop Singles 1955-1996 (softcover)		$69.95	
11. Pop Hits 1940-1954 (hardcover)		$44.95	
12. Pop Annual 1955-1994 (hardcover)		$69.95	
13. Pop Annual 1955-1994 (softcover)		$59.95	
14. Top Country Singles 1944-1997 (hardcover)		$64.95	
15. Country Annual 1944-1997 (hardcover)		$64.95	
16. Top Country Albums 1964-1997 (hardcover)		$49.95	
17. Top R&B Singles 1942-1995 (hardcover)		$64.95	
18. Top R&B Albums 1965-1998 (hardcover)		$49.95	
19. Pop Memories 1890-1954 (hardcover)		$59.95	
20. Bubbling Under Singles And Albums 1998 Edition (softcover)		$49.95	
21. Top Adult Contemporary 1961-1993 (hardcover)		$39.95	
22. Top 10 Charts 1958-1997 (hardcover)		$39.95	
23. Top 10 Album Charts 1963-1998 (hardcover)		$39.95	
24. Rock Tracks (softcover)		$34.95	
25. Billboard Top 1000 x 5 1996 Edition (softcover)		$29.95	
26. Daily #1 Hits 1940-1992 (softcover)		$24.95	
27. Music Yearbooks (softcover)		$34.95 each	

☐ 1998   ☐ 1997   ☐ 1996   ☐ 1995

28. Music Yearbooks (softcover) .... $29.95 each _____

☐ 1994   ☐ 1993   ☐ 1992   ☐ 1991   ☐ 1990

Shipping & Handling (see below) ...... _____

Wisconsin Residents Only (add 5.1% sales tax)...... _____

SHIPPING & HANDLING:

If your order subtotals:	U.S.	Foreign
Up to $30.00	$5.00	$5.00
$30.01 - $50.00	$6.00	$6.00
$50.01 - $80.00	$7.50	$7.50
$80.01 - $130.00	$8.50	$10.00
$130.01 - $180.00	$9.00	$12.50
$180.01 - $230.00	$10.00	$16.00
$230.01 - $300.00	$11.50	$21.00
Over $300.00	$13.00	$25.00

TOTAL PAYMENT ....$_____

PAYMENT METHOD:

☐ MasterCard   ☐ Check

☐ VISA   ☐ Money Order

☐ American Express

Credit Card
Expiration Date: _____ / _____
                  Mo.   Yr.

U.S. orders shipped via UPS (please give complete street address). Foreign orders shipped via surface mail; allow 8-12 weeks for delivery. Must be paid in U.S. dollars and drawn on a U.S. bank. Call for special air shipping information/rates.

Credit Card #   __ __ __ __   __ __ __ __   __ __ __ __   __ __ __ __

Signature _____

To charge your order by phone, call **414-251-5408** or fax **414-251-9452** (office hours: 8 a.m.-noon & 1-5 p.m. CST) or e-mail to: **record@execpc.com** or mail to: **Record Research Inc., P.O. Box 200, Menomonee Falls, WI 53052-0200 U.S.A.**

Name _____

Company Name _____

Address _____ Apt/Suite # _____

City _____ State/Province _____

ZIP/Postal Code _____ Country _____